D0330317

Central
Europe

Lisa Dunford,
Brett Atkinson, Neal Bedford, Steve Fallon, Tim Richards,
Caroline Sieg, Ryan Ver Berkmoes, Nicola Williams

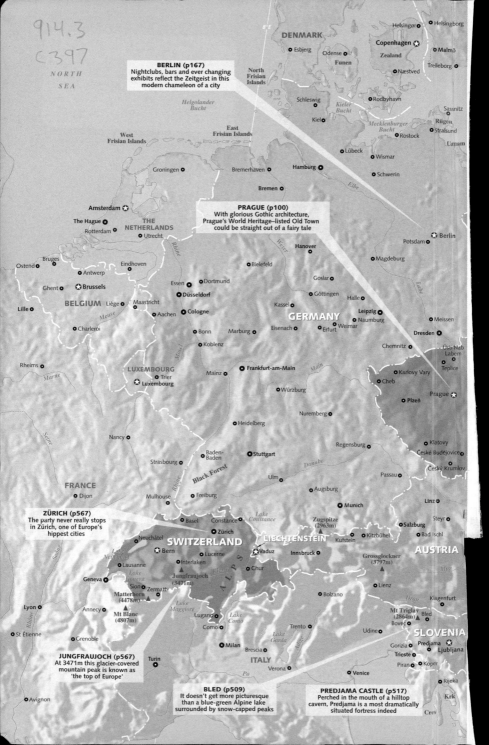

914.3
C397

NORTH
SEA

DENMARK

Helsingør · Helsingborg

Copenhagen · Malmö

Zealand

Trelleborg

Næstved

Sassnitz

Rügen · Stralsund

Usnam

North
Frisian
Islands

Helgolander
Bucht

Esbjerg · Odense · Funen

Rødbyhavn

Kiel

Mecklenburger
Bucht

Rostock

Schleswig

Kieler
Bucht

Lübeck · Wismar

Schwerin

BERLIN (p167)
Nightclubs, bars and ever changing
exhibits reflect the Zeitgeist in this
modern chameleon of a city

East
Frisian Islands

West
Frisian Islands

Groningen

Bremerhaven · Hamburg

Bremen

Elbe

Amsterdam

The Hague

Rotterdam

THE
NETHERLANDS

Utrecht

PRAGUE (p100)
With glorious Gothic architecture,
Prague's World Heritage–listed Old Town
could be straight out of a fairy tale

Hanover

Potsdam · Berlin

Bruges

Ostend

Antwerp

Ghent · Brussels

Lille

BELGIUM

Eindhoven

Essen · Dortmund

Düsseldorf

Liège · Maastricht

Aachen · Cologne

Charleroi

Bonn

Koblenz

Marburg

Bielefeld

Goslar

Göttingen · Halle

Kassel

Eisenach · Erfurt · Weimar

GERMANY

Magdeburg

Hanover

Leipzig · Naumburg

Meissen

Dresden

Ústí Nad
Labem

Teplice

Rheims

Marne

Seine

LUXEMBOURG

Trier

Luxembourg

Mosel

Mainz · Frankfurt-am-Main

Main

Würzburg

Nuremberg

Chemnitz

Cheb · Karlovy Vary

Plzeň

Prague

Nancy

Baden-
Baden · Stuttgart

Strasbourg

Black Forest

Heidelberg

Regensburg

Klatovy

České Budějovice

Český Krumlov

FRANCE

Dijon

Mulhouse · Freiburg

Basel · Constance

Ulm

Danube

Augsburg

Munich

Passau

Linz

ZÜRICH (p567)
The party never really stops
in Zürich, one of Europe's
hippest cities

Neuchâtel

Lake
Neuchâtel · Bern

Lausanne

Geneva

Lake
Geneva · Sion · Zermatt

Matterhorn
(4478m)

Lake
Constance

Zürich

SWITZERLAND

Interlaken

Jungfraujoch
(3471m)

Lucerne

ALPS

Chur

LIECHTENSTEIN

Vaduz

Innsbruck · Kufstein

Zugspitze
(2963m)

Kitzbühel

Grossglockner
(3797m)

Salzburg · Bad Ischl

Steyr

AUSTRIA

Lienz

Bolzano

Klagenfurt

Mt Triglav
(2864m) · Bled

Bovec

Lyon

Annecy

Mt Blanc
(4807m)

St Étienne

Grenoble

Lake
Maggiore

Lugano · Lake
Como

Como

Milan

Brescia

ITALY

Verona

Po

JUNGFRAUJOCH (p567)
At 3471m this glacier-covered
mountain peak is known as
'the top of Europe'

Turin

Trento

Lake
Garda

Adige

Udine

Gorizia · Predjama

Trieste · Ljubljana

Piran · Koper

SLOVENIA

Venice

Rijeka

Krk

Cres

BLED (p509)
It doesn't get more picturesque
than a blue-green Alpine lake
surrounded by snow-capped peaks

PREDJAMA CASTLE (p517)
Perched in the mouth of a hilltop
cavern, Predjama is a most dramatically
situated fortress indeed

Avignon

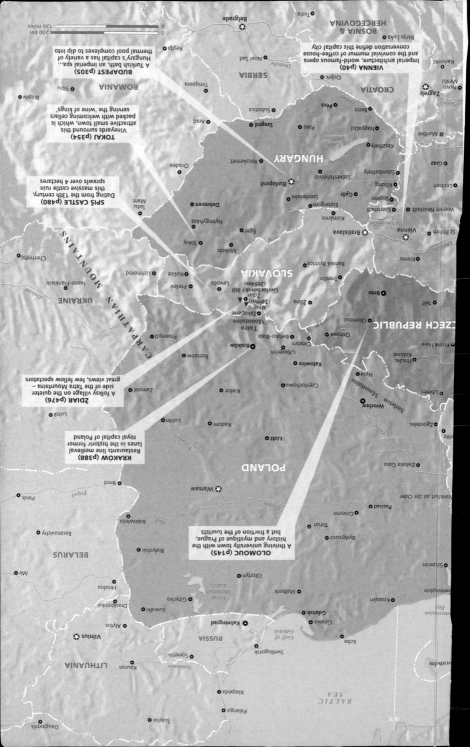

BUDAPEST (p305) A Turkish bath, an imperial spa... Hungary's capital has a variety of thermal pool complexes to dip into

VIENNA (p40) Imperial architecture, world-famous opera and the convivial murmur of coffee-house conversation define this capital city

TOKAJ (p354) Vineyards surround this attractive small town, which is packed with welcoming cellars serving the 'wine of kings'

SPIŠ CASTLE (p480) Dating from the 13th century, this massive castle ruin sprawls over 4 hectares

ŽDIAR (p476) A folksy village on the quieter side of the Tatra Mountains – great views, few fellow spectators

KRAKÓW (p388) Restaurants line the medieval lanes in the historic former royal capital of Poland

OLOMOUC (p145) A thriving university town with the history and mystique of Prague, but a fraction of the tourists

Central Europe Highlights

Central Europe can't be easily labelled. It extends from the Adriatic Sea in the south to the Baltic and North Seas in the north, and contains some of Europe's most iconic sights and evocative cities. Many of the countries here have changed enormously since the fall of the Berlin Wall, but all offer lofty mountain peaks, gut-hugging cuisine and tipples worth a hearty cheer. Following are some top tips and experiences from travellers, Lonely Planet staff and authors. If you come back with your own highlights, we'd love to hear about them.

① THE ALPS, SLOVENIA

More often than not, even serial visitors to Slovenia, like myself, just stop and stare, mesmerised by the sheer beauty of this land. With so much splendour strewn across the country, it's high on to impossible to choose a *stevilka ena* (that's 'number one' to you) absolute favourite top place. OK, OK, it's the Vršič Pass (p514), which stands head and shoulders above the rest, and leads me past Mt Triglav, then down to sunny Primorska province and the bluer-than-blue Soča River in a hair-raising, spine-tingling hour.

Steve Fallon, Lonely Planet Author

BUDAPEST, HUNGARY

We wandered down Castle Hill in Budapest (p305) in search of a sweet afternoon snack, and landed in an outdoor cafe sublimely shaded by massive trees, and overlooking the Danube and the majestic parliament building across the river. Ten minutes later we were all silence and smiles – drinking iced coffees and relishing each bite of our cream-filled pastries.

Jo Potts, Lonely Planet Staff

MARTIN MOOS

2

NA ZDROWIE (CHEERS!), POLAND

Kraków (p388), the jewel of Poland. Also freezing cold. Find a dark pub off ul Floriańska, gather some new Polish friends, order a round of vodka shots and be merry. This will also help solve any colds you've picked up along the way.

PetraJW, Traveller

BRUCE BI

3

KRZYSZTOF DYD

4 CRUSHED BY BEAR, GERMANY

There I was with 100,000 of my new best friends at Munich's Oktoberfest (p213). Despite oodles of beer tents the size of aircraft hangers, we only found table space after being absorbed by a mob of drunken revellers. One was a huge fellow from Hamburg named Bear, who took a sloppy liking to my friend Angela. She wasn't charmed so I did my best to rescue her by diverting Bear's attention. He was in the mood for love and after several hours of nonstop drinking wasn't very discriminating. He sat on my lap, nuzzled my ear and slurred something that may have been 'you're cute'. I looked around in alarm but my friends had vanished.

Ryan Ver Berkmoes, Lonely Planet Author

WAYNE WALTON

5 ŽDIAR, SLOVAKIA

Whether snow is lying quietly on the hillsides or heather is blooming in the fields, there's something so tranquil about Ždiar (p476), a traditional Slovak village snuggled beneath the Tatra Mountains. Is it the hand-painted designs on the log cottages, the fire burning in each of the handful of restaurants, or the nature surrounding you on every side? Yes – all of the above.

Lisa Dunford, Lonely Planet Author

GROSSGLOCKNER HOCHALPENSTRASSE, AUSTRIA

Leaving from Zell am See, which sits at a *mere* 757m, the snaking stretch of road (p83) quickly begins its ascent, taking me past alpine meadows, cascading waterfalls, sheer drops and immense peaks, and flinging me in my tiny rental car around 36 switchbacks. The road peaks at 2577m; I get out of my car and gaze at the breathtaking scene before me, which includes Grossglockner, Austria's highest peak, and then have a quick chat with a crazy (and obviously very fit) Czech cyclist. It feels like a fast and furious drive down the other side to Heiligenblut, where I stop for lunch. And it's then that I notice the burning smell. My brakes...

Neal Bedford, Lonely Planet Author

6

GARETH MCCORMACK

LJUBLJANA, SLOVENIA

I loved the compact nature of Ljubljana (p497) – everything was so easy to reach and accessible. I wandered through its tiny streets, past picturesque squares and hopping cafes. And as I climbed up the hill to the castle I caught an amazing view of the grand Julian Alps, standing tall over the pocket-sized city.

Clifton Wilkinson, Lonely Planet Staff

7

JOHN ELK III

SHOPPING FOR AMBER, POLAND

What I enjoyed most of all was shopping for amber jewellery in Gdańsk (p423). It was great fun scouring the lovely Old Town for the perfect orange earrings or green pendant. The prices were so good – why not buy one more amber brooch?

**Fayette Fox,
Traveller**

8 ## FRIBOURG, SWITZERLAND, OR FREIBURG, GERMANY?

I was taking a train from France to Freiburg (p239), Germany. My friend had made the booking in amateur French. No big deal, I thought, that my ticket said Fribourg rather than Freiburg. Alighting from the train, I sat waiting for my friend. After 20 minutes there was no sign of her, and I decided to give her a call. For some reason I couldn't get her mobile number to work. Eventually I called directory, which advised me to dial +49 for international calls to Germany. 'Oh no,' I assured the woman, 'I'm already in Germany.' 'Oh no,' she informed me, 'You're in Switzerland.' Thankfully, a couple of trains later, I was in the *right* Freiburg, downing a delicious *Hefeweizen* (wheat beer) with banana.

Leonie Starnawski, Lonely Planet Staff

9

10 ## ACROSS THE DANUBE, HUNGARY

I remember looking over the Danube at Visegrád (p326), thinking how remarkable it was that I was gazing at the ancient border of the Roman Empire. Just for a moment, I had an overwhelming sense of all the kingdoms and people who'd come and gone since that distant time in the past.

Tim Richards, Lonely Planet Author

THE ALPINE MICRONATION, LIECHTENSTEIN

I hike up to the castle on the hill, trying to get my head around the fact that the royal family actually lives here! As I wander down the quiet streets of Vaduz (p365), taking in the rocky mountain peaks and breathing in the fresh air, I know this gorgeous, tiny country is much more than just the largest exporter of dentures.

Helene Wanner, Traveller

VARIO IMAGES GMBH & CO.KG / ALAMY

11

THE OTHER EIFFEL, CZECH REPUBLIC

I hopped on the funicular in Prague (p100), zipping up the hill to a wooded and tranquil oasis. The calm on Petřín Hill was a welcome respite after the crowds on the Charles Bridge. Then I spotted…the Eiffel Tower? What? I'm in Prague. How much beer *had* I consumed last night? A few enquiries revealed it was an imitation. Well, hey, I've never been to Paris, so I suppose this is a sneak peek!

Lucy Monie, Lonely Planet Staff

CHRISTER FREDRIKSSON

12

STRALSUND, GERMANY

After being wowed by the red-brick architecture and lively market of Stralsund (p206), I walked off my fresh-off-the-boat seafood sandwich along the Baltic harbour and then ducked into the snazzy aquarium.

Caroline Sieg, Lonely Planet Author

13

IMAGEBROKE

IN THE SHADOW OF THE ASTRONOMER, POLAND

Whenever I arrive in Toruń (p431), I start to relax. This beautiful Gothic city has a great vibe, and just the right balance between sightseeing and chilling. I like to grab a *zapiekanka* (toasted roll topped with mushrooms, cheese and tomato sauce) from the milk bar just off the main square, then saunter past the locals to check out the curious statuary around the square's edge, waving hello to my old friend Copernicus on his plinth. To finish a warm summer's day in one of the fancy beer-garden decks perched on the cobble-stones is perfection itself.

**Brett Atkinson,
Lonely Planet Author**

14

CRAIG PERSHOUSE

JOHN EL

15

CASTLES & BEER, CZECH REPUBLIC

In the pretty West Bohemian town of Loket (p129), all of the Czech Republic's different attractions come together. The town sits improbably on a serpentine bend in the Ohře River, and is crowned by a dramatic castle. It's a good starting point for river adventures or a day hike to the spa scene at nearby Karlovy Vary. And when you come back from tasting the spa town's mineral-laden waters, Loket's Pivovar Sv Florian microbrewery is one of the country's best.

Brett Atkinson, Lonely Planet Author

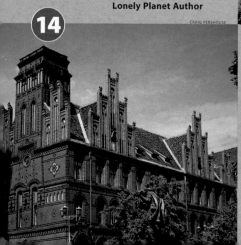

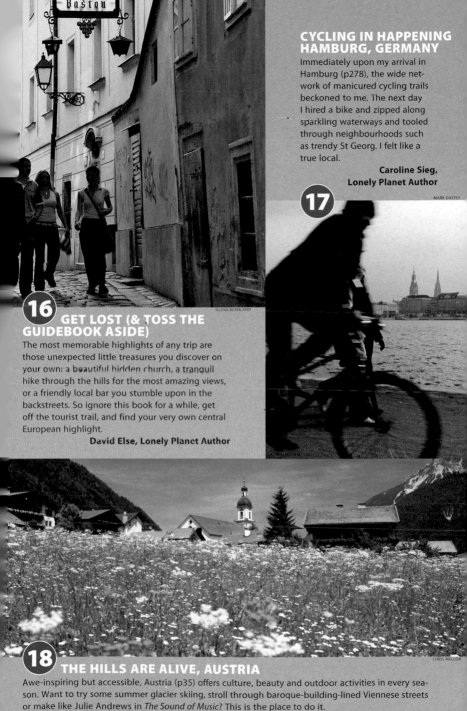

CYCLING IN HAPPENING HAMBURG, GERMANY

Immediately upon my arrival in Hamburg (p278), the wide network of manicured cycling trails beckoned to me. The next day I hired a bike and zipped along sparkling waterways and tooled through neighbourhoods such as trendy St Georg. I felt like a true local.

**Caroline Sieg,
Lonely Planet Author**

17

MARK DAFFEY

16 GLENN BEANLAND

GET LOST (& TOSS THE GUIDEBOOK ASIDE)

The most memorable highlights of any trip are those unexpected little treasures you discover on your own: a beautiful hidden church, a tranquil hike through the hills for the most amazing views, or a friendly local bar you stumble upon in the backstreets. So ignore this book for a while, get off the tourist trail, and find your very own central European highlight.

David Else, Lonely Planet Author

CHRIS MELLOR

18 THE HILLS ARE ALIVE, AUSTRIA

Awe-inspiring but accessible, Austria (p35) offers culture, beauty and outdoor activities in every season. Want to try some summer glacier skiing, stroll through baroque-building-lined Viennese streets or make like Julie Andrews in *The Sound of Music*? This is the place to do it.

Paula Hardy, Lonely Planet Staff

19 DETOURS, CZECH REPUBLIC

The ancient train lumbered its way out of Nuremburg station, heading towards Prague, and we looked at each other, sniffing the train carriage. Musty, stuffy, unpleasant. Find alcohol? Yes. On the way to the restaurant carriage, an announcement mumbled something about construction and a bus. We shrugged it off over a few beers, bought at the lace-curtained bar. A few hours later, we piled into a bus, grateful that we'd bought extra beer. 'We're going to arrive late in Prague', we lamented, thinking about all the things we'd planned to do on our first night. Then the bus pulled away and we rode through wheat-coloured fields, snaking our way through tiny villages, glimpsing farmers walking to the pub and women cycling down unpaved roads. It was gorgeous. The detours are so often the best parts of a trip.

Agnes Biernacki, Traveller

20 FERME MONTAVON, THE JURA, SWITZERLAND

Sleeping above a herd of bell-jangling goats is not as rough as it sounds. In fact, our night spent kipping in the eaves of Ferme Montavon (p553) between bales of hay and spiky straw stacked like sugar cubes was disarmingly romantic. It was far too nippy to stick so much as a little finger out of the sleeping bag, and getting dressed in the morning felt like a race against frostbite. We're talking late October, when the remote Jura hills sit lost in swirling mist until 10am, at which time the autumnal blue sky suddenly breaks through in crystal-clear song.

Nicola Williams, Lonely Planet Author

Contents

Regional Map Contents

Destination Central Europe

The bright lights of Paris, the towering history of London…been there, done that. You're looking for the hidden heart of Europe – the chance to savour both vibrant folk traditions and city street parties, to witness the architectural legacies of fallen dynasties and revel in a diverse range of landscapes. Well, you've come to the right place – central Europe has all this and more.

Cultural treasures are spread across all nine of the central European nations, as attested by the 80-plus Unesco World Heritage–listed sites in the region. Medieval Old Towns, ancient ruins, richly embellished opera houses and castles galore dot the landscape. Some of the world's great composers were born here, as was the oompah band. Lovers of the arts can trace the origins and accomplishments of favourite musicians, writers and painters by visiting their birthplaces, drinking in their haunts and enjoying their output in concert halls, cinemas, bookshops and galleries.

For those seeking pleasures that are more down to earth, the region's natural beauty provides more than enough opportunity for adventure. You can ride the rails up to a Swiss mountain peak, hike the Black Forest or bike past aquamarine glacial lakes in Alpine Austria. Alternatively, you can watch migrant cranes roost on the Hungarian plains, canoe in a Polish lake or climb up sandstone fissures in the Czech Republic. And since central Europe stretches from coast to coast, you might also choose to bask on a Baltic Sea beach in Poland or enjoy freshly caught calamari along the Adriatic in Slovenia.

If you want big-city excitement, you can have that too: beer-loving Munich, mystical Prague, imperial Vienna and design-driven Zürich are all attractions of the region.

In some ways, the territories of today's central Europe had more in common pre–WWI than they do post. The royal house of Habsburg had influence in every country in the region at some point or another (save for Poland), whether through confederation or crown. In 1914, when Habsburg archduke Franz Ferdinand's murder precipitated WWI, the Czech Republic, Slovenia, Slovakia, Hungary and Austria were all part of the Austro-Hungarian empire.

After WWII the rise of nation states and the creation of the Iron Curtain separated central Europe into distinct entities, East and West. Forty-plus years of communist rule left an industrial concrete mark on the easternmost nations, but that period of history has long since gone. (Restoration work on the Berlin Wall art began in mid-2009 – after all, it had been 20 years since the barrier crumbled and artists celebrated.) Though you'll see vestiges of the old East–West divide – environmentally aware tourist infrastructure is more developed in the West, for example – boundaries have blurred. Prices are rapidly equalising, and the hold-outs from the EU are Switzerland and Liechtenstein, not the eastern nations.

In fact, not only have all the eastern central European states joined the EU, they've become part of the reduced border controls implemented under the Schengen Agreement. At the time of writing, Germany, Austria, Slovakia and Slovenia use the euro as their currency, while Poland, the Czech Republic and Hungary are expected to convert within the next few years.

The development of a united Europe has not always gone smoothly here, however. A no-confidence vote by the Czech parliament in 2009 came halfway through that nation's six-month term as EU president and some questioned its fitness to lead the union. But it was the economy that was the hot topic across Europe in 2008–09, as credit crunches, bank rescues and lay-offs hit hard. In Germany, for example, the question of whether to prop up the ailing car manufacturer Opel dominated the political scene in an election year. Even fiscally conservative Switzerland took action, with the central bank buying up foreign currencies to stem the Swiss franc's appreciation against the euro. (The government also agreed it would respond to overseas requests for information in tax-evasion cases, eliminating a smidge of the country's famous banking anonymity.) According to a report by the Economic Intelligence Unit, Poland was the only European country with an economy expected to expand in 2009.

Whether or not collapsing economies fuel xenophobic fires can be debated, but central European nations all have issues with racism to greater or lesser degrees. In 2009 Slovak policemen were caught on tape humiliating four Roma boys who'd allegedly robbed and injured an elderly lady; Amnesty International judged that Austria's judicial system was plagued with racism; and *Der Spiegel* reported that neo-Nazism was on the rise in Germany.

During tough times spectator sports are a great diversion, and central Europe is rife with football fever: Germany hosted the FIFA World Cup in 2006, Austria and Switzerland cohosted Europe 2008, and Poland will be one of the sites of the Europe 2012 tournament. Ice hockey comes close to rivalling football for popularity in several countries in the region, particularly in the Czech Republic and Slovakia; the latter is gearing up to host the IIHF World Championships in 2011. Given the mountainous geography here, it's no surprise that central European nations fair well in winter sports; you can watch the Ski-Jumping World Cup Championships in Slovenia every March.

At least for now, snow is very much on the mind of those that make their living from Alpine tourism. According to a study by the Organisation for Economic Co-Operation and Development (OECD), climate change could affect two-thirds of the ski areas across the Alps by 2050, rendering skiing impossible under 1500m. So it's understandable that the Alpine nations have a particularly strong environmental focus. Recycling and green building practices are already big in Germany, Austria and Liechtenstein, while the Swiss have developed carbon-free ski resorts to offset the environmental impact of their ski-crazy country.

So there's no better time to get to Central Europe than today, really – with cheaper beer and still-abundant winter snow, what more could you want? After all, whether you're wandering among high-meadow wildflowers or along the narrow lanes of a former Venetian port, listening to traditional folk music in a village or operatic falsetto in a city, skiing in Slovakia's High Tatras or Austria's Alps, you're in the heart of the heart of Europe.

Getting Started

With few bureaucratic hurdles to jump in central Europe, you can easily plan for a trip here as much or as little as you like. All of the countries in this book participate in the Schengen Agreement, which reduced intra-European border controls. Of the EU member states (all countries included here except Switzerland and tiny Liechtenstein), only Poland, Hungary and the Czech Republic have not yet converted to the euro.

During blow-out festivals and the summer holidays (from June through to August), some amount of booking ahead may be warranted if you're particular about the places you stay. And plotting out at least a general course can steer you toward money savings (hint: minimise time in Swiss cities and maximise time in rural Slovakia). No matter what you decide, we always recommend leaving some time to wander – life's best adventures are often unexpected.

WHEN TO GO

See Climate Charts (p594) for more information.

Mild weather and less crowds make May (spring flowers) and September (new wine) ideal months to visit the countries of central Europe. July and August are the hottest months, and the busiest in terms of tourists, but they offer the fullest range of activities, events and services available. Cultural festivals take place year-round, so you'll never lack for something to do. In general, prices climb during summer (at least from June through to August) and at Christmas and Easter times. By travelling outside of peak seasons, you may snag lodging bargains, but some attractions in the easternmost countries close between October and April.

If skiing is your thing, the wintry months from December to April are for you – be it atop the continent's most dramatic peaks (Switzerland) or at some of its most affordable ski resorts (Slovenia and Slovakia). Note that the highest trails may not open for hiking until June or July.

COSTS & MONEY

This stretch of the continent may indeed leave you scratching your head over the vagaries of capitalism – just how can the same item differ in price so much over a few hundred kilometres? *Vive la difference,* indeed! That said, although it was once a truism that Eastern European countries were cheaper than those in the west of the continent, the rise of the EU has certainly challenged this assertion. Lodging prices in Bratislava, Slovakia, for example, have climbed close to the levels of neighbouring Vienna (without offering a commensurate setting).

A bare-bones day of hostels and store-bought food can usually be had for €45 per person. To allow for stays in medium-range accommodation, restaurant-cooked meals and regular visits to museums and bars, plan on spending from €100 per day in less-expensive destinations to a *minimum* of €150 per day elsewhere when travelling solo. (Note that two or more people sharing a hotel room will cut these costs.) Accommodation is likely to make up the bulk of your daily expenditure but some excursions and travel fares (most noticeably in Switzerland) can munch through a daily budget in a trice. Families and friends travelling together should look into group train passes (see p615). Shopping at local markets and cooking in self-catering apartments (which often have multiple beds) is another great way to save money if travelling en masse.

ATMs are easy to find in towns (not in villages) throughout most of the region. The most popular currencies are the euro, US dollar and British pound; it's possible to exchange other currencies in the capitals and large cities. Credit cards (Visa and MasterCard, mostly) are widely accepted, although you won't be able to solely rely on these in rural parts of the region's eastern countries. Travellers cheques are also accepted across the region, though they are a dying breed.

TRAVELLING RESPONSIBLY

Central Europe contains vast areas of pristine Alpine landscape, thick forests and delicate ecosystems worth protecting. In general, the countries in the western part of the region have well-established green initiatives and ecological protections. According to the 2008 Environmental Performance Index, Switzerland tops the global list of countries ranked by environmental performance, with its advanced and dense railway system, carbon-free ski resorts and 169 marked routes for hikers and cyclists. Germany and Austria are not far behind in their own green initiatives. Further east, while there is a deep bond felt with nature, systemic eco-enterprise has only just begun.

To find long- and short-term volunteer opportunities in Europe, check in at www.volunteerabroad.com.

Getting There & Away

Though low cost carriers continue to proliferate in central Europe, so do the associated carbon gasses. All but the furthest outposts of the region are well connected by rail to the UK, Western Europe and beyond. Intercontinental travellers will have a tougher time of getting there green. If you opt for short air hops, consider offsetting your carbon emissions through websites such as www.climatecare.org and www.carbonneutral.com.

Slow Travel

If you have time, consider taking it slooooooow. The countries in this book all have marked cycling trails. Not only will you be going green by cycling across Europe, you get to connect with local communities in a way that's impossible on a fly-by. Follow the **Eurovelo 6** (www.eurovelo6.org) track and you could make your way through parts of Switzerland, Germany, Austria, Slovakia and Hungary. **Eurovelo 9** (www.eurovelo.org), the Amber Route, starts at the Black Sea in Gdańsk, Poland, and wends it's way through the Czech Republic, Austria and Slovenia before making its way to the Adriatic. For more on bike tours, see p592. Too fast for you? Hike instead of bike. The E3 European walking route traverses Germany, the Czech Republic, Poland, Slovakia and Hungary.

DON'T LEAVE HOME WITHOUT...

You can buy almost anything in the countries of central Europe that you might have left at home, but if you require specific medicines, it's best to stock up on these before your departure. Consider notifying your bank and your credit card companies to expect charges and withdrawals from abroad. Most visitors will be able to travel visa-free for 90 days, but if you're from a far remote land, double check (see p601). Other things to think about bringing:

- A Swiss Army knife with bottle opener/cork screw (they're pricey in-country!).
- Lonely Planet's *Central European Phrasebook* – so you don't get an offal surprise when ordering from a menu.
- Flip-flops and a towel – de rigueur at thermal baths and pools regionwide (they also come in handy at hostels).
- Herbal teas or instant decaf; in-room hot-pot options are usually highly caffeinated.

SUSTAINABLE SLEEPS

■ **L'Aubier, Val de Travers, Switzerland** The glowing white-and-natural rooms at this small hotel look out on the associated organic farm in a green mountain valley. Try the site-made carrot cheese for a treat; see p551.

■ **Naturfreundehaus, Grindelwald, Switzerland** Attend environmental awareness seminars and visit the owners' pet trout at the 'House of Nature' chalet; see p565.

■ **Lint Hotel, Cologne, Germany** Rooftop solar collectors provide heat and hot water at this 18-room lodging in the centre of Cologne's Old Town pedestrian district; see p265.

■ **Die Fabrik, Berlin, Germany** An old factory has been recycled into a partially solar-powered hostel-like hotel with no TVs or phones in the room to waste resources; see p179.

■ **Aquacity, Poprad, Slovakia** This sprawling geothermal- and solar-run waterpark and its hotels and apartments garnered recognition as a World's Leading Green Resort in 2008 from the World Travel Awards; see p477.

Accommodation & Food

More and more lodgings these days use energy-efficient lighting and offer not to wash your sheets daily (whether out of activism or economic interest). For those using more stringent green criteria, once again there is a bit of a geographic divide. Ecohotels and resorts are more common in Switzerland, Germany and Austria. Wherever you travel, guest houses and small inns are character-filled options, and are usually more likely to be locally owned than big chain hotels. Camping is another viable alternative. In Germany, look out for ecologically responsible camping grounds sporting the Green Leaf award from the Allgemeiner Deutscher Automobil-Club (ADAC) motoring association.

Shopping at local vegetable and fruit markets also helps support the community, and produce is primarily organic. Restaurants serving locally sourced and organic meals are not uncommon in the westernmost countries of the region – heck, you can even have organic meat in your schnitzel at some places. Elsewhere, you're most likely to find wholefoods served at vegetarian and vegan restaurants, which are more prevalent in the capital cities in the easternmost countries.

> Train is the only way to travel between major cities in environmentally friendly Austria; they don't want no stinkin' carbon-emitting long-distance buses.

Responsible Travel Organisations

Backroads (www.backroads.com) Environmentally committed tour company that organises biking, hiking, multisport, and single and multicountry trips (cycle the Czech Republic and Austria or walk your way through Hungary, Poland and Slovakia etc).

Bio-Hotels (www.biohotels.info) Started in Austria, this association of hotels provides wholefoods and organic-oriented options; it now has members across central Europe.

Connected Traveler (http://connectedtraveler.com) Educates travellers on how to discern the best ecotourism options and standards. Lists guides in Europe.

Europcar (www.europcar.com) Has one of the lowest emissions car-hire fleets in the world. They have Smart Cars, hybrids, and ethanol-powered autos for hire, and work with a carbon-offsetting partner.

European Centre for Eco Agro Tourism (www.eceat.org) A network of more than 1300 small-scale lodges and farms that provide rural, ecofriendly lodging. Also certifies environmentally friendly establishments throughout Europe.

International Ecotourism Society (www.ecotourism.org) Provides training for emerging ecotourism businesses, lists eco-outfitters and offers discount trips available by auction.

Linblad Expeditions (www.expeditions.com) Tour company that encourages travel philanthropy, supports local microbusinesses and sources food locally. One itinerary starts in Prague and then cruises the Danube through Germany, Austria, Slovakia and Hungary.

> Learn how you can live – and travel – more responsibly at the World Wildlife Federation's site www.panda.org/how _you_can_help/

Sustainable Travel International (www.sustainabletravelinternational.org) Maintains an eco-directory of sustainable tour operators, runs an environmental certification program and facilitates carbon offsetting and other environmental donation programs.

World Wide Opportunities on Organic Farms (www.wwoof.org) In return for your volunteer labour you can learn organic ways while you stay down on the farm in Austria, Germany, Switzerland and the Czech Republic.

TRAVEL LITERATURE

- *Alpine Points of View: A Collection of Images of the Alps* (2004), by Kev Reynolds, entices armchair travellers with engaging short text and stunning photos.
- *Routledge Companion to Central and Eastern Europe since 1919* (2008), by Adrian Webb, should help clear the cobwebs of confusion surrounding recent history.
- *Between Past and Future: The Roma of Central and Eastern Europe* (2002), by Will Guy, comprises essays examining the fate, and speculating on the future of, one of Europe's most maligned and fascinating ethnic groups.
- *Kaffeehaus* (2002), by Rick Rodgers, is a delightful look at Prague, Vienna and Budapest — from inside their splendid coffee shops. Recipes galore included.
- *New Europe* (2007), by Michael Palin, details the BBC author's journey through former communist countries for his TV travel series.
- *Historical Atlas of Central Europe* (2002), by Robert Magocsi, visually illustrates how boundaries in the region have shifted, from tribal origins to modern times.
- *Court, Cloister & City: The Art and Culture of Central Europe, 1450–1800* (1997), by Thomas Kaufmann, provides a multilayered context for all those museums, castles and monasteries.
- *National Geographic Jewish Heritage Travel: A Guide to Eastern Europe* (2007), by Ruth Ellen Gruber, is the perfect companion piece for anyone travelling in the area in search of lost and remaining Jewish culture.

A satirical travel guide and deft Lonely Planet send-up, *Molvania: A Land Untouched by Modern Dentistry* (by Santo Cilauro et al) creates a fictitious land in Europe that's the 'next big thing'.

INTERNET RESOURCES

Central Europe Online (www.centraleurope.com) Subscription site with the region's news headlines, updated daily.

Lonely Planet (www.lonelyplanet.com) Book buying, hotel booking and the Thorn Tree travellers forum for shared traveller's tips.

Central Europe Experience (www.gotocentraleurope.com) Regional introduction and travel specifics for Germany, Czech Republic, Poland, Slovakia, Hungary and Austria.

Gemut.com (www.gemut.com) Travel features on Austria, Germany and Switzerland.

In Your Pocket (www.inyourpocket.com) A snappily written, up-to-date compendium of events and listings in Germany, Poland, Czech Republic, Hungary and Slovenia, among others.

Real Beer (www.realbeer.com/edu/central_europe) Czech and German beer news dominates the central European page.

The acclaimed *Stalin's Nose* (1992), by Rory MacLean, is the surreal and darkly funny tale of the author's travels through Germany, Czechoslovakia, Hungary and Poland mere weeks after the toppling of the Berlin Wall.

MUST-SEE MOVIES

- *Goodbye Lenin* (2003) In this crowd-pleasing comedy set in East Berlin, a young woman falls into a coma just before the onslaught of capitalism. When she wakes up, her family shields her from the shock and hilariously goes about restoring the old communist ways, pretending the Wall never fell.
- *The Sound of Music* (1965) Sure, you've seen it 14 times already, but you need to practise your lines before prancing around Salzburg's

AN ENVIRONMENTALLY FRIENDLY WAY TO TRAVEL

Long a passionate advocate for the environment, Gabor Oban started his career as a science and environmental studies teacher before deciding to create and become managing director of **Ecotours Ltd** (www.ecotours.hu) in the late 1990s. The tour company has since branched out from his home country of Hungary to offer eco-oriented nature and adventure itineraries in central and Eastern Europe, and the Americas.

Have you seen a rise in environmentally aware travel recently in central Europe? Definitely, ecotourism is stronger year by year in this region. Before 1989 hardly any ecotourists dared to venture to the eastern part of Europe. After political changes the most curious and adventurous started to come, first in relatively small numbers. They spread the word. In the past five years there are more and more ecotour operators and also young NGOs, clubs and associations who organise different activities.

What types of experiences are most sought-after? Visitors come to the region mainly for the following ecotourism activities: bird-watching, wildflower/botanical tours, large mammal-watching tours (bear, red deer, elk, wolf, bison); and bat tours are becoming more and more popular. Butterfly and dragonfly tours are relatively new, but quickly became favourites. However there are regional differences in the countries we work in: the Czech Republic, Slovakia and Poland are very strong in hiking, rock climbing and rafting possibilities, as well as mountain birding and wildlife watching. Besides the above activities, the Mediterranean Sea and caving are strong magnets in Slovenia. Austria has excellent biking routes and well-organised kayaking and canoeing. Hungary additionally offers really great birding and butterfly watching, plus botany tours with special Pannonian endemic flora and a strong horse riding tradition.

What advice do you have for readers who want to travel more responsibly?
Stay and eat at local, family-owned accommodations and restaurants, preferably those who care about the local environment; reuse and recycle; consume local, natural products and bio-food whenever possible; and buy folklore and souvenir items from local people, not at supermarkets. Also support ecotourism operators who can ensure all the above points, plus are involved in local environmental projects and spend part of their profit on habitat and species protection.

Schloss Mirabell gardens. C'mon, all together now: 'Doe, a deer, a female deer…'

- *Kafka* (1991) Not much to do with the real Kafka, but Prague and its castle never looked so beautiful in black-and-white surrealism. Jeremy Irons plays the role of an insurance clerk with a secret passion for writing. He seeks to uncover a dastardly plot in the bowels of the castle.
- *Latcho Drom* (1993) Tony Gatlif's hauntingly beautiful musical travelogue follows the historical migration of Roma culture across modern-day Eastern and central Europe. Eschewing dialogue, subjects sing and dance their story.
- *Schindler's List* (1993) Steven Spielberg's film is considered one of the greatest of all time for the skilful and uncontrived way it tells the tale of one man who saved hundreds of Jews from certain death. Considered to be *the* film made about the Holocaust.
- *The Pianist* (2002) Your trip to Poland won't be the same after this stirring film featuring Oscar-winner Adrian Brody as the last pianist to play live on Polish radio before the Nazis arrive in the Warsaw ghetto. This touching masterpiece by Roman Polański doesn't glorify its protagonist as a hero; he is but a lucky and wilful survivor.
- *Heidi* (1968) Follow cloyingly sweet Heidi on her quest to be reunited with her beloved grandfather in this, the most popular version of the pigtailed legend. You'll want to re-enact scenes from this classic groaner about the poor orphan while skipping though the Swiss Alps: 'Grandpa – wherefore art thou?'
- *The Third Man* (1939) Trying to find some remnants of post-WWII Vienna will become an obsession after this great film noir by Carol

Wildflower fanatics should scope out which Alpine blooms sprout when at www.alpine flowers.net.

Reed. Joseph Cotton is an alcoholic author of pulp novels who falls into the pit of intrigue and suspicion that the shattered city has become. It begins with the line, 'I knew the old Vienna, before the war…'

■ *Zentropa* (1991) Lars von Trier's mesmerising film captures the engulfing creepiness in the air in post-WWII Germany. The action takes place in the subconscious, or perhaps in a dream, as we follow Jean-Marc Barr as a second-generation German-American who arrives in war-torn Germany and finds himself over his head in unfathomable intrigue.

■ *Kráska v nesnázich* (Beauty in Trouble; 2006) This delightful and insightful drama follows a Czech family as three generations try to navigate the tumultuous transition from communism. Their troubled existence is disrupted when they cross paths with a kind-hearted and wealthy émigré who has returned to settle his dead mother's estate.

Endangered reptiles were relocated to new habitats before construction of the environmentally aware Brandenburg International Airport was begun outside Berlin.

Events Calendar

Attending a festival can be a great way to go local: mingle with residents, experience the culture, eat local foods and hear some great music. Crowd-a-phobes may want to steer clear, though! Below we've listed some of the region's top picks; look for more events in each country section.

FEBRUARY

KURENTOVANJE   Tue before Lent
This parade (p525), including its horned-and-feathered, sheepskin-covered Carnival characters with painted masks, highlights the 10-day celebration leading up to Shrove Tuesday in Ptuj, Slovenia.

KARNEVAL/FASCHING   Tue before Lent
The pre-Lenten season is celebrated in Germany along the Rhine and in the Black Forest and Munich (p291).

MARCH–APRIL

BUDAPEST SPRING FESTIVAL   Mar
Hungary's capital welcomes spring with a cornucopia of popular opera, classical music and ballet, performed both in gilt concert halls and on open-air stages (p314).

EASTER FESTIVAL OF SACRED MUSIC   2 weeks leading up to Easter
Petrov Cathedral serves as the blessed background for six Lenten concerts held in Brno, Czech Republic (p143).

MAY

PRAGUE SPRING   mid-May–early Jun
Czech composer Bedřich Smetana inspired this Prague classical-music festival (p111). It kicks off with a parade from Smetana's grave to the performance hall where his opera *Má vlast* is staged.

VIENNA FESTIVAL   mid-May–mid-Jun
Opera plays a key role in the wide-ranging program of arts that is held in Vienna, Austria, every summer (p49).

DRUGA GODBA   late May-early Jun
Ljubljana, Slovenia, hosts a festival of alternative and world music (p503) at a sprawling monastic complex that dates back to the 13th century.

KHAMORO   last week in May
Traditional and contemporary music, and 'Gypsy jazz' performances are part of this festival celebrating Roma culture (p111) in Prague.

JUNE

WROCŁAW NON STOP   Jun-Jul
Quirky art installations, alternative movies, music, theatre and dance are all part of this month-long festival (p415) in Wrocław, Poland.

ROCK OTOČEC   late Jun or early Jul
Slovenia's biggest open-air concert (p527) rocks for three days each summer in Novo Mesto.

VÝCHODNÁ FOLKLORE FESTIVAL   late Jun or early Jul
Folk dancers and musicians from across Europe perform at Východná and several other small towns in eastern Slovakia, for one weekend each July (p490).

CHRISTOPHER STREET DAY   last weekend in Jun
Begun in 1978, this Berlin celebration (p291) is one of the oldest gay and lesbian festivals in the world.

BRATISLAVA CULTURAL SUMMER FESTIVAL   Jun-Sep
More a series of concerts and performances than a true festival. Slovakia's capital has its cultural dance card filled all summer long (p461).

JULY

JEWISH CULTURE FESTIVAL   1st week in Jul
Scholarly discussions, concerts, films, theatre performances, art and memorial sightseeing are all part of the week-long celebration of Jewish culture (p394) in Kraków, Poland.

KARLOVY VARY INTERNATIONAL FILM FESTIVAL early Jul
International celebrities often appear at this Czech Republic festival (p126), which screens more than 200 films each year.

MONTREUX JAZZ FESTIVAL early–mid-Jul
A distinct air of glamour surrounds this famously fabulous Swiss festival (p549), during which the world's biggest names in the jazz scene play to rapt audiences for two weeks.

BAŽANT POHODA mid-Jul
Rock, pop, alternative, hip hop, techno, world music – for one weekend you can hear it all in Trenčín, at Slovakia's open-air music festival (p466).

WARSAW SUMMER JAZZ DAYS 3 weeks in Jul
This summer concert series (p381) attracts international artists such as Wynton Marsalis and Natalie Cole, as well as Polish performers.

LJUBLJANA FESTIVAL Jul-Aug
Slovenia's top cultural event (p503) includes music, dance and theatre performances in and around the city's historic sights.

SALZBURG FESTIVAL late Jul-Aug
Some 250,000 people crowd into the quaint city of Salzburg, Austria, for this world-renowned classical music and theatre festival (p68), which began in 1920.

AUGUST

ZÜRICH STREET PARADE early Aug
Love mobiles cruise along the street while about a million ravers and revellers lap up the fun in a giant Swiss celebration of life, love and techno music (p570).

SZIGET MUSIC FESTIVAL mid-Aug
The week-long outdoor international-music bash (p314), complete with camping, on Óbuda Shipbuilding Island in Budapest features world music (including Romani), rock, ska, indie and hip hop – pretty much a little of everything.

DEBRECEN FLOWER FESTIVAL mid-Aug
Flower-clad floats parade through town as part of a week-long street fair with international music and food in eastern Hungary (p355).

ST DOMINIC'S FAIR 3 weeks in Aug
Craftspeople and artists exhibit their wares while orchestras, street performers and cabarets round out the party atmosphere in Gdańsk, Poland (p426).

SEPTEMBER–OCTOBER

ARS ELECTRONICA FESTIVAL early Sep
Science and art collide in a very cool and techie way during this futuristic, five-day festival (p59) in Linz, Austria.

COWS' BALL mid-Sep
A zany weekend of folk dance, music, eating and drinking marks the return of the cows from high pastures to the valleys in Bohinj, Slovenia (p513).

OKTOBERFEST mid-Sep–early Oct
What might just be the biggest public festival in the world: some six million people guzzle 5 million litres of beer and 400,000 sausages each year in Munich, Germany (p213). Music and madness abound.

NOVEMBER–DECEMBER

CHRISTMAS MARKETS late Nov-Dec
Winter Christmas Markets are held across central Europe. The most famous are in Vienna (p49) and Nuremberg (p223), Germany, but just about every Old Town has at least a small crafts fair. Drink mulled wine and find a unique (or kitschy) present for that special someone.

Itineraries
CLASSIC ROUTES

A CAPITAL TOUR
Two Weeks / Berlin to Bern

Spend the first few days of your whirlwind tour (two to three days per capital) in the dynamic, delightfully idiosyncratic party city of **Berlin** (p167), the capital of reunited Germany. Then ride the rails to sprawling **Warsaw** (p375); its reconstructed Old Town first became the capital of the Commonwealth of Poland and Lithuania in the mid-16th century. After a few days, travel south to view mystical architectural beauty (not to mention savour great beer) in **Prague** (p100), the Czech seat of power. The imperial opulence of the long-reigning Habsburg Empire is still evident in Austria's capital, **Vienna** (p40). But don't satiate yourself on coffeehouse culture here, because awaiting you are the cafes of Hungary's capital, **Budapest** (p305, where modern and momentous buildings sit side by side. If you have time, detour to **Ljubljana** (p497) in Slovenia and tiny **Vaduz** (p365) in Liechtenstein; otherwise World Heritage–listed **Bern** (p555), the Swiss capital fought over by Holy Roman and Habsburg Empires alike, is your next (and final) stop. It's so beautiful, it's no wonder everyone wanted a piece of it.

> This 3000km tour will introduce you to the region's contemporary urban life and at the same time give you a feel for its grand history.

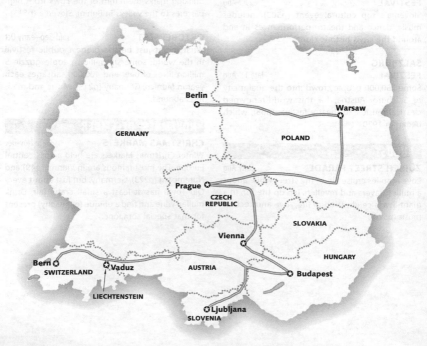

THE GREEN DANUBE   Two Weeks / Regensburg to Budapest

Build on Johann Strauss' classical attempt to capture the mood of the central European terrain by travelling green (instead of blue) in a slow-travel exploration of this wide and wonderful watercourse. Begin your trip with a riverview meal in Germany's **Regensburg** (p224), a city replete with historic constructions, including a Gothic church hewn from limestone. You'll have to bike to Passau, Austria (OK, there are trains, too), where you can board a boat to **Linz** (p58). Visit its stunning riverside art gallery riverside before cruising on to **Melk** (p57), which is dominated by an intimidating Benedictine monastery. The most beautiful castle- and vineyard-crowded river section, the **Danube Valley** (p57), begins here and stretches on to **Krems an der Donau** (p57), which has a pretty cobblestone centre. Meandering on, **Vienna** (p40) is your next port of call. Take a break to tour the imperial city and maybe have a splash in the Alte Danube before boating on to the Slovakian capital of **Bratislava** (p456), where on one side of the river there's some strikingly ugly communist real estate, while on the other there's the rabbit-warren Old Town and the city's ancient castle. Follow the Danube east as it marks out the border between Slovakia and Hungary before sweeping south in the grand arc called the **Danube Bend** (p322), where there's prime birdwatching. At **Esztergom** (p327) you can gaze up at the awesome walled basilica high above. From here you and the Danube flow south to **Budapest** (p305). Renting a bike and tootling around the park on Margaret Island, midriver, seems a fitting end to your Danube adventure.

Go with the flow and follow the course of the Danube as it surges 770km from the south of Germany through Austria and Slovakia to Hungary. Medieval townships, thriving modern cities and diverse landscapes compete for your attention along the way.

WORLD HERITAGE SIGHTS

Three Weeks / Bellinzona to Białowieża National Park

Unesco's World Heritage list contains more than 80 of central Europe's cultural and natural gems, and a sampling takes you to all the region's states but one (alas, little Liechtenstein has yet to garner recognition). Start in Switzerland at the lovely trio of lakefront castles in **Bellinzona** (p577), located at the conversion of several valleys. When you've moved on to Germany, you can compare these with the timber-and-stone **Wartburg** (p197) in Eisenach, where composer Johann Sebastian Bach was born. You'll want to get to Potsdam early, since daily tickets to see its celebrated rococo palace, **Schloss Sanssouci** (p184), often sell out. Pressing on, the medieval townscape of **Kutná Hora** (p121), outside Prague, awaits. Silver ore mined here was minted into the hard currency for central Europe in the 14th century. To the south in Austria, Salzburg's **historic centre** (p64) has more baroque architecture than entire countries do – of course it made the list. The Unesco roll-call continues when you arrive in Slovenia at the **Škocjan Caves** (p517), where you cross an unimaginably deep chasm by footbridge. You'll likely have to pass through Vienna to get to Győr and the incredible collection of ancient texts at **Pannonhalma Abbey** (p330). Continue your medieval history lesson in **Bardejov** (p487), Slovakia's well-preserved Gothic-Renaissance town with 15th-century walls. Traverse the Tatra Mountains to get to the eight listed sites around **Kraków** (p388). The Old Town and the salt-sculpture-filled Wieliczka Salt Mines are interesting, but the Auschwitz and Birkenau concentration camps are the most chilling. Your last stop? The region's farthest eastern reaches, at **Białowieża National Park** (p387). The major drawcard is the magnificent European bison, once extinct outside zoos, which has been successfully reintroduced here.

Soaring mountains, plunging caves, medieval towns, ancient fortresses, national parks – what don't you see in the course of this 3900km tour of central Europe's World Heritage sites? Consider this Unesco's best of the best.

ROADS LESS TRAVELLED

EASTWARD BOUND
One Month / Leipzig to Piran

Avoid the tourist hordes by taking this tour into lovely, little-populated areas in the eastern stretches of several countries. Start in **Leipzig** (p192) and find out why Bach, Wagner and Goethe all lived here. Make a brief stop in the reconstructed baroque city of **Dresden** (p186) before slipping into the Czech Republic, where you can sample contemporary Moravian life without the crowds in the university town of **Brno** (p140). From here, travel east to **Olomouc** (p145), a small town that has an astronomical clock and architecture on par with Prague's. And if you like medieval construction, you'll love **Kraków** (p388), nearby in Poland. From here catch an overnight train north to the lively Baltic Sea town of **Gdańsk** (p423) and the beaches beyond. You'll have to backtrack through Kraków before spending several days enjoying nature (and reasonable prices) in **Zakopane** (p406) and across the Slovakian border in **Ždiar** (p476), both in the in Tatra Mountains. Stopping at every footpath cafe along the Old Town streets will keep you busy for a day or two once you've moved on to **Bratislava** (p456). If you're lucky, a street fair will be going on in **Kecskemét** (p346), where you can admire the Secessionist architecture and eat apricot jam. You'll need to transfer in Budapest if you're taking the trip down to pleasant little **Ljubljana** (p497). Though Slovenia's green-space-filled capital is still relatively undiscovered (and you now know the difference between Slovenia and Slovakia), your real goal is the Adriatic shore. Your journey ends in the romantic port of **Piran** (p520), dining on fresh seafood and wandering Venetian alleyways.

This 2900km-long, eastern-oriented trip offers less glitz, but fewer tourist groups to contend with. Small-town surprises, interesting architecture and lively port towns characterise this road less travelled.

TAILORED TRIPS

CASTLE SPOTTING

Anyone harbouring a fortress fetish will love central Europe, where a mixture of monarchic egotism and a centuries-old siege mentality has resulted in an abundance of impressive – if not downright intimidating – castle architecture. Start big, with the magnificent 1100-year-old bulk of **Prague Castle** (p108). Once you've finished marvelling at St Vitus Cathedral and strolling down Golden Lane, check out the stunning confines of **Wawel Castle** (p389) in Poland's capital, Kraków, and the World Heritage–listed **Wartburg** (p197) in Eisenach, Germany. For a more whimsical experience, have a look at the Bavarian follies of **Neuschwanstein** (p226) and **Hohenschwangau** (p226), near the town of Füssen. In Slovenia, search no further than the oh-so-picturesque clifftop **Bled Castle** (p510). **Eger Castle** (p351) offers fine views of the surrounding Hungarian countryside, while a similarly grand vista is offered from **Schloss Vaduz** (p365) in Liechtenstein. Montreux's lovely **Château de Chillon** (p549) and Salzburg's **Festung Hohensalzburg** (p64) are completely lit up at night. Follow the torchlight parade during summertime night tours, complete with medieval-costumed guides, at **Trenčín Castle** (p465) in western Slovakia, or attend the festival of ghouls and ghosts at the fairy-tale-like **Bojnice Castle** (p468), further east.

LIQUID DELIGHTS

A sipping (or slurping) tour of the region doesn't have to mean the continuous elimination of brain cells and a throbbing head each morning. Conducted with a sense of moderation and an awareness of the consequences of overindulgence, a tipple tour of central Europe will instead initiate you into some memorable local social customs. *Pivo* (beer) is the mother of all drinks in the Czech Republic. Pay your respects to this fine fluid by visiting **Plzeň** (p130), the birthplace of pilsner. For another beery treat, visit Munich at the end of September to chug your way through **Oktoberfest** (p213). Germany's **Moselle Valley** (p244) makes a different but just as pleasing impression on the palate with its trademark wines. In Hungary you can acquire a taste for Bull's Blood, the medium-bodied red table wine produced in **Eger** (p351), or for the sweet dessert white produced **Tokaj** (p354). Meanwhile, a trip to the Slovenian plateau of **Karst** (p516) will leave your lips stained ruby with Teran wine. Up the alcoholic ante in Austria's lovely **Mayrhofen** (p80) with a sip of schnapps. After the lifting of a 100-year-old embargo, the potent drink absinthe is now being distilled in **Val de Travers** (p550), Switzerland. The stand-out drop in **Poland** (p369) is vodka – sample it countrywide.

NATURAL HIGHS

Central Europe's beautiful countryside accommodates numerous exhilarating activities, from hiking under forest canopies and paddling slowly down wide rivers to snowboarding down steep, powdery slopes. Hikers can stride through **Bohemian Switzerland National Park** (p125) in the Czech Republic or follow challenging ladder-assisted trails up waterfall-filled gorges in **Slovenský raj National Park** (p482). Speaking of climbing, those who love hauling themselves up sheer rock faces should head for the **Adršpach-Teplice Rocks** (p139) in the Czech Republic, while mountaineers should try their hands at scaling the **Bavarian Alps** (p226) in Germany. Water sports in the region include kayaking around the glacier-gouged **Great Masurian Lakes** (p439) in Poland, and swimming at Hungary's **Lake Balaton** (p335), one of Europe's largest lakes – when it freezes over in winter, skating becomes the activity of choice. Cyclists can spin their wheels around Germany's **Rügen Island** (p208). The more adventurous can try canyoning or mountain biking at **Bovec** (p515) in Slovenia, or skydiving or night sledding at **Interlaken** (p563) in Switzerland. Skiing and snowboarding is offered at **Stubai Glacier** (p77) near Innsbruck, Austria, but life can't go downhill any faster than it does in Switzerland's **Jungfrau Region** (p564) or in the shadow of the Matterhorn at **Zermatt** (p553). Of course, it's cheaper to shoosh the slopes in Slovakia's **High Tatras** (p474).

A HISTORY LESSON

Transport yourself back in time to significant events and periods in recent central European history by tackling the following history-soaked itinerary. To most visitors **Bad Ischl** (p72) is simply a relaxing spa resort in Austria's Lake District, but it was here in 1914 that WWI was declared by a holidaying emperor. Another place with a strong WWI connection is **Kobarid** (p515), a town that bore witness to the fierce fighting in Slovenia's Soča Valley. WWII reached its nadir at **Terezín** (p123), a concentration camp in the Czech Republic where 35,000 people died, most of them Jews. A less grim historical episode can be reimagined in Bern's **Einstein Museum** (p556), where a guy by the name of Albert decided that some things are relative. In the outer Kraków suburb of **Nowa Huta** (p394) you can get a glimpse of a communist-era version of paradise, and in **Malá Fatra National Park** (p468) you can learn all about Slovakia's 18th-century version of Robin Hood, Juraj Jánošík. The most recent momentous event in the region's history can be invoked by tracing the ruins of the notorious **Berlin Wall** (p174).

Austria

Julie Andrews lied – the hills weren't alive with music. If she'd taken a few minutes from twirling around she'd have noticed that she was in the heart of alpine country, a land where tall, snowy *mountains* dominate and hills are passé. And honestly, there isn't much singing going on in the mountains and valleys anyway; that's left to Austria's westerly neighbour. Instead, this is a land of outdoor pursuits – whether you're into gentle walks, strenuous hikes, free-wheel pedalling, challenging mountain-biking, testing rock-climbing, downhill skiing, fearless snowboarding, or wet 'n' wild rafting, you'll find it here.

Venture into the cobbled backstreets of Vienna and Salzburg – two cities with more baroque architecture than some countries – and it's a different matter altogether. The sweet sounds of classical music and opera waft from open windows, and quality classical concerts are daily occurrences. The cultural extravaganza offered by the two cities is legendary, extending to their cakes, coffee houses, confectionary shops, castles, and, in Vienna's case, clubbing.

Then there's Austria's less well known drawcards. Graz, a student town with drive and energy, hides contemporary architectural gems, while Innsbruck, a city with an intact medieval centre, proudly sits among towering, alpine ranges. Then there's the lakes and peaks of the Salzkammergut, meadows and mountains of Vorarlberg, and sunshine and wine of the Wachau.

We shouldn't be so hard on Julie though; after all, she turned the spotlight on a country that assuredly deserves more attention – one that should be on anyone's European itinerary.

FAST FACTS

- **Area** 83,855 sq km
- **Capital** Vienna
- **Currency** euro (€); US$1 = €0.73; UK£1 = €1.06; A$1 = €0.50; ¥100 = €0.76; NZ$1 = €0.41
- **Famous for** apple strudel, Wiener schnitzel, Adolf Hitler, Arnold Schwarzenegger, Freud, Mozart, *The Sound of Music*
- **Official language** German (Slovene, Croat and Hungarian are also official languages in some southern states)
- **Phrases** *Grüss Gott* (hello); S*ervus* (hello and goodbye); *Ba Ba* (bye bye)
- **Population** 8.3 million
- **Telephone codes** country code ☎ 43; international access code ☎ 00
- **Visas** not required for stays up to three months for US, Canadian, Australian or New Zealand citizens; no time limit for European Union and Swiss nationals; see p89

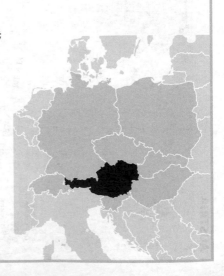

AUSTRIA

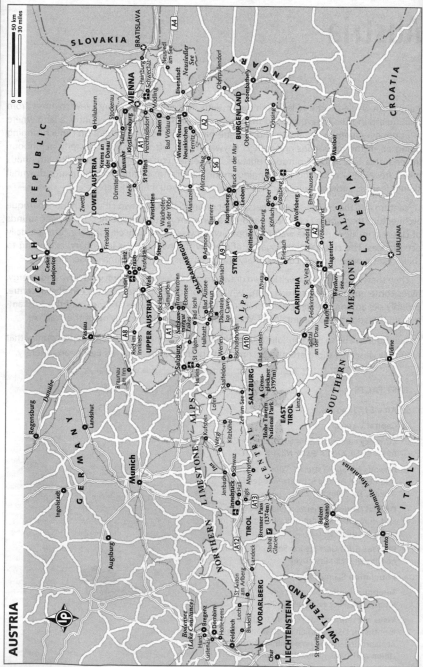

AUSTRIA

HIGHLIGHTS

- Discover the classical, kitsch, and contemporary corners of Austria's evocative capital, **Vienna** (p40).
- Bathe in the baroque beauty of **Salzburg** (p64), and – if you must – relive scenes from *The Sound of Music*.
- Experience Tyrolean culture with plenty of recreation opportunities and nightlife in **Innsbruck** (p75) or **Mayrhofen** (p80).
- Road-trip through the Hohe Tauern National Park along one of the world's most scenic highways, the **Grossglockner Hochalpenstrasse** (p83).
- Take a dip in one of a plethora of lakes in **Salzkammergut** (p71), Austria's summer playground.

ITINERARIES

- **Two days** Spend this entire time in Vienna, making sure to visit the Habsburg palaces and Stephansdom before cosying up in a *Kaffeehaus* (coffee house). At night check out the pumping bar scene or catch an opera at the celebrated opera house.
- **One week** Spend two days in Vienna, plus another day exploring the Wachau wine region, a day each in Salzburg and Innsbruck, one day exploring the Salzkammergut lakes, and finally one day at Mayrhofen hiking or skiing (depending on the season).

CLIMATE & WHEN TO GO

Austria has a typical central European climate, with Vienna enjoying an average maximum of 2°C (35°F) in January and 25°C (77°F) in July. Some people find the *Föhn* – a hot, dry wind that sweeps down from the mountains in early spring and autumn – rather uncomfortable. For more information, see p595.

Austria hangs out its *Zimmer frei* (rooms vacant) signs year-round, but its high seasons are July and August, and Christmas to New Year. Christmas to late February is the peak skiing time. Alpine resorts can be pretty dead between seasons, ie May, June and November.

HISTORY

Austria is a small nation with a big past. It may be hard to believe that this diminutive, landlocked Alpine country was once the epicentre of the mighty Habsburg empire and, in the 20th century, a pivotal player in the outbreak

CONNECTIONS: MOVING ON FROM AUSTRIA

Due to its central location, Austria has plenty of connections to all parts of Europe. Trains (p56) from Vienna run to many Eastern European destinations, including Bratislava, Budapest, Prague and Warsaw; there are also connections south to Italy via Klagenfurt (p63) and north to Berlin. Salzburg is within sight of the Bavarian border, and there are many trains Munich-bound and beyond from the baroque city (p70). Innsbruck is on the main train line connecting Austria to Switzerland, and there are a handful of trains from Bregenz to the bigger Swiss cities.

of WWI. For centuries the Habsburgs used strategic marriages to maintain their hold over a territory that encompassed much of central and Eastern Europe and, for a period, even Germany. But defeat in WWI brought that to an end, when the republic of Austria was formed in 1918.

Like so many European countries, Austria has experienced invasions and struggles since time immemorial. There are traces of human occupation since the ice age, but it was the Celts who made the first substantial mark on Austria around 450 BC. The Romans followed 400 years later, who in turn were followed by Bavarians, and, in 1278, the House of Habsburg who took control of the country by defeating the head of the Bavarian royalty.

The 16th and 17th centuries saw the Ottoman threat reach the gates of Vienna, and in 1805 Napoleon defeated Austria at Austerlitz. Austrian Chancellor Metternich cleverly reconsolidated Austria's power in 1815 after Waterloo, but the loss of the 1866 Austro-Prussian War, and creation of the Austro-Hungarian empire in 1867, diminished the Habsburg's influence in Europe.

However, these setbacks pale beside Archduke Franz Ferdinand's assassination by Slavic separatists in Sarajevo on 28 June 1914. When his uncle, the Austro-Hungarian emperor Franz Josef, declared war on Serbia in response, the ensuing 'Great War' (WWI) would prove the Habsburgs' downfall.

During the 1930s Nazis began to influence Austrian politics and by 1938 the recession-hit country was ripe for picking. Invading

AUSTRIA

HOW MUCH?

- **1L milk** €1.10
- **Loaf of bread** €1 to €3
- **Bottle of house white wine market/ restaurant** from €3/10
- **Newspaper** €0.70 to €1.30
- **Short taxi ride** €7

LONELY PLANET INDEX

- **1L petrol** €0.95
- **1L bottled water** €0.45 to €0.65
- **Bottle of beer** €3 to €3.50
- **Souvenir T-shirt** €15
- **Street snack (wurst)** €3

German troops met little resistance and Hitler was greeted on Heldenplatz as a hero by 200,000 Viennese.

Austria was heavily bombed during WWII, but the country recovered well, largely through the Marshall Plan and sound political and economic decisions (excluding its foray with the far-right Freedom Party and its controversial leader, Jörg Haider, in the '90s). Austria has maintained a neutral stance since 1955, been home to a number of international organisations, including the UN, since 1979, and joined the EU in 1995.

PEOPLE

At first glance, Austrians can seem reserved and even slightly suspicious of strangers. Not generally regarded for outward displays of friendliness, this changes when you get to know them better. Then most are friendly and exhibit genuine interest in sharing a multifaceted culture with the rest of the world. Politeness and formality are highly esteemed and expected, especially among the older generation.

Within the country, Vienna has always been a paradox, mixing Austrian conservatism with a large dollop of decadence. The scene you might get at Viennese balls of grand old society dames flirting with drag queens aptly reflects this. The capital's pervading humour, *Wiener Schmäh,* is quite ironic and cutting, but is also meant to be charming.

Nearly one-fifth of the Austrian population lives in Vienna, but other cities are small, so more than two-thirds live in small towns or in rural areas.

RELIGION

Austria is a largely Christian nation. Some 80% of the population is Catholic while the rest is Protestant, concentrated in Burgenland and Carinthia. Austria, and particularly Vienna, once had a sizable Jewish community, but their numbers have been reduced to around 7000 today.

ARTS

Austria's musical heritage tends to elbow most of its other artistic achievements off the page. European composers were drawn to the country by the Habsburgs' generous patronage during the 18th and 19th centuries: Beethoven, Brahms, Haydn, Mozart and Schubert all made Vienna their home during this period. The waltz originated in the city, perfected by Johann Strauss Jr (1825–99).

However, Vienna at the end of the 19th century was also a city of design and painting. The Austrian Secessionist movement, the local equivalent of art nouveau (*Jugendstil*), turned out such talents as the painter Gustav Klimt and architect Otto Wagner. Expressionist painters Egon Schiele and Oskar Kokoschka and modernist architect Adolf Loos followed.

While Austrian literature is not well known in the outside world, Arthur Schnitzler's *Dream Story (Traumnovelle)* inspired the Stanley Kubrick film *Eyes Wide Shut.* Football fans should be familiar with one famous work by Carinthian novelist Peter Handke, *The Goalie's Fear of the Penalty Kick (Der Angst des Tormanns beim Elfmeter).*

Today Austria's fine musical tradition has moved in the wholly different direction of chilled, eclectic electronica and dub lounge. Celebrity DJs Kruder & Dorfmeister have had the greatest global success, but the scene is loaded with other talent, including Pulsinger & Tunakan, the Vienna Scientists and the Sofa Surfers.

Meanwhile, expert film director Michael Haneke has also been creating a splash with his controversial *Funny Games* (1997) and the twisted romance of the much-lauded *The Piano Teacher* (2001). The country's most famous TV export is the detective series *Inspector Rex (Kommisar Rex).* As well as being big in Germany and Australia, Rex, a

German shepherd dog who regularly proves invaluable to his police owners, apparently has a cult following in some 93 countries. In recent times perhaps the most noteworthy Austrian imprint to be stamped on the world (and in particular the USA) is former professional bodybuilder/actor turned politician, and current governor of the state of California, Arnold Schwarzenegger, who was born near Graz.

ENVIRONMENT

More than half of Austria's 83,855 sq km is mountainous. Three chains run west to east: the Northern Limestone Alps; the Central (or High) Alps, which have the tallest peaks in Austria, including the 3797m Grossglockner; and the Southern Limestone Alps. They are banded around the middle and the south of the country, occupying most of its western half, and leaving flats around the Danube Valley and Vienna in the northeast, and Graz to the southeast.

Meadows and forests cover much of the country. Although Austria is home to Europe's largest national park, Hohe Tauern, only 3% of its landmass is protected. These wilderness areas are good places to spot wildlife, such as marmots. Hohe Tauern itself has many species of alpine wildflower, and the bearded vulture and lyre-horned ibex were reintroduced in recent years.

Austrians are highly environmentally conscious and rarely spoil the pristine landscape by littering. Recycling and biocompost bins are ubiquitous throughout the country.

Changing weather patterns are beginning to take their toll on the Alps and Austria's ski regions. It is estimated that 75% of the country's glaciers will disappear within the next 45 years, and most of Austria's low-lying ski resorts will receive no snow by 2030. The knock-on effect could mean more erosion, floods, and an increased risk of avalanches.

FOOD & DRINK
Staples & Specialities

There's more to Austrian cuisine than *Wiener schnitzel* (a veal or pork cutlet coated in breadcrumbs). Traces of the country's wider historical reach endure in the Hungarian paprika used to flavour several dishes, including *Gulasch* (beef stew), and in the Styrian polenta and pumpkin-seed oil popular in Italian and Slovenian cuisine respectively. Some staples like wurst (sausage) and regional dishes, such as *Tiroler Bauernschmaus* – a selection of meats served with sauerkraut, potatoes and dumplings – can be very fatty and stodgy. However, hearty soups often include *Knödel* (dumplings) or pasta.

Besides strudel (filo pastry filled with a variety of fruits, poppy seeds or cheese), *Salzburger Nockerl* (a fluffy soufflé) is a popular Austrian dessert.

Known for its lager beer – from brands like Gösser, Schwechater, Stiegl and Zipfer to *Weizenbier* (wheat beer) – Austria also produces some excellent wines in the east and southeast. *Heuriger* wine is the latest vintage, and is avidly consumed, even in autumn while still semifermented (called *Sturm*).

Where to Eat & Drink

Restaurants are found throughout the country, and in the countryside they often go by the name *Gasthaus* or *Gasthof*. Most open between 11am and midnight; some stop serving food (or shut up shop) from 2.30pm to 6pm. In Vienna a traditional inn is called a *Beisl* (from the Hebrew word for 'house'), where hearty Austrian fare fills the menu, and in the city's wine areas you'll find *Heurigen*, wine taverns where wine is served by the litre and food is available buffet-style. Some are tourist haunts, while others, located further from public transport, cater solely to locals.

Of course, lots of Asian restaurants and pizzerias dot the countryside. These, in addition to the dumplings in local cuisine, mean that vegetarians shouldn't have too much trouble finding satisfying meals.

For cheap food, try *Mensens* (university canteens). Another way to save money on food is to make lunch the main meal of the day (as many Austrians do); many restaurants provide a good-value *Tagesteller* or *Tagesmenu* (set meal) at this time.

In January 2009 Austria introduced new smoking laws for restaurants and cafes, which state that all establishments over 80 sq metres in size must provide a nonsmoking section. Those smaller than 50 sq metres can choose whether to be smoking or nonsmoking, and for those in between the authorities will determine if patrons are able to puff away or not. In practice, however, the new laws are taking some time to have an effect, and at the time of writing few places had provided a partitioned nonsmoking area.

AUSTRIA

VIENNA

☎ 01 / pop 1.66 million

Vienna is a city that straddles the past and present with ease. No other city effortlessly combines a rich history that has left behind such remarkable gifts as gothic Stephansdom or baroque Schloss Schönbrunn with contemporary gems like the Leopold Museum or Museums Quartier. Here you can spend your days marvelling at one historical building after the next, and evenings clubbing to electronic beats.

The cultural output of this Austrian capital is not limited to architectural delights however. Vienna has for centuries been a busy intersection of ethnicities, beliefs and peoples, and this heady mix has attracted a mine of artists, musicians and thinkers. Gustav, Schiele, Beethoven, Mozart, Strauss and Freud (to name but a few) all practised their arts here, and their efforts can be seen and heard in various museums throughout the city.

But thankfully it's just as easy to avoid Vienna's cultural trappings as it is to indulge in them. Take a stroll down the Naschmarkt, the city's main market, grab a coffee in a coffee house, head for a *Heurigen* on the edge of the Vienna Woods, or take a dip in the *Alte Donau* (Old Danube) – and this is just the icing on a very rich cake.

HISTORY

Vienna probably began life as a Celtic camp but the first solid foundations of the city were laid by the Romans who arrived here in 15 BC. They named their settlement Vindobona, after the Celtic tribe Vinid, and by the 3rd century it had developed into a town. It was first officially recorded as 'Wenia' in 881 and became a Babenberg stronghold in the 11th century. The Babenberg's ruled for 200 years until the Habsburgs took control of the city's reigns and held them firm until the end of WWI.

Over the centuries Vienna suffered Ottoman sieges in 1529 and 1683 and occupation in 1805 and 1809 by Napoleon and his armies. In the years in between, it received a major baroque makeover, the remnants of which can be seen in many buildings throughout the city. The mid-1800s saw Vienna blossom again, and the royal coffers were emptied to build the celebrated Ringstrasse and accompanying buildings.

Between the two world wars Vienna's political pendulum swung from one extreme to the other – the '20s saw the influx of socialism and the '30s the rise of fascism. The city suffered heavily under Allied bombing in WWII and was liberated by the Russians on 11 April 1945. By 1955 it was once again a free city, and since then it has gone from sitting on the edge of the Iron Curtain to occupying a central position in the EU.

ORIENTATION

Many of the historic sights are in the old city, the Innere Stadt. The Danube Canal (Donaukanal) is located to the northeast and a series of broad boulevards called the Ring or Ringstrasse encircle it.

Most of the attractions in the city centre are within walking distance of each other. Stephansdom (St Stephen's Cathedral), in the heart of the city, is the principal landmark.

In addresses, the number of a building within a street *follows* the street name. Any number *before* the street name denotes the district, of which there are 23. District 1 (the Innere Stadt) is the central region, mostly within the Ring. Generally, the higher the district number, the further it is from the city centre. The middle two digits of postcodes refer to the district, hence places with a postcode 1010 are in district 1, and 1230 means district 23.

The main train stations are Franz Josefs Bahnhof to the north, Westbahnhof to the west and Südbahnhof to the south; transferring between them is easy. Most hotels and pensions (B&Bs) are in the city centre and to the west.

INFORMATION
Bookshops
British Bookshop (Map pp46-7; ☎ 512 19 45; www .britishbookshop.at; 01, Weihburggasse 24-6) Stocks English-language titles.

Freytag & Berndt (Map pp46-7; ☎ 533 86 85; www .freytagberndt.at; 01, Kohlmarkt 9) The best map and guidebook stockist in the city.

Discount Cards
Vienna Card (€18.50) Admission discounts and a free 72-hour travel pass; available at tourist offices and hotels.

Internet Access
Bignet (Map pp46-7; ☎ 533 29 39; 01, Hoher Markt 8-9; per hr €5.90)

Speednet Café (Map pp46-7; ☎ 532 57 50; 01 Morzin-platz 4; per hr €4.60)
Surfland Internetcafé (Map pp46-7; ☎ 512 77 01; 01, Krugerstrasse 10; initial charge €1.50, per min €0.09)

Medical Services
Allgemeines Krankenhaus (General Hospital; Map pp42-3; ☎ 40 400-0; 09, Währinger Gürtel 18-20; ☺ 24hr)
Dental Treatment (☎ 512 20 78; ☺ 24hr) German-speaking only.

Money
Banks and currency-exchange offices can be found across town, the latter in the main train stations. *Bankomats* (ATMs) are everywhere.
Amex (Map pp46-7; ☎ 515 11 500; 01, Kärntner Strasse 21-23; ☺ 9am-5.30pm Mon-Fri, 9am-noon Sat)

Post
Main Post Office (Map pp46-7; ☎ 577 67-71010; 01, Fleischmarkt 19; ☺ 6am-10pm) Other post offices with extended opening hours are at Südbahnhof, Franz Josefs Bahnhof and Westbahnhof.

Tourist Information
Information & Hotel Reservation Counters Westbahnhof (☺ 5.30am-9pm); Airport arrivals hall (☺ 7am-10pm)
Jugendinfo (Vienna Youth Information; Map pp46-7; ☎ 17 99; www.wienxtra.at; 01, Babenbergerstrasse 1; ☺ noon-7pm Mon-Sat) Offers various reduced-price tickets for 14- to 26-year-olds.
Tourist Info Wien (Map pp46-7; ☎ 24 555; www .wien.info; 01, cnr Am Albertinaplatz & Maysedergasse; ☺ 9am-7pm) Near the state opera house, with loads of regional information.

SIGHTS
Vienna's ostentatious buildings and beautifully tended parks make it a lovely city for strolling. The Ringstrasse (the road circling the city centre) is the perfect place to acquire a taste for the city, and an hour's walk will bring you past the neo-Gothic **Rathaus** (city hall; Map pp46-7), the Greek Revival-style **Parliament** (Map pp46-7) and the 19th-century **Burgtheater** (Map pp46-7), among others. You can even glimpse the baroque **Karlskirche** (St Charles' Church; Map pp46-7) on your meander.

Strolling along the pedestrian-only Kärntner Strasse will take you past plush shops, cafes and street entertainers. The main point of interest in Graben is the knobbly **Pestsäule** (Plague Column; Map pp46-7), designed by Fischer von Erlach and built to commemorate the end of the Great Plague. There's also a concrete

Holocaust memorial (Map pp46-7) by Rachel Whiteread in Judenplatz, Austria's first monument of its kind. Look closely and you'll notice that the sides are constructed of cement books facing open-end out, perhaps to convey a lack of closure coupled with an enduring remembrance for the victims of the Holocaust.

Interesting buildings in the city centre include **Loos Haus** (Map pp46-7), now a Raiffeisen bank, across from the Hofburg. The art nouveau **Postsparkasse** (Savings Bank; Map pp46-7; Georg Coch Platz) and **Stadtbahn Pavilions** (train station pavilions; Map pp46-7; Karlsplatz) are by architect Otto Wagner.

Stephansdom
The prominent latticework spire and geometric patterned roof tiles of **Stephansdom** (St Stephen's Cathedral; Map pp46-7; ☎ 515 52-0; www .stephanskirche.at; 01, Stephansplatz; admission free; ☺ 6am-10pm Mon-Sat, 7am-10pm Sun; ☒ U-Bahn Stephansplatz) make this 13th-century Gothic masterpiece one of the city's key points of orientation. The interior is nothing to scoff at either, complete with a 16th-century stone pulpit and gigantic baroque high altar. Bearing in mind the significance of the church in daily medieval commerce, run your fingers across over-200-year-old rudimentary circular grooves on the cathedral's face (right side of front), once used for standardising and regulating exact measurements of bread loaves, and over two horizontally fastened iron bars at one time utilised for gauging proper lengths of cloth.

Inside, you can take the lift up the **north tower** (adult/child €4.50/1.50; ☺ 8.30am-5.30pm), tackle the 343 steps to the top of the **south tower** (adult/child €3.50/1; ☺ 9am-5.30pm), and explore the church's **Katakomben** (catacombs; adult/child €4.50/1.50;

VIENNA IN TWO DAYS

Start with **Stephansdom** (above), then head to the **Hofburg** (p44) via Graben and the Kohlmarkt. After a coffee-house lunch break, hop on tram 1 around the Ringstrasse before alighting near the **Museums Quartier** (p44). Spend the evening in the **opera** (p54) or head to a club such as **Flex** (p54).

On your second morning explore a few galleries or museums, then spend a lazy afternoon at **Schloss Schönnbrunn** (p45). At night, venture into the suburbs to Vienna's *Heurigen* (p53).

VIENNA

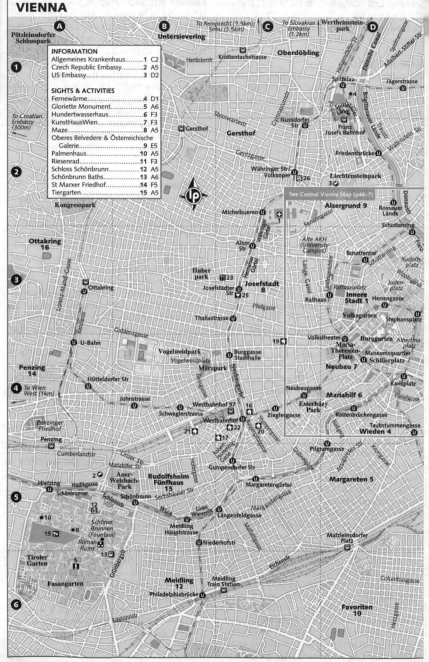

See Central Vienna Map (p46-7)

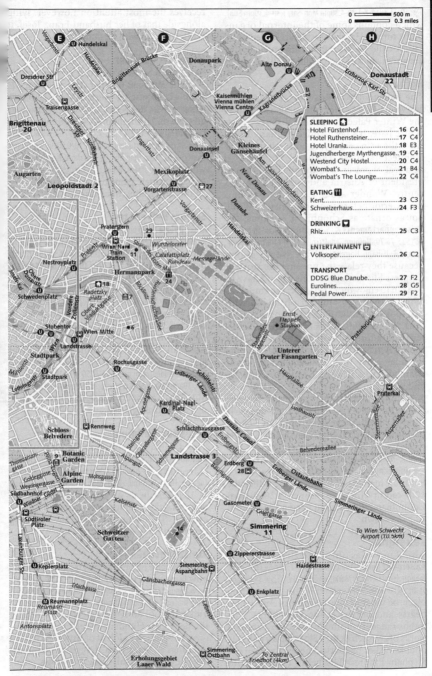

0 _____ 500 m
0 _____ 0.3 miles

SLEEPING
Hotel Fürstenhof....................16 C4
Hotel Ruthensteiner................17 C4
Hotel Urania.........................18 E3
Jugendherberge Myrthengasse...19 C4
Westend City Hostel...............20 C4
Wombat's.............................21 B4
Wombat's The Lounge............22 C4

EATING
Kent....................................23 C3
Schweizerhaus......................24 F3

DRINKING
Rhiz....................................25 C3

ENTERTAINMENT
Volksoper............................26 C2

TRANSPORT
DDSG Blue Danube................27 F2
Eurolines.............................28 G5
Pedal Power.........................29 F2

🕙 10-11.30am & 1.30-4.30pm Mon-Sat, 1.30-4.30pm Sun), which contains some of the internal organs of the former Habsburgs rulers. Guided tours (adult/child €4.50/1.50) are also available, as are audio guides (adult/child €3.50/1).

Hofburg

The **Hofburg** (Imperial Palace; Map pp46-7; www.hofburg-wien.at; 🚇 U-Bahn Herrengasse), also known as the Winter Palace, was the Habsburgs' city-centre base. It's been added to many times since the 13th century, resulting in a mix of architectural styles. The palace continues to be a seat of power, housing the office of the president of Austria and a major congress centre. Wander around a bit and admire the exterior before venturing inside. While not as ornate as Schönbrunn's rooms, the **Kaiserappartements & 'Sissi' Museum** (Map pp46-7; 🕾 535 75 70; Hofburg; adult/child €9.90/4.90; 🕙 9am-5pm; 🚇 U-Bahn Herrengasse) are worth seeing because they relate the unusual life story of Empress Elisabeth (Sissi). You don't have to be a fan to enjoy the experience: the empress's 19th-century gym and her obsession with her looks are attention-grabbing enough. Plus, the museum helps explain why Sissi's face still adorns shop windows in Vienna today. A ticket to the Kaiserappartements includes entry to the **Silberkammer** (silver chamber), which is home to fine silverware and porcelain.

Among several other points of interest within the Hofburg you'll find the **Burgkapelle** (Royal Chapel), where the Vienna Boys' Choir performs (see p55), the **Spanish Riding School** (p54), and the **Schatzkammer** (Treasury; Map pp46-7; 🕾 525 24-0; Schweizerhof; adult/child €10/7.50; 🕙 10am-6pm Wed-Mon; 🚇 U-Bahn Herrengasse), which holds all manner of wonders, including the 10th-century Imperial Crown, a 2860-carat Columbian emerald, and even a thorn from Christ's crown.

Kaisergruft

Also known as the Kapuzinergruft, the **Kaisergruft** (Imperial Vault; Map pp46-7; 🕾 512 68 53; 01, Tegetthofstrasse/Neuer Markt; adult/child €4/1.50; 🕙 10am-6pm; 🚇 U-Bahn Stephansplatz) is the final resting place of most of the Habsburg elite (their hearts and organs reside elsewhere). The tombs range from simple affairs to elaborate works of art, such as the 18th-century baroque double casket of Maria Theresia and Franz Stephan. Empress Elisabeth's ('Sissi') coffin

receives the most attention however: lying alongside that of her husband Franz Josef, it is often strewn with fresh flowers.

Museums Quartier

Small guidebooks have been written on the popular **Museums Quartier** (Map pp46-7; 🕾 523 58 81; www.mqw.at; 07, Museumsplatz 1; 🚇 U-Bahn Museumsquartier, Volkstheater), so only a taster can be given here. The highpoint is undoubtedly the **Leopold Museum** (Map pp46-7; 🕾 525 700; www.leopoldmuseum.org; adult/student/senior €10/6.50/9; 🕙 10am-6pm Fri-Wed, 10am-9pm Thu; 🚇 U-Bahn Museumsquartier), which houses the world's largest collection of Egon Schiele paintings, with some minor Klimts and Kokoschkas thrown in.

Schloss Belvedere

This **palace** (Map pp46-7; 🕾 79 557-0; www.belvedere.at; combined ticket adult/student/senior €12.50/8.50/9.50; 🚋 D or 71 to Belvedere) consists of two main buildings. The first is the **Oberes Belvedere & Österreichische Galerie** (Upper Belvedere & Austrian Gallery; Map pp42-3; 03, Prinz Eugen Strasse 37; adult/student/senior €9.50/6/7.50; 🕙 10am-6pm), where you'll find instantly recognisable works, such as Gustav Klimt's *The Kiss*, which is accompanied by other late-19th to early-20th-century Austrian works. The second is the **Unteres Belvedere** (Lower Belvedere; Map pp46-7; 03, Rennweg 6A; adult/student/senior €9.50/6/7.50; 🕙 10am-6pm Thu-Tue, 10am-9pm Wed), which contains a baroque museum. The buildings sit at opposite ends of a manicured garden.

Secession Building

This popular art nouveau 'temple of art' **building** (Map pp46-7; 🕾 587 53 07; www.secession.at; 01, Friedrichstrasse 12; adult/student €6/3.50; 🕙 10am-6pm Tue-Sun, 10am-8pm Thu; 🚇 U-Bahn Karlsplatz) was built in 1898 and bears an intricately woven gilt dome that the Viennese nickname the 'golden cabbage'. The highlight inside is the 34m-long *Beethoven Frieze* by Klimt.

KunstHausWien

This formerly inconspicuous factory building, now fairy-tale **art gallery** (Map pp42-3; 🕾 712 04 91; www.hundertwasser.at; 03, Untere Weissgerberstrasse 13; adult/student €9/7, Mon half-price; 🕙 10am-7pm; 🚋 N or O to Radetzkyplatz) designed and transformed by Friedensreich Hundertwasser into a repository for his art, is redolent of Antonio Gaudi's buildings in Barcelona. Irregular elements, like uneven floors, misshapen windows, amalgamations of glass, metal, brick and ceramic tile, almost literally sweep you off your feet. Down the road there's a block of residential flats by Hundertwasser, the **Hundertwasserhaus** (Map pp42-3; 03, cnr Löwengasse & Kegelgasse; Ⓡ N to Löwengasse). In the north of the city is another of Hundertwasser's fantastical creations, the architecturally unique **Fernewärme** (Map pp42-3; ☎ 313 26; 09, Spittelauer Lände 45; admission free; ☻ tours by appointment only; Ⓤ U-Bahn Spittelau). It's towering, golden-tiled smoke stack tops one of the most colourful rubbish incinerator's you'll ever see.

Albertina

Simply reading the highlights among its enormous collection – several Michelangelos, some Raphaels and Albrecht Dürer's *Hare* – should have any art fan lining up for entry into this **gallery** (Map pp46-7; ☎ 53 483-0; www .albertina.at; 01, Albertinaplatz 1a; adult/student/senior €9.50/7/8; ☻ 10am-6pm Thu-Tue, 10am-9pm Wed; Ⓡ U-Bahn Karlsplatz). As the collection is so large (1.5 million prints and 50,000 drawings), exhibitions change regularly so check the website to find out what's on show.

In addition to the mostly temporary exhibitions, a series of Habsburg staterooms are always open.

Schloss Schönbrunn

The single attraction most readily associated with Vienna is the Habsburgs' **summer palace** (Map pp42-3; ☎ 81 113-0; www.schoenbrunn.at; 13, Schönbrunner Schlossstrasse 47; self-guided 22-/40-room tour €9.50/12.90; ☻ 8.30am-5pm Apr-Oct, 8.30am-6pm Jul & Aug, 8.30am-4.30pm Nov-Mar; Ⓡ U-Bahn Schönbrunn). Despite being a vast complex, the sumptuous 1441-room palace can at times be uncomfortably crowded, so it's best to arrive early to avoid the throngs. Students receive a slight discount.

Inside you'll traipse through progressively more luxurious apartments. The most impressive, the **Audience Rooms**, are only included in the 40-room grand tour.

The grounds are more enjoyable and are home to the world's oldest zoo, the **Tiergarten** (www.zoovienna.at; adult/child under 6yr/senior & student €12/free/5), founded in 1752. Other highlights include the formal gardens and fountains, the **maze** (admission €2.90), the **Palmenhaus** (greenhouse; admission €3.30) and the **Gloriette Monument** (admission €2), whose roof offers a wonderful view over the palace grounds and beyond.

Liechtenstein Museum

The collection of Duke Hans-Adam II of Liechtenstein is on show at Vienna's gorgeous baroque **Liechtenstein Palace** (Map pp46-7; ☎ 319 57 67-0; www.liechtensteinmuseum.at; 09, Fürstengasse 1; adult/child €10/free; ☻ 10am-5pm Fri-Tue; Ⓡ D to Bauernfeldplatz). It's one of the largest private collections in the world, and boasts a plethora of classical paintings, including some Rubens.

Kunsthistorisches Museum

When it comes to classical works of art, nothing comes close to the **Kunsthistorisches Museum** (Museum of Fine Arts; Map pp46-7; ☎ 52 524-0; www .khm.at; 01, Maria Theresien Platz; adult/student €10/7.50; ☻ 10am-6pm Tue, Wed & Fri-Sun, 10am-9pm Thu; Ⓡ U-Bahn Volkstheater or Museumsquartier). It houses a huge range of art amassed by the Habsburgs and includes works by Rubens, Van Dyck, Holbein and Caravaggio. Paintings by Peter Brueghel the Elder, including *Hunters in the Snow*, also feature. There is an entire wing of ornaments, clocks and glassware, and Greek, Roman and Egyptian antiquities.

Other Museums

Vienna has so many museums that you might overlook the superlative **Haus der Musik** (House of Music; Map pp46-7; ☎ 51 648; www.haus-der-musik-wien .at; 01, Seilerstätte 30; adult/student €10/8.50; ☻ 10am-10pm; Ⓡ U-Bahn Karlsplatz or Stephansplatz). But try not to. Interactive electronic displays allow you to create different forms of music through movement and touch, and to connect with something a lot deeper than just your inner child.

Some former homes of the great composers, including one of Mozart's, are open to the public; ask at the tourist office. There is also the fairly low-key **Sigmund Freud Museum** (Map pp46-7; ☎ 319 15 96; www.freud-museum.at; 09, Berggasse 19; adult/student €7/4.50; ☻ 9am-6pm Jul-Sep, 9am-5pm Oct-Jun; Ⓡ U-Bahn Rossauer or Schottentor).

The **Wien Museum** (Map pp46-7; ☎ 505 87 47-0; www .wienmuseum.at; 04, Karlsplatz 5; adult/student/senior €6/3/4, permanent exhibition Sun free; ☻ 9am-6pm Tue-Sun; Ⓡ U-Bahn Karlsplatz) is also worthwhile; it provides a snapshot of the city's history, and contains a handsome art collection.

Cemeteries

The **Zentralfriedhof** (Central Cemetery; off Map pp42-3; 11, Simmeringer Hauptstrasse 232-244; admission free; ☻ 7am-7pm May-Aug, 7am-6pm Mar, Apr, Sep & Oct, 8am-5pm Nov-Feb; Ⓡ 6 or 71 to Zentralfriedhof), about 4km

AUSTRIA

CENTRAL VIENNA

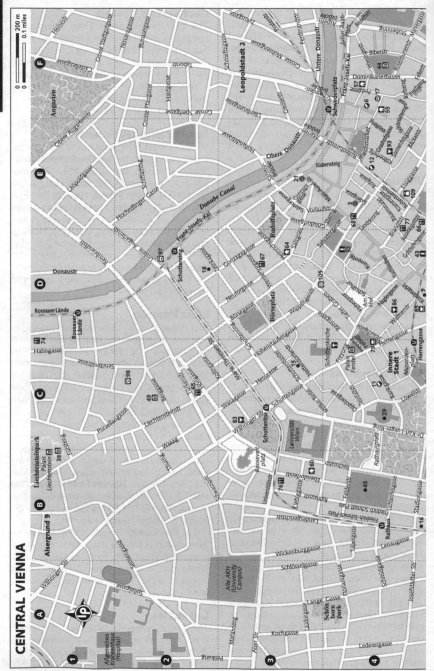

0 200 m
0 0.1 miles

Leopoldstadt 2

Augarten

Donaustr

Rossauer Lände

Hahngasse

Alsergrund 9

Liechtensteinpark
Palais
Liechtenstein

Alte AKH
(University
Campus)

Schönborn
park

Innere
Stadt 1

Universität
Wien

Rathaus

Franz-Josefs-Kai

Schwedenplatz

Rudolfsplatz

Börseplatz

Schottentor

Roosevelt
platz

Friedrich-Schmidt-Platz

Rathausplatz

Dr.Karl-Lueger-Ring

Schottenring

Danube Canal

Obere Donaustr

Untere Donaustr

Dominikanerbastei

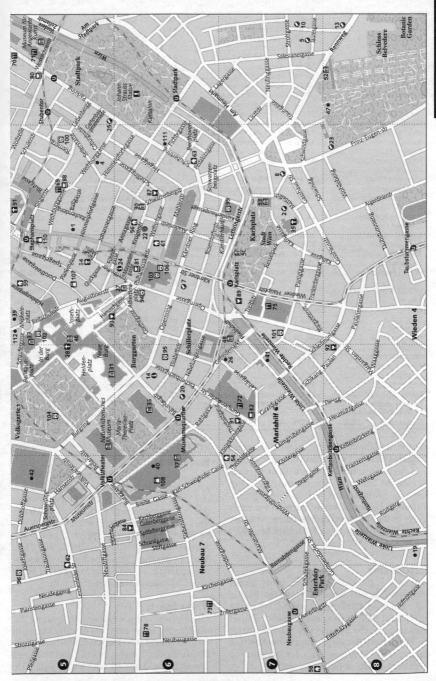

AUSTRIA

southeast of the city centre, is one of Europe's largest, greater in size than the Innere Stadt and home to more 'residents' than Vienna. Beethoven, Schubert, Brahms and Schönberg have memorial tombs here, as does Mozart, although he was actually buried in a mass grave in the **St Marxer Friedhof** (Cemetery of St Mark; Map pp42-3; 03, Leberstrasse 6-8; admission free; 🚋 71 to Liftassstrasse).

Naschmarkt

Saturday is the best day to visit this **market** (Map pp46-7; 06, Linke Wienzeile; 🕑 6am-6pm Mon-Sat; 🚇 U-Bahn Karlsplatz or Kettenbrückengasse), when the usual food stalls and occasional tacky clothes stall are joined by a proper flea market. Curios and trinkets sit beside produce from Austrian farms, plus there are cafes for an alfresco breakfast, lunch or refuelling stop.

ACTIVITIES

Riesenrad

In theory, riding the **Riesenrad** (giant wheel; Map pp42-3; www.wienerriesenrad.com; adult/child/student €8/3.50/7; 🕑 10am-7.45pm; 🚇 U-Bahn Praterstern) in the Prater amusement park allows you to re-live a classic film moment: when Orson Welles ad libbed his immortal speech about peace, Switzerland and cuckoo clocks in *The Third Man*. In practice, you'll be too distracted by other passengers and by the views as the Ferris wheel languidly takes you 65m aloft.

Water Sports

There's swimming, sailboarding, boating and windsurfing in the stretches of water known as the Alte Donau (Old Danube), northeast of the Donau Insel (Danube Island), and the Neue Donau (New Danube), which runs parallel to and just north of the Donaukanal (Danube Canal). There are stretches of river bank that offer unrestricted access. Alternatively, visit the **Schönbrunn baths** (Map pp42-3; Schönbrunner Schlossstrasse 47; full day/afternoon incl locker €9/7; ⏰ 8.30am-10pm Jun–mid-Aug, 8.30am-8pm mid-Aug–late-Aug, 8.30am-7pm May & Sep; 🚇 U-Bahn Schönbrunn), within the Schloss Schönbrunn grounds.

TOURS

The tourist office publishes a monthly list of guided walks, called *Wiener Spaziergänge* – online information can be found at www.wien guide.at. **Vienna Walks** (☎ 774 89 01; www.vienna walks.tix.at) organises **Third Man tours** (tour €17; ⏰ 4pm Mon & Fri), which explore the locations of the film, and a tour of **Jewish Vienna** (tour €13; ⏰ 1.30pm Mon).

FESTIVALS & EVENTS

The **Vienna Festival**, from mid-May to mid-June, has a wide-ranging arts program. Contact **Wiener Festwochen** (Map pp46-7; ☎ 589 22-22; www.festwochen.or.at; 06, Lehárgasse 11; ⏰ Jan–mid-Jun) for details.

The extremely popular **Vienna Spring Marathon** (www.vienna-marathon.com) is held in April/May and Vienna's **Summer of Music** runs from mid-July to mid-September; contact **KlangBoden** (Map pp46-7; ☎ 40 00-8410; 01, Stadiongasse 9).

Look out for free rock, jazz and folk concerts during the **Donauinselfest** (www.don auinselfest.at, in German), held at the beginning of September. The free open-air **Opera Film es-**

FREE THRILLS

Not many things in Vienna are free, but at least there are some:

- **Stephansdom** (p41) Only the nave is free, but what a nave!
- **Schönbrunn Gardens** (p45) Wander the immaculate gardens like an emperor or empress.
- **Inner City** An open-air museum and deserved Unesco-listed site.
- **Zentralfriedhof** (p45) One of Europe's finest cemeteries, and burial place to some of Vienna's most celebrated burghers.
- **Wien Museum** (p45) Perfect snapshot of Vienna in all its guises; free Sunday.

---

tival on Rathausplatz runs throughout July and August.

Each year Vienna's traditional **Christkindlmarkt** (Christmas market) takes place in front of the Rathaus between mid-November and 24 December; it's one of a number scattered across the city.

SLEEPING
Budget

Vienna has its fair share of budget options, but none are located in the very heart of the city. Rooms fill quickly in summer, so book ahead when possible.

Wien West (off Map pp42-3; ☎ 914 23 14; www.wien camping.at; 14, Hüttelbergstrasse 80; camp site per adult/tent Sep-Jun €5.90/4.50, Jul & Aug €6.90/5.50, 2-/4-person cabin Apr-Oct €35/50; ⏰ Mar-Jan; 🖥) On the edges of the Wiener Wald (Vienna Woods), but just 30 minutes from the city centre, this well-equipped camping ground has modern facilities, bike hire, and even a wi-fi hotspot. Take U4 or the S-Bahn to Hütteldorf, then bus 148 or 152.

our pick **Hostel Ruthensteiner** (Map pp42-3; ☎ 893 42 02; www.hostelruthensteiner.com; 15, Robert Hamerling Gasse 24; dm/d from €16/50; 🖥) This laid-back and friendly independent hostel is one of the top finds in central Europe. Facilities are modern (renovations took place only a few years back) and the common areas are a pleasure to hang out in – think beautifully handmade wooden bar, chilled music–lounge room, and private garden. Some rooms are a little pokey, but they're highly functional and immaculately clean. Book ahead in summer.

Jugendherberge Myrthengasse (Map pp42-3; ☎ 523 63 16; hostel@chello.at; 07, Myrthengasse 7; dm from €17; 🖥) This small Hostelling International (HI) hostel is the closest hostel to the city centre, and one of the more chilled. As expected, it's all fairly basic inside, but there's a lovely inner courtyard to enjoy. Breakfast is included; towels aren't.

Westend City Hostel (Map pp42-3; ☎ 597 67 29; www .westendhostel.at; 6, Fügergasse 3; dm from €19.50, s/d from €52/62; 🖥) The pale purple facade of this former bordello fronts a spick-and-span hostel suitable for families and backpackers looking for a quiet night's rest. Despite the colourful frontage, rooms are pretty bland, but each has an en-suite bathroom and lockers for every guest. Prices include breakfast.

Wombat's (Map pp42-3; ☎ 897 23 36; www.wombats .at; 15, Grangasse 6; dm/d €21/25; 🖥) Top-flight

AUSTRIA

cleanliness and comfort fuse with a gregarious party bar to make Wombat's immensely popular. The mixed-gender dorms have secured entry, wooden bunk beds and modern bathrooms. There's also a second location called The Lounge just around the corner (15, Mariahilfer Strasse 137).

Pension Hargita (Map pp46–7; ☎ 526 19 28; www .hargita.at; 07, Andreasgasse 1; s/d with shared bathroom from €38/52, with private bathroom €55/66) One of the cleanest and most charming budget pensions in Vienna. Rooms have aqua blue or sunny yellow features, the friendly Hungarian owner keeps things spotless, and breakfast is included.

Schweizer Pension (Map pp46–7; ☎ 533 81 56; www .schwiezerpension.com; 01, Heinrichsgasse 2; s/d with shared bathroom from €42/62) The Schweizer isn't overly modern but who cares when the beds are still comfy and you're paying a pittance for such a great location. And they're big on the environment too – energy-saving bulbs are employed throughout and organic produce is used for breakfasts. Book ahead as there are only 11 rooms.

Midrange

There are loads of charming guest houses and small hotels in this price bracket.

Pension Dr Geissler (Map pp46–7; ☎ 533 28 03; www .hotelpension.at; 01, Postgasse 14; s/d with shared bathroom from €32/43, with private bathroom from €47/60) Don't let the slow lift deter you: when you do make it to your floor, you'll find rooms are an eclectic mix of faux baroque and 1950s retro. The airport bus to Schwedenplatz almost brings you to the door, making it handy for jet-lag rehab.

Hotel Post (Map pp46–7; ☎ 51 583-0; www.hotel -post-wien.at; 01, Fleischmarkt 24; s/d with shared bathroom €40/66, with private bathroom from €70/97; 💻) The strongest feature of this hotel is its location, right in the heart of things. With its parquet flooring in the rooms, long, carpeted hallways and decorative cast-iron lift, it feels like a grand, if somewhat faded, 19th-century boarding house.

Pension Wild (Map pp46–7; ☎ 406 51 74; www.pension -wild.com; 08, Langegasse 10; s/d with shared bathroom from €41/53, with private bathroom €65/97) Most of the rooms at this gay-friendly pension have been given a substantial makeover, but some cheaper accommodation remains, with shared showers and toilets. All guests can prepare snacks in the small kitchenette on each floor.

Hotel Fürstenhof (Map pp42–3; ☎ 523 32 67; www .hotel-fuerstenhof.com; 07, Neubaugurtel 4; s/d with shared bathroom from €46/65, with private bathroom €69/110; 💻) Family-run Fürsthenhof still retains a few of its 1906 original fittings, such as the gorgeous lift, but its rooms are suitably modern and often spacious. Service is friendly, the hotel is handy to Westbahnhof, and there are excellent public transport connections to the city.

Hotel Urania (Map pp42–3; ☎ 713 17 11; www.hotel -urania.at; 03, Obere Weissgerberstrasse 7; s/d/tr/q from €48/70/95/120) This hotel is tacky, but fun. Episodes of various Austrian TV series (eg *Inspector Rex*) have been filmed here, and as a guest you'll feel you're in one, too. Not all of the eclectic rooms will be to everyone's taste (a knight's boudoir with animal skins on the floor, anyone?). Others, such as the Hundertwasser and Japanese rooms, are actually quite chic. The hotel is quiet, but central.

Pension Residenz (Map pp46–7; ☎ 406 47 86-0; www .pension-residenz.co.at; 01, Ebendorferstrasse 10; s/d €70/100; 💻) This pension is a model of restraint. Decorated in a traditional style, with white, light-coloured fittings, it has a pleasant, if not overly personal, feel. Its location near the university is also handy.

Pension Suzanne (Map pp46–7; ☎ 513 25 07; www .pension-suzanne.at; 01, Walfischgasse 4; s/d €77/100; 💻) Suzanne is only a few steps off Kärnter Strasse and just around the corner from the Staatsoper. Rooms are a little on the small side but this is mitigated somewhat by attractive antique furniture.

Hotel zur Wiener Staatsoper (Map pp46–7; ☎ 513 12 74; www.zurwienerstaatsoper.at; 01, Krugerstrasse 11; s/d from €80/113) Famous for its appealing neobaroque facade, this hotel's rooms are small, but its prices are great value for the central location.

Pension Pertschy (Map pp46-7; ☎ 534 49-0; www
.pertschy.com; 01, Habsburgergasse 5; s/d from €90/113; 🖳)
Pertschy is a gem of a pension with a peaceful location in the heart of the city. Rooms
are large, warm and inviting, and staff will
welcome both adults and children with
equal enthusiasm.

Top End
Vienna has a glut of four- and five-star hotels.
Every major chain is represented and even the
city's most recognisable names now belong to
one of these groups.

Schubertring (Map pp46-7; ☎ 717 02-0; www.schuber
tring.at; 01, Schubertring 11; s/d from €99/128; 🐾) This
sought-after address has rooms in Biedermeier
or art-nouveau style and views of the celebrated Ring. Advance bookings advisable.

Das Tyrol (Map pp46-7; ☎ 587 54 15; 06, www.das
-tyrol.at; Mariahilfer Strasse 15; s/d from €109/149; 🐾 🖳)
For the price, this boutique hotel has some
of the best rooms in town. Expect to find
modern and cosy rooms bathed in warm
hues and sporting personal touches such as
fresh flowers. It's handily located on a major
shopping throughfare and close to the
Museums Quartier.

EATING
The city's signature dish, *Wiener schnitzel*,
is widely available and Vienna is renowned
for its excellent pastries. There are plenty
of options, however, if you're not into
Austrian cuisine. You can buy groceries outside normal shopping hours at Südbahnhof
and Westbahnhof.

Restaurants
Der Wiener Deewan (Map pp46-7; 09, Liechtensteinstrasse
10; ⊗ Mon-Sat) Pakistani curries – three vegetarian and two meat – are prepared daily and
served buffet-style at this easygoing eatery.
There's no set price here, just eat as much as
you like and pay as much as you like, although
the food's so good you'll want to fork over a
decent amount of cash.

Kent (Map pp42-3; 16, Brunnengasse 67; mains €4-9)
Authentic Turkish cuisine and one of the largest gardens in the city make Kent a hugely
popular choice with locals of all ethnic backgrounds. After your meal, take a wander along
the nearby Brunnen market and pick up some
fresh fruit for dessert.

Zu den 2 Leiserln (Map pp46-7; 07, Burggasse 63; schnitzel from €6) A classic *Beisl* if ever there was one.

Leiserln has been serving enormous schnitzels
for over 100 years to politicians, blue-collar
workers, and everyone in between. Take a seat
and appreciate a true Viennese institution.

St Josef (Map pp46-7; 07, Mondscheingasse 10; mains
€6-7.20; ⊗ Mon-Sat) St Josef is the choice of the
healthy diner. It only serves wholly organic
and vegetarian cuisine, and the menu changes
daily.

Ra'mien (Map pp46-7; ☎ 585 47 98; 06, Gumpendorfer
Strasse 9; mains €7-10; ⊗ Tue-Sun) This Asian diner
specialises in noodle soups and dishes, but offers a handful of rice specialities to mix things
up. Evening time its cellar transforms into a
thumping bar-club.

Immervoll (Map pp46-7; ☎ 513 52 88; 01 Weihburggasse
17; mains €8-17) Run by a famous Austrian actor,
Immervoll (literally, 'always full') attracts an
arty crowd to its uncluttered interior. The
menu changes daily, the delicious food often
has Hungarian and Italian influences.

our pick Stomach (Map pp46-7; ☎ 310 20 99; 09,
Seegasse 26; mains €10-18; ⊗ dinner Wed-Sat, lunch & dinner
Sun) Many vegetarian dishes have dropped off
the menu at Styrian-style Stomach, but some
remain, and the quaint, ramshackle rooms
and the courtyard create a rustic outpost in
the big city.

Schweizerhaus (Map pp42-3; 02, Strasse des Ersten
Mai 116; mains €10-20; ⊗ mid-Mar–Oct) In the Prater
park, this place serves *Hintere Schweinsstelze*
(roasted pork hocks) and the like to a rowdy
crowd of international travellers who wash it
all down with huge mugs of Czech beer fresh
from the barrel.

Wrenkh (Map pp46-7; 01, Bauernmarkt 10; mains €11)
Quiche, mung beans and nut roast are *not*
on the menu at this vegetarian restaurant.
Instead this is an upmarket affair, with
sleek-looking customers and lip-smacking
Mediterranean, Austrian and Asian fare that
ranges from risotto to tofu.

Österreicher im MAK (Map pp46-7; ☎ 714 01 21;
01, Stubenring 5; lunch menu €6.40, mains €12-22) Top
chef Helmut Österreicher has channelled his
considerable talents into creating a menu
here filled with measured portions of classic
Viennese dishes and modern takes on traditional Austrian cuisine.

Indochine 21 (Map pp46-7; ☎ 513 76 60; 01, Stubenring
18; mains €15-40) This is one of Vienna's finest restaurants, obtaining the Best Asian
Restaurant award in the city a few years back.
The food is trendy French-Vietnamese, while
red-lacquered umbrellas hang on the walls

AUSTRIA

and exotic potted plants evoke a vaguely colonial ambience.

DO & CO (Map pp46-7; ☎ 535 39 69; 01, Haas Haus, Stephansplatz 12; mains €15-30) The food and the views from seven floors above Stephansplatz keep this elegant restaurant in business. Contemporary Viennese dishes are highlighted, but it also serves Austrian classics, Uruguayan beef and Asian specialities. The service is flawless. Book ahead.

En (Map pp46-7; ☎ 532 44 90; 01, Werdertorgasse 8; lunch menu €8-10, meals about €20) En offers some of the best sushi in the entire city, and its lunch menus are an absolute bargain considering the quality. Outdoor seating is available in summer; in winter take a pew inside at the bar and watch the skilled sushi-makers prepare your meal.

Quick Eats & Self-Catering

Sausages are the fast-food choice of many Viennese (especially at the end of a night out), and sausage stands dot the city: **Würstelstand am Hoher Markt** (Map pp46-7; 01, Hoher Markt) is often rated at the best in Vienna. There are plenty of supermarkets throughout the city, and many have delicatessens that make cheap sandwiches on request.

Cheap student cafeterias include **Technical University Mensa** (Map pp46-7; 04, Resselgasse 7-9; mains €3.50-5; ☷ 11am-2pm Mon-Fri) and **Universität Mensa** (Map pp46-7; 7th fl, 01, Universitätsstrasse 7; mains €4.50-5; ☷ 11am-2pm Mon-Fri). Though the latter is closed in July and August, its adjoining **cafe** (☷ 8am-3pm Mon-Fri) remains open for business year-round.

DRINKING
Bars

The area near Schwedenplatz, dubbed the **Bermudadreieck** (Bermuda Triangle; Map pp46-7), may still attract plenty of drinkers (mainly they're drunk teenagers and out-of-towners), but the real scene has moved out of the centre to the likes of the Naschmarkt, along the Danube Canal (summer only), Schleifmühlgasse area (Map pp46-7), and along the Gürtel (Map pp42-3). There is, however, a plethora of great *Lokals* (bars) located in every neighbourhood.

Flanagans (Map pp46-7; ☎ 513 73 78; 01, Schwarzenberg Strasse 1-3) With plenty of TVs featuring live English football and international rugby, along with Guinness and Stella on tap, Flanagans pulls in the expat crowd like no

other pub in Vienna. Friday and Saturday nights here can be a spectacle.

Palmenhaus (Map pp46-7; ☎ 533 10 33; 01, Burggarten) Housed in a beautifully restored Victorian palm house, the Palmenhaus is among the most elaborate bar-restaurants in the city. In summer, tables spill out onto the pavement overlooking the green of the Burggarten.

Kunsthallencafé (Map pp46-7; ☎ 587 00 73; 04, Treitlstrasse 2) The ubercool Kunsthallencafé is a mecca for BoBos and students, offering slick surrounds, comfy couches, regular DJs, and a massive summer terrace. Surprisingly, the desserts here are divine.

Das Möbel (Map pp46-7; ☎ 524 94 97; 07, Burggasse 10) The interior is never dull at this bar near the Museums Quartier. It's remarkable for its funky decor and furniture – cube stools, assorted moulded lamps – and everything is up for sale.

Café Stein (Map pp46-7; ☎ 319 72 41; 09, Währinger Strasse 6-8; ⌨) This trendy, student cafe-bar-cum-diner offers a smoke-free environment in which to curl up with a good book or surf the internet. It also hosts poetry slams and modern-art exhibitions.

Also recommended:

Phil (Map pp46-7; ☎ 581 04 89; 06, Gumpendorferstrasse 10-12) Retro bookshop-bar with a bohemian slant and easygoing vibe.

Rhiz (Map pp42-3; ☎ 409 25 05; 08, Lechenfelder Gürtel 37-38) A mecca for Vienna's electronic music scene; it's in the U-Bahn arches.

Schikaneder (Map pp46-7; ☎ 585 58 88; 04, Margaretenstrasse 22-4) Alternative bar-cinema attracting students and black-clad folk.

Coffee Houses

Vienna's famous *Kaffeehäuser* (coffee houses) are like economic forecasts; ask two people for a recommendation and you'll get four answers. Following are a few local favourites – a full-sized coffee will cost roughly €3 to €3.50, but you can take as long as you like to drink it without being moved on.

our pick **Café Sperl** (Map pp46-7; ☎ 586 41 58; 06, Gumpendorfer Strasse 11) With its scuffed but original 19th-century fittings and cast of slacker patrons playing chess and reading newspapers, this is exactly how you expect an Austrian coffee house to be. Under the high ceiling and old-fashioned lights, wooden panelling reaches up to meet mustard-coloured wallpaper, while battered wooden

WHAT'S ON A COFFEE DRINKER'S MIND?

From the way customers linger over their cappuccino, *Grosser Brauner* or *Melange* in a Viennese *Kaffeehaus* (coffee house), it's easy to believe Austrians have always been born with a coffee spoon in their mouths. How did the tradition take such a hold here?

Local schoolchildren are taught that the beverage entered their country after the Ottoman Empire's siege of Vienna in 1683. Polish merchant Georg Kolschitzky smuggled a message out of his adopted city to the Polish king, who eventually came to Vienna's rescue; and Kolschitzky asked to be rewarded with the sacks of coffee beans abandoned by Kara Mustafa's retreating army. As historian Simon Schama put it, Austria managed to 'resist the Turkish siege but (was) defenceless against the coffee bean'.

Only much later, from the 18th century, did the tradition of spending long hours in coffee houses truly become entrenched. To escape Vienna's mostly unheated apartments, impoverished artists and intellectuals would set up shop at their coffee-house tables, writing and holding meetings and debates. Sigmund Freud and Leon Trotsky spent hours at Café Central (below), plotting, playing chess and running up a tab for hot drinks. When the Russian Revolution started, Trotsky left Vienna (much to the chagrin of the head waiter) without paying his bill.

Today coffee drinking remains a central part of Viennese, and to a lesser extent Austrian, life. It goes beyond a simple Starbucks culture (but surprisingly that chain now exists here, too). The true coffee house is still a place for music, exhibitions and cultural events; see what's on at the **Viennese Coffee House** (www.wiener-kaffeehaus.at). Above all, in the birthplace of psychoanalysis, it's somewhere to offset the stresses of the everyday. As the owner of a Viennese coffee shop once theorised to the *Guardian* newspaper, 'The coffee is the medicine, the waiters, the therapists'.

---

legs hold up red-patterned chairs and a few billiard tables add a modern twist.

Café Prückel (Map pp46-7; ☎ 512 61 15; 01, Stubenring 24) Juxtaposing Vienna's formal cafes, this 1950s-style cafe is the epitome of shabby chic. Enjoy the delightful cakes, friendly waiters, and nonsmoking section out back.

Café Central (Map pp46-7; ☎ 533 37 63; 01, Herrengasse 14) A lot more commercialised than when Herrs Trotsky, Freud and Beethoven drank here, we dare say, but still appealing with vaulted ceilings, palms and baroque architecture.

Also noteworthy:

Café Sacher (Map pp46-7; ☎ 514 56-661; 01, Philharmoniker strasse 4) An institution for its world-famous chocolate cake – the Sacher Torte, baked here since 1832. Expensive treat, but well worth the little extra.

Demel (Map pp46-7; ☎ 535 17 17; 01, Kohlmarkt 14) In operation since 1786. Stop by and gaze longingly at the incredible cake creations in the window.

Kleines Café (Map pp46-7; 01, Franziskanerplatz 3) Tiny bohemian cafe with wonderful summer seating on Franziskanerplatz.

Heurigen (Wine Taverns)

Vienna's *Heurigen* are a good way to see another side of the city. Selling 'new' wine produced on the premises, they have a lively atmosphere, especially as the evening progresses. Outside tables and picnic benches are common, as is buffet food.

Because *Heurigen* tend to be clustered together, it's best just to head for the wine-growing suburbs to the north, northeast, south and west of the city and to look for the green wreath or branch hanging over the door that identifies a *Heuriger*. Opening times are approximately from 4pm to 11pm, and wine costs less than €2.50 per *Viertel* (250mL).

The *Heurigen* areas of Nussdorf and Heiligenstadt are near each other at the terminus of tram D, north of the city centre. In 1817 Beethoven lived at 19, Pfarrplatz 3, Heiligenstadt in what is now known as Beethovenhaus. Further up into the hills (bus 38A from Heiligenstadt or tram 38 from the Ring) is Grinzing, an area favoured by tour groups.

Reinprecht (off Map pp42-3; ☎ 320 14 71; 19, Cobenzlgasse 22; ☺ mid-Feb–Dec) Reinprecht is the best option in the row of *Heurigen* where Cobenzlgasse and Sandgasse meet in Grinzing. It's in a former monastery and boasts a large paved courtyard and a lively, if somewhat touristy, atmosphere.

Sirbu (off Map pp42-3; ☎ 320 59 28; 19, Kahlenberger Strasse 210; ☺ Mon-Sat Apr-Oct) This spot has great views of the Danube. Catch bus 38A east to the final stop at Kahlenberg, from where it is a 15-minute walk downhill.

City *Heurigen:*

Esterházykeller (Map pp46-7; ☎ 533 34 82; 01, Haarhof 1) Dating from 1683 (and allegedly used for provision storage during the Turkish siege), this cellar *Heurigen* is well below the street level.

Zwölf Apostelkeller (Map pp46-7; ☎ 512 67 77; 01, Sonnenfelsgasse 3) Another atmospheric cellar haunt with as many levels as Dante's *Inferno.*

ENTERTAINMENT

Check listings magazine *Falter* (€2.40, in German) for weekly updates. The tourist office has copies of *Vienna Scene* and produces monthly events listings.

Cinemas & Theatre

Burgkino (Map pp46-7; ☎ 587 84 06; 01, Opernring 19) Screens *The Third Man* every Friday evening, and also on Sunday, Tuesday, Wednesday and Thursday afternoons, if you want to revisit this classic movie while in Vienna. Seats are cheapest on Monday.

There are performances in English at the **English Theatre** (Map pp46-7; ☎ 402 12 60-0; www .englishtheatre.at; 08, Josefsgasse 12) and **International Theatre** (Map pp46-7; ☎ 319 62 72; www.international theatre.at; 09, Porzellangasse 8).

Classical Music

The cheapest deals are the standing-room tickets that go on sale at each venue around an hour before performances. However, you may need to queue three hours before that for major productions.

Staatsoper (State Opera; Map pp46-7; ☎ 513 1513; www .staatsoper.at; 01, Opernring 2; standing room €2-3.50, seats €7-254) Performances are lavish, formal affairs, where people dress up.

Volksoper (People's Opera; Map pp42-3; ☎ 514 44-3318; www.volksoper.at; 09, Währinger Strasse 78; standing room €1.50-4, seats €4-150) Productions are more modern here and the atmosphere is a little more relaxed.

Musikverein (Map pp46-7; ☎ 505 18 90; www.musik verein.at; 01, Bösendorferstrasse 12; standing room €4-6, seats €17-118) The opulent and acoustically perfect (unofficial) home of the Vienna Philharmonic Orchestra. You can buy standing-room tickets three weeks in advance at the box office to hear this world-class orchestra.

The state ticket office, **Bundestheaterkassen** (Map pp46-7; ☎ 514 44-7880; www.bundestheater.at; 01, Goethegasse 1), sells tickets without commission

for both the Staatsoper and Volksoper. In the hut by the Staatsoper, **Wien Ticket** (Map pp46-7; ☎ 58 885; www.wien-ticket.at, in German; 01, Kärntner Strasse 40) also charges little or no commission for cash sales.

There are no performances in July and August. Ask at the tourist office for details of free concerts at the Rathaus or in churches.

Nightclubs

our pick **Flex** (Map pp46-7; ☎ 533 75 25; www.flex.at; 01, Donaukanal/Augartenbrücke) The stairwell leading from the U-Bahn stop to its doors constantly reeks of urine, and the circling dealers are an annoyance, but Flex is still the finest club in the city. Time after time this uninhibited shrine to music (it has one of the best sound systems in Europe) puts on great live shows and features the top DJs from Vienna and abroad. Each night is a different theme, with Crazy on Tuesday and London Calling on Wednesday among the most popular.

Porgy n Bess (Map pp46-7; ☎ 512 88 11; www .porgy.at; 01, Riemergasse 11; ☺ 7pm-late) Vienna's best spot to catch modern, local and international jazz acts. It has a relaxed and sophisticated atmosphere that attracts a professional crowd.

Volksgarten (Map pp46-7; ☎ 532 42 41; www .volksgarten.at; 01, Burgring 1) In the middle of the park of the same name, this place is very popular. There's modern dance and an atmospheric 1950s-style salon that was once a former *Walzer Dancing* venue. Friday and Saturday are the big nights, although it's open other evenings, too.

Roxy (Map pp46-7; www.roxyclub.at; 04, Operngasse 24; ☺ Wed-Sun) Often leading the way, or at least keeping pace, with Vienna's progressive clubbing scene. Its tiny dance floor is therefore regularly bursting at the seams. The sounds range from jazz to world music.

Why Not? (Map pp46-7; ☎ 535 11 58; www.why-not .at; 01, Tiefer Graben 22; ☺ Fri & Sat) A popular gay bar-disco for like-minded people.

Spanish Riding School

The famous Lipizzaner stallions strut their stuff at the **Spanish Riding School** (Map pp46-7; ☎ 533 90 31-0; www.srs.at; 01, Michaelerplatz 1; standing room €20-28, seats €35-165) behind the Hofburg. Performances are sold out months in advance, but you can book online or over the phone. On the day, unclaimed tickets are sold 45 minutes before performances. Travel

HAPPY SNAPS

Vienna is the perfect place to (re)discover your love of photography, with a Russian-designed camera of course. The city is the home of Lomo, plastic compacts that, for example, put nine identical images in one frame or that capture a sequence of four actions in one picture. Although originally a Russian brand, they are now designed in Vienna, which also hosts the Lomographic World Archive in **Lomography Society International** (www.lomography.com). The **Lomo Shop** (Map pp46–7; ☎ 523 70 16; MuseumsQuartier; ☒ 11am-7pm), next to the Kunsthalle, is eminently browsable, as you can just admire the artistic photos on its walls.

agents usually charge commission on top of the listed prices.

Same-day **tickets** (adult/senior/student €12/9/6, with entry to the Lipizzaner Museum €25/19/12; ☒ 10am-noon Tue-Sat Feb-Jun & Sep-Dec) can be bought to watch the horses train. The best riders go first and queues disappear by 11am.

Vienna Boys' Choir

Never mind bands like Take That and 'N Sync; the Vienna Boys' Choir *(Wiener Sängerknaben)* is *the* original boy band. The first troupe was put together back in 1498 and the latest bunch of cherubic angels in sailor suits still holds a fond place in Austrian hearts.

The choir performs weekly at the **Burgkapelle** (Music Chapel; Map pp46–7; ☎ 533 99 27; whmk@chello .at; 01, Hofburg, Rennweg 1; standing-room free, seats €5-29, ☒ tickets Fri & 8.15am Sun) at 9.15am on Sunday, except from July to mid-September. Concerts are routinely sold out (tickets can be booked in advance via telephone or email) and there's often a crush of fans wanting to meet the choir afterwards. The group also performs regularly in the Musikverein (opposite) – check www .wsk.at for more information.

SHOPPING

The Innere Stadt is generally reserved for designer labels and overpriced jewellery – most Viennese head to Mariahilfer Strasse (Map pp42–3) for their High St shopping.

Manner (Map pp46–7; ☎ 513 70 18; 01; Stephansplatz 7) Manner has been producing Vienna's fa-vourite sweets, *Manner Schnitten* (wafers filled with hazelnut cream), since 1898, and after one bite, you'll too be hooked. Buy a backpack-full here.

Österreiche Werkstätten (Map pp46–7; ☎ 512 24 18; 01, Kärntner Strasse 6) Good for art deco–type jewellery and household objects in the Viennese tradition; other local specialities include lamps, handmade dolls, and wrought-iron and leather goods.

Dorotheum (Map pp46–7; ☎ 515 60-0; www.dorotheum .com; 01, Dorotheergasse 17) One of Europe's largest auction houses, where surprisingly not every item is priced out of this world. Stop by and simply browse – it's as entertaining as visiting many of the Vienna's museums.

GETTING THERE & AWAY
Air

Austrian Airlines (OS; ☎ 051 766 1000; www.aua.com; Vienna Schwechat airport) regularly links Vienna with Linz, Salzburg, Innsbruck, Klagenfurt and Graz, but considering the size of Austria, travelling by train is a highly viable option. There are also daily nonstop flights to all major European destinations. For further details, see p89.

Boat

Fast hydrofoils travel eastwards to Bratislava (one-way €16 to €28, return €32 to €48, bike extra €6, 1¼ hours), daily from April to October and on Saturdays and Sundays in March and Budapest (one-way/return €89/109, bike extra €20, 5½ hours) daily. Bookings can be made through **DDSG Blue Danube** (Map pp42–3; ☎ 58 880-0; www.ddsg-blue-danube .at; 02, Handelskai 265).

Heading west, a series of boats plies the Danube between Krems and Melk, with a handful of services originating in Vienna. Two respectable operators include DDSG Blue Danube and **Brandner** (☎ 07433-25 90; www.brandner.at), the latter located in Wallsee. Both run trips from April through October that start at around €11 one way. For trips into Germany, contact **Donauschiffahrt Wurk + Köck** (☎ 0732 783607; www.donauschiffahrt.de; Untere Donaulände 1, Linz).

Bus

Eurolines (Map pp42–3; ☎ 798 29 00; 03, Erdbergstrasse 202; ☒ 6.30am-9pm) is the main bus company operating out of Vienna. Most buses, including those destined for Bratislava (one way/return €5/10,

AUSTRIA

one hour), Budapest (one way/return €23/36, three hours), Prague (one way/return €19/35, 4¼ hours) Split (one way/return €41/74, 12½ hours) and Warsaw (one way/return €35/63, 12 hours), leave from Erdbergstrasse, but some buses can be picked up at Südbahnhof, Schwedenplatz, and Praterstern.

Car & Motorcycle

The Gürtel is an outer ring road that joins up with the A22 on the north bank of the Danube and the A23 southeast of town. All the main road routes intersect with this system, including the A1 from Linz and Salzburg, and the A2 from Graz.

Train

International trains leave from Westbahnhof (Map pp42–3) or Südbahnhof (Map pp42–3), both of which will be receiving major renovations for the life of this book. Westbahnhof's main concourse will remain closed, and access to trains is through a temporary entrance to the south of the station where ticket desks, left luggage and other services are located. Train timetables, however, will not be affected. Between 2009 and 2013 Südbahnhof will be demolished and a modern station, Wien Hauptbahnhof, will be built in its place. At the time of writing, it was not clear how train services would be affected.

Westbahnhof has trains to northern and Western Europe, and to western Austria. Services to Salzburg (€44, three hours) leave roughly hourly, where a change is normally required if travelling on to Munich (€77, 5½ hours). To Zürich there are two trains during the day (€91, 8¾ hours) and one night train (€91 plus charge for fold-down seat/couchette); Paris is served by two daytime (€216, 12 hours) and three overnight trains (€174, 13 to 15½ hours); all require a change in either Germany or Switzerland. Ten direct trains daily go to Budapest (€34.20, three hours). Wien-Mitte Bahnhof handles local trains only, and Franz Josefs Bahnhof has local and regional trains.

For train information, call ☎ 05-17 17.

GETTING AROUND
To/From the Airport

It is 19km from the city centre to **Wien Schwechat airport**. The **City Airport Train** (CAT; ☎ 25 250; www.cityairporttrain.com) takes 16 minutes between Schwechat and Wien Mitte (one way/return

€9/16). The **S-Bahn (S7)** does the same journey (single €3.40) but in 26 minutes.

Buses run every 20 or 30 minutes, between 5am and midnight, from the airport (one way/return €7/13). Services run to Südtiroler Platz, Südbahnhof and Westbahnhof, UNO City, and Schwedenplatz.

Taxis cost about €35. **C&K Airport Service** (☎ 44 444) charges €27 one way for shared vans.

Bicycle

Vienna is serviced by **CityBike** (☎ 0810-500 500; www.citybikewien.at; 1st hr free, 2nd hr €1, 3rd hr €2, per hr thereafter €4), which offers a series of more than 50 bicycle stands across the city. You'll need a Visa, MasterCard or JCB credit card, or a Tourist Card available from **Royal Tours** (Map pp46–7; ☎ 710 4606; 01, Herrengasse 1-3; card €2; ☒ 9-11.30am & 1-6pm) to be able to use the payment machines.

You'll pay a lot more for bike hire at **Pedal Power** (Map pp42–3; ☎ 729 72 34; www.pedalpower.at; 02, Ausstellungsstrasse 3; per half-/full day €17/27), the city's dominant operator, but the tourist office should be able to point to others near your hostel or hotel. *Tips für Radfahrer*, available from the tourist office, shows circular bike tours.

Car & Motorcycle

Parking is difficult in the city centre and the Viennese are impatient drivers. Blue parking zones (labelled *Kurzparkzone*) allow a maximum stop of 1½ or two hours from 9am to 10pm on weekdays.

Parking vouchers (€0.80/2.40 per one/two hours) for these times can be purchased in *Tabak* (tobacconist) shops and banks. The cheapest parking garage in the city centre is at Museumsplatz.

Fiakers

Before hiring a *Fiaker* (horse-drawn carriage) by the Stephansdom for a ride around the city, it's worth asking yourself whether these are pony traps or tourist traps. Sure, they're kind of cute, but at around €65/95 for a 30-/60-minute ride…well, you do the maths.

Public Transport

Vienna has a unified public transport network that encompasses trains, trams, buses, and underground (U-Bahn) and suburban (S-Bahn) trains. Routes are outlined on the free tourist-office map.

Before use, all advance-purchase tickets must be validated at the entrance to U-Bahn stations or on trams and buses. Tickets are cheaper to buy from ticket machines in U-Bahn stations or from *Tabak* shops, where single tickets cost €1.70. On board, they cost €2.20. Singles are valid for an hour, and you may change lines on the same trip.

Daily passes *(Stunden-Netzkarte)* cost €5.70 (valid 24 hours from first use); a three-day pass costs €13.60; and an eight-day multiple-user pass *(8-Tage-Karte)* costs €27.20 (validate the ticket once per day per person). Weekly tickets (valid Monday to Sunday) cost €14; the Vienna Card (€18.50) includes travel on public transport for up to three days.

Children under six years travel free; those under 16 travel free on Sunday, public holidays and during Vienna school holidays (photo ID necessary). Senior citizens should ask about discounts.

Ticket inspections are not very frequent, but fare dodgers pay an on-the-spot fine of €62. Austrian and European rail passes (see p615) are valid on the S-Bahn only. Public transport finishes around midnight, but there's also a comprehensive night-bus service, for which all tickets are valid.

Taxi

Taxis are metered for city journeys and cost €2.50 flag fall during the day and €2.60 at night, plus from €0.87 per kilometre. It's safe to hail taxis from the street, and there's generally an abundance of choice.

THE DANUBE VALLEY

The stretch of Danube between Krems and Melk, known locally as the Wachau, is arguably the loveliest along the entire length of the mighty river. Both banks are dotted with ruined castles, medieval towns, and lined with terraced vineyards. Further upstream is the industrial city of Linz which has more going for it than first appearances let on.

KREMS AN DER DONAU
☎ 02732 / pop 24,000
Krems is the gateway to the Danube Valley. Despite its pretty cobbled centre and attractive position on the northern bank of the Danube, most people only see it during a stopover on a boat or bike trip through the Danube Valley. The **tourist office** (☎ 82

676; www.tiscover.com/krems; Kloster Und, Undstrasse 6; ⏰ 9am-6pm Mon-Fri, 9am-5pm Sat, 9am-4pm Sun May-Oct, 9am-5pm Mon-Fri Nov-Apr) can offer accommodation details, otherwise head for the riverside **ÖAMTC Camping Krems** (☎ 84 455; donaucampingkrems@aon.at; Wiedengasse 7; camp site per person & tent €5.50; ⏰ Easter–mid-Oct) or central HI **Jugendherberge** (☎ 83 452; oejhv.noe.krems@aon .at; Ringstrasse 77; dm from €18.20; ⏰ Apr-Oct).

The *Schiffsstation* (boat station) is a 20-minute walk west from the train station along Donaulände. Three buses leave daily from outside the train station to Melk (€6.50, 56 minutes), and frequent trains head in the opposite direction to Vienna (€14, one hour).

DÜRNSTEIN
☎ 02711 / pop 900
This pretty town, on a curve in the Danube, is not only noted for its beautiful buildings but also for the castle above the town, which at one time imprisoned English king Richard I (the Lion-Heart) in 1192. His unscheduled stopover on the way home from the Crusades came courtesy of Austrian archduke Leopold V, whom he had insulted.

There's not much left of **Künringerburg castle** today. It's basically just a pile of rubble. Still, it's worth snapping a picture and the views from the top are breathtaking.

For more about Dürnstein, contact the **tourist office** (☎ 200; www.duernstein.at; Dürnstein Bahnhof; ⏰ 2-6pm Mon-Sat mid-Mar–mid-Nov) in the train station. Dürnstein can be reached from Krems by train (€3, 10 minutes) on an hourly basis.

MELK
☎ 02752 / pop 5200
With its imposing abbey-fortress rising above the Danube and a small, cobbled town, Melk is the highlight of the Danube Valley. Featured in the epic medieval German poem *Nibelungenlied* and Umberto Eco's best-selling novel *The Name of the Rose*, the impressive Benedictine monastery endures as a major Wachau landmark. It's an essential stop along the Danube Valley route, however, so be prepared to fight through loads of tourists to explore the place.

Orientation & Information
The train station is 300m from the town centre. Walk straight ahead from the train station along Bahnhofstrasse, turning right into Abt Karl Strasse if you're going to the hostel

AUSTRIA

or continuing ahead for the town. The quickest way to the central Rathausplatz is through the small Bahngasse path (to the right of the cow's-head mural at the bottom of the hill), rather than veering left into Hauptplatz.

Turn right from Bahngasse into Rathausplatz and then right again at the end, following the signs to the **tourist office** (☎ 52 307-410; www .tiscover.com/melk; Babenbergerstrasse 1; 9am-noon & 2-6pm Mon-Fri, 10am-noon Sat Apr, plus 10am-noon & 4-6pm Sat & Sun May, Jun & Sep, 9am-7pm Mon-Sat, 10am-noon & 5-7pm Sun Jul & Aug, 9am-noon & 2-5pm Mon-Fri, 10am-noon Sat Oct).

Sights & Activities

On a hill overlooking the town is the ornate golden abbey **Stift Melk** (☎ 555 232; www.stiftmelk .at; adult/student €7.70/4.50, with guided tour €9.50/6.30; 9am-5.30pm May-Sep, 9am-4.30pm mid-Mar–Apr 7 Oct, guided tours only Nov-Mar). Home to monks since the 11th century, the current building was erected in the 18th century after a devastating fire. Consequently, it's an elaborate example of baroque architecture, most often lauded for its imposing marble hall and beautiful library, but just as unforgettable for the curved terrace connecting these two rooms. The **Abbey Museum** on the grounds outlines the history of the building and the church with its exhibition topic entitled 'The Path from Yesterday to Today – Melk in its Past and Present'. Various rooms using computer animation, sound and multimedia accurately narrate the 910-year-plus Benedictine monastic history of Melk.

It's helpful to phone ahead if you want a tour in English.

Sleeping & Eating

Camping Melk (☎ 53 291; Kolomaniau 3; camp site per person/car/tent €3/2/3.50; Mar-Oct) Located on the west bank of the canal that joins the Danube, this camping ground is a tranquil spot. If you get hungry, there is an attached restaurant, where you'll also find reception.

Jugendherberge (☎ 52 681; melk@noejhw.at; Karl Strasse 42; dm €20; check-in 4-9pm) This HI hostel is modern and comfy and only 10-minutes' walk from the train station.

Gasthof Goldener Stern (☎ 52 214; www.sternmelk .at; Sterngasse 17; s/d from €35/42) This charming guest house sports individually decorated rooms with more than a touch of romance about them. Expect to find four-poster beds, anti-allergy duvets and sheets, and warm

colour schemes. It's located above the main square and also has a fine restaurant.

Self-caterers should stock up at the **Spar** supermarket (Rathausplatz 9), but those wanting a meal befitting the Wachau can head to **Tom's Restaurant** (☎ 52 475; Hauptplatz 1; mains €20), whose menu heavily features seasonal cuisine and fab regional wines.

Getting There & Away

Boats leave from the canal by Pionierstrasse, 400m behind the monastery. There are hourly direct trains to Vienna's Westbahnhof (€16.10, 1¼ hours) daily.

LINZ

☎ 0732 / pop 189,000

In Linz beginnt's (it begins in Linz) goes the Austrian saying, but at first glance it's unsure what began here. On closer inspection, however, it soon becomes clear. Linz is blessed with a leading-edge cyber centre and world-class contemporary-art gallery, both of which are signs that the country's technological industry got its kick start in the Upper Austrian capital. And even though Linz is essentially industrial by nature, there's plenty of culture to contend with, so much so that it gained the title of European Capital of Culture 2009.

Orientation

Most of the city is on the south bank of the Danube. The main square, Hauptplatz, is reached from the train station on trams 1, 2 and 3. To walk here, turn right (northeast) out of the station forecourt, Bahnhofplatz, and continue straight ahead until you come to a park on the left. Turn left here into Landstrasse and continue for 10 minutes to get to Hauptplatz.

Information

Ars Electronica Center (☎ 72 720; www.aec.at; Hauptstrasse 2; 9am-5pm Wed-Fri, 10am-6pm Sat & Sun) Offers free internet access.

Linz City Ticket Premium (€20) Free public transport, sightseeing discounts and a meal valued at €10; available at the tourist office.

Main post office (Bahnhofplatz 11-13; 7am-9pm Mon-Fri, 9am-6pm Sat, 9am-1pm Sun)

Tourist office (☎ 7070-1777; www.linz.at; Hauptplatz 1; 8am-7pm Mon-Fri, 10am-7pm Sat & Sun May-Oct, 8am-6pm Mon-Fri, 10am-6pm Sat & Sun Nov-Apr)

WORTH THE TRIP: MAUTHAUSEN

It may not be everyone's cup of tea, but **KZ Mauthausen** (☎ 07238-2269; Erinnerrungstrasse 1; adult/concession €2/1; ⊙ 9am-5.30pm) is an important reminder of a dark period in Austrian history and a testament to the depths of human cruelty. From 1938 to 1945 the Nazis used this former quarry site as a concentration camp and went about murdering 100,000 prisoners who passed through its gates. Parts of the original camp remain intact, including cramped living quarters and the disturbing gas chambers. Artefacts, photos, and camp documents are also on display.

Frequent buses and trains connect Mauthausen with Linz (€7.80, 30 minutes). The camp site is 5km west of the train station; thankfully bicycles can be hired here.

Sights & Activities

Architecturally eye-catching and artistically impressive, the riverside **Lentos Kunstmuseum Linz** (☎ 7070 3614; www.lentos.at, in German; Ernst Koref Promenade 1; adult/concession €6.50/4.50; ⊙ 10am-6pm Fri-Wed, till 9pm Thu) is a must-see. Built a little like an asymmetric tray table, with legs on either side, the building looks particularly spectacular at night when it's lit up. Behind its partially reflective glass facade lie works by artists such as Klimt, Schiele, Picasso, Kokoschka, Matisse, Haring and Warhol.

Across the Danube is the **Ars Electronica Center** (☎ 72 72-0; www.aec.at; Hauptstrasse 2; adult/student €6/3; ⊙ 9am-5pm Wed-Fri, 10am-6pm Sat & Sun), the city's centre for technological wizardry. Spend the afternoon strapped into a flight simulator over Linz, or use 'Gulliver's World' to rearrange the world a mountain range at a time.

A ride on the **Pöstlingbergbahn** (funicular railway; adult/child €4/2; ⊙ 5.40am-8.20pm Mon-Sat, 7.15am-8.20pm Sun) offers great views and is bound to keep kids of all ages happy. It looks like a quaint street trolley from a movie and climbs slowly to the ornate twin-spired church and **children's grotto railway** (☎ 3400 7506; adult/child €4.50/2.30; ⊙ 10am-6pm Jun-Aug, 10am-5pm Mar-May & Sep-Nov) atop the Pöstlingberg hill. To reach the Pöstlingbergbahn take tram 3 to Bergbahnof Urfahr.

Festivals & Events

The **Ars Electronica Festival** (☎ 72 72-0; www.aec.at) in early September showcases cyberart, computer music, and other marriages of technology and art. This leads into the **Brucknerfest** (☎ 775 230; www.bruckerhaus.at, in German; Brucknerhaus Kasse, Untere Donaulände, A-4010 Linz), which pays homage to native son Anton Bruckner with a month of classical music between mid-September and mid-October. Book early for this.

Sleeping

The tourist office offers a free accommodation-booking service for visitors, but only face-to-face and not over the phone.

Jugendgästehaus (☎ 664 434; www.oejhv.or.at; Stanglhofweg 3; dm/s/d €19.50/29.50/44) This modern and comfortable hostel offers half- and full-board options. Its only drawback is its location, 1.5km west of the city centre; board bus 17, 19 or 27 to get them.

Wilder Mann (☎ 656 078; wilder-mann@aon.at; Goethestrasse 14; s/d with shared bathroom €25/42, with private bathroom €30/50) Despite first impressions at this boarding house–style place, the rooms are reasonably comfy and the bathrooms clean. Try to avoid the top floor, where frosted-glass door panels let in hall light. Breakfast is an extra €6.

Goldener Anker (☎ 771 088; goldener.anker.linz@aon.at; Hofgasse 5; s/d from €50/80) A tastefully decorated family run *Gasthof* (guest house) inside Linz's oldest pub, rooms here are comfortable and quaint. It's also well located just off the main square.

Hotel Wolfinger (☎ 773 291-0; www.hotelwolfinger.at; Hauptplatz 19; s/d €87/126) Originally a cloister, Wolfinger has been renovated in baroque style. Its front rooms have commanding views over the Hauptplatz and all are bedecked with period furniture and touches of charm.

Eating

Café Traximayr (☎ 773 353; Promenadestrasse 16; snacks from €5; ⊙ 8am-10pm Mon-Fri, 8am-8pm Sat, 9am-6pm Sun) An elegant coffee house, with only a few snooker tables breaking up the formal environment of white walls, marble, mirrors and chandeliers. Try the Linzer torte – this heavy, nutty-tasting sponge filled with strawberry jam isn't on the menu but it is on the cake trolley, so just ask.

p'aa (☎ 776 461; Altstadt 28; mains €8-12; ⊙ Mon-Sat) The menu here is an eclectic mix of Tibetan,

Indian and Mexican cuisine, most of which is vegetarian. Sit on the cobblestones outside or inside under low arched ceilings.

Stiegelbräu zum Klosterhof (Landstrasse 30; mains €10-18) Klosterhof has earned a fine gastronomic reputation with its Austrian classics and seasonal specialities. In summer the huge beer garden is a favourite of half the town.

Getting There & Around

Low-cost Ryanair flies to **Linz airport** (LNZ; ☎ 07221-600-0; www.linz-airport.at) four times weekly from London Stansted; a shuttle bus (€2.50, 20 minutes) links the airport to the main train station.

Linz is halfway between Salzburg and Vienna on the main road and rail routes. Trains to Salzburg (€20.70) and Vienna (€29.10) take between 1¼ and two hours and leave approximately hourly.

City transport tickets are bought before you board: €0.80 per journeys up to four stops, €1.70 for anything over that, and €3.40 for a day card. Some of the bus services stop early in the evening.

THE SOUTH

Austria's two main southern states, Styria (Steiermark) and Carinthia (Kärnten), often feel worlds apart from the rest of the country, both in climate and attitude. Elements of Italian, Slovenian and Hungarian culture are present here, and residents have historical connections with each of those countries. Styria is a blissful amalgamation of genteel architecture, rolling green hills, vine-covered slopes and soaring mountains. Its capital, Graz, is one of Austria's most attractive cities.

A jet-setting, fashion-conscious crowd heads to sun-drenched Carinthia for summer holidays. The region (right on the border with Italy) exudes an atmosphere that's as close to Mediterranean as this staunch country gets.

GRAZ
☎ 0316 / pop 248,000
For many, Graz is Austria's number-two city, not simply because it's the country's second-largest city. This Styrian capital wins the hearts and minds of locals and tourists alike with its laid-back, almost Mediterranean, atmosphere, student-fuelled nightlife, mix of modern architectural gems and Renaissance

flourishes, and captivating museums. Pop in for a visit and Graz is sure to leave an indelible impression on you too.

Orientation

Graz is dominated by its *Schlossberg* (castle hill) looming above the city centre. The River Mur runs in a north–south path in front (west) of the hill, separating the city centre from the main train station (Hauptbahnhof). Trams 3 and 6 run from the train station to the central Hauptplatz. Several streets radiate from this square, including cafe-lined Sporgasse and the primary pedestrian thoroughfare, Herrengasse. The latter leads to Jakominiplatz, a major transport hub.

Information

Graz Tourismus (☎ 80 75-0; www.graztourismus.at; Herrengasse 16; ☼ 10am-5pm Mon-Fri, 10am-4pm Sat & Sun Jan-Mar & Nov, 10am-6pm Mon-Sat, 10am-4pm Sun Apr-Jun, Sep-Oct & Dec, 10am-7pm Mon-Fri, 10am-6pm Sat & Sun Jul & Aug) Also has an information stand and terminal in the train station (open 8.30am to 5pm Monday to Saturday) which has a free hotline to the main tourist office.
High Speed Internet-Selfstore (Herrengasse 3; per hr €3; ☼ 7am-1pm) Also offers wi-fi connection.
Main post office (Neutorgasse 46; ☼ 8am-8pm Mon-Fri)

Sights & Activities

Graz is a city easily enjoyed by simply wandering aimlessly, discovering its plethora of museums, galleries, grandiose architecture, churches and unusual surprises. If you'd prefer more direction, the tourist office organises **guided walks** (from €9.50), 2.30pm daily mid-March to October and on Saturday the rest of the year.

Most visitors first head for the **Schlossberg** to get an overview of the city and explore what remains of its fortress. This includes the medieval **clock tower**, plus a **bell tower**, **bastion** and **garrison museum** (☎ 827 348; adult/child €1/free; ☼ 10am-4pm Tue-Sun). There are three main ways to ascend: the glass **Schlossberglift** (adult/child €0.60/0.30), hewn through the hill; the **Schlossbergbahn** (funicular railway €1.70, free with 24-hour public ticket); and the 260 steps near the lift (free).

From this vantage point, you can't help but notice the striking bubble-shaped **Kunsthaus Graz** (☎ 8017 9200; www.kunsthausgraz.at; Lendkai 1; adult/student €7/3; ☼ 10am-6pm Tue-Sun). This creation by UK architects Colin Fournier and Peter

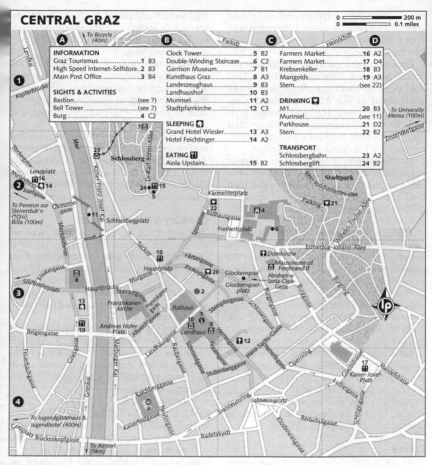

CENTRAL GRAZ

0 — 200 m
0 — 0.1 miles

INFORMATION		
Graz Tourismus	1	B3
High Speed Internet-Selfstore	2	B3
Main Post Office	3	B4

SIGHTS & ACTIVITIES		
Bastion	(see 7)	
Bell Tower	(see 7)	
Burg	4	C2

Clock Tower	5	B2
Double-Winding Staircase	6	C2
Garrison Museum	7	B1
Kunsthaus Graz	8	A3
Landeszeughaus	9	B3
Landhaushof	10	B3
Murinsel	11	A2
Stadtpfarrkirche	12	C3

SLEEPING		
Grand Hotel Wiesler	13	A3
Hotel Feichtinger	14	A2

EATING		
Aiola Upstairs	15	B2

Farmers Market	16	A2
Farmers Market	17	D4
Krebsenkeller	18	B3
Mangolds	19	A3
Stern	(see 22)	

DRINKING		
M1	20	B3
Murinsel	(see 11)	
Parkhouse	21	D2
Stern	22	B2

TRANSPORT		
Schlossbergbahn	23	A2
Schlossberglift	24	B2

Cook is referred to as the 'friendly alien' and is one of Europe's leading modern buildings. Whatever the temporary exhibitions – and these are often very good – it's the structure that's the star.

Likewise, the **Murinsel** (24hr), an artificial island in the River Mur connected to both banks, will surprise and delight. This open seashell of glass, concrete and steel, by New York artist Vito Acconic, houses an amphitheatre and trendy cafe-bar in aqua blue.

The heart of the Old Town has its fair share of triumphs. The **Landhaushof**, through an archway on Herrengasse by the tourist office, is one of the most celebrated examples of Italian Renaissance architecture in Austria, while the nearby **Landeszeughaus** (8017 9810; Herrengasse 16;

adult/student €7/3; 10am-6pm mid-Mar–Oct, 10am-5pm Mon-Sat, 10am-4pm Sun Nov–mid-Mar) will leave anyone with even a slight medieval-armour fetish in pure ecstasy. The **Stadtpfarrkirche** (Herrengasse 23; admission free; dawn-dusk) is famous for the stained-glass window behind the altar that depicts Hitler and Mussolini looking on as Jesus is tortured. Enjoying an elevated position above the Old Town is the **Burg** (Hofgasse); to the left of the door marked 'Stiege III' there's a **double-winding staircase** that twists in and out of itself.

Sleeping
Jugendgästehaus & Jugendhotel (708 3-210; www.jfgh.at; Idlhofgasse 74; dm/s/d €22/33/52;)
Ultramodern and comfortable, with en-suite

AUSTRIA

rooms, spacious reception/and restaurant areas, full wheelchair access, bike rental, and even a climbing wall. It's about 10 minutes on foot from the train station.

Pension Zur Steirerstub'n (☎ 716 855; www.pension -graz.at; Lendplatz 8; s/d/tr from €41/74/111) This neat pension looks for all the world like a *gästehaus* in the Austrian countryside. The sizable rooms are modern however, and the Styrian restaurant on the ground floor serves tasty food on a pleasant terrace overlooking Lendplatz.

Hotel Feichtinger (☎ 724 100; www.hotel-feichtinger .at; Lendplatz 1a; s/d from €51/96; 🖳) It may not ooze character, but this newer hotel offers a high level of comfort and is very good value for money. It's also within easy walking distance of the Old Town and Kunsthaus.

our pick **Hotel Daniel** (☎ 711 080; www.hoteldaniel .com; Europlatz 1; r €59-79; 🖳) Daniel may look like just another ugly train-station hotel from the outside, but inside it's an immaculate shrine to modern design and living. Rooms come in 'Smart' and 'Loggia' – both are bedecked with clean, minimalist furniture and fittings, however the latter are larger and come with balcony. Vespas are available to guests for €15 per day.

Grand Hotel Wiesler (☎ 70 66-0; www.hotelwiesler .com; Grieskai 4; s/d from €185/245; 🖳) The best of the top-end hotels in town, the Grand Wiesler is a beautiful art-nouveau affair with equally beautiful rooms and impeccable five-star service. Rooms are regularly discounted, so call ahead to check the going price.

Eating

With green, leafy salads dressed in delicious pumpkin-seed oil, lots of polenta, fish specialities and *Pfand'l* (pan-grilled) dishes, Styrian cuisine feels lighter and healthier than most regional Austrian cooking.

Mangolds (Griesgasse 11; meals €5-10; ☉ 11am-7pm Mon-Fri, 11am-4pm Sat) An ultrahealthy and cheap vegetarian buffet, with loads of salads and hot dishes to choose from. A 30% discount is offered after 5pm.

Stern (☎ 818 400; Sporgasse 38; mains €5-14; ☉ 9am-3am) Fill up on fine salads, wok specialities, and pasta dishes here during the day and early evening, then finish off the night with a cocktail on the large terrace or a boogie to DJs inside.

Krebsenkeller (☎ 829 377; Sackstrasse 12; mains €8-13) The Krebsenkeller is a regular favourite

with tourists and locals alike for its traditional surrounds, including a peaceful inner courtyard, and mix of hearty Austrian and lighter Styrian specialities.

Aiola Upstairs (☎ 818 797; Schlossberg 2; mains €9-20; ☉ 9am-midnight) Perched atop of Schlossberg, Aiola has the best views of any restaurant in the city. The scene is completed with quality international cuisine, attentive service, and an extensive wine list.

Self-caterers can avail of Graz's two morning **farmers markets** (Kaiser-Franz-Josef Platz & Lendplatz; ☉ 4.30am-1pm Mon-Sat), the **Billa** at Lendplatz 30, and the **Spar** in the train station. For cheap, filling meals, head to the main **university Mensa** (Sonnenfelsplatz 1; menus €5; ☉ 11am-2.30pm Mon-Fri).

Drinking & Entertainment

The bar scene in Graz is split between three areas: around the university, adjacent to the Kunsthaus, and stretching from Karmeliterplatz to Prokopgasse in the Old Town. In the last, 3rd-floor **M1** (Färbergasse 1) is favoured by the beautiful – and invariably young – people, while Stern (left) attracts a student crowd ready to party.

Murinsel (☎ 818 669; ☉ 9am-11pm Sun-Wed, 9am-2am Thu-Sat) You'll never again drink anywhere quite like the Murinsel, so at least start the evening in this shimmering, fluorescent-lit platform in the middle of the river. There are DJs on some evenings.

Parkhouse (☎ 827 434; Stadtpark 2; ☉ 11am-4am) Join the crowd at this atmospheric and friendly place in the city park if you're looking to party minus any type of pretentious vibe.

Dom in Berg (www.domimberg.at, in German; Schlossbergplatz) Located in the bowels of the Schlossberg, this nightclub and concert venue occupies tunnels once used as air-raid shelters and has a superb sound system.

Getting There & Away

Ryanair has regular flights from London Stansted and Barcelona to **Graz airport** (GRZ; ☎ 29 02-0; www.flughafen-graz.at, in German), while Intersky connects the city with Berlin and Friedrichshafen six times a week, and TUIfly with Cologne five times. Direct Intercity (IC) trains to Vienna's Südbahnhof depart every two hours (€31.40, 2¾ hours). Trains depart every two hours to Salzburg (€44.20, four hours), either direct or changing at Bischofshofen. Two daily, direct trains depart for Ljubljana (€34, 3⅓ hours), and one for Budapest (€47, 5¾ hours), although many more travel via Szombathely. Trains to Klagenfurt (€33, 2¾ hours) go via Bruck an der Mur. The A2 autobahn from Vienna to Klagenfurt passes a few kilometres south of the city.

Getting Around
Public transport tickets cover trams, buses, the Schlossbergbahn, and the hourly train to the airport from the train station. Tickets cost €1.70 each, or €3.70 for a 24-hour pass. Bicycles can be hired from aptly named **Bicycle** (☎ 821 357-0; Körösistrasse 5) from €10/49 per day/week.

KLAGENFURT
☎ 0463 / pop 92,000
With its salacious location on Wörthersee and more Renaissance than baroque beauty, Carinthia's capital Klagenfurt has a distinct Mediterranean feel. While there isn't a huge amount here to see, it makes a handy base for exploring Wörthersee's lakeside villages and elegant medieval towns to the north.

Orientation
The heart of the city is Neuer Platz, which is 1km north of the main train station. Walk straight down Bahnhofstrasse and turn left into Paradiesergasse to get there, or take buses 40 or 41 to Heiligengeistplatz, just around the corner from Neuer Platz.

Information
Gates Cafebar (Waagplatz 7; per 10min €1; ☼ 9am-1am Mon-Fri, 7pm-1am Sat & Sun) Offers internet access.
Main post office (Dr Hermann Gasse 4; ☼ 7.30am-6pm Mon-Fri, 8am-noon Sat)
Tourist office (☎ 537 22 23; www.klagenfurt-tourismus.at; Rathaus, Neuer Platz; ☼ 8am-6pm Mon-Fri, 10am-5pm Sat, 10am-3pm Sun)

Sights & Activities
The **Wörthersee**, 4km west of the city centre, is one of the region's warmer lakes, thanks to subterranean thermal springs: the average water temperature between June and September is 21°C (69°F). Events from go-kart rallies to avant-garde festivals of tattoo and body painting ensure you'll never be left without something to see. The 50km **cycle path** around the lake is one of the 'Top 10' in Austria. There is a *Fahrad Verleih* (bike hire) scheme from May to September: hire a stand-

ard bicycle at one of several outlets around the lake or the tourist office and return it at any other outlet (three hours/24 hours/one week costs €6/10/40). Mountain bikes (€12/19/85) are also available.

Also near the lake, Europa Park has various attractions, including the theme park **Minimundus** (☎ 21 194-0; Villacher Strasse 241; adult/student €12/11; ☼ Apr-Oct), which displays more than 150 models of famous international buildings on a 1:25 scale.

Sleeping & Eating
When you check into your accommodation in Klagenfurt, ask for a *Gästekarte* (guest card), which entitles you to a range of discounts.
Jugendherberge (☎ 230 020; jgh.klagenfurt@oejhv.or.at; Neckheimgasse 6; dm €20, r €28; ☐) A large, modern salmon-shaded hostel close to the university and Europa Park, and within walking distance to the lake. Some rooms come with balconies, and in summer it's often full with kids' groups.
Hotel Garni Blumenstöckl (☎ 577 93; www.blumenstoeckl.at; 10-Oktober-Strasse 11; s/d €47/76) Blumenstöckl is about as cheap as accommodation comes in downtown Klagenfurt. Rooms aren't particularly modern but they're centred on a lovely inner courtyard and staff are supremely friendly.
Hotel Geyer (☎ 578 86; www.hotelgeyer.com; Priesterhausgasse 5; s/d from €55/80) Everyone's favourite Klagenfurt hotel. The public areas are quite funky, with loads of modern art on the walls, and rooms are compact yet comfortable. A generous breakfast buffet is included.
Zum Augustin (☎ 513 992; Pfarrhofgasse 2; mains €8-18) This brewery is not only popular for its solid Austrian fare but also for the large range of beer on tap, including a couple of varieties from its own barrels. Grab a *krügel* (large beer) and enjoy the atmospheric cobbled courtyard.

Getting There & Around
Klagenfurt airport (KLU; ☎ 41 500; www.klagenfurt-airport.com) is served by Ryanair from London Stansted and Frankfurt-am-Main, and TUIfly from Berlin, Cologne, Hamburg and Hanover. Trains to Graz (€33, 2½ to 3½ hours) go via Bruck an der Mur and depart at least every two hours. Trains to western Austria, Italy and Germany go via Villach (€7.80, 30 minutes).

AUSTRIA

Bus drivers sell single tickets (€1.70), while daily/weekly passes cost €4/13. For the Europa Park vicinity, take bus 10, 11, 12, 20, 21 or 22 from Heiligengeistplatz in the city centre. To the airport, take bus 40 to Annabichl and change to bus 45; a taxi from the centre costs around €10. Bikes can be hired from **Zweirad Impulse** (☎ 516 310; 24-hr hire adult/child €10/7).

SALZBURG

☎ 0662 / pop 149,000

The joke 'if it's baroque, don't fix it' is a perfect maxim for Salzburg; the tranquil Old Town burrowed in below steep hills looks much as it did when Mozart lived here 250 years ago. Second only to Vienna in numbers of visitors, this compact city is centred on a tight grouping of narrow, cobbled streets overshadowed by ornate 17th-century buildings, which are in turn dominated by the medieval Hohensalzburg fortress from high above. Across the fast-flowing Salzach River rests the baroque Schloss Mirabell, surrounded by gorgeous manicured gardens.

If this doesn't whet your appetite, then bypass the grandeur and head straight for kitsch-country by joining a tour of *The Sound of Music* film locations.

ORIENTATION

The pedestrianised Old Town is on the south bank of the Salzach River, wedged between the river and Mönchsberg behind it. Many attractions and the shopping street of Getreidegasse are here. On the north bank is Mozart's Wohnhaus and Schloss Mirabell, as well as the new city centre, with most of the cheaper hotels. Buses 3 and 5 will take you from the main train station (Hauptbahnhof) to the city centre. To walk (about 10 minutes), turn left out of the train station into Rainerstrasse and follow it (taking the second, not the first tunnel under the railway) to Mirabellplatz.

INFORMATION

Tourist offices and hotels sell the Salzburg Card (€21/29/34 for 24/48/72 hours), which provides free museum entry and public transport, and offers various reductions. The tourist office's commission for hotel reservations is €2.20.

Amex (Map p66; ☎ 80 80; Mozartplatz 5; ☼ 9am-5.30pm Mon-Fri, 9am-noon Sat) For travel agency information.

Isis Internet Café (Map p65; Hauptbahnhof; per hr €3; ☼ 8am-midnight) Also offers cheap calls.

Landeskrankenhaus (Hospital; Map p65; ☎ 44 82-0; Müllner Hauptstrasse 48)

Main post office (Map p66; Residenzplatz 9; ☼ 7am-6.30pm Mon-Fri, 8-10am Sat)

Post office (Map p65; Hauptbahnhof; ☼ 7am-8.30pm Mon-Fri, 8am-2pm Sat, 1-6pm Sun) At the train station.

Salzburg Internet Café (Map p66; Gstättengasse 3; per hr €2; ☼ 10am-10pm) Cheap internet access and calls.

STA Travel (Map p66; ☎ 458 733; Rainerstrasse 2; ☼ 9am-6pm Mon-Fri)

Tourist Information Counter (Map p65; Platform 2A, Hauptbahnhof; ☼ 9am-8pm) Opening hours vary throughout the year.

Tourist office (Map p66; ☎ information 88-987 330, hotel reservations 88-987 314; www.salzburg.info; Mozartplatz 5; ☼ 9am-6pm Mon-Sat Jan-Apr & mid-Oct–Nov, 9am-7pm May–mid-Oct & Dec) A mine of information on the city. Hands out free maps.

SIGHTS

A Unesco World Heritage site, Salzburg's Old Town centre is equally entrancing whether viewed from ground level or the hills above.

Residenzplatz is a good starting point for a wander. The **Dom** (cathedral; Map p66; Domplatz; admission free; ☼ 6.30am-5pm Mon-Sat, 8am-5pm Sun), just to the south, is worth checking out for the three bronze doors symbolising faith, hope and charity, and excavations of a medieval cathedral and **Roman remains** (adult/student €2.50/1.50; ☼ 9am-5pm). From here, head west along Franziskanergasse and turn left into a courtyard for **St Peterskirche** (Map p66; St Peter Bezirk 1/2; admission free; ☼ 8am-noon & 2.30-6.30pm), an abbey dating from AD 847. Among lovingly tended graves in the abbey's grounds you'll find the entrance to the **Katakomben** (catacombs; Map p66; adult/student €1/0.60; ☼ 10.30am-5pm May-Sep, 10.30am-3.30pm Wed & Thu, 10.30am-4pm Fri-Sun Oct-Apr). The western end of Franziskanergasse opens out into Max Reinhardt Platz, where you'll see the back of Fisher von Erlach's **Universitätskirche** (Map p66; Universitätsplatz; admission free; ☼ dawn-dusk), an outstanding example of baroque architecture. The **Stift Nonnberg** (Nonnberg Abbey; Map p66; admission free; ☼ 7am-dusk), where *The Sound of Music* first encounters Maria, is back in the other direction, a short climb up the hill to the east of the Festung Hohensalzburg.

Festung Hohensalzburg

This **castle fortress** (Map p66; ☎ 842 430-11; www.salzburg-burgen.at; Mönchsberg 34; adult/student €10/9.10;

SALZBURG

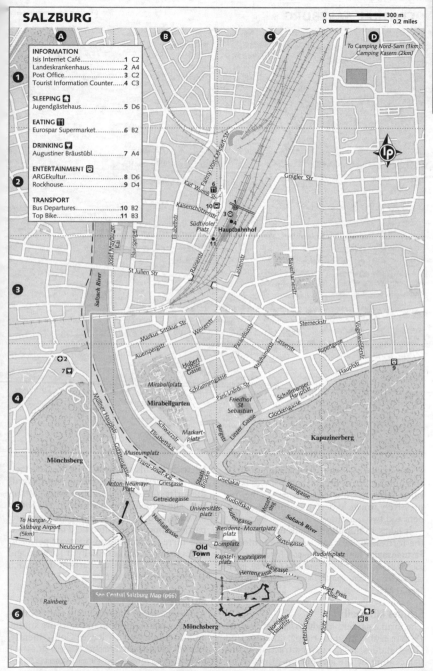

0 ————————— 300 m
0 ————————— 0.2 miles

INFORMATION
Isis Internet Café.........................1 C2
Landeskrankenhaus....................2 A4
Post Office.................................3 C2
Tourist Information Counter......4 C3

SLEEPING 🏠
Jugendgästehaus........................5 D6

EATING 🍴
Eurospar Supermarket................6 B2

DRINKING 🍷
Augustiner Bräustübl.................7 A4

ENTERTAINMENT 🎭
ARGEkultur................................8 D6
Rockhouse.................................9 D4

TRANSPORT
Bus Departures.........................10 B2
Top Bike..................................11 B3

To Camping Nord-Sam (1km);
Camping Kasern (2km)

Gnigler Str

Hauptbahnhof

Südtiroler
Platz

Kaiserschützenstr

Karl-Wurmb-Str

Fanny-von-Lehnert-Str

St Julien Str

Josef-Mayburger-Kai

Salzach River

Elisabethkai

Rainerstr

Lastenstr

Bayerhamerstr

Sterneckstr

Markus-Sittikus-Str

Weiserstr

Auerspergstr

Vogelweiderstr

Paracelsusstr

Stelzhamerstr

Lasserstr

Rupertgasse

Hauptstr

Hubert-
Sattler-
Gasse

Mirabellplatz

Schrannengasse

Franz-Josef-Str

Friedhof
St
Sebastian

Mirabellgarten

Schwarzstr

Bergstr

Linzer Gasse

Glockengasse

Kapuzinerberg

Markart-
platz

Müllner Hauptstr

Museumplatz

Franz-Josef-Kai

Gstättengasse

Staats-
Brücke

Giselakai

Schallmooser
Hauptstr

Steingasse

Mönchsberg

Anton-Neumayr-
Platz

Griesgasse

Getreidegasse

Rudolfskai

Mozart-
steg

Salzach River

To Hangar-7;
Salzburg Airport
(5km)

Hofstallgasse

Universitäts-
platz

Judengasse

Residenz-
platz

Mozartplatz

Basteigasse

Rudolfsplatz

Neutorstr

Old
Town

Domplatz

Kapitel-
platz

Kapitelgasse

Herrengasse

Kaigasse

Josef-
Preis-
Allee

See Central Salzburg Map (p66)

Rainberg

Mönchsberg

Nonnteler Hauptstr

Petersbrunnstr

Kliz-Str

AUSTRIA

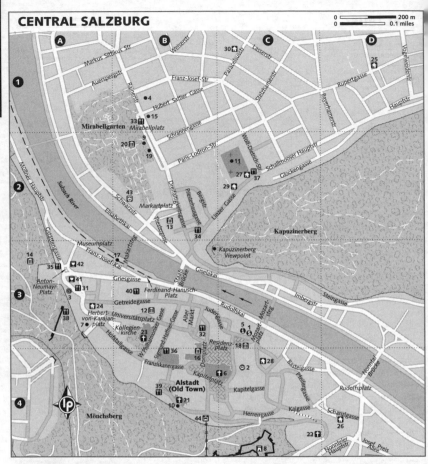

CENTRAL SALZBURG

Dietrich for his mistress in 1606. The view from the western end (looking east towards the fortress) is one of Salzburg's most attractive. The gardens were featured in *The Sound of Music*, and are now popular with wedding parties. Concerts are often held in the palace, and there are sometimes open-air performances in the garden (normally at 10.30am and 8.30pm May to August). Parts of the garden are off-limits in winter.

9am-7pm May-Sep, 9am-5pm Oct-Apr), built in 1077, was home to many archbishop-princes (who ruled Salzburg from 798). Inside are the impressively ornate staterooms, torture chambers and two museums.

It takes 15 minutes to walk up the hill to the fortress, or you can catch the funicular **Festungsbahn funicular** (Map p66; Festungsgasse 4; adult/child one way €2.10/1.10, return €3.40/1.80, incl in castle ticket; 9am-10pm May-Aug, 9am-9pm Sep, 9am-5pm Oct-Apr).

Schloss Mirabell

The formal gardens of **Schloss Mirabell** (Map p66; dawn-dusk), with their tulips, crocuses and Greek statues, are the main attraction at this palace built by the archbishop-prince Wolf

Museums

Although Mozart is now a major tourist drawcard, the man himself found Salzburg stifling and couldn't wait to leave. Consequently, **Mozart's Geburtshaus** (birthplace; Map p66; ☎ 844 313; www.mozarteum.at; Getreidegasse 9; adult/student €6.50/5.50;

🕒 9am-6pm Sep-Jun, 9am-7pm Jul & Aug, last entry 30min before closing) and **Mozart's Wohnhaus** (residence; Map p66; ☎ 874 227; Makartplatz 8; adult/student €6.50/5.50; 🕒 9am-6pm Sep-Jun, 9am-7pm Jul & Aug, last entry 30min before closing) cover only his early years as a prodigy and young adult, until he left town in 1780 at 24 years of age. A combined ticket to both houses is €10 (students and seniors €8). The Wohnhaus is more extensive, and houses the **Mozart Sound & Film Museum** (Map p66; admission free; 🕒 9am-1pm Mon, Tue, & Fri, 1-5pm Wed & Thu).

In the **Residenz State Rooms & Gallery** (Map p66; ☎ 80 42-2690; www.salzburg-burgen.at; Residenzplatz 1; adult/student €8.20/6.20; 🕒 10am-5pm, gallery closed Mon) you can visit the archbishops' baroque staterooms and a gallery housing fine 16th- and 17th-century Dutch and Flemish paintings.

The latest entry on Salzburg's list of museums is the aptly named **Salzburg Museum** (Map p66; ☎ 620 808-700; www.salzburgmuseum.at; in German; Mozartplatz 1; adult/student Tue-Sat €7/6, Sun €5.50/4.50; 🕒 9am-5pm Tue, Wed & Fri-Sun, 9am-8pm Thu, plus 9am-5pm Mon Jul, Aug, & Dec), which covers the city and its favourite citizens in an interactive way and presents contemporary art exhibitions on a regular basis. The **Museum der Moderne** (Map p66; ☎ 842 220-403; www.museumdermoderne .at; Mönchsberg; adult/student €8/6; 🕒 10am-6pm Tue & Thu-Sun, 10am-9pm Wed) adds a further contemporary touch to historic Salzburg with rotating modern-art shows.

Mausoleum of Wolf Dietrich

In the **graveyard** (Map p66; Linzer Gasse; admission free; 🕒 9am-6.30pm Apr-Oct, 9am-4pm Nov-Mar) of the 16th-century St Sebastian's Church sits Wolf Dietrich's not so humble **memorial** to himself. Both Mozart's father and his widow are also buried in the graveyard.

TOURS
Sound of Music Tours

Although these are the tours that interest the greatest number of visitors, how much fun you have depends on whether your fellow passengers enter into the necessary kitsch, tongue-in-cheek attitude. If you can, try to get together your own little posse. Otherwise, hope to find yourself among manic Julie Andrews impersonators flouncing in the fields, screeching 'the hills are alive' or some such thing.

Tours take three to four hours and usually spend most time in neighbouring Salzkammergut, rather than Salzburg itself. Following are some recommended operators:

Fräulein Maria's Bicycle Tours (Map p66; ☎ 0676-342 62 97; www.mariasbicycletours.com; Mirabellplatz; adult/child €22/15; 🕒 9.30am May-Sep) Near main entrance to Schloss Mirabell.

Panorama Tours (Map p66; ☎ 874 029; www .panoramatours.com; Mirabellplatz; adult/child €37/18; 🕒 9.30am & 2pm)

Salzburg Sightseeing Tours (Map p66; ☎ 881 616; www.salzburg-sightseeingtours.at; Mirabellplatz; adult/child €37/18; 🕒 9.30am & 2pm)

River Tours

Boats operated by **Salzburg Schiffahrt** (☎ 825 769-12; www.salzburgschifffahrt.at) cruise along the Salzach (adult/child €13/7, 40 minutes) leaving half-hourly to hourly from around

AUSTRIA

HANG(AR)TIME AT THE SALZBURG AIRPORT

If you have time to kill at the airport it's worth a trip to **Hangar-7** (off Map p65; ☎ 21 97; www.hangar-7.com; Wilhelm-Spazier-strasse 7a, Salzburg airport; admission free; ☒ 9am-10pm). This huge, clear plexi-enclosed airplane hangar is large enough to house a Douglas DC6 jumbo jet, a B-52 bomber, a plethora of assorted Red Bull Team Formula One racing cars, motorcycles and other historical aircraft. There's also an expensive but excellent cafe where you can recharge your engine. The hangar is owned by Red Bull founder and motor sports/aviation enthusiast, Dietrich Mateschitz.

10.45am to 6pm April to October. Others go to Schloss Hellbrunn (adult/child €16/10), departing at 12.45pm April to September, with an extra sailing at 10.45am in July and August. The company also has atmospheric tours by night in late July and August.

Boats leave from the Salzach Insel, on the city side of the Makart bridge.

FESTIVALS & EVENTS

Austria's most renowned classical music festival, the **Salzburg Festival** (www.salzburgfestival.at), attracts international stars from late July to the end of August. Book on its website before January, or ask the **Festspielhäuser ticket office** (☎ 80 45; Herbert von Karajan Platz 11; ☒ from 9am) about cancellations during the festival.

SLEEPING

Ask for the tourist office's hotel brochure, which gives prices for hotels, pensions, hostels and camping grounds. Accommodation is at a premium during festivals.

Budget

International Youth Hotel (YoHo; Map p66; ☎ 879 649; www.yoho.at; Paracelsusstrasse 9; dm with shared bathroom from €17, s/d/tr with private bathroom €29/44/60; ☐) If you're hankering after a lively bar scene with cheap beer, friendly staff and regular events, including daily screenings of *The Sound of Music*, this hostel is for you. Book ahead on its website – phone reservations are accepted only one day in advance. Rooms were undergoing renovation at the time of research, but expect them to be clean and spartan.

Jugendgästehaus (Map p65; ☎ 842 670; salzburg@jfgh.at; Josef Preis Allee 18; dm from €18.90, d from €31; ☒ check-in from 11am, access to rooms from 1pm; ☐) Lots of Austrians, families and backpackers stay at this comfy HI hostel. The eight-bed dorms feel a bit like boarding school, but the en-suite four-bed dorms and doubles on the floors above could belong to a nice budget hotel. There's a small cafe on-site and bike rental for €9.50 per day.

ourpick Institut St Sebastian (Map p66; ☎ 871 386; www.st-sebastian-salzburg.at; Linzer Gasse 41; dm €19, s/d with shared bathroom €32/51, with private bathroom €40/64) Just a few minutes walk from the bridge, through the gate marked 'Feuerwache Bruderhof', on Linzer Gasse, Institut St Sebastian is closer to the action than any other Salzburg hostel-style accommodation. In fact, when the church bells ring next door, you might find this student abode is almost too close to the action. Don't expect much of a social atmosphere, but (aside from the church bells) you'll be guaranteed of some peace and quiet. There is a roof terrace and kitchen for guest use.

Gasthaus Hinterbrühl (Map p66; ☎ 846 798; www.fam-wagner.at; Schanzlgasse 12; s/d €42/58) This small guest house may be a bit frayed around the edges, but its central, cheap, and can trace its history back to the 14th century. Room 14, with private bathroom and balcony, is the best.

Also worth considering:

Naturfreundehaus (Map p66; ☎ 841 729; Mönchsberg 19) Undergoing major renovation at the time of research. Whatever the result, its position atop Mönchsberg hill makes it an excellent choice. Call ahead or check with the tourist office for information.

Camping Kasern (off Map p65; ☎ 450 576; www.camping-kasern-salzburg.com; Carl Zuckmayer Strasse 4; camp site per adult/car & tent €6/5, bungalow tent per person €10; ☒ Apr-Oct; ☐) Just north of the A1 Nord exit. Bungalow tents are excellent value for money, but you need your own bedding.

Camping Nord-Sam (off Map p65; ☎ 660 494; www.camping-nord-sam.com; Samstrasse 22a; camp site per adult/car & tent €7.50/10; ☒ Easter & mid-Apr–Sep) Slightly closer to the city. Has a pool, shop, and bike rental.

Midrange & Top End

Salzburg has a fair number of options in these price brackets.

Bergland Hotel (Map p66; ☎ 872 318; www.berglandhotel.at; Rupertgasse 15; s/d/tr/f €65/95/110/140; ☐) Plenty of care has been taken with the recent renovation of this excellent midrange hotel. The comfy rooms are coloured in warm hues, and art adorns most walls. Bergland is about a 15-minute walk from the Old Town, or hire a bike for €6.

Hotel Wolf (Map p66; ☎ 843 453-0; www.hotelwolf .com; Kaigasse 7; s/d from €80/110; 🖵) With its neat living room set off from the main entrance hall, this family-owned hotel immediately feels like a real home. Austrian country-style bedrooms have been reconstructed in this 500-year-old abode, which has none of the mustiness of most buildings its age.

Arthotel Blaue Gans (Map p66; ☎ 842 491-0; www .blauegans.at; Getreidegasse 41-43; r from €135; 🖵) The 'Blue Goose' may be one of Salzburg's oldest inns, but these days it's a contemporary hotel housing modernist art pieces and sleek yet comfortable rooms.

Also noteworthy is **Hotel Amadeus** (Map p66; ☎ 871 401; www.hotelamadeus.at; Linzer Gasse 43; s/d €92/180; 🖵), a boutique hotel with spacious rooms and huge buffet breakfast.

EATING
Restaurants
Most Salzburg restaurants cater to the Austrian palette, but there are a few worldly choices on its cobbled streets. To avoid a large dining bill, make lunch your main meal, or grab a *Bosna* (€2.80), a spicy hotdog particular to the city. Sausage stands are scattered around Salzburg.

SKS Spicy Spices (Map p66; Wolf-Dietrich-Strasse 1; mains €6) If you're into healthy eating don't pass over this tiny eatery that specialises in vegan and vegetarian food from the Indian sub-continent.

Il Sole (Map p66; Gstättengasse 15; mains €6-15) Fill up on tasty pasta dishes and wood-fired pizzas at Il Sole, a small trattoria with a lively buzz and superfriendly staff.

Wilder Mann (Map p66; ☎ 841 787; Getreidegasse 20; mains €8-11; 🕑 Mon Sat) Traditional Austrian food in a friendly, bustling environment, located in the passageway off Getreidegasse. Tables, both inside and out, are often so packed it's almost impossible not to get chatting with fellow diners.

ourpick **Afro Cafe** (Map p66; ☎ 844 888; Bürgerspitalplatz 5; mains €10-20; 🕑 Mon-Sat) It's a shock to find Afro Cafe in the heart of traditional Salzburg. This vibrant, multicoloured restaurant-cafe-bar is bedecked with retro furniture, palm trees, and junk art, and its full menu features the likes of Pemba Island

prawns and ostrich kebabs. A delightful, unpretentious eatery.

Stiftskeller St Peter (Map p66; ☎ 841 268-34; St Peter Bezirk 1/4; mains €13-23) A favourite of locals and tourists alike, this Stiftskeller is a special spot for its renowned Austrian specialities, vine-clad courtyard, and baroque main salon. It's best to reserve a table on warm summer evenings.

Other good dining options:

Mensa Toscana (Map p66; Sigmund-Haffner-Gasse 11; meals €4.10-4.80; 🕑 8.30am-5pm Mon-Thu, 8.30am-3pm Fri) University mensa in the heart of the Old Town.

Gablerbräu (Map p66; ☎ 88 965; Linzer Gasse 9; mains €10-20) Low-key and pleasant; Austrian and Styrian specialities and its own beer.

Cafés
Café Konditorei Fürst (Map p66; Brodgasse 13, Alter Markt; confections from €3) Café Konditorei Fürst boasts that its *Mozartkugeln* chocolates – wrapped in blue and silver paper instead of the usual red and gold – are the original 'Mozart's Balls'. They're still made here from an age-old recipe.

Stadtalm (Map p66; Mönchsberg 19c; mains €7-11; 🕑 mid-May–mid-Sep) The dishes here are standard Austrian fare – wurst, *Wiener schnitzel* and *Tafelspitz* (boiled beef) – but the view of the Old Town from Mönchsberg is far from standard.

Quick Eats & Self-Catering
Salzburg has no shortage of markets, with a **fruit and vegetable market** (Map p66; Mirabellplatz) on Thursday morning, and market stalls and fast-food stands on Universitätsplatz and Kapitelplatz Monday to Saturday. There's a **Eurospar supermarket** (Map p65; 🕑 Mon-Sat) opposite the train station.

DRINKING
Salzburg's most famous stretch of bars, clubs and discos remains Rudolfskai, but it's largely patronised by teenagers. Those who've already hit their 20s (or beyond) will probably prefer the scene around Anton Neumayr Platz, where things keep going until 4am on weekends.

Augustiner Bräustübl (Map p65; ☎ 431 246; Augustinergasse 4-6; 🕑 3-11pm Mon-Fri, 2.30-11pm Sat & Sun) Known locally as Müllnerbräu (after its neighbourhood), this hillside complex of beer halls and gardens is not to be missed. The local monks' brew keeps the huge crowd of up to 2800 humming.

Humboldt Stub'n (Map p66; ☎ 843 171; Gstättengasse 4-6) Perennial favourite with students – particularly on Wednesday nights when beers are €2.50. The decor is particularly wacky, featuring cartoons and purple antelope horns.

Republic (Map p66; ☎ 841 613; Anton Neumayr Platz 2) A hip, American bar-brasserie that features regular club nights.

ENTERTAINMENT

High-brow entertainment venues include the **Schlosskonzerte** (Map p66; ☎ 848 586; www.salzburger -schlosskonzerte.at) in Schloss Mirabell, and the **Mozarteum** (Map p66; ☎ 873 154; www.mozarteum.at; Schwarzstrasse 26). Most bands with a modern bent will invariably play at either the **Rockhouse** (Map p65; ☎ 884 914; www.rockhouse.at, in German; Schallmooser Hauptstrasse 46) or **ARGEkultur** (Map p65; ☎ 848 784-0; www.argekultur.at, in German; Josef-Preis-Allee 16); the latter also doubles as a popular student bar.

GETTING THERE & AWAY
Air

Salzburg airport (off Map p65; SZG; ☎ 85 80-0; www .salzburg-airport.com) receives scheduled flights from as near as Munich to as far away as Dublin. Ryanair provides connections between Salzburg and London Stansted and the Irish capital; British Airways serves London Gatwick; and TUIfly serves Berlin, Hamburg, Hanover, and Cologne. There are also a number of charter flights to the Mediterranean during the summer months.

Bus

Bus services to the Salzkammergut region leave from just to the left of the main Hauptbahnhof exit (Map p66). Destinations include Bad Ischl (€8.70, 1½ hours), Mondsee (€5.40, 50 minutes), St Gilgen (€5.40, 45 minutes) and St Wolfgang (€7.90, 1½ hours; change normally required at Strobl).

There are timetable boards at each departure point and a bus information office in the train station.

Car & Motorcycle

Three autobahns converge on Salzburg and form a loop around the city: the A1 from Linz, Vienna and the east; the A8/E52 from Munich and the west; and the A10/E55 from Villach and the south. Heading south to Carinthia on the A10, there are two tunnels through the mountains; the combined toll is €10 (€7 for motorcycles).

Train

Fast trains leave for Vienna (€44, three hours) via Linz (€20.70, 1¼ hours) hourly. The express service to Klagenfurt (€33, 3¼ hours) goes via Villach. The quickest way to Innsbruck (€35.20, two hours) is by the 'corridor' train through Germany via Kufstein; trains depart at least every two hours. There are trains every hour or so to Munich (€28, two hours).

GETTING AROUND

Salzburg airport is located 4km west of the city centre. Bus 2 goes there from the Hauptbahnhof (€1.80). A taxi costs about €14.

Bus drivers sell single bus tickets for €1.80. Other tickets must be bought from the automatic machines at major stops, *Tabak* shops or tourist offices. Day passes cost €4.20 and weeklies €12.40. Children aged six to 15 years travel half-price; those under six travel free.

The majority of the Old Town is pedestrianised. The nearest central parking area is the Altstadt Garage under the Mönchsberg. Attended car parks cost €1.40 to €2.40 per hour. On streets with automatic ticket machines (blue zones), a three-hour maximum applies (€0.50 for 30 minutes) between 9am and 7pm Monday to Friday and 9am and 4pm Saturday.

Bicycle hire is available from **Top Bike** (Map p65; ☎ 0676-476 72 59; www.topbike.at; 2hr/4hr/day €6/10/15, 20% discount with all train tickets), which is located just outside the Hauptbahnhof.

For a taxi, call ☎ 81 11, or go to the ranks at Hanuschplatz, Residenzplatz or the Hauptbahnhof.

AROUND SALZBURG

SCHLOSS HELLBRUNN

Four kilometres south of Salzburg's Old Town centre is the popular **Schloss Hellbrunn** (☎ 820 372-0; www.hellbrunn.at; Fürstenweg 37; adult/student €8.50/6; ⏰ 9am-10pm Jul & Aug, 9am-5.30pm May, Jun & Sep, 9am-4.30pm Mar, Apr & Oct). Built by bishop Markus Sittikus, this 17th-century castle is known for its ingenious trick fountains and water-powered figures. When the tour guides set them off, expect to get wet! Admission includes a tour of the baroque palace. Other parts of the garden (without fountains) are open year-round and free to visit.

City bus 25 runs to the palace every 30 minutes from Salzburg's Hauptbahnhof, via Rudolfskai in the Old Town. Salzburg tickets are valid.

WERFEN

☎ 06468 / pop 3000

It may be small, but Werfen, 40km south of Salzburg, is big on attractions – its home to the world's largest accessible ice caves and a fortress not to be messed with. Both attractions can be visited as a day trip from Salzburg if you start early (tour the caves first and be at the castle by 3pm for the falconry show), otherwise consult the **tourist office** (☎ 53 88; www.werfen.at; Markt 24; ☒ 9am-7pm Mon-Fri, 5-7pm Sat mid-Jul–mid-Aug, 9am-5pm Mon-Fri mid-Aug–mid-Jul) for accommodation options.

More than 1000m above the village in the Tennengebirge mountains is the **Eisriesenwelt Höhle** (Giant Ice Caves; ☎ 52 48; www.eisriesenwelt.at; adult/student without cable-car ride €8.50/7.50, with cable-car ride €19/17; ☒ 9am-3.30pm May-Jun & Sep-Oct, 9am-4.30pm Jul-Aug). Its 42km of passageways houses elaborate and beautiful ice formations; take warm clothes because it gets cold inside and the tour lasts 1¼ hours – you also need to be reasonably fit.

The **Hohenwerfen Fortress** (☎ 76 03; adult/student €13/7; ☒ 9am-6pm Jul & Aug, 9am-5pm May-Jun, 9.30am-4.30pm Apr, Oct & Nov, closed Mon Apr) stands on the hill above the village. It was originally built in 1077, although the present building dates from the 16th century. Admission includes an exhibition, a guided tour of the interior and a dramatic falconry show, in which birds of prey swoop low over the heads of the crowd. The walk up from the village takes 20 minutes.

Werfen can be reached from Salzburg along the A10. By train it takes 50 minutes and costs €8.60. The village is a five-minute walk from Werfen train station. Getting to the caves is a bit more complicated, though scenic. A minibus service (€5.80 return) from the train station operates along the steep, 6km road to the car park, which is as far as cars can go. A 15-minute walk then brings you to the cable car (€10.50 return), from where it is a further 15-minute walk to the caves. Allow four hours return from the train station, or three hours from the car park (keep in mind that peak-season queues may add an hour). The whole route can be hiked, but it is a very hard four-hour ascent, rising 1100m above the village.

SALZKAMMERGUT

A picture-perfect wonderland of glassy blue lakes and tall craggy peaks, Austria's Lake District is a long-time favourite holiday destination attracting visitors in droves from Salzburg and beyond.

Whether you're looking for a way to entertain the kids or hoping to just commune with nature, the area is big on variety. The peaceful lakes offer limitless opportunities for boating, fishing, swimming, or just lazing on the shore. Favourite waterside beauty spots include the picturesque villages of Hallstatt and St Wolfgang, and the Riviera-style port of Gmunden. You can also tour the salt mines that made the region wealthy or plunge into the depths of the fantastic Dachstein caves, where glittering towers of ice are masterfully illuminated in the depths of a mountain.

Getting There & Around

The major rail routes bypass the heart of Salzkammergut, but regional trains cross the area north to south. This route begins at Attnang-Puchheim on the Salzburg–Linz line. The track from here connects to Bad Ischl, Hallstatt and Obertraun in one direction and Gmunden in another. At small, unstaffed stations *(unbesetzter Bahnhof)*, tickets can be bought on the train; no surcharge applies.

After Obertraun, the railway continues eastwards via Bad Aussee before connecting with the main Bischofshofen–Graz line at Stainach-Irdning.

Regular buses connect the region's towns and villages, though less frequently on weekends. Timetables are displayed at stops, and tickets can be bought from the driver.

Passenger boats ply the waters of the Attersee, Traunsee, Mondsee, Hallstätter See and Wolfgangsee.

To reach Salzkammergut from Salzburg by car or motorcycle, take the A1 or Hwy 158.

TIP

Throughout the year resorts have a *Gästekarte* (guest card) offering region-wide discounts; ask at your hotel, hostel or camping ground. Alternatively, buy the Salzkammergut Card (€4.90; available May to October), which provides a 30% discount on sights, ferries, cable cars and some buses.

AUSTRIA

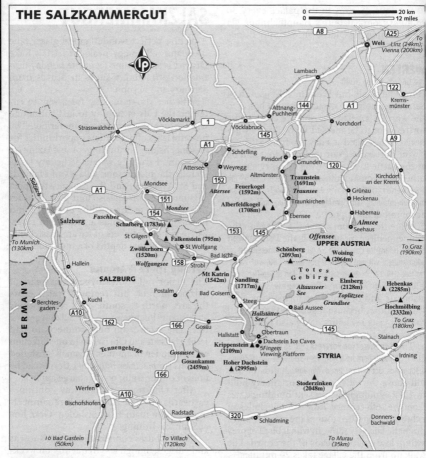

THE SALZKAMMERGUT

BAD ISCHL

☎ 06132 / pop 14,000

During the last century of the Habsburg reign, Bad Ischl became the favourite summertime retreat for the imperial family and their entourage. Today the town and many of its dignified buildings still wear an imperial aura, while a shockingly high proportion of the local women still go about their daily business in *Dirndl* (Austria's traditional full, pleated skirt). It makes a good base for exploring the entire Salzkammergut region.

Orientation

The town centre rests within a bend of the Traun River. To head into town, turn left into the main road as you come out of the train station; you'll pass the tourist office and post office.

Information

Post office (Aübockplatz 4; ☼ 8am-6pm Mon-Fri, 9am-noon Sat)

Salzkammergut Touristik (☎ 24 000-0; www.salzkammergut.co.at; Götzstrasse 12; ☼ 9am-8pm) Has internet access (per hour €4.50) and bike rental (per 24 hour €13).

Tourist office (Kurdirektion; ☎ 27 757-0; www.badischl.at; Bahnhofstrasse 6; ☼ 8am-6pm Mon-Fri, 9am-3pm Sat, 10am-1pm Sun)

Sights & Activities

The **Kaiservilla** (☎ 23 241; www.kaiservilla.at; Kaiserpark; adult/student €11/10, grounds only €4/3; ☼ 9.30am-4.45pm May-Oct, 10am-4pm Wed Jan-Apr) was Franz osef's summer residence and shows that ne loved huntin', shootin' and fishin' – t's decorated with an obscene number of animal trophies. It can be visited only by guided tour, during which you'll pick up little gems, like the fact that Franz Josef was conceived in Bad Ischl after his mother, Princess Sophie, took a treatment to cure her infertility in 1828, and it was here that the Kaiser signed the letter declaring war on Serbia, which lead to WWI.

The teahouse of Franz Josef's wife, Elisabeth, is now a **photo museum** (☎ 244 422; adult/child €2/1.50; ☽ 9.30am-5pm Apr-Oct).

Bad Ischl has downhill skiing from **Mt Katrin** (day pass €23); however, there are only three trails. It also has various cross-country skiing routes. In summer the Mt Katrin cable car costs €14.20 return.

Free *Kurkonzerte* (spa concerts) are held regularly during summer; the tourist office has venues and times. The **Lehár Festival** (www .leharfestival.at), which features operas and operettas, takes place in July and August.

Sleeping & Eating

Jugendgästehaus (☎ 26 577; www.oejhv.or.at; Am Rechensteg 5; dm €15, s/d €30/44; ☽ reception 8am-1pm Mon-Fri, 5-7pm daily ▯) For an Austrian youth hostel, this is a rather bland example. However, you can count on clean, simple rooms and a quiet night's sleep. Look for it in the town centre behind Kreuzplatz.

Hotel Garni Sonnhof (☎ 23 078; www.sonnhof .at; Bahnhofstrasse 4; s/d from €65/90) Nestled into a leafy glade of maple trees next to the train station, this is an excellent option – it has cosy, traditional decor, a lovely garden, sunny conservatory, and large bedrooms with attractive antique furniture and wooden floors. There's also a billiard room, sauna and a steam bath on-site.

K.u.K. Hofbeisl (☎ 27 271; Wirerstrasse 4; mains €5-15; ☽ 8am-4am) For quality grub at a decent price, it's hard to beat this simple eatery. It doubles as a lively bar come sundown.

Restaurant Zauner Esplanade (☎ 23 722; Hasner Allee 2; mains €7-18; ☽ 10am-9pm May-Oct, 10am-8pm Wed-Sun Dec–mid-Apr) Zauner occupies a prime location – right on the banks of the Traun River – and is the perfect place for summer dining. The restaurant's Austrian cuisine is of the highest standard, and often employs organic produce. Café Zauner, its older sister at Pfarrgasse 7, has changed little since

imperial times, retaining glittering chandeliers, marble floors and fantastical displays of confectionary. Founded in 1832, it was Franz Josef's bakery of choice – his mistress ordered their morning pastries here when he was in residence.

Weinhaus Attwenger (☎ 23 327; Lehárkai 12; mains €7-20; ☽ Tue-Sun) High-quality Austrian food is served at this quaint chalet with a relaxing garden next to the river. The menu changes seasonally, with wines to match. Set-course meals are also offered (from €31).

Bad Ischl also has its fair share of quality private rooms, including those at **Haus Rothauer** (☎ 23 628; Kaltenbachstrasse 12; s/d €25/44); both tourist offices can help with accommodation.

Getting There & Around

The quickest and cheapest way to get to Bad Ischl from Salzburg is by bus (€8.70, 1½ hours); these run hourly between 6am and 10.30pm via St Gilgen (€4.40, 40 minutes). Buses run approximately every hour to St Wolfgang (€3.40, 30 minutes), and Hallstatt every couple of hours (€4.50, 30 minutes).

Trains on to Hallstatt depart roughly hourly between 6am and 6pm (€4.50, 30 minutes); be aware that the train station is on the opposite side of the lake from the village (see p74).

Salzkammergut Touristik (opposite) has bikes for hire.

HALLSTATT

☎ 06134 / pop 900

With pastel-hued homes, swans and towering mountains on either side of a glassy green lake, Hallstatt looks like some kind of greeting card for tranquillity. Boats chug lazily across the water from the train station to the village itself, which clings precariously to a tiny bit of land between mountain and shore. So small is the patch of land occupied by the village that its annual Corpus Christi procession takes place largely in small boats on the lake.

Orientation & Information

Seestrasse is the main street. Turn left from the ferry to reach the **tourist office** (☎ 82 08; www.hallstatt.net; Seestrasse 169; ☽ 9am-noon & 2-5pm Mon-Fri year-round, 9am-5pm Mon-Fri, 10am-5pm Sat Jul & Aug). The **post office** (Seestrasse 160) is a couple of doors away.

AUSTRIA

Sights & Activities

Hallstatt has been classified a Unesco World Heritage site for its natural beauty and for evidence of human settlement dating back 4500 years. Over 2000 graves have been discovered in and around the village, most dating from 1000 to 500 BC, but the most interesting examples of human remains aren't nearly so old. The macabre **Beinhaus** (Bone House; ☎ 82 79; Kirchenweg 40; adult/child €1.50/0.50; ☉ 10am-6pm May-Oct), near the village parish church, contains rows of stacked skulls painted with flowery designs and the names of the deceased. The old Celtic pagan custom of mass burial has been practised here since 1600 (mainly due to the lack of graveyard space), and the latest skull to be added to the collection dates from 1995.

Mining salt in the peak above the village was the main activity for thousands of years, but these days the mine earns its keep through tourists. The **Salzbergwerk** (Saltworks; ☎ 06132-200 2400; adult/student €16/10; ☉ 9am-4.30pm late Apr–mid-Sep, 9am-3pm mid-Sep–Oct) can be reached by funicular (one way/return adult €10/6, student €6/4), otherwise ask the tourist office about the two scenic hiking trails you could take to get there.

At nearby **Obertraun** you'll find the intriguing **Dachstein Rieseneishöhle** (Giant Ice Caves; ☎ 06131-53 10; www.dachsteinwelterbe.at; cable car return plus 2 caves adult/child €29.30/16.70, cable car return plus 1 cave €24.20/14.10, 2 caves only €14.90/8.40, 1 cave only €9.80/5.80; ☉ May–late Oct, tours 9.20am-4pm). The caves are millions of years old and extend into the mountain for almost 80km in places. The ice itself is no more than 500 years old, but is increasing in thickness each year – the 'ice mountain' is 8m high, twice as high now as it was when the caves were first explored in 1910.

From Obertraun it's also possible to catch a cable car to **Krippenstein** (2109m; return adult/child €21.80/14.70) where you'll find the freaky **5Fingers viewing platform**, which protrudes out over a sheer cliff face. Not for sufferers of vertigo.

Sleeping & Eating

Hallstatt's steep footpaths certainly help you work up an appetite for a hearty meal, after which you will be in need of a good rest. Some private rooms are available during the busiest months of July and August only; others require a minimum three-night stay. The tourist office will phone around for you without charge.

Campingplatz Krausner-Höll (☎ 83 22; www.cam ing.hallstatt.net, in German; Lahnstrasse 7; per adult/car/ten €7/3/4; ☉ mid-Apr–mid-Oct; ☐) This camping ground is conveniently located south of the town centre.

Gasthaus zur Mühle (☎ 83 18; toeroe.f@magnet.at, Kirchenweg 36; dm €13) On the Hallstatt hillside and overlooking the lake, this place is popular with independent travellers. Dorms are rather basic. Below the hostel, the restaurant has a fine range of pastas, pizzas and Austrian dishes (mains €6 to €12). Dine inside on cold days, or make use of the large terrace when the weather's favourable.

our pick Gasthof Hallberg (☎ 82 86; www.pension -hallberg.at.tf; Seestrasse 113; s/d from €40/70) At this excellent-value guest house, the best rooms are light and airy, furnished with pale wood and boasting superb lake views on both sides. Even the more ordinary rooms are still great quality, with many featuring quaintly sloping ceilings and mountain views.

Bräu Gasthof (☎ 82 21; Seestrasse 120; mains €8-15; ☉ May-Oct) Served in vaulted rooms or on tables by the lake, the menu promises hearty local fare and turns out dishes like sirloin steak with onions (€15) or game goulash (€12), as well as a few salads.

Getting There & Away

There are five buses daily to/from Bad Ischl (€4.50, 30 minutes), the last leaving Bad Ischl at 6.10pm. You alight at 'Lahn', just south of the road tunnel. There are up to 12 train services daily from Bad Ischl (€4.50, 30 minutes). The train station is across the lake from the village, but the ferry captain waits for trains to arrive before making the short crossing (€2, six minutes). Though trains run later, the last ferry departs from the train station at 6.29pm (leaving Hallstatt at 6.15pm). Parking in the village is free if you're staying the night and therefore have a guest card.

WOLFGANGSEE

Wolfgangsee is a hugely popular place to spend the summer swimming, boating, walking, or simply lazing by its soothing waters. Its two main resorts are St Wolfgang and St Gilgen, the first of which takes first prize in the beauty stakes.

Coming from Salzburg, the first town you come across is **St Gilgen**. It's a fine point from which to explore the surrounding region, and its **tourist office** (☎ 06227-23 48; www.wolfgangsee.at;

ondsee Bundesstrasse 1a; ☾ 9am-noon & 2-6pm Mon-Fri,
am-noon Sat Apr-May & mid-Sep–Oct, 9am-8pm Mon-Fri,
am-7pm Sat, 10am-5pm Sun Jun–mid-Sep, 9am-noon & 2-
pm Mon-Fri Nov-Mar) can help with accommoda-
ion and activities.

St Wolfgang, towards the southern end of
Wolfgangsee, is squeezed between the north-
rn shoreline of the lake and the towering peak
f Schafberg (1783m). Its **tourist office** (☎ 06138-
239-0; info@stwolfgang.at; ☾ 9am-6pm Mon-Fri, 9am-noon
at Oct-May, 9am-6pm Mon-Fri, 9am-noon & 2-6pm Sat Jun &
ep, 9am-8pm Mon-Fri, 9am-noon & 2-6pm Sat, 2-6pm Sun Jul
& Aug) has plenty of information for travellers.

In the heart of the village is the 14th-century
Pilgrimage Church (donation €1; ☾ 9am-6pm), a highly
ornate example which still attracts pilgrims.
Reaching the top of **Scharfberg** is an easy exercise – from May to October, a cog-wheel
railway climbs to its summit in 40 minutes
(one way/return €14.70/26.90). Otherwise it's
a three- to four-hour walk.

Both St Wolfgang and St Gilgen have numerous pensions, starting from about €25 per
person; the local tourist offices have details.

On the lakefront, 1km east of St Wolfgang,
Camping Appesbach (☎ 06138-22 06; www.appesbach
.at; Au 99; adult/tent & car €6/7) is a favourite with
Austrian holidaymakers.

The **Jugendgästehaus Schafbergblick** (☎ 06227-
23 65; www.oejhv.or.at; Mondseestrasse 7; dm/d from
€17.50/40; ☾ reception 8am-1pm & 5-7pm Mon-Fri, 8-9am
& 5-7pm Sat & Sun) is in St Gilgen and very handy
to the lake and town's swimming beach. It's
a place to kick back and relax, and rooms on
the top level have views of the lake.

A ferry operates from Strobl to St Gilgen,
stopping at various points en route, including St Wolfgang. Services run from late April
to early November, but are more frequent
from early July to early September. The ferry
journey from St Wolfgang to St Gilgen takes
45 minutes (€6), with boats sailing during
the high season approximately twice hourly
between 8.45am and 6.55pm.

Buses from St Wolfgang to St Gilgen and
Salzburg go via Strobl on the east side of the
lake. From St Gilgen the bus to Salzburg
(€5.40, 45 minutes) departs hourly until
8.05pm; from St Wolfgang (€7.90, 1½ hours)
hourly until 7.17pm.

NORTHERN SALZKAMMERGUT

Mondsee is popular for two reasons – its close
proximity to Salzburg (only 30km) and its
warm water. The main village on the lake,
also called Mondsee, is home to an attractive
15th-century church that was used in the
wedding scene of *The Sound of Music* and a
small and helpful **tourist office** (☎ 06232-22 70;
www.mondsee.at; Dr Franz Müller Strasse 3; ☾ 8am-6pm
Mon-Fri, plus 9am-7pm Sat & Sun Jul & Aug).

Lying to the east of Mondsee is **Attersee**,
Salzkammergut's largest lake and a favourite with sailors. East again from Attersee
you'll find **Traunsee** and its three main resorts: Gmunden, Traunkirchen and Ebensee.
Gmunden is famous for its twin castles, linked
by a causeway on the lake, and its green and
white ceramics. Contact the local **tourist office** (☎ 07612-643 05; www.traunsee.at; Toscanapark 1;
☾ 8am-6pm Mon-Fri, plus 10am-7pm Sat & Sun Jul & Aug)
for information on accommodation and activities on and around the lake.

Buses run every hour to Mondsee from
Salzburg (€6.20, 50 minutes). Gmunden is
connected to Salzburg by train (€15.10, 1½
hours), via Attnang-Puchheim.

TIROL

With converging mountain ranges behind
lofty pastures and tranquil meadows, Tirol
(also Tyrol) captures a quintessential Alpine
panoramic view. Occupying a central position is Innsbruck, the region's jewel, while
in the northeast and southwest are superb
ski resorts. In the southeast, separated
somewhat from the main state since part of
South Tirol was ceded to Italy at the end of
WWI, lies the protected natural landscape
of the Hohe Tauern National Park, which
is home to 30 peaks over 3000m, including the country's highest, the Grossglockner
(3797m).

INNSBRUCK
☎ 0512 / pop 118,000
Tirol's capital is a sight to behold. The mountains are so close that, within 25 minutes, its
possible travel from the heart of the city to
over 2000m above sea level. Summer and
winter outdoor activities abound, and it's
understandable why some visitors only take
a peek at Innsbruck proper before heading for the hills. But to do so is a shame,
for Innsbruck has its own share of gems,
including an authentic medieval Altstadt (Old
Town), inventive architecture, and vibrant
student-driven nightlife.

AUSTRIA

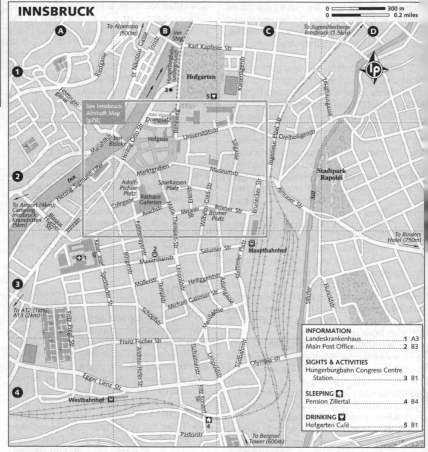

INNSBRUCK

INFORMATION
Landeskrankenhaus.............................1 A3
Main Post Office...................................2 B3

SIGHTS & ACTIVITIES
Hungerburgbahn Congress Centre
     Station.......................................3 B1

SLEEPING 🏠
Pension Zillertal.................................4 B4

DRINKING 🍺
Hofgarten Café...................................5 B1

Orientation

Innsbruck, in the valley of the Inn River, is scenically squeezed between the northern chain of the Alps and the Tuxer mountains to the south. The city centre is compact, with the Hauptbahnhof only a 10-minute walk from the pedestrian-only Altstadt centre. Herzog Friedrich Strasse is the Altstadt's main street.

Information

Bubble Point Waschsalon (Map p78; ☎ 565 007; Brixner Strasse 1; per load €4, internet access per hr €6) Internet cafe and laundrette combined.

Landeskrankenhaus (Map p76; University Clinic; ☎ 50 504-0; Anichstrasse 35) For medical treatment.

Main post office (Map p76; Maximilianstrasse 2;

🕐 7am-9pm Mon-Fri, 7am-3pm Sat, 8am-7.30pm Sun) There is another branch in the Hauptbahnhof.

Innsbruck Information (Map p78; ☎ 53 56, hotel reservations 562 00; www.innsbruck.info; Burggraben 3; 🕐 9am-6pm Apr-Oct, 8am-6pm Nov-Mar) Sells ski passes, hands out free maps, books accommodation, and has loads of info on the city and its surrounds.

Tourist counter (Map p78; Hauptbahnhof, lower concourse; 🕐 9am-7pm)

Sights

OLD TOWN

Innsbruck's atmospheric, medieval Altstadt is ideal for a lazy stroll. A good starting point is the famous **Goldenes Dachl** (Map p78; Golden Roof; Herzog Friedrich Strasse), which comprises 2657 gilded copper tiles. It was built by Emperor

Maximilian I in the 16th century as a display of wealth.

Close by is another former royal dwelling, the **Hofburg** (Imperial Palace; Map p78; ☎ 587 186; Rennweg 1; adult/student €5.50/4; ⊗ 9am-5pm). A favourite of Maria Theresia, these state apartments betray the wealth of the Habsburgs – each room is lavishly adorned in rococo splendour, the highlight of which is the Riesensaal (Giant's Hall).

The **Hofkirche** (Imperial Church; Map p78; Universitätsstrasse 2; adult/child €4/2; ⊗ 9am-5pm Mon-Sat, 10am-5pm Sun) contains a memorial to Maximilian, and although his 'sarcophagus' has been restored, it's actually empty. Perhaps more memorable are the 28 giant statues of Habsburgs lining either side of the cask. You're now forbidden to touch the statues, but numerous inquisitive hands have already polished parts of the dull bronze, including Kaiser Rudolf's codpiece!

BERGISEL TOWER

If you've ever wondered what it feels like to stand on top of an Olympic-sized ski jump, you'll leave the **Bergisel tower** (off Map p76; ☎ 589 259; adult/child €8.30/4; ⊗ 10am-6.30pm) with a better idea. And if you've never been curious about such death-defying feats, you'll still be rewarded with truly fantastic views; the tower sits 3km south of the city centre on the crest of the refurbished Winter Olympics ski-jump stadium, overlooking Innsbruck. A reminder of the perils of ski-jumping – in the shape of a cemetery – lies directly over the lip of the hill.

The tower evinces the curving design typical of its designer – Iraqi-born, British-based Zaha Hadid (who also designed the new Hungerburgbahn). For the full experience, stop for coffee in the **Café im Turm** (meals €8.50-16.60), whose panorama windows give a whole new meaning to the term 'caffeine high'. The stadium is still used for ski-jumping in June and January.

To get here, take tram 1 (direction Bergisel) from Museumstrasse and then follow the signs to Bergisel – it's a fairly steep path for 15 minutes.

ALPENZOO

The **Alpenzoo** (Alpine Zoo; off Map p76; ☎ 292 323; www.alpenzoo.at, in German; Weiherburggasse 37; adult/child/student €7/3.50/5, incl return ticket on Hungerburgbahn €9/4.50/7.50; ⊗ 9am-6pm) houses a comprehensive collection of alpine animals, including ibexes, bears, an eagle and a bearded vulture. Walk up the hill to get there or take the revamped Hungerburgbahn.

OTHER SIGHTS

The **Nordkettenbahn** (Northpark cable car; ☎ 293 344; www.nordpark.com) connects the centre of Innsbruck with the Hafelekar peak (2256m) in a staggering 25 minutes. The ride is split into three parts: the new **Hungerburgbahn** (Map p76; one way/return €3.40/5.60; ⊗ 7am-7.30pm Mon-Fri, 8am-7.30pm Sat & Sun), displaying the tell-tale signs of its designer, Zaha Hadid, runs from the Congress Centre to Hungerburg (860m); the **Seegrube cable car** (Innsbruck-Seegrube one way/return €13.20/22; ⊗ 8.30am-5.30pm) connects Hungerburg with the Seegrube station (1905m); and the **Hafelekar cable car** (Innsbruck-Hafelekar one way/return €14.70/24.50; ⊗ 9am-5pm) hauls you up the last leg. The views are breathtaking.

The **Landesmuseum Ferdinandeum** (Map p78; ☎ 59 489; Museumstrasse 15; adult/student €8/4; ⊗ 9am-6pm Tue-Sun) has a massive collection of Gothic statues and altarpieces. Tours of the city are possible with the 'hop on, hop off' **Sightseer bus** (adult/concession day ticket €8/6.20; ⊗ services every half-hr 9am-5.30pm May-Oct, 10am-5pm Nov-Apr), which makes getting to some of the more remote sights easier. Pick up a brochure at the tourist office.

Activities

Skiing is a major winter activity around Innsbruck, and the area is constantly being improved each year. Three/seven day passes cost

---

MORE FOR YOUR MONEY

If you plan to experience Innsbruck fully, consider purchasing the **Innsbruck Card** (€25/30/35 for 24/48/72 hours), which allows you visit to most major attractions, one return journey on cable cars, and free use of public transport. It's available from the main tourist office.

Those staying in Innsbruck are entitled to the **Club Innsbruck Card**, available at your hostel or hotel, which gives discounts on transport, admission fees, and includes free guided mountain hikes. The hiking program runs from June to the beginning of October, and includes day hikes, sunrise hikes, and night-time lantern walks. For more information, contact the tourist office.

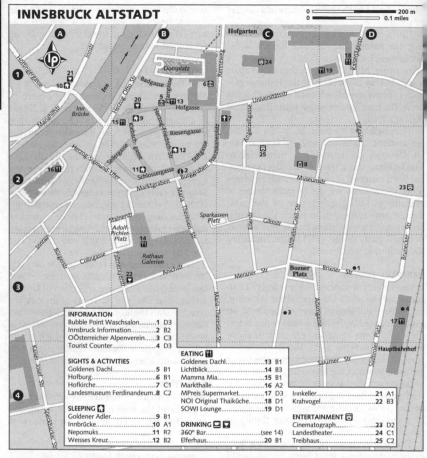

INNSBRUCK ALTSTADT

0 ——— 200 m
0 ——— 0.1 miles

INFORMATION
Bubble Point Waschsalon.........1 D3
Innsbruck Information............2 B2
OÖsterreicher Alpenverein.....3 C3
Tourist Counter....................4 D3

SIGHTS & ACTIVITIES
Goldenes Dachl....................5 B1
Hofburg..............................6 B1
Hofkirche.............................7 C1
Landesmuseum Ferdinandeum..8 C2

SLEEPING
Goldener Adler.....................9 B1
Innbrücke...........................10 A1
Nepomuks..........................11 B2
Weisses Kreuz......................12 B2

EATING
Goldenes Dachl...................13 B1
Lichtblick...........................14 B3
Mamma Mia.......................15 B1
Markthalle..........................16 A2
MPreis Supermarket............17 D3
NOI Original Thaiküche........18 D1
SOWI Lounge......................19 D1

DRINKING
360° Bar..........................(see 14)
Elferhaus...........................20 B1

Innkeller.............................21 A1
Krahvogel...........................22 B3

ENTERTAINMENT
Cinematograph....................23 D2
Landestheater.....................24 C1
Treibhaus...........................25 C2

€99/188, and equipment hire starts at around €20 per day. However, it's not just a winter pastime in this region – year-round skiing is available at **Stubai Glacier**. The tourist office offers a package for €54 for one day which includes transport, passes and equipment hire; buses leave from the Hauptbahnhof, with the journey taking about 80 minutes. The last bus back leaves at 5.30pm. It's a good deal in summer, however in winter there's a free ski bus leaving from various hotels, so compare going it alone with taking the tourist-office package first.

The mountains around Innsbruck are crisscrossed with well-marked trails, making them a target for **hiking** in summer. The tourist office offers guided hikes, and the Nordkettenbahn

(p77) allows hikers to access the mountains with minimum fuss.

Sleeping

The tourist office has lists of private rooms in Innsbruck from €35 per person.

Camping Innsbruck Kranebitten (off Map p76; ☎ 284 180; www.campinginnsbruck.com; Kranebitter Allee 214; adult/tent & car €5.40/3.40; 💻) In an idyllic location under the mountains 5km from the Altstadt, this camping ground is open year-round. It has a restaurant and bike hire, and offers a shuttle service into the city.

Jugendherberge Innsbruck (off Map p76; ☎ 346 179; www.jugendherberge-innsbruck.at; Reichenauerstrasse 147; dm from €16.50, s/d €33/50; 💻) Seen from afar, this hostel resembles a building from the former

USSR – a huge, concrete monstrosity. Up close the picture is a bit prettier – its dorms are actually quite modestly sized. Prices include breakfast. To get here, take bus O (direction Olympisches Dorf/Josef Kerschbaumer Strasse) from Museumstrasse.

our pick **Nepomuks** (Map p78; ☎ 584 118; www.nepomuks.at; Kiebachgasse 16; dm/d €20/50) This wonderful establishment has oodles of charm, with CD players and books in rooms and a thoroughly warm welcome. The staircase has been around since the year 1800, but the spotless rooms are remodelled (only 10), and the excellent breakfast in the attached patisserie downstairs will get your day off to a grand start.

Pension Zillertal (Map p76; ☎ 582 129; www.pensionzillertal.com; Fritz Konzert Strasse 7; s/d/tr from €25/46/64) A family-run B&B in a converted apartment building, south of the city and close to the Bergisel tower. Very good value; the rooms are spotless, and have TVs and phones.

Innbrücke (Map p78; ☎ 281 934; www.gasthofinnbruecke.at; Innstrasse 1; s/d from €32/55; 🖳) It may be a little run down and the staff a tad unconventional, but the Innbrücke is a solid option and you can't beat the location/price ratio.

Weisses Kreuz (Map p78; ☎ 59 479; www.weisseskreuz.at; Herzog Friedrich Strasse 31; s/d with shared bathroom from €36/66, with private bathroom from €64/100) It's had the honour of hosting Mozart, and this creaky, atmospheric hotel remains comfortable to this day. Parking costs €10.

Binders Hotel (off Map p76; ☎ 33 436; www.binders.at; Dr Glatz Strasse 20; s/d from €59/78; 🖳) Brightly coloured lampshades, pillows and armchairs create a splash against a neutral, modern background in this small hotel with a touch of art design. It's a 20-minute walk, or short ride on tram 3, east of the train station.

Goldener Adler (Map p78; ☎ 571 111; www.goldeneradler.com; Herzog Friedrich Strasse 6; s/d from €84/120; 🖳) The grand dame of Innsbruck's hotel scene, the Goldener Adler has been around in one form or another since 1390. The rooms are suitably plush and the location impossible to beat.

Eating
NOI Original Thaiküche (Map p78; ☎ 589 777; Kaiserjägerstrasse 1; mains €4-11, midday menu €8; ☺ Mon-Fri, dinner Sat) The whiff of Thai spices – and the reasonable prices – attracts both students and business lunchers to this tiny eatery. Expect delicious Thai staples, such as soups,

noodle dishes and curries, and outdoor tables in summer.

SOWI Lounge (Map p78; Universitätstrasse 15; meals around €5; ☺ 8am-9pm Mon-Thu, 8am-6pm Fri) University mensa with an ever-changing menu but always a good selection of dishes.

Mamma Mia (Map p78; ☎ 562 902; Kiebachgasse 2; mains €6.40-7) This cheap and cheerful Italian serves generous helpings of pizza and pasta in the heart of the Altstadt. Its sunny terrace is perfect in summer.

Lichtblick (Map p78; ☎ 566 550; 7th fl, Maria Theresien Strasse 18; daytime snacks €7-11, dinner menu €35-45; ☺ Mon-Sat) This is the city's hot ticket, and little wonder, given both the fabulous views of the surrounding mountains and the delicious modern international food. It's a romantic setting at night. After dinner grab a drink across the foyer in the 360 Bar (below).

Goldenes Dachl (Map p70; ☎ 589 370; Hofgasse 1; mains €10-18) The menu features Tirolean specialities, such as *Bauerngröstl*, a pork, bacon, potato and egg concoction served with salad, along with *Wiener schnitzel* and various types of *Braten* (roasts).

There is an **MPreis Supermarket** (Map p78; ☺ 6am-9pm) in the Hauptbahnhof and a large indoor food market by the river in **Markthalle** (Map p78; Herzog-Siegmund-Ufer; ☺ 7am-6.30pm Mon-Fri, 7am-1pm Sat).

Drinking
Elferhaus (Map p78; ☎ 582 875; Herzog Friedrich Strasse 11) Tunnelling into a slab of rock, this cool *Bierhaus* (beer house) has a vibe that gets lively late when the mostly college crowd shows up.

Hofgarten Café (Map p76; ☎ 588 871; Rennweg 6a) If you're looking for a green, tree-shaded spot outdoors in which to enjoy a drink, while DJs spin tunes in the background, then Hofgarten will more than suffice.

360° Bar (Map p78; ☎ 566 550; 7th fl, Maria Theresien Strasse 18; ☺ Mon-Sat) As the name suggests, it's all about the views. This hip wine bar across from Lichtblick has perhaps the best views of the city. Relax in the plush surroundings and lounge in style swathed in ultramodern comfort with excellent service.

Also worth recommending:

Krahvogel (Map p78; ☎ 5801 4971; Anichstrasse 12) Favourite student haunt which gets busy after 10pm.

Innkeller (Map p78; ☎ 291 508; Innstrasse 1) Party spot for its electronic tunes and outdoor terrace on busy Innstrasse.

WORTH THE TRIP: AROUND INNSBRUCK

Within a 30-minute radius of the Tirolean capital is an unusual world of crystals, a gruesome collection of saintly bones, and a town with an intact medieval centre.

Crystal Worlds (☎ 05224-51 080; www.swarovski.com/kristallwelten; Kristallweltenstrasse 1; adult/child €9.50/free; ☼ 9am-5.30pm), located in **Wattens**, is the work of crystal makers Swarovski. The centre features elaborate installations by – or based on – leading artists, including Eno, Warhol and Dali, but the giant cranium at the entrance, complete with sparkling crystalline eyes and waterfall-spewing mouth, steals the show. Juxtaposing such sparkling beauty is the 13th-century **Pfarrkirche** (Oberer Stadtplatz; admission free; ☼ dawn-dusk) in **Hall in Tirol**. It's home to a collection of 45 skulls and 12 bones, removed from the skeletons of minor saints by Florian Waldauf, advisor to Maximilian I. The spectacle is sure to repulse and fascinate. **Schwaz**, some 18km east of Innsbruck, was, in the 15th century, Austria's second-largest city after Vienna. Now it's a sleepy town, but the labyrinth of pretty cobbled streets at its medieval heart is testament to the wealth it accumulated from silver mines over the centuries.

Wattens is best reached by bus (€3.90 return, 20 minutes) from Innsbruck, as is Hall in Tirol (€2.80, 30 minutes). The train to Schwaz (€5.20, 20 minutes) is the quickest option.

Entertainment

The tourist office sells tickets for 'Tirolean evenings' (adult/child €22/10 for alpine music, folk dancing, yodelling and one drink), classical concerts and performances in the **Landestheater** (Map p78; ☎ 520 744; www.landestheater.at, in German, Rennweg 2). For more entertainment options, pick up a copy of *Innsider*, found in cafes across town.

Cinematograph (Map p78; ☎ 578 500; Museumstrasse 31) screens independent films in their original language.

The arty, community-minded **Treibhaus** (Map p78; ☎ 572 000; Angerzellgasse 8) hosts live music ranging from urban groove to ska, short-film festivals and the like. Attracts students and those with an alternative bent.

Getting There & Away

EasyJet flies twice a week from London Gatwick to **Innsbruck airport** (off Map p76; IIN; ☎ 22 525-0; www.innsbruck-airport.com), while Austrian Airlines, TUIfly, and Welcome Air connect the city with a handful of other European destinations.

The A12 and the parallel Hwy 171 are the main roads to the east and west respectively. Hwy 177 heads north to Germany and Munich. The A13 motorway is a toll road (€8) southwards through the Brenner Pass to Italy; it includes the impressive Europabrücke (Europe Bridge), several kilometres south of the city. Toll-free Hwy 182 follows the same route, passing under the bridge.

Fast trains depart eight times daily for Bregenz (€29.20, 2½ hours) and every two hours to Salzburg (€35.20, two hours) and Kitzbühel (€17.90, one hour). On many trains to Lienz (€30.10, 3¼ hours), people travelling on Austrian rail passes must pay a surcharge for travelling through Italy. Ask before boarding or call ☎ 05-17 17, available 24 hours.

Getting Around

The airport is 4km west of the city centre. To get there, take bus F, which departs from opposite the Hauptbahnhof half-hourly (hourly on Saturday afternoon and Sunday) and passes through Maria Theresien Strasse. A taxi from the main train station to the airport costs around €10.

Single bus tickets, including to the airport, cost €1.70. A 24-hour pass is €3.80.

Street parking is very limited in the city centre. Parking garages (eg under the Altstadt) cost €10 and upwards per day.

MAYRHOFEN
☎ 05285 / pop 3800

Tirol is ribbed by beautiful valleys, but the Zillertal is rated among the best. This long thin, alpine paradise is bristling with high mountain peaks, peaceful meadows, and rural farmhouses. It also has its fair share of towns, villages, and, naturally, tourists, many of whom head for Mayrhofen, a centre where you can base yourself for skiing year-round.

The town's **tourist office** (☎ 676 00; www.mayrhofen.at; Europahaus; ☼ 8am-7pm Mon-Fri, 9am-5pm Sat & Sun) has loads of comprehensive information, including free *Info von A–Z* booklets for both summer and winter in English. There are good **walks** originating from the village; ask at the tourist office for maps or about guided trips. Mayrhofen is home to the steepest piste in Austria, known as the HariKari, and there is year-round **skiing** on nearby **Hintertux Glacier**. A pass costs €39/32 per day in winter/summer; inquire at the tourist office.

To work your taste buds instead of your legs, pay a visit to **Erlebnis Sennerei** (☎ 627 13; www.sennerei-zillertal.at; Hollenzen 116; admission with/without tasting €11.20/5.80; ☽ 10-11.30am & 12.30-3pm), a grass-roots dairy. See how local cheeses are made on the production facility tour and then enjoy the chance to taste them. There's also a fine **restaurant** (mains €7-14; ☽ 10am-6pm) on-site.

The tourist office has a handy booklet listing all the accommodation in the town and its surrounds. **Traudl** (☎ 625 69; info@traudl .at; Dornaustrasse 612; s/d from €40/70; ☐) is a solid Austrian pension, and close to both village amenities and cable cars.

For local grub, try the evergreen drinking and eating hole **Mo's** (Hauptstrasse 417; mains €6-20), which offers a selection of fast food from around the world and occasional live music, or **Mamma Mia's** (Einfahrt Mitte 432; mains €7-10), where pasta and pizza fill the menu.

To reach Mayrhofen from Innsbruck (€13.40, 1½ hours), a change is required at Jenbach (€5.60, one hour). Trains run at least hourly.

KITZBÜHEL
☎ 05356 / pop 8500

Kitzbühel began life in the 16th century as a silver and copper mining town and today continues to preserve a charming medieval centre despite its other persona - as a fashionable and prosperous winter resort. It's renowned for the white-knuckled Hahnenkamm downhill ski race in January and the excellence of its slopes.

Orientation & Information

The main train station is 1km north of the town centre; after emerging onto Bahnhofstrasse, walk straight ahead and then turn left into Josef Pirchl Strasse, then take the right fork (no entry for cars), which is still Josef Pirchl Strasse, and continue past the **post office** (☽ 8am-6pm Mon-Fri). Following this road will eventually take you to the **tourist office** (☎ 777; www.kitzbuehel.com; Hinterstadt 18; ☽ 8.30am-6pm Mon-Fri, 9am-6pm Sat, 10am-noon & 4-

6pm Sun Jul-Sep & Christmas-Easter, 8.30am-6pm Mon-Fri, 9am-1pm Sat rest of year).

Activities
SKIING

In winter there is good intermediate skiing on Kitzbüheler Horn to the north and Hahnenkamm to the south of town. A one-day ski pass costs €35, though some pensions and hotels offer 'Ski Hit' reductions before mid-December or after mid-March.

HIKING

Dozens of summer hiking trails surround Kitzbühel; the tourist office gives free maps and free guided hikes (for those overnighting in the town). Get a head start to the heights with a one- or three-day cable-car pass for €15.70/37.50.

There is an alpine flower garden (free) on the slopes of the Kitzbüheler Horn (a toll road for drivers). The scenic Schwarzsee, 3km to the northwest, is a fine location for summer swimming.

Sleeping & Eating

The tourist office can help with accommodation, but its best to book well ahead in winter.

Snow Bunnys (☎ 0676-794 0233; www.snowbun nys.co.uk; Bichstrasse 30; dm/d from €28/70; ☐) Don't let the cramped common area downstairs put you off this small and friendly independent hostel. The rooms upstairs are spacious, bright, colourful, and some come with attached balcony. DIY breakfast is included in the price, as is the company of two resident cats.

Pension Mühlbergerhof (☎ 628 35; muehlberger hof@tirol.com; Schwarzseestrasse 6; s/d from €38/76) A warm, homely feel is one of the winning features of Pension Mühlbergerhof. Others include large rooms with balconies and views of the Hahenhkamm, and breakfasts using the owner's very own farm produce.

Pension Schmidinger (☎ 631 34-0; www.schmidinger .cc; Ehrenbachgasse 3; s/d €45/90) Only a few minutes' south of the centre is this comfy pension with spotless rooms decorated in a pleasant country style.

Huberbräu Stüberl (Vorderstadt 18; mains €7-13) This is a Kitzbühel 'must', although so many diners come for the Austrian food and beer that the service is sometimes rather off-hand and slow.

WORTH THE TRIP: KRIMML FALLS

At the northwestern corner of the Hohe Tauern National Park, on Hwy 168 (which becomes Hwy 165), is the spectacular, triple-level **Krimml Falls** (adult/child €2/0.50; ☺ ticket office 8am-6pm mid-Apr–Oct). At 380m it's Europe's highest waterfall, and one of Austria's most unforgettable sights. The village of Krimml has a handful of places to sleep and eat – contact the **tourist office** (☎ 06564-72 39; www.krimml.at; ☺ 8am-noon & 2.30-5.30pm Mon-Fri, 8.30-10.30am Sat) for more information.

Buses run to the falls from Zell am See (€7.90, 1½ hours) year-round.

La Fonda (Hinterstadt 13; mains €8-13; ☺ 5-midnight) The kitschy Tex-Mex decor makes this place a popular choice, as does the kitchen which stays open until midnight for those wanting to dine late on nachos, burritos and enchiladas.

For self-caterers, there's a **Spar supermarket** (Bichlstrasse 22).

Getting There & Away

Direct trains to Innsbruck (€17.90, one to 1½ hours) leave Kitzbühel every two hours, but there are hourly services to Wörgl (€7.80, 30 minutes), where you can change for Innsbruck. Trains to Salzburg (€25, two to 2½ hours) leave roughly hourly and normally require a change in Wörgl. Slower trains stop at Kitzbühel-Hahnenkamm, which is closer to the town centre than the main Kitzbühel stop.

The train connection to Lienz is terrible; bus (€13.20, two hours) is the way to go. Six run Monday to Friday and four Saturday and Sunday.

Heading south to Lienz, you pass through some marvellous scenery. Hwy 108 (the Felber Tauern Tunnel) and Hwy 107 (the Grossglockner mountain road; closed in winter) both have toll sections.

LIENZ

☎ 04852 / pop 12,000

Lienz is the last major Ost Tirol outpost before Italy, only 40km to the southwest. With its pretty centre and busy squares, many visitors find it a charming town, but it's the Dolomite mountain range engulfing the southern skyline that people really come here for. Lienz is also a stopover for skiers and hikers passing through or on the way to the Hohe Tauern National Park.

Orientation & Information

The town centre is within the junction of the Isel and Drau Rivers. To reach Hauptplatz from the train station cross the road (or take the 'Zur Stadt' exit) and follow the street past the post office. The **tourist office** (☎ 652 65; www.lienz-tourismus.at; Europaplatz 1; ☺ 8am-6pm Mon-Fri, 9am-noon & 5-7pm Sat Jul–mid-Sep, 8am-6pm Mon-Fri, 10.30am-noon Sun Jul & Aug) will find rooms free of charge, or you can use the hotel board (free telephone) outside. Free internet access is available at the local **library** (Muchargasse 1; ☺ 9am-noon & 3-7pm Tue & Thu, 9am-noon & 3-6pm Wed & Fri, 9am-noon Sat).

Sights & Activities

Lienz has its fair share of hiking and skiing possibilities right on its doorstep. A €30 day pass covers skiing on the nearby **Zettersfeld** and **Hochstein** peaks; however, the area around Lienz is more renowned for its cross-country skiing; the town fills up for the annual **Dolomitenlauf** cross-country skiing race in mid-January.

Cable cars are in action from June to September, and lift passes for either Zettersfeld or Hochstein cost around €10. It's also possible to tackle the area in the company of llamas – contact **Dolomiten Lamatrekking** (☎ 680 87; www.dolomitenlama.at) for more details.

Sleeping & Eating

Comfort-Camping Falken (☎ 64 022; Eichholz 7; www.camping-falken.com, in German; camp site per adult/child/tent €5.50/4/9; ☺ mid-Dec–Oct; 🖳) Just 10-minutes' walk south of town, this camping ground has wonderful mountain views, a restaurant and good laundry facilities.

Altstadthotel Eck (☎ 647 85; altstadthotel.eck@uta net.at; Hauptplatz 20; s/d €42/74) Atmospheric and spacious, Altstadthotel Eck provides all the comfort you'd expect from one of the town's top hotels.

Adlerstüberl (☎ 625 50; Andrä Kranz Gasse 5; mains €8-14; ☺ 11am-3pm & 6pm-midnight) A central option where tourists and locals alike grab a table to avail of the array of Austrian dishes. The two-course midday menu (€11) will keep you going for days.

There is an **ADEG supermarket** at Hauptplatz 12 and a few sausage and kebab stands scattered around town.

Getting There & Away

Except for the 'corridor' route through Italy to Innsbruck, trains to the rest of Austria connect via Spittal Millstättersee to the east. Trains to Salzburg (€31.40) take at least 3½ hours, to Klagenfurt (€22.60) two hours. Villach, east of Klagenfurt, is a main junction for rail routes to the south. To head south by car, you must first divert west or east along Hwy 100.

HOHE TAUERN NATIONAL PARK

You wouldn't guess from its small stature, but little Austria actually contains the largest national park in the Alps. Straddling Tirol, Salzburg and Carinthia, the Hohe Tauern National Park stretches over 1786 sq km. At the heart of this protected oasis of flora and fauna (including marmots and some rare ibexes) lies the **Grossglockner** (3797m), Austria's highest mountain. The Grossglockner towers over the 10km-long Pasterze Glacier, which is best seen from the outlook at **Franz Josefs Höhe** (2369m).

The portion of the **Grossglockner Hochalpenstrasse** (Hwy 107; www.grossglockner.at, in German) running through the park is considered one of the most scenic in the world. It winds upwards 2000m past waterfalls, glaciers and Alpine meadows. The highway runs between Lienz and Zell am See, and if you catch a bus from Lienz to Franz Josef's Höhe, you'll be traversing the southern part of this route. If you have your own vehicle, you'll have more flexibility, although the road is open only between May and mid-September, and you must pay tolls (per car/motorcycle €28/18).

The major village on the Grossglockner Rd is **Heiligenblut**, which is dominated not only by mountain peaks, but also by the steep spire of a 15th-century pilgrimage church. Here you'll find a **tourist office** (☎ 04824-20 01; www .heiligenblut.at; ☯ 9am-6pm Mon-Fri, 9am-noon & 4-6pm Sat Jul, Aug & Dec-Mar, 9am-noon & 2-5pm Mon-Fri Apr, May & Sep-Nov), restaurants, and a spick-and-span **Jugendherberge** (☎ 04824-22 59; www.oejhv.or.at; Hof 36; dm/r €19/26; ☯ reception 7-10am, 5-8pm). Although camping is not allowed in the park, there are mountain huts and hiking trails open from May until the first snow fall; the tourist office in Heiligenblut has details.

Eight buses connect Lienz and Heiligenblut from Monday to Saturday year-round (€7.40, one hour); from late June to late September buses make the trip between Heiligenblut and Franz Josefs Höhe (€4.10, 30 minutes, four daily Monday to Friday, three daily Saturday and Sunday). Between mid-June and late September, two buses daily (€10.60, two hours) head north from Franz Josef Höhe to Zell am See, a major holiday resort in the region. Timetables change regularly here though, so it's best to check with the tourist office in Lienz (opposite) before setting off.

VORARLBERG

Vorarlberg has always been a little different. Cut off from the rest of Austria by the snow-capped Arlberg massif, this westerly region has often associated itself more with Switzerland than Vienna far to the east, and it citizens have developed a strong dialect Tiroleans even find hard to decipher.

Alluringly beautiful, this region is an aesthetic mix of mountains, hills and valleys. Trickling down from the Alps to the shores of Lake Constance (Bodensee), Vorarlberg is a destination in its own right, attracting everyone from classical-music buffs to skiers. It's also a gateway, by rail or water, to Germany, Liechtenstein and Switzerland.

BREGENZ

☎ 05574 / pop 27,000

Bregenz has been a ritzy address for generations, which is not surprising considering its pretty location on the shores of Lake Constance. Boating, cycling, and lounging on the lake's shores are the general activities here, and many time a visit to Vorarlberg's capital to catch the annual Bregenzer Festspiele (Bregenz Festival) in summer.

Orientation

Bregenz is on Lake Constance's eastern shore. Turn left at the main train station exit and take Bahnhofstrasse to the city centre (five minutes). Buses for the city leave from outside the train station.

Information

Cockpit Café (Seegalerie, Bahnhofstrasse 10; per 30min €2.40, per hr wi-fi €3; ☯ 8am-7pm Mon-Fri, 8am-6pm Sat) Internet access, printing and scanning services.

WORTH THE TRIP: BREGENZERWALD

Only a few kilometres east of Bregenz begins the Bregenzerwald, a region of spectacular limestone peaks, velvet-green pastures, and alpine dairies. In summer it's a glorious place to spend a few days hiking the hills and filling up on all manner of home-made cheeses and other Bregenzerwald delectables. Winter brings plenty of snow, and the area is noted for its downhill and cross-country skiing.

The **Bregenzerwald tourist office** (☎ 05512-23 65; www.bregenzerwald.at; Gerbe 1135, Egg; ☼ 9am-5pm Mon-Fri, 8am-1pm Sat & Sun) has information on the region, and cheese-lovers can consult www.kaesestrasse.at for the low-down on Bregenzerwald's **Cheese Road**. From Bregenz, buses travel to Egg (€3.70, 45 minutes) and Bezau (€4.40, one hour), two of the region's main villages, every two hours.

Post office (Seestrasse 5; ☼ 7am-7pm Mon-Fri, 8am-noon Sat)

Tourist office (☎ 49 59-0; www.bregenz.at, in German; Rathausstrasse 35a; ☼ 8.30am-6pm Mon-Fri, till noon Sat, to 7pm Mon-Sat during the Bregenzer Festspiele) Can help with accommodation and activities in the area.

Sights & Activities

Most tourists who arrive in Bregenz are drawn almost instinctively to the **Bodensee**, a major summer-holiday destination for Austrians, Swiss and Germans, all of whom take advantage of the many water sports and attractions lining its banks. Boats operate on the lake; see opposite for more details. Otherwise take matters into your own hands (and feet) and hire a bike from **Fahrradverleih Bregenz** (☎ 0650-541 300; Am Blumenmolo; per 12/24 hr €12/16.50; ☼ 9am-7pm May-Sep) on the lakefront or a canoe from **La Canoa** (☎ 73 260; Hechtweg 4; per hr/day €10/25) at Mexico Camping, 1km west of the train station.

Bregenz itself has notable architecture, including the impressive edifice of the **Kunsthaus** (☎ 485 94-0; www.kunsthaus-bregenz.at; Karl-tizian-Platz; adult/concession €8/6; ☼ 10am-6pm Tue, Wed & Fri-Sun, 10am-9pm Thu) by award-winning Swiss architect Peter Zumthor. Set high above the modern centre is the charming **Oberstadt**, the medieval heart of the town; look for the enormous onion dome of the **Martinsturm** (St Martin's Tower; Martinsgasse 3; adult/child €1/0.50; ☼ 9am-6.30pm Tue-Sun May–mid-Oct), reputedly the largest in central Europe.

For spectacular views of the lake and town catch the **Pfänder cable car** (☎ 42 160-0; www.pfaenderbahn.at; adult/concession €6/5.50; ☼ 9am-7pm, closed 2 weeks in Nov) which rises to 1064m.

Festivals & Events

A feature that makes the **Bregenzer Festspiele** (Bregenz Festival; www.bregenzerfestspiele.com; tickets €26-

280) in July and August so remarkable is its setting. During the four-week program, operas and classical works are performed from a floating stage on the lake's edge. For tickets, contact the **Kartenbüro** (☎ 407-6; Postfach 311, A-6901) about nine months beforehand, or ask about cancellations on the day.

Sleeping & Eating

The tourist office can help with private rooms (€20 to €40 per person) if none of the following options sound appealing. Expect prices during the festival to be higher than those quoted here.

Jugendgästehaus Bregenz (☎ 42 867; www.jgh .at/bregenz; Mehrerauerstrasse 5; dm from €23.30; ☐) In a former needle factory, this HI hostel is a lively place, with larger than average dorms boasting only six beds plus en suite. There's also a decent restaurant on the premises. The hostel is near the skateboard park; take the 'Zum See' exit from the train station and pass the casino.

Pension Sonne (☎ 42 572; www.bbn.at/sonne; Kaiserstrasse 8; s/d with shared bathroom from €36/68, with private bathroom €45/80) This family-run pension is very basic and rooms are small, but it's cheap and supremely central. Ask to see a few rooms; some have nicer decor than others.

Pension Matt (☎ 71 777; www.gasthofmatt.at, in German; Wuhrbaumweg 36; s/d from €40/64; ☐) The comfy, spacious, and cosy rooms at this lovely pension are some of the best value for money in town. There's also a restaurant on-site that serves up seasonal specialities. Only thing, it's 20 minutes' walk west of the centre.

Deuring-Schlössle (☎ 47 800; www.deuring-schloessle .at, in German; Ehregutaplatz 4; s/d €95/105; ☐) Bregenz's best rooms are found in this fabulously renovated old castle. Each one is decorated differently, but all have loads of medieval charm and grace. Its restaurant (mains around €20) is also the best in Bregenz, with a sophisticated look and a gourmet menu.

Cafesito (Maurachgasse 6; smoothies & bagels €3-4; ☺ 7.45am-7pm Mon-Fri, 9am-4.30pm Sat) A tiny, chilled cafe on the way up (or even better, on the way down) to the Oberstadt, with imaginative takes on bagels, smoothies and drinks.

Gösserbräu (☎ 42 467; Anton Schneider Strasse 1; mains €8-12; ☺ 9am-1pm Mon-Thu, 9am-2pm Fri & Sat) Solid Austrian fare, simple and hearty, but not too stodgy, can be taken in either modern surrounds, typically traditional rooms (complete with wood panelling), or on the terrace.

Getting There & Away

Trains to Munich (€40.20, 2½ hours) go via Lindau. There are also three departures daily to St Gallen (€11.20, 35 minutes) and Zürich (€25, 1½ hours). Trains to Innsbruck (€29.20, 2½ hours) depart every two hours. From April to mid-October, boats connect Bregenz to a number of towns and cities on Bodensee, including Constance (one way €12.80, 4¼ hours, up to six times daily) in Switzerland and Friedrichshafen (€11, two hours, up to eight times daily) in Germany. For information call ☎ 42 868 or consult www.bodensee schifffahrt.at (in German).

ARLBERG REGION

The Arlberg region, shared by Vorarlberg and neighbouring Tirol, has some of the best skiing in Austria. In summer, however, you'll find most restaurants and bars closed.

St Anton am Arlberg is the largest resort, and Austria's prime skiing destination, attracting eager skiers from across Europe with good intermediate to advanced runs, nursery slopes on Gampen and Kapall, and legendary après-ski festivities. The **tourist office** (☎ 05446-22 690; www.stantonamarlberg.com; Arlberghaus; ☺ 8am-6pm Mon-Fri, 9am-noon Sat & Sun summer, 8.30am-6pm Mon-Fri, 9am-6pm Sat, 9am-noon & 2-5pm Sun winter), diagonally left from the train station on the main street, can help with accommodation and activity information.

A **ski pass** (www.skiarlberg.at) that's valid for 85 ski lifts in St Anton and neighbouring St Christoph Lech, Zürs and Stuben costs €42.50/224 for one day/week (reductions for children and seniors). Naturally hiking is the number-one summer pastime: the **Wanderpass** (€32 for seven days) allows unlimited access to all lifts.

Despite a seemingly endless array of accommodation options, it can be almost impossible to find something in winter, and stays of less than a week are generally not possible. In summer you'll have no problem finding a place to crash.

St Anton has no hostel; the closest is in Lech. **Tiroler Frieden** (☎ 05446-2247; tiroler.frieden@ st-anton.at; Dorfstrasse 75; s/d €29/58) has an authentic Tirolean feel, with plenty of wood panelling and clean, simple rooms, while **Haus Moostal** (☎ 05446-2831; www.hausmoostal.at; Marktstrasse 14; s/d €45/90; 🖵) is another fine choice; its rooms are big and bright, and there's a small sauna on-site.

When hunger hits, there is a **Spar supermarket** (☺ 7am-7pm Mon-Fri, 7am-1pm Sat) on the main road if you want to do your own thing, and decent pizza and pasta dishes at **Pomodoro** (Dorfstrasse 5; mains from €8; ☺ dinner Dec-Apr).

The following bars are huge tourist haunts, but there's no better place to party when you're done with the slopes. All are open December to April only. Loud, bawdy and very English, **Piccadilly** (Walter-Schuler-Weg 2) often has live music, while further up the piste, **Krazy Kanguruh** (Mooserweg 19) and **Mooserwirt** (Unterer Mooserweg 2) are full to overflowing with merry skiers all day long.

Getting There & Away

St Anton is situated on the main railway route between Bregenz (€16.90, 1½ hours) and Innsbruck (€20, 1¼ hours). St Anton is close to the eastern entrance of the Arlberg Tunnel, the toll road connecting Vorarlberg and Tirol. The tunnel toll is €8.50 one way. You can avoid the toll by taking the B197, but no vehicles with trailers are allowed on this winding road.

AUSTRIA DIRECTORY

ACCOMMODATION

Reservations are recommended at Christmas and Easter, along with July and August in cities and December to April in ski resorts. They are binding on both parties, so if you don't take a reserved room, the price could still be deducted from your credit card. Hostels tend to be more flexible; however, small groups booking into hostels might find their reservation for a four-bed room translated into four separate beds on arrival.

Tourist offices can supply lists of all types of accommodation and will generally make reservations – sometimes for a small fee.

Many resort towns hand out a *Gästekarte* (guest card) to people staying overnight. This card is funded by a resort tax of around €1 to €2 per night, added to the accommodation tariff, and it offers useful discounts on transport, sporting facilities and museums. Check with the tourist office if you're not offered one at your resort accommodation. In smaller towns, the first night's accommodation can cost slightly more than subsequent nights.

There are over 500 camping grounds in Austria, but most close in winter. If you pitch a tent outside an established camping ground you need the property owner's approval; on public land it's illegal. Outside Vienna, Tirol and protected areas, free camping is allowed in a campervan, but only if you don't set up equipment outside the van. The **Austrian Camping Club** (Österreichischer Camping Club; Map p46-7; ☎ 01-713 6151; www.campingclub.at; Schubertring 1-3, A-1010 Vienna) has information.

In the mountains, hikers can take a break from camping by spending the night in an alpine hut. See right for further details.

There are a couple of HI-affiliated hostelling associations operating within the country: **Österreichischer Jugendherbergsverband** (Map pp46-7; ☎ 01-533 53 53; www.oejhv.or.at; Gonzagagasse 22, A-1010 Vienna) and **Junge Hostels Austria** (Map pp46-7; ☎ 01-533 18 33; www.jungehotels.at; Helferstorferstrasse 4, A-1010 Vienna). Prices generally range from €15 to €20 per night.

It's quite common for house owners to rent out rooms in their home (€18 to €40 per person, per night). Look out for the ubiquitous *Zimmer frei* (rooms vacant) signs.

The cheapest budget hotels start at around €25/40 for singles/doubles with a shared bathroom, and €35/60 for those with private facilities. Most midrange hotels start at around €55/90 for rooms with private facilities.

For this chapter we've defined places costing less than €45 as budget, while midrange options cost €45 to €100 and top-end hotels start at €100 per person.

Accommodation prices quoted in this chapter are for the high summer season (or for winter in ski resorts) and include all taxes. Unless otherwise stated, all rooms have private bathrooms, and include breakfast in their price.

ACTIVITIES
Hiking & Mountaineering

Walking and climbing are popular activities with visitors and Austrians alike, and most tourist offices sell maps of hiking routes. Mountain paths have direction indicators and often markers indicating their level of difficulty. Those with a red-white-red marker mean you need sturdy hiking boots and a pole; a blue-white-blue marker indicates the need for mountaineering equipment. There are 10 long-distance national hiking routes, while three European routes pass through Austria. Options include the northern Alpine route from Lake Constance to Vienna, via Dachstein, or the central route from Feldkirch to Hainburger Pforte, via Hohe Tauern National Park.

Don't try mountaineering without having the proper equipment or experience. The **Österreichischer Alpenverein** (ÖAV; Austrian Alpine Club; Map p78; ☎ 0512-59 547; www.alpenverein-ibk.at, in German; Wilhelm Greil Strasse 15, A-6010 Innsbruck) has touring programs and also maintains a list of alpine huts in hill-walking regions. These provide inexpensive accommodation and often have meals or cooking facilities. Members of the club take priority but anyone can stay. It's a good idea to book huts. Listing your next intended destination in the hut book on departure provides you with an extra measure of safety, as search-and-rescue teams will be alerted should a problem arise.

Skiing & Snowboarding

Austria has some of the world's best skiing and snowboarding. The most popular regions are Vorarlberg and Tirol, but Salzburg province and Carinthia offer cheaper possibilities. Unusually, skiing is possible year-round at the famous Stubai Glacier near Innsbruck (see p77).

The skiing season starts in December and lasts well into April at higher-altitude resorts. Count on spending €20 to €40 for a daily ski pass (to ride the ski lifts). Rental generally starts at €20 for downhill equipment or €15 for cross-country skis; rates drop for multiple days.

Spa Resorts

There are spa resorts throughout the country, identifiable by the prefix *Bad* (bath). While perfect for the self-indulgent pampering that stressed-out city-dwellers today so often crave, they also promise more traditional healing cures for respiratory, circulatory and other ailments. The **Austrian National Tourist Office** (www.austria.info) can provide details, as can the **Österreichischer Heilbäder & Kurortverband** (Austrian Thermal Baths & Spa Association; ☎ 01-512 19 04; oehkv@newsclub.at).

BUSINESS HOURS

Shops usually open 9am to 6pm Monday to Friday, and 9am to 1pm or 5pm on Saturday; in smaller cities, there's sometimes a two-hour closure over lunch. In the larger centres some stay open late on a Thursday or Friday night, to either 7.30pm or 8pm. Supermarkets are open 7.30am to 7pm Monday to Thursday till 7.30pm Friday, and till 1pm or 6pm Saturday.

Banks keep short hours, usually opening from 9am to 12.30pm, and 1.30pm to 3pm Monday to Friday, with 'late' (5.30pm) closing on Thursday. Information offices are generally open from 9am to 5pm Monday to Saturday. Restaurants normally open around 11am till 2.30pm and 6pm till 11pm; many stop serving food around 10pm however. Most bars open sometime around noon, while clubs don't start rocking until after 10pm.

EMBASSIES & CONSULATES

Only *Botschaften* (embassies) and *Konsulate* (consulates) in Vienna issue visas. In case of an emergency, you might be redirected to a limited-hours consulate in a nearer city. The following diplomatic missions are located in Vienna unless otherwise stated:

Australia (Map pp46-7; ☎ 01-506 740; www.australian -embassy.at; 04, Mattiellistrasse 2-4)
Canada (Map pp46-7; ☎ 01-53 138-3000; www.kanada .at; 01, Laurenzerberg 2)
Croatia (off Map pp42-3; ☎ 01-484 87 83-0; 17, Heuberggasse 10)
Czech Republic (Map pp42-3; ☎ 01-899 58-111; www .mzv.cz/vienna; 14, Penzingerstrasse 11-13)
France (Map pp46-7; ☎ 01-50 275-0; www.ambafrance -at.org; 04, Technikerstrasse 2)
Germany (Map pp46-7; ☎ 01-71 154-0; www.wien .diplo.de; 03, Metternichgasse 3)
Hungary (Map pp46-7; ☎ 01-53 780-300; 01, Bankgasse 4-6)
Ireland (Map pp46-7; ☎ 01-715 42 46-0; 01, Rotenturmstrasse16-18)
Italy (Map pp46-7; ☎ 01-712 51 21; www.ambvienna .esteri.it; 03, Rennweg 27)

Netherlands (Map pp46-7; ☎ 01-58 939; www.mfa .nl/wen; 01, Opernring 5)
New Zealand (Map pp170-1; ☎ 49-30 20 621-0; www .nzembassy.com; Friedrichstrasse 60, D-10117 Berlin, Germany) Berlin has the nearest New Zealand embassy.
Slovakia (off Map pp42-3; ☎ 01-318 90 55-200; www .vienna.mfa.sk; 19, Armbrustergasse 24)
Slovenia (Map pp46-7; ☎ 01-586 13 09; 01, Niebelungengasse 13)
Switzerland (Map pp46-7; ☎ 01-79 505-0; www.eda .admin.ch/wien; 03, Prinz Eugen Strasse 7)
UK (Map pp46-7; ☎ 01-71 613-0; www.britishembassy .at; 03, Jauresgasse 12)
USA Embassy (Map pp42-3; ☎ 01-31 339-0; www .usembassy.at; 09, Boltzmanngasse 16); Consulate (Map pp46-7; ☎ 512 58 35; 01, Parkring 12a) Visas at the consulate only.

FESTIVALS & EVENTS

The **Austrian National Tourist Office Vienna** (ANTO; www.austria.info) has a list of annual and one-off events on its website; click on 'Themed Holidays' and then 'Events'. Following is a list of major festivals.

February
Fasching This Shrovetide carnival before Lent involves parties, waltzes and a parade; celebrated countrywide.

May/June
Vienna Festival (Vienna; www.festwochen.or.at) The Wiener Festwochen focuses on classical music, theatre and other performing arts.
Lifeball (Vienna; www.lifeball.org) One of the final – and flamboyant – balls of the season, this is a huge gay/straight AIDS fundraising gala that attracts celebrity guests.

July/August
Bregenzer Festspiele (Bregenz; www.bregenzerfest spiele.com) Opera with a difference – performed on a floating stage on Lake Constance.
Salzburg Festival (Salzburg; www.salzburgfestival .at) Austria's leading classical-music festival attracts major stars, like Simon Rattle and Placido Domingo.

September
Ars Electronica Festival (Linz, www.aec.at) This is a celebration of weird and wonderful technological art and computer music.
Bruckner Fest (Linz; www.brucknerhaus.at) This highbrow classical-music festival pays homage to native Linz son Bruckner.

November
St Martin's Day (11 November) Feasts of goose and wine mark the day of St Martin.

December
Christmas Markets (particularly Vienna & Salzburg) Quaint stalls selling traditional decorations, foodstuffs, mulled wine and all manner of presents heralding the arrival of the festive season.
Krampus (Innsbruck & elsewhere) St Nicholas, his friend Krampus (Black Peter) and an array of masked creatures cause merriment and mischief in a parade that harks back to pagan celebrations.
Kaiserball (Vienna) The Imperial Ball kicks off Vienna's three-month season of balls, combining glamour and high society with camp decadence.

GAY & LESBIAN TRAVELLERS
Public attitudes to homosexuality are less tolerant than in most European countries, except perhaps in Vienna. A good information centre and meeting point in Vienna is **Rosa Lila Villa** (Map pp46-7; ☎ 01-586 81 50; www.villa.at; 06, Linke Wienzeile 102). The age of consent for gay men is 18; for everyone else it's 14. Vienna has a Pride march, the Rainbow Parade, at the end of June/beginning of July.

HOLIDAYS
New Year's Day 1 January
Epiphany 6 January
Easter Monday March/April
May Day 1 May
Ascension Five and a half weeks after Easter
Whit Monday Seven weeks after Easter
Corpus Christi Ten days after Whit Monday
Assumption of the Virgin Mary 15 August
National Day 26 October
All Saints' Day 1 November
Immaculate Conception 8 December
Christmas Day 25 December
St Stephen's Day 26 December

LANGUAGE
Although Austrians understand Hochdeutsch ('high' German), they use different words, and dialects are different everywhere. In some parts of the country dialects are so strong that even other Austrians have trouble understanding their compatriots. Austrians generally join their Bavarian cousins in forming the diminutive with '-erl' instead of the northern German '-chen'. Therefore when Austrians say *ein Bisserl*, they mean *ein Bisschen* (a little),

and they use the word *Mäderl* (girl) instead of *Mädchen*.

English is generally widely spoken, especially by the younger generation.

MONEY
The currency is the euro, although you may still hear some references to its Austrian predecessor, the Schilling, from both young and old. Major train stations have currency offices, and there are plenty of banks, *bureaux de change* and *Bankomats* (ATMs) across the country.

Costs
Expenses in Austria are average for western central Europe, with prices highest in big cities and ski resorts. Budget travellers can possibly scrape by on €45 a day, after railcard costs; double this amount if you intend to avoid self-catering or staying in hostels.

Taxes & Refunds
Value-added tax (*Mehrwertsteuer* or MwSt) is charged at either 10% (eg travel, food and museum entry) or 20% (drinks and luxury goods). Prices always include taxes. For purchases over €75, non-EU residents can reclaim the MwSt either upon leaving the EU or afterwards. (Note that one-third of your refund will be absorbed in charges.) Ensure the shop has the forms to be filled out at the time of purchase, and present the documentation to customs on departure for checking and stamping.

The airports at Vienna, Salzburg, Innsbruck, Linz and Graz have counters for instant refunds, as do some land crossings. You can also reclaim by post.

Tipping & Bargaining
Austrian waiters aren't renowned for friendly or speedy service, but it's still rude not to round off the bill so that it includes a 10% tip. Pay it directly to the server; don't leave it on the table. Taxi drivers will also expect tips of 10%. Bargaining is unheard of, but you could try your luck in Vienna's markets.

POST
Post-office hours vary: typical hours in smaller towns are 8am to noon and 2pm to 6pm Monday to Friday (money exchange to 5pm), and 8am to 11am Saturday, but a few main post offices in big cities are open daily

until late, or even 24 hours. Stamps are also available in *Tabak* (tobacco) shops. Postcards and standard letters (up to 20g) cost €0.55 within Austria and €0.65 to Europe.

TELEPHONE

Don't worry if a telephone number you are given has only four digits, as many as nine digits, or some odd number in between. The Austrian system often adds direct-dial (DW) extensions to the main number after a hyphen. Thus, say ☎ 12 345 is a main number, ☎ 12 345-67 will be an extension. Generally, a 0 will give you the switchboard operator.

From a public phone, it costs €0.12 per minute to call anywhere in Austria. **Telekom Austria** (☎ 0800-100 100; www.aon.at, in German) is Austria's main telecommunications provider. Telekom maintains the public phones throughout the country, which take either coins or phonecards and cost a minimum of €0.20 for a local call. It's also possible to make calls from phone booths inside post offices – cheaper rates are available for both national and international calls between 6pm and 8am Monday to Friday and on weekends. Additionally, major centres are sprinkled with call centres which offer competitive rates.

Austria's country code is ☎ 0043 and international directory assistance is available on ☎ 0900 11 88 77.

Mobile Phones

Mobile phones *(Handy)* in Austria operate on GSM 900/1800, which is compatible with other European countries and Australia, but not with the North American GSM 1900 system or the system used in Japan. *Handy* numbers start with 0699, 0676, 0664, 0660 and 0650.

If you're staying for a while, it's possible to buy SIM cards from the major providers for €30 or €39 (available in phone stores; refills can be purchased in supermarkets).

EMERGENCY NUMBERS

- Alpine Rescue ☎ 140
- Ambulance ☎ 144
- Fire ☎ 122
- Police ☎ 133

Phonecards

Austria has a wide range of phonecards *(Telefon-Wertkarte)* available from post offices, trains stations and newsstands.

TOURIST INFORMATION

Tourist offices, which are dispersed far and wide in Austria, tend to adjust their hours from one year to the next, so the hours listed in this chapter are a guide only and may have changed slightly by the time you arrive.

The **Austrian National Tourist Office** (ANTO; www .austria.info) has a number of overseas offices. There is a comprehensive listing on the ANTO website.

VISAS

Visas are not required for stays up to three months for US, Canadian, Australian or New Zealand citizens. There are no time limits for European Union and Swiss nationals, but they should register with the police before taking up residency. Most African and Arab nationals require a visa.

TRANSPORT IN AUSTRIA

GETTING THERE & AWAY
Air

The national carrier, Austrian Airlines, has an excellent safety record and specialises in linking numerous Eastern European cities to the West via Vienna.

Low-cost airlines also serve Austria. Niki, Austria's home-grown budget carrier, has flights from Vienna to major destinations throughout Western Europe and even as far as Thailand and South Africa. It also connects Innsbruck to a handful of European cities. Ryanair flies from London to Graz, Klagenfurt, Linz and Salzburg; Air Berlin flies to Vienna from a plethora of destinations in Europe and beyond; easyJet connects Vienna and Innsbruck with London; and germanwings has services to Germany's major cities and a handful of other countries. Central European low-cost carrier Sky Europe flies to many destinations, including Croatia, France, Hungary, Italy and Poland. Be warned, however, that its 'Vienna' airport is far from the city – in Slovakia's capital, Bratislava. It also has a service from Innsbruck to Bratislava.

Following are the key international airports in Austria:

Graz (GRZ; ☎ 0316-29 02-0; www.flughafen-graz.at)
Innsbruck (INN; ☎ 0512-22 525-0; www.innsbruck -airport.com)
Klagenfurt (KLU; ☎ 0463-41 500; www.klagenfurt -airport.com)
Linz (LNZ; ☎ 07221-600-0; www.linz-airport.at)
Salzburg (SZG; ☎ 0662-85 80-0; www.salzburg-airport .com)
Vienna (VIE; ☎ 01-70 07-0; www.viennaairport.com)

Major international airlines, reputable regional carriers and low-cost airlines flying to and from Austria include the following:

Air Berlin (AB; ☎ 0820-600 830; www.airberlin.com)
Air France (AF; ☎ 01-50 222-2400; www.airfrance.com)
Alitalia (AZ; ☎ 01-505 17 07; www.alitalia.com)
Austrian Airlines (OS; ☎ 05-17 66-1000; www.aua.com)
British Airways (BA; ☎ 01-79 567-567; www.ba.com)
CSA (OK; ☎ 01-512 38 05-0; www.czechairlines.com)
easyJet (U2; www.easyjet.com)
germanwings (4U; ☎ 0820-240 554; www.german wings.com)
Iberia (IB; ☎ 01-795 677-2; www.iberia.com)
Intersky (3L; ☎ 05575-488 00-46; www.intersky.biz)
KLM (KL; ☎ 0810-310 890; www.klm.com)
LOT Polish Airlines (LO; ☎ 0810-810 885; www.lot.com)
Lufthansa (LH; ☎ 0810-1025 8080; www.lufthansa.com)
Niki (HG; ☎ 0820-737 800; www.flyniki.com)
Ryanair (FR; ☎ 0900-210 240; www.ryanair.com)
SAS (SK; ☎ 0810-977 980; www.flysas.com)
SkyEurope Airlines (NE; ☎ 0910-160 696; www .skyeurope.com)
Swiss International Air Lines (LX; ☎ 0810-810 840; www.swiss.com)
TUIfly (X3; ☎ 0820 820 033; www.tuifly.com)

Land

BORDER CROSSINGS

As Austria now resides in the middle of an enlarged European Union, border controls are very lax. There are many entry points from the Czech Republic, Hungary, Slovakia, Slovenia, Switzerland, Italy and Germany, all of which are normally open 24 hours.

BUS

Buses depart from Austria for as far afield as England, the Baltic countries, the Netherlands, Germany and Switzerland. But most significantly, they provide access to Eastern European cities small and large – from the likes of Sofia and Warsaw, to Banja Luka, Mostar and Sarajevo.

Services operated by **Eurolines** (www.eurolines .at) leave from Vienna (see p55) and from several regional cities.

CAR & MOTORCYCLE

Austria levies fees for its entire motorway network. Therefore tourists need to choose between a 10-day pass (motorcycle/car €4.40/7.70), a two-month pass (€11.10/22.20) or a yearly pass (€29.50/73.80) and then clearly display the chosen toll label (*Vignette*) on their vehicle. Passes are available at borders, on freeways or from service stations. Without one, you'll face an on-the-spot fine of up to €300 or, if you don't pay immediately, up to a €3000 fine. See **Asfinag** (www.oesag.at, in German) for details.

TRAIN

The main rail services in and out of the country from the west normally pass through Bregenz, Innsbruck or Salzburg on their way to Vienna's Westbahnhof. Trains to Eastern Europe invariably leave from Südbahnhof in Vienna. Express services to Italy go via Innsbruck or Villach; trains to Slovenia are routed through Graz.

For Austrian rail passes that extend into other countries, see p92.

Aside from Economy and First Class, Austrian Rail now offers **Railjet** (www.railjet.at), a new service introducing Premium Class. Premium provides more comfort, above-par cuisine and working space. At the time of writing, Premium was only available between Vienna, Munich and Budapest, but expect it to expand.

River & Lake

Hydrofoils run to Bratislava and Budapest from Vienna; slower boats cruise the Danube between the capital and Passau (see p55). Germany and Switzerland can be reached from Bregenz (see p85).

GETTING AROUND

Air

Austrian Airlines (OS; ☎ 05-17 66-1000; www.aua.com) and its subsidiary, Tyrolean Airlines, operate regular internal flights, while Austria's budget airline, **Niki** (HG; ☎ 0820-737 800; www .flyniki.com), connects Vienna with Innsbruck. This is a small country, though, so train, bus and car travel is likely to suffice.

Bicycle

Austria is a pleasure to tour by bicycle – the country is criss-crossed by designated cycle paths and bikes can be transported by trains: on slow trains it costs €2.90/7.50/22.50 for a daily/weekly/monthly ticket, and on fast trains €6.80 per day, if space allows. Booking is advisable, because if there's no space in the passenger carriages, you will have to send your bike as registered luggage (€21.40). If a group of you are travelling with bikes, ask about the '1-Plus Freizeitticket' (passenger plus bike).

Private operators and hostels hire bikes; expect to pay anything from €7 to €10 per day. Vienna has cut-price city bikes (p56).

Boat

Services along the Danube are mainly scenic pleasure cruises, but provide a leisurely way of getting from A to B. For more information on boat services along the river, see p55.

Bus

Both *Posthuses* and *Bahnbuses* are now operated by the railways, ÖBB. Bus services are generally limited to less-accessible regions, such as the Salzkammergut or Hohe Tauern National Park. Between major cities in environmentally friendly Austria, only train services exist.

Buses are single class, clean, efficient and run on time. Generally you can only buy tickets from the drivers. Call ☎ 01-711 01 (between 7am and 8pm) for inquiries.

Car & Motorcycle

AUTOMOBILE ASSOCIATIONS

The **Austrian Automobile Club** (Österreichischer Automobil, Motorrad und Touring Club; ÖAMTC; Map pp46-7; ☎ 0810-120 120; www.oeamtc.at; Schubertring 1-3, A-1010 Vienna) provides emergency breakdown assistance via its **24-hour phone line** (☎ 120). Nonmembers are charged an initial call-out fee of €112/135 per day/night, on top of other service charges.

BRING YOUR OWN VEHICLE

Cars can be transported on trains; Vienna is linked by a daily motorail service to Innsbruck, Salzburg and Villach.

DRIVING LICENCE

Visitors from the EU and the USA can drive using their home driving licence; those from elsewhere require an International Driving Permit.

FUEL & SPARE PARTS

Motorway service stations are found at regular intervals. Basic spare parts are widely available. Ordering more specialised parts, especially for non-European models, takes time and can be costly.

HIRE

Multinational car-hire firms **Avis** (www.avis .at), **Budget** (www.budget.at), **Europcar** (www.europcar .co.at) and **Hertz** (www.hertz.at) all have offices in major cities; ask at tourist offices for details. The minimum age for hiring small cars is 19 years, or 25 years for larger, 'prestige' cars. Customers must have held a driving licence for at least a year. Many contracts forbid customers to take cars outside Austria, particularly into Eastern Europe.

ROAD CONDITIONS

Roads are generally good, but care is needed on difficult mountain routes. Snow chains are highly recommended in winter. There are tolls (usually €2.50 to €10) for some mountain tunnels.

ROAD RULES

Vehicles drive on the right-hand side, and you must give way to traffic on the right. On mountain roads, buses always have priority; otherwise, priority lies with uphill traffic. The usual speed limits are 50km/h in towns, 130km/h on motorways and 100km/h on other roads. There's a steep on-the-spot fine for drink-driving (over 0.05% blood-alcohol content) and your driving licence may be confiscated. If you plan to drive on motorways, you must pay a tax and affix a *Vignette* to your windscreen (see opposite).

Many city streets have restricted parking (called 'blue zones' or 'short-stay parking zones') during shopping hours. Parking is unrestricted on unmarked streets.

Motorcyclists must have their headlights on during the day, and crash helmets are compulsory for riders and passengers.

Hitching

It's illegal to hitchhike on Austrian motorways (and for minors under 16 years of age to hitch anywhere in Burgenland, Upper Austria, Styria and Vorarlberg).

AUSTRIA

Train

The efficient state network, **ÖBB** (☎ 05-17 17; www.oebb.at), is supplemented by a few private lines. Eurail and Inter-Rail passes are always valid on the state network, but only valid sometimes on private lines. There is no supplement on Eurail and Inter-Rail passes for national travel on faster EC (Eurocity) and IC (Intercity) trains. Tickets purchased on the train cost €3 extra. Fares quoted in this chapter are for 2nd-class tickets.

Before arriving in Austria, EU residents can buy an **InterRail One Country Pass** (www.interrail .net) for Austria for €109/139/189/229 covering three/four/six/eight days travel within a month.

Available to non-EU residents are the Eurail Austria Pass (€100 for three days unlimited travel within a 15-day period; €15 for

each extra day up to eight days in total) and a variety of Eurail regional passes, including the Austria-Switzerland Pass, Austria-Germany Pass and Austria–Czech Republic Pass. Each allows between four and 10 days unlimited 1st-class travel within a two-month period; for more information see www.eurail.com.

Within Austria, anyone can buy a Vorteilscard (adult/under 26 years/senior €100/20/27), which reduces fares by at least 45% and is valid for a year.

Tram

Many of Austria's larger cities supplement bus systems with convenient and environmentally friendly trams. Most towns have an integrated transport system, meaning you can switch between bus and tram routes on the same ticket.

Czech Republic

Two decades after the fall of the Berlin Wall, an atlas-full of European countries and cities are touted to travellers as the 'new Prague', or the 'next Czech Republic'. The focus may have shifted slightly to other up-and-coming destinations, but the original Prague and Czech Republic remain essential stops on any European sojourn.

Prague's inevitable transition from communist capital to modern metropolis is now complete, as centuries of history and architectural overachievement compete with energy and impetus. And now, more than ever, is the time to explore the Czech Republic beyond Prague.

Elsewhere, castles and chateaux abound, illuminating the stories of powerful families and individuals whose influence was felt well beyond the nation's current borders. Unravel the history of Bohemia and Moravia and you're delving into the legacy of Europe itself.

Beautifully preserved Renaissance towns that withstood ravages of the communist era link the centuries, and idiosyncratic landscapes provide a stage for active adventures.

Highlights include the audacious cliff-top chateau at Český Krumlov, the discreetly confident university town of Olomouc, and Brno's cosmpolitan buzz. Venture further to quieter gems such as Loket, Telč, Mikulov and Slavonice to uncover the true essence of the Czech Republic.

You'll discover the Czech Republic is more than a match for any new challengers.

FAST FACTS

- **Area** 78,864 sq km
- **Capital** Prague
- **Currency** Czech crown (Kč); €1 = 27Kč; US$1= 20Kč; UK£1 = 28Kč; A$1 = 14Kč; ¥100 = 20Kč; NZ$1 = 11Kč
- **Famous for** beer, ice hockey, Kafka, supermodels
- **Official Language** Czech
- **Phrases** *dobrý den*/*ahoj* (hello/hi); *na shledanou* (goodbye); *děkuji* (thank you); *promiňte* (excuse me)
- **Population** 10.2 million
- **Telephone codes** country code ☎ 420; international access code ☎ 00
- **Visas** citizens of Australia, Canada, Israel, Japan, New Zealand, South Korea, the USA and 23 other countries can stay for up to 90 days without a visa; see p154 for details

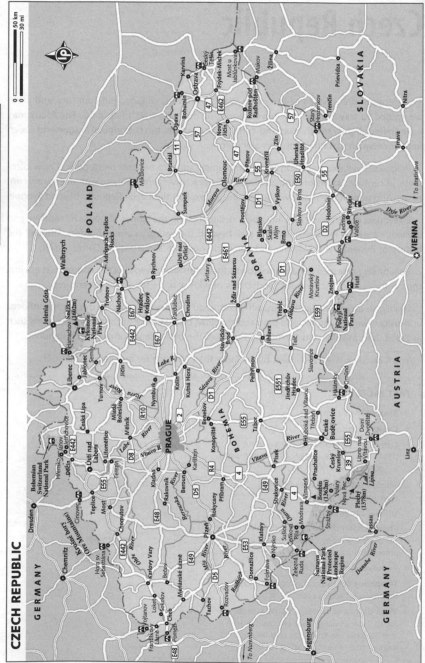

HIGHLIGHTS

- Experience the glorious old-world heritage of **Prague** (p100), but also dive into the emerging arts, music, and nightlife scenes in hip neighbourhoods like Vinohrady and Žižkov.
- Savour the tasty future of Czech beer at the best of the country's **microbreweries** (p100).
- Spend a lazy day on the Vltava River around **Český Krumlov,** (p135) before getting active in the **Šumava** (p139) region.
- Explore the spectacular rock formations and sinuous river valleys of the **Bohemian Switzerland National Park** (p125).
- Relax in the beautiful town square in **Olomouc** (p145) and try and keep its easy-going vibe to yourself.

ITINERARIES

- **One week** Experience Prague's exciting combination of a tumultuous past and an energetic present. Take an essential day trip to Terezín, and then head south to Český Krumlov for a few days of riverside R&R.
- **Two weeks** Begin in Prague before heading west for the spa scenes at Mariánské Lázně or Karlovy Vary. Balance the virtue and vice ledger with a few Bohemian brews in Plzeň before heading south for relaxation and rigour around Český Krumlov. Head east through České Budějovice en route to the Renaissance grandeur of Telč and Brno's cosmpolitan galleries and museums. Use the Moravian capital as a base for exploring the Moravian Karst caves and Mikulov's wine country, before continuing to under-rated Olomouc to admire the Holy Trinity Column. From Olomouc it's an easy trip back to Prague, or on to Poland.

CLIMATE & WHEN TO GO

The Czech climate has cool, humid winters, warm summers and distinct spring and autumn seasons. July and August are very busy so try and visit in May, June or September. Easter, Christmas and New Year are also busy. During the Prague Spring festival (in May), accommodation in Prague can be scarce.

HISTORY

Czech history is the story of a people surviving occupation, and Czechs are more interested in their rebels and heretics than the kings, emperors and dictators who oppressed them.

Located in central Europe, the Czechs have been invaded by the Habsburgs, the Nazis and the Soviets. The country's location has meant domestic upheavals have not stayed local for long. Their rejection of Catholicism in 1418 resulted in the Hussite Wars. The 1618 revolt against Habsburg rule ignited the Thirty Years' War, and the German annexation of the Sudetenland in 1938 helped fuel WWII. The liberal reforms of 1968's Prague Spring led to tanks rolling in from across the Eastern Bloc, and the peaceful ousting of the government during 1989's Velvet Revolution is a model for freedom-seekers everywhere.

Bohemian Beginnings

Ringed by hills, the ancient Czech lands of Bohemia and Moravia have formed natural territories since earliest times. A Celtic tribe called the Boii gave Bohemia its name, while Moravia comes from the Morava River, a Germanic name meaning 'marsh water'.

Slavic tribes from the east settled these territories, and they united from 830 to 907 in the Great Moravian Empire. Christianity was adopted after the arrival in 863 of the Thessalonian missionaries Cyril and Methodius, who created the first Slavic (Cyrillic) alphabet.

In the 9th century, the first home-grown dynasty, the Přemysls, erected some huts in what was to become Prague. This dysfunctional clan gave the Czechs their first martyred saints – Ludmila, killed by her daughter-in-law in 874,

---

CONNECTIONS: MOVING ON FROM THE CZECH REPUBLIC

The Czech Republic is a convenient hub for exploring neighbouring countries. Prague (p118) is well connected to Berlin, Nuremberg and Hamburg, and Plzeň (p132) is on the main train line from Nuremberg via Prague to Munich. From Český Krumlov (p139) it's a short distance to Linz in Austria, with connections to Vienna, and Budapest in Hungary. For travel to Poland, Olomouc (p148) is a key transit point for trains to Warsaw and Kraków, and the eastern city of Brno (p144) has regular bus and train services to Vienna and the Slovakian capital, Bratislava.

CZECH REPUBLIC

HOW MUCH?

- **Night in hostel** 400Kč
- **Double room in pension** 1100Kč
- **Oplátkly (spa wafer)** 10Kč
- **Two hours' rafting** 250Kč
- **Postcard home** 15Kč

LONELY PLANET INDEX

- **1L petrol** 25Kč
- **1L bottled water** 45Kč
- **500mL beer** 35Kč
- **Souvenir T-shirt** 250Kč
- **Street snack (sausage & mustard)** 30Kč

and her grandson, the pious Prince Václav (or Good 'King' Wenceslas; r 921–29), murdered by his brother Boleslav the Cruel.

The Přemysls' rule ended in 1306, and in 1310 John of Luxembourg came to the Bohemian throne through marriage, and annexed the kingdom to the German empire. The reign of his son, Charles IV (1346–78), who became Holy Roman Emperor, saw the first of Bohemia's two 'Golden Ages'. Charles founded Prague's St Vitus Cathedral, built Charles Bridge, and established Charles University. The second was the reign of Rudolf II (1576–1612), who made Prague the capital of the Habsburg Empire and attracted artists, scholars and scientists to his court. Bohemia and Moravia remained under Habsburg dominion for almost four centuries.

Under the Habsburg Thumb

In 1415 the Protestant religious reformer Jan Hus, rector of Charles University, was burnt at the stake for heresy. Hus led a movement that espoused letting the congregation taste the sacramental wine as well as the host. He inspired the nationalist Hussite movement which plunged Bohemia into civil war (1419–34).

When the Austrian and Catholic Habsburg dynasty ascended the Bohemian throne in 1526, the fury of the Counter-Reformation was unleashed when Protestants threw two Habsburg councillors from a Prague Castle window. This escalated into the Catholic–Protestant Thirty Years' War (1618–48), which devastated much of central Europe.

The defeat of the Protestants at the Battle of White Mountain in 1620 marked the start of a long period of forced re-Catholicisation, Germanisation and oppression of Czech language and culture. The baroque architectural style of the time symbolised the Catholic victory.

National Reawakening

The Czechs starting rediscovering their linguistic and cultural roots at the start of the 19th century, during the so-called Národní obrození (National Revival). Overt political activity was banned, so the revival was culturally based. Important figures included historian Josef Palacký and composer Bedřich Smetana.

An independent Czech and Slovak state was realised after WWI, when the Habsburg empire's demise saw the creation of the Czechoslovak Republic on 28 October 1918. The first president was Tomáš Garrigue Masaryk. Three-quarters of the Austro-Hungarian empire's industrial power was inherited by Czechoslovakia, as were three million Germans, mostly in the border areas of Bohemia (the pohraniči, known in German as the Sudetenland).

The Czechs' elation was to be short-lived. Under the Munich Pact of September 1938, Britain and France accepted the annexation of the Sudetenland by Nazi Germany, and in March 1939 the Germans occupied the rest of the country (calling it the Protectorate of Bohemia and Moravia).

Most of the Czech intelligentsia and 80,000 Jews died at the hands of the Nazis. When Czech paratroopers assassinated the Nazi governor Reinhardt Heydrich in 1942, the entire town of Lidice was wiped out in revenge.

Communist Coup

After the war, the Czechoslovak government expelled 2.5 million Sudeten Germans – including antifascists who had fought the Nazis – from the Czech borderlands and confiscated their property. During the forced marches from Czechoslovakia many were interned in concentration camps and tens of thousands died. In 1997 Czech Prime Minister Václav Klaus and German chancellor Helmut Kohl signed a declaration of mutual apology, but many Sudeten Germans are still campaigning for the restitution of lost land and houses.

In 1947 a power struggle began between the communist and democratic forces, and in early 1948 the Social Democrats withdrew from the postwar coalition. The result was the Soviet-backed coup d'état of 25 February 1948, known as *Vítězný únor* (Victorious February). The new communist-led government established the dictatorship of the proletariat.

The 1950s were repressive years and thousands of noncommunists fled the country. Many were imprisoned and hundreds were executed or died in labour camps.

Prague Spring & Velvet Revolution

In April 1968 the new first secretary of the Communist Party, Alexander Dubček, introduced liberalising reforms to create 'socialism with a human face' – known as the 'Prague Spring'. Censorship ended, political prisoners were released, and economic decentralisation began. Moscow was not happy, but Dubček refused to buckle and Soviet tanks entered Prague on 20 August 1968, closely followed by 200,000 Soviet and Warsaw Pact soldiers.

Many Communist Party functionaries were expelled and 500,000 party members lost their jobs after the dictatorship was re-established. Dissidents were summarily imprisoned and educated professionals were made manual labourers.

The 1977 trial of the rock group the Plastic People of the Universe inspired the formation of the human-rights group Charter 77. (The communists saw the musicians as threatening the status quo, but others viewed the trial as an assault on human rights.) Charter 77's group of Prague intellectuals, including the playwright/philosopher Václav Havel, continued their underground opposition throughout the 1980s.

By 1989 Gorbachev's perestroika and the fall of the Berlin Wall on 9 November raised expectations of change. On 17 November an official student march in Prague was smashed by police. Daily demonstrations followed, culminating in a general strike on 27 November. Dissidents led by Havel formed the Anti-Communist Civic Forum and negotiated the resignation of the Communist government on 3 December, less than a month after the fall of the Berlin Wall.

A 'Government of National Understanding' was formed, with Havel elected president on 29 December. With no casualties, the days after 17 November became known as *Sametová revoluce* (the 'Velvet Revolution').

Velvet Divorce

Following the end of communist central authority, antagonisms between Slovakia and Prague re-emerged. The federal parliament granted both the Czech and Slovak Republics full federal status within a Czech and Slovak Federated Republic (ČSFR), but this failed to satisfy Slovak nationalists. The Civic Forum split into two factions: the centrist Civic Movement and the more right-wing Civic Democratic Party (ODS).

Elections in June 1992 sealed Czechoslovakia's fate. Václav Klaus' ODS took 48 seats in the 150-seat federal parliament; while 24 went to the Movement for a Democratic Slovakia (HZDS), a left-leaning Slovak nationalist party led by Vladimír Mečiar.

In July, goaded by Mečiar's rhetoric, the Slovak parliament declared sovereignty. Compromise couldn't be reached, and on 1 January 1993 Czechoslovakia ceased to exist for the second time. Prague became capital of the new Czech Republic, and Havel was elected its first president.

A New Country

Thanks to booming tourism and a solid industrial base, the Czech Republic started strongly. Unemployment was negligible, shops were full and, by 2003, Prague enjoyed Eastern Europe's highest living standards. Capitalism also meant a lack of affordable housing, rising crime and a deteriorating health system.

Since then the Czech Republic has continued as one of the economic success stories from the communist bloc, and in 2006 it was awarded the status of 'Developed Country' by the World Bank, the only former Comecon (an organisation of communist states from 1949 to 1991) nation to achieve this.

Annual growth in GDP is around 6%, and for a few years economic growth occurred despite government instability. In 2003, Václav Havel was replaced as president by former prime minister Václav Klaus; it took three elections for Czechs to confirm this appointment. Further government instability followed inconclusive elections in June 2006, which left the Czech Republic's lower house equally divided between the left and the right. The country's next general election is planned for 2009, and at the time of writing, Mirek Topolánek of the ODS was prime minister.

MIND YOUR MANNERS

It's customary to say *dobrý den* (good day) when entering a shop, cafe or quiet bar, and *na shledanou* (goodbye) when leaving.

The Czech Republic became a member of NATO in 1999, and joined the EU on 1 May 2004. With EU membership, greater numbers of younger Czechs are now working and studying abroad, seizing opportunities their parents didn't have. The Czech Republic is currently scheduled to adopt the euro in 2012.

PEOPLE

The population of the Czech Republic is 10.2 million; 95% of the population are Czech and 3% are Slovak. Only 150,000 of the three million Sudeten Germans evicted after WWII remain. A significant Roma population (0.3%) is subject to hostility and racism, suffering from poverty and unemployment. There are an estimated 55,000 Vietnamese in the Czech Republic, the biggest ethnic minority, at around 0.5% of the total population.

RELIGION

Most Czechs are atheist (39.8%) or nominally Roman Catholic (39.2%), but church attendance is low. There are small Protestant (4.6%) and Orthodox (3%) congregations. The Jewish community (1% in 1918) today numbers only a few thousand. Religious tolerance is accepted and the Catholic Church abstains from political interference.

ARTS
Literature

Franz Kafka and other German-speaking Jewish writers strongly influenced Prague's literary scene in the early 20th century.

After WWI Jaroslav Hašek devoted himself to lampooning the Habsburg empire. His folk masterpiece *The Good Soldier Švejk* is a riotous story of a Czech soldier during WWI.

Bohumil Hrabal (1914–97), one of the finest Czech novelists of the 20th century, wrote *The Little Town Where Time Stood Still*, a gentle portrayal of the machinations of small-town life.

Milan Kundera (b 1929) is the most renowned Czech writer internationally, with his novel *The Unbearable Lightness of Being* being adapted as a film. His first work *The Joke* explores the communist era's paranoia.

Jáchym Topol is the contemporary rock-lyricist author of *Sister City Silver*, an exhilarating exploration of post-communist Prague.

Cinema

The films of Jan Hřebejk (b 1967), *Musíme si pomáhat* (Divided We Fall, 2000), *Pupendo* (2003), and *Horem pádem* (Up and Down, 2004) all cover different times in the country's tumultuous 20th-century history.

Jiří Menzel's take on writer Bohumil Hrabal's *I Served the King of England* (2006) enjoyed art-house success, and *Občan Havel* (Citizen Havel, 2008) is a documentary about Václav Havel that enjoyed huge domestic support.

Buy Czech films on DVD at Kino Světozor (p118).

Music

Bedřich Smetana (1824–84), an icon of Czech pride, incorporated folk songs and dances into his classical compositions. His best-known pieces are the operas *Prodaná Nevěsta* (The Bartered Bride) and *Dalibor a Libuše* (Dalibor and Libuše), and the symphonic-poem cycle *Má vlast* (My Homeland).

Antonín Dvořák's (1841–1904) most popular works include the symphony *From the New World*, his *Slavonic Dances* of 1878 and 1881, the operas *The Devil & Kate* and *Rusalka*, and his religious masterpiece *Stabat Mater*.

More recently the Plastic People of the Universe influenced 1989's Velvet Revolution in 1989 and still play the occasional live gig. Jaromír Nohavica is a Dylanesque singer-songwriter, and Traband integrate Jewish klezmer music and Roma styles.

In recent years, Czech musician Markéta Irglová won an Academy Award for Best Song for the movie *Once* (2006).

Visual Arts

Though he is associated with the French art-nouveau movement, Alfons Mucha's (1860–1939) heart remained at home in Bohemia. Much of his work reflects themes of Slavic suffering, courage and cross-nation brotherhood. Most outstanding are 20 large, cinematic canvasses called the *Slav Epic* (see p108), and his interior decoration in Prague's Municipal House (p107).

David Černý (b 1967) is a contemporary Czech sculptor. His controversial work includes the statue of St Wenceslas riding an upside-down horse in Prague's pasáž Lucerna and the giant babies crawling up the Žižkov TV tower in Prague; see p107.

ENVIRONMENT
The Land
The landlocked Czech Republic is bordered by Germany, Austria, Slovakia and Poland. The land is made up of two river basins: Bohemia in the west, drained by the Labe (Elbe) River flowing north into Germany; and Moravia in the east, drained by the Morava River flowing southeast into the Danube. Each basin is ringed by low, forest-clad hills, notably the Šumava range along the Bavarian-Austrian border in the southwest, the Krušné hory (Ore Mountains) along the northwestern border with Germany, and the Krkonoše mountains along the Polish border east of Liberec. The country's highest peak, Sněžka (1602m), is in the Krkonoše. Interspersed with farmland, spruce, oak and beech forests cover one-third of the country.

South Bohemia has hundreds of linked fishponds and artificial lakes, including the 4870-hectare Lake Lipno. East Bohemia is home to the striking 'rock towns' of the Adršpach-Teplice Rocks.

National Parks
National parks and protected landscape areas cover 15% of the country, with the emphasis on both visitor use and species and landscape protection. Key areas include the Bohemian Switzerland and Šumava national parks, and the Adršpach-Teplice Protected Landscape Area.

Environmental Issues
Now regenerating, the forests of northern Bohemia and Moravia were devastated by acid rain created by the burning of brown coal. Industrial emissions have been cleaned up in recent years following the adoption of EU environmental codes.

In 2008, the Czech environmental group Friends of the Earth made a formal complaint to the EU that German and Austrian clear-felling of forest just across the border from the Šumava national park, was also threatening forests in the Czech Republic.

FOOD & DRINK
Czech food is similar to German or Polish food, with lots of meat served with knedlíky (dumplings) and cabbage. A few differences make Czech food special though. Have svíčková (roast beef with a sour-cream sauce and spices) with fluffy knedlíky and you'll be wondering why you haven't heard more about this cuisine.

Staples & Specialities
Traditional Czech cuisine is strong on meat, knedlíky and gravy and weak on fresh vegetables. The classic Bohemian dish is knedlo-zelo-vepřo – bread dumplings, sauerkraut and roast pork. Also look out for cesneková (garlic soup), svíčková na smetaně (roast beef with sour-cream sauce and cranberries), and kapr na kmíní (fried or baked carp with caraway seed). Ovocné knedlíky (fruit dumplings) are a delicious dessert served with cottage cheese or crushed poppy seeds and melted butter.

One of the first words of Czech you'll learn is pivo (beer). The most famous brands are Budvar (see p132) and Pilsner Urquell (see p130), but beyond the 'Big Two' there's a whole hoppy world of other regional and local brews to be discovered.

The South Moravian vineyards (p150) produce improving bílé víno (white wines).

Where to Eat & Drink
A bufet or samoobsluha is a self-service, cafeteria with chlebíčky (open sandwiches), salads, klobásy (spicy sausages), špekačky (mild pork sausages), párky (frankfurters), guláš (goulash) and of course knedlíky. Some of these places are tucked to the side of potraviny (food shops). A bageteria serves made-to-order sandwiches and baguettes.

A pivnice is a pub without food, while a hospoda or hostinec is a pub or beer hall serving basic meals. A vinárna (wine bar) has anything from snacks to a full-blown menu. The occasional kavárna (cafe) has a full menu but most only serve snacks and desserts. A restaurace is any restaurant.

Restaurants open as early as 11am and carry on till midnight; some take a break between lunch and dinner. Main dishes may stop being served well before the advertised closing time, with only snacks and drinks after that.

Fearing public disapproval, the Czech Republic goverment has been slow to ban smoking in bars and restaurants. Despite this,

TOP FIVE CZECH MICROBREWERIES

Czech beer is not just about Pilsner Urquell and Budvar. There are an increasing number of excellent microbreweries also worth investigating. Buy the 'Good Beer Guide to Prague & the Czech Republic' by longtime Prague resident Evan Rail. It's available at Prague's Big Ben Bookshop (right), the Globe Café & Bookstore (opposite) or Shakespeare & Sons (opposite). Online, see www.amazon.com or www.amazon.co.uk.

- Pivovarský Dům, Prague (p115)
- Pivnice Dačický, Kutná Hora (p123)
- Pivovar Sv Florian, Loket (p130)
- Pivnice Pegas, Brno (p144)
- Moritz, Olomouc (p148)

a growing number of food and drink outlets are establishing special nonsmoking areas. Look out for signs saying *Kouření zakázano*.

Vegetarians & Vegans

In Prague and other main cities, you'll find vegetarian restaurants, but smaller towns remain limited. Vegans will find life difficult. There are a few standard *bezmasá jídla* (meatless dishes) served by most restaurants. The most common are *smažený sýr* (fried cheese) and vegetables cooked with cheese sauce.

Habits & Customs

Most beer halls have a system of marking everything you eat or drink on a small piece of paper that is left on your table, then totted up when you pay (say *zaplatím, prosím* – I'd like to pay, please).

In a pub, always ask if a chair is free before sitting down (*Je tu volno?*). The standard toast involves clinking together first the tops, then the bottoms of glasses, then touching the glass to the table. Most people say *Na zdraví* (To health).

PRAGUE

pop 1.22 million

It's the perfect irony of Prague. You are lured there by the past, but compelled to linger by the present and the future. Fill your days with its artistic and architectural heritage – from Gothic and Renaissance to art nouveau and cubist – but after dark move your focus to the here and now in the lively restaurants, bars and clubs in emerging neighbourhoods like Vinohrady and Žižkov. And if Prague's seasonal army of tourists sometimes wears you down, that's OK. Just drink a glass of the country's legendary Bohemian lager, relax and be reassured that quiet moments still exist: a private dawn on Charles Bridge, a chilled beer in Letná as you gaze upon the glorious cityscape of Staré Město or getting reassuringly lost in the intimate lanes of Malá Strana or Josefov. Everyday you'll uncover plenty of reasons to reinforce Prague's reputation as one of Europe's most exciting cities.

ORIENTATION

Central Prague nestles on the Vltava River, separating Hradčany (the medieval castle district) and Malá Strana (Little Quarter) on the west bank, from Staré Město (Old Town) and Nové Město (New Town) on the east.

Prague Castle overlooks Malá Strana, while the twin Gothic spires of Týn Church dominate Old Town Sq (Staroměstské nám). The broad avenue of Wenceslas Sq (Václavské nám) stretches southeast from Staré Město towards the National Museum and main train station.

Walk from Praha-hlavní nádraží (Prague's main train station) to Old Town Sq in 10 minutes. Some international trains stop at Praha-Holešovice, where it is 10 minutes by metro to Old Town Sq. From Florenc bus station take Line B (yellow) to Můstek for the city centre.

Prague's up-and-coming neighbourhoods include leafy Vinohrady with good cafes and restaurants, and the grungier, more energtic after dark scene of Žižkov.

Maps

Good maps include Marco Polo's *Praha – centrum* (1:5000) and SHOCart's GeoClub *Praha – plán města* (1:15,000), both available from city bookshops. The Prague Information Service (p103) offers maps of the city centre on request.

INFORMATION
Bookshops

Anagram (Map pp104–5; ☎ 224 895 737; www .anagram.cz; Týn 4, Staré Město; ☿ 10am–8pm Mon-Sat, to 7pm Sun) History and culture books. Another branch at Prague's Ruzyně airport.

Big Ben Bookshop (Map pp104–5; ☎ 224 826 565; www.bigbenbookshop.com; Malá Štupartská 5, Staré

Město; ☽ 9am-7pm Mon-Fri, 10am-6pm Sat, noon-5pm Sun) English-language books, magazines and newspapers. Also carries *Provokátor,* a free magazine listing Prague events.

Globe Café & Bookstore (Map pp104-5; ☎ 224 934 203; www.globebookstore.cz; Pštrossova 6, Nové Město; ☽ 9.30am-midnight) Books in English and German, international magazines and newspapers.

Kiwi (Map pp104-5; ☎ 224 948 455; Jungmannova 23, Nové Město; ☽ 9am-6.30pm Mon-Fri, 10am-2pm Sat) Maps and guidebooks.

Neo Luxor (Map pp104-5; ☎ 221 111 364; Václavské nám 41, Nové Město; ☽ 8am-8pm Mon-Fri, 9am-7pm Sat, 10am-7pm Sun) Books and magazines in English, German and French and internet access (1Kč per minute). Another branch in Prague's main train station.

Shakespeare & Sons (Map pp102-3; ☎ 271 740 839; www.shakes.cz; Krymská 12; ☽ 10am-7pm) More than books with a cafe, poetry readings and live jazz.

Emergency

If your passport or valuables are stolen, obtain a police report and crime number from the **Prague 1 Police Station** (Map pp104-5; ☎ 224 222 558; Jungmannovo nám 9, Nové Město; ☽ 24hr). You'll need this for an insurance claim. There's usually an English-speaker on hand. The emergency phone number for the police is ☎ 158.

Internet Access

Many hotels, bars, fast-food restaurants and internet cafes provide wi-fi hotspots.

Globe Café & Bookstore (Map pp104-5, ☎ 224 934 203; www.globebookstore.cz; Pštrossova 6, Nové Město; per min 1.50Kč; ☽ 9.30am-midnight) Weekly (800Kč) and monthly (2250Kč) rates with your own laptop.

Mobilarium (Map pp104-5; ☎ 221 967 327; Rathova Pasaž, Na příkopě 23, Nové Město; per min 1.50Kč; ☽ 10am-7pm Mon-Fri, 11am-6pm Sat) Also cheap international phone calls.

Planeta (Map pp102-3; ☎ 267 311 182; Vinohradská 102, Vinohrady; per min 0.45-1Kč; ☽ 8am-11pm) Also CD photo downloads and Skype.

Internet Resources

Dopravní podnik (www.dpp.cz) Infor… public transport in Prague. Includes section … travellers.

Prague Information Service (www.pis.cz) O… tourist office site.

Prague Post (www.praguepost.cz) News, events and visitor information.

Prague TV (www.prague.tv) Events, arts and nightlife.

Laundry

Laundrettes charge around 250Kč to wash and dry a 9kg load of laundry.

Laundryland (Map pp104-5; ☎ 221 014 637; Na příkopě 12, Nové Město; ☽ 9am-8pm Mon-Fri, 9am-7pm Sat, 11am-7pm Sun) On the 1st floor of Černá Růže shopping centre, above the Panská entrance. Last wash two hours before closing.

Prague Cyber Laundromat (Map pp104-5; ☎ 222 510 180; Korunní 14, Vinohrady; ☽ 8am-8pm) Near Námĕsti Míru metro station. Friendly place with internet cafe (20Kč per 30 minutes) and kids' play area.

Left Luggage

Florenc bus station (per bag per day 35Kč; ☽ 5am-11pm) Upstairs on the left beyond the main ticket hall.

Main train station (per small/large bag per day 15/30Kč; ☽ 24hr) On Level 1. Also lockers (80Kč).

Medical Services

Canadian Medical Care (off Map pp102-3; ☎ 235 360 133, after hr 724 300 301; www.cmcpraha.cz; Veleslavínská 1, Veleslavín; ☽ 8am-6pm Mon, Wed & Fri, to 8pm Tue & Thu) Expat centre with English-speaking doctors, 24-hour medical aid and pharmacy.

Na Homolce Hospital (off Map pp102-3; ☎ 257 271 111, after hr 257 272 527; www.homolka.cz; 5th fl, Foreign Pavilion, Roentgenova 2, Motol) Prague's main casualty department.

Polyclinic at Národní (Map pp104-5; ☎ 222 075 120; 24hr emergencies 720 427 634; www.poliklinika.narodni.cz; Národní třída 9, Nové Město; ☽ 8.30am-5pm Mon-Fri) English-, French- and German-speaking staff.

CZECH REPUBLIC

PRAGUE IN TWO DAYS

Beat the tourist hordes with an early-morning stroll across **Charles Bridge** (p111) and continue uphill to Hradčany and the glories of **Prague Castle** (p108). Head back down to the **Franz Kafka Museum** (p111), and cross the river again to the **Charles Bridge Museum** (p108).

On day two, explore **Josefov** (p107), Prague's original Jewish quarter, and then pack a hilltop picnic for the view-friendly fortress at **Vyšehrad** (p111). Make time for a few Czech brews, either at the relaxed beer garden at **Letenské sady** (p116), or at the excellent **Pivovarský Klub** (p115), before kicking on for robust Czech food at **Kolkovna** (p114) or **Na Verandách** (p114). For a nightcap head to an effortlessly cool late-night bar like **Hapu** (p115) or **Bukowski's** (p115).

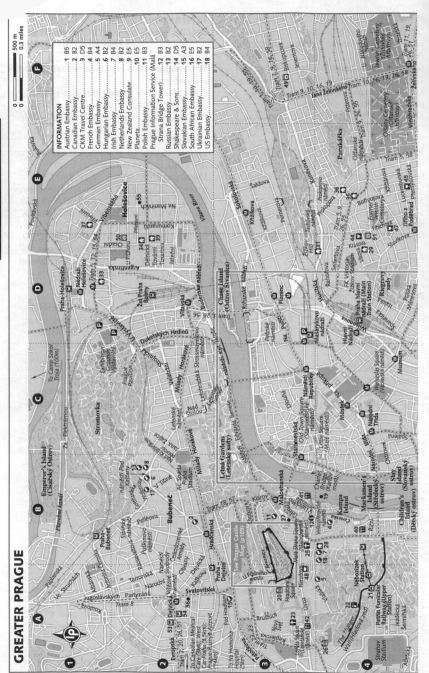

GREATER PRAGUE

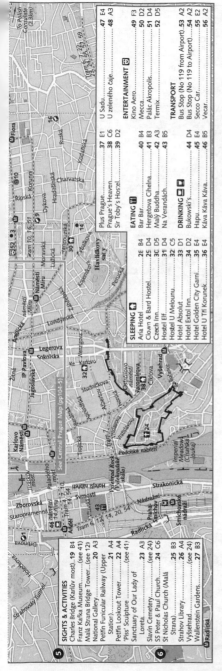

	........47 E4
	........48 A3
U Sadu........49 F3	
U zeleného čaje........	

ENTERTAINMENT
Kino Aero........50 D2
Mecca........51 D4
Palác Akropolis........52 D5
Termix........

Plus Prague........37 E1
Prague's Heaven........38 C6
Sir Toby's Hostel........39 D2

TRANSPORT
Bus Stop (No 119 from Airport)........53 A2
Bus Stop (No 119 to Airport)........54 A2
Secco Car........55 E2
Vecar........56 A2

EATING
Bar Bar........40 B4
Hergetova Cihelna........41 B3
Malý Buddha........42 D4
Na Verandách........43 B5

SLEEPING
Aria Hotel........2E B4
Clown & Bard Hostel........25 D4
Czech Inn........3C D5
Hostel Elf........31 D4
Hostel U Melounu........32 C5
Hotel Absolut........33 D1
Hotel Extol Inn........34 D2
Hotel Golden City Garni........35 E4
Hotel U Tří Korunek........36 E4

DRINKING
Bukowski's........44 D4
Hapu........45 E4
Káva Káva Káva........46 B5

SIGHTS & ACTIVITIES
Charles Bridge (Karlův most)........19 B4
Franz Kafka Museum........(see 41)
Malá Strana Bridge Tower........(see 12)
National Gallery........20 A3
Petřín Funicular Railway (Upper Station)........21 A4
Petřín Lookout Tower........22 A4
'Piis' Sculpture........(see 41)
Sanctuary of Our Lady of Loreta........23 A3
Slavín Cemetery........(see 24)
SS Peter & Paul Church........24 C6
St Nicholas Church (Malá Strana)........25 B3
Strahov Library........(see 24)
Vyšehrad........(see 24)
Wallenstein Gardens........27 B3

CZECH REPUBLIC

Praha lékárna (Map pp104-5; ☎ 224 946 982; Palackého 5, Nové Město) A 24-hour pharmacy; for emergency service after business hours, ring the bell.

Money

The major banks are best for changing cash, but using a debit card in an ATM gives a better rate of exchange. Avoid *směnárna* (private exchange booths), which advertise misleading rates and have exorbitant charges.
Česká spořitelna (Map pp104-5; Václavské nám 16, Nové Město)
ČSOB (Map pp104-5; Na příkopě 14, Nové Město)
Komerční banka (Map pp104-5; Václavské nám 42, Nové Město)
Živnostenská banka (Map pp104-5; Na příkopě 20, Nové Město)

Post

At the **main post office** (Map pp104-5; Jindřišská 14, Nové Město; ✆ 2am-midnight), collect a ticket from the automated machines outside the main hall (press 1 for stamps and parcels, 4 for Express Mail Service – EMS). Wait until your *lístek číslo* (number) comes up on the electronic boards inside and go to the window indicated.

Pick up poste restante mail at window 1 and buy phonecards at window 28. International and EMS parcels are sent from window 7 to 10 (closed from noon Saturday and all day Sunday).

Telephone

There's a 24-hour telephone centre to the left of the right-hand entrance to the central post office. Most internet cafes have Skype.

Tourist Information

The **Prague Information Service** (Pražská informační služba, PIS; ☎ 12 444, in English & German 221 714 444; www.pis.cz) provides free tourist information with good maps and detailed brochures including accommodation.

There are three PIS offices:
Czech Tourism (Map pp104-5; www.czechtourism.com; Staroměstské nám, Staré Město; ✆ 9am-5pm Mon-Fri) Has an office in Prague's Old Town Sq.
Main train station (Praha hlavní nádraží; Map pp104-5; Wilsonova 2, Nové Město; ✆ 9am-7pm Mon-Fri, to 6pm Sat & Sun)
Malá Strana Bridge Tower (Map pp102-3; Charles Bridge; ✆ 10am-6pm Apr-Oct)
Old Town Hall (Map pp104-5; Staroměstské nám 5, Staré Město; ✆ 9am-7pm Mon-Fri, to 6pm Sat & Sun Apr-Oct, to 6pm Mon-Fri, to 5pm Sat & Sun Nov-Mar) The main branch.

CZECH REPUBLIC

CENTRAL PRAGUE

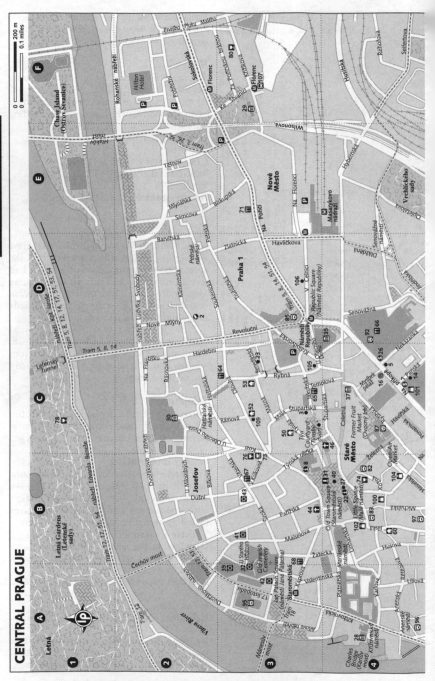

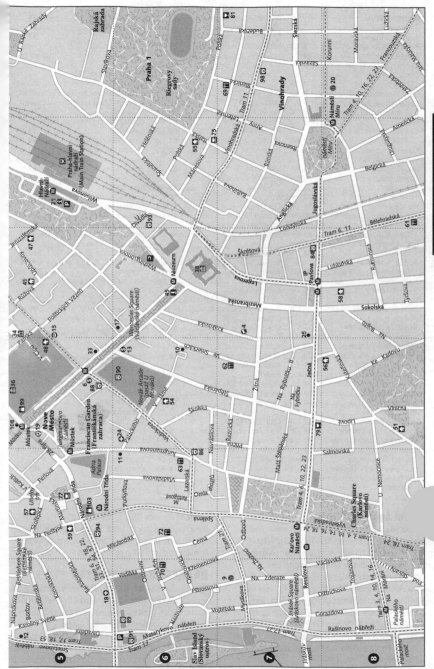

CZECH REPUBLIC

...vel Agencies

...ok (Map pp104–5; ☎ 800 112 112; www.cedok
.cz; Na příkopě 18, Nové Město; ☽ 9am-7pm Mon-Fri,
9.30am-1pm Sat) Travel agency; also books accommodation, concert and theatre tickets and rental cars.

CKM Travel Centre (Map pp102–3; ☎ 222 721 595;
www.ckm.cz; Mánesova 77, Vinohrady; ☽ 10am-6pm
Mon-Thu, to 4pm Fri) Discounts for those aged under 26. Sells youth cards.

GTS International (Map pp104–5; ☎ 222 119 700;
www.gtstravel.cz; Ve Smečkách 33, Nové Město; ☽ 9am-
6pm Mon-Fri, 10am-3pm Sat) Youth cards and air, bus and
train tickets.

Student Agency (Map pp104–5; ☎ 0800 100 1300;
www.studentagency.cz; Ječná 37, Vinohrady; ☽ 9am-
6pm Mon-Fri, to 1pm Sat) Air and bus tickets. Office at
Florenc bus station (Map pp104–5) also.

DANGERS & ANNOYANCES

Pickpockets work the crowds at the astronomical clock, Prague Castle and Charles Bridge,
and on the central metro and tram lines, especially crowded trams 9, 22 and 23.

Most taxi drivers are honest, but some operating from tourist areas overcharge their
customers (even Czechs). Phone a reputable

taxi company (see p121), or look for the red and yellow signs for the 'Taxi Fair Place' scheme, indicating authorised taxi stands.

The park outside the main train station is a hang-out for dodgy types and worth avoiding late at night. Slightly less dodgy, but often as drunk, are occasional groups of stag-party boozers around Wenceslas Sq and the Old Town.

Scams

Bogus police sometimes approach tourists and ask to see their money, claiming they're looking for counterfeit notes. They then run off with the cash. If in doubt, just ask the 'policeman' to accompany you to the nearest police station.

SIGHTS

All the main sights are in the city centre, and are easily reached on foot. You can take in the Castle, Charles Bridge and Old Town Sq in a couple of days.

Staré Město

Kick off in Prague's **Old Town Square** (Staroměstské nám), dominated by the twin Gothic steeples of **Týn Church** (Map pp104–5; 1365), the baroque **St Nicholas Church** (Map pp104–5; 1730s; not to be confused with the more famous St Nicholas Church in Malá Strana) and the **Old Town Hall clock tower** (Map pp104–5; ☎ 224 228 456; Staroměstské nám 12; adult/child 60/40Kč; ☯ 11am-6pm Mon, 9am-6pm Tue-Sun). From the top spy on the crowds below watching the **astronomical clock** (Map pp104–5; 1410), which springs to life every hour with assorted apostles and a bell-ringing skeleton. Don't be too surprised to hear random mutterings of the 'Is that it?' variety. In the square's centre is the **Jan Hus Monument**, erected in 1915 on the 500th anniversary of the religious reformer's execution.

The shopping street of Celetná leads east to the art-nouveau **Municipal House** (Obecní dům; Map pp104–5; www.obecni-dum.cz; nám Republiky 5; guided tours adult/child 190/140Kč; ☯ 11am-5pm), decorated by the early 20th century's finest Czech artists. Included in the guided tour are the impressive Smetana Concert Hall and other beautifully decorated rooms.

To the south of the Old Town Sq is the neoclassical **Estates Theatre** (Stavovské divadlo; Map pp104–5; 1783), where Mozart's *Don Giovanni* was premiered on 29 October 1787, with the maestro himself conducting.

North and northwest of the Old Town Sq, **Josefov**, was Prague's Jewish Quarter. Six mon-

uments form the **Prague Jewish Museum** (☎ 221 711 511; www.jewishmuseum.cz; adult/child 300/200Kč; ☯ 9am-6pm Sun-Fri Apr-Oct, to 4.30pm Nov-Mar). The museum's collection exists only because in 1942 the Nazis gathered objects from 153 Jewish communities in Bohemia and Moravia, planning a 'museum of an extinct race' after completing their extermination program.

Part of the museum, the **Klaus Synagogue** (Map pp104–5; U Starého hřbitova 1) features an exhibition on Jewish customs and traditions, and the **Pinkas Synagogue** (Map pp104–5; Široká 3) is now a memorial to the Holocaust. Its walls are inscribed with the names of 77,297 Czech Jews, including Franz Kafka's three sisters. A few blocks northeast is the **Spanish Synagogue** (Map pp104–5; Dušní 12), built in a Moorish style in 1868. Now the ornate interior is used occasionally for concerts.

The oldest still-functioning synagogue in Europe, the early Gothic **Old-New Synagogue** (Map pp104–5; Červená 1; adult/child 200/140Kč; ☯ 9.30am-5pm Sun-Thu, 9am-1pm Fri), dates from 1270. Opposite is the Jewish town hall with its picturesque 16th-century clock tower. A combined ticket (adult/child 480/320Kč) is available for entry to the Prague Jewish Museum and the Old-New Synagogue.

The **Old Jewish Cemetery** (Map pp104–5; entered from the Pinkas Synagogue) is Josefov's most evocative corner. The oldest of its 12,000 graves date from 1439. Use of the cemetery ceased in 1787 as it was becoming so crowded that burials were up to 12 layers deep.

Tucked away in the northern part of Staré Město's narrow streets is one of Prague's oldest Gothic structures, the magnificent **Convent of St Agnes** (Map pp104–5; ☎ 221 879 111; www.ngprague .cz; U Milosrdných 17; adult/child 150/80Kč; ☯ 10am-6pm Tue-Sun), now housing the National Gallery's collection of Bohemian and Central European medieval art, dating from the 13th to the mid-16th centuries.

THE CHALLENGING MR CĚRNÝ

David Cěrný is the kind of artist whose work polarises people. In the art-nouveau Lucerna pasáž, (p108), he's hung St Wenceslas and his horse upside down, and across the river, Cěrný's 'Piss' sculpture (p111) invites contributions by SMS. Rising above the city, like a faded relic from *Star Wars*, is the Žižkov Tower with Cěrný's giant babies crawling up the exterior.

More contemporary is the **Museum of Czech Cubism** (Map pp104–5; ☎ 221 301 003; www.ngprague.cz; Ovocný trh 19; adult/child 100/50Kč; ☒ 10am-6pm Tue-Sun). Located in Josef Gočár's House of the Black Madonna, the angular collection of art and furniture is yet another branch of Prague's National Gallery. On the ground floor is the Grand Café Orient (p116).

Nové Město

Dating from 1348, Nové Město (New Town) is only 'new' when compared with the even older Staré Město. The sloping avenue of **Wenceslas Sq** (Václavské nám; Map pp104–5), lined with shops, banks and restaurants, is dominated by a **statue of St Wenceslas** (Map pp104–5) on horseback. Wenceslas Sq has always been a focus for demonstrations and public gatherings. Beneath the statue is a shrine to the victims of communism, including students Jan Palach and Jan Zajíc, who burned themselves alive in 1969 protesting against the Soviet invasion.

The nearby **Lucerna pasáž** (Map pp104–5; Lucerna Passage) is an art-nouveau shopping arcade now graced with David Černý's (p107) 'Horse' sculpture; a sly upside-down reflection of the statue of St Wenceslas in the square.

At the uphill end of the square is the imposing **National Museum** (Map pp104–5; ☎ 224 497 111; www.nm.cz; Václavské nám 68; adult/child 100/50Kč; ☒ 10am-6pm May-Sep, to 5pm Oct-Apr, closed 1st Tue of month). The ho-hum collections cover prehistory, mineralogy and stuffed animals, but the grand interior is worth seeing for the pantheon of Czech historical luminaries. In 2009, a new annex was due to open across the street; in 2011 the museum is scheduled to close for five years for major renovations.

Fans of artist Alfons Mucha, renowned for his art-nouveau posters of garlanded Slavic maidens, can admire his work at the **Mucha Museum** (Map pp104–5; ☎ 221 451 333; www.mucha.cz; Panská 7; adult/child 120/60Kč; ☒ 10am-6pm), including an interesting video on his life and art. Mucha also painted the magnificent *Slav Epic*, a monumental series of paintings the size of billboards depicting Slavic history and mythology. The canvases were due to be moved from the small Moravian town of Moravský Krumlov to a purpose-built space somewhere in Prague sometime after 2009. Ask at the Mucha Museum for an update.

The **City of Prague Museum** (Map pp104–5; ☎ 224 227 490; www.muzeumprahy.cz; Na Poříčí 52; Karlín; adult/

child 100/40Kč; ☒ 9am-6pm Tue-Sun), housed in a grand, neo-Renaissance building near Florenc metro station, charts Prague's evolution from prehistory to the 19th century, culminating in a huge scale model of Prague in 1826–37.

The **Museum of Communism** (Map pp104–5; ☎ 224 212 966; www.muzeumkomunismu.cz; Na příkopě 10; Nové Město; adult/child 180/140Kč; ☒ 9am-9pm) is tucked (ironically) behind McDonald's. The exhibition is fascinating through its use of simple everyday objects to illuminate the restrictions of life under communism. Unfortunately, 1989's momentous Velvet Revolution is given a once-over-lightly treatment.

Before or after strolling across Charles Bridge (p111), examine the history of the Vltava's most famous crossing at Prague's newest museum, the **Charles Bridge Museum** (Map pp104–5; ☎ 739 309 551; www.muzeumkarlovamostu.cz; Křížovnické nám; Staré Město; adult/child 150/100Kč; ☒ 10am-8pm). When you know the bridge's tumultuous 650-year history, it's surprising it's still standing.

Prague Castle

The biggest castle complex in the world, **Prague Castle** (Pražský hrad; Map p109; ☎ 224 373 368; www.hrad.cz; ☒ castle 9am-5pm Apr-Oct, 9am-4pm Nov-Mar, grounds 5am-midnight Apr-Oct, 9am-11pm Nov-Mar) feels more like a small town. It's the seat of Czech power, housing the president's office and the ancient Bohemian crown jewels.

The **long tour** (adult/child 350/175Kč) includes the Old Royal Palace, the Story of Prague Castle exhibit, Basilica of St George, Convent of St George and Golden Lane with Daliborka Tower. The **short tour** (adult/child 250/125Kč) omits a visit to the Old Royal Palace. Buy tickets at the **Castle Information Centre** in the Second Courtyard. Most areas are wheelchair accessible. Count on about three hours for the long tour and two hours for the short tour. Tickets are valid for two days, but you can only visit each attraction once. DIY audio guides can also be rented. Entry to the castle courtyards and the gardens is free.

The main entrance is at the western end. The **changing of the guard**, with stylish uniforms created by Theodor Pistek (costume designer

for the film *Amadeus*) takes place every hour, on the hour. At noon a band plays from the windows above.

The **Matthias Gate** leads to the Second Courtyard and the **Chapel of the Holy Cross** (concert tickets on sale here). On the north side is the **Prague Castle Picture Gallery** (adult/child 150/80Kč; 🕙 9am-5pm Apr-Oct, to 4pm Nov-Mar), with a collection of European baroque art.

The Third Courtyard is dominated by **St Vitus Cathedral**, a French Gothic structure begun in 1344 by Emperor Charles IV, but not completed until 1929. Stained-glass windows created by early-20th-century Czech artists illuminate the interior, including one by Alfons Mucha (third chapel on the left as you enter the cathedral) featuring SS Cyril and

CZECH REPUBLIC

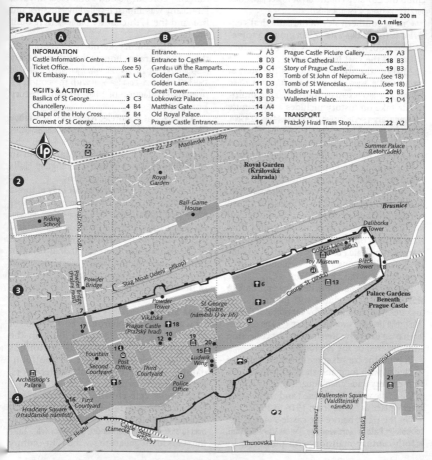

PRAGUE CASTLE

0 ———————— 200 m
0 ———————— 0.1 miles

INFORMATION
Castle Information Centre............**1** B4
Ticket Office....................(see 5)
UK Embassy.........................**2** C4

SIGHTS & ACTIVITIES
Basilica of St George................**3** C3
Chancellery..........................**4** B4
Chapel of the Holy Cross........**5** B4
Convent of St George...............**6** C3

Entrance..............................**7** A3
Entrance to Castle..................**8** D3
Garden on the Ramparts........**9** C4
Golden Gate.........................**10** B3
Golden Lane.........................**11** D3
Great Tower.........................**12** B3
Lobkowicz Palace..................**13** D3
Matthias Gate......................**14** A4
Old Royal Palace...................**15** B4
Prague Castle Entrance.........**16** A4

Prague Castle Picture Gallery.........**17** A3
St Vitus Cathedral..................**18** B3
Story of Prague Castle...........**19** B3
Tomb of St John of Nepomuk........(see 18)
Tomb of St Wenceslas................(see 18)
Vladislav Hall.......................**20** B3
Wallenstein Palace.................**21** D4

TRANSPORT
Pražský Hrad Tram Stop................**22** A2

Methodius. In the apse is the **tomb of St John of Nepomuk** – two tons of baroque silver watched over by hovering cherubs.

The 14th-century chapel on the cathedral's southern side with the black imperial eagle on the door contains the **tomb of St Wenceslas**, the Czechs' patron saint and the Good King Wenceslas of Christmas carol fame. Wenceslas' zeal in spreading Christianity and his submission to the German King Henry I saw him murdered by his brother, Boleslav I. According to legend he was stabbed to death clinging to the Romanesque lion's-head handle that graces the chapel door. The smaller door on the far side, beside the windows, leads to the Bohemian crown jewels (not open to the public). On the other side of the transept, climb the 287 steps of the **Great Tower** (adult/child 50/25Kč; 9am-4.15pm Apr-Oct).

On the southern side of the cathedral's exterior is the **Golden Gate** (Zlatá brána) a triple-arched doorway topped by a 14th-century mosaic of the Last Judgment.

Also on the southern side is the **Story of Prague Castle** (www.story-castle.cz; adult/child 140/70Kč, incl with long tour tickets) exhibition. This multimedia take on history includes a 40-minute **documentary** (in English 9.45am, 11.14am, 12.45pm, 2.15pm & 3.45pm). The exhibit is a good way to get a handle on Prague Castle's sprawling location and history before or after you go exploring.

Opposite is the entrance to the **Old Royal Palace** (included with long and short tour tickets) with the elegantly vaulted **Vladislav Hall**, built between 1486 and 1502. Horsemen used to ride into the hall up the ramp at the far end for indoor jousts. Two Catholic councillors were thrown out the window of the adjacent **Chancellery** by irate Protestant nobles on 23 May 1618. This infamous Second Defenestration of Prague ignited the Thirty Years' War.

Leaving the palace, the Romanesque **Basilica of St George** (1142; included with long and short tour tickets), and the nearby **Convent of St George** (adult/child 100/50Kč; www.ngprague.cz; 1am-6pm Tue-Sun) has an extensive Renaissance art collection administered by the National Gallery.

Beyond, the crowds surge into the **Golden Lane** (included with long and short tour tickets), a 16th-century tradesmen's quarter of tiny houses in the castle walls. Kafka lived and wrote at his sister's place at No 22 from 1916 to 1917.

On the right, before the castle's exit, is the **Lobkowicz Palace** (admission free; 10.30am-6.30pm), a 16th-century mansion with paintings by Brueghel and Canaletto, and manuscripts from Beethoven and Mozart. From the castle's eastern end, the Old Castle Steps lead to Malostranská metro station, or turn sharp right to wind through the **Garden on the Ramparts**.

There are two main routes to the castle. Either catch the metro to Malostranská or tram 12, 20, 22 or 23 to Malostranska nám and look forward to a brisk walk up Nerudova. Alternatively take tram 22 or 23 to the Pražský hrad stop, where you can enter at the Second Courtyard.

Hradčany

The Hradčany area west from Prague Castle is mainly residential, with shops and restaurants on Loretánská and Pohořelec. In 1598, Hradčany was almost levelled by Hussites and fire, and the 17th-century palaces were built on the ruins.

The 18th-century Šternberg Palace outside the castle entrance houses the **National Gallery** (Map pp102-3; 220 514 598; www.ngprague.cz; adult/child 150/80Kč; 10am-6pm Tue-Sun) with the country's principal collection of 14th- to 18th-century European art.

A passage at Pohořelec 8 leads to the **Strahov Library** (Map pp102-3; 233 107 718; www.strahovskyklaster .cz; adult/child 80/50Kč; 9am-noon & 1-5pm), the country's largest monastic library, built in 1679. The Philosophy and Theological Halls feature gorgeous frescoed ceilings.

The baroque **Sanctuary of Our Lady of Loreta** (Map pp102-3; 220 516 789; www.loreta.cz; Loretánské nám 7; adult/child 110/90Kč; 9.15am-4.30pm Tue-Sun) showcases precious religious artefacts, and the cloister houses a 17th-century replica of the Santa Casa from the Italian town of Loreta, reputedly the Virgin Mary's house in Nazareth, and transported to Italy by angels in the 13th century.

Malá Strana

Downhill are the baroque backstreets of Malá Strana (Little Quarter), built in the 17th and 18th centuries by victorious Catholic clerics and nobles on the foundations of their Protestant predecessors' Renaissance palaces.

Near the cafe-crowded main square of Malostranské nám is the beautiful baroque **St Nicholas Church** (Map pp102-3; www.psalterium.cz; adult/child 70/35Kč; 9am-5pm Mar-Oct, to 4pm Nov-Feb). Take the stairs to the gallery to see the 17th-century

Passion Cycle paintings. From April to October the church is used for **classical music concerts** (adult/child 490/300Kč; 🕑 6pm Wed-Mon).

East along Tomâšská, is the **Wallenstein Palace** (Map p109; Valdštejnský palác; admission free; 🕑 10am-4pm Sat & Sun), built in 1630 and now home to the Czech Republic's Senate. Albrecht von Wallenstein, a notorious general in the Thirty Years' War, defected from the Protestants to the Catholics and built this palace with his former comrades' expropriated wealth. In 1634 the Habsburg Emperor Ferdinand II learned that Wallenstein was about to switch sides again and had him assassinated.

The **Wallenstein Gardens** (Map pp102-3; admission free; 🕑 10am-6pm Apr-Oct) boast a Renaissance loggia and bronze (replica) sculptures by Adrian de Vries (the Swedish army looted the originals in 1648 and they're in Stockholm).

Malá Strana is linked to Staré Město by **Charles Bridge** (Karlův most; Map pp102-3). Built in 1357, and graced by 30 18th-century statues, until 1841 it was the city's only bridge. Climb the **Malá Strana bridge tower** (Map pp102-3; adult/child 50/30Kč; 🕑 10am-6pm Apr-Nov) for excellent views. In the middle of the bridge is a bronze statue (1683) of St John of Nepomuk, a priest thrown to his death from the bridge in 1393 for refusing to reveal the queen's confessions to King Wenceslas IV. Visit the bridge at dawn before the tourist hordes arrive. An after-dark crossing with an illuminated Prague Castle is also an essential Prague experience. From 2006 to 2010, Charles Bridge has undergone significant reconstruction. Visit the **Charles Bridge Museum** (p108) to understand why, after 650 years of history, a makeover was overdue.

North of Charles Bridge is the **Franz Kafka Museum** (Map pp102-3 ☎ 257 535 507; www.kafkamuseum.cz; Cihelná 2b; adult/child 120/60Kč; 🕑 10am-6pm). Kafka's diaries, letters and first editions provide a poignant balance to the T-shirt cliché the writer has become in tourist shops.

In front is the **'Piss' sculpture** by Czech artist David Černý (p107) with two animatronic figures piddling in a puddle shaped like the Czech Republic. Interrupt the flow of famous Prague literary quotations by sending your own message via SMS to ☎ 420 724 370 770.

Escape the tourist throngs on the **funicular railway** (Map pp102-3; tram ticket 26Kč; 🕑 every 10-20 min 9.15am-8.45pm) from Újezd to the rose gardens on **Petřín Hill**. Cimb 299 steps to the top of the view-friendly iron-framed **Petřín Lookout Tower**

(Map pp102-3; adult/child 50/40Kč; 🕑 10am-10pm May-Sep, to 7pm Apr & Oct, to 5pm Sat & Sun Nov-Mar), built in 1891 in imitation of the Eiffel Tower. Behind the tower a staircase leads to lanes winding back to Malostranské nám.

Vyšehrad

Pack a picnic and take the metro (Vyšehrad station) to the ancient clifftop fortress **Vyšehrad** (Map pp102-3; www.praha-vysehrad.cz; admission free; 🕑 9.30am-6pm Apr-Oct, to 5pm Nov-Mar), perched above the Vltava. Dominated by the towers of **SS Peter & Paul Church** (Map pp102-3) and founded in the 11th century, Vyšehrad was rebuilt in the neo-Gothic style between 1885 and 1903. Don't miss the art-nouveau murals inside. The adjacent **Slavín Cemetery** (Map pp102-3), contains the graves of many Czechs, including the composers Smetana and Dvořák. The view from the citadel's southern battlements is superb.

TOURS

Prague Tours (☎ 777 816 849; www.praguer.com; per person 300-450Kč) Including an Old Town Pub Tour and Ghost Trail.

Prague Walks (☎ 608 339 099; www.praguewalks .com; per person 300-450Kč) From Franz Kafka to microbreweries, communism, and a 'Fashion Tour' (300Kč).

Pražské Benátky (☎ 776 776 749; www.prazske benatky.cz; adult/child 350/175Kč; 🕑 10.30am-11pm Jul & Aug, to 8pm Mar-Jun, Sep & Oct, to 6pm Nov-Feb) Runs 45-minute cruises under the arches of Charles Bridge.

Wittmann Tours (☎ 603 426 564; www.wittmann -tours.com; per person from 750Kč) Specialises in tours of Jewish interest, including day trips (1150Kč) to the Museum of the Ghetto at Terezín.

To explore Prague on two wheels, see p119.

FESTIVALS & EVENTS

Prague Spring (www.festival.cz) From 12 May to 3 June, classical music kicks off summer.

Prague Fringe Festival (www.praguefringe.com) Eclectic action in late May.

Khamoro (www.khamoro.cz) Late May's annual celebration of Roma culture.

United Islands (www.unitedislands.cz) World music in mid-June.

Prague Autumn (www.pragueautumn.cz) Celebrates summer's end from 12 September to 1 October.

Prague International Jazz Festival (www.jazzfestival praha.cz) Late November.

Christmas Market 1 to 24 December in the Old Town Sq.
New Year's Eve Castle fireworks.

CZECH REPUBLIC

SLEEPING

At New Year, Christmas or Easter, or from May to September, book in advance. Prices quoted are for the high season, generally April to October. Rates can increase up to 15%, notably at Christmas, New Year, Easter and during the Prague Spring festival. Some hotels lower rates in July and August. Rates normally decrease by 20% to 40% from November to March. Consider an apartment for stays longer than a couple of nights.

Accommodation agencies include the following:

Ave Hotels (☎ 800 046 385; www.avehotels.cz; ✆ 8am-6pm) Online and telephone booking service.

Hostel.cz (☎ 415 658 580; www.hostel.cz) Around 60 hostels with online booking.

Mary's Travel & Tourist Service (Map pp104-5; ☎ 222 254 007; www.marys.cz; Italská 31, Vinohrady; ✆ 9am-9pm) Private rooms, hostels, apartments and hotels.

Prague Apartments (☎ 224 990 900; www.prague -apartments.com) Web-based offering of furnished apartments.

Budget

Camp Sokol Troja (off Map pp102-3; ☎ 233 542 908; www .camp-sokol-troja.cz; Trojská 171a, Troja 102, camp sites per person/car 130/90Kč; 🖳) Riverside campground with kitchen and laundry in Troja, 15 minutes north of the centre on tram 5, 14 or 17.

Czech Inn (Map pp102-3; ☎ 267 267 600; www.czech-inn .com; Francouzská 76, Vinohrady; dm 295-545Kč, s/d/tw from 990/1320/1320Kč, apt from 1650Kč; 🖳) From dorms to private apartments, everything's covered at this designer hostel with good transport links. There are no kitchen facilities, but Vinohrady's restaurants and cheap eats are minutes away. Breakfast costs an additional 140Kč.

Clown & Bard Hostel (Map pp102-3; ☎ 222 716 453; www.clownandbard.com; Bořivojova 102, Žižkov; dm 300-380Kč, d 1000-1160Kč; 🖳) Party hard in the basement bar and recharge at the all-you-can-eat breakfast any time until 2pm. Double rooms offer (slightly) more seclusion.

Prague's Heaven (Map pp102-3; ☎ 603 153 617; www .hostelpraha.eu; Jaromírova 20, Vyšehrad; dm 320-350Kč, s/d/tr/q from 850/1300/1500/1980; 🖳) This quieter spot in Vyšehrad is ideal for travellers not interested in Prague's reputation as a party town. Apartment-style rooms and shiny new bathrooms huddle around a central lounge. It's a 15-minute journey to central Prague on tram 7, 18 or 24. Credit cards not accepted.

Hostel Elf (Map pp102-3; ☎ 222 540 963; www.hostelelf .com; Husitská 11, Žižkov; dm 320-390Kč, s/d/tr 750/950/1450Kč;

🖳) Have the best of both worlds at this hip hostel near Žižkov's bars. Swap tales in the beer garden or grab quiet time in the hidden nooks and crannies. More expensive rooms have private bathrooms.

Hostel AZ (Map pp104-5; ☎ 246 052 409; www.hostel -az.com; Jindřišská 5, Nové Město; dm 320-350Kč, s/d/tr/q 950/1000/1450/1600Kč; 🖳) This smaller, homely hostel enjoys a central location near Wenceslas Sq, an in-house laundromat, and seven-bed dorms. It's down a shopping arcade so is relatively quiet after dark. Breakfast is an extra 80Kč.

Sir Toby's Hostel (Map pp102-3; ☎ 283 870 635; www .sirtobys.com; Dělnická 24, Holešovice; dm 330-470Kč, s/d/tw/tr 1150/1400/1600/1800Kč; 🖳) In an up-and-coming suburb a 10-minute tram ride from the city centre, Sir Toby's is in a refurbished apartment building on a quiet street. The staff is friendly and knowledgeable and there is a shared kitchen and lounge.

Plus Prague (Map pp102-3; ☎ 246 052 409; www.plus prague.com; Přívozní 1, Holešovice; dm 350-520Kč; 🖳 🖳) The rooms are a bit clinical and it's a preferred stop of backpacker tour groups, but this 540-bed place in Holešovice includes a pool, on-site bar and restaurant, and separate accomodation for women. Recommended for the younger, social traveller.

Hostel U Melounu (Map pp102-3; ☎ 224 918 322; www.hostelumelounu.cz; Ke Karlovu 7, Vinohrady; dm/s/d 400/750/1200Kč; 🖳) An attractive hostel in an historic building on a quiet street, U Melounu features a sunny barbecue area, plus shared kitchen and laundry facilities. A few pricier rooms have private bathrooms.

Hostel Týn (Map pp104-5; ☎ 224 808 333; www .tyn.prague-hostels.cz; Týnská 19, Staré Město; dm/s/d/tr 420/1240/1240/1410Kč; 🖳) In a quiet lane metres from Old Town Sq, you'll struggle to find better-value central accommodation. Look forward to occasional church bells.

Hostel Rosemary (Map pp104-5; ☎ 222 211 124; www .praguecityhostel.cz; Růžová 5, Nové Město; dm 450-500Kč, s/tw/tr from 900/1400/1650Kč; 🖳) Hostel Rosemary enjoys a quiet location near Wenceslas Sq and Prague's main railway station. Rooms are light and airy with high ceilings; some include a private bathroom and kitchen.

Midrange

Miss Sophie's (Map pp104-5; ☎ 296 303 530; www.miss -sophies.com; Melounova 3; dm 560Kč, s/d from 1790/2050Kč, apt from 2290Kč; 🖳) 'Boutique hostel' sums up this converted apartment building. Polished oncrete blends with oak flooring, and the asement lounge is all bricks and black leather. ;ood restaurants await outside.

Hotel Extol Inn (Map pp102-3; ☎ 220 876 541; www xtolinn.cz; Přístavní 2, Holešovice; s/d from 820/1400Kč; 🖵) The reader-recommended rooms here re all excellent value. The cheapest rooms /ith shared bathrooms are no-frills but spicknd-span, while the three-star rooms with rivate bathroom include use of the sauna nd spa. Breakfast is included, and the city is 0 minutes by tram.

Pension Březina (Map pp104-5; ☎ 296 188 888; www orezina.cz; Legerova 39-41; Nové Město; s/d economy 400/1600Kč, luxury 2700/2900Kč) A friendly pension n a converted art-nouveau apartment block vith a small garden. Ask for a quieter room at :he back. The economy rooms are great value 'or budget travellers.

Hotel Golden City Garni (Map pp102-3; ☎ 222 711 008; www.goldencity.cz; Táboritská 3, Žižkov; s/d/tr 1900/2700/2900Kč, apts 3100-4100Kč; 🖵) This 19th-century apartment block has clean Ikeafurnished rooms, buffet breakfasts and easy access to the city centre on tram 5, 9 or 26. Family apartments with small kitchenettes are also on offer.

Dasha (Map pp104-5; ☎ 602 210 716; www.accommoda tion-dasha.cz; Jeruzalémská 10; Nové Město; s/d from €30/40, apt €70-90) A restored apartment building 200m from the main train station has private rooms and apartments for up to 10 people. With kitchen facilities the apartments are a good choice for larger groups or families. Advance bookings are essential.

Old Prague Hotel (Map pp104-5; ☎ 224 211 801; www .pragueexpreshotel.cz; Skořepka 5, Staré Město; s/d from 1800/3000Kč; 🖵) The decor's chintzy, but a central location amid winding lanes and hidden squares maximises Prague's reputation as a walking city. Cheaper rooms with shared bathrooms are also available (single/double 1200/1600Kč).

Penzión u Medvídků (Map pp104-5; ☎ 224 211 916; www.umedvidku.cz; Na Perštýně 7, Staré Město; s/d 1950/3000Kč) 'At the Little Bear' is a pub and restaurant with attractive rooms upstairs. Romantic types should choose an historic attic room with exposed wooden beams. Just mind your head after having a few in the microbrewery downstairs.

Hotel Antik (Map pp104-5; ☎ 222 322 288; www.antik hotels.com; Dlouhá 22; Staré Město; s/d 2590/2990Kč) A recent makeover has given the popular Antik a modern tinge, but heritage fans can still celebrate its 15th-century building (no lift) beside an antique shop. It's a great area for bars and restaurants, so ask for a quieter back room. Breakfast is served in a garden courtyard.

Hotel Absolut (Map pp102-3; ☎ 221 634 100; www.ab soluthotel.cz; Jablonského 639; Vinohrady; d from €100; 🖵) This smart new opening combines modern bathrooms, wi-fi and cosmopolitan style. The area's a bit characterless, but there's an excellent on-site restaurant, and trams and the Holešovice metro are just 200m away.

Hotel 16 U sv Kateřiny (Map pp104-5; ☎ 224 920 636; www.hotel16.cz; Kateřinská 16, Nové Město; s/d incl breakfast from 2900/3700Kč; 🖵) Near the Botanic Gardens and five minutes' walk from Karlovo nám metro station; most days you'll wake up to birdsong at this family-run spot with a quiet garden and cosy bar.

Hotel U Tří Korunek (Map pp102-3; ☎ 222 781 112; www .three-crowns-hotel-prague.com; Cimburkova 28; Žižkov; s/d/tr from €85/105/130) The 'Three Crowns' rambles across three buildings. It's worth upgrading to a superior room with wooden floors and designer furniture (around €20 extra). Up-and-coming Žižkov is a good area for bars, and the city centre is just a few tram stops away.

Top End

Savic Hotel (Map pp104-5; ☎ 233 920 118; www.hotelsavic .cz; Jilská 7; Staré Město; d €149-159; 🖵) Looking for somewhere romantic and central? Originally a Dominican convent, the Savic's combination of 14th-century heritage and 21st-century amenities avoids the chintzy overkill of other top-end places. Rooms are cheaper from Sunday to Thursday.

Hotel Josef (Map pp104-5; ☎ 221 700 111; www.hoteljosef .cz; Rybná 20, Staré Město; s/d from €153/174; 🖵) Sleekly modern in old-world Staré Město, this boutique hotel combines top-class linen, a newly completed massage room and massive showerheads for effortless luxury.

ourpick Icon Hotel (Map pp104-5; ☎ 221 634 100; www .iconhotel.eu; V jámě 6; Nové Město; d €165-210; 🖵) Here's design-savvy cool concealed down a quiet laneway. The handmade beds are extra-wide, and the crew at reception is unpretentious and hip. Linger in the downstairs bar before exploring Prague's nightlife.

Aria Hotel (Map pp102-3; ☎ 225 334 111; www.ariahotel .net; Tržiště 9, Malá Strana; d from €215; 🖵) Choose your favourite composer or musician and stay in a luxury themed room with a selection of their tunes in a music database. Check online for interesting packages.

EATING

Prague has many cuisines and price ranges. Choose from good-value beer halls with no-nonsense fare, or enjoy a chic riverside restaurant with a high-flying clientele and prices to match. Increasing numbers of ethnic restaurants makes the cloistered days of communism a fading memory.

Eating in Prague's tourist areas is pricey, but cheaper eats are available just a block or two away. Pubs offer both snacks and full meals, and there are stands in Wenceslas Sq selling street snacks such as *párek* (hot dog) or *bramborák* (potato pancake). A late night/early morning plate of *smažený sýr* (fried cheese) is an essential Prague experience.

Prague has good vegetarian restaurants, and most restaurants have a few vegie options. Most restaurants open from 11am to 11pm.

Staré Město

Country Life Nové Město (Map pp104-5; ☎ 224 247 280; Jungmannova 1; ⏰ 9.30am-6.30pm Mon-Thu, 9am-6pm Fri); Staré Město (Map pp104-5; ☎ 224 213 366; Melantrichova 15; mains 75-150Kč; ⏰ 9am-8.30pm Mon-Thu, 9am-6pm Fri, 11am-8.30pm Sat & Sun) This all-vegan cafeteria features inexpensive salads, sandwiches, soy drinks and sunflower-seed burgers.

Kolkovna (Map pp104-5; ☎ 224 819 701; Kolkovně 8, Staré Město; meals 160-400Kč) Kolkovna's contemporary spin on the traditional beer hall serves up classy versions of Czech dishes like *gula*š and roast pork. Try Pilsner Urquell's delicious unpastuerised *tankovna* beer.

Dahab (Map pp104-5; ☎ 224 837 375; Dlouhá 33, Staré Město; mains 200-400Kč; ⏰ noon-1am) Morocco meets the Middle East amid Dahab's softly lit souk-like ambience. Relax with a mint tea and a hookah (water pipe) before diving into tagines and couscous. There's also takeaway falafel and shawarma wraps for on-the-go dining.

Tucked away in an Old Town courtyard, **Beas** (Map pp104-5; ☎ 608 035 727; Týnská 19, Staré Město; mains 90-120Kč; ⏰ 11am-10pm Mon-Sat, 11am-6pm Sun) dishes up good-value Indian vegetarian food. There's another good-value incense-infused **branch** (Map pp104-5; ☎ 608 035 727; Bělehradská 90, Vinohrady; ⏰ 11am-9pm Mon-Fri, noon-8pm Sat, noon-6pm Sun) near the IP Pavlova metro station.

Nové Město

Café Vesmírna (Map pp104-5; ☎ 222 212 363; Ve Smečkách 5, Nové Město; snacks 30-70Kč; ⏰ 9am-10pm Mon-Fri, noon-8pm Sat) Vesmírna provides training and opportunities for people with special needs. There's healthy snacks like savoury crêpes and a 'how do I choose?' selection of teas and coffees.

Velryba (Map pp104-5; ☎ 224 912 484; Opatovick 24, Nové Město; mains 80-150Kč; ⏰ closed Sun) Goo salads, pasta and vegetarian dishes feature a this student fave with an attached art gallery Dig out your black polo-neck jumper for th back-streets-of-Prague bohemian vibe.

Pizzeria Kmotra (Map pp104-5; ☎ 224 934 100; Jirchářích 12; Nové Město; pizza 100-150Kč) More tha 30 varieties feature at this cellar pizzeria tha gets superbusy after 8pm.

Giallo Rossa (Map pp104-5; ☎ 604 898 989; Jabuská mains 100-180Kč; 🖳) Dine in on rustic pizza an pasta or duck next door to the takeaway win dow and grab a few late night/early mornin slices (from 30Kč) of Neapolitan-style pizza Another deal you can't refuse is free interne with your pizza.

Café FX (Map pp104-5; ☎ 224 254 776; Bělehradsk 120, Vinohrady; mains 120-230Kč; ⏰ 11.30am-2am Café FX is chiffon and chandelier chic with Prague's best vegetarian flavours from Mexico, India and Thailand. The kitchen stays open until the wee small hours. Relax at weekend brunch and lose yourself in the adjacent CD store.

Modrý Zub (Map pp104-5; ☎ 222 212 622; Jindřišská 5, Nové Město; mains 120-280Kč) Sometimes all you want is healthy Asian food. The 'Blue Tooth' turns out authentic versions of pad Thai and satay you'll recall from your favourite Asian food hall back home.

Kogo (Map pp104-5; ☎ 224 451 259; Slovanský dům; Na příkopě 22, Nové Město; pizzas 150-250Kč, mains 200-450Kč) Concealed in a leafy garden behind a ritzy shopping arcade, Kogo's classy pizza, pasta, steak and seafood are favourites of Prague's business elite.

Na Verandách (Map pp102-3; ☎ 257 191 200; Nádražní 84, Smíchov; meals 150-300Kč) Across the river in Smíchov, the Staropramen brewery's restaurant is a modern spot crowded with locals enjoying superior versions of favourite Czech dishes, and an 'it could be a long night' selection of different brews. Na Verandách is a short walk from Anděl metro station.

Pastička (Map pp102-3; ☎ 222 253 228; Blanická 24, Vinohrady; mains 150-350Kč; ⏰ 11am-midnight Mon-Fri, from 5pm Sat & Sun) Vinohrady's emerging dining scene around Mánesova now features the unpretentious 'Mousetrap'. Locals come for excellent Bernard beer, eat huge meaty meals, and feel good about living in the funky part of town.

Siam Orchid (Map pp104-5; ☎ 222 319 410; Na ořičí 21; Nové Město; mains 160-280Kč) The waiter's Cambodian, but that doesn't stop this tiny Thai restaurant from being Prague's most authentic Asian eatery.

La Bodeguita del Medio (Map pp104-5; ☎ 224 813 22; Kaprova 5, Staré Město; mains 200-550Kč; ☉ 10am-2am) Crammed energetically into a heritage pace near Old Town Sq, this Cuban-themed place includes the mojito-fuelled bar you've only dreamed about, and zesty food like chilli prawns.

Hradčany & Malá Strana

Malý Buddha (Map pp102-3; ☎ 220 513 894; Úvoz 46, Hradčany; mains 70-220Kč) Malý ('Little') Buddha is an incense-infused haven atop Hradčany hill. When the castle's crowds wear you down, restore your chi with restorative wines, healing tea and pan-Asian food. Credit cards are not accepted.

Bar Bar (Map pp102-3; ☎ 257 312 246; Všhrdova 17, Malá Strana; mains 120-240Kč) Despite the double-barrelled name, this spot – a pleasant riverside walk from Malá Strana's tourist bustle – is actually a good-value local restaurant. Look forward to rustic comfort food such as risotto and savoury crêpes.

Hergetova Cihelna (Map pp102-3; ☎ 257 535 534; Cihelná 2b, Malá Strana; mains 220-550Kč; ☉ 9am-2am) A restored *cihelná* (brickworks) is now a hip space with a riverside terrace looking back to Charles Bridge and Staré Město. Come for steak, seafood or pizza, and linger for the sublime view.

DRINKING

Bohemian beers are among the world's best. The most famous brands are Budvar, Plzeňský Prazdroj (Pilsner Urquell), and Prague's own Staropramen. An increasing number of independent microbreweries also offer a more unique drinking experience.

Avoid the tourist areas, and you'll find local bars selling half-litres for 35Kč or less. Traditional pubs open from 11am to 11pm. More stylish modern bars open from noon to 1am, and often stay open till 3am or 4am on Friday and Saturday.

Bars & Pubs

our pick **Pivovarský Dům** (Map pp104-5; ☎ 296 216 666; cnr Ječná & Lipová, Nové Město) The 'Brewery House' microbrewery conjures everything from a refreshing wheat beer to coffee and banana-

flavoured styles – even a beer 'champagne'. The classic Czech lager is a hops-laden marvel. Really keen beer fans are directed to their associated Pivovarský Klub (see below).

Pivovarský Klub (Map pp104-5; ☎ 222 315 777; Křižíkova 17, Karlín) Submit to your inner hophead at this pub-restaurant–beer shop with interesting limited-volume draught beers, and bottled brews from around the Czech Republic. Come for lunch, as it gets full of loyal regulars later on. It's right beside Florenc metro station.

Čili Bar (Map pp104-5; Kozná 10, Staré Město; ☉ from 5pm) This raffish bar is more Žižkov than Staré Město, with cool cocktails and a grungy tinge in welcome contrast to the crystal shops and Russian dolls around the corner.

Kozička (Map pp104-5; ☎ 224 818 308; Kozí 1, Staré Město) The 'Little Goat' rocks in standing-room-only fashion until well after midnight in a buzzing basement bar. Your need for midnight munchies will be answered by the late-night kitchen.

U Medvídků (Map pp104-5; ☎ 296 216 666; Na Perštýně 7, Staré Město; ☉ beer museum noon-10pm) A microbrewery with the emphasis on 'micro', this place specialises in X-Beer, an 11.8% 'knocks-your-socks-off' dark lager.

Bukowski's (Map pp102-3; Bořvojova 86, Žižkov; ☉ from 6pm) This new late-night cocktail bar is driving grungy Žižkov's inevitable transformation into Prague's hottest after-dark neighbourhood. Leave the Old Town English pubs to the easyJet masses, and sip on cool concoctions here instead.

U Sadu (Map pp102-3; ☎ 222 727 072; Škroupovo nám, Žižkov) Escape the overpriced tyranny of central Prague at this neighbourhood pub in up-and-coming Žižkov. With its ragtag collection of memorabilia, including communist-era posters of forgotten politicians, nothing's really changed here in a few decades. An essential stop before or after gigs at the Palác Akropolis (p117).

Hapu (Map pp102-3; 222 770 158 Orlická 8; Vinohrady; ☉ from 6pm) 'Pop round for a drink after work.' Well, that's what it feels like at this shabby but chic basement bar that's a dead ringer for a friend's front room. That's if you had mates with superb mixologist skills.

U Sudu (Map pp104-5; ☎ 222 232 20; Vodičkova 10, Nové Město) Moravian wines are growing in reputation and this labyrinth of cellar bars and lounges is a good spot to fast-track your knowledge of the local wine scene.

Letenské sady (Map pp104-5; Letna Gardens, Bubeneč) This garden bar has views across the river of the Old Town and southwest to the castle. In summer it's packed with a young crowd enjoying cheap beer and grilled sausages. Sometimes the simple things in life are the best.

Cafes

Prague's summer streets are crammed with outdoor tables, and good-quality tea and coffee are widely available.

Grand Café Orient (Map pp104-5; ☎ 224 224 240; Ovocný trh 19, Nové Město; ☻ 9am-10pm Mon-Fri, from 10am Sat & Sun) In the 'House of the Black Madonna', Josef Gočár's cubist gem, the reborn Grand Café Orient also features Gočár-designed lampshades and furnishings. He had nothing to do with the coffee, but it's also pretty good.

Káva.Káva.Káva (Map pp104-5; ☎ 224 228 862; Národní třída 37, Nové Město; ☻ 7am-10pm Mon-Fri, 9am-10pm Sat & Sun; ▢) In the Platýz courtyard, this cafe offers huge smoothies and tasty nibbles such as chocolate brownies. Access the internet (2Kč per minute or 15 minutes free with a purchase) or hitch your laptop to the wi-fi hot spot. There's another branch in Smichov (Map pp102-3; ☎ 257 314 277; Lidicka 42).

Bakeshop Praha (Map pp104-5; ☎ 224 329 060; Kozí 1; snacks 40-180Kč; ☻ 7am-7pm) Bakeshop's corner spot offers innovative salads, superior pies and almost healthy quiche. Service can be hit or miss, but it's worth grabbing a coffee and watching Prague's cinematic scroll outside.

Kaaba (Map pp104-5; ☎ 224 254 021; Mánesova 20; Vinohrady; snacks 50-80Kč; ☻ 8am-10pm Mon-Sat, 10am-10pm Sun) Vinohrady's hipsters park themselves on 1950s-style furniture and recharge with snappy espressos, beer, wine and tasty snacks. The decor may be retro, but the cool staff are definitely not old-school surly.

U zeleného čaje (Map pp102-3; ☎ 257 530 027; Nerudova 19, Malá Strana) Linger at this tiny wooden-floored tea-haven on the way to the castle, or grab a speciality tea to go for the final push up the hill. Sandwiches and wine are also available.

ENTERTAINMENT

From clubbing to classical music, puppetry to performance art, Prague offers plenty of entertainment. It's an established centre of classical music and jazz, and is now also famed for its dance and rock scenes. For current listings, see *Culture in Prague* (available from PIS offices; see p103), www.prague.tv, or the monthly free

Provokátor magazine (www.provokator.org; from clubs, cafes, and art-house cinemas.

For classical music, opera, ballet, theatre and some rock concerts – even the most 'sold-out' *vyprodáno* (events) – you can often find tickets on sale at the box office around 30 minutes before the performance starts. Ticket agencies sell the same tickets with a high commission.

Tickets can cost as little as 100Kč for standing room only to over 1000Kč for the best seats; the average price is about 600Kč. Be wary of touts selling concert tickets in the street. You may end up sitting on stacking chairs in a cramped hall listening to amateur musicians, rather than in the grand concert hall that was implied.

Try the following ticket agencies:

Bohemia Ticket International (☎ 224 227 832; www.ticketsbti.cz) Nové Město (Map pp104-5; Na příkopě 16, ☻ 10am-7pm Mon-Fri, to 5pm Sat, to 3pm Sun); Staré Město (Map pp104-5; Malé nám 13; ☻ 9am-5pm Mon-Fri, to 1pm Sat)

FOK Box Office (Map pp104-5; ☎ 222 002 336; www .fok.cz; U obecního domu 2, Staré Město; ☻ 10am-6pm Mon-Fri) For classical concert tickets.

Ticketpro (Map pp104-5; ☎ 296 333 333; www.ticket pro.cz; Lucerna pasáž, Šětěpánská 61, Nové Město; ☻ 9am-12.30pm & 1-5pm Mon-Fri) Also has branches in PIS offices (p103).

Ticketstream (www.ticketstream.cz) Online bookings for events in Prague and the Czech Republic.

Performing Arts

You'll see fliers advertising concerts for tourists. It's a good chance to relax in old churches and historic buildings, but performances can be of mediocre quality. Prices begin around 400Kč.

Rudolfinum (Map pp104-5; ☎ 227 059 352; www.rudolf inum.cz; nám Jana Palacha, Staré Město; ☻ box office 10am-12.30pm & 1.20-6pm Mon-Fri plus 1hr before performances) One of Prague's main concert venues is the Dvořák Hall in the neo-Renaissance Ruldolfinum, and home to the Czech Philharmonic Orchestra.

Smetana Hall (Obecní dům; Map pp104-5; ☎ 222 002 101; www.obecni-dum.cz; nám Republiky 5, Staré Město; ☻ box office 10am-6pm Mon-Fri) Another main concert venue is Smetana Hall in the art-nouveau Municipal House. A highlight is the opening of the Prague Spring festival.

Prague State Opera (Státní opera Praha; Map pp104-5; ☎ 224 227 266; www.opera.cz; Legerova 75, Nové Město; ☻ box office 10am-5.30pm, 10am-noon & 1-5pm Sat & Sun) Opera, ballet and classical drama (in Czech)

re performed at this neo-Renaissance theatre. The box office is at Wilsonova 4.

National Theatre (Národní divadlo; Map pp104-5; ☎ 224 901 377; www.narodni-divadlo.cz; Národní třída 2, ové Město; ◷ box office 10am-6pm) Classical drama, opera and ballet.

Laterna Magika (Map pp104-5; ☎ 224 931 482; www laterna.cz; Nová Scéna, Národní třída 4, Nové Město; tickets 40-680Kč; ◷ box office 10am-8pm Mon-Sat) A multimedia show combining dance, opera, music and film.

Estates Theatre (Stavovské divadlo; Map pp104-5; ☎ 224 902 322; www.estatestheatre.cz; Ovocný trh 1, Staré Město; ◷ box office 10am-6pm) Every night from mid-July to the end of August Opera Mozart (☎ 271 741 403; www.mozart-praha.cz) performs *Don Giovanni*, which premiered here in 1787.

Divadlo Hybernia (Hybernia divadlo; Map pp104-5; ☎ 221 419 420; www.divadlo-hybernia.cz; nám Republiky 4, Nové Město; ◷ box office 10am-7pm Mon-Sat, to 3pm Sun) Originally a 17th-century church for Irish monks, the Hybernia now showcases musical theatre with tourist-friendly themes like the Jewish legend of Golem.

Black Theatre of Jiří Srnec (Map pp104-5; ☎ 257 921 835; www.blacktheatresrnec.cz; Reduta Theatre, Národní 20, Nové Město; tickets 620Kč; ◷ box office 3-7pm Mon-Fri, shows at 9.30pm) Prague is awash in 'black light theatre' shows combining mime, ballet, animated film and puppetry. Jiří Srnec's Black Theatre is the original and the least touristy.

Theatre on the Balustrade (Divadlo na zábradlí; Map pp104-5; ☎ 222 868 868; www.nazabradli.cz; Anenské nám 5, Staré Město; ◷ box office 2-8pm Mon-Fri, 2hr before show Sat & Sun) Plays by former president Václav Havel are often staged (in Czech) here.

Divadlo Minor (Map pp104-5; ☎ 222 231 351; www.minor .cz; Vodičkova 6, Nové Město; ◷ box office 9am-1.30pm & 2.30-8pm Mon-Fri, 11am-6pm Sat & Sun) Kid-friendly shows including puppets and pantomime.

Nightclubs

Mecca (Map pp102-3; ☎ 283 870 522; www.mecca.cz; U Průhonu 3, Holešovice; admission 100-400Kč; ◷ 10pm-6am Wed-Sat) Prague's most fashionable dance club attracts film stars, fashionistas and fab types, plus occasional gigs by name DJs.

Club Radost FX (Map pp104-5; ☎ 224 254 776; www .radostfx.cz; Bělehradská 120, Vinohrady; admission 120-280Kč; ◷ 10pm-6am) Prague's most stylish, self-assured club remains hip for its bohemian-boudoir decor and its popular Thursday hip-hop night FXBounce (www.fxbounce.com).

Roxy (Map pp104-5; ☎ 224 826 296; www.roxy.cz; Dlouhá 33, Staré Město; admission 120-280Kč; ◷ 10pm-6am) In a

resurrected old cinema, the Roxy presents innovative DJs and the occasional global act. 'Free Mondays' will give you more money for beer.

Live Music

Prague has jazz clubs varying in style from traditional to avant-garde.

Lucerna Music Bar (Map pp104-5; ☎ 224 217 108; www.musicbar.cz; Lucerna pasaž, Vodičkova 36, Nové Město; ◷ 8pm-3am) Lucerna features local bands and almost-famous international acts. Jettison your musical snobbery at the wildy popular '80s and '90s nights (admission 100Kč; Friday and Saturday).

Palác Akropolis (Map pp102-3; ☎ 296 330 911; www .palacakropolis.cz; Kubelikova 27, Žižkov; ◷ club 7pm-5am) Get lost in the labyrinth of theatre, live music, clubbing, drinking and eating that makes up Prague's coolest venue. Hip hop, house, reggae, or rocking Roma bands from Romania – anything goes. Kick your night off nearby at the quirky U Sadu pub (p115).

Reduta Jazz Club (Map pp104-5; ☎ 224 912 246; www .redutajazzclub.cz; Národní třída 20, Nové Město; ◷ 9pm-3am) Founded in 1958 and one of the oldest jazz clubs in Europe. Bill Clinton jammed here in 1994.

USP Jazz Lounge (Map pp104-5; ☎ 603 551 680; www .jazzlounge.cz; Michalská 9, Staré Město; ◷ 8pm-3am) A less traditional venue with modern jazz from 10pm. DJs kick on from midnight.

AghaRTA Jazz Centrum (Map pp104-5; ☎ 222 221 275; www.agharta.cz; Železná 16, Staré Město; admission 200Kč; ◷ 6pm-1am) Rock up early for a table in the medieval cellar or book online the day before.

Gay & Lesbian Venues

The inner suburb of Vinohrady is developing as a gay quarter, and the city enjoys a relaxed scene.

Prague Saints (Map pp104-5; ☎ 222 250 326; www .praguesaints.cz; Polska 32; Vinohrady) Online information on Prague's gay scene. The on-site Saints Bar (open from 5pm to 4am) is a good intro to what's happening. Thursdays from 8pm is lesbian night.

Termix (Map pp102-3; ☎ 222 710 462; www.club-termix .cz; Třebízkého 4A, Vinohrady; ◷ 8pm-5am Wed-Sun) A friendly mixed gay-and-lesbian scene with an industrial/high-tech vibe. Wednesdays are good fun with retro Czech pop.

Valentino (Map pp104-5; ☎ 222 513 491; www.club -valentino.cz; Vinohradská 40, Vinohrady; ◷ from 11am)

Welcome to Prague's gay superclub, with three floors concealing two dance areas, four bars, and other rooms with exceedingly low lighting. Weekends get interestingly busy.

Cinemas

Most films are screened in their original language with Czech subtitles (*české titulky*), but Hollywood blockbusters are often dubbed into Czech (*dabing*); look for the labels 'tit.' or 'dab.' on listings. Tickets are around 180/140Kč for adult/child.

Kino Aero (Map pp102-3; ☎ 271 771 349; www.kinoaero .cz; Biskupcova 31, Žižkov) An art-house cinema, with themed weeks and retrospectives; often with English subtitles.

Kino Světozor (Map pp104-5; ☎ 224 946 824; www.kino svetozor.cz; Vodičkova 41, Nové Město) Your best bet for Czech films with English subtitles; under the same management as Kino Aero but more central, plus it includes a cool DVD and movie poster shop.

Palace Cinemas (Map pp104-5; ☎ 257 181 212; www .palacecinemas.cz; Slovanský dům, Na příkopě 22, Nové Město) A 10-screen multiplex showing current Hollywood films.

SHOPPING

Prague's main shopping streets are in Nové Město – Wenceslas Sq, Na příkopě, 28.října and Národní třída – and there are many tourist-oriented shops on Celetná, the Old Town Sq, Pařížská and Karlova in Staré Město. Local souvenirs include Bohemian crystal, ceramics, marionettes and garnet jewellery.

Crystal

Moser (Map pp104-5; ☎ 224 211 293; Na příkopě 12, Nové Město; ☺ 10am-8pm Mon-Fri, to 7pm Sat & Sun) Top-quality Bohemian crystal.

Rott Crystal (Map pp104-5; ☎ 224 229 529; Malé nám 3, Staré Město; ☺ 10am-8pm) Housed in a neo-Renaissance building that's worth a look even if you're just browsing.

Department Stores

The **Tesco Department Store** (Map pp104-5; ☎ 222 003 111; Národní třída 26, Nové Město; ☺ 8am-9pm Mon-Fri, 9am-8pm Sat, 10am-7pm Sun) has clothes, electrical and household goods, plus a **supermarket** (☺ 7am-10pm Mon-Fri, 8am-8pm Sat, 9am-7pm Sun).

Handicrafts, Antiques & Ceramics

Manufaktura (Map pp104-5; ☎ 221 632 480; www.manu faktura.biz; Melantrichova 17, Staré Město) Sells traditional Czech handicrafts, wooden toys and handmade cosmetics.

Near the Old Town Sq, explore the antique shops of Týnská and Týnská ulička. For traditional Moravian folk cermaics, see **Tupes' lidová keramika** (Map pp104-5; ☎ 224 210 728; Havelsk 21, Staré Město)

Music

Bontonland (Map pp104-5; ☎ 224 473 080; Václavské nám 1 Nové Město; ☺ 9am-8pm Mon-Sat, 10am-7pm Sun) A megastore stocking all genres, including lots of contemporary Czech music.

GETTING THERE & AWAY

See also p154.

Bus

The main terminal for international and domestic buses is **Florenc Bus Station** (ÚAN Florenc; Map pp104-5; ☎ 12 999; Křižíkova 4, Karlín), 600m northeast of the main train station (ÚAN is short for *Ústřední autobusové nádraží*, or 'central bus station'). Some regional buses depart from near metro stations Anděl, Dejvická, Černý Most, Nádraží Holešovice, Smíchovské Nádraží and Želivského. Check timetables and departure points at www.idos.cz.

At Florenc get information at **windows 6 to 21** (☺ 6am-9pm), or use the touch-screen computer.

Short-haul tickets are sold on the bus. Long-distance domestic tickets are sold at the station from AMS windows 1 to 4 in the central hall, or direct from the nearby Student Agency (www.studentagency.cz) or Megabus (www.megabus.cz) offices.

More buses depart in the mornings. Buses sometimes leave early, so be there at least 10 minutes before departure time. If you're not seated five minutes before departure, you could lose your reservation. Many services don't operate at weekends, so trains can often be a better option.

There are direct services from Florenc to Brno (180Kč, 2½ hours, hourly), České Budějovice (130Kč, 2¾ hours, four daily), Karlovy Vary (130Kč, 2¼ hours, eight daily) and Plzeň (90Kč, 1½ hours, hourly). Student Agency's bus from Florenc to Karlovy Vary travels via Prague's Ruzyně airport.

International services from Florenc include Amsterdam (14 to 16 hours), Bern (12 hours), Berlin (five hours), Dusseldorf (12 hours), Frankfurt (seven to eight hours), Hamburg

12 hours), Munich (six hours), London (20 hours), Geneva (15 hours), Oslo (11 hours), 'aris (15 hours), Rotterdam (16 hours), Salzburg 7½ hours), Stockholm (12 hours) and Vienna five hours). In summer, these buses run at least laily, while service may be less frequent at other imes of year. Most of these routes originate in 3rno. There are also buses that go to Naples (24 hours) via Venice, Florence and Rome.

Other buses from Prague to České 3udějovice (130Kč, 2½ hours, 16 daily) and Český Krumlov (140Kč, three hours, seven daily) depart from Ná Knížecí bus station, at Anděl metro's southern entrance, or from outside Roztyly metro station.

Companies include the following:

Eurolines (Map pp104-5; ☎ 245 005 245; www.bei.cz; ÚAN Florenc Bus Station; ⊙ 8am-7pm Mon-Fri) Buses to all over Europe.

Megabus Central Prague (Map pp104-5; ☎ 234 704 977; Shop 12, Můstek metro station, Nove Město; ⊙ 8.30am-7pm Mon-Fri) Florenc (☎ 777 320 102; www.megabus.cz; ⊙ 7am-7pm Mon-Fri) Linking Prague with Karlovy Vary, Plzeň and Brno. Also has a branch at Ruzyně airport.

Student Agency Central Prague (Map pp104-5; ☎ 224 999 666; Ječná 37; Nove Město ⊙ 9am-6pm Mon-Fri); Florenc (☎ 224 894 430; www.studentagency.cz; ⊙ 9am-6pm Mon-Fri) Linking major Czech cities and services throughout Europe. Also has a branch at Ruzyně airport.

Train

Prague's main train station is **Praha-hlavní nádraží** (Map pp104-5; ☎ 221 111 122; Wilsonova, Nové Město). Domestic tickets and seat reservations are sold on level 2 at even-numbered windows from 10 to 24 to the right of the stairs leading up to level 3. International tickets are sold on level 3 at windows 26 to 36. At the time of writing Praha-hlavní nádraží was undergoing major redevelopment and the station layout may be different when you read this.

Some international trains stop at Praha-Holešovice station on the northern side of the city, while some domestic services terminate at Praha-Masarykovo in Nové Město, or Praha-Smíchov south of Malá Strana. Also buy train tickets and get timetable information from **ČD Centrum** (⊙ 6am-7.30pm) at the southern end of level 2 in Praha-hlavní nádraží.

There are direct trains from Praha-hlavní nádraží to Brno (314Kč, three hours, eight daily), České Budějovice (211Kč, 2½ hours, hourly), Karlovy Vary (292Kč, three hours, three daily), Kutná Hora (95Kč, 55 minutes, seven daily) and Plzeň (145Kč, 1½ hours, eight

daily). There are also SC Pend speed) daily departures to Brno (S. from Praha-Holešovice.

Sample one-way fares to Prague from other European cities include the following:
Basel €113, 14 hours
Berlin €51, five hours
Bratislava €20, 4¾ hours
Budapest €88, seven hours
Hamburg €106, 7½ hours
Frankfurt €78, 7½ hours
Kraków €29, 8½ hours
Munich €66, six hours
Salzburg €44, eight hours
Vienna €38, 4½ hours
Warsaw €43, 9½ hours

Check train timetables and depature points online at www.idos.cz.

GETTING AROUND
To/From the Airport

Prague's Ruzyně airport is 17km west of the city centre. To get into town, buy a ticket from the public transport (Dopravní podnik; DPP) desk in arrivals and take bus 119 (26Kč, 20 minutes, every 15 minutes) to the end of the line (Dejvická), then continue by metro into the city centre (another 10 minutes; no extra ticket needed). You'll also need a half-fare (13Kč) ticket for your backpack or suitcase if it's larger than 25cm by 45cm by 70cm.

Alternatively, the **Airport Express** (adult/child 45/25Kč; ⊙ 5am-9pm) bus service goes direct to the Holešovice metro station. Luggage is free on this service; buy your ticket from the driver.

The **Cedaz minibus** (☎ 221 111 111; www.cedaz.cz) leaves from outside arrivals (20 minutes, every half-hour from 6am to 9pm). Buy your ticket from the driver. The minibus stops at the **Czech Airlines** (Map pp104-5; V Celnici 5) office near the Hilton around nám Republiky (120Kč) or further out at the Dejvická metro station (90Kč). You can also get a Cedaz minibus from your hotel or any other address (480Kč for one to four people, 960Kč for five to eight).

Prague Airport Taxis, with airport-regulated prices, charge 650Kč into central Prague. Drivers speak good English. **AAA Taxis** (☎ 14 014; www.aaataxi.cz) is also reputable.

Bicycle

City Bike (Map pp104-5; ☎ 776 180 284; www.citybike-prague .com; Královdvorská 5, Staré Město; ⊙ 9am-7pm May-Sep)

Two- to three-hour tours cost 540Kč, departing at 10.30am, 1.30pm and 4.30pm. Independent hire is 300Kč for the first two hours and 500Kč for all day.

Praha Bike (Map pp104–5; ☎ 732 388 880; www.praha bike.cz; Dlouhá 24, Staré Město; ☉ 9am-8pm) A range of different tour routes including rail and bike combos to Karlštejn Castle.

Car & Motorcycle

Challenges to driving in Prague include cobblestones, trams and one-way streets. Try not to arrive or leave on a Friday or Sunday afternoon or evening, when Prague folk are travelling to and from their weekend houses.

Central Prague has many pedestrian-only streets, marked with Pěší Zoná (Pedestrian Zone) signs, where only service vehicles and taxis are allowed; parking can be a nightmare. Meter time limits range from two to six hours at around 50Kč per hour. Parking in one-way streets is normally only allowed on the right-hand side. Traffic inspectors are strict, and you could be clamped or towed. There are several car parks at the edges of Staré Město, and Park-and-Ride car parks around the outer city (most are marked on city maps), close to metro stations.

Public Transport

All public transport is operated by **Dopravní podnik hl. m. Prahy** (DPP; ☎ 800 191 817; www.dpp .cz), with information desks at **Ruzyně airport** (☉ 7am to 7pm) and in four metro stations – **Muzeum** (☉ 7am to 9pm), **Můstek** (☉ 7am to 6pm), **Anděl** (☉ 7am to 6pm) and **Nádraží Holešovice** (☉ 7am to 6pm) – where you can get tickets, directions, a multilingual system map, a map of Noční provoz (night services) and a detailed English-language guide to the whole system.

Buy a ticket before boarding a bus, tram or metro. Tickets are sold from machines at metro stations and major tram stops, at newsstands, Trafiky snack shops, PNS and other tobacco kiosks, hotels, all metro station ticket offices and DPP information offices.

A jízdenka (transfer ticket) is valid on tram, metro, bus and the Petřín funicular and costs 26Kč (half-price for six- to 15-year-olds); large suitcases and backpacks (anything larger than 25cm by 45cm by 70cm) also need a 13Kč ticket. Kids under six ride free. Validate (punch) your ticket by sticking it in the little yellow machine in the metro station lobby or

on the bus or tram the first time you board this stamps the time and date on it. Onc validated, tickets remain valid for 75 min utes from the time of stamping, if validate between 5am and 10pm on weekdays, and fo 90 minutes at other times. Within this period you can make unlimited transfers between al types of public transport (you don't need to punch the ticket again).

There's also a short-hop 18/9Kč adult. child ticket, valid for 20 minutes on buses and trams, or for up to five metro stations. No transfers are allowed with these, and they're not valid on the Petřín funicular or on night trams (51 to 58) or night buses (501 to 512). Being caught without a valid ticket entails a 400Kč on-the-spot fine (100Kč for not having a luggage ticket). The inspectors travel incognito, but will show a badge when they ask for your ticket. A few may demand a higher fine from foreigners and pocket the difference, so insist on a doklad (receipt) before paying.

Tickets for 24 hours (100Kč) and three/five days (330/500Kč) are also available. If you're staying for longer and will be travelling a lot, consider a monthly pass (550Kč). All passes must be validated on first use only. If a ticket is stamped twice, it becomes invalid. Before shelling out on a pass, note much of central Prague can be explored on foot.

On metro trains and newer trams and buses, an electronic display shows the route number and the name of the next stop, and a recorded voice announces each station or stop. As the train, tram or bus pulls away, it says: Příští stanice (or zastávka)… meaning 'The next station (or stop) is…', perhaps noting that it's a přestupní stanice (transfer station). At metro stations, signs point you towards the výstup (exit) or to a přestup (transfer to another line).

The metro operates from 5am to midnight daily. Line A runs from northwest Prague at Dejvická to the east at Depo Hostivař; line B runs from the southwest at Zličín to the northeast at Černý Most; and line C runs from the north at Letňany to the southeast at Háje. Line A intersects line C at Muzeum, line B intersects line C at Florenc and line A intersects line B at Můstek.

After the metro closes, night trams (51 to 59) and buses (501 to 512) travel about every 40 minutes. Check if one of these services passes near where you're staying.

Taxi

Try to avoid getting a taxi in tourist areas such as Wenceslas Sq. To avoid being ripped off, phone a reliable company such as **AAA** (☎ 14 014; www.aaa.radiotaxi.cz) or **City Taxi** (☎ 257 257 257; www.citytaxi.cz). Both companies also offer online bookings.

Prague recently introduced the 'Taxi Fair Place' scheme, with authorised taxis in tourist areas. Drivers can charge a maximum of 28Kč/km and must announce the estimated price in advance. Look for the yellow and red signs.

If you do feel cheated, keep the receipt and email the details to taxi@cityofprague.cz.

AROUND PRAGUE

Visit the following places on day trips using public transport.

KARLŠTEJN

Erected by the Emperor Charles IV in the mid-14th century, **Karlštejn Castle** (☎ 274 008 154; www.hradkarlstejn.cz; Karlštejn; ◷ 9am-6pm Tue-Sun Jul & Aug, to 5pm May, Jun & Sep, to 4pm Apr & Oct, to 3pm Mar & Nov, closed Jan, Feb & Dec), crowns a ridge above Karlštejn village. It's a 20-minute walk from the train station.

The highlight is the **Chapel of the Holy Rood**, where the Bohemian crown jewels were kept until 1420. The 55-minute guided tours (in English) on Route I costs 200/120Kč for adult/child tickets. Route II, which includes the chapel (June to October only), are 300/150Kč adult/child and must be prebooked.

Trains from Praha-hlavní nádraží station to Beroun stop at Karlštejn (46Kč, 45 minutes, hourly).

KONOPIŠTĚ

The assassination of the heir to the Austro-Hungarian throne, Archduke Franz Ferdinand d'Este, sparked off WWI. For the last 20 years of his life he hid away southeast of Prague in **Konopiště Chateau**, his country retreat.

Three guided tours are available. **Tour III** (adult/child 300/200Kč) is the most interesting, visiting the archduke's private apartments, unchanged since the state took over the chateau in 1921. **Tour II** (adult/child 190/110Kč) takes in the **Great Armoury**, one of Europe's most impressive collections.

The castle is a testament to the archduke's twin obsessions of hunting and St George. Having renovated the massive Gothic and Renaissance building in the 1890s, Franz Ferdinand decorated his home with some of his 300,000 hunting kills. About 100,000 of them adorn the walls, marked with when and where it was slain. The **Trophy Corridor** and **Chamois Room** (both on Tour III) are truly bizarre.

His collection of St George–related artefacts includes 3750 items, many displayed in the **Muzeum sv Jiří** (adult/child 30/15Kč) at the front of the castle. From June to September weekend concerts are sometimes held in the castle's grounds.

There are direct trains from Prague's hlavní nádraží to Benešov u Prahy (66Kč, 1¼ hours, hourly). Buses depart from Florenc or the Roztyly metro station to Benešov on a regular basis (48Kč, 1¼ hours)

Konopiště is 2.5km west of Benešov. Local bus 2 (11Kč, six minutes, hourly) runs from a stop on Dukelská, 400m north of the train station (turn left out of the station, then first right on Tyršova and first left) to the castle car park. Otherwise it's a 30-minute walk. Turn left out of the train station, go left across the bridge over the railway, and follow Konopišťská street west for 2km.

KUTNÁ HORA

In the 14th century, the silver-rich ore under Kutná Hora gave the now-sleepy town an importance in Bohemia second only to Prague. The local mines and mint turned out silver *groschen* for use as the hard currency of central Europe. The silver ore ran out in 1726, leaving the medieval townscape largely unaltered. Now with several fascinating and unusual historical attractions, the Unesco World Heritage–listed town is a popular day trip from Prague.

Orientation & Information

Kutná Hora hlavní nádraží (the main train station) is 3km northeast of the Old Town centre. The bus station is more conveniently located on the Old Town's northeastern edge.

To visit Kutná Hora on a day trip, arrive on a morning train from Prague, then make the 10-minute walk from Kutná Hora hlavní nádraží to Sedlec Ossuary. From there it's another 2km walk or a five-minute bus ride into town. A bus leaves Prague Florenc at 8.10am for an early start.

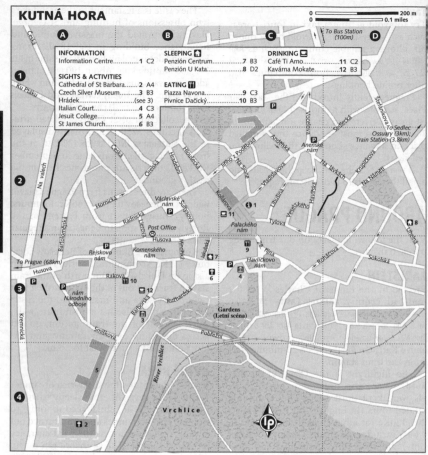

KUTNÁ HORA

0 ——————— 200 m
0 ——————— 0.1 miles

INFORMATION
Information Centre.............**1** C2

SIGHTS & ACTIVITIES
Cathedral of St Barbara.......**2** A4
Czech Silver Museum..........**3** B3
Hrádek.....................(see 3)
Italian Court.................**4** C3
Jesuit College................**5** A4
St James Church..............**6** B3

SLEEPING 🏠
Penzión Centrum...............**7** B3
Penzión U Kata................**8** D2

EATING 🍴
Piazza Navona.................**9** C3
Pivnice Dačický...............**10** B3

DRINKING 🍷
Café Ti Amo...................**11** C2
Kavárna Mokate..............**12** B3

To Bus Station (100m)

To Sedlec Ossuary (3km); Train Station (3.8km)

To Prague (68km)

Gardens (Letní scéna)

Vrchlice

The **information centre** (☎ 327 512 378; www .kutnahora.cz; Palackého nám 377; ☺ 9am-6pm Apr-Sep, 9am-5pm Mon-Fri, 10am-4pm Sat & Sun Oct-Mar) books accommodation, provides internet access (1Kč per minute), and rents bicycles (220Kč per day).

In early June, the town hosts an **International Music Festival** (www.mfkh.cz), with chamber-music recitals in venues, including the soaring Cathedral of St Barbara.

Sights

Walk 10-minutes south from Kutná Hora hlavní nádraží to the remarkable **Sedlec Ossuary** (Kostnice; ☎ 327 561 143; www.kostnice.cz; adult/child 50/30Kč; ☺ 8am-6pm Apr-Sep, 9am-noon & 1-5pm Oct & Mar, 9am-noon & 1-4pm Nov-Mar). When

the Schwarzenberg family purchased Sedlec monastery in 1870, a local woodcarver got creative with the bones of 40,000 people from the centuries-old crypt. Skulls and femurs are strung from the vaulted ceiling, and the central chandelier contains at least one of each bone in the human body. Four giant pyramids of stacked bones squat in the corner chapels, and crosses of bone adorn the altar.

From the Kutná Hora bus station catch bus 1B and get off at the 'Tabak' stop. From Sedlec it's another 2km walk (or five-minute bus ride) to central Kutná Hora.

The Old Town lies south of **Palackého nám**, the main square. From the square's western end, Jakubská leads to **St James Church** (1330).

Further east is the **Italian Court** (Vlašský dvůr; ☎ 327 512 873; Havlíčkovo nám 552; adult/child 100/80Kč; ☽ 9am-6pm Apr-Sep, 10am-5pm Mar & Oct, 10am-4pm Nov-Feb), the former Royal Mint. Florentine craftsmen began stamping silver coins here in 1300. It houses a mint museum and a 15th-century **Audience Hall** with 19th-century murals depicting the election of Vladislav Jagiello as King of Bohemia in 1471 and the Decree of Kutná Hora being proclaimed by Wenceslas IV and Jan Hus in 1409.

From the southern side of St James Church, Ruthardská leads to the **Hrádek** (Little Castle), a 15th-century palace housing the **Czech Silver Museum** (České Muzeum Stříbra; ☎ 327 512 159; www .cms-kh.cz; adult/child 60/30Kč, English-speaking guide 400Kč; ☽ 10am-6pm Jul & Aug, 9am-6pm May, Jun & Sep, 9am-5pm Apr & Oct, 10am-4pm Sat & Sun Nov, closed Mon year-round). Don a miner's helmet to join the 1½-hour 'Way of Silver' tour (adult/child 110/70Kč) through 500m of medieval mine shafts beneath the town. Kids need to be at least seven for this tour. A combination ticket for the museum and the mine tour (adult/child 130/80Kč) is also available.

Beyond the Hrádek is a 17th-century former **Jesuit college**, with a terrace featuring 13 baroque sculptures of saints, inspired by those on Prague's Charles Bridge. The second one along of a woman holding a chalice is St Barbara, the patron saint of miners and Kutná Hora.

At the terrace's far end is the Gothic **Cathedral of St Barbara** (☎ 327 512 115; adult/child 50/30Kč; ☽ 9am-5.30pm Tue-Sun, 10am-4pm Mon May-Sep, 10am-4pm Oct-Apr). Rivalling Prague's St Vitus in magnificence, its soaring nave culminates in elegant, six-petalled ribbed vaulting. The ambulatory chapels preserve original 15th-century frescos, some showing miners at work. Outside there are fine views.

Sleeping

Penzión U Kata (☎ 327 515 096; www.ukata.cz; Uhelná 596; s/d/tr 500/760/1140Kč) You won't lose your head over the rates at this good-value family hotel called 'The Executioner'. Bikes can be rented for 200Kč per hour and it's a short stroll from the bus station.

Penzión Centrum (☎ 327 514 218; Jakubská 57; d incl breakfast 800Kč) A quiet, central location with snug rooms – what more could you want? How about pancakes and coffee in the grassy courtyard? Just around the corner are the best of Kutná Hora's galleries.

Eating & Drinking

Pivnice Dačický (☎ 327 512 248; Rakova 8; mains 90-240Kč) Try Kutná Hora's dark beer at this traditional beer hall. Rustle up three drinking buddies and order the Gamekeepers Reserve, a huge platter that demands at least a second beer. There are six different brews available, so try not to miss your bus back to Prague.

Piazza Navona (☎ 327 512 588; Palackého nám 90; mains 100-140Kč) Have authentic pizza by an authentic Italian on Kutná Hora's main square. Finish with gelati in summer and hot chocolate in winter.

Café Ti Amo (Kollárova 9; snacks 65-70Kč) This cosmopolitan cafe with outdoor tables, excellent coffee and wine is a popular meeting spot for locals. It's a couple of blocks from the main square tourist hubbub.

Kavárna Mokate (Baborská 7; coffee & cake 70-80Kč; ☽ 8.30am-9.30pm Mon-Thu, 9am-midnight Fri & Sat, noon-7pm Sun) It's not just good coffee at this place with rustic tiled floors, and mismatched furniture from your last student flat. A global array of teas complements yummy cakes.

Getting There & Away

There are direct trains from Prague's hlavní nádraží to Kutná Hora hlavní nádraží (98Kč, 55 minutes, seven daily).

Buses to Kutná Hora from Prague (62Kč, 1¼ hours, hourly) depart Florenc bus station; services are less frequent at weekends.

BOHEMIA

The ancient land of Bohemia makes up the western two-thirds of the Czech Republic. The modern term 'bohemian' comes to us via the French, who thought that Roma came from Bohemia; the word *bohémien* was later applied to people living an unconventional lifestyle. The term gained currency in the wake of Puccini's opera *La Bohème* about poverty-stricken artists in Paris.

TEREZÍN

The massive fortress at Terezín (Theriesenstadt in German) was built by the Habsburgs in the 18th century to repel the Prussian army, but the place is better known as a notorious WWII prison and concentration camp. Around 150,000 men, women and children, mostly Jews, passed through en route to the extermination camps of Auschwitz-Birkenau: 35,000 of them died here of hunger, disease or suicide, and only 4000 survived. From 1945 to 1948 the fortress served as an internment camp for the Sudeten Germans, who were expelled from Czechoslovakia after the war.

Ironically, Terezín played a tragic role in deceiving the world of the ultimate goals of the Nazi's 'Final Solution'. Official visitors were immersed in a charade, with Terezín being presented as a Jewish 'refuge', complete with shops, schools and cultural organisations – even an autonomous Jewish 'government'. As late as April 1945, Red Cross visitors espoused positive reports.

The **Terezín Memorial** (☎ 416 782 225; www .pamatnik-terezin.cz) consists of the Museum of the Ghetto in the Main Fortress, and the Lesser Fortress, a 10-minute walk east across the Ohře River. Admission to one part costs 160/130Kč; a combined ticket is 200/150Kč. At the ticket office, ask about historical films in the museum's cinema.

The **Museum of the Ghetto** (Muzeum ghetta; ☾ 9am-6pm Apr-Oct, to 5.30pm Nov-Mar) records daily life in the camp during WWII, through moving displays of paintings, letters and personal possessions. Entry to the Museum of the Ghetto includes entry to the Magdeburg Barracks and vice versa.

Around 32,000 prisoners, many of them Czech partisans, were incarcerated in the **Lesser Fortress** (Malá pevnost; ☾ 8am-6pm Apr-Oct, to 4.30pm Nov-Mar). Take the grimly fascinating self-guided tour through the prison barracks, workshops, morgues and mass graves, before arriving at the bleak execution grounds where more than 250 prisoners were shot.

At the **Magdeburg Barracks** (Magdeburská kasárna; cnr Tyršova & Vodárenská; ☾ 9am- 6pm Apr-Oct, to 5.30pm Nov-Mar), the former base of the Jewish 'government', are exhibits on the rich cultural life – music, theatre, fine arts and literature – that flourished against this backdrop of fear. Most poignant are the copies of *Vedem* ('In the Lead') magazine, published by 100 boys from 1942 to 1944. Only 15 of the boys survived the war.

Terezín is northwest of Prague and 3km south of Litoměřice. Buses between Prague and Litoměřice stop at both the main square and the Lesser Fortress. There are frequent buses between Litoměřice bus station and Terezín (10Kč, 10 minutes). Many Prague tour companies offer day trips to Terezín.

LITOMĚŘICE
pop 25,100

Founded by German colonists in the 13th century, Litoměřice prospered in the 18th century as a royal seat and bishopric. The town centre features picturesque buildings and churches, some designed by the locally born baroque architect Ottavio Broggio.

The Old Town lies across the road to the west of the train and bus stations, guarded by the remnants of the 14th-century town walls. Walk along Dlouhá to the central square, Mírové nám.

The **information centre** (☎ 416 732 440; www .litomerice.cz; Mírové nám 15/7; ☾ 8am-6pm Mon-Sat, 9.30am-4pm Sun May-Sep, 8am-4pm Mon-Fri, 8-11am Sat Oct-Apr) in the town hall books accommodation and runs **walking tours** (adult/child 60/40Kč; ☾ 9am-4.30pm Mon-Sat, 9.30am-3.30pm Sun, May-Sep, 8.30am-3.30pm Mon-Fri Apr & Oct).

Internet Club Centrum (1st Flor, Mírové nám 25; ☾ noon-midnight Mon-Sat, 2-8pm Sun) is down an arcade opposite the information centre.

Sights

The main square is lined with Gothic arcades and facades dominated by the tower of **All Saints Church**, the step-gabled **Old Town Hall** and the distinctive **House at the Chalice** (Dům U Kalicha), housing the present town hall. Sprouting from the roof is a copper chalice, the traditional symbol of the Hussite church. The slim baroque facade at the square's elevated end is the **House of Ottavio Broggio**.

Along Michalská on the square's southwest corner is another Broggio design, the **North Bohemia Fine Arts Gallery** (☎ 416 732 382; Michalská 7; adult/child 32/18Kč; ☾ 9am-noon & 1-6pm Tue-Sun Apr-Sep, 9am-noon & 1-5pm Oct-Mar) with the priceless Renaissance panels of the Litoměřice Altarpiece.

Turn left on Michalská and follow Domská to Domské nám on Cathedral Hill, passing the baroque **St Wenceslas Church**, on a side street to the right. Atop the hill is the town's oldest church, the 11th-century **St Stephen Cathedral**.

Follow the arch on the cathedral's left and descend down steep and cobbled Máchova. At the foot of the hill turn left then first right, up the zigzag steps to the **Old Town walls**. Follow the walls right to the next street, Jezuitská, then turn left back to the square.

Sleeping

Autocamp Slavoj (☎ 416 734 481; kemp.litomerice@post.cz; per tent/bungalow 80/220Kč; ⏰ May-Sep; 💻) South of the train station is this rudimentary camping ground on Střelecký ostrov (Marksmen Island).

U Svatého Václava (☎ 416 737 500; www.upfront.cz/penzion; Svatovaclavská 12; s/d incl breakfast 700/1200Kč) Beside St Wenceslas Church, this popular haven has well-equipped rooms, hearty cooked breakfasts, and owners whose English is better than they think.

Pension Prislin (☎ 416 735 833; www.prislin.cz; Na Kocandě 12; s/d/tr/q incl breakfast 750/1260/1570/1880Kč) Pension Prislin has a friendly dog called Baltimore and a switched-on owner who's decorated his pension in bright colours. The spacious apartments take up to five travellers.

Hotel Salva Guarda (☎ 416 732 506; www.salva-garda.cz; Mírové nám 12; s/d 1220/1750Kč) With old maps in reception, it's a shame they keep the lights so low. However, the spotless rooms are well lit in this classy hotel that's housed in a *sgraffito* building from 1566. Breakfast is 140Kč.

Eating

U Štěpána Pizzeria (☎ 728 928 804, Dlouhá 43; pizza 45-145Kč) At the downhill end of the square, this spot has a monk as a logo, but there's definitely nothing frugal about the pizza toppings.

Music Club Viva (☎ 606 437 783; Mezibrani; mains 100-235Kč) Shared wooden tables ensures conversation flows as naturally as the drinks in this hip spot in the Old Town bastion.

Radniční sklípek (☎ 416 731 142; Mírové nám 21; mains 110-250Kč) Keep your head down in this underground labyrinth that does great grills accompanied by a good wine list. In summer, the meaty action spills onto the main square.

Gurmănie (☎ 416 532 305; Novobranská 14; mains 110-250Kč; ⏰ 9am-5pm Mon-Fri, 9am-3pm Sat) At the top end of the square, Gurmănie has tasty ciabatta sandwiches for on-the-go dining, and salads and pasta. Say *ahoj* to Litoměřice's best coffee.

Pekárna Kodys & Hamele (Novobranská 18) has all your favourite baked goodies in one place.

Getting There & Away

Direct buses from Prague to Litoměřice (75Kč, one hour, hourly) depart from station 17 at Florenc bus station (final destination Ustí nad Labem).

BOHEMIAN SWITZERLAND NATIONAL PARK

The main road and rail route between Prague and Dresden follows the fast-flowing Labe (Elbe) River, gouging a sinuous, steep-sided valley through a sandstone plateau on the border between the Czech Republic and Germany. The landscape of sandstone pinnacles, giddy gorges, dark forests and high meadows is the Bohemian Switzerland National Park (Národní park České Švýcarsko), named after two 19th-century Swiss artists who settled here.

Sights & Activities

Just south of the German border, **Hřensko** is a cute village of half-timbered houses crammed into a sandstone gorge where the Kamenice River joins the Labe. It's overrun with German day trippers on summer weekends, but upstream peaceful hiking trails begin.

A signposted 16km (five to six hours) circular hike explores the main sights. From Hřensko's eastern end a trail leads via ledges, walkways and tunnels through the mossy chasms of the **Kamenice River Gorge**.

Two sections – **Edmundova Soutěska** (Edmund's Gorge; ⏰ 9am-6pm May-Aug, Sat & Sun only Apr, Sep & Oct) and **Divoká Soutěska** (Savage Gorge; ⏰ 9am-5pm May-Aug, Sat & Sun only Apr, Sep & Oct) – have been dammed. Continue by punt and a ferryman through a canyon 5m wide and 50m to 150m deep. Each ferry trip costs 60/30Kč per adult/child.

The **Hřensko information office** (☎ 414 554 286; www.ceskosaske-svycarsko.cz; ⏰ 9am-6pm Apr-Oct) on the road from Děčín organises canoeing trips (per person €20).

A kilometre beyond the end of the second boat trip, a blue-marked trail leads uphill to the Hotel Mezní Louka. Across the road, a red-marked trail continues through the forest to the spectacular rock formation **Pravčická Brána** (www.pbrana.cz; adult/child 75/25Kč; ⏰ 10am-6pm Apr-Oct, to 4pm Sat & Sun Nov-Mar), the largest natural arch in Europe. Crouched beneath is the **Falcon's Nest**, a 19th-century chateau housing a national park museum and restaurant. From here the red trail descends westward back to Hřensko.

The area is also popular with climbers. Ask at the Hřensko information office about climbing day trips, and hire gear from **Hudy Sport** (⏰ 9am-5.30pm) around 400m up the Kamenice River Gorge road.

CZECH REPUBLIC

Sleeping & Eating

Pension Lugano (☎ 412 554 146; www.hrensko-lugano
.cz; Hřensko; s/d incl breakfast 500/1000Kč) A cheerful
place in the centre of Hřensko serving terrific
breakfasts at a riverside restaurant.

In the hills, **Hotel Mezní Louka** (☎ 412 554 220;
www.mezni-louka.cz; Mezní Louka 71; s/d 900/1450Kč) is
a 19th-century hiking lodge with a decent
restaurant (mains 90Kč to 170Kč). Across the
road is **Camp Mezní Louka** (☎ 412 554 084; r.kolarova@
npcs.cz; camp sites per tent/bungalow 110/510Kč).

With your own car, base yourself in either
Janov or Jetřichovice. In Janov **Pension Pastis**
(☎ 142 554 037; www.pastis.cz; Janov 22; s/d incl breakfast
540/1080Kč; 🖳) has an excellent restaurant; in
Jetřichovice try **Pension Dřevák** (☎ 412 555 015; s/d
incl breakfast 700/1050Kč), housed in a 19th-century
wooden building. Bookings can be made at
www.ceskosaske-svycarsko.cz.

Getting There & Away

From Prague, take a bus from Florenc (120Kč,
1¾ hours, five daily) to Děčín, then another to
Hřensko (18Kč, 25 minutes, four daily).

Alternatively, catch a Dresden-bound train
and get off at Bad Schandau (280Kč, two hours,
eight daily), in Germany, and then a local train
back to Schöna (€1.80, 12 minutes, every half-
hour) on the German bank of the river opposite Hřensko. From the station, a ferry (20Kč,
three minutes, from 6am to 10pm April to
September and from 8am to 6pm October to
March) crosses to Hřensko on demand.

On weekdays there are three buses a day
(year-round) between Hřensko and Mezní
Louka (8Kč, 10 minutes), and two a day at weekends (July to September only). In summer, keep
an eye out for the big red **Nationalpark Express**, a
heritage double-decker bus that crosses over
from Germany and provides regular transport
to Pravčická Brána and Mezní Louka.

If you're heading on to Germany, either do
the river crossing to Schöna described above
and catch a local train to Bad Schandau,
or catch a local bus from Hřensko back to
Děčín and then catch a direct train to Dresden
(110Kč, 50 minutes, 10 daily). Most of these
trains also carry on to Berlin or Hamburg.
See ww.idos.cz.

KARLOVY VARY
pop 60,000

According to legend, Emperor Charles IV
discovered Karlovy Vary's hot springs accidentally in 1350 when one of his hunting
dogs fell into the waters. Now the fashionable
town is the closest the Czech Republic has to a
glam resort, but Karlovy Vary is definitely glam
with a small 'g'. Well-heeled hypochondriacs
from Germany, Austria and (especially) Russia
make the pilgrimage for courses of lymphatic
drainage, hydrocolonotherapy, and other
treatments that sound more like weapons of
mass destruction. Preferred form is to sip on
the mineral-laden waters from a dainty porcelain cup, but the caffeine-laden offerings from
the town's cafes are actually much tastier.

The **Karlovy Vary International Film Festival** in
early July is well worth attending. More than
200 films are shown, tickets are easy to get, and
a funky array of concurrent events, including
buskers and world-music concerts, gives the
genteel town an annual energy transfusion. It's
also your chance to spy international visitors
such as Robert De Niro and John Malkovich.

Orientation

Karlovy Vary has two train stations: Dolní
nádraží (Lower Station), beside the main bus
station, and Horní nádraží (Upper Station),
across the Ohře River the the north.

Trains from Prague arrive at Horní nádraží.
Take bus 11, 12 or 13 (12Kč) from across the
road to the Tržnice station; 11 continues to
Divadelni nám in the spa district.

Alternatively, it's 10 minutes on foot: cross
the road outside the station and go right,
then first left on a path that leads downhill
under the highway. At its foot, turn right on
U Spořitelny, then left at the far end of the
big building and head for the river bridge.

The Tržnice bus stop is three blocks east
of Dolní nádraží, in the middle of the town's
modern commercial district. Pedestrianised
TG Masaryka leads east to the Teplá River;
from here the old spa district stretches
upstream for 2km along a steep-sided valley.

Information

Infocentrum Dolni nádraží (☎ 353 232 838; www
.karlovyvary.cz; Západni; 🕑 9am-5pm Mon-Fri, 10am-
4pm Sat & Sun); Lázeňská (☎ 353 224 097; Lázeňská
1; 🕑 10am-6pm Mon-Fri, to 5pm Sat & Sun) Loads of
information on the town, plus maps, accommodation help
and pricey internet (per minute 2Kč).
Main post office (TG Masaryka 1)
Moonstorm Internet (TG Masaryka 31; per min 1Kč;
🕑 9am-9pm)

There's free wi-fi at Kino Panasonic (p129).

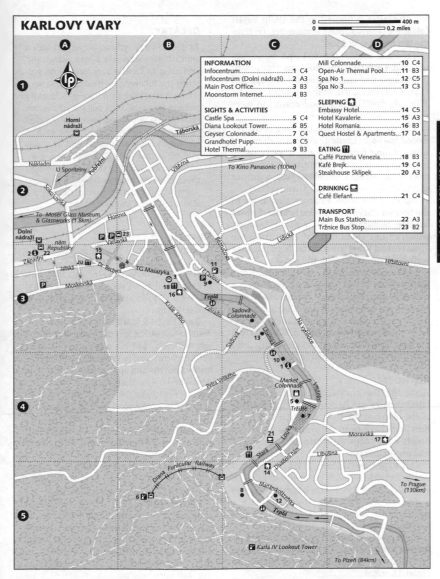

KARLOVY VARY

0 — 400 m
0 — 0.2 miles

INFORMATION	
Infocentrum	1 C4
Infocentrum (Dolní nádraží)	2 A3
Main Post Office	3 B3
Moonstorm Internet	4 B3

SIGHTS & ACTIVITIES	
Castle Spa	5 C4
Diana Lookout Tower	6 B5
Geyser Colonnade	7 C4
Grandhotel Pupp	8 C5
Hotel Thermal	9 B3

Mill Colonnade	10 C4
Open-Air Thermal Pool	11 B3
Spa No 1	12 C5
Spa No 3	13 C3

SLEEPING	
Embassy Hotel	14 C5
Hotel Kavalerie	15 A3
Hotel Romania	16 B3
Quest Hostel & Apartments	17 D4

EATING	
Caffé Pizzeria Venezia	18 B3
Kafé Brejk	19 C4
Steakhouse Sklipek	20 A3

DRINKING	
Café Elefant	21 C4

TRANSPORT	
Main Bus Station	22 A3
Tržnice Bus Stop	23 B2

CZECH REPUBLIC

Sights

At the central spa district is the neoclassical **Mill Colonnade** (Mlýnská Kolonáda), with occasional summer concerts. Other elegant colonnades and 19th-century spa buildings are scattered along the Teplá River, with the 1970s concrete **Hotel Thermal** spoiling the effect slightly.

Purchase a *lázenské pohár* (spa cup) and some *oplátky* (spa wafers; p128) and sample the various hot springs (free). Infocentrum has a leaflet describing the 12 springs in the 'drinking cure', ranging from the **Rock Spring** (Skalní Pramen), which dribbles just 1.3L per minute, to the robust **Geyser** (Vřídlo), which spurts 2000L per minute in a 14m-high jet. The latter is housed in the 1970s **Geyser Colonnade** (Vřídelní Kolonáda; admission free; ⏱ 10am-6pm Mon-Fri, to 4pm Sat & Sun).

To look inside the old spa buildings without enduring the dubious rigours of *proktologie* and *endoskopie*, nip into **Spa No 3** (Lázně III) just north of the Mill Colonnade. The cafe upstairs is a good reason to have a look.

The most splendid spa building is the restored **Spa No 1** (Lázně I) at the south end of town, dating from 1895 and once housing Emperor Franz Josef's private baths. Across the river is the baroque **Grandhotel Pupp**, a former meeting place of European aristocrats.

North of the hotel, a narrow alley leads to the bottom station of the **Diana Funicular Railway** (adult one-way/return 36/60Kč, child 18/30Kč; ⏱ 9am-6pm), which climbs 166m to great views from the **Diana Lookout Tower** (admission free). It's a pleasant walk back down through the forest.

Just out of town, the newly expanded **Moser Glass Museum** (Sklářské muzeum Moser; ☎ 353 416 242, www.moser-glass.com; Kpt Jaroše 19; adult/child 80/50Kč; ⏱ 9am-5pm) has more than 2000 items on display. Afterwards get hot under the collar at the adjacent **glassworks** (adult/child 120/70Kč; ⏱ 9am-2.30pm). Combined tickets (adult/child 180/100Kč) are also available.

Activities

Although the surviving traditional *lázně* (spa) centres are basically medical institutions, many of the town's old spa and hotel buildings have been renovated as 'wellness' hotels with cosmetic treatments, massages and aromatherapy.

Castle Spa (Zámecké Lázně; ☎ 353 222 649; http://english.edenhotels.cz; Zámechý vrch; treatments from €25; ⏱ 7.30am-7.30pm Mon-Fri, from 8.30am Sat & Sun) is a modernised spa centre, complete with a subterranean thermal pool. It still retains a heritage ambience.

For a cheaper paddle head to the **open-air thermal pool** (per hr 80Kč; ⏱ 8am-8pm Mon-Sat, to 9pm Sun). Follow the 'Bazén' signs up the hill behind Hotel Thermal.

Festivals & Events

Karlovy Vary International Film Festival (www.kviff.com) Early July.

International Student Film Festival (www.freshfilmfest.net) Late August.

Karlovy Vary Folklore Festival Early September.

Dvořák Autumn September; classical music festival.

OPLÁTKY

To quote Monty Python: 'Do you get wafers with it?' The answer is a resounding 'yes' according to Karlovy Vary locals, who prescribe the following method of taking your spring water: have a sip from your *lázeňský pohárek* (spa cup), then dull the sulphurous taste with a big, round sweet wafer called *oplátky*. *Oplátky* are sold for 10Kč each at spa hotels, speciality shops and at a stall in front of the Hotel Thermal. Steer clear of the fancy chocolate or hazelnut flavours though; they're never as crunchily fresh and warm as the standard flavour. *Oplátky* are also a big hit in Mariánské Lázně.

Sleeping

Accommodation is pricey, and can be tight during weekends and festivals; definitely book ahead. Infocentrum (p126) can find hostel, pension and hotel rooms. Consider staying in Loket (p130) and visiting Karlovy Vary as a day trip.

Quest Hostel & Apartments (☎ 353 820 030; www.hostel-karlovy-vary.cz; Moravská 44; dm from 410Kč, s/tw from 845/1090Kč; 🖳) It's a long uphill walk to get here, but you're rewarded with well-run budget dorms and apartments with two, four or six beds. Alternatively catch bus 8 (12Kč) from Tržnice to the Černý Kůn stop (five stops). Cross the road behind you and walk down the steps 100m to your right.

Hotel Kavalerie (☎ 353 229 613; www.kavalerie.cz; TG Masaryka 43; s/d incl breakfast from 950/1225Kč) Friendly staff abound in this cosy spot above a cafe. It's located near the bus and train stations, and nearby eateries can help you avoid the spa district's high restaurant prices.

Hotel Romania (☎ 353 222 822; www.romania.cz; Zahradni 49; s/d incl breakfast 1950/1650Kč) Don't be put off by the ugly Hotel Thermal dominating the views from this good-value, reader-recommended spot. Just squint a little, because the rooms are spacious and the English-speaking staff very helpful.

Embassy Hotel (☎ 353 221 161; www.embassy.cz; Nová Luka 21; s/d incl breakfast from 2260/3130Kč; 🖳) KV's not short of top-end hotels, but most lack the personal touch inherent in the Embassy's family-owned combination of a riverside location and perfectly pitched heritage rooms. Downstairs, the Embassy Pub has seen visits from a DVD store full of Film Fest luminaries.

Eating & Drinking

Caffé Pizzeria Venezia (☎ 353 229 721; Zahradní 43; pizza 95-120Kč) After an espresso and pizza, blur your eyes through your designer sunnies and see if you can spot any gondoliers from this pretty-in-pink spot looking out on the Teplá River.

Steakhouse Sklipek (☎ 353 229 197; Zeyerova 1; meals 140-180Kč) Red-checked tablecloths and an emphasis on good steaks, fish and pasta give this place an honest, rustic ambience missing from the more expensive chichi spots down the hill in the spa district.

Also recommended:

Café Elefant (☎ 353 223 406; Stará Louka 30; coffee 50Kč) Classy old-school spot for coffee and cake. A tad touristy, but still elegant and refined.

Kafé Brejk (Stará Louka 62; coffee 45Kč, baguettes 60Kč; ⏲ 9am-5pm) Trendy new-school spot for takeaway coffees and design-your-own baguettes.

Entertainment

Kino Panasonic (☎ 353 233 933; www.kinopanasonic.cz; Vítězná 48; 🖵) This compact art-house cinema showcases Karlovy Vary's film-festival credentials year-round. The coffee's good, and there's free wi-fi access.

Getting There & Around

Student Agency (www.studentagency.cz) and **Megabus** (www.megabus.cz) run frequent buses to/from Prague Florenc (130Kč, 2¼ hours, eight daily) departing from the main bus station beside Dolní nádraží train station. There are direct buses to Plzeň (84Kč, 1½ hours, hourly).

There are direct (but slow) trains from Karlovy Vary to Prague Holešovice (288Kč, three hours). Heading west from Karlovy Vary to Nuremberg, Germany (4½ hours, two a day), and beyond, you'll have to change at Cheb (Eger in German). Check online at www.idos.cz and www.bahn.de.

Buses to/from Loket, a recommended base for visiting Karlovy Vary, run throughout the day (26Kč, 20 minutes).

LOKET

Nestled in a bend of the Ohře River, Loket is a gorgeous little place that's attracted many famous visitors from nearby Karlovy Vary. A plaque on the facade of the Hostinec Bílý Kůň on the chocolate-box town square commemorates Goethe's seven visits. Loket even scored a cameo role in the 2006 James Bond movie, *Casino Royale*.

Most people visit Loket as a day trip from Karlovy Vary, but it's also a sleepy place to ease off the travel accelerator for a few days, especially when the day trippers have all departed. Loket also makes a good base for visiting Karlovy Vary.

The bus arriving from Karlovy Vary stops across the bridge from the Old Town. Walk across the bridge to reach the castle, accommodation and **Infocentrum** (☎ 352 684 123; www.loket.cz; TG Masaryka 12; ⏲ 10.30am-5pm). The Hrnčírna Galerie Café (see p130) has internet access.

In the second half of July, the annual **Loket Summer Cultural Festival** (www.loketfestival.info) features classical music and opera on an outdoor stage near the river with the castle as a dramatic backdrop.

WORTH THE TRIP: MARIÁNSKÉ LÁZNĚ & CHODOVÁ PLANÁ

For a more relaxed Bohemian spa experience than bustling Karlovy Vary, consider Mariánské Lázně. Perched at the southern edge of the Slavkov Forest (Slavkovský Les), the spa town formerly known as Marienbad drew luminaries such as Goethe, Thomas Edison and King Edward VII. Even old misery-guts Franz Kafka was a regular visitor, enjoying the pure waters and getting active on the walking trails that criss-cross the rolling forest. In contemporary times the appeal of spa services, heritage hotels and gentle exercise is complemented by a busy summertime cultural program, including mid-August's **Chopin Music Festival** (www.chopinfestival.cz). You can also catch a local bus (18Kč, 20 minutes) to nearby Chodová Planá and bath in giant hoppy tubs of lager in the Czech Republic's only **beer spa** (www.chodovar.cz).

From Prague, Mariánské Lázně can be reached by train (390Kč, five hours) via Cheb from Prague's main train station (Praha-hlavní nádraží). Buses (160Kč, three hours) run from platform 18 at Prague's Florenc bus station. There are also trains (98Kč, 1½ hours, eight per day) and buses (69Kč, one hour, four daily) to/from Plzeň. From the adjacent bus and train stations at the southern end of Mariánské Lázně, catch trolleybus 5 to the spa area's main bus stop. The **information office** (www.marianskelazne.cz) is 200m uphill on the left.

CZECH REPUBLIC

CZECH REPUBLIC

Sights & Activities

Perched above the river, the **castle** (☎ 352 684 104; adult/child with English guide 90/60Kč, with English text 80/45Kč; ✇ 9am-4.30pm Apr-Oct, to 3.30pm Nov-Mar) has a museum dedicated to locally produced porcelain. The nearby **Black Gate Tower** (Černá Věž; TG Masaryka; admission 20Kč; ✇ 11am-5pm Jul & Aug, Fri-Sun only May, Jun & Sep) provides great views.

Ask at Infocentrum about short walks in the surrounding forests. You can also walk from Karlovy Vary to Loket along a 17km (three hours) blue-marked trail, starting at the Diana lookout (p128).

Karlovy Vary is the destination for one-day rafting trips along the Ohře River with either **Dronte** (☎ 274 779 828; www.dronte.cz) or **Petr Putzer** (☎ 606 902 310; www.putzer.cz). Rafting on the Ohře is a quieter alternative to Český Krumlov and the Vltava River. Costs including transport are around 1200Kč per person. Ask at Infocentrum.

Sleeping & Eating

Lazy River Hostel (☎ 352 684 587; www.lazyriverhostel .com; Kostelní 61; dm/d/tr 300/750/1125Kč) Friendly expat owner Doug is a long-term Loket resident, and his new, more spacious digs for Lazy River have a heritage ambience with ancient wooden floors and Old Town views. He's got a castle-full of ideas for day trips, so look forward to staying longer than planned.

Penzion Ve Skalé (☎ 352 624 936; www.penzion veskale.cz; Nádražní 232; 61; s/d 650/1200Kč) Spacious and romantic rooms feature at this new pension just up the hill from the train station. You're forgoing an Old Town location, but the excellent-value rooms more than compensate. Discounts kick in on your second night.

Pizzeria na Růžka (☎ 606 433 282; cnr TG Masaryka & Kostelní; pizza 130Kč) Has a sunny Mediterranean ambience and excellent thin-crust wood-fired pizzas.

Hrnčírna Galerie Café (☎ 352 684 459; TG Masaryka 32; ✇ 2pm-6pm Mon-Fri, 10am-6pm Sat & Sun; 🖳) This funky main-square cafe conceals an art space for local artists and a cosy garden. Loket's best coffee and internet access comes as standard.

Pivovar Sv Florian (☎ 352 225 959; TG Masaryka 81) In the basement of the restored Hotel Císař Ferdinand, a few enthusiastic locals brew what could be Bohemia's best beer. Well, that's according to in-depth research by one guidebook writer anyway.

Getting There & Away

Buses run frequently from Karlovy Vary to Loket (26Kč, 20 minutes).

PLZEŇ

pop 175,000

Plzeň (Pilsen in German) is the hometown of Pilsner Urquell (Plzeňský prazdroj), the world's original lager beer. 'Urquell' (in German; *prazdroj* in Czech) means 'original source' or 'fountainhead', and the local style is now imitated across the world.

Pilsner Urquell is now owned by international conglomerate SAB-Miller, and some beer buffs claim the brew's not as good as before. One taste of the town's tasty *nefiltrované pivo* (unfiltered beer) will have you disputing that claim, and the original brewery is still an essential stop for beer aficionados.

The capital of West Bohemia is a sprawling industrial city, but has an attractive Old Town wrapped in tree-lined gardens. Plzeň's industrial heritage includes the massive Škoda Engineering Works. These armament factories were bombed heavily during WWII and now make machinery and locomotives.

Plzeň is an easy day trip from Prague, but the buzzing pubs of this university town also reward an overnight stay.

Orientation

The main bus station is west of the centre on Husova. Plzeň-hlavní nádraží, the main train station, is on the eastern side of town, 10 minutes' walk from nám Republiky, the Old Town square. Tram 2 (12Kč) goes from the train station through the centre of town and on to the bus station.

Information

There are left-luggage facilities at the **bus station** (per small/large bag 15Kč/25Kč; ✇ 6am-8pm) and the **train station** (per small/large bag 12/23Kč; ✇ 7am-7pm). Lockers at the train station are 30Kč per 24 hours.

City Information Centre (www.plzen.eu) nám Republiky (městské informační středisko; ☎ 378 035 330; nám Republiky 41; ✇ 9am-6pm); train station (☎ 972 524 313; ✇ 9am-7pm Apr-Sep, to 6pm Oct-Mar) Arranges accommodation.

Main post office (Solní 20)

Matrix Internet (Sedláčkova, per hr 40Kč; ✇ 8.30am-8pm Mon-Thu, 10am-8pm Fri, noon-10pm Sat & Sun) Down the arcade beside Oberbank.

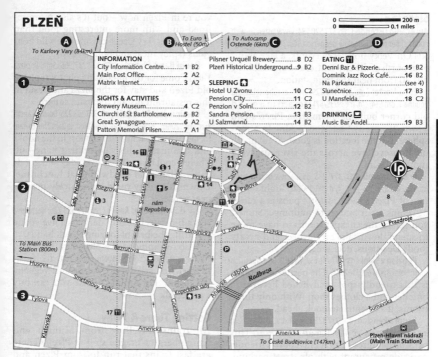

PLZEŇ

| | | | 0 ————— 200 m |
| | | | 0 ————— 0.1 miles |

INFORMATION		Pilsner Urquell Brewery..........8 D2	EATING 🍴
City Information Centre.........1 B2		Plzeň Historical Underground...9 B2	Denní Bar & Pizzerie...........15 B2
Main Post Office.................2 A2			Dominik Jazz Rock Café.........16 B2
Matrix Internet..................3 A2		SLEEPING 🛏	Na Parkanu....................(see 4)
		Hotel U Zvonu...................10 C2	Slunečnice.....................17 B3
SIGHTS & ACTIVITIES		Pension City...................11 C2	U Mansfelda....................18 C2
Brewery Museum..................4 C2		Penzion v Solní................12 B2	
Church of St Bartholomew........5 B2		Sandra Pension.................13 B3	DRINKING 🍷
Great Synagogue.................6 A2		U Salzmannů....................14 B2	Music Bar Anděl................19 B3
Patton Memorial Pilsen..........7 A1			

CZECH REPUBLIC

Sights

In summer people congregate at the outdoor beer bar in nám Republiky, the sunny Old Town square, beneath the Gothic **Church of St Bartholomew** (adult/child 20/10Kč; 🕙 10am-6pm Wed-Sat Apr-Sep, to 6pm Wed-Fri Oct-Dec). Inside the 13th-century structure there's a Gothic *Madonna* (1390) on the high altar and fine stained-glass windows. Climb the 102m church **tower** (adult/child 30/10Kč; 🕙 10am-6pm, weather dependent), the highest in Bohemia, for great views of Plzeň's rugged sprawl. Ask at the city information centre about guided tours of the church.

The **Brewery Museum** (☎ 377 235 574; www .prazdroj.cz; Veleslavínova 6; guided tour adult/child 120/100Kč, with text 100/60Kč; 🕙 10am-6pm Apr-Dec, to 5pm Jan-Mar) is in a medieval malt house. A combined entry (adult/child 250/130Kč) including the Pilsner Urquell Brewery is also available.

In previous centuries beer was brewed, stored, and served in the tunnels beneath the Old Town. The earliest were dug in the 14th century and the latest date from the 19th century. Take a 30-minute guided tour through 500m of tunnels at the **Plzeň Historical Underground** (☎ 377 225 214; Perlová 4; adult/child 55/35Kč; 🕙 9am-5pm Tue-Sun Jul-Sep, Wed-Sun Apr-Jun, Oct & Nov). The temperature is a chilly 10°C, so wrap up and bring a torch (flashlight).

The **Great Synagogue** (☎ 377 223 346; Sady Pětatřicátníků 11; adult/child 55/35Kč; 🕙 10am-6pm Mon-Sun Apr-Oct), west of the Old Town, is the third-largest in the world – only those in Jerusalem and Budapest are bigger. It was built in the Moorish style in 1892 by the 2000 Jews who lived in Plzeň at the time. English guides cost 500Kč extra. The building is often used for concerts and art and photography exhibitions.

North of the Great Synagogue is the **Patton Memorial Pilsen** (☎ 377 320 414; Podřezní 10; adult/child 45/30Kč; 🕙 9am-1pm & 2-5pm Tue-Sun), with an interesting and poignant display on the liberation of Plzeň in 1945 by the American army under General George Patton. Look for the jeep parked outside.

Beer fans should make the pilgrimage east across the river to the famous **Pilsner Urquell Brewery** (☎ 377 062 888; www.prazdroj.cz; guided tour adult/child 150/80Kč; 🕙 10am-6pm). A combined entry (adult/child 250/130Kč) including the Brewery Museum is also available.

Sleeping

Autocamp Ostende (☎ 377 520 194; www.ostende-web node.cz; per tent/bungalow per person 100/300Kč; ☺ May-Sep) On Velký Bolevecký rybník, a lake about 6km north of the city centre, and accessible by bus 20 from near the train station.

Euro Hostel (☎ 377 373 729; www.eurohostel.cz; Na Roudne 1; dm €14, s/d/tr €39/39/57) Housed in a grand old corner building 400m from Plzeň's Old Town. It's pretty basic and lacking in atmosphere, but the location is good. Walk north on Rooseveltova across the river and veer right on Luční.

U Salzmannů (☎ 377 235 855; www.usalzmannu .cz; Pražská 8; s 550-1350Kč, d 700-1900Kč) Right above one of Plzeň's most historic pubs is a range of rooms from budget to midrange. Should you go for the cheaper rooms to have more to spend downstairs on the beer and hearty food? Decisions, decisions.

Penzion v Solní (☎ 377 236 652; www.volny.cz/pension solni; Solní 8; s/d 600/1020Kč) The best deal in town is this friendly spot sandwiched between a butcher and a clothes shop. With only three rooms, it's essential to book ahead.

Sandra Pension (☎ 377 325 358; sandra.101@seznam .cz; Kopeckého sady 15; s/d incl breakfast 990/1260Kč) This pension has three clean rooms above a friendly parkside restaurant with off-street parking. Family rooms for four people are 2200Kč.

Pension City (☎ 377 326 069; www.pensioncityplzen .cz; Sady 5 kvetna 52; s/d incl breakfast 1050/1450Kč) On a quiet street near the river, the City is popular with both local and overseas guests. The welcoming English-speaking staff are a good source of local information.

Hotel U Zvonu (☎ 378 011 855; www.hotel-uzvonu .cz; Pražská 27; s/d 1850/2710Kč; 🖵) Owned by Czech ice-hockey legend Martin Straka, the four-star U Zvonu is at the edge of the Old Town and has modern rooms and facilities galore for business travellers. The flash 'Apartment 31' (3950Kč) is decorated with memorabilia from the owner's 18 seasons in the NHL.

Eating & Drinking

Na Parkanu (Veleslavínova 4; mains 100-150Kč) Attached to the Brewery Museum, Na Parkanu lures a mix of tourists and locals with good-value meals and a summer garden. Don't leave without trying the *nefiltrované pivo* (unfiltered beer). It's not our fault if you stay for another.

U Mansfelda (☎ 37 333 844; cnr Dřevěna & Křížíkovy sady; mains 110-160Kč) Sure, it's a pub – remember you're in Plzeň now – but it's also more refined and with more interesting food than other places. Try Czech cuisine like wild boar *gulaš* (spicy meat and potato soup).

Denní Bar & Pizzerie (☎ 377 237 965; Solní 9; pizza 110Kč) Come for the interesting photographs of old Plzeň and stay for the pizza and pasta in this restaurant just off the main square.

Dominik Jazz Rock Café (☎ 377 323 226; Dominikánská 3; mains 120Kč; ☺ 10am-11pm Mon-Wed, to 2am Thu, to 4am Fri, 1pm-2am Sat, 1pm-10pm Sun) Get lost in the nooks and crannies of this vast student hang-out. There's cool beats all day everyday and good-value salads and sandwiches at lunchtime. Downstairs they've added a nicely grungy beer garden.

By day **Music Bar Anděl** (☎ 377 323 226; Bezručova 7) is a hip cafe, but after dark it's a live venue featuring the best of touring Czech bands.

Also recommended is **Slunečnice** (Jungmanova 10; baguettes 60Kč; ☺ 7.30am-6pm) for its fresh sandwiches, self-service salads and vegetarian dishes. For around 100Kč you can buy a plate-full.

Getting There & Away

All trains travelling from Munich and Nuremberg to Prague stop at Plzeň. There are fast trains that run to/from Plzeň and Prague Smíchov (140Kč, 1½ hours, eight daily) and České Budějovice (172Kč, two hours, five daily).

If you're heading for Karlovy Vary, take a bus (80Kč, 1¾ hours, five daily). There are express buses to Prague (90Kč, 1½ hours, hourly), and trains (98Kč, 1½ hours, eight daily) and buses (69Kč, one hour, four daily) to/from Mariánské Lázně .

ČESKÉ BUDĚJOVICE
pop 100,000

After Plzeň, conduct the ultimate Bohemian beer taste test at České Budějovice (Budweis in German), the home of Budvar lager. The regional capital of South Bohemia is also a picturesque medieval city. Arcing from the town square are 18th-century arcades leading to bars that get raffishly rowdy on weekends – most fuelled by the town's prized export, of course.

Orientation

From the train station it's a 10-minute walk west down Lannova třída, then Kanovnická, to nám Přemysla Otakara II, the main

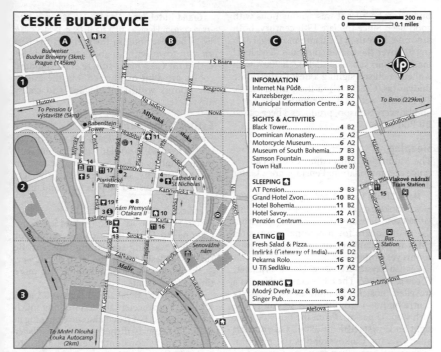

ČESKÉ BUDĚJOVICE

INFORMATION
Internet Na Půdě.............................1 B2
Kanzelsberger................................2 B2
Municipal Information Centre...3 A2

SIGHTS & ACTIVITIES
Black Tower....................................4 B2
Dominican Monastery..................5 A2
Motorcycle Museum....................6 A2
Museum of South Bohemia.......7 B3
Samson Fountain..........................8 B2
Town Hall....................................(see 3)

SLEEPING
AT Pension.....................................9 B3
Grand Hotel Zvon......................10 B2
Hotel Bohemia...........................11 B2
Hotel Savoy................................12 A1
Penzión Centrum......................13 A2

EATING
Fresh Salad & Pizza..................14 A2
Indická (Gateway of India)......15 D2
Pekarna Rolo..............................16 B2
U Tří Sedláků.............................17 A2

DRINKING
Modrý Dveře Jazz & Blues......18 A2
Singer Pub..................................19 A2

square. České Budějovice's flash new bus station is 300m southeast of the train station above the Mercury Central shopping centre on Dvořákova.

Information

Internet Na Půdě (Krajinská 28; 8am-10pm)
Kanzelsberger (386 352 584; Hroznová 17) English-language books.
Left luggage (per small/large bag 12/25Kč) bus station (6am-8pm); train station (2.30am-11pm)
Municipal Information Centre (Městské Informarční Centrum; 386 801 413; www.c-budejovice.cz; nám Přemysla Otakara II 2; 8.30am-6pm Mon-Fri, 8.30am-5pm Sat, 10am-4pm Sun May-Sep, 9am-5pm Mon-Fri, to 1pm Sat Oct-Apr) Books tickets, tours and accommodation, and has free internet.

Sights

The broad expanse of **Nám Přemysla Otakara II**, centred on the **Samson Fountain** (1727) and surrounded by 18th-century arcades, is one of the largest town squares in Europe. On the western side stands the baroque **town hall** (1731), topped with figures of the cardinal virtues: Justice, Wisdom, Courage and Prudence.

On the square's opposite corner is the 72m-tall **Black Tower** (adult/child 25/15Kč; 10am-6pm daily Jul & Aug, closed Mon Apr-Jun, Sep & Oct, closed Nov-Mar), dating from 1553.

The streets around the square, especially Česká, are lined with old burgher houses. West near the river is the former **Dominican monastery** (1265) with a tall tower and a splendid pulpit. Adjacent is the **Motorcycle Museum** (723 247 104; Piaristické nám; adult/child 50/20Kč; 10am-6pm Tue-Sun), with a fine collection of Czech Jawas and WWII Harley-Davidsons. The **Museum of South Bohemia** (Jihočeské muzeum; 387 929 328; adult/child 60/30Kč; 9am-12.30pm & 1-5.30pm Tue-Sun) showcases history, books, coins, weapons and wildlife.

The **Budweiser Budvar Brewery** (387 705 341; www.budvar.cz; cnr Pražská & K Světlé; adult/child 100/50Kč; 9am-4pm) is 3km north of the main square. Group tours run every day and the 2pm tour (Monday to Friday only) is open to individual travellers. The highlight is a glass of real-deal Budvar deep in the brewery's chilly cellars. Catch bus 2 to the Budvar stop (12Kč).

In 1876, the founders of US brewer Anheuser-Busch chose the brand name

Budweiser because it was synonymous with good beer. Since the late 19th century, both breweries have used the name and a legal arm wrestle over the brand continues. The legal machinations subsided slightly in 2007, with Anheuser-Busch signing a deal to distribute Budvar (as 'Czechvar') in the United States. To confuse matters, České Budějovice's second brewery Samson, produces a beer called BB Budweiser.

Sleeping

The Municipal Information Centre can arrange accommodation. Pensions are a better deal than hotels.

Motel Dlouhá Louka Autocamp (☎ 387 203 601; www.dlouhalouka.cz; Stromovka 8; camp sites per tent/s/d 75/750/1000Kč) Take bus 6 to 'Autocamping' from the main square for functional camp sites (May to September), or uninspiring motel rooms year-round.

Pension U výstavište (☎ 387 240 148; U výzstavište 17; r per person 270Kč) The city's closest thing to a travellers' hostel is 20 minutes from the city centre on bus 1 from the bus station to the fifth stop (U parku). From the bus stop veer right on U výstavište for 250m. On your left after crossing Čajkovského is the pension. New arrivals after 9pm won't be accepted.

AT Pension (☎ 603 441 069; www.atpension.cz; Dukelská 15; s/d 490/750Kč) In a quiet riverside neighbourhood a leafy stroll from the Old Town, this great-value spot still has the Czech Republic's biggest breakfasts (50Kč). Don't go making plans for a big lunch.

Penzión Centrum (☎ 387 311 801; www.penzion centrum.cz; Biskupská 130/3; s/d incl breakfast 1000/1400Kč) Huge rooms with queen-size beds and crisp linen make this an excellent reader-recommended spot near the main square. Right next door there's a good organic restaurant.

Hotel Savoy (☎ 387 201 719; www.hotel-savoy -cb.cz; B Smetany; s/d/tr 1350/1850/2350Kč; 🖳) Newly opened, the Savoy is already making an impression with spacious, modern rooms decorated with art deco–style furniture – trust us, the combination works – and a quiet location just outside the Old Town.

Hotel Bohemia (☎ 386 360 691; www.bohemiacb .cz; Hradební 20; s/d incl breakfast 1490/1790Kč) Carved wooden doors open to a restful interior in two old burghers' houses down a quiet street. The restaurant comes recommended by the tourist information office.

Grand Hotel Zvon (☎ 387 311 384; www.hotel -zvon.cz; nám Přemysla Otakara II 28; d 1800-3900Kč; 🖳) The best hotel in town enjoys the best view in town with an absolute ringside location on CB's main square. The standard rooms are a bit overpriced, but the executive rooms would be elegant and classy anywhere.

Eating & Drinking

Fresh Salad & Pizza (☎ 387 200 991; Hroznová 21; salads 70-90Kč, pizza 100-130Kč) This lunch spot with outdoor tables does exactly what it says on the tin; healthy salads and (slightly) less healthy pizza dished up by a fresh and funky youthful crew.

Indická (Gateway of India; ☎ 386 359 355; 1st fl, Chelčického 11; mains 100-150Kč; 😋 closed Sun) From Chennai to České, here comes respite for travellers wanting something different. Be sure to request spicy if you want it that way, as the kitchen is used to dealing with more timid Czech palates.

U Tři Sedláku (☎ 387 222 303; Hroznová 488; mains 101-170Kč) Locals celebrate that nothing much has changed at U Tři Sedláku since opening in 1897. Tasty meaty dishes go with the Pilsner Urquell that's constantly being shuffled to busy tables.

Pekarna Rolo (Dr Stejskala 7; 😋 7.30am-6pm Mon-Fri, 7am-noon Sat) Superb baked goods, open sandwiches and fresh fruit cover all the bases for an on-the-go combination of eating and strolling.

Singer Pub (Česká 55) With Czech and Irish beers, plus good cocktails, don't be surprised if you get the urge to rustle up something on the Singer sewing machines on every table. If not, challenge the regulars to a game of *foosball* with a soundtrack of noisy rock.

modrý dveře jazz & blues (☎ 386 359 958; Biskupská 1) By day modrý dveře is a welcoming bar-cafe with vintage pics of Sinatra. At dusk the lights dim for regular jazz piano gigs on Wednesdays (from 7pm) and live blues and jazz on Thursdays (from 8pm). Tell them Frank sent you.

Getting There & Away

There are trains from České Budějovice to Prague (211Kč, 2½ hours, hourly) and Plzeň (172Kč, two hours, five daily). Frequent trains trundle to Český Krumlov (44Kč, 45 minutes).

WORTH THE TRIP: TÁBOR

The Old Town of Tábor was a formidable natural defence against invasion. Six centuries ago, the Hussite religious sect founded Tábor as a military bastion in defiance of Catholic Europe. Based on the biblical concept that 'nothing is mine and nothing is yours, because everyone owns the community equally', all Hussites participated in communal work, and possessions were allocated equally in the town's main square. This exceptional nonconformism gave the word 'bohemian' the connotations we associate with it today. Religious structures dating from the 15th century line the town square and it's possible to visit the 650m stretch of underground tunnels the Hussites used for refuge in times of war.

Penzión Alfa (☎ 381 256 165; www.pensionalfa.zde.cz; Klokotská; s/d/tr 570/900/1300Kč) occupies a cosy corner just metres from the main square. Downstairs get your Geronimojo back at the funky Native American–themed cafe.

The annual **Tabor Meetings Festival** is held on the second weekend in September. Expect medieval merriment with lots of food, drink and colourfully dressed locals celebrating their Hussite heritage. See www.tabor.cz for more information.

Travel to Tábor by bus, either from Prague Florenc (86Kč, 1½ hours, eight daily) or České Budějovice (62Kč, one hour, 15 daily).

Heading for Vienna (620Kč, four hours, two daily) you'll have to change at Gmünd, or take a direct train to Linz (420Kč, 2¼ hours, one daily) and change there.

The bus to Brno (194Kč, 3½ to 4½ hours, four daily) travels via Telč (92Kč, two hours). Buses regularly shuttle south to Český Krumlov (32Kč, 45 minutes).

HLUBOKÁ NAD VLTAVOU

Hluboká nad Vltavou's neo-Gothic **chateau** (☎ 387 843 911; www.zamek-hluboka.eu; 9am-5pm Jul & Aug, to 5pm Tue-Sun May-Jun, to 4.30pm Apr, Sep & Oct), was rebuilt by the Schwarzenberg family in 1841–71 with turrets and crenellations inspired by England's Windsor Castle. The palace's 144 rooms remained in use up to WWII.

There are three English-language tours available. Tour 1 (adult/child 220/150Kč) focuses on the castle's public areas, while Tour 2 (adult/child 230/150Kč) goes behind the scenes in the castle apartments. Tour 3 (adult/child 170/80Kč) explores the kitchens. Tours in Czech are 90Kč cheaper. The park is open throughout the year (no admission charge). The **information centre** (☎ 387 966 164; www.visithluboka.cz; Masarykova 35) can help with accommodation, but Hluboká is an easy day trip from České Budějovice by local bus (18Kč, 20 minutes, two hourly).

ČESKÝ KRUMLOV

pop 14,600

Crowned by a stunning castle, and centred on an elegant Old Town square, Český Krumlov's

Renaissance and baroque buildings enclose the meandering arc of the Vltava river.

During summer, countless photographic memory cards are filled as pigeons dart through busloads of day-tripping tourists exploring the town's narrow lanes and footbridges. Either side of July and August, the town is (slightly) more subdued and secluded. Come in winter to experience the castle blanketed in snow.

The town's original Gothic fortress was rebuilt as an imposing Renaissance chateau in the 16th century. Since the 18th century the town's appearance is largely unchanged, and careful renovation and restoration has replaced the architectural neglect of the communist era. In 1992 Český Krumlov was granted Unesco World Heritage status.

For too many travellers, Český Krumlov is just a hurried day trip, but its combination of glorious architecture and watery fun on the Vltava deserve more attention. Add in the rugged attractions of the nearby Šumava region, and you can easily fill three days.

Orientation

The bus station is east of the town centre, but if you're arriving from České Budějovice get off at the Špičák bus stop (the first in the town centre, just after you pass beneath a road bridge). The train station is 1.5km north of the town centre; buses 1, 2 and 3 go from the station to the Špičák bus stop. From the bridge over the main road beside the bus stop, Latrán leads south into town.

ČESKÝ KRUMLOV

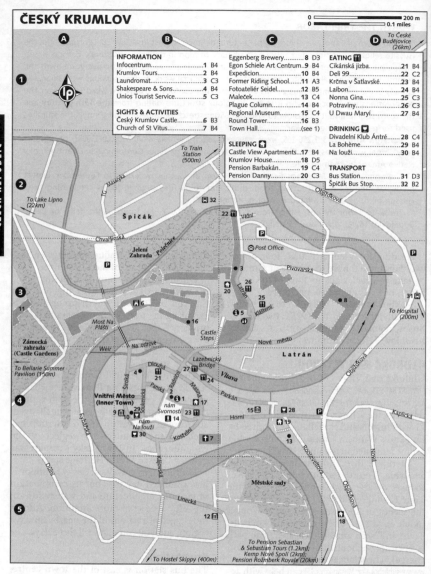

INFORMATION	
Infocentrum	**1** B4
Krumlov Tours	**2** B4
Laundromat	**3** C3
Shakespeare & Sons	**4** B4
Unios Tourist Service	**5** C3
SIGHTS & ACTIVITIES	
Český Krumlov Castle	**6** B3
Church of St Vitus	**7** B4

Eggenberg Brewery	**8** D3
Egon Schiele Art Centrum	**9** B4
Expedicion	**10** B4
Former Riding School	**11** A3
Fotoateliér Seidel	**12** B5
Maleček	**13** C4
Plague Column	**14** B4
Regional Museum	**15** C4
Round Tower	**16** B3
Town Hall	(see 1)

SLEEPING	
Castle View Apartments	**17** B4
Krumlov House	**18** D5
Pension Barbakán	**19** C4
Pension Danny	**20** C3

EATING	
Cikánská jizba	**21** B4
Deli 99	**22** C2
Krčma v Šatlavské	**23** B4
Laibon	**24** B4
Nonna Gina	**25** C3
Potraviny	**26** C3
U Dwau Maryí	**27** B4

DRINKING	
Divadelní Klub Ántré	**28** C4
La Bohème	**29** B4
Na louži	**30** B4

TRANSPORT	
Bus Station	**31** D3
Špičák Bus Stop	**32** B2

Don't take a car into the centre of the Old Town; use one of the car parks around the perimeter. The Chvalšinská car-park, north of the Old Town, is most convenient.

Information

There is wi-fi at Egon Schiele Art Centrum cafe (opposite) and Deli 99 (p138).

Infocentrum (☎ 380 704 622; www.ckrumlov.cz; nám Svornosti 1; 🕘 9am-6pm) Transport and accommodation info, maps, internet access (5Kč per five minutes) and audio guides (100Kč per hour). A guide for disabled visitors is available. A good source of information on the Šumava region.

Krumlov Tours (☎ 723 069 561; www.krumlovtours .com; nám Svornosti; per person 200-250Kč) Has walking tours with regular departure times; good for solo travellers.

Laundromat (☎ 380 713 153; Pension Lobo, Latrán 73; per load 140Kč; 9am-noon & 1-4pm Mon-Fri, 9-11am Sat)

Oldřiška Baloušková (oldriskab@gmail.com) Offers tailored tours (per hr 450Kč).

Shakespeare & Sons (☎ 380 711 203; Soukenická 44; 11am-7pm) Good for English-language paperbacks.

Unios Tourist Service (☎ 380 725 110; www.visit ceskykrumlov.cz; Zámek 57; 9am-6pm) Accommodation and an internet cafe with international calling.

Sights

The Old Town, almost encircled by the Vltava River, is watched over by **Český Krumlov Castle** (☎ 380 704 721; www.castle.ckrumlov.cz; 9am-6pm Tue-Sun Jun-Aug, to 5pm Apr, May, Sep & Oct) and its ornately decorated **Round Tower** (45/30Kč). Three different guided tours are on offer: **Tour I** (adult/child 230/130Kč) takes in the Renaissance and baroque apartments that the aristocratic Rožmberk and Schwarzenberg families called home; **Tour II** (adult/child 180/100Kč) visits the Schwarzenberg apartments used in the 19th century; and the **Theatre Tour** (adult/child 350/200Kč; 10am-4pm Tue-Sun May-Oct) explores the chateau's remarkable rococo theatre, complete with original stage machinery. Wandering through the courtyards and gardens is free.

The path beyond the fourth courtyard leads across the spectacular **Most ná Plášti** to the castle gardens. A ramp to the right leads to the **former riding school**, now a restaurant. The relief above the door shows cherubs offering the head and boots of a vanquished Turk – a reference to Adolf von Schwarzenberg, who conquered the Turkish fortress of Raab in the 16th century. From here the Italian-style **Zámecká zahrada** (castle gardens) stretch away towards the **Bellarie summer pavilion**.

Across the river is nám Svornosti, the Old Town square, overlooked by the Gothic **town hall** and a baroque **plague column** (1716). Above is the striking Gothic **Church of St Vitus** (1439), and nearby is the **Regional Museum** (☎ 380 711 674; Horní 152; adult/child 50/25Kč; 10am-6pm Jul & Aug, 10am-5pm May, Jun & Sep, 9am-4pm Tue-Fri, 1-4pm Sat & Sun, Mar, Apr & Oct-Dec), with an interactive model of the town c 1800.

The **Egon Schiele Art Centrum** (☎ 380 704 011; www.schielartcentrum.cz; Široká 70-72; adult/child 120/700Kč; 10am-6pm) is an excellent gallery showcasing the Viennese painter Egon Schiele (1890–1918). The attached **cafe** (10am-7pm) is appropriately arty and has a good selection of Moravian wines.

Newly opened in 2008, the **Fotoateliér Seidel** (☎ 380 704 611; Linecká 272; www.seidel.ckrumlov.cz; admission 130Kč; 9am-6pm) presents a retrospective of the work of local photographers Josef Seidel and his son František. Especially poignant are the images recording early-20th-century life in nearby mountain villages.

The **Eggenberg Brewery** (☎ 380 711 225; www .eggenberg.cz; Latrán 27; tours with/without tasting 130/100Kč; tours 11am) is also where most canoeing and rafting trips end. Relive your experiences on the Vltava's gentle rapids in the brewery's beer garden. Book brewery tours at Infocentrum.

Activities

Rent canoes, rafts and rubber rings from **Maleček** (☎ 380 712 508; http://en.malecek.cz; Rooseveltova 28; 9am-5pm). A half-hour splash in a two-person canoe costs 350Kč, or you can rent a canoe for a full day trip down the river from Rožmberk (850Kč, six to eight hours). Maleček also has sedate river trips through Český Krumlov on giant wooden rafts seating up to 36 people (290Kč, 45 minutes).

Sebastian Tours (☎ 607 100 234; www.sebastianck -tours.com; 5 Května Ul, Plešivec; per person 450Kč) can get you discovering southern Bohemia on guided tours including stops at Hluboká nad Vltavou and České Budějovice.

Expedicion (☎ 607 963 868; www.expedicion.cz; Soukenická 33; 9am- 7pm) rents bikes (280Kč a day), arranges horse-riding (250Kč an hour) and operates action-packed day trips (1680Kč including lunch) incorporating horse-riding, fishing, mountain biking and rafting in the nearby Šumava region.

Festivals & Events

Infocentrum sells tickets to most festivals.

Five-Petalled Rose Festival In mid-June; features two days of street performers, medieval games.

Chamber Music Festival Late June to early July.

Český Krumlov International Music Festival (www .festivalkrumlov.cz) July to August.

Jazz at Summer's End Festival (www.jazz-krumlov .cz) Mid-September.

Sleeping

Kemp Nové Spolí (☎ 380 728 305; www.kempkrumlov.cz; camp sites per person 70Kč; Jun-Aug) Located on the Vltava River about 2km south of town, with basic facilities but an idyllic location. Take bus 3 from the train or bus station to the Spolí mat. šk. stop, otherwise it's a half-hour walk from the Old Town.

CZECH REPUBLIC

Krumlov House (☎ 380 711 935; www.krumlovhostel .com; Rooseveltova 68; dm/d 300/650Kč) Perched above the river, Krumlov House is friendly and comfortable and has plenty of books, DVDs and local info to feed your inner backpacker. Lots of day trips are also on offer.

Hostel Skippy (☎ 380 728 380; www.skippy.wz.cz; Plesivecka 123; dm/d 300/650Kč) Smaller and less boisterous than some other CK hostels, Skippy is more like staying at a friend's place. The creative owner, 'Skippy', is an arty muso type, so you might be surprised with an impromptu jam session in the front room.

our pick **Pension Sebastian** (☎ 608 357 581; www .sebastianck.com; 5 Května Ul, Plešivec; s/d/tr incl breakfast 790/990/1490Kč; ☯ Apr-Oct) An excellent option just 10 minutes' walk from the Old Town, and therefore slightly cheaper. Larger four-bed rooms (1780Kč) are good for families and there's a pretty garden for end-of-day drinks and diary writing. The well-travelled owners also run tours of the surrounding region (p137).

Pension Rožmberk Royale (☎ 380 727 858; www .pensionroyale.cz; Rožmberk nad Vltavou; s/d 800/1300Kč) This new pension has an absolute riverfront location in the sleepy village of Rožmberk nad Vltavou. A castle looms above the village, and it's a short, scenic bus ride from Český Krumlov (28Kč, 35 minutes, seven daily). A pleasant stroll just around the river reveals a good fish restaurant.

Pension Danny (☎ 380 712 710; www.pensiondanny .cz; Latrán 72; d incl breakfast from 990Kč) Exposed timber beams and refurbished bathrooms add up to a good-value Old Town location. Have breakfast in your room and enjoy views of romantic CK at the same time.

Pension Barbakán (☎ 380 717 017; www.barbakan.cz; Horní 26; s/d incl breakfast from 1700Kč; ☐) Originally the town's gunpowder arsenal, Barbakán now creates fireworks of its own, with supercomfy rooms featuring bright and cosy wooden decor. Sit in the grill restaurant (mains 140Kč to 210Kč) and watch the tubing and rafting action below.

Castle View Apartments (☎ 731 108 677; http:// accommodation-cesky-krumlov.castleview.cz; Satlavska; d incl breakfast 2900-3500Kč) Furnished apartments are better value than top-end hotels in Český Krumlov. Castle View has seven apartments with spacious bathrooms and decor combining sophistication and romance in equal measure. Five of the apartments can sleep up to five people.

Infocentrum can also recommend other furnished apartments, easily Krumlov's best option for romantic couples.

Eating

Booking for dinner in July and August is recommended.

our pick **Laibon** (☎ 728 676 654; Parkán 105; mains 90-180Kč) Candles and vaulted ceilings create a great boho ambience in the best little vegetarian teahouse in Bohemia. The riverside setting's pretty fine as well. Order the blueberry dumplings for dessert and don't miss the special 'yeast beer' from the Bernard brewery. Ask David, the well-travelled owner, where he's headed next.

Nonna Gina (☎ 380 717 187; Klášteriní ul 52; pizza 90-155Kč) Authentic Italian flavours from the authentic Italian Massaro family feature in this pizzeria down a quiet lane. Grab an outdoor table and pretend you're in Naples.

Krčma v Šatlavské (☎ 380 713 344; Horní 157; mains 100-150Kč) Nirvana for meat-lovers, this medieval barbecue cellar serves sizzling platters in a funky labyrinth illuminated by candles and the flickering flames of open grills.

U Dwau Maryí (☎ 380 717 228; Parkán 104; mains 100-200Kč) The 'Two Marys' medieval tavern recreates old recipes and is your best chance to try dishes made with buckwheat and millet; all tastier than they sound. Wash the food down with a goblet of mead (a drink made with honey) or a 21st-century Pilsner. In summer it's a tad touristy, but the stunning riverside castle views easily compensate.

Cikánská jizba (☎ 380 717 585; Dlouhá 31; mains 120-210Kč; ☯ 3pm-midnight Mon-Sat) At 'The Gypsy Room' there's live Roma music at the weekends to go with the menu of meaty Czech favourites.

Also recommended:

Deli 99 (Latrán 106; snacks 50-80Kč; ☯ 7am-7pm Mon-Sat, 8am-5pm Sun) Bagels, sandwiches, organic juices and wi-fi internet all tick the box marked 'Slightly Homesick Traveller'.

Potraviny (supermarket; Latrán 55) Self-catering central, especially if you're going rafting.

Drinking

Na louži (☎ 380 711 280; Kájovská 66) Nothing's changed in this wood-panelled *pivo* parlour for almost a century. Locals and tourists pack Na louži for huge meals and tasty dark beer from the Eggenberg brewery.

La Bohème (Soukenická 34; ☯ from 5pm) With art-deco styling, La Bohème is your best bet or a quieter spot with good cocktails. It's a favourite for locals avoiding the tourist rush. From 5pm to 8pm, there's a 30% 'Happy Hour' discount.

Divadelní Klub Ántré (☎ 602 336 320; Horní Braná 2; www.klubantre.cz) This arty cafe-bar in the town theatre has a sprawling terrace overlooking the river. There's free wi-fi, and it's always worth dropping by to see if any music gigs are scheduled.

Getting There & Away

Buses depart from Prague Florenc to Český Krumlov (160Kč, three hours, daily) via České Budějovice. **Student Agency** (www.student agency.cz) leaves from Prague Ná Knížecí (140Kč). In July and August this route is very popular and booking a couple of days ahead is recommended.

Local buses (32Kč, 50 minutes, seven daily) and trains (46Kč, one hour, eight daily) run to České Budějovice, for onward travel to Brno or Plzeň.

The most straighforward way to Austria are the direct shuttle buses offered by several Český Krumlov companies. Stiff competition keeps prices relatively low; Vienna (1100Kč), Salzburg (1100Kč) and Linz (350Kč). From Linz there are regular trains to Vienna, Salzburg and Munich. Public transport to Austria involves heading to north to České Budějovice and catching a train to Linz (two hours).

ŠUMAVA

The Šumava region's forested hills stretch for 125km along the border with Austria and Germany. The highest summit is Plechý (1378m), west of Horní Planá. Before 1989 the range was divided by the Iron Curtain, a line of fences, watchtowers, armed guards and dog patrols between Western Europe and the communist East. Many Czechs made a bid for freedom by creeping through the forests at night. In a different era, the hills are popular for hiking, cycling and cross-country skiing.

The **Povydří trail** along the Vydra (Otter) River in the northern Šumava is one of the national park's most popular walk. It's an easy 7km hike along a deep, forested river valley between Čeňkova Pila and Antýgl. Buses run between Sušice and Modrava, stopping at Čeňkova Pila and Antýgl. Plenty of pension accommodation is available.

Around the peak of **Boubín** (1362m), the 46-hectare *prales* (virgin forest) is the only part of the Šumava forest that is largely untouched by human activity. The trailhead is 2km north-east of the zastávka Zátoň train stop (not Zátoň town train station) at Kaplice, where there is car parking as well as basic camping facilities. From here it's an easy 2.5km to U pralesa Lake on a blue and green marked trail. Remain on the blue trail for a further 7.5km to reach the summit of Boubín. Return by following the trail southwest. The complete loop takes about five hours.

If you'd rather use wheels, the **Šumava Trail** is a weeklong bike ride through dense forests and past mountain streams from Český Krumlov to Domažlice.

If lying in the sun sounds more fun, head to **Lake Lipno**, a 30km-long reservoir south of Český Krumlov. Known as 'the Czech Riviera', it's lined with camping grounds, swimming areas and water-sports centres; there's even a yacht marina at Lipno nad Vltavou.

Infocentrum (p136) in Český Krumlov has a wall-full of Šumava suggestions.

A nightly train runs from České Budějovice (121Kč, three hours) and Český Krumlov (83Kč, one hour 40 minutes), to Volary, calling at Horní Planá and Nová Pec on Lake Lipno. From May to August, buses cover a similar route (80Kč, two hours).

From Volary, trains continue north to Strakonice via Zátoň (28Kč, 30 minutes, four daily).

The Povydří trail is best approached from Sušice, which can be reached by direct bus from Prague Ná Knížecí (121Kč, 2½ hours, two daily). Another bus links Sušice with Čeňkova Pila and Antýgl (46Kč, one hour, two or three daily).

See Infocentrum (p136) in Český Krumlov for detailed transport information.

ADRŠPACH-TEPLICE ROCKS

The Czech Republic's most extraordinary scenery lies near Poland, in a protected landscape region known as the Adršpach-Teplice Rocks (Adršpašsko-Teplické skály). Thick layers of stratified sandstone have been eroded and fissured by water and frost to form giant towers and deep, narrow chasms. Discovered by mountaineers in the 19th century, the region is popular with rock climbers and hikers. Sandy trails lead through pine-scented forests and loop through the

CZECH REPUBLIC

pinnacles, assisted occasionally by ladders and stairs.

Two main formations – **Adršpach Rock Town** (Adršpašské skalní město) and **Teplice Rock Town** (Teplické skalní město) – comprise a single nature reserve. At each entrance there's a **ticket booth** (adult/child 60/30Kč; ☾ 8am-6pm Apr-Nov) with handy 1:25,000 trail maps on offer. Outside the official opening hours, enter for free. It's an additional 25Kč for a boat trip on a compact lake secreted in the rocks. Buy tickets on the boat.

There's a small **information office** (☎ 491 586 012; www.skalyadrspach.cz; ☾ 8am-12.30pm & 1-5pm Apr-Oct) near Adršpach train station. In summer the trails are busy; book accommodation at least a week ahead. In winter – snow lingers to mid-April – you'll have the area mainly to yourself but some trails may be closed. Try and avoid weekends, when Polish busloads visit on day trips.

If you're pushed for time, walk the green loop trail (1½ hours), starting at Adršpach and progressing through deep mossy ravines and soaring rock towers to the **Great Lookout** (Velké panorama). Admire the view of pinnacles escalating above the pines, before threading through the **Mouse Hole** (Myší dírá), a vast vertical fissure barely a shoulder-width wide.

The blue loop trail (2½ hours), starting at Teplice, passes a metal staircase leading strenuously to **Střmen**, a rock tower once occupied by an outlaw's timber castle, before continuing through the area's most spectacular pinnacles to the chilly ravine of **Siberia** (Sibiř). An excellent day hike (four to five hours), taking in the region's highlights, links the head of the Teplice trail, beyond Sibiř, to Adršpach via the **Wolf Gorge** (Vlčí rokle). Return from Adršpach to Teplice by walking along the road (one hour) or by train (10 minutes).

To experience the rock towns more closely, contact Tomas Pycha at **Tomadventure** (☎ 775 158 838; www.tomadventure.org, climbing per hr 200Kč). Climbing instruction for beginners to advanced is available, and Tomas also rents out bicycles for 250Kč per day.

Sleeping & Eating

In Teplice nad Metují-Skály, the **Hotel Orlík** (☎ 491 581 025; www.orlik.hotel-cz.com; s/d incl breakfast 450/900Kč) is a good place to recharge with a popular bar. Nearby **Pension Skály** (☎ 491

581 174; www.adrspach-skaly.cz; Střmenské Podhradi 132; s/d incl breakfast 500/1000Kč) has cosy rooms for post-hike relaxation.

Eating at the rock towns is limited to a few over-priced fast-food emporia, and you're better off to eat where you're staying.

In Adršpach, the new **Hotel Javor** (☎ 491 586 182; www.hotel-adrspach.cz; s/d incl breakfast 850/1700Kč; ▣) has 41 smart rooms decked out in modern furniture with skylights galore. Downstairs the restaurant also achieves a lighter touch with good salads and pasta. If you're really hungry after hiking, they can also whistle you up a meaty mixed grill.

In a quiet setting between Teplice and Adršpach, the **Skalní Mlýn** (☎ 491 586 961; www.skalni-mlyn.cz; s/d incl breakfast 500/1000Kč) has rustic rooms and friendly dogs in a restored river mill. It's best if you have your own transport to get here.

Getting There & Away

There are direct buses from Prague's Černý Most metro station to Trutnov (152Kč, 2¾ hours, hourly).

Trains (eight daily) rattle from Trutnov to Adršpach (40Kč, one hour) and Teplice nad Metují (46Kč, 1¼ hours).

MORAVIA

Away from the tourist commotion of Prague and Bohemia, Moravia provides a quietly authentic experience. Olomouc and Telč are two of the country's prettiest towns, and bustling Brno serves up Czech urban ambience, without the tourists. Mildly active travellers can explore the stunning landscapes of the Moravian Karst region and everyone can celebrate with a good vintage from the Moravian wine country.

BRNO
pop 387,200

The attractions of Brno may not seem that obvious after the showy buzz of Prague, but after a short stay you'll see the traditional Moravian reserve melting away in the Old Town's bars and restaurants. Leave the touristy commotion back west in the capital – you'll have a stellar array of museums and galleries almost to yourself. Despite having a population of less than 400,000, Brno behaves just like the confident, cosmopolitan capital (ie of Moravia) that it is.

BRNO

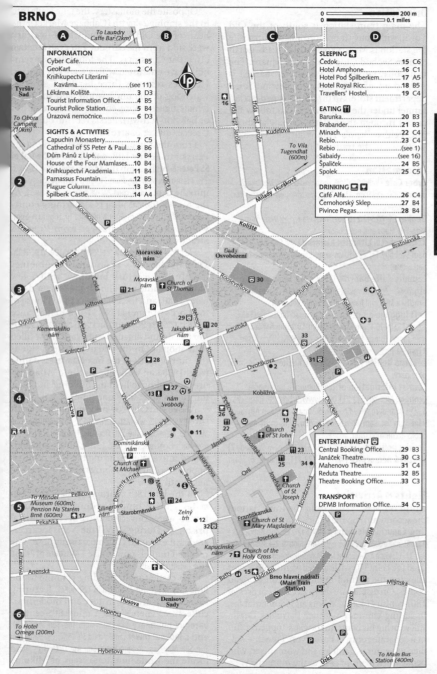

CZECH REPUBLIC

Orientation

The main train station is south of the Old Town, with a busy tram stop outside. Opposite the station is Masarykova, which leads north to nám Svobody, the city's main square. The main bus station (Brno ÚAN Zvonařka) is 800m south of the train station, beyond Tesco department store. Go through the pedestrian tunnel under the train tracks, and follow the crowd through the Galerie Vaňkovka shopping centre. Brno's Tuřany airport is 7.5km southeast of the train station.

Information

Cyber Cafe (Velký Spalicek shopping centre, Mečova 2; per hr 60Kč; 9am-11pm) Also provides wi-fi access for laptop toters.
Geokart (542 216 561; Vachova 8; 9am-6pm Mon-Fri) Maps and guidebooks.
Knihkupectví Literární Kavárna (542 217 954; nám Svobody 13; 10am-7pm) English-language books and a cafe.
Laundry Caffe Bar (775 602 167; Skřivanova 1; per 6kg 70Kč; 2pm-midnight) Catch tram 6 or 7 to the Hrnčířská stop and have a drink while you wait.
Left luggage bus station (per day small/big bag 9/18Kč; 5.15am-10.15pm Mon-Fri, 6am-10.15pm Sat & Sun); train station (ground fl; lockers per 24hr 90Kč; closed 11pm-4am)
Lékárna Koliště (545 424 811; Koliště 47) A 24-hour pharmacy.
Tourist information office (Kulturní a Informační Centrum; KIC; 542 211 090; www.ticbrno.cz; Radnická 8; 8am-6pm Mon-Fri, 9am-5.30pm Sat & Sun Apr-Sep, 9am-5pm Sat, 9am-3pm Sun Nov-Mar) Sells maps and books accommodation.
Tourist police station (974 626 100; nám Svobody 7)
Úrazová nemocnice (545 538 111; Ponávka 6) Main hospital.

Sights & Activities

North on Masarykova from the train station, the second turn on the left leads to the compelling **Capuchin Monastery** (542 213 232; Kapucínské nám 5; adult/child 60/30Kč; 9am-noon & 2-4.30pm Mon-Sat, 11-11.45am & 2-4.30pm Sun May-Sep, closed Mon Oct-Apr, closed Dec 15-Jan 31), with a well-ventilated crypt allowing the natural mummification of dead bodies. On display are the desiccated corpses of 18th-century monks, abbots and local notables, including chimney-sweeper Barnabas Orelli, still wearing his boots. In the glass-topped coffin in a separate room is Baron von Trenck – soldier, adventurer, gambler and womaniser, who bequeathed loads of cash to the monastery.

Opposite the monastery, the lane leads into to the sloping **Zelný trh** (Cabbage Market), the heart of the Old Town, and where live carp were sold from the baroque **Parnassus Fountain** (1695) at Christmas. The fountain is a symbolic cave encrusted with allegorical figures. Hercules restrains three-headed Cerberus, watchdog of the underworld, and the three female figures represent the ancient empires of Babylon (crown), Persia (cornucopia) and Greece (quiver of arrows).

From the top of the Cabbage Market take Petrská to Petrov Hill, site of the **Cathedral of SS Peter & Paul**. Climb the **tower** (adult/child 35/30Kč; 11am-6pm Mon-Sat, from 11.45am Sun) or descend into the **crypt** (adult/child 20/10Kč; as per tower). At the foot of the cathdral is a charming courtyard **cafe** (11am-9pm Mon-Thu, to 10pm Fri-Sun), which serves excellent beer from Prague's Strahov monastery.

Having survived a recent spruce up, **Nám Svobody**, the city's main square, combines mainly 19th-century buildings with a few older monuments. The **plague column** dates from 1680, and the **Dům Pánů z Lipé** (House of the Lords of Lipé) at No 17 is a Renaissance palace (1589–96) with a 19th-century *sgraffito* facade and arcaded courtyard (now filled with shops). On the square's eastern side is the quirky **House of the Four Mamlases**, dating from 1928 and with four moronic 'Atlas' figures struggling to hold the building and their loincloths up at the same time.

Above the Old Town looms **Špilberk Castle** (542 215 012; www.spilberk.cz; 9am-6pm Tue-Sun May-Sep, 9am-5pm Tue-Sun Oct-Apr, 10am-5pm Wed-Sun Nov-Mar). Founded in the 13th century and converted into a citadel during the 17th century, opponents of the Habsburgs were imprisoned here until 1855.

In the late 18th century, parts of the **casemates** – brick tunnels within the fortifications – were converted into cells for political prisoners. During WWII the Nazis incarcerated and executed Czech partisans here. The restored tunnels now house a **Museum of Prison Life** (adult/child 70/35Kč).

The castle's main building is home to the **Brno City Museum** (adult/child 120/60Kč), featuring Renaissance art, city history and modern architecture. There's also a mid-18th-century **baroque pharmacy** (9am-6pm Tue-Sun May-Sep), and a **lookout tower** (adult/child 30/15Kč; 9am-6pm Tue-Sun May-Sep, to 5pm Sat & Sun Apr-Oct). Try and locate the white limestone crags of Mikulov on the southern horizon. A combined ticket (adult/child 120/60Kč) allows admission to the casemates, museum and tower.

Gregor Mendel (1822–84), the Augustinian monk whose studies of peas and bees at Brno's Abbey of St Thomas established modern genetics, is commemorated in the **Mendel Museum** (☎ 543 424 043; www.mendel-museum.org; Mendlovo nám 1; adult/child 60/30Kč; ☯ 10am-6pm Tue-Sun Apr-Oct, to 5pm Nov-Mar), housed in the Abbey itself. In the garden are the foundations of Mendel's original greenhouse.

Fans of modern architecture will love Brno's cubist, functionalist and internationalist styles. The finest is the functionalist **Vila Tugendhat** (☎ 545 212 118; www.tugendhat-villa.cz; Černopolni 45; adult/child 120/60Kč; ☯ 10am-6pm Wed-Sun), northeast of town, and designed by Mies van der Rohe in 1930. Catch tram 3, 5 or 11 to the Dětská nemocnice stop. Advance booking is essential.

Ask at the tourist information office about Brno's many other museums and art galleries.

Festivals & Events

During Easter, there's the **Festival of Sacred Music** (www.mhf-brno.cz). The noisiest event is mid-August's **Moto Grand Prix** (www.motogp.com), when the city packs out with motorbike fans. The race circuit is off the D1 road to Prague, 10km west of Brno. Accommodation can be difficult to find on race weekend.

Only slightly less noisy is the **Ignis Brunensis Fireworks Festival** (www.ignisbrunensis.cz; ☯ late May-early Jun) with fireworks geeks from around the world.

Sleeping

Accommodation increases in cost and demand when major trade fairs are on, especially IBF (mid-April) and MSV (mid-September). See www.bvv.cz for a calendar of events.

Čedok (☎ 542 321 267; Nádražní 10/12) Books accommodation in student dormitories during July and August.

Obora Camping (☎ 546 223 334; www.autocamp obora.cz; per tent/bungalow per person 80/230Kč; ☯ May-Sep) At the Brněnská přehrada (Brno dam), northwest of the city centre. Take tram 1 from the train station to the zoo and change to bus 103 alighting at the seventh stop.

Travellers' Hostel (☎ 542 213 573; www.travellers.cz; Jánská 22; dm incl breakfast 290Kč; ☯ Jul & Aug) Set in the heart of the Old Town, this place provides the most central cheap beds in the city – for July and August anyway.

Hotel Omega (☎ 543 213 876; www.hotelomega.cz; Křídloviská 19b; s/d incl breakfast 950/1450Kč; ☐) In a quiet neighbourhood, 1km from the centre, this tourist information favourite has spacious rooms with modern pine furniture. A couple of three- and four-bed rooms cater to travelling families. Catch tram 1 from the railway station to the Václavská stop.

Penzion Na Starém Brně (☎ 543 247 872; www .pension-brno.com; Mendlovo nám 1a; s/d incl breakfast 960/1290Kč) An atmospheric Augustinian monastery conceals five compact rooms that come reader-recommended. Just metres away there's a Moravian wine bar.

Hotel Amphone (☎ 545 428 310; www.amphone.cz; trída kpt Jaroše 29; s/d incl breakfast from 990/1390Kč; ☐) On an elegant tree-lined street, the friendly Amphone has bright and airy rooms around a garden. New carpet and a lick of paint wouldn't go amiss though.

Hotel Pod Špilberkem (☎ 543 235 003; www .hotelpodspilberkem.cz; Pekařská 10; s/d incl breakfast 1400/1550Kč) Tucked away near the castle are quiet rooms clustered around a central courtyard. The secure car-park is a good option for self-drive travellers.

Hotel Royal Ricc (☎ 542 219 262; www.romantichotels .cz; Starobrněnská 10; s/d incl breakfast from 3500/3900Kč; ☒ ☐) An utterly captivating mix of traditional and modern, this intimate Old Town hotel with 29 rooms would be right at home in Paris or Venice. Rates fall by around 25% on weekends.

Eating

Rebio (☎ 542 211 110; Orli 16; mains 70-100Kč; ☯ 8am-8pm Mon-Fri, 10am-3pm Sat) Healthy risottos and vegie pies stand out in this self-service spot. There's another all-veg branch (open 9am to 9pm Monday to Friday, 10am to 10pm Saturday and Sunday) on the 1st floor of the Velký Spalicek shopping centre.

Spolek (☎ 542 213 002; Orli 22; mains 70-100Kč; ☯ closed Sun) The service is unpretentious at this coolly bohemian – yes, we are in Moravia – haven with interesting salads, soups, pasta and wine.

Sabaidy (☎ 545 428 310; trída kpt Jaroše 29; mains 100-220Kč; ☯ 5pm-11pm Mon-Fri) With decor incorporating Buddhist statues and a talented Lao chef delivering authentic flavours, Sabaidy delivers both 'ommm' and 'mmmm'. After lots of 'same same' Czech food, this really is different.

Špaliček (☎ 542 215 526; Zelný trh 12; mains 140–300Kč)
Brno's oldest (and just maybe its meatiest)
restaurant sits on the edge of the Cabbage
Market. Ignore the irony and dig into the huge
Moravian meals.

Brabander (☎ 542 211 922; Joštova 4; mains 150–340Kč)
This cellar restaurant serves up innovative
food – on a Brno scale anyway – with a lighter
Mediterranean and Asian touch. A good wine
list adds to the appeal of one of Brno's best.

Also recommended:

Barunka (Běhounská 20; snacks 15–25Kč; ⊙ 7am-7pm
Mon-Fri, 8am-noon Sat) A sunny spot for open sandwiches,
salads, coffee, beer and wine.

Minach (Poštovská 6; per chocolate 13Kč; ⊙ 10am-7pm
Mon-Sat, from 2pm Sun) More than 50 kinds of handmade
chocolates and bracing coffee make this an essential mid-
morning or mid-afternoon detour.

Drinking

Pivnice Pegas (Jakubská 4) *Pivo* melts that old
Moravian reserve as the locals become pleasantly noisy. Don't miss the wheat beer with a
slice of lemon. Good luck finding a table, or
grab a spot at Brno's longest bar.

Café Alfa (Poštovská 6; ⊙ 8am-midnight Mon-Sat,
3-11pm Sun) This groovy spot has an arty vibe,
but also welcomes the not-so-hip. Start the
day with coffee and return for Alfa's nocturnal
transformation into a funky bar.

Černohorský Sklep (nám Svobody 5; ⊙ closed Sun)
Try the Black Hill aperitif beer or the honey-
infused Kvasar brew at the Black Mountain
Brewery's Brno outpost.

Entertainment

Brno offers excellent theatre and classical
music. Find entertainment listings in the
free monthly *Metropolis*, ask at the tourist information office or see the website
of the Národní' Divadlo Brno (National
Theatre Brno; www.ndb.cz).

Theatre Booking Office (předprodej; ☎ 542 321 285;
www.ndb.cz; Dvořákova 11; ⊙ 8am-5.30pm Mon-Fri, 9am-
noon Sat) Sells tickets for performances at the
Reduta, Mahenovo and Janáček Theatres.

Central Booking Office (Centrální předprodej; ☎ 542
210 863; Běhounská 17; ⊙ 10am-6pm Mon-Fri) Tickets to
rock, folk and classical concerts.

Janáček Theatre (Janáčkovo divadlo; Sady Osvobození)
Opera and ballet are performed at the
modern theatre.

Mahenovo Theatre (Mahenovo divadlo; Dvořákovo 11)
The neo-baroque Mahenovo Theatre presents
classical drama in Czech, and operettas.

Reduta Theatre (Reduta divadlo; Zelný trh 4) The
restored Reduta showcases Mozart's work (he
played there in 1767).

Getting There & Away

There are frequent buses from Brno to Prague
(130Kč, 2½ hours, hourly), Bratislava (110Kč,
2¼ hours, hourly) and Vienna (200Kč, 2½
hours, two daily). The departure point is either the bus station or near the railway station opposite the Grand Hotel. Check your
ticket. Private companies **Student Agency** (www
.studentagency.cz) and **Megabus** (www.megabus.cz)
both leave from their ticket booths opposite
the Grand Hotel.

There are trains to Prague (160Kč, three
hours) every two hours. Direct Eurocity trains
from Brno to Vienna (5725Kč, 1¾ hours, five
daily) arrive at Vienna's Südbahnhof. There
are frequent trains to Bratislava in Slovakia
(188Kč, two hours), and direct trains to Berlin
(€72, 7½ hours), Dresden (€43, five hours) and
Hamburg (€120, 10½ hours) in Germany. See
www.idos.cz for bus and train information.

ČSA (www.csa.cz) flies from Prague and **Ryan
Air** (www.ryanair.com) flies daily from London.
Smart Wings (www.smartwings.net) flies to Moscow
twice a week.

Getting Around

Buy public transport tickets from vending machines, news-stands or at the **DPMB Information
Office** (☎ 543 174 317; www.dpmb.cz; Novobranská 18;
⊙ 6am-6pm Mon-Fri, 8am-3.30pm Sat). Tickets are
valid for 60/90 minutes, cost 15/21Kč, and
allow unlimited transfers; 24-hour tickets are
60Kč. A 10-minute, no-transfer ticket is 10Kč.
For taxis, try **City Taxis** (☎ 542 321 321).

AROUND BRNO
Slavkov u Brna

Slavkov u Brna is better known in history by
its Austrian name, **Austerlitz**. On 2 December
1805 the Battle of the Three Emperors was
fought here, when Napoleon Bonaparte's
Grande Armée defeated the combined
forces of Emperor Franz I (Austria) and
Tsar Alexander I (Russia). During lulls in the
fighting, Napoleon stayed at **Slavkov Chateau**
(zámek Slavkov; ☎ 544 221 204; www.zamek-slavkov.cz;
tours adult/child 60/40Kč, in English 105/85Kč; ⊙ 9am-
5pm Jun-Aug, Tue-Sun May & Sep, to 4pm Tue-Sun Apr,
Oct & Nov).

The battle was decided at **Pracký kopec**, 12km
west of Slavkov, now marked by the **Cairn of**

Peace (Mohyla míru; adult/child 75/35Kč; ☻ 9am-6pm Jul & Aug, to 5pm May, Jun & Sep, Tue-Sun Apr, to 3.30pm Tue-Sun Oct-Mar) with a museum on the conflict which claimed 20,000 lives. Annual re-enactments take place around 2 December.

Slavkov is 21km east of Brno and reached by bus (29Kč, 25 minutes) or train (40Kč, 35 minutes). Pracký kopec is awkward by public transport. Take a local train from Brno to Ponětovice (26Kč, 20 minutes) and walk 3.5km southeast through Prace.

Moravian Karst

A good day trip from Brno, the limestone plateau of the Moravian Karst (Moravský kras) is riddled with caves and canyons carved by the subterranean Punkva River. There's a car park at Skalní Mlýn with an information desk and ticket office. A **mini-train** (adult/child return 70/60Kč; ☻ Apr-Sep) travels along the 1.5km between the car park and the caves. Otherwise it's a 20-minute stroll through forest.

The **Punkva Caves tour** (Punkevní jeskyně; ☎ 516 418 602; www.smk.cz; adult/child 150/70Kč; ☻ 8.20am-3.50pm Apr-Sep, 8.40am-2pm Mon-Fri, 8.40am-3.40pm Sat & Sun Oct, 8.40am-2pm Nov-Mar) involves a 1km walk through limestone caverns to the bottom of the **Macocha Abyss**, a 140m-deep sinkhole. Small, electric-powered boats then cruise along the underground river back to the entrance. On weekends and in July and August tickets for cave tours can sell out in advance, so book ahead.

Beyond the Punkva Caves entrance, a **cable car** (adult/child return 80/70Kč, combined tourist train & cable-car ticket 120/100Kč) travels to the upper rim of the Macocha Abyss. Afterwards, wander down on the blue-marked trail (2km).

Kateřinská Cave (Kateřinská eskyně; ☎ 516 413 161; adult/child 60/50Kč; ☻ 8.20am-4pm Apr-Sep, to 2pm Oct, 10am, noon & 2pm Feb-Mar) is 300m from the Skalní Mlýn car park. Usually less crowded, the 30-minute tour explores two massive chambers.

From Brno trains run to Blansko (33Kč, 30 minutes, hourly). Bus 226 departs from platform 742 at Blansko bus station (across the bridge from the train station) to Skalní Mlýn (16Kč, 15 minutes, five daily April to September).

Get an early start from Brno and catch one of the two buses (9.15am and 11.15am) departing to Blansko before noon, and you can easily visit the caves as a day trip. You can also hike an 8km trail from Blansko to Skalní Mlýn (two hours).

OLOMOUC
pop 105,000

While show-offs Prague, Karlovy Vary and Český Krumlov are constantly praised, Olomouc (pronounced olla-moats) goes quietly about its authentically Moravian business, and emerges as the Czech Republic's most under-rated destination.

An Old Town square rivalling Prague's Old Town Sq combines with the graceful campus of the country's second-oldest university. Moravia's most impressive religious structures play host to a thrilling history and one of the Czech Republic's best museums. And, with tourist numbers at a relative trickle, Olomouc is a great-value destination.

Orientation

The main train station (hlavní nádraží) is 2km east of the Old Town, over the Morava and Bystřice rivers (tram 2 or 6). The bus station is 1km further east (tram 4).

The Old Town comprises the two linked squares of Horní (Upper) and Dolní (Lower) nám. The Přemysl Palace is along Ostružinická and třída 1 máje.

Information

Internet U Dominika (Slovesnská 12; per min 1Kč; ☻ 9am-9pm Mon-Fri, from 10am Sat & Sun) Includes wi-fi for laptop travellers.

Knihy Dobrovský (☎ 585 393 252; Horní nám) Bookshop with English-language paperbacks and good maps.

Main tourist information office (Olomoucká informační služba; ☎ 585 513 385; www.olomouc-tourism.cz; Horní nám; ☻ 9am-7pm) Sells maps and makes accommodation bookings. Audio guides (150Kč for three hours) include a map detailing 28 points of interest.

Olomouc Tours (☎ 775 345 570; www.olomouctours .com; by donation Jul & Aug, rest of year 200Kč) Two-hour walking tours with the guys from Poet's Corner Hostel leave from the astronomical clock daily at 10am from July to August. During other months you'll need to book. Cycling tours (350Kč, two hours) are also available.

Sights & Activities

HORNÍ NÁM & AROUND

The splendid **town hall** was built in 1378, though its present appearance and **tower** (věž; admission 15Kč; ☻ tours 11am & 3pm Mar-Oct) date from 1607. Don't miss the **astronomical clock** on the north side, remodelled in communist style, so that each hour is announced by ideologically pure workers instead of pious saints. The best display is at

OLOMOUC

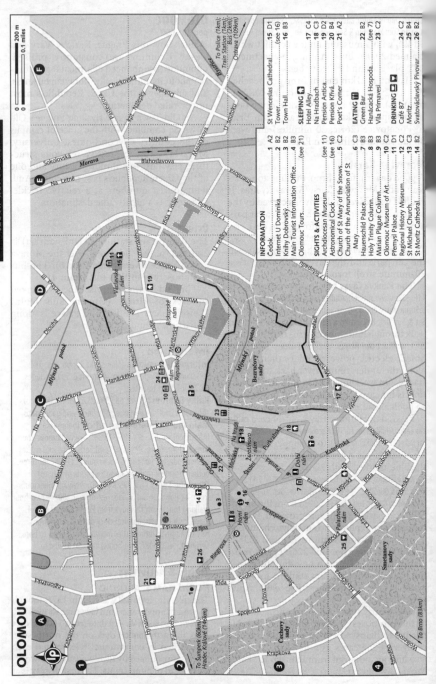

INFORMATION
Cedok................................	**1** A2
Internet U Dominika...........	**2** B2
Knihy Dobrovský................	**3** B2
Main Tourist Information Office...	**4** B3
Olomouc Tours...................	(see 21)

SIGHTS & ACTIVITIES
Archdiocesan Museum........	(see 11)
Astronomical Clock............	(see 16)
Church of St Mary of the Snows...	**5** C2
Church of the Annunciation of St	
Mary.................................	**6** C3
Hauenschild Palace............	**7** B3
Holy Trinity Column...........	**8** B3
Marian Plague Column........	**9** B3
Olomouc Museum of Art.....	**10** D1
Přemysl Palace..................	**11** D1
Regional History Museum...	**12** C3
St Michael Church..............	**13** C3
St Moritz Cathedral............	**14** B2
St Wenceslas Cathedral......	**15** D1
Tower................................	(see 16)
Town Hall.........................	**16** B3

SLEEPING 🛏
Hotel Alley........................	**17** C4
Na Hradbach.....................	**18** C3
Pension Antica...................	**19** D2
Pension Křivá....................	**20** B4
Poet's Corner....................	**21** A2

EATING 🍴
Green Bar..........................	**22** B2
Hanácecká Hospoda...........	(see 7)
Vila Primavesi...................	**23** C2

DRINKING 🍷
Café 87.............................	**24** C2
Moritz...............................	**25** B4
Svatováclavský Pivovar.......	**26** B2

noon. In front of the town hall, a brass model of Olomouc will help you get your bearings.

Across the square is the Unesco World Heritage–listed **Holy Trinity Column** (Sousoší Nejsvětější trojice). Built between 1716 and 1754, the baroque structure is reminiscent of the Buddhist stupa. During summer, a friendly nun explains the meaning of the interior sculptures. The square is ringed by historic facades and features two of the city's six baroque fountains. The tourist information office has a good brochure about the distinctive fountains.

Down Opletalova is the immense, Gothic **St Moritz Cathedral** (chrám sv Mořice), built slowly from 1412 to 1530. The cathedral's peace is shattered every September with an International Organ Festival; the cathedral's own organ is Moravia's mightiest.

DOLNÍ NÁM

The 1661 **Church of the Annunciation of St Mary** (kostel Zvěstování Panny Marie) has a beautifully sober interior. In contrast is the opulent 16th-century Renaissance **Hauenschild Palace** (not open to the public), and the **Marian Plague Column** (Mariánský morový sloup).

Picturesque lanes thread northeast to the green-domed **St Michael Church** (kostel sv Michala). The baroque interior includes a rare painting of a pregnant Virgin Mary. Draped around the entire block is an active Dominican seminary (Dominikánský klášter).

NÁM REPUBLIKY & AROUND

The original Jesuit college complex, founded in 1573, stretched along Universitní and into nám Republiky, and includes the **Church of St Mary of the Snows** (kostel Panny Marie Sněžné), with many fine frescos.

Opposite is the **Regional History Museum** (Vlastivědné muzeum; ☎ 585 515 111; www.vmo.cz; nám Republiky 5; adult/child 40/20Kč; ⓨ 9am-6pm Tue-Sun Apr-Sep, 10am-5pm Wed-Sun Oct-Mar) with historical, geographical and zoological displays. Adjacent is the **Olomouc Museum of Art** (Olomoucký muzeum umění; ☎ 585 514 111; www.olumart.cz; Denisov 47; adult/child 50/25Kč; ⓨ 10am-6pm Tue-Sun), with an excellent collection of 20th-century Czech painting and sculpture. Admission includes entry to the Archdiocesan Museum (see right).

PŘEMYSL PALACE & ST WENCESLAS CATHEDRAL

To the northeast, the pocket-sized Václavské nám has Olomouc's most venerable buildings, now converted into one of the Czech Republic's finest museums.

The early-12th-century **Přemysl Palace** (Přemyslovský palác) is now the **Archdiocesan Museum** (☎ 585 514 111; www.olumart.cz; Václavské nám 3; adult/child 50/25Kč; ⓨ 10am-6pm Tue-Sun) with treasures from the 12th to the 18th centuries, when Olomouc was the Moravian capital. A thoughtful makeover showcases the site's diverse architecture from several centuries and many of the ecclesiastical treasures are superb. Don't miss the magnificent Troyer Coach, definitely the stretch limo of the 18th century. Admission includes entry to the Olomouc Museum of Art.

Originally a Romanesque basilica first consecrated in 1131, the adjacent **St Wenceslas Cathedral** (dóm sv Václava) was rebuilt several times before having a 'neo-Gothic' makeover in the 1880s.

Sleeping

The information office can book private and hotel rooms.

Poet's Corner (☎ 777 570 730; www.hostelolomouc.com; 3rd fl, Sokolská 1; dm/tw/tr/q 350/900/1200/1600Kč) Aussie owners Greg and Francie are a wealth of local information at this friendly and well-run hostel. Bicycles can be hired for 100Kč per day. In summer there's a two-night minimum stay, but Olomouc's definitely worth it.

Na Hradbach (☎ 585 233 243; nahradbach@quick.cz; Hrnčířská 3; s/d 600/800Kč) On a pretty street sits Olomouc's best-value pension, with two good restaurants across the lane. Be sure to book ahead.

Pension Křivá (☎ 585 209 204; www.pension-kriva.cz; Křivá 8; s/d 1450/1950Kč) This new opening gets a lot of things right: spacious rooms with cherrywood furniture, flash bathrooms with even flasher toiletries, plus a cosy cafe downstairs. The quiet laneway location doesn't hurt either.

Pension Antica (☎ 731 560 264; www.pension.antica.cz; Wurmova 1; apt 1450-2000Kč) With antique furniture, crisp white duvets and Oriental rugs on wooden floors, the Antica is a spacious and splurge-worthy romantic getaway. Catch bus 2 or 6 from the train station or bus 4 from the bus station. Get off at the U Domú stop.

Hotel Alley (☎ 585 209 204; www.hotel-alley.cz; Křivá 8; s/d 2800/3100Kč) The preferred digs of rock stars – well, Suzanne Vega stayed here anyway – the Hotel Alley combines solid four-star

CZECH REPUBLIC

business cred and an in-house spa-massage centre. Slightly characterless, but the best digs in town. From Friday to Sunday there's a 30% discount.

Eating & Drinking

Café 87 (Denisova 87; chocolate pie 40Kč, coffee 40Kč; ⏰ 8am-9pm) Locals flock to this funky cafe beside the Museum of Art for coffee and the famous chocolate pie. Some locals still prefer the dark chocolate to the white chocolate. When will they learn? It's a top spot for breakfast too.

our pick Hanácacká Hospoda (☎ 582 237 186; Dolní nám 38; mains 70-100Kč) In the same building as the Hauenschild palace; the menu lists everything in the local Haná dialect. It's worth persevering though, as the huge Moravian meals are tasty and supreme value. They've got an English menu if you're still coming up to speed with Haná.

Green Bar (☎ 777 749 274; Ztacená 3; meals 100Kč; ⏰ 10am-5pm Mon-Fri, to 2pm Sat) Around 100Kč will get you a feast of salads, couscous and veg lasagna at this self-service vegetarian cafe. It's popular with a cosmoplitan mix of overseas students.

Moritz (☎ 585 205 560; Nešverova 2; mains 100-180Kč) This microbrewery and restaurant quickly became a local favourite after opening in 2007. We reckon it's a combination of the terrific beers, good-value food and a praise-worthy 'No smoking' policy.

Svatováclavský Pivovar (☎ 585 203 641; Riegrova 22; meals 140-200Kč) Another new microbrewery – what's in the water in Olomouc? – the Svatováclavský has a buzzy beerhall ambience. Try the zingy wheat beer with the stinky Olomouc cheese.

Vila Primavesi (☎ 777 749 288; Universtiní 7; mains 180-250Kč) In an art-nouveau villa that played host to Austrian artist Gustav Klimt in the early 20th century, the Vila Primavesi is Olomouc's newest eatery. On summer evenings enjoy meals such as tuna steak and risotto in the lovely gardens.

Getting There & Away

From Brno, there are 15 buses (83Kč, 1¼ hours) and five direct fast trains (120Kč, 1½ hours) daily. Trains from Prague (324Kč, 3¼ hours) leave from Praha-hlavní nádraží. Faster SC Pendolino trains (634Kč, 2¼ hours) stop at Olomouc en route from Praha-Holešovice to Ostrava. See www.idos.cz.

From Olomouc to Poland there is one direct train to Warsaw at 12.57pm daily (750Kč, six hours), and one to Kraków at 4.57pm (430Kč, 4½ hours).

Direct trains link Olomouc to Košice at 1.57pm (538Kč, 5½ hours) in Slovakia, but for Bratislava you'll need to change at Břeclav.

TELČ
pop 6000

Telč is a quiet town, with a gorgeous old centre ringed by medieval fish ponds and unspoilt by modern buildings. Unwind with a good book and a glass of Moravian wine at one of the local cafes.

The bus and train stations are a few hundred metres apart on the eastern side of town. A 10-minute walk along Masarykova leads to nám Zachariáše z Hradce, the Old Town square.

The **information office** (☎ 567 243 145; www .telc-etc.cz; nám Zachariáše z Hradce 10; ⏰ 8am-5pm Mon-Fri, 10am-5pm Sat & Sun) books accommodation in private homes (around 350Kč to 400Kč per person). Internet access is 1Kč per minute.

Sights

In a country full of gorgeous Old Town squares, Telč's Unesco World Heritage–listed and cobblestoned **nám Zachariáše z Hradce** may outshine the lot. When the day trippers have departed, the Gothic arcades and elegant Renaissance facades are a magical setting.

At the square's northwestern end is the **Water Chateau** (☎ 567 243 943; www.zamek-telc.cz). **Tour A** (1hr adult/child90/45Kč, in English 180Kč; ⏰ 9am-5pm Tue-Sun May-Sep, to 4pm Apr & Oct) visits the Renaissance halls, while **Tour B** (45min adult/child 80/40Kč; ⏰ 9am-5pm Tue-Sun May-Sep) visits the private apartments, inhabited by the aristocratic owners until 1945. A new exhibition focuses on the chateau's **portrait gallery** (adult/child 40/20Kč; ⏰ 9am-5pm Tue-Sun May-Sep, to 4pm Apr & Oct, to 3pm Nov-Mar).

At the castle's entrance is the **Chapel of All Saints**, where trumpeting angels guard the tombs of Zacharias of Hradec, the castle's founder, and his wife. The **historical museum** (adult/child 30/15Kč; ⏰ 9am-5pm Tue-Sun May-Sep, to 4pm Apr & Oct), in the courtyard, has a model of Telč from 1895. More than a century later, not much has changed.

Sleeping & Eating

Penzión u Rudolfa (☎ 567 243 094; nám Zachariáše z Hradce 58; s/d 300/600Kč; ⏰ Jul & Aug) A pretty

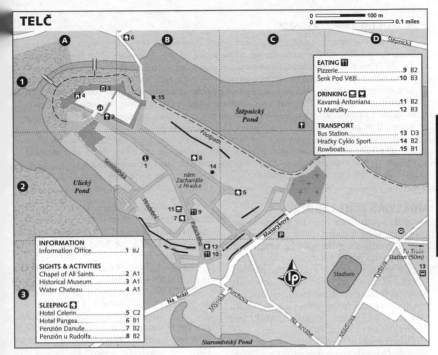

TELČ

merchant's house on the main square conceals a friendly pension with shared kitchen facilities.

Penzlón Danuše (☎ 567 213 945; www.telc-etc.cz/cz/privat/danuse; Hradebni 25; s/d 450/900Kč, 4-bed apt 2000Kč) Discreet wrought-iron balconies and wooden window boxes provide a touch of class just off the main square.

Hotel Celerin (☎ 567 243 477; www.hotelcelerin.cz; nám Zachariáše z Hradce 43; s/d incl breakfast from 980/1530Kč; 🖥) Three-star charm showcases 12 romantic rooms wth decor varying from cosy wood to wedding-cake kitsch. Have a look before you hand over your passport.

Hotel Pangea (☎ 567 213 122; www.pangea.cz; Na Baště 450; s/d incl breakfast 1200/1600Kč; 🎟 🖥 📷) Huge buffet breakfasts and loads of facilities make the functional Pangea good value. Ask the friendly hotel dog for a discount outside of July and August.

Kavarná Antoniana (☎ 605 519 903; nám Zachariáše z Hradce; coffee & cake 70Kč; 🕙 8am-2am) Documentary-style photography from around the world will get you planning your next trip at this modern refuge from the Renaissance glories outside. Have a coffee or something stronger.

Šenk Pod Věži (☎ 603 526 999; Palackého 116; mains 100-200Kč; 🕙 11am-3pm & 6-9pm Mon-Sat, 11am-4pm Sun) Sizzling grills and live music are the big drawcards at this cosy restaurant under the tower.

U Marušky (☎ 605 870 854; Palackého) Telč's hipper younger citizens crowd this buzzy bar for cool jazz and tasty eats.

Order in pizza from **Pizzerie** (☎ 567 223 246; nám Zachariáše z Hradce 32; pizza 75-140Kč) just across the square.

Getting There & Away

Five buses daily travel from Prague Roztyly to Telč (124Kč, 2½ hours). Buses running between České Budějovice and Brno also stop at Telč (92Kč, two hours, two daily). Trains rumble south to the beautiful village of Slavonice.

Getting Around

Hračky Cyklo Sport (nám Zachariáše z Hradce 23; per day 100Kč; 🕙 8am-5pm Mon-Fri, 9am-noon Sat) rents bicycles.

Rent **rowboats** (per 30min 20Kč; 🕙 10am-6pm Jul & Aug) from outside the East gate.

CZECH REPUBLIC

WORTH THE TRIP: SLAVONICE

Barely hanging onto the Czech Republic's coat-tails – the border with Austria is just 1km away – Slavonice is a little town any country would be proud to own. Slavonice's initial prosperity during the Thirty Years' War produced two squares dotted with stunning Renaissance architecture. Economic isolation followed when the main road linking Prague and Vienna was diverted in the 18th century, and in the 20th century, Slavonice's proximity to the Cold War border with Austria maintained its isolation. The town's architectural treasures were spared the socialist makeover other parts of the country endured and now, once the Austrian day trippers have left, Slavonice resurrects its compellingly moody atmosphere like nowhere else.

Slavonice is on a little-used train line from Telč (43Kč, one hour). The sleepy **tourist office** (☎ 384 493 320; www.mesto-slavonice.cz) is on the main square, nám Miru. Just off nám Miru, **Bešidka** (☎ 606 212 070; www.besidka.cz; d 1290-1490Kč) has spacious loft-style rooms and a cosmopolitan downstairs cafe that might just serve the Czech Republic's best wood-fired pizzas.

MORAVIAN WINE COUNTRY

Heading south from Brno to Vienna is the Moravian wine country. Czech wine has improved greatly since the fall of communism in 1989, with small producers concentrating on the high-quality end of the market. Czech red wines, such as the local speciality Svatovavřinecké (St Lawrence), are mediocre, but dry and fruity whites can be good, especially the Riesling *(Vlašský Ryzlink)* and Müller-Thurgau varietals.

There are lots of *vinné sklepy* (wine cellars), *vinoteky* (wine shops) and *vinárny* (wine bars) to explore, as well as spectacular chateaux. The terrain is relatively flat, so cycling is a leisurely way to get around.

Mikulov

Described by Czech poet Jan Skácel as a 'piece of Italy moved to Moravia by God's hand', Mikulov is an excellent base to explore the neighbouring Lednice-Valtice Cultural Landscape. The nearby Palava Hills are a mecca for hiking and cycling. If you're travelling from Brno to Vienna, Mikulov is a good stopping-off point.

The **tourist information office** (☎ 519 510 855; www.mikulov.cz; Nám 30; 🕑 8am-6pm Mon-Fri, 9am-6pm Sat & Sun Jun-Sep, 8am-noon & 12.30-5pm Mon-Fri, 9am-4pm Sat & Sun Apr, May & Oct, 8am-noon & 1-4pm Mon-Fri Nov-Mar) is beneath the impressive Renaissance **chateau** (☎ 519 510 255; adult/child 70/35Kč; 🕑 9am-5pm Tue-Sun May-Sep, 9am-4pm Apr & Oct), seat of the Dietrichstein and Liechtenstein families.

Bicycles and cycle-touring information are available from **Půjčovna Kol** (Husova 42; per day 120Kč). If no-one's around, ask at the Hotel Templ next door.

Spend the afternoon wine-tasting at the **Vinařské Centrum** (☎ 519 51 368; www.obchodsvinem .cz; Nám 11, per tasting glass 15-25Kč; 🕑 10am-5.30pm Sun-Thu, to 8pm Fri & Sat). Wines from across the region are available.

Mikulov has some excellent boutique hotels in the old Jewish quarter.

our pick **Hotel Templ** (☎ 519 323 095; www.templ .cz; Husova 50; s/d incl breakfast from 1390/1650Kč) has discreetly furnished rooms and a stylish restaurant in a restored Renaissance mansion.

A few doors up, **Pension Reisten** (☎ 519 324 327; www.pensionreisten.cz; Husova 44; d incl breakfast 1400-2400Kč) effortlessly combines modern furniture with beautifully resurrected rooms with exposed brick walls and wooden floors.

More affordable is the **Fajka Vinárna & Pension** (☎ 732 833 147; www.fajka-mikulov.cz; Alfonse Mucha 18; s/d 400/800Kč), with comfortable rooms above a cosy wine bar. Out back is a garden restaurant if you really, really like the local wine.

There are regular buses from Brno to Mikulov (55Kč, one hour, 14 daily), and less frequent buses between Mikulov and Vienna (180Kč, two hours, two daily).

Lednice & Valtice

A few kilometres east, the **Lednice-Valtice Cultural Landscape** consists of 200 sq km of woodland, artificial lakes and tree-lined avenues dotted with baroque, neoclassical and neo-Gothic chateaux. Effectively Europe's biggest landscaped garden, it was created over several centuries by the dukes of Liechtenstein and is now a Unesco World Heritage site.

The massive neo-Gothic **Lednice Chateau** (☎ 519 340 128; www.lednice.cz; 🕑 9am-6pm Tue-Sun May-Aug, to 5pm Tue-Sun Sep, to 4pm Sat & Sun Apr & Oct), was the Liechtensteins' summer palace.

Studded with battlements, pinnacles and gargoyles, it gazes across an island-dotted artificial lake. **Tour 1** (adult/child 80/40Kč, 45 min) visits the major rooms, while **Tour 2** (adult/child 100/50Kč, 45 min) concentrates on the Liechtenstein apartments. Visit the gardens for free, or cruise on a **pleasure boat** (9.30am-5pm Jul & Aug, Tue-Sun May, Jun & Sep, Sat & Sun Apr & Oct). Routes include between the chateau and an incongruous minaret (adult/child 80/40Kč) and between the minaret and nearby Janův castle (adult/child 120/60Kč).

During summer the **Birds of Prey show** (www .zayferus.cz; adult/child 90/45Kč) presents birds soaring and hunting above Lednice's meadows.

Valtice's huge baroque chateau houses the **National Wine Salon** (Národní salon vín; 519 352 072; www.salonvin.cz; Zámek 1; 9.30am-5pm Tue-Thu, 10.30am-6pm Fri & Sat, 10.30am-5pm Sun Jun-Sep), with wine tasting sessions from 120Kč to 399Kč per person (minimum five people).

There are five buses daily from Mikulov to Lednice (31Kč, 40 minutes), and one daily at 11am from Brno (68Kč, 1¾ hours). Regular buses shuttle the short distance between Lednice and Valtice (14Kč, 15 minutes).

CZECH REPUBLIC DIRECTORY

ACCOMMODATION

Accommodation reviews in this chapter are listed in order of price, from cheapest to most expensive. Budget means less than 1400Kč for a double, midrange is 1400Kč to 3500Kč, and top end is more than 3500Kč. Unless otherwise stated, rooms in this chapter include private bathroom.

You usually have to show your passport when checking in at accommodation in the Czech Republic. There is no law banning smoking in rooms, but a growing number of midrange and top-end options can provide nonsmoking accommodation.

There are several hundred camping grounds spread around the country; most are open from May to September only and charge around 70Kč to 100Kč per person. Camping on public land is prohibited.

Klub mladých cestovatelů (KMC Young Travellers Club; Map pp104-5; 222 220 347; Karolíny Světlé 30, Prague 1) is the HI affiliate in Prague, and can book hostel accommodation throughout the country. In July and August many student dormitories become temporary hostels, and some in Prague are also year-round backpacker hostels. Prague and Český Krumlov are the only places with a solid choice of backpacker-oriented hostels. Dorm beds costs around 400Kč in Prague and 300Kč to 350Kč elsewhere; it's best to book ahead. An HI-membership card is not usually needed, although it will often get you a reduced rate. An ISIC, ITIC, IYTC or Euro26 card may also get you a discount.

Another category of hostel accommodation is *turistické ubytovny* (tourist hostels), which provide very basic dormitory accommodation (200Kč to 300Kč); rooms can usually be booked through the local tourist information office or KMC branch. Look for signs advertising private rooms (*privát* or *Zimmer frei* – like B&Bs without the breakfast). Most tourist information offices can book them for you. Expect to pay from 400Kč to 550Kč per person outside Prague. Some have a three-night minimum-stay requirement.

Pensions (*penzióny*) are a step up: small, homely, often family-run, but offering rooms with private bathroom, often including breakfast. Rates range from 900Kč to 1500Kč for a double room (1800Kč to 2500Kč in Prague).

Hotels in central Prague, Český Krumlov and Brno can be expensive, but smaller towns are usually significantly cheaper. Two-star hotels offer reasonable comfort for 900Kč to 1000Kč for a double, or 1100Kč to 1500Kč with private bathroom (50% higher in Prague).

ACTIVITIES

There is good hiking among the hills of the Šumava (p139) south of Český Krumlov, in the forests around Karlovy Vary, in the Moravian Karst and in the Adršpach-Teplice Rocks (p139). Climbing is also excellent in these last two. Canoeing and rafting are popular on the Vltava River around Český Krumlov (p137) and the whole country is ideal for cycling and cycle touring. Especially good for cycling are the Šumava region (p139) and the Moravian Wine Country. A recent introduction are beer and wine tours.

The following companies provide activities-based tours:

Ave Bicycle Tours (251 551 011; www.bicycle-tours .cz) Cycle touring specialists.
E-Tours (572 557 191; www.etours.cz) Nature, wildlife and photography tours.

Greenways Travel Club (☎ 519 511 572; www.visit greenways.com) From cycling and walking to beer and wine, Czech glass and Czech music tours.

Top Bicycle (☎ 519 513 745; www.topbicycle.com) Biking and multisport tours.

BUSINESS HOURS

Outside Prague, almost everything closes on Saturday afternoon and all day Sunday. Most restaurants are open every day; most museums, castles and chateaux are closed on Mondays year-round. Banks open from 8am to 4.30pm Monday to Friday, while post office operate from 8am to 6pm Monday to Friday and to noon Saturdays. Shops are generally open from 8.30am to 5pm or 6pm Monday to Friday and to noon or 1pm Saturday. Restaurant opening hours are 11am to 11pm daily; bars operate from 11am to midnight daily.

COURSES

The **Institute for Language & Preparatory Studies** (Ústav jazykové a odborné přípravy; ☎ 224 990 411; www .ujop.cuni.cz) runs six-week Czech language courses for foreigners (€610). The **London School of Modern Languages** (☎ 226 096 140; www .londonschool.cz) offers one-on-one Czech language tuition (350Kč per 45 minutes), while the **Prague School** (☎ 257 534 013; www.filmschool.cz) runs four-week intensive film-making workshops in summer.

DANGERS & ANNOYANCES

Pickpocketing can be a problem in Prague's tourist zone and there are occasional reports of robberies on overnight international trains. There is racism towards the local Roma population, but Prague's increasingly cosmopolitan society means that abuse directed at darker-skinned visitors is rapidly becoming less prevalent.

EMBASSIES & CONSULATES

Most embassies and consulates are open at least 9am to noon Monday to Friday.

Australia (Map pp104-5; ☎ 296 578 350; www.embassy .gov.au/cz.html; 6th fl, Klimentská 10, Nové Město) Honorary consulate for emergency assistance only; nearest Australian embassy is in Vienna.

Austria (Map pp102-3; ☎ 257 090 511; www.austria.cz, in German & Czech; Viktora Huga 10, Smíchov)

Bulgaria (Map pp104-5; ☎ 222 211 258; bulvelv@mbox .vol.cz; Krakovská 6, Nové Město)

Canada (Map pp102-3; ☎ 272 101 800; www.canada.cz; Muchova 6, Bubeneč)

France (Map pp102-3; ☎ 251 171 711; www.france.cz, in French & Czech; Velkopřerovské nám 2, Malá Strana)

Germany (Map pp102-3; ☎ 257 113 111; www.deutsch land.cz, in German & Czech; Vlašská 19, Malá Strana)

Hungary (Map pp102-3; ☎ 233 324 454; huembprg@ vol.cz; Českomalínská 20, Bubeneč)

Ireland (Map pp102-3; ☎ 257 530 061; www.embassyof ireland.cz; Tržiště 13, Malá Strana)

Netherlands (Map pp102-3; ☎ 233 015 200; www .netherlandsembassy.cz; Gotthardská 6/27, Bubeneč)

New Zealand (Map pp102-3; ☎ 222 514 672; eger mayer@nzconsul.cz; Dykova 19, Vinohrady) Honorary consulate providing emergency assistance only; the nearest NZ embassy is in Berlin. Visits only by appointment.

Poland consulate (off Map pp102-3; ☎ 224 228 722; konspol@mbox.vol.cz; Vúžlabině 14, Strašnice); embassy (Map pp102-3; ☎ 257 099 500; www.ambpol.cz; Valdštejnská 8, Malá Strana) Go to the consulate for visas.

Russia (Map pp102-3; ☎ 233 374 100; rusembas@ bohem-net.cz; Pod Kaštany 1, Bubeneč)

Slovakia (Map pp102-3; ☎ 233 113 051; www .slovakemb.cz, in Slovak; Pod Hradbami 1, Dejvice)

South Africa (Map pp102-3; ☎ 267 311 114; www .saprague.cz; Ruská 65, Vršovice)

UK (Map p109; ☎ 257 402 111; www.britain.cz; Thunovská 14, Malá Strana)

Ukraine (Map pp102-3; ☎ 233 342 000; emb_cz@mfa .gov.ua; Charlese de Gaulla 29, Bubeneč)

USA (Map pp102-3; ☎ 257 022 000; www.usembassy.cz; Tržiště 15, Malá Strana)

GAY & LESBIAN TRAVELLERS

Homosexuality is legal in the Czech Republic (the age of consent is 15), but Czechs are not yet used to seeing public displays of affection; it's best to be discreet. In July 2006 same-sex civil unions became legal. **Prague Saints** (www.prague saints.cz) has comprehensive English-language information, and links to gay-friendly accommodation and bars. Also worth checking out are www.gay.cz and www.prague.gayguide.net.

HOLIDAYS

New Year's Day 1 January; also anniversary of the founding of the Czech Republic.

Easter Monday March/April

Labour Day 1 May

Liberation Day 8 May

SS Cyril and Methodius Day 5 July

Jan Hus Day 6 July

Czech Statehood Day 28 September

Republic Day 28 October

Struggle for Freedom and Democracy Day 17 November

Christmas 24 to 26 December

INTERNET RESOURCES

ABC Prague (www.abcprague.com) English-language news.
Czech Tourism (www.czechtourism.com) Official tourist information.
Czech.cz (www.czech.cz) Informative government site on travel and tourism, including visa requirements.
IDOS (www.idos.cz) Train and bus timetables.
Mapy (www.mapy.cz) Online maps.
Prague Information Service (www.prague-info.cz) Official tourist site for Prague.
PragueTV (www.praguetv.cz) Prague events and entertainment listings.
Radio Prague (www.radio.cz) Dedicated to Czech news, language and culture (in English, French, German, Spanish and Russian).

MONEY

Currency

Czech crown (Koruna česká, or Kč) banknotes come in denominations of 20, 50, 100, 200, 500, 1000, 2000 and 5000Kč, and coins in one, two, five, 10, 20 and 50Kč.

Keep small change handy for use in public toilets, telephones and tram-ticket machines, and try to keep some small denomination notes for shops, cafés and restaurants. Changing larger notes from ATMs can be a problem.

The Czech crown (Koruna česká) has appreciated against other currencies in recent years and Prague is no longer a budget destination.

Some businesses quote prices in euros; prices in this chapter conform to quotes of individual businesses.

Exchanging Money

There is no black market, and anyone who offers to change money in the street is a thief.

There's a good network of *bankomaty* (ATMs). The main banks are the best places to change cash and travellers cheques or get a cash advance on Visa or MasterCard.

EMERGENCY NUMBERS

- Ambulance ☎ 155
- Fire ☎ 150
- Motoring Assistance (ÚAMK) ☎ 1230
- Municipal Police ☎ 156
- State Police ☎ 158

American Express (Amex) and Travelex offices change their own cheques without commission. Credit cards are widely accepted in petrol stations, midrange and top-end hotels, restaurants and shops.

Beware of *směnárna* (private exchange offices), especially in Prague – they advertise misleading rates, and often charge exorbitant commissions or 'handling fees'.

Tipping

Tipping in restaurants is optional, but increasingly expected in Prague. If there is no service charge you should certainly round up the bill to the next 10 or 20Kč (5% to 10% is normal in Prague). The same applies to tipping taxi drivers. When you're a buying a beer, it's customary to leave leftover small change as a tip.

POST

General delivery mail can be addressed to Poste Restante, Pošta 1, in most major cities. For Prague, the address is Poste Restante, Jindřišská 14, 11000 Praha 1, Czech Republic. International postcards cost 15Kč.

TELEPHONE

All Czech phone numbers have nine digits – you have to dial all nine for any call, local or long distance. Make international calls at main post offices or directly from phonecard booths. The international access code is ☎ 00. The Czech Republic's country code is ☎ 420.

Payphones are widespread, some taking coins and some phonecards. Buy phonecards from post offices, hotels, news-stands and department stores for 150Kč or 1000Kč.

Mobile-phone coverage (GSM 900) is excellent. If you're from Europe, Australia or New Zealand, your own mobile phone should be compatible. It's best to purchase a Czech SIM card from any mobile-phone shop for around 500Kč (including 300Kč of calling credit) and make local calls at local rates. In this case you can't use your existing mobile number.

Local mobile phone numbers start with the following numbers; 601 to 608 and 720 to 779.

TOURIST INFORMATION

Czech Tourism (www.czechtourism.com) offices provide information about tourism, culture and business in the Czech Republic.

TRAVELLERS WITH DISABILITIES

Ramps for wheelchair users are becoming more common, but cobbled streets, steep hills and stairways often make getting around difficult. Public transport is still problematic, but a growing number of trains and trams have wheelchair access. See www.dpp.cz for more information (listed under 'Barrier Free'). Major tourist attractions such as Prague Castle also offer wheelchair access. Anything described as *bezbariérová* is 'barrier-free'.

Czech Tourism (Map pp104-5 ☎ 221 580 111; www .czechtourism.com; Vinohradská 46; Vinohrady; ◷ 8.30am-noon & 1-4pm) can supply 'Wheeling the Czech Republic' brochure with a list of wheelchair-friendly accommodation and attractions. See also the 'Holidays Suitable for the Disabled' section on www.czechtourism.com

Prague Wheelchair Users Organisation (Map pp104-5; Pražská organizace vozíčkářů; ☎ 224 827 210; www.pov .cz, in Czech; Benediktská 6, Staré Město) has a CD-ROM guide 'Prague for the Disabled' in Czech, English and German.

VISAS

Everyone requires a valid passport (or identity card for EU citizens) to enter the Czech Republic.

Since March 2008, the Czech Republic has been part of the Schengen Agreement, and citizens of EU and EEA countries do not need visas. Citizens of Australia, Canada, Israel, Japan, New Zealand, Singapore, the USA and 23 other countries can stay for up to 90 days in a six-month period without a visa. If you are also travelling in other Schengen Agreement countries, you can still only stay for a maximum of 90 days in any six-month period.

For travellers from other countries, a Schengen Visa is required. You can only do this from your country of residence. Most Schengen Agreement countries will honour Schengen Visas issued by other member countries. Visa regulations change from time to time, so check www.czech.cz for the latest information.

TRANSPORT IN THE CZECH REPUBLIC

GETTING THERE & AWAY
Air
The Czech Republic's main international airport is **Prague-Ruzyně** (☎ 220 113 314; www.csl.cz/en).

The national carrier, **Czech Airlines** (ČSA; Map pp104-5; ☎ 239 007 007; www.csa.cz; V celnici 5, Nové Město), has direct flights to Prague from many European cities.

The main international airlines serving Prague:

Aer Lingus (EI; ☎ 224 815 373; www.aerlingus.com)
Aeroflot (SU; ☎ 227 020 020; www.aeroflot.ru)
Air France (AF; ☎ 223 090 933; www.airfrance.cz)
Alitalia (AZ; ☎ 224 194 150; www.alitalia.com)
Austrian Airlines (OS; ☎ 227 231 231; www .aua.com)
bmibaby (WW; www.bmibaby.com)
British Airways (BA; ☎ 239 000 299; www .ba.com)
Brussels Airlines (SN; ☎ 220 114 323; www .flysn.com)
Croatia Airlines (OU; ☎ 222 222 235; www .croatiaairlines.com)
Czech Airlines (OK; ☎ 239 007 007; www.csa.cz)
Delta (DL; www.delta.com)
easyJet (EZY; www.easyjet.com)
El Al (LY; ☎ 224 226 624; www.elal.co.il)
germanwings (4U; www.germanwings.com)
JAT Airways (JU; ☎ 224 942 654; www.jat.com)
Jet2.com (LS; www.jet2.com)
KLM (KL; ☎ 233 090 933; www.klm.com)
LOT (LO; ☎ 222 317 524; www.lot.com)
Lufthansa (LH; ☎ 234 008 234; www.lufthansa.com)
Malev (MA; ☎ 841 182 182; www.malev.com)
Ryanair (FR; www.ryanair.com)
SAS (SK; ☎ 220 116 031; www.flysas.com)
SkyEurope (NE; ☎ 246 096 096; www.skyeurope .com)
SmartWings (QS; ☎ 900 166 565; www.smart wings.net)
Turkish Airlines (TK; ☎ 234 708 708; www.thy.com)

Land
If you're travelling overland into the Czech Republic, note that under the Schengen Agreement there's no border control between the Czech Republic and surrounding countries.

BUS
Prague's main international bus terminal is Florenc Bus Station, 600m north of the main train station. The peak season for bus travel is mid-June to the end of September, with daily buses to major European cities. Outside this season, frequency falls to two or three a week. See p118 for services from Prague. Other international services include shuttle buses to Austria from Český Krumlov

(p139), and buses from Brno (p144) to Austria and Slovakia.

CAR & MOTORCYCLE

Motorists can enter the country at any of the many border crossings marked on most road maps; see the map on p94 for all major 24-hour crossings.

You will need to buy a *nálepka* (motorway tax coupon) – on sale at border crossings, petrol stations and post offices – in order to use Czech motorways (220/330Kč for one week/month). See www.ceskedalnice.cz for more information.

TRAIN

International trains arrive at Prague's main train station (Praha-hlavní nádraží, or Praha hl. n.), or the outlying Holešovice (Praha Hol.) and Smíchov (Praha Smv.) stations. See p119 for further information on services.

Trains between Prague and Germany stop at Plzeň (p132), while Brno (p144) has services to Austria, Slovakia and Germany. Other international services include trains to Poland and Slovakia from Olomouc (p148).

You can buy tickets in advance from Czech Railways (České dráhy, or ČD) ticket offices and various travel agencies. Seat reservations are compulsory on international trains. International tickets are valid for two months with unlimited stopovers. Inter-Rail (Zone D) passes are valid in the Czech Republic, and in 2009 the country became part of the Eurail network.

GETTING AROUND
Bicycle

The Czech Republic offers good opportunities for cycle touring. Cyclists should be careful as minor roads are often narrow and potholed. In towns, cobblestones and tram tracks can be a dangerous combination, especially after rain. Theft is a problem, especially in Prague and other large cities, so always lock up your bike.

It's fairly easy to transport your bike on Czech trains. First purchase your train ticket and then take it with your bicycle to the railway luggage office. There you fill out a card, which will be attached to your bike; on the card you should write your name, address, departure station and destination.

The cost of transporting a bicycle is 60Kč to 80Kč, depending on the length of the journey. You can also transport bicycles on most buses

if they are not too crowded and if the bus driver is willing.

Czech Railway also provides a handy bicycle hire service in areas best explored on two wheels. See www.cd.cz/static/eng /bikehireservice.htm.

Bus

Within the Czech Republic buses are often faster, cheaper and more convenient than trains, though not as comfortable. Many bus routes have reduced frequency (or none) at weekends. Buses occasionally leave early, so get to the station at least 15 minutes before the official departure time.

Most services are operated by the national bus company **ČSAD** (☎ information line 900 144 444). Check bus timetables and prices at www.idos .cz. Ticketing at main bus stations is computerised, so you can often book a seat ahead and be sure of a comfortable trip. Other stations are rarely computerised and you must line up and pay the driver.

Private companies include **Student Agency** (www.studentagency.cz), with destinations including Prague, Brno, České Budějovice, Český Krumlov, Karlovy Vary and Plzeň, and **Megabus** (www.megabus.cz), linking Prague with Karlovy Vary, Brno and Plzeň.

The footnotes on printed timetables may drive you crazy. Note the following: crossed hammers means the bus runs on *pracovní dny* (working days; ie Monday to Friday only); a Christian cross means it runs on Sundays and public holidays; and numbers in circles refer to particular days of the week (1 is Monday, 2 Tuesday etc). *Jede* means 'runs', *nejede* means 'doesn't run' and *jede denne* means 'runs daily'. *V* is 'on', *od* is 'from' and *do* is 'to' or 'until'.

Fares are very reasonable; expect to pay around 80Kč for a 100km trip.

Car & Motorcycle
DRIVING LICENCE

Foreign driving licences are valid for up to 90 days. Strictly speaking, licences that do not include photo identification need an International Driving Permit as well, although this rule is rarely enforced. Ordinary UK licences without a photo are normally accepted without comment.

FUEL

There are plenty of petrol stations, many open 24/7. Leaded petrol is available as *special*

(91 octane) and *super* (96 octane), and un-leaded as *natural* (95 octane) or *natural plus* (98 octane). The Czech for diesel is *nafta* or just *diesel*. *Autoplyn* (LPG gas) is available in every major town but at very few outlets.

HIRE

The main international car-rental chains all have offices in Prague. Small local companies offer better prices, but are less likely to have fluent, English-speaking staff. It's often easier to book by email than by phone. Typical rates for a Škoda Fabia are around 800Kč a day including unlimited kilometres, collision-damage waiver and value-added tax (VAT). Reputable local companies include the following:

Secco Car (Map pp102-3; ☎ 220 802 361; www .seccocar.cz; Přístavní 39, Holešovice)

Vecar (Map pp102-3; ☎ 224 314 361; www.vecar.org; Svatovítská 7, Dejvice)

West Car Praha (off Map pp102-3; ☎ 235 365 307; www.westcarpraha.cz, in Czech; Veleslavínská 17, Veleslavín)

ROAD RULES

Road rules are the same as the rest of Europe. A vehicle must be equipped with a first-aid kit, a red-and-white warning triangle and a nationality sticker on the rear; the use of seat belts is compulsory. Drinking and driving is strictly forbidden – the legal blood-alcohol level is zero. Police can hit you with on-the-spot fines of up to 2000Kč for speeding and other traffic offences (be sure to insist on a receipt).

Speed limits are 30km/h or 50km/h in built-up areas, 90km/h on open roads and 130km/h on motorways; motorbikes are limited to 80km/h. At level crossings over railway lines the speed limit is 30km/h. Beware of speed traps.

You need a motorway tax coupon to use the motorways. This is included with most rental cars.

Local Transport

City buses and trams operate from around 4.30am to midnight daily. Tickets must be purchased in advance – they're sold at bus and train stations, news-stands and vending machines – and must be validated in the time-stamping machines found on buses and trams and at the entrance to metro stations. Tickets are hard to find at night, on weekends and out in residential areas, so carry a good supply.

Taxis have meters – ensure they're switched on.

Train

Czech Railways provides efficient train services to almost every part of the country. Fares are based on distance: one-way, 2nd-class fares cost around 80/150/275/500Kč for 50/100/200/400km. For travel within the Czech Republic only, the Czech Flexipass is available (from US$112 to US$268 for three to eight days travel in a 15-day period). The sales clerks at ticket counters outside of Prague may not speak English, so write down your destination with the date and time you wish to travel. If you're paying by credit card, let them know *before* they issue the ticket.

Train categories include the following:

EC (EuroCity) Fast, comfortable international trains, stopping at main stations only, with 1st- and 2nd-class coaches; supplementary charge of 60Kč, reservations recommended. Includes 1st-class only SC Pendolino trains which run from Prague to Olomouc, Brno and Ostrava, with links to Vienna and Braitslava.

Ex (express) As for IC, but no supplementary charge.

IC (InterCity) Long-distance and international trains with 1st- and 2nd-class coaches; supplement of 40Kč, reservations recommended.

Os *(osobní)* Slow trains using older rolling stock that stop in every one-horse town; 2nd-class only.

R *(rychlík)* The main domestic network of fast trains with 1st- and 2nd-class coaches and sleeper services; no supplement except for sleepers; express and *rychlík* trains are usually marked in red on timetables.

Sp *(spěšný)* Slower and cheaper than *rychlík* trains; 2nd class only.

If you need to purchase a ticket or pay a supplement on the train, advise the conductor *before* they ask for your ticket or you'll have to pay a fine. Some Czech train conductors may try to intimidate foreigners by pretending there's something wrong with their ticket. Don't pay any 'fine', 'supplement' or 'reservation fee' unless you first get a *doklad* (written receipt).

Germany

Beer or wine? That sums up the German conundrum. One is at the heart of a pilsner-swilling culture that draws kegloads of visitors annually, is the very reason for one of the world's great parties (Oktoberfest) and is consumed with pleasure across the land. The other is exported worldwide, is responsible for gorgeous vine-covered valleys and is enjoyed everywhere, often from cute little green-stemmed glasses.

And the questions about Germany continue. Berlin or Munich? Castle or club? Ski or hike? East or west? BMW or Mercedes? In fact, the answers are simple: both. Why decide? The beauty of Germany is that rather than choosing, you can revel in the contrasts (except maybe with the car question…). Exploring this country and all its facets can keep visitors happy for weeks.

Berlin, edgy and vibrant, is a grand capital in a constant state of reinvention. At the other end, Munich perches atop Bavaria, the centre of national traditions. Half-timbered villages can't help but bring smiles as you wander their cobblestoned and castle-shadowed lanes. Cities of all sizes boast some of Europe's best clubs, as you'd expect from the home of techno. Enjoying the outdoors, from skiing Alpine peaks to hiking carefully preserved forests, is essential. And compare the ancient traditions of the east, as beautiful Dresden adjusts to the 21st century, with Cologne, where decades of prosperity burnish its grand heritage.

FAST FACTS

- **Area** 356,866 sq km
- **Capital** Berlin
- **Currency** euro (€); US$1 = €0.73; UK£1 = €1.06; A$1 = €0.50; ¥100 = €0.76; NZ$1 = €0.41
- **Famous for** sausages, Oktoberfest, culture, cars, history
- **Official language** German
- **Phrases** *Guten Tag* (good day); *Auf Wiedersehen* (goodbye); *Ja/Nein* (yes/no); *Danke* (thank you); *Sprechen Sie Englisch?* (Do you speak English?)
- **Population** 83 million
- **Telephone codes** country code ☎ 49; international access code ☎ 00
- **Visas** not required for citizens of the EU, Australia, USA, Japan and most other Western nations; see p293

HIGHLIGHTS

- Party day and night in **Berlin** (p167); save sleep for somewhere else as there's no time with the clubs, museums, bars and ever-changing Zeitgeist.
- Time your journey for **Oktoberfest** (p213), Munich's orgy of suds, or just hang out in a beer garden.
- Go slow in Germany's alluring small towns like **Bamberg** (p220), with winding lanes, smoked beer (!) and a lack of cliché.
- Go cuckoo in the **Black Forest** (p236), discovering its chilly crags, misty peaks and endless trails.
- Get into the swing of **Dresden** (p186), with a creative culture beyond the restorations.

ITINERARIES

- **One week** Starting in Berlin spend three days in and around the city, then head south through the wonderful little Thuringian town of Weimar before ending up in Munich.
- **Two weeks** Start in Munich for some Bavarian joy, then head up to the goofy castles in Füssen. Take in some of the Bavarian Alps and the fun of Freiburg. Explore the Black Forest, soak up Baden-Baden and settle in for a boat voyage down the Rhine in Mainz. Pop up to Hamburg and Lübeck then south to the old East and Weimar and Dresden. Finish it all in Berlin.

CLIMATE & WHEN TO GO

German weather can be variable, so it's best to be prepared for many conditions throughout the year. The most reliable weather is from May to October, coinciding with the standard tourist season (except for skiing). The shoulder periods (late March to May and September to October) can bring fewer tourists and surprisingly pleasant weather. See p595 for climate charts for Berlin.

HISTORY

Events in Germany have often dominated the European stage, but the country itself is a relatively recent invention: for most of its history Germany has been a patchwork of semi-independent principalities and city-states, occupied first by the Roman Empire, then the Holy Roman Empire and finally the

---

> **CONNECTIONS: MOVING ON FROM GERMANY**
>
> At the heart of Europe, Germany's superb railway (p293) is well linked to surrounding countries. Freiburg and Stuttgart have services south to Switzerland and Italy, Munich is close to Austria and the Czech Republic, Berlin is close to Poland, Hamburg has frequent services to Denmark, Cologne is good for both the Netherlands and Belgium, and Frankfurt is the base for fast trains to France and Paris (four hours).

Austrian Habsburgs. Perhaps because of this, many Germans retain a strong regional identity, despite the momentous events that have occurred since.

The most significant medieval events in Germany were pan-European in nature – Martin Luther brought on the Protestant Reformation with his criticism of the Catholic Church in Wittenberg in 1517, a movement that sparked the Thirty Years' War. Germany became the battlefield of Europe, only regaining stability after the Napoleonic Wars with increasing industrialisation and the rise of the Kingdom of Prussia. In 1866 legendary Prussian 'Iron Chancellor' Otto von Bismarck brought the German states together, largely by force, and a united Germany emerged for the first time in 1871, under Kaiser Wilhelm I.

WWI & the Rise of Hitler

With the advent of the 20th century, Germany's rapid growth soon overtaxed the political talents of Kaiser Wilhelm II and led to mounting tensions with England, Russia and France. When war broke out in 1914, Germany's only ally was a weakened Austria-Hungary. Gruelling trench warfare on two fronts sapped the nation's resources, and by late 1918 Germany sued for peace. The kaiser abdicated and escaped to the Netherlands. Amid widespread public anger and unrest, a new republic, which became known as the Weimar Republic, was proclaimed.

The Treaty of Versailles in 1919 chopped huge areas off Germany and imposed heavy reparation payments. These were impossible to meet, and when France and Belgium occupied the Rhineland to ensure continued payments, the subsequent hyperinflation and miserable economic conditions provided

HOW MUCH?

- **Budget hotel room** €60
- **Tasty sausage meal** €6
- **Bratwurst** €2
- **Bottle of Rhine wine** €6
- **U-Bahn ticket** €2

LONELY PLANET INDEX

- **1L petrol** €1.19
- **1L bottled water** €1
- **Beer (0.3L local Pils)** €2
- **Souvenir T-shirt** €15
- **Doner kebab** €2

fertile ground for political extremists. One of these was Adolf Hitler, an Austrian drifter, would-be artist and German army veteran.

Led by Hitler, the National Socialist German Workers' Party (or Nazi Party) staged an abortive coup in Munich in 1923. This landed Hitler in prison for nine months, during which time he wrote *Mein Kampf*.

From 1929 the worldwide economic Depression hit Germany hard, leading to unemployment, strikes and demonstrations. The Communist Party under Ernst Thälmann gained strength, but wealthy industrialists began to support the Nazis and police turned a blind eye to Nazi street thugs.

The Nazis increased their strength in general elections and in 1933 replaced the Social Democrats as the largest party in the Reichstag (parliament), with about one-third of the seats. Hitler was appointed chancellor and one year later assumed absolute control as führer (leader).

WWII & the Division of Germany

From 1935 Germany began to re-arm and build its way out of the economic depression with strategic public works such as the *autobahns* (freeways). Hitler reoccupied the Rhineland in 1936, and in 1938 annexed Austria and, following a compromise agreement with Britain and France, parts of Czechoslovakia.

All of this took place against a backdrop of growing racism at home. The Nuremberg Laws of 1935 deprived non-Aryans – mostly Jews and Roma (sometimes called Gypsies) –

of their German citizenship and many other rights. On 9 November 1938 the horror escalated into *Kristallnacht* (night of broken glass), in which synagogues and Jewish cemeteries, property and businesses across Germany were desecrated, burned or demolished.

In September 1939, after signing a pact that allowed both Stalin and himself a free hand in the east of Europe, Hitler attacked Poland, which led to war with Britain and France. Germany quickly occupied large parts of Europe, but after 1942 began to suffer increasingly heavy losses. Massive bombing reduced Germany's cities to rubble, and the country lost 10% of its population. Germany surrendered unconditionally in May 1945, soon after Hitler's suicide.

At the end of the war, the full scale of Nazi racism was exposed. 'Concentration camps', intended to rid Europe of people considered undesirable according to Nazi doctrine, had exterminated some six million Jews and one million more Roma, communists, homosexuals and others in what has come to be known as the Holocaust, history's first 'assembly line' genocide.

At conferences in Yalta and Potsdam, the Allies (the Soviet Union, the USA, the UK and France) redrew the borders of Germany, making it around 25% smaller than it had become after the Treaty of Versailles 26 years earlier. Germany was divided into four occupation zones.

In the Soviet zone of the country, the communist Socialist Unity Party (SED) won the 1946 elections and began a rapid nationalisation of industry. In September 1949 the Federal Republic of Germany (FRG) was created out of the three western zones; in response the German Democratic Republic (GDR) was founded in the Soviet zone the following month, with (East) Berlin as its capital.

From Division to Unity

As the West's bulwark against communism, the FRG received massive injections of US capital, and experienced rapid economic development (the *Wirschaftswunder* or 'economic miracle') under the leadership of Konrad Adenauer. The GDR, on the other hand, had to pay US$10 billion in war reparations to the Soviet Union and rebuild itself from scratch.

A better life in the west increasingly attracted skilled workers away from the miserable economic conditions in the east. As these were people the GDR could ill afford to lose, it built a wall around West Berlin in 1961 and sealed its border with the FRG.

In 1971 a change to the more flexible leadership of Erich Honecker in the east, combined with the *Ostpolitik* (East Politics) of FRG chancellor Willy Brandt, allowed an easier political relationship between the two Germanys. In the same year the four occupying powers formally accepted the division of Berlin.

Honecker's policies produced higher living standards in the GDR, yet East Germany barely managed to achieve a level of prosperity half that of the FRG. After Mikhail Gorbachev came to power in the Soviet Union in March 1985, the East German communists gradually lost Soviet backing.

Events in 1989 rapidly overtook the GDR government, which resisted pressure to introduce reforms. When Hungary relaxed its border controls in May 1989, East Germans began crossing to the west. Tighter travel controls resulted in would-be defectors taking refuge in the FRG's embassy in Prague. Meanwhile, mass demonstrations in Leipzig spread to other cities and Honecker was replaced by his security chief, Egon Krenz, who introduced cosmetic reforms. Then suddenly on 9 November 1989, a decision to allow direct travel to the west was mistakenly interpreted as the immediate opening of all GDR borders with West Germany. That same night thousands of people streamed into the west past stunned border guards. Millions more followed in the next few days, and the dismantling of the Berlin Wall began soon thereafter.

The trend at first was to reform the GDR but, in East German elections held in early 1990, citizens voted clearly in favour of the pro-reunification Christian Democratic Union (CDU). A Unification Treaty was drawn up to integrate East Germany into the Federal Republic of Germany, enacted on 3 October 1990. All-German elections were held on 2 December that year and, in the midst of national euphoria, the CDU-led coalition, which strongly favoured reunification, soundly defeated the Social Democrat opposition. CDU-leader Helmut Kohl earned the enviable position of 'unification chancellor'.

Two Decades Somewhat Whole

In 1998 a coalition of Social Democrats, led by Gerhard Schröder, and Bündnis 90/die Grünen (the Greens party) took political office from Kohl and the CDU amid allegations of widespread financial corruption in the unification-era government.

Schröder and the SDP-Greens only narrowly managed to retain office in the 2002 general election. In 2004 things looked even worse. The slashing of university funding brought students out in protest for several weeks, and a botched reform of the public-health-insurance system was one of the most unpopular pieces of legislation ever, resulting in massive gains for the supposedly discredited CDU at subsequent local elections.

These advances paid off in September 2005 as a fumbling Schröder went down in national elections, although just barely. The winner by a very narrow margin was Angela Merkel and the CDU. Not only is Merkel the first woman chancellor in German history but she is also the first one who grew up in the old GDR.

During her first term in office, Merkel proved to be a cautious leader, forming a coalition with the SPD. Her style, devoid of even a trace of drama-queen, struck a chord with many Germans and her popularity remained at over 50% even as the CDU's fell somewhat on increasingly harsh economic times. One move which won her plaudits was the frosty reception she gave efforts at a summit neck rub by the US president George W Bush, a man deeply unpopular in Germany.

Meanwhile Germany's export-based economy has been battered by global recession and the mood is glum. Two decades after reunification, the overall stereotypes of the west and the old east – that the *Wessis* are arrogant while the *Ossis* simply bitch – had become ingrained in German culture. But now both agree on one thing: times used to be better.

PEOPLE

Germany has a population of around 83 million, making it the most populous in central Europe. Germany's main native minority is the tiny group of Slavonic Sorbs in the eastern states of Saxony and Brandenburg, who maintain their own folk traditions. In political and economic terms, Germany is Europe's most decentralised nation, but considerable variation in population density exists. The Ruhr district in the northern Rhineland has

GERMANY

Germany's densest concentration of people and industry, while Mecklenburg-Western Pomerania in the northeastern corner is relatively sparsely settled. About one-third of the population lives in 84 cities, each with more than 100,000 people.

Immigration compensates for the extremely low birth rate among the established German population, and more than seven million foreigners now live in Germany. Most hail from Turkey, Italy, Greece and the former Yugoslavia, and have arrived as 'guest workers' in the west since the early 1960s to work in lower-paid jobs. In 1999 archaic immigration laws dating back to 1913 were changed to make it easier for residents without German ancestry to gain citizenship. Integration is generally fairly successful, although larger immigrant communities tend to stick together.

Recently Poles, freed by EU regulations, have been drawn by the relatively brighter lights of Germany, especially in the more affordable east.

RELIGION

The majority religions in Germany are Protestantism and Catholicism, which claim roughly equal numbers of followers. Some regions have higher concentrations of one branch – Bavaria is staunchly Catholic, for example.

The most significant minority religion is Islam, with about 1.8 million adherents, many of them immigrants. Around 60,000 Jews also live in Germany, little more than a tenth of pre-WWII numbers. Many are actually from the former Soviet Union, attracted by the relaxed immigration and citizenship deals offered around the time of reunification.

Germans who belong to a registered denomination have to pay a church tax on top of their income tax, usually around 10% of their salary. Unsurprisingly, fewer and fewer people are choosing to declare their religious affiliation.

ARTS

Germany's meticulously creative population has made major contributions to international culture, particularly during the 18th century when the Saxon courts at Weimar and Dresden attracted some of the greatest minds of Europe. With such rich traditions to fall back on, inspiration has seldom been in short supply for the new generations of German artists, despite the upheavals of the country's recent history.

Literature

The undisputed colossus of the German arts was Johann Wolfgang von Goethe: poet, dramatist, painter, politician, scientist, philosopher, landscape gardener and perhaps the last European to achieve the Renaissance ideal of excellence in many fields. His greatest work, the drama *Faust*, is the definitive version of the legend, showing the archetypal human search for meaning and knowledge.

Goethe's close friend Friedrich Schiller was a poet, dramatist and novelist. His most famous work is the dramatic cycle *Wallenstein,* based on the life of a treacherous general of the Thirty Years War who plotted to make himself arbiter of the empire. Schiller's other great play, *Wilhelm Tell,* dealt with the right of the oppressed to rise against tyranny.

On the scientific side, Alexander von Humboldt contributed much to environmentalism through his studies of the relationship of plants and animals to their physical surroundings. His contemporary, the philosopher Georg Wilhelm Friedrich Hegel, created an all-embracing classical philosophy that is still influential today.

Postwar literature was influenced by the politically focused Gruppe 47. It included writers such as Günter Grass, winner of the 1999 Nobel Prize for Literature, whose modern classic, *Die Blechtrommel* (The Tin Drum), humorously follows German history through the eyes of a young boy who refuses to grow up. Christa Wolf, an East German novelist and Gruppe 47 writer, won high esteem throughout Germany. Her 1963 story *Der geteilte Himmel* (Divided Heaven) tells of a young woman whose fiancé abandons her for life in the west.

A wave of recent novelists has addressed modern history in a lighter fashion. *Helden wie wir* (Heroes Like Us) by Thomas Brussig, an eastern German, tells the story of a man whose penis brings about the collapse of the Berlin Wall, while the GDR's demise is almost incidental to the eponymous barfly in Sven Regener's *Herr Lehmann* (Mr Lehmann). Also from Berlin is Russian-born Wladimir Kaminer (a possible mayoral candidate in 2011), whose books document stranger-than-fiction lives in the capital. His *Russian Disco* has been translated into English.

Bitterness in the east over the reunification is given a full airing in the darkly satirical *New Lives* by Ingo Schulze. The same subject matter is given a more entertaining take in *Settlement* by Christoph Hein, which follows the rise of Germany's richest man. Meanwhile the explicit tales of an 18-year-old girl, *Wetlands* by Charlotte Roche, set tongues wagging even in nonprudish Germany.

Cinema & TV

Since the foundation of the UFA studios in Potsdam in 1917, Germany has had an active and successful film industry. Marlene Dietrich (1901–92) became the country's first international superstar and sex symbol, starting out in silent films and later moving to Hollywood. Director Fritz Lang also made a name for himself, with complex films like *Metropolis* (1926) and *M* (1931).

During the Third Reich, the arts were devoted mainly to propaganda, with grandiose projects and realist art extolling the virtues of German nationhood. The best-known Nazi-era director was Leni Riefenstahl (1902–2003), whose *Triumph of the Will* (1934), depicting the Nuremberg rallies, won great acclaim but later rendered her unemployable. The controversy surrounding her personal politics dogged her for much of her life.

The 1960s and 1970s saw a great revival of German cinema, spearheaded by energetic, politically aware young directors such as Rainer Werner Fassbinder, Wim Wenders, Volker Schlöndorff and Margarethe von Trotta.

Most recently, Wolfgang Becker's GDR comedy *Good Bye Lenin!* (2003) was a surprise smash hit worldwide. One of the most powerful recent movies has been Marc Rothemund's *Sophie Scholl: The Final Days* (2006). It's a harrowing true story about a woman who protested against the Nazis in Munich and paid the ultimate price. And not to be missed is *The Lives of Others* (2006), the brilliant film about mistrust and betrayal in the old GDR. It won the Oscar for Best Foreign Film.

Meanwhile, German TV still shows a real predilection for showing musical variety shows long on hokum and schmaltz. After a few beers they're a hoot.

Music

Forget brass bands and oompah music – few countries can claim the impressive musical heritage of Germany. Even a partial list of household names would have to include Johann Sebastian Bach, Georg Friedrich Handel, Ludwig van Beethoven, Richard Strauss, Robert Schumann, Johannes Brahms, Felix Mendelssohn-Bartholdy, Richard Wagner and Gustav Mahler, all of whom are celebrated in museums, exhibitions and festivals around the country.

These musical traditions continue to thrive: the Berlin Philharmonic, Dresden Opera and Leipzig Orchestra are known around the world, and musical performances are hosted almost daily in every major theatre in the country.

Germany has also made significant contributions to the contemporary-music scene. Internationally renowned artists include punk icon Nina Hagen, '80s balloon girl Nena, and rock bands from the Scorpions to Die Toten Hosen and current darlings Wir sind Helden. Gothic and hard rock have a disproportionally large following in Germany, largely thanks to the success of death-obsessed growlers Rammstein.

For real innovation, though, the German dance-music scene is second to none, particularly in Frankfurt-am-Main and Berlin. Kraftwerk pioneered the original electronic sounds, which were then popularised in raves and clubs such as Berlin's Tresor in the early '90s. Paul van Dyk was among the first proponents of euphoric trance, which pushed club music firmly into the commercial mainstream; DJs such as Ian Pooley, Westbam and Ellen Allien now play all over the world. Germany has the largest electronic-music scene in the world and it is on full display (in every way) at the annual Love Parade in Berlin (p291).

The German pop scene is led by the goth-punk-boy-band fusion Tokio Hotel. Their chart-topping songs are led by the big-haired and androgynous Bill Kaulitz. Their appeal crosses borders: they won MTV's video music award for Best New Artist in 2008.

Architecture

The scope of German architecture is such that it could easily be the focus of an entire visit. The first great wave of buildings came with the Romanesque period (800–1200), examples of which can be found at Trier Cathedral,

GERMANY

the churches of Cologne and the chapel of Charlemagne's palace in Aachen.

The Gothic style (1200–1500) is best viewed at Freiburg's Münster cathedral, Cologne's Dom (cathedral) and the Marienkirche in Lübeck. Red-brick Gothic structures are common in the north of Germany, with buildings such as Schwerin's Dom and Stralsund's Nikolaikirche.

For classic baroque, Balthasar Neumann's superb Residenz in Würzburg, the magnificent cathedral in Passau and the many classics of Dresden's old centre are must-sees. The neoclassical period of the 19th century was led by Karl Friedrich Schinkel, whose name crops up all over Germany.

In 1919 Walter Gropius founded the Bauhaus movement in an attempt to meld theoretical concerns of architecture with the practical problems faced by artists and craftspeople. The Bauhaus flourished in Dessau, but with the arrival of the Nazis, Gropius left for Harvard University.

Albert Speer was Hitler's favourite architect, known for his pompous neoclassical buildings and grand plans to change the face of Berlin. Most of his epic works ended up unbuilt or flattened by WWII.

Frankfurt shows Germany's take on the modern high-rise. For a glimpse of the future of German architecture, head to Potsdamer Platz, Leipziger Platz and the new government area north of the Reichstag in Berlin, which are glitzy swathes of glass, concrete and chrome.

Visual Arts

The Renaissance came late to Germany but flourished once it took hold, replacing the predominant Gothic style. The draughtsman Albrecht Dürer of Nuremberg was one of the world's finest portraitists, as was the prolific Lucas Cranach the Elder, who worked in Wittenberg for more than 45 years. The baroque period brought great sculpture, including works by Andreas Schlüter in Berlin, while romanticism produced some of Germany's most famous paintings, best exemplified by Caspar David Friedrich and Otto Runge.

At the turn of the 20th century, expressionism established itself with great names like Swiss-born Paul Klee and the Russian-born painter Wassily Kandinsky, who were also associated with the Bauhaus design school. By the 1920s, art had become more radical and political, with artists like George Grosz, Otto Dix and Max Ernst exploring the new concepts of Dada and surrealism. Käthe Kollwitz is one of the era's few major female artists, known for her social-realist drawings.

The only works encouraged by the Nazis were of the epic style of propaganda artists like Mjölnir; nonconforming artists such as sculptor Ernst Barlach and painter Emil Nolde were declared 'degenerate' and their pieces destroyed or appropriated for secret private collections.

Since 1945 abstract art has been a mainstay of the German scene, with key figures like Joseph Beuys, Monica Bonviciniand and Anselm Kiefer achieving worldwide reputations. Leipzig is a hot spot for art. Figurative painters like Neo Rauch are generating much acclaim.

Theatre & Dance

In the 1920s Berlin was the theatrical capital of Germany; its most famous practitioner was the poet and playwright Bertolt Brecht (1898–1956). Brecht introduced Marxist concepts into his plays, aiming to encourage moral debate by detaching the audience from what was happening on stage.

Today Berlin once again has the most dynamic theatre scene in the country, as Volksbühne director Frank Castorf vies with Schaubühne head Thomas Ostermeier to capture the attention of young audiences neglected by the major stages, choosing mainly modern, provocative works. Dance, too, is undergoing a renaissance – although it is in Frankfurt. American William Forsythe has put together what is possibly the world's most innovative dance troupe, the Forsythe Company (www.theforsythecompany.de), which tours almost constantly – often in Dresden.

SPORT

Football (soccer) is the number-one spectator sport in Germany, as in most other European countries. Germany hosted the cup in 2006 in new or rebuilt stadiums all over the country. Although Germany finished third (Italy beat France in the final in Berlin), it was widely praised for hosting a fantastic series of matches, and many Germans took great pride in their time on the world stage.

Germany did one better at Euro 2008, although it lost to Spain in the final in Vienna. The Bundesliga is the top national league, with seasons running from September to June; notable top-flight teams include Bayern München, Borussia Dortmund and VfB Stuttgart. The DFB (www.dfb.de) is the national body responsible for all levels of the game.

International sports are also very well attended, especially when the relevant national teams are in form; major tennis, athletics, Grand Prix, swimming, cycling and water-polo events are all features of the German sporting calendar.

ENVIRONMENT
The Land

Germany covers 356,866 sq km and can be divided from north to south into several geographical regions.

The Northern Lowlands are a broad expanse of flat, low-lying land that sweeps across the northern third of the country from the Netherlands into Poland. The landscape is characterised by moist heaths interspersed with pastures and farmland.

The complex Central Uplands region divides northern Germany from the south. Extending from the deep schisms of the Rhineland massifs to the Black Forest, the Bavarian Forest, the Ore Mountains and the Harz Mountains, these low mountain ranges are Germany's heartland. The Rhine and Main Rivers, important waterways for inland shipping, cut through the southwest of this region. With large deposits of coal as well as favourable transport conditions, this was one of the first regions in Germany to undergo industrialisation.

The Alpine Foothills, wedged between the Danube and the Alps, are typified by sub-alpine plateaus and rolling hills, and moors in eastern regions around the Danube.

Germany's Alps lie entirely within Bavaria and stretch from the large, glacially formed Lake Constance in the west to Berchtesgaden in Germany's southeastern corner. Though lower than the mountains to their south, many summits are well above 2000m, rising dramatically from the Alpine Foothills to the 2962m Zugspitze, Germany's highest mountain.

Wildlife

Few species of flora and fauna are unique to Germany. However, what is unique is the importance Germans place on their forests, the prettiest of which are mixed-species decidu-

---

SMALL PARKS FOR THE PEOPLE

You see them by the thousands from trains: small individual gardens in clusters on odd bits of land near towns and cities, at railways junctions and in the shadow of roads. Called *Schrebergarten* (literally 'small gardens'), they are private patches of green splendour for their owners, who escape their urban flats to spend countless hours lavishing attention on their creations through the year. More than simply a place to grow cucumbers and tomatoes, the patches are often elaborate, with little cottages, pea-sized lawns and barbeques. Although tenants are there when they are off their jobs, you may glimpse their permanent inhabitants: garden gnomes.

---

ous forests planted with beech, oak, maple and birch. You'll find that many cities even have their own *Stadtwald* (city forest). Alpine regions bloom in spring with orchids, cyclamen, gentians, edelweiss and more; and the heather blossom on the Lüneburg Heath, north of Hanover, is stunning in August.

Apart from human beings, common mammals include deer, wild pigs, rabbits, foxes and hares. The chances of seeing these in summer are fairly good, especially in eastern Germany. On the coasts you will find seals and, throughout Germany, falcons, hawks, storks and migratory geese are a common sight.

National Parks

Berchtesgaden (in the Bavarian Alps), the Wattenmeer parks in Schleswig-Holstein, Lower Saxony and Hamburg, and the Unteres Odertal, a joint German-Polish endeavour, are highlights among Germany's 14 national parks.

There are 32 Unesco-listed sites in Germany. These include Bamberg (p220), Cologne's cathedral (p264), Lübeck (p286), Trier's monuments (p246) and Stralsund's centre (p206).

Environmental Issues

Germans are wholly on board with various green schemes. Households and businesses participate enthusiastically in waste-recycling programs. A refund system applies to a wide range of glass bottles and jars, while containers for waste paper and glass can be found in

GERMANY

each neighbourhood. The government is a signatory of the major international treaties on climate change and runs its own campaigns to save energy and reduce CO_2 emissions domestically. Despite a somewhat hostile climate for such schemes, requirements for solar power in residential and commercial buildings are proliferating.

FOOD & DRINK
Staples & Specialities
Wurst (sausage), in its hundreds of forms, is by far the most universal main dish. Regional favourites include bratwurst (spiced sausage), *Weisswurst* (veal sausage) and *Blutwurst* (blood sausage). Other popular main dishes include *Rippenspeer* (spare ribs), *Rotwurst* (black pudding), *Rostbrätl* (grilled meat), *Putenbrust* (turkey breast) and many forms of schnitzel (breaded pork or veal cutlet).

Potatoes feature prominently in German meals, as *Bratkartoffeln* (fried), *Kartoffelpüree* (mashed), Swiss-style rösti (grated then fried) or *Pommes Frites* (French fries); a Thuringian speciality is *Klösse*, a ball of mashed and raw potato that is then cooked into a dumpling. A similar Bavarian version is the *Knödel*. *Spätzle*, a noodle variety from Baden-Württemberg, is a common alternative.

Germans are keen on rich desserts. Popular choices are the *Schwarzwälder Kirschtorte* (Black Forest cherry cake) – one worthwhile tourist trap – as well as endless varieties of *Apfeltasche* (apple pastry). In the north you're likely to find berry *Mus*, a sort of compote. Desserts and pastries are also often enjoyed during another German tradition, the 4pm coffee break.

Beer is the national beverage and it's one cultural phenomenon that must be fully explored. The beer is excellent and relatively cheap. Each region and brewery has its own distinctive taste and body.

Vollbier is 4% alcohol by volume, *Export* is 5% and *Bockbier* is 6%. *Helles Bier* is light beer, while *dunkles Bier* is dark. *Export* is similar to, but much better than, typical international brews, while the *Pils* is more bitter. *Alt* is darker and more full-bodied. A speciality is *Weizenbier*, which is made with wheat instead of barley malt and served in a tall, 500mL glass. Nonalcoholic beers such as Clausthaler are also popular.

Eastern Germany's best beers hail from Saxony, especially Radeberger from near Dresden and Wernesgrüner from the Erzgebirge on the Czech border. Berliner Weisse is a low-alcohol wheat beer mixed with woodruff or raspberry syrup, seen as a bit of a tourist drink by locals. The breweries of Cologne produce Kölsch, always served in 200mL glasses to keep it fresh; in Bamberg Schlenkerla Rauchbier is smoked to a dark-red colour.

German wines are exported around the world, and for good reason. They are inexpensive and typically white, light and intensely fruity. A *Weinschorle* or *Spritzer* is white wine mixed with mineral water. The Rhine and Moselle Valleys are the classic wine-growing regions.

The most popular nonalcoholic choices are mineral water and soft drinks, coffee, and fruit or black tea. Bottled water almost always comes bubbly *(mit Kohlensäure)* – order *ohne Kohlensäure* if you're bothered by bubbles.

Where to Eat & Drink
German towns of any size have bright and modern bistro-type restaurants serving a wide range of fresh and creative food. In addition you'll find no shortage of ethnic foods; Italian, Turkish, Greek and Chinese are all popular. Most pubs serve basic German food. If you're on a low budget, you can get a feed at stand-up food stalls *(Schnellimbiss* or *Imbiss)*. The food is usually reasonable and filling, ranging from doner kebabs to traditional German sausages to the ubiquitous *Currywurst* (sausage served sliced, swimming in ketchup and sprinkled with curry powder) with beer.

Much of the German daily and social life revolves around daytime cafes, which often serve meals and alcohol as well as coffee. The late-opening variety are good places to meet people. See p290 for standard opening hours.

For self-caterers, supermarkets are inexpensive and have a decent range. Make a point of buying your drinks in supermarkets if your budget is tight. Most city centres have open-air food markets one or more days a week.

Students can eat cheaply (though not always well) at university *Mensa* (cafeterias). ID is not always checked.

Eating venues are supposed to be nonsmoking though this is not always followed.

Vegetarians & Vegans
Most German restaurants will have at least a couple of vegetarian dishes on the menu, although it is advisable to check anything that

doesn't specifically say it's meat-free, as bacon and chicken stock both seem to be common undeclared ingredients in German cuisine. Asian and Indian restaurants will generally be quite happy to make vegetarian dishes on demand. Vegans may find themselves having to explain exactly what they do and don't eat to get something suitable.

Habits & Customs
Restaurants always display their menus outside with prices, but watch for daily or lunch specials chalked onto blackboards. Lunch is the main meal of the day; getting a main meal in the evening is never a problem, but you may find that the dish or menu of the day only applies to lunch.

Rather than leaving money on the table, tip when you pay by stating a rounded-up figure or saying 'es stimmt so' (that's the right amount). A tip of 10% is generally about right.

BERLIN

☎ 030 / pop 3.41 million

Something old, something new. Reminders of Berlin's once-divided past sit side by side with its united present – Norman Foster's Reichstag dome, Peter Eisenman's Holocaust Memorial and the iconic Brandenburg Gate are all contained within a few neighbouring blocks of each other. Potsdamer Platz and its shiny Sony Centre host the star-studded Berlin Film Festival each year, a stone's throw from where only 20 years ago you could climb up a viewing platform in the west and peer over the wall to glimpse the alternate reality of the east. Casually strolling along Bernauerstrasse near trendy Prenzlauer Berg, you suddenly place your foot on a brick-marked line in the pavement marking where the wall once stood.

Renowned for its diversity and its tolerance, its alternative culture and its night-owl stamina, the best thing about the German capital is the way it reinvents itself and isn't shackled by its mind-numbing history. And the world is catching on – as evidenced by the surge of expatriates and steady increase of out-of-towners coming to see what all the fuss is about.

Meanwhile, freelancers and creative types flock here to write that book, paint their hearts out or simply live the ultimate bohemian life (though its the low price tag that often inspires these romantic lifestyle choices). Still, in Berlin nobody questions artistic intentions, experimental philosophies or lofty ideas, and it's perfectly fine to try, fail and try again. Some arrive seeking (and finding) Hemingway's Paris or Warhol's New York, but everyone unearths something extraordinary that often makes home seem, well, banal.

In the midst of it all, students rub shoulders with Russian émigrés, fashion boutiques inhabit monumental GDR buildings, Turkish residents live next door to famous DJs and the nightlife has long left the American sector as edgy clubbers watch the sun rise over the neon-lit Universal Music headquarters in the city's east.

In short, all human life is here, and don't expect to get much sleep.

HISTORY
United, divided, united again, Berlin has a rollercoaster past. The merger of two medieval trading posts, it enjoyed its first stint as a capital when in 1701 it became the leading city of the state of Brandenburg-Prussia. Under Prussian King Friedrich I and his son, Friedrich II, it flourished culturally and politically.

The Industrial Revolution, when commercial giants such as Siemens emerged, also boosted the city. As workers flooded to Berlin's factories, its population doubled between 1850 and 1870. 'Deutschland' was a latecomer to the table of nationhood, but in 1871 Berlin was again proclaimed a capital, this time of the newly unified Germany.

By 1900 the city was home to almost two million people, but after WWI it fell into decline and like the rest of Germany it suffered an economic crisis and hyperinflation. There was a brief, early communist uprising in the capital, led by Karl Liebknecht and Rosa Luxemburg (whose names now adorn Berlin streets). However, that was quickly squashed, and during the following Weimar Republic (1919–33) Berlin gained a reputation for decadence. Cabaret, the savage political theatre of Bertolt Brecht, expressionist art and jazz all flourished as Berliners partied to forget their troubles.

In the mid-1930s Berlin became a centrepiece of Nazi power and suffered heavily during WWII. During the 'Battle of Berlin' from August 1943 to March 1944, British bombers

GERMANY

GREATER BERLIN

targeted the city nightly. The Soviets also shelled Berlin and invaded from the east.

The Potsdam Conference took place in August 1945 and split the capital into zones occupied by the four victorious powers – the USA, Britain, France and the Soviet Union. In June 1948 the three Western Allies introduced a separate currency and administration in their sectors. In response, the Soviets blockaded West Berlin. Only a huge airlift by the Allies managed to keep the city stocked with food and supplies. In October 1949 East Berlin became the capital of the GDR, the German Democratic Republic.

The Berlin Wall, built in August 1961, was originally intended to prevent the drain of skilled labour from the East, but soon became a Cold War symbol. For decades East Berlin and West Berlin developed separately, until Hungarians breached the Iron Curtain in May 1989 and the Berlin Wall followed on 9 November. By 1 July 1990 the wall was being hacked to pieces. The Unification Treaty signed on 3 October that year designated Berlin the official capital of Germany, and in June 1991 the parliament voted to move the

seat of government from Bonn back to Berlin. In 1999 that was finally achieved.

Times, however, have been tough. Without the huge national subsidies provided during the decades of division, the newly unified Berlin has struggled economically. In 2001 the centre-right mayor resigned amid corruption allegations, leaving the city effectively bankrupt. Current centre-left and openly gay mayor Klaus Wowereit first came into power in 2001 and was re-elected in 2006 – he is popular and passionately dedicated to his city, but has made few inroads into the crisis. But Wowereit remains undaunted and tries to look on the bright side, constantly reminding us of his now-famous proclamation, 'Berlin is poor, but sexy'.

ORIENTATION

Standing at Berlin's Brandenburg Gate, on the former east–west divide, you can see many major sights. Looking east, your eye follows the road Unter den Linden, past the Museumsinsel (Museum Island) in the Spree River, to the needle-shaped Fernsehturm (TV tower) at Alexanderplatz.

If you turn west, you face the golden Siegessäule (Victory Column) along the equally huge thoroughfare of Strasse des 17 Juni, which cuts through the middle of Berlin's central park, the Tiergarten. To your right, just near the Brandenburg Gate, is the glass-domed Reichstag and beyond that the new government district and the snazzy Hauptbahnhof (main train station). The cluster of skyscrapers diagonally off to the left, with the unusual circus-tent roof, is Potsdamer Platz.

On the other, far west side of the Tiergarten, out of sight near Zoo station, sits the one-time centre of West Berlin, including the shopping street of the Kurfürstendamm (or 'Ku'damm').

Although wealthier, more mature Berliners still happily frequent the west, the eastern districts are the most happening. Even Mitte, or the centre, now lies east of the former Wall. As Mitte heads northeast, it merges into the trendy district of Prenzlauer Berg. Friedrichshain, another popular neighbourhood, is found several kilometres east of the centre, around Ostbahnhof.

Kreuzberg, south of Mitte, has two sides: Western Kreuzberg was the alternative hub of West Berlin and is still hanging in there, with some interesting restaurants and bars; eastern Kreuzberg is grungier, hopping and definitely where the 'kool kids' – and adults – hang out. Farther east and south is the rapidly gentrifying Kreuzköln, which is loosely defined as the area where Kreuzberg and neighbouring Neuköln overlap. The upscale southwestern districts of Charlottenburg, Schöneberg and Wilmersdorf offer nice restaurants and a calm atmosphere, though some may find it a tad sterile in comparison with places further east.

INFORMATION

Internet access is a breeze to find in Berlin – and the entire Sony Center at Potsdamerplatz (p174) is a free public hot spot.

Al Hamra (Map pp170-1; ☎ 4285 0095; Raumerstrasse 16; per hr €1; ☺ 9am-4am; Ⓜ Eberswalder Strasse) Internet access.

Berlin Tourismus (☎ 250 025; www.berlin-tour ist-information.de) Alexanderplatz (Map pp170-1; Alexa Shopping Centre; ☺ 10am-6pm); Brandenburger Tor (Map pp170-1; ☺ 10am-6pm); Hauptbahnhof/Main Train Station (Map pp170-1; Ground fl/Europa Platz Entrance; ☺ 8am-10pm); Reichstag (Map pp170-1; ☺ 10am-6pm); Zoologisher Garten Station (Map p176; Kurfürstendamm 21; ☺ 10am-8pm Mon-Sat, to 6pm Sun)

Berlin Welcome Card (www.berlin-welcomecard.de; 48/72hr €16.50/21.50, incl Potsdam & up to 3 children €18/24.50) Free public transport, plus museum and entertainment discounts.

Kassenärztliche Bereitschaftsdienst (Public Physicians' Emergency Service; ☎ 310 031; www.kvberlin.de, in German) Phone referral service.

Post office (Map pp170-1; Rathausstrasse 5; ☺ 8am-7pm Mon-Fri, to 4pm Sat; Ⓜ Alexanderplatz).

Surf & Sushi (Map pp170-1; ☎ 2838 4898; www .surfandsushi.de; Oranienburger Strasse 17; per hr €2; ☺ from noon Mon-Sat, from 1pm Sun; Ⓜ Oranienburger Strasse or Hackescher Markt) Internet access – free if you eat a bite of sushi.

SIGHTS

Unless otherwise indicated, where sights are grouped together they are all accessed by the same station listed at the beginning of the section.

Brandenburg Gate

Finished in 1791 as one of 18 city gates, the neoclassical **Brandenburg Gate** (Brandenburger Tor; Map pp170-1; Pariser Platz; Ⓜ S-Bahn Unter den Linden)

GERMANY

BERLIN IN TWO DAYS

Investigate the **Brandenburg Gate** (above) area, including the **Reichstag** (p172) and the **Holocaust Memorial** (p172). Walk east along Unter den Linden, stopping at the **Bebelplatz book-burning memorial** (p172). Veer through the **Museumsinsel** (p172) for window-shopping and cafe-hopping through **Hackescher Markt** (p173). In the evening, explore the bars of Prenzlauer Berg, along Kastanieanallee and Pappelallee. Stop for a drink in **Fleischmöbel** (p181).

Start the next day at the **East Side Gallery** (p174) remnant of the Berlin Wall, before heading to **Checkpoint Charlie** (p174) and the nearby **Jewish Museum** (p176). Take the U-Bahn to **Kurfürstendamm** (p176) and catch scenic bus 100 back to the **Fernsehturm** (p173). Later, explore Kreuzberg nightlife around Kottbusser Tor and go clubbing – **Berghain/Panorama Bar** (p181) is best if you are short on time. Alternatively, head for the **Berliner Ensemble** (p182).

MITTE & PRENZLAUER BERG

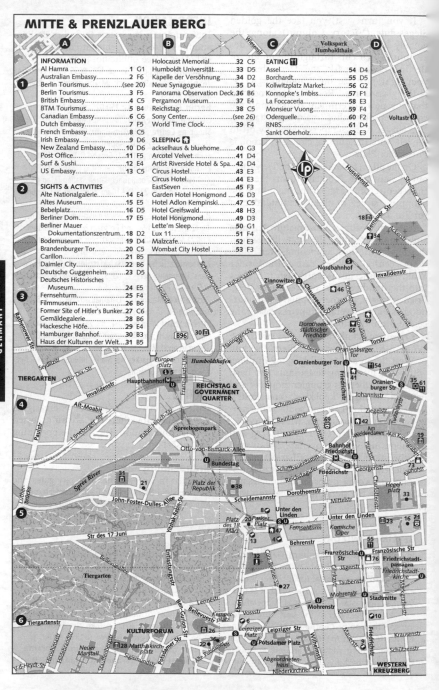

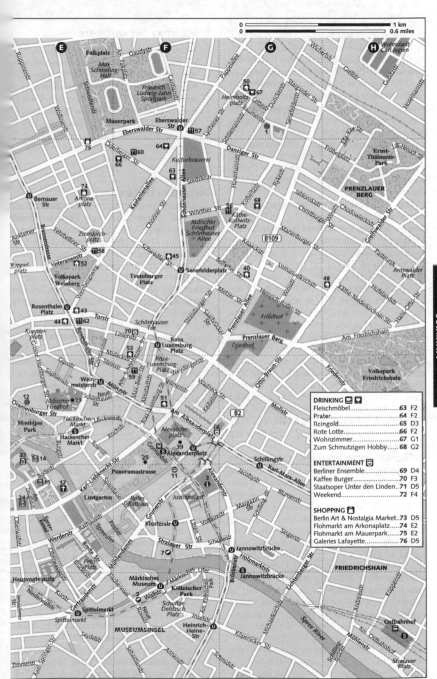

GERMANY

DRINKING 🍺 🍷
Fleischmöbel.............................**63** F2
Prater.......................................**64** F2
Reingold...................................**65** D3
Rote Lotte................................**66** F2
Wohnzimmer...........................**67** G1
Zum Schmutzigen Hobby......**68** G2

ENTERTAINMENT 🎭
Berliner Ensemble....................**69** D4
Kaffee Burger...........................**70** F3
Staatsoper Unter den Linden..**71** D5
Weekend...................................**72** F4

SHOPPING 🛍
Berlin Art & Nostalgia Market..**73** D5
Flohmarkt am Arkonaplatz.....**74** E2
Flohmarkt am Mauerpark.......**75** E2
Galeries Lafayette....................**76** D5

became an east–west crossing point after the Berlin Wall was built in 1961. A symbol of Berlin's division, it was a place US presidents loved to grandstand. John F Kennedy passed by in 1963. Ronald Reagan appeared in 1987 to appeal to the Russian leader, 'Mr Gorbachev, tear down this wall!'. In 1989 more than 100,000 Germans poured through it as the wall fell. Five years later, Bill Clinton somewhat belatedly noted: 'Berlin is free'. The crowning Quadriga statue, a winged goddess in a horse-drawn chariot (once kidnapped by Napoleon and briefly taken to Paris), was cleaned in 2000 along with the rest of the structure.

Just to the west stands the glass-domed **Reichstag** (Parliament; Map pp170-1; ☎ 2273 2152; www.bundestag.de; Platz der Republik 1; admission free; ☷ 8am-midnight, last admission 10pm), with four national flags fluttering. A fire here in 1933 allowed Hitler to blame the communists and grab power, while the Soviets raised their flag here in 1945 to signal Nazi Germany's defeat. Today the building is once again the German seat of power, but it's the glass cupola added during the 1999 refurbishment that some 10,000 people a day flock to see. Walking along the internal spiral walkway by British star architect Lord Norman Foster feels like being in a postmodern beehive. To beat the queues, book a table at the rooftop restaurant **Käfer** (☎ 2262 9935; www.feinkost-kaefer.de), which uses a separate entrance. With young children in tow, you're allowed to bypass the queue, too.

The Reichstag overlooks the **Tiergarten** (see opposite) and further south again is the **Holocaust Memorial** (Denkmal für die ermordeten Juden Europas; Map pp170-1; ☎ 2639 4336; www.stiftung-denkmal.de; Cora-Berliner-Strasse 1; admission free; ☷ field 24hr, information centre 10am-8pm Tue-Sun, last entry 7.15pm Apr-Sep, 10am-7pm Tue-Sun, last entry 6.15pm Oct-Mar; Ⓜ Potsdamer Platz/S-Bahn Unter den Linden) a grid of 2711 'stelae' or differently shaped concrete columns set over 19,000 sq metres of gently undulating ground. This slate grey expanse of walkways and pillars can be entered from any side, but presents varied sombre perspectives as you move through it. For historical background, designer Peter Eisenman has created an underground information centre in the southeast corner of the site. Highly recommended are the weekly **English tours** (€3; ☷ tours 4pm Sun).

NIGHT AT THE MUSEUMS

All museums listed on www.smb.museum are free on Thursday for four hours before closing time – this includes the **Pergamon Museum** (below) and the **Altes Museum** (below). Alternatively, museumophiles will love the **SchauLust Museen Berlin Pass** (☎ 250 025). A mere €15 gives you free admission to more than 70 museums (not including Checkpoint Charlie or the DDR Museum) over three days.

Unter den Linden

Celebrated in literature and lined with lime (or linden) trees, the street **Unter den Linden** (Map pp170-1) was the fashionable avenue of old Berlin. Today, after decades of communist neglect, it's been rebuilt and regained that status. The thoroughfare stretches east from the Brandenburger Tor to the Museuminsel, passing shops, embassies, operas, the **Deutsche Guggenheim** (Map pp170-1; ☎ 202 0930; www.deutsche-guggenheim.de; Unter den Linden 13-15; adult/concession €4/3, Mon free; ☷ 11am-8pm, to 10pm Thu; Ⓜ Französische Strasse) and the **Humboldt Universität** (Map pp170-1; Ⓜ S-Bahn Friedrichstrasse).

Stop by **Bebelplatz** (Map pp170-1; Ⓜ Französische Strasse), opposite the university, where there's a **book-burning memorial** – a reminder of the first major Nazi book-burning, which occurred in May 1933. A transparent window tile in the stone pavement reveals empty bookshelves below.

Museumsinsel

Lying along the Spree River, the **Museumsinsel** (Museums Island; Map pp170-1; ☎ all museums 2090 5577; www.smb.museum; adult/concession per museum €8/4, combined ticket for all museums €12/6, last 4hr Thu free; ☷ 10am-6pm Tue-Sun, to 10pm Thu; Ⓜ S-Bahn Hackescher Markt) contains the **Pergamonmuseum** (Map pp170-1; Am Kupfergraben 5), which is to Berlin what the British Museum is to London: a feast of Mesopotamian, Greek and Roman antiquities looted by archaeologists. The museum takes its name from the Pergamon Altar inside, but the real highlight of the collection is the Ishtar Gate from Babylon.

Meanwhile, the **Alte Nationalgalerie** (Old National Gallery; Map pp170-1; Bodestrasse 1-3) houses 19th-century European sculpture and painting; the **Altes Museum** (Map pp170-1; Am Lustgarten) has art from ancient Rome and Greece, including the spectacular bust of Nefertiti, housed here temporarily until she moves to the Neues Museum next door in late 2009; and the **Bodemuseum** (Map pp170-1; Monbijoubrücke) houses sculpture, Byzantine art and painting from the Middle Ages to the 19th century. Watch for special exhibitions at each.

Overlooking the 'island' is the **Berliner Dom** (Berlin Cathedral; Map pp170-1; ☎ 2026 9136 www.ber liner-dom.de; adult/under 14/concession €5/free/3; ☻ 9am-8pm Mon-Sat, from noon Sun, to 7pm Oct-Mar). The nearby **Deutsches Historisches Museum** (German History Museum; Map pp170-1; ☎ 203 040; www.dhm .de; Unter den Linden 2; admission €4, ☻ 10am-6pm) has a permanent exhibition on German history, but is still arguably most notable for the glass-walled spiral staircase by modernist architect IM Pei (creator of the Louvre's glass pyramid).

The entire Museumsinsel is currently being renovated and redeveloped – a new main visitor reception area is in the works and construction is expected to last until 2015. One of the most exciting projects is the reopening of the Neues Museum, which was reduced to rubble during WWII. It has now been fully rebuilt and is set to open in late 2009. The Neues Museum will house Queen Nefertiti and the rest of the Egyptian museum (currently part of the Altes Museum); the Museum of Pre- and Early History, currently living at Schloss Charlottenberg, will also relocate here. See www.museumsinsel-berlin.de for details.

Hackescher Markt

A complex of shops and apartments around eight courtyards, the **Hackesche Höfe** (Map pp170-1; Ⓜ S-Bahn Hackescher Markt) is commercial and touristy, but it's definitely good fun to wander around the big-name brand shops and smaller boutiques or simply people-watch in the cafes and restaurants – the atmosphere is always lively. You'll also find the **Neue Synagogue** (Map pp170-1; ☎ 8802 8300; www .cjudaicum.de; Oranienburger Strasse 28-30; adult/concession €3/2; ☻ 10am-8pm Sun & Mon, to 6pm Tue-Thu, to 5pm Fri, reduced hr Nov-Apr), with its history of local Jewish life.

Further north, the contemporary-art museum **Hamburger Bahnhof** (Map pp170-1; ☎ 3978 3439; www.hamburgerbahnhof.de; Invalidenstrasse 50, Mitte; adult/concession €8/4, last 4hr Thu free; ☻ 10am-6pm Tue-Fri, 11am-8pm Sat, 11am-6pm Sun; Ⓜ Hauptbahnhof/Lehrter Stadtbahnhof) is housed in a former neoclassical train station and showcases works by

Warhol, Lichtenstein, Cy Twombly and Keith Haring.

TV Tower

Call it Freudian or call it *Ostalgie* (nostalgia for the communist East or *Ost*), but Berlin's once-mocked socialist **Fernsehturm** (Map pp170-1; ☎ 242 3333; www.berlinerfernsehturm.de; adult/concession €9.50/4.50; ☻ 9am-midnight Mar-Oct, from 10am Nov-Feb; Ⓜ Alexanderplatz) is fast becoming its most-loved symbol. Originally erected in 1969 and the city's tallest structure, its central bauble was decorated as a giant football for the 2006 Fifa World Cup, while its 368m outline still pops up in numerous souvenirs. That said, ascending 207m to the revolving (but musty) Telecafé is a less singular experience than visiting the Reichstag dome.

The Turm dominates **Alexanderplatz**, a former livestock and wool market that became the low-life district chronicled by Alfred Döblin's 1929 novel *Berlin Alexanderplatz* and then developed as a 1960s communist showpiece.

Even in a city so often described as one big building site, today's Alexanderplatz is an unusual hive of construction activity as it is transformed into the next Potsdamer Platz–style development. However, its communist past still echoes through the retro **World Time Clock** (Map pp170–1) and along the portentous **Karl-Marx-Allee**, which leads several kilometres east from the square to Friedrichshain.

Tiergarten

From the Reichstag (see opposite), the Tiergarten park's **carillon** (Map pp170-1; John-Foster-Dulles-Allee; ☒ 100 or 200) and the **Haus der Kulturen der Welt** (House of World Cultures; Map pp170-1; John-Foster-Dulles-Allee) are clearly visible. The latter was the US contribution to the 1957 International Building Exposition and it's easy to see why locals call it the 'pregnant oyster'.

Further west, the wings of the **Siegessäule** (Victory Column; Map p176; ☒ 100 or 200) were the *Wings of Desire* in that famous Wim Wenders film. This golden angel was built to commemorate Prussian military victories in the 19th century. Today, as the end point of the annual Christopher Street Parade, she's also a gay icon. However, there are better views than those at the column's peak.

A short walk south from here is a cluster of interesting embassy buildings and museums,

IF WALLS COULD TALK

Today's remnants of the 155km wall are scattered across the city, but you can follow all or sections of its former path along the 160km-long **Berliner Mauerweg** (Berlin Wall Trail; www.berlin .de/mauer), a signposted walking and cycling path that follows the former border fortifications, either along customs-patrol roads in West Berlin or border-control roads used by GDR guards. Along the route, 40 multilingual information stations provide historical context, highlight dramatic events and relate stories about daily life in the divided city.

The longest surviving stretch is the **East Side Gallery** (Map p175; www.eastsidegallery.com; Mühlenstrasse; Ⓜ S-Bahn Warschauer Strasse) in Friedrichshain. Panels along this 1.3km of graffiti and art include the famous portrait of Soviet leader Brezhnev kissing GDR leader Erich Hönecker and a Trabant car seemingly bursting through the (now crumbling) concrete.

The sombre **Berliner Mauer Dokumentationszentrum** (Berlin Wall Documentation Centre; Map pp170-1; ☎ 464 1030; www.berliner-mauer-dokumentationszentrum.de; Bernauer Strasse 111; admission free; Ⓨ 10am-6pm Tue-Sun Apr-Oct, to 5pm Nov-Mar; Ⓜ U-Bahn Bernauersrasse) is a memorial containing a section of the original wall, photos of the surrounding area (before and during the lifespan of the wall), newspaper clippings and listening stations featuring old West and East Berlin radio programs as well as eyewitness testimonies. Be sure to climb the tower for a view of an artistic re-creation of no-man's land as well as the **Kapelle der Versöhnung** (Chapel of Reconciliation), a modern round structure of pressed earth and slim wooden planks built on the site of an 1894 red-brick church blown up in 1985 in order to widen the border strip. A 15-minute remembrance service for those killed while attempting to flee from east to west is held at noon Tuesday to Friday.

In Kreuzberg, the famous sign at **Checkpoint Charlie** (Map p175) still boasts 'You are now leaving the American sector'. But it and the reconstructed US guardhouse are just tourist attractions now. For a less light-hearted view of the past, visit **Haus am Checkpoint Charlie** (Map p175; ☎ 253 7250; www.mauer-museum.com; Friedrichstrasse 43-45; adult/concession €12.50/9.50; Ⓨ 9am-10pm; Ⓜ Kochstrasse/Stadtmitte). Tales of spectacular escape attempts include through tunnels, in hot-air balloons and even using a one-man submarine.

GERMANY

including the **Bauhaus Archiv** (Map p176; ☎ 254 0020; www.bauhaus.de; Klingelhöferstrasse 14; adult/concession Sat-Mon €7/4, Wed-Fri €6/3; Ⓨ 10am-5pm Wed-Mon; Ⓜ Nollendorfplatz) with drawings, chairs and other Modernist objects from the famous Bauhaus school of design – as well as a very tempting shop. The school itself survives in Dessau (see p202).

More museums are found a little east in the **Kulturforum** (Map pp170-1). These include the spectacular **Gemäldegalerie** (Picture Gallery; Map pp170-1; ☎ 266 2951; www.gemaelde galerie-berlin.de; Matthäikirchplatz 4-6; adult/concession €8/4; Ⓨ 10am-6pm Tue, Wed & Fri-Sun, to 10pm Thu; Ⓜ S-Bahn Potsdamer Platz) showing European painting from the 13th to the 18th centuries. Nearby is the **Neue Nationalgalerie** (Map p175; ☎ 266 2951; www .neue-nationalgalerie.de; Potsdamer Strasse 50; adult/concession €8/4; Ⓨ 10am-6pm Tue, Wed & Fri, to 10pm Thu, 11am-6pm Sat & Sun; Ⓜ S-Bahn Potsdamer Platz). Twentieth-century works by Picasso, Klee, Munch, Dalì, Kandinsky and many German expressionists are housed in an exquisite 'temple of light and glass' built by Bauhaus-director Ludwig Mies van der Rohe.

Potsdamer Platz

The lid was symbolically sealed on capitalism's victory over socialism in Berlin when this postmodern temple to Mammon was erected in 2000 over the former death strip. Under the big-top, glass-tent roof of the **Sony Center** (Map pp170-1; Ⓜ S-Bahn Potsdamer Platz) and along the malls of the Legolike **Daimler City** (Map pp170-1), people swarm in and around shops, restaurants, offices, loft apartments, clubs, a cinema, a luxury hotel and a casino – all revitalising what was the busiest square in prewar Europe.

During the International Film Festival Berlin (see p177), Potsdamer Platz welcomes Hollywood A-listers. In between you can rub shoulders with German cinematic heroes – particularly Marlene Dietrich – at the **Filmmuseum** (Map pp170-1; ☎ 300 9030; www .filmmuseum-berlin.de; Potsdamer Strasse 2, Tiergarten; adult/concession €6/4.50; Ⓨ 10am-6pm Tue, Wed & Fri-Sun, to 8pm Thu). There's also 'Europe's fastest' lift to the 100m-high **Panorama Observation Deck** (Map pp170-1; www.panoramapunkt.de; adult/concession €3.50/2.50; Ⓨ 11am-8pm).

KREUZBERG & FRIEDRICHSHAIN

See Mitte & Prer:lauer Berg Map (pp176–1)

GERMANY

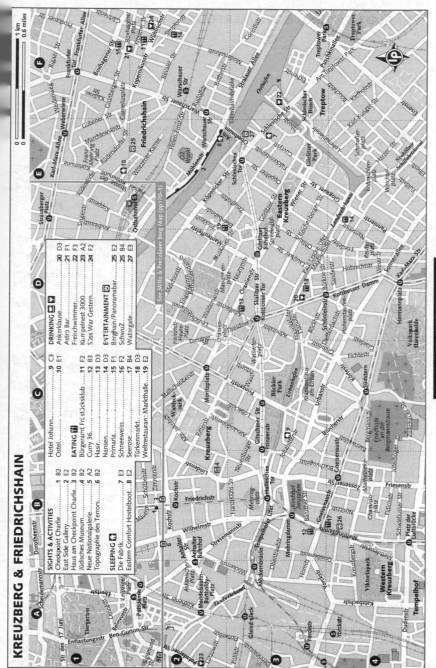

GERMANY

CHARLOTTENBURG & WILMERSDORF

INFORMATION		
Berlin Tourismus...................1 B2	EATING	SHOPPING
	Café Einstein Stammhaus..........6 D3	KaDeWe..................11 C3
SIGHTS & ACTIVITIES	Schwarzes Café.......................7 B2	
Bauhaus Archiv.....................2 D2	Winterfeldtplatz Farmers Market..8 D3	TRANSPORT
Kaiser-Wilhelm-Gedächtniskirche.3 C2		ADM Mitfahrzentrale.........12 B2
Siegessäule.........................4 D1	DRINKING	ADM Mitfahrzentrale.........13 C2
	Green Door.............................9 D3	
SLEEPING	Hafen.....................................10 D3	
Hotel Bogota.......................5 A3		

But, as ever in Berlin, the past refuses to go quietly. Just north of Potsdamer Platz lies the **former site of Hitler's Bunker** (Map pp170–1). A little southeast lies the **Topographie des Terrors** (Map p175; ☎ 2548 6703; www.topographie.de; Niederkirchner Strasse 8; admission free; ☉ 10am-8pm May-Sep, to dusk Oct-Apr), a shockingly graphic collection of text and images mounted on the ruins of the Gestapo and SS headquarters.

Jewish Museum
The Daniel Libeskind building that is the **Jüdisches Museum** (Map p175; ☎ 2599 3300; www.juedisches-museum-berlin.de; Lindenstrasse 9-14; adult/concession €5/2.50; ☉ 10am-10pm Mon, to 8pm Tue-Sun, last entry 1hr before closing; Ⓜ Hallesches Tor) is as much the attraction as the Jewish-German history

collection within. Designed to disorientate and unbalance with its 'voids', cul-de-sacs, barbed metal fittings, slit windows and uneven floors, this still-somehow-beautiful structure swiftly conveys the uncertainty and sometime terror of past Jewish life in Germany. It's a visceral experience, after which the huge collection itself demands your concentration. The building's footprint is a ripped-apart Star of David.

Kurfürstendamm
West Berlin's legendary shopping thoroughfare, the Ku'damm has lost some of its cachet since the wall fell, but is worth visiting. You will find the **Kaiser-Wilhelm-Gedächtniskirche** (Map p176; ☎ 218 5023; www.gedaechtniskirche-berlin

.de; Breitscheidplatz; ⏳ Memorial Hall 10am-4pm Mon-Sat, Hall of Worship 9am-7pm) here, which remains in ruins – just as British bombers left it on 22 November 1943 – as an antiwar memorial. Only the broken west tower still stands. In 1961 the modern hall of worship was built adjacent to the church.

Stasi Museum

The imposing compound, formerly the secret police headquarters, now contains the **Stasi Museum** (Map p168; ☎ 553 6854; House 1, Ruschestrasse 103; adult/concession €4/3; ⏳ 11am-6pm Tue-Fri, 2-6pm Sat & Sun; Ⓜ Magdalenenstrasse). It's largely in German, but well worth it to get a sense of the impact the Stasi had on the daily lives of GDR citizens through its extensive photos and displays of the astounding range of surveillance devices, as well as exhibits of the tightly sealed jars used to retain cloths containing body-odour samples.

Tours

Guided tours are phenomenally popular; you can choose Third Reich, Wall, bunker, communist, boat or bicycle tours, as well as guided pub crawls. Expect to pay around €15 and up.

New Berlin (☎ 017-9973 0397; www.newberlintours .com) even offers free (yup, free) 3½-hour introductory walking tours. These leave at 10:30am and 12:30pm from the Dunkin' Donuts opposite the Zoologisher Garten train station, and 11am and 1pm outside the Starbucks at Pariser Platz near the Brandenburg Gate. Guides are enthusiastic, knowledgeable…and accept tips.

Alternatively, you can tool around Berlin in a Trabant car. **Trabi Safari** (☎ 275 2273; www .trabi-safari.de; €30-60) operates from the Berlin Hi-Flyer near Checkpoint Charlie (see p174).

Other operators:

Insider Tours (☎ 692 3149; www.insidertour.com)
Original Berlin Walks (☎ 301 9194; www.berlin walks.com)

FESTIVALS & EVENTS

International Film Festival Berlin (☎ 259 200; www.berlinale.de) The Berlinale, held in February, is Germany's answer to the Cannes and Venice film festivals.
Christopher Street Day (☎ 2362 8632; www.csd-ber lin.de) Held on the last weekend in June, Germany's largest gay event celebrated its 30th anniversary in 2008.
B-Parade (www.b-parade.eu) Held each July, Berlin's huge techno street parade is the successor to the Love Parade.
Fuckparade (www.fuckparade.org) Each August, this anti-establishment, antigentrification demonstration dances to its own noncommercial techno beat.

SLEEPING
Mitte & Prenzlauer Berg
BUDGET

Berlin's independent hostels are far superior to the standard DJH (www.jugendherberge .de) locations in town.

Lette'm Sleep (Map pp170-1; ☎ 4473 3623; www .backpackers.de; Lettestrasse 7; dm from €11, tw with shared bathroom from €40, apt from €69; Ⓜ Eberswalder Strasse; 🖳) Located within stumbling distance of the Prenzlauer Berg nightlife action, this colourful and convenient party hostel is simply groovy, baby, groovy.

EastSeven (Map pp170-1; ☎ 9362 2240; www.east seven.de; Schwedter Strasse 7; dm from €13, s/d/tr/q per person

GERMANY

FREE PICKS

Welcome news for budget travellers: in comparison to other European capitals, Berlin is generally quite inexpensive, and several key sights and experiences are completely free:

- **Brandenburg Gate** (p169) The symbol of Berlin and of reunified Germany is a must-see on any Berlin itinerary.
- **Kaiser-Wilhelm-Gedächtniskirche** (opposite) This left-as-it-was-bombed church on the Ku'damm is a vivid reminder of WWII.
- **Tiergarten** (p173) Let yourself get lost in this oasis of green.
- **New Berlin city tours** (above) They're free, and guides are chock-full of information about their beloved city.
- **Holocaust Memorial** (p172) An experiential monument to the victims of the Holocaust.
- **East Side Gallery** (p174) The longest remaining section of the wall is a memorial to freedom.

from €30/21/17/16.50, bedding €3; **M** Senefelder Platz; 💻)
Retro and homey with spotless rooms and sturdy pine furniture, there is a youthful elegance here rarely present in hostels. The lovely garden is perfect for summer barbecues.

Circus Hostel (Map pp170-1; ☎ 2839 1433; www .circus-hostel.de; Weinbergsweg 1a; dm €19-25, s/d with shared bathroom €40/56, with private bathroom €50/70, 2-/4-person apt €85/140; **M** U-Bahn Rosenthaler Platz; 💻) This stalwart is one of the most popular hostels in town, with great central location, friendly staff and tastefully decorated rooms in cheerful colours. There's a two-night minimum stay for apartments.

Wombat City Hostel (Map pp170-1; ☎ 8471 0820; www.wombats-hostels.com; Alte Schönhauser Strasse 2; dm/d €21/58, apt with kitchen €100; **M** Rosa-Luxemburg-Platz; 💻) A new addition to the Mitte hostel scene, rooms and dorms (all en suite) are decorated Ikea-style and doubles offer long balconies. A hopping lounge and all-you-can-eat breakfast buffet (€3.50) round out the package. Discounts are available from November to February.

Hotel Greifswald (Map pp170-1; ☎ 4442 7888; www .hotel-greifswald.de; Greifswalderstrasse 211; s/d/tr/apt from €57/69/90/75; **M** Senefelder Platz; 💻) You'd never guess this informal, quiet hotel set back from the street around a sweet courtyard is regularly home to bands and even rock stars – until you see their photos in the lobby. We love the sumptuous breakfast buffet (€7.50) served until noon.

MIDRANGE & TOP END

Circus Hotel (Map pp170-1; ☎ 2000 3939; www.circus -berlin.de; Rosenthalerstrasse 1; s €68, d from €78, ste €98, apt €110-160; **M** U-Bahn Rosenthaler Platz; 💻) The fancier younger sister to the Circus Hostel (above) across the intersection, this brand-spanking new hotel has given careful attention to every detail – the result is a retro twist on minimalism, airy rooms, bold-coloured walls and supershiny wood flooring.

Malzcafe (Map pp170-1; ☎ 702 21357; www.malzcafe .de; Veteranenstrasse 10; s/d/q €69/99/139, apt from €109; **M** Rosenthaler Platz; 💻) A small hotel above an adjoining cafe, here you'll be made to feel right at home in minimalist rooms with soft, soothing tones, high ceilings and plenty of space. A pleasant terrace is divine in warm weather, and you're a short hop to both the heart of Mitte and Prenzlauer Berg.

Artist Riverside Hotel & Spa (Map pp170-1; ☎ 284 900; www.great-hotel.de; Friedrichstrasse 106; d €80-300;

M Friedrichstrasse; 💻 🛁) Colourful rooms with class, regardless of what level of luxury and price range you choose (there are five). All guests receive 50% off the popular adjoining day spa and discount on massages. Breakfast costs €5 to €19.50.

our pick ackselhaus & bluehome (Map pp170-1; ☎ 4433 7633; www.ackselhaus.de; Belforter Strasse 21; ste from €90, apt €140-260; **M** Senefelder Platz; 💻) This Zen oasis, spread out across two buildings, offers exquisitely designed suites or apartments (most with kitchenettes); each has a different theme, from Italian to Hollywood; all exude an element of exquisite class, calm and humour – the African suite, for example, has stuffed-animal heads mounted on the wall.

Arcotel Velvet (Map pp170-1; ☎ 278 7530; www .arcotel.at; Oranienburger Strasse 52; d €130-220, ste €135-155; **M** Oranienburger Tor) Floor-to-ceiling windows give front rooms a bird's-eye view of the bustling street and, combined with bathrooms separated only by gauze curtains, create a feeling of loft living. If you plan to retire before 2am, request a room facing the back. Breakfast is €16.

Lux 11 (Map pp170-1; ☎ 936 2800; www.lux-eleven .com; Rosa-Luxemburg-Strasse 9-13; r/ste from €165/255; **M** Weinmeisterstrasse/Alexanderplatz; 💻) A liberal use of white makes this slick, streamlined hotel a haven of unpretentious minimalism.

Hotel Honigmond (Map pp170-1; ☎ 284 4550; www .honigmond-berlin.de; Tieckstrasse 12; s €95-149, d €89-199; **M** Oranienburger Tor; 💻) is a perfect choice for a romantic weekend (or simply those seeing a touch of elegance and class). This tasteful hotel is all creaky wooden floors and four-poster beds. Sister property **Garden Hotel Honigmond** (Map pp170-1; ☎ 2844 5577; www .honigmond-berlin.de; Invalidenstrasse 122; s/d from €99/109; **M** Zinnowitzer Strasse; 💻) offers similar rooms but includes a tranquil back garden.

Still remembered for being the site of Michael Jackson's baby-dangling episode, the luxurious **Hotel Adlon Kempinski** (Map pp170-1; ☎ 226 10; www.hotel-adlon.de; Am Pariser Platz, Unter den Linden 77; r from €450; 🖩 💻 🛁) is situated on the doorstep of the Brandenburg Gate.

Kreuzberg & Friedrichshain

Ostel (Map p175; ☎ 2576 8660; www.ostel.eu; Wriezener Karree 5; dm/d €9/61, apt €120; **M** Ostbahnhof; 💻) *Ostalgie* – nostalgia for the communist East – is taken to a whole new level at this hostel/ hotel with original socialist GDR furnishings and portraits of Honecker and other former socialist leaders. You can even stay in a 'bugged' Stasi Suite. You might think you've entered a surreal time machine – until you access the free wi-fi in the lobby, that is.

Eastern Comfort Hostelboot (Map p175; ☎ 6676 3806; www.eastern-comfort.com; Mühlenstrasse 73-77; dm €16, s/d from €54/76, bedding €5; Ⓜ S-Bahn Warschauer Strasse; 🖳) This moored boat-turned-hostel is close to the East Side Gallery, is convenient for both Kreuzberg and Friedrichshain and features cosy rooms and dorms (all en suite). If it's full, campers can pitch a tent on the deck for €12 a night or ask about the 18 units in the Western Comfort boat across the river (check-in at Eastern Comfort). Free wi-fi.

our pick Die Fabrik (Map p175; ☎ 611 7716; www .diefabrik.com; Schlesischestrasse 18; dm €18, s/d/tr/q from €38/52/69/84; Ⓜ Schlesisches Tor; 🖳) A cross between a hostel and a hotel (feels more like the latter), these tidy and simple rooms are a steal. Plenty of spotless shower and toilet facilities are located on each floor and larger doubles come with washbasins and tiny sitting areas – oh, and solar power heats 100% of your hot water in the sunny months (and a smaller percentage in other seasons).

Hotel Johann (Map p175; ☎ 225 0740; www.hotel -johann-berlin.de; Johanniterstrasse 8; d €90-100; Ⓜ Prinzenstrasse, Hallesches Tor; 🖳) A design hotel with a comfortable feel, Johann features include exposed brick walls, tall arched ceilings and a lovely garden.

Charlottenburg & Schöneberg

Berliner Bed & Breakfast (off Map p176; ☎ 2437 3962; www.berliner-bed-and-breakfast.de; Langenscheidtstrasse 5; s/d/tr/q with shared bathroom €30/50/65/75; Ⓜ Kleistpark). Lofty ceilings and gorgeous wood floors dominate in this small, unique space with themed rooms (Asia, retro, fashionable). Excellent breakfast food is left for guests each day, which you prepare yourself in the communal kitchen.

Hotel Bogota (Map p176; ☎ 881 5001; www.bogota.de; Schlüterstrasse 45; d with shared bathroom €64-77, with private bathroom €90-150; Ⓜ Uhlandstrasse) With oodles of charm and character at affordable prices, this is a must for vintage-furniture lovers. Ask about the landmark building's fascinating fashion history (which will explain the snazzy photos adorning the walls).

Propellor Island City Lodge (off Map p176; ☎ 891 9016; www.propeller-island.de; Albrecht-Achilles-Strasse 58; r per person €69-190; Ⓜ Adenauer Platz; 🖳) Keen to sleep in a bed suspended by ropes, or in a

coffin or on a pile of chopped logs? If you've dreamed it you can probably find it in one of the 31 themed rooms (oh, and slightly more standard spaces are available too).

EATING

Berliners love to eat out – it's relaxed and affordable and patrons often linger long after finishing their meals – in fact, many of the best finds are in the budget category. Restaurants usually open from 11am to midnight, with varying *Ruhetage* or rest days. Cafes often close around 8pm, though equal numbers stay open until 2am or later.

Berlin is a snacker's paradise, with Turkish (your best bet), wurst (sausage), Greek, Italian, and Chinese *Imbiss* stalls throughout the city. Meat-eaters should not leave the city without trying Berlin's famous *Currywurst*.

There's the excellent organic **Kollwitzplatz market** (Map pp170-1; 🕐 9am-4pm Sat & Sun), the relaxed **Winterfeldtplatz farmers market** (Map p176; 🕐 Wed & Sat) and the bustling, ultracheap **Türkenmarkt** (Turkish market; Map p175; 🕐 noon-6:30pm Tue & Fri).

Mitte & Prenzlauer Berg

La Focacceria (Map pp170-1; ☎ 4403 2771; Fehrbelliner Strasse 24; slices €1.50; 🕐 11am-11pm; Ⓜ Rosenthaler Platz) A character-filled focaccia and pizza joint with an intense local following – perfect for an afternoon snack after a hard day's shopping or sightseeing.

Konnopke's Imbiss (Map pp170-1; Schönhauser Allee 44a; snacks €1.50-5; 🕐 6am-8pm Mon-Fri, noon-7pm Sat; Ⓜ Eberswalder Strasse) The quintessential wurst stand under the elevated U-Bahn tracks. We think Konnopke's serves the best *Currywurst* in town.

RNBS (Map pp170-1; ☎ 540 2505; Oranienburger Strasse 50; mains €3.50-6; Ⓜ Oranienburger Strasse/ Hackescher Markt) The Asian soups and noodle dishes served up by this tiny orange-and-white outlet are as delicious as they are healthy: no preservatives, no MSG, no artificial flavourings.

Sankt Oberholz (Map pp170-1; ☎ 2408 5586; Rosenthaler Strasse 72a; dishes €4-7; Ⓜ Rosenthaler Platz) Berlin's 'Urbanen Pennern' (officeless, self-employed creative types) have been flocking here for years with their laptops for the free wi-fi access, but we like it for the people-watching – especially from the lofty lifeguard chairs out front. Soups, sandwiches and salads are always satisfying.

our pick **Assel** (Map pp170-1; ☎ 281 2056; Oranienburgerstrasse 61; mains €5-15; Ⓜ Oranienburger Strasse or Hackescher Markt) One of the few exceptional picks on a particularly touristy and busy stretch of Mitte. Come for coffee, a bite or a full meal and stretch out in the wooden booths made from old S-Bahn seats. Plus, the toilets are entertaining (you'll see).

Monsieur Vuong (Map pp170-1; ☎ 3087 2643; Alte Schönhauser Strasse 46; mains €6.90; Ⓜ Weinmeisterstrasse, Rosa-Luxemburg-Platz or Alexanderplatz) Berlin's original designer Asian soup den is trendy, packed and consistently serves amazing Vietnamese fare. Arrive early to avoid queuing.

Oderquelle (Map pp170-1; ☎ 4400 8080; Oderberger Strasse 27; mains €8-16; ☯ dinner; Ⓜ Eberswalder Strasse) Modern German food in such mellow, convivial digs is rare, almost as rare as snagging a table here after 7pm, so be sure to reserve.

Borchardt (Map pp170-1; ☎ 8188 6250; Französische Strasse 47; mains €18-40; Ⓜ Französische Strasse) On every Berlin *promi*'s (celeb's) speed-dial list, this refined French-German bistro also tolerates ordinary civilians.

Kreuzberg & Friedrichshain

Bürgeramt Früstücksklub (Map p175; Krossenerstrasse 22; burgers €2-4; ☯ from 11am Mon-Fri, from 10am Sat & Sun; Ⓜ Samariterstrasse) A mere 13 types of burgers, including chicken and vegie versions, are cooked up with love and a smile in this wee space – if you can't snag a seat head to the tree-filled square opposite. Hearty breakfast fare is also available.

Curry 36 (Map p175; ☎ 881 4710; Mehringdamm 36; snacks €2-6; ☯ 9am-4pm Mon-Sat, to 3pm Sun; Ⓜ Mehringdamm) This is Kreuzberg's most popular sausage stand, as evidenced by the daily queues (yes, it really is worth the wait).

Primaria (Map p175; ☎ 2904 4976; Boxhagener Strasse 26; mains €2-6; Ⓜ Frankfurter Tor) Mostly meatless Bulgarian fare (salads, casseroles, lots of feta) in cosy digs, and a friendly, helpful staff.

Hasir (Map p175; Adalbertstrasse 10; mains €5-10; ☯ 24hr; Ⓜ Kottbusser Tor) Local lore says this is the birthplace of Berlin's doner kebab – we haven't seen proof but we do know it tastes fantastic and we can indulge on proper chairs.

Schneeweiss (Map p175; ☎ 2904 9704; Simplonstrasse 16; day menu €7-10, mains €10-20; Ⓜ S-Bahn Warschauer Strasse) Subtly embossed vanilla wallpaper, rectangular glass lights along the long, central table and parquet flooring keep neutral 'Snow White' feeling more après-ski than icy. The vaguely German 'Alpine' food is excellent.

Seerose (Map p175; ☎ 6981 5927; Mehringdamm 47; dishes €7.50-8; Ⓜ Mehringdamm) One of the most popular vegie restaurants in town serves imaginative organic fare – pastas, soups and salads.

Nansen (Map p175; ☎ 301 1438; Maybachufer 39; mains €10-19; ☯ dinner; Ⓜ Schönlein Strasse) A newcomer in a rapidly changing area, here you can dine on seasonal modern German cuisine in a romantic, candlelit space – most menu items are sourced locally.

Weltrestaurant Markthalle (Map p175; ☎ 617 5502; Pücklerstrasse 34; mains €11.50-17; Ⓜ Görlitzer Bahnhof) This wood-lined, century-old pub draws a mixed clientele of ageing hipsters and neighbourhood folk with its relaxed vibe and interesting German fare.

Charlottenburg & Schöneberg

Schwarzes Café (Map p176; ☎ 313 8038; Kantstrasse 148; dishes €4.50-10; Ⓜ S-Bahn Zoo or Savignyplatz) Founded in 1978, this 24-hour food 'n' booze institution must have seen half of Berlin pass through it (or out in it) at some point. Don't leave without checking out the toilets.

Petite Europe (off Map p176; ☎ 781 2964; Langenscheidtstrasse 1; mains €5-12; ☯ dinner; Ⓜ Kleist park) Pizzas, pastas and other straightforward Italian fare are still going strong at this 40-year-old institution.

Café Einstein Stammhaus (Map p176; ☎ 261 5096; www.cafeeinstein.com, in German; Kurfürstenstrasse 58; breakfast €6-15, mains €15-23; ☯ 9am-1am; Ⓜ Nollendorfplatz) You'll think you've hopped to another capital at this Viennese coffee house. Choose from schnitzel, strudel and other Austrian fare in the polished, palatial digs.

Engelbecken (off Map p176; ☎ 615 2810; Witzlebenstrasse 31; mains €8-18; ☯ dinner Mon-Sat, lunch & dinner Sun; Ⓜ Sophie Charlotte Platz) Come here for what many rate as Berlin's best Bavarian food, with *Schweinbraten* (pork sausages), schnitzels, dumplings and sauerkraut. All meats are organic.

DRINKING

Gemütlichkeit, which roughly translates as 'cosy, warm and friendly, with a decided lack of anything hectic', dominates the upscale bars of the west as well as the hipper, more underground venues in the east. Prenzlauer Berg, the first GDR sector to develop a happening nightlife, still attracts visitors, creative types and gay customers, but as its residents have aged (and produced many, many babies) its nightlife has become more subdued. Clubs and bars in Mitte around Hackescher Markt cater to a cool, slightly older and wealthier crowd. Friedrichshain boasts a young hipster feel and Kreuzberg remains the alternative hub, becoming grungier as you move east. Charlottenburg and Winterfeldtplatz are fairly upmarket and mature, but liberal.

Bars without food open between 5pm and 8pm and may close as late as 5am (if at all).

Astrobar (Map p175; ☎ 2966 1615; Simon-Dach-Strasse 40; **M** S-Bahn Warschauer Strasse) The Astro offers the future as it looked in the 1960s, with spaceships, robots and classic computer games in the back room. DJs start spinning after 10pm.

Rote Lotte (Map pp170-1; ☎ 017 7345 3693; Oderbergerstrasse 38; **M** Eberswalder Strasse) Plush sofas and booths have an old-world feel in this stylish crowd-pleaser – perfect for a quiet, civilised drink.

Kumpelnest 3000 (Map p175; ☎ 0891 7960, Lützowstrasse 23; **M** Kurfürstenstrasse) Once a brothel, always an experience: the Kumpelnest has been famed since the '80s for its wild, inhibition-free nights. Much of the original whorehouse decor remains intact. We've had reports that pickpockets operate here – be aware.

Prater (Map pp170-1; ☎ Kastanienallee 7-9; **M** Eberswalder Strasse) A summer institution, Berlin's oldest beer garden (since 1837) invites you in for a tall chilled draft under the canopy of chestnut trees.

Green Door (Map p176; ☎ 215 2515; Winterfeldtstrasse 50; **M** Nollendorfplatz) Ring the doorbell to get them to open the namesake green door and let you into this tiny neighbourhood bar. Cocktails are on offer.

Wohnzimmer (Living Room; Map pp170-1; ☎ 445 5458; Lettestrasse 6; ☼ 10am-4am; **M** Eberswalder Strasse) The vintage furnishings often match up well with the style of its patrons in this laid-back Prenlauer Berg stalwart.

Fleischmöbel (Meat Furniture; Map pp170-1; Oder berger Strasse 2; ☼ from noon; **M** Eberswalder Strasse). Despite its odd name, the furniture is merely secondhand at this loungy cafe. It morphs into a convivial drinking den after dark, with serious locals engaging in intense conversations.

Ankerklause (Map p175; ☎ 693 5649; Kottbusser Damm 104; **M** Kottbusser Tor) Slightly kitsch but always a winner, this nautical-themed bar in an old harbour-master's house is worthy of a brew or two. Thursdays it turns into a casual dance floor with music suiting most tastes.

our pick **Freischwimmer** (Free Swimmer; Map p175; ☎ 6107 4309; Vor dem Schlesischen Tor 2a; ☼ from 2pm Mon-Fri, from 11am Sat & Sun, reduced hours in winter; **M** Schlesisches Tor). It was a boathouse, now it's a bar that entices with its chill vibe and a view of the tranquil canal.

Reingold (Map p170-1; ☎ 2838 7676; Novalisstrasse 11; **M** Oranienburger Tor). Gold walls and sleek furnishings manage to be both glam and retro in this recently revamped Mitte bar. Pricey (but exceptional) cocktails contain freshly squeezed juices and house-made fruit syrups.

Süss War Gestern (Yesterday Was Sweet; Map p175; Wülischstrasse 43; **M** S-Bahn Ostkreuz). Street-art covered walls, 1970s decorations and comfortable sofas make this outpost worth the trek. Most nights feature a DJ spinning anything from funk to soul to electric music.

ENTERTAINMENT

Berlin's legendary nightlife needs little introduction. Whether alternative, underground, cutting edge, saucy, flamboyant or even highbrow, it all crops up here.

Nightclubs

Few club opens before 11pm (and if you arrive before midnight you may be dancing solo) but they stay open well into the early hours – usually sunrise at least. As the scene changes so rapidly, it's always wise to double-check listings magazines or ask locals. Admission charges, when they apply, range from €5 to €15.

Berghain/Panoramabar (Map p175; www.berghain .de; Wrienzer Bahnhof; ☼ from midnight Thu-Sat; **M** Ostbahnhof) If you only make it to one club in Berlin, this is where you need to go. The upper floor (Panoramabar, aka 'Pannebar'; open both days) is all about house; the big factory hall below (Berghain) goes hardcore techno. Expect cutting-edge sounds in industrial surrounds.

Kaffee Burger (Map pp170-1; ☎ 2804 6495; www .kaffeeburger.de; Torstrasse 60; **M** Rosa-Luxemburg-Platz) The original GDR '60s wallpaper is part of the decor at this arty-bar, club and music venue in Mitte. Burger hosts popular monthly readings by local (mainly expat) writers in English, but many come here for indie, rock, punk and cult author Wladimir Kaminer's fortnightly *Russendisko* (Russian disco; www.russendisko.de).

Watergate (Map p175; ☎ 6128 0394; www.water -gate.de; Falckensteinstrasse 49a; ☼ from 11pm Fri & Sat;

GERMANY

GERMANY

GAY & LESBIAN BERLIN

Berlin boasts a liberal – no, wild is more like it – gay scene where anything goes. Still going strong since the 1920s, Schöneberg is the original gay area, but these days Prenzlauer Berg is the trendiest; Friedrichshain also has a small studenty gay scene. Skim through **Berlin Gay Web** (http://berlin.gay-web.de, in German) for all things gay in Berlin or **Girl Ports** (www.girlports.com/lesbian-travel/destinations/berlin), a lesbian travel magazine.

SchwuZ (Map p175; ☎ 693 7025; www.schwuz.de; Mehringdamm 61; ☒ from 11pm Fri & Sat; Ⓜ Mehringdamm) is one of the longest-running mixed institutions; there's a cafe here all week too.

Hafen (Map p176; ☎ 211 4118; Motzstrasse 19; Ⓜ Nollendorfplatz) is a Schöneberg staple with a consistent party scene. There's also an eclectic quiz night on Mondays (in English first Monday of the month).

A popular bar attracting a mixed crowd is **Zum Schmutzigen Hobby** (Map pp170-1; Rykestrasse 45; ☒ from 5pm; Ⓜ Eberswalder Strasse) run by well-known drag queen Nina Queer.

Ⓜ Schlesisches Tor) Watch the sun rise over the Spree River through the floor-to-ceiling windows of this fantastic lounge. The music is mainly electro, drum'n'bass and hip hop.

Weekend (Map pp170-1; www.week-end-berlin.de; Am Alexanderplatz 5; ☒ from 11pm Thu-Sat; Ⓜ Alexanderplatz) Tear your eyes from the beautiful people and gaze through the 12th-floor windows, across the *Bladerunner* landscape of dug-up Alexanderplatz and over Berlin. (Alexanderplatz 5 is the one with the Sanyo logo.) Thursdays are best, while Saturdays see an invasion of suburban weekend warriors.

Berlin also has a thriving scene of no-holds-barred sex clubs. The notorious **Kit Kat Club** (off Map p176; ☎ 7889 9704; Bessemerstrasse 14; Ⓜ Alt-Tempelhof) is the original and best.

Music & Theatre

Staatsoper Unter den Linden (Map pp170-1; ☎ information 203 540, tickets 2035 4555; www.staatsoper-berlin.de; Unter den Linden 5-7; Ⓜ S-Bahn Unter den Linden) This is the handiest and most prestigious of Berlin's three opera houses, where unsold seats go on sale cheap an hour before curtains-up.

Berliner Ensemble (Map pp170-1; ☎ information 284 080, tickets 2840 8155; www.berliner-ensemble.de; Bertolt-Brecht-Platz 1; Ⓜ Friedrichstrasse) 'Mack the Knife' had its first public airing here, during the *Threepenny Opera's* premiere in 1928. Bertolt Brecht's former theatrical home continues to present his plays.

SHOPPING

KaDeWe (Map p176; ☎ 212 10; www.kadewe.de; Tauentzienstrasse 21-24; ☒ 10am-8pm Mon-Thu, to 9pm Fri, 9.30am-8pm Sat; Ⓜ U-Bahn Wittenbergplatz) is Germany's most renowned retail emporium, equivalent to Harrods. The 6th-floor gourmet food halls are extraordinary, and the store is near the principal western shopping thoroughfare of Kurfürstendamm. Famous Parisian department store **Galeries Lafayette** (Map pp170-1; ☎ 2094 8280; www.galeries-lafayette.de; Friedrichstrasse 76-78; ☒ 10am-8pm Mon-Sat; Ⓜ U-Bahn Französische Strasse) also has a branch in Mitte, including a floor of fancy French food and swanky spots to grab a tipple after a hard day's shop.

While Hackescher Markt (p173) is increasingly commercial, plenty of cutting-edge boutiques are found in Prenzlauer Berg (especially along Kastanienallee and Stargarder Strasse) and in the side streets of Kreuzberg.

Flea market–hopping is a popular local pastime on the weekend, particularly Sundays. The **Berlin Art & Nostalgia Market** (Map pp170-1; Georgenstrasse, Mitte; ☒ 8am-5pm Sat & Sun; Ⓜ S-Bahn Friedrichstrasse) is heavy on collectibles, books, ethnic crafts and GDR memorabilia; the **Flohmarkt am Mauerpark** (Map pp170-1; Bernauer Strasse 63, Mauerpark; ☒ 10am-5pm Sun; Ⓜ Eberwalder Strasse) is known for it's vintage wear and young-designer retro fashions; and the **Flohmarkt am Arkonaplatz** (Map pp170-1; Arkonaplatz; ☒ 10am-5pm Sun; Ⓜ Bernauerstrasse) is best for 1960s and 1970s furniture and accessories.

GETTING THERE & AWAY
Air

Berlin has two international airports, reflecting the legacy of the divided city. The larger one is in the northwestern suburb of Tegel (TXL), about 8km from the city centre; the other is in Schönefeld (SXF), about 22km southeast of town. For information about either, go to www.berlin-airport.de or call ☎ 0180-500 0186.

Berlin will eventually get its own major international airport, as Schönefeld is being expanded into Berlin Brandenburg International (BBI); estimated completion date is 2011.

Bus

Berlin is well connected to the rest of Europe by a network of long-distance buses. Most buses arrive at and depart from the **Zentraler Omnibusbahnhof** (ZOB; off Map p176; ☎ 302 5361; Masurenallee 4-6; Ⓜ Kaiserdamm/Witzleben), opposite the Funkturm radio tower. Tickets are available from travel agencies or at the bus station.

Car

Lifts can be organised by **ADM Mitfahrzentrale** (ride-share agencies; www.mitfahrzentralen.org, in German) Hardenbergplatz (Map p176; ☎ 194 240; Hardenbergplatz 14; ⊙ 9am-8pm Mon-Fri, 10am-2pm Sat, 10am-4pm Sun); Zoo station (Map p176; ☎ 194 40; ⊙ 9am-8pm Mon-Fri, 10am-6pm Sat & Sun).

Train

Regular long-distance services arrive at the architecturally spectacular Hauptbahnhof (also called Lehrter Bahnhof), with many continuing east to Ostbahnhof and Lichtenberg. ICE and IC trains leave hourly to every major city in Germany and there are also connections to central Europe. Sample fares include to Leipzig (€34, 1¼ hours), Hamburg (€65, 1½ to two hours), Stralsund (€35 to €44, 2¾ to 3¼ hours) and Prague (€56.80, 4½ to five hours).

Unfortunately the few lockers available are hidden in the parking garage.

GETTING AROUND

Berlin's public transport system is excellent – leave your car at home. The comprehensive network of U-Bahn and S-Bahn trains, buses, trams and ferries covers most corners.

To/From the Airport
SCHÖNEFELD

The S9 travels through all the major downtown stations, taking 40 minutes to Alexanderplatz.

The faster 'Airport Express' trains travel the same route half-hourly to Bahnhof Zoo (30 minutes), Friedrichstrasse (23 minutes), Alexanderplatz (20 minutes) and Ostbahnhof (15 minutes). Note that these are regular regional RE or RB trains designated as Airport Express in the timetable. Trains stop about 400m from the terminals, which are served by

a free shuttle bus every 10 minutes. Walking takes five to 10 minutes.

Buses 171 and X7 link the terminals directly with the U-Bahn station Rudow (U7), with onward connections to central Berlin.

The fare for any of these trips is €2.80 (ABC tariff). A taxi to central Berlin costs about €35.

TEGEL

Tegel (TXL) is connected to Mitte by the JetExpressBus TXL (30 minutes) and to Bahnhof Zoo (Zoo Station) in Charlottenburg by express bus X9 (20 minutes). Bus 109 serves the western city – it's slower but useful if you're headed somewhere along Kurfürstendamm (30 minutes). Tegel is not directly served by the U-Bahn, but both bus 109 and X9 stop at Jakob-Kaiser-Platz (U7), the station closest to the airport.

Any of these trips costs €2.10. Taxi rides cost about €20 to Bahnhof Zoo and €23 to Alexanderplatz.

Bicycle

Flat and bike-friendly, with special bike lanes, abundant green spaces and peaceful waterways, Berlin is best explored by tooling around on two wheels. For details on following the course of the former Berlin Wall by bike along the marked Berliner Mauerweg, see p174. Bicycles (*Fahrräder*) may be taken aboard designated U-Bahn and S-Bahn cars (though not on buses) for the price of a reduced single ticket (see p184).

Many hostels and hotels rent bicycles to their guests or can refer you to an agency. Expect to pay from €10 per day and €50 per week. A minimum cash deposit and/or ID is required. One reliable outfit with English-speaking staff and six branches throughout central Berlin is **Fahrradstation** (☎ central reservations 0180-510 8000; www.fahrradstation.de).

Car & Motorcycle

Garage parking is expensive (about €2 per hour) and vehicles entering the environmental zone (within the S-Bahn rail ring) must display a special sticker (*Umweltplakette*; €5 to €15). Order it online at www.berlin.de/labo /kfz/dienstleistungen/feinstaubplakette.php. Non-German-speakers can also order it at www.umweltplakette.de, operated by a private company that charges around €37. The fine for getting caught without the sticker is €40.

GERMANY

GERMANY

PUBLIC TRANSPORT TICKETS

Three tariff zones exist – A, B and C. Unless venturing to Potsdam or the outer suburbs, you'll only need an AB ticket.

Ticket	AB (€)	BC (€)	ABC (€)
Single	2.10	2.50	2.80
Day pass	6.10	6.30	6.50
Group day pass (up to 5 people)	15.40	15.90	16.10
7-day pass	26.20	27.00	32.30

Public Transport

One type of ticket is valid on all transport – including the U-Bahn, buses, trams and ferries run by **Berliner Verkehrsbetriebe** (☎ 194 49; www.bvg.de) as well as the S-Bahn and regional RE, SE and RB trains operated by **Deutsche Bahn** (www.bahn.de).

For ticket prices and zones, see the boxed text, above.

Most tickets are available from vending machines located in the stations, but must be validated before use. If you're caught without a validated ticket, there's a €40 on-the-spot fine.

Services operate from 4am until just after midnight on weekdays, with many *Nachtbus* (night bus) services in between. At weekends, they run all night long (except the U4).

Taxi

Taxi stands are located at all main train stations and throughout the city. Order a taxi on ☎ 0800-222 2255.

BRANDENBURG

Although it surrounds bustling Berlin, the Brandenburg state of mind is quiet, rural and gentle with vast expanses of unspoilt scenery, much of it in protected nature reserves. Its landscape is quilted in myriad shades, from emerald beech forest to golden fields of rapeseed and sunflowers, but it's also rather flat, windswept and perhaps even a bit melancholic.

POTSDAM

☎ 0331 / pop 150,000

Featuring ornate palaces and manicured gardens dotted around a huge riverside park, the Prussian royal seat of Potsdam is the most popular day trip from Berlin. Elector Friedrich Wilhelm of Brandenburg laid the ground for the town's success when he made it his second residence in the 17th century. But Friedrich II (Frederick the Great) commissioned most of the palaces in the mid-18th century.

In August 1945 the victorious WWII Allies chose nearby Schloss Cecilienhof for the Potsdam Conference, which set the stage for the division of Berlin and Germany into occupation zones.

Orientation

Potsdam Hauptbahnhof is just southeast of the city centre, across the Havel River. As this is still quite a way – 2km – from Sansoucci Park, you might like to change here for a train going one or two stops to Charlottenhof (for Schloss Sanssouci) or Sanssouci (for Neues Palais). Some RB trains from Berlin stop at all three stations.

Information

Potsdam Tourist Office (☎ 275 580; www.potsdam tourismus.de; Brandenburger Strasse 3; 9.30am-6pm Mon-Fri, 9.30am-4pm Sat & Sun Apr-Oct, 10am-6pm Mon-Fri, 9.30am-2pm Sat & Sun Nov-Mar) Near the Hauptbahnhof.

Sanssouci Besucherzentrum (☎ 969 4202; www.spsg .de; An der Orangerie 1; 8.30am-5pm Mar-Oct, 9am-4pm Nov-Feb) Near the windmill and Schloss Sanssouci.

Sights
PARK SANSSOUCI

At the heart of **Park Sanssouci** (admission free; dawn to dusk) lies a celebrated rococo palace, **Schloss Sanssouci** (☎ 969 4190; adult/concession Apr-Oct €12/8, Nov-Mar €8/5; 10am-6pm Tue-Sun Apr-Oct, to 5pm Nov-Mar). Built in 1747, it has some glorious interiors. Only 2000 visitors are allowed entry each day (a Unesco rule), so tickets are usually sold by 2.30pm, even in quiet seasons. Tours run by the tourist office guarantee entry.

The late-baroque **Neues Palais** (New Palace; ☎ 969 4255; adult/concession €6/5; 10am-6pm Wed-Mon Apr-Oct, to 5pm Nov-Mar) was built in 1769 as the royal family's summer residence. It's one of the most imposing buildings in the park and the one to see if your time is limited.

The **Bildergalerie** (Picture Gallery; ☎ 969 4181; adult/concession €3/2.50; 10am-6pm Tue-Sun mid-May–Oct) contains a rich collection of 17th-century paintings by Rubens, Caravaggio and other big names.

Many consider the **Chinesisches Haus** (Chinese House; ☎ 969 4222; admission €2; ⏲ 10am-6pm Tue-Sun mid-May–Oct) to be the pearl of the park. It's a circular pavilion of gilded columns, palm trees and figures of Chinese musicians and animals, built in 1757.

NEUER GARTEN

When outgoing British Prime Minister Winston Churchill and his accompanying successor Clement Attlee arrived at **Schloss Cecilienhof** (☎ 969 4244; tours adult/concession €6/5; ⏲ 9am-6pm Tue-Sun, to 5pm Nov-Mar) in 1945 they must have immediately felt at home. Located in the separate New Garden, northeast of the centre on the bank of the Heiliger See, this is an incongruously English-style country manor in rococo-heavy Potsdam.

FILMPARK BABELSBERG

Germany's **UFA Film Studios** (☎ 721 2755; www.filmpark.de; Grossbeerenstrasse; adult/child/concession €19/13/16; ⏲ 10am-6pm Apr–Oct) was where Fritz Lang's *Metropolis* was shot and FW Murnau filmed the first Dracula movie, *Nosferatu*. Since a relaunch in 1999, it's helped Berlin regain its

film-making crown, with Roman Polanski's *The Pianist* made here, and at research time, Quentin Tarantino's *Inglorious Bastards* starring Brad Pitt was making local headlines. The visitor experience includes theme-park rides and a studio tour – the daily stunt show (2pm) is worth catching. The studios are east of the city centre.

ALTSTADT

The **Brandenburger Tor** (Brandenburg Gate) at the western end of the Old Town on Luisenplatz isn't a patch on the one in Berlin but it is older, dating from 1770. From here, pedestrian Brandenburger Strasse runs due east, providing the town's main eating strip.

Standing out from its surrounds is the pretty **Holländisches Viertel** (Dutch Quarter). Towards the northern end of Friedrich-Ebert-Strasse, it has 134 gabled red-brick houses, built for Dutch workers who came to Potsdam in the 1730s at the invitation of Friedrich Wilhelm I. The homes have been well restored and now house all kinds of interesting galleries, cafes and restaurants.

GERMANY

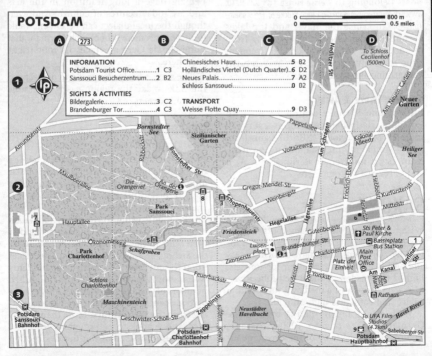

WORTH THE TRIP: SACHSENHAUSEN CONCENTRATION CAMP

In 1936 the Nazis opened a *Konzentrationslager* (concentration camp) for men in a disused brewery in Sachsenhausen, some 35km north of Berlin. By 1945 about 220,000 prisoners had passed through the gates – labelled, as at Auschwitz in Poland, *Arbeit Macht Frei* (Work Sets You Free). About 100,000 were murdered here.

After the war the Soviets and the communist leaders of the new GDR set up Speziallager No 7 (Special Camp No 7) for political prisoners, ex-Nazis, monarchists and others, jailing 60,000 and killing up to 12,000.

The **Sachsenhausen Memorial and Museum** (☎ 03301-200 200; www.gedenkstaette-sachsenhausen .de; admission free; ⌚ 8.30am-6pm mid-Mar–mid-Oct, to 4pm mid-Oct–mid-Mar) consists of several parts. The **Neues Museum** (New Museum) includes a history of anti-Semitism and audiovisual material. East of it are **Barracks 38 and 39**, reconstructions of two typical huts housing most of the 6000 Jewish prisoners brought to Sachsenhausen after Kristallnacht (9–10 November 1938). Number 38 was rebuilt after being torched by neo-Nazis in September 1992. North of here is the prison and prison yard, where you find a **memorial** to the homosexuals who died here. The recently revamped **Lagermuseum** (Camp Museum), situated in what was once the camp kitchen, houses exhibits illustrating the everyday life in the camp during its various phases, including some artwork produced by the inmates. Left of the tall **monument** (1961), erected by the GDR in memory of political prisoners interned here, is the **crematorium** and **Station Z extermination site**, a pit for shooting prisoners in the neck with a wooden 'catch' where bullets could be retrieved and recycled.

The easiest way to get to Sachsenhausen from Berlin is to take the frequent S1 to Oranienburg (€2.80, 50 minutes). The walled camp is a signposted 20-minute walk from Oranienburg station.

Tours

Boats belonging to **Weisse Flotte** (☎ 275 9210; www.schiffahrt-in-potsdam.de; Lange Brücke 6; ⌚ 9.45am-7pm Apr-Oct) cruise the Havel and the lakes around Potsdam, departing regularly from the dock near Lange Brücke, with frequent trips to Wannsee (€8/11 one way/return) and around the castles (€10).

Getting There & Away

S-Bahn line S7 links central Berlin with Potsdam Hauptbahnhof about every 10 minutes. Some regional (RB/RE) trains from Berlin stop at all three stations in Potsdam. Your ticket must cover Berlin Zones A, B and C (€2.80) to come here.

SAXONY

With its restored 'old German' roots, Saxony has emerged as one of the biggest draws for visitors. Dresden is the flavour of the decade and is a major destination for tourists. Linked to Dresden by the fabled Elbe River, Meissen is a gem of a medieval town with a palace and cathedral high on a hill.

With a long history dating back to the Germanic tribes of over 1000 years ago, Saxony embodies many of the classic quali-

ties associated with Germany. Dresden and Leipzig have a long tradition in the arts and are today centres of culture. And even though the local dialect can be impenetrable to those with mere schoolbook German, that same classic German traces its roots right back here.

The state is fairly compact and high-speed rail links make the region easily accessible from all corners of Germany.

DRESDEN

☎ 0351 / pop 484,000

Proof that there is life after death, Dresden has become one of Germany's most popular attractions, and for good reason. Restorations have returned the city to its glory when it was famous throughout Europe as 'Florence on the Elbe', owing to the efforts of Italian artists, musicians, actors and master craftsmen who flocked to the court of Augustus the Strong, bestowing countless masterpieces upon the city. But then death came suddenly when, shortly before the end of WWII, Allied bombers blasted and incinerated much of the baroque centre, a beautiful jewel-like area dating from the 18th century. More than 35,000 died, and in bookstores throughout town you can peruse books showing the destruction (or read about it in Kurt Vonnegut's classic *Slaughterhouse Five*).

Rebuilding began under the communist regime in the 1950s and accelerated greatly after reunification. The city celebrated its 800th anniversary in 2006 and while much focus is on the restored centre, you should cross the River Elbe to the Neustadt, where edgy new clubs and cafes open every week, joining the 150 already there.

Orientation

The Elbe River splits the town in a rough V-shape, with the Neustadt to the north and the Altstadt (old city) to the south.

Dresden has two main train stations: the beautifully restored Hauptbahnhof on the southern side of town, and the contemporary Dresden-Neustadt north of the river. Most trains stop at both. Dresden-Mitte is little more than a forlorn platform between the two.

From the Hauptbahnhof, pedestrian-only Prager Strasse leads north into the Altstadt. Here there's a mix of communist-era triumphalism and modern-day commercialism. The lovely Brühlsche Terrasse runs along the Elbe between the Albertinum and the Zwinger, with boat docks below. The Altmarkt-Galerie is a vast urban mall.

In the Neustadt, home to much of the city's nightlife, the main attractions for visitors are the Albertplatz and Antonstadt quarters. In and around Louisenstrasse you'll find all manner of shops, galleries, funky boutiques and dozens of cafes, bars and clubs. Hauptstrasse is pedestrianised and connects Albertplatz with the Augustusbrücke.

Information

Dresden Information Prager Strasse 2 (☎ 4919 2100; www.dresden.de; ☉ 10am-7pm Mon-Sat); Theaterplatz 2 (☉ 10am-6pm Mon-Fri, to 4pm Sat & Sun) Discount cards from €21.

Haus Des Buches (☎ 497 369; Dr-Külz-Ring 12) Bookshop with huge selection on local history and culture.

K&E Callshop (Wiener Passage; per hr €2; ☉ 10am-10pm) Internet access; located in the subterranean passageway outside the Hauptbahnhof.

Sights

MONUMENTS & LANDMARKS

One of Dresden's most beloved icons, the **Frauenkirche** (Church of Our Lady; ☎ 439 3934; www.frauenkirche-dresden.org; Neumarkt; ☉ 10am-6pm) was rebuilt in time for the city's 800th anniversary celebrations in 2006. Initially built between 1726 and 1743 under the direction of baroque architect George Bähr, it was Germany's greatest Protestant church until February 1945, when bombing raids flattened it. The communists decided to leave the rubble as a war memorial; after reunification, calls for reconstruction prevailed, although the paucity of charcoal-tinged original stones shows just how much is new.

Look for the very few blackened stones on the exterior, these were salvaged from the rubble of the original. Otherwise – not surprisingly – the church feels brand new, especially inside. Most moving is the melted cross from the original. You can also climb to the top for good views. The surrounding Neumarkt is part of a massive redevelopment designed to evoke prewar Dresden.

The neo-Renaissance opera house, **Semperoper** (☎ 491 1496; www.semperoper.de; Theaterplatz; tour adult/child €7/3.50; ☉ varies), designed by Gustav Semper, *is* Dresden. The original building opened in 1841 but burned down less than three decades later. Rebuilt in 1878, it was pummelled in WWII and reopened in 1985 after the communists invested a fortune restoring it. The best way to appreciate it is through one of the many performances.

The **Schloss** (☎ 491 4619; Schlossplatz), a massive neo-Renaissance palace, has ongoing restoration projects. Its many features include the **Hausmannsturm** (Servants' Tower; adult/child €3/2; ☉ 10am-6pm Wed-Mon), which has sobering pictures of the WWII destruction, and the baroque Catholic **Hofkirche** (☉ 9am-5pm Mon-Thu, 1-5pm Fri, 10am-5pm Sat, noon-4pm Sun), which contains the heart of Augustus the Strong. Outside, you'd need a really wide-angle lens to get a shot of Wulhelm Walther's amazing 102m-long tiled mural, the **Fürstenzug** (Procession of Princes; Augustusstrasse), on the wall of the former Stendehaus (Royal Stables). The scene, a long row of royalty on horses, was painted in 1876 and then transferred to some 24,000 Meissen porcelain tiles in 1906. The Schloss also houses museums, see p189.

MUSEUMS

For information on most of Dresden's museums, see the website www.skd-dresden.de. Allow at least two full days for a sampling of what's on offer.

DRESDEN

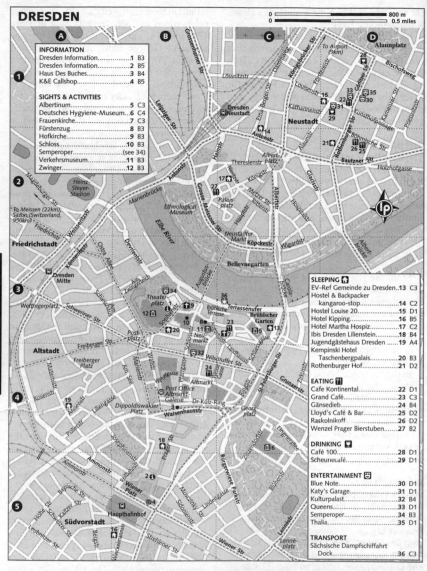

0   800 m
0   0.5 miles

The imposing block **Albertinum** (☎ 491 4619; Brühlsche Terrasse) houses many of Dresden's art treasures, including the **Münzkabinett** collection of antique coins and medals, and the **Skulpturensammlung**, which includes classical and Egyptian works. The **Galerie Neue Meister** has renowned 19th- and 20th-century paintings from leading French and German

Impressionists. The complex is meant to re-open in 2010 after a massive reconstruction.

Dresden's elaborate 1728 fortress **Zwinger** (☎ 491 4622; Theaterplatz 1; 🕙 10am-6pm Tue-Sun) is an attraction in its own right, with a popular ornamental courtyard, and also houses six major museums. The most important is the **Galerie Alte Meister** (adult/child incl entry to Rüstkammer

€7/4.50), which features masterpieces including Raphael's *Sistine Madonna*. The **Rüstkammer** (armoury) has a superb collection of ceremonial weapons. The dazzling **Porzelansammlung** (Porcelain Collection; adult/child €6/3.50) is filled with flamboyant breakables.

Located in the Schloss, the **Grünes Gewölbe** (Green Vault; adult/child €7/3.50; 10am-6pm Wed-Mon) is one of the world's finest collections of jewel-encrusted precious objects. Treasures include the world's biggest green diamond, tiny pearl sculptures and a stunning group of 137 gem-studded figures by Johann Melchior Dinglinger, court jeweller of Augustus the Strong.

Also in the Schloss, the **Verkehrsmuseum** (Transport Museum; 864 40; Augustusstrasse 1; adult/child €4.50/2.50; 10am-5pm Tue-Sun) is fittingly located in the Johanneum, the old stables. Motoring back towards the 20th century, this is a fascinating collection including penny farthings, trams, dirigibles and carriages. Included in the admission is a melancholy 40-minute film with original black-and-white footage of 1930s Dresden.

One of the oddest museums is the product of a mouthwash baron. The **Deutsches Hygiene-Museum** (484 6670; Lingnerplatz 1; adult/child €6/3; 10am-6pm Tue-Sun) is awash in displays relating to the ravages of venereal disease, the theory of eugenics and reasons to bathe.

Tours

Cruise the Elbe on the world's oldest fleet of paddle-wheel steamers with **Sächsische Dampfschiffahrt** (866 090; www.saechsische-dampf schiffahrt.de; adult/child €16/8). Ninety-minute tours leave from the Terrassenufer dock several times daily in summer. There's also service to villages along the river such as Meissen (p191).

Sleeping

Accommodation in Dresden can be very expensive in the high season. Luckily, several good-value budget places can be found in the lively Neustadt; although rising property values in the area are taking a toll, some quirky places, such as Raskolnikoff (p190), continue to soldier on.

BUDGET

Jugendgästehaus Dresden (492 620; www.jugendher berge.de; Maternistrasse 22; dm €19;) This tower block was once a Communist Party training

centre; now it's a huge hostel (HI), with 480 beds in small dorms and a bistro (breakfast included). Take tram 7 or 10 to the corner of Ammonstrasse and Freiberger Strasse.

Hostel & Backpacker kangaroo-stop (314 3455; www.kangaroo-stop.de; Erna-Berger-Strasse 8-10; dm/s/d/ from €13/29/38;) Welcoming and low-key, with rooms spread over two buildings: one for backpackers and the other for families. So which will see more immature behaviour? The internet is free and the big breakfast buffet costs €5. Dresden-Neustadt station is nearby.

Hostel Louise 20 (889 4894; www.louise20.de; Louisenstrasse 20; dm/s/d from €14/30/40;) Rooms are divided between two buildings here. Basic ones are off a courtyard at the back, while more expensive – and Ikea-styled – units are up front. Families can rent entire suites of rooms. The Dresden-Neustadt station is 10-minute walk

EV-Ref Gemeinde zu Dresden (438 230; www .ev-ref-gem-dresden.de; Brühlscher Garten 4; s/d €60/75) The name is not a marketer's dream, but this pension (guest house) is amazing value in a great location – right across from the Albertinum and on the river. This historic retirement home makes rooms available for travellers whenever a resident has permanently 'checked out'. Rooms have showers and TV and often great views; breakfast is included.

MIDRANGE & TOP END

Ibis Dresden Lillenstein (4856 6663; www.ibishotel .com; Prager Strasse 13; r €50-120;) Together with the adjoining Ibis Dresden Bastei and the Ibis Dresden Königstein, this enormous communist-era complex has more than 900 rooms. The decor has been redone 'cheap and cheerful' and pluses include wi-fi and a good chance at a vacancy in summer. The €10 breakfast buffet is vast.

Hotel Martha Hospiz (817 60; www.hotel -martha-hospiz.de; Nieritzstrasse 11; s/d €55/120;) Hospitality is taken very seriously at this lovely quiet inn, which is close to the lively Königstrasse. Newer rooms are decked out in Biedermeier style; there's wi-fi. Breakfast is €10.

Rothenburger Hof (812 60; www.rothenburger hof.de; Rothenburger Strasse 15-17; r €75-160, apt €140-180;) This mannered launch pad for Neustadt explorations counts among its assets apartments with kitchenette and balcony, a Moorish-style steam room and a free extra-lavish breakfast.

Hotel Kipping (☎ 478 500; www.hotel-kipping.de; Winckelmannstrasse 6; s/d from €80/95; 💻) Just south of the Hauptbahnhof, this is a family-run, family-friendly hotel that comes with 20 comfortable rooms in a house right out of the *Addams Family*. The bar and cafe are especially appealing and there's wi-fi.

Kempinski Hotel Taschenbergpalais (☎ 491 20; www.kempinski-dresden.de; Taschenberg 3; r €200-400; 🔀 💻 🐾) This restored 18th-century mansion is Dresden's heavyweight, with views over the Zwinger, incredibly quiet corridors, and doors that seem impervious to anything outside, protecting the 214 rooms and suites. In winter the courtyard turns into an ice rink.

Eating

It's no problem finding somewhere to eat in the Neustadt, with oodles of cafes and restaurants found along Königstrasse and the streets north of Albertplatz. This is definitely the most interesting part of town at night. South of the river, look near the Altmarkt, and Münzgasse/Terrassengasse, between Brühlsche Terrasse and the Frauenkirche, for restaurants representing all kinds of local and international cuisine.

ʎ **Raskolnikoff** (☎ 804 5706; www.raskolnikoff.de; Böhmische Strasse 34; mains €4-12) This bohemian cafe in a former artists' squat was one of the Neustadt's first post-Wende pubs. The menu is sorted by compass direction (borscht to quiche Lorraine to smoked fish) and there's an ivy-lined, sweet beer garden out back, and a gallery and pension (rooms €40 to €55) upstairs.

Cafe Kontinental (☎ 801 3531; Görlitzer Strasse 1; mains €5-15; 🕙 24hr; 💻) A bustling place open around the clock, this trendy cafe caters to a broad swath of Neustadt characters.

Lloyd's Café & Bar (☎ 5018774; Martin-Luther-Strasse 17; mains €6-10) Across a square from the Martin Luther Kirche, this swanky place is a bargain given the creamy leather seating, high style and year-round gelato sales. Breakfast is served all day. There's also salads, panini and pasta.

Wenzel Prager Bierstuben (☎ 804 2010; Königstrasse 1; mains €7-20; 🕙 11am-midnight) This busy beer hall serves up oceans of Czech lager under arched brick ceilings. Always crowded, the menu leans towards traditional meaty mains.

The garlic soup is sublime, the cured pork with horseradish a delight.

Gänsedieb (☎ 485 0905; Weisse Gasse 1; mains €8-15) One of nearly a dozen choices on Weisse Gasse, the 'Goose Thief' serves hearty schnitzels, goulash and steaks alongside a full range of Bavarian Paulaner beers. The name was inspired by the fountain outside.

Grand Café (☎ 496 2444; An der Frauenkirche 12; mains €10-20; 🕙 10am-1am) Yummy cakes and more ambitious mains in the gold-trimmed Coselpalais, plus tables on a large patio and good views of Frauenkirche.

Drinking & Entertainment

Dresden's nightlife is ever changing and still has plenty of that proletariat/GDR vibe: grunge beats swank every time. As elsewhere, many of the places listed under Eating are also good just for a drink.

Café 100 (☎ 801 7729; Alaunstrasse 100) Off a courtyard. You'll pass hundreds of empty bottles on the way in, a foreshadowing of the lengthy wine list and delights that follow. Candles give the underground space a romantic yet edgy glow.

Scheunecafé (☎ 802 6619; Alaunstrasse 36-40) Set back from the street, Indian food (mains €7 to €12), a vast beer garden, live music and deejays all combine here for a fun and funky stew.

Katy's Garage (☎ 656 7701; Alaunstrasse 48) This place, a key venue for indie gigs and club nights throughout the week, is in a former tyre shop.

Queens (☎ 810 8108; Görlitzerstrasse 3) This hopping gay bar-lounge-disco is a good first stop to find out what's happening locally.

Thalia (☎ 652 4703; www.thalia-dresden.de; Görlitzer Strasse 6) The motto is 'Cinema, Coffee, Cigarettes' at this art house–cum-cafe. Full program of films not found elsewhere and drinks to heighten the appreciation.

Blue Note (☎ 801 4275; www.jazzdepartment.com; Görlitzer Strasse 2b; 🕙 until 5am) Small, smoky and smooth, this converted smithy has live jazz almost nightly until 11pm, then turns into a night-owl magnet until the wee hours. The talent is mostly regional.

Dresden is synonymous with opera, and performances at the spectacular **Semperoper** (☎ 491 1496; www.semperoper.de; Theaterplatz) are brilliant. Tickets cost from €10, but they're usually booked out well in advance. Some performances by the renowned philharmonic are also held there, but most are in the communist-

era **Kulturpalast** (☎ 486 60; www.kulturpalast-dresden
.de; Schlossstrasse 2), which hosts a wide range of
concerts and events.

Getting There & Around

Dresden's **airport** (DRS; www.dresden-airport.de),
served by Lufthansa and Air Berlin among
others, is 9km north of the city centre, on S-
Bahn line 2 (€1.70, 30 minutes). The Airport
City Liner bus serves Dresden-Neustadt (€4)
and the Hauptbahnhof (€5), with stops at
key points in town. A taxi to the centre is
about €20.

Dresden is well linked with regular services
through the day to Leipzig (€26, 70 minutes),
Berlin-Hauptbahnhof by IC/EC train (€36,
2¼ hours) and Frankfurt-am-Main by ICE
(€85, 4½ hours).

Dresden's **public transport network** (www.dvbag
.de) charges €1.80 for a single-trip ticket; day
tickets cost €4.50. Tram 3, 7, 8 and 9 provide good links between the Hauptbahnhof
and Neustadt.

AROUND DRESDEN
Meissen

☎ 03521 / pop 29,000

Some 27km northwest of Dresden, Meissen
is a compact, perfectly preserved Old Town
and the centre of a rich wine-growing region.
It makes for a good day trip out of Dresden
by train or boat and beguiles with its red-tiled
roofs and old Saxon charm.

Like Dresden, Meissen straddles the Elbe
River, with the Old Town on the western bank
and the train station on the eastern. Both sides
were struck by record flood levels in 2002,
with water pushing quite a distance into the
Altstadt; look out for plaques marking the
highest points. Cafes line the streets and are
popular on warm days.

The tourist office is at **Meissen-Information**
(☎ 419 40; www.touristinfo-meissen.de; Markt 3; ☺ 10am-
6pm Mon-Fri, to 4pm Sat & Sun Apr-Oct, 10am-5pm Mon-Fri,
to 3pm Sat Nov-Mar). Staff can help find accommodation. The Markt (square) is framed by
the **Rathaus** (1472) and the Gothic **Frauenkirche**,
which – fittingly – has a porcelain carillon.

SIGHTS

Meissen's medieval fortress, the 15th-century
Albrechtsburg (☎ 470 70; Domplatz 1; adult/child €4/3;
☺ 10am-6pm Mar-Oct, to 5pm Nov-Feb), crowns a ridge
high above the Elbe River and is reached by
steep lanes. It contains the former ducal palace

and Meissen Cathedral, a magnificent Gothic
structure. It is widely seen as the birthplace of
Schloss architecture, with its ingenious system
of internal arches. Augustus the Strong of
Saxony created Europe's first porcelain factory here in 1710.

Next door, the towering 13th-century
Albrechtsburg Cathedral (☎ 452 490; Domplatz 7;
adult/child €3.50/2; ☺ 10am-6pm Mar-Oct, to 4pm Nov-
Feb) contains an altarpiece by Lucas Cranach
the Elder.

Meissen has long been renowned for its
chinaware, with its trademark insignia of
blue crossed swords. Meissen's porcelain
factory is now 1km southwest of the Altstadt
in an appropriately beautiful building, the
Porzellan-Museum (☎ 468 700; Talstrasse 9; adult/child
€8/4; ☺ 9am-6pm May-Oct, to 5pm Nov-Apr), which
dates to 1916. There are often long queues
for the workshop demonstrations, but you
can view the porcelain collection upstairs at
your leisure.

GETTING THERE & AWAY

Half-hourly S-Bahn trains run from Dresden's
Hauptbahnhof and Neustadt train stations
(€5.50, 40 minutes). To visit the porcelain
factory, get off at Meissen-Triebischtal (one
stop after Meissen).

A more pleasant way to get here is by
steamer (between May and September).
Boats leave from the **Sächsische Dampfschiffahrt**
(☎ 866 090; www.saechsische-dampfschiffahrt.de) dock in
Dresden once daily (€17 return, two hours).

Saxon Switzerland

Sächsische Schweiz (Saxon Switzerland) is
a 275-sq-km national park 50km south of
Dresden, near the Czech border. Its wonderfully wild, craggy country is dotted with
castles and tiny towns along the mighty
Elbe River. The landscape varies unexpect-
edly and radically: its forests can look de-
ceptively tropical, while the worn cliffs and
plateaux recall the parched expanses of New
Mexico or central Spain (generally without
the searing heat).

The highlight of the park is the **Bastei**
lookout, on the Elbe River some 28km
southeast of Dresden. One of the most
breathtaking spots in the whole of Germany,
it features fluted pinnacles 305m high and
unparalleled views of the surrounding forests, cliffs and mountains, not to mention a
sweeping view along the river itself.

There's 15,000 routes for hiking (and biking). Get here on the S1 train to Königstein, which makes a good base.

LEIPZIG

☎ 0341 / pop 498,500

Leipzig is the busiest city in Saxony, a bustling, more commercial alternative to Dresden. Although it lacks the capital's busload of museums, Leipzig in many ways feels more vibrant in an everyday sense. It's not weighed down by the past, and like its shopping passages, it invites exploration.

Leipzig also has some of the finest classical music and opera in the country, and its art and literary scenes are flourishing. Once home to Bach, Wagner and Mendelssohn, and to Goethe (who set a key scene of *Faust* in the cellar of his favourite watering hole), it more recently earned the sobriquet *Stadt der Helden* (City of Heroes) for its leading role in the 1989 democratic revolution.

Fill a day or more wandering the compact centre.

Orientation

Leipzig's centre lies within a ring road that outlines the town's medieval fortifications. To reach the city centre from the Hauptbahnhof, cross Willy-Brandt-Platz and continue south along Nikolaistrasse for five minutes.

The central Markt, which was being redeveloped for a new underground station at the time of research, is a couple of blocks southwest, and east down Grimmiasche Strasse is the massive Augustusplatz, home to some of the city's most important (if not prettiest) GDR-era buildings and also the modern MDR Tower.

The Hauptbahnhof contains a modern mall with over 140 shops and (radically for Germany) it is open from 6am to 10pm daily. You'll find good bookshops, a post office, banks and much more.

Information

Internetcafé (☎ 993 9530; Reichsstrasse 18; per 30min €1; 10am-10pm) A full-service internet shop for CD burning plus cheap calls and copies.

Leipzig Tourist Service (☎ 710 4260; www.leipzig.de; Richard-Wagner-Strasse 1; 9.30am-6pm Mon-Fri, to 4pm Sat, to 3pm Sun) One of the most helpful in Germany, with discount cards from €9.

Sights

Don't rush from sight to sight – wandering around Leipzig is a pleasure in itself, with many of the blocks around the central Markt criss-crossed by old internal shopping passages. Four good ones: **Steibs Hof** (100-year-old blue tiles and classic cafes), **Specs Hof** (soaring atrium, bookshops, cafes), **Jägerhofpassage** (galleries, theatre, antiques) and the classic **Mädlerpassage** (grand design, the famous Auerbachs Keller, see p194).

MONUMENTS & LANDMARKS

Off the southern ring road is the 108m-high tower of the baroque **Neues Rathaus** (New Town Hall; ☎ 1230; Martin-Luther-Ring; 7am-4.30pm Mon-Fri). Though the origins date to the 16th century, its current manifestation was completed in 1905. The interior makes it one of the finest municipal buildings in Germany; the lobby houses rotating exhibitions, mostly on historical themes.

Some 100,000 soldiers died in the epic 1813 battle that led to the decisive victory of Prussian, Austrian and Russian forces over Napoleon's army. Built a century later, the **Völkerschlachtdenkmal** (Battle of Nations Monument; ☎ 878 0471; Prager Strasse; adult/child €5/3; 10am-6pm Apr-Oct, to 4pm Nov-Mar) is a sombre and imposing 91m colossus that towers above southeastern Leipzig, not far from the actual killing fields. Climb the 500 steps for a view of the region. Take tram 15 from the station (direction: Meusdorf).

MUSEUMS

Leipzig's finest museum, the **Museum der Bildenden Künste** (Museum of Fine Arts; ☎ 216 990; Grimmaische Strasse 1-7; adult/child €5/3.50; 10am-6pm Tue & Thu-Sun, noon-8pm Wed), is housed in a stunning glass cube of a building that provides both a dramatic – and echoey – backdrop to its collection, which spans old masters and the latest efforts of local artists.

Haunting and uplifting by turns, the **Zeitgeschichtliches Forum** (Forum of Contemporary History; ☎ 222 20; Grimmaische Strasse 6; admission free; 9am-6pm Tue-Fri, 10am-6pm Sat & Sun) tells the story of the GDR from division and dictatorship to resistance and reform. It does a good job of chronicling the 1989 revolution, which started here, and it captures the tragic drama of the original Iron Curtain division.

Former headquarters of the East German secret police, the **Stasi Museum** (☎ 961 2443;

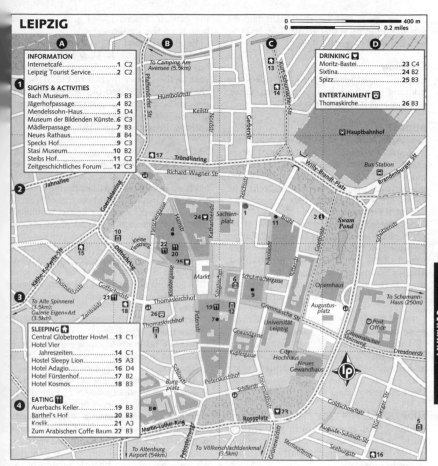

LEIPZIG

Dittrichring 24; admission free; 10am-6pm) has exhibits on propaganda, amazingly hokey disguises, surveillance photos and other forms of 'intelligence', all part of the chilling machinations of the GDR's all-out zeal for controlling, manipulating and repressing its own people.

Opposite the Thomaskirche is the **Bach Museum** (964 110; Thomaskirchhof 16; admission free; 11am-6pm), where JS Bach worked from 1723 until his death in 1750. This collection focuses on the composer's busy life in Leipzig. Things are temporary while restorations continue.

Other stars of the real, real, real oldies beat in Leipzig include Felix Mendelssohn-Bartholdy, who lived (and died) in the **Mendelssohn-Haus** (127 0294; www.mendelssohn-stiftung.de; Goldschmidtstrasse 12; admission €3.50; 10am-

6pm); and Robert Schumann, who spent the first four years of his marriage to Leipzig pianist Clara Wieck in the **Schumann-Haus** (393 9620; www.schumann-verein.de; Inselstrasse 18; admission €3; 2-5pm Wed-Fri, 10am-5pm Sat & Sun).

ART

'Cotton to culture' is the motto of the **Alte Spinnerei** (498 0270; www.spinnerei.de; Spinnereistrasse 7; 11am-6pm Tue-Sat), a 19th-century cotton-spinning factory turned artist colony. Around 80 New Leipzig School artists, including Neo Rauch, have their studios in this huge pile of red-brick buildings, alongside designers, architects, goldsmiths and other creative types. Their work is displayed in about 10 galleries, including **Galerie Eigen+Art** (960

GERMANY

7886; www.eigen-art.com), internationally famous for championing young artists. Take tram 14 to S-Bahnhof Plagwitz.

Sleeping

Leipzig Tourist Service (see p192) offers free booking in private homes near the centre. Average cost is from €35 to €50.

BUDGET

Camping Am Auensee (☎ 465 1600; www.motel-auensee .de; Gustav-Esche-Strasse 5; camp sites per person from €5, cabins €35-60) This camping ground is in a pleasant wooded spot on the city's northwestern outskirts (take tram 10 or 11 to Wahren). The cabins are A-frame bungalows.

Central Globetrotter Hostel (☎ 149 8960; www .globetrotter-leipzig.de; Kurt-Schumacher-Strasse 41; dm €13-15, s/d €24/36, linen €2; 🖳) In a busy location just north of the train station, this 80-room hostel offers bare-bones accommodation, although some rooms boast murals, albeit ones that won't win any scholarships to the Art Academy of Leipzig. Breakfast is €4 extra.

Hostel Sleepy Lion (☎ 993 9480; www.hostel-leip zig.de; Käthe-Kollwitz-Strasse 3; dm from €14, s/d €30/45; 🖳) Budget-minded nomads will feel welcome at this low-key hostel, with 60 clean and comfy beds in cheerfully painted rooms with private facilities. Major sights are just steps away; breakfast is €4.

MIDRANGE & TOP END

Midrange accommodation in the centre is fairly unexciting and usually the preserve of the big chains (particularly the many Accor brands).

Hotel Kosmos (☎ 233 4422; www.hotel-kosmos.de; Gottschedstrasse 1; s/d from €50/80) Right on a street with burgeoning nightlife, this low-key place in a grand building combines GDR-era furniture with murals in themed rooms. The murals next to the bed in the Marilyn Monroe room may fool the foolhardy.

Hotel Vier Jahreszeiten (☎ 985 10; www.guen newig.de; Kurt-Schumacher-Strasse 23-29; s €73-114, d €92-150; 🖳) Close to the train station, this anonymous place has wi-fi in all 67 comfortable rooms and serves up a good buffet breakfast in the atrium.

Hotel Adagio (☎ 216 699; www.hotel-adagio.de; Seeburgstrasse 96; r €74-100) The 32 rooms here are smartly decked out with a cream-and-green theme. You can enjoy the free breakfast in

the garden. Trams 10, 11 and 16 get you here from the station.

Hotel Fürstenhof (☎ 1400; www.starwood.de; Tröndlinring 8; r €230-300; 🐛 🖳 🖳) This intimate but grand hotel, with a 200-year pedigree, is part of the luxury branch of the Starwood chain. It has updated old-world flair, impeccable service, a gourmet restaurant and an oh-so-soothing grotto-style pool and spa. Breakfast costs €19.

Eating

Zum Arabischen Coffe Baum (☎ 965 1321; Kleine Fleischergasse 4; mains €6-15) Leipzig's oldest coffee bar has a restaurant and cafe offering excellent meals over three floors, plus a free coffee museum at the top. Composer Robert Schumann met friends here, and if you ask nicely you can sit at his regular table.

Barthel's Hof (☎ 141 310; Hainstrasse 1; mains €7-22) This is a sprawling place with outdoor seating in a courtyard, lots of roasts with thick, oniony sauces and quirky Saxon dishes such as *Heubraten* (marinated lamb roasted on hay).

Koslik (☎ 998 5993; Zentralstrasse 1; mains €8-14; ☘ 9am-1am) A stylish wood interior complements the tasty world cuisine offered here, with great breakfasts and meals from pizza to Thai soup to Swiss potato rösti.

Auerbachs Keller (☎ 216 100; www.auerbachs-kel ler-leipzig.de; Mädlerpassage; mains €14-22) Founded in 1525, Auerbachs Keller is one of Germany's classic restaurants, serving typically hearty fare. Goethe's *Faust – Part I* includes a scene here, in which Mephistopheles and Faust carouse with some students before they ride off on a barrel. The historic section of the restaurant includes the Goethe room and the *Fasskeller*; note the carved tree trunk in the latter, depicting the whole barrel-riding adventure. Excellent trad chow.

Drinking & Entertainment

Barfussgässchen and Kleine Flieschergasse, west of the Markt, form one of Leipzig's two 'pub miles', packed with outdoor tables that fill up the second the weather turns warm. The other is on Gottschedstrasse, a wider nightlife strip just west of the Altstadt.

Moritz-Bastei (☎ 702 590; www.moritzbastei.de; Universitätsstrasse 9) One of the best student clubs in Germany, in a spacious cellar below the old city walls. It has live music or DJs most nights and runs films outside in summer.

Sixtina (☎ 017-476 4855; Katharinenstrasse 11) At some point in the last few years the word 'absinthe' has ceased to mean 'bad idea', and the result is places like Sixtina, wholly dedicated to the deadly green fairy. Part the foliage on the way in.

our pick **Spizz** (☎ 960 8043; Markt 9) Classic brass instruments dangle above the stage at this city slicker, where you might catch some cool jazz. It has three levels, a good range of wines and beers, and a fine sidewalk cafe that's good day or night.

To hear the works of native-born Bach and others, try the 18th-century **Thomaskirche** (☎ 212 4676; Thomaskirchhof 18), which has frequent recitals and other performances.

Getting There & Away

Leipzig-Halle airport (LEJ; www.leipzig-halle-airport .de) has only a few flights. Ryanair serves tiny **Altenburg airport** (ADC; www.flughafen-altenburg.de), some 53km from Leipzig. There's a shuttle bus (€12, 1¾ hours) timed to coincide with the flights to/from London.

Leipzig is an important rail hub and fittingly has a monumental Hauptbahnhof. Regular services through the day include Dresden (€26, 70 minutes), Munich by ICE (€84, five hours), Berlin-Hauptbahnhof by ICE (€40, 70 minutes) and Frankfurt-am-Main (€63, 3½ hours).

Getting Around

Trams are the main public-transport option, with most lines running via the Hauptbahnhof. The S-Bahn circles the city's outer suburbs. A single ticket costs €2 and a day card €5.20. The vast project of building an S-Bahn line under the city centre is due for completion in 2012.

THURINGIA

Thuringa likes to trade on its reputation as the 'Green Heart' of Germany, an honour helped by the former-GDR's dodgy economy, which limited development. These days its main towns of Erfurt and Weimar are popular for their historic centres and long histories. In fact the latter is a microcosm of German history – high and low – over the last 500 years.

While the communist era may have been relatively benign, the previous decades were not. The Nazis had numerous concentration camps here, including the notorious Buchenwald and the nightmare of Mittelbau Dora. But yet again, in contrast, Weimar was the place where Germany tried a liberal democracy in the 1920s and in previous centuries it was home to notables such as Bach, Schiller, Goethe, Thomas Mann and many more.

ERFURT

☎ 0361 / pop 203,000

Thuringia's capital was founded by St Boniface as a bishopric in 742. In the Middle Ages the city shot to prominence and prosperity as an important trading post. The Altstadt's many well-preserved 16th-century and later buildings attest to its wealth.

The damage sustained in WWII was extensive, and the GDR regime did little to restore the city's former glories. Over the past decade, however, Erfurt has spiffed up what it has, and a stroll through the old streets and across the rivers can occupy several hours.

Orientation

Most of the car traffic is routed around the Altstadt via two ring roads, making it a pleasure to walk between the main sights. The train and bus stations are just beyond the southeastern edge of the town centre, and were undergoing a massive reconstruction at the time of research. It's a five-minute walk north along Bahnhofstrasse to Anger, the main shopping and business artery. The little Gera River bisects the Altstadt, spilling off into numerous creeks.

Information

Erfurt Tourismus (☎ 664 00; www.erfurt-tourist-info .de; Benediktsplatz 1; ☼ 10am-7pm Mon-Fri, to 4pm Sat & Sun) Has a discount card from €9.90.

Tourist Thüringen (☎ 374 2388; Willy-Brandt-Platz 1; ☼ 9am-7pm Mon-Fri, 10am-4pm Sat & Sun) Regional tourism office is directly in front of the station.

Sights

It's hard to miss Erfurt's cathedral, **Dom St Marien** (☎ 646 1265; Domplatz; tours adult/child €2.50/1.50; ☼ 9am-5pm Mon-Fri, to 4.30pm Sat, 1-5pm Sun, short hours in winter), which casts its massive shadow over Domplatz from an artificial hill built specially to hold it. Ironically, it was originally only planned as a simple chapel in 752; by the time it was completed it was the

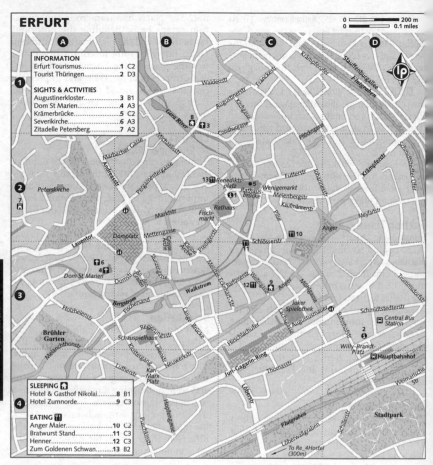

ERFURT

0	200 m
0	0.1 miles

INFORMATION
Erfurt Tourismus..................1 C2
Tourist Thüringen..................2 D3

SIGHTS & ACTIVITIES
Augustinerkloster..................3 B1
Dom St Marien......................4 A3
Krämerbrücke.......................5 C2
Severikirche.........................6 A3
Zitadelle Petersberg...............7 A2

SLEEPING
Hotel & Gasthof Nikolai..........8 B1
Hotel Zumnorde....................9 C3

EATING
Anger Maier..........................10 C2
Bratwurst Stand......................11 C3
Henner................................12 C3
Zum Goldenen Schwan..........13 B2

rather strange, huge amalgam you see today (if only a divine hand could reach down and rearrange things a bit…). In July the stone steps leading up to the cathedral are the site of the **Domstufenfestspiele**, where operas are performed against the dramatic background.

Next to the cathedral, the 1280 **Severikirche** (☎ 576 960; ⌚ 9am-12.30pm & 1.30-5pm Mon-Fri, shorter hours in winter) is an impressive five-aisled church hall boasting a stone Madonna (1345) and a 15m-high baptismal font (1467), as well as the sarcophagus of St Severus, whose remains were brought to Erfurt in 836.

The **Augustinerkloster** (☎ 576 600; Augustinerstrasse; adult/child €8/6; ⌚ tours 10am-noon & 2-5pm Tue-Sat, 11am-2pm Sun), now a nunnery, has a strong pedigree: Martin Luther was a monk here from 1505 to

1511 and, after being ordained in the chapel, read his first Mass. You can view Luther's cell and an exhibit on the Reformation. The grounds and church are free.

North of the Dom complex and west of Andreasstrasse, many of the city's lesser churches were demolished to erect the impressively tough-looking **Zitadelle Petersberg** (Petersberg fortress; ☎ 211 5270) – hence the reason why Erfurt has so many steeples without churches attached. There is a fascinating series of subterranean tunnels within the thick walls, which can only be seen on a guided tour from the tourist office.

Unique in this part of Europe, the medieval **Krämerbrücke** (Merchants' Bridge) is an 18m-wide, 120m-long curiosity spanning the Gera

River. Quaint houses and shops line both sides of the narrow road.

Sleeping

Re_4Hostel (☎ 6000 110; www.re4hostel.de; Puschkinstrasse 21; dm €13-16, s/d €26/52; 🖳) Rooms in this former police station range from hotel-like twins to hostel-like dorms. Bedding and towels cost extra. Breakfast and bike rentals both cost €5 (the latter per day).

Hotel & Gasthof Nikolai (☎ 5981 7119; www.hotel-nikolai-erfurt.com; Augustinerstrasse 30; r €80-100) The location alongside the river, the overall high standard of the 17 rooms, and the friendly owners make this a prime choice. The restaurant is good and there's a fine garden plus a beautiful curved wooden staircase.

Hotel Zumnorde (☎ 568 00; www.hotel-zumnorde.de; Anger 50/51; s €100-140, d €120-170; 🕱) The 50 rooms and suites are modern, quite large and avoid decoration-overload in this fine hotel in the centre. There's a pretty garden hiding behind the noble facade. Enter from Weitergasse.

Eating

Look for interesting and trendy restaurants and cafes along Michaelisstrasse and Marbacher Gasse.

Henner (☎ 654 6691; www.henner-sandwiches.de; Weitergasse 8; sandwiches from €2.50; 🕑 closed Sun) This stylish sandwich bar has sleek orange colours and delicious food.

Zum Goldenen Schwann (☎ 2623 742; Michaelisstrasse 9; mains €5-12.50) It's not so much the unpretentious traditional food that makes this place popular locally, rather the highly rated unfiltered boutique beer.

Anger Maier (☎ 566 1058; Schlösserstrasse 8; meals €6-12) This tunnel-like restaurant is an Erfurt student institution, with cheap, quality eats in a busy, smoky old warren. Set your lungs free in the leafy beer garden.

For a quick treat, have a *Thuringer Bratwurst* hot off the grill from a **stand** (☎ 793 5250; Schlösserstrasse; meal €1.50) near a small waterfall.

Getting There & Around

Erfurt's flashy Hauptbahnhof is on a line with frequent services linking Leipzig (€25, one hour) and Weimar (€7.50, 15 minutes). Hourly ICE/IC services go to Frankfurt (€48, 2¼ hours) and Berlin-Hauptbahnhof (€54, 2½ hours).

You can easily walk everywhere in Erfurt.

AROUND ERFURT

Eisenach is home to the Wartburg, the only German castle to be named a Unesco World Heritage site. Composer Johann Sebastian Bach was born here but he plays second fiddle to the awe-inspiring edifice in stone and half-timber high on the hill.

The small town has a good **tourist office** (☎ 792 30; www.eisenach.de; Markt 9; 🕑 10am-6pm Mon-Fri, 10am-4pm Sat year-round, plus 11am-1pm Sun Apr-Oct), which can help you find accommodation if your day trip gets extended.

The **Wartburg** (☎ 2500; www.wartburg-eisenach.de; tour adult/child €7/4; 🕑 tours 8.30am-5pm Mar-Oct, 9am-3.30pm Nov-Feb), parts of which date from the 11th century, is perched high above the town on a wooded hill. It is said to go back to Count Ludwig der Springer (the Jumper); you'll hear the story of how the castle got its name many times, but listen out for how Ludwig got his peculiar moniker as well.

The castle owes its huge popularity to Martin Luther, who went into hiding here from 1521 to 1522 after being excommunicated; during this time he translated the entire New Testament from Greek into German, contributing enormously to the development of the written German language. His modest, wood-panelled **study** is part of the guided tour (available in English), which is the only way to view the interior. The **museum** houses the famous Cranach paintings of Luther and important Christian artefacts from all over Germany. Most of the rooms you'll see here are extravagant 19th-century impressions of medieval life rather than original fittings; the re-imagined Great Hall inspired Richard Wagner's opera *Tannhäuser*. Between Easter and October crowds can be horrendous; arrive before 11am.

Frequent direct trains run to Erfurt (€11 to €14, 30 to 45 minutes) and most continue on the short distance to Weimar.

WEIMAR

☎ 03643 / pop 65,200

Maybe it's because eggheads consider wax museums declassé that Weimar doesn't have one, otherwise the pantheon of intellectual and creative giants who lived and worked here amounts to a virtual Germanic hall of fame: Cranach the Elder, Johann Sebastian Bach, Wieland, Schiller, Herder, Goethe, Liszt, Nietzsche, Gropius, Feininger, Kandinsky, Klee…the list goes on.

GERMANY

Weimar is not impressive on first glance. There are no vast cathedrals or palaces, nor are there any world-renowned museums. But spend a little time wandering its enchanting old streets and immersing yourself in its epochs of culture and you'll be seduced.

The town is best known as the place where Germany's first republican constitution was drafted in 1919, though there are few reminders of this historic moment (which was centred on the Deutsches Nationaltheater). The ghostly ruins of the Buchenwald concentration camp (p200), on the other hand, still provide haunting evidence of the terrors of the Nazi regime. The Bauhaus and classical Weimar sites are protected as Unesco World Heritage sites.

Orientation

Weimar's compact and walkable centre is a 20-minute jaunt downhill from the station.

Information

There are scores of little book and music shops in town.

Die Eule (☎ 850 388; Frauentorstrasse 9-11; per 30min €1; ☻ 10am-6pm Mon-Fri, to 1pm Sat) Internet access.

Tourist information (☎ 240 00; www.weimar.de; Markt 10; ☻ 9.30am-6pm Mon-Fri, to 4pm Sat & Sun) Discount cards start at €10.

Sights

A good place to begin a tour is in front of the neo-Gothic 1841 **Rathaus** on the Markt. Directly east is the **Cranachhaus**, where painter Lucas Cranach the Elder lived for two years before his death in 1553. Just south is the other extreme of local history, the Nazi-era Hotel Elephant (p200).

For in-depth museum information and high-end souvenirs try the **Stiftung Weimarer Klassik** (Weimar Classics Foundation; ☎ 545 401; www .swkk.de; Frauentorstrasse 4; ☻ 10am-6pm Mon-Sat, 11am-4pm Sun).

The **Goethe Nationalmuseum** (☎ 545 347; Frauenplan 1; adult/child €8.50/6.50; ☻ 9am-6pm Tue-Sun) focuses not so much on the man but his movement, offering a broad overview of German classicism, from its proponents to its patrons. The adjoining **Goethe Haus**, where such works as *Faust* were written, focuses much more on the man himself. He lived here from 1775 until his death in 1832. Goethe's original 1st-floor living quarters are reached via an expansive Italian Renaissance staircase decorated with sculpture and paintings brought back from

his travels to Italy. You'll see his dining room, study and the bedroom with his deathbed. Because demand often exceeds capacity, you'll be given a time slot to enter. Once inside, you can stay as long as you want. The **Faustina Café** has a controversial Christoph Hodgson mural depicting Weimar's famous and infamous.

Goethes Gartenhaus was his beloved retreat and stands in the **Park an der Ilm**.

The Bauhaus School and movement were founded here in 1919 by Walter Gropius, who managed to draw artists including Kandinsky, Klee, Feininger and Schlemmer as teachers. The exhibition at the **Bauhaus Museum** (☎ 545 961; Theaterplatz; adult/child €5/4; ☻ 10am-6pm) chronicles the evolution of the group and explains its design innovations, which continue to shape our lives. In 1925 the Bauhaus moved to Dessau and in 1932 to Berlin, where it was dissolved by the Nazis the following year. Once the form is in line with its function, a much grander museum is planned.

Housed in the **Stadtschloss**, the former residence of the ducal family of Saxe-Weimar, the **Schlossmuseum** (☎ 545 960; Burgplatz 4; adult/child €5/4; ☻ 10am-6pm Tue-Sun Apr-Oct, 10am-4pm Nov-Mar) boasts the Cranach Gallery, several portraits by Albrecht Dürer and collections of Dutch masters and German romanticists. A €90-million project for a full restoration is now in the works. Note that the courtyard was used by both the Nazis and the communists for interrogating political prisoners.

Goethe's fellow dramatist Friedrich von Schiller lived in Weimar from 1799 until his early death in 1805; his house is now the **Schiller Museum** (☎ 545 350; Schillerstrasse 12; adult/child €4/3; ☻ 9am-6pm Wed-Mon). The study at the end of the 2nd floor contains the desk where he penned *Wilhelm Tell* and other works.

Liszt Haus (☎ 545 388; Marienstrasse 17; adult/child €4/3; ☻ 10am-6pm Tue-Sun Apr-Oct) is on the western edge of Park an der Ilm. Composer and pianist Franz Liszt lived here in 1848 and again from 1869 to 1886, when he wrote *Hungarian Rhapsody* and *Faust Symphony*.

Sleeping

The tourist office can help find accommodation, especially at busy times. There are many pensions scattered about the centre, which is where you should stay.

Hababusch (☎ 850 737; www.hababusch.de; Geleitstrasse 4; dm/s/d from €10/15/26) Get in touch with

WEIMAR

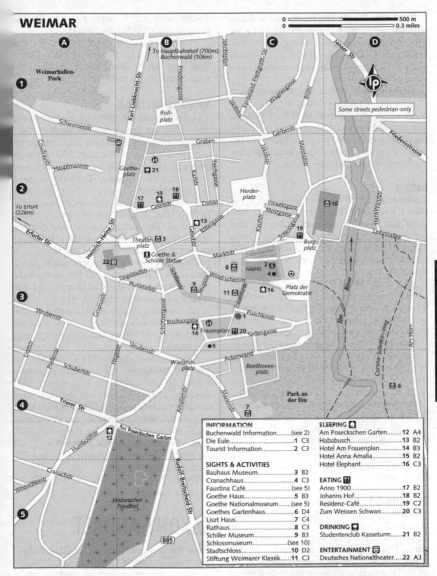

INFORMATION
Buchenwald Information	(see 2)
Die Eule	**1** C3
Tourist Information	**2** C3

SIGHTS & ACTIVITIES
Bauhaus Museum	**3** B2
Cranachhaus	**4** C3
Faustina Café	(see 5)
Goethe Haus	**5** B3
Goethe Nationalmuseum	(see 5)
Goethes Gartenhaus	**6** D4
Liszt Haus	**7** C4
Rathaus	**8** C3
Schiller Museum	**9** B3
Schlossmuseum	(see 10)
Stadtschloss	**10** D2
Stiftung Weimarer Klassik	**11** C3

SLEEPING
Am Poseckschen Garten	**12** A4
Hababusch	**13** B2
Hotel Am Frauenplan	**14** B3
Hotel Anna Amalia	**15** B2
Hotel Elephant	**16** C3

EATING
Anno 1900	**17** B2
Johanns Hof	**18** B2
Residenz-Café	**19** C2
Zum Weissen Schwan	**20** C3

DRINKING
Studentenclub Kasseturm	**21** B2

ENTERTAINMENT
Deutsches Nationaltheater	**22** A3

GERMANY

the town's past at this unrestored 19th-century house. Hababusch is run – and furnished – by students. Perfectly located with no shortage of funky charm. Cook your own brekkie in the kitchen.

Am Poseckschen Garten (☎ 850 792; www.weimar -posgarten.jugendherberge.de; Humboldtstrasse 17; dm from €24; 🖳) An official DJH/HI hostel in a vin-

tage building near the Historischer Friedhof. Dorms have eight to 10 beds.

Hotel Am Frauenplan (☎ 494 40; www.hotel-am -frauenplan.de; Brauhausgasse 10; r €45-80; 🖳) A classic, vintage German building that's no nonsense inside and out. The 46 rooms are clean; interior details are kept to a minimum although breakfast is included.

Hotel Anna Amalia (☎ 495 60; www.hotel-anna-amalia.de; Geleitstrasse 8-12; r €60-100; 🖥) The 51 rooms are very spacious and quiet in this hotel near Goetheplatz. It's all light woods and pastels. There's wi-fi, and breakfast in the cheery dining room is free.

Hotel Elephant (☎ 8020; www.starwood.de; Markt 19; r €100-250; 🖥) A true classic, the 1937 marble Bauhaus-deco splendour of the 99-room, five-star Elephant has seen most of Weimar's great and good come and go; just to make the point, a golden Thomas Mann looks out over the Markt from a balcony in front.

Eating

Residenz-Café (☎ 594 08; www.residenz-café.de; Grüner Markt 4; mains €5-15) For over 160 years, the 'Resi' has been an enduring favourite, and for good reason: everyone finds something for their taste here. Meaty platters let you sample local specialities – all best accented with local mustard.

Johanns Hof (☎ 493 617; Scherfgasse 1; mains €6-16) Large windows punctuate the maroon walls in this historic and stylish cafe. The long wine list specialises in German white wines. Creative dishes include many changing specials.

Anno 1900 (☎ 903 571; www.anno1900-weimar.de; Geleitstrasse 12a; mains €8-15) On the scene since 1920, this attractive cafe in an art-nouveau-style conservatory is a lovely stopover; it has some vegetarian offerings and fine desserts.

Zum Weissen Schwan (☎ 908 751; Frauentorstrasse 23; mains €10-18; 🕑 noon-midnight Wed-Sun) Goethe's favourite dish is served here (broiled beef with herby Frankfurt green sauce, red beet salad and potatoes). Schiller and lots of others have apparently graced the tables of this traditional classic, too.

Drinking & Entertainment

Studentenclub Kasseturm (☎ 851 670; www.kasseturm.de; Goetheplatz 10; 🕑 6pm-late) A classic, the Kasseturm is a historic round tower with three floors of live music, DJs, cabaret and €2 beers.

Deutsches Nationaltheater (German National Theatre; ☎ 755 334; www.nationaltheater-weimar.de; Theaterplatz; 🕑 closed Jul & Aug) This historic venue hosts a mix of classic and contemporary plays, plus ballet, opera and classical concerts.

Getting There & Away

Weimar's Hauptbahnhof is on a line with frequent services linking Leipzig (€22, one hour) and Erfurt (€7.50, 15 minutes).

Two-hourly ICE/IC services go to Berlin-Hauptbahnhof (€51, 2¼ hours).

Most buses serve Goetheplatz, on the northwestern edge of the Altstadt. Don't have time for the 20-minute walk before the next train? A cab costs €6.

AROUND WEIMAR

The **Buchenwald** (☎ 03643-4300; www.buchenwald.de; 🕑 9am-6pm Apr-Oct, 9am-4pm Nov-Mar) concentration-camp museum and memorial are 10km north of Weimar. The contrast between the brutality of the former and the liberal humanism of the latter is hard to comprehend.

Between 1937 and 1945, more than one-fifth of the 250,000 people incarcerated here died. The location on the side of a hill only added to the torture of the inmates, as there are sweeping views of the region – a place where people were free while those here died. Various parts of the camp have been restored and there is an essential **museum** with excellent exhibits. There's also a heart-breaking display of art created by the prisoners. Murals of flowers speak volumes about what was lost. A visit can occupy several hours.

After the war, the Soviets turned the tables but continued the brutality by establishing Special Camp No 2, in which 7000 so-called anticommunists and ex-Nazis were literally worked to death. Their bodies were found after the reunification in mass graves north of the camp, near the Hauptbahnhof.

In Weimar, **Buchenwald Information** (☎ 430 200; Markt 10; 🕑 9.30am-6pm Mon-Fri, to 3pm Sat & Sun) is an excellent resource.

To reach the camp, take bus 6 (€1.70, 15 minutes, hourly).

SAXONY-ANHALT

Once the smog-filled heart of GDR industry, Saxony-Anhalt (Sachsen-Anhalt) isn't on everyone's must-visit list. In fact, while the landscape is looking much greener these days, the flow of human traffic is mainly in an outbound direction, as many young people look west in search of jobs.

Still, the state has some strong drawcards: this is the home of the Bauhaus legacy and the wonderful bordering landscape of the Harz region.

MAGDEBURG
☎ 0391 / pop 230,000

Something old, something new: Magdeburg is constantly characterised by the juxtaposition of those two. Home to Germany's most ancient cathedral, the city also boasts the last of Austrian architect Friedensreich Hundertwasser's bonkers buildings and is a model of GDR-style wide boulevards and enormous *Plattenbauten* (concrete tower blocks) apartments. Last, a small enclave of early-20th-century terraces and cobbled streets around Hasselbachplatz stands out so remarkably that entering and leaving this historic district is like being transported in a time machine.

Orientation
To reach the centre from the Hauptbahnhof, take the city exit, skirt left around the Cinemaxx movie theatre into Ernst-Reuter-Allee, and continue ahead until you come to the city's main north–south artery, Breiter Weg. The tourist office is just after this intersection, on the left side of Ernst-Reuter-Allee.

Northwards, Breiter Weg leads to Universitätsplatz; heading south it takes you to the cathedral and Hasselbachplatz.

Information
Tourist Information Magdeburg (☎ 194 33; www.magdeburg-tourist.de; Ernst-Reuter-Allee 12; ♥ 10am-6.30pm Mon-Fri Apr-Dec, to 6pm Jan-Mar, 10am-3pm Sat).

Sights
Magdeburg is most famous for its 13th-century **Dom** (☎ 543 2414; Domplatz; admission free; ♥ 10am-4pm Mon-Sat, 11.30am-4pm Sun), which is apparently the oldest on German soil. However, the town also has a 21st-century attraction in Friedensreich Hundertwasser's **Green Citadel** (Grüne Zitadelle; ☎ 400 9650; www .gruene-zitadelle.de; Breiter Weg 8-10; German tours €6; ♥ information office 10am-6pm, tours 11am, 3pm & 5pm Mon-Fri, hourly 10am-5pm Sat & Sun). The last design by the famous Austrian architect, this apartment and shopping complex was completed in 2005, five years after his death. It evinces all his signature features – irregular windows, free-form walls and golden domes. The building is pink, but derives its name from its natural architecture and grass-covered roof.

The historic area surrounding **Hasselbachplatz** is an attraction in its own right and full of bars, clubs and restaurants.

Sleeping & Eating
DJH Magdeburg (☎ 532 101; www.jugendherberge .de; Leiterstrasse 10; dm €19-23, s €29; 🖵) The smart, modern premises, generous space, good facilities and quiet but central location make this a winner.

our pick **Green Citadel** (☎ 620 780; www.hotel zitadelle.de; Breiter Weg 9; s/d/ste from €105/125/145; 🖵) Fans of Hundertwasser can ponder the architect's penchant for uneven, organic forms in the elegant rooms of this hotel. The attached cafe (dishes €4 to €5, open 7am to 7pm) is open to the public, serving breakfast and light meals.

Liebig (☎ 555 6754; Liebigstrasse 1-3; snacks €3-10, meals €5.50-14; ♥ 10am-late) Private alcoves and pleated curtains lining the walls create a feeling of warmth and privacy amid this trendy bar-cafe-restaurant. Mediterranean fare, curries and steaks are all served.

Amsterdam (☎ 662 8680; Olvenstedter Strasse 9; dishes €7.50-14.50; ♥ 10am-1am Sun-Thu, 10am-2am Fri, 3pm-2am Sat) There's nothing Dutch about this welcoming bistro, with food ranging from bruschetta and panini to tuna steaks, a dedicated vegetarian selection and sumptuous breakfasts served until 5pm on weekdays and 6pm on Sundays.

Getting There & Away
There are trains to/from Berlin (€23.70, one hour and 40 minutes, hourly), while regular IC and RE trains run to Leipzig (€20.20, 1¼ hours, 1¾ to every two hours).

DESSAU
☎ 0340 / pop 77,200

'Less is more' and 'form follows function' – both these dictums were taught in Dessau, home of the influential Bauhaus School. Between 1925 and 1932, some of the century's greatest artists and architects breathed life into the ground-breaking principles of modernism here, among them Walter Gropius, Paul Klee, Wassily Kandinsky and Ludwig Mies Van der Rohe. Their legacy still stands proud, in the immaculate Bauhaus School building, the lecturers' purpose-built homes and other pioneering constructions.

The Bauhaus was born in Weimar in 1919, and it sought brief respite in Berlin (see p174)

GERMANY

before being disbanded by the Nazis in 1933. But as the site of the movement's heyday and the 'built manifesto of Bauhaus ideas', Dessau is the true keeper of the flame.

Orientation

The leading Bauhaus sights are west of the Hauptbahnhof, clearly signposted and within easy walking distance. The town centre lies east, also reachable on foot.

Information

Bauhaus Foundation (☎ 650 8251; www.bau haus-dessau.de; Gropiusallee 38; ☼ 10am-6pm) Offers educational info on, and tours of, Bauhaus buildings, sometimes in English.

Tourist office (☎ 204 1442, accommodation reservations 220 3003; www.dessau-tourismus.de; Zerbster Strasse 2c; ☼ 9am-6pm Mon-Fri, to 1pm Sat Apr-Oct, 9am-5pm Mon-Fri, 10am-1pm Sat Nov-Mar) Offers city tours and sells a three-day discount card (€8).

Sights

Bauhaus founder Walter Gropius considered architecture the ultimate creative expression. So his first realised project, the **Bauhaus Gebäude** (Bauhaus Building; ☎ 650 8251; www.bauhaus-dessau.de; Gropiusallee 38; exhibition hall adult/concession €5/4, with Meisterhäuser €12/8, tours €4/3; ☼ 10am-6pm, German tours 11am & 2pm, extra tours Sat & Sun), is extremely significant. Once home to the Hochschule für Gestaltung (Institute for Design) where the architect and his colleagues taught, today it houses a postgraduate college. You can visit the changing exhibitions and wander through a small section. However, taking a tour is best; it gets you into otherwise closed rooms, even if you don't understand German.

Since a key Bauhaus aim was to 'design for living', the three white, concrete **Meisterhäuser** (Master Craftsmen's Houses; www.meisterhaeuser.de; Ebertallee 63-71; admission to all 3 adult/concession €5/3; ☼ 10am-6pm Tue-Sun mid-Feb–Oct, to 5pm Nov–mid-Feb) are a fascinating insight into this philosophy and style of living.

Sleeping & Eating

In Dessau, you really can eat, drink and sleep Bauhaus. For a different diet, investigate the main thoroughfare of Zerbster Strasse.

Bauhaus dorms (☎ 650 8318; kaatz@bauhaus-dessau .de; Gropiusallee 38; r per person from €30) Since the Bauhaus school was renovated in 2006, you can really live the modernist dream by hiring the former students' dorms inside.

An den 7 Säulen (☎ 619 620; Ebertallee 66; s €47-56 d €62-74) This relaxed pension has a spa and a glass-fronted breakfast room overlooking the Meisterhäuser across the leafy street.

Bauhaus Klub (☎ 650 8444; Gropiusallee 38; mains €3-7) Starting to see a pattern here? The occasional cool dude in black polo-neck jumper and horn-rimmed glasses can be seen among the broad mix of people in this basement bar of the Bauhaus school.

Kornhaus (☎ 640 4141; Kornhausstrasse 146; mains €7.50-14.50) This is Bauhaus gone a touch upscale on the edge of the Elbe River where you can lounge on the wide balcony and contemplate the curve of the river and the building all at once.

In the same building as the Klub, student favourite **Bauhaus Mensa** (☎ 650 8421; Gropiusallee 38; mains €2.50-5.50; ☼ 8am-2pm Mon-Fri) offers cheaper cafeteria-style meals.

Getting There & Away

RE trains run to Berlin twice every one to two hours (€20, 1¾ hours). Dessau is equidistant from Leipzig and Magdeburg (both €9.90, 45 minutes to one hour), with frequent services to each.

MECKLENBURG-WESTERN POMERANIA

Mecklenburg-Vorpommern combines historic Hanseatic-era towns like Schwerin, Wismar and Stralsund with holiday areas such as Warnemünde and Rügen Island. It is off the path for many travellers, but in summer it seems like half the country is here in some state of undress lolling on the sands. Outside of these somewhat mild times (this is a region where the beaches are dotted with large, wicker beach baskets to provide shelter) the intrepid visitor is rewarded with journeys far from the maddening crowds.

SCHWERIN

☎ 0385 / pop 95,900

State capital Schwerin has a modest dignity befitting its status. The oldest city in Mecklenburg-Western Pomerania, it has numerous lakes, including one that is the town's centrepiece. Buildings are an interesting mix of 16th- to 19th-century architecture. It's small nough to explore on foot, and if you're on the move, you can see it as part of a half-day break on a train journey. But Schwerin's beauty and charm are invariably infectious, and few people regret spending extra time here.

Orientation

The Altstadt is a 10-minute walk south from the Hauptbahnhof along Wismarsche Strasse. A couple of blocks east of the Hauptbahnhof is the rectangular Pfaffenteich, a pretty artificial pond with the garish apricot-coloured 1840 Arsenal (now government offices) at its southwest corner. Heading east from here will take you to the central Markt.

Information

Call-Shop (☎ 572 7946; Martin Strasse 4; per hr €1; ⏰ 10am-10pm Mon-Fri, noon-10pm Sat & Sun) Internet access.

Schwerin-Information (☎ 592 5212; www.schwerin.de; Markt 14; ⏰ 9am-6pm Mon-Fri, 10am-4pm Sat & Sun)

Sights

Southeast of the Alter Garten, over the causeway on the Burginsel (Burg Island), the striking neo-Gothic **Schloss Schwerin** (☎ 525 2920; www.schloss-schwerin.de; adult/child €6/4; ⏰ 10am-6pm mid-Apr–mid-Oct, 10am-5pm Tue-Sun mid-Oct–mid-Apr) was built in the mid-1800s around the chapel of a 16th-century ducal castle and is quite rightly the first attraction visitors head to upon arrival. The causeway is overlooked by a statue of **Niklot**, an early Slavic prince, who was defeated by Heinrich der Löwe (Henry the Lion) in 1160. The huge, graphic picture of his death is a highlight of the castle's interior.

You don't get better examples of north German red-brick architecture than the 14th-century Gothic **Dom** (☎ 565 014; Am Dom 4; tower adult/child €1.50/.50; ⏰ 10am-5pm Mon-Fri, noon-5pm Sun), towering above the Markt. You can climb up to the platform in the 19th-century tower.

The enormous neoclassical building in the Alter Garten, the **Staatliches Museum** (☎ 595 80; www.museum-schwerin.de; Alter Garten 3; adult/concession €5/4; ⏰ 10am-6pm mid-Apr–mid-Oct, 10am-5pm Tue-Sun mid-Oct–mid-Apr) permanently displays old Dutch masters including Rembrandt, Rubens and Brueghel, as well as oils by Lucas Cranach the Elder and collections of more modern works by Marcel Duchamp and Ernst Barlach.

Sleeping & Eating

DJH Hostel (☎ 326 0006; www.jugendherberge.de; Waldschulweg 3; dm €17.50-20.50) This basic hostel is about 4km south of the city centre, just opposite the zoo. Take tram 1 to Marienplatz, then bus 14 to the last stop, Jugendherberge.

Hotel Nordlicht (☎ 558 150; www.hotel-nordlicht.de; Apothekerstrasse 2; s €46-54, d €65-77, apt €74.50-120; 🖥) Simple furnishings, helpful staff, spotless rooms (some with balconies) and walls covered with interesting old photos of Schwerin round out this excellent budget choice in a quiet part of town.

Hotel Niederländischer Hof (☎ 591 100; www.niederlaendischer-hof.de; Karl-Marx-Strasse 12-13; s/d/tr from €94/125/158, apt €147) You can't beat the Pfaffenteich location or the elegant rooms and marble bathrooms at this exceedingly classy hotel. There's even a library with an open fire for those contemplative German winters.

our pick **Friedrich's** (☎ 555 473; Friedrichstrasse 2; mains €8-15) Overlooking the Pfaffenteich, this Parisian-style cafe has a casual atmosphere, a classy, friendly bar area and an uncomplicated selection of salads, fish, grills and vegetarian dishes. The waterfront terrace is divine in warm weather.

Historisches Weinhaus Wöhler (☎ 555 830; www.weinhaus-woehler.com; Puschkinstrasse 26; mains €9-21) Stained-glass windows tell you that this place is indeed historic. Open since 1895, the building dates to the 18th century. The restaurant offers classic Mecklenburg specialities and there's even a fun tapas bar for a quick non-Germanic bite. The beer garden is alluring and you can sleep it off in the comfortable rooms (€80 to €150) upstairs.

Getting There & Away

Schwerin is on the line linking Hamburg (€20.70 to €25, 50 minutes to 1¼ hours) with Stralsund (€31, two hours). Services to Rostock (€14.60 to €18.50, one hour) are frequent, as are those to Wismar (€6.60, 30 minutes). There are RE trains to Berlin-Hauptbahnhof (€31.10, 2¼ hours).

WISMAR

☎ 03841 / pop 45,000

Wismar, a Hanseatic gem that's fast being discovered, joined the powerful trading league in the 13th century – the first town east of Lübeck to do so. For centuries it was in and out of Swedish control – hence the 'Swedish heads' dotted across town. Quieter than Rostock or Stralsund, Wismar can fill up with visitors quickly in high season; it's definitely worth an overnight stay, and is also the gateway to **Poel Island**, a lovely little piece of green to the north.

Orientation & Information

The Altstadt is built up around the Markt, which is the largest medieval town square in northern Germany. The Bahnhof is at the northeastern corner of the Altstadt and the Alter Hafen port is in the northwest.

In the Altstadt you'll find **tourist information** (☎ 251 3025; www.wismar.de; Am Markt 11; ☒ 9am-6pm Mon-Sat, 10am-4pm Sun Jan-Mar).

Sights & Activities

The old harbour, **Alter Hafen**, with old boats swaying in the breeze, evokes trading days from centuries ago. Featured in the 1922 film *Nosferatu*, it is still a focal point of activity in Wismar. **Clermont Reederei** (☎ 224 646; www .reederei-clermont.de; adult/child €8/4) operates hour-long harbour cruises 12 times daily from May to October, four times daily in April and four times on Saturday and Sunday in March, leaving from Alter Hafen. Daily boats also go to Poel Island (adult/child €13/6 return, May to September). Various other companies run tours on historic ships during summer; contact the harbour for details.

Running through town, the **Grube** (channel) is the last artificial medieval waterway in the north and should be a part of any stroll through the historic quarter. The **Wasserkunst** is a 12-sided well from 1602 that anchors a corner of the attractive **Markt**.

The town's historical museum **Schabbellhaus** (☎ 282 350; www.schabbellhaus.de; Schweinsbrücke 8; adult/ child €2/1, Fri free; ☒ 10am-8pm Tue-Sun May-Oct, to 5pm Tue-Sun Nov-Apr) has taken over a former Renaissance brewery (1571), just south of the St-Nikolai-Kirche across the canal. The museum's pride and joy is the large 16th-century tapestry *Die Königin von Saba vor König Salomon* (The Queen of Sheba before King Solomon).

Wismar was a target for Anglo-American bombers just weeks before the end of WWII. Of the three great red-brick churches that once rose above the rooftops, only **St-Nikolai-Kirche** (St-Nikolai-Kirchhof; admission €1; ☒ 8am-8pm May-Sep, 10am-6pm Apr & Oct, 11am-4pm Nov-Mar), built from 1381 to 1487, remains intact. Massive **St-Georgen-Kirche** is being restored for use as a church, concert hall and exhibition space with

a much-doubted completion date of 2010. The great brick **steeple** (☒ 10am-8pm Apr-Oct), buil in 1339, of the 13th-century **St-Marien-Kirche** towers above the city.

Sleeping & Eating

Pension Chez Fasan (☎ 213 425; www.pension-chez -fasan.de; Bademutterstrasse 20a; s with shared/private bathroom €21/24, d with private bathroom €45) This is the best budget deal in town. Rooms in the three-building complex come with private bathrooms, satellite TV and a great central location. Breakfast costs €5.

DJH Hostel Wismar (☎ 32 680; www.jugendherberge .de; Juri Gagarin Ring 30a; dm €22) Popular with large groups, this hostel is simple and clean. It's a 15-minute walk from the train station; alternatively take bus D to Philip Müller Strasse.

Bio Hotel Reingard (☎ 284 972; www.reingard .de; Weberstrasse 18; s €58-62, d €86-88) Foodies should dump their luggage quickly in their charming room – individually decorated with antique furnishings – before heading straight to the lauded organic restaurant here. Added bonus: a delightful garden filled with apple trees and the cutest little bar you've ever seen. Breakfast is €8, and worth every euro.

Zur Reblaus Wein- und Kaffeestube (☎ 40 556; www.zur-reblaus.de; Neustadt 9; snacks €3-10; ☒ 2-10pm May-Sep, closed Sun Oct-Apr) A snug wine bar and cafe where locals come for a drink or a *Kaffeeklatsch* (chat over coffee); try their house speciality pie, the *Trummertorte*. Rooms are also available upstairs in the attached pension (single/double from €30/54).

Brauhaus am Lohberg (☎ 250 238; Kleine Hohe Strasse 15; mains €7-13) Spread over a series of warehouses dating back to the 16th century, this popular spot is honouring Wismar's long tradition of brewing by once again making its own beer. There's a good seafood menu.

Getting There & Away

Trains travel the coastal branch lines to Rostock (€9.90, 70 minutes, hourly) and Schwerin (€6.60, 30 minutes, hourly).

ROSTOCK & WARNEMÜNDE

☎ 0381 / pop 200,400

Rostock, the largest city in sparsely populated northeastern Germany, is a major Baltic port and shipbuilding centre. Its chief suburb – and chief attraction – is Warnemünde, 12km north of the centre. Counted among eastern Germany's most popular beach resorts, it's

GERMANY

hard to see it as a small fishing village these days, but the boats still bring in their catches, and some charming streets and buildings persist amid the tourist clutter.

First mentioned in 1161 as a Danish settlement, Rostock began taking shape as a German fishing village around 1200. In the 14th and 15th centuries, it was an important Hanseatic trading city; parts of the city centre, especially along Kröpeliner Strasse, retain the flavour of this period.

Orientation & Information

The city begins at the Südstadt (Southern City), south of the Hauptbahnhof, and extends north to Warnemünde on the Baltic Sea. Much of the city is on the western side of the Warnow River, which creates a long shipping channel due north to the sea.

The Altstadt is an oval area approximately 1.5km north of the Hauptbahnhof. Rosa-Luxemburg-Strasse runs north from the station to Steintor, which unofficially marks the southern boundary of the Old Town.

Tourist Information (☎ 381 2222; www.rostock.de; Neuer Markt 3; ☺ 10am-7pm Mon-Fri, to 4pm Sat & Sun Jun-Aug, 10am-6pm Mon-Fri, to 4pm Sat & Sun May & Sep, 10am-6pm Mon-Fri, to 3pm Sat, closed Sun Oct-Apr)

Warnemünde-Information (☎ 548 000; www .warnemuende.de; Am Strom 59; ☺ 9am-6pm Mon-Fri, 10am-4pm Sat & Sun Mar-Oct, 10am-5pm Mon-Fri, to 3pm Sat Nov-Feb)

Sights

Lined with 15th- and 16th-century burghers' houses, Kröpeliner Strasse is a lively, cobbled pedestrian street that runs west from Neuer Markt to the **Kröpeliner Tor**, a 55m-high tower you can climb (☎ 454 177; adult/child €2/1; ☺ 10am-6pm).

The **Kloster Zum Heiligen Kreuz** (Holy Cross Convent; ☎ 203 590; Klosterhof 18) was established in 1270 by Queen Margrethe I of Denmark; today it houses the **Cultural History Museum** (admission free; ☺ 10am-6pm Tue-Sun), with an excellent and varied collection including large numbers of everyday items used by locals over the centuries.

Rostock's pride and joy, the **Marienkirche** (☎ 453 325; Am Ziegenmarkt; ☺ 10am-6pm Mon-Sat, 11.15am-5pm Sun May-Sep, 10am-4pm Mon-Sat, 11.15am-12.15pm Sun Oct-Apr), built in 1290, was the only one of Rostock's four main churches to survive WWII unscathed. The long north–south transept was added after the ceiling collapsed

in 1398. Notable features include the 12m-high astrological clock (1470–72) and the Gothic bronze baptismal font (1290).

Warnemünde, the lively seafront to the north lined with hotels and restaurants, is where the tourists congregate. Its broad, sandy beach stretches west from the **lighthouse** (1898) and the **Teepott** exhibition centre, and is chock-a-block with bathers on hot summer days.

Sleeping

our pick **Bräckföst Hostel** (☎ 444 3858; www.braeck foest.de; Beginenberg 25, Rostock; dm €13-20, s €25-35, d €20-30, apt €30-40, linen €2.50; 🖳) Open since 2006 in a landmark building, this palatial place features rooms with moulded ceilings and lots of space. Breakfast is €3.60.

DJH hostel Warnemünde (☎ 548 170; www.djh -mv.de; Parkstrasse 47; dm €32.70-26.70; 🖳) Opened in 2001, this fantastic hostel is in a converted weather station just minutes from the western end of the Warnemünde beach, near Diedrichshagen. The tower rooms are particularly popular with families, who tend to dominate in the July and August holiday period.

City-Pension (☎ 252 260; www.city-pension-rostock .de; Krönkenhagen 3, Rostock; s €39-58, d €60-96) This is a small family *pension* occupying a lovely quiet street near the harbour, in the heart of the old-fashioned northern Altstadt. Rooms are simple but comfortable.

Pension Zum Steuermann (☎ 511 68; www .pension-zum-steuermann.de; Alexandrinenstrasse 57, Warnemünde; apt €40-115) These cheerful blue and white former fishermen's houses are tucked away down a side street and have a relaxed, beachy feel and are popular with families.

Hotel Kleine Sonne (☎ 497 3153; www.die-kleine -sonne.de; Steinstrasse 7, Rostock; r €52-72; 🖳) The bargain offshoot of the swanky Steigenberger Hotel Sonne across the street, rooms are simple business-hotel standard, and the €9 buffet breakfast is gargantuan.

Steigenberger Hotel Sonne (☎ 497 30; www .hotel-sonne-rostock.de; Neuer Markt 2, Rostock; s €110-130, d €130-160; 🖳) It's hard for the interior to compete with the ornate facade at this hotel – a confection of stepped gables and iron lacework topped with a golden 'sun'. However, the rooms do their best in tones of brown, red and yellow, and there's a clutch of classy restaurants.

Eating

Krahnstöver Likörfabrik (☎ 252 3551; Grosse Wasserstrasse 30/Grubenstrasse 1; mains €6-12) This late-15th-century, old liquor factory is an excellent example of late-Gothic architecture. The wine bar has an inventive menu; around the corner, the Kneipe seems as old as the building and dishes up hearty fare.

Zur Kogge (☎ 493 4493; Wokrenterstrasse 27, Rostock; mains €8-15) Touristy but still unmissable, this is Rostock's oldest restaurant. Cosy wooden booths are lined with stained-glass decorations of Hanseatic coats of armour and monster fish threatening sailing ships, while life preservers hang from the walls. The menu is dominated by fish, but you can enjoy coffee and cake between meal times if you want to avoid the crowds.

Café Kloster (☎ 375 7950; Klosterhof 6, Rostock; mains €9-15; ☿ closed Sun) This sweet bistro offers soups, salads and plenty of veggie fare in its art-filled interior or in its hidden garden under a massive pear tree.

Seekist zur Krim (☎ 521 14; Am Strom 47, Warnemünde; mains €9-20) On a tree-shaded and quiet stretch of Am Strom, this restaurant serves schnitzel and seafood. Try a platter of the latter for €15. There's a nice patio.

Weineckeck Krahnstöver (☎ 490 2004; Grosse Wasser Strasse 30, Rostock; mains €9-18; ☿ closed Sun) One side is a wine bar with a pub feel, the other side a proper restaurant: both sides have a loyal local following and offer a lengthy list of wines which you sip in the warm, old-fashioned atmosphere between dark wood walls.

Additionally, excellent fish and wurst stalls set up shop on Rostock's Neuer Markt and Warnemünde's harbour most mornings.

Getting There & Around

Rostock is on the busy line that links Hamburg (€29.70 to €38, 1¾ to 2½ hours) to Stralsund (€12.80, one hour). Services to/from Schwerin (€14.60 to €18.50, one hour) are frequent as is the branch line to Wismar (€9.90, 70 minutes, hourly). There are RE trains to Berlin-Hauptbahnhof (€33.80, 2½ to 2¾ hours, every two hours).

Various ferry companies operate from Rostock seaport. **Scandlines** (☎ 673 1217; www .scandlines.de) has daily services to Trelleborg in Sweden (€21, 5¾ hours) and Gedser in Denmark (€6, 1¾ hours). **TT-Line** (☎ 670 790; www.ttline.de) departs for Trelleborg several times daily (€30, four to six hours).

There are frequent S-Bahn services linking Rostock to Warnemünde (€1.70, 20 minutes). In Rostock, tram lines 3, 4 and 6 link the train station with the centre. The area lends itself to bike touring. **Radstation** (☎ 240 1153; www.radstation-rostock.de; Hauptbahnhof; per day from €7; ☿ 10am-6pm Mon-Fri, to 1pm Sat) is convenient for rentals.

STRALSUND
☎ 03831 / pop 58,000

You instantly know you're next to the sea here. Possessing an unmistakable medieval profile, Stralsund was the second-most powerful member of the medieval Hanseatic League, after Lübeck. In 1648 Stralsund, Rügen Island and Pomerania came under the control of the Swedes – who had helped in their defence. The city remained Swedish until 1815, when it was incorporated into Prussia.

An attractive town of imposing churches and elegant town houses, Stralsund boasts more examples of classic red-brick Gothic gabled architecture than almost anywhere else in northern Germany. It has some excellent sights, including the fantastic new aquarium Ozeaneum. This is great place if you want to feel the culture of the Baltic.

Orientation

The Altstadt is effectively on its own island, surrounded by lakes and the sea. Its main hubs are Alter Markt in the north and Neuer Markt in the south. The Hauptbahnhof is about a 20-minute walk across the Tribseer Damm causeway, west of the Neuer Markt. The harbour is on the Altstadt's eastern side.

Information

Toffi's Web Cafe (☎ 309 385; Am Lobshagen 8a; per hr €3; ☿ noon-10pm) Surf the net with a bottle of beer or cup of coffee or tea.

Tourismuszentrale (☎ 246 90; www.stralsundtourismus.de; Alter Markt 9; ☿ 10am-6pm Mon-Fri, to 4pm Sat & Sun May-Sep, 10am-5pm Mon-Fri, to 4pm Sat, closed Sun Nov-Apr)

Sights

ALTER MARKT & NEUER MARKT

One of the two structures dominating the Alter Markt is the gorgeous 14th-century **Rathaus**, with its late-Gothic decorative facade. The upper portion has slender copper turrets and gables that have openings to prevent strong winds from knocking over the facade; this ornate design was Stralsund's answer

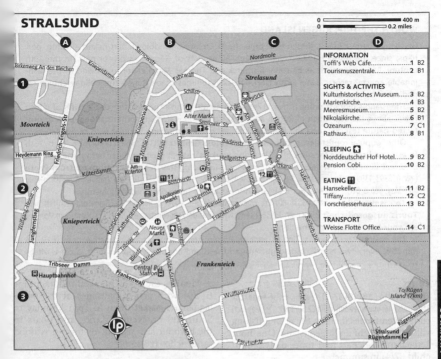

STRALSUND

INFORMATION	
Toffi's Web Cafe.....................1	B2
Tourismuszentrale.................2	B1
SIGHTS & ACTIVITIES	
Kulturhistorisches Museum......3	B2
Marienkirche........................4	B3
Meeresmuseum.....................5	B2
Nikolaikirche........................6	B1
Ozeanum.............................7	C1
Rathaus...............................8	B1
SLEEPING	
Norddeutscher Hof Hotel........9	B2
Pension Cobi.......................10	B2
EATING	
Hansekeller........................11	B2
Tiffany...............................12	C2
Torschliesserhaus................13	B2
TRANSPORT	
Weisse Flotte Office.............14	C1

to its rival city, Lübeck, which has a similar town hall. The sky-lit gallery overhanging the vaulted walkway is held aloft by shiny black pillars on carved and painted bases.

Exit through the eastern walkway to the main portal of the other dominant presence in the Alter Markt, the 1270 **Nikolaikirche** (☎ 299 799; Alter Markt; ☽ 10am-4pm Mon-Sat, 2-4pm Sun). Modelled after the Marienkirche in Lübeck (p287) and bearing a fleeting resemblance to Notre Dame, it's filled with art treasures. Also worth a closer look are the **high altar** (1470), 6.7m wide and 4.2m tall, showing Jesus' entire life, and the mostly inaccurate **astronomical clock** (1394), allegedly the oldest in the world.

The Neuer Markt is dominated by the massive 14th-century **Marienkirche** (☎ 298 965; Neuer Markt; ☽ 10am-5pm), another superb example of north German red-brick construction. Check out the huge **F Stellwagen organ** (1659), festooned with music-making cherubs. You can climb the steep wooden steps up the **tower** (adult/concession €4/2) for a sweeping view of the town and Rügen Island. Ongoing renovations through to 2011 are intended to restore the church to its original look.

MUSEUMS

North of Neuer Markt, a 13th-century convent church is now the **Meeresmuseum** (Oceanographic Museum; ☎ 265 010; www.meeres museum.de; Katharinenberg 14-20; adult/child €7.50/5, combination ticket incl Ozeaneum adult/child €18/11; ☽ 10am-6pm Jun-Sep, 10am-5pm Oct-May), which showcases displays on local sea life and the people who catch it. The massive white swirl of a structure on the harbour is the new **Ozeaneum** (☎ 265 0610; www.ozeaneum.de; Hafeninsel Stralsund; adult/child €14/8, combination ticket incl Meeresmuseum adult/child €18/11; ☽ 9.30am-7pm, to 9pm Jun-Sep), where aquariums take you on a spectacular journey through the ecosystems of the Baltic, the North Sea and the North Atlantic.

Stralsund's cultural-history museum, **Kulturhistorisches Museum** (☎ 287 90; Mönchstrasse 25-27; adult/child €4/2; ☽ 10am-5pm Tue-Sun), has a large historical collection, paintings by Caspar David Friedrich and Philipp Otto Runge, faience (tin-glazed earthenware), playing cards and Gothic altars, as well as various outlying exhibitions in restored houses.

GERMANY

WORTH THE TRIP: RÜGEN ISLAND

Germany's largest island, Rügen is at times hectic, relaxed, windblown and naked – fitting, perhaps, since the resort tradition here reflects all aspects of Germany's recent past. In the 19th century, luminaries such as Einstein, Bismarck and Thomas Mann came to unwind in the fashionable coastal resorts. Later both Nazi and GDR regimes made Rügen the holiday choice for dedicated comrades.

The island's highest point is the 117m **Königsstuhl** (king's throne), the **chalk cliffs** of which tower above the sea. Much of Rügen and its surrounding waters are either national park or protected nature reserves, and the **Bodden** inlet area is a bird refuge popular with birdwatchers.

Other popular tourist destinations are **Jagdschloss Granitz** (1834), which is surrounded by lush forest, and **Prora**, the location of a 2km-long workers' retreat built by Hitler before the war. It is a surreal sight and is home to several museums including the **Dokumentationszentrum Prora** (☎ 038393-13991; www.proradok.de; Objektstrasse 1; adult/concession €5/4; ☑ 9.30am-7pm Jun-Aug, 10am-6pm Mar-May, Sep & Oct, 11am-4pm Nov-Feb), which looks at the huge construction's history.

Tourismus Rügen (☎ 03838-807 70; www.ruegen.de; Am Markt 4, Bergen; ☑ 8am-6pm Mon-Fri) and **Tourismusgesellschaft Binz** (☎ 03838-134 60; www.binz.de; Zeppelinstrasse 7, Binz; ☑ 10am-6pm Mon-Fri) are your best bets for information.

The main resort town is Binz in eastern Rügen; trains from Stralsund arrive here (€12, 45 minutes, every two hours), but to get around the island and really appreciate it, a car is vital.

Tours

Weisse Flotte (☎ 0180-321 2120; www.weisse-flotte.com; Fährstrasse 16; one way adult/child €2.50/1.30; ☑ May-Oct) runs seven ferries daily to the scenic fishing village of Altefähr on Rügen Island. One-hour **harbour cruises** depart four times daily (adult/child €7/4) in summer.

Sleeping & Eating

Pension Cobi (☎ 278 288; www.pension-cobi.de; Jakobiturmstrasse 15; s €35-45, d €50-70) In the shadow of the Jakobikirche, this is a great location for exploring the Altstadt. The 14 rooms are smart and clean, and some have balconies.

Norddeutscher Hof Hotel (☎ 293 161; www.nd-hof .de; Neuer Markt 22; r €40-90) This maroon vision has a great central location and 13 historic rooms. Some have ancient roof beams plunging through the walls. All are comfortable. The restaurant is a stylish melange of tin walls and carved wood.

Tiffany (☎ 309 0088; Am Langenwall; buffet €6.50; ☑ 9am-6pm Tue-Sun) This loosely themed breakfast bar is simply fantastic, darling.

Hansekeller (☎ 703 840; Mönchstrasse 48; mains €8-13) A simple exterior belies the fact that this underground place lies within. It serves up hearty regional dishes at moderate prices in its vaulted brick cellar.

Torschliesserhaus (☎ 293 032; Am Kütertor 1; mains €8-16) In a 1281 building right by a fragment of the city wall, this restaurant-pub has a good beer garden and tasty local fare heavy on seafood.

Finally, there's a great stand (sausage €1.80) with grilled sausages at the **morning farmers market** (8am to 1pm Monday to Saturday) on Neuer Markt, and boats in the harbour sell just-out-of-the-sea seafood sandwiches (€3 to €5).

Getting There & Away

Stralsund is on the line to Hamburg (€47, three hours) via Rostock (€12.80, one hour) and Schwerin (€31, two hours). Direct trains go to Berlin (€35 to €44, 2¾ to 3¼ hours).

BAVARIA

Bavaria (Bayern) can seem like every German stereotype rolled into one. Lederhosen, beer halls, oompah bands and romantic castles are just some Bavarian clichés associated with Germany as a whole. But as any Bavarian will tell you, the state thinks of itself as Bavarian first and German second. And as any German outside of Bavaria will tell you, the *Bavarian* stereotypes aren't representative of the rest of Germany. It's a mostly Catholic place and the politics are often conservative, even if people drink serious quantities of beer (almost 90 years ago this was the land of beer-hall putsches).

Bavaria was ruled for centuries as a duchy under the line founded by Otto I of Wittelsbach, and eventually graduated to the status of kingdom in 1806. The region suffered amid numerous power struggles between Prussia and Austria and was finally brought into the German empire in 1871 by Bismarck. The last king of Bavaria was Ludwig II (1845–86), who earned the epithet 'the mad king' due to his obsession with building fantastic fairy-tale castles at enormous expense. He was found drowned in Starnberger See in suspicious circumstances and left no heirs.

Bavaria draws visitors year-round. If you only have time for one part of Germany after Berlin, this is it. Munich, the capital, is the heart and soul. The Bavarian Alps, Nuremberg and the medieval towns on the Romantic Road are other important attractions.

MUNICH
☎ 089 / pop 1.25 million

Munich (München) is truly the capital of all things Bavarian. It's a heady mix of world-class museums, historic sites, cosmopolitan shopping, exhausting nightlife, trendy restaurants, roaring beer halls, vast parks and, of course, Oktoberfest.

Navigating and enjoying all of this blue-and-white-checked fun (the colours of Bavaria) will take a few days. The efficient public transport system can whisk you around town – although if you stay above ground you might be surprised at how walkable the centre really is. Against all this urban life is the backdrop of the Alps, peaks that exude an allure that many locals – and visitors – find inescapable.

No visit to Germany is complete without at least some time spent in this storied city.

History

Originally settled by monks from the Benedictine monastery at Tegernsee in the 7th and 8th century, the city itself wasn't founded until 1158 by Heinrich der Löwe. In 1255 Munich became the home for the Wittelsbach dukes, princes and kings who ruled for the next 700 years. The city suffered through the Black Plague, first in 1348 and again in 1623, when two-thirds of the population died.

Munich has been the capital of Bavaria since 1503, but didn't really achieve prominence until the 19th century under the guiding hand of Ludwig I. Ludwig became more conservative and repressive, and carried on an affair with the actress and dancer Lola

Montez. He was forced to abdicate in favour of his son, Maximilian II, who started a building renaissance, promoting science, industry and education.

At the turn of the last century there were half-a-million residents, but in the aftermath of WWI Munich became a hotbed of right-wing political ferment. Hitler staged a failed coup attempt in Munich in 1923, but the National Socialists seized power only a decade later. WWII brought bombing and more than 6000 civilian deaths until American forces entered the city in 1945. Then, in 1972, the Munich Olympics turned disastrous when 11 Israeli athletes were murdered.

Today it is the centre of major German industries such as Siemens and BMW.

Orientation

The main train station is just west of the city centre. From the station, head east along Bayerstrasse, through Karlsplatz, and then along Neuhauser Strasse and Kaufingerstrasse to Marienplatz, the hub of Munich.

North of Marienplatz are the Residenz (the former royal palace), Schwabing (the famous student section) and the parklands of the Englischer Garten through which the Isar River runs. East of Marienplatz is the Platzl quarter for beer houses and restaurants, as well as Maximilianstrasse, a fashionable street that is ideal for simply strolling and window-shopping.

Information

For late-night shopping and services such as pharmacies and currency exchange, the Hauptbahnhof's multilevel shopping arcades cannot be beaten.

BOOKSHOPS

Hugendubel Marienplatz (☎ 484 484; Marienplatz 22); Salvatorplatz (☎ 484 484; Salvatorplatz 2) Marienplatz has a good selection of guides and maps (and good Glockenspiel views from the top floor); the Salvatorplatz outlet has all English titles.
Max&Milian (☎ 260 3320; Ickstattstrasse 2) Gay bookshop and unofficial community centre.

DISCOUNT CARDS

City Tour Card (www.citytourcard.com; 1/3 days €9.80/18.80) Includes transport and discounts of between 10% and 50% for about 30 attractions. Available at some hotels, MVV (Munich public transport authority) offices and U-Bahn and S-Bahn vending machines.

GERMANY

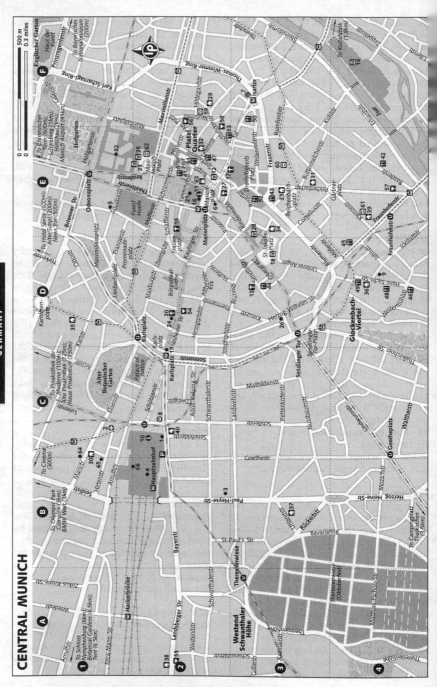

CENTRAL MUNICH

INTERNET ACCESS

Internet + Callshop (☎ 2423 1767; Thomas-Wimmer-Ring 1; per 30min €1; ☻ 9am-11pm) Full service shop and office for Munich Walk Tours (p212).

INTERNET RESOURCES

www.muenchen-tourist.de Munich's official website.
www.munichfound.com Munich's expat magazine.
www.mvv-muenchen.de Everything about Munich's transport system.
www.toytowngermany.com English-language community website with specialised Munich pages.

LAUNDRY

City SB-Waschcenter (Paul-Heysestrasse 21; per load €6; ☻ 7am-11pm) Close to the Hauptbahnhof.

MEDICAL SERVICES

Bahnhof-Apotheke (☎ 598 119; Bahnhofplatz 2, Ludwigsvorstadt)
Bereitschaftsdienst der Münchner Ärzte (☎ 01805-191 212; Elisenhof; ☻ 24hr) Nonemergency medical services with English-speaking doctors.

POST

Main post office (Bahnhofplatz 1; ☻ 7.30am-8pm Mon-Fri, 9am-4pm Sat) The poste-restante address is Hauptpost-lagernd (Poste Restante), Bahnhofplatz 1, 80074 München.

TOURIST INFORMATION

EurAide (☎ 593 889; www.euraide.de; Hauptbahnhof; ☻ 8am-noon & 1-4pm, longer hours in summer) Has desks in the Travel Centre and near the Subway (sandwich shop, not the U-Bahn). Validates rail passes, sells train tickets and tours, and dispenses savvy advice in English.

Tourist office (☎ 2339 6500; www.muenchen.de) Hauptbahnhof (Bahnhofplatz 2; ☻ 9.30am-6.30pm Mon-Sat, 10am-6pm Sun, longer hours in summer & during holidays); Marienplatz (Neues Rathaus, Marienplatz 8; ☻ 10am-8pm Mon-Fri, to 4pm Sat) Be sure to ask for the excellent and free guides *Young and About in Munich*, *National Socialism in Munich* and various neighbourhood guides.

Sights
PALACES

The huge **Residenz** (Max-Joseph-Platz 3) housed Bavarian rulers from 1385 to 1918 and features more than 500 years of architectural history. Apart from the palace itself, the **Residenzmuseum** (☎ 290 671; www.residenz-muenchen.de; entrance on Max-Joseph-Platz; adult/child €6/free; ☻ 9am-6pm Apr–mid-Oct, 10am-5pm mid-Oct–Mar) has an extraordinary array of 100 rooms containing no end of treasures and artworks. In the same building, the **Schatzkammer** (Treasure Chamber; adult/child €6/free; ☻ 9am-6pm Apr–mid-Oct, 10am-5pm mid-Oct–Mar) exhibits jewels, crowns and ornate gold.

If this doesn't satisfy your passion for palaces, visit **Schloss Nymphenburg** (☎ 179 080; adult/child Apr–mid-Oct €10/8, mid-Oct–Mar €8/6; ☻ 9am-6pm Apr–mid-Oct, 10am-4pm mid-Oct–Mar), north-west of the city centre via tram 17 from the Hauptbahnhof. This was the royal family's equally impressive summer home. Parts date from 17th century. The surrounding park deserves a long, regal stroll.

ART GALLERIES

A treasure house of European masters from the 14th to 18th centuries, recently renovated **Alte Pinakothek** (☎ 2380 5216; www.pinakothek.de; Barer Strasse 27, enter from Theresienstrasse; adult/child €5.50/free, Sun €1; ☉ 10am-8pm Tue, to 6pm Wed-Sun), a stroll northeast of the city, includes highlights such as Dürer's Christ-like *Self Portrait* and his *Four Apostles*, Rogier van der Weyden's *Adoration of the Magi* and Botticelli's *Pietà*.

Immediately north of the Alte Pinakothek, the **Neue Pinakothek** (☎ 2380 5195; www.pinakothek .de/; Barer Strasse 29, enter from Theresienstrasse; adult/child €5.50/free, Sun €1; ☉ 10am-5pm Thu-Mon, to 8pm Wed, closed Tue) contains mainly 19th-century works, including Van Gogh's *Sunflowers*, and sculpture.

Located one block east of the Alte Pinakothek, the **Pinakothek der Moderne** (☎ 2380 5360; www.pinakothek.de; Barer Strasse 40, enter from Theresienstrasse; adult/child €8/free, Sun €1; ☉ 10am-6pm Tue, Wed & Fri-Sun, 10am-8pm Thu) displays four collections of modern art, graphic art, applied art and architecture in one suitably arresting 2002 building.

MUSEUMS

An enormous science and technology museum, **Deutsches Museum** (☎ 217 91; www.deut sches-museum.de; Museumsinsel 1; adult/child €8.50/3; ☉ 9am-5pm) celebrates the many achievements of Germans, and humans in general. Kids become gleeful kids as they interact with the exhibits. So do adults. Many get a charge out of the shocking electrical displays. Take the S-Bahn to Isartor.

The **Bayerisches Nationalmuseum** (☎ 211 2401; www.bayerisches-nationalmuseum.de; Prinzregentenstrasse 3; adult/child €5/free, Sun €1; ☉ 10am-5pm Tue, Wed & Fri-Sun, to 8pm Thu), east of the Hofgarten, shows the lives of old Bavarians, from peasants to knights.

Tracing the lives of local Jews before, during and after the Holocaust, the **Jüdisches Museum** (☎ 2339 6096; www.juedisches-museum.muenchen.de; St-Jakobs-Platz 16; adult/child €6/3; ☉ 10am-6pm Tue-Sun) offers insight into Jewish history, life and culture in Munich. The Nazi era is dealt with, but the accent of this recently opened museum is clearly on contemporary Jewish culture.

North of the city, auto-fetishists can thrill to the gargantuan **BMW Welt** (www.bmw-welt.de; admission free, tours adult/child €6/3; ☉ 9am-8pm), adjacent to the BMW headquarters. As part of the corporate-image arms race among German carmakers (see p231), BMW has this temple to its brand (plus a nearby museum shaped like a bowl). Take the U3 to Olympiazentrum.

PARKS & GARDENS

One of the largest city parks in Europe, the **Englischer Garten**, west of the city centre, is a great place for strolling, especially along the Schwabinger Bach. In summer nude sunbathing is the rule rather than the exception. It's not unusual for hundreds of naked people to be in the park during a normal business day, with their clothing stacked primly on the grass. If they're not doing this, they're probably drinking merrily at one of the park's three beer gardens (p216).

Munich's beautiful **Botanical Gardens** (☎ 1786 1350; www.botmuc.de; Menzinger Strasse 65; adult/child €3/free; ☉ varies with season, generally 9am-6pm) are two stops past Schloss Nymphenburg on tram 17.

OLYMPIA PARK COMPLEX

If you like heights, then take a ride up the lift of the 290m **Olympiaturm** (tower) situated in the **Olympia Park Complex** (☎ 3067 2750; adult/child €4/2.50; ☉ 9am-midnight, last trip 11.30pm). And if you fancy a swim, then the **Olympic Pool Complex** (☎ 3067 2290; Olympic Park; admission €3.60; ☉ 7am-11pm) will have you feeling like Mark Spitz while you imagine seven gold medals around your neck – or just work on your breaststroke. Take the U3 to Olympia Zentrum.

Tours

The hordes of visitors and plethora of sights mean there's lots of people willing to show you around – an excellent way to gain background and context on what you see.

Mike's Bike Tours (☎ 2554 3987; www.mikesbike tours.com; tours from €24) Enjoyable (and leisurely) city cycling tours in English. Tours depart from the archway at the Altes Rathaus on Marienplatz.

Munich Walk Tours (☎ 2423 1767; www.munichwalk tours.de; Thomas-Wimmer-Ring 1; tours from €10) Walking tours of the city and a tour focused on 'beer, brewing and boozing'.

New Munich Free Tour (www.newmunich.com; tours free; ☉ 10.45am & 1pm) English-language walking tours tick off all of Munich's central landmarks and historical milestones in three hours. Guides are well informed and work only for tips. Tours depart from Marienplatz by Mary's Column.

MUNICH WALKING TOUR

The pivotal **Marienplatz** is a good starting point for a walking tour of Munich. Dominating the square is the towering neo-Gothic **Neues Rathaus** (new town hall; Marienplatz), with its ever-dancing **Glockenspiel** (carillon), which performs at 11am and noon (also at 5pm from March to October), bringing the square to an expectant standstill (note the fate of the Austrian knight...). Two important churches are on this square: the baroque star **St Peterskirche** (260 4828; Rindermarkt 1; church free, tower adult/child €1.50/0.30; ☾ 9am-7pm Apr-Oct, to 6pm Nov-Mar) and, behind the **Altes Rathaus**, the often forgotten **Heiliggeistkirche** (Tal 77; ☾ 7am-6pm). Head west along shopping street Kaufingerstrasse to the landmark of Munich, the late-Gothic **Frauenkirche** (Church of Our Lady; ☎ 290 0820; Frauenplatz 1; admission free; ☾ 7am-7pm Sat-Wed, 7am-8.30pm Thu, 7am-6pm Fri) with its then-trendy 16th-century twin onion domes. Go inside and join the hordes gazing at the grandeur of the place, or climb the tower for majestic views of Munich. Continue west to the large, grey 16th-century **Michaelskirche** (☎ 609 0224; Neuhauserstrasse 52; ☾ 8am-7pm), Germany's earliest and grandest Renaissance church.

Further west is the **Richard Strauss Fountain** and the medieval **Karlstor**, an old city gate. Double back towards Marienplatz and turn right onto Eisenmannstrasse, which becomes Kreuzstrasse and converges with Herzog-Wilhelm-Strasse at the medieval gate of **Sendlinger Tor**. Go down the shopping street Sendlinger Strasse to the **Asamkirche** (Sendlinger Strasse 34), a flamboyant 17th-century church designed by brothers Cosmas Damian and Egid Quirin Asam. The ornate marble facade won't prepare you for the opulence inside, where scarcely an inch is left unembellished.

Continue along Sendlinger Strasse and turn right on Hermann-Sack-Strasse to reach the **Stadtmuseum** (☎ 2332 2370; www.stadtmuseum-online.de; St-Jakobs-Platz 1; adult/child €4/2, Sun free; ☾ 10am-6pm Tue-Sun), where a mixed but good bag of exhibits cover beer-brewing, fashion, musical instruments, photography and puppets (who *don't* get top billing).

Festivals & Events

Hordes come to Munich for **Oktoberfest** (www .oktoberfest.de; ☾ 10am-11.30pm, from 9am Sat & Sun), running the 15 days before the first Sunday in October. Reserve accommodation well ahead and go early in the day so you can grab a seat in one of the hangar-sized beer 'tents'. The action takes place at the Theresienwiese grounds, about a 10-minute walk southwest of the Hauptbahnhof. While there is no entrance fee, those €8 1L steins of beer (called *mass*) add up fast. Although its origins are in the marriage celebrations of Crown Prince Ludwig in 1810, there's nothing regal about this beery bacchanalia now; expect mobs, expect to meet new and drunken friends, expect decorum to vanish as night sets in and you'll have a blast.

A few tips: locals call it *Weisn* (meadow), the Hofbrauzelt tent is big with tourists while Augustinerzelt draws traditionalists. Traditional Oktoberfest beer should be a rich copper colour, although the masses demand pale lager.

Sleeping

Munich has no shortage of places to stay – except at Oktoberfest or during some busy summer periods, when the wise (meaning those with a room) will have booked. Many of the budget and midrange places can be found in the anonymous streets around the train station. There's no good reason to stay in this area if you can avoid it as you'll find more charm and atmosphere elsewhere.

BUDGET

Munich's youth hostels that are DJH- and HI-affiliated do not accept guests over age 26, except group leaders or parents accompanying a child.

Campingplatz Thalkirchen (☎ 7243 0808; www .camping-muenchen.de; Zentralländstrasse 49; camp sites per person/tent €5/4, cabin per person €13; ☾ mid-Mar–end Oct) To get to this camping ground, southwest of the city centre, take the U3 to Thalkirchen and catch bus 57 (about 20 minutes).

Tent (☎ 141 4300; www.the-tent.com; In den Kirschen 30; camp sites €5.50 plus per person €5.50, bed in main tent €11; ☾ Jun-Sep) Pads and blankets provided for the bagless; bring your own lock for the lockers. Take tram 17 to the Botanic Gardens then follow the signs to a legendary international party.

Wombat's (☎ 5998 9180; www.wombats-hostels.com; Senefelderstrasse 1; dm €12-24, r from €68; 🖳) Style, comfort and location are hallmarks of this hotel-cum-hostel. You'll sleep well in pine beds with real mattresses (free linen), reading lamps in doubles, and dorms with en suite bathrooms. Breakfast is an extra €4.

Meininger City Hostel & Hotel (☎ 420 956 053; www .meininger-hostels.de; Landsbergerstrasse 20; dm/s/d from €17/43/62; 🖳) This hotel-hostel combo scores big points for three reasons: location, amenities and service. Just west of the Hauptbahnhof, it has 380 beds in 95 cheerful rooms ranging in size from singles to 12-bed dorms. Rates include a generous buffet breakfast and wi-fi throughout.

Hotel Alcron (☎ 228 3511; Ledererstrasse 13; www .hotel-alcron.de, in German; s €60-70, d €80-95, tr €90-105; 🖳) Within stumbling distance of the Hofbräuhaus, this quaint hotel has a dizzying spiral staircase leading up to traditionally furnished rooms that don't spoil you with space. Beds, though, are comfortable enough to sleep off any excesses.

MIDRANGE & TOP END

our pick **Hotel am Viktualienmarkt** (☎ 231 1090; www .hotel-am-viktualienmarkt.de; Utzschneiderstrasse 14; s/d from €48/98) Owner Elke and her daughter Stephanie run this good-value property with panache and a sunny attitude. A steep staircase (no lift) leads to rooms, the nicest of which have wooden floors and framed poster art. Book far ahead.

Creatif Hotel Elephant (☎ 555 785; www.creatif -hotel-elephant.com; Lämmerstrasse 6; r €50-150; 🖳) The Creatif is a polychromatic and friendly place bursting with flowers. Its 44 rooms are stylish and comfortable, in an Ikea sort of way and there's free wi-fi.

Hotel Savoy (☎ 287 870; www.pension-haydn.de; Amalienstrasse 25; r €60-150; 🖳) In a Maxvorstadt area thick with modest hotels and cafes, the Savoy stands out for good service, a lift and 74 large rooms with wi-fi. Big windows look across to other inns so you can compare rooms. Breakfast is extra.

Hotel Blauer Bock (☎ 231 780; www.hotelblauerbock .de; Sebastiansplatz 9; s €64-72, d €100-120; 🖳) A whiff of roasted almonds away from the Viktualienmarkt, this no-nonsense hotel once provided shelter for Benedictine monks and has a location that's the envy of more prestigious abodes. It's comfy, familiar and spacious and has free wi-fi. Cheaper rooms share bathrooms.

Pension Gärtnerplatz (☎ 202 5170; www.pension-gaertnerplatztheater.de; Klenzestrasse 45; s/d from €70/95; 🖳) Escape the tourist rabble, or reality altogether, in this eccentric establishment where rooms are a stylish interpretation of Alpine pomp. The one named 'Sisi' will have you sleeping in a canopy bed guarded by a giant porcelain mastiff. There's free wi-fi.

Hotel Uhland (☎ 543 350; www.hotel-uhland .de; Uhlandstrasse 1; s €75-140, d €85-185; 🖳) The Uhland is an enduring favourite with regulars who expect their hotel to feel like a home away from home. Three generations of family members are constantly finding ways to improve their guests' experience, be it with wi-fi, bike rentals or mix-your-own breakfast muesli.

Hotel Marienbad (☎ 595 585; www.hotelmarienbad .de; Barer Strasse 11, Maxvorstadt; r incl breakfast €80-135) Back in the 19th century, Wagner, Puccini and Rilke shacked up in what once ranked among Munich's finest hotels. Still friendly and well maintained, it now flaunts an endearing alchemy of styles, from playful art nouveau to campy 1960s utilitarian.

Deutsche Eiche (☎ 231 1660; www.deutsche-eiche. com; Reichenbachstrasse 13; r incl breakfast €80-180; 🖳) Traditionally it's been a gay outpost, but style junkies of all sexual persuasions should enjoy the plushly designed rooms. Older rooms downstairs are cheaper. There's wi-fi and free breakfast. Also on the premises: a bathhouse.

Hotel Olympic (☎ 231 890; www.hotel-olympic.de; Hans-Sachs-Strasse 4; r €90-180; ⬚ 🖳) If you're into designer decor, Frette linens and chocolates on your pillow, go elsewhere. But if you like a hip location, public areas doubling as an art gallery, and 38 spacious rooms (with wi-fi), give this one a try. Rooms facing the inner courtyard are quieter.

Apartments & Hotel Maximilian (☎ 242 580; www .maximilian-munich.com; Hochbrückenstrasse 18; r €160-300; ⬚ 🖳) This stylish place has 54 studios and apartments in a great location. All units come with kitchen facilities and wi-fi. There's a garden out back and the staff are tops. This is a great place for longer stays or for those sick of hotel rooms. Look for deals.

Eating

Clusters of restaurants can be found anywhere there's pedestrian life. The streets in and around Gärtnerplatz and Glockenbach-Viertel are the flavour of the moment. You can always do well in and around Marienplatz and the wonderful Viktualienmarkt, while Schwabing is always full of eating delights.

RESTAURANTS

Dönertier (Sendlinger Strasse 31; doner €3.60-4.20; ☺ 10.30am-8.30pm Mon-Fri, 11am-8pm Sat) This spacey doner bar takes the humble snack to new heights. Go classic or try the 'deluxe' version with *rucola* (rocket) and mozzarella. Definitely top it off with the refreshing mango yoghurt.

Fraunhofer (☎ 266 460; Fraunhoferstrasse 9; mains €5-14; ☺ 4.30pm-1am) This classic brewpub brings tradition into the 21st century. The olde-worlde atmosphere (mounted animal heads and a portrait of Ludwig II) contrasts with the clued-in, intergenerational crowd and a menu that offers progressive takes on classical fare.

Saf Deli (☎ 1892 2813; Ledererstrasse 3; mains from €6; 11am-7pm Mon-Sat) Vegan fair is served in this stylish cafe right in the heart of roasted-meat land. The curried pea soup's a winner as is the huge range of salads and sandwiches. It's the perfect start after a long night.

Riva (☎ 220 240; Tal 44; mains €7-14) Straight from fashionable Milan, this authentic pizza place packs 'em in for wood-fired treats. Wait for a table inside or out at the long bar up front, and toss a *ciao* or two to the cheery chefs.

Weisses Brauhaus (☎ 290 1380; Tal 7; mains €9-20) The place for classic Bavarian fare in an ancient beer-hall setting. Everything from *Weissewurst* (beloved local white sausage) to hearty traditional fare such as boiled ox cheeks is on offer.

Der Pschorr (☎ 5181 8500; Viktualienmarkt 15; mains €10 15) Shining like a jewel box across a square, this modern high-ceilinged restaurant operated by one of the main local brewers is more bistro than beer hall. Dishes, many with Mediterranean flair, issue forth by the score from the open kitchen.

Haxnbauer (☎ 216 6540; Sparkassenstrasse; mains €10-22) Meats of all kinds roast in the windows of this modern take on a trad restaurant. The wood is dark as are the crispy bits on the much-favoured roast goose. Always popular; excellent quality.

CAFES

News Bar (☎ 281 787; Amalienstrasse 55; breakfast €3-10; ☺ 7.30am-2am) From tousled students to young managers and greying professors, everybody loves their news, especially at this stylish Maxvorstadt cafe that also sells international papers and mags.

Nil (☎ 265 545; Hans-Sachs-Strasse 2; meals €7-12; ☺ 8am-4am) Right in trendy Glockenbach-Viertel, this hip place draws a straight and gay crowd in the know. Tables outside are packed when the sun shines, inside it's packed all night long.

Kranz (☎ 2166 8250; Hans-Sache-Strasse 12; mains €8-16) A luxe cafe in the heart of the edgy and trendy streets of the Glockenbach-Viertel. Posh desserts beg you go easy on the organic burgers etc. Excellent sidewalk tables.

Baader Café (☎ 201 0638; Baaderstrasse 47; ☺ 9.30am-1am) This literary think-and-drink place gets everyone from short skirts to tweed jackets to mingle beneath the conversation-fuelling map of the world. Lines form early for Sunday brunch.

Götterspeise (☎ 2388 7374; Jahnstrasse 30; ☺ 8am-7pm Mon-Fri, 9am-6pm Sat) If the Aztecs thought of chocolate as the elixir of the gods, then this shop-cum-cafe must be heaven. Cocoa addicts satisfy their cravings with rave-worthy French chocolate cake, thick, hot drinking chocolate and chocolate-flavoured 'body paint' for those wishing to double their sins.

SELF-CATERING

Alois Dallmayr (☎ 213 50; Dienerstrasse 14) You'll find one of the world's great delicatessens behind the mustard yellow awnings, with sparkling cases filled with fine foods. This is the place to come if you want a pet crayfish (see their fountain home).

our pick Viktualienmarkt (☺ Mon-Fri & morning Sat), just south of Marienplatz, is a large open-air market, where you can put together a picnic feast to take to the Englischer Garten. The fresh produce, cheese and baked goods are hard to resist. Or relax here under the trees, at tables provided by one of the many beer and sausage vendors. This is the place to see the German's love of all things organic.

Drinking

Apart from the beer halls and gardens, Munich has no shortage of lively pubs. Schwabing and Glockenback-Viertel are good places to follow your ears. Many places serve food. Most are open until 1am or later on weekends.

Alter Simpl (☎ 272 3083; Türkenstrasse 57, Maxvorstadt) Thomas Mann and Hermann Hesse used to knock 'em back at this legendary thirst parlour. Alter Simpl is also a good place to satisfy midnight munchies as bar bites are available until one hour before closing time.

BEER HALLS & BEER GARDENS

Beer-drinking is not just an integral part of Munich's entertainment scene, it's a reason to visit. Germans drink an average of 130L of the amber liquid each per year, while Munich residents manage to drink much more. Locals will be happy to help ensure that you don't bring down the average.

Beer halls can be vast boozy affairs seating thousands, or much more modest neighbourhood hang-outs. The same goes for beer gardens. Both come in all shapes and sizes. What's common is a certain camaraderie among strangers, huge litre glasses of beer (try putting one of those in your carry on) and lots of cheap food – the saltier the better. Note that in beer gardens tradition allows you to bring your own food, a boon if you want an alternative to pretzels, sausages and the huge white radishes served with, you guessed it, salt.

On a warm day there's nothing better than sitting and sipping among the greenery at one of the Englischer Garten's classic beer gardens. **Chinesischer Turm** (☎ 383 8730) is justifiably popular while the nearby **Hirschau** (☎ 369 942) on the banks of Kleinhesseloher See is less crowded.

our pick **Augustiner Bräustuben** (☎ 507 047; Landsberger Strasse 19) Depending on the wind, an aroma of hops envelops you as you approach this ultra-authentic beer hall inside the actual Augustiner brewery. The Bavarian grub here is superb, especially the *Schweinshaxe* (pork knuckles). Giant black draft horses are stabled behind glass on your way to the loo.

Augustiner Bierhalle (☎ 5519 9257; Neuhauser Strasse 27) What you probably imagine an old-style Munich beer hall looks like, filled with laughter, smoke and clinking glasses.

Zum Dürnbrau (☎ 222 195; Tal 21) Tucked into a corner off Tal, this is a great and authentic little alternative to the Hofbräuhaus. There's a small beer garden, and drinkers of dark drafts enjoy pewter-topped mugs.

Hofbräuhaus (☎ 2901 3610; Am Platzl 9) The ultimate cliché of Munich beer halls. Tourists arrive by the busload but no one seems to mind that this could be Disneyland (although the theme park wasn't once home to Hitler's early speeches, like this place was).

Morizz (☎ 201 6776; Klenzestrasse 43) This mod art deco–style lounge with red leather armchairs and mirrors for posing and preening goes for a more moneyed clientele and even gets the occasional local celebrity drop-in. Packed on weekends.

Trachtenvogl (☎ 201 5160; Reichenbachstrasse 47, Gärtnerplatzviertel; ☼ 10am-1am) At night you'll have to shoehorn your way into this buzzy lair favoured by a chatty, boozy crowd of scenesters, artists and students. Daytimes are mellower at this former folkloric garment shop.

Entertainment

CINEMAS & THEATRE

Munich is one of the cultural capitals of Germany; the publications and websites listed on p211 can guide you to the best events. For tickets, try **Munchën Ticket** (☎ 5481 8154; www.muenchenticket.de).

Residenztheater (☎ 2185 1920; Max-Joseph-Platz 2) is home of the **Bavarian State Opera** (www .staatsoper.de) and also the site of many cultural events (particularly during the opera festival in July).

Cult and current films in English are screened at **Cinema** (☎ 555 255; www.cinema-muenchen.com; Nymphenburger Strasse 31). Take the U1 to Stiglmaier Platz, exit at Nymphenburgerstrasse.

NIGHTCLUBS

Jazzbar Vogler (☎ 294 662; Rumfordstrasse 17, Gärtnerplatzviertel) This intimate watering hole brings some of Munich's baddest cats to the stage. You never know who'll show up for Monday's blues-jazz-Latin jam session.

Kultafabrik (www.kultafabrik.de; Grafingerstrasse 6; ☼ 8pm-6am) There's over 25 clubs in this old potato factory that you can sample before you end up mashed or fried. Electro and house beats charge up the crowd at the loungy apartment 11, the Asian-themed Koi and at the small and red cocktail cantina called Die Bar. It's close to the Ostbahnhof station.

Atomic Café (☎ 228 3054; www.atomic.de; Neuturmstrasse 5; ☼ 10pm-4am, 9pm on concert nights Tue-Sun) This bastion of indie sounds with funky '60s decor is known for bookers with a knack for catching upwardly hopeful bands before their big break.

GAY & LESBIAN VENUES

Much of Munich's gay and lesbian nightlife is around Gärtnerplatz and the Glockenback-Viertel. Any of the places in this area listed earlier (such as Nil) will have a mixed crowd. *Our Munich* and *Sergej* are monthly guides easily found in this neighbourhood. Another good resource is Max&Milian (p209).

Many nightspots are mixed. Morizz (p215) is a good place to start. Deutsche Eiche is a good place to stay (p214). Nil (p215) is good by day.

Shopping

All shoppers converge on the Marienplatz to buy designer shoes or kitschy souvenirs. The stylish department store **Ludwig Beck** (☎ 236 910; Marienplatz 11) has something for everyone. Bypass Calvin et al for more unusual European choices.

To truly 'unchain' yourself, though, you should hit the Gärtnerplatzviertel and Glockenbach-Viertel, bastions of well-edited indie stores and local-designer boutiques. Hans-Sachs-Strasse and Reichenbachstrasse are especially promising. Maxvorstadt, especially Türkenstrasse, also has an interesting line-up of stores with stuff you won't find on the high street back home.

Munich has eight Christmas markets from late November, including a big one on Marienplatz. For more on these popular events, see p223.

Getting There & Away

AIR

Munich's sparkling white **airport** (MUC; www.munich-airport.de) is second in importance only to Frankfurt-am-Main for international and national connections. Flights will take you to all major destinations worldwide. Main German cities are serviced by at least half-a-dozen flights daily. easyJet is a major budget carrier here.

BUS

Munich is linked to the Romantic Road by the popular **Deutsche-Touring** (☎ 8898 9513; www.touring.com; Hirtenallee 14) Munich–Frankfurt service (see p218). Buses stop along the northern side of the train station on Arnulfstrasse.

CAR & MOTORCYCLE

Munich has *autobahns* (freeways) radiating out on all sides. Take the A9 to Nuremberg, the A92 to Passau, the A8 east to Salzburg, the A95 to Garmisch-Partenkirchen and the A8 to Ulm or Stuttgart. The main hire companies have counters together on the second level of the Hauptbahnhof. For arranged rides, the **Mitfahrzentrale** (☎ 194 40; www.mitfahrzentrale.de; Lämmerstrasse 6; ☺ 8am-8pm) is near the Hauptbahnhof. The cost is split with the driver and you can reach most parts of Germany for well under €40.

TRAIN

Train services to/from Munich are excellent. There are rapid connections at least every two hours to all major cities in Germany, as well as daily trains to other European cities such as Paris (€135, 6¼ hours), Vienna (€76, four hours) and Zürich (€64, 4¼ hours).

High-speed ICE services from Munich run to Frankfurt (€89, three hours, hourly), Hamburg (€115, 5½ hours, hourly) and Berlin (€113, 5¾ hours, every two hours).

Getting Around

TO/FROM THE AIRPORT

Munich's international airport is connected by the S8 and the S1 to Marienplatz and the Hauptbahnhof (€9.20). The service takes about 40 minutes and there is a train every 10 minutes from 4am until around 12.30am. The S8 route is slightly faster. For €10 you can get a ticket that's good all day.

Taxis make the long haul for at least €60.

BICYCLE

Pedal power is popular in relatively flat Munich. **Radius Bike Rental** (☎ 596 113; www.radiustours.com; Hauptbahnhof near track 32; ☺ 10am-6pm May-Sep) rents out two-wheelers from €15 per day.

CAR & MOTORCYCLE

It's not worth driving in the city centre – many streets are pedestrian only. The tourist office has a map that shows city parking places (€2 or more per hour).

PUBLIC TRANSPORT

Munich's excellent **public transport network** (MVV; www.mvv-muenchen.de) is zone-based, and most places of interest to tourists (except Dachau and the airport) are within the 'blue' inner zone (*Innenraum;* €2.30). MVV tickets are valid for the S-Bahn, U-Bahn, trams and buses, but they must be validated before use.

GERMANY

The U-Bahn ceases operating around 12.30am Monday to Friday and 1.30am on Saturday and Sunday, but there are some later buses and S-Bahns. Rail passes are valid exclusively on the S-Bahn.

Kurzstrecke (short rides) cost €1.20 and are good for no more than four stops on buses and trams, and two stops on the U- and S-Bahns. *Tageskarte* (day passes) for the inner zone cost €5, while three-day tickets cost €12.30.

Bus 100, the Museenlinie, runs a route past scores of museums, including all the Pinokotheks, between the Hauptbahnhof (north side) and the Ostbahnhof.

TAXI

Taxis are expensive and not much more convenient than public transport. For a radio-dispatched taxi dial ☎ 216 10.

DACHAU

The first Nazi concentration camp was **Dachau** (☎ 08131-669 970; www.kz-gedenkstaette-dachau.de; Alte-Roemerstrasse 75; admission free; ☺ 9am-5pm Tue-Sun), built in March 1933. Jews, political prisoners, homosexuals and others deemed 'undesirable' by the Third Reich were imprisoned in the camp. More than 200,000 people were sent here; more than 30,000 died at Dachau, and countless others died after being transferred to other death camps. An English-language documentary is shown at 11.30am and 3.30pm. A visit includes camp relics, memorials and a very sobering museum. Take the S2 (direction: Petershausen) to Dachau and then bus 726 to the camp. A Munich XXL day ticket (€6.70) will cover the trip.

ROMANTIC ROAD

The popular and schmaltzily named Romantic Road (Romantische Strasse) links a series of picturesque Bavarian towns and cities. It's not actually one road per se, but rather a 353km route chosen to highlight as many quaint towns and cities as possible in western Bavaria.

From north to south it includes the following major stops:

- Würzburg (opposite) – Starting point and featuring 18th-century artistic splendour among the vineyards.
- Rothenburg ob der Tauber (p221) – The medieval walled hub of cutesy picturesque Bavarian touring.
- Dinkelsbühl – Another medieval walled town replete with moat and watchtowers; a smaller Rothenberg. The town is best reached by bus or car.
- Augsburg (p225) – A medieval and Renaissance city with many good places for a beer.
- Wieskirche – Stunning Unesco-recognised church (p226).
- Füssen (p225) – The southern end of the route, and the cute and over-run home of mad King Ludwig's castles.

In addition to these principal stops, more than a dozen little towns clamour for attention – and your money. A good first stop is the info-packed English-language website www.romanticroad.de.

Getting There & Around

The principal cities and towns listed above are all easily reached by train – see the individual listings for details. But to really explore the route, you are best off with your own transportation. The entire length is copiously marked with brown signs in German, English and Japanese. With a car, you can blow through places of little interest and linger at those that attract.

A popular way to tour the Romantic Road is the **Deutsche-Touring Romantic Road bus** (www .deutsche-touring.com). Starting in Frankfurt in the north and Füssen in the south, a bus runs in each direction each day covering the entire route between Würzburg and Füssen. However, seeing the whole thing in one day is only for those with unusual fortitude and a love of buses. Stops are brief (17 minutes for Wieskirche, *Schnell!* 35 minutes for Rothenburg, *Schnell!* etc) so you'll want to choose places where you can break the trip for a day (stopovers are allowed). But of course this leads you to decide between a 30-minute visit and a 24-hour one.

The buses depart April to October south from Frankfurt Hauptbahnhof at 8am and north from Füssen at 8am and Munich Hauptbahnhof (north side) at 11am, and take about 11 hours. The total fare (tickets are bought on board) is a pricey €150. Railpass-holders get a paltry 20% discount. You can also just ride for individual segments (eg Rothenberg to Augsburg costs €31), which may be the best use.

GERMANY

WÜRZBURG

☎ 0931 / pop 131,000

Nestled among river valleys lined with vineyards, Würzburg beguiles even before you reach the city centre. Three of the four largest wine-growing estates in all of Germany are here and most of the delicate whites produced locally never leave the region – the locals will always reach for a wine glass first. Over 1300 years old, Würzburg was rebuilt after bombings late in the war (it took only 17 minutes to almost completely destroy the city). The grand buildings are amazing, even if the town itself is a tad drab.

The **tourist office** (☎ 372 398; www.wuerzburg.de; Marktplatz; ☉ 10am-6pm Mon-Fri, 10am-2pm Sat & Sun May-Oct, reduced hours & closed Sun other times), in the rococo masterpiece Falkenhaus, runs 90-minute English-language **city walks** (€6; ☉ 1pm Sat May-Oct, plus 6.30pm Sun-Fri mid-Jun–mid-Sep).

Sights

The magnificent, sprawling Unesco-listed **Residenz** (☎ 355 170; Balthasar-Neumann-Promenade; adult/child €5/4; ☉ 9am-6pm Apr-Oct, 10am-4pm Oct-Mar), a baroque masterpiece by Neumann, took a generation to build and boasts the world's largest ceiling fresco (graphic artists take note: he didn't need Photoshop); the **Hofgarten** at the back is a beautiful spot. The interior of the **Dom St Kilian** (☎ 3866 5600; museum €5; ☉ 10am-7pm Tue-Sun Apr-Oct, to 5pm Tue-Sun Nov-Mar) and the adjacent **Neumünster**, an 11th-century church in the Old Town housing the bones of St Kilian, the patron saint of Würzburg, continue the baroque themes of the Residenz.

Neumann's fortified **Alter Kranen** (old crane), which serviced a dock on the riverbank south of Friedensbrücke, is now the **Haus des Frankenweins** (☎ 390 1111; Kranenkai 1), where you can taste Franconian wines (for around €3 per glass).

The medieval fortress **Marienberg**, across the river on the hill, is reached by crossing the 15th-century stone **Alte Mainbrücke** (old bridge) from the city and walking up Tellstiege, a small alley. It encloses the **Fürstenbau Museum** (☎ 355 1753; adult/child €4/3; ☉ 9am-6pm Tue-Sun Apr-Oct), featuring the Episcopal apartments, and the regional **Mainfränkisches Museum** (☎ 205 940; Festung Marienberg; adult/child €3/1.50; ☉ 10am-5pm Tue-Sun Apr-Oct, to 4pm Tue-Sun Nov-Mar). For a simple thrill, wander the walls enjoying the panoramic views.

Sleeping & Eating

Würzburg's many *Weinstuben* (cozy places to enjoy wine in a traditional setting) are excellent places to sample the local vintages. Look for crests of gilded grapes over entrances. Sanderstrasse has a good strip of lively bars.

Kanu-Club (☎ 725 36; Mergentheimer Strasse 13b; camp sites per tent €6, plus per person €6; ☉ Apr-Sep) A camping ground on the west bank of the Main; take tram 3 or 5 to Jugendbühlweg.

Babelfish Hostel (☎ 304 0430; www.babelfish-hostel.de; Prymstrasse 3; dm €16-18; ▢) This green-powered independent hostel is operated by two fun-loving locals. Facilities include spotless dorms, a chilled commonroom/kitchen, free wi-fi, and bike rental (€5 per day). It's a hop, skip and a jump from the train station; enter via Haugerring. Parking's free.

Pension Spehnkuch (☎ 547 52; www.pension-spehnkuch.de; Röntgenring 7; r €32-65; ▢) This little *pension* 100m from the train station has few frills (except wi-fi), but the seven rooms are clean. Breakfast is served in a sunny room with a balcony.

Hotel Till Eulenspiegel (☎ 355 840; www.hotel-till-eulenspiegel.de; Sanderstrasse 1a; r €66-110; ▢) Oxygen lovers celebrate: this is a nonsmoking hotel. Run by the gregarious Johannes, the 18 rooms are comfortable, have wi-fi and some have sunny balconies. There's also a small but good *weinstube* and a pub serving unusual Bavarian microbrews.

Kult (☎ 531 43; Landwehrstrasse 10; mains €5.50-8.50) Old washing machine and dryer drums have been turned into light fittings at this cafe that draws an alternative crowd for its organic food, steaming mugs of Ovaltine and good beer.

Weinstuben Juliusspital (☎ 540 80; Juliuspromenade 19; mains €8-20) This rambling place serves up a long list of wines (especially local whites). You can have a meal or just a drink at one of the many old wooden tables.

Zum Stachel (☎ 527 70; www.weinhaus-stachel.de; Gressengasse 1; mains €12-22; ☉ closed Sun) There's a restaurant at this 15th-century watering hole, but better yet is to just enjoy a drink on one of its stone balconies overlooking the Romeo-and-Juliet–like Renaissance courtyard.

Getting There & Away

Würzburg is served by frequent ICE trains from Frankfurt (€32, 70 minutes) and Nuremberg (€32, 69 minutes). It's a major

GERMANY

stop for the ICE trains on the Hamburg–Munich line. It is also on the Deutsche-Touring Romantic Road bus route (€14, 1½ hours to/from Rothenburg). The stop is in front of the train station.

BAMBERG

☎ 0951 / pop 71,000

Off the major tourist routes, Bamberg is worshipped by those in the know. It boasts a beautifully preserved collection of 17th- and 18th-century buildings, palaces and churches. It is bisected by a large canal and a fast-flowing river that are spanned by cute little bridges, and it even has its own local style of beer. No wonder it has been recognised by Unesco as a World Heritage site. Could it be the best small town in Germany?

Start your visit at the **tourist office** (☎ 297 6200; www.bamberg.info; Geyersworthstrasse 3; ☒ 9.30am-6pm Mon-Fri, to 2.30pm Sat year-round, plus 9.30am-2.30pm Sun Apr-Dec). The Bamberg Card (€8.50) is good for 48 hours of admission to attractions and more.

Sights

Bamberg's main appeal is its fine buildings – the sheer number, their jumble of styles and the ambience this creates. Most attractions are spread either side of the Regnitz River, but the **Altes Rathaus** (Obere Brücke) is actually solidly perched on its own islet. Its lavish murals are among many around town.

The princely and ecclesiastical district is centred on Domplatz, where the Romanesque and Gothic **cathedral** (Domplatz; ☒ 8am-6pm Apr-Sep, to 5pm Oct-Mar), housing the statue of the chivalric king-knight, the *Bamberger Reiter*, is the biggest attraction. Look for the enigmatic statue, the *Lächelnde Engel* (Smiling Angel).

Across the square, the imposing 17th-century **Neue Residenz** (☎ 519 390; Domplatz 8; adult/child €4/3; ☒ 9am-6pm Apr-Sep, 10am-4pm Oct-Mar) has 40 rooms filled with treasures and opulent decor.

Above Domplatz is the former Benedictine monastery of St Michael, at the top of Michaelsberg. The **Kirche St Michael** (Franziskanergasse 2; ☒ 9am-6pm) is a must-see for its baroque art and the herbal compendium painted on its ceiling. The garden terraces afford another marvellous overview of the city's splendour.

Sleeping

Bamberg's unique style of beer is called *Rauchbier*, which literally means smoked beer. With a bacon flavour at first, it is a smooth brew that goes down easily. Happily, many of the local breweries also rent rooms.

Campingplatz Insel (☎ 563 20; www.campinginsel .de; Am Campingplatz 1; adult €3, camp site €3.50-7) A well-equipped place in a tranquil spot right on the river. Take bus 18 to Campingplatz.

Backpackers Bamberg (☎ 2221718; www.backpackers bamberg.de; Memmelsdorfer Strasse 21; dm €16-19) This little eight-bed hostel is set within an old half-timbered house. You can cook in the kitchen and dine on the rooftop terrace, before bedding down in spotless dorms. It's a five-minute walk to the Hauptbahnhof. Book ahead.

Brauereigasthof Fässla (☎ 265 16; www.faessla .de; Obere Königstrasse 19-21; r €40-70) Rooms at this snug guest house are a mere staircase up from the pub-brewery and covered courtyard. Chairs at the on-site restaurant (mains €7 to €10, closed Sunday) are embossed with Fässla's cute coat of arms – a gnome rolling a giant beer barrel.

Hotel Sankt Nepomuk (☎ 984 20; www.hotel-nep omuk.de; Obere Mühlbrücke 9; r €85-130; ☒) This is a classy yet family-friendly establishment in a half-timbered former mill right on the Regnitz. It has a superb restaurant (mains €15 to €30) and comfy rustic rooms with wi-fi.

Eating & Drinking

Brauerei Spezial (☎ 243 04; www.brauerei-spezial .de; Obere Königstrasse 10; mains €8-15) Across from Fässla, this half-timbered brewery has cosy drinking and dining areas featuring old tile stoves. The seven rooms (€25 to €60) are simple but comfortable.

Klosterbräu (☎ 522 65; Obere Mühlbrücke 3; ☒ Thu-Tue) This beautiful half-timbered brewery is Bamberg's oldest, with a young, fun crowd and friendly staff.

our pick **Schlenkerla** (☎ 560 60; Dominikanerstrasse 6; ☒ Wed-Mon) Decked out with lamps fashioned from antlers, this 16th-century restaurant is famous for tasty Franconian specialities and *Rauchbier*, served directly from oak barrels.

Getting There & Away

Two trains per hour go to/from both Würzburg (€15.50, one hour) and Nuremberg (€18, one hour). Bamberg is also served by ICE trains running between Munich (€56, two hours) and Berlin (€72, 3¾ hours) every two hours.

ROTHENBURG OB DER TAUBER
☎ 09861 / pop 12,000
In the Middle Ages, Rothenburg's town fathers built strong walls to protect the town from siege; today they are the reason the town is under siege from tourists. The most stereotypical of all German walled towns, Rothenburg can't help being so cute.

Granted 'free imperial city' status in 1274, it's a confection of twisting cobbled lanes and pretty architecture enclosed by towered stone walls. The **tourist office** (☎ 194 12; www.rothenburg .de; Marktplatz 2; ⏱ 9am-6pm Mon-Fri, 10am-3pm Sat & Sun Apr-Oct, 9am-5pm Mon-Fri, 10am-1pm Sat Nov-Mar) can help you find a room, a splendid idea because after dark the streets are quiet and the underlying charm oozes out.

Note that the gaggle of Christmas shops and 'museums' are quite wiley – once in you have to walk the entire labyrinth in order to escape.

Sights
The **Rathaus on Markt** was commenced in Gothic style in the 14th century but completed in Renaissance style. The **tower** (admission €1) gives a majestic view over the town and the Tauber Valley. According to legend, the town was saved during the Thirty Years War when the mayor won a challenge by the Imperial General Tilly and downed more than 3L of wine at a gulp. The **Meistertrunk** scene is re-enacted by the clock figures on the tourist office building (eight times daily in summer). Actors re-enact other famous scenes from the past (but not the mythical assault on the tour bus by fudge vendors) at 6.30pm Friday, May to September.

Totally uncommercial, **Jakobskirche** (☎ 700 60; Klingengasse 1; adult/child €2/1; ⏱ 9am-4pm) is sober and Gothic. Marvel at the carved *Heilige Blut Altar* (Holy Blood Altar).

The **Reichsstadt Museum** (☎ 939 043; Klosterhof 5; adult/under 18yr €3/2; ⏱ 10am-5pm Apr-Oct, 1-4pm Nov-Mar), in the former convent, features the superb 1494 *Rothenburger Passion* in 12 panels.

Sleeping & Eating
Resist the temptation to try a *Schneeball*, a crumbly ball of bland dough with the taste and consistency of chalk – surely one of Europe's worst 'local specialities'.

Pension Raidel (☎ 3115; www.romanticroad.com/ raidel; Wenggasse 3; r €25-60) This half-timbered inn has 500-year-old exposed beams studded with wooden nails, and musical instruments for guests to play. Some rooms share bathrooms.

Gasthof Goldener Greifen (☎ 2281; www.gasthof -greifen-rothenburg.de; Obere Schmiedgasse 5; mains €8-16) Classic regional fare focusing on schnitzel, sausages and especially pork (fried, roasted, breaded etc) is dished up in this homey restaurant in the heart of the Altstadt. There are also comfy rooms upstairs (€50 to €90).

Restaurant Bürgerkeller (☎ 2126; Herrngasse 24; mains €8-16; ⏱ Thu-Tue) Down a short flight of steps in a frescoed 16th-century cellar, this hidden spot serves local, seasonal fare.

Getting There & Away
There are hourly trains to/from Steinach, a transfer point for service to Würzburg (total journey €12, 70 minutes). Rothenburg is a crossroad for tourist buses. Deutsche-Touring Romantic Road buses pause here for 35 minutes.

NUREMBERG
☎ 0911 / pop 498,000
Nuremberg (Nürnberg) woos visitors with its wonderfully restored medieval Altstadt, its grand castle and its magical *Christkindlesmarkt* (Christmas market). Thriving traditions also include sizzling *Nürnberger Bratwürste* (finger-sized sausages) and *Lebkuchen* – large, soft gingerbread cookies, traditionally eaten at Christmastime but available here year-round. Both within and beyond the high stone wall encircling the Altstadt is a wealth of major museums that shed light on Nuremberg's significant history.

Nuremberg played a major role during the Nazi years, as documented in Leni Riefenstahl's film *Triumph of the Will*, and during the war-crimes trials afterwards. The city has done an admirable job of confronting this ugly past with museums and exhibits.

Orientation
The main train station is situated just outside the city walls of the Old Town. The main artery, the mostly pedestrian Königstrasse, takes you through the Old Town and its major squares. Breite Gasse, Königsstrasse and Karolinenstrasse are the main shopping streets.

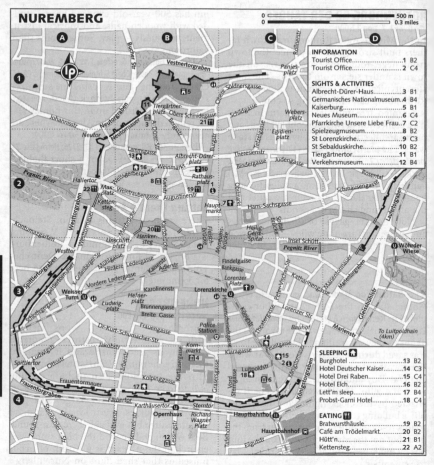

NUREMBERG

INFORMATION
Tourist Office...............................1 B2
Tourist Office...............................2 C4

SIGHTS & ACTIVITIES
Albrecht-Dürer-Haus....................3 B1
Germanisches Nationalmuseum...4 B4
Kaiserburg...................................5 B1
Neues Museum............................6 C4
Pfarrkirche Unsere Liebe Frau....7 C2
Spielzeugmuseum........................8 C3
St Lorenzkirche...........................9 C3
St Sebalduskirche......................10 B2
Tiergärtnertor...........................11 B1
Verkehrsmuseum.......................12 B4

SLEEPING
Burghotel..................................13 B2
Hotel Deutscher Kaiser.............14 C3
Hotel Drei Raben.......................15 B2
Hotel Elch.................................16 B2
Lett'm sleep..............................17 B4
Probst-Garni Hotel....................18 C4

EATING
Bratwursthäusle........................19 B2
Café am Trödelmarkt.................20 B2
Hütt'n......................................21 B1
Kettensteg................................22 A2

Information

The Hauptbahnhof has several internet cafes, most serving beer so you can email things you later regret.

Staff at the **tourist office** (www.tourismus.nuernberg.de) Hauptmarkt (☎ 2336 135; Hauptmarkt 18; 9am-6pm Mon-Sat, 10am-4pm Sun May-Oct, 9am-6pm Mon-Sat Nov & Jan-Apr, 10am-7pm daily during Christkindlesmarkt); Künstlerhaus (☎ 233 6131; Königstrasse 93; 9am-7pm Mon-Sat year-round, plus 10am-4pm Sun during Christkindlesmarkt) sell the Nürnberg + Fürth Card (€19), which is good for two days of unlimited public transport and admissions.

Sights

The scenic **Altstadt** is easily covered on foot. On Lorenzer Platz there's the **St Lorenzkirche**, noted

for the 15th-century tabernacle that climbs like a vine up a pillar to the vaulted ceiling.

To the north is the bustling **Hauptmarkt**, where the most famous **Christkindlmarkt** in Germany is held from the Friday before Advent to Christmas Eve (opposite). The church here is the ornate **Pfarrkirche Unsere Liebe Frau**; the clock's figures go strolling at noon. Near the Rathaus is **St Sebalduskirche**, Nuremberg's oldest church (dating from the 13th century), with the shrine of St Sebaldus.

Climb up Burgstrasse to the enormous 15th-century **Kaiserburg** (☎ 200 9540; adult/child incl museum €6/5; 9am-6pm Apr-Sep, 10am-4pm Oct-Mar) for good views of the city. The walls spread west to the tunnel-gate of **Tiergärtnertor**, where you can stroll behind the castle to the gardens.

Nearby is the renovated **Albrecht-Dürer-Haus** (☎ 231 2568; Albrecht-Dürer-Strasse 39; adult/child €5/2.50; ☷ 10am-5pm Fri-Wed, to 8pm Thu), where Dürer, Germany's renowned Renaissance draughtsman, lived from 1509 to 1528.

The stunning **Germanisches Nationalmuseum** (☎ 133 10; Kartäusergasse 1; adult/child €6/4; ☷ 10am-6pm Tue & Thu-Sun, to 9pm Wed) is the most important general museum of German culture in the country. It displays works by German painters and sculptors, an archaeological collection, arms and armour, musical and scientific instruments and toys.

Close by, the sleekly curving **Neues Museum** (☎ 240 200; Luitpoldstrasse 5; adult/child €4/3; ☷ 10am-8pm Tue-Fri, to 6pm Sat & Sun) contains a superb collection of contemporary art and design.

Nuremberg has a lot of toy companies and the **Spielzeugmuseum** (Toy Museum; ☎ 231 3164; Karlstrasse 13-15; adult/child €4/2; ☷ 10am-5pm Tue-Fri, to 6pm Sat & Sun) presents them in their infinite variety. The **Verkehrsmuseum** (Transportation Museum; ☎ 01804-442 233; www.dbmuseum.de; Lessingstrasse 6; adult/child €4/2; ☷ 10am-3pm Mon, 1-5pm Thu, 10am-5pm Sun) has a trainload of exhibits on the German railways.

Nuremberg's role during the Third Reich is well known. The Nazis chose this city as their propaganda centre and for mass rallies, which were held at **Luitpoldhain**, a (never completed) sports complex of megalomaniac proportions. After the war, the Allies deliberately chose Nuremberg as the site for the trials of Nazi war criminals. Don't miss the **Dokumentationzentrum** (☎ 231 5666; www.museen .nuernberg.de; Bayernstrasse 110; adult/child €5/2.50; ☷ 9am-6pm Mon-Fri, 10am-6pm Sat & Sun) in the north wing of the massive unfinished Congress Hall, which would have held 50,000 people for Hitler's spectacles. The museum's absorbing exhibits trace the rise of Hitler and the Nazis, and the important role Nuremberg played in the mythology. Take tram 9 or 6 to Doku-Zentrum.

Sleeping

Lette 'm Sleep (☎ 992 8128; www.backpackers.de; Frauentormauer 42; dm €16-25, linen €3, s/d from €30/50; ☐) A backpacker favourite, this independent hostel is just five minutes' walk from the Hauptbahnhof, with a laundry, colourfully painted dorms and wi-fi.

Probst-Garni Hotel (☎ 203 433; www.hotel-garni -probst.de; Luitpoldstrasse 9; r €35-110) Nuremberg's most reasonably priced pension is squeezed on the 3rd floor of a vintage building. Some singles are tiny and some share bathrooms. The letters from happy guests are sweet.

Hotel Elch (☎ 249 2980; www.hotel-elch.com; Irrerstrasse 9; r €55-110; ☐) Tucked up in the antiques quarter, this 14th-century, half-timbered house has morphed into a snug, romantic little 12-room hotel. A couple of rooms (Nos 2 and 7) have half-timbered walls and ceilings too, and modern touches include glazed terracotta bathrooms and free wi-fi.

Burghotel (☎ 238 890; www.burghotel-nuernberg .de; Lammsgasse 3; r €80-185; ☐ ☒) Immaculate rooms at this friendly hotel span small singles and doubles with '50s-style built-in timber furniture reminiscent of old-fashioned train carriages. All 57 rooms are appealing and have wi-fi. All guests can use the basement heated swimming pool and sauna.

Hotel Deutscher Kaiser (☎ 242 660; www.deut scher-kaiser-hotel.de; Königstrasse 55; r €90-125; ☐) A grand sandstone staircase leads to 52 ornately decorated rooms (equipped with wi-fi) in this 1880s-built hotel. Bathrooms are equipped with bidets and there's a lavish buffet breakfast.

Hotel Drei Raben (☎ 274 380; www.hotel3raben. de; Königstrasse 63; r €100-185; ☐) The design of this original hotel builds upon the legend of the three ravens perched on the building's chimney stack. Each of the 'mythology' rooms tells a particular tale – from the life of Albrecht Dürer to the history of the local football club.

CHRISTMAS MARKETS

Beginning in late November every year, central squares across Germany – especially those in Bavaria – are transformed into Christmas markets or *Christkindlmarkts* (also known as *Weihnachtsmärkte*). Folks stamp about between the wooden stalls, perusing seasonal trinkets (from treasures to schlock) while warming themselves with tasty *glühwein* (mulled, spiced red wine) and treats such as sausages and potato pancakes. The markets are popular with tourists but locals love 'em too, and bundle themselves up and carouse for hours. Nuremberg's **market** (www.chriskindlesmarkt. de) fills much of the centre and attracts two million people.

Eating

Don't leave Nuremberg without trying its famous *Nürnberger Bratwürste*. Order 'em by the dozen with *Meerrettich* (horseradish) on the side. Restaurants line the hilly lanes above the Burgstrasse.

Café am Trödelmarkt (☎ 208 877; Trödelmarkt 42; dishes €3-5; ☻ 9am-6pm) A gorgeous place on a sunny day, this multilevel waterfront cafe overlooks the covered Henkersteg bridge. It's popular for its fresh and tasty continental breakfasts.

our pick **Bratwursthäusle** (☎ 227 695; Rathausplatz 2; meals €6-12) A local legend and *the* place for flame-grilled and scrumptious local sausages. Get them with *Kartoffelsalat* (potato salad). There are also nice tree-shaded tables outside.

Hütt'n (☎ 201 9881; Burgstrasse 19; mains €8-15; ☻ from 4pm Mon-Wed) Be prepared to queue for a table at this local haunt. The special here is the *ofenfrische Krustenbraten:* roast pork with crackling, dumplings and sauerkraut salad. There's also a near-endless variety of schnapps and beers.

Kettensteg (☎ 221 081; Maxplatz 35; mains €7-15) Right by the river and with its own suspension bridge to the other side, this beer garden and restaurant is fine on a summer day and cosy in winter. The basic fare is tasty and absorbs lots of beer.

Getting There & Around

Nuremberg's **airport** (NUE; www.airport-nuernberg .de) is a hub for budget carrier Air Berlin, which has services throughout Germany, as well as flights to London. There's frequent service to the airport on the S-2 line (€2, 12 minutes).

The city is also a hub for train services. ICE trains run to/from Berlin-Hauptbahnhof (€89, 4½ hours, every two hours), Frankfurt-am-Main (€48, two hours, hourly) and on the new fast line to Munich (€49, one hour, hourly). Trains run hourly to Stuttgart (€38, 2¼ hours).

Tickets on the bus, tram and U-Bahn system cost €1.80 each. Day passes are €4.

REGENSBURG

☎ 0941 / pop 129,000

On the wide Danube River, Regensburg has relics of all periods as far back as the Romans, yet doesn't have the tourist mobs you'll find in other equally attractive German cities.

Oh well, their loss. The centre escaped the war's carpet bombing, and Renaissance towers that could be in Florence mix with half-timbered charm. Some 25,000 students keep things lively.

Orientation & Information

From the main train station, walk up Maximilianstrasse for 10 minutes to reach the centre. There's internet access at coin-operated terminals (€1 per 15 minutes) on the top level of the train station. Visit the centrally located **tourist office** (☎ 507 4410; www .regensburg.de; Altes Rathaus; ☻ 9am-6pm Mon-Fri, to 4pm Sat & Sun).

Sights

A veritable miracle of engineering in its time, the **Steinerne Brücke** (Stone Bridge) was cobbled together between 1135 and 1146. For centuries it remained the only solid crossing along the entire Danube.

Lording over Regensburg, **Dom St Peter** (☎ 597 1002; Domplatz; admission free; ☻ 6.30am-6pm Apr-Oct, to 5pm Nov-Mar) ranks among Bavaria's grandest Gothic cathedrals. Construction of this green-hued twin-spired landmark began in the late 13th century, mostly to flaunt the city's prosperity. The cavernous interior's prized possessions include kaleidoscopic stained-glass windows.

The **Altes Rathaus** (507 4411; adult/child incl museum €6/3; ☻ tours in English 3pm Apr-Oct, 2pm Nov, Dec & Mar) was progressively extended from medieval to baroque times and remained the seat of the Reichstag for almost 150 years.

The **Roman wall**, with its **Porta Praetoria** arch, follows Unter den Schwibbögen onto Dr-Martin-Luther-Strasse.

Lavish **Schloss Thurn und Taxis** (☎ 504 8133; www .thurnundtaxis.de; Emmeramsplatz 5; tours adult/child €11.50/9; ☻ 11am-5pm Mon-Fri, 10am-5pm Sat & Sun) is near the train station and includes the castle proper (Schloss) and the royal stables *(Marstall).* The adjoining **Basilika St Emmeram** (☎ 510 30; Emmeramsplatz; ☻ 10am-4.30pm) is a riot of rococo and has a perfect cloister.

Sleeping & Eating

Azur-Camping (☎ 270 025; www.azur-camping.de; Weinweg 40; per person €5.50-7, camp sites €6-8) Bus 6 from the train station goes to the entrance of this beautiful riverside site.

Brook Lane Hostel (☎ 690 0966; www.hostel-regens burg.de, in German; Obere Bachgasse 21; dm €15, d with shared bathroom €35). This ever-expanding indie hostel in the heart of town has a full kitchen, colourful dorms with timber bunks, and a small supermarket downstairs.

Goldenes Kreuz (☎ 558 12; www.hotel-goldeneskreuz .de; Haidplatz 7; s €75-105, d €95-125; 🖳) Dating back to at least 1531, and frequented by emperors, nobles and other luminaries (such as yourself), this ancient inn has been painstakingly renovated into a choice little nine-room hotel. Wi-fi is available.

Spaghetteria (☎ 563 695; Am Römling 12; mains €6-12) Lit by huge candelabras suspended from its cross-vaulted ceiling, this one-time Gothic chapel cooks up a plethora of perfect pastas. Its antipasti buffet is as colourful as a Michelangelo painting.

ourpick Historische Wurstküche (☎ 466 210; Thundorferstrasse 3; meals €7) The Danube rushes past this little house that's been cooking up the addictive local version of Nuremberg sausages (slightly spicier) since 1135.

Restaurant Künstlerhaus (☎ 830 5998; Andreasstrasse 28; mains €8-18; 🏵 closed Mon) Overlooking the river, this stylish bistro boasts art produced by artists occupying the atelier above. Fresh, seasonal and locally sourced produce is prepared in creative ways.

Getting There & Away

Regensburg is on the train line between Nuremberg (€18 to €24, one hour, hourly) and Vienna, Austria (€70, four hours). There are hourly trains to Munich (€24, 1½ hours).

AUGSBURG

☎ 0821 / pop 260,000

Originally established by the Romans in 15 BC, Augsburg later became a centre of Luther's Reformation. Today it's a lively provincial city, criss-crossed by little streams, that has an appealing ambience and vitality. It makes a good day trip from Munich.

The **tourist office** (☎ 502 0724; www.augsburg -tourismus.de; Maximilian Strasse 57; 🏵 9am-5pm Mon-Fri, 10am-2pm Sat) can help with accommodation.

Sights

Look for the very impressive onion-shaped towers on the 17th-century **Rathaus** (☎ 3240; Rathausplatz; 🏵 10am-6pm) and the adjacent **Perlachturm**, a former guard tower. North of here is the 10th-century **Dom Maria Heim-**

suchung (Hoher Weg; 🏵 10am-6pm Mon-Sat), which has more 'modern' additions, such as the 14th-century doors showing scenes from the Old Testament.

The Fuggers – a 16th-century banking family – left their mark everywhere. They have lavish tombs inside **St Anna Kirche** (☎ 392 92; Im Annahof 2, off Annastrasse; 🏵 10am-noon Tue-Sat, 3-5pm Tue-Sun), a place also known for being a Martin Luther bolt-hole. The 16th-century **Fuggerei** (no laughing!) was built with banking riches to house the poor. The excellent **museum** (☎ 319 881; Mittlere Gasse 13; adult/child €2/1; 🏵 9am-6pm) shows how they lived.

Sleeping & Eating

Jakoberhof (☎ 510 030; www.jakoberhof.de; Jakoberhofstrasse 41; r €40-80; 🖳) Rooms at this dignified corner inn are sparsely decorated, which makes it easier not to lose something. Look for this temple of good value (which has wi-fi) under its own onion dome.

Ratskeller (☎ 3198 8238; Rathausplatz 2; mains €7-15) Ambiently lit corners, ante-rooms and mezzanines are strewn with comfy lounges, and there's a wide terrace out back. Ratskeller's kitchen is renowned for its *Schweinebraten* – roast pork with dumplings and red-cabbage sauerkraut.

Bauerntanz (☎ 153 644; Bauerntanzgässchen 1; mains €9-16) Framed by lace curtains, this dark-timber place with copper lamps serves big portions of creative Swabian and Bavarian food. There's outdoor seating.

Getting There & Away

Trains between Munich and Augsburg are frequent (€12 to €20, 40 minutes). The Deutsche-Touring Romantic Road bus stops at the train station and the Rathaus.

FÜSSEN

☎ 08362 / pop 14,000

Never have so many come to a place with so few inhabitants by comparison. Close to the Austrian border and the foothills of the Alps, Füssen has some splendid baroque architecture, but that is overlooked by the mobs swarming the two castles associated with King Ludwig II in nearby Schwangau. The **tourist office** (☎ 938 50; www.fuessen.de; Kaiser-Maximillian-Platz 1; 🏵 9am-5pm Mon-Fri, 10am-2pm Sat, 10am-noon Sun) is often overrun.

GERMANY

WORTH THE TRIP: WEISKIRCHE

This Unesco World Heritage **church** (☎ 08862 932 930; www.wieskirche.de; ☒ 8am-7pm May-Oct, to 5pm Nov-Apr) is a truly amazing work of 18th-century rococo excess. Its white pillars tower over a tiny village 25km northeast of Füssen. The church can be reached by the Romantic Road bus (p218) or via RVO bus 9606 (www.rvo-bus.de), which runs between Füssen and Garmisch-Partenkirchen via Weiskirche and Oberammergau (five to six daily).

Sights

Neuschwanstein and **Hohenschwangau castles** provide a fascinating glimpse into the romantic king's state of mind (or lack thereof) and well-developed ego. Hohenschwangau is where Ludwig lived as a child. It's not as cute, even though both castles are 19th-century constructions, but it draws less crowds and visits are more relaxed. The adjacent Neuschwanstein is Ludwig's own creation (albeit with the help of a theatrical designer). Although it was unfinished when he died in 1886, there is plenty of evidence of Ludwig's twin obsessions: swans and Wagnerian operas. The sugary pastiche of architectural styles, alternatively overwhelmingly beautiful and just a little too much, reputedly inspired Disney's Fantasyland castle.

Tickets may only be bought from the **ticket centre** (☎ 930 830; www.ticket-center-hohenschwangau.de; Alpseestrasse 12, Hohenschwangau; adult/child €9/8, incl Schloss Hohenschwangau €17/15; ☒ tickets 8am-5pm Apr-Sep, 9am-3pm Oct-Mar). In summer it's worth the €1.80 surcharge each to reserve ahead. To walk to Hohenschwangau takes 20 minutes while Neuschwanstein is a 45-minute steep hike. Horse-drawn carriages (€6) and shuttle buses (€2) shorten but don't eliminate the hike. The walk between the castles is a piney 45-minute stroll.

Take the bus from Füssen train station (€2, 15 minutes, hourly) or share a taxi (☎ 7700; €10 for up to four people). Go early to avoid the worst of the rush.

And remember, as soon as you leave the main trails, you're in beautiful and untrammelled Alpine wilderness.

Sleeping & Eating

A pavilion near the tourist office has a computerised list of vacant rooms in town; most of the cheapest rooms, at around €15 per person, are in private homes just a few minutes from the Altstadt. Füssen is a pretty quiet place after dark and most people will stay only long enough to see the castles. There are a couple of cafes in the centre where you can grab lunch.

Altstadt Hotel zum Hechten (☎ 916 00; www.hotel-hechten.com; Ritterstrasse 6; r €50-90) Set around a quiet inner courtyard, this child-friendly place is one of Füssen's oldest Altstadt hotels, with rustic public areas and bright, modern guest rooms.

Ritterstub'n (☎ 7759; Ritter-Strasse 4; mains €7-12) Local specialities and lake fish are on offer at this historic restaurant, which is always good for a beer.

Getting There & Away

Train connections to Munich (€24, two hours) run every two hours. Füssen is the start of the Romantic Road. Deutsche-Touring buses (p218) start here and are the best way to reach Wieskirche (left; €9, 50 minutes) if you don't have a car.

RVO bus 9606 (www.rvo-bus.de) connects Füssen, via Weiskirche and Oberammergau, with Garmisch-Partenkirchen (€10, two hours, five to six daily).

BAVARIAN ALPS

While not quite as high as their sister summits further south in Austria and Switzerland, the Bavarian Alps (Bayerische Alpen) still are standouts, owing to their abrupt rise from the rolling Bavarian foothills. Stretching westward from Germany's southeastern corner to the Allgäu region near Lake Constance, the Alps take in most of the mountainous country fringing the southern border with Austria.

Getting There & Around

While the public transport network is good, the mountain geography means there are few direct routes between main centres; sometimes a short cut via Austria is quicker (such as between Füssen and Garmisch-Partenkirchen). Road rather than rail routes are often more practical. For those driving, the German Alpine Rd (Deutsche Alpenstrasse) is a scenic way to go.

BERCHTESGADEN

☎ 08652 / pop 7900

Steeped in myth and legend, the Berchtes-gadener Land enjoys a natural beauty so abundant that it's almost preternatural. Framed by six formidable mountain ranges and home to Germany's second-highest mountain, the Watzmann (2713m), the dreamy, fir-lined valleys are filled with gurgling streams and peaceful Alpine villages.

Much of the terrain is protected by law as the Nationalpark Berchtesgaden, which embraces the pristine Königssee, one of Germany's most photogenic lakes. Yet, Berchtesgaden's history is also indelibly entwined with the Nazi period as chronicled at the Dokumentation Obersalzberg. The Eagle's Nest, a mountaintop lodge built for Hitler, is now a major tourist attraction.

The **tourist office** (☎ 9670; www.berchtesgaden .de; Königsseer Strasse 2; ☼ 8.30am-6pm Mon-Fri, to 5pm Sat, 9am-3pm Sun mid-Jun–Sep, reduced hours other times) is just across the river from the train station and has internet access.

Sights & Activities

In 1933 quiet Obersalzberg (some 3km from Berchtesgaden) became the southern headquarters of Hitler's government, a dark period that's given the full historical treatment at the **Dokumentation Obersalzberg** (☎ 947 960; www .obersalzberg.de; Salzbergstrasse 41, Obersalzberg; adult/child & student €3/free; ☼ 9am-5pm daily Apr-Oct, 10am-3pm Tue-Sun Nov-Apr). To get there take bus 838 from the Hauptbahnhof in Berchtesgaden.

Berchtesgaden's creepiest – yet impressive – draw is the **Eagle's Nest** atop Mt Kehlstein, a sheer-sided peak at Obersalzberg. Perched at

---

HOT & COLD FUN IN THE ALPS

The Bavarian Alps are extraordinarily well organised for outdoor pursuits, with skiing, snowboarding and hiking being the most popular. The ski season usually runs from mid-December to April. Ski gear is available for hire in all the resorts, with the lowest daily/weekly rates including skis, boots and stocks at around €15/50. Five-day skiing courses start from €100.

During the warmer months, the activities include kayaking, rafting, cycling and paragliding. Tourist offices can always advise on hikes long and short.

1834m, the innocent-looking lodge (called Kehlsteinhaus in German) has sweeping views across the mountains and down into the valley where the Königssee shimmers. Ironically, Hitler is said to have suffered from vertigo and rarely enjoyed the spectacular views himself.

Drive or take bus 849 from the Berchtesgaden Hauptbahnhof to the Kehlstein stop, where you board a special **bus** (www.kehlstein haus.de; adult/child €13/12) that drives you up the mountain. It runs between 7.20am and 4pm, and takes 35 minutes.

Eagle's Nest Tours (☎ 649 71; www.eagles-nest -tours.com; adult/6-12yr €45/30; ☼ 1.30pm mid-May–Oct) has four-hour tours in English that cover the war years.

Change themes with a tour of the **Salzbergwerk** (☎ 600 20; adult/child €14/9; ☼ 9am-5pm May-Oct, 11.30am-3.30pm Nov-Apr), which combines history with a carnival. Visitors descend into the salt mine for a 1½-hour tour.

Crossing the beautiful, emerald green Königssee, a beautiful alpine lake situated 5km south of Berchtesgaden (and linked by hourly buses in summer) is sublime. There are frequent boat tours across the lake to the pixel-perfect chapel at St Bartholomä (€12).

The wilds of Berchtesgaden National Park offer some of the best **hiking** in Germany. A good introduction to the area is a 2km path up from St Bartholomä beside the Königssee to the Watzmann-Ostwand, a massive 2000m-high rock face where scores of overly ambitious mountaineers have died.

Sleeping & Eating

Of the five camping grounds around Berchtesgaden, the nicest are at Königssee.

Grafenlehen (☎ 4140; www.camping-grafenlehen .de; Königsseerfussweg 71, Schönau; per camp site/person €6.50/5.50) This place has a playground and mountain views.

Jugendherberge (☎ 943 70; www.berchtesgaden .jugendherberge.de; Struberweg 6, Bischofswiesen; dm €16-20, s/d from €24/40; ☼ closed Nov–late Dec) A 25-minute hike or bus 839 brings you to this busy HI hostel.

Hotel Krone (☎ 946 00; Am Rad 5; www.hotel-krone -berchtesgaden.de; s €37-42, d €68-104; 🖳) In a quiet spot, yet close to the centre, this family-run property offers great extras (including wi-fi, a sauna and steam room) at very reasonable prices. The cosiest rooms are the lodge-style ones, which are clad in knotty pine. The best rooms have stunning mountain panoramas.

Getting There & Away

There is hourly service to Berchtesgaden from Munich (€34, 2½ hours), which usually requires a change in Frilassing. There are hourly services to nearby Salzburg in Austria (€9, one hour).

GARMISCH-PARTENKIRCHEN

☎ 08821 / pop 26,500

The Alpine towns of Garmisch and Partenkirchen were merged for the 1936 Winter Olympics. Munich residents' favourite getaway spot, this often-snooty, year-round resort is also a big draw for skiers, snowboarders, hikers and mountaineers.

The **tourist office** (☎ 180 700; www.garmisch-partenkirchen.de; Richard-Strauss-Platz 1, Garmisch; ☼ 8am-6pm Mon-Sat, 10am-noon Sun) sells the **Zugspitzcard** (www.zugspitzcard.com), which includes cable-car rides, admission to museums and fun pools and other activities in Garmisch-Partenkirchen and surrounding villages. The three-day version costs €39/24 per adult/child.

Sights & Activities

The huge **ski stadium** outside town hosted the Olympics. From the pedestrian Am Kurpark, walk up Klammstrasse, cross the tracks and veer left on the first path to reach the stadium and enjoy the spectacular views.

An excellent short hike from Garmisch is to the **Partnachklamm gorge**, via a winding path above a stream and underneath the waterfalls. You take the Graseck cable car and follow the signs.

An excursion to the **Zugspitze** summit, Germany's highest peak (2962m), is a spectacular outing from Garmisch. There are various ways up, including by the **Bayerische Zugspitzbahn rack-railway** (www.zugspitze.de, with live cams), just west of the main train station, summit cable car or Eibsee cable car. You can use any combination of these modes for €38 round-trip. Or you can scale it in two days. For detailed information concerning guided hiking or mountaineering courses, check with **Bergsteigerschule Zugspitze** (☎ 589 99; www.bergsteigerschule-zugspitze.de; Dreitorspitzstrasse 13, Garmisch).

Garmisch is bounded by three separate ski areas – **Zugspitze plateau** (the highest), **Alpspitze/Hausberg** (the largest) and **Eckbauer** (the cheapest). Day ski passes range from €18 for Eckbauer to €36 for Zugspitze. The optimistically named Happy Ski Card is a pass for the entire region (from €95 for three days). A web of cross-country ski trails runs along the main valleys.

Skischule Alpin (☎ 945 676; www.skischulealpin.de; Reintalstrasse 8, Partenkirchen; 1-day group lessons €30, ski gear €18) and **Skischule Garmisch-Partenkirchen** (☎ 4931, 74260; www.skischule-gap.de; Am Hausberg 8, Garmisch; 1-day group lessons €35, ski gear €25) have good reps.

Sleeping & Eating

Jugendherberge (☎ 967 050; www.garmisch.jugendherberge.de; Jochstrasse 10; dm €20.50-26.50; ☐) Amenities at this revamped hostel in a gorgeous creekside spot are as good as at basic chain hotels. It has 205 beds in brightly pigmented rooms with modern furnishings.

Hotel Staudacherhof (☎ 9290; www.staudacherhof.de; Höllentalstrasse 48, Garmisch; r €50-150; ☐ ☒) Rooms at this elegant inn are done up in pastels and come with balconies. Head to the spa for an extended relaxation session or go active with yoga, pilates or aqua-fitness.

Bräustüberl (☎ 2312; Fürstenstrasse 23, Garmisch; mains €6-17) Conversation flows as freely as the beer at this quintessential Bavarian brewpub, complete with enormous enamel coal-burning stove and dirndl-clad waitresses. In summer locals and tourists share tables in the beer garden.

Getting There & Away

From Garmish there is train service to Munich (€18, 80 minutes, hourly) and to Innsbruck, Austria via Mittenwald (€14, 80 minutes, every two hours). RVO bus 9606 (www.rvo-bus.de), from in front of the train station, runs to Füssen, via Oberammergau and Weiskirche (€10, two hours, five to six daily).

OBERAMMERGAU

☎ 08822 / pop 5400

A blend of genuine piety, religious kitsch and monumental commercial greed, Oberammergau sometimes seems to sink under the weight of day trippers. Sadly, the crush of humanity may distract from the town's triple charms: its gorgeous valley setting below the jagged Kofel peak, a 500-year-old woodcarving tradition and a wealth of houses painted with *Lüftlmalerei* (idealised murals painted on outside walls).

About 20km north of Garmisch-Partenkirchen, Oberammergau is known worldwide for hosting the famous **Passion

Play, acted out by much of the townsfolk roughly every 10 years since 1634 to give thanks for being spared from the plague. The next one is in 2010.

Performances are at the 4720-seat **Passionstheater** (☎ 923 10; Passionswiese 1). About one year before the curtain goes up, over 2000 townsfolk are chosen for various roles. In the past this has resulted in a lot of local strife depending on who got plum roles. Tickets go on sale about a year before performances and are popular among the faithful and those who want to be part of one of Europe's most unusual and longest-running spectacles.

Tickets (☎ 923 10; www.passionplay-oberammergau .com) cost from €50 to €165. Performances are held on most days from May 15 to October 3. The play is presented in two acts, the first from 2.30pm to 5pm and the second from 8pm to 10:30pm. Various hotel packages start at €200 per person per night, including tickets to the show.

For local information, contact the **tourist office** (☎ 923 10; www.oberammergau.de; Eugen-Papst-Strasse 9a; ☯ 9am-6pm Mon-Fri, 9am-noon Sat year-round, plus 10am-noon Sun Jun-Oct).

Hourly trains connect Munich with Oberammergau with a change at Murnau (€17, 1¾ hours). RVO bus 9606 (www.rvo -bus.de) links Oberammergau with Füssen and the Wieskirche as well as Garmisch-Partenkirchen five to six times daily.

BADEN-WÜRTTEMBERG

With the exception of cuckoo clocks in the Black Forest, Baden-Württemberg runs a distant second in the cliché race to Bavaria. But that's really all the better, as it leaves more for you to discover on your own.

It's a pretty land of misty hills, shadowy conifers and cute villages that rewards exploration. If you want a big and quaint German village with lots of history, then there's Heidelberg. Baden-Baden is the sybaritic playground for spa-goers, and Freiburg has youthful vibrance in an intriguing package. Finally, Lake Constance is a misty redoubt bordering Switzerland and has all the pleasures a large body of water can offer.

The prosperous modern state of Baden-Württemberg was created in 1951 out of three smaller regions: Baden, Württemberg

and Hohenzollern (thank goodness the names stopped at two).

STUTTGART

☎ 0711 / pop 590,000

Hemmed in by vine-covered hills, comfortable Stuttgart enjoys a quality of life funded by its fabled car companies: Porsche and Mercedes. Nevertheless it is Baden-Württemberg's state capital and the hub of its industries. At the forefront of Germany's economic recovery from the ravages of WWII, Stuttgart started life less auspiciously in 950 as a horse stud farm. About 80% of the city centre was destroyed in the war, but there are a few historical buildings left and – no surprise – car museums. Mostly, however, it is a good hub for exploring other parts of the state.

Information

Königstrasse is the spine of central Stuttgart, with most of the major stores and malls.

Coffee Fellows (Hauptbahnhof; per hr €2; ☯ 8am-11pm) Has computers and free wi-fi across from track 4.

Tourist office (☎ 222 80; www.stuttgart-tourist.de; Königstrasse 1a; ☯ 9am-8pm Mon-Fri, 9am-6pm Sat, 11am-6pm Sun) Sells the three-day Stuttcard discount card for €18.

Wittwer (☎ 250 70; Königstrasse 30) A bookshop with large English-language and travel sections. Excellent outdoor cafe.

Sights

The tower at the daggy main train station sports a revolving three-pointed star of the Mercedes-Benz. Get up close and personal and enjoy great views as part of the **TurmForum** (Hauptbahnhof; admission free; ☯ 10am-9pm Apr-Sep, to 6pm Oct-Mar), an exhibition promoting a radical new train station scheme for Stuttgart.

Stretching southwest from the Neckar River to the city centre is the **Schlossgarten**, an extensive strip of parkland divided into three sections (Unterer, Mittlerer and Oberer), complete with ponds, swans, street entertainers and modern sculptures. At the gardens' southern end they encompass the sprawling baroque **Neues Schloss** (Schlossplatz) and the beautiful Renaissance **Altes Schloss**.

Next to the Altes Schloss is the city's oldest square, Schillerplatz, with its **Friedrich Schiller statue** in honour of the poet, and the 12th-century **Stiftskirche** (Stiftstrasse 12) with its twin 61m-high late-Gothic towers

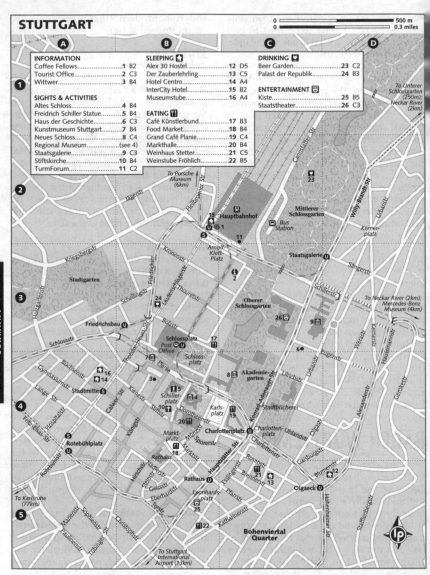

STUTTGART

INFORMATION		
Coffee Fellows	1	B2
Tourist Office	2	C3
Wittwer	3	B4

SIGHTS & ACTIVITIES		
Altes Schloss	4	B4
Friedrich Schiller Statue	5	B4
Haus der Geschichte	6	C3
Kunstmuseum Stuttgart	7	B4
Neues Schloss	8	C4
Regional Museum	(see 4)	
Staatsgalerie	9	C3
Stiftskirche	10	B4
TurmForum	11	C2

SLEEPING		
Alex 30 Hostel	12	D5
Der Zauberlehrling	13	C5
Hotel Centro	14	A4
InterCity Hotel	15	B2
Museumstube	16	A4

EATING		
Café Künstlerbund	17	B3
Food Market	18	B4
Grand Café Planie	19	C4
Markthalle	20	B4
Weinhaus Stetter	21	C5
Weinstube Fröhlich	22	B5

DRINKING		
Beer Garden	23	C2
Palast der Republik	24	B3

ENTERTAINMENT		
Kiste	25	B5
Staatstheater	26	C3

MUSEUMS & GALLERIES

The Altes Schloss houses the **regional museum** (☎ 279 3400; Schillerplatz 6; adult/child €3/2; ⏰ 10am-5pm Tue-Sun) where exhibits include Roman-era discoveries.

Possibly more beautiful than the works within, the **Kunstmuseum Stuttgart** (☎ 216 2188; www.kunstmuseum-stuttgart.de; Kleiner Schlossplatz 1; adult/

child €5/3.50; ⏰ 10am-6pm Tue, Thu, Sat & Sun, to 9pm Wed & Fri) glows like a radioactive sugarcube at night. Highlights include works by Otto Dix, Dieter Roth and Willi Baumeister.

Adjoining the Schlossgarten you'll find the renovated and enlarged **Staatsgalerie** (☎ 212 4050; www.staatsgalerie.de; Konrad-Adenauer-Strasse 30; adult/child €4.50/3; ⏰ 10am-6pm Tue-Sun, to 9pm Thu), which houses an excellent collection from the Middle Ages to the present. It's especially rich in old German masters from the surrounding Swabia region.

Next door there's the **Haus der Geschichte** (House of History; ☎ 212 3950; Urbansplatz 2; admission €3; ◷ 10am-6pm Tue-Sun, to 9pm Thu). This is an eye-catching postmodern museum that covers the past 200 years of the local area with edgy film, photography, documents and multimedia.

MOTOR MUSEUMS
An arms race has broken out between the local auto giants, with both building new and costly monuments to themselves.

The motor car was first developed by Gottlieb Daimler and Carl Benz at the end of the 19th century. The impressive **Mercedes-Benz Museum** (☎ 172 2578; Mercedesstrasse 137; adult/child €8/4; ◷ 9am-6pm Tue-Sun) is in the suburb of Bad-Cannstatt; take S-Bahn 1 to Neckarstadion. Don't mention Chrysler.

For even faster cars, cruise over to the striking **Porsche Museum** (☎ 911 5685; Porscheplatz 1; adult/child €8/4; ◷ 9am-6pm Tue-Sun); take S-Bahn 6 to Neuwirtshaus, north of the city. No word yet on if they'll be adding a VW wing.

Sleeping
Alex 30 Hostel (838 8950; www.alex30-hostel.de; Alexanderstrasse 30; dm €22, r €35-100; ▣) Tidy and orderly in an interesting neighbourhood. Take U-Bahn lines 5, 6 or 7 to Olgaeck.

Museumstube (☎ 296 810; www.museumstube.de; Hospitalstrasse 9; s/d from €32/47) A modest, family-run place with 14 rooms that are clean and functional, like that generic Ford you rented many years back. Confirm that reception will be open when you arrive.

Hotel Centro (☎ 585 3315; www.hotelcentro.de, in German; Büchsenstrasse 24; s/d from €60/95) A central hotel, the 11 rooms of which are practical and compact, sort of like an old VW Beetle. A singles with shared bathroom go for €40.

InterCity Hotel (☎ 222 8233; www.intercityhotel .com; Hauptbahnhof; r €65-180; ▣) Right in the train station, the 112 large rooms have wi-fi; otherwise they're utilitarian. This is the perfect location if you plan a quick getaway or late arrival.

Der Zauberlehrling (☎ 237 7770; www.zauberlehr ling.de; Rosenstrasse 38; r €115-280; ▣) This ultra-chic 'design hotel' has 17 named rooms, each unique and each a design sensation. Amenities abound, including wi-fi, a breakfast garden and more.

Eating
Stuttgart is a great place to sample Swabian specialities such as *Spätzle* (homemade noodles) and *Maultaschen* (a hearty ravioli in broth).

Weinhaus Stetter (☎ 240 163; Rosenstrasse 32; mains €5-10; ◷ dinner Mon-Fri, lunch Sat) The results of all those grapes you see growing in the hills line the wine list here. Locals jam the place for the *Maultaschen*.

Grand Café Planie (☎ 292 553; Charlottenplatz 17; mains €5-15) Fully luxe, like a loaded E-class sedan, this fin de siècle cafe features a print of the 'Grossstadt' triptych by the realist Otto Dix. You may wish the realism didn't extend to the lavish array of tortes in a long case but have one anyway.

Café Künstlerbund (☎ 227 0036; Schlossplatz 2; mains €7-10) Shelter under the arches facing the park or out in the sunshine at this funky cafe that's part of a large gallery. The drinks menu is huge, as are the choices for breakfast. When the weather gets nasty, duck into the groovy upstairs room.

our pick Weinstube Fröhlich (☎ 242 471; Leonhardstrasse 5; mains €8-15) Hard in the midst of Stuttgart's paltry red-light district, this restaurant is traditional but not a period piece. Creative takes on local standards include superb *Maultaschen* and plate-covering schnitzel.

Self-caterers can try the **food market** (Marktplatz; ◷ 7.30am-1pm Tue, Thu & Sat) and the **Markthalle** (market hall; Dorotheenstrasse 4; ◷ 7am-6.30pm Mon-Fri, 7am-4pm Sat), which sells picnic fix-in's and has Italian and Swabian restaurants.

Drinking & Entertainment
Though in German, *Lift Stuttgart* (€1), a comprehensive guide to local entertainment and events, is useful.

Palast der Republik (☎ 226 4887; Friedrichstrasse 27) A legendary and tiny pillbox of a bar that pulls a huge crowd of laid-back, genial drinkers. Statuary and stickers abound.

Kiste (☎ 553 2805; Hauptstätter Strasse 35; ◷ 4pm-2am Mon-Thu, to 3am Fri & Sat) This hole-in-the-wall bar, often jam-packed, is the city's leading jazz venue, with concerts nightly except Sunday, starting at 9.30pm or 10pm.

Staatstheater (☎ 202 090; www.staatstheater.stutt gart.de; Oberer Schlossgarten 6) Home of the famous Stuttgart Ballet, this theatre holds regular symphony, ballet and opera performances.

A **beer garden** (☎ 226 1274; Canstatterstr 18) in the Mittlerer Schlossgarten northeast of the main train station has beautiful views over the city.

GERMANY

Getting There & Around

Stuttgart's international **airport** (SGT; www.stuttgart -airport.com) is south of the city and includes service from Air Berlin (Germany), Germanwings (Germany, London, Eastern Europe and the Mediterranean) and Lufthansa. It's served by S2 and S3 trains (€3.10, 30 minutes from the Hauptbahnhof).

There are frequent train departures for all major German, and many international, cities. ICE trains run to Frankfurt (€56, 1¼ hours, hourly) and Munich (€39 to €52, 2¼ hours, two hourly). Trains run hourly to Nuremberg (€38, 2¼ hours).

One-way fares on Stuttgart's public transport network (www.vvs.de) are €2 in the central zone; a central zone day pass is €5.80.

TÜBINGEN

☎ 07071 / pop 83,200

Tübingen, 40km south of Stuttgart, mixes all the charms of a late-medieval city – such as a hilltop fortress, cobbled alleys and lots of half-timbered houses – with the erudition and mischief of a real university town. Wander winding alleys of half-timbered houses and old stone walls, then take a boat ride down the Neckar River.

The **tourist office** (☎ 913 60; www.tuebingen-info .de; An der Neckarbrücke 1; ☺ 9am-7pm Mon-Fri, 9am-5pm Sat, 11am-4pm Sun May-Oct) is beside the bridge.

On **Marktplatz**, the centre of town, is the 1435 **Rathaus** with its baroque facade and astronomical clock. The nearby late-Gothic **Stiftkirche** (Am Holz-markt; ☺ 9am-5pm Feb-Oct, to 4pm Nov-Jan) houses the tombs of the Württemberg dukes and has excellent medieval stained-glass windows. From the heights of the Renaissance **Schloss Hohentübingen** (Burgsteig 11), now part of the university, there are fine views over the steep, red-tiled rooftops of the Old Town and a museum.

Just a block up the hill from Am Markt, friendly **Hotel Hospiz Tübingen** (☎ 9240; www.hotel -hospiz.de; Neckarhalde 2; r €70-115) is painted a remarkable ochre-pink colour and has 50 attractive medium-sized rooms.

Stroll up a hill for fine local foods sourced from organic farmers at **Wurstküche** (☎ 927 50; Am Lustnauer Tor 8; mains €7-12). That sausage you savoured was never fresher.

No one has said this before: get shlossed at the **Schloss Café** (☎ 965 153), a fine student hang-out with live music and poetry.

There are half-hourly RE trains between Tübingen and Stuttgart (€11.30, one hour).

HEIDELBERG

☎ 06221 / pop 143,000

Heidelberg's baroque Old Town, lively university atmosphere, excellent pubs and evocative half-ruined castle make it hugely popular with visitors, 3.5 million of whom flock here each year. They are following in the footsteps of the 19th-century romantics, most notably the poet Goethe. Britain's William Turner also loved the city, which inspired him to paint some of his greatest landscapes.

Less starry-eyed was Mark Twain (www .mark-twain-in-heidelberg.de), who in 1878 began his European travels with a three-month stay in Heidelberg, recounting his bemused observations in *A Tramp Abroad*.

Orientation

Heidelberg's captivating Old Town starts to reveal itself after a 15-minute walk that will interest few west of the main train station, along the Kurfürsten-Anlage. Hauptstrasse is the long pedestrian spine leading eastwards through the heart of the Altstadt from Bismarckplatz via Marktplatz to Karlstor.

Information

There's internet places in the train station. **Buchhandlung Schmitt & Hahn** (☎ 845 196; Hauptstrasse 8) Classy bookshop with lots of English titles. **Tourist office** (☎ 194 33; www.heidelberg-marketing .de) Hauptbahnhof (Willy-Brandt-Platz 1; ☺ 9am-7pm Mon-Sat year-round, 10am-6pm Sun Apr-Nov); Marktplatz (☺ 8am-5pm Mon-Fri, 10am-5pm Sat) The €10 Heidelberg Card offers discounts and free admission to many sights.

Sights

Heidelberg's imposing **Schloss** (☎ 538 421; adult/child €4/2, tours €4; ☺ 10am-5.30pm) is one of Germany's finest examples of grand Gothic-Renaissance architecture. The building's half-ruined state only enhances its romantic appeal (Twain called it 'the Lear of inanimate nature'). Seen from anywhere in the Altstadt, this striking red-sandstone castle dominates the hillside. The entry fee covers the castle, the **Grosses Fass** (Great Vat), an enormous 18th-century keg capable of holding 221,726L, and the **Deutsches Apothekenmuseum** (German Pharmaceutical Museum; ☎ 258 80; Schlosshof 1).

You can take the **funicular railway** (one-way adult/child €3/2; ☺ 9am-8pm summer, to 5pm other times) to the castle from lower Kornmarkt station, or enjoy an invigorating 15-minute walk up steep, stone-laid lanes. Either way be sure to walk down, especially through the less crowded paths to the east. The funicular continues up to the **Königstuhl**, where there are good views (adult/child €5/4).

Dominating Universitätsplatz are the 18th-century **Alte Universität** and the **Neue Universität**. On the backside (!), find the **Studentenkarzer** (student jail; ☎ 543 554; Augustinergasse 2; adult/child €3/2; ☺ 10am-6pm Tue-Sun Apr-Sep, 10am-4pm Tue-Sat Oct-Mar). From 1778 to 1914 this jail was used for misbehaved students (crimes included drinking, singing and womanising). The **Marstall** is the former arsenal, now a student *Mensa*.

The **Kurpfälzisches Museum** (Palatinate Museum; ☎ 583 402; Hauptstrasse 97; adult/child €3/2; ☺ 10am-6pm Tue-Sun) contains paintings, sculptures and the jawbone of the 600,000-year-old Heidelberg Man.

The Heidelberg region has been a major global supplier of printing equipment, much of it used to create packaging for products. The **Deutsches Verpackungs-Museum** (German Museum of Packaging; ☎ 213 61; Hauptstrasse 22; adult/child €3.50/2.50; ☺ 1-6pm Wed-Fri, 11am-6pm Sat & Sun) celebrates classic packages such as the Nivea jar as well as less successful items such as Titanic-brand cigarettes.

A stroll along the **Philosophenweg**, north of the Neckar River, gives a welcome respite from Heidelberg's tourist hordes.

The tourist office runs English-language **guided tours** (adult/student €7/5; ☺ tours 10.30am Fri & Sat Apr-Oct) that depart from the Löwenbrunnen (Lions Fountain) at Universtätsplatz.

Sleeping

Finding any accommodation during Heidelberg's high season can be difficult. Arrive early in the day or book ahead.

Camping Haide (☎ 802 506; www.camping-heidelberg .de; Schlierbacher Landstrasse 151; camp sites per person €6, tent €3.50-6) These grounds are in a pretty spot on the river. Take bus 35 to Orthopädie.

Sudpfanne (☎ 163 636; www.heidelberger-sudpfanne .de; Hauptstrasse 223; dm/s/d €20/30/60; 🖳) Right in the centre of things, the mood is set by the wine-barrel entrance (it's also a cafe). Bathrooms are shared and it's all rather bare-bones (there is wi-fi), but you can't beat the price.

Pension Jeske (☎ 237 33; www.pension-jeske-hei delberg.de; Mittelbadgasse 2; r €25-65) Large, colour-ful and decorated with flair, the rooms in this 250-year-old house are the antithesis of cookie-cutter, chain-hotel blandness. The cheapest singles share bathrooms.

Hotel Am Kornmarkt (☎ 905 830; www.hotelamkorn markt.de; Kornmarkt 7; r €40-110) Discreet and under-stated, this Altstadt favourite has 20 pleasant, well-kept rooms. The pricier rooms have great views of the Kornmarkt, while cheaper ones share spotless hall showers. Hardwood floors add to the modern appeal.

Hotel Goldener Hecht (☎ 536 80; www.hotel-gold ener-hecht.de; Steingasse 2; r €62-100; 🖳) Goethe al-most slept here: the hotel would have kept the famous author had the clerk on duty not been so uppity. Ever since, guests at this family-run place have received a warm welcome. Some of the 13 sparkling rooms (with wi-fi), each unique, have views of the Neckar River.

Hotel Zum Pfalzgrafen (☎ 204 89; www.hotel -zum-pfalzgrafen.de; Kettengasse 21; r €70-110) Polished pine floors are a nice touch at this family-run place, which has 24 well-appointed rooms. The breakfast buffet is included.

Eating

Try heading down small streets away from Marktplatz to increase your ratio of locals.

Grey Stones (☎ 588 0280; Steingasse 16a; meals €4-10) A new age cafe with comfy tables out front for hanging out over long, shared breakfasts. Inside there's a techno beat that lasts well into the night.

Brauhaus Vetter (☎ 165 850; Steingasse 9; mains €5-12) A popular brewery that serves up lots of hearty fare to absorb the suds. The cop-per kettles gleam. Groups of six or more can order the Brewer's feast, a sausage, pretzels, radishes, meat and cheese smorgasbord.

Kulturbrauerei Heidelberg (☎ 502 980; Leyergasse 6; mains €8-15) The classic-looking Kulturbrauerei has an excellent beer garden. It's a big, bright and airy place and is always busy.

Zur Herrenmühle (☎ 602 909; Hauptstrasse 239; mains €9-23; ☺ 6-11pm Mon-Sat) Serves traditional, classic south-German food and international cuisine under the ancient wood beams of a 17th-century mill. Rustically elegant, with geraniums hanging over the windows.

Drinking & Entertainment

'German university life is a very free life; it seems to have no restraints.' So observed Mark Twain, and two centuries later little has changed; you won't have to go far to

GERMANY

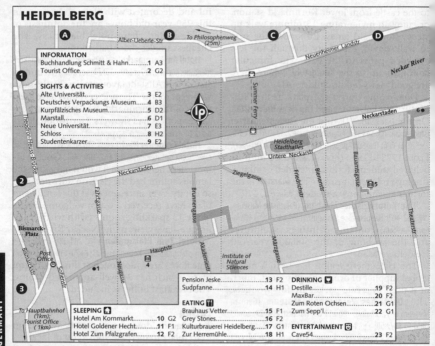

HEIDELBERG

INFORMATION
Buchhandlung Schmitt & Hahn..........1 A3
Tourist Office..................................2 G2

SIGHTS & ACTIVITIES
Alte Universität...............................3 E2
Deutsches Verpackungs Museum......4 B3
Kurpfälzisches Museum....................5 D2
Marstall...6 D1
Neue Universität.............................7 E3
Schloss..8 H2
Studentenkarzer..............................9 E2

SLEEPING
Hotel Am Kornmarkt.....................10 G2
Hotel Goldener Hecht....................11 F1
Hotel Zum Pfalzgrafen...................12 F2

Pension Jeske................................13 F2
Sudpfanne....................................14 H1

EATING
Brauhaus Vetter............................15 F1
Grey Stones..................................16 F2
Kulturbrauerei Heidelberg..............17 G1
Zur Herremühle.............................18 H1

DRINKING
Destille...19 F2
MaxBar...20 F2
Zum Roten Ochsen........................21 G1
Zum Sepp'l...................................22 G1

ENTERTAINMENT
Cave54...23 F2

find a happening backstreet bar. Lots of the action centres on Unterestrasse.

MaxBar (244 19; Marktplatz 5t) A French-style cafe with classic views of the Marktplatz. Perfect for a beer or a pastis, it's especially popular on weekend nights.

Destille (228 08; Untere Strasse 16) Known for the tree trunk behind the bar, this mellow and hugely popular pub pours stiff drinks that inspire chess openings among the players heretofore never seen.

Cave54 (278 40; www.cave54.de; Krämerpetrolse 2; Thu-Sun) For live jazz and blues, head to this stone cellar that oozes character. Some nights there's a DJ.

Two ancient pubs, **Zum Roten Oschen** (209 77; Hauptstrasse 213) and **Zum Sepp'l** (230 85; Hauptstrasse 217), are now filled with tourists reliving the uni days they never had.

Getting There & Around

There are IC trains to/from Frankfurt (€19, one hour, hourly) and Stuttgart (€24, 40 minutes, hourly) The frequent service to Mannheim (€5, 15 minutes) has connections to cities throughout Germany.

Bismarckplatz is the main public transport hub. One-way tickets for the excellent bus and tram system are €2.10. Greatly shorten the trek from the train station to the Altstadt with bus 32 or 33 to the Bergbahn stop.

BADEN-BADEN

07221 / pop 54,900

What kind of person wants to bathe naked with a bunch of strangers? That's the question at the heart of the matter in Baden-Baden, the storied and ritzy spa town. The answer, of course, should be anyone who wants to enjoy a truly self-indulgent experience.

And let's see, shall we call them, well, prudes, can still get a bit of the pleasure while staying suited and segregated. The natural hot springs have attracted visitors since Roman times, but this small city only really became fashionable in the 19th century, when it became a destination of royalty. It is stately, closely cropped and salubrious. Take the 69°C plunge.

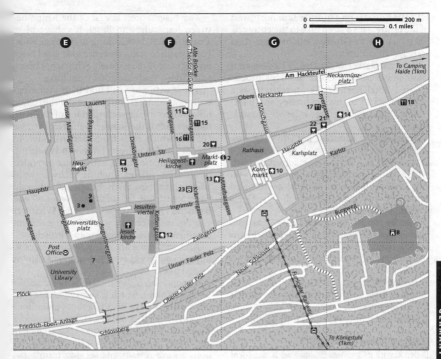

Orientation & Information

The train station is 7km northwest of town. Leopoldplatz and Sophienstrasse are the hubs. North of here are the baths, the Stiftskirche and the Neues Schloss. Across the little river to the west you will find the *Trinkhalle* (pump room) and the tourist office, and past Goetheplatz both the *Kurhaus* (casino) and *Spielhalle* (games hall). Unless noted, everything listed below is within the centre.

Internet cafe (Lange Strasse 54; per hr €2; 10am-10pm) Internet access at the northern edge of the pedestrianised centre.

Tourist office (275 200; www.baden-baden.com; Kaiserallee 3; 10am-5pm Mon-Sat, 2-5pm Sun) In the *Trinkhalle*. Drink from the source of it all here for €0.20 (it's warm and salty).

Sights & Activities

The 19th-century **Friedrichsbad** (275 920; www.roemisch-irisches-bad.de; Römerplatz 1; bathing program €21-29; 9am-10pm) is the reason for your journey. It's decadently Roman in style and provides a muscle-melting 16-step bathing program. No clothing is allowed inside, and several bathing sections are mixed on most days. The more modern **Caracalla-Therme** (275 940; Römerplatz 11; per 2hr €13; 8am-10pm) is a vast, modern complex of outdoor and indoor pools, hot- and cold-water grottoes. You must wear a bathing suit and bring your own towel.

The 2000-year-old **Römische Badruinen** (Roman Bath Ruins; 275 934; Römerplatz 1; adult/child €2/1; 11am-5pm) are worth a quick look, but for a real taste of Baden-Baden head to the **Kurhaus**, built in the 1820s, which houses the opulent **casino** (302 40; Kaiserallee 1; admission €3, guided tours adult/child €4/2; tours 9.30am-noon, gambling after 2pm), which inspired Dostoyevsky to write *The Gambler*. Wear what you want for tours; for gambling men wear a coat and tie (rentals €11).

Sleeping & Eating

Most restaurants huddle in the pedestrianised stretch around Leopoldsplatz. Nightlife is low-key.

Jugendherberge (522 23; www.jugendherberge-baden-baden.de; Hardbergstrasse 34; dm 1st/subsequent night €18.70/15.40) This modern three-storey

HI/DJH hostel is on a hillside 3km northwest of the centre – it's a steep hike to the entrance. Take bus 201 to Grosse Dollenstrasse then walk for 10 minutes.

Hotel am Markt (☎ 270 40; www.hotel-am-markt -baden.de; Marktplatz 18; r €30-80; 💻) This peach-fronted hotel next to the Stiftskirche is a real find. Its 23 rooms are homey and bath-rooms squeaky clean. Free internet access is a bonus.

Steigenberger Badischer Hof (☎ 93 40; www .badischer-hof.steigenberger.com; Lange Strasse 47; r €125-260; 💻 🍴) Perfect for splashing out, with swanky quarters. In some rooms you can choose between mineral water and tap water – in your bathtub, that is. Deals available off-season.

Jensens (☎ 397 900; Sophienstrasse 45; light meals €5-8) Opposite Caracalla-Therme, this bistro with a patio has a hip feel with its pepper red walls, wood floors and jazzy tunes. Wi-fi is available.

Aumatt (☎ 337 55; Aumattstrasse 36a; mains €7.50-15) Families flock to this riverside beer garden for its playground, sandpit and kids' meals. Fondue and schnitzel staples top the menu.

Getting There & Around

Baden Airpark (FKB; www.badenairpark.de) is the local airport. It has daily Ryanair service (Dublin, London and Rome) but like many tiny airports served by the budget carrier, getting to/from the airport can be a challenge. Consult the airport website for details on the sketchy service.

Baden-Baden is on the busy Mannheim–Basel train line. Frequent local trains serve Karlsruhe (€8, 15 minutes) and Offenburg (€9, 20 minutes), from where you can make connections to much of Germany.

Buses 201, 205 and 216 run frequently to/from Leopoldsplatz (€2).

BLACK FOREST

The Black Forest (Schwarzwald) gets its name from the dark canopy of evergreens, which evoke mystery and allure in many. Although some parts heave with visitors, a 20-minute walk from even the most crowded spots will put you in quiet countryside interspersed with enormous traditional farmhouses and patrolled by amiable dairy cows. It's not nature wild and remote, but bucolic and picturesque.

The Black Forest is east of the Rhine between Karlsruhe and Basel. It's shaped like a bean, about 160km long and 50km wide. From north to south there are four good bases for your visit: Freudenstadt, Schiltach, Triberg and Titisee. Each has good train links.

Those with a car will find their visit especially rewarding, as you can wander the rolling hills and deep valleys at will. One of the main tourist roads is the Schwarzwald-Hochstrasse (B500), which runs from Baden-Baden to Freudenstadt and from Triberg to Waldshut. Other thematic roads with maps provided by tourist offices include Schwarzwald Bäderstrasse (spa town route), Schwarzwald Panoramastrasse (panoramic view route) and Badische Weinstrasse (wine route). Whatever you do, make certain you have an excellent commercial regional road map with you.

And, yes, there are many, many places to buy cuckoo clocks (you pay at least €150 for a good one).

Regional specialities include *Schwarz wälder Schinken* (ham), which is smoked and served in a variety of ways. Rivalling those ubiquitous clocks in fame (but not price), *Schwarzwälder Kirschtorte* (Black Forest cake) is a chocolate and cherry concoction. Most hotels and guest houses have restaurants serving traditional hearty (but expensive) German fare. Wash it all down with Rothaus, the crisp local pilsener.

FREUDENSTADT

☎ 07441 / pop 23,000

Freudenstadt is a good base for exploring the northern Black Forest and hikes into the surrounding countryside. It's most notable feature is a vast **marketplace** that is the largest in the country. The **tourist office** (☎ 8640; www .freudenstadt.de; Marktplatz 64; 🕑 9am-6pm Mon-Fri, 10am-2pm Sat & Sun May-Oct, 10am-5pm Mon-Fri, 10am-1pm Sat, 11am-1pm Sun Nov-Apr) has internet access and is good for local hiking ideas.

The **DJH Hostel** (☎ 7720; www.jugendherberge. de; Eugen-Nägele-Strasse 69; dm €19) has 138 beds in a central and classic 1960s building. **Hotel Schwanen** (☎ 915 50; www.schwanen-freudenstadt .de in German; Forststrasse 2; r €40-90; 💻) has spruced up rooms with wi-fi. The Markt has many excellent cafes, some with wi-fi.

From Freudenstadt, hourly trains run south to Schiltach (€7, 30 minutes) and north to the important transfer point of Karlsruhe (€16, 1½ hours). Stuttgart has hourly trains (€16, 1½ hours).

BLACK FOREST (SCHWARZWALD)

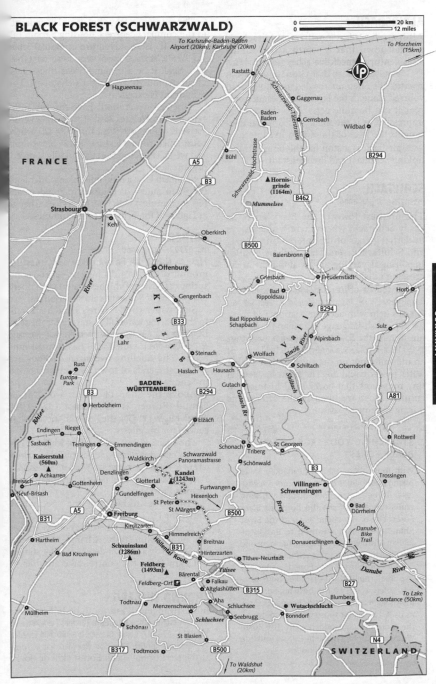

ALPIRSBACH

Alpirsbach, 10km north of Schiltach, is a small town that is worth a trip for its 12th-century **Benedictine abbey** (adult/child €3/2; ☺ 10am-4.30pm Mon-Sat, 11am-4.30pm Sun, shorter hours in winter). It's often uncrowded and if you find yourself alone in the large Romanesque complex it can be quite eerie. The cloisters are impressive, as is the small museum that documents the lives of those who lived here.

Alpirsbach is a stop for the hourly trains linking Schiltach and Freudenstadt.

SCHILTACH

☎ 07836 / pop 4000

The prettiest town in the Black Forest is easily Schiltach, where there is the always underlying roar of the intersecting Kinzig and Schiltach Rivers. Half-timbered buildings lean at varying angles along the crisscrossing hillside lanes.

The **tourist office** (☎ 5850; www.schiltach.de; Hauptstrasse 5; ☺ 10am-5pm Mon-Fri, to 2pm Sat Apr-Oct) can help with accommodation and has a lot of English-language information. Be sure not to miss the **Schüttesäge-museum** (Hauptstrasse 1; ☺ 11am-5pm Tue-Sun Apr-Oct), which is part of an old mill built on the river. It shows what water power could do. The **Markt** has several tiny museums that cover local history and culture. Most are open in the afternoons during the tourist season.

STRETCHING YOUR LEGS IN THE BLACK FOREST

With more than 7000km of marked trails, hiking possibilities during summer are endless. Three classic long-distance **hiking trails** run south from the northern Black Forest city of Pforzheim as far as the Swiss Rhine: the 280km Westweg to Basel; the 230km Mittelweg to Waldhut-Tiengen; and the 240km Ostweg to Schaffhausen.

The southern Black Forest, especially the area around the 1493m Feldberg summit, offers some of the best hiking; small towns such as Todtmoos or Bonndorf serve as useful bases for those wanting to get off the more heavily trodden trails. The 10km Wutachschlucht (Wutach Gorge) outside Bonndorf is justifiably famous.

There are numerous hotels and restaurant in the compact centre. Choosing a room (all with wi-fi) is an adventure at **Gasthof Sonne** (☎ 957 570; Marktplatz 3; www.sonneschiltach.de; r €43-80 🖳). Shall it be a romantic rose-tinged nest or an armour-filled knight's chamber? The restaurant is excellent.

Nineteen generations have run the 16th-century inn **Weysses Rössle** (☎ 387; www.weysses-roessle.de; Schenkenzeller Strasse 42; r €50-70; 🖳), where countrified rooms feature snazzy bathrooms and wi-fi. The restaurant uses locally sourced, organic fare.

Schiltach is on a train line linking Offenburg (€8, 45 minutes) via Hausach to Freudenstadt (€5, 30 minutes) with hourly services. Change at Hausach for Triberg (€7, 50 minutes).

TRIBERG

☎ 07722 / pop 5400

Heir to the Black Forest cake recipe, nesting ground of the world's biggest cuckoos and spring of Germany's highest waterfall – Triberg is a torrent of Schwarzwald superlatives.

Start with a stroll. There's a one-hour walk to the roaring **waterfall**; it starts near the **tourist office** (☎ 866 490; www.triberg.de; Wallfahrtstrasse 4; ☺ 10am-5pm), which also has a small museum. The duelling oversized cuckoos are at opposite ends of town (we prefer the one in Schonach).

Above the shop of master woodcarver Gerald Burger is **Kukucksnest** (☎ 869 487; Wallfahrtstrasse 15; r €50), the beautiful nest he has carved for his guests.

The Black Forest cake at **Café Schäfer** (☎ 44 65; www.cafe-schaefer-triberg.de; Hauptstrasse 33; coffee & cake €4-6; ☺ 9am-6pm Mon, Tue, Wed & Fri, 8am-6pm Sat, 11am-6pm Sun) is the real deal; it has the original recipe to prove it.

Triberg is midway on the spectacular Karlsruhe (€22, 1½ hours) to Konstanz (€22, 1½ hours) train line. There are hourly services and good connections. Change at Hausach for Schiltach and Freudenstadt. The station is 1.7km from the centre; take any bus to the Markt.

AROUND TRIBERG

In Furtwangen, 17km south of Triberg, visit the **Deutsches Uhrenmuseum** (German Clock Museum; ☎ 07723-920 117; Gerwigstrasse 11; adult/child €5/2.50; ☺ 9am-6pm Apr-Oct, 10am-5pm Nov-Mar) for a look at the traditional Black Forest skill of clock-

---

WORTH THE TRIP: HEAVEN & HOLE

Just south of Furtwangen, look for a tiny road off to the west evocatively called the **Hexenloch** (Witch's Hole). This narrow road penetrates deep into a narrow valley of rushing white water and tall trees. It alone is worth the cost of a car hire – which is the only way to enjoy the hole. Even on warm days it's cold as a witch's … you know what, down here. The road follows the bends in the river and you'll see shaded banks of snow months after it has melted elsewhere. Look for small roadhouses with little spinning water wheels.

West of the south end of the Hexenloch road, **St Peter** is a tiny town that offers redemption with a big church. Two onion-domed towers mark the town's namesake old abbey. It's an 18th-century vision in gold, glitter and gilt that would do any Las Vegas designer proud. You can ponder your own place in heaven at the cute little cafes out front.

---

making. A fun demo shows what puts the 'cuc' and the 'koo' in the namesake clock. Buses from Triberg stop here.

TITISEE-NEUSTADT
☎ 07651 / pop 12,000
The iconic glacial lake here draws no shortage of visitors to the busy village of Titisee-Neustadt. Walking around Titisee or paddle-boating across it are major activities. If you have wheels, ride or drive into the surrounding rolling meadows to see some of the truly enormous traditional house-barn combos.

The **tourist office** (☎ 980 40; www.titisee-neustadt .de; Strandbadstrasse 4; 9am-6pm Mon-Fri, 10am-1pm Sat & Sun May-Oct, 9am-noon & 1.30-5pm Mon-Fri Nov-Apr) can help you arrange a farm stay.

There are four campgrounds around the lake. **Jugendherberge Veltishof am Titisee** (☎ 07652-?38; www.jugendherberge-titisee-veltishof.de; Bruderhalde 27; dm from €20) is in a huge farmhouse and is reached by bus 7300 from Titisee or by foot (30 minutes).

Bergseeblick (☎ 8257; www.bergseeblick-titisee.de; Erlenweg 3; s €24-30, d 48-58), near the church, offers quiet rooms and gnomes themed for Snow White and her Seven Dwarves.

Titisee is linked to Freiburg by frequent train services (€10, 40 minutes). To reach Triberg to the north, there are scenic hourly connections via Neustadt and Donaueschigen (€16, two hours).

AROUND TITISEE
The Black Forest **ski season** runs from late December to March. While there is good downhill skiing, the area is more suited to cross-country skiing. The centre for winter sports is around Titisee, with uncrowded downhill ski runs at **Feldberg** (www

.liftverbund-feldberg.de; day pass adult/child €25/13, rental equipment available) and numerous graded cross-country trails.

In summer you can use the lifts to reach the summit of the sallow-sloped Feldberg (1493m) for a wondrous panorama that stretches to the Alps.

Feldberg is 15km south of Titisee. It can be reached by bus 7300 from Titisee (€4, 12 minutes, hourly) or in season by free ski shuttles.

FREIBURG
☎ 0761 / pop 213,500
Nestled between hills and vineyards, Freiburg im Breisgau has a medieval Altstadt made timeless by a thriving university community. There's a sense of fun here exemplified by the *bächle* (tiny medieval canals) running down the middle of streets. Perhaps being Germany's sunniest city contributes to the mood.

Founded in 1120 and ruled for centuries by the Austrian Habsburgs, Freiburg has retained many traditional features, although major reconstruction was necessary following WWII. The monumental 13th-century cathedral is the city's key landmark but the real attractions are the vibrant cafes, bars and street life, plus the local wines. The best times for tasting are July for the four days of *Weinfest* (Wine Festival), or August for the nine days of *Weinkost* (wine tasting).

Orientation
The city centre is a convenient 10-minute walk from the train station. Walk east along Eisenbahnstrasse to the tourist office, then continue through the bustling pedestrian zone to Münsterplatz, dominated by the red-stone cathedral.

GERMANY

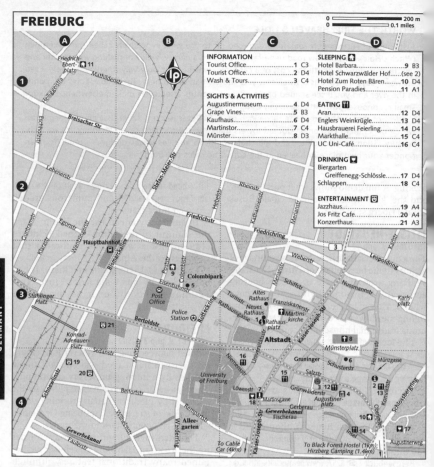

FREIBURG

INFORMATION
Tourist Office.................1 C3
Tourist Office.................2 D4
Wash & Tours.................3 C4

SIGHTS & ACTIVITIES
Augustinermuseum.................4 D4
Grape Vines.................5 B3
Kaufhaus.................6 D4
Martinstor.................7 C4
Münster.................8 D3

SLEEPING
Hotel Barbara.................9 B3
Hotel Schwarzwälder Hof.....(see 2)
Hotel Zum Roten Bären.................10 D4
Pension Paradies.................11 A1

EATING
Aran.................12 D4
Englers Weinkrügle.................13 D4
Hausbrauerei Feierling.................14 D4
Markthalle.................15 C4
UC Uni-Café.................16 C4

DRINKING
Biergarten
 Greiffenegg-Schlössle.................17 D4
Schlappen.................18 C4

ENTERTAINMENT
Jazzhaus.................19 A4
Jos Fritz Cafe.................20 A3
Konzerthaus.................21 A3

GERMANY

Information
Tourist office (☎ 388 1880; www.freiburg.de; Rathaus-platz 2-4; ⏱ 8am-8pm Mon-Fri, 9.30am-5pm Sat, 10am-noon Sun Jun-Sep, 8am-6pm Mon-Fri, 9.30am-2.30pm Sat, 10am-noon Sun Oct-May) Well stocked with hiking and cycling maps to the region.

Wash & Tours (☎ 288 866; Salzstrasse 22; wash €5, internet per hr €2.50; ⏱ 9am-7pm) There's a drop-off laundry downstairs and an internet cafe upstairs.

Sights
The major sight in Freiburg is the 700-year-old **Münster** (Cathedral; Münsterplatz; tower adult/child €1.50/1; ⏱ 9.30am-5pm Mon-Sat, 1-5pm Sun), a classic example of both high- and late-Gothic architecture that looms over Münsterplatz, Freiburg's market square. Ascend the west

tower to the stunning pierced spire for great views of Freiburg and, on a clear day, the Kaiserstuhl wine region and the Vosages Mountains to the west. South of the Münster stands the solid red **Kaufhaus**, the 16th-century merchants' hall.

The bustling **university quarter** is northwest of the **Martinstor** (one of the old city gates). On the walk in from the station, note the field of **grape vines** from around the world.

Freiburg's main museum, the **Augustinermuseum** (☎ 201 2531; Salzstrasse 32; ⏱ 10am-5pm Tue-Sun) has a fine collection of medieval art, including some lavish stained-glass windows.

The popular trip by **cable car** (one way/return adult €8/12, child €5/7; ⏱ 9am-5pm Jan-Jun, to 6pm Julep, 9.30am-5pm Oct-Dec) to the **Schauinsland peak** (1284m) is a quick way to reach the Black Forest highlands. Numerous easy and well-marked trails make the Schauinsland area ideal for day walks. From Freiburg take tram 4 south to Günterstal and then bus 21 to Talstation.

Sleeping

Hirzberg Camping (☎ 350 54; www.freiburg-camping.de; Kartäuserstrasse 99; camp sites per adult/tent €6/3.50; 🖳) Pitch a tent at this serene woodland camp site 1.5km east of Schwabentor.

Black Forest Hostel (☎ 881 7870; www.blackforest-hostel.de; Kartäuserstrasse 33; dm €13-21, s/d €30/50; 🖳) Freiburg's funkiest budget digs are five minutes' stroll from the centre. Overlooking vineyards, this former factory has been lovingly revamped as a industrial-themed hostel. Bike hire costs €5 per day.

Pension Paradies (☎ 273 700; www.paradies-freiburg.de; Friedrich-Ebert-Platz; r €36-75; 🖳) This treasure over the train tracks (take tram 4) has simple but stylish rooms. There is a vast cafe with vegetarian specials and a large terrace.

Hotel Schwarzwälder Hof (☎ 380 30; www.schwarzwaelder-hof.eu; Herrenstrasse 43; r €45-120; 🖳) This bijou hotel has an unrivalled style-for-euro ratio. A wrought-iron staircase sweeps up to snazzy rooms, some with postcard views of the Altstadt. Bargain singles share bathrooms.

Hotel Barbara (☎ 296 250; www.hotel-barbara.de; Poststrasse 4; s €72-120; 🖳) Tucked down a quiet street, this town house oozes art-nouveau charm with its high ceilings and twisting staircase. The pastel-hued rooms offer old-style comfort and wi-fi charm.

Hotel zum Roten Bären (☎ 387 870; www.roter-baeren.de; Oberlinden 12; s €100-170; 🖳) Billed as Germany's oldest guest house, this blush-wine-pink hotel near Schwabentor dates to 1120. Though the vaulted cellar is medieval, rooms are modern with sleek wood furnishings and wi-fi.

Eating & Drinking

There's a good selection of wurst and other quick eats from stalls set up in the market square during lunchtime.

Aran (☎ 790 9664; Salzstrasse 28; meals €2-5) This organic cafe has a terrace facing Augustinerplatz that's perfect for chilling. Locals pile in for fresh juices, thick soups and creative sandwiches.

UC Uni-Café (☎ 383 355; Niemensstrasse 7; meals €3-7) A popular hang-out that serves snacks on its see-and-be-seen outdoor terrace.

Markthalle (Grünwälderstrasse 2; meals €3-8; 🕑 7am-7pm) A dozen stands selling ethnic food cluster around a bar selling local wine. A fun and fine deal.

Biergarten Greiffenegg-Schlössle (☎ 327 28; Schlossbergring 3; mains €5) Perched above Freiburg, this terrace beer garden is great for watching the sun set over the city's red rooftops. The restaurant inside the villa is posh.

Hausbrauerei Feierling (☎ 243 480; Gerberau 46; mains €6-12) Starring one of Freiburg's best beer gardens, this brewpub serves great vegetarian options and humungous schnitzels with *Brägele* (chipped potatoes). If you drink one too many, take care not to fall in the stream or you may become dinner for the open-jawed *Krokodil*.

Englers Weinkrügle (☎ 383 115; Konviktstrasse 12; mains €8-15; 🕑 Tue-Sun) A warm, woody *Weinstube* with wisteria growing out front and regional flavours on the menu. The trout in various guises is delicious.

ourpick Schlappen (☎ 334 94; Löwenstrasse 2; 🕑 11am-1am Mon-Thu, to 3am Fri & Sat, 3pm-1am Sun) With its jazz-themed back room and poster-plastered walls, this student watering hole is a perennial fave. Try a *Flammkuche* (tasty, crispy Alsatian pizza), then forget about it with absinthe.

Entertainment

Konzerthaus (☎ 388 8552; Konrad-Adenauer-Platz 1) This concert hall has an impressive range of orchestral performances.

Jazzhaus (☎ 349 73; www.jazzhaus.de; Schnewlinstrasse 1) Under the brick arches of a wine cellar, this venue hosts first-rate jazz, rock and hip-hop concerts (€10 to €30) at 8pm at least three nights a week. It morphs into a club on weekends.

Jos Fritz Cafe (☎ 300 19; www.josfritzcafe.de; Wilhelmstrasse 15) Down a little alley past the recycling bins, this cafe hosts concerts of alternative bands and events such as political discussions (stir things up with 'Is Merkel too liberal?').

Getting There & Around

Freiburg is on the busy Mannheim to Basel, Switzerland (€22, 45 minutes, hourly) train line. ICE services include Frankfurt (€61, two hours, hourly). Freiburg is linked to Titisee by frequent trains (€10, 40 minutes).

Cut across the Rhine to France's cute Colmar. SBG bus 1076 (www.suedbadenbus .de) makes the run two to three times daily (€11, 1¼ hours).

Single rides on the efficient local bus and tram system cost €2. A 24-hour pass costs €5. Trams depart from the bridge over the train tracks.

LAKE CONSTANCE

Lake Constance (Bodensee) is an oasis in landlocked southern Germany. Even if you never make contact with the water, this giant bulge in the sinewy course of the Rhine can offer a splash of refreshment. There are many historic towns around its periphery, which can be explored by boat or bicycle and on foot. While sun is nice, the lake is best on one of the many misty days when it is shrouded in mystery.

Constance's southern side belongs to Switzerland and Austria, where the snow-capped Alps provide a perfect backdrop when viewed from the northern shore. The German side of Lake Constance features three often-crowded tourist centres in Constance, Meersburg and the island of Lindau. It's essentially a summer area, when it abounds with aquatic joy.

Getting There & Around

Trains link Lindau and Constance, and buses fill in the gaps to places like Meersburg. By car, the B31 hugs the northern shore of Lake Constance, but it can get rather busy. The Constance–Meersburg car ferry run by BSB ferries (opposite) provides a vital link for those who don't want to circumnavigate the entire lake.

The most enjoyable, albeit slowest, way to get around is on the **Bodensee-Schiffsbetriebe boats** (BSB; www.bsb-online.com), which, from Easter to late October, call several times a day at the larger towns along the lake; there are discounts for rail pass–holders.

The **Erlebniskarte** (3 days/1 week €69/89) is a handy pass that allows free boat travel and free access to a host of activities around the lake. Numerous other discount cards are available. Ask at tourist information offices.

WHEELING AROUND LAKE CONSTANCE

A 270km international bike track circumnavigates Lake Constance through Germany, Austria and Switzerland, tracing the often-steep shoreline beside vineyards and pebble beaches. The route is well signposted, but you may want one of the many widely sold cycling maps. The tourist booklet *Rad Urlaub am Bodensee* lists routes, hire places and a wealth of other information about the region.

In Constance, **Kultur-Rädle** (☎ 07531-273 10; www.kultur-raedle.de; Bahnhofplatz 29; ⏰ 9am-12.30pm & 2.30-6pm Mon-Fri, 10am-4pm Sat year-round, 10am-12.30pm Sun Apr-Oct) rents out bikes (€10 per day) and organises cycling tours.

CONSTANCE

☎ 07531 / pop 81,000

Constance (Konstanz) sits right on the Swiss border. It's a tidy lake town and is a good place for gazing across the misty waters. Its main attraction is fittingly named Mainau Island.

It achieved historical significance in 1414, when the Council of Constance convened to try to heal huge rifts in the Catholic Church. The consequent burning at the stake of the religious reformer Jan Hus as a heretic, and the scattering of his ashes over the lake, did nothing to block the Reformation.

The **tourist office** (☎ 133 030; www.konstanz.de/tourismus; Bahnhofplatz 13; ⏰ 9am-6.30pm Mon-Fri, to 4pm Sat, 10am-1pm Sun Apr-Oct, 9.30am-12.30pm & 2-6pm Mon-Fri Nov-Mar) is 150m to the right from the train station exit. Across the street, **TelCenter** (☎ 284 266; Bahnhofplatz 6; per 30min €1; ⏰ 10am-10pm) has internet access.

Sights & Activities

The city's most visible feature is the Gothic spire of the cathedral, added in 1856 to a church that was started in 1052, which has excellent views over the Old Town. Visit the **Niederburg quarter** or relax in the parklands of the **Stadtgarten**. Head across to **Mainau Island** (☎ 3030; www.mainau.de; adult/child €14/8; ⏰ 7am-8pm mid-Mar–Nov, 9am-6pm Nov–mid-Mar), with its baroque castle set in vast and gorgeous gardens that include a butterfly house. Take bus 4 (€2, 20 minutes) or a BSB ferry from the harbour behind the station (€6, one hour, hourly). Five rocky shore areas optimistically called **beaches** are open from May to September, including the Strandbad Horn (the best and most crowded), with bush-enclosed nude bathing. Take bus 5 or walk for 20 minutes north around the shore.

Sleeping & Eating

Campingplatz Bruderhofer (☎ 31 388; www.camping platz-konstanz.de; Fohrenbühlweg 45; camp sites per adult/ car/tent €4/3/4) This modern camping ground, in Constance's northeastern suburb of Staad, is 3km northeast of the Altstadt and 800m south of the Meersburg car-ferry dock.

Jugendherberge Konstanz (☎ 322 60; www.ju gendherberge-konstanz.de; Zur Allmannshöhe 18; dm €25) This 178-bed hostel, in a white cylindrical one-time water tower, is in Allmannsdorf, 4km northeast of the Altstadt and 1.2km northwest of the Meersburg car-ferry dock. Take bus 4 (to Jugendherberge)

Hotel Barbarossa (☎ 128 990; www.barbarossa-hotel .com; Obermarkt 8-12; r €50-120; 🖳) Charming old place, carefully restored (although the floors still creak). White walls set off beautiful wooden antiques. The art deco restaurant (mains €8 to €20) has fine local specialities.

Hotel Sonnenhof (☎ 222 57; www.hotel-sonnenhof -konstanz.de; Otto-Raggenbass-Strasse 3; r €55-90) This simple, comfortable, family-run guest house is on a quiet residential street midway between Bodanstrasse and the Swiss border.

Radieschen (☎ 228 87; Hohenhausgasse 1; mains €6-10) The name means radish and you'll find the namesakes on the heaping salads. The menu mixes local seafood with excellent Turkish fare that goes beyond that served up to drunks from stalls. Excellent and spicy grilled meats are a treat.

Brauhaus Johann Albrecht (☎ 250 45; Konradigasse 2; mains €8-16) A rambling beer hall with a rustic menu featuring daily specials. The food here offers good value and the beer, brewed on the premises in copper vats, goes down fine.

Getting There & Away

Constance has trains to Offenburg via Triberg in the Black Forest (€29, 2¼ hours, hourly) and connections via Singen to Stuttgart (€38, 2¼ hours, every two hours). There are good connections into Switzerland (which is 200m south!) including Zürich (€17, 1¼ hours, hourly).

BSB Ferries (www.bsb-online.com) on various schedules serves numerous destinations including Meersburg (€5, 30 minutes) and Lindau (€14, three to four hours).

MEERSBURG

☎ 07532 / pop 5300

Constance is the big city compared to Meersburg across the lake. The winding cobblestone streets, vine-patterned hills and a sunny lakeside promenade make it a good stop if travelling by ferry or car.

The helpful **tourist office** (☎ 440 400; www.meers burg.de; Kirchstrasse 4; 🕑 9am-6pm Mon-Fri, 10am-2pm Sat, reduced hours in winter) is in the Altstadt and can help find accommodation if you decide to stay.

Steigstrasse is lined with delightful half-timbered houses, each boasting a gift shop. The modest 11th-century **Altes Schloss** (☎ 800 00; adult/child €7/5; 🕑 9am-6.30pm) is the oldest structurally intact castle in Germany.

The useful Constance to Meersburg **car ferry** (☎ 07531-803 666; www.bsb-online.com; person/ car €2.50/8) runs every 15 minutes year-round from the northeastern Constance suburb of Staad and takes half an hour. BSB ferries stop on their shore-hugging voyages between Constance (€5, 30 minutes) and Lindau (€13, 2½ to three hours).

LINDAU

☎ 08382 / pop 26,500

A forgotten corner of Bavaria, most people assume the medieval little island-city is part of Baden-Württemberg but it's not. Here you'll see the blue and white Bavarian state colours, and sudsy brews trump the wines found elsewhere on the lake.

The **tourist office** (☎ 260 030; www.lindau.de; Ludwigstrasse 68; 🕑 9am-1pm & 2-7pm Mon-Fri, 2-7pm Sat & Sun May-Sep, 9am-1pm & 2-5pm Mon-Fri Oct-Apr) is opposite the train station. Footsteps away from here is Lindau's little harbour, which is guarded by a **lighthouse**.

Connected to the nearby lakeshore by bridges, this is a charming, nearly car-free town. Key sights (often adorned with murals) include **Altes Rathaus** (Reichsplatz), the **city theatre** (Barfüsser-platz) and the harbour's **Seepromenade**, with its Bavarian Lion monument. When the haze clears, the Alps provide a stunning backdrop for watersports that include wind-surfing and rowing.

Park Camping Lindau am See (☎ 722 36; www.park -camping.de; Fraunhoferstrasse 20; 2-person camp sites €20) has a beach 3km southeast of Lindau. Take bus 1 or 2 to the bus station, then bus 3.

GERMANY

The attractive-looking facade of **Hotel Gasthof Goldenes Lamm** (☎ 5732; www.goldenes-lamm-lindau.de; Schafgasse 3; r €60-120) is mirrored by the 21 comfortable rooms inside. The rustic restaurant is good and has many fish dishes.

Grand hotels garland the lake, but tucked in among them, the **Hotel Schreier** (☎ 944 484; www.hotel-schreier.de; Fäbergasse 2; r €75-160; ▯) is a little-known treat with nine boutique rooms (with wi-fi) named after flavours of ice cream served at its ice-cream shop-cafe below. 'Vanilla' has a sunlounge-strewn terrace overlooking the lake, for example.

Carving through the centre of the island, Lindau's cobbled main street, **Maximilianstrasse**, is lined with elegant cafes, restaurants and crêperies.

Lindau has trains to Ulm on the Munich–Stuttgart line (€22, 1¾ hours, hourly), Munich (€38, 2¼ hours, every two hours) and direct to Zürich (€25, four times daily). Trains to nearby Bregenz (€4.20, nine minutes, two hourly) let you connect to the rest of Austria and Switzerland.

BSB Ferries (www.bsb-online.com) on various schedules serve destinations including Meersburg (€13, 2½ to three hours) and Constance (€14, three to four hours).

RHINELAND-PALATINATE

Rhineland-Palatinate (Rheinland-Pfalz) is deeply riven by rivers, the names of which, like Rhine and Moselle, are synonymous with the wines made from the grapes growing on its hillsides. Created after WWII from parts of the former Rhineland and Rhenish Palatinate regions, its turbulent history goes all the way back to the Romans, as seen in Trier (p246). In recent centuries it was hotly contested by the French and a variety of German states, which led to many of its now-crumbling fortresses.

This land of wine and great natural beauty reaches its apex in the verdant Moselle Valley towns such as Cochem, and along the heavily touristed Rhine, where rich hillside vineyards provide a backdrop for noble castles and looming medieval fortresses. For this part of Germany, focus your attention on the water, the land it courses through and the fruit of the vines on its hillsides.

MOSELLE VALLEY

Exploring the vineyards and wineries of the Moselle (Mosel) Valley is an ideal way to get a taste of German culture and people – and, of course, the crisp, light wines. Take the time to slow down and savour a glass or two.

The Moselle is bursting at the seams with historical sites and picturesque towns built along the sinuous river below steep rocky cliffs planted with vineyards (they say locals are born with one leg shorter than the other so that they can easily work the vines). It's one of the country's most scenic regions, with a constant succession of views rewarding the intrepid hikers who brave the hilly trails.

Many wine-makers have their own small pensions but accommodation is hard to find in May, on summer weekends or during the local wine harvest (mid-September to mid-October). Note also that much of the region – like the vines themselves – goes into a deep slumber from November to March, albeit after an autumn explosion of colour.

GETTING THERE & AROUND

The most scenic part of the Moselle Valley runs 195km northeast from Trier to Koblenz; it's most practical to begin your Moselle Valley trip from either of these two.

It is not possible to travel the banks of the Moselle River via rail. Local and fast trains run every hour between Trier and Koblenz, but the only riverside stretch of this line is between Cochem and Koblenz (however it's a scenic dandy). Apart from this run – and the scenic Moselweinbahn line taking tourists between Bullay and Traben-Trarbach – travellers must use buses, ferries, bicycles or cars to travel between most of the upper Moselle towns.

Moselbahn (☎ 0651-147 750; www.moselbahn.de) runs eight buses on weekdays (fewer at weekends) between Trier and Bullay (three hours each way), a pretty route following the river's winding course and passing through numerous quaint villages. Buses leave from outside the train stations in Trier and Bullay.

A great way to explore the Moselle in the high season is by boat. Between May and early October, **Köln-Düsseldorfer (KD) Line** (☎ 0221-208 8318; www.k-d.com) ferries sail daily between Koblenz and Cochem (€24 one way, 5¼ hours upstream, 4¼ hours downstream). Various smaller ferry companies also operate on the Moselle from some of the towns. Eurail and

German Rail passes are valid for all normal KD Line services, and travel on your birthday is free.

The Moselle is a popular area among cyclists, and for much of the river's course there's a separate 'Moselroute' bike track. Most towns have a rental shop or two; ask at the tourist offices. Many of the Moselbahn buses also carry bikes.

Koblenz
☎ 0261 / pop 109,000

Koblenz is an important ferry and train junction at the confluence of the Rhine and Moselle Rivers. The **tourist office** (☎ 303 880; www.koblenz.de; Bahnhofsplatz 7; ☼ 9am-6pm Mon-Sat year-round, plus 10am-6pm Sun Apr-Oct) is in a modern building in front of the Hauptbahnhof.

The **Deutsches Eck** is a park at the dramatic meeting point of the rivers. It's dedicated to German unity and is a good reason for a riverside stroll.

South of Koblenz, at the head of the beautiful Eltz Valley, **Burg Eltz** (☎ 02672-950 500; adult/child €8/5.50; ☼ 9.30am-5.30pm Apr-Oct) is not to be missed. Towering over the surrounding hills, this superb medieval castle has frescoes, paintings, furniture and ornately decorated rooms. Burg Eltz is best reached by train to Moselkern on the Trier line, from where it's a 50-minute walk up through the forest. Alternatively, a shuttle bus runs in peak season.

In town, Altenhof and the area around Münzplatz in the Altstadt offer a variety of good eating options. The small towns in either river valley offer more atmospheric accommodation than those in town.

The busy KD Line ferry dock is a 10-minute walk from the train station. Trains fan out in all directions: up the Moselle to Trier (€20, 1½ hours, hourly) via Cochem and Bullay; north along the Rhine to Cologne (€20, one hour, two hourly) and south on the Rhine to Mainz (€20, one hour, two hourly).

Cochem
☎ 02671 / pop 5400

This often-crowded German town has narrow alleyways and one of the most beautiful castles in the region. It's also a good base for hikes into the hills. The staff are a joy at the **tourist office** (☎ 600 40; www.cochem.de; Endertplatz; ☼ 9am-5pm Mon-Sat, 10am-noon Sun, reduced hours in winter), next to the Moselbrücke bridge.

For a great view, head up to the **Pinnerkreuz** with the chairlift on Endertstrasse (€5). The perfect crown on the 100m-high hill, **Reichsburg Castle** (☎ 255; ☼ 9am-5pm mid-Mar–mid-Nov) is a 15-minute walk from town. Its idealised form can be credited to its 1877 construction (it was never needed to actually *function* as a castle). There are regular daily tours (adult/child €4.50/2.50).

Many local vineyards offer tours which include a chance to wander the vines, enjoy the views, have a picnic, sample some cheese, visit the gift shop and, oh, try the wine.

Moseltal-Jugendherberge (☎ 8633; www.djh .de; Klottener Strasse 9; dm/s/d €19/31/48; ☐) is beautifully situated on the banks of the river. The 148 beds are mostly in spotless four-bed rooms with wi-fi.

Hotel-Pension Garni Villa Tummelchen (☎ 910 520; www.villa-tummelchen.com; Schlossstrasse 22; s/d from €52/72; ☐) is a bit up the hill from town and thus has sweeping Moselle vistas. It's worth an extra couple of euros to get a room with a balcony and a view.

Tucked away uphill from the Markt and its fountain, **Zom Stüffje** (☎ 7260; www.zom-stuef fje.de; Oberbachstrasse 14; mains €8-18; ☼ Wed-Mon) is richly decorated with dark timber and murals, and serves classic German fare and, get this, Moselle wine!

This is the terminus for KD Line boats from Koblenz. Trains on the Trier–Koblenz line run twice hourly to Bullay (€5, 10 minutes), where you can pick up the Moselbahn bus.

Cochem to Trier

Take the train from Cochem to Bullay where you can catch the Moselbahn bus for the little river towns the rest of the way upstream to Trier.

Full of fanciful art-nouveau villas, the double town of **Traben-Trarbach** is a welcome relief from the 'romantic-half-timbered-town' circuit. Pick up a map of the town at the **tourist office** (☎ 06531 839 80; www.traben-trarbach.de; Bahnstrasse 22).

The twin town of **Bernkastel-Kues** is at the heart of the middle Moselle region. On the right bank, Bernkastel has a charming **Markt**, a romantic ensemble of half-timbered houses with beautifully decorated gables. For a primer on the local vino, try Bernkastel's **Weingut Dr Willkomm** (☎ 06531 8054; Gestade 1). Located in a lovely old arched cellar, the vineyard also distils its own brandy. The **tourist office** (☎ 06531 4023; www.bernkastel-kues.de; Am Gestade 6) is in Bernkastel.

GERMANY

TRIER

☎ 0651 / pop 100,000

Trier is touted as Germany's oldest town and you'll find more Roman ruins here than anywhere else north of the Alps. Although settlement of the site dates back to 400 BC, Trier itself was founded around 16 BC as Augusta Treverorum, the capital of Gaul, and was second in importance only to Rome in the Western Roman Empire. Its proximity to France can be tasted in its cuisine, while its large student population injects life among the ruins.

Orientation & Information

From the main train station head west along Bahnhofstrasse and Theodor-Heuss-Allee to the Porta Nigra, where you'll find Trier's **tourist office** (☎ 978 080; www.trier.de; ⏰ 9am-6pm Mon-Sat, 10am-5pm Sun May-Oct, reduced hours winter). There are good two-hour guided **city walking tours** (adult/child €7/3.50; ⏰ 1.30pm Sat May-Oct) in English. The Trier-Card (€9) offers discounts and free public transport.

From Porta Nigra, walk along Simeonstrasse's pedestrian zone to Hauptmarkt, the heart of the old city. Most of the sights are within this area of roughly 1 sq km. Several places around the station offer internet access.

Sights

The town's chief landmark is the **Porta Nigra** (adult/child €2.10/1; ⏰ 9am-6pm Apr-Sep, to 5pm Mar & Oct, to 4pm Nov-Feb), the imposing city gate on the northern edge of the town centre, which dates back to the 2nd century AD. Nearby, **Städtisches Museum** (☎ 718 1459; Simeonstrasse 60; adult/child €5/3; ⏰ 9.30am-5.30pm Tue-Sun) fills a renovated 11th-century Trier monastery with two millennia of Trier history.

Trier's massive (and massively restored) Romanesque **Dom** (www.dominformation.de; Liebfrauenstrasse 12; ⏰ 6.30am-6pm Apr-Oct, to 5.30pm Nov-Mar) shares a 1600-year history with the nearby and equally impressive **Konstantin Basilika** (☎ 724 68; Konstantinplatz; ⏰ 10am-6pm Mon-Fri, noon-6pm Sun Apr-Oct).

Additional Roman sites include the **Amphitheater** (Olewigerstrasse; adult/child €2.10/1; ⏰ 9am-6pm Apr-Sep, to 5pm Mar & Oct, to 4pm Nov-Feb) and the gloomy underground caverns of the **Kaiserthermen** (Im Palastgarten).

The early-Gothic **Dreikönigenhaus** (Simeonstrasse 19) was built around 1230 as a protective tower; the original entrance was on the second level, accessible only by way of a retractable rope ladder.

The **Karl Marx Haus** (☎ 970 680; Brückenstrasse 10; adult/child €3/1.50; ⏰ 10am-6pm daily Apr-Oct, to 5pm Tue-Sun Nov-Mar) is the suitably modest birthplace of the man. It is a major pilgrimage stop for the growing numbers of mainland Chinese tourists to Europe. The walls are lined with manifestos.

Sleeping

Camping Treviris (☎ 869 21; Luxemburger Strasse 81; camp sites per person/tent/car €6/5/5; ⏰ Apr-Oct) This camping ground is central and beside the Moselle River.

Hille's Hostel (☎ 710 2785; www.hilles-hostel-trier.de; Gartenfeldstrasse 7; dm €15-18, s/d €40/50; 🖳) The rooms here are furnished with Ikea bunk beds and are set back from the road amid some hardy palms. There's free internet and the chance to ponder the mugs of previous guests that line the walls.

Warsberger Hof (☎ 975 250; www.warsberger-hof.de; Dietrichstrasse 42; dm/s/d €23/30/50; 🖳) In a foundation-run hotel aimed at young people, the 150 beds are scattered about a vintage building that's ideally located. Bathrooms are shared and there's a fine outdoor cafe in the courtyard.

Hotel Pieper (☎ 230 08; www.hotel-pieper-trier.de; Thebäerstrasse 39; r €50-120; 🖳) An excellent family-run hotel on a residential street with a few neighbourhood cafes. Rooms are comfy and have free wi-fi. Best of all is the bounteous breakfast buffet that includes treats such as fresh pineapple.

Hotel Römischer Kaiser (☎ 977 00; www.friedrich-hotels.de; Am Porta-Nigra-Platz 6; s/d €67/98; 🖳) The Kaiser is in an elegant, old corner building. Rooms are comfortable, decorated in soft colours and have wi-fi; some have balconies. Ceilings are regally high.

Eating

The narrow and historic Judengasse, near the Markt, has several small bars and clubs. There's a cluster of stylish places on Viehmarktplatz and another bunch in front of the Dom.

Astarix (☎ 722 39; Karl-Marx-Strasse 11; mains from €5) Popular student hang-out with good pizza and hot specials. The bar out front sometimes has live jazz.

Walderdorff's (☎ 9946 9212; Domfreihof 1a; mains €8-16) A high-concept wine bar and cafe

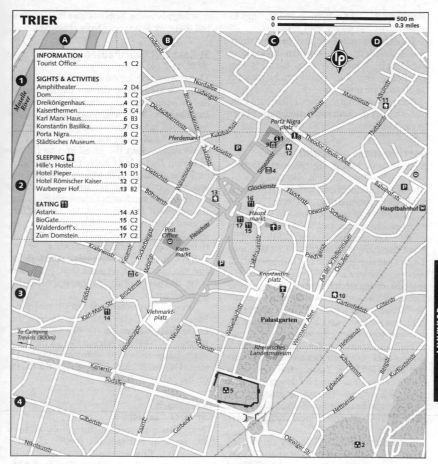

TRIER

0 _____ 500 m
0 _____ 0.3 miles

INFORMATION
Tourist Office..................1 C2

SIGHTS & ACTIVITIES
Amphitheater...................2 D4
Dom.................................3 C2
Dreikönigenhaus..............4 C2
Kaiserthermen.................5 C4
Karl Marx Haus.................6 B3
Konstantin Basilika..........7 C3
Porta Nigra.....................8 C2
Städtisches Museum........9 C2

SLEEPING
Hille's Hostel.................10 D3
Hotel Pieper..................11 D1
Hotel Römischer Kaiser...12 C2
Warberger Hof...............13 B2

EATING
Astarix..........................14 A3
BioGate.........................15 C2
Walderdorff's.................16 C2
Zum Domstein...............17 C2

across from the Dom. Score one of the dozens of tables out front or inside in the stylish surrounds.

Zum Domstein (☎ 744 90; Am Hauptmarkt 5; mains €9.50-18.50, Roman dinner €15-33) A touristy but fun German-style bistro where you can either feast like the ancient Romans or dine on more conventional German and international fare. Avoid indecision and have a wine flight (sampler).

Gather up organic and healthy picnic fare at **BioGate** (☎ 912 0820; Palastrasse 3).

Getting There & Away

Trier has a train service to Koblenz (€20, 1½ hours, hourly) via Bullay and Cochem, as well as to Luxembourg (€16, 50 minutes, hourly).

RHINE VALLEY – KOBLENZ TO MAINZ

A trip along the Rhine is a highlight for most travellers, as it should be. The section between Koblenz and Mainz provides vistas of steep vineyard-covered mountains punctuated by scores of castles. It really is rather magical. Spring and autumn are the best times to visit the Rhine Valley; in summer it's overrun and in winter most towns go into hibernation. For information on Koblenz, see p245.

ACTIVITIES

The Koblenz-to-Mainz section of the Rhine Valley is great for wine tasting, with Bacharach, 45km south of Koblenz, being one of the top choices for sipping. For tastings in other towns just follow your instincts.

Though the trails here may be a bit more crowded with day-trippers than those along the Moselle, hiking along the Rhine is also excellent. The slopes and trails around Bacharach are justly famous.

Every town along the route offers cute little places to stay or camp and atmospheric places to eat and drink.

GETTING THERE & AROUND

Koblenz and Mainz are the best starting points. The Rhine Valley is also easily accessible from Frankfurt on a long day trip, but it could drive you to drink, as it were.

Each mode of transport on the Rhine has its own advantages and all are equally enjoyable. Try combining several of them. The **Köln-Düsseldorfer (KD) Line** (☎ 0221-208 83 18; www .k-d.com) runs several slow and fast boats daily between Koblenz and Mainz (as well as the less-interesting stretch between Cologne and Koblenz). The journey takes about four hours downstream and about 5½ hours upstream (€45, free with rail pass). Boats stop at various riverside towns along the way.

Frequent train services operate on both sides of the Rhine River, but are more convenient on the left bank. You can travel nonstop on IC/EC trains or travel by slower regional RB or RE services. The ride is amazing; sit on the right heading north and on the left heading south. Note that most stations don't have lockers.

Touring the Rhine Valley by car is also good. The route between Koblenz and Mainz is short enough for a car to be rented and returned to either city. There are no bridge crossings between Koblenz and Rüdesheim, but there are several car-ferry crossings.

St Goar & St Goarshausen
☎ 06741 / pop 3100

These two towns are on opposite sides of the Rhine; St Goar is on the left bank. One of the most impressive castles on the river is **Burg Rheinfels** (☎ 383; adult/child €5/2.50; ⏰ 9am-6pm Apr-Oct, 11am-5pm Sat & Sun in good weather Nov-Mar) in St Goar. An absolute must-see, the labyrinthine ruins reflect the greed and ambition of Count Dieter V of Katzenelnbogen, who built the castle in 1245 to help levy tolls on passing ships ('African or European?'). Across the river, just south of St Goarshausen, is the Rhine's most famous sight, the **Loreley Cliff**. Legend has it that a maiden sang sailors to their deaths against its base. It's worth the trek to the top of the Loreley for the view.

For camping, **Campingplatz Loreleyblick** (☎ 2066; camp sites €3, per person €2.50; ⏰ Mar-Oct) is on the banks of the Rhine, opposite the legendary rock.

St Goar's **Jugendherberge** (☎ 388; www.djh.de; Bismarckweg 17; dm/s/d €18/30/50) is right below the castle. **Hotel Hauser** (☎ 333; www.hotelhauser.de; Heerstrasse 77; r €40-80) is relaxed like an old easy chair. Large restaurant windows and the 13 rooms all overlook the Rhine. Have a drink on the patio.

Bacharach
☎ 06743 / pop 2400

Walk beneath one of the thick-arched gateways in Bacharach's medieval walls and you'll find yourself in a beautifully preserved medieval village. The **tourist office** (☎ 919 303; www.bacharach.de; Oberstrasse 45; ⏰ 9am-5pm Mon-Fri, 10am-4pm Sat Apr-Oct) will mind day-trippers' bags.

Bacharach's **Jugendherberge** (☎ 1266; www .djh.de; dm €19) is a legendary facility housed in the Burg Stahleck castle. The **Hotel Kranenturm** (☎ 1308; www.kranenturm.com; Langstrasse 30; s/d from €45/90; ⏰) is a turreted fantasy of stone. Trainspot your way through the filling meals.

Part of the old ramparts, the **Rhein Hotel** (☎ 1243; www.rhein-hotel-bacharach.de; Langstrasse 50; r €55-100; ⏰ ⏰) has 14 well-lit, soundproofed rooms with compact bathrooms and original artwork. The restaurant (mains €9 to €17; closed Tuesday) serves regional dishes.

GERMANY

RHINE TOWNS

Besides those listed in this section, here's the low-down on some other towns along the Rhine route. All have train and boat service.

Boppard Roman walls and ruins (left bank).

Oberwesel Numerous towers and walkable walls of a ruined castle (left bank).

Assmannshausen Small, relatively untouristed village with nice hotels and sweeping views; good hikes (right bank).

Rüdesheim Overrated and overvisited town of trinkets and hype.

Mainz

☎ 06131 / pop 184,000

A short train ride from Frankfurt, Mainz has an attractive Old Town that makes for a good day trip. Though it can't compare to the compact beauty of the nearby towns along the Rhine, Mainz impresses with its massive **Dom** (☎ 253 412; Domstrasse 3; ⏰ 9am-6pm Tue-Fri, to 4pm Sat, 1-3pm Sun), which has a smorgasbord of architecture: Romanesque, Gothic and baroque. **St Stephanskirche** (Weisspetrolse 12; ⏰ 10am-noon & 2-5pm) has stained-glass windows by Marc Chagall. Mainz's museums include the standout **Gutenberg Museum** (☎ 122 640; Liebfrauenplatz 5; adult/child €5/3; ⏰ 9am-5pm Tue-Sat, 11am-3pm Sun), which contains two namesake copies of the first printed Bible. For more information on attractions in Mainz, visit the **tourist office** (☎ 286 210; www .indo-mainz.de; Brückenturm am Rathaus; ⏰ 9am-6pm Mon-Fri, 10am-3pm Sat)

Trains along the Rhine to Koblenz (€20, one hour) run twice hourly. Heidelberg (€20, one hour, hourly) is an easy trip, as is Frankfurt via the Frankfurt airport (€10, 40 minutes, several per hour).

HESSE

The Hessians, a Frankish tribe, were among the first to convert to Lutheranism in the early 16th century. Apart from a brief period of unity in that same century under Philip the Magnanimous, Hesse (Hessen) remained a motley collection of principalities and, later, of Prussian administrative districts until proclaimed a state in 1945. Its main cities are Frankfurt-am-Main, Kassel and the capital, Wiesbaden.

As well as being a transport hub, Frankfurt-am-Main offers its own diversions, although the rest of Germany will soon beckon.

FRANKFURT-AM-MAIN

☎ 069 / pop 643,000

Called 'Mainhattan' and 'Bankfurt', and much more, Frankfurt is on the Main (pronounced 'mine') River, and, after London, it is Europe's centre of finance. Both sobriquets also refer to the city's soaring skyline of bank-owned skyscrapers.

But while all seems cosmopolitan, it is often just a small town at heart. Streets get quiet in the evenings and the long list of museums is devoid of any really outstanding stars. Then again, it has cute old pubs you would only ever find in a small town. Mind you, when a major trade fair is in town, such as the Frankfurt Book Fair (p291), it feels as jammed as any metropolis.

Frankfurt-am-Main is Germany's most important transport hub for air, train and road connections, so you will probably end up here at some point. Note that it is generally referred to as Frankfurt-am-Main, or Frankfurt/Main, since there is another Frankfurt (Frankfurt-an-der-Oder) located near the Polish border.

Orientation

The airport is 11 minutes by train southwest of the city centre. The Hauptbahnhof is on the western side of the city, but it's still within walking distance of the city centre.

The best route to the city centre through the sleazy train-station area is along Kaiserstrasse. This leads to Kaiserplatz and on to a large square called An der Hauptwache. This is the retail hub with stores stretching along in all directions.

The area between the former prison/police station (Hauptwache) and the Römerberg, in the tiny vestige of Frankfurt's original old city, is the centre of Frankfurt. The Main River flows just south of the Altstadt, with several bridges leading to one of the city's more charming areas, Sachsenhausen. Its northeastern corner, known as Alt-Sachsenhausen, is full of quaint old houses and narrow alleyways.

Information

BOOKSHOPS

The Hauptbahnhof is an excellent place to go book shopping. Stores near tracks 7 and 17 have scores of English-language books and periodicals, as well as guidebooks and maps.

INTERNET ACCESS

The underground forecourt of the Hauptbahnhof has places with internet access and cheap calls as does the first block of the Kaiserstrasse.

CyberRyder (☎ 396 754; Töngesgasse 31; per 30min €3; ⏰ 9am-8pm Mon-Sat) A professional, full-service shop.

GERMANY

GERMANY

FRANKFURT-AM-MAIN

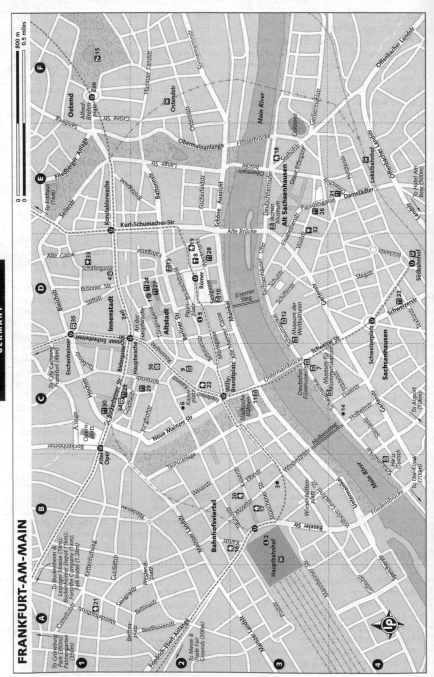

LAUNDRY

Miele Wash World (Moselstrasse 17; wash/dry €4/1; ☺ 6am-11pm)

MEDICAL SERVICES

Doctor Referral Service (☎ 192 92; ☺ 24hr)
Uni-Klinik (☎ 630 10; Theodor Stern Kai, Sachsen-hausen; ☺ 24hr)

MONEY

Reisebank airport (Terminal 1, arrival hall B; ☺ 6am-11pm); Hauptbahnhof (☺ 7am-9pm) The train-station branch is at the head of platform 1.

POST

Post office airport (departure lounge B; ☺ 7am-9pm); Hauptbahnhof (☺ 7am-7.30pm Mon-Fri, 8am-4pm Sat); Innenstadt (Zeil 90, ground fl, Karstadt department store; ☺ 9.30am-8pm)

TOURIST INFORMATION

Main tourist office (☎ 212 388 00; www.frankfurt-tourismus.de; ☺ 8am-9pm Mon-Fri, 9am-6pm Sat & Sun) In the main hall of the train station. For its efficient room-finding service the charge is €3.
Römer tourist office (Römerberg 27; ☺ 9.30am-5.30pm Mon-Fri, 10am-4pm Sat & Sun) Northwest corner of the Römerberg square. The Frankfurt-am-Main Card (one day/two days €9/13) gives 50% off admission to important attractions and unlimited travel on public transport.

Sights

Frankfurt has the most skyscraper-filled skyline in Europe. Banks and related firms have erected a phalanx of egotistical edifices along Mainzer Landstrasse and the Taunusanlange. Tallest at 259m is the pudgy yet pinnacled **Commerzbank Building** on Kaiserplatz. It was designed by Sir Norman Foster.

Frankfurt has room for all these high-rises as about 80% of the old city was wiped off the map by two Allied bombing raids in March 1944. Although postwar reconstruction was subject to the hurried demands of the new age, rebuilding efforts were more thoughtful in the **Römerberg**, the old central area of Frankfurt west of the cathedral, where ersatz 14th- and 15th-century buildings provide a glimpse of the beautiful city this once was. The old town hall, or **Römer**, is in the northwestern corner of Römerberg and consists of three 15th-century houses topped with Frankfurt's trademark stepped gables.

East of Römerberg, behind the Historischer Garten (which has the remains of Roman and Carolingian foundations), is the **Frankfurter Dom** (Domplatz 14; museum adult/child €3/2; ☺ 9am-noon & 2.30-6pm), the coronation site of Holy Roman emperors from 1562 to 1792. It's dominated by the elegant 15th-century Gothic **tower** – one of the few structures left standing after the 1944 raids (see the pictures inside).

'Few people have the imagination for reality' uttered the ever-pithy Johann Wolfgang von Goethe. Read more quotes at the **Goethe Haus** (☎ 138 800; Grosser Hirschgraben 23-25; adult/child €5/3; ☺ 10am-6pm Mon-Sat, to 5.30pm Sat & Sun), where he was born in 1749.

A little further afield, there's the botanical **Palmengarten** (☎ 2123 6689; Siesmayerstrasse 63; adult/child €5/2; ☺ 9am-6pm), next door to **Grüneburg Park**. The **Zoo** (☎ 212 337 35; Alfred-Brehm-Platz 16; adult/child €8/4; ☺ 9am-7pm, to 5pm Oct-Apr) is also a good place to unwind.

Walk the banks of the Main and you'll find plenty of benches popular for BYO frivolity. There's a vast **flea market** (☺ 8am-2pm Sat) along Museumsufer where true tat competes with just junk for sales.

GERMANY

Frankfurt's museum list is long but a mixed bag. To sample them all, buy a 48-hour Museumsufer ticket (€12). North of the cathedral, the excellent **Museum für Moderne Kunst** (☎ 2123 0447; Domstrasse 10; adult/child €8/4; 🕑 10am-8pm Tue-Sun) features works of modern art by Joseph Beuys, Claes Oldenburg and many others. Nearby, the **Historisches Museum** (☎ 2123 5599; Saalgasse 19; adult/child €4/1; 🕑 10am-6pm Tue & Thu-Sun, to 8pm Wed) has a model showing the vast extent of prewar medieval Frankfurt.

Also on the north bank there's the **Jüdisches Museum** (Jewish Museum; ☎ 2123 5000; Untermainkai 14-15; adult/child €4/2; 🕑 10am-5pm Tue & Thu-Sun, to 8pm Wed), a huge place with exhibits on the city's rich Jewish life before WWII.

Numerous museums line the south bank of the Main River along the so-called Museumsufer (Museum Embankment). Pick of the crop is the **Städelsches Kunstinstitut** (☎ 605 0980; Schaumainkai 63; adult/child €10/free; 🕑 10am-5pm Tue & Fri-Sun, to 9pm Wed & Thu), with a world-class collection of paintings by artists from the Renaissance to the 20th century, including Botticelli, Dürer, Van Eyck, Rubens, Rembrandt, Vermeer, Cézanne and Renoir.

Other museums among the gaggle include the fascinating, design-oriented **Museum für Angewandte Kunst** (Museum of Applied Arts; ☎ 2123 4037; Schaumainkai 17; adult/child €5/2.50; 🕑 10am-5pm Tue & Thu-Sun, to 8pm Wed) and the **Deutsches Architekturmuseum** (☎ 2123 8844; Schaumainkai 43; adult/child €6/3; 🕑 11am-6pm Tue & Thu-Sun, to 8pm Wed).

ON TRACK FOR A BUZZ

Why not enjoy Frankfurt's iconic apple wine while seeing the city? The **Ebbelwei-Express** (www.ebbelwei-express.com; adult €6, apple wine extra; 🕑 1.30-5.30pm Sat & Sun) is a special tram that makes a circuit of all the city's principal sights every weekend year-round. The trams are decades old but the wood seats are the perfect venue for quaffing, munching a fresh pretzel and enjoying the sites. There's a reason every time you see one of these go by everyone on board has a huge grin. The trams stop all over town; get a schedule from the tourist offices.

Sleeping

Predictably, most of Frankfurt's budget accommodation is in the grotty Bahnhofsviertel, which surrounds the station. The streets between here and the Messe (convention centre) are convenient for early departures or meetings. During large trade fairs the town is booked out months in advance and rates soar.

BUDGET

If you're thinking of a place near the train station, check some rooms first as some are total dumps.

City Camp Frankfurt (☎ 570 332; www.city-camp -frankfurt.de; An der Sandelmühle 35; camp sites €5, plus per person/car €6/5; 🖳) This camping ground is in the Heddernheim district northwest of the city centre. It's a 15-minute ride on the U1, U2 or U3 from the Hauptwache U-Bahn station – get off at Heddernheim.

Frankfurt Hostel (☎ 247 5130; www.frankfurt-hostel .com; Kaiserstrasse 74; dm €18-22, s/d from €50/60; 🖳) A good indie hostel in a grand old building. Rooms have private bathrooms and there's a lively international crowd.

Haus der Jugend (☎ 610 0150; www.djh.de; Deutschherrnufer 12; dm from €22) Within walking distance of the city and Sachsenhausen's nightspots, this HI hostel is a good choice. From the train station take bus 46 to Frankensteinerplatz, or take S-Bahn lines S3, S4, S5 or S6 to Lokalbahnhof, then walk north for 10 minutes. Check-in begins at 1pm, curfew is 2am.

Pension Backer (☎ 747 992; Mendelssohnstrasse 92; s/d from €25/50) The Backer has 25 basic rooms with shared bathrooms; it's in a nice residential neighbourhood.

MIDRANGE & TOP END

Hotel Am Berg (☎ 660 5370; www.hotel-am-berg -ffm.de; Grethenweg 23; r €35-100) Located in a sandstone building in the quiet backstreets of Sachsenhausen, this hotel close to the Südbahnhof has large rooms (some sharing bathrooms) that could have been sets for a '70s porn movie. Seek refuge out back.

Hotel Kaiserhof (☎ 256 1790; www.kaiserhof-frank furt.de; Kaiserstrasse 62; s/d from €65/80; 🖳 🖳) This sprightly hotel three minutes from the Hauptbahnhof has 42 rooms that are easy on the eyes and have wi-fi. Those on the top floor have a small terrace. Some have air-con.

(Continued on page 261)

EXPERIENCING CENTRAL EUROPE

Natural beauty abounds in the heart of the heart of Europe: incomparable mountains, vast forests, two sea coasts… The ebb and flow of empires has also left an impression here in the form of culture and castles. But it's not all strictly high brow – these lands flow with beer, wine and coffee. Whether you're into the outdoors, plan to do some serious history study or are ready to party hard, central Europe has the experience for you.

Iconic Images

What is it about a photograph that can sum up a place so well? Snow-capped peaks, hilltop fortresses and imperial dancing stallions – plus reminders of past oppression – are all images to bring back from central Europe.

3

4

1 Bled, Slovenia

George Eastman (the founder of Kodak) couldn't have designed a more picturesque setting than the Slovenian municipality of Bled (p509), where the Julian Alps surround a sparkling aquamarine lake containing a small island and a quaint church.

2 Berlin Wall, Germany

Today you can follow the ruins of the 160km-long wall (p174) that separated West Berlin from East. The graffiti-covered segment still standing in the East Side Gallery is prime for a picture.

3 Auschwitz, Poland

Thirty surviving brick buildings are a sobering reminder that Auschwitz (p399) was the largest Nazi-run concentration camp during WWII. It's the piles of victims' eyeglasses and artificial legs that truly tell the tale.

4 Prague Castle, Czech Republic

Prague Castle (p108) is the world's largest, spreading more than seven football fields in length. Early morning is the time to capture the magic of the courtyards, gardens and Gothic spires around the castle's church, St Vitus Cathedral.

5 Spanish Riding School, Austria

The stunning white Lipizzaner stallions were first bred for the Habsburg monarchy in 1580. Today you can watch the high-stepping breed perform choreographed routines at the Spanish Riding School (p54) in Vienna.

6 Postage Stamps, Liechtenstein

How fitting that the biggest thing to do in Vaduz, the capital of stamp-sized Liechtenstein, is buy a stamp and postcard to send home. The Postmuseum (p365) showcases all the mini works of art issued since 1912.

Scenic Surrounds

From 3741m above ground to 163m below, central Europe has stunning scenery on every level. Glacial lakes, mountain vistas, evergreen forests, waterfall-filled gorges – and underground rivers and caverns – are just some of the natural wonders you'll encounter.

③

① Jungfrau Region, Switzerland

Cowbells echo in the lush green valleys below the peaks of the Jungfrau Region (p564). Take the train ride up its namesake, Jungfraujoch (3741m), to be surrounded by swirling glaciers and rock pinnacles.

② Black Forest, Germany

Scattered below a dark evergreen canopy, small towns and farms create a bucolic scene in Germany's Black Forest (p236). Get off the cuckoo-clock tourist circuit and trek more than 7000km of trails.

③ Karst Region, Slovenia

The fantastic stalagmites and stalactites of Postojna Cave (p516) in Slovenia's Karst region are impressive. But the sheer depth of the underground chasm in the Škocjan Caves (p517) is even more stupendous.

④ Slovenský Raj National Park, Slovakia

Craggy limestone gorges are so steep in Slovenský raj National Park (p481) that ladders, chains and metal footholds have been installed to help hikers on the one-way trails. Climbing up as rushing waterfalls crash down is well worth the effort.

⑤ Kiskunsági Nemzeti Park, Hungary

Hungarian cowboys once roamed the broad, flat prairie expanses of the Great Plain – and they still do during the horse show at Bugac in Kiskunsági Nemzeti Park (p348).

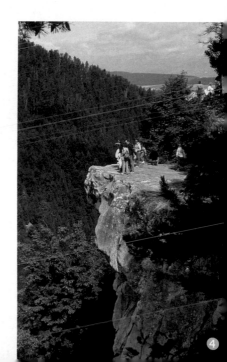

④

Castles & More Castles

Centuries of royal rule left hundreds of residences behind. Romantic castles and gilt-encrusted summer palaces define the character of many a central European city, and coming upon a craggy hilltop fortress shadowing a river far below can be the high point of any visit.

3

❶ Spiš Castle, Slovakia

More a monument to what might have been than an intact fortress, the Unesco-listed Spiš Castle ruins (p480) spread across more than 4 hectares. Whether wildflowers are blooming or the hillside below is covered in snow, the sight is dramatic.

❷ Schloss Schönbrunn, Austria

The Habsburg imperial summer palace (p45), located outside Vienna, contains a mere 1441 gold-clad, art-covered, crystal-dripping rooms. Amazingly, the gardens, fountains, maze and zoo are just as noteworthy.

❸ Neuschwanstein, Germany

A king's folly if there ever was one, the crenellations, turrets and towers of Neuschwanstein (p226) are something to see. You decide if King Ludwig II was truly mad – in addition to indulging a Wagnerian swan obsession, he installed running water on every floor (then practically unheard of).

❹ Château de Chillon, Switzerland

Lord Byron brought Château de Chillon (p549) on the shores of Lake Geneva to the world's attention when he penned *The Prisoner of Chillon* in 1816. The lakeside visage is impressive, but it was the castle's dungeons that inspired him.

❺ Schloss Vaduz, Liechtenstein

The silhouette of Liechtenstein's still inhabited royal castle (p365) graces every second traveller's postcard home – and no wonder, given its dramatic perch and Alpine backdrop. Views from the hilltop trails are jaw dropping.

Drink & Be Merry

German and Czech brews are known worldwide, but there are also plenty of other options to quench your thirst. Eminently drinkable wines are available direct from the vintners' cellars, and coffee and pastries are an afternoon tradition not to be missed. If you're looking for more action with your imbibing, the region's nightclubs can provide it.

① Beer Gardens & Halls

The Czech beers Budvar and Pilsner Urquell were born in Bohemia (p123), and spending time in a beer garden there is rivalled only by the experience of enjoying vats of lager with a few hundred new friends in a Bavarian beer hall (p216).

② Coffee Houses

The sumptuous tradition of ornate coffee houses and indulgent tortes dates back to the days of the Austro-Hungarian Empire. Today the grandest of the gilt-clad cafes are to be found in Vienna (p52) and Budapest (p318).

③ Wineries

Oenophiles have ample options, including sipping new wine at a Viennese tavern (p53), tasting a sweet white in a centuries-old Tokaj cellar (p355), or indulging in a medium-bodied red in Eger's Szépasszony völgy (Valley of the Beautiful Women; p352).

④ Capital Clubs

From Berlin (p181) to Warsaw (p384) to Bern (p558), nightclubs in the cities of central Europe pulse with energy. Whether you're after edgy or upscale, straight shots or swirly cocktails, you can have whatever late-night (or early-morning) experience you desire.

(Continued from page 252)

Concorde Hotel (☎ 242 4220; www.hotelconcorde
.de; Karlstrasse 9; r €65-120; ✗ ⌨) Understated and
friendly, this establishment in a restored art
deco building near the Hauptbahnhof is a
good choice any time, but especially on weekends. Rooms have free wi-fi.

Falk Hotel (☎ 7191 8870; www.hotel-falk.de; Falkstrasse
38; r from €70-120; ✗ ⌨) This small hotel located
on a quiet street in Bockenheim is popular for
its 29 nicely appointed rooms (with wi-fi). It's
near the Bockenheim shops. Take the U-Bahn
to Leipziger Strasse.

Hotel am Dom (☎ 138 1030; www.hotelamdom
.de; Kannengiessergasse 3; r €90-120; ⌨) This unpre-
possessing hotel offers immaculate rooms,
suites and apartments just a few paces from
the Frankfurter Dom. There's wi-fi and a large
breakfast buffet is included.

Steigenberger Frankfurter Hof (☎ 215 02; www
.steigenberger.de; Am Kaiserplatz; r from €160; ✗ ⌨)
Schopenhauer used to lunch here but his
pessimism is unlikely to dampen your enthusiasm for this cosmopolitan and elegant
19th-century neo-Renaissance institution,
Frankfurt's most gracious and traditionally
luxurious hotel.

Eating
Known to the locals as Fressgasse (Munch-
Alley), the Kalbächer Petrolse and Grosse
Bockenheimer Strasse area, between Opernplatz
and Börsenstrasse, has some medium-
priced restaurants and fast-food places with
outdoor tables in summer.

Wallstrasse and the surrounding streets
in Alt-Sachsenhausen also have lots of lively
midpriced restaurants.

Look for a plethora of outdoor stands serving food and drinks to gregarious crowds during April to October in the streets south of
the Zeil.

RESTAURANTS
Eckhaus (☎ 491 197; Bornheimer Landstrasse 45; mains
€8-14) The smoke-stained walls, the iron fan
above the door and those ancient floorboards
all suggest an inelegant, long-toothed past.
The hallmark rösti have been served in this
restaurant-bar for over 100 years. Take the
U-4 to Merianplatz.

Scialpi (☎ 282 226; Hochstrasse 51; mains €8-16)
Excellent Italian fare. The pizzas are as thin
as Milan models and as tasty... er, they are

delicious. Tables outside vie with the stylish
interior for your favour.

Mutter Ernst (☎ 28 38 22; Alte Rothofstrasse 12;
mains €9-18; ☽ closed Sun) The ancient amber-
coloured glass windows look into a timeless
dining room. Grab a wooden table among
the panelled walls for some excellent trad
German fare.

CAFES
Café Mozart (☎ 291 954; Töngesgasse 23; cakes from €1)
Sample Frankfurt's traditional torte scene
by joining the travellers who beat a path
to this popular cafe to linger over coffee
for hours on end.

Ebert's (☎ 973 877; Grosse Bockenheimer Strasse 31;
mains €5-20) A minor deli and cafe empire right
on the Fressgasse. Scores of tables outside
await diners ready for fresh and creative soups,
sandwiches and more elaborate snacks such as
caviar. Some champagne perhaps?

Metropol (☎ 288 287; Weckmarkt 13-15; mains €7)
Near the Dom, this popular place serves up
cafe fare until late. Savour a soothing beverage while reading a book.

APPLE-WINE TAVERNS
Apple-wine taverns are a Frankfurt's great
local tradition. They serve *Ebbelwoi* (Frankfurt
dialect for *Apfelwein*), an alcoholic apple cider,
along with local specialities like *Handkäse mit
Musik* (literally, 'hand-cheese with music').
This is a round cheese soaked in oil and vinegar and topped with onions; your bowel supplies the music. Anything with the sensational
local sauce made from herbs, *Grünesauce*, is
a winner. Some good *Ebbelwoi* taverns are
situated in Alt-Sachsenhausen.

Zur Germania (☎ 613 336; Textorstrasse 16; meals
€7-15) This Sachsenhausen apple-wine tavern
has a good outdoor area and is well-known
for its huge pork roasts.

our pick Fichte Kränzi (☎ 612 778; Wallstrasse 5;
mains €7-15) Just superb. A smallish place down
an alley with a large, shady tree outside. The
schnitzels are tops as is the patter from
the waiters.

Adolf Wagner (☎ 612 565; Schweizer Strasse 71; meals
€8-15) This old place has one of the most atmospheric interiors in Sachsenhausen. The
garden is appealing as well.

SELF-CATERING
Off Hasenpetrolse, **Kleinmarkthalle** (Hasengasse 5-7;
☽ 7.30am-6pm Mon-Fri, to 3pm Sat) is a great produce

market with loads of fruit, vegetables, meats and hot food.

Drinking

Many of the places listed under Eating are good for a drink, especially the apple-wine joints. Wander the streets of Alt-Sachsenhausen to hear the echoes of the millions of American military personnel who drank at the gaudy bars here during the Cold War.

Lobster (☎ 612 920; Wallstrasse 21) A scenester bar located in the heart of Sachsenhausen. Tables out front give smokers freedom, while the techno tunes beat away in the intimate interior.

Zum Schwejk (☎ 293 166; Schafergasse 20) This is a popular gay bar and one of several on this street.

Entertainment

Ballet, opera and theatre are strong features of Frankfurt's entertainment scene. Free *Frizz* has good listings (in German) of what's on in town.

Forsythe Company (☎ 2123 7586; www.theforsythe company.de; Bockenheimer Depot; Carlo-Schmid-Platz 1) Easily the world's most talked-about dance company; the work of William Forsythe is often on tour.

Turm-Palast (☎ 281 787; Am Eschenheimer Turm) A multiscreen cinema with films in English.

Jazzkeller (☎ 288 537; Kleine Bockenheimer Strasse 18a) This club attracts top acts.

U60311 (☎ 297 060 311; Rossmarkt 6) A top club for techno, U60311 draws the best talent from around Europe. It's underground, literally, and often still going at noon from the night before.

Getting There & Away

AIR

Germany's largest airport is **Frankfurt airport** (FRA; ☎ 6901; www.frankfurt-airport.com), a vast labyrinth with connections throughout the world. It's served by most major airlines, although not many budget ones.

Only cynics like Ryanair would say that Frankfurt has another airport. **Frankfurt-Hahn airport** (HHN; www.hahn-airport.de) is 70km west of Frankfurt. Buses from Frankfurt's Hauptbahnhof take about 2¼ hours – longer than the flight from London. Given the journey time it's fitting the bus company is called **Bohr** (☎ 06543-501 90; www.bohr-omnibusse.de; adult/ child €12/6; ☉ hourly).

BUS

The Deutsche-Touring Romantic Road bus (see p218) leaves from the south side of the Hauptbahnhof.

CAR

Frankfurt-am-Main features the famed Frankfurter Kreuz, the biggest *autobahn* intersection in the country. All the main car-hire companies have offices in the main hall of the Hauptbahnhof and at the airport.

TRAIN

The Hauptbahnhof handles more departures and arrivals than any station in Germany. Among the myriad services: Berlin (€111, four hours, hourly), Hamburg (€106, 3½ hours, hourly) and Munich (€89, 3¼ hours). For Cologne take the fast (€63, 75 minutes) ICE line or the slower and more scenic line along the Rhine (€41, 2½ hours, hourly).

Many long-distance trains also serve the airport. This station, *Fernbahnhof*, is beyond the S-Bahn station under Terminal 1.

Getting Around

TO/FROM THE AIRPORT

S-Bahn lines S8 and S9 run every 15 minutes between the airport and Frankfurt Hauptbahnhof (€3.60, 11 minutes, 4.15am to 1am), usually continuing via Hauptwache and Konstablerwache. Taxis (about €35) take 30 minutes without traffic jams.

The airport train station has two sections: platforms 1 to 3 (below Terminal 1, hall B) handle S-Bahn connections, while IC and ICE connections are in the long-distance train station *(Fernbahnhof)* 300m distant.

PUBLIC TRANSPORT

Both single or day tickets for Frankfurt's excellent **transport network** (RMV; www.traffiq.de) can be purchased from automatic machines at almost any train station or stop. The peak period short-trip tickets *(Kurzstrecken)* cost €1.35, single tickets cost €2.20 and a *Tageskarte* (24-hour ticket) costs €5.60 (€8.90 with the airport).

TAXI

Taxis are slow compared to public transport and expensive at €2.75 flag fall plus a minimum of €1.65 per km (more at night). There are numerous taxi ranks throughout the city, or you can book a cab (☎ 230 001, 25 00 01, 54 50 11).

NORTH RHINE-WESTPHALIA

From vibrant Cologne to elegant Düsseldorf to stately Bonn, the heavily populated Rhine-Ruhr region goes far beyond its coal and steels industries and offers historic towns and cities each with a distinct life and atmosphere.

COLOGNE

☎ 0221 / pop 1 million

Cologne (Köln) seems almost ridiculously proud to be home to Germany's largest cathedral; the twin-tower shape of its weather-beaten Gothic hulk adorns the strangest souvenirs – from egg cosies and slippers to glassware and expensive jewellery. However, this bustling Rhine-side metropolis has much more to offer than its most recognisable and ubiquitous symbol. As early as the 1st century AD, Colonia Agrippinensis was an important Roman trading settlement. Today it's one of Germany's most multicultural spots, with a vibrant nightlife only partly fuelled by the local *Kölsch* beer.

Orientation

The Dom (cathedral) is smack in your face as soon as you exit the train station. A few steps away you'll find the pedestrianised Hohe Strasse – best avoided on the weekends,

GERMANY

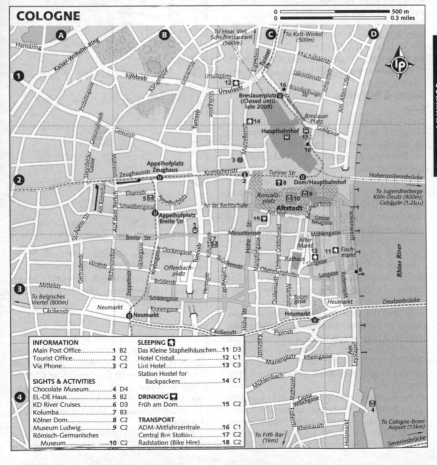

COLOGNE

0   500 m
0   0.3 miles

INFORMATION		
Main Post Office	1	B2
Tourist Office	2	C2
Via Phone	3	C2

SIGHTS & ACTIVITIES		
Chocolate Museum	4	D4
EL-DE Haus	5	B2
KD River Cruises	6	D3
Kolumba	7	B3
Kölner Dom	8	C2
Museum Ludwig	9	C2
Römisch-Germanisches Museum	10	C2

SLEEPING		
Das Kleine Staphelhäuschen	11	D3
Hotel Cristall	12	C1
Lint Hotel	13	C2
Station Hostel for Backpackers	14	C1

DRINKING		
Früh am Dom	15	C2

TRANSPORT		
ADM-Mitfahrzentrale	16	C1
Central Bus Station	17	C2
Radstation (Bike Hire)	18	C2

unless you relish fighting your way at a snail's pace through throngs of shoppers – the parallel streets are a far calmer way to navigate your way south to the Old Town. Alternatively, there's a pleasant riverfront stroll 500m to the east.

The nightlife hubs of the Belgisches Viertel (tram 3, 4 or 5 to Friesenplatz) and the Zülpicher Viertel (tram 9 to Zülpicherplatz/Bahnhof Süd) are several kilometres southwest.

Information

Köln Welcome Card (€9/14/19 for 24/48/72hr) Discount card that includes free public transport (including Bonn) and discounted museum admission. Available from the tourist office.

Main post office (☎ 01802-3333; WDR Centre, Breite Strasse 6-26; ☑ 9am-7pm Mon-Fri, to 2pm Sat)

Tourist office (☎ 2213 0400; www.koelntourismus.de; Unter Fettenhennen 19; ☑ 9am-8pm Mon-Sat, 10am-5pm Sun & holidays).

Via Phone (☎ 1399 6200; Marzellenstrasse 3-5; per hr €1; ☑ 9am-midnight Mon-Sat, from 10am Sun) Internet access.

Sights & Activities
DOM

As easy as it is to get church-fatigue in Germany, the huge **Kölner Dom** (www.koelner-dom.de; admission free; ☑ 6am-7.30pm, no visitors during services) is one you shouldn't miss. Blackened with age, this gargoyle-festooned Gothic cathedral has a footprint of 12,470 sq metres, with twin spires soaring to 157m. Although its ground stone was laid in 1248, stop-start construction meant it wasn't finished until 1880, as a symbol of Prussia's drive for unification. Just over 60 years later it escaped WWII's heavy night-bombing largely intact.

Sunshine filtering softly through stained-glass windows and the weak glow of candles are the only illumination in the moody, high-ceilinged interior.

Behind the altar lies the cathedral's most precious reliquary, the **Shrine of the Three Magi** (c 1150–1210), which reputedly contains the bones of the Three Wise Men. Brought to Cologne from Milan in the 12th century, it can just be glimpsed through the gates to the inner choir.

To see the shrine properly, you need to take a **guided tour** (adult/concession €6/4; ☑ 10.30am & 2.30pm Mon-Sat, 2.30pm Sun in English). Alternatively, you can embark on the seriously strenuous endeavour of climbing the 509 steps of the

ZÜLPICHER & BELGISCHES VIERTEL

SLEEPING 🏠	
Hotel Hopper et cetera	1 A3
Pension Jansen	2 A3

EATING 🍴	
Alcazar	3 A2
Feynsinn	4 A4
MoschMosch	5 B3
Weinstube Bacchus	6 A4

DRINKING 🍷	
Hotelux	7 A4
M20	8 A3
Päffgen	9 B2

Dom's **south tower** (adult/concession €2.50/1; ☑ 9am-6pm May-Sep, to 5pm Oct, Mar & Apr, to 4pm Nov-Feb). You pass the 24-tonne **Peter Bell**, the world's largest working clanger, before emerging at 98.25m to magnificent views.

MUSEUMS

South along the riverbank is the glass-walled **Chocolate Museum** (☎ 931 8880; www.schokoladenmuseum.de; Am Schokoladenmuseum 1a; adult/concession €7.50/5; ☑ 10am-6pm Tue-Fri, 11am-7pm Sat & Sun, last entry 1hr before closing), where you nibble on samples while learning the history and process of chocolate-making. Don't miss the 'Cult chocolate' floor.

Two prominent museums sit right next to the cathedral. The **Römisch-Germanisches**

Museum (Roman Germanic Museum; ☎ 2212 2304; www
.museenkoeln.de; Roncalliplatz 4; adult/concession €5/3;
⊗ 10am-5pm Tue-Sun) displays artefacts from the
Roman settlement in the Rhine Valley. The
Museum Ludwig (☎ 2212 6165; www.museenkoeln.de;
Bischofsgartenstrasse 1; adult/concession €9/6, 50% off after
5pm first Thu of each month; ⊗ 10am-6pm Tue-Sun, to 10pm
first Thu of each month) has an astoundingly good
collection of 1960s pop art, German expressionism and Russian avant-garde painting, as
well as photography.

The sombre **EL-DE Haus** (NS-Dokumentationszentrum;
☎ 2212 6331; www.nsdok.de, in German; Appellhofplatz 23-
25; adult/concession €3.60/1.50; ⊗ 10am-4pm Tue, Wed
& Fri, to 6pm Thu, 11am-4pm Sat & Sun) documents
Cologne's Nazi era.

Take a Gothic church, excavated ruins and
a modern space – all cleverly designed and
renovated by Swiss architect Peter Zumthor –
add art spanning the past 2000 years designed
to inspire and suggest you contemplate art
and culture in relation to time, and you get
Kolumba (☎ 933 1930; www.kolumba.de; Kolumbastrasse 4;
adult/concession €5/3; ⊗ noon-5pm Wed-Sun), Cologne's
newest museum.

Tours

Day cruises and Rhine journeys can be organised through **KD River Cruises** (☎ 208 8318;
www.k-d.com; Frankenwerft 35). Day trips (10.30am,
noon, 2pm and 6pm) cost €7.20. Sample one-
way fares to Bonn are €12.20.

Festivals & Events

Held just before Lent in late February or early
March, Cologne's **Carnival** (Karneval) rivals
Munich's Oktoberfest for exuberance, as
people dress in creative costumes and party
in the streets. Things kick off the Thursday
before the seventh Sunday before Easter and
last until Monday (Rosenmontag), when there
are formal and informal parades.

Sleeping

Accommodation prices in Cologne increase
by at least 20% when fairs are on. For more
options, see the tourist office, which offers a
room-finding service (€3).

Station Hostel for Backpackers (☎ 912 5301; www.
hostel-cologne.de; Marzellenstrasse 44-56; dm €17-22, s €32-
39, d €55; ⊒) You can't get more convenient
than this friendly six-floor hostel around the
corner from the train station. The rooms
could use some sprucing up but they're perfectly simple and clean. Breakfast costs €3.

Jugendherberge Köln-Deutz (☎ 814 711; www
.jugendherberge.de; Siegesstrasse 5a; dm/s €25/42) This is
a behemoth of a hostel and while there's not
much character in its green-grey rooms, those
on the top floors have great views. Plus, everything feels clean and spanking new. It's a relatively easy 15-minute walk east from the main
train station over the Hohenzollernbrücke.

Das Kleine Stapelhäuschen (☎ 272 7777; www
.koeln-altstadt.de/stapelhaeuschen; Fischmarkt 1-3; s/d from
€40/67; ⊒) A small, friendly hotel housed in a
historic 12th-century building in the centre of
the Old Town just off the riverbank. Exposed
beams, antique furnishings and simple but
cosy touches give rooms a homey feel.

Pension Jansen (☎ 251 85; www.pensionjansen.de;
2nd fl, Richard Wagner Strasse 18; s/d with shared bathroom
from €45/65) This cute, well-cared-for pension
has six individually decorated rooms with
cheerful colours and motifs. Details like handmade wreaths hanging on aqua walls – or a
big red rose screen-printed on the bed linen –
convey a homey atmosphere. Book early.

Hotel Hopper et cetera (☎ 924 400; www.hopper
.de; Brüsseler Strasse 26; s/d/ste from €80/120/150; ⊒)
Parquet flooring, white linen and red chairs
lend an elegant simplicity to this former monastery's rooms. The package is rounded off
with a bar and sauna in separate parts of the
vaulted cellar.

Lint Hotel (☎ 920 550; www.lint-hotel.de; Lintgasse 7;
s/d €95/150) Modern, clean rooms with parquet
flooring and light, white bedspreads fill this
ecofriendly hotel in the heart of the Old Town.
The staff will be happy to tell you all about
their solar panels and how they keep waste
to a minimum.

Hotel Cristall (☎ 163 00; www.hotelcristall.de;
Ursulaplatz 9-11; s/d/tr €105/135/165; ⊒) Angular
red, orange and purple sofas also greet you
in the lobby of this recently expanded boutique hotel. Rooms in the newest wing feature luxuriously minimalist spaces with slate
showers and black carpeting; the main building has simpler rooms with a stylish but less
modern look.

Eating

While Cologne's beer halls serve excellent
meals, the city overflows with restaurants –
for the largest variety and the most happening atmosphere, head to the Zülpicher and
Belgisches Viertels.

Alcazar (☎ 515 733; Bismarckstrasse 39; snacks €4-
9, mains €10-15) The food and atmosphere are

GERMANY

both hearty and warming at this old-school, slightly hippie pub. The changing menu always has one veggie option.

Hoai Viet Schnellrestaurant (☎ 139 3093; Weidengasse 68; mains €5-8) Exceptional and affordable Vietnamese and Thai staples are served in this sublime, brick-lined space. Small touches like bamboo and flowers give it a Zen feel. Takeaway is also available.

MoschMosch (☎ 965 7767; Pfeilstrasse 25-27; dishes €7-10; ⏱ 11am-11pm) This sleek Japanese noodle bar offers flavourful ramen noodle soups and teppanyaki dishes in a candlelit space in the heart of the trendy Belgishes Viertel.

our pick **Feynsinn** (☎ 240 9210; Rathenauplatz 7; mains €7-18) The glint of artfully arranged glasses behind the mirrored bar will catch your eye from the street, as will the broken-glass chandeliers. Inside under murals, students, creative types and tourists tuck into seasonal cuisine (menu changes weekly) as well as traditional Cologne fare like *Himmel & Aad* (literally 'Heaven & Earth', which is mashed potatoes and apple sauce).

Weinstube Bacchus (☎ 217 986; Rathenauplatz 17; mains €8-19; ⏱ dinner) Dark-wood tables, yellow walls that are lined with paintings by local artists (all pieces are for sale), a seasonal international menu, and an almost exclusively German wine list make this casual wine bar–restaurant popular among the locals. Look for the special wine table – any bottle is €13, and if you don't like it they guarantee a refund.

Drinking & Entertainment

As in Munich, beer in Cologne reigns supreme. More than 20 local breweries turn out a variety called *Kölsch*, which is relatively light and slightly bitter. The breweries run their own beer halls and serve their wares in skinny 200ml glasses.

BEER HALLS

Früh am Dom (☎ 258 0394; Am Hof 12-14) This three-storey beer hall and restaurant (including cellar bar) is the most central, with black-and-white flooring, copper pans and tiled ovens keeping it real, despite the souvenir shop. It's open for breakfast.

Päffgen (☎ 135 461; Friesenstrasse 64-66) Another favourite, this thrumming wood-lined room has its own beer garden. It's not far from the bars of the Belgisches Viertel.

BARS

For more options, take a tram to Zülpicherplat and explore.

Katt-Winkel (☎ 990 1214; Greesbergstrasse 2 Housed in a cool, triangular space, this ga cafe-bar welcomes everyone. It's a relaxin spot to unwind to mellow music with a expertly mixed cocktail.

Fiffi Bar (☎ 340 6211; Rolandstrasse 99) Loo for the pink-lei wearing bull-terrier statu mounted above the entrance of this hilari ous retro, red-vinyl, dog-themed joint. W personally recommend ordering the Froze Setter (cuervo, pineapple and lemon) bu perhaps you'd prefer the Sweet Lassie (rum banana and cream)?

Hotelux (☎ 241 136; Rathenauplatz 22) Red walls red booths and red lights; Hotelux serve cocktails and over 30 types of 'Soviet water' (ie vodka) to students and intellectual types.

Gebäude 9 (☎ 814 637; Deutz-Mülheimer Strasse 127-129) Once a factory, this is now a Cologne nightlife stalwart spinning drum'n' bass, indie pop, gypsy music and '60s trash to film noir and puppets.

M20 (☎ 519 666; Maastrichter Strasse 20) This popular retro cocktail bar sports cube-shaped lights and brown leather sofas. Regular DJ evenings favour indie guitar rock, but some live acts play more laid-back Latin music.

Getting There & Away

AIR

Cologne-Bonn airport (CGN; www.airport-cgn.de) is growing in importance. There are now direct flights to New York, while budget airlines **German Wings** (www.germanwings.com) and **easyjet** (www.easyjet.com) fly here, among others. Alternatively, low-cost carrier Ryanair flies to **Niederrhein (Weeze) airport** (NRN; www.flughafen-nied errhein.de). A shuttle bus (☎ 06543-501 90; www.bohr -omnibusse.de) to Cologne (€21, 2¼ hours) leaves soon after the planes' scheduled arrivals.

CAR

The city is on a main north–south *autobahn* route and is easily accessible for drivers and hitchhikers. The **ADM-Mitfahrzentrale** (☎ 194 40; www.citynetz-mitfahrzentrale.de; Maximinen Strasse 2) is near the train station.

TRAIN

There are frequent RE services operating to Düsseldorf (€10.50 to €16, 25 to 30 minutes) and Aachen (€13.80, 50 minutes to one hour).

Frequent EC, IC, or ICE trains go to Hanover (€54 to €61, 2¾ to three hours), Frankfurt-am-Main (€39 to €61, one to 2¼ hours, three hourly) and Berlin (€102, 4¼ hours, hourly). Frequent Thalys high-speed services connect Cologne to Paris (€91, four hours) via Brussels, and ICE trains go to Amsterdam (€56, 2½ hours).

Getting Around

S-Bahn 13 runs between Cologne-Bonn airport and the main train station every 15 minutes from 5.30am to 11.20pm daily (€2.30, 20 minutes). Bus 670 goes to Bonn every half-hour.

Buses and trams serve the inner city, with local trains handling trips up to 50km away, including Bonn. A one-day pass costs €6.90 if you're staying near the city (one or two zones), €8.40 for most of the Cologne area including Bonn. Single city trips cost €1.60, while 1½-hour two-zone tickets are €2.

Cologne is flat and cycle-friendly. Bicycle hire is available next to the main train station at **Radstation** (☎ 139 7190; www.radstationkoeln .de; Am Hauptbahnhof/Breslauerplatz; per 3hr/1/3/7 days €5/10/20/40; ☉ 5.30am-10.30pm Mon-Fri, 6.30am-8pm Sat, 8am-8pm Sun).

BONN

☎ 0228 / pop 315,000

South of Cologne on the Rhine's banks, Beethoven's birthplace became West Germany's temporary capital in 1949. But exactly 50 years later it was demoted when most (but not all) government departments returned to Berlin. These days several large company headquarters reside here, including telecommunications giant Deutsche Telekom, Deutsche Post World Net (German postal service plus international express mail service DHL) and reknowned German TV broadcaster Deutsche Welle.

An excellent collection of museums and a quiet, compact Old Town filled with 18th-century baroque architecture make Bonn a worthwhile day trip.

The **tourist office** (☎ 775 000; www.bonn-regio .de; Windeckstrasse 1; ☉ 9am-6.30pm Mon-Fri, to 4pm Sat, 10am-2pm Sun) is a three-minute walk along Poststrasse from the Hauptbahnhof, and can fill you in with any extra details.

Ludwig van Beethoven fans will head straight to the **Beethoven-Haus** (☎ 981 7525; www .beethoven-haus-bonn.de; Bonngasse 24-26; adult/concession €5/4; ☉ 10am-6pm Mon-Sat, 11am-6pm Sun Apr-Oct, to 5pm Nov-Mar), where the composer was born in 1770.

The house contains memorabilia concerning his life and music, including his last piano, with an amplified sounding board to accommodate his deafness. The annual Beethoven Festival takes place August to September.

The **Haus der Geschichte der Bundesrepublik Deutschland** (FRG History Museum; ☎ 916 50; www.hdg .de; Willy-Brandt-Allee 14; admission free; ☉ 9am-7pm Tue-Sun) presents Germany's postwar history. It is part of the **Museumsmeile**, four museums that also includes the **Kunstmuseum Bonn** (☎ 776 260; www.kunstmuseum-bonn.de; Friedrich-Ebert-Allee 2; adult/concession €5/2.50; ☉ 10am-6pm Tue & Thu-Sun, to 9pm Wed) and the **Kunst-und Ausstellungshalle der Bundesrepublik Deutschland** (☎ 917 1200; www .bundeskunsthalle.de; Friedrich-Ebert-Allee 2; adult/concession €8/5; ☉ 10am-9pm Tue & Wed, to 7pm Thu-Sun).

From Cologne, it's quicker to take an RE train to Bonn (€6.30, 20 minutes) than a tram (€8.40 day pass, 55 minutes each way). For river trips, see p265.

DÜSSELDORF

☎ 0211 / pop 585,000

'D-Town' or 'The City D', as local magazine editors like to call Düsseldorf, is Germany's fashion capital. But that means Jil Sander and Wolfgang Joop rather than cutting-edge streetwear, as you'll soon discover observing fur-clad *Mesdames* with tiny dogs along the ritzy shopping boulevard of the Königsallee.

Indeed, this elegant and wealthy town could feel stiflingly bourgeois if it weren't for its lively old-town pubs, its position on the Rhine, its excellent art galleries and the postmodern architecture of its Mediahafen.

Orientation

The train station lies at the southeastern edge of the Old Town, about 1km east of the Rhine River. The Mediahafen and Rheinturm are much further south, on the riverbank.

Information

Düsseldorf Welcome Card (24/48/72hr €9/14/19) Discount card offering free public transport and discounted museum admission. Available from the tourist office.

Telesurf (Graf-Adolf-Strasse 102; per hr €2; ☉ 10am-2am Mon-Sat, to midnight Sun) Minutes left of the train station.

Tourist office (www.duesseldorf-tourismus.de) main office (☎ 172 0222; Immermannstrasse 65b; ☉ 9.30am-7pm Mon-Sat); Old Town (☎ 1720 2840; Marktstrasse/Ecke Rheinstrasse; ☉ noon-6pm).

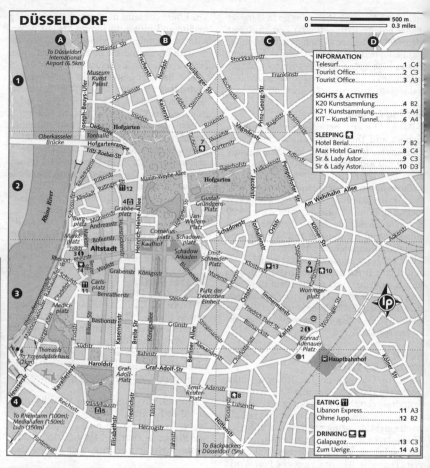

DÜSSELDORF

0 — 500 m
0 — 0.3 miles

INFORMATION	
Telesurf............................1	C4
Tourist Office....................2	C3
Tourist Office....................3	A3

SIGHTS & ACTIVITIES	
K20 Kunstsammlung...........4	B2
K21 Kunstsammlung...........5	A4
KIT – Kunst im Tunnel........6	A4

SLEEPING	
Hotel Berial.....................7	B2
Max Hotel Garni...............8	C4
Sir & Lady Astor...............9	C3
Sir & Lady Astor..............10	D3

EATING	
Libanon Express...............11	A3
Ohme Jupp......................12	B2

DRINKING	
Galapagoz.......................13	C3
Zum Uerige.....................14	A3

Sights & Activities

Düsseldorf has a lively **Altstadt** (Old Town), which is filled with enough restaurants, beer halls and pubs to have earned it the slightly exaggerated title of the 'longest bar in the world'. In the central **Marktplatz** you'll find a statue of the former ruler, or elector, Jan Wellem.

What really sets the city apart, however, is the contemporary architecture of its **Mediahafen**. Here, in the city's south, docks have been transformed into an interesting commercial park, most notably including the **Neuer Zollhof**, three typically curved and twisting buildings by Bilbao Guggenheim architect Frank Gehry. You'll find a map of the park on a billboard located behind

(ie on the street side of) the red-brick Gehry building.

For a bird's-eye view of the Mediahafen, and indeed all of Düsseldorf, catch the express elevator to the 168m viewing platform of the neighbouring **Rheinturm** (adult/child €3.50/1.50; ☺ 10am-11.30pm). There's also a revolving restaurant and cocktail bar a level above, at 172.5m.

It's a pleasant stroll between the Mediahafen and the Altstadt along the riverside **Rheinuferpromenade**. Alternatively, you can join the city's elite window-shopping along the **Königsallee**, or 'Kö' – Düsseldorf's answer to Rodeo Drive.

Three excellent galleries, two sharing the same collection, form the backbone of Düsseldorf's reputation as a city of art.

Due to reopen in summer 2010, **K20** (☎ 838 ‹0; www.kunstsammlung.de; Grabbeplatz 5; adult/concession €6.50/4.50, combination ticket K20 & K21 €10/8; ☻ 10am-›pm Tue-Fri, 11am-6pm Sat & Sun) will feature a brand-new wing and early-20th-century masters, including an extensive Paul Klee collection.

K21 (☎ 838 1600; www.kunstsammlung.de; Stän-dehausstrasse 1; adult/concession €6.50/4.50, combination ticket K20 & K21 €10/8) concentrates on art from 1990 onwards. Highlights include Nam June Paik's *TV Garden*, local artists Katarina Fritsch's giant black mouse sitting on a sleeping man, the psychedelically decorated bar and the glassed-in roof.

KIT – Kunst Im Tunnel (☎ 892 0769; www.kunst -im-tunnel.de; Mannesmannufer 1b; adult/concession €4/3) literally translates to 'Art in the Tunnel', which is exactly what you get in the former road tunnel onwards. Revolving exhibits – often by local students from the Düsseldorfer Art Academy – line the concrete curved walls of this surreal, subterranean space. The riverside cafe upstairs is a popular drinking spot during clement weather.

Sleeping

Backpackers-Düsseldorf (☎ 302 0848; www.backpack ers-duesseldorf.de; Fürstenwall 180; dm €22; ☐) This modern hostel adds bright colours and table football to soft beds and free wi-fi to come out a real winner. Near the Mediahafen, it's reached from the train station by bus 725 to Kirchplatz, from where there are several trams into town.

Jugendgästehaus (☎ 557 310; www.jugendherberge .de; Düsseldorfer Strasse 1; dm €22, s/d from €26/48; ☐) Situated in posh Oberkassel, recent renovations turned this 368-room hostel into a snazzy modern place that feels more like a boutique hotel. All rooms are en suite and breakfast is served in a large, airy space over-looking the Rhine.

Hotel Berial (☎ 490 0490; Gartenstrasse 30; www.ho telberial.de; s/d from €47/67; ☐) An inviting ambi-ence reigns here, thanks to the friendly staff and the contemporary furnishings. Decor fea-tures lots of blue, blond wood, glass bathroom doors and some bright prints. The breakfast buffet is truly gargantuan. Free wi-fi.

Max Hotel Garni (☎ 386 800; www.max-hotelgarni .de; Adersstrasse 65; s/d/tr €69/80/96; ☐) With touches of lime green walls, red carpet along the wall of one hall and some squiggly original por-traits, this lovely modern place has a youthful atmosphere. Rates include a regional trans-

port pass and free coffee, tea and soft drinks in the lobby.

Sir & Lady Astor (☎ 173 370; www.sir-astor.de; Kurfürstenstrasse 18 & 23; s/d €88/110; ☐) The twin-hotel features two parts across the street from each other: Sir Astor features only African and Scottish motifs but Lady Astor is more international and themed rooms evoke Asia, the Middle East and beyond.

Eating & Drinking

Libanon Express (☎ 134 917; Berger Strasse 19-21; cafe €3-14, restaurant €10-19) Crammed with mir-rors and tiles – and with recommendations stickered on the window – this cafe serves great kebabs, falafel and other Middle Eastern specialities.

Ohme Jupp (☎ 326 406; Ratinger Strasse 19; dishes €5-8; ☻ 8am-1am) Casual, artsy cafe serving break-fast and seasonal blackboard specials; also a popular after-work drinking den.

Zum Uerige (☎ 866 990; Berger Strasse 1) In this noisy, cavernous place, the trademark Uerige Alt beer (a dark and semisweet brew typical of Düsseldorf) flows so quickly that the waiters just carry around trays and give you a glass whenever they spy one empty.

Galapagoz (☎ 355 8983; www.galapagoz.de; Kloster-strasse 68a) Tuck into this tiny cafe-bar for fan-tastic cocktails, wines and snacks (the menu is written on the slate tiles that wrap their way around) in a laid-back South American space.

Lido (☎ 1576 8730; www.lido1960.de; Am Handelshafen 15) A glass and steel cube extends out over the water in the Mediahafen and its smooth outdoor lounge-deck is *the* place to see and be seen on a hot summer night.

Getting There & Away

From **Düsseldorf International Airport** (DUS: www .duesseldorf-international.de), trains go directly to other German cities, while frequent S-Bahn services (1 and 7) head to Düsseldorf train station.

Low-cost carrier Ryanair flies to **Niederrhein (Weeze) airport** (NRN; www.flughafen-niederrhein.de). A **shuttle bus** (☎ 06543-501 90; www.bohr-omnibusse .de) to Düsseldorf (€14, 1¼ hours) leaves soon after the planes' scheduled arrivals.

The many train services from Düsseldorf include to Cologne (€10.50 to €16, 25 to 30 minutes), Frankfurt-am-Main (€70, 1½ to 1¾ hours), Hanover (€53, 2½ hours) and Berlin (€97, 4¼ hours).

GERMANY

Getting Around

The metro, trams and buses are useful to cover Düsseldorf's distances. Up to three stops (Kurzstrecke) costs €1.30, a ticket for the centre €2.20 and for the greater city €4.30. Day passes start at €5.20.

AACHEN

☎ 0241 / pop 253,000

A spa town with a hopping student population and tremendous amounts of character, Aachen has narrow cobbled streets, quirky fountains, shops full of delectable Printen (local biscuit, a bit like gingerbread), and a pretty cathedral, which make for an excellent day trip from Cologne or Düsseldorf or a worthy overnight.

Orientation

Aachen's compact centre is contained within two ring roads roughly tracing the old city walls. The inner ring road, or Grabenring, changes names – most ending in 'graben' – and encloses the old city proper. To get to the tourist office from the Hauptbahnhof, cross Römerstrasse, follow Bahnhofstrasse north and then go left along Theaterstrasse to Kapuzinergraben.

Information

Tourist office (☎ 180 2960/1; www.aachen.de; Atrium Elisenbrunnen, Kapuzinergraben; ☉ 9am-6pm Mon-Fri, to 2pm Sat year-round, plus to 3pm Sat, 10am-2pm Sun Apr-Dec)

Web (☎ 997 9210; Kleinmarschierstrasse 74-76; per 10min €0.50; ☉ 10am-3pm Mon-Thu, to 3am Fri & Sat, 11am-10pm Sun)

Sights

OLD TOWN & FOUNTAINS

Next to the tourist office is the **Elisenbrunnen**; despite its sulphuric 'rotten eggs' smell, you can drink it – it's supposedly good for the digestion.

In the far left-hand corner of the park behind the Elisenbrunnen, you'll find the **Geldbrunnen**, which represents the circulation of money. The comical figures around the pool clutch their coins or purses while the water is sucked down the central plughole (jokingly known as 'the taxman').

Head east along the top of the park here, towards Forum M, and turn left into Buchkremerstrasse. Soon you'll reach a fountain with a scary-looking creature. This is the mythological **Bahkauv**, which was rumoured to jump on the backs of those returning late from the pub and demand a lift all the way home.

Buchkremerstrasse becomes Buchel. Turn left just past Leo van den Daele (see opposite), then right again, and you'll come to Hühnermarkt, with its **Hühnerdiebbrunnen** (Chicken-thief fountain). The hasty thief hasn't noticed one of his stolen chickens is a rooster and is about to unmask him by crowing.

From here, Aachen's main **Markt** is visible just to the northeast. The 14th-century **Rathaus** (adult/concession €2/1; ☉ 10am-5pm Mon-Fri, 10am-1pm & 2-5pm Sat & Sun) overlooks the Markt, while a fountain statue of **Charlemagne** is in the middle.

Head back down the hill along Krämerstrasse until you come to the **Puppenbrunnen** (Puppet fountain), where you're allowed to play with the movable bronze figures.

Continuing in the same direction for 50m, you'll arrive at Aachen's famous Dom.

DOM

While Cologne's cathedral wows you with its size and atmosphere, Aachen's similarly Unesco-listed **Dom** (Kaiserdom or Münster; www .aachendom.de; ☉ 7am-7pm Apr-Oct, to 6pm Nov-Mar) impresses with its shiny neatness. The small, Byzantine-inspired **octagon** at the building's heart dates from 805 but was refurbished in 2003, so its ceiling mosaics glitter and its marble columns gleam.

The building's historical significance stems not just from Charlemagne's having ordered it built, but that 30 Holy Roman emperors were crowned here from 936 to 1531.

The brass **chandelier** hanging in the centre was donated by Emperor Friedrich Barbarossa in 1165. Meanwhile, standing at the main altar and looking back towards the door, it's just possible to glimpse Charlemagne's simple marble throne. The man himself lies in the golden **shrine** behind the altar. The cathedral became a site of pilgrimage after his death.

THERMAL BATHS

The 8th-century Franks were first lured to Aachen for its thermal springs. And just over 1200 years later, the state-of-the-art **Carolus Thermen** (Carolus Thermal Baths; ☎ 182 740; www.carolus -thermen.de; Stadtgarten/Passstrasse 79; ☉ 9am-11pm; with/ without sauna from €20/10) are still reeling them in.

That's hardly surprising, for the complex is part therapeutic spa – good for rheumatism etc – and part swimming centre. Quirky currents whiz you around one pool, water jets bubble up in another, and taps pour out cold water in yet another. Only diehard fans should pay for the sauna, as there's – bizarrely – a steam room accessible to all.

The baths are in the city garden, northeast of the centre.

Sleeping

Jugendgästehaus (☎ 711 010; www.jugendherberge .de; Maria-Theresia-Allee 260; dm/s €23/37; 🖵) This modern DJH outpost sits on a hill overlooking the city, and gets lots of school groups. Take bus 2 to Ronheide.

Hotel Marx (☎ 375 41; www.hotel-marx.de; Hubertusstrasse 33-35; s/d with shared bathroom from €37/70, with private bathroom from €54/79; 🖵) There's a garden with a pond out of the back of this traditional family-run place. Inside, the rooms are decent, even if the bathrooms are a little cramped.

Hotel Benelux (☎ 400 030; www.hotel-benelux.de; Franzstrasse 21-23; s €88, d €103-148) This well-run hotel is clean and uncluttered with tasteful art in all its rooms. The rooftop garden with the enclosed gazebo is a bonus.

Eating & Drinking

Leo van den Daele (☎ 357 24; Büchel 18; dishes €5-9.50) A warren of 17th-century rooms linked by crooked stairs across four merchants' homes, this nationally renowned cafe specialises in gingerbread, or *Printen*. Yet you can also enjoy light meals – soups, sandwiches, quiches and *pastetchen* (vol au vents) – among its tiled stoves and antique knick-knacks.

Kaiser Wetter (☎ 9437 9950; www.kaiserwetter-aachen.de; Hof 5; mains €5-15) Stop by for a drink, a snack or a light meal of salads and pizzas at this restaurant-lounge in the centre of town. Relax at the outdoor tables under the shadow of giant roman pillars or step inside the modern interior.

Anna's Tafel (☎ 5593 5537; Pontstrasse 62; mains €10-14) This tiny, quiet wine bar–restaurant with unfinished wood tables and romantic candelabras serves seasonal French specialities, cheese and charcuterie plates and decadent desserts. A great escape from the student crowds just up the road.

Aachen's students have their own 'Latin Quarter' along Pontstrasse, with dozens of

> ### NOT QUITE GINGERBREAD
>
> It comes in all shapes and sizes – a porcupine, a dog, Santa Claus or the Easter Bunny. It tastes like gingerbread, sort of. It's a little bit like *Lebkuchen,* but firmer. Window displays of **Aachener Printen** greet you all over town and we're certain you'll give in and buy a bag while you're in town. The exact recipe is a closely guarded secret, but generally involves cinnamon, ginger, clove and allspice and makes a fantastic gift to bring home. Leo Van Deele (left) sells some of the best *Printen* around.

bars and cheap eats. The street heads northeast off the Markt and runs for nearly a kilometre. The laid-back sandwich king **Vitaminbar** (☎ 409 3912; Alexaniergraben 13-15; dishes €3-7) is an excellent budget choice

Getting There & Around

There are frequent trains to Cologne (€13.80 to €19.50, 30 minutes to one hour) and twice-hourly service to Düsseldorf (€17.10, 70 minutes to 1½ hours). The high-speed Thalys train passes through regularly on its way to Brussels and Paris (€85, three hours).

Buses cost €1.50 (trip of a few stops only), €2.20 (regular single) or €6.10 (day pass).

LOWER SAXONY

Lower Saxony (Niedersachsen) likes to make much of its half-timbered towns. Hamelin is certainly a true fairy-tale beauty, and leaning Lüneberg is quite unlike any other town you'll see. The state is also home to the global headquarters of Volkswagen and the business-minded capital, Hanover, as well as the pretty Harz mountains.

HANOVER

☎ 0511 / pop 517,000

German comedians – yes, they do exist – like to dismiss Hanover as 'the *autobahn* exit between Göttingen and Walsrode'. However, the capital of Lower Saxony is far livelier than its reputation assumes, and its residents are remarkably friendly and proud of their small town. While it's famous for hosting trade fairs, particularly the huge

GERMANY

CEBIT computer show in March, it also boasts acres of greenery in the Versailles-like Herrenhäuser Gärten (gardens).

Parts of the central Altstadt look medieval, but few of them are. They're mostly clever fakes built after intense WWII bombing.

Information

Hannover Tourismus (☎ information 1234 5111, room reservations 1234 555; www.hannover.de; Ernst-August-Platz 8; ☒ 9am-6pm Mon-Fri, to 2pm Sat)

Hannover Welcome Card (24/72hr for €9/15) Discount card offering free public transport and discounted museum admission. Available from the tourist office.

Teleklick Hannover (Schillerstrasse 23; ☒ 10am-11pm Mon-Sat, noon-10pm Sun) Internet access.

Sights & Activities

The enormous **Grosser Garten** (Large Garden; admission €3, free in winter) is the highlight of the **Herrenhäuser Gärten** (☎ 1684 7576; www.herrenhaeuer -gaerten.de; ☒ 9am-sunset). It has a small maze and Europe's tallest fountain. Check the website in summer for Wasserspiele, when all fountains are synchronised, and the night-time **Illuminations**. The **Niki de Saint Phalle Grotto** is a magical showcase of the artist's work. She was French – her colourful figures adorn the famous Stravinsky fountain outside the Centre Pompidou in Paris – but developed a special relationship with Hanover. There's a popular beer garden in the Grosser Garten. Alternatively, the flora of the **Berggarten** (Mountain Garden; admission €2, combined entry with Grosser Garten €4) is interesting. Adjacent lies the new **Sea Life Hannover** (☎ 56 669 0101; adult/ child €13.95/9.95, incl Grosser Garten & Berggarten adult/ child €14.50/10.95; ☒ 10am-5pm), a 3500-sq-metre educational aquarium with friendly staff and clever displays.

The **Neues Rathaus** (new town hall) was built between 1901 and 1913. Town models in the foyer reveal the extent of WWII devastation. Further east lies the Leine River and, since 1974, **Die Nanas** live here – three fluorescent-coloured, earth-mama sculptures by de Saint Phalle. They're best seen on Saturday, when there's a flea market at their feet.

In summer, the **Machsee** (lake) has ferries (crossing €3, tour €6) and numerous boats for hire. There's a free public **swimming beach** on the southeast shore.

Sleeping

The tourist office only finds private rooms during trade fairs but can arrange hotel bookings year-round for €7.

Jugendherberge (☎ 131 7674; www.jugendherberge .de; Ferdinand-Wilhelm-Fricke-Weg 1; dm €21; ☒) This large space-lab-looking structure houses a modern hostel with breakfast room and terrace bar overlooking the river in an area that feels more country than city. Take U3 or U7 to Fischerhof, cross the mini, red suspension bridge and turn right.

GästeResidenz PelikanViertel (☎ 399 90; Pelikanstrasse 11; s €46-240, d €66-240, tr €92-300; ☒) Upmarket student residence meets budget hotel, this huge complex (located in the former Pelikan fountain-pen factory) has a wide range of Ikea-style rooms, all with kitchenettes. Prices skyrocket during trade-fair periods. Take U3, U7 or U9 to Pelikanstrasse.

City Hotel am Thielenplatz (☎ 327 691; www .smartcityhotel.de; Thielenplatz 2; s from €55, d from €62; ☒) Recently renovated rooms contain crisp, white, retro furnishings and high ceilings. Some bathrooms are miniscule but overall this place is excellent value and only a short walk from the train station. The reception desk is located in the popular downstairs bar.

City Hotel Flamme (☎ 388 8004; www.cityhotel flamme.de; Lammstrasse 3; s from €65, d/apt €99/109; ☒) This art hotel features endearing touches such as goodnight stories on bedside tables. Rooms are arranged around a tropical-feeling atrium that has an inviting bar. Accommodation is spotless and the staff is friendly.

Eating & Drinking

Markthalle (Karmarschstrasse 49; dishes €3.50-10; ☒ 7am-8pm Mon-Wed, to 10pm Thu & Fri, to 4pm Sat) This huge covered market of food stalls (sausages, sushi, tapas and more), gourmet delis and standing-only 'bars' is a no-nonsense, atmospheric place for a quick bite. It's also heaving each Friday evening with people proclaiming *Prost!* (Cheers!) to the start of the weekend.

Maestro (☎ 300 8575; www.maestro-hannover.de; Sophienstrasse 2; mains €7-14.50) This atmospheric subterranean restaurant offers an all-you-can-eat vegetarian buffet (€7) at lunch daily and surprises you with its hidden courtyard beer garden.

LÜNEBURG: THE WOBBLY TOWN

With an off-kilter church steeple, buildings leaning on each other and houses with swollen 'beer-belly' facades, it's as if charming Lüneburg has drunk too much of the Pilsener lager it used to brew.

Of course, the city's wobbly angles and uneven pavements have a more prosaic cause. For centuries until 1980, Lüneburg was a salt-mining town, and as this 'white gold' was extracted from the earth, ground shifts and subsidence knocked many buildings sideways. Inadequate drying of the plaster in the now-swollen facades merely added to this asymmetry.

But knowing the scientific explanation never detracts from the pleasure of being on Lüneburg's comic-book crooked streets.

Between Hanover (€26, one hour) and Hamburg (€13.20, 30 minutes), the city's an undemanding day trip from either. From the train station, head west into town towards the highly visible, 14th-century **St Johanniskirche**, the 106m-high spire of which leans 2.2m off true. Local legend has it that the architect tried to kill himself by jumping off it. (He fell into a hay cart and was saved, but celebrating his escape later in the pub he drank himself into a stupor, fell over, hit his head and died after all.)

The church stands at the eastern end of the city's oldest square, **Am Sande**, full of typically Hanseatic stepped gables. At the western end stands the beautiful black-and-white **Industrie und Handelskammer** (Trade and Industry Chamber).

Continue one block past the Handelskammer and turn right into restaurant-lined Schröderstrasse, which leads to the **Markt**, where the ornate **Rathaus** contains the tourist office (☎ 207 6620; www.lueneburg.de; ☺ 9am-6pm Mon-Fri, to 4pm Sat, 10am-4pm Sun May-Sep, 9am-5pm Mon-Fri, to 2pm Sat Oct-Apr).

Admire the square before continuing west along Waagestrasse and down our favourite Lüneburg street, **Auf dem Meere**, en route to the **St Michaeliskirche**. Here the wonky facades and wavy pavements are like something from a Tim Burton film.

It's too late now to regain your equilibrium, so head back along Am Flock for the pubs along **Am Stintmarkt** on the bank of the Ilmenau River.

Café-Bar Celona (☎ 353 8576; Knochenhauerstrasse 47; mains €7-16) Latin-themed and plant-filled, this cafe bar is fine any time of day (or night) for a bite, a drink, or both – but book ahead for its massive (and massively popular) all-you-can-eat Sunday brunch (€8.95).

Mr Phung Kabuki (☎ 215 7609; Friedrichswall 10; sushi €3, mains €8-15) Boats bob by on the water-based sushi chain, but you can order all manner of pan-Asian and wok dishes in this airy, trendy restaurant with an enormous range of spirits.

Getting There & Around

Hanover's **airport** (HAJ; www.hannover-airport.de) has many connections, including on low-cost carrier **Air Berlin** (www.airberlin.com).

There are frequent IC/ICE train services running to/from Hamburg (€34 to €39, 1¼ to 1½ hours), Berlin (€53 to €58, 1½ to two hours), Cologne (€54 to €61, 2¾ to 3¼ hours) and to Munich (€112, 4¼ to 4¾ hours), among other destinations.

U-Bahn lines from the Hauptbahnhof are boarded in the station's north (follow the signs towards Raschplatz), except the U10 and U17, which are overground trams leaving near the tourist office.

Most visitors only travel in the central 'Hannover' zone. Single tickets are €2.10 and day passes €4.10.

The S-Bahn (S5) takes 17 minutes to the airport (€2.80).

AROUND HANOVER
Celle
☎ 05141 / pop 70,700

With row upon row of ornate half-timbered houses, all decorated with scrolls and allegorical figures, Celle is a pleasant place for a leisurely day trip. Even the tourist office, **Tourismus Region Celle** (☎ 1212; www.region-celle .com; Markt 14; ☺ 9am-6pm Mon-Fri, 10am-4pm Sat, 11am-2pm Sun May-Sep, 9am-5pm Mon-Fri, 10am-1pm Sat Oct-Apr), is located in a striking building, the **Altes Rathaus** (1561–79), which boasts a wonderful

GERMANY

BEWITCHING HARZ

The **Harz Mountains** constitute a mini-Alpine region straddling Saxony-Anhalt and Lower Saxony. Here, medieval castles overlook fairy-tale historic towns, while there are caves, mines and numerous hiking trails to explore.

The region's highest – and most famous – mountain is the Brocken, where one-time visitor Johann Wolfgang von Goethe set the 'Walpurgisnacht' chapter of his play *Faust*. His inspiration in turn came from folk tales depicting *Walpurgisnacht*, or *Hexennacht* (witches' night) as an annual witches' coven. Every 30 April to 1 May it's celebrated enthusiastically across the Harz region.

Goslar

Goslar is a truly stunning 1000-year-old city with beautifully preserved half-timbered buildings and an impressive **Markt**. The town's **Kaiserpfalz** is a reconstructed Romanesque 11th-century palace. Just below there's the restored **Domvorhalle**, which displays the 11th-century 'Kaiserstuhl' throne, used by German emperors.

Brocken's summit is an easy day trip from Goslar. Take a bus (810) or train (faster) from Goslar to Bad Harzburg and then a bus (820) to Torfhaus, where the 8km Goetheweg trail begins.

If climbing a mountain is not your thing, a mere wander around town and a stroll along the circumference of town, a green space dotted with bucolic lakes and bits of the old city wall, makes for a fine day.

The **tourist office** (☎ 05321-780 60; www.goslar.de; Markt 7; ☺ 9.15am-6pm Mon-Fri, 9.30am-4pm Sat, to 2pm Sun Apr-Oct, 9.15am-5pm Mon-Fri, 9.30am-2pm Sat Nov-Mar) can help with accommoda-

---

Weser Renaissance stepped gable, topped with the ducal coat of arms and a golden weather vane.

Lying just west of the Rathaus is the 13th-century **Stadtkirche** (☎ 7735; An der Stadtkirche 8; ☺ 10am-6pm Tue-Sat Apr-Dec, to 5pm Jan-Mar, tower 10-11.45am & 2-4.45pm Tue-Sat). You can climb up the 235 steps to the top of the church steeple for a view of the city, or just watch as the city trumpeter climbs the 220 steps to the white tower below the steeple for a trumpet fanfare in all four directions. The spectacle is most entertaining and takes place daily at 9.30am and 5.30pm (sometimes more frequently during the summer months – enquire at the tourist office).

Further west lies the magnificently proportioned wedding-cake **Schloss** (Ducal Palace; ☎ 123 73; Schlossplatz; tours adult/concession €4/3; ☺ tours hourly 11am-3pm Tue-Sun Apr-Oct, 11am & 3pm Tue-Sun, plus 1pm Sat & Sun Nov-Mar). Built in 1292 by Otto Der Strenge (Otto the Strict) as a town fortification, the building was expanded and turned into a residence in 1378. The last duke to live here was Georg Wilhelm (1624–1705), and the last royal was Queen Caroline-Mathilde of Denmark, who died here in 1775.

The Schloss can only be visited on guided tours (in German), but there are explanatory brochures in English for sale. Highlights include the magnificent baroque theatre, the private apartment of Caroline-Mathilde and, above all, the chapel. Its original Gothic form is evident in the high windows and vaulted ceiling, but the rest of the intricate interior is pure Renaissance. The duke's pew was above; the shutters were added later so His Highness could snooze during the three-hour services.

Across from the palace stands Celle's **Kunstmuseum** (Art Museum; ☎ 123 55; www.kunst.celle.de; Schlossplatz 7; adult/concession incl Museum €5/4, Fri free; ☺ 10am-5pm Tue-Fri, to 6pm Sat & Sun), which bills itself as 'the world's first 24-hour museum'. It's claiming this after a €4-million refurbishment created a transparent glass facade that showcases electric-light installations right through the evening – the exterior colour changes from red, orange, purple, gold and blue during the last few hours of darkness. During the day, you can visit the contemporary German paintings, sculptures and objects of collector Robert Simon.

In the older building adjacent, you'll still find the regional history **Bomann Museum** (☎ 125 44; www.bomann-museum.de; Schlossplatz 7; adult/concession incl Kunstmuseum €5/4; ☺ 10am-5pm Tue-Sun, last entry 4.15pm). Here, among other things,

GERMANY

tion, which includes a **DJH Hostel** (☎ 05321-222 40; www.jugendherberge.de; Rammelsbergerstrasse 25; dm €20.50-23.50) and hotels **Die Tanne** (☎ 05321-343 90; www.die-tanne.de; Bäringerstrasse 10; s €40-65, d €65-100) and the fancier **Kaiserworth** (☎ 05321-7090; www.kaiserworth.de; Markt 3; s €80-101, d €122-207, apt €182-252; 🖳). For a special experience, don't miss **Fortezza** (☎ 05321-4803; Thomasstrasse 2; mains €8-17), a Spanish restaurant ensconced in a 16th-century tower attached to the old city wall.

As well as being serviced by buses (www.rbb-bus.de), Goslar is connected by train to Hanover (€15.20, one hour and 10 minutes).

Quedlinburg

The Unesco World Heritage town of Quedlinburg is best known for its spectacular castle district, perched on a 25m-high plateau above its historic half-timbered buildings. Originally established during the reign of Heinrich I (919–936), the present-day Renaissance **Schloss** dates from the 16th century. Its centrepiece is the restored baroque **Blauer Saal** (Blue Hall).

Contact **Quedlinburg-Tourismus** (☎ 03946-905 625; www.quedlinburg.de; Markt 2; 🕑 9.30am-6.30pm Mon-Fri, to 4pm Sat, to 3pm Sun Apr–mid-Oct, 9.30am-5pm Mon-Fri, to 2pm Sat mid-Oct–Mar) for more information. Lodgings include a **DJH hostel** (☎ 03946-811 703; www.jugendherberge.de; Neuendorf 28; dm €16.50-19.50, bedding €3) and the hotels **Pension Zum Altstadtwinkel** (☎ 03946-91 9975; www .altstadtwinkel.de; Hohe Stasse 15; s/d/apt €35/66/120) and **Romantik Hotel Theophano** (☎ 03946-963 00; www.hoteltheophano.de; Markt 13-14; s/d from €69/79).

There are frequent trains to Magdeburg (€13.30, one hour and 10 minutes, hourly).

you can wander through rooms furnished in 19th-century style.

Various train services to Celle run from Hanover (€8.40 to €10.50, 20 to 35 minutes) and Hamburg (€23.80 to €28, one to 1½ hours). The Altstadt is about a 15-minute walk east of the Hauptbahnhof.

Hamelin

☎ 05151 / pop 58,900

If you were to believe *The Pied Piper of Hamelin* fairy tale, this quaint, ornate town on the Weser River ought to be devoid of both rats and children. According to legend, the Pied Piper *(Der Rattenfänger)* was employed by Hamelin's townsfolk to lure their pesky rodents into the river in the 13th century. When they refused to pay him, however, he picked up his flute again and led their kids away.

However, it is a bedtime story, after all; international tourism means the reality is very different. Everywhere you look along Hamelin's cobbled streets are – you guessed it – fake rats and happy young children.

The train station is about 800m east of the centre. To get to **Hameln Tourist Information** (☎ 957 823; www.hameln.de/touristinfo; Diesterallee 1; 🕑 9am-6pm Mon-Fri year-round, 9.30am-4pm Sat, 9.30am-

1pm Sun May-Sep, 9.30am-1pm Sat Oct-Apr) take bus 2, 3, 4, 21, or 33.

The best way to explore is to follow the **Pied Piper trail** – the line of white rats drawn on the pavements. There are information posts at various points. They're in German, but at least you know when to stop to admire the various restored 16th- to 18th-century half-timbered houses.

The detailed Weser Renaissance style dominates the Altstadt – the **Rattenfängerhaus** (Rat Catcher's House; Osterstrasse 28), from 1602, is perhaps the finest example, with its steep and richly decorated gable. Also not to be missed is the **Hochzeitshaus** (1610–17) at the Markt end of Osterstrasse. The **Rattenfänger Glockenspiel** at the far end chimes daily at 9.35am and 11.35am, while a **carousel of Pied Piper figures** twirls at 1.05pm, 3.35pm and 5.35pm.

Between May and September you can watch the **Pied Piper open-air play** at noon on Sunday and the comic musical *Rats* on Wednesday at 4.30pm; both are free and are performed at the Hochzeitshausplatz in the centre of town – contact the tourist office for details.

Frequent S-Bahn trains (S5) head from Hanover to Hamelin (€10.30, 45 minutes). By car, take the B217 to/from Hanover.

GERMANY

VOLKSWAGEN CITY

Volkswagen *is* the Lower Saxon town of **Wolfsburg** – and the huge VW emblem adorning the company's global headquarters (and a factory the size of a small country) won't let you forget it. 'Golfsburg', as it's nicknamed after one of it's most successful models, does a nice sideline in modern architecture. But really, the top reason people come here is to experience the theme park called Autostadt, which tells you everything you ever wanted to know about VW.

Spread across 25 hectares, **Autostadt** (Car City; ☎ 0800-2886 782 38; www.autostadt.de; Stadtbrücke; adult/child/concession/family €15/6/12/38, incl Phaeno adult/child/family €18/11/56; ☺ 9am-6pm) is a celebration of all things Volkswagen. Exhibitions run the gamut of automotive design and engineering, the history of the Beetle and the marketing of individual marques, including VW itself, Audi, Bentley, Lamborghini, Seat and Skoda.

Included in the admission price is the **CarTower Discovery**, a fun glass lift that whisks you up to the 20th floor as if you were an actual car (vehicles are stored inside the towers). At the top you have a sweeping view of the city and complex. Most exciting for wannabe race-car-drivers, there are obstacle courses and safety training (€25 to €28) where you can take an adrenalin-fuelled spin.

The space-age building beside the train station is **Phaeno** (☎ 0180-106 0600; www.phaeno.de; Willy Brandt-Platz 1; adult/child/concession/family €12/7.50/9/26.50, incl Phaeno adult/child/family €18/11/56; ☺ 9am-5pm Mon-Fri, 10am-6pm Sat & Sun), a science centre designed by British-based Iraqi architect Zaha Hadid. Some 250 hands-on exhibits and experiments – wind up your own rocket, watch thermal images of your body – provide hours of fun. It's very physical, but also requires concentration. Instructions and explanations come in German and English.

Wolfsburg's centre lies just southeast of the Hauptbahnhof. Autostadt is north across the train tracks. Head through the 'tunnel' under the Phaeno science centre, and you'll see the footbridge. **Wolfsburg tourist office** (☎ 899 930; www.wolfsburg.de; Willy Brandt-Platz 3; ☺ 9am-6pm Mon-Fri, 10am-3pm Sat & Sun) is in the train station.

Frequent RE/IC/ICE train services arrive from Hanover (€12.80 to €20.50, 30 minutes to one hour) and Berlin (€34 to €42, one to 1¼ hours).

BREMEN

☎ 0421 / pop 547,000

It's a shame the donkey, dog, cat and rooster in Grimm's *Die Bremerstadmusikanten* (Town Musicians of Bremen) never actually made it here – they would have fallen in love with it. This little city is big on charm, from the statues of the famous fairy-tale characters to the jaw-dropping art-nouveau lane to the impressive Markt. On top of that, the waterfront promenade along the Weser River is a relaxing refuge filled with outdoor cafes, and the student district along Ostertorsteinweg knows it's got a good thing going and leaves little to be desired.

ORIENTATION

Head south (straight ahead) from the train station to reach the centre, on banks of the Weser River. The Schlachte waterfront promenade is west of the centre; the Schnoor district lies just east. The student and nightlife district is further east still, along Ostertorsteinweg.

INFORMATION

Internet Café (☎ 168 440; Bahnhofstr 10; per hr €1; ☺ 10am-10pm Mon-Fri, 11am-10pm Sat, noon-10pm Sun)
Tourist office (☎ 01805-101030; www.bremen-tourism.de) Hauptbahnhof (☺ 9am-7pm Mon-Fri, 9.30am-6pm Sat & Sun); branch office (Obernstrasse/Liebfrauenkirchhof; ☺ 10am-6.30pm Mon-Fri, to 4pm Sat & Sun) Sells the ErlebnisCARD (family one/two days costs €7.90/9.90), which offers free public transport and discounts on sights. Also organises daily city tours.

SIGHTS & ACTIVITIES

Bremen's **Markt** is striking, particularly its ornate, gabled **Rathaus** (town hall). In front stands a 13m-tall medieval statue of the knight **Roland**, Bremen's protector. On the building's western side, you'll find a sculpture of the **Town Musicians of Bremen** (1951). Local artist Gerhard Marcks has cast them in their most famous pose, scaring the robbers who invaded their house, with the rooster atop the cat, perched on the dog, on the shoulders of the donkey.

Also on the Markt is the twin-towered **Dom St Petri**, the most interesting – and slightly macabre – feature of which is its **Bleikeller** (Lead Cellar; ☎ 365 0441; adult/concession €1.50/1; ☒ 10am-5pm Mon-Fri, 10am-2pm Sat, noon-5pm Sun Apr-Oct) Here, open coffins reveal eight corpses that have mummified in the dry underground air. The Bleikeller has its own entrance, south of the main cathedral door.

If the Markt is memorable, then nearby **Böttcherstrasse** is unique. It's an opulent art deco alley commissioned by Ludwig Roselius, the inventor of decaffeinated coffee and founder of the company Hag. He later managed to save it from the Nazis, who thought it 'degenerate'. Under the golden relief you enter a world of tall brick houses, shops, galleries, restaurants, a **Glockenspiel** and several museums (which can easily be skipped). If you can,

peek in the back door of 'Haus Atlantis' (aka the Hilton hotel), for its phantasmagorical, multicoloured, glass-walled **spiral staircase**.

The maze of narrow winding alleys known as the **Schnoorviertel** was once the fishermen's quarter and then the red-light district. Now its dollhouse-sized cottages are souvenir shops and restaurants. The cute **Schnoor Teestübchen** (Teashop; Wüste Stätte 1) serves Frisian tea and cakes.

With more time, make a visit to **Beck's Brewery** (☎ 5094 5555; Am Deich 18-19; tours in German & English €8.50; ☒ tours 10am-5pm Tue-Sat, to 3pm Sun, in English 11am Tue-Sun) or the oyster-shaped **Universum Science Center** (☎ 334 60; www.usc-bremen .de; Wiener Strasse 2; adult/concession & child €15.50/10.50, incl special exhibits €18.50/12.50; ☒ 9am-6pm Mon-Fri, 10am-7pm Sat & Sun, last entry 90min before closing).

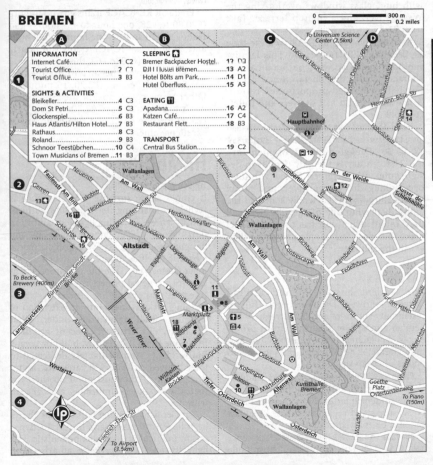

BREMEN

INFORMATION
Internet Café.....................1 C2
Tourist Office.....................2 C2
Tourist Office.....................3 B3

SIGHTS & ACTIVITIES
Bleikeller.........................4 C3
Dom St Petri......................5 C3
Glockenspiel......................6 B3
Haus Atlantis/Hilton Hotel......7 B3
Rathaus...........................8 C3
Roland............................9 B3
Schnoor Teestübchen...........10 C4
Town Musicians of Bremen ...11 B3

SLEEPING 🛏
Bremer Backpacker Hostel......12 D3
DJH Hostel Bremen..............13 A2
Hotel Bölts am Park............14 D1
Hotel Überfluss..................15 A3

EATING 🍴
Apadana..........................16 A2
Katzen Café......................17 C4
Restaurant Flett.................18 B3

TRANSPORT
Central Bus Station.............19 C2

To Universum Science Center (2.5km)

To Beck's Brewery (400m)

To Airport (3.5km)

To Piano (150m)

GERMANY

SLEEPING

Bremer Backpacker Hostel (☎ 223 8057; www.bremer -backpacker-hostel.de; Emil-Waldmannstrasse 5-6; dm €17-23, s €28, bedding €3; ⌨) A friendly place five minutes from the train station, here you'll find simply furnished but spotless rooms spread out over several levels (each floor is named after a continent), a full kitchen and living room.

DJH Hostel Bremen (☎ 163 820; www.jugendher berge.de; Kalkstrasse 6; dm €23.50-26.50, s/d €33.50/38.50; ⌨) Looking like a work of art from the exterior, with a yellow and orange Plexiglas facade and slit rectangular windows, this refurbished building looks more like a museum than a hostel. Comfortable dorms are all en suite, there's a bar–breakfast room with huge glass windows overlooking the Weser River, and a rooftop terrace. Take tram 3 or 5 to Am Brill.

Hotel Bölts am Park (☎ 346 110; www.hotel-boelts .de; Slevogtstrasse 23; s/d €65/95; ⌨) This family-run hotel in a leafy neighbourhood has real character, from the old-fashioned breakfast hall to its well-proportioned rooms. A few singles with hall showers and toilets cost €48.

Hotel Überfluss (☎ 322 860; www.hotel-ueberfluss .com; Langenstrasse 72/Schlachte; s/d/ste €139/184/359; ⌧ ⌨ ⌦) Dragging quaint Bremen into the 21st century is this jaw-dropping design hotel. It's all green-tinted windows overlooking the Weser River, and shiny black bathrooms. The friendly staff and the lobby displaying bits of the old city wall they found when constructing the hotel make this place feel unique and more than worth the splurge.

EATING

The student quarter in and around Ostertorsteinweg, Das Viertel, is full of restaurants and cafes and has a vaguely bohemian atmosphere. The waterfront promenade, Schlachte, is more expensive and mainstream. The Marktplatz is home to oodles of cheap snack stands.

Piano (☎ 785 46; Fehrfeld 64; mains €5.50-10.50) One of the most enduringly popular cafes in the student quarter, Piano serves pizza, pasta, steaks and vegie casseroles. Breakfast can also be enjoyed until 4pm.

Apadana (☎ 577 5997; Heinkenstrasse & Faulenstrasse; mains €6.50-13.50) This family-run, hospitable Persian restaurant serves lovingly prepared, traditional fare in a simple, quiet space.

Restaurant Flett (☎ 320 995; Böttcherstrasse 3-5; mains €8-16) Despite all the tourists, this is the best place in Bremen to try local specialities like *Labskaus* (a hash of beef or pork with potatoes, onion and herring) or *Knipp* (fried hash and oats).

Katzen Café (☎ 326 621; Schnoor 38; mains €9-17.50) This Moulin Rouge–style restaurant opens out into a rear sunken terrace bedecked with flowers. The menu runs the gamut from Alsatian to Norwegian, with seafood a strong theme.

GETTING THERE & AROUND

Flights from **Bremen airport** (BRE: www.airport -bremen.de) include low-cost carrier **Air Berlin** (www.airberlin.com).

Frequent RE/IC/ICE trains go to Hamburg (€20.80 to €28, one hour to 1¼ hours) and Hanover (€21 to €30, one hour to one hour and 20 minutes); IC/ICE trains run hourly from Cologne (€60 to €62, three hours).

Tram 6 leaves the airport frequently, heading to the centre (€2.20, 16 minutes). Other trams cover most of the city. Single bus/tram tickets cost €2.20, a day pass (€5.90 for one adult and two children) is excellent value.

HAMBURG

☎ 040 / pop 1.76 million

It comes as no surprise that Hamburg is stylishly expanding itself by 40% without batting an eyelid – this is where ambition flows through the ubiquitous waterways and designer-clad residents cycle to their media jobs with a self-assurance unmatched by any other German city. The site of Europe's largest urban renewal project is a never-ending forest of cranes that are efficiently transforming old city docks into an extension of the city – it all makes you wonder 'What *can't* this city achieve?' Decent weather, that's one thing it can't buy, build or create. But residents are passionately dedicated to their beloved city and will rarely fret about drizzly skies – they just open up their artistically designed umbrellas and get on with it.

But Germany's leading port city has always been forward-thinking and liberal. Its dynamism, multiculturalism and hedonistic redlight district, the *Reeperbahn*, all arise from its maritime history. Joining the Hanseatic League trading bloc in the Middle Ages, Hamburg has been enthusiastically doing business with the rest of the world ever since. In the 1960s it nurtured the musical talent of the Beatles. Nowadays, it's also a media capital and the wealthiest city in Germany.

ORIENTATION

The Hauptbahnhof is quite central, near the Binnenalster and Aussenalster (Inner and Outer Alster Lakes); the Speicherstadt and port lie south/southwest of these, on the Elbe River. The nightlife districts of St Pauli (containing the *Reeperbahn*) and the Schanzenviertel are further west. The city's sprawl means using public transport is necessary.

INFORMATION

EMERGENCY
Police station Hauptbahnhof (Kirchenallee exit); St Pauli (Davidwache, Spielbudenplatz 31; Ⓜ Reeperbahn)

INTERNET ACCESS
Internet Café (☎ 2800 3898; Adenauerallee 10; per hr €1.50; Ⓨ 10am-midnight Mon-Sat, to 1pm Sun; Ⓜ Hauptbahnhof)
Tele-Time (☎ 4131 4730; Schulterblatt 39; per hr €2; Ⓨ 10am-midnight; Ⓜ Feldstrasse or Sternschanze) Behind the hookah lounge.

POST
Main post office (☎ 01802-3333; Dammtorstrasse 14; Ⓨ 8.30am-6pm Mon-Fri, 9am-noon Sat; Ⓜ Jungfernstieg)
Post office (☎ 01802-3333; Mönckebergstrasse 7; Ⓨ 9am-7pm Mon-Fri, to 3pm Sat; Ⓜ Hauptbahnhof)

TOURIST INFORMATION
Hamburg Tourismus Hauptbahnhof (☎ information 3005 1200, hotel bookings 3005 1300; www.hamburg -tourismus.de; Kirchenallee exit; Ⓨ 8am-9pm Mon-Sat, 10am-6pm Sun); Landungsbrücken (btwn piers 4 & 5; Ⓨ 8am-6pm Apr-Oct, 10am-6pm Nov-Mar; Ⓜ Landungsbrücken); airport (☎ 5075 1010; Ⓨ 6am-11pm) Sells the Hamburg Card (€9/19/35 for one/three/five days) Free public transport and museum discounts.

DANGERS & ANNOYANCES

Although safe, Hamburg contains several red-light districts around the train station and *Reeperbahn*. The Hansaplatz in St Georg can feel a bit dicey after dark. Fortunately, there's a strong police presence in these areas.

SIGHTS & ACTIVITIES
Old Town

Hamburg's medieval **Rathaus** (☎ 4283 120 10; tours adult/child €3/.50, Ⓨ tours in English hourly 10.15am-3.15pm Mon-Thu, to 1.15pm Fri, to 5.15pm Sat, to 4.15 Sun; Ⓜ Rathausmarkt or Jungfernstieg) is one of Europe's most opulent. North of here, you can wander through the **Alsterarkaden**, the Renaissance-style arcades sheltering shops and cafes alongside a canal or 'fleet'.

For many visitors, however, the city's most memorable building is south in the Merchants' District. The 1920s, brown-brick **Chile Haus** (cnr Burchardstrasse & Johanniswall; Ⓜ Mönckebergstrasse/ Messberg) is shaped like an ocean liner, with remarkable curved walls meeting in the shape of a ship's bow and staggered balconies that look like decks.

Alster Lakes

A cruise on the Binnenalster and Aussenalster is one of the best ways to appreciate the elegant side of the city. **ATG Alster-Touristik** (☎ 3574 2419; www.alstertouristik.de; 2hr trip adult/child €10/5; Ⓨ Apr-Oct; Ⓜ Jungfernstieg) is a good bet. The company also offers 'fleet' tours and winter tours through the icy waters.

Better yet, hire your own rowboat or canoe. Opposite the Atlantic Hotel you'll find **Segelschule Pieper** (☎ 247 578; www.segel schule-pieper.de; An der Alster; per hr from €13; Ⓨ Apr-Oct; Ⓜ Hauptbahnhof).

Speicherstadt & Harbour

The beautiful red-brick, neo-Gothic warehouses lining the Elbe archipelago south of the Altstadt once stored exotic goods from around the world. Now the so-called **Speicherstadt** (Ⓜ Messberg/Baumwall) is a popular sightseeing attraction. It's best appreciated by simply wandering through its streets or taking a Barkassen boat up its canals. **Kapitän Prüsse** (☎ 313 130; www.kapitaen-pruesse.de; Landungsbrücke No 3; adult/child from €10/5) offers regular Speicherstadt tours, leaving from the port. Other Barkassen operators simply tout for business opposite the archipelago.

Another way to see the Speicherstadt is from the **High-Flyer Hot Air Balloon** (☎ 3008 6968; www.highflyer-hamburg.de; per 15min €15; Ⓨ 10am-midnight, to 10pm winter, weather permitting) moored nearby.

The Speicherstadt merges into the **HafenCity**, an area where the old docks are being transformed into a 155 hectare extension of the city –

GERMANY

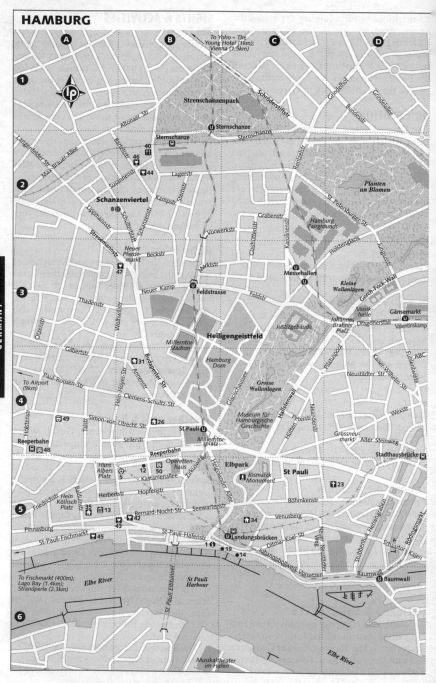

HAMBURG

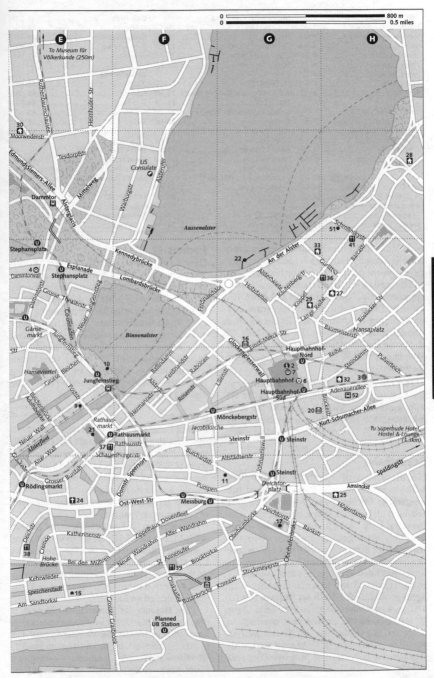

what looks like a never-ending construction zone is actually Europe's largest inner-city development project; when finished, the area will house a new U-Bahn station, a university, approximately 5500 apartments and more. It's estimated that it will extend the centre city of Hamburg by about 40%. Get details and ponder models detailing the magnitude of the project at the **HafenCity InfoCenter** (☎ 3690 1799; Am Sandtorkai 30; 🕙 10am-6pm Tue-Sun, to 8pm Thu May-Sep).

Port and Elbe River cruises start in summer at the St Pauli Landungsbrücken. **Hadag** (☎ 311 7070; www.hadag.de; Brücke 2; 1hr harbour trip adult/child from €9/4.50) offers some of the best deals and cruises.

Reeperbahn

No discussion of Hamburg is complete without mentioning St Pauli, home of the **Reeperbahn** (Ⓜ Reeperbahn), Europe's biggest red-light district. Sex shops, peep shows, dim bars and strip clubs line the streets, which generally start getting crowded with the masses after 8pm or 9pm. This is also where the notorious **Herbertstrasse** is located (a block-long street lined with brothels that's off-limits to men under 18 and to female visitors of all ages) as well as the **Erotic Art Museum** (☎ 317 4757; www.eroticartmuseum.de; Bernhard-Nocht-Strasse 69; adult/concession €8/5; 🕙 noon-10pm, to midnight Fri & Sat), and the **Condomerie** (☎ 319 3100; www.con domerie.de; Spielbudenplatz 18; 🕙 noon-midnight), with its extensive collection of prophylactics and sex toys.

Fischmarkt

Here's the perfect excuse to stay up all Saturday night. Every Sunday between 5am and 10am, curious tourists join locals of every age and walk of life at the famous Fischmarkt in St Pauli. The market has been running since 1703, and its undisputed stars are the boisterous *Marktschreier* (market criers) who hawk their wares at full volume. Live bands also entertainingly crank out cover versions of ancient German pop songs in the adjoining *Fischauktionshalle* (Fish Auction Hall). Take bus 112 to Hafentreppe.

Museums

Four of Hamburg's dozens of museums stand out. The **Hamburger Kunsthalle** (☎ 428 131 200; www.hamburger-kunsthalle.de; Glockengiesserwall; adult/concession €8.50/5; 🕙 10am-6pm Tue, Wed & Fri-Sun, to 9pm Thu; Ⓜ Hauptbahnhof) consists of two buildings – an old one housing old masters and 19th-century art, and a new white concrete cube of contemporary works.

The **Museum für Kunst und Gewerbe** (Museum of Arts & Crafts; ☎ 428 542 732; www.mkg-hamburg.de; Steintorplatz 1; adult/concession €8/5, from 5pm Tue, Wed & Thu €5; 🕙 11am-6pm Tue, Fri-Sun, to 9pm Wed & Thu; Ⓜ Hauptbahnhof) offers something for everyone with its period rooms, photography, posters, graphic design and textiles.

The **Museum für Völkerkunde** (Museum of Ethnology; ☎ 01805-308 888; www.voelkerkundemuseum .com; Rothenbaumchaussee 64; admission €5, after 4pm Fri free; 🕙 10am-6pm Tue, Wed & Fri-Sun, to 9pm Thu; Ⓜ Hallerstrasse or Dammtor) demonstrates sea-going Hamburg's acute awareness and aims to promote respect of the world and its cultures. You'll be awestruck by the giant statues from Papua New Guinea at the top of the stairs.

The **International Maritime Museum** (☎ 300 93 300; www.internationales-maritimes-museum.de; Koreastrasse 1; adult/concession €10/7; ☒ 10am-6pm Tue, Wed & Fri-Sun, to 8pm Thu; Ⓜ Messberg) is the newest addition to Hamburg's **HafenCity** (p279). This nine-floor, enormous space examines 3000 years of maritime history through displays of model ships, naval paintings, navigation tools and educational exhibits explaining the seas and its tides and currents. Added bonus: sweeping views of the HafenCity development project greet you at every window.

Churches

From the tower of the **St Michaeliskirche** (tower adult/concession €3/1.50; ☒ 10am-6pm Apr-Oct, to 5pm Nov-Mar; Ⓜ Stadthausbrücke), or 'Der Michel' as it's commonly called, you have panoramic views.

The WWII-damaged **St-Nikolai-Kirche** (Ost-West-Strasse; adult/child €3.50/2; ☒ 10.30am-5.30pm; Ⓜ Rödingsmarkt) is now an antiwar memorial, with some chilling photos of the then-bombed-out city.

SLEEPING
Budget

A & O City Hauptbahnhof Hostel(☎ 644 2104 5600; www .aohostel.com; Amsinckstrasse 6-10; dm €13-16, s/d from €29/32, bedding €3; ☒ ; Ⓜ Hauptbahnhof) New, clean, but rather sterile and characterless, this huge hostel is nevertheless excellent value and convenient. Breakfast costs €5; A & O also offers bike hire (€10 per day).

ourpick Superbude Hotel, Hostel & Lounge (☎ 380 8780, www.superbude.de; Spaldingstrasse 152; dm €16-22, d €59-89, q €91-133; ☒ ; Ⓜ Berliner Tor) This new addition near St Georg is just about the snazziest hotel-hostel we've ever seen. Housed in a former printer, the modern, spacious dorms and rooms feel like trendy loft spaces. Quirky touches include plungers used as wall 'hooks', a metallic polka-dot entrance, slate stone flooring, cow-hide rugs and two entertainment rooms (one with Nintendo, Wii and table football; the other is a mini cinema). Breakfast is €7.

Jugendherberge-Auf dem Stintfang (☎ 313 488; www.jugendherberge.de; Alfred-Wegener-Weg 5; dm €19.90-22.70, d €59; ☒ ; Ⓜ Landungsbrücken) Modern, clean and convenient (head out of the U-Bahn station, up the steps to the massive modern complex at the top of the hill), this DJH hostel

overlooks the Elbe River and the harbour. With lots of large, noisy school groups, however, it's very keen on rules, and you're locked out part of the day.

Kogge (☎ 312 872; www.kogge-hamburg.de; Bernhard-Nocht-Strasse 59; s/d/q with shared bathroom from €29.50/49.50/78; Ⓜ Landungsbrücken or Reeperbahn; ☒) This friendly, fun rock 'n' roll bar and hotel sits on a quite street around the corner from the noisy *Reeperbahn* territory; themed rooms include the rooms named 'Bollywood', 'Punk Royal', 'Disco Dream' and all share shower and toilet facilities. Popular with musicians and perfect for travellers planning to party all night and sleep until late (standard check out is 2pm).

Hotel Annenhof (☎ 243 426; www.hotelannenhof .de; Lange Reihe 23; s/d from €40/65; Ⓜ Hauptbahnhof) The Annenhof's attractive, cheerful rooms have polished wooden floorboards and clean, simple furnishings. There's no breakfast but plenty of cafes nearby.

Midrange & Top End

Hotel Village (☎ 480 6490; www.hotel-village.de; Steindamm 4; s €50-75, d €65-100; Ⓜ Hauptbahnhof; ☒) A former bordello going straight, it has boudoirs that feature various mixes of red velvet, gold flock wallpaper, leopard prints and sometimes even blue-neon-lit bathrooms or mirrors above the bed – don't be surprised if you stumble upon a photo shoot during your stay. It's a fun, functional space a stone's throw from the main train station.

Hotel Fresena (☎ 410 4892; www.hotelfresena .de; Moorweidenstrasse 34; s €65-85, d €88; Ⓜ Dammtor; ☒) Palatial, clean, modern rooms, high ceilings, African statues and cool theatre photographs give this place character without clutter. If it's full, the building houses four other pensions and the friendly staff will help you find a room elsewhere. Breakfast is €9.

Hotel Wedina (☎ 280 8900; www.wedina.de; Gurlittstrasse 23; s €70-148, d €118-168; Ⓜ Hauptbahnhof) You might find a novel instead of a chocolate on your pillow at Wedina, a hotel that's a must for bookworms and literary groupies. Jonathan Franzen, Vladimir Nabokov and JK Rowling are just some of the authors who've stayed and left behind signed books. Young and friendly, the hotel is spread over four buildings, offering a choice of traditional decor in the main red building or modern, urban living in its green, blue and yellow houses. The hotel also offers bike hire (€8 per day).

CRAZY ABOUT EEL

Tired of wurst and dumplings? Well, you're in a port city now so specialities generally involve seafood and definitely veer away from stereotypical German fare. *Labskaus* is a dish of boiled marinated beef put through the grinder with mashed potatoes and herring and served with a fried egg, red beets and pickles. Or perhaps you'd prefer *Aalsuppe* (eel soup) spiced with dried fruit, ham, vegetables and herbs? **Deichgraf** (☎ 364 208; www.deichgraf-hamburg.de; Deichstrasse 23; mains €17-27; ☻ lunch Mon-Sat, dinner Sat) is one leading local restaurant that can acquaint you with these and other local dishes.

Hotel St Annen (☎ 317 7130; www.hotel-st-annen.de; Annenstrasse 5; s €78-98, d €88-139; M St Pauli or Feldstrasse; 💻) An oasis of middle-class comfort tucked away in one of the few quiet streets between the *Reeperbahn* and Schanzenviertel, this is a favourite with businesspeople and mainstream travellers for its stylish modern rooms and its pleasant back garden.

YoHo – The Young Hotel (☎ 284 1910; www.yoho-hamburg.de; Moorkamp 5; s/d €85/99, under 26yr €62/75; M Schlumpf; 💻) Tasteful with retro chairs, simple white bedspreads and a minimalist feel. Breakfast costs €12. Excellent value and immensely popular – book early.

Galerie-Hotel Sarah Petersen (☎ 249 826, 0173 200 0746; www.galerie-hotel-sarah-petersen.de; Lange Reihe 50; s €86-155, d €109-165; M Hauptbahnhof; ✂ 💻) Sarah Petersen's professional paintings decorate the walls, and the rooms mix contemporary to 1950s French to classic Biedermeier styles. Some rooms are like suites, with rooftop terraces and separate living areas, but those with external bathrooms are much cheaper (single/double €49/69).

East (☎ 309 933; www.east-hamburg.de; Simon-von-Utrecht-Strasse 31; d €155-215, ste €250-420, apt €150-550; M St Pauli) Pillars, walls and lamps emulate organic forms in the public areas of this warm, richly decorated design hotel. Floors are themed by plants and spices.

George (☎ 280 0300; www.thegeorge-hotel.de; Barcastrasse 3; r from €159; M Hauptbahnhof; ✂) New design hotel decorated in a 'Brittish style' reminiscent of a traditional London gentlemen's club in the heart of hopping St Georg.

EATING

frank und frei (☎ 430 0573; Schanzenstrasse 93; mains €4-15; M Sternschanze) Big, bustling and laid-back restaurant-pub offering simple German fare, salads and pastas with brick walls, wooden booths, shiny pillars and a stylish curved wood bar. A great place to unwind with a beer, a bite or a full meal.

Café Koppel (☎ 249 235; Lange Reihe 66; dishes €4.50-9) Set back from busy Lange Reihe, with a garden in summer, this largely vegie cafe is a refined oasis in an airy space housing galleries and artists workshops. The menu includes great breakfasts, lots of salads, stews, jacket potatoes, curries and pasta.

Fleetschlösschen (☎ 3039 3210; Brooktorkai 17; snacks €7-10; ☻ 8am-8pm Mon-Fri, 11am-6pm Sat & Sun; M Messburg) This former customs post overlooks a Speicherstadt canal and the HafenCity development and has a narrow, steel spiral staircase to the toilets. There's barely room for 20 inside, but its several outdoor seating areas are brilliant in sunny weather.

Geel Haus (☎ 280 3660; Koppel 76; €8-15; ☻ from 6pm; M Hauptbahnhof) A casual, homey neighbourhood favourite tucked away on a quiet street in St Georg with an emphasis on Austrian and German fare, plus plenty of vegie options.

Café Paris (☎ 3252 7777; Rathausstrasse 4; mains €9-17; ☻ from 9am Mon-Fri, from 10am Sat & Sun; M Rathausmarkt) At this stalwart in the city centre, be sure to admire the spectacular maritime-and-industry-themed ceiling murals and tiles. On weekends breakfast is served until 4pm in this bustling French brasserie.

Vienna (☎ 439 9182; Fettstrasse 2; mains €10.50-19; ☻ bistro service from 2pm, meals from 7pm Tue-Sun) Even though it looks like a French country-cottage restaurant, particularly with the overgrown garden hiding its outdoor terrace, the schnitzels, venison and fish are distinctly authentic.

The **Schanzenviertel** (M Feldstrasse/Schanzenstern) swarms with cheap eateries; try **Schulterblatt** for Portuguese outlets or **Susanenstrasse** for Asian and Turkish. Be aware that many fish restaurants around the Landungsbrücken are over-rated and touristy. **St Georg's** Lange Reihe (M Hauptbahnhof) offers many character-full eating spots to suit every budget, and there is a seemingly endless selection of simple but quality, high-value sushi joints all over town.

DRINKING & ENTERTAINMENT

Zoë 2 (Neuer Pferdemarkt 17; ☺ from noon; Ⓜ Feldstrasse) The sister living room to the original Zoë in Berlin (which, sadly, has closed), this one is alive and kicking with battered sofas, rough-hewn walls and old lampshades.

ourpick **Südhang** (☎ 4309 9099; www.suedhang -hamburg.de; Susannenstrasse 29; ☺ from noon Mon-Sat, from 4pm Sun; Ⓜ Sternschanze) Walk through the shoe store, head up the stairs and enter this friendly wine bar with polished mahogany tables and low-lighting perched right above the hustle of the neighbourhood.

20up (☎ 311 190; Bernard-Nocht Strasse 97; ☺ from 6pm; Ⓜ Reeperbahn) Sink in to the plush chairs and absorb the sweeping view of Hamburg through 7m-high floor-to-ceiling windows on the 20th floor of the Empire Hotel.

Elbwerk (☎ 6579 1420; Bernard-Nocht Strasse 68; ☺ from 11am; Ⓜ Landungsbrücken) Although this swanky cafe-lounge serves lite bites, this place is best for a cocktail at sunset and to admire its exceptional view over the Elbe River.

Fritz Bauch (☎ 430 0194; Bartelstrasse 6; ☺ from 5pm; Ⓜ Sternschanze) A down-to-earth neighbourhood bar in the middle of the Schanzenviertel with yellow and pale pink walls, wooden arched ceilings, basic, no-nonsense drinks and hopping music.

Meanie Bar/Molotow Club (☎ 310 845; www .molotowclub.com; Spielbudenplatz 5; ☺ from 6pm; Ⓜ Reeperbahn) One of the few venues along the *Reeperbahn* with real local cred, retro Meanie Bar sits above the Molotow Club, where an independent-music scene thrives.

Grosse Freiheit 36/Kaiserkeller (☎ 3177 7811; Grosse Freiheit 36; ☺ from 10pm Tue-Sat; Ⓜ Reeperbahn) Wedged between live-sex theatres and peep shows, this is popular for live rock and pop, particularly as the Beatles played in the basement Kaiserkeller.

China Lounge (☎ 3197 6622; www.china-lounge.de; Nobistor 14; ☺ from 11pm Wed-Fri, Sat, from 10pm Thu; Ⓜ Reeperbahn) This leading club has four areas playing electro, house, hip hop and R&B – the main floor is under a huge laughing Buddha. On Thursdays students pay no cover charge.

GETTING THERE & AWAY

Air

Hamburg's **airport** (HAM: www.flughafen-hamburg .de) has frequent flights to domestic and European cities, including on low-cost carrier **Air Berlin** (www.airberlin.com).

For flights to/from Ryanair's so-called 'Hamburg-Lübeck' see p288.

Bus

The **Zentral Omnibus Busbahnhof** (ZOB, central bus station; ☎ 247 5765; www.zob-hamburg.de; Adenauer Allee 78) is most popular for services to central and eastern Europe. **Eurolines** (☎ 4024 7106; www.eurolines.com) has buses to Prague (€64) and Vilnius (€84).

Car & Motorcycle

The A1 (Bremen–Lübeck) and A7 (Hanover–Kiel) cross south of the Elbe River.

Train

When reading train timetables, remember that there are two main train stations: Hamburg Hauptbahnhof and Hamburg-Altona. There are frequent RE/RB trains to Lübeck (€11.50, 45 minutes), as well as various services to Hanover (€35 to €40, 1¼ to 1½ hours) and Bremen (€20.80 to €28, one to 1¼ hours). In addition there are EC/ICE trains to Berlin (€65, 1½ to two hours), Cologne (€78, four hours) and Munich (€127, 5½ to six hours) as well as EC trains to Copenhagen (€78.80, 4¾ hours).

LIFE'S A BEACH BAR

Following the trend in Paris, Zürich and Berlin, beach bars in Hamburg are *the* place to be in the summer. The city beach season kicks off around April and lasts until at least September, as patrons come to drink, listen to music, dance and generally hang out on the waterfront. A few leading venues, open daily, include **Lago Bay** (www.lago.cc, in German; Grosse Elbstrasse 150; Ⓜ Königstrasse), a stylish retreat where you can actually swim while free exercise classes will help you keep fit, er, between cocktails. **StrandPauli** (www.strandpauli.de, in German; St-Pauli Hafenstrasse 84; bus 112) is a more laid-back stretch of sand with a youthful feel, and **Strandperle** (www.strandperle-hamburg.de, in German; Övelgönne 1; bus 112) is the original Hamburg beach bar. Little more than a kiosk, but the people-watching is tops, as patrons linger over the newspaper with a drink or a coffee – think of it as a sandy, alfresco cafe-lounge.

THE TREND COKE

Created in response to a deep dissatisfaction with 'mainstream cola', fritz-cola was concocted in 2002 by a few anti-establishment blokes (Lorenz Hampl and Mirco Wiegert) in Hamburg. Their edge over the corporate behemoths of the soda world? Caffeine. Each bottle of fritz-cola contains the maximum amount of caffeine allowed by German law (25mg per 100ml). The result is a soda with a punch, served only in small bottles, that tastes vaguely less sweet than the competition. The soda is easy to find – two mega-grinning faces (hyper from the hefty dose of caffeine, perhaps?) flank every 0.33L bottle and often pop up in corner stores in Hamburg and other major German cities. Recently, fritz-cola has branched out to include variations like melon lemonade and carbonated apple juice, but it's the original that dominates the shelves and enjoys enormous popularity. For the full buzz, check out www.fritz-cola.de.

GETTING AROUND
To/From the Airport
The **Airport Express** (☎ 227 1060; www.jasper-hamburg.de) runs between the Hauptbahnhof and airport (€5, 25 minutes, every 10 to 20 minutes from 5.45am to midnight). You can also take the U1 or S1 to Ohlsdorf, then change to bus 110.

Bicycle
Hamburg is a fantastic place to explore by bike, with extensive cycle lanes (many along the water). For bike hire, try **Fahrradladen St Georg** (☎ 243 908; Schmilinskystrasse 6; per day €10).

Public Transport
There is an integrated system of buses, U-Bahn and S-Bahn trains. Day tickets, bought from machines before boarding, cost €6, or €5.10 after 9am. From midnight to dawn the night-bus network takes over from the trains, converging on the main metropolitan bus station at Rathausmarkt.

SCHLESWIG-HOLSTEIN

Sandwiched between the North and Baltic Seas, Schleswig-Holstein is Germany's answer to the Côte d'Azur. Of course, the weather here often makes it a pretty funny sort of answer, as dark clouds and strong winds whip in across the flat peninsula. Still, people flock to the beaches on the coasts, and the countryside in between has a stark beauty.

LÜBECK
☎ 0451 / pop 213,800
Two pointed cylindrical towers of Lübeck's Holstentor (gate) greet you upon arrival – if you think they're a tad crooked, you're not

seeing things: they lean towards each other across the stepped gable that joins them. Right behind them, the streets are lined with medieval merchants' homes and spired churches forming the city's so-called 'crown'. It's hardly surprising that this 12th-century gem is on Unesco's World Heritage List.

Orientation & Information
Lübeck's Old Town is set on an island ringed by the canalised Trave River, a 10-minute walk east of the Hauptbahnhof. Leaving the station, head through the bus station and veer left along Hansestrasse. The tourist office is just across the Puppenbrücke (Doll Bridge), near the Holstentor. Staff at the **Lübeck Travemünde Tourismus** (☎ 01805 882 233; www.lubeck-tourism.de; Holstentorplatz 1; ☯ 10am-6pm Apr-Dec, 11am-7pm Tue-Sun Jan-Mar) can organise city tours and sell discount cards.

Sights
The impossibly cute city gate or **Holstentor** (☎ 122 4129; adult/concession €5/2.50; ☯ 10am-5pm Tue-Sun Apr-Sep, to 4pm Tue-Sun Oct-Mar) serves as Lübeck's museum as well as its symbol. The six gabled brick buildings east of the Holstentor are the **Salzspeicher**, once used to store the salt from Lüneburg that was pivotal to Lübeck's Hanseatic trade.

Behind these warehouses, the Trave River forms a moat around the Old Town, and if you do one thing in Lübeck in summer, it should be a boat tour. From April to September, **Maak-Linie** (☎ 706 3859; www.maak-linie.de) and **Quandt-Linie** (☎ 777 99; www.quandt-linie.de) depart regularly from either side of the Holstentorbrücke. Prices are €8/4/6.50 per adult/child/student.

Each of Lübeck's churches offers something different. The shattered bells of the

Marienkirche (Schüsselbuden 13; ☉ 10am-6pm Apr-Oct, to 5pm Tue-Sun Nov-Mar) still lie on the floor where they fell after a bombing raid. There's also a little devil sculpture outside, with an amusing fairy tale (in English). The tower lift in the **Petrikirche** (☎ 397 730; Schüsselbuden 13; www.st-petri -luebeck.de, in German; adult/concession €3/2; ☉ 9am-9pm Apr-Sep, 10am-7pm Oct-Mar) affords superb views.

The **Rathaus** (town hall; ☎ 122 1005; Breite Strasse 64; adult/concession €4/2; ☉ tours 11am, noon & 3pm Mon-Fri) is ornate, but all the tours are in German. If you have a sweet tooth, head across the street to **JG Niederegger shop and cafe** (Breite Strasse 89) and pick up a chocolate-coated marzipan treat, a gift, or both.

Lübeck has some 90 lovely *Gänge* (walkways) and *Höfe* (courtyards) tucked away behind its main streets, the most famous being the **Füchtingshof** (Glockengiesserstrasse 25; ☉ 9am-noon & 3-6pm); renovations on the delightful **Glandorps Gang** (Glockengiesserstrasse 41-51) should be finished by the time you read this.

A few steps further, fans of *The Tin Drum* (*Die Blechtrommel*) shouldn't miss the **Günter Grass-Haus** (☎ 122 4192; www.guenter-grass-haus.de; Glockengiesserstrasse 21; adult/concession €5/2.50, 'Kombi' card with Buddenbrookhaus €7/4; ☉ 10am-5pm Apr-Dec, 11am-5pm Jan-Mar), which includes a fine collection of manuscripts and sculptures. Fellow Nobel Prize–winning author Thomas Mann (*Death in Venice*) was born in Lübeck and he's commemorated in the award-winning **Buddenbrookhaus** (☎ 122 4190; www.buddenbrookhaus .de; Mengstrasse 4; adult/concession €5/2.50; 'Kombi' card with Buddenbrookhaus €7/4; ☉ 10am-6pm Apr-Dec, 11am-5pm Jan-Mar).

For children, there's a fantastic **Theater Figuren Museum** (☎ 786 26; www.tfm-luebeck.com; Am Kolk 14; adult/child/concession €4/1.50/3; ☉ 10am-6pm). It's a private collection of some 1200 puppets, props, posters and more, from Europe, Asia and Africa. The adjoining cafe is also a good place to refuel. Alternatively, ask the tourist office about the nearby seaside resort of **Travemünde**.

Sleeping

DJH Hostel Vor dem Burgtor (☎ 334 33; www.jugend herberge.de; Am Gertrudenkirchhof 4; dm €16.40-18.40; ☐) Those fussier about their furnishings might prefer this huge, modern place; however, it's popular with school groups, and outside the Old Town – just.

DJH Hostel Altstadt (☎ 702 0399; www.jugendher berge.de; Mengstrasse 33; dm €18.70-21.70) Standard hostel in the Old Town – it isn't particularly new, but it's cosy and central.

Hotel zur Alten Stadtmauer (☎ 737 02; www.ho telstadtmauer.de; An der Mauer 57; s/d with shared bathroom from €37/60, with private bathroom €42/70) With pine furniture and splashes of red or yellow, this simple, 25-room hotel is bright and cheerful. The wooden flooring means sound carries, but customers tend not to be quieter types. Back rooms overlook the river.

Hotel Lindenhof (☎ 872 100; www.lindenhof-lue beck.de; Lindenstrasse 1a; s €64-95, d €80-135, f €100-165, ste €120-160; ☐) Its rooms are businesslike and small, but a healthy breakfast buffet, friendly service and little extras (free biscuits, newspapers, and a 6am to midnight snack service) propel the Lindenhof into a superior league.

Hotel Jensen (☎ 702 490; www.hotel-jensen.de; An der Obertrave 4-5; s €75-90, d €87-115, ste €135-179; ☐) Classic and romantic, this old *Patrizierhaus* (mansion house) is conveniently located facing the Salzspeicher across the Trave River. Its seafood restaurant, Yachtzimmer, is also excellent.

Two very cheap and basic places are **Sleep-Inn** (☎ 719 20; www.cvjm-luebeck.de; Grosse Petersgrube 11; dm €12.50) and the **Hotel Am Dom** (☎ 399 9430; www.cvjm-luebeck.de; Dankwartsgrube 43; s/d €36/68).

Eating

Suppentopf (☎ 400 8136; Fleischerstrasse 36; soups €3.50; ☉ 11am-4pm Mon-Fri) It's always bustling here, so join Lübeck's office workers for a stand-up lunch of delicious, often spicy, soup.

Tlpasa (☎ 706 0451; Schlumacherstrasse 12-14; mains €5-16) Pizzas, curries and other budget meals are served below the faux caveman frescos of animals and Australian Aboriginal dot paintings.

Schiffergesellschaft (☎ 767 76; www.schifferges ellschaft.de; Breite Strasse 2; mains €10.50-23) The fact it's a tourist magnet can't detract from this 500-year-old guildhall's thrilling atmosphere. Seafood-heavy Frisian specialities and local beer are the way to go here.

Markgraf (☎ 706 0343; www.markgraf-luebeck.de, in German; Fischergrube 18; mains €12.50-19.50; ☉ dinner Tue-Sun) This historic restaurant is the epitome of elegance, with white tablecloths and silverware laid out under the chandeliers and black ceiling beams of this 14th-century house. The cuisine displays Mediterranean and Asian influences.

GERMANY

Getting There & Away

Lübeck's **airport** (LBC; www.flughafen-luebeck.de) is linked to London by budget carriers **Ryanair** (www.ryanair.com) and **easyJet** (www.easyjet.com).

To head into town, catch scheduled bus 6 to the Hauptbahnhof and the neighbouring central bus station (one way €2.40, 20 minutes). If you're flying on Ryanair to 'Hamburg-Lübeck' there are synchronised shuttle buses to Hamburg (one way €8, 1¼ hours).

Trains head to Hamburg at least hourly (€11.50, 45 minutes).

NORTH FRISIAN ISLANDS

Part playground of the rich and famous, part nature-lovers' utopia, the grass-covered dunes, ochre cliffs, traditional reed-thatched cottages and just-off-the-boat seafood of Germany's North Frisian Islands provide a restorative escape from the everyday. Pondering the sunset on a windy stretch of beach, the gusts of wind blow away every inch of whatever may plague you on the mainland. Sylt, the largest island of the Frisian archipelago, is the northernmost point in the country and sees the most action. Quieter and more remote, Amrum and Föhr lie just to the south and east.

SYLT

☎ 04651 / pop 21,200

Sylt can't be labelled without scratching your head. Downtown Westerland, the largest town, is largely filled with high-rises that obscure views of the beach, although some pretty thatched houses and simple brick homes dot the outskirts. Additionally, some of the **world's best windsurfing** is also off this shore.

Further north, pretty Kampen is largely where the wealth is most obvious, with ritzy restaurants and celebrity guests. But it's also home to the 52.5m-tall, ochre-coloured **Uwe Dune**. Climb the wooden steps to the top for a stunning 360-degree view.

Towards List, on the island's northern tip, is the popular **Wanderdünengebiet**, where people hike between grass-covered dunes. Or try List's **beach-side sauna**.

Inside the Westerland train station, there's an **information pavilion** (☎ 846 1029; ☺ 9am-4pm, reduced hr winter) or try **Westerland Tourism**

(☎ 9980, 0180 550 9980; www.westerland.de; ☺ 9am-5pm Mon-Sat, 11am to 2pm Sun).

Accommodation is at a premium in summer, but ask the tourist office about cheaper private rooms. Significant discounts can be found outside the summer months. Beware that credit cards are not always accepted – even in some midrange hotels. A small *Kurtaxe*, or resort tax, will be added to your bill.

Hostels include the Hörnum **DJH Hostel** (☎ 880 294; www.jugendherberge.de; Friesenplatz 2; dm €18.20), in the south of the island, and List's **DJH Hostel** (☎ 870 397; www.jugendherberge.de; List; dm €19.20). Neither is very central, but bus services bring you close.

Mirrors like portholes, unpolished wood and painted cane chairs exude simple but elegant, beachy comfort at **Long Island House Sylt** (☎ 04651-995 9550; www.sylthotel.de; Eidumweg 13, Westerland; s €88-116, d €128-176, ste €196; ☐). There's a spacious garden and breakfast includes local specialities and traditional Frisian tea.

Single Pension (☎ 920 70; www.singlepension.de; Trift 26, Westerland; s €39-54, d €70-79) happily welcomes singles and pairs, and the mainly over-50 clientele unwind over tea in the garden, or during the walking and cycling tours offered. Rooms are humble, but the location central and the atmosphere relaxed. Cheaper rooms share bathrooms.

The **Gosch** (fish sandwiches €3-6, meals €7-12) fastfish chain has colonised mainland Germany, but it originated in Sylt and remains here in force.

Giant mugs of coffee or Frisian tea and enormous, homemade slices of cake are de rigueur at **Kupferkanne** (☎ 410 10; Stapelhooger Wai, Kampen; meals €5.50-14), a World War II bunker–turned-cafe. Dine outdoors on wooden tables surrounded by a maze of low bramble hedges overlooking the Wadden Sea, or inside where it's easy (and fun) to get lost in its cavernous nooks and crannies.

Reservations are a must at **Sansibar** (☎ 964 646; Hörnumer Strasse 80; Rantum; mains €12-29). This airy grass-roof pavilion on the beach north of Hörnum is ideal for a drink or dinner at sunset.

Getting There & Around

Sylt is connected to the mainland by a narrow causeway exclusively for trains. Regular services travel from Hamburg (Altona and

> **MUDDY WATERS**
>
> It's a tad messy but a ton of fun. The best *Wattwandern*, walking on tidal flats from one point to another (the same as Dutch *Wadlopen*), is between the islands of Amrum and Föhr. Full-day excursions (from €25) can be combined with various boat trips. Contact **Westerland Tourism** (opposite).

Hauptbahnhof) to Westerland (€30.50 to €42 return, three to 3¼ hours).

If driving, you must load your vehicle onto a **car train** (☎ 995 0565; www.syltshuttle.de; return €80) in Niebüll near the Danish border. There are constant crossings (usually at least once an hour) in both directions, and no reservations can be made.

There's also a **car ferry** (☎ 0180-310 3030; www.sylt-faehre.de; return from €61) from Havneby, Denmark to List on the north of the island.

Air Berlin (www.airberlin.com) has several services a week from Berlin and Düsseldorf, among others, to **Sylt/Westerland airport** (GWT; www.flughafen-sylt.de); **Lufthansa** (www.lufthansa.com) arrives from Frankfurt, Hamburg and Munich.

Sylt's two north–south bus lines run every 20 to 30 minutes, and three other frequent lines cover the rest of the island.

AMRUM & FÖHR

Tiny Amrum is renowned for its fine white *Kniepsand* (sand bank). There's a 10km stroll from the tall **lighthouse** at Wittdün to the village of Norddorf, and an 8km return hike along the beach. The **tourist office** (☎ 04682-94 030; www.amrum.de; ferry landing, Wittdün; ☷ 8.30am-5pm Mon-Thu, to 5.30pm Fri, 9am-12.30pm Sat, 9am-12.30pm & 4pm-5.30pm Sun) can provide accommodation.

The 'green isle' of Föhr is interesting for its Frisian culture. Its main village, Wyk, boasts plenty of windmills, there are 16 northern hamlets tucked behind dikes up to 7m tall, and there's the large 12th-century church of **St Johannis** in Nieblum. The **Föhr information service** (☎ 04681-300; www.foehr.de) can help with more details. There is no camping here.

Getting There & Around

WDR (☎ 800; www.wdr-wyk.de) has ferries to Föhr (€6, 45 minutes) and Amrum (€8.45, two hours) from Dagebüll Hafen.

Adler-Schiffe (☎ 04651-987 00; www.adler-schiffe.de; Boysenstrasse 13, Westerland; return adult/child €25/13) offers day cruises from Hörnum harbour in Sylt, and has quicker journeys on its *Adler Express* ship.

On Amrum, there are buses between the ferry terminal in Wittdün and Norddorf.

GERMANY DIRECTORY

ACCOMMODATION

Germany has all types of places to unpack your suitcase, from hostels, camping grounds and family hotels to chains, business hotels and luxury resorts. Reservations are a good idea, especially if you're travelling in the busy summer season (June to September). Local tourist offices will often go out of their way to find something in your price range.

In this book, options are listed in budget order, with the cheapest first. Accommodation usually includes breakfast, except in camping grounds and holiday apartments. Prices include private bathrooms unless otherwise specified and are quoted at peak season.

Private rooms and guest houses can be excellent value, especially for lone travellers, with prices starting as low as €30. Budget hotels and pensions typically charge under €70 for a double room (under €60 with shared bathroom), while good-value midrange options come in around €70 to €150. Anything over €150 can generally be considered top end, and should offer enough amenities to justify the price – spa facilities are a common extra.

Renting an apartment for a week or more is a popular option, particularly for small groups. Again, tourist offices are generally the best source of information.

Germany has more than 2000 organised camping grounds, several hundred of which stay open throughout the year. Prices are around €3 to €5 for an adult, plus €3 to €7 for a car and/or tent. Look out for ecologically responsible camping grounds sporting the Green Leaf award from the ADAC motoring association.

Deutsches Jugendherbergswerk (DJH; www.djh.de) coordinates the official Hostelling International (HI) hostels in Germany. Rates in gender-segregated dorms or in family rooms range from €13 to €25 per person,

---

SLEEPING WITH PIGS: FARMSTAYS

A holiday on a working farm is a big hit with kids who love interacting with their favourite barnyard animals and helping with everyday chores. Accommodation ranges from bare-bones rooms with shared facilities to fully furnished holiday flats. Minimum stays of three days are common. For details, check www.landtourismus.de or www.bauernho furlaub.com (in German).

---

including linen and breakfast. People over 27 are charged an extra €3 or €4.

Unless you're a member of your home country's HI association, you need to buy a Hostelling International Card for €15.50 (valid for one year) when you check in.

Indie hostels are more relaxed and can be found in large cities, including Berlin, Munich and Frankfurt.

ACTIVITIES

Germany, with its rugged Alps, picturesque uplands and fairy-tale forests, is ideal for hiking and mountaineering. There are well-marked trails criss-crossing the countryside, especially in popular areas such as the Black Forest (see p238), the Harz Mountains (p274), the Saxon Switzerland area (p191) and the Thuringian Forest. The Bavarian Alps (p227) offer the most dramatic and inspiring scenery, however, and are the centre of mountaineering in Germany. Good sources of information on hiking and mountaineering are **Verband Deutscher Gebirgs-und Wandervereine** (Federation of German Hiking Clubs; ☎ 0561-938 730; www.wanderverband .de); and **Deutscher Alpenverein** (German Alpine Club; ☎ 089-140 030; www.alpenverein.de).

The Bavarian Alps are the most extensive area for winter sports. Cross-country skiing is also good in the Black Forest and Harz Mountains. Ski equipment starts at around €15 per day, and daily ski-lift passes start at around €15. Local tourist offices are the best sources of information.

Cyclists will often find marked cycling routes, and eastern Germany has much to offer in the way of lightly travelled back roads. There's an extensive cycling trail along the Elbe River, and islands like Rügen Island (p208) are also good for cycling. For more details and tips, see p294.

BOOKS

For a more detailed guide to the country, pick up a copy of Lonely Planet's *Germany*. Lonely Planet also publishes *Munich, Bavaria & the Black Forest*, and *Berlin*.

BUSINESS HOURS

Shops are permitted to be open until 8pm Monday to Saturday but – except for a few in the big city centres – most lock up at 6pm or 6.30pm (1pm or 2pm on Saturday). But this is changing and in large cities more places are finding ways to open on Sunday.

Banks do business from 8.30am to 4pm Monday to Friday (sometimes 6pm Thursday). Government offices close for the weekend and at 1pm or 3pm on Friday. Museums are often closed on Monday; opening hours vary greatly, although many are open later one evening per week.

Restaurants are usually open from 11am to midnight, with varying *Ruhetage* (closing days); many close for lunch during the day from 3pm to 6pm. Cafes often close around 8pm, though equal numbers stay open until 2am or later. Bars that don't serve food open between 5pm and 8pm and may close as late as 5am (if at all) in the larger cities.

DANGERS & ANNOYANCES

Although the usual cautions should be taken, theft and other crimes against travellers are relatively rare in Germany. Africans, Asians and southern Europeans may encounter racial prejudice, especially in eastern Germany, where they can be singled out as convenient scapegoats for economic hardship. However, the animosity is usually directed against immigrants, not tourists.

DISCOUNT CARDS

Many cities offer discount cards. These cards will usually combine up to three days' free use of public transport with free or reduced admission to major local museums and attractions. They're generally a good deal if you want to fit a lot in; see the Information section under the relevant destination and ask at tourist offices for full details.

EMBASSIES & CONSULATES

The following embassies are all in Berlin. Many countries also have consulates in cities such as Frankfurt-am-Main and Munich.

Australia (Map pp170-1; ☎ 030-880 0880; www
.australian-embassy.de; Wallstrasse 76-79)
Canada (Map pp170-1; ☎ 030-203 120; www.kanada
.info.de; Leipziger Platz 17)
France (Map pp170-1; ☎ 030-590 039 000; www
.botschaft-frankreich.de; Pariser Platz 5)
Ireland (Map pp170-1; ☎ 030-220 720; www
.botschaft-irland.de; Friedrichstrasse 200)
Netherlands (Map pp170-1; ☎ 030-209 560; www
.dutchembassy.de; Klosterstrasse 50)
New Zealand (Map pp170-1; ☎ 030-206 210; www
.nzembassy.com; Friedrichstrasse 60)
UK (Map pp170-1; ☎ 030-204 570; www.britischebot
schaft.de; Wilhelmstrasse 70)
USA (Map pp170-1; ☎ 030-238 5174; www.us-bot
schaft.de; Pariser Platz 2)

FESTIVALS & EVENTS

January & February
Karneval/Fasching (Carnival) The pre-Lent season is
celebrated with costumed street partying, parades, satirical shows and general revelry, mostly in cities that are
located along the Rhine such as Düsseldorf, Cologne and
Mainz, but also in the Black Forest and Munich.

April
Walpurgisnacht Celebrated on 30 April throughout the
Harz, this festival of pagan origin has villages roaring to
life; young and old dress up as witches and warlocks and
parade through the streets.

May
Maifest (May Festival) Villagers celebrate the end of
winter by chopping down a tree (*Maibaum*), painting,
carving and decorating it, and staging a merry revelry with
traditional costumes.
Rhein in Flammen (Rhine in Flames) Huge fireworks
festival in Rhine villages; May to September.

June
Christopher Street Day (www.csd-germany.de) Major
gay celebration with wild street parades and raucous
partying, especially in Berlin, Cologne and Hamburg but
also in Dresden, Munich, Stuttgart and Frankfurt.

July & August
Love Parade (www.loveparade.net) All types of electronic music at the world's largest rave in mid-July; Berlin.

September, October & November
Oktoberfest (www.oktoberfest.de) Legendary beer-
swilling party, enough said. Actually starts in mid-
September; Munich (p213).

Frankfurt Book Fair (Frankfurter Buchmesse; www
.buchmesse.de) October sees the world's largest book fair,
with 1800 exhibitors from 100 countries.

December
Christmas Markets Popular across the country (p223).
Silvester The German New Year's Eve is called Silvester in
honour of the 4th-century pope under whom the Romans
adopted Christianity as their official religion; there's partying all night long.

GAY & LESBIAN TRAVELLERS

Overall, Germans are tolerant of gays
(*Schwule*) and lesbians (*Lesben*) although, as
elsewhere in the world, cities (Berlin!) are
more liberal than rural areas, and younger
people tend to be more open-minded than
older generations. Discrimination is more
likely in eastern Germany and in the conservative south where gays and lesbians tend
to keep a lower profile.

HOLIDAYS

Germany observes eight religious and three
secular holidays nationwide. Shops, banks,
government offices and post offices are
closed on these days. States with predominantly Catholic populations, such as Bavaria
and Baden-Württemberg, also celebrate
Epiphany (6 January), Corpus Christi (10
days after Pentecost), Assumption Day (15
August) and All Saints' Day (1 November).
Reformation Day (31 October) is only observed in eastern Germany.

The following are *gesetzliche Feiertage*
(public holidays):
Neujahrstag (New Year's Day) 1 January
Ostern (Easter) March/April – Good Friday, Easter Sunday
and Easter Monday
Christi Himmelfahrt (Ascension Day) Forty days after
Easter.
Maifeiertag/Tag der Arbeit (Labour Day) 1 May
Pfingsten (Whit/Pentecost Sunday & Monday) May/June;
50 days after Easter.
Tag der Deutschen Einheit (Day of German Unity) 3
October
Weihnachtstag (Christmas Day) 25 December
Zweite Weihnachtstag (Boxing Day) 26 December

LEGAL MATTERS

Germany's federal ban on smoking in public
places is really just a lot of smoke. In 2008

GERMANY

the federal court overturned the ban in small bars and restaurants, and left the final determination and enforcement of the ban up to the individual states. Although a majority of cafes and nightspots remain nonsmoking, you'll encounter a few where smokers can light up.

MEDIA

The most widely read newspapers in Germany are *Die Welt, Frankfurter Allgemeine,* Munich's *Süddeutsche Zeitung* and the left-leaning *Die Tageszeitung (Taz). Bild* is Germany's favourite sensationalist tabloid.

Germany's most popular news magazines are *Der Spiegel, Focus* and *Stern.*

Germany's two national TV channels are the government-funded ARD and ZDF. They are augmented by a plethora of regional broadcasters, plus private cable channels, which show a lot of dubbed US series and films with long ad breaks.

Websites excellent for German news:

Deutsche Welle (www.dw-world.de)
Local (www.thelocal.de)

MONEY

See the Regional Directory (p598) for a full discussion of all things monetary in the region.

The easiest places to change cash in Germany are the banks or foreign-exchange counters at airports and train stations, particularly those of the Reisebank. The main banks in larger cities generally have money-changing machines for after-hours use, although they don't often offer reasonable rates.

There are international ATMs virtually everywhere in Germany. Travellers cheques can be cashed at any bank. A percentage commission (usually a minimum of €5) is charged by most banks on any travellers cheque, even those issued in euros.

Restaurant bills always include a service charge *(Bedienung)* but most people add 5% or 10% unless the service was truly abhorrent. At hotels, bellhops get about €1 per bag and it's also nice to leave a few euros for the room cleaners. Tip bartenders about 5% and taxi drivers around 10%.

POST

Standard post office hours are 8am to 6pm weekdays and to noon on Saturday. Many train-station post offices stay open later o. offer limited services outside these hours.

Letters sent within Germany take one tc two days; those to destinations within Europe or to North America take four to six days anc those to Australasia five to seven days.

TELEPHONE

See p600 for more info on using phones in central Europe.

German phone numbers consist of an area code followed by the local number, which can be between three and nine digits long. The country code for Germany is ☎ 49. To ring abroad from Germany, dial ☎ 00 followed by the country code, area code and number.

An operator can be reached on ☎ 0180-200 1033. **Deutsche Telekom directory assistance** (☎ 118 37 for an English-speaking operator) charges a ridiculous €1.39 per minute for numbers within Germany and €1.99 for numbers outside Germany (☎ 118 34). Get the same information for free at www.telefonbuch.de.

Mobile Phones

Mobile phones ('Handys') are ubiquitous in Germany; the main operators are T-Mobile, Vodafone, O2 and E-Plus. You can pick up a prepay SIM card for around €30; top-up cards are available from kiosks, various shops and vending machines. Mobile numbers generally begin with a ☎ 016 or ☎ 017 prefix.

Phonecards

Most pay phones in Germany accept only phonecards, available for €5, €10 and €20 at post offices, news kiosks, tourist offices and banks. One call unit costs a little more than €0.06 from a private telephone and €0.10 from a public phone.

TRAVELLERS WITH DISABILITIES

Germany is fair at best (but better than much of Europe) for the needs of physically disabled

---

EMERGENCY NUMBERS

■ ADAC breakdown service ☎ 0180-222 2222

■ Ambulance ☎ 112

■ Fire ☎ 112

■ Police ☎ 110

travellers, with access ramps for wheelchairs and/or lifts in some public buildings.

Deutsche Bahn operates a **Mobility Service Centre** (☎ 01805-512 512; ☾ 8am-8pm Mon-Fri, to 2pm Sat) whose operators can answer questions about station and train access. With one day's notice, they can also arrange for someone to meet you at your destination.

VISAS

See the Regional Directory (p601) for a full discussion about visas in the region.

TRANSPORT IN GERMANY

GETTING THERE & AWAY

Air

The main arrival and departure points in Germany used to be Frankfurt-am-Main (p262) and Munich (p217). But with the explosion of budget carriers, almost any town with a tarmac seems to be getting a few flights. Places such as Düsseldorf, Berlin, Nuremberg and even Baden-Baden have cheap flights to parts of Europe. See p605 for details on how you can find cheap flights within Europe.

Ryanair, easyJet, Air Berlin and Germanwings are among the foremost cheap options in Germany, but don't count Lufthansa out: it has been aggressively competing on price as well.

The following airlines all fly to Germany from across Europe (see p605 for a list of international carriers):

Air Berlin (AB; ☎ 01805-737 800; www.airberlin.de)
British Airways (BA; ☎ 01805-266 522; www.britishairways.com)
Czech Airlines (OK; ☎ 01805-006 737; www.csa.cz)
easyJet (BH; ☎ 01803-654 321; www.easyjet.com)
germanwings (4U; ☎ 01805-955 855; www.germanwings.com)
Iberia (IB; ☎ 01803-000 613; www.iberia.es)
Lufthansa (LH; ☎ 01803-803 803; www.lufthansa.com)
Ryanair (FR; ☎ 0190-170 100; www.ryanair.com)
SAS (SK; ☎ 01803-234 023; www.flysas.com)
Wizzair (W6; www.wizzair.com)

Land

BUS

Travelling by bus between Germany and the rest of Europe is cheaper than by train or plane, but journeys will take a lot longer.

Eurolines is a consortium of national bus companies operating routes throughout the continent. Sample one-way fares and travel times:

Route	Price	Duration (hr)
London-Frankfurt	€85	16
Amsterdam-Berlin	€58	10
Paris-Munich	€61	13

Eurolines has a discounted youth fare for those under 26 that saves you around 10%. Tickets can be purchased throughout Germany at most train stations. Eurolines' German arm is **Deutsche-Touring** (☎ 069-790 350; www.deutsche-touring.com).

CAR & MOTORCYCLE

Germany is served by an excellent highway system. If you're coming from the UK, the quickest option is the Channel Tunnel. Ferries take longer but are cheaper. You can be in Germany three hours after the ferry docks.

Within Europe, *autobahns* and highways become jammed on weekends in summer and before and after holidays. For details on road rules when driving in Germany, see p295.

TRAIN

A favourite way to get to Germany from elsewhere in Europe is by train. See p614 for details on trains in central Europe.

Conventional long-distance trains between major German cities and other countries are often called EuroCity (EC) trains. The main German hubs with the best connections for major European cities are Hamburg (Scandinavia); Cologne (high-speed Thalys trains to France, Belgium and the Netherlands, with Eurostar connections from Brussels going on to London); Frankfurt (high-speed trains to Paris); Munich (high-speed trains to Paris and regular trains to southern and southeastern Europe) and Stuttgart (high-speed Cisalpino trains to Italy and Switzerland).

Often longer international routes are served by at least one day train and sometimes a night train as well.

Sea

Germany's main ferry ports are Kiel, Lübeck and Travemünde in Schleswig-Holstein, and Rostock and Sassnitz (on Rügen Island) in

GERMANY

Mecklenburg-Western Pomerania. All have services to Scandinavia and the Baltic states.

GETTING AROUND

Air

There are lots of flights within the country, many by budget carriers such as Air Berlin and Germanwings. See p293 for additional details. Note that with check-in and transit times, flying is rarely as efficient as a fast train.

Bicycle

Radwandern (bicycle touring) is very popular in Germany. Pavements are often divided into separate sections for pedestrians and cyclists – be warned that these divisions are taken very seriously. Favoured routes include the Rhine, Moselle, Elbe and Danube Rivers and the Lake Constance area.

Simple three-gear bicycles can be hired from around €15/40 per day/week, and more robust mountain bikes from €20/50.

Cycling is allowed on all roads and highways but not on the *autobahns*. Cyclists must follow the same rules of the road as vehicles. Helmets are not compulsory, not even for children, but wearing one is still a good idea.

Bicycles may be taken on most trains but you must buy a separate *Fahrradkarte* (bicycle ticket). These cost €9 on long-distance trains and €4.50 on regional trains (RB, RE and S-Bahn, valid all day). Bicycles are not allowed on high-speed ICE trains. There is no charge at all on some trains; for specifics enquire at a local station or call Deutsche Bahn on the **DB Radfahrer-Hotline** (bicycle hotline; ☎ 01805-151 415). Free lines are also listed in DB's complimentary *Bahn & Bike* brochure (in German), as are the almost 250 stations throughout the country where you can hire bikes for between €3 and €13.

Germany's main cycling organisation is the **Allgemeiner Deutscher Fahrrad Club** (ADFC; ☎ 0421-346 290; www.adfc.de).

Boat

Boats are most likely to be used for basic transport when travelling to or between the Frisian Islands, though tours along the Rhine, Elbe and Moselle Rivers are also popular. During summer there are frequent services on Lake Constance but, with the exception of the Constance–Meersburg and the Friedrichshafen–Romanshorn car ferries, these boats are really more tourist crafts than a transport option. From April to October, excursion boats ply lakes and rivers in Germany and can be a lovely way to see the country.

Bus

The bus network in Germany functions primarily in support of the train network. Bus stations or stops are usually located near the train station in any town. Consider using buses when you want to cut across two train lines and avoid long train rides to and from a transfer point. A good example of where to do this is in the Alps, where the best way to follow the peaks is by bus.

Within Germany **Eurolines** (☎ 069-790 350) operates as Deutsche-Touring GmbH; services include the Romantic Road bus in southern Germany, as well as organised bus tours of Germany lasting a week or more.

Car & Motorcycle

AUTOMOBILE ASSOCIATIONS

Germany's main motoring organisation, the **Allgemeiner Deutscher Automobil-Club** (ADAC; ☎ for roadside assistance 0180-222 2222, if calling from mobile phone 222 222; www.adac.de, in German) offers roadside assistance to members of its affiliates, including British AA, American AAA and Canadian CAA.

DRIVING LICENCE

Visitors do not need an international driving licence to drive in Germany; technically you should carry an official translation of your licence with you, but in practice this is rarely necessary.

HIRE

You usually must be at least 21 years of age to hire a car in Germany. You'll need to show your licence and passport, and make sure you keep the insurance certificate for the vehicle with you at all times.

Germany's four main rental companies, **Avis** (☎ 0180-555 77; www.avis.de), **Europcar** (☎ 0180-580 00; www.europcar.de), **Hertz** (☎ 0180-533 3535; www.hertz.de) and **Sixt** (☎ 0180-526 0250; www.sixt.de), have offices or affiliates from Aschaffenburg to Zwiesel.

INSURANCE

You must have third-party insurance to enter Germany with a vehicle.

ROAD CONDITIONS

The *autobahn* system of motorways runs throughout Germany. Road signs (and most motoring maps) indicate national *autobahn* routes in blue with an 'A' number, while international routes have green signs with an 'E'. Though efficient, the *autobahns* are often busy, and visitors frequently have trouble coping with the high speeds. Secondary roads (usually designated with a 'B' number) are easier on the nerves and much more scenic, but can be slow going.

Cars are impractical in urban areas. Vending machines on many streets sell parking vouchers that must be displayed clearly behind the windscreen. Leaving your car in a central *Parkhaus* (car park) costs roughly €10 per day or €1.50 per hour.

ROAD RULES

Road rules are easy to understand, and standard international signs are in use. You drive on the right, and most cars are right-hand drive. Right of way is usually signed, with major roads given priority, but on unmarked intersections traffic coming from the right always has right of way.

The usual speed limits are 50km/h in built-up areas and 100km/h on the open road. The speed on *autobahns* is unlimited, though there's an advisory speed of 130km/h; exceptions are clearly signposted.

The blood-alcohol limit for drivers is 0.05%. Obey the road rules carefully: the German police are very efficient and issue heavy on-the-spot fines. Germany also has one of the highest concentrations of speed cameras in Europe.

Public Transport

Public transport is excellent within big cities and small towns, and is generally based on buses, *Strassenbahn* (trams), S-Bahn and/or U-Bahn (underground trains). Tickets cover all forms of transit; fares are determined by zones or time travelled, sometimes both. Multiticket strips and day passes are generally available offering better value than single-ride tickets.

Make certain that you have a ticket when boarding – only buses and some trams let you buy tickets from the driver. In some cases you will have to validate it on the platform or once aboard. Ticket inspections are frequent (especially at night and on holidays) and the fine is a non-negotiable €50 or more.

Train

Operated almost entirely by **Deutsche Bahn** (DB; www.bahn.de), the German train system is the finest in Europe, and is generally the best way to get around the country. There are a few independent operators, such as ALX which runs between Munich and Regensburg.

Trains run on an interval system, so wherever you're heading, you can count on a service at least every two hours. Schedules are integrated throughout the country so that connections between trains are time-saving and tight, often only five minutes. Of course this means that when a train is late, connections are missed and you can find yourself stuck waiting for the next train.

CLASSES

It's rarely worth buying a 1st-class ticket on German trains; 2nd class is usually quite comfortable. There's more difference between the train classifications – basically the faster a train travels, the plusher it is.

Train types include the following:

CNL, EN, D These are night trains, although an occasional D may be an extra daytime train.

ICE InterCityExpress services run at speeds up to 300km/h. The trains are very comfortable and feature cafe cars.

IC/EC Called InterCity or EuroCity, these are the premier conventional trains of DB. When trains are crowded, the open-seating coaches are much more comfortable than the older carriages with compartments.

RE RegionalExpress trains are local trains that make limited stops. They are fairly fast and run at one- or two-hourly intervals.

RB RegionalBahn are the slowest DB trains, not missing a single cow or town.

S-Bahn These DB-operated trains run frequent services in larger urban areas. Not to be confused with U-Bahns, which are run by local authorities who don't honour rail passes.

COSTS

Standard DB ticket prices are distance-based. You will usually be sold a ticket for the shortest distance to your destination.

Sample fares for one-way, 2nd-class ICE travel include Hamburg–Frankfurt €106, Frankfurt-am-Main–Berlin €111 and Frankfurt-am-Main–Munich €89. Regular full-fare tickets are good for four days from the day you tell the agent your journey will begin, and you can make unlimited stopovers along your route during that time. In this chapter train fares given between towns are all undiscounted 2nd class.

GERMANY

DB sells Savings Fares that discount the high cost of regular tickets and are sold like airline tickets (ie trains with light loads may have tickets available at a discount, others none). Ask at the ticket counters, use the vending machines or visit www.bahn.de.

The following are among the most popular discounts offered by DB (2nd class):

BahnCard 25/50/100 Only worthwhile for extended visits to Germany, these discount cards entitle holders to 25/50/100% off regular fares and cost €57/225/3650.

Savings Fare 25 Round-trip tickets bought three or more days in advance and restricted to particular trains save 25%.

Savings Fare 50 Same conditions as the fare above but also including a Saturday night stay.

Schönes Wochenende 'Happy Weekend' tickets allow unlimited use of RE, RB and S-Bahn trains on a Saturday or Sunday between midnight and 3am the next day, for up to five people travelling together, or one or both parents and all their children/grandchildren for €37. They are best suited to weekend day trips from urban areas.

RESERVATIONS

During peak periods, a seat reservation (€3.50) on a long-distance train can mean the difference between squatting near the toilet or relaxing in your own seat. Reservations can be made using vending machines or the web.

SCHEDULE INFORMATION

The **DB website** (www.bahn.de) is excellent. There is extensive info in English and you can use it to sort out all the discount offers and schemes. In addition it has an excellent schedule feature that works not just for Germany but the rest of Europe.

Telephone information is also available: reservations ☎ 118 61; toll-free automated timetable ☎ 0800-150 7090.

TICKETS

Many train stations have a *Reisezentrum* (travel centre) where staff sell tickets and can help you plan an itinerary (ask for an English-speaking agent). Smaller stations may only have a few ticket windows and the smallest ones aren't staffed at all. In this case, you must buy tickets from multilingual vending machines. These are also plentiful at staffed stations and convenient if you don't want to queue at a ticket counter. Both agents and machines accept major credit cards.

Buying your ticket on the train carries a surcharge (€3 to €8). Not having a ticket carries a stiff penalty.

TRAIN PASSES

Agencies outside Germany sell German Rail passes for unlimited travel on all DB trains for a set number of days within a 30-day period. Sample 2nd-class prices for adults/under-26 are €160/130 for four days. Most Eurail and Inter-Rail passes are valid in Germany.

Hungary

Where else but Hungary can you laze about in an open-air thermal spa while snow patches glisten around you, then head to a local bar where a Romani band yelps while a crazed crowd whacks its boot heels, as commanded by Hungarian tradition? And where else could you go clubbing in an ancient bathhouse, where everyone dances in swimsuits, waist-deep in the healing waters?

If these pursuits don't appeal, there are always Roman ruins, ancient castles, and Turkish minarets in baroque cities such as Pécs and Eger. In the countryside you can experience the joy of seeing cowboys riding astride five horses, storks nesting on streetlamps, and a sea of apricot trees blooming.

Not that urban pleasures are neglected. Cosmopolitan Budapest is replete with world-class operas, monumental historical buildings, and the mighty Danube River flowing through its centre. Prices here are somewhere in the middle: not nearly as high as in Austria nor as inexpensive as in Ukraine. However, the focus is slowly turning from quantity to quality. Boutique hotels are popping up in Budapest and Balaton; world-class restaurants are spreading out from the capital to smaller enclaves; and superior thermal retreats are replacing dated communist-era eyesores.

Despite the rising tide of commericalism, Hungary has held onto the one factor that makes it special – being Hungarian. Having established itself as a state in the year 1000, Hungary has a long history, a rich culture and strong folk traditions that are well worth exploring.

FAST FACTS

- **Area** 93,000 sq km
- **Capital** Budapest
- **Currency** forint (Ft); €1 = 306Ft;
  US$1 = 225Ft; UK£1 = 325Ft; A$1 = 155Ft;
  ¥100 = 234Ft; NZ$1 = 126Ft
- **Famous for** paprika, Bull's Blood and *csárda* music
- **Official language** Hungarian (Magyar)
- **Phrases** *jo napot kivanok* (good day); *szia* (hi/bye); *köszönöm* (thank you)
- **Population** 10 million
- **Telephone codes** country code ☎ 36; international access code ☎ 00; intercity access code ☎ 06
- **Visa** no visa needed for most nationalities if you stay less than 90 days; see p360

HUNGARY

HUNGARY

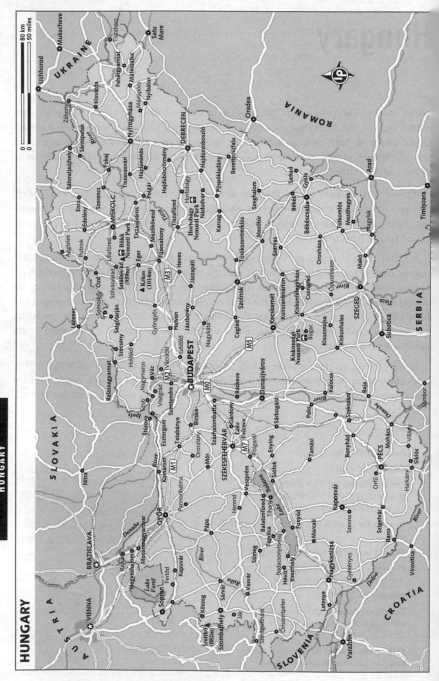

HIGHLIGHTS

- Ease your aching muscles in the warm waters of Budapest's **thermal baths** (p310), and try a spa treatment for good measure.
- Learn about the defiance **Eger** (p351) showed to Turkish invaders, and how the city's Bull's Blood wine got its name.
- Watch the cowboys ride at Bugac in **Kiskunsági Nemzeti Park** (p348), in the heart of the Hungarian *puszta* (plain).
- Absorb the Mediterranean climate and historic architecture of the southern city of **Pécs** (p342), including its intriguing Mosque Church.
- Take a pleasure cruise across (or a dip in) Central Europe's largest body of fresh water, **Lake Balaton** (p335).

ITINERARIES

- **One week** Make sure that you spend at least four days in Budapest, checking out the sights, museums and pavement cafes. On your fifth day take a day trip to a Danube Bend town: see the open-air museum in Szentendre or the cathedral at Esztergom. Day six can be spent getting a morning train to Pécs and seeing the lovely Turkish remains, and checking out the many galleries in town. Let your hair down on day seven and try some local wine in Eger, a baroque town set in red-wine country.
- **Two weeks** If you're here in summer, make sure you spend some time exploring the towns around Lake Balaton, or just chill out on the beach by the side of this popular lake. Tihany is a rambling hillside village filled with craftsmen's houses, set on a peninsula that is a protected nature zone. Keszthely is an old town with a great palace in addition to a beach. Alternatively, head south to Pécs and see more of the Great Plain. Szeged is on the Tisza River, and Kecskemét is further north. Finish your trip in Tokaj, home of Hungary's most famous wine.

CLIMATE & WHEN TO GO

Hungary has a temperate continental climate. July and August are the warmest months, and when the thermometer hits 27°C it can feel much hotter, given that most places don't have air-con. Spring is unpredictable, but usually arrives in April. November is already rainy and chilly; January and February are the coldest, dreariest months, with temperatures dropping below 0°C. September, with loads of sunshine, mild temperatures and grape-harvest festivals in the countryside, may be the best time to visit. May, with a profusion of flowers and sunshine, is a close second. See p595 for climate charts.

The busiest tourist season is July and August (Lake Balaton is especially crowded), but hotels quote high-season prices from April to October. In provincial and smaller towns, attractions are often closed, or have reduced hours, from October to May.

HISTORY
Pre-Hungarian Hungary

The plains of the Carpathian Basin attracted waves of migration, from both east and west, long before the Magyar tribes decided to settle there. The Celts occupied the area in the 3rd century BC, but the Romans conquered and expelled them just before the Christian era. The lands west of the Danube (Transdanubia) in today's Hungary became part of the Roman province of Pannonia, where a Roman legion was stationed at the town of Aquincum (now called Óbuda). The Romans brought writing, planted the first vineyards and built baths near some of the region's many thermal springs.

A new surge of nomadic tribespeople, the Huns, who lent Hungary its present-day name, arrived on the scene with a leader who would become legendary in Hungarian history. By AD 441, Attila and his brother Bleda had conquered the Romans and acquired a reputation as great warriors. This reputation

---

CONNECTIONS: MOVING ON FROM HUNGARY

Hungary's landlocked status ensures plenty of possibilities for onward travel overland. There are direct train connections (p321) from Budapest to major cities in all of Hungary's neighbours, including Vienna, Bratislava, Bucharest, Kyiv (continuing to Moscow), Zagreb, Belgrade and Ljubljana. International buses head in all directions (p321), including localities across the border in Serbia, Croatia and Romania. And in the warmer months, you can take a ferry along the Danube to reach Bratislava or Vienna (p320).

HUNGARY

still runs strong and you will notice that many Hungarians carry the name Attila, even though the Huns have no connection with present-day Hungarians and the Huns' short-lived empire did not outlast Attila's death (453), when remaining tribespeople fled back from whence they came. Many tribes filled the vacuum left by the Huns and settled in the area, such as the Goths, Longobards and the Avars, a powerful Turkic people who controlled parts of the area from the 5th to the 8th centuries. The Avars were subdued by Charlemagne in 796, leaving space for the Franks and Slavs to move in.

The Conquest

Magyar (Hungarian) tribes are said to have moved in around 896, when Árpád led the alliance of seven tribes into the region. The Magyars, a fierce warrior tribe, terrorised much of Europe with raids reaching as far as Spain. They were stopped at the Battle of Augsburg in 955 and subsequently converted to Christianity. Hungary's first king and its patron saint, István (Stephen), was crowned on Christmas Day in 1000, marking the foundation of the Hungarian state.

Medieval Hungary was a powerful kingdom that included Transylvania (now in Romania), Transcarpathia (now in Ukraine), modern-day Slovakia and Croatia. Under King Matthias Corvinus (1458–90), Hungary experienced a brief flowering of Renaissance culture. However, in 1526 the Ottomans defeated the Hungarian army at Mohács and by 1541 Buda Castle had been seized and Hungary sliced in three. The central part, including Buda, was controlled by the Ottomans, while Transdanubia, present-day Slovakia, and parts of Transcarpathia were ruled by Hungarian nobility based in Pozsony (Bratislava) under the auspices of the Austrian House of Habsburg. The principality of Transylvania, east of the Tisza, prospered as a vassal state of the Ottoman Empire.

Habsburg Hegemony & the Wars

After the Ottomans were evicted from Buda in 1686, the Habsburg domination of Hungary began. The 'enlightened absolutism' of the Habsburg monarchs Maria Theresa (r 1740–80) and her son Joseph II (r 1780–90) helped the country leap forward economically and culturally. Rumblings of Hungarian independence surfaced off and on, but it was the unsuccessful 1848 Hungarian revolution that really started to shake the Habsburg oligarchy. After Austria was defeated in war by Prussia in 1866, a weakened empire struck a compromise with Hungary in 1867, creating a dual monarchy. The two states would be self-governing in domestic affairs, but act jointly in matters of common interest, such as foreign relations. The Austro-Hungarian monarchy lasted until WWI.

After WWI and the collapse of the Habsburg Empire in November 1918, Hungary was proclaimed a republic. But she had been on the losing side of the war. The 1920 Treaty of Trianon stripped the country of more than two-thirds of its territory – a hot topic of conversation to this day.

In 1941 Hungary's attempts to recover lost territories saw the nation in war, on the side of Nazi Germany. When leftists tried to negotiate a separate peace in 1944, the Germans occupied Hungary and brought the fascist Arrow Cross Party to power. The Arrow Cross immediately began deporting hundreds of thousands of Jews to Auschwitz. By early April 1945, all of Hungary was liberated by the Soviet army.

Communism

By 1947 the communists assumed complete control of the government and began nationalising industry and dividing up large estates among the peasantry. On 23 October 1956, student demonstrators demanding the withdrawal of Soviet troops were fired upon. The next day Imre Nagy, the reformist minister of agriculture, was named prime minister. On 28 October Nagy's government offered an amnesty to all those involved in the violence and promised to abolish the hated secret police, the ÁVH (known as ÁVO until 1949). On 4 November Soviet tanks moved into Budapest, crushing the uprising. By the time the fighting ended on 11 November, some 25,000 people were dead. Then the reprisals began: an estimated 20,000 people were arrested; 2000 were executed, including Nagy; another 250,000 fled to Austria.

By the 1970s Hungary had abandoned strict central economic control in favour of a limited market system, often referred to as 'Goulash Communism'. In June 1987 Károly Grósz took over as premier and Hungary began moving towards full democracy. The huge numbers of East Germans who were able to slip through the Iron Curtain by leaving via Hungary contributed to the eventual crumbling of the Berlin Wall.

The Republic

At their party congress in February 1989 the Hungarian communists agreed to surrender their monopoly on power. The Republic of Hungary was proclaimed in October, and democratic elections were scheduled for March 1990. Hungary changed its political system with scarcely a murmur, and the last Soviet troops left the country in June 1991.

The painful transition to a full market economy resulted in declining living standards for most people and a recession in the early 1990s, but the early years of the 21st century saw astonishing growth. Hungary became a fully fledged member of NATO in 1999. In a national referendum during April 2003, the Hungarian people voted to join the European Union (EU), and the country became a member on 1 May 2004.

In April 2006 the Socialist-led coalition won the parliamentary elections, becoming the first government to win consecutive terms in office since the restoration of democracy in 1990. The incoming prime minister, multimillionaire businessman Ferenc Gyurcsány, was chosen by the Socialist Party to succeed the former prime minister, Peter Medgyessy. His efforts to rein in Hungary's large budget deficit by introducing austerity measures caused riots on the streets later that year.

In December 2007 Hungary joined the Schengen zone of European countries, abandoning border controls with its EU neighbours Austria, Slovakia and Slovenia. Late in 2008, reeling from the fallout of the global financial crisis, Hungary was forced to approach the International Monetary Fund for economic assistance. Hungary originally aimed to adopt the euro by 2010, but the effects of the crisis have since obliged the government to delay adoption until at least 2012.

PEOPLE

Some 10.2 million people live within the national borders, and another five million Hungarians and their descendants are abroad. The estimated 1.45 million Hungarians in Transylvania constitute the largest ethnic minority in Europe, and there are another 530,000 in Slovakia, 293,000 in Serbia, 156,000 in Ukraine and 40,500 in Austria.

Ethnic Magyars make up approximately 93% of the population. Many minority groups estimate their numbers to be significantly higher than official counts. There are 13 recognised minorities in the country, including Germans (2.6%), Serbs and other South Slavs (2%), Slovaks (0.8%) and Romanians (0.7%). The number of Roma is officially put at 1.9% of the population, though some sources place the figure as high as 4%.

RELIGION

Of those Hungarians declaring religious affiliation, about 52% are Roman Catholic, 16% Reformed (Calvinist) Protestant, 3% Evangelical (Lutheran) Protestant, and 2.6% Greek Catholic and Orthodox. Hungary's Jews number around 100,000, down from a prewar population of nearly eight times that amount.

ARTS

Budapest is Hungary's artistic heart, but the provinces resound with the arts too. The country (and the capital in particular) is known for its traditional culture, with a strong emphasis on the classical – and for good reason. The history of Hungarian arts and literature includes world-renowned

HUNGARY

composers such as Béla Bartók and Franz Liszt, and the Nobel prize–winning writer Imre Kértesz and his innovative contemporary Peter Esterházy. Hungary's proximity to classical music hub Vienna, as well as the legacy of the Soviet regard for the 'proper arts', means that opera, symphony and ballet are high on the entertainment agenda, and even provincial towns have decent companies.

For the more contemporary branches of artistic life, Budapest is the focus, containing many art galleries and theatre and dance companies. The capital is also a centre for folk music and crafts that have grown out of village life or minority culture.

Literature

Hungary has some excellent writers, both of poetry and prose. Sándor Petőfi (1823–49) is Hungary's most celebrated poet. A line from his work National Song became the rallying cry for the War of Independence between 1848 and 1849, in which he fought and is commonly thought to have died. His comrade-in-arms, János Arany (1817–82), wrote epic poetry. The prolific novelist and playwright Mór Jókai (1825–1904) gave expression to heroism and honesty in works such as The Man with the Golden Touch. Lyric poet Endre Ady (1877–1919) attacked narrow materialism; poet Attila József (1905–37) expresses the alienation felt by individuals in the modern age; and novelist Zsigmond Móricz (1879–1942) examines the harsh reality of peasant life in Hungary.

Contemporary Hungarian writers whose work has been translated into English and are worth a read include Tibor Fischer, Péter Esterházy and Sándor Márai. The most celebrated Hungarian writer is the 2002 Nobel prize winner Imre Kertész. Among his novels available in English are Fatelessness (1975), Detective Story (1977), Kaddish for an Unborn Child (1990) and Liquidation (2003). Another prominent contemporary writer, who died in 2007 at age 90, was Magda Szabó (Katalin Street, 1969; The Door, 1975).

Music

As you will no doubt see from the street names in every Hungarian town and city, the country celebrates and reveres its most influential musician, composer and pianist, Franz (or Ferenc) Liszt (1811–86). The eccentric Liszt described himself as 'part Gypsy', and in his Hungarian Rhapsodies, as well as in other works, he does indeed weave Romani motifs into his compositions.

Ferenc Erkel (1810–93) is the father of Hungarian opera, and his stirringly nationalist Bánk Bán is a standard at the Hungarian State Opera House in Budapest. Béla Bartók (1881–1945) and Zoltán Kodály (1882–1967) made the first systematic study of Hungarian folk music; both integrated some of their findings into their compositions.

Hungarian folk musicians play violins, zithers, hurdy-gurdies, bagpipes and lutes on a five-tone diatonic scale. Look out for Muzsikás; Marta Sebestyén; Ghymes, a Hungarian folk band from Slovakia; and the Hungarian group Vujicsics, which mixes in elements of southern Slav music. Another folk musician with eclectic tastes is the Paris-trained Bea Pálya, who combines such sounds as traditional Bulgarian and Indian music with Hungarian folk.

Romani music, found in restaurants in its schmaltzy form (best avoided), has become a fashionable thing among the young, with Romani bands playing 'the real thing' in trendy bars till the wee hours: a dynamic, hopping mix of fiddles, bass and cymbalom (a stringed instrument played with sticks). An instrument a Romani band would never be seen without is the tin milk bottle used as a drum, which gives Hungarian Roma music its characteristic sound. It's reminiscent of traditional Indian music, an influence that perhaps harks back to the Roma's Asian roots. Some modern Romani music groups – Kalyi Jag (Black Fire) from northeastern Hungary, Romano Drom (Gypsy Road) and Romani Rota (Gypsy Wheels) – have added guitars, percussion and even electronics to create a whole new sound.

Klezmer music (traditional Eastern European Jewish music) has also made a comeback in the playlists of the young and trendy.

Pop music is as popular here as anywhere – indeed, Hungary has one of Europe's biggest pop spectacles, the annual Sziget Music Festival (p314). It has more than 1000 performances over a week and attracts an audience of up to 385,000 people. Popular Hungarian musical artists to look out for include pop singers Magdi Rúzsa and Laci Gáspár, and pop/folk band Nox.

Visual Arts

Favourite painters from the 19th century include realist Mihály Munkácsy (1844–1900), the so-called painter of the plains, and Tivadar Kosztka Csontváry (1853–1919). Győző Vásárhelyi (1908–97), who changed his name to Victor Vasarely when he emigrated to Paris, is considered the 'father of op art'. Contemporary painters to keep an eye out for include Árpád Müller and the late Endre Szász (1926–2003).

In the 19th and early 20th centuries, the Zsolnay family created world-renowned decorative art in porcelain. Ceramic artist Margit Kovac (1902–1977) produced a large number of statues and ceramic objects during her career. The traditional embroidery, weavings and ceramics of the nation's *népművészet* (folk art) endures, and there is at least one handicraft store in every town.

SPORT

The Hungarian Formula One Grand Prix, held in mid-August, is the year's biggest sporting event. The **Hungaroring** (www.hungaroring.hu) track is 19km north of Budapest, in Mogyoród, but hotels in the capital fill up and prices skyrocket during the event.

ENVIRONMENT
The Land

Hungary occupies the Carpathian Basin to the southwest of the Carpathian Mountains. Water dominates much of the country's geography. The Duna (Danube River) divides the Nagyalföld (Great Plain) in the east from the Dunántúl (Transdanubia) in the west. The Tisza (597km in Hungary) is the country's longest river, and historically has been prone to flooding. Hungary has hundreds of small lakes and is riddled with thermal springs. Lake Balaton (596 sq km, 77km long), in the west, is the largest freshwater lake in Europe outside Scandinavia. Hungary's 'mountains' to the north are merely hills, with the country's highest peak being Kékes (1014m) in the Mátra Range.

Wildlife

There are a lot of common European animals in Hungary (deer, hares, wild boars and foxes), as well as some rare species (wild cat, lake bat and Pannonian lizard), but most of the country's wildlife comes from the avian family. Hungary is a premier European spot for birdwatching. Around 75% of the country's 480 known vertebrates are birds, for the most part waterfowl attracted by the rivers, lakes and wetlands. The rare black stork, a smaller, darker version of its common cousin, also spends time in Hungary on its migration from Africa to Europe.

National Parks

There are 10 national parks in Hungary. Bükk Nemzeti Park, north of Eger, is a mountainous limestone area of forest and caves. Kiskunsági Nemzeti Park and Bugac, near Kecskemét, and Hortobágy Nemzeti Park (www.hnp.hu) in the Hortobágy Puszta (a World Heritage site), outside Debrecen, protect the unique grassland environment of the plains.

Environmental Issues

In the past decade there has been a marked improvement in both the public's awareness of environmental issues and the government's dedication to environmental safety. Air pollution has long been a problem due to emissions from inefficient coal-fired power plants and the nation's ancient car fleet. Many of the plants have been shut down in recent years, resulting in the reduction of the country's sulphur dioxide emissions by a third. Additionally, the government has forced many polluting autos off the road and introduced lead- and sulphur-free petrol.

To cut down your carbon emissions, consider travelling to Hungary by train (p361) or bus (p360), rather than flying.

FOOD & DRINK
Staples & Specialities

The omnipresent seasoning in Hungarian cooking is paprika, a mild red pepper that appears on restaurant tables as a condiment beside the salt and black pepper, as well as in many recipes. *Pörkölt*, a paprika-infused stew, can be made from different meats, including *borju* (veal), and usually it has no vegetables. *Galuska* (small, gnocchi-like dumplings) are a good accompaniment to soak up the sauce. The well-known *paprikas csirke* (chicken paprikash) is stewed chicken in a tomato-cream-paprika sauce (not as common here as in Hungarian restaurants abroad). *Töltött káposzta* (cabbage rolls stuffed with meat and rice) is cooked in a roux made with paprika, and topped with sour cream, as is *székelygulyás* (stewed

HUNGARY

pork and sour cabbage). Another local favourite is *halászlé* (fisher's soup), a rich mix of several kinds of poached freshwater fish, tomatoes, green peppers and (you guessed it) paprika.

Leves (soup) is the start to any main meal in a Hungarian home; some claim that you will develop stomach disorders if you don't eat a hot, daily helping. *Gulyás* (goulash), although served as a stew outside Hungary, is a soup here, cooked with beef, onions and tomatoes. Traditional cooking methods are far from health-conscious, but they are tasty. Frying is a nationwide obsession, and you'll often find fried turkey, pork and veal schnitzels on the menu.

For dessert you might try the cold *gyümölcs leves* (fruit soup) made with sour cherries and other berries, or *palincsinta* (crêpes) filled with jam, sweet cheese or chocolate sauce. A good food-stand snack is *lángos,* fried dough that can be topped with cheese and/or *tejföl* (sour cream).

Two Hungarian wines are known internationally: the sweet, dessert wine Tokaji Aszú and Egri Bikavér (Eger Bull's Blood), the full-bodied red, high in acid and tannin. But the country produces a number of other eminently drinkable wines. Hungarian beers sold nationally include Dreher and Kőbanyai; Borosodi is a decent amber brew. For the harder stuff, try *pálinka*, a strong, firewater-like brandy distilled from a variety of fruits, but most commonly plums or apricots. Zwack distillery produces Unicum, a bitter aperitif that has been around since 1790; it tastes a bit like the medicine doctors give you to induce vomiting – but it's popular.

Where to Eat & Drink

An *étterem* is a restaurant with a large selection, formal service and formal prices. A *vendéglő* is smaller, more casual and serves homestyle regional dishes. The overused term *csárda*, which originally meant a rustic country inn with Romani music, can now mean anything – including 'tourist trap'. To keep prices down, look for *étkezde* (a tiny eating place that may have a counter or sit-down service), *önkiszolgáló* (a self-service canteen), *kinai gyorsbüfé* (Chinese fast food), *grill* (which generally serves gyros or kebabs and other grilled meats from the counter) or a *szendvicsbar* (which has open-faced sandwiches to go).

There are still a number of stuffy Hungarian restaurants with condescending waiters, formal service and Romani music from another era. For the most part, avoiding places with tuxedoed waiters is a good bet.

Wine has been produced in Hungary for thousands of years, and you'll find it available by the glass or bottle everywhere. There are plenty of pseudo-British/Irish/Belgian pubs, smoky *sörözök* (Hungarian pubs, often in a cellar, where drinking is taken very seriously), *borozók* (wine bars, usually a dive) and nightclubs, but the most pleasant place to imbibe a cocktail or coffee may be in a cafe. A *kávéház* may primarily be an old-world dessert shop, or it may be a bar with an extensive drinks menu; either way they sell alcoholic beverages in addition to coffee. In spring, pavement tables sprout up alongside the new flowers.

Restaurants generally open from 11am to 11pm, and bars and cafes open from 11am to midnight.

Though Hungarian bars and restaurants are required to have separate smoking and nonsmoking sections, their often compact size means that passive smoking is inevitable. However, at the time of research the government was bravely set on introducing a total ban on smoking in public places.

Vegetarians & Vegans

Traditional Hungarian cuisine and vegetarianism are definitely not a match made in heaven. However, things are changing and there are places even in the provinces that serve good vegetarian meals. Where there are no vegetarian restaurants, you'll have to make do with what's on the regular menu or shop for ingredients in the markets.

Some not very light, but widely available dishes for vegetarians to look for are *rántott sajt* (fried cheese), *gombafejek rántva* (fried mushroom caps), *gomba leves* (mushroom soup) and *túrós* or *káposzta csusza* (short, wide pasta with cheese or cabbage). *Bableves* (bean soup) usually contains meat.

Habits & Customs

The Magyar are a polite people and their language is filled with courtesies. To toast someone's health before drinking, say *egéségére* (egg-eh-shaig-eh-ray), and to wish them a good appetite before eating, *jo étvágat* (yo ate-vad-yaht). If you're invited to someone's home, always bring a bunch of flowers and/or a bottle of good local wine.

BUDAPEST

☎ 1 / pop 1.7 million

There's no other Hungarian city like Budapest in terms of size and importance. Home to almost 20% of the national population, Hungary's capital (*főváros*, or main city) is the nation's administrative, business and cultural centre; everything of importance starts or finishes here.

But it's the beauty of Budapest – both natural and constructed – that makes it stand apart. Straddling a gentle curve in the Danube, the city is flanked by the Buda Hills on the west bank and the beginnings of the Great Plain to the east. Architecturally, it is a gem, with enough baroque, neoclassical, eclectic and art nouveau elements to satisfy anyone.

In recent years, Budapest has taken on the role of the region's party town. In the warmer months outdoor entertainment areas called *kertek* (gardens) are heaving with party-makers, and the world-class Sziget Music Festival in August is a cultural magnet. And you need not venture out for fun; the city's scores of new hostels offer some of the best facilities and most convivial company in Europe.

Budapest does have an ugly side, with organised crime, pollution, ubiquitous fast-food chain eateries, and mindless graffiti covering much of its gorgeous architecture. But come dusk on a fine day, cross the Danube on foot and you'll see why unique, passionate, vibrant Budapest remains unmissable.

HISTORY

Strictly speaking, the story of Budapest begins only in 1873 with the administrative union of three cities that had grown together: Buda, west of the Danube; Óbuda (Buda's oldest neighbourhood) to the north; and Pest on the eastern side of the river. But the area had already been occupied for thousands of years.

The Romans built a settlement at Aquincum (Óbuda) during the first centuries of the Common Era. In the 1500s, the Turks arrived uninvited and stayed for almost 150 years. The Habsburg Austrians helped kick the invaders out, but then made themselves at home for 200 more years.

In the late 19th century, under the dual Austro-Hungarian monarchy, the population of Budapest soared. Many notable buildings date from that boom period. The city suffered some damage in the two world wars, and the 1956 revolution left structures pockmarked with bullet holes. Today many of the city's grand buildings have been restored, and Budapest is the sophisticated capital of a proud nation with a distinctive heritage.

ORIENTATION

The city's aquatic artery, the Danube, is spanned by nine bridges that link hilly, residential Buda with bustling, commercial and very flat Pest. Two ring roads link three of the bridges across the Danube and essentially define central Pest. Important boulevards such as Rákóczi út and leafy Andrássy út fan out from these, creating large squares and circles. The most central square in Pest is Deák tér, where the three metro lines meet. Buda is dominated by Castle and Gellért Hills; its main square is Moszkva tér.

Budapest is divided into 23 *kerület* (districts). The Roman numeral appearing before each street address signifies the district. Central Buda is district I; central Pest is district V, and fans out to districts VI and VII. You can also tell the district by reading its postal code:

HUNGARY

BUDAPEST IN TWO DAYS

The best way to start your day in Budapest is to have an early-morning soak alfresco at **Széchenyi Baths** (p311). Then stroll down Andrássy út and grab a late breakfast or coffee at **Lukács** (p319), next to the infamous and ever-popular spy museum, the **Terror House** (p313). Take an afternoon tour around the grand **Hungarian State Opera House** (p313) and have cake at the legendary **Gerbeaud** (p319), before hitting the shops on **Váci utca** (p313). Then go dancing at **Merlin** (p320).

On day two grab breakfast at **Centrál Kávéház** (p319), before getting the funicular to **Castle Hill** (p309) in Buda. Tour **Matthias Church** (p309) and explore the many museums, including the **Budapest History Museum** (p310). In the evening, back in Pest, walk along the waterfront and have a meal at any of the boat restaurant-pubs, before going Hungarian dancing at **Fonó Budai Zeneház** (p320).

INFORMATION		Memento Park	**15** A6	DRINKING🍷	
Australian Embassy	**1** A4	Museum of Fine Arts	**16** C3	Kisrabló	**29** B4
Dutch Embassy	**2** B3	Palace of Art	**17** C3		
Hungarian Federation of Disabled		Széchenyi Baths	**18** C3	ENTERTAINMENT 🎭	
Persons' Associations	**3** B2	Sétacikli	**19** B3	Fonó Buda Zeneház	**30** B5
Romanian Embassy	**4** C3	Transport Museum	**20** C3		
Serbian Embassy	**5** C3	Vájdahunyad Castle	**21** C3	SHOPPING 🛍	
Slovakian Embassy	**6** D3			Városligeti Bolhapiac	**31** C3
Slovenian Embassy	**7** A2	SLEEPING 🛏			
South African Embassy	**8** A3	Back Pack Guesthouse	**22** B5	TRANSPORT	
Ukrainian Embassy	**9** D3	Boat Hotel Fortuna	**23** B3	Árpád Híd Bus Station	**32** C2
		Martos Hostel	**24** B4	BKV Passenger Ferry	**33** C4
SIGHTS & ACTIVITIES		Papillon Hotel	**25** B3	Népliget Bus Station	**34** D5
Aquincum Museum	**10** B1			Stadionok Bus Station	**35** D4
Buda Hills	**11** A3	EATING 🍴			
City Park	**12** C3	Bagolyvár	**26** C3		
Cog Railway	**13** A3	Kisbuda Gyöngye	**27** B2		
Hősök tere	**14** C3	Marcello	**28** B4		

the two numbers after the initial one signify the district (ie H-1114 is in the XI district).

INFORMATION
Bookshops
Bestsellers (Map p312; V Október 6 utca 11; 🕙 9am-6.30pm Mon-Fri, 10am-5pm Sat, 10am-4pm Sun) The best English-language bookshop in town.

Irók Boltja (Map p312; VI Andrássy út 45; 🕙 10am-7pm Mon-Fri, to 1pm Sat) Good selection of Hungarian writers in translation.

Red Bus Second-hand Bookstore (Map p312; V Sem-melweiss utca 14; 🕙 11am-6pm Mon-Fri, 10am-2pm Sat) Sells used English-language books.

Treehugger Dan's Bookstore (Map p312; VI Csengery utca 48; 🕙 10am-7pm Mon-Fri, 10am-5pm Sat) New kid on the block sells thousands of secondhand English-language books, does trade-ins and serves organic fair trade coffee.

Discount Cards
See p358 for details on the Hungary Card.

Budapest Card (☎ 266 0479; www.budapestinfo.hu; 48/72hr card 6500/8000Ft) Offers access to many museums; unlimited public transport; and discounts on tours and other services. Buy it at hotels, travel agencies, large metro station kiosks and tourist offices.

Emergency
For emergency numbers, see p360.

District V Police Station (Map p312; ☎ 373 1000; V Szalay utca 11-13) Pest's most central police station.

Internet Access
The majority of hostels offer internet access, often free of charge. Among the most accessible internet cafes in Budapest are the following:

Electric Café (Map p312; VII Dohány utca 37; per hr 200Ft; 🕙 9am-midnight) Huge place, very popular with travellers.

Plastic Web (Map p312; V Irány utca 1; per hr 390Ft; 🕙 9.30am-11.30pm) This friendly place is about as central as you'll find in Pest.

Medical Services
FirstMed Centers (Map p308; ☎ 224 9090; I Hattyú utca 14, 5th fl; 🕙 8am-8pm Mon-Fri, 9am-2pm Sat) On call 24/7 for emergencies.

SOS Dent (Map p312; ☎ 269 6010; VI Király utca 14; 🕙 24hr) Around-the-clock dental care.

Teréz Patika (Map p312; ☎ 311 4439; VI Teréz körút 41; 🕙 8am-8pm Mon-Fri, 8am-2pm Sat) Pharmacy.

Money
You'll find ATMs everywhere.

K&H Bank (Map p312; V Váci utca 40) Quite central.

OTP Bank (Map p312; V Deák Ferenc utca 7-9) Favourable rates.

Post
Main post office (Map p312; V Petőfi Sándor utca 13-15; 🕙 8am-8pm Mon-Fri, to 2pm Sat) Just minutes from Deák Ferenc tér.

Tourist Information
Tourinform main office (Map p312; ☎ 438 8080; V Sütő utca 2; 🕙 8am-8pm); Castle Hill (Map p308; ☎ 488 0475; I Szentháromság tér; 🕙 9am-7pm May-Oct, 10am-6pm Nov-Apr); Liszt Ferenc Square (Map p312; ☎ 322 4098; VI Liszt Ferenc tér 11; 🕙 10am-6pm Mon-Fri)

Travel Agencies
Discover Budapest (Map p312; ☎ 269 3843; VI Lázár utca 16; 🕙 9.30am-6.30pm Mon-Fri, 10am-4pm Sat & Sun) Visit this one-stop shop for helpful tips and advice, accommodation bookings, internet access, and cycling and walking tours.

Express (Map p312; ☎ 327 7298; www.express-travel .hu; VII Dohány utca 30/a & Kazinczy utca 3/b; 🕙 8.30am-5pm Mon-Fri, 9am-1pm Sat) The main office of this

HUNGARY

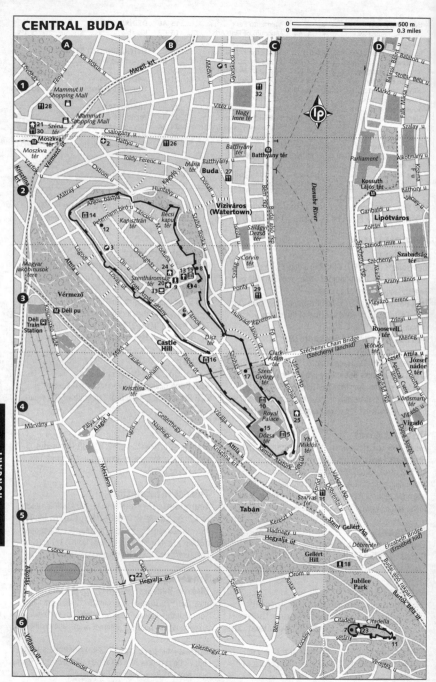

CENTRAL BUDA

youth-oriented agency can book accommodation in Budapest, particularly in hostels and colleges, and sells transport tickets.

Ibusz (Map p312; ☎ 501 4910; www.ibusz.hu; V Ferenciek tere 10; 🕙 9am-6pm Mon-Fri, to 1pm Sat) The main branch of this national agency has an exchange office, sells transport train tickets and books accommodation.

DANGERS & ANNOYANCES

Overall, Hungary is a very safe country with little violent crime, but scams can be a problem in the capital. Those involving attractive young women, gullible guys, expensive drinks in nightclubs and a frogmarch to the nearest ATM accompanied by in-house security have been all the rage in Budapest for well over a decade now, so be aware. Overcharging in taxis is also not unknown.

Watch out for pickpockets: the usual method is for someone to distract you (by running into you, or dropping something) while an accomplice makes off with your goods. Pickpocketing is most common in markets, the Castle District, Váci utca and Hősök tere, near major hotels, and on certain popular buses (eg 7) and trams (2, 4, 6, 47 and 49).

As for personal security, some locals now avoid Margaret Island after dark during the low season, and both residents and visitors give the dodgier parts of the VIII and IX districts (areas of prostitution activity) a wide berth.

SIGHTS & ACTIVITIES

Budapest is an excellent city for sightseeing, especially on foot. The Castle District in Buda contains a number of museums, both major and minor, but the lion's share is in Pest. Think of Margaret Island as a green buffer between the two – short on things to see, but a great place for a breather.

Buda

CASTLE HILL

Surfacing at the M2 metro station of the Socialist-style Moszkva tér, continue left up Várfok utca, or board bus 16A to reach **Castle Hill** (Várhegy; Map p308) where most of Budapest's remaining medieval buildings are clustered. Castle Hill is high above the glistening Danube, and wandering the old streets and enjoying the city views is part of the attraction, so get off at the first stop after the Vienna Gate and walk.

Magdalene Tower (Magdolona toronye; Map p308; Kapisztrán tér) is all that's left of a Gothic church destroyed here during WWII. The white neoclassical building facing the square is the **Military History Museum** (Hadtörténeti Múzeum; Map p308; I Tóth Árpád sétány 40; adult/concession 700/350Ft; 🕙 10am-6pm Tue-Sun Apr-Sep, to 4pm Tue-Sun Oct-Mar).

For a peek into the life of the Budapest bourgeoisie, check out the mansions of the Buda Hills to the south of the ramparts promenade. Follow the third alleyway to your left and you reach Szentháromság tér and the **Holy Trinity statue** (Szentháromság szobor; Map p308) at its centre.

Don't miss the gorgeous, neo-Gothic **Matthias Church** (Mátyás Templom; Map p308; www .matyas-templom.hu; I Szentháromság tér 2; adult/concession 700/480Ft; 🕙 9am-5pm Mon-Sat, 1-5pm Sun), with a colourful tiled roof and lovely murals inside. Franz Liszt's *Hungarian Coronation Mass* was played here for the first time at the coronation of Franz Joseph and Elizabeth in 1867.

Step across the square, under the gaze of Hungary's first king, immortalised in the equestrian **St Stephen statue** (Szent István szobor; Map p308). Behind the monument, walk along **Fishermen's Bastion** (Halászbástya; Map p308; I Szentháromság tér; adult/concession 330/160Ft; 🕙 8.30am-11pm). The fanciful, neo-Gothic arcade built on the fortification wall is prime picture-taking

HUNGARY

territory, with views of the river and the parliament beyond.

Tárnok utca runs southeast to Dísz tér, past which is the entrance for the **Sikló** (Map p308; I Szent György tér; one way/return adult 800/1400Ft, child 500/900Ft; ⊗ 7.30am-10pm, closed 1st & 3rd Mon of month), a funicular railway. The views from the little capsule, across the Danube and over to Pest, are glorious. The Sikló takes you down the hill to Clark Ádám tér. The massive **Royal Palace** (Királyi Palota; Map p308) occupies the far end of Castle Hill; inside are the **Hungarian National Gallery** (Nemzeti Galéria; www.mng.hu; I Szent György tér 6; adult/concession 800/400Ft; ⊗ 10am-6pm Tue-Sun) and the **Budapest History Museum** (Budapesti Történeti Múzeum; www.btm.hu; I Szent György tér 2; adult/concession 900/450Ft; ⊗ 10am-6pm daily mid-Mar–mid-Sep, 10am-4pm Wed-Mon mid-Sep–mid-Mar).

Nearby is the **Royal Wine House & Wine Cellar Museum** (Borház és Pincemúzeum; Map p308; www.kiralyi borok.com; I Szent György tér, Nyugati sétány; adult/concession 900/500Ft; ⊗ noon-8pm), situated in what were once the royal cellars, dating back to the 13th century. Tastings cost 1350/1800/2700Ft for three/four/six wines. You can also elect to try various types of Hungarian champagne and *pálinka* (fruit brandy).

GELLÉRT HILL

The 'other peak' overlooking the Danube, south of Castle Hill, is Gellért Hill. The **Liberty Monument** (Szabadság szobor; Map p308), a gigantic statue of a lady with a palm frond proclaiming freedom throughout the city, sits at its top and is visible from almost anywhere in town. The monument was erected as a tribute to the Soviet soldiers who died liberating Hungary in 1945, but the victims' names in Cyrillic letters that used to adorn the plinth, as well as the memorial statues of Soviet soldiers, were removed in 1992.

West of the monument is the **Citadella** (Map p308; www.citadella.hu; admission free; ⊗ 24hr). Built by the Habsburgs after the 1848 revolution to 'defend' the city from further Hungarian insurrection, it was never used as a fortress. Excellent views, exhibits, a restaurant and a hotel can be enjoyed here. Take tram 19 along the riverfront from Clark Ádám tér and climb the stairs behind the waterfall and **St Gellért statue** (Szent Gellért szobor; Map p308), then follow the path through the park opposite the entrance to the Danubius Hotel Gellért. Or take bus 27, which runs almost to the top of the hill from XI Móricz Zsigmond

körtér, a square located southwest of the Gellért Hotel and accessible using trams 18, 19, 47 or 49.

Bellow Gellért Hill is the city's most famous thermal spa, the **Gellért Baths** (Gellért Fürdő; Map p312; ☎ 466 6166; Danubius Hotel Gellért, XI Kelenhegyi út; admission 3400Ft; ⊗ 6am-7pm May-Sep, 6am-7pm Mon-Fri & 6am-5pm Sat & Sun Oct-Apr), where majestic domes hang above healing waters. This art nouveau palace has dreamy spas where you can soak for hours while enjoying its elegant and historic architecture.

MEMENTO PARK

In Buda's southwest is **Memento Park** (Map p306; www.mementopark.hu; XXII Balatoni út 16; adult/concession 1500/1000Ft; ⊗ 10am-dusk), a kind of historical dumping ground for socialist statues deemed unsuitable since the early '90s. It's a major tourist attraction and there's a direct bus from Deák tér in Pest at 11am daily (adult/concession return 3950/2450Ft, including admission). To go independently, take tram 19 from Clark Ádám tér to the XI Etele tér Terminus, then catch bus 150 to the park.

AQUINCUM

Seven kilometres north of Buda's centre, in Óbuda, is the **Aquincum Museum** (Aquincumi Múzeum; Map p306; www.aquincum.hu; III Szentendre út 139; adult/concession 900/450Ft; ⊗ 10am-6pm May-Sep, 10am-5pm Tue-Sun Oct-Apr), containing the most complete ruins of a 2nd-century Roman civilian town left in Hungary. Take the HÉV from the Batthyány tér metro stop.

BUDA HILLS

With 'peaks' up to 500m, a comprehensive system of trails and no lack of unusual conveyances to get you around, the **Buda Hills** (Map p306) are the city's playground and are a welcome respite from hot, dusty Pest in summer.

Heading for the hills is more than half the fun. From Moszkva tér metro station on the M2 line in Buda, walk westward along Szilágyi Erzsébet fasor for 10 minutes (or take tram 18 or 56 for two stops) to the circular Hotel Budapest at Szilágyi Erzsébet fasor 47. Directly opposite is the terminus of the **Cog Railway** (Fogaskerekű vasút; Map p306; www.bkv.hu; Szilágyi Erzsébet fasor 14-16; admission 270Ft; ⊗ 5am-11pm). Built in 1874, the cog climbs for 3.6km in 14 minutes three or four times an hour to Széchenyi-hegy (427m), one of the prettiest residential areas in Buda.

At Széchenyi-hegy, you can stop for a picnic in the attractive park south of the old-time station or board the narrow-gauge **Children's Railway** (Gyermekvasút; off Map p306; www .gyermekvasut.hu; adult/child section 450/250Ft, entire line 600/300Ft; closed Mon Sep-Apr), two minutes to the south on Hegyhát út. The railway, with eight stops, was built in 1951 by Pioneers (social-ist Scouts) and is now staffed entirely by schoolchildren aged 10 to 14 – the engineer excepted. The little train chugs along for 12km, terminating at Hűvösvölgy. Departure times vary widely depending on the day or the week and the season – but count on one every hour or so between 9am or 10am and 5pm or 6pm.

There are walks fanning out from all of the stops along the Children's Railway line, or you can return to Moszkva tér on tram 56 from Hűvösvölgy. A more interesting way down, however, is to get off at János-hegy, the fourth stop on the Children's Railway and the highest point (527m) in the hills. About 700m to the east is a **chairlift** (libegő; off Map p306; adult/child 500/400Ft; 9.30am-5pm mid-May–mid-Sep, 10am-4pm mid-Sep–mid-May, closed 2nd & 4th Monday each month), which will take you down to Zugligeti út. From here, bus 291 returns to Moszkva tér.

Margaret Island

Neither Buda nor Pest, 2.5km-long **Margaret Island** (Margit-sziget; Map p306) in the mid-dle of the Danube was the domain of one religious order or another until the Turks came and turned what was then called the Island of Rabbits into – of all things – a harem. It's been a public park since the mid-19th century. Like the Buda Hills, the island is a recreational rather than educational experience.

Cross over to Margaret Island from Pest or Buda via trams 4 or 6. Bus 26 covers the length of the island as it makes the run between Nyugati train station and Árpád Bridge bus station. Cars are allowed on Margaret Island from Árpád Bridge only as far as the two big hotels at the northeast-ern end; the rest is reserved for pedestrians and cyclists.

You can hire a bicycle from one of several stands, including **Sétacikli** (Map p306; 06 30 966 6453; per hr 650Ft; 9am-dusk), which is on the western side just before the athletics stadium as you walk from Margaret Bridge.

Pest

HŐSÖK TERE & AROUND

The leafy Andrássy út, Pest's northeastern artery, is the best place to start your sight-seeing. From Deák tér, Bajcsy-Zsilinszky ut becomes Andrássy út, which ends at the wide, tiled **Hősök tere** (Heroes' Sq; Map p306). This public space holds a sprawling monument constructed to honour the millennial anni-versary (in 1896) of the Magyar conquest of the Carpathian Basin.

Continental Europe's oldest underground – Budapest's M1 yellow line metro, constructed in the 19th century – runs beneath Andrássy út. Start your Hősök tere sightseeing from the metro station of the same name. The tall green monument on the square showcases statues of important moustachioed tribal leaders, kings and statesmen. Across the street, the **Museum of Fine Arts** (Szépművészeti Múzeum; Map p306; www .mfab.hu; XIV Dózsa György út 41; adult/concession 1200/600Ft; 10am-5.30pm Tue, Wed & Fri-Sun, 10am-10pm Thu) houses a collection of foreign art, including an impressive number of El Grecos. Don't miss the **Palace of Art** (Műcsarnok; Map p306; www.mucsarnok .hu; XIV Hősök tere; adult/concession 1200/600Ft; 10am-6pm Tue-Wed & Fri-Sun, to 8pm Thu), a large contemporary-art gallery, opposite the museum.

Adjacent is the oasis of **City Park** (Városliget; Map p306), which has boating on a small lake in the summer, ice skating in winter, and duck-feeding year round. The park's schizo-phrenic **Vájdahunyad Castle** (Vájdahunyad Vár; Map p306) was built in varied architectural styles typical of historic Hungary, including baroque, Romanesque, Gothic and Tudor. Nearby, the varied exhibits of the **Transport Museum** (Közlekedési Múzeum; Map p306; XIV Városligeti körút 11; adult/concession 800/400Ft; 10am-5pm May-Sep, to 4pm Oct-Apr) make it one of the most enjoyable museums in Budapest, and a great place for kids. In the park's northern corner is **Széchenyi Baths** (Széchenyi Fürdő; Map p306; 363 3210; XIV Állatkerti út 11; admission 2600Ft; 6am-10pm), its cupola visible from any-where in the park. Built in 1908, this place has a dozen thermal baths and five swimming pools. The peaceful atmosphere of the indoor thermal baths, saunas and massage area contrasts with the buzzing atmosphere of the main pool.

Walk southwest from Hősök tere on Andrássy út to see many grand, World Heritage–listed 19th-century buildings. Stop for coffee and cake at Lukács (p319), the old haunt of the dreaded secret police, whose head-quarters have now been turned into the **Terror**

HUNGARY

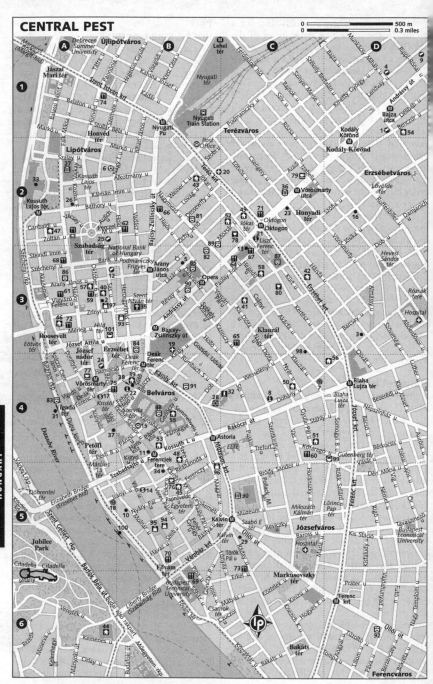

CENTRAL PEST

INFORMATION	
Austrian Embassy	**1** D1
Bestsellers	**2** A3
Centre of Rural Tourism	**3** D3
Croatian Embassy	**4** D1
Discover Budapest	**5** B3
District V Police Station	**6** A2
Electric Café	**7** C4
Express	**8** C4
French Embassy	**9** D1
Hungarian Youth Hostels Association	**10** B5
Ibusz	**11** B4
Irish Embassy	**12** A3
Írok Boltja	**13** C3
K&H Bank	**14** B5
Main Post Office	**15** B4
National Federation of Rural & Agrotourism	**16** D2
OTP Bank	**17** A4
Plastic Web	**18** A5
Red Bus Second-hand Bookstore	(see 55)
SOS Dent	**19** B3
Teréz Patika	**20** B2
Tourinform (Liszt Ferenc Square)	**21** C2
Tourinform (Main Office)	**22** B4
Treehugger Dan's Bookstore	**23** C2
UK Embassy	**24** A4
US Embassy	**25** A2

SIGHTS & ACTIVITIES	
Debrecen Summer University Branch	**26** A2
Ethnography Museum	**27** A2
Gellért Baths	(see 44)
Great Synagogue	**28** B4
Hungarian Equestrian Tourism Association	**29** C5
Hungarian National Museum	**30** C5
Hungarian State Opera House	(see 85)
Mahart PassNave	**31** A4

Memorial of the Hungarian Jewish Martyrs	**32** C4
Parliament	**33** A2
Pegazus Tours	**34** B5
St Stephen's Basilica	**35** B3
Terror House	**36** C2
Váci utca	**37** A4
Yellow Zebra Bikes	**38** B4

SLEEPING ⬛	
Best Hotel Service	**39** B4
Central Backpack King Hostel	**40** A3
Connection Guest House	**41** C3
Corinthia Grand Hotel Royal	**42** C3
Cotton House	**43** B2
Danubius Hotel Gellért	**44** A6
Erzsébet Hotel	**45** B5
Four Seasons Gresham Palace Hotel	**46** A3
Garibaldi Guesthouse	**47** A2
Gingko Hostel	**48** B4
Home-Made Hostel	**49** C2
Hostel Marco Polo	**50** C4
Hotel Anna	**51** C4
Hotel Medosz	**52** C2
Leo Panzió	**53** B4
Radio Inn	**54** D1
Red Bus Hostel	**55** B4
Soho Hotel	**56** D4
To-Ma Travel Agency	**57** A3
Unity Hostel	**58** C3

EATING ⬛	
Első Pesti Rétesház	**59** A3
Fülemüle	**60** C4
Govinda	**61** A3
Hold utca Market	**62** B2
Iguana	**63** A2
Klassz	**64** C3
Köleves	**65** C3
Marquis de Salade	**66** B2
Menza	**67** C3
Momotaro Ramen	**68** A3

Nagycsarnok	**69** B6
Pireus Rembetiko Taverna	**70** B5
Rothschild Supermarket	**71** C2
Salaam Bombay	**72** A3
Soul Café	**73** C5
Szeráj	**74** A1
Vapiano	**75** A4

DRINKING ⬛ ⬛	
Centrál Kávéház	**76** B5
Gerbeaud	**77** A4
Kiadó Kocsma	**78** C2
Lukács	**79** C2
Szimpla	**80** C3

ENTERTAINMENT ⬛	
Alter Ego	**81** B2
Café Eklektika	**82** B3
Columbus Jazzklub	**83** A4
Gödör Klub	**84** B3
Hungarian State Opera House	**85** B3
Kalamajka Táncház	**86** A3
Liszt Ferenc Zeneakadémia	**87** C3
Merlin	**88** B4
Symphony Ticket Office	**89** B2
Ticket Express	**90** B3
Ticket Pro	**91** B4
Trafó Bár Tangó	**92** D6

SHOPPING ⬛	
Bortársaság	**93** B3
Folkart Centrum	**94** B5
Intuita	**95** B5
Központi Antikvárium	**96** B5
Mester Pálinka	**97** A3

TRANSPORT	
BKV Office	**98** C3
Kenguru	**99** D4
Mahart PassNave	(see 31)
Mahart PassNave Ticket Office	**100** B5
MÁV-Start Passenger Service Centre	**101** A3

House (Terror Háza; Map p312; www.terrorhaza.hu; VI Andrássy út 60; adult/concession 1500/750Ft; ☽ 10am-6pm Tue-Fri, to 7.30pm Sat & Sun), almost next door. The museum focuses on the crimes and atrocities committed by Hungary's fascist and Stalinist regimes. The years leading up to the 1956 uprising get the lion's share of the exhibition space.

Further down on Andrássy út, the opulence of the 1884 neo-Renaissance **Hungarian State Opera House** (Magyar Állami Operaház; Map p312, ☎ 332 8197; www.operavisit.hu; VI Andrássy út 22; tours adult/concession 2800/1400Ft; ☽ 3pm & 4pm) is a real treat; try to make it to an evening performance here. **Váci utca**, in Pest's touristy centre, is an extensive pedestrian shopping street. It begins at the southwest terminus of the yellow line, Vörösmarty tér.

PARLIAMENT & AROUND

The huge, riverfront **Parliament** (Parlament; Map p312; ☎ 441 4904; www.parlament.hu; V Kossuth Lajos tér 1-3; adult/concession 2520/1260Ft; ☽ 8am-6pm Mon & Wed-Fri, 8am-2pm Sun May-Sep, 8am-4pm Mon & Wed-Sat, 8am-2pm Sun Oct-Apr) dominates Kossuth Lajos tér. English-language tours are at 10am, noon and 2pm daily.

Across the park is the **Ethnography Museum** (Néprajzi Múzeum; Map p312; www.neprajz.hu; V Kossuth Lajos tér 12; adult/concession 800/400Ft; ☽ 10am-6pm Tue-Sun), which has an extensive collection of national costumes among the permanent displays on folk life and art. Look for the mummified right hand of St Stephen in the chapel of the colossal **St Stephen's Basilica** (Szent István Bazilika; Map p312; V Szent István tér; adult/concession 400/300Ft; ☽ 9am-5pm Apr-Sep, 10am-4pm Oct-Mar) near Bajcsy-Zsilinszky út.

JEWISH QUARTER

Northeast of the Astoria metro stop is what remains of the Jewish quarter. The twin-towered,

HUNGARY

1859 **Great Synagogue** (Nagy Zsinagóga; Map p312; VII Dohány utca 2; synagogue & museum adult/concession 1600/750Ft; ☺ 10am-6.30pm Mon-Thu, to 2pm Fri, to 5.30pm Sun mid-Apr–Oct, 10am-3pm Mon-Thu, to 2pm Fri, to 4pm Sun Nov–mid-Apr) has a museum with a harrowing exhibit on the Holocaust, and behind the synagogue is the **Memorial of the Hungarian Jewish Martyrs** (p312) in the shape of a weeping willow. Funded by the actor Tony Curtis, it's dedicated to those who perished in the death camps. A few blocks south along the *kis körút* (little ring road) is the **Hungarian National Museum** (Magyar Nemzeti Múzeum; Map p312; www.hnm .hu; VIII Múzeum körút 14-16; adult/concession 1000/500Ft; ☺ 10am-6pm Tue-Sun), with its historic relics, from archaeological finds to coronation regalia.

TOURS

To tour the Danube, hop on one of the cruises operated by **Mahart PassNave** (Map p312; ☎ 484 4005; www.mahartpassnave.hu; Vigadó tér Pier; ☺ Apr-Oct). There are regular two-hour sightseeing cruises (adult/concession 2900/1490Ft), and lunch-and dinner-buffet cruises (adult/concession 5990/2990Ft). Tickets can be purchased at the pier before departure.

For a fun way to tour Budapest, day or night, **Yellow Zebra Bikes** (Map p312; ☎ 266 8777; www .yellowzebrabikes.com; V Sütő utca 2, courtyard; ☺ 8.30am-8pm Apr-Oct, 10am-6pm Nov-Mar) offers cycling tours (adult/concession 5000/4500Ft) of the city. The same company runs **Absolute Walking Tours** (☎ 266 8777; www.absolutetours.com), whose repertoire includes an entertaining 3½-hour city walking tour (adult/concession 4000/3500Ft), the Hammer & Sickle Tour (adult/concession 5000/4500 Ft), the 1956 Revolution Walk (6000/3000Ft) and the Absolute Hungaro Gastro Tour (7000/3500Ft).

FESTIVALS & EVENTS

Many festivals and events are held in and around Budapest. Look out for the tourist board's annual *Events Calendar* for a complete listing.

Budapest Spring Festival (www.springfestival.hu) In March.

Sziget Music Festival (www.sziget.hu) On Óbudai hajógyári-sziget (Óbuda Shipbuilding Island), from late July to early August.

Hungarian Formula One Grand Prix (www.hungaro ring.hu) At Mogyoród, 24km northeast of Budapest, in mid-August.

Budapest International Wine Festival (www .winefestival.hu) Held in September.

> **FREE THRILLS**
>
> If you're on a budget, take advantage of these no-cost Budapest attractions:
>
> ■ Stroll through the historic **Castle Hill** area (p309).
>
> ■ Investigate the heroic monuments of **Hősök tere** (p311).
>
> ■ Take in the impressive views from the **Citadella** (p310).
>
> ■ Go people-watching in the attractive surrounds of **City Park** (p311).
>
> ■ Enjoy the flea-market bustle and browsing of the **Ecseri Piac** (p320).

Budapest International Marathon (www.budapest marathon.com) In October.

SLEEPING

Accommodation prices and standards are pretty reasonable in Budapest. Many year-round hostels occupy middle floors of old apartment buildings (with or without a lift) in central Pest. Come summer (July to late August), student dormitories at colleges and universities open to travellers. The travel agency Express (p307) can help book these rooms.

Private rooms in Budapest homes generally cost 6000Ft to 7500Ft for a single, 7000Ft to 8500Ft for a double, and 9000Ft to 13,000Ft for a small apartment. Ibusz (p309) has the most extensive listings in town (some with photos on its website). Two other private-room brokers:

Best Hotel Service (Map p312; ☎ 318 4848; www .besthotelservice.hu; V Sütő utca 2; ☺ 8am-8pm)

To-Ma Travel Agency (Map p312; ☎ 353 0819; www .tomatour.hu; V Október 6 utca 22; ☺ 9am-noon & 1-8pm Mon-Fri, 9am-5pm Sat & Sun)

Buda

BUDGET

Zugligeti Niche Camping (off Map p306; ☎ 200 8346; www.campingniche.hu; XII Zugligeti út 101; camp sites per person 1800Ft, small/big tents 1500/2000, campervans 3200Ft) An excellent option for mixing a city break with a hiking holiday: the camp's in the Buda Hills at the bottom station of a chairlift. Take bus 158 from Moszkva tér to the terminus.

our pick **Back Pack Guesthouse** (Map p306; ☎ 385 8946; www.backpackbudapest.hu; XI Takács Menyhért utca 33;

beds in yurt 2500Ft, large/small dm 3000/3500Ft, d 9000Ft; 🖳) A hippyish, friendly place, though relatively small, with just 50 beds. There's a lush garden in the back with a hammock stretched invitingly between trees. Take bus 7 (from Erzsébet híd or Keleti train station in Pest), tram 49 from the *kis körút* in central Pest, or tram 19 from Batthyány tér in Buda.

Hotel Citadella (Map p308; ☎ 466 5794; www.citadella .hu; XI Citadella sétány, Gellért Hill; dm 3200Ft, r from 10,500Ft) What could be better than sleeping in a historic old fortress? Well, OK, this hotel in the fortress atop Gellért-hegy is pretty threadbare, though the dozen guestrooms are extra large, retain some of their original features and each has its own shower. Take bus 27 from XI Móricz Zsigmond körtér in Buda, then hike about 500m uphill from the stop near the Búsuló Juhász restaurant on Kelenhegyi út.

Martos Hostel (Map p306; ☎ 209 4883; http://hotel .martos.bme.hu; XI Sztoczek utca 5-7; s/d/tr/q/apt from 4000 /6000/9000/12,000/15,000Ft; 🖳) Primarily student accommodation, Martos is open year-round to all. It's a few minutes' walk from Petőfi Bridge (or take tram 4 or 6).

MIDRANGE & TOP END

Papillon Hotel (Map p306; ☎ 212 4750; www.hotelpapil lon.hu; II Rózsahegy utca 3/b; s/d/tr/apt from €31/41/56/72; 🞩 🖳 🞷) This small 20-room hotel in Rózsadomb has a delightful back garden with a small swimming pool, and some rooms have balconies. There are also four apartments available in the same building, one of which has a lovely roof terrace.

Büro Panzió (Map p308; ☎ 212 2929; www.buropanzio .hu; II Dékán utca 3; s/d/tr/q from €42/56/72/82; 🞩 🖳) This pension looks basic from the outside, but its 10 compact rooms are comfortable and have TV and telephone. The central Moszkva tér transportation hub – metro stop, tram stations – is seconds away.

Charles Hotel & Apartments (Map p308; ☎ 212 9169; www.charleshotel.hu; I Hegyalja út 23; d/tr/apt from €45/60/75; 🖳) Somewhat off the beaten track (a train line runs right past it), the Charles has 70 inexpensive 'studios' (larger-than-average rooms) with tiny kitchens and weary-looking furniture, as well as two-room apartments. Bike hire is available for 2000Ft per day.

Hotel Kulturinnov (Map p308; ☎ 224 8102; www .mka.hu; I Szentháromság tér 6; s/d/tr €60/75/100; 🞩) A small hotel sitting in the belly of the grandiose Hungarian Culture Foundation, a neo-Gothic structure dating back to 1904. The rooms are

unimpressive, but you can't beat the scenic locale, on top of Castle Hill.

Danubius Hotel Gellért (Map p312; ☎ 889 5500; www .danubiusgroup.com/gellert; XI Szent Gellért tér 1; s/d/ste from €67/135/233; 🞩 🖳 🞷) Peek through the doors of this turn-of-the-20th-century grand dame, even if you don't choose to stay here. The 234-room, four-star hotel has loads of character, and its famous thermal baths (p310) are free for guests. Prices depend on your room's view and the quality of its bathroom.

Burg Hotel (Map p308; ☎ 212 0269; www.burghotel budapest.com; I Szentháromság tér 7-8; s/d/ste from €85/99/109; 🞩 🖳) The affordable Burg is at the centre of Castle Hill, just opposite Matthias Church. Ask for a room overlooking Matthias Church for a truly historic wake-up view. The 26 partly refurbished rooms are fairly ordinary, but location is everything here.

our pick **Lánchíd 19** (Map p308; ☎ 419 1900; www.lanchid19hotel.hu; I Lánchíd utca 19; s/d/ste from €120/140/300; 🞩 🖳) This new boutique number facing the Danube won the European Hotel Design Award for Best Architecture in 2008. Its facade features images created by special sensors that reflect the movement of the Danube, and its rooms are equally impressive, containing distinctive artwork and unique chairs designed by art students.

Pest

BUDGET

Home-Made Hostel (Map p312; ☎ 302 2103; www .homemadehostel.com; VI Teréz körút 22; dm/d/q from €8/40/56; 🖳) This cosy, extremely welcoming hostel has unique decor, with recycled tables hanging upside down from the ceiling, and old valises serving as lockers. The old-style kitchen is also a blast from the past.

Hostel Marco Polo (Map p312; ☎ 413 2555; www .marcopolohostel.com; VII Nyár utca 6; dm/s/d/tr/q from 3000/ 10,000/12,000/15,000/18,000; 🖳) Very central flagship hostel with swish, powder-blue rooms. All rooms other than dorms have telephones and TVs, and there's a lovely courtyard.

Unity Hostel (Map p312; ☎ 413 7377; www.unity hostel.com; VI Király utca 60; dm/d from €12/36; 🖳) Hostel located in the heart of party town, with a roof terrace taking in breathtaking views of the Liszt Music Academy. There are 24 beds in five rooms over two levels.

Gingko Hostel (Map p312; ☎ 266 6107; www.gingko .hu; V Szép utca 5; dm/d/q 3500/11,000/18,000Ft; 🖳) This very green hostel is one of the best kept in

HUNGARY

town and the fount-of-all-knowledge manager keeps it so clean you could eat off the floor. There are books to share, bikes to hire (per day 2500Ft) and a positively enormous double giving on to Reáltanoda utca.

Red Bus Hostel (Map p312; ☎ 266 0136; www .redbusbudapest.hu; V Semmelweiss utca 14; dm/s/d/tr 3900/9900/9900/13,000Ft; 🖳) Red Bus is a central and well-managed place, with large and airy dorms as well as five private rooms. It's a quiet spot with a fair number of rules – the full 16 are listed in reception – so don't expect to party here.

Central Backpack King Hostel (Map p312; ☎ 06 30 200 7184; centralbpk@freemail.hu; V Október 6 utca 15; dm/d/tr/q from €15/54/66/84; 🖳) This upbeat place has dorm rooms with between seven and nine beds on one floor, and doubles, triples and quads on another. There's a small but scrupulously clean kitchen, and a large and very bright common room.

Boat Hotel Fortuna (Map p306; ☎ 288 8100; www .fortunahajo.hu; XIII Szent István Park, Pesti alsó rakpart; s/d/tr from €20/30/40; 🌣 🖳) Sleeping on this one-time river ferry anchored in the Danube is a unique experience. The best choices on this 'boatel' are the air-conditioned rooms with shower and toilet at water level.

MIDRANGE

Garibaldi Guesthouse (Map p312; ☎ 302 3457; garibaldi guest@hotmail.com; V Garibaldi utca 5; s/d €28/36, apt per person €25-45) This old building belongs to a gregarious owner who has many apartments available over several floors, as well as private rooms in apartments with shared bathroom and kitchen.

Connection Guest House (Map p312; ☎ 267 7104; www.connectionguesthouse.com; VII Király utca 41; s/d from €45/50; 🖳) This central gay-friendly pension above a leafy courtyard attracts a young crowd due to its proximity to nightlife venues. Three of the seven rooms share bathroom facilities.

Hotel Medosz (Map p312; ☎ 3753 1700; www.medosz hotel.hu; VI Jókai tér 9; s/d/tr/ste from €49/59/69/89) Well priced for its central location, the Medosz is opposite the restaurants and bars of Liszt Ferenc tér. Its rooms are well worn but slated for a revamp at the time of research.

Leo Panzió (Map p312; ☎ 266 9041; www.leopanzio.hu; V Kossuth Lajos utca 2/a; s/d from €49/76; 🌣) Just steps from Váci utca, this B&B with a lion motif is in the middle of everything. A dozen of its 14 immaculate rooms look down on busy Kossuth Lajos utca, but they all have double glazing and are quiet.

Radio Inn (Map p312; ☎ 342 8347; www.radioinn.hu; VI Benczúr utca 19; s/d/apt from €65/78/80) Spacious apartments with full kitchens, sitting areas and one or two bedrooms are the drawcard here, perfect for a longer stay. Embassies are your neighbours on the quiet, tree-lined street near Bajza utca metro stop (M1 yellow line).

Hotel Anna (Map p312; ☎ 327 2000; www.anna hotel.hu; VIII Gyulai Pál utca; s/d/ste from €66/82/88) Anna has 42 fairly basic rooms scattered over three floors of two 18th-century buildings that surround an enormous courtyard and garden. It's not the greatest value for money in town, but the rooms are quiet and the location is great.

Cotton House (Map p312; ☎ 354 2600; www.cotton house.hu; Jókai utca 26; r €70-150; 🖳) This 23-room guest house has a jazz/speakeasy theme, complete with old radios and vintage telephones that actually work. Prices vary, depending on the season and whether there's a shower, tub or spa in the bathroom.

Erzsébet Hotel (Map p312; ☎ 889 3700; www.danubius group.com/erzsebet; V Károlyi Mihály utca 11-15; s/d from €72/84; 🌣 🖳) The Erzsébet is in a very good location in the centre of the university district, within easy walking distance of the pubs and bars of Ráday utca. The 123 rooms – mostly twins – are spread across eight floors. They tend to be small and somewhat dark, but they're comfortable enough.

TOP END

Soho Hotel (Map p312; ☎ 872 8292; www.sohohotel .hu; VII Dohány utca 64; s/d/ste from €99/109/169; 🌣 🖳) This delightfully stylish boutique hotel sports a foyer bar in eye-popping reds, blues and lime greens. The nonallergenic rooms have bamboo matting on the walls, parquet floors and a music/film theme throughout (check out the portraits of Bono, George Michael and Marilyn).

Corinthia Grand Hotel Royal (Map p312; ☎ 479 4000; www.corinthia.hu; VII Erzsébet körút 43-49; r/ste from €179/310; 🌣 🖳 🖳) Decades in the remaking, this five-star beauty has been carefully reconstructed in the Austro-Hungarian style of heavy drapes, sparkling chandeliers and large, luxurious ballrooms. Its restored Royal Spa, dating from 1886 but now as modern as tomorrow, is a legend reborn.

Four Seasons Gresham Palace Hotel (Map p312; ☎ 268 6000; www.fourseasons.com; V Roosevelt tér 5-6;

s/d/ste from €305/340/1090; ⊠ ⊠) Restored to its bygone elegance, with mushroom-shape windows, whimsical ironwork and glittering gold decorative tiles on the exterior, the Four Seasons inhabits the art nouveau Gresham Palace (1907) and provides superb views of the Danube through Roosevelt Park.

EATING

Very roughly, a cheap two-course sit-down meal for one person with a glass of wine or beer in Budapest costs 3000Ft, while the same meal in a midrange eatery would be 6500Ft. An expensive meal ranges up to 10,000Ft. Unless otherwise stated, restaurants listed below are open from 10am or 11am to 11pm or midnight. It's always best to arrive by 9pm or 10pm at the latest, though, to ensure being served. It is advisable to book tables at medium-priced to expensive restaurants, especially at the weekend.

Ráday utca and Liszt Ferenc tér are the two most popular traffic-free streets. The moment the weather warms up, tables and umbrellas spring up on the pavements and the people of Budapest crowd the streets. Both areas have oodles of cafes, restaurants, snack shops and bars.

International fast-food places are a dime a dozen in Budapest, but old-style self-service restaurants, the mainstay of both white- and blue-collar workers under the old regime, are disappearing fast. As everywhere else, pizzerias are on an upward spiral.

Buda

Éden (Map p308; ☎ 06 20 337 7575; I Iskola utca 31; mains 790-990Ft; ☽ 8am-9pm Mon-Thu, 8am-6pm Fri, 11am-9pm Sun) Located in an 1811 town house just below Castle Hill, this self-service place offers solid but healthy vegetarian fare.

Új Lanzhou (Map p308; ☎ 201 9247; II Fő utca 71; mains 1190-3290Ft; ☽ noon-11pm) Many diners think this is the most authentic Chinese restaurant in Budapest. Make up your own mind while sampling the excellent soups, the relatively large choice of vegetarian dishes, and the stylish surrounds.

Szent Jupát (Map p308; ☎ 212 2923; II Dékán utca 3; mains 1490-3380Ft; ☽ noon-2am Sun-Thu, to 4am Fri & Sat) This is the classic late-night choice for solid Hungarian fare, and there's half a dozen vegetarian choices too. It's just north of Moszkva tér and opposite the Fény utca market – enter from II Retek utca 16.

Kisbuda Gyöngye (Map p306; ☎ 368 6402; III Kenyeres utca 34; mains 1880-4680Ft; ☽ noon-midnight Mon-Sat) A traditional and very elegant Hungarian restaurant in Óbuda, with an antique-cluttered dining room evoking a fin de siècle atmosphere.

Marcello (Map p306; ☎ 466 6231; XI Bartók Béla út 40; mains 2000Ft; ☽ noon-10pm Mon-Sat) Popular with students from the nearby university for over two decades, this family-owned eatery has good Italian fare at affordable prices.

Le Jardin de Paris (Map p308; ☎ 201 0047; II Fő utca 20; mains 2200-4700Ft; ☽ noon-midnight) A regular haunt of staff from the French Institute across the road, the Parisian Garden is located in a wonderful old town house abutting an ancient castle wall. The back garden is a delight in the warmer months. Set lunch is 1500Ft.

Tabáni Terasz (Map p308; ☎ 201 1086; I Apród utca 10; mains 2600-4900Ft; ☽ noon-midnight) This delightful terrace and cellar restaurant at the foot of Castle Hill has a modern take on Hungarian cuisine, with lighter dishes and an excellent wine selection. Set lunch is a snip at under 1200Ft.

Csalogány 26 (Map p308; ☎ 201 7892; I Csalogány utca 26; mains 2800-4000Ft; noon-3pm & 7pm-midnight Tue-Sat) One of the best restaurants in Budapest turns out superb international dishes. Try the tenderloin of *mangalica* (a kind of pork) with puy lentils (2800Ft). A three-course set lunch is 1400Ft.

For self-catering in Buda, visit the **Fény utca market** (Fény utcai piac; Map p308; II Fény utca; ☽ 6am-6pm Mon-Fri, 6am-2pm Sat), just next to the Mammut shopping mall.

Pest

BUDGET

Govinda (Map p312; ☎ 269 1625; V Vigyázó Ferenc utca 4; mains 230-490Ft; ☽ 11.30am-8pm Mon-Fri, noon-9pm Sat) This basement restaurant northeast of the Chain Bridge serves wholesome salads, soups and desserts as well as a daily set menu for 1550/1850Ft (small/large).

Első Pesti Rétesház (Map p312; V Október 6 utca 22; strudels 240-290Ft; ☽ 9am-11pm Mon-Fri, 11am-11pm Sat & Sun) The decor may resemble a Magyar Disneyland, with olde-worlde counters, painted plates on the walls and curios embedded in plexiglass washbasins. However, the First Strudel House of Pest is just the place to taste this Hungarian pastry filled with apple, cheese, poppy seeds or sour cherries.

Szeráj (Map p312; ☎ 311 6690; XIII Szent István körút 13; mains 450-1400Ft, ☽ 9am-4am Mon-Thu, to 5am Fri &

HUNGARY

Sat, to 2am Sun) A very inexpensive self-service Turkish place for *lahmacun* (or 'Turkish pizza'), falafel and kebabs, with up to a dozen varieties on offer.

Vapiano (Map p312; ☎ 411 0864; V Bécsi utca 5; mains 1200-1950Ft) A very welcome addition is this pizza and pasta bar where everything is prepared on site. You'll be in and out in no time, but the taste will pleasantly linger.

Köleves (Map p312; ☎ 322 1011; Kazinczy utca 35 & Dob utca 26; mains 1280-3680Ft; ☻ noon-midnight) Always buzzing, 'Stone Soup' attracts a young crowd with its delicious matzo-ball soup, tapas, lively decor and reasonable prices. It's a great place to first try Hungarian food.

Iguana (Map p312; ☎ 331 4352; V Zoltán utca 16; mains 1390-3990Ft; ☻ 11.30am-12.30am) Iguana serves decent-enough Mexican food, but it's hard to say whether the pull is the enchilada and burrito combination plates, the fajitas or the frenetic party atmosphere.

A self-catering option is the **Hold utca market** (Map p312; V Hold utca 11; ☻ 6am-5pm Mon, 6.30am-6pm Tue-Fri, 6.30am-2pm Sat) near Szabadság tér. The **Nagycsarnok** (Great Market; Map p312; IX Vámház körút 1-3; ☻ 6am-5pm Mon, to 6pm Tue-Fri, to 2pm Sat) is a vast market built of steel and glass. Head here for fruit, vegetables, deli items, fish and meat.

A nonstop supermarket in Pest is the **Rothschild Supermarket** (Map p312; VI Teréz körút 19; ☻ 24hr), near Oktogon.

MIDRANGE

ourpick Klassz (Map p312; ☎ 413 1545; www.klassz.eu; VI Andrássy út 41; mains 1490-3490Ft; ☻ 11.30am-11pm Mon-Sat, 11.30am-6pm Sun) Klassz is focused on wine, but the food is also of a high standard. Varieties of foie gras and native *mangalica* pork are permanent stars on the menu, with dishes such as Burgundy-style leg of rabbit and lamb trotters with vegetable ragout playing cameo roles.

Momotaro Ramen (Map p312; ☎ 269 3802; V Széchenyi utca 16; mains 1500-3600Ft; ☻ 11am-10pm) This is a favourite pit stop for Chinese and Japanese noodles and dumplings when the *pálinka* has been a-flowing the night before. But it's also good for more-substantial dishes.

Menza (Map p312; ☎ 413 1482; VI Liszt Ferenc tér 2; mains 1890-2490Ft; ☻ 10am-1am) This stylish restaurant on Budapest's most lively square takes its name from the Hungarian for a drab school canteen – something it is anything but. It's always packed with diners who come for its simply but perfectly cooked Hungarian classics with a modern twist. Weekday two-course set lunches are just 890Ft.

Pireus Rembetiko Taverna (Map p312; ☎ 266 0292; V Fóvám tér 2-3; mains 1890-4990Ft; ☻ noon-midnight) Overlooking the Nagycsarnok (Great Market) at the foot of Liberty Bridge, this place serves reasonably priced and pretty authentic Greek fare.

Fülemüle (Map p312; ☎ 266 7947; VIII Kőfaragó utca 5; mains 1900-4800Ft; ☻ noon-10pm Sun-Thu, noon-11pm Fri & Sat) Quaint Hungarian restaurant that seems frozen in time in the interwar period. Dishes mingle Hungarian and international tastes with some old-style Jewish favourites.

Soul Café (Map p312; ☎ 217 6986; IX Ráday utca 11-13; mains 1990-4390Ft; ☻ noon-11.30pm) One of the better choices along a street heaving with so-so restaurants and iffy cafes, the Soul has inventive European cuisine and decor and a great terrace on both sides of the street.

Salam Bombay (Map p312; ☎ 411 1252; V Mérleg utca 6; mains 2190-3990Ft; ☻ noon-3pm & 6-11pm) If you hanker after a fix of authentic curry or tandoori in a bright, upbeat environment, look no further than this attractive eatery just east of Roosevelt tér. As would be expected, there's a wide choice of vegetarian dishes.

TOP END

Marquis de Salade (Map p312; ☎ 302 4086; VI Hajós utca 43; mains 2400-3400Ft; ☻ noon-midnight) Taking its cue from its odd name, this basement restaurant is a strange hybrid of a place, with dishes from Russia and Azerbaijan as well as Hungary. There are lots of quality vegetarian choices on the menu.

Bagolyvár (Map p306; ☎ 468 3110; XIV Állatkerti út 2; mains 2850-4250Ft; ☻ noon-11pm) Serving imaginatively reworked Hungarian classics, the 'Owl's Castle' attracts the Budapest foodie cognoscenti. It's staffed entirely by women – in the kitchen, at table, and front of house.

DRINKING

One of Budapest's ceaseless wonders is the number of bars, cellars, cafes, clubs and general places to drink.

Budapest in the 19th century rivalled Vienna in its cafe culture, though cafe numbers waned under communism. The majority of the surviving traditional cafes are in Pest, but Buda can still lay claim to a handful.

HUNGARY

Budapest is also loaded with pubs and bars, and there's enough variation to satisfy all tastes. In summer the preferred drinking venues are the *kerteks*, outdoor entertainment zones.

The best places to drink are in Pest (Buda's too sleepy to stay up all night), especially along Liszt Ferenc tér and Radáy utca, which have a positively festive feel during the summer.

Buda

Kisrabló (Map p306; XI Zenta utca 3; ☾ 11am-2am Mon-Sat) Attractive and well-run pub that's very popular with students. Take tram 19 or 49 one stop past Danubius Hotel Gellért.

Ruszwurm (Map p308; I Szentháromság utca 7; ☾ 10am-7pm) This is the perfect place for coffee and cake in the Castle District, though it can get pretty crowded.

Pest

Kiadó Kocsma (Map p312; VI Jókai tér 3; ☾ 10am-2am Mon-Fri, noon-2am Sat & Sun) The 'Pub for Rent' is a great place for a swift pint and a quick bite (salads and pasta), and is just a stone's throw away from Liszt Ferenc tér.

Szimpla (Map p312; VII Kertész utca 48; ☾ 10am-2am Mon-Fri, noon-2am Sat, noon-midnight Sun) This distressed-looking, very unflashy place remains one of the most popular drinking venues south of Liszt Ferenc tér. There's live music in the evenings from Tuesday to Thursday.

Centrál Kávéház (Map p312; V Károlyi Mihály utca 9; ☾ 8am-midnight) One of the finest coffee houses in the city, with high, decorated ceilings, lace curtains, pot plants, elegant coffee cups and professional service. You can have an omelette breakfast here, eat a full-on meal, or just sit down with a coffee or beer and enjoy the atmosphere.

For more coffee in exquisite art nouveau surroundings, two places are particularly noteworthy. **Gerbeaud** (Map p312; V Vörösmarty tér 7; ☾ 9am-9pm; ☒), Budapest's cake-and-coffee-culture king, has been serving since 1870. Or station yourself where Hungary's dreaded ÁVH secret police once had its HQ, at **Lukács** (Map p312; VI Andrássy út 70; ☾ 8.30am-8pm Mon-Fri, 9am-8pm Sat, 9.30am-8pm Sun).

ENTERTAINMENT

Budapest has a nightlife that can keep you up for days on end – and not just because the techno beat from the club next to your hotel is keeping you awake. There are nightclubs, bars,

live concerts (classical and folk), Hungarian traditional dancing nights, opera treats, ballet, DJ bars and random **Cinetrip** (www.cinetrip.hu) club nights at the thermal spas. It's usually not difficult getting tickets or getting in; the hard part is deciding what to do.

To find out what's on, check out the free **Budapest Funzine** (www.funzine.hu) published every second Thursday and available at hotels, bars, cinemas and various tourist spots. More comprehensive is the freebie **PestiEst** (www.est.hu, in Hungarian) and the ultrathorough **Pesti Műsor** (Budapest Program; www.pestimusor.hu, in Hungarian; 295Ft), with everything from clubs and films to art exhibitions and classical music. Both appear every Thursday.

The free *Koncert Kalendárium*, published monthly (bimonthly in summer), covers the performing arts, including classical concerts, opera and dance. A hip little publication with all sorts of insider's tips is the *Budapest City Spy Map*. It's available free at pubs and bars.

Gay & Lesbian Venues

Alter Ego (Map p312; www.alteregoclub.hu; VI Dessewffy utca 33; ☾ 10pm-5am Fri & Sat) Budapest's premier gay club, with the coolest crowd (think attitude) and the best dance music.

Café Eklektika (Map p312; V Semmelweis utca 21; ☾ noon-midnight) This lesbian-owned cafe and restaurant (lunch buffet 990Ft) in stunning new digs is a great place for a meal and a little LGBT information gathering. Attracts a youthful, arty crowd.

Performing Arts

Magyar Állami Operaház (Hungarian State Opera House; Map p312; ☎ 331 2550; www.opera.hu; VI Andrássy út 22) Take in a performance while admiring the incredibly rich interior decoration. The ballet company performs here as well.

Liszt Ferenc Zeneakadémia (Liszt Academy of Music; Map p312; ☎ 342 0179; VI Liszt Ferenc tér 8) You can hear the musicians practising from outside this magnificent concert hall, which hosts classical music performances.

Classical concerts are held regularly in the city's churches, including Matthias Church (p309) on Castle Hill in Buda.

A useful ticket broker, with outlets across town, is **Ticket Express** (Map p312; ☎ 312 0000; www.tex.hu; VI Andrássy út 18; ☾ 10am-6.30pm Mon-Fri, to 3pm Sat). **Ticket Pro** (Map p312; ☎ 555 5155; www.ticketpro.hu; VII Károly körút 9; ☾ 9am-9pm Mon-Fri, 10am-2pm Sat) also sells tickets to plays, concerts and sporting events, while the **Symphony Ticket Office** (Szimfonikus Jegyiroda; Map p312; ☎ 302 3841; VI Nagymező utca 19; ☉ 10am-6pm Mon-Fri, 10am-2pm Sat) specialises in classical-music events.

Live Music

Kalamajka Táncház (Map p312; ☎ 354 3400; V Arany János utca 10; ☉ 8.30pm-midnight Sat) The Kalamajka is an excellent place to hear authentic Hungarian music, especially on its dance nights, when everyone gets up and takes part.

Fonó Budai Zeneház (Map p306; ☎ 206 5300; www .fono.hu; XI Sztregova utca 3; ☉ 2-10pm Wed-Fri, 7-10pm Sat) The best place in Budapest for folk music of any kind, including the diverse sounds of Hungarian, Transylvanian, Balkan, Romani, klezmer and tango. You might even strike a didgeridoo night.

Columbus Jazzklub (Map p312; ☎ 266 9013; www .majazz.hu; V Pesti alsó rakpart at Lánchíd bridgehead; ☉ 4pm-midnight) Jazz venue located on a boat moored in the Danube, just off the northern end of V Vigadó tér, hosting big-name local and international performers. Music starts at 8pm nightly.

Nightclubs

Not all clubs and music bars in Budapest levy a cover charge, but those that do will ask for between 1000Ft and 2500Ft at the door. Nightclubs usually open from 4pm to 2am Sunday to Thursday and until 4am on Friday and Saturday; some only open on weekends.

Merlin (Map p312; www.merlinbudapest.org; V Gerlóczy utca 4; ☉ 10am-midnight Sun-Thu, to 5am Fri & Sat) One of those something-for-everyone places, with everything from jazz and breakbeat to techno and house. It's most visitors' first port of call in Budapest.

Gödör Klub (Map p312; V Erzsébet tér; ☉ 9am-late) This large underground club is a real mixed bag, offering a mix of folk, world, rock and pop, played to an audience of all ages.

Trafó Bár Tangó (Map p312; IX Lilliom utca 41; ☉ 6pm-4am) An arty crowd makes the scene beneath this cultural house and exhibition space, enjoying some of the best DJs in town.

SHOPPING

As well as the usual folk arts, wines, spirits, food and music, Budapest has more distinctive items such as hand-blown glassware and antique books. But there are those who consider the city's flea markets their shopping

highlight – and they certainly are a distinctive Budapest experience. Shops are generally open from 9am or 10am to 6pm during the week, and till 1pm on Saturday.

Folkart Centrum (Map p312; ☎ 318 4697; V Váci utca 58; ☉ 10am-7pm) Everything Magyar – whether made here or in China – is available here, from embroidered waistcoats and tablecloths to painted eggs and plates.

Intuita (Map p312; ☎ 266 5864; V Váci utca 67; ☉ 11am-6pm) Purveyor of modern Hungarian crafted items such as hand-blown glass, jewellery, ceramics and bound books.

Központi Antikvárium (Map p312; ☎ 317 3514; V Múzeum körút 13-15) For antique and secondhand books, try the Central Antiquarian, which was established in 1885.

There's an excellent selection of Hungarian wines at **Bortársaság** (Map p312; ☎ 328 0341; V Szent István tér 3; ☉ noon-8pm Mon-Fri, 10am-4pm Sat) in Pest, and you can pick up the Hungarian fruit-flavoured brandy *pálinka* at **Mester Pálinka** (Map p312; ☎ 374 0388; V Zrínyi utca 18).

Two major flea markets take place in Budapest during the week. The closest to the city centre is **Városligeti Bolhapiac** (Map p306; ☉ 7am-2pm Sat & Sun) in City Park. There's junk and antiques, and the best things are to be found early in the morning. The real market mamma, though, is the **Ecseri Piac** (off Map p306; XIX Nagykőrösi út 156; ☉ 8am-4pm Mon-Fri, 6am-3pm Sat, 8am-1pm Sun), on the edge of town. International antiques dealers come to scout on Saturdays, so things can get pricey. Take bus 54 from Boráros tér in Pest or, for a quicker journey, the red-numbered express bus 84E, 89E or 94E from the Határ utca stop on the M3 metro line and get off at the Fiume utca stop. Then follow the crowds over the pedestrian bridge.

GETTING THERE & AWAY
Air

The main international carriers fly in and out of Terminal 2 at Budapest's **Ferihegy airport** (www.bud.hu), 24km southeast of the centre on Hwy 4; low-cost airlines use the older Terminal 1 next door. For carriers flying to Hungary, see p360.

Boat

Mahart PassNave (Map p312; www.marhartpassnave.hu; Belgrád rakpart ☎ 484 4010; Vigadó tér Pier ☎ 484 4005), with two docks, runs ferries and hydrofoils from Budapest. A hydrofoil service on the Danube River between Budapest and Vienna

5½ to 6½ hours) operates daily from late April to early October; passengers can disembark at Bratislava with advance notice (four hours). Adult one-way/return fares for Vienna are €89/109 and for Bratislava €79/99. Students with ISIC cards receive a €10 discount, and children between two and 14 years of age travel for half-price. Boats leave from the Nemzetközi hajóállomás (International Ferry Pier).

There are ferries departing at 10.30am daily for Szentendre (one way/return 1490/2235Ft, 1½ hours) from May to September, decreasing to 9am departures on weekends only in April and October.

Vác (one way/return 1990/2990Ft, 40 minutes), Visegrád (one way/return 2690/3990Ft, one hour) and Esztergom (one way/return 3290/4990Ft, 1½ hours) can be reached by fast hydrofoil from Budapest at 9.30am on weekends between May and September (and also on Friday from June to August). There are also slower daily ferries at 8am from Budapest to Vác (one way/return 1490/2235Ft, 2½ hours), Visegrád (one way/return 1590/2385Ft, 3½ hours) and Esztergom (one way/return 1990/2985Ft, 5½ hours) between June and August. Services run on Friday and weekends in May, and weekends only in September.

When day-tripping to the Danube Bend by ferry, remember to check the return departure time when you arrive at your destination. Most sail to Budapest between 4.30pm and 6.45pm.

Bus

Volánbusz (☎ 382 0888; www.volanbusz.hu), the national bus line, has an extensive list of destinations from Budapest. All international buses and some buses to/from southern Hungary use **Népliget bus station** (Map p306; IX Üllői út 131). **Stadionok bus station** (Map p306; XIV Hungária körút 48-52) generally serves places to the east of Budapest. Most buses to the northern Danube Bend arrive at and leave from the **Árpád híd bus station** (Map p306; off XIII Róbert Károly körút). All stations are on metro lines, and all are in Pest. If the ticket office is closed, you can buy your ticket on the bus.

Buses depart from Budapest for Vienna (5900Ft, 3½ hours, five daily); Bratislava, Slovakia (in Hungarian, Pozsony; 3700Ft, four hours, one daily); Subotica in Serbia (in Hungarian, Szabadka; 3900Ft, 4½ hours, one daily); Rijeka in Croatia (9900Ft, 8¼ hours,

one weekly), Prague in the Czech Republic (9900Ft, 7½ hours, two weekly); and Sofia in Bulgaria (12,500Ft, 13½ hours, three weekly). Other countries serviced include Belgium, Denmark, France, Germany, Great Britain, Italy, Netherlands, Sweden and Switzerland; sample destinations include Frankfurt (22,900Ft, 18 hours, daily), Munich (14,900Ft, 10 hours, four weekly), Paris (24,900Ft, 21 hours, three weekly), London (30,900Ft, 27 hours, four weekly) and Rome (24,900Ft, 22½ hours, twice weekly) via Florence (19,900Ft, 19 hours, twice weekly).

Car & Motorcycle

Car rental is not recommended if you are staying in Budapest. The public transport network is extensive and cheap, whereas parking is scarce and road congestion is high.

If you want to venture into the countryside, travelling by car is an option. Daily rates start at around €60 per day with unlimited kilometres included. If the company does not have an office at the airport, it will usually provide free pick-up and delivery within Budapest or at the airport during office hours. All the major international chains have branches in Terminal 2 at Ferihegy airport.

Two good options:

Anselport (☎ 362 6080; www.anselport.hu; ☒ 9am-6pm) Reliable outfit.

Fox Autorent (☎ 382 9000; www.foxautorent.com; ☒ 8am-6pm) Another good bet.

Train

The Hungarian State Railways, **MÁV** (☎ 06 40 494949; www.mav.hu) covers the country well and has its schedule online. The **MÁV-Start passenger service centre** (Map p312; ☎ 512 7921; www.mav-start.hu; V József Attila utca 16) provides information and sells domestic and international train tickets and makes seat reservations (though you can also buy tickets at the busy stations).

Keleti train station (Eastern; Map p306; VIII Kerepesi út 2-4) handles international trains from Vienna and most other points west, plus domestic trains to/from the north and northeast. For some Romanian destinations, as well as domestic ones to/from the northwest and the Danube Bend, head for **Nyugati train station** (Western; Map p312; VI Nyugati tér). For trains bound for Lake Balaton and the south, go to **Déli train station** (Southern; Map p308; I Krisztina körút 37). All three train stations are on metro lines.

HUNGARY

Some direct train connections from Budapest include Vienna (€26, three hours), Austria; Bratislava (€16, 2½ hours), Slovakia; Bucharest (€82, 13 to 15 hours), Romania; Csop (4½ hours) and Kyiv (€96, 24 hours), Ukraine, continuing to Moscow (37 hours); Berlin (€58, 12 hours), Frankfurt (€78, 15 hours) and Munich (€58, seven to nine hours), Germany; Ljubljana (€39, 8½ hours), Slovenia; Prague (€38, seven hours), Czech Republic; Warsaw (€58, 12 hours), Poland; Zürich (€78, 12 hours), Switzerland; Venice (€55, 14 hours), Italy; Sofia (€77, 18 hours), Bulgaria; and Thessaloniki, Greece (23 hours).

GETTING AROUND
To/From the Airport

The simplest way to get to town is to take the **Airport Minibus** (☎ 296 8555; www.airportshuttle .hu; one way/return 2990/4990Ft) directly to the place you're staying. Buy tickets at the clearly marked stands in the arrivals halls.

An alternative is travelling with **Zóna Taxi** (☎ 365 5555), which has the monopoly on picking up taxi passengers from the airport. Fares to most central locations range from 5100Ft to 5700Ft. Of course, you can take any taxi *to* the airport, and several companies offer a flat fare (between 4600Ft and 5100Ft) to/from Ferihegy.

The cheapest (and slowest) way to get into the city centre from Terminal 2A and 2B is to take city bus 200 (270Ft, or 350Ft on the bus), which terminates at the Kőbánya-Kispest metro station. Look for the stop on the footpath between terminals 2A and 2B. From its final stop, take the M3 metro into the city centre. The total cost is 540Ft to 620Ft.

Bus 93 runs from Terminal 1 to Kőbánya-Kispest metro station. Trains also link Terminal 1 with Nyugati station. They run between one and six times an hour between 4am and 11pm and cost 300Ft (or 520Ft if you board the hourly IC train). The journey takes 20 minutes.

Boat

From May to August, the **BKV passenger ferry** (Map p306; ☎ 461 6500; www.bkv.hu) departs from Boráros tér Terminus beside Petőfi Bridge, south of the centre, and heads for III Pünkösdfürdő in Óbuda, a 2¼-hour trip with 14 stops along the way. Tickets (adult/concession 900/450Ft from end to end) are sold on board. The ferry stop closest to the Castle

District is Batthyány tér, and Petőfi tér is no far from Vörösmarty tér, a convenient plac to pick up the boat on the Pest side.

Public Transport

Public transport is run by **BKV** (☎ 461 6500; www .bkv.hu). The three underground metro lines (M1 yellow, M2 red, M3 blue) meet at Deák tér ir Pest. The HÉV above-ground suburban railway runs north from Batthyány tér in Buda. A *turista* transport pass is only good on the HÉV within the city limits (south of the Békásmegyer stop). There's also an extensive network of buses, trams and trolleybuses. Public transport operates from 4.30am until 11.30pm, and 35 night buses run along main roads.

A single ticket for all forms of transport is 270Ft (60 minutes of uninterrupted travel on the same metro, bus, trolleybus or tram line *without* transferring/changing). A transfer ticket (420Ft) is valid for one trip with one validated transfer within 90 minutes. The three-day *turista* pass (3400Ft) or the seven-day pass (4000Ft) make things easier, allowing unlimited travel inside the city limits. Keep your ticket or pass handy; the fine for 'riding black' is 6000Ft on the spot, or 12,000Ft if you pay later at the **BKV Office** (Map p312; ☎ 461 6800; VII Akácfa utca 22; ☒ 6am-8pm Mon-Fri, 8am-1.45pm Sat).

Taxi

Taxi drivers overcharging foreigners in Budapest has been a problem for some time. Never get into a taxi that lacks an official yellow licence plate, the logo of the taxi firm, and a visible table of fares. If you have to take a taxi, it's best to call one; this costs less than if you flag one down. Make sure you know the number of the landline phone you're calling from, as that's how the dispatcher establishes your address (though you can call from a mobile as well). Dispatchers usually speak English. **City** (☎ 211 1111), **Fő** (☎ 222 2222) and **Rádió** (☎ 377 7777) are reliable companies.

THE DANUBE BEND

North of Budapest, the Danube breaks through the Pilis and Börzsöny Hills in a sharp bend before continuing along the Slovak border. The Roman Empire had its northern border here, and medieval kings ruled Hungary from majestic palaces overlooking the river at Esztergom and Visegrád. East of Visegrád

he river divides, with Szentendre and Vác on
different branches. Today the easy access to
historic monuments, rolling green scenery –
and vast numbers of souvenir craft shops – lure
many day trippers from Budapest.

SZENTENDRE
☎ 26 / pop 24,000

Once an artists colony, now a popular day
trip 19km north of Budapest, pretty little Szentendre (*sen*-ten-dreh) has narrow,
winding streets and is a favourite with sou-
venir-shoppers. The charming old centre has
plentiful cafes and art-and-craft galleries, and
there are several Orthodox churches that are
worth a peek. Expect things to get crowded
in summer and at weekends. Outside town
is the largest open-air village museum in
the country.

Orientation & Information
From the HÉV train and bus stations, walk
under the subway and up Kossuth Lajos utca
to Fő tér, the centre of the Old Town. The
Duna korzó and the river embankment is a
block east of this square. The Mahart ferry pier

is about 1km northeast on Czóbel sétány, off
Duna korzó. There are no left-luggage offices
at the HÉV train or bus stations.

Tourinform (☎ 317 965; szentendre@tourinform.hu;
Dumtsa Jenő utca 22; ☽ 9.30am-4.30pm Mon-Fri year-round,
10am-2pm Sat & Sun mid-Mar–Oct) has information
about the numerous small museums and galleries in town. The **OTP Bank** (Dumtsa Jenő utca 6) is
just off Fő tér, and the **main post office** (Kossuth
Lajos utca 23-25) is across from the bus and train
stations. **Silver Blue** (Dunakanyar Körút 14; per hr 400Ft;
☽ 10am-8pm Mon-Sat) is an internet cafe near the
train and bus terminals.

Sights
Begin your sightseeing at the colourful Fő tér,
the town's main square. Here you'll find many
structures from the 18th century, including
the 1763 **Memorial Cross** (Emlékkereszt) and the
1752 Serbian Orthodox **Blagoveštenska Church**
(Blagoveštenska Templom; Fő tér; admission 250Ft; ☽ 10am-
5pm Tue-Sun), which is small but stunning.

All the pedestrian lanes surrounding the
square burst with shops, the merchandise spilling out into displays on the streets. Downhill
to the east, off a side street on the way to the

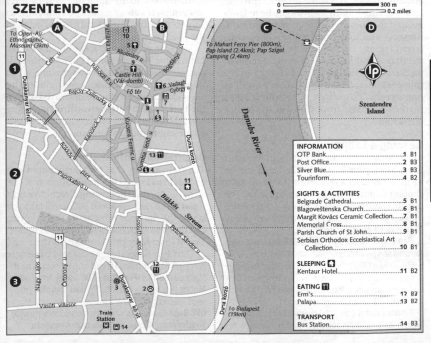

SZENTENDRE

0 ——— 300 m
0 ——— 0.2 miles

HUNGARY

Danube, is the **Margit Kovács Ceramic Collection** (Kovács Margit Kerámiagyüjtemény; Vastagh György utca 1; adult/concession 700/350Ft; ✆ 10am-6pm). Kovács (1902–77) was a ceramicist who combined Hungarian folk, religious and modern themes with a hint of Gothic to create her figures. Uphill to the northwest, a narrow passageway leads up from between Fő tér 8 and 9 to Castle Hill (Vár-domb) and the **Parish Church of St John** (Szent Janos Plébánia Templom; Várhegy), rebuilt in 1710, from where you get great views of the town and the Danube. Nearby, the tall red tower of the Serbian **Belgrade Cathedral** (Belgradi Székesegyház; Pátriárka utca 5; ✆ 10am-4pm Fri-Sun Jan & Feb, 10am-4pm Tue-Sun Mar, Apr & Oct-Dec, 10am-6pm Tue-Sun May-Sep), from 1764, casts its shadow. You can hear beautiful chanting wafting from the open doors during services. The **Serbian Orthodox Ecclesiastical Art Collection** (Szerb Ortodox Egyháztörnténeti Gyűjtemény; Pátriárka utca 5; adult/concession 500/250Ft; ✆ 10am-6pm Tue-Sun Mar-Sep, 10am-4pm Tue-Sun Oct-Dec, 10am-4pm Fri-Sun Jan & Feb) is in the courtyard.

Don't miss the extensive **Open-Air Ethnographic Museum** (Szabadtéri Néprajzi Múzeum; www.skanzen.hu; Sztaravodai út; adult/concession 1000/500Ft; ✆ 9am-5pm Tue-Sun late Mar-Oct), 3.5km outside town. Walking through the fully furnished ancient wooden and stone homes, churches and working buildings brought here from around the country, you can see what rural life was – and sometimes still is – like in different regions of Hungary. In the centre of the park stand Roman-era ruins. Frequent weekend festivals give you a chance to see folk costumes, music and dance, as well as home crafts. To get here, take hourly buses marked 'Skansen' from stop 7 at the town's bus station.

Sleeping & Eating

Seeing Szentendre on a day trip from Budapest is probably your best bet. The town can be easily covered in a day, even if you spend a couple of hours at the open-air museum. For private rooms in town, visit the Tourinform office. Being a tourist town, there are plenty of places to grab a bite to eat.

Pap-sziget Camping (✆ 310 697; www.pap-sziget.hu; camp sites per adult/concession 1000/600Ft, tents 2920Ft, bungalows from 8200Ft; ✆ May–mid-Oct; ✇) Has large shady trees, a sandy beach and numerous tent and caravan sites. Bungalows are fairly basic. Take bus 11 from Szentendre.

Kentaur Hotel (✆ 312 125; www.hotels.hu/kentaur; Marx tér 3; s/d 11,700/14,500Ft) After receiving a re-

cent makeover, this hotel is a fine choice close to the action. Rooms are neat and tidy, and staff are eager to please.

Erm's (✆ 303 388; Kossuth Lajos utca 22; mains aroun 2000Ft) Unpretentious spot serving Hungarian specialities, and even some vegetarian choices. The simple wooden tables dressed in lacy cloth are reminiscent of yesteryear.

For a change from Hungarian cuisine, try the varied dishes of **Palapa** (✆ 302 418; Batthyány utca 4; mains 1500-3000Ft; ✆ 5pm-midnight Mon-Fri, noon-midnight Sat & Sun).

Getting There & Away

The most convenient way to get to Szentendre is to take the commuter HÉV train from Buda's Batthyány tér metro station to the end of the line (one way 370Ft, 45 minutes, every 10 to 15 minutes).

For ferry services from Budapest, see p321.

VÁC

✆ 27 / pop 33,300

Lying on the eastern bank of the river, Vác is an unpretentious town with interesting historic relics, from its collection of baroque town houses to its vault of 18th-century mummies. It's also the place to view glorious sunsets over the Börzsöny Hills, reflected in the Danube.

Vác is an old town. Uvcenum – the town's Latin name – is mentioned in Ptolemy's 2nd-century *Geographia* as a river crossing on an important road. The town's medieval centre and Gothic cathedral were destroyed during the Turkish occupation; reconstruction under several bishops in the 18th century gave Vác its present baroque appearance.

Orientation & Information

The train station is at the northeastern end of Széchenyi utca, the bus station is a few steps southwest. Following Széchenyi utca towards the river for about 500m will take you across the ring road (Dr Csányi László körút) and down to Március 15 tér, the main square. The Mahart ferry pier is at the northern end of Liszt Ferenc sétány; the car and passenger ferry to Szentendre Island is just south of it.

Main post office (Posta Park 2) Off Görgey Artúr utca.

Matrix (Rév köz; per hr 280Ft; ✆ 9am-1pm Mon-Fri) Small internet cafe.

OTP Bank (Dunakanyar shopping centre, Széchenyi utca)

Tourinform (✆ 316 160; www.tourinformvac.hu;

THE AQUATIC HIGHWAY

No other river in Europe is as evocative as the Danube. It has been immortalised in legends, tales, songs, paintings, and movies through the ages, and has played an essential role in the cultural and economic life of millions of people since the earliest human cultures settled along its banks.

Originating in Germany's Black Forest, the river cuts an unrelenting path through – or along the border of – 10 countries, and after 2800km, empties itself into the Black Sea in Romania. It is second only in length to the Volga in Europe (although, at 6400km, the Amazon dwarfs both), and contrary to popular belief, is green-brown rather than blue. Around 2400km of its length is navigable, making it a major transport route across the continent.

Even though only 12% of the river's length is located in its territory, Hungary is greatly influenced by the Danube. The entire country lies within the Danube river basin, and being so flat, it is highly prone to flooding. As early as the 16th century, massive dyke systems were built for flood protection. However, it's hard to stop water running where it wants to – as recently as 2006 the river burst its banks, threatening to fill Budapest's metro system and putting the homes of 32,000 people in danger.

Despite the potential danger the river is much beloved, and has even been awarded its own day. On 29 June every year cities along the Danube host festivals, family events and conferences in honour of the mighty waterway. If you'd like to join in, visit www.danubeday.org for more information.

Március 15 tér 17; 10am-7pm Mon-Fri, 10am-2pm Sat mid-Jun–Aug, 9am-5pm Mon-Fri, 10am-noon Sat Sep–mid-Jun) On the main square.

Sights

Március 15 tér, the main square, has the most colourful buildings in Vác. Here you'll find a **crypt** (Március 15 tér; admission 240Ft; 9am-5pm May-Sep), the only remnant of the medieval St Michael's Church. It contains a brief history of the church and town in the Middle Ages.

Dominating the square is the **Dominican church** (Fehérek temploma; Március 15 tér 19; admission free), below which you can meet some fascinating mummies (see boxed text, p326). Also of note is another baroque masterpiece, the **Town Hall** (1764; Március 15 tér 11). Opposite is the former **Bishop's Palace** (Március 15 tér 6). Next door, the **Vác Diocesan Museum** (Március 15 tér 4; adult/concession 500/200Ft; 2-6pm Wed-Fri, 10am-6pm Sat & Sun) displays a tiny portion of the treasures the Catholic Church amassed in Vác over the centuries.

North of the main square is the **Triumphal Arch** (Diadalív-kapu), the only such structure in Hungary. It was built by Bishop Migazzi in honour of a visit by Empress Maria Theresa and her husband Francis of Lorraine in 1764. From here, dip down one of the narrow side streets (such as Molnár utca) to the west for a stroll along the Danube. The **old city walls** and Gothic **Pointed Tower**

(now a private home) are near Liszt Ferenc sétány 12.

Tree-lined Konstantin tér to the southeast is dominated by colossal **Vác Cathedral** (Váci székesegyház; admission free; 10am-noon & 1.30-5pm Mon-Sat, 7.30am-7pm Sun), which dates from 1775 and was one of the first examples of neoclassical architecture in Hungary.

If you continue walking south along Budapesti főút, you'll reach the small stone **Gombás Stream Bridge** (Gombás-patak hídja; 1757), lined with the statues of seven saints – Vác's modest response to Charles Bridge in Prague.

Sleeping & Eating

Vác is an easy day trip from Budapest, but here are some accommodation and dining options if you want to stay over.

Alt Gyuláné (316 860; altvendeghaz@invitel .hu; Tabán utca 25; s/d 5000/12,000Ft;) Staying at this small pension is like staying with (nice) family. Rooms are kitschy but very cosy, and there's a fully equipped kitchen and private garden.

Fónagy & Walter (310 682; www.fonagy.hu; Budapesti főút 36; r 8500Ft) Fónagy & Walter is a pension from the 'homely' mould – rooms are lovingly prepared, and the wine selection from the private cellar is outstanding.

Vörössipka (501 055; okktart@netelek.hu; Honvéd utca 14; s/d 9000/14,000Ft) If the previous two are full, consider this plain hotel located away from

---

THE MUMMIES OF VÁC

Between 1731 and 1801 the original crypt of the Dominican church functioned as a place of burial for the general public, but it was later bricked up and forgotten. The microclimatic conditions underground were perfect for mummification – a cool temperature and minimal ventilation allowed the bodies of the deceased to remain in exceptional condition for centuries. When renovation work on the church began in 1994, the crypt was rediscovered. Of the 262 bodies exhumed over the ensuing months, 166 were easily identified through church records. It was a goldmine for historians; the clothing, jewellery and general appearance of the corpses helped to shed light on the burial practices and the local way of life in the 18th century.

The majority of mummies now reside in the vaults of the Hungarian National Museum (p314) in Budapest but three are on display in the **Memento Mori exhibition** (Március 15 tér 19; adult/concession 800/400Ft; ☺ 10am-6pm Tue-Sun) below the church. It also showcases some colourfully painted coffins, clothes and jewellery of the deceased, a registry of those buried, and a brief history of the church and its crypt.

---

the centre. Rooms lack character, but they're clean and definitely adequate for a night.

Barlang Bar (☎ 501 760; Március 15 tér 12; mains 1000-2800Ft; ☺ 11am-11pm Sun-Thu, to 1am Fri & Sat) With its fluorescent lighting and red booths, this cellar restaurant/bar looks like it would be more at home in New York. Its international menu is appealing, and there's outdoor seating on the square in summer.

Váci Remete (☎ 302 199; Fürdő utca; mains 1800-2600Ft) This eatery impresses with views of the Danube from its terrace, a top-notch wine selection, and a fine choice of Hungarian specialities.

Duna Presszó (Március 15 tér 13) Duna is the quintessential cafe: dark-wood furniture, chandeliers, excellent cake and ice cream, and the occasional resident drunk. Good for coffee during the day and something stronger at night.

Entertainment

Imre Madách Cultural Centre (☎ 316 411; Dr Csányi László körút 63) This circular centre can help you with what's on in Vác, such as theatre, concerts and kids' shows.

Getting There & Away

Car ferries (1200/400/400/330Ft per car/bicycle/adult/concession, hourly 6am to 8pm) cross over to Szentendre Island; a bridge connects the island's west bank with the mainland at Tahitótfalu. From there hourly buses run to Szentendre. You can also catch half-hourly buses (450Ft, 50 minutes) and trains (525Ft, 40 minutes) from Vác to Budapest.

For ferry services from Budapest, see p321.

VISEGRÁD

☎ 26 / pop 1700

The spectacular vista from the ruins of Visegrád's (*vish*-eh-grahd) 13th-century citadel, high on a hill above a curve in the Danube, is what pulls visitors to this sleepy town. The first fortress here was built by the Romans as a border defence in the 4th century. Hungarian kings constructed a mighty citadel on the hilltop, and a lower castle near the river, after the 13th-century Mongol invasions. In the 14th century a royal palace was built on the flood plain at the foot of the hills, and in 1323 King Charles Robert of Anjou, whose claim to the local throne was being fiercely contested in Buda, moved the royal household here. For nearly two centuries Hungarian royalty alternated between Visegrád and Buda.

The destruction of Visegrád came first at the hands of the occupying Turks and then at the hands of the Habsburgs, who destroyed the citadel to prevent Hungarian independence fighters from using it. All trace of the palace was lost until 1934 when archaeologists, by following descriptions in literary sources, uncovered the ruins that you can visit today.

The small town has two distinct areas: one to the north around Mahart ferry pier and another, the main town, about 1km to the south.

Sights & Activities

The partial reconstruction of the **Royal Palace** (Királyi Palota; Fő utca 29; adult/concession 1000/500Ft; ☺ 9am-5pm Tue-Sun), 400m south of the Mahart pier, only hints at its former magnificence.

nside, a small museum is devoted to the history of the palace and its excavation and reconstruction.

The palace's original Gothic fountain, along with town-history exhibits, is in the museum at **Solomon's Tower** (Salamon Torony; adult/concession 600/300Ft; ☻ 9am-5pm Tue-Sun May-Sep), a few hundred metres north of the palace. The tower was part of a lower castle controlling river traffic. From here you can climb the very steep path uphill to the **Visegrád Citadel** (Visegrád Cittadella; adult/concession 1400/700Ft; ☻ 9.30am-5.30pm daily mid-Mar–mid-Oct, 9.30am-5.30pm Sat & Sun mid-Oct–mid-Mar) directly above. While the citadel (1259) ruins themselves are not as spectacular as their history, the view of the Danube Bend from the walls is well worth the climb. From the town centre a trail leads to the citadel from behind the Catholic church on Fő tér; this is less steep than the arduous climb from Solomon's Tower.

Sleeping & Eating

As with the other towns in the Danube Bend, Visegrád is an easy day trip from Budapest, so it's not necessary to stay over if you don't want to. **Visegrád Tours** (☎ 398 160; Rév utca 15; ☻ 8am-5.30pm), a travel agency in the town centre, provides information and books private rooms for around 5000Ft per person per night.

Jurta Camping (☎ 398 217; camp sites per adult/concession/tent 800/500/650Ft; ☻ May-Sep) On Mogyoróhegy (Hazelnut Hill), about 2km northeast of the citadel, this camping ground is pretty and green. There's a taxi-van service (2500Ft for up to six passengers) between the Mahart ferry pier and the citadel via the Nagymaros ferry pier and Jurta Camping, available on request from April to September.

Hotel Honti (☎ 398 120; www.hotelhonti.hu; Fő utca 66; s/d from €40/55; 🖳) Honti is a friendly pension filled with homey rooms. Its large garden and table tennis are available for guest use, and bicycles can be hired for 2000Ft per day.

Reneszánsz (☎ 398 081; Fő utca 11; mains 2000-4000Ft) Step through this restaurant's doors to be greeted by a medieval banquet and men in tights with silly hats. In the right mood, it can be quite a hoot.

Kovács-kert (☎ 398 123; Rév utca 4; mains 1300-2500Ft) A more down-to-earth dining option close to the Nagymaros ferry. The large menu covers a fine array of Hungarian standards, and its terrace seating is a welcome relief in the warmer summer months.

Getting There & Away

Frequent buses go to Visegrád from Budapest's Árpád híd bus station (525Ft, 1¼ hours, hourly), the Szentendre HÉV station (375Ft, 45 minutes, every 45 minutes) and Esztergom (375Ft, 40 minutes, hourly).

For ferry services from Budapest, see p321.

ESZTERGOM

☎ 33 / pop 29,800

It's easy to see the attraction of Esztergom, even from a distance. The city's massive basilica, sitting high above the town and Danube River, is an incredible sight, rising magnificently from its rural setting.

The significance of this town is greater than its architectural appeal. The 2nd-century Roman emperor-to-be Marcus Aurelius wrote his famous *Meditations* while he camped here. In the 10th century, Stephen I, founder of the Hungarian state, was born and crowned at the cathedral. From the late 10th to the mid-13th centuries Esztergom served as the Hungarian royal seat. In 1543 the Turks ravaged the town and much of it was destroyed, only to be rebuilt in the 18th and 19th centuries. Nowadays it's an attractive riverside town, with much spiritual and temporal attraction for both Hungarians and international visitors.

Orientation & Information

The train station is on the southern edge of town, about a 15-minute walk (1.2km) south of the bus station. From the train station, walk north on Baross Gábor út, then along Ady Endre utca to Símor János utca, past the bus station to the town centre.

OTP Bank (Rákóczi tér 2-4) does foreign-exchange transactions. The **post office** (Arany János utca 2) is just off Széchenyi tér. **Gran Tours** (☎ 502 001; Rákóczi tér 25; ☻ 8am-5pm Mon-Fri, 9am-noon Sat Jun-Aug, 8am-4pm Mon-Fri Sep-May) is the best source of information in town.

Sights & Activities

Hungary's largest church is the **Esztergom Basilica** (Esztergomi Bazilika; www.bazilika-esztergom.hu; Szent István tér 1; ☻ 6am-6pm). Perched on Castle Hill, its 72m-high central dome can be seen for many kilometres around. Reconstructed in the neoclassical style, much of the building dates from the 19th century; the oldest section is the red-marble **Bakócz Chapel** (Bakócz

HUNGARY

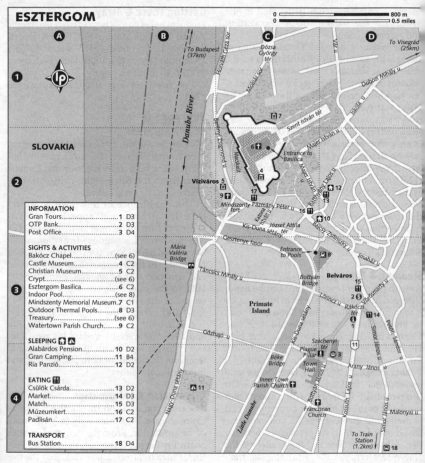

ESZTERGOM

Kápolna; 1510). The **treasury** (kincsház; adult/concession 600/300Ft; 9am-4.30pm Mar-Oct, 11am-3.30pm Sat & Sun Nov-Dec) contains priceless objects, including ornate vestments and the 13th-century Hungarian coronation cross. Among those buried in the **crypt** (altemplom; admission 150Ft; 9am-4.45pm) under the cathedral is the controversial Cardinal Mindszenty, who was imprisoned by the communists for refusing to allow Hungary's Catholic schools to be secularised (see boxed text, opposite).

At the southern end of the hill is the **Castle Museum** (Vár Múzeum; adult/concession 800/400Ft; 10am-6pm Tue-Sun Apr-Oct, 10am-4pm Tue-Sun Nov-Mar), inside the reconstructed remnants of the medieval royal palace (1215), which was built upon previous castles. The earliest exca-

vated sections on the hill date from the 2nd to 3rd centuries.

Southwest of the cathedral along the banks of the Little Danube, narrow streets wind through the Víziváros (Watertown) district, home to the **Watertown Parish Church** (Víziváros Plébánia Templom; 1738) at the start of Berényi Zsigmond utca. The **Christian Museum** (Keresztény Múzeum; www.christianmuseum .hu; Berényi Zsigmond utca 2; adult/concession 700/350Ft; 10am-6pm Wed-Sun May-Oct, 11am-3pm Tue-Sun Nov, Dec, Mar & Apr) is in the adjacent Primate's Palace (1882). The stunning collection of medieval religious art includes a statue of the Virgin Mary from the 11th century.

Cross the bridge south of Watertown Parish Church, and about 100m further down is **Mária**

aléria Bridge. Destroyed during WWII, it again connects Esztergom with Slovakia and the city of Štúrovo. Just east of the Little Danube are **outdoor thermal pools** (Kis-Duna sétány 1; adult/concession 1100/800Ft; 9am-7pm May-Sep) and stretches of grass 'beach'. You can use the **indoor pool** 6am-6pm Mon-Sat, 8am-4pm Sun) year-round.

Sleeping & Eating

Although frequent transportation connections make Esztergom an easy day trip from Budapest, you might want to stop a night if you are going on to Slovakia. Contact Gran Tours (p327) about private rooms (3000Ft to 4000Ft per person) or apartments (from 9000Ft).

Gran Camping (402 513; www.grancamping-fortanex.hu; Nagy-Duna sétány 3; camp sites per adult/concession/tent/tent & car 1500/750/1000/1600Ft, bungalows 12,000-16,000Ft, dm/d/tr 1900/8500/9500Ft; May-Sep;) Small but centrally located, this camping ground has space for 500 souls in various forms of accommodation, as well as a good-size swimming pool. It's a 10-minute walk along the Danube from the cathedral.

Alabárdos Panzió (312 640; www.alabardospanzio.hu; Bajcsy-Zsilinszky utca 49; s/d 7500/11,500Ft) Alabárdos isn't flashy but it does provide neat, tidy and sizeable accommodation. The breakfast is big, as is the friendly guard dog. The location is great if you want to be close to the cathedral: the hotel is at the base of Castle Hill.

Ria Panzió (313 115; www.riapanzio.com; Battyány Lajos utca 11; s/d 9000/12,000Ft;) This is a family-run place in a converted town house just down from the basilica. Relax on the terrace or arrange an adventure through the owners: you can rent a bicycle or take a waterskiing trip on the Danube in summer.

Padlisán (311 212; Pázmány Péter utca 21; mains 1500-3000Ft) With a sheer rock face topped by a castle bastion as its backdrop, Padlisán has a dramatic setting. Thankfully its menu doesn't let the show down, featuring modern Hungarian dishes and imaginative salads.

Csülök Csárda (412 420; Battyány Lajos utca 9; mains 1800-3900Ft) The Pork Knuckle Inn – guess the speciality here – is a charming eatery popular with visitors and locals alike. It serves up good home cooking (try the bean soup), with huge portions.

Múzeumkert (Battyány Lajos utca 1; 9am-midnight Apr-Oct, 9am-10pm Nov-Mar) For a drink, alcoholic or otherwise, head to this modern cocktail lounge serving the best cakes and pastries in Esztergom.

Self-caterers can shop at the **Match** (Bajcsy-Zsilinszky utca; 6.30am-8pm Mon-Fri, 6.30am-6pm Sat, 8am-noon Sun), next to the OTP Bank, or the small town **market** on Simor János utca.

Getting There & Away

Buses run to/from Budapest's Árpád híd bus station (675Ft, 1½ hours) and to/

CARDINAL MINDSZENTY

Born József Pehm in 1892, Mindszenty was politically active from the time of his ordination in 1915. Imprisoned under the short-lived regime of communist Béla Kun in 1919 and again when the fascist Arrow Cross came to power in 1944, Mindszenty was made archbishop of Esztergom – and thus primate of Hungary – in 1945, and cardinal the following year.

In 1948, when he refused to secularise Hungary's Roman Catholic schools under the new communist regime, Mindszenty was arrested, tortured and sentenced to life imprisonment for treason. Released during the 1956 Uprising, he took refuge in the US Embassy on Szabadság tér when the communists returned to power. He remained there until September 1971.

As relations between the Kádár regime and the Holy See began to improve in the late 1960s, the Vatican made several requests for the cardinal to leave Hungary, which he refused to do. Following the intervention of US President Richard Nixon, Mindszenty left for Vienna, where he continued to criticise the Vatican's relations with the regime in Hungary. He retired in 1974 and died the following year. But as he had vowed not to return to his homeland until the last Soviet soldier had left Hungarian soil, Mindszenty's remains were not returned until May 1991. This was actually several weeks before the last soldier had been repatriated.

If you wish to know more about one of Hungary's most controversial figures, visit the **Mindszenty Memorial Museum** (Mindszenty Emlékmúzeum; Szent István tér 4; adult/concession 400/200Ft; 9am-5pm Wed-Sun May-Dec), northeast of the basilica, which displays a handful of his personal items and shows a short film on his life and times.

from Visegrád (375Ft, 45 minutes) at least hourly. Hourly buses also link Esztergom to Szentendre (750Ft, 1½ hours).

The most comfortable way to get to Esztergom from Budapest is by rail. Trains depart from Budapest's Nyugati train station (900Ft, 1½ hours) at least hourly. Cross the Mária Valéria Bridge into Štúrovo, Slovakia, and you can catch a train to Bratislava, which is an hour and a half away.

For ferry services from Budapest, see p321.

NORTHWESTERN HUNGARY

A visit to this region is a boon for anyone wishing to see remnants of Hungary's Roman legacy, medieval heritage and baroque splendour. This swath of land was fortunate in largely avoiding the Ottoman destruction wrought on the country in the 16th and 17th centuries. Its seminal towns – Sopron and Győr – managed to save their medieval centres from total devastation, and exploring their cobbled streets and hidden courtyards is a magical experience. They also house a cornucopia of baroque architecture, something rare in Hungary. Equally rewarding are reminders of Roman settlement, and the region's natural beauty.

GYŐR

☎ 96 / pop 128,000

Not many tourists make the effort to stop at Győr (German: Raab), which is all the more reason to visit. This large city with the tricky name (pronounced *jyeur*) is a surprisingly splendid place, with a medieval heart hidden behind a commercial facade.

Midway between Budapest and Vienna Győr sits at the point where the Mosoni Danube, Rábca and Rába Rivers meet. This wa the site of a Roman town named Arrabona. I the 11th century, Stephen I established a bisho pric here, and in the 16th century a fortress wa erected to hold back the Turks. The Ottoman captured Győr in 1594 but were able to hold or to it for only four years. For that reason Győ is known as the 'dear guard', watching ove the nation through the centuries.

Orientation & Information

The large neobaroque City Hall (1898) is the prominent structure opposite the train station. Baross Gábor utca, which leads to the Old Town and the rivers, lies diagonally opposite this building. Much of central Győr is pedestrianised, making walking easy.

Main post office (Bajcsy-Zsilinszky út 46; ☒ 8am-6pm Mon-Fri)

Mandala (Sarkantyú köz 7; per hr 300Ft; ☒ 10am-10pm Mon-Thu, 10am-11pm Fri & Sat, 2-9pm Sun) Internet access on one computer.

OTP Bank (Baross Gábor 16)

Tourinform (☎ 311 771; www.gyortourism.hu; Árpad út 32; ☒ 9am-6pm Jun-Aug, 9am-5pm Mon-Fri, 9am-1pm Sat Sep-May) Small but helpful tourist office.

Sights & Activities

The enchanting 1725 **Carmelite Church** (Karmelita Templom; Bécsí kapu tér) and many fine baroque palaces line riverfront Bécsí kapu tér. On the northwestern side of the square are the fortifications built in the 16th century to stop the Turks. A short distance to the east is **Napoleon House** (Napoleon-ház; Király utca 4), named after the French dictator (see p332). Walk the old streets and stop in at a pavement cafe or two.

North up Káptalan-domb (Chapter Hill), in the oldest part of Győr, is the solid baroque

---

WORTH THE TRIP: PANNONHALMI ABBEY

Take half a day and make the short trip to the ancient and impressive **Pannonhalma Abbey** (Pannonhalmi Főapátság; ☎ 570 191; www.bences.hu; Vár utca 1; foreign-language tours adult/student/family 2400/1500/6000Ft; ☒ 9am-4pm Tue-Sun Apr & Oct–mid-Nov, 9am-4pm Jun-Sep, 10am-3pm Tue-Sun mid-Nov–Mar), now a Unesco World Heritage site. Most buildings in the complex date from the 13th to the 18th centuries; highlights include the Romanesque basilica (1225), the Gothic cloister (1486) and the impressive collection of ancient texts in the library. Because it's an active monastery, the abbey must be visited with a guide. English and German tours leave at 11.20am and 1.20pm from April to September, with an extra tour at 3.20pm from June to September. Between October and March, foreign-language tours must be booked in advance.

There are frequent buses to/from Győr (375Ft, 30 minutes, 21km, half-hourly).

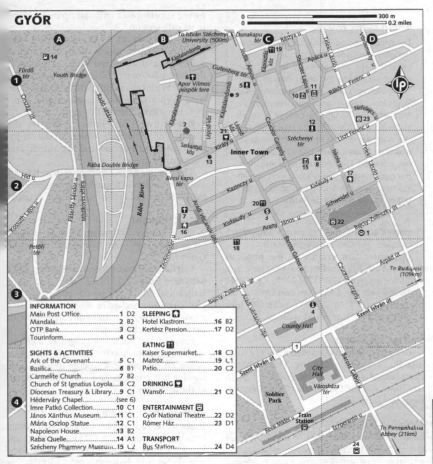

GYŐR

Basilica (Bazilika; Apor Vilmos püspök tere; 8am-noon & 2-6pm). Situated on the hill, it was originally Romanesque, but most of what you see inside dates from the 17th and 18th centuries. Don't miss the Gothic **Héderváry Chapel** (Héderváry-kápolna) on the southern side of the cathedral, which contains a glittering 15th-century bust of King (and St) Ladislas.

East of the Basilica is the **Diocesan Treasury & Library** (Egyházmegyei Kincstár és Kkönyvtár; adult/concession 700/400Ft; 10am-4pm Tue-Sun Mar-Oct). Of particular value in its collection are the Gothic chalices and Renaissance mitre embroidered with pearls, but stealing the show is the precious library, containing almost 70,000 volumes printed before 1850. At the bottom of the hill on Jedlik Ányos utca is the **Ark of the Covenant**

(Frigyláda), a statue dating from 1731. From here you can head north to a bridge overlooking the junction of the city's three rivers.

In Széchenyi tér, the heart of Győr, is the fine **Church of St Ignatius Loyola** (Szent Ignác Templom; 1641) and the **Column of the Virgin Mary** (Mária-ozlop; 1686). Cross the square to the **Xántus János Múzeum** (János Xántus Museum; Széchenyi tér 5; adult/concession 650/300Ft; 10am-6pm Tue-Sun Apr-Sep, 1-5pm Tue-Sun Oct-Mar), built in 1743, to see exhibits on the city's history. Next door is the **Patkó Imre Gyűjtemény** (Imre Patkó Collection; Széchenyi tér 5; adult/concession 550/300Ft; 10am-6pm Tue-Sun Apr-Sep, 1-5pm Tue-Sun Oct-Mar), a fine small museum in a 17th-century house. Collections include 20th-century Asian and African art. Look out for the highly decorated baroque ceiling at the **Szécheny**

HUNGARY

NAPOLEONIC PAUSE

The great Napoleon once spent a night in Hungary – in Győr to be precise. The great general slept over at Király utca 4, due east of Bécsi kapu tér, on 31 August 1809. The building is now called Napoleon-ház (Napoleon House), appropriately enough. And why did Bonaparte choose Győr to make his grand entrée into Hungary? The city was near the site of the Battle of Raab, which had taken place just 11 weeks earlier, between Franco-Italian and Austrian-Hungarian armies. Boney's side won, and an inscription on the Arc de Triomphe in Paris still recalls 'la bataille de Raab'.

Pharmacy Museum (Szécheny Patikamúzeum; Széchenyi tér 9; admission free; ☺ 7.40am-4pm Mon-Fri) nearby.

The water temperature in the pools at thermal bath **Rába Quelle** (☎ 514 900; Fürdő tér 1; adult/concession per day 1950/1350Ft, per 3hr 1550/1100Ft; ☺ thermal baths 9am-8.30pm, pool 8am-8pm Mon-Sat) ranges from 29°C to 38°C. You can also take advantage of its fitness and wellness centres.

Festivals & Events

Győr has a couple of festivals held every summer that are worth catching. The **Hungarian Dance Festival** (www.magyartancfesztival.hu) is held in late June, and the **Győr Summer Cultural Festival** from late June to late July.

Sleeping & Eating

István Széchenyi University (☎ 503 447; Hédervári út 3; dm 3100Ft) Dormitory accommodation is available year-round at this huge academic institution north of the town centre.

Kertész Pension (☎ 317 461; www.kertesz-panzio.hu; Iskola utca 11; s/d/tr/q 7000/11,000/14,000/16,000Ft) The Gardener has very simple rooms on offer, but it's well located in downtown Győr and staff couldn't be friendlier.

Hotel Klastrom (☎ 516 910; www.klastrom.hu; Zechmeister utca 1; s/d/tr 14,700/18,700/21,400Ft; 💻) This delightful three-star hotel occupies a 300-year-old Carmelite convent south of Bécsi kapu tér. Rooms are charming and bright, and extras include a sauna, a solarium, a pub with a vaulted ceiling, and a restaurant with seating in a leafy and peaceful garden.

Patio (☎ 310 096; Baross Gábor utca 12; mains 1000-2000Ft) This restaurant's dining area serves up Hungarian dishes, which are overshadowed by the superb cakes and marzipan creations in its cafe section.

our pick Matróz (☎ 336 208; Dunakapu tér 3; mains 1080-1700Ft) Matróz makes the best damn fish dishes around, from warming carp soup to delicate pike-perch fillets. The handsome vaulted brick cellar, complete with dark-blue tiled oven and nautical memorabilia, completes this wonderful little eatery.

Wansör (Lépcső köz) Have a night on the tiles at this cellar pub, which attracts a jovial crowd with occasional live music and inexpensive drinks.

The massive **Kaiser supermarket** (Arany János utca 16; ☺ 7am-7pm Mon-Fri, 6.30am-3pm Sat, 8am-1pm Sun) is the place to head for self-catering purposes.

Entertainment

A good source of information for what's on in Győr is the free fortnightly magazine *Győri Est*.

Győr National Theatre (Győri Nemzeti Színház; ☎ 520 600; Czuczor Gergely utca 7) The celebrated Győr Ballet and the city's opera company and philharmonic orchestra all perform at this modern venue. Tourinform can help with performance schedules.

Rómer Ház (☎ 550 850; www.romerhaz.eu; László Teleki utca 21) One-stop shop for entertainment, featuring an independent cinema upstairs, and regular live concerts and club nights down in the dungeon.

Getting There & Away

Buses travel to Budapest (2040Ft, two hours, hourly), Pannonhalma (375Ft, 30 minutes, half-hourly), Esztergom (1770Ft, 2½ hours, one daily) and Balatonfüred (1500Ft, 2½ hours, six daily).

Győr is well connected by express train to Budapest's Keleti and Déli train stations (2040Ft, 1½ hours, half-hourly), and ten daily trains connect Győr with Vienna's Westbahnhof (2750Ft, 1½ hours).

SOPRON

☎ 99 / pop 56,400

It's true – many visitors to Sopron (*shop*-ron) are Austrians seeking inexpensive dental work and cheap haircuts. However, Sopron is also one of Hungary's most beautiful towns, with a Gothic town centre enclosed by medieval walls, narrow streets and mysterious passages. Many have called it 'little Prague', and rightly so. Once you've strolled through its

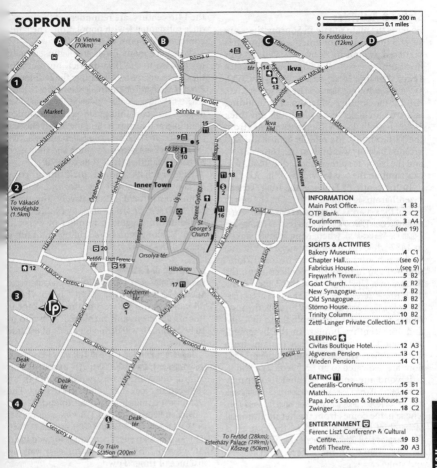

SOPRON

INFORMATION	
Main Post Office	1 B3
OTP Bank	2 C2
Tourinform	3 A4
Tourinform	(see 19)

SIGHTS & ACTIVITIES	
Bakery Museum	4 C1
Chapter Hall	(see 6)
Fabricius House	(see 9)
Firewatch Tower	5 B2
Goat Church	6 B2
New Synagogue	7 B2
Old Synagogue	8 B2
Storno House	9 B2
Trinity Column	10 B2
Zettl-Langer Private Collection	11 C1

SLEEPING	
Civitas Boutique Hotel	12 A3
Jégverem Pension	13 C1
Wieden Pension	14 C1

EATING	
Generális-Corvinus	15 B1
Match	16 C2
Papa Joe's Saloon & Steakhouse	17 B3
Zwinger	18 C2

ENTERTAINMENT	
Ferenc Liszt Conference & Cultural Centre	19 B3
Petőfi Theatre	20 A3

quiet backstreets, you can opt for a glass or two of the local wine, or head out of town and enjoy nature's offerings.

The Mongols and Turks never got this far, so unlike many Hungarian cities, numerous medieval buildings remain in use. The town sits on the Austrian border, only 69km south of Vienna. In 1921 the town's residents voted in a referendum to remain part of Hungary, while the rest of Bürgenland (the region to which Sopron used to belong) went to Austria. The region is known for producing good red wines such as Kékfrancos, which you can sample in local cafes and restaurants.

Sopron Festival Weeks (www.prokultura.hu) run from late June to mid-July.

Orientation & Information

From the main train station, walk north on Mátyás Király utca, which becomes Várkerület, part of a loop following the line of the former city walls. Előkapu (Front Gate) and Hátsókapu (Back Gate) are the two main entrances in the walls. The bus station is northwest of the Old Town on Lackner Kristóf utca.

Main post office (Széchenyi tér 7-10)

OTP Bank (Várkerület 96/a)

Tourinform main branch (☎ 517 560; sopron@tourin form.hu; Liszt Ferenc utca 1; ☉ 9am-6pm daily mid-Jun–Aug, 9am-5pm Mon-Fri, 9am-noon Sat Sep–mid-Jun); southern branch (☎ 505 438; Deák tér 45; ☉ 9am-5pm Mon-Fri, 9am-noon Apr-Oct) Both branches offer free internet access and a plethora of tourist information.

HUNGARY

Sights & Activities

Fő tér is the main square in Sopron; there are several museums, monuments and churches scattered around it. Above the Old Town's northern gate rises the 60m-high **Firewatch Tower** (Tűztorony; Fő tér; adult/concession 700/350Ft; 10am-8pm May-Aug, 10am-6pm Tue-Sun Apr, Sep & Oct), run by the Soproni Múzeum. The building is a true architectural hybrid: the 2m-thick square base, built on a Roman gate, dates from the 12th century, the middle cylindrical and arcaded balcony was built in the 16th century and the baroque spire was added in 1680. You can climb to the top for views of the Alps.

In the centre of Fő tér is the **Trinity Column** (Szentháromság Oszlop; 1701). On the north side of the square is **Storno House** (Storno Ház; Fő tér 8; adult/concession 1000/500Ft; 10am-6pm Tue-Sun Apr-Sep, 2-6pm Tue-Sun Oct-Mar), where King Mátyás stayed in 1482 while his armies lay siege to Vienna. Today it houses a so-so local history exhibition, with an impressive art collection on the floor above. Upstairs at **Fabricius House** (Fabricius Ház; Fő tér 6; adult/concession 700/350Ft; 10am-6pm Tue-Sun Apr-Sep, 10am-2pm Tue-Sun Oct-Mar), walk through rooms re-created to resemble those in 17th- and 18th-century homes. In the basement see stone sculptures and other remains from Roman times. The back rooms of the ground floor are dedicated to an archaeology exhibit.

Beyond the square is the 13th-century **Goat Church** (Kecske Templom; Templom utca 1; admission free; 8am-9pm mid-Apr–Sep, 8am-6pm Oct–mid-Apr), whose name comes from the heraldic animal of its chief benefactor. Below the church is the **Chapter Hall** (Káptalan Terem), part of a 14th-century Franciscan monastery, with frescos and stone carvings.

The **New Synagogue** (Új Zsinagóga; Új utca 11) and **Old Synagogue** (Ó Zsinagóga; Új utca 22; adult/concession 600/300Ft; 10am-6pm Tue-Sun May-Oct), both built in the 14th century, are reminders of the town's once substantial Jewish population. The latter contains a museum of Jewish life.

There are many other small museums in town. Two in the Ikva district, northeast of the centre, are quite interesting: the **Zettl-Langer Private Collection** (Zettl-Langer Gyűjtemény; Balfi út 11; admission 500Ft; 10am-noon Tue-Sun Apr-Oct, 10am-noon Fri-Sun Nov-Jan & Mar), containing antiquities, ceramics, paintings and furniture; and the **Bakery Museum** (Pék Múzeum; 311 327; Bécsi út 5; adult/concession 400/200Ft, 2-6pm Tue-Sun Apr-Sep), in a house and shop used by bakers' families from 1686 to 1970.

Avid cyclists should pick up a copy of the brochure *Cycling Around Sopron* from Tourinform. Alternatively, the pamphlet *Green Sopron*, also available from Tourinform, suggests a number of walks in the hills, along with horse riding and sailing possibilities nearby.

Sleeping & Eating

Vákació Vendégház (338 502; www.vakacio-vendeghazak.hu; Ady Endre út 31; dm 2800Ft) Cheap, cheerful lodgings not far west of the town centre. Rooms are clean and furnished with two to 10 beds; bus 10 will drop you off right outside the door.

Jégverem Pension (510 113; www.jegverem.hu; Jégverem utca 1; s/d 6900/8900Ft) An excellent and central bet, with five suitelike rooms in an 18th-century ice cellar in the Ikva district. The restaurant comes highly recommended.

Wieden Pension (523 222; www.wieden.hu; Sas tér 13; s/d/tr from 7700/10,900/12,900Ft; apt from 11,900Ft;) Sopron's loveliest pension is located in an attractive old town house within easy walking distance of Inner Town.

Civitas Boutique Hotel (788 228; www.civitashotel.com; s/d/apt from €40/63/80;) A thoroughly modern hotel within easy striking distance of

---

WORTH THE TRIP: ESTERHÁZY PALACE

Don't miss **Esterházy Palace** (Esterházye Kasthély; Joseph Haydn utca 2; Palace Museum tour adult/concession 1500/750Ft, Great Palace tour 2500/2000Ft; 10am-6pm Tue-Sun mid-Mar–Oct, 10am-4pm Fri-Sun Nov–mid-Mar), a magnificent, Versailles-style baroque extravaganza 28km outside town in Fertőd. Built in 1766, this 126-room palace was owned by one of the nation's foremost families. You have to put on felt booties and slip around the marble floors under gilt chandeliers with a Hungarian guide, but information sheets in various languages are on hand. The Haydn Festival of the Budapest Strings happens here in July, followed by the Haydn Festival in late August/early September. The Tourinform (p330) office in Győr can help you with performance schedules.

Fertőd is easily accessible from Sopron by bus (450Ft, 45 minutes, hourly); the town is dominated by the palace and its grounds.

he centre. Rooms feature smart furniture and flat-screen TVs.

Generális-Corvinus (☎ 505 035; Fő tér 7-8; mains 990-2100Ft; ☽ 9am-11pm) This large restaurant is in reality two eateries – one serving decent Hungarian cuisine and guarded by a very camp general, the other dishing up pizzas under the gaze of a black crow. In summer its tables on the main square are *the* place to dine.

Papa Joe's Saloon & Steak House (☎ 340 933; Várkerület 108; mains 2000Ft; ☽ 11am-midnight Sun-Wed, 11am-2am Thu-Sat) If you insist on dining at a Wild West–themed pub/restaurant while in Hungary, this is the one to choose.

Zwinger (Várkerület 92; ☽ 8am-7pm) Sidling up to the old city walls down a narrow alleyway is this old-fashioned cafe. Its pink, purple and flowery decor may not be to everyone's liking, but its winter garden and homemade cakes are a different matter.

For self-catering supplies, head for **Match** (Várkerület 100; ☽ 6.30am-7pm Mon-Fri, 6.30am-3pm Sat) supermarket.

Entertainment
Ferenc Liszt Conference & Cultural Centre (Liszt Ferenc Kulturális Központ; ☎ 517 517; Liszt Ferenc tér) A concert hall, cafe and exhibition space all rolled into one. The information desk has the latest on classical music and other cultural events in town.

Petőfi Theatre (☎ 517 517; www.prokultura.hu; Petőfi tér 1) This beautiful building with mosaics on its facade is Sopron's leading theatre.

Getting There & Away
There are two buses a day to Budapest (3010Ft, 3¾ hours), and seven to Győr (1350Ft, two hours). Trains run to Budapest's Keleti train station (3390Ft, 2¾ hours, eight daily) via Győr. You can also travel to Vienna's Südbahnhof station (3750Ft, 1¼ hours, up to 15 daily).

LAKE BALATON

Central Europe's largest expanse of fresh water is Lake Balaton, covering 600 sq km. Hungarians flock here to enjoy the obvious activities – swimming, sailing, sunbathing, fishing and relaxing.

The southern shore is mostly a forgettable jumble of tacky resorts, with the exception of party town Siófok. The northern

shore, however, is yin to the southern's yang. Here the pace of life is more gentle and refined, and the forested hills of the Balaton Uplands National Park create a wonderful backdrop. Historical towns such as Keszthely and Balatonfüred dot the landscape, while Tihany, a peninsula cutting the lake almost in half, is home to an important historical church.

But the best thing about the Lake Balaton region is the lake itself. Spend some time here, and before you know it you'll have fallen under its spell, like so many artists and holiday-makers have over the centuries.

SIÓFOK
☎ 84 / pop 23,900
Siófok is officially known as 'Hungary's summer capital' – unofficially it's called 'Hungary's Ibiza'. In July and August, nowhere in the country parties as hard or stays up as late as this lakeside resort, which attracts an ever-increasing number of international DJs and their avid followers. Outside the summer months Siófok returns to relative normality, and is largely undistinguishable from the other resorts on the southern shore.

Orientation & Information
Greater Siófok stretches for some 17km, as far as the resort of Balatonvilágos (once reserved exclusively for communist honchos) to the east and Balatonszéplak to the west. Szabadság tér, the centre of Siófok, is to the east of the Sió Canal and about 500m southeast of the ferry pier. The bus and train stations are in Millennium Park just off Fő utca, the main drag.
Main post office (Fő utca 186)
OTP Bank (Szabadság tér 10/a)
Tourinform (☎ 310 117; tourinform@siofokportal.hu; Szabadság tér; ☽ 8am-7pm Mon-Fri, 10am-7pm Sat & Sun mid-Jun–mid-Sep, 8am-4pm Mon-Fri, 9am-noon Sat mid-Sep–mid-Jun) Based in the old *víztorony* (water tower).

Sights & Activities
There's not a whole lot to see of cultural or historical importance in a place where hedonism rules the roost. However, if you walk north on narrow Hock János köz, you'll reach the **Imre Kálmán Museum** (Kálmán Imre sétány 5; adult/concession 300/150Ft; ☽ 9am-4pm Tue-Sun). It's devoted to the life and works of a composer of popular operettas who was born in Siófok in 1882.

HUNGARY

For an overview of the town and lake beyond, climb the wooden **water tower** (víztorony; Szabadság tér; adult/concession 200/100Ft; ☻ 8am-7pm Mon-Fri, 10am-7pm Sat & Sun mid-Jun–mid-Sep, 8am-4pm Mon-Fri, 9am-noon Sat mid-Sep–mid-Jun). It was built in 1912.

Nagy Strand (adult/concession 750/500Ft), Siófok's 'Big Beach', is centre stage on Petőfi sétány; free concerts are often held here on summer evenings. There are many more managed swimming areas along the lakeshore which cost around the same as Nagy Strand.

There are rowing boats and sailing **boats** for hire at various locations along the lake, including Nagy Strand. **Lake cruises** run from late May to mid-September, generally daily at 10am, 11.30am, 1pm, 2.30pm, 4pm, and 5.30pm. There are additional cruises at 11am, 2pm and 4pm daily from late April to late May.

Siófok's newest attraction, **Galerius** (☎ 506 580; www.galerius-furdo.hu, in Hungarian; Szent László utca 183; swimming pools adult/concession 2000/1300Ft, sauna & swimming pools adult 2300Ft; ☻ 9am-9pm), is 4km west of downtown Siófok. It offers a plethora of indoor thermal pools, saunas and massages.

Sleeping & Eating

Prices quoted below are for the high season in July and August. Tourinform can help find you a private room (€12 to €20 per person), or an apartment for slightly more.

Siófok Város College (☎ 312 244; www.siofokvaros kollegiuma.sulinet.hu; Petőfi sétány 1; dm 2530Ft) Close to the action in central Siófok, it's hard to beat this basic college accommodation for price and location.

Hotel Yacht Club (☎ 311 161; www.hotel -yachtclub.hu; Vitorlás utca 14; s/d €58/92; ✵ 🖳 🖭) Overlooking the harbour is this excellent little hotel with cosy rooms, some of which have balconies overlooking the lake, and a new wellness centre. Bicycles can be hired.

our pick **Mala Garden** (☎ 506 687; www.mala garden.hu; Petőfi sétány 15/a; r 18,900-26,900Ft; ✵) Most of Siófok's accommodation options pale in comparison with this gorgeous boutique hotel. It's reminiscent of Bali, with Indonesian art lining the walls, a small manicured flower garden at the rear of the hotel, and a quality restaurant serving Asian cuisine.

Roxy (☎ 506 573; Szabadság tér; mains 990-3000Ft) This pseudo-rustic restaurant-pub on busy Szabadság tér attracts diners with its wide range of international cuisine and surprisingly imaginative Hungarian mains. Don't arrive too late in the evening or you'll be hard-pressed to find a table.

Entertainment

South Balaton Cultural Centre (☎ 311 855; Fő tér 2). Siófok's main cultural venue, stages concerts, dance performances and plays. However, most visitors to Siófok are interested in more-energetic entertainment. Turnover of bars and clubs is high, but the following manage to attract punters year after year:

Flört (www.flort.hu; Sió utca 4) Well-established club with trippy light shows.

Palace (www.palace.hu; Deák Ferencutca 2) Hugely popular club. Accessible by free bus from outside Tourinform between 9pm and 5am daily from May to mid-September.

Renegade (Petőfi sétány 9) Wild pub near the beach where table dancing and live music are common.

Getting There & Away

From April to October, four daily Mahart ferries run between Siófok and Balatonfüred (1280Ft, 55 minutes), two of which carry on to Tihany. Up to eight ferries follow the same route in July and August.

Buses serve a lot of destinations from Siófok, but you'll find the more frequent train connections of more use. Trains to Nagykanizsa pass through all the resorts on the southern edge of the lake, and there are eight daily train connections to and from Budapest (1770Ft, two hours).

BALATONFÜRED

☎ 87 / pop 13,000

Walking the hillside streets, you'll catch glimpses of the easy grace that 18th- and 19th-century Balatonfüred (bal-ah-tahn fuhr-ed) enjoyed. In those days the wealthy and famous built large villas on its tree-lined streets, hoping to take advantage of the health benefits of the town's famous thermal waters. In more recent times, the lake frontage has received a massive makeover and now sports the most stylish marina on the lake. The hotels here are a bit cheaper than those on the neighbouring Tihany peninsula, making this a good base for exploring.

Orientation & Information

The adjacent bus and train stations are on Dobó István utca, 1km from the lake.

BALATONFÜRED

INFORMATION
OTP Bank	.....1 C3
Post Office	.....2 D3
Tourinform	.....3 D3

SIGHTS & ACTIVITIES
Disco Boat	....(see 15)
Kossuth Pump House	.....4 D3
Mór Jókai Museum	.....5 D3
Pleasure Cruise	....(see 15)
Round Church	.....6 D3

SLEEPING
Fontaine Room Service	.....7 C4
Hotel Blaha Luiza	.....8 D3
Sun City Tours	.....9 C3

EATING
Balaton	.....10 D3
Bazsalikom	....(see 11)
Karolina	.....11 D4
Stefánia Vitorlás	.....12 D4

ENTERTAINMENT
Cultural Centre	.....13 A2

TRANSPORT
Bus Station	.....14 B3
Mahart Ferry Pier	.....15 D4
Tempo 21	.....16 C3

OTP Bank (Petőfi Sándor utca 8)

Post office (Zsigmond utca 14; 🕑 8am-4pm Mon-Fri)

Tourinform (☎ 580 480; balatonfured@tourinform.hu; Kisfaludy utca 1; 🕑 9am-7pm Mon-Fri, to 6pm Sat, to 1pm Sun Jul & Aug, 9am-5pm Mon-Fri, to 1pm Sat Jun & Sep, 9am-4pm Mon-Fri Oct-May) Helpful tourist office.

Sights & Activities

The park along the central shore, near the ferry pier, is worth a promenade. You can take a one-hour **pleasure cruise** (☎ 342 230; www.balatonihajozas.hu; Mahart ferry pier; adult/concession 1250/625Ft) five times a day, from late May to mid-September. The **disco boat** (disco hajo; ☎ 342 230; www.balatonihajozas.hu; Mahart ferry pier; cruise 1600Ft), a two-hour cruise with music and drinks, leaves at 9pm Tuesday, Wednesday, Friday and Saturday in July and August.

Kisfaludy Strand (Aranyhíd sétány; adult/concession 375/275Ft; 🕑 8am-6pm mid-May–mid-Sep), along the footpath 800m northeast of the pier, is a relatively sandy beach. You can explore the waterfront by bike (see p338).

North of the pier is the renovated 1846 **Round Church** (Kerek Templom; cnr Jókai Mór & Honvéd utca). **Mór Jókai Museum** (Jókai Mór Múzeum; Honvéd utca 1) commemorates the life of the acclaimed novelist in what was once his summer house (1871), though at the time of research it was closed for renovation. The heart of the old spa town is Gyógy tér, where **Kossuth Forrásvíz** (Kossuth Spring, 1853) dispenses slightly sulphurous water that people actually drink for health. Don't stray far from a bathroom afterwards.

HUNGARY

On the lake, sprawling the length of Zákonyi Ferenc utca, is Balatonfüred's biggest development in years. Explore the sparkling new **marina** and its stylish cafes, fashionable restaurants and boutique shops.

Sleeping

Prices fluctuate throughout the year and usually peak between early July and late August; high-season prices are quoted below.

As elsewhere around Lake Balaton, private room prices are rather inflated. **Sun City Tours** (☎ 06 30 947 2679; Csokonai utca 1) can help with finding you a place, as can **Fontaine Room Service** (☎ 343 673; Honvéd utca 11). There are lots of houses with rooms for rent on the streets north of Kisfaludy Beach.

Füred Camping (☎ 580 241; fured@balatontourist .hu; Széchenyi utca 24; camp sites per adult/concession/tent 1600/1200/5500Ft; bungalows/caravans from 17,000/23,000Ft; ☺ mid-Apr–early Oct) Sprawling beachfront complex 1km west of the centre, with water-sport rentals, swimming pools, tennis courts, a restaurant and a convenience store.

Villa Balaton (☎ 06 30 223 6453; www.villabalaton .hu; Deák Ferenc utca 38; s/d 6000/12,000Ft) The large, bright rooms of this pastel-yellow villa uphill from the lake are available for rent. Each has its own balcony overlooking a sunny garden and grapevines, and guests can make use of the well-equipped kitchen.

Hotel Blaha Lujza (☎ 581 210; www.hotelblaha .hu; Blaha Lujza utca 4; s/d €37/50) This was once the holiday home of the much-loved 19th-century Hungarian actress-singer Blaha Lujza. Its rooms are a little compact but very comfy.

Eating & Drinking

Balaton (☎ 481 319; Kisfaludy utca 5; mains 1000-3000Ft) This cool, leafy oasis amid all the hubbub is set back from the lake in a shaded park area. It serves generous portions and, like so many restaurants in town, has an extensive fish selection.

Bazsalikom (☎ 06 30 538 0690; Zákonyi Ferenc sétány 4; mains 1500-3000Ft) Taking pride of place on the new marina's waterfront is Bazsalikom, a restaurant that combines fine dining and a relaxed atmosphere. Pasta and pizza are the mainstays of the menu, but don't overlook the daily blackboard specials.

Stefánia Vitorlás (☎ 343 407; Tagore sétány 1; mains 1500-3000Ft) Enormous wooden eatery sitting right on the lake's edge at the foot of the pier. Watch the yachts sail in and out of the harbour while enjoying Hungarian cuisine and local wine.

our pick **Karolina** (Zákonyi Ferenc sétány 4) Karolina is a sophisticated cafe-bar that serves excellent coffee, teas and local wines.

Getting There & Around

Buses to Tihany (250Ft, 30 minutes) leave every 30 minutes or so throughout the day. Seven buses daily head to the northwestern lakeshore towns including Keszthely (1050Ft, 1½ hours).

Budapest-bound buses (2040Ft) depart from Balatonfüred four times daily and take between two and three hours to get there. Trains (1690Ft, three daily) take about as long. There are a number of towns on the train line with 'Balaton' or 'Füred' somewhere in their name, so double-check which station you're getting off at.

From April to September, four daily ferries ply the water from Balatonfüred to Tihany (930Ft, 20 minutes) and Siófok (1280Ft, 55 minutes).

A good way to explore the waterfront is to rent a bike from **Tempo 21** (☎ 06 20 924 4995; Deák Ferenc utca 56; per hr/day 350/2400Ft; ☺ 9am-7pm mid-May–mid-Sep).

TIHANY
☎ 87 / pop 1500

The place with the greatest historical significance on Lake Balaton is Tihany, a peninsula jutting 5km into the lake. Activity here is centred on the tiny town of the same name, which is home to the celebrated Abbey Church. Contrasting with this are the hills and marshy meadows of the peninsula's nature reserve, which has an isolated, almost wild feel to it.

The peninsula has beaches on both its eastern and western coasts, and a big resort complex on its southern tip. However, you can easily shake off the tourist hordes by going hiking. Birdwatchers, bring your binoculars: the trails have abundant avian life.

Orientation & Information

The harbour where ferries heading to and from Balatonfüred dock is a couple of kilometres downhill from the village of Tihany. Buses pull up in the heart of town, outside the post office on Kossuth Lajos utca.

Tourinform (☎ 448 804; tihany@tourinform.hu; Kossuth Lajos utca 20; ☺ 9am-7pm Mon-Fri, 10am-6pm Sat

& Sun mid-Jun–mid-Sep, 9am-5pm Mon-Fri, 10am-4pm Sat mid-Apr–mid-Jun & late Sep, 10am-4pm Mon-Fri Oct–mid-Apr) sells hiking maps and film, and provides tourist information.

Sights & Activities

You can spot Tihany's twin-towered **Abbey Church** (Apátság Templom; adult/concession 700/300Ft; 9am-6pm May-Sep, 10am-5pm Apr & Oct, 10am-3pm Nov-Mar), dating from 1754, from a long way off. Entombed in the church's crypt is the abbey's founder, King Andrew I. The admission fee includes entry to the attached **Abbey Museum** (Apátsági Múzeum). The path behind the church leads to outstanding views.

Follow the pathway along the ridge north from the church in the village to reach the tiny **Open-air Folk Museum** (Szabadtéri Néprajzi Múzeum; Pisky sétány 10; adult/concession 350/250Ft; 10am-6pm May-Sep).

Back at the clearing in front of the church, there's a large hiking map that has all of Tihany's trails marked. Following the green trail northeast of the church for an hour will bring you to a Russian well (oroszkút) and the ruins of the Old Castle (Óvár), where Russian Orthodox monks, brought to Tihany by Andrew I, hollowed out cells in the soft basalt walls.

Sleeping & Eating

Tihany is an easy day trip from Balatonfüred, so there's no reason to stay over unless you're hiking. If you are looking for lodgings, one option is to look for a 'Zimmer frei' (German for 'room for rent') sign on the small streets north of the church.

Adler (☎ 538 000; www.adler-tihany.hu; Felsőkopaszhegyi utca 1/a; r €41-52, apt €68-95;) Features large, whitewashed rooms with balconies, and there's a spa bath, sauna and restaurant on the premises.

our pick **Ferenc Pince** (☎ 448 575; Cser-hegy 9; mains from 1500Ft; noon-11pm Wed-Mon) Ferenc is a wine and food lover's dream. During the day, its open terrace offers expansive views of the lake, while at night the twinkling lights of the southern shore are in full view. It's about 2km south of the abbey church.

Rege Cafe (Kossuth Lajos utca 22; 10am-6pm) From its high vantage point near the Benedictine abbey, this modern cafe has an unsurpassed panoramic view of Lake Balaton. On a sunny day, there is no better place to enjoy coffee, cake and the sparkling waters.

Getting There & Away

Buses travel along the 14km of mostly lakeside road between Tihany village and Balatonfüred's train and bus stations (250Ft, 30 minutes) at least 13 times a day.

Passenger ferries sail between Tihany and Balatonfüred from April to September (930Ft, 20 minutes, seven daily). You can follow a steep path up to the village from the pier to reach the Abbey Church.

KESZTHELY

☎ 83 / pop 21,800

At the very western end of the Balaton sits Keszthely (kest-hey), a place of grand town houses and a gentle ambience far removed from the lake's tourist hot spots. Its small, shallow beaches are well suited to families, and there are enough accommodation options to suit most holidaymakers. Of its handful of museums and historical buildings, nothing tops the Festetics Palace, a lavish baroque residence. The town lies just over 1km northwest of the lake and with the exception of a few guest houses, almost everything stays open year-round. If you visit in May, you might catch the town's annual Balaton Festival.

Orientation & Information

The bus and train stations, side by side at the end of Mártírok útja, are fairly close to the ferry pier. Walk northeast on Kazinczy utca and you'll see the water to your right in a few hundred metres. To get to town, turn left and head towards Kossuth Lajos utca.

Tourinform (☎ 314 144, keszthely@tourinform.hu; Kossuth Lajos utca 28; 9am-8pm Mon-Fri, to 6pm Sat mid-Jun–mid-Sep, 9am-5pm Mon-Fri, to 12.30pm Sat mid-Sep–mid-Jun) has information on the whole Lake Balaton area.

There's a huge **OTP Bank** (Kossuth Lajos utca) facing the park south of the church, and close by is the **main post office** (Kossuth Lajos utca 48).

Sights & Activities

The glimmering white, 100-room **Festetics Palace** (Festetics Kastély; ☎ 312 190; Kastély utca 1; adult/concession 1650/800Ft; 9am-6pm Jul-Aug, 10am-4pm Sep-Jun) was first built in 1745; the wings were extended out from the original building 150 years later. About a dozen rooms in the one-time residence have been turned into a museum. Many of the decorative arts in the gilt salons were imported from England in the mid-1800s. The **Helikon Library** (Helikon

HUNGARY

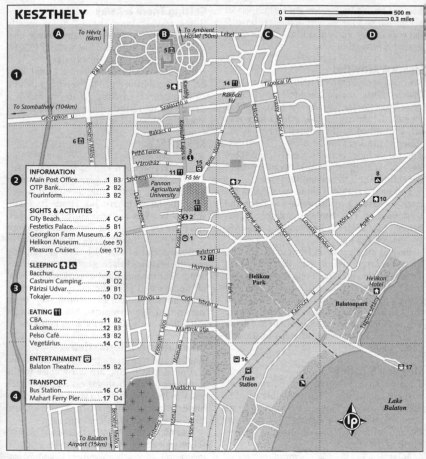

KESZTHELY

INFORMATION
Main Post Office............1 B3
OTP Bank...................2 B2
Tourinform.................3 B2

SIGHTS & ACTIVITIES
City Beach.................4 C4
Festetics Palace...........5 B1
Georgikon Farm Museum......6 A2
Helikon Museum.........(see 5)
Pleasure Cruises.......(see 17)

SLEEPING
Bacchus...................7 C2
Castrum Camping...........8 D2
Párizsi Udvar.............9 B1
Tokajer..................10 D2

EATING
CBA......................11 B2
Lakoma...................12 B3
Pelso Café...............13 B2
Vegetárius...............14 C1

ENTERTAINMENT
Balaton Theatre..........15 B2

TRANSPORT
Bus Station..............16 C4
Mahart Ferry Pier........17 D4

Könyvtár), in the baroque south wing, is known for its 100,000 volumes and its hand-carved furniture, crafted by a local artisan. To reach the palace, follow Kossuth Lajos utca, the long pedestrian street in the centre of the Old Town.

In 1797 Count György Festetics, an uncle of the reformer István Széchenyi, founded Europe's first agricultural institute, the Georgikon, in Keszthely. Part of the original school is now the **Georgikon Farm Museum** (Georgikon Major Múzeum; Bercsényi Miklós utca 67; adult/concession 500/250Ft; 10am-5pm Tue-Sun May-Sep, 10am-5pm Mon-Fri Apr & Oct).

The lakeside area centres on the long Mahart ferry pier. From March to October you can take a one-hour **pleasure cruise** (312 093; www.balatoni

hajozas.hu; Mahart ferry pier; adult/concession 1250/625Ft) on the lake at 11am, 1pm, 3pm and 5pm daily. If you're feeling like a swim, **City Beach** (Városi Strand) is not far west of the pier, near plenty of beer stands and food booths. There are other beaches you can explore further afield; some hotels have private shore access.

Sleeping

Tourinform can help find private rooms (from 3000Ft per person). Otherwise, strike out on your own (particularly along Móra Ferenc utca) and keep an eye out for 'szoba kiadó' or 'Zimmer frei' signs (Hungarian and German, respectively, for 'room for rent').

Castrum Camping (312 120; www.castrum-group .hu; Móra Ferenc utca 48; camp sites per adult/concession/

tent 1200/900/1800Ft; Apr-Oct;) North of the stations, this large camping ground is green and spacious, but the management seems to prefer caravans to tents. Unfortunately you have to cross the railway tracks to reach the lake.

Ambient Hostel (06 30 460 3536; hostel-accom modation.fw.hu; Sopron utca 10; dm/d from 2900/6800Ft;) Only a short walk north of the palace is this new hostel with basic, cheap dorms, each of which comes with its own bathroom. Laundry service is available 3pm to 5pm, from Monday to Friday.

Tokajer (319 875; www.pensiontokajer.hu; Apát utca 21; s/d/apt from €33/50/58;) Spread over four buildings in a quiet area of town, Tokajer has slightly dated rooms, but they're still in good condition. Extras include a mini–wellness centre and free use of bicycles.

Párizsi Udvar (311 202; parizsiudvar@freemail.hu; Kastély utca 5; d/tr/apt 9400/11,400/15,000Ft) Large basic rooms share kitchen facilities in what was once part of the Festetics Kastély complex. The central courtyard adds to the quiet of the place.

Bacchus (510 450; www.bacchushotel.hu; Erzsébet királyné utca 18; s/d/apt 12,300/16,500/24,800Ft) Bacchus' central position and immaculate rooms make it a popular choice with travellers. Equally pleasing is its atmospheric cellar, which is divided between a fine restaurant and a wine museum (admission free, open 11am to 11pm) where tastings are available.

Eating

Pelso Café (Fő tér; coffee & cake from 290Ft; 9am-9pm) This modern two-level cafe at the southern end of the main square does decent coffee, cake and cocktails, has a selection of teas from

around the world, and attracts both young and old.

Vegetárius (311 023; Rákóczi tér 3; mains 800-1000Ft; 11am-4pm Mon-Fri) This small vegetarian restaurant down the hill from the palace has a good vibe and plenty of healthy choices during the midweek lunch-hour rush.

Lakoma (313 129; Balaton utca 9; mains 1000-2600Ft) With a good fish selection, grill/roast specialities and a back garden that transforms itself into a leafy dining area in the summer months, it's hard to go wrong with Lakoma.

If you need groceries, shop while admiring the beautiful stained-glass windows of the **CBA** (Kossuth Lajos utca 35) supermarket on the main street.

Entertainment

The biweekly *ZalaEst* booklet, available from Tourinform, is a good source of information on entertainment activities in Keszthely.

Balaton Theatre (515 230; www.balatonsz inhaz.hu, in Hungarian, Fő tér 3) Catch the latest in theatre performances at this venue on the main square.

Getting There & Away

Balaton airport (354 256; www.flybalaton.hu), 15km southwest of Keszthely at Sármellék, receives Ryanair flights from Düsseldorf, Frankfurt and London Stansted. There's no public transport between the airport and Keszthely, but transfers can be arranged with **FlyBalaton Airport Transfer** (554 055; www.balatonairporttransfer .com; one way/return €6/10).

Back on the ground, buses from Keszthely to Hévíz (200Ft, 15 minutes) leave at least every 30 minutes during the day. Other places served by buses include Balatonfüred (1050Ft,

---

WORTH THE TRIP: HÉVÍZ

Just 6km northwest of Keszthely is the spa town of Hévíz. People have utilised the warm mineral water here for centuries, first for tanning in the Middle Ages and later for curative purposes (it was developed as a private resort in 1795). One of Europe's largest thermal lakes, the 5-hectare **Gyógytó** (Thermal Lake; www.spaheviz.hu; day pass 2900Ft; 8am-6pm May-Sep, 9am-4pm Oct-Apr) gurgles up in the middle of town. The hot spring is a crater some 40m deep that disgorges up to 80 million litres of warm water a day. The surface temperature here averages 33°C and never drops below 26°C, allowing bathing year-round. You can rent towels, inner tubes and even swimsuits. Both the water and the bottom mud are slightly radioactive; the minerals are said to alleviate various medical conditions.

To get here, take the bus from Keszthely station (200Ft, 15 minutes, half-hourly). The lake park is across Deák tér from the Hévíz bus station. Walk right around the park to get to the closest year-round entrance in the east.

1½ hours, seven daily) and Budapest (2780Ft, three hours, seven daily).

Keszthely is on a railway branch line linking the lake's southeastern shore with Budapest (2780Ft, four hours, six daily). To reach towns along Lake Balaton's northern shore by train, you have to change at Tapolca (375Ft, 30 minutes, hourly). A more extravagant rail option is the vintage steam train operated by **MÁV Nostalgia** (www.mavnosztalgia.hu) from Keszthely to Badacsonytomaj (one way 1170Ft, 1¾ hours) from late June to late August at 9.50am every Tuesday, Thursday and Saturday, returning at 2.53pm.

From April to September, **Mahart ferries** (www.balatonihajozas.hu) link Keszthely with Badacsonytomaj (1430Ft, two hours, four daily) and other, smaller lake towns.

SOUTH CENTRAL HUNGARY

Southern Hungary is a region of calm, a place to savour life at a slower pace. It's only marginally touched by tourism, and touring through the countryside is like travelling back in time. Passing through the region, you'll spot whitewashed farmhouses whose thatched roofs and long colonnaded porticoes decorated with floral patterns seem unchanged over the centuries.

Historically, the area bordering Croatia and Serbia has often been 'shared' between Hungary and these countries, and it's here that the remnants of the 150-year Turkish occupation can be most strongly felt.

The region is bounded by the Danube River to the east, the Dráva River to the south and west, and Lake Balaton to the north. Generally flat, the Mecsek and Villány Hills rise up in isolation from the plain. The weather always seems to be a few degrees warmer here than in other parts of the country; the sunny clime is great for grape growing, and oak-aged Villány reds are well regarded, if highly tannic.

PÉCS

☎ 72 / pop 156,000

Blessed with a mild climate, an illustrious past and a number of fine museums and monuments, Pécs (pronounced *paich*) is one of the most pleasant and interesting cities to visit in Hungary. For those reasons and more – a handful of universities, the nearby Mecsek Hills, a lively nightlife – many travellers put it second only to Budapest on their Hungary must-see list.

Lying equidistant from the Danube to the east and the Dráva to the south, Pécs enjoys a microclimate that lengthens the summer and is ideal for viticulture and fruit production (especially almonds). An especially fine time to visit is during a warm *indián nyár* (Indian summer), when the light seems to take on a special quality.

History has far from ignored Pécs. The Roman settlement of Sopianae on this site was the capital of the province of Lower Pannonia for 400 years. Christianity flourished here in the 4th century and in 1009 Stephen I made Pécs a bishopric. The first Hungarian university was founded here in the mid-14th century. City walls were erected after the Mongol invasion of 1241, but 1543 marked the start of almost a century and a half of Turkish domination. In the 19th century the manufacture of Zsolnay porcelain and other goods, such as Pannonia sparkling wine, helped put Pécs back on the map.

Orientation & Information

The train station is a little over 1km south of the old town centre. Walk up Jókai Mór utca to the town centre. The bus station is a few blocks closer, next to the market. Follow Bajcsy-Zsilinszky utca north to get to the centre. **Tourinform** (☎ 213 315; baranya-m@tourinform.hu; Széchenyi tér 9; 🕑 8am-6pm Mon-Fri, 10am-8pm Sat & Sun Jun-Aug, 8am-5.30pm Mon-Fri, 10am-2pm Sat May, Sep & Oct, 8am-4pm Mon-Fri Nov-Apr) has internet access (100Ft per hour) and tons of local info, including a list of museums. The **main post office** (Jókai Mór utca 10) is in a beautiful art nouveau building (1904) with a colourful Zsolnay porcelain roof. There are plenty of banks and ATMs scattered around town. The **Ibusz** (☎ 211 011; www.ibusz.hu; Király utca 11; 🕑 8am-5pm Mon-Fri, 8am-noon Sat) travel agency offers a currency-exchange booth, rents private rooms and books transport tickets.

Sights & Activities

The curiously named **Mosque Church** (Mecset Templom; Széchenyi tér; 🕑 10am-4pm Mon-Sat, 11.30am-4pm Sun mid-Apr–mid-Oct, 10am-noon Mon-Sat, 11.30am-2pm Sun mid-Oct–mid-Apr) dominates the city's central square. It has no minaret and has

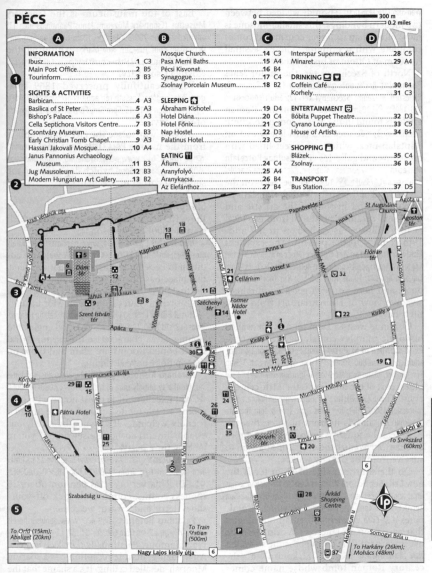

PÉCS

0 — 300 m
0 — 0.2 miles

INFORMATION
Ibusz....................................1 C3
Main Post Office....................2 B5
Tourinform............................3 B3

SIGHTS & ACTIVITIES
Barbican...............................4 A3
Basilica of St Peter.................5 A3
Bishop's Palace.....................6 A3
Cella Septichora Visitors Centre...7 B3
Csontváry Museum.................8 B3
Early Christian Tomb Chapel....9 A3
Hassan Jakovali Mosque.........10 A4
Janus Pannonius Archaeology
　Museum............................11 B3
Jug Mausoleum....................12 B3
Modern Hungarian Art Gallery...13 B2

Mosque Church....................14 C3
Pasa Memi Baths...................15 A4
Pécsi Kisvonat......................16 B4
Synagogue...........................17 C4
Zsolnay Porcelain Museum.....18 B2

SLEEPING
Ábraham Kishotel..................19 D4
Hotel Diána..........................20 C4
Hotel Főnix...........................21 C3
Nap Hostel...........................22 D3
Palatinus Hotel.....................23 C3

EATING
Áfium..................................24 C4
Aranyfolyó...........................25 A4
Aranykacsa..........................26 B4
Az Elefánthoz.......................27 B4

Interspar Supermarket............28 C5
Minaret................................29 A4

DRINKING
Coffein Café.........................30 B4
Korhely...............................31 C3

ENTERTAINMENT
Bóbita Puppet Theatre............32 D3
Cyrano Lounge......................33 C5
House of Artists.....................34 B4

SHOPPING
Blázek.................................35 C4
Zsolnay...............................36 B4

TRANSPORT
Bus Station..........................37 D5

HUNGARY

been a Christian place of worship for a long time, but the Islamic elements inside, such as the mihrab on the southeastern wall, reveal its original identity. Constructed in the mid-16th century from the stones of an earlier church, the mosque underwent several changes of appearance over the years – including the addition of a steeple. In the

late 1930s the building was restored to its medieval form.

West along Ferencesek utcája, you'll pass the ruins of the 16th-century Turkish **Pasa Memi Baths** (Memi Pasa Fürdője) before you turn south on Rákóczi utca to get to the 16th-century **Hassan Jakovali Mosque** (Hassan Jakovali Mecset; adult/concession 500/250Ft; 🕘 9.30am-5.30pm

Wed-Sun late Mar-Oct). Though wedged between two modern buildings, this smaller mosque is more intact than its larger cousin and comes complete with a minaret. There's a small museum of Ottoman history inside.

North of Széchenyi tér, the minor **Janus Pannonius Archaeology Museum** (Janus Pannonius Régészeti Múzeum; Széchenyi tér 12; adult/concession 350/180Ft; 🕑 10am-2pm Tue-Sat) contains Roman artefacts found in the area. From here, climb Szepessy Ignéc utca and turn left (west) on Káptalan utca, which is a street lined with museums and galleries. The **Zsolnay Porcelain Museum** (Zsolnay Porcélan Múzeum; Káptalan utca 2; adult/concession 700/350Ft; 🕑 10am-5pm Tue-Sun) is on the eastern end of this strip. English translations provide a good history of the artistic and functional ceramics produced from this local factory's illustrious early days in the mid-19th century to the present. The excellent **Modern Hungarian Art Gallery** (Modern Magyar Képtár; Káptalan utca 4; adult/concession 460/230Ft; 🕑 noon-6pm Tue-Sun Apr-Oct, 10am-4pm Tue-Sun Nov-Mar) is next door, and here you can get a comprehensive overview of Hungarian art from 1850 till today.

Continue west to Dóm tér and the walled bishopric complex containing the four-towered **Basilica of St Peter** (Szent Péter Bazilika; Dóm tér; adult/concession 800/500Ft; 🕑 9am-5pm Mon-Sat, 1-5pm Sun Apr-Oct, 10am-4pm Mon-Sat, 1-4pm Sun Nov-Mar). The oldest part of the building is the 11th-century crypt. The 1770 **Bishop's Palace** (Püspöki Palota; adult/concession 1500/700Ft; 🕑 tours 2pm, 3pm & 4pm Thu late Jun–mid-Sep) stands in front of the cathedral. Also near the square is a nearby 15th-century **barbican** (barbakán), the only stone bastion to survive from the old city walls.

On the southern side of Dom tér is the new **Cella Septichora Visitors Centre** (Janus Pannonius utca; adult/concession 1500/800Ft; 🕑 10am-6pm Tue-Sun Apr-Oct, 10am-4pm Tue-Sun Nov-Mar), which illuminates a series of early-Christian burial sites that have been on Unesco's World Heritage list since 2000. The highlight is the so-called **Jug Mausoleum** (Korsós Sírkamra), a 4th-century Roman tomb whose name comes from a painting of a large drinking vessel with vines.

Across Janus Pannonius utca from the centre, the **early Christian tomb chapel** (Ókeresztény sírkápolna; Szent István tér 12; adult/concession 400/200Ft; 🕑 10am-6pm Tue-Sun Apr-Oct, 10am-4pm Tue-Sun Nov-Mar) dates from about AD 350 and has frescos of Adam and Eve, and Daniel in the lion's den.

East of the mausoleum is the **Csontváry Museum** (Csontváry Múzeum; Janus Pannonius utca 11; adult/concession 700/350Ft; 🕑 10am-6pm Tue-Sun Apr-Oct, 10am-4pm Tue-Sun Nov-Mar), exhibiting the works of master 19th-century painter Tivadar Kosztka Csontváry.

Pécs' beautifully preserved 1869 **synagogue** (zsinagóga; Kossuth tér; adult/concession 500/300Ft; 🕑 10am-noon & 12.45-5pm Sun-Fri May-Oct) is south of Széchenyi tér.

An easy way to see the city's highlights is from the mobile **Pécs Little Train** (Pécsi Kisvonat; ☎ 06 70 454 5610; www.pecsikisvonat.hu; adult/concession 950/500Ft; 🕑 10am-5pm), which departs from the southeast corner of Széchenyi tér.

Sleeping

Ibusz (p342) arranges private rooms, which start at 3500Ft per person.

Nap Hostel (☎ 950 684; www.naphostel.com; Király utca 23-25; dm/d from 2400/9600Ft; 🖳) A welcome addition to Pécs' budget accommodation scene, this place has dorms and a double room on the first floor of a former bank. There's also a large kitchen. Enter from Szent Mór utca.

Hotel Főnix (☎ 311 682; www.fonixhotel.hu; Hunyadi János út 2; s/d 7790/12,590Ft; 🍴 🖳) Odd angles and sloping eaves characterise the asymmetrical Hotel Főnix. Rooms are plain and those on the top floor have skylights.

Ábrahám Kishotel (☎ 510 422; www.abrahamhotel .hu; Munkácsy Mihály utca 8; s/d/tr 9100/12,000/14,000Ft; 🍴 🖳) Excellent little guest house with blue rooms, a well-tended, peaceful garden and a friendly welcome. It's owned by a religious establishment, so head elsewhere if you're looking for a party.

Hotel Diána (☎ 328 594; www.hoteldiana.hu; Tímár utca 4/a; s/d/tr/q from 9500/13,000/18,300/20,000Ft; 🍴 🖳) This very central pension offers 20 spotless rooms, comfortable kick-off-your-shoes decor and a warm welcome.

Palatinus Hotel (☎ 889 400; www.danubiushotels .com; Király utca 5; s/d from €60/80; 🍴 🖳) For art nouveau glamour, Palatinus is the place in Pécs. An amazing, marble reception has a soaring Moorish-detailed ceiling. It's a shame that the rooms are not as luxurious, but still, in Pécs, it's as good as it gets.

Eating & Drinking

Pubs, cafes and fast-food eateries line pedestrian-only Király utca.

Aranyfolyó (☎ 212 269; Váradi Antal utca 9; mains 450-750Ft; 🕑 11.30am-10pm) The two Chinese dragons guarding the door of this restaurant are a hint about the in-house cuisine. Rice and noodle dishes are a snip at 450Ft to 2100Ft.

Minaret (☎ 311 338; Ferencesek utcája 35; mains 1200-2100Ft; 🕑 noon-4pm Sun-Mon, to 9pm Tue-Thu, to 11pm Fri & Sat) Boasting one of the loveliest gardens in the city, this eatery in the shadow of the Pasa Memi Baths serves tasty Hungarian favourites.

our pick Áfium (☎ 511 434; Irgalmasok utca 2; mains 1400-1900Ft; 🕑 11am-1am) With Croatia and Serbia so close, it's a wonder that more restaurants don't offer cuisine from south of the border. Don't miss the bean soup with trotters. Set lunch is 520Ft during the week.

Az Elefánthoz (☎ 216 055; Jókai tér 6; mains 1600-2100Ft) With its enormous terrace and quality Italian cuisine, this place is a sure bet for first-rate food in the centre of town. It has a wood-burning stove for making pizzas.

Aranykacsa (☎ 518 860; Teréz utca 4; mains 1620-3240Ft; 🕑 11.30am-10pm Tue-Thu, to midnight Fri & Sat, to 3pm Sun) This stunning wine restaurant takes pride in its silver service and beautiful venue. The menu offers at least eight duck dishes, including such memorables as duck ragout with honey and vegetables.

Korhely (Boltív köz 2; 🕑 11am-midnight) This outrageously popular *csapszék* (tavern) has peanuts on the table, shells on the floor, a half-dozen beers on tap and a sort of 'retro socialist meets Latin American' decor. It works.

Coffein Café (Széchenyi tér 9; 🕑 8am-midnight Mon-Thu, 8am-2am Fri & Sat, 10am-10pm Sun) For the best views across Széchenyi tér to the Mosque Church and Király utca, find a perch at this cool cafe done up in the warmest of colours.

Get self-catering supplies at the **Interspar supermarket** (Bajcsy-Zsilinszky utca 11; 🕑 7am-9pm Mon-Thu & Sat, 7am-10pm Fri, 8am-7pm Sun) in the basement of the Árkád shopping centre.

Entertainment

Pécs has well-established opera and ballet companies as well as a symphony orchestra. Tourinform has schedule information. The free biweekly *Pécsi Est* also lists what's on around town.

House of Artists (Művészetek Háza; ☎ 522 834; www.pmh.hu; Széchenyi tér 7-8) This is a cultural venue that hosts classical-music performances. A schedule is posted outside.

Bóbita Puppet Theatre (Bóbita Bábszínház; ☎ 210 301; www.bobita.hu; Mária utca 18) Somewhere John Malkovich would be proud to perform, the Bóbita is not just for kids.

Cyrano Lounge (Czindery utca 6; 🕑 8pm-5am Fri & Sat) A big nightclub, popular with the in crowd, next to the big Árkád shopping centre.

Shopping

Pécs has been known for its leatherwork since Turkish times, and you can pick up a few bargains around the city. Try **Blázek** (☎ 332 460; Teréz utca 1), which deals mainly in handbags and wallets. **Zsolnay** (☎ 310 220; Jókai tér 2) has a porcelain outlet south of Széchenyi tér.

Getting There & Away

Buses for Harkány (900Ft, 1½ hours) leave regularly throughout the day. At least five buses a day connect Pécs with Budapest (3010Ft, 4½ hours), three with Siófok (2040Ft, three hours) and eight with Szeged (3010Ft, 4½ hours).

Pécs is on a main rail line with Budapest's Déli train station (3230Ft, 3½ hours, nine daily). Three daily trains run from Pécs to Osijek (two hours) in Croatia, with one continuing to the Bosnian capital, Sarajevo (nine hours).

AROUND PÉCS

The hot springs at **Harkány** (www.harkany.hu, in Hungarian), 26km south of Pécs, have medicinal waters with the richest sulphuric content in Hungary. The indoor and outdoor baths and pools of **Gyógyfürdő** (Thermal Baths; ☎ 480 251; www.harkanyfurdo.hu; Kossuth Lajos utca 7; adult/concession 2250/1590Ft; 🕑 9am-6pm) range in temperature from 26°C to 33°C in summer and from 33°C to 35°C in winter. Consider booking a spa service, mud bath or massage. The town is basically the thermal bath complex in a 12-hectare park surrounded by hotels and restaurants. Buses between Harkány and Pécs (900Ft, 1½ hours) depart at least half-hourly. The Harkány bus station is at the southeast corner of the park.

SOUTHEASTERN HUNGARY

Like the Outback for Australians or the Old West for Americans, the Nagyalföld (Great Plain) holds a romantic appeal for Hungarians. Images of shepherds guiding their flocks with moplike *puli* dogs and cowboys riding across the *puszta* are scattered throughout the nation's poetry and painting. The Great Plain covers some 45,000 sq km east and southeast of Budapest. Beyond its big sky country appeal, the Great Plain is also home to cities of graceful architecture, winding rivers and easygoing afternoons.

KECSKEMÉT

☎ 76 / pop 103,000

Located about halfway between Budapest and Szeged, Kecskemét (*kech*-kah-mate) is a green, pedestrian-friendly city with interesting art nouveau architecture. Colourful buildings, fine small museums and the region's excellent *barackpálinka* (apricot brandy) beckon. And Kiskunsági Nemzeti Park, the *puszta* of the Southern Plain, is right at the back door. Day-trip opportunities include hiking in the sandy, juniper-covered hills, a horse show at Bugac, or a visit to one of the area's many horse farms.

Orientation & Information

Central Kecskemét is made up of squares that run into one another, and consequently it's hard to tell them apart. The main bus and train stations are opposite each other

in József Katona Park. A 10-minute walk southwest along Nagykőrösi utca brings you to the first of the squares, Szabadság tér.

Datanet Internet Café (Kossuth tér 6-7; per hr 300Ft; ⊗ 9am-10pm) Internet access.

Ibusz (☎ 486 955; Malom Centre, Korona utca 2; ⊗ 8am-5pm Mon-Fri Sep-Jun, 8am-5pm Mon-Fri, 9am-1pm Sat Jul-Aug) Arranges private rooms.

Main post office (Kálvin tér 10)

OTP Bank (Malom Centre, Korona utca 2)

Tourinform (☎ 481 065; kecskemet@tourinform.hu; Kossuth tér 1; ⊗ 8am-7pm Mon-Fri, 10am-8pm Sat & Sun Jul-Aug, 8am-6pm Mon-Fri Sep-Jun) In the northeastern corner of the large Town Hall.

Sights

Walk around the parklike squares, starting at Szabadság tér, and admire the eclectic buildings, including the Technicolor art nouveau style of the 1902 **Ornamental Palace** (Cifrapalota; Rákóczi út 1), recently refurbished and covered in multicoloured majolica tiles. Check out the wonderful interiors of the **Kecskemét Gallery** (Kecskeméti Képtár; Rákóczi út 1; adult/concession 300/150Ft; ⊗ 10am-5pm Tue-Sat, 1.30-5pm Sun) here. Across the street, the Moorish building is the

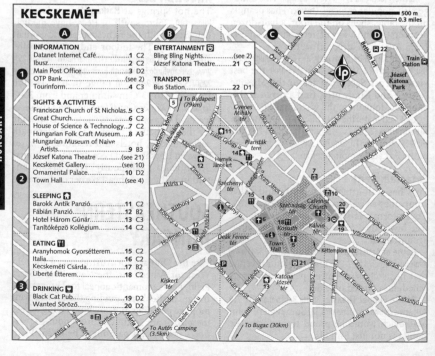

KECSKEMÉT

0 — 500 m
0 — 0.3 miles

INFORMATION	
Datanet Internet Café	1 C2
Ibusz	2 C2
Main Post Office	3 D2
OTP Bank	(see 2)
Tourinform	4 C3

SIGHTS & ACTIVITIES	
Franciscan Church of St Nicholas	5 C3
Great Church	6 C2
House of Science & Technology	7 C2
Hungarian Folk Craft Museum	8 A3
Hungarian Museum of Naïve Artists	9 B3
József Katona Theatre	(see 21)
Kecskemét Gallery	(see 10)
Ornamental Palace	10 D2
Town Hall	(see 4)

SLEEPING	
Barokk Antik Panzió	11 C2
Fábián Panzió	12 B2
Hotel Három Gúnár	13 C3
Tanítóképző Kollégium	14 C2

EATING	
Aranyhomok Gyorsétterem	15 C2
Italia	16 C2
Kecskeméti Csárda	17 B2
Liberté Étterem	18 C2

DRINKING	
Black Cat Pub	19 D2
Wanted Söröző	20 D2

ENTERTAINMENT	
Bling Bling Nights	(see 2)
József Katona Theatre	21 C3

TRANSPORT	
Bus Station	22 D1

House of Science & Technology (Tudomány és Technika Háza; Rákóczi út 2; adult/concession 200/100Ft; 8am-4pm Mon-Fri). This former synagogue is now an exhibition hall.

Kossuth tér is dominated by the massive 1897 art nouveau **Town Hall** (Városháza), which is flanked by the baroque **Great Church** (Nagytemplom; Kossuth tér 2; 9am-noon & 3-6pm Tue-Sun May-Sep, 9am-noon Tue-Sun Oct-Apr) and the earlier **Franciscan Church of St Nicholas** (Szent Miklós Templom), dating from the 13th century. Nearby is the magnificent 1896 **József Katona Theatre** (Katona József Színház; ☎ 483 283; Katona József tér 5), a neobaroque performance venue with a statue of the Trinity (1742) in front of it.

The town's museums are scattered around the main squares' periphery. Go first to the **Hungarian Museum of Naive Artists** (Magyar Naiv Müvészek; Gáspár András utca 11; adult/concession 200/100Ft; 10am-5pm Tue-Sun mid-Mar–Oct), in the Stork House (1730) northwest off Petőfi Sándor utca. It has an impressive small collection. Further to the southwest, the **Hungarian Folk Craft Museum** (Népi Iparmüvészeti Múzeum; Serfőző utca 19/a; adult/concession 300/150Ft; 10am-5pm Tue-Sat Feb-Nov) has a definitive collection of regional embroidery, weaving and textiles, as well as some furniture, woodcarving and agricultural tools. A few handicrafts are for sale at the entrance.

Sleeping

Tourinform can help you locate the numerous colleges that offer dormitory accommodation in July and August, and the Ibusz agency arranges private rooms (see opposite).

Autós Camping (☎ 329 398; Csabay Géza körút 5; camp sites per person/tent 800/700Ft; bungalows 5000-8000Ft; May-Sep) Neat rows of tents and bungalows (with kitchen and bathroom, but no hot water) line this camping ground near the Aqua Park, 3km from centre. Don't expect much shade. Take bus 1 to get southwest of town.

Tanítóképző Kollégium (Teachers' College; ☎ 486 977; loveikollegium@tfk.kefo.hu; Piaristák tere 4; s/d 2500/5000Ft; mid-Jun–Aug) A good choice among the academic accommodation options, with a central location.

Barokk Antik Panzió (☎ 260 3215; www.barokk antik-panzio.hu; Fráter György utca 17; s/d 7500/10,500Ft) A sombre painting or two lends a bit of an old-world feel, but we wouldn't say the rooms have actual antiques. Thankfully, they do have minibars and very modern bathrooms.

our pick **Fábián Panzió** (☎ 477 677; www.panzio fabian.hu; Kápolna utca 14; s/d from 8800/11,000Ft;) The world-travelling family that owns this pretty-in-pink guest house knows how to treat a visitor well. Friendly staff help their guests plan each day's excursions, teapots are available for in-room use, wireless internet is free, and bikes are available for hire. Simply luvverly.

Hotel Három Gúnár (☎ 483 611; Batthyány utca 1; s/d 10,500/13,800Ft;) Four multihued town houses – flowerboxes and all – have been transformed to contain 49 smallish rooms (the best are Nos 306 to 308). Simple veneer furnishings in the rooms are less cheery than the exterior facade. There's an on-site restaurant.

Eating & Drinking

Aranyhomok Gyorsétterem (☎ 503 730; Kossuth tér 3; mains 300-600Ft; 24hr) Locals love this quick and tasty self-service cafeteria on the ground floor of the city's ugliest hotel. The staff keep the food fresh, despite being open round the clock.

Italia (☎ 484 627; Hornyik János körút 4; mains 1200-1400Ft) Italia is a little short on atmosphere but does a roaring trade with students from the nearby Teachers' College. Order pizza, pasta or any fried-pork variation you can imagine.

our pick **Liberté Étterem** (☎ 509 175; Szabadság tér 2; mains 1200-2000Ft) Artistic presentations come with your order, whether it's the traditional stuffed cabbage or the mixed sautéed chicken with aubergine. This is modern Hungarian done well. Its outside tables have the best seats in town for people-watching.

Kecskeméti Csárda (☎ 488 686; Kölcsey utca 7; mains 1500-2000Ft) Restaurant trading on folksy charm. It goes over the top with rustic fishing gear on the walls and Romani music at weekends.

For drinkies, the Western-themed pub **Wanted Söröző** (Csányi János körút 4; 10am-midnight Mon-Sat, from 4pm Sun) sits handily across from the more alternative **Black Cat Pub** (Csányi János körút 6; 11am-midnight Sun-Thu, to 2am Fri & Sat), making for quite the convivial corner.

Entertainment

Tourinform has a list of what concerts and performances are on, or check out the free weekly magazine *Kecskeméti Est*.

József Katona Theatre (Katona József Színház; ☎ 483 283; www.katonaj.hu; Katona József tér 5) Experience operettas and symphony performances in this grand 19th-century building.

Bling Bling Nights (www.blingblingnights.hu; Malom, Korona tér 2) Hip hop, house, R&B – the nightclub atop Malom Shopping Centre is definitely eclectic. DJs host most nights, but there are occasional live concerts.

Getting There & Away

Frequent buses depart for Budapest (1350Ft, 1½ hours, hourly) and for Szeged (1350Ft, 1¾ hours, hourly). A direct rail line links Kecskemét to Budapest's Nyugati train station (1770Ft, 1½ hours, hourly) and Szeged (1350Ft, one hour, hourly).

KISKUNSÁGI NEMZETI PARK

Totalling 76,000 hectares, **Kiskunsági Nemzeti Park** (Kiskunság National Park; www.knp.hu) consists of half a dozen 'islands' of protected land. Much of the park's alkaline ponds and sand dunes are off limits. Bugac (boo-gats) village, about 30km southwest of Kecskemét, is the most accessible part of the park.

From the village, walk, drive, or ride a **horse-driven carriage** (adult/concession incl horse show 2900/1700Ft; ☼ 11.15pm & 12.15pm May-Oct) along the 1.5km-long sandy track to the **Herder Museum** (admission free; ☼ 10am-5pm May-Oct), a circular structure designed to look like a horse-driven dry mill. The highlight of the museum is the popular **horse show** (admission 1400Ft; ☼ 12.15pm & 1.15pm May-Oct, extra show 3.15pm Jun-Aug). Once the show starts, the horse herders crack their whips, race one another bareback and ride 'five-in-hand', a breathtaking performance in which one csikós (cowboy) gallops five horses at full speed while standing on the backs of the rear two.

Afterwards, the food is surprisingly good at the kitschy **Bugaci Karikás Csárda** (☎ 575 112; Nagybugac 135; mains 1600-2100Ft; ☼ 8am-8pm May-Oct), next to the park entrance. The gulyás is hearty and the accompanying folk-music ensemble will get your feet tapping on the terrace.

The best way to get to Bugac is by bus from Kecskemét (600Ft, 50 minutes). The 11am bus from the main terminal gets you to the park entrance around noon. A bus returns directly from Bugac to Kecskemét at 3.50pm on weekdays. Otherwise catch a bus to Kiskunfélegyháza or Jakabszállás, and change there for Kecskemét (approximately hourly).

SZEGED

☎ 62 / pop 177,000

It's hard to decide what's most appealing about Szeged (seh-ged). Perhaps it's the shady green main square, perhaps the abundant sidewalk cafe seating in its pedestrian zone that seems to stretch on forever or perhaps it's the stimulating architecture of its attractive palaces. But it could also be its lively vibe – a product of year-round cultural performances and its energetic student population.

Szeged sits astride the Tisza River, which almost wiped the city off the map in 1879 via a major flood. However, the town bounced back with a vengeance and an eye for uniform architecture.

Orientation & Information

The train station is south of the city centre on Indóház tér; from here, tram 1 takes you along Boldogasszony sugárút into the centre of town. The bus station, on Mars tér, is west of the centre within easy walking distance via pedestrian-only Mikszáth Kálmán utca.

Tourinform (☎ 488 699; http://tip.szegedvaros.hu; Dugonics tér 2; ☼ 9am-5pm Mon-Fri, to 1pm Sat) Tourist office hidden in a courtyard.

Cyber Arena (Híd utca 1; per hr 400Ft; ☼ 24hr) Internet access with Skype set-ups and cheap international phonecards.

Main post office (Széchenyi tér 1)

OTP Bank (Klauzál tér 4)

Sights & Activities

East of Széchenyi tér, the huge, neoclassical **Ferenc Móra Museum** (Móra Ferenc Múzeum; www.mfm .u-szeged.hu; Roosevelt tér 1; adult/concession 600/300Ft; ☼ 10am-5pm Tue-Sun) overlooks the Tisza River. The museum contains a colourful collection of folk art from Csongrád County with descriptions in several languages and an exhibit of 7th-century gold work by the Avar, a mysterious people who are thought to have originated somewhere in Central Asia. But the best exhibit showcases an even more obscure group, the Sarmatians, who originated in present-day Iran.

To the west, the **New Synagogue** (Új Zsinagóga; www.zsinagoga.szeged.hu; Gutenberg utca 13; adult/concession 300/150Ft; ☼ 10am-noon & 1-5pm Sun-Fri Apr-Sep, 10am-2pm Sun-Fri Oct-Mar) is the most beautiful Jewish house of worship in Hungary and is still in use. An ornate blue and gold-painted interior graces the 1903 art nouveau building. The nearby **Old Synagogue** (Ó Zsinagóga; Hajnóczy utca 12) was built in 1843.

The **Szeged Open-Air Festival** (☎ 541 205; www .szegediszabadteri.hu) is held in Dom tér from mid-July to late August. Running along three sides

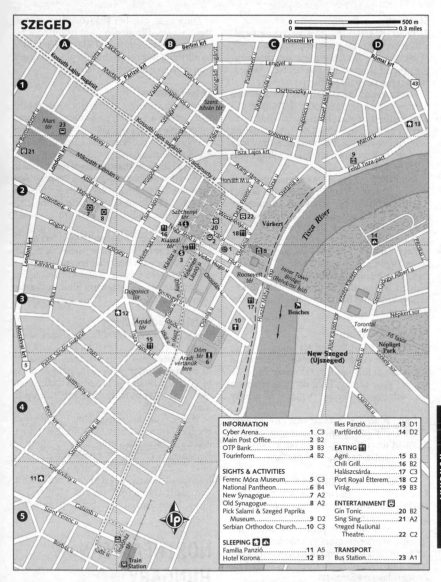

SZEGED

INFORMATION		
Cyber Arena	1	C3
Main Post Office	2	B2
OTP Bank	3	B3
Tourinform	4	B2

SIGHTS & ACTIVITIES		
Ferenc Móra Museum	5	C3
National Pantheon	6	B4
New Synagogue	7	A2
Old Synagogue	8	A2
Pick Salami & Szeged Paprika		
Museum	9	D2
Serbian Orthodox Church	10	C3

SLEEPING		
Família Panzió	11	A5
Hotel Korona	12	B3

Illes Panzió	13	D1
Partfürdő	14	D2

EATING		
Agni	15	B3
Chili Grill	16	B2
Halászcsárda	17	C3
Port Royal Étterem	18	C2
Virág	19	B3

ENTERTAINMENT		
Gin Tonic	20	B2
Sing Sing	21	A2
Szeged National		
Theatre	22	C2

TRANSPORT		
Bus Station	23	A1

of the square is the **National Pantheon** (Nemzeti Emlékcsarnok), with statues and reliefs of 80 Hungarian notables. One block northeast, inside the **Serbian Orthodox Church** (Szerb Ortodox Templom; adult/concession 200/150Ft; 8am-4pm), have a look at the fantastic iconostasis – a central gold 'tree' with 60 icons hanging off its branches.

Just north of the Old Town ring road is the **Pick Salami & Szeged Paprika Museum** (Pick Szalámi és Szegedi Paprika Múzeum; Felső Tisza-part 10; adult/concession 3 50/250Ft; 3-6pm Mon, 9am-5pm Tue-Fri, 9am-noon Sat). Two floors of exhibits show traditional methods of salami production. There's a small gift stand in the museum and a butcher shop around the corner in this factory building.

Sleeping

Partfürdő (☎ 430 843; Közép-kikötő sor; camp sites per person/tent 990/350Ft, r 4600-6900Ft, bungalows 8,000-12,000Ft; 🕙 mid-May–Sep; 🐾) This green, grassy camping ground is across the river in New Szeged. Bungalows sleep up to four people.

Família Panzió (☎ 411 122; www.familiapanzio.hu; Szentháromság utca 71; s/d/tr 8000/10,000/15,000Ft; 🐾) This family-run guest house with contemporary furnishings in a great Old Town building is often booked up. The reception area may be dim, but rooms have high ceilings and loads of light.

Illes Panzió (☎ 315 641; www.illespanzio-vadaszet terem.hu; Maros utca 37; r 9900-12,900Ft; 🐾 💻 🐾) This refurbished old mansion 10 minutes north of the centre has fresh, clean rooms with wood panels, cool tiled floors, TVs and polished woodwork.

Hotel Korona (☎ 555 787; www.hotelkoronaszeged. hu; Petőfi Sándor sgt 4; s/d 13,800/18,000Ft; 🐾) You can hardly see the original 1883 building outlines hidden within this modern hotel. Lemon yellow walls and blond wood accentuate the up-to-date vibe.

Eating & Drinking

Chili Grill (☎ 317 344; Nagy Jenő utca 4; mains 600-1000Ft; 🕙 11am-10pm Mon-Fri, 11am-6pm Sat) There *are* a few tables at this modern takeaway, but why not eat your turkey, bean or chilli wrap on the park benches under the trees of nearby Széchenyi tér?

Agni (☎ 477 739; Tisza Lajos körút 76; mains 1000-1300Ft) Daily lunch specials round out the menu at this little vegetarian restaurant. Try the substantial paprika-and-mushroom stew with millet.

our pick Port Royal Étterem (☎ 547 988; Stefánia 4; mains 1300-2200Ft; 🕙 11am-midnight Mon-Thu, 11am-2am Fri & Sat, 11am-11pm Sun) Tropical plants and live parrots are enough reason to make this eatery's pleasant patio your destination on a steamy summer evening. The modern kitchen turns out tasty traditional dishes, international faves and vegie options. Cocktails served till 2am Friday and Saturday.

Halászcsárda (☎ 555 980; Roosevelt tér 14; mains 2000-3500Ft) An institution that knows how to prepare the best fish dish in town – whole roasted pike with garlic, accompanied by pan-fried frog legs and fillet of carp soup. Although there are white tablecloths and waiters are dressed to the nines, the outdoor terrace is pretty casual.

Since 1922, cafe-bar **Virág** (Klauzál tér 1; 🕙 8am-10pm) has steadily grown until its outdoor tables have taken over half of Klauzál tér. Lots of locals think this is still the best place to linger over coffee, or something harder.

Entertainment

Szeged's status as a university town means that there's a vast array of bars, clubs and other nightspots, especially around Dugonics tér. Nightclub programs are listed in the free *Szegedi Est* magazine.

Szeged National Theatre (Szegedi Nemzeti Színház; ☎ 479 279; www.szinhaz.szeged.hu, in Hungarian; Deák Ferenc utca 12-14) Since 1886, this venue has been the centre of cultural life in the city. Opera, ballet and drama performances take to its stage.

Sing Sing (Mars tér C pavilion; 🕙 11pm-5am Wed, Fri & Sat) Huge warehouse rave parties take place here, replete with sexy themes and dancers.

Gin Tonic (Széchenyi tér 1; 🕙 10pm-4am Wed-Fri) This central dance club pulses to a funk, house and techno beat.

Getting There & Away

Buses run to Pécs (2780Ft, 4¼ hours, seven daily) and Debrecen (3230Ft, five hours, two daily). Buses also head for Arad, across the Romanian border, daily at 6.30am Monday to Saturday. Buses run to Serbian destinations Novi Sad at 4pm daily, and Subotica up to four times daily.

Szeged is on the main rail line to Budapest's Nyugati train station (2780Ft, 2¾ hours, hourly); trains also stop halfway along in Kecskemét (1770Ft, 1¼ hours, hourly). You have to change in Békéscsaba (1500Ft, two hours, half-hourly) to get to Arad in Romania. Two daily trains (6.50am and 12.30pm) go direct from Szeged to Subotica (two hours) in Serbia.

NORTHEASTERN HUNGARY

If ever a Hungarian wine were world-famous, it would be tokay. And this is where it comes from, a region of Hungary containing microclimates conducive to wine production. The chain of wooded hills in the northeast constitutes the foothills of the Carpathian Mountains, which stretch along the Hungarian border with Slovakia. Though you'll definitely notice the rise in elevation, Hungary's highest peak of Kékes is still only a proverbial bump in the road at 1014m. The highlights here are wine towns Eger and Tokaj, and Szilvásvárad – the Hungarian home of the snow-white Lipizzaner horse.

EGER

☎ 36 / pop 58,300

Filled with wonderfully preserved baroque architecture, Eger (*egg*-air) is a jewel box of a town containing gems aplenty. Explore the bloody history of Turkish conquest and defeat at its hilltop castle, climb a Turkish minaret, hear an organ performance at the ornate basilica…but best of all, go from cellar to cellar in the Valley of Beautiful Women (yes, it's really called that), tasting the celebrated Bull's Blood wine where it's made.

It was here in 1552 that Hungarian defenders temporarily stopped the Turkish advance into Western Europe and helped preserve Hungary's identity (see boxed text, p353). However, the persistent Ottomans returned in 1596 and finally captured Eger Castle. They were evicted in 1687.

In the 18th century, Eger played a central role in Ferenc Rákóczi II's attempt to overthrow the Habsburgs, and it was then that a large part of the castle was razed by the Austrians. Eger has some of Hungary's finest architecture, especially examples of Copf (Zopf in Hungarian), a transitional style between late baroque and neoclassicism found only in central Europe.

Orientation & Information

The main train station is a 15-minute walk south of town, on Vasút utca, just east of Deák Ferenc utca. Egervár train station, which serves Szilvásvárad and other points north, is a five-minute walk north of the castle along Vécseyvölgy utca. The bus station is west of Széchenyi István utca, Eger's main drag.

Egri Est Café (Széchenyi István utca 16; per hr 300Ft; ☺ 11am-midnight Sun-Thu, to 2am Fri & Sat) Cafe-bar with internet access.

OTP Bank (Széchenyi István utca 2)

Post office (Széchenyi István utca 22; ☺ 8am-8pm Mon-Fri, to 1pm Sat)

Tourinform (☎ 517 715; eger@tourinform.hu; Bajcsy-Zsilinszky utca 9; ☺ 9am-5pm Mon-Fri, to 1pm Sat & Sun mid-Jun–mid-Sep, closed Sun mid-Sep–mid-Jun)

Sights & Activities

The most striking attraction and the best views of town are from **Eger Castle** (Egri Vár; www.egrivar .hu; Vár 1; adult/concession incl museum 1200/600Ft; ☺ 9am-5pm Tue-Sun Apr-Oct, 10am-4pm Tue-Sun Nov-Mar), a huge walled complex at the top of the hill off Dósza tér. First fortified after an early Mongol invasion in the 13th century, the earliest ruins on site are the foundations of St John's Cathedral, built in the 12th century and destroyed by the Turks. The excellent **István Dobó Castle Museum** (Dobó István Vármuzeum), inside the Bishop's Palace (1470) within the castle grounds, explores the history and development of the castle and the town. Other onsite exhibits such as the **Waxworks** (Panoptikum; adult/concession 400/300Ft) and the **Minting Exhibit** (Éremverde; adult/concession 400/300Ft) cost extra. Even on days when the museums are closed, you can walk around the grounds and battlements and enjoy the views if you buy a *sétaljegy* (strolling ticket, adult/concession 400/200Ft).

A surprise awaits you west of the castle hill: a 40m-high **minaret** (Knézich Károly utca; admission 200Ft; ☺ 10am-6pm Apr-Oct), minus the mosque, is allegedly Europe's northernmost remains of the Ottoman invasion in the 16th century. The **Minorite Church** (Minorita Templom; Dobó István tér; admission free; ☺ 9am-5pm Tue-Sun), built in 1771, is a glorious baroque building. In the square in front are statues of national hero István Dobó and his comrades-in-arms routing the Turks in 1552.

The first thing you see as you come into town from the bus or train station is the neoclassical **Eger Basilica** (Egri Bazilika; Pyrker János tér 1), built in 1836. Directly opposite is the Copf-style **Lyceum** (Líceum; Esterházy tér 1; admission free; ☺ 9.30am-3.30pm Tue-Sun Apr-Sep, 9.30am-1pm Sat & Sun Oct-Mar), dating from 1765, with a 20,000-volume frescoed **library** (könyvtár; adult/concession 700/350Ft) on the 1st floor and an 18th-century observatory in the **Astronomy Museum** (Csillagászati Múzeum; adult/concession 800/650Ft) on the 6th floor. Climb three more floors up to the observation deck for a great view of the city and to try out the camera obscura, the 'eye of Eger', designed in 1776 to entertain the locals.

The Archbishop's Garden was once the private reserve of papal princes, but today the park is open to the public. Inside the park, the **City Thermal Baths** (Városi Térmalfürdő; ☎ 413 356; Fürdő utca 1 3; adult/concession 1250/1050Ft; ☺ 6am-8pm Apr-Oct, 9am-7pm Nov-Mar) has both open-air and

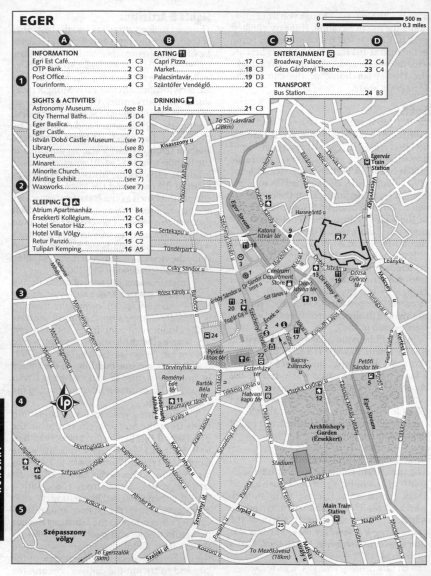

EGER

0 ———————— 500 m
0 ———————— 0.3 miles

covered pools with different temperatures and mineral contents. From June to August you can pay 700Ft extra to get into the modern 'adventure' complex with bubbling massage pools and a castle-themed kids' pool. By the time you read this, the 1617 Turkish Bath (Török Fürdő) should have reopened after a total reconstruction.

To sample Eger's wine, visit the extravagantly named **Szépasszony völgy** (Valley of the Beautiful Women; off Király utca), home to dozens of small wine cellars that truck in, store and sell Bull's Blood and other regional red and white wines. Walk the horseshoe-shaped street through the valley and stop in front of one that strikes your fancy and ask ('*meg-*

AS STRONG AS A BULL

The story of the Turkish attempt to take Eger Castle is the stuff of legend. Under the command of István Dobó, a mixed bag of 2000 soldiers held out against more than 100,000 Turks for a month in 1552. As every Hungarian kid in short trousers can tell you, the women of Eger played a crucial role in the battle, pouring boiling oil and pitch on the invaders from the ramparts.

If we're to believe the tale, it seems that Dobó sustained his weary troops with a ruby-red vintage of the town's wine. When they fought on with increased vigour – and stained beards – rumours began to circulate among the Turks that the defenders were gaining strength by drinking the blood of bulls. The invaders departed, and the legend of Bikavér (Bull's Blood) was born.

---

kosztólhatok?') to taste their wares (100Ft per decilitre). If you want wine to go, you can bring an empty bottle and have it filled for about 350Ft per litre. The cellar's outdoor tables fill up on a late summer afternoon as locals cook *gulyás* in the park and strains from a gypsy violinist float up from the restaurants at the valley's entrance. A taxi back to the centre costs about 1000Ft.

Sleeping

Tourinform has a glossy booklet of accommodation, including private rooms, for the city and the surrounding area.

Tulipán Kemping (☎ 410 580; Szépasszony völgy utca 71; camp sites per person 1450Ft, bungalows 6000Ft; 🔊) Many of the camping sites here are in an open, shadeless field, but you're surrounded by vineyards and are stumbling distance from the valley wine cellars. The bungalows are simple cabins, without bathrooms or kitchens.

Érsekkerti Kollégium (Archbishop's Garden College; ☎ 520 432; Klapka György utca 12; dm 3000Ft) A number of colleges offer dormitory accommodation from June to August; this is the most central option, in an Old Town building full of character.

our pick Retur Panzió (☎ 416 650; www.returven deghaz.hu; Knézich Károly utca 18; s/d 4000/6000Ft) You couldn't find sweeter hosts than the daughter and mother who own this pension. It's in a central location and has a cheery shared kitchen/eating area and a huge garden with tables and fire pit at your disposal.

Atrium Apartmanház (☎ 418 427; www.atriumapart ment.eu; Neumayer János út 8; s/d/tr apt 6500/10,000/12,500Ft; 🔊 🖳) Your home in the city. Each loft apartment has at least one bedroom, a kitchenette, and cool tile floors.

Hotel Villa Völgy (☎ 321 664; www.hotelvillavolgy .hu; Tulipánkert utca 5; s/d 12,900/17,500Ft; 🔊) Awaken to a view of the vineyards in this classy,

modern-design villa situated in the wine valley. Neoclassical columns surround the glass-enclosed pool.

Hotel Senator Ház (☎ 320 466; www.senatorhaz.hu; Dobó István tér 11; s/d 15,000/19,000Ft; 🔊) Warm and cosy rooms with traditional white furnishings fill the upper floors of this delightful 18th-century inn on Eger's main square. The ground floor is shared by a quality restaurant and a reception area that could easily moonlight as a history museum.

Eating & Drinking

At the base of Szépasszony völgy utca there are numerous small terrace *büfé* (snack bars) that resemble food stands but employ a waiter to serve you at your picnic table. There are also lots of restaurants and cafes along pedestrianised Széchenyi István utca in town. The area is known for its *pistrang* (trout) dishes.

Capri Pizza (☎ 410 877; Bajcsy-Zsilinszky utca 4; mains 550-1100Ft) Beans feature on a surprising number of the pizzas at this hole-in-the-wall eatery. White pizzas (sans sauce) and vegetarian options available.

our pick Palacsintavár (☎ 413 986; Dobó István utca 9; mains 1400-1600Ft) Pop art lines the walls, and groovy music provides the soundtrack to this eclectic eatery. Entrée-sized *palacsintak* (crêpelike pancakes) are served with an abundance of fresh vegetables and range in flavour from Asian to Italian.

Szántófer Vendéglő (☎ 517 298; Bródy utca 3; mains 1400-1800Ft; ☽ 8am-10pm) The best choice in town for hearty, homestyle Hungarian food. Farming equipment and cooking utensils hang on the walls, and the covered courtyard out back is perfect for escaping the heat.

La Isla (cnr Széchenyi & Foglár utca; ☽ 10am-midnight Sun-Thu, to 2am Fri & Sat) As much a Latin cocktail bar as a cafe, this is a fine place to kick back after a hard day's sightseeing.

HUNGARY

Head to the covered **market** (piac; Katona István tér; ☿ 6am-6pm Mon-Fri, to 1pm Sat, to 10am Sun) to buy fruit, vegetables, meat and bread.

Entertainment

The Tourinform office can tell you what concerts and musicals are on. The free *Egri Est* magazine has nightlife listings.

Géza Gárdonyi Theatre (Gárdonyi Géza Színház; ☎ 310 026; Hatvani kapu tér 4) Dance, opera and drama are staged at this theatre.

Broadway Palace (Pyrker János tér 3; ☿ 10pm-6am Wed, Fri & Sat) This bizarre, cavernous dance club beneath the cathedral's steps parties hard on weekends.

Getting There & Away

Hourly buses make the trip from Eger to Szilvásvárad (450Ft, 45 minutes). Other destinations include Kecskemét (2060Ft, 4½ hours, three daily) and Szeged (3220Ft, 5¾ hours, two daily). To get to Tokaj by bus, you have to go past it to Nyíregyháza and get another bus back.

Up to seven direct trains a day head to Budapest's Keleti train station (2290Ft, 2½ hours). Otherwise, Eger is on a minor train line linking Putnok and Füzesabony, so you have to change at the latter for Debrecen (1770Ft, three hours). You can also catch infrequent trains to Szilvásvárad (525Ft, one hour, six daily), but at the time of research this service was threatened with discontinuation.

SZILVÁSVÁRAD

☎ 36 / pop 1750

Home to graceful white stallions, carriage races, a narrow-gauge train and forest trails, Szilvásvárad makes an excellent day's excursion from Eger, 28km to the south. The town hides in the Bükk Hills, most of which fall within the 43,000-hectare **Bükk Nemzeti Park**. The village has an **information stand** (www.szil vasvarad.hu; Szalajka-völgy; ☿ 10am-6pm Jun-Oct) in high season; at other times, check with the Tourinform office in Eger (p351).

The bus from Eger will drop you off in the centre on Egri út. You get off the train at Szilvásvárad-Szalajkavölgy, the first of the town's two stations. Follow Egri út east and then north for about 10 minutes into town. At the turn, if you go right instead, you'll get to the valley.

Learn more about the famous Lipizzaner horses at the **Lipcsai Múzeum** (☎ 355 135; Park utca 8; adult/concession 400/200Ft; ☿ 9am-noon & 1-4pm Thu-Sun). Exhibits focus on bloodlines, but the real sight is the breeding mares who live here in an 18th-century stable.

Call a day ahead to arrange a carriage (from 5000Ft per hour) or a horseback ride at the **Lipizzaner State Stud Farm** (Lipicai Állami Ménesgazdaság; ☎ 564 400; www.menesgazdasag.hu; Fenyves utca; adult/concession 300/200Ft; ☿ 10am-noon & 2-4pm Thu-Sun).

At the entrance of Szalajka völgy there are restaurants, souvenir shops and tracks where Lipizzaner coaches race some summer weekends. You can park here for 100Ft per hour. Hike from here further into the valley, or take a ride on the **narrow-gauge railway** (keskeny nyomtávú vasút; Szalajka-völgy 6; adult/concession one-way 300/150Ft; ☿ Apr-Oct). The train makes the journey seven times daily from May to September (10 times daily on the weekend). Departures in April and October leave when enough people gather.

Hourly buses connect Szilvásvárad and Eger (405Ft, 45 minutes), but there's been talk of discontinuing service on the rail line from Eger (525Ft, one hour). At the time of research, there were six trains a day, but none between 10am and 2pm.

TOKAJ

☎ 47 / pop 5100

The sweet and sultry wines produced here have been around for centuries, thanks to the area's volcanic soil and unique microclimate, which promotes the growth of *Botrytis cinerea* (noble rot) on the grapes. The result is Tokaji Aszú, a world-class dessert wine.

Today Tokaj is a picturesque little town of old buildings, wine cellars and nesting storks. The 66-sq-km Tokaj-Hegyalja wine-producing region, a microclimate along the southern and eastern edges of the Zemplén Hills, was declared a World Heritage site in 2002.

Orientation & Information

Trains arrive 1200m south of the town centre; walk north on Baross Gábor utca and turn left on Bajcsy-Zsilinszky út, which turns into Rákóczi út, the main thoroughfare. The bus station is much more convenient, in town on Seráz utca. **Tourinform** (☎ 552 070; www.tokaj .hu; Serház utca 1; ☿ 9am-6pm Mon-Fri, 10am-7pm Sat & Sun Jun-Aug, 9am-5pm Mon-Fri Sep-May) is just off Rákóczi út.

Sights & Activities

Start at the **Tokaj Museum** (Tokaji Múzeum; Bethlen Gábor utca 13; adult/concession 400/200Ft; 🕑 10am-4pm Tue-Sun), which leaves nothing unsaid about the history of Tokaj, the region and its wines. After you're thoroughly knowledgeable, head to the 600-year-old **Rákóczi Cellar** (Rákóczi Pince; Kossuth tér 15; 🕑 11am-7pm) for a tasting and a tour. Bottles of wine mature underground in the long cavelike corridors (one measures 28m by 10m). A flight of six Tokaj wines costs about 2600Ft. The correct order of sampling Tokaj wines is: Furmint, dry Szamorodni, sweet Szamorodni and then the Aszú wines, moving from three to six *puttony*, the measurement used for sweetness. Six, by the way, is the sweetest.

Smaller cellars line Hegyalja utca, off Bajcsy-Zsilinszky utca at the base of the vine-covered hill above the train station. A small, wheeled **wine train** (per ride 500Ft; 🕑 May-Oct) departs from Tourinform at varying hours and rolls around town, allowing time to visit cellars.

Other town attractions include the 19th-century eclectic **Great Synagogue** (Nagy Zsinagóga; Serház utca 55). Having been used as a German barracks during WWII, it's once again gleaming after a thorough renovation.

Sleeping & Eating

Private rooms on offer along Hegyalja utca are convenient to the train station and are surrounded by vineyards.

Tutajos Beach Camping (🕾 06 20 969 1088; Honfoglalás 24; per person camp sites/bungalows 300/2200Ft; 🕑 Apr-Oct) Shady tent sites and basic bungalows are adjacent to a beach with boat rental. Showers cost 100Ft for four minutes.

Huli Panzió (🕾 352 791; www.hulipanzio.hu; Rákóczi út 16; s/d 4000/8000Ft; 🕲) Bright pension with 12 down-to-earth rooms. Enjoy breakfast (800Ft) at the ground-floor restaurant.

Vaskó Panzió (🕾 352 107; http://vaskopanzio.fw.hu; Rákóczi út 12; r 8000Ft) The supremely central Vaskó has eight cute rooms, and windowsills bedecked with flowerpots. It's above a private wine cellar and the proprietor can organise tastings.

Millennium Hotel (🕾 352 247; www.tokajmillennium .hu; Bajcsy-Zsilinszky utca 34; s/d 13,000/15,900Ft; 🕲 🖳) Equidistant from the train station and town centre, the only drawback to this hotel's location is the busy road out front. Pleasant beer garden, though.

Huli Panzió Grill Büfé (🕾 352 791; Rákóczi út 16; mains 1100-1600Ft; 🕑 8am-10pm) When everything in Tokaj seems touristy and over the top, step into this simple counter-service eatery for a hot breakfast or grilled meat meal.

our pick **Degenfeld** (🕾 553 050; Kossuth tér 1; mains 1650-2500Ft) Experts' wine pairings accompany each exquisite dish, such as the pork loin medallions with wild mushroom stew, on this restaurant's two set menus.

Shopping

You can buy wine at any of the places mentioned for tasting, or stop at the **Furmint Vinotéka** (🕾 353 340; Bethlen Gábor utca 12; 🕑 9am-6pm) wine shop for a large local selection.

Getting There & Away

No direct buses connect Tokaj with Budapest or Eger; train travel is your best option here. Up to 16 trains a day head west to Budapest Keleti (3750Ft; 2½ hours), and east to Debrecen (1480Ft, two hours).

DEBRECEN

🕾 52 / pop 215,000

Flanked by the golden Great Church and historic Aranybika Hotel, the main square of Hungary's second city is quite pretty; a surprise given the unattractive industrial zones and apartment blocks you pass when arriving by bus or train. During summer, street festivals fill the pedestrian core with revellers, and the city's array of museums and its town thermal baths will keep you busy for a day or two. The **Debrecen Flower Festival** happens in late August; Debrecen Jazz Days, in September.

The area around Debrecen has been settled since the earliest times. Debrecen's wealth, based on salt, the fur trade and cattle-raising, grew steadily through the Middle Ages and increased during the Turkish occupation. Debrecen played a pivotal role in the 1848 revolt, and it experienced a major building boom in the late 19th and early 20th centuries.

Orientation & Information

A ring road, built on the city's original earthen walls, encloses the Belváros, or Inner Town. This is bisected by Piac utca, which runs northward from the train station (Petőfi tér) to Kálvin tér, site of the Great Church and Debrecen's centre. The bus station (Külső-Vásártér) is on the 'outer marketplace' at the western end of Széchenyi utca.

HUNGARY

Data Net Cafe (Kossuth utca 8; per hr 900Ft; ☿ 9am-midnight) Internet and cheap international calls.

Ibusz (☎ 415 555; Révész tér 2; ☿ 8am-5pm Mon-Fr, 9am-1pm Sat) Travel agency renting private apartments.

Main post office (Hatvan utca 5-9)

OTP Bank (Piac utca 16 & 45) Both have ATMs.

Tourinform (☎ 412 250; www.gotodebrecen.hu) town hall office (Piac utca 20; ☿ 9am-8pm Mon-Fri, 9am-5pm Sun Jun-Aug, 9am-5pm Mon-Fri Sep-May); summer booth (Kossuth tér; ☿ 10am-6pm daily Jun-Sep)

Sights & Activities

Many of the town's big sights are at the northern end of Piac utca, including the yellow neoclassical **Great Church** (Kálvin tér; adult/concession 300/200Ft; ☿ 9am-4pm Mon-Fri, 9am-1pm Sat, noon-4pm Sun Apr-Oct, 10am-1pm Mon-Sat, 11.30am-1pm Sun Nov-Mar). Built in 1821, it has become so synonymous with Debrecen that mirages of its twin clock towers were reportedly seen on the Great Plain early last century. Climb the 210 steps to the top of the west clock tower for grand views over the city.

North of the church stands the 1816 **Reformed College** (Református Kollégium; Kálvin tér 16; adult/concession 500/200Ft; English-language tours 3000Ft; ☿ 10am-4pm Tue-Sat, to 1pm Sun), the site of a prestigious secondary school and theological college since the Middle Ages. It houses exhibits on religious art and sacred objects (including a 17th-century chalice made from a coconut) and on the school's history.

Folklore exhibits at the **Déri Museum** (Déri tér 1; adult/concession 1000/500Ft; ☿ 10am-4pm Tue-Sun Nov-Mar, to 6pm Apr-Oct), a short walk west of the Reformed College, offer excellent insights into the lives of both the proletarian and bourgeois citizens of Debrecen up to the 19th century. The museum's entrance is flanked by four superb bronzes by sculptor Ferenc Medgyessy (1881–1958), a local boy who merits his own **Medgyessy Museum** (Péterfia utca 28; adult/concession 500/250Ft; ☿ 10am-4pm Tue-Sun) in an old burgher house to the northeast.

Just walking along Piac utca and down some of the side streets, with their array of neoclassical, baroque and art nouveau buildings, is a treat. Kossuth utca and its continuation, Széchenyi utca, are especially interesting. Check out the baroque Calvinist **Little Church** (Révész tér 2; admission free; ☿ 9am-noon Mon-Fri & Sun), completed in 1726, with its bastion-like tower.

You can wander along leafy trails and rent a **paddle boat** (per hr 1000Ft; ☿ 9am-8pm Jun-Aug) in

Nagyerdei Park, north of the centre. But the main attraction here is **Aquaticum** (www.aquaticum.hu; adult/concession 2100/1600Ft; ☿ 10am-10pm), a complex of 'Mediterranean Enjoyment Baths' offering all manner of slides and waterfalls, spouts and grottoes within its pools.

Sleeping

Loads of dormitory accommodation is available in July and August; ask at Tourinform for details.

Maróthi György College (☎ 502 780; Blaháné utca 15; s/d 3000/6000Ft) Right across from the Votive Church, this is a central place to stay. Rooms are fairly basic (containing just a bed and a desk), and facilities are shared. There are simple kitchens available, along with a courtyard and a basketball court for guest use.

our pick Szi Panzió (☎ 322 200; www.szivpanzio.hu; Szív utca 11; s/d 6000/7800Ft) Guest house on a tree-lined street not far from the train station. Warm colours enliven the simple, fresh rooms with low-slung beds (and well-stocked minibars).

Centrum Panzió (☎ 442 843; www.panziocentrum.hu; Péterfia utca 37/a; s/d 8500/10,500Ft; ▢) A bit like your grandmother's apartment, if she collected Victorian bric-a-brac. All rooms have fridges and microwaves.

Aranybika (☎ 508 600; www.civishotels.hu; Piac utca 11-15; s/d from €60/85; ☒ ▣) This landmark art nouveau hotel has been *the* place to stay in Debrecen since construction in 1915. Superior rooms have a bit more space than standard, as well as reproduction antique furnishings.

Aquaticum Wellness Hotel (☎ 514 111; www.aquaticum.hu; Nagyerdei park 1; s/d €80/95; ☒ ▢ ▣) Kids' programs, babysitting, bike rental, spa services, a swimming pool, and loads of other amenities make Aquaticum attractive to both adults and children.

Eating & Drinking

Klári Salátabár (☎ 412 203; Bajcsy-Zsilinszky utca 3; per 100g 100-300Ft; ☿ 9am-7pm Mon-Fri) Broccoli egg rolls, fried mushrooms, peas and white rice – the dishes at this self-service storefront are mostly vegetarian.

Pompeji Étterem (☎ 416 988; Batthyány utca 4; mains 1300-1800Ft) Despite the Italian name and murals, the menu is a delicious smorgasbord. Sautéed chicken might be topped with mozzarella and tomato sauce, or with

Greek yoghurt dip and olives. The wood-fired pizzas are great, too.

Csokonai Söröző (☎ 410 802; Kossuth utca 21; mains 1600-2000Ft) Medieval decor, sharp service and excellent Hungarian specialities all help to create one of Debrecen's best eating experiences. This cellar pub-restaurant also serves the odd international dish, like turkey enchiladas with beans.

Teaház a Vörös Oroszlánhaz (Bajcsy-Zsilinszky utca 14; ☉ 1-11pm Mon-Sat, 3-11pm Sun) Hushed conversations and the smell of incense rises from this esoteric teahouse, which has dozens of cold and hot choices.

There's a **grocery shop** (Piac utca 75; ☉ 24hr) within walking distance of the train station and a small covered **fruit and vegetable market** (Csapó utca; ☉ 5am-3pm Mon-Sat, to 11am Sun) right in the centre.

Entertainment

Pick up a copy of the biweekly entertainment freebie *Debreceni Est* (www.est.hu) for music listings.

Csokonai Theatre (☎ 455 075; www.csokonaiszinhaz .hu; Kossuth utca 10) Three-tiered gilt balconies, ornate ceiling frescos, and elaborate chandeliers: the Csokonai is everything a 19th-century theatre should be. Musicals and operas are staged here.

Club Silence (Bajcsy-Zsilinszky utca 3-5; cover charge 1000Ft) DJs spin house and techno tunes here most weekends, but some Saturdays see theme parties.

Getting There & Away

Buses are quickest if you're going directly to Eger (2040Ft, 2½ hours) or Szeged (3220Ft, five hours, three daily). Frequently departing trains will get you to Budapest (3750Ft, 3¼ hours) and Tokaj (1350Ft, 1½ hours).

Trains also depart Debrecen to Satu Marie (2½ hours) in Romania at 3.30pm daily. The night train from Budapest to Moscow stops here at 9pm.

HUNGARY DIRECTORY

ACCOMMODATION

Budapest has the widest variety of lodging prices, but even in provincial towns you can find camping grounds, hostels and private rooms in the budget range (under 7500Ft per double per night in the provinces; under

13,500Ft in Budapest); *panziók* (pensions), guest houses and small hotels in the mid-range (between 7500Ft and 15,500Ft in the country; 13,500Ft and 30,000Ft in Budapest); and multiamenity hotels at the top end (over 16,000Ft outside Budapest; over 30,000Ft in Budapest). Reviews in this chapter are ordered according to price. Unless otherwise stated, rooms in this chapter include private bathroom.

Hungary's more than 400 camping grounds are listed in Tourinform's *Camping Hungary* map/brochure (www.camping.hu). Facilities are generally open May to October and can be difficult to reach without a car.

The **Hungarian Youth Hostels Association** (MISZSZ; www.miszsz.hu) keeps a list of year-round hostels throughout Hungary. In general, year-round hostels have a communal kitchen, laundry and internet service, and sometimes a lounge; a basic bread-and-jam breakfast may be included. Having an HI card is not required, but it may get you a 10% discount. Useful websites with online booking include www .youthhostels.hu and www.hiho stels.hu.

From July to August, students vacate college and university dorms, and administration opens them to travellers. Facilities are usually – but not always – basic and shared. Local Tourinform offices can help you locate such places.

Renting a private room in a Hungarian home is a good budget option and can be a great opportunity to get up close and personal with the culture. You generally share a bathroom with the family. Prices outside Budapest run from 3000Ft to 6000Ft per person per night. Tourinform offices can usually help with finding these; otherwise look for houses with signs reading '*szoba kiadó*' or '*Zimmer frei*'.

Midrange accommodation may or may not have a private bathroom, satellite TV and in-room phone, but all top-end places do. A cold breakfast buffet is usually included in the price at pensions, and there are hot breakfasts included at hotels. A reasonable place might bill itself as a *kishotel* (small hotel) because it has satellite TV and a minibar. Air-conditioning is scarce nationwide, but you're more likely to find it at higher-priced establishments.

An engaging alternative is to stay in a rural village or farmhouse, but only if you have wheels: most of these places are truly remote. Contact Tourinform, the **National**

Federation of Rural & Agrotourism (FATOSZ; Map p312; ☎ 1-352 9804; VII Király utca 93) or the **Centre of Rural Tourism** (Map p306; ☎ 1-321 2426; www.falutur .hu; VII Dohány utca 86) in Budapest.

ACTIVITIES

Hungary has more than 100 thermal baths open to the public, and many are attached to hotels with well-being packages. For locations, ask Tourinform for the *Spa & Wellness* booklet. For more about Budapest spas, check out www.spasbudapest.com.

There's also a helpful HNTO *Riding in Hungary* booklet on equestrian tourism, or you could contact the **Hungarian Equestrian Tourism Association** (Map p312; MLTSZ; ☎ 1-456 0444; www.equi.hu; IX Ráday utca 8, Budapest). **Pegazus Tours** (Map p312; ☎ 1-317 1644; www.pegazus.hu; V Ferenciek tere 5, Budapest) organises horse-riding tours, and occasionally bicycle tours as well.

Hiking enthusiasts may enjoy the trails around Tihany at Lake Balaton, the Bükk Hills north of Eger or the plains at Bugac Puszta south of Kecskemét. Hiking maps usually have yellow borders. Birdwatchers could explore these same paths or take a tour with **Birding Hungary** (www.birdinghungary.com).

Hungary's flat terrain makes it ideal for cycling. **Velo-Touring** (☎ 1-319 0571; www.velo -touring.hu) has a great selection of seven-night trips in all regions, from a senior-friendly Danube Bend tour (€690) to a bike ride between spas on the Great Plain (€750).

For canoeists, **Ecotours** (☎ 1-361-0438; www.eco tours.hu) leads seven day Danube River canoe-camping trips (tent rental and food extra) for about €500, as well as shorter Danube Bend and Tisza River trips.

BUSINESS HOURS

With some rare exceptions, opening hours (*nyitvatartás*) are posted on the front door of establishments; *nyitva* means 'open' and *zárva* is 'closed'. Grocery stores and supermarkets open from about 6am or 7am to 6pm or 7pm Monday to Friday and 7am to 3pm Saturday; an ever-increasing number also open 7am to noon Sunday. Smaller ones, especially in Budapest, may be open on Sunday or holidays as well. Most towns have a 'nonstop' convenience store, and many have 'hyper-markets', such as Tesco, which are open 24 hours. Main post offices are open 8am to 6pm weekdays, and to noon Saturday. Banks are generally open from 8am to 4pm weekdays. Most restaurants open from 11am to 11pm, and bars and cafes open from 11am to midnight. Nightclubs usually open from 4pm to 2am Sunday to Thursday and until 4am on Friday and Saturday; some only open on weekends.

COURSES

The granddaddy of all Hungarian language schools, **Debreceni Nyári Egyetem** (Debrecen Summer University; ☎ 52-532 594; www.nyariegyetem.hu; Egyetem tér 1, Debrecen), in eastern Hungary, is the most well known and the most respected. It organises intensive two- and four-week courses during July and August and 80-hour, two-week advanced courses during winter. The **Debrecen Summer University Branch** (Map p312; ☎ 1-320 5751; www.nyariegyetem.hu/bp; V Báthory utca 4) in Budapest puts on regular and intensive courses.

DISCOUNT CARDS

Those planning extensive travel in Hungary might consider the **Hungary Card** (☎ 1-266 3741; www.hungarycard.hu; 6540Ft), which gives 50% discounts on six return train fares and some bus and boat travel; free entry to many museums; up to 20% off selected accommodation; and 50% off the price of the Budapest Card (p307). It's available at Tourinform offices.

EMBASSIES & CONSULATES

Embassies in Budapest (phone code ☎ 1) include the following. Most embassies are open to the public from 9am to 4pm on weekdays, though some only open in the morning.
Australia (Map p306; ☎ 457 9777; XII Királyhágó tér 8-9)
Austria (Map p312; ☎ 413 0240; VI Benczúr utca 16)
Canada (Map p308; ☎ 392 3360; II Ganz utca 12-14)
Croatia (Map p312; ☎ 269 5657; VI Munkácsy Mihály utca 15)
France (Map p312; ☎ 374 1100; VI Lendvay utca 27)
Germany (Map p308; ☎ 488 3505; I Úri utca 64-66)
Ireland (Map p312; ☎ 301 4960; V Szabadság tér 7-9)
Netherlands (Map p306; ☎ 336 6300; II Füge utca 5-7)
Romania (Map p306; ☎ 220 1666; XIV Thököly út 72)
Serbia (Map p306; ☎ 322 1436; VI Dózsa György út 92/a)
Slovakia (Map p306; ☎ 273 3500; XIV Gervay utca 44)
Slovenia (Map p306; ☎ 438 5600; II Csatárka köz 9)
South Africa (Map p306; ☎ 392 0999; II Gárdonyi Géza út 17)
UK (Map p312; ☎ 266 2888; V Harmincad utca 6)
Ukraine (Map p306; ☎ 422 4122; XIV Stefánia út 77)
USA (Map p312; ☎ 475 4164; V Szabadság tér 12)

GAY & LESBIAN TRAVELLERS

There is little openly antigay sentiment in Hungary, but neither is there a large openly gay population. The organisations and night-clubs that do exist are generally in Budapest, though the Budapest-biased freebie pamphlet **Na Végre!** (At Last!; www.navegre.hu) lists a handful of venues in the countryside. For up-to-date information on venues, events, groups etc, contact **Budapest gayguide.net** (☎ 06 30 932 3334; ✆ 4-8pm Mon-Fri).

HOLIDAYS

Hungary's public holidays:

New Year's Day 1 January
1848 Revolution Day 15 March
Easter Monday March/April
International Labour Day 1 May
Whit Monday May/June
St Stephen's Day 20 August
1956 Remembrance Day 23 October
All Saints' Day 1 November
Christmas Holidays 25 and 26 December

MEDIA

Budapest has three English-language weeklies: the expat-oriented *Budapest Sun* (399Ft), with a useful arts and entertainment supplement; the *Budapest Business Journal* (1250Ft); and the *Budapest Times* (580Ft), containing interesting reviews and opinion pieces.

MONEY

The unit of currency is the Hungarian forint (Ft). Coins come in denominations of five, 10, 20, 50 and 100Ft, and notes are denominated in 200, 500, 1000, 2000, 5000, 10,000 and 20,000Ft. ATMs accepting most credit and cash cards are everywhere in Hungary, even in small villages. Some businesses quote prices in euros, as reflected in this chapter. Hungary is a very tip-conscious society, and everyone routinely tips waiters, hairdressers and taxi drivers approximately 10% of the bill.

POST

Postcards and letters up to 30g sent within Hungary cost 70Ft (100Ft for priority mail), while to the rest of Europe letters up to 20g cost 200Ft (230Ft priority) and postcards 150Ft (170Ft priority). To addresses outside Europe, expect to pay 220Ft (250Ft priority) for letters up to 20g, and 170Ft (190Ft priority) for postcards.

Mail addressed to poste restante in any town or city will go to the main post office (*főposta*). When collecting poste-restante mail, look for the sign '*postán maradó küldemények*'.

TELEPHONE & FAX

Hungary's country code is ☎ 36. To make an outgoing international call, dial ☎ 00 first. To dial city-to-city (and all mobile phones) within the country, first dial ☎ 06, wait for the second dial tone and then dial the city code and phone number. All localities in Hungary have a two-digit city code, except for Budapest, whose code is ☎ 1.

In Hungary you must always dial ☎ 06 when ringing mobile telephones, which have specific area codes depending on the telecom company: **Pannon GSM** (☎ 06 20; www.pgsm.hu), **T-Mobile** (☎ 06 30; www.t-mobile.hu) or **Vodafone** (☎ 06 70; www.voda fone.hu).

If you have a GSM mobile phone, check with your service provider about using it in Hungary, and beware of calls being routed internationally. If you're going to spend more than just a few days here, consider buying a rechargeable SIM card. Pannon offers prepaid SIMs for 2600/3900Ft with 1300/2500Ft worth of credit; T-Mobile 4000Ft with 2500Ft worth of credit; and Vodafone 1680Ft with 500Ft worth of credit. Recharge cards, available from mobile phone stores and supermarkets, come in denominations of 900Ft, 1800Ft and 3600Ft. Local calls using a local SIM card cost between 25Ft and 40Ft per minute.

There's also a plethora of phonecards on offer, including T-Com's **Barangoló**, which come in denominations of 1000Ft and 5000Ft; **NeoPhone** (www.neophone.hu), with cards also valued at 1000Ft and 5000F; and **Pannon**, offering cards for 1000Ft, 3000Ft and 5000Ft. It can cost as little as 8Ft per minute to call the USA, Australia and New Zealand using such cards. Telephone boxes with a black-and-white arrow and red target on the door and the word '*Visszahívható*' display a telephone number, so you can be phoned back.

TOURIST INFORMATION

The **Hungarian National Tourist Office** (HNTO; www.hungarytourism.hu) has a chain of over 140 **Tourinform** (☎ hotline 30 30 30 600; www.tourinform.hu) information offices across the country. These are the best places to ask general questions and pick up brochures.

EMERGENCY NUMBERS

■ Ambulance ☎ 104

■ Fire ☎ 105

■ Police ☎ 107

■ Roadside assistance ☎ 188

If your query is about private rooms, flights or international train travel, you could ask a commercial travel agency. The oldest, **Ibusz** (www.ibusz.hu), is arguably the best for private accommodation.

TRAVELLERS WITH DISABILITIES

Hungary has made great strides in recent years in making public areas and facilities more accessible to people with disabilities. Wheelchair ramps and toilets fitted for people with disabilities do exist, though not as commonly as in Western Europe, and audible traffic signals are becoming commonplace in cities. For more information, contact the **Hungarian Federation of Disabled Persons' Associations** (MEOSZ; Map p306; ☎ 1-388 5529; www.meoszinfo.hu; III San Marco utca 76) in Budapest.

VISAS

EU citizens do not need visas to visit Hungary and can stay indefinitely. Citizens of the USA, Canada, Israel, Japan, New Zealand and Australia do not require visas to visit Hungary for stays of up to 90 days.

However, since Hungary's entry into the Schengen zone of European nations in December 2007, the 90-day visa-free entry period includes stays in all Schengen countries; so if travelling from Hungary through Austria and Germany, for example, you can't exceed 90 days in total. Once your 90 days is up, you must leave the Schengen zone for a minimum of 90 days before you can once again enter it visa-free.

South Africans do still require a visa. Check with the **Ministry for Foreign Affairs** (www.mfa.gov.hu) for an up-to-date list of which country nationals require visas.

Visas are issued at Hungarian consulates or missions, most international highway border crossings, Ferihegy airport and the International Ferry Pier in Budapest. However, visas are never issued on trains and rarely on international buses.

TRANSPORT IN HUNGARY

GETTING THERE & AWAY

Air

The vast majority of international flights land at **Ferihegy International Airport** (☎ 1-296 7000; www.bud.hu) on the outskirts of Budapest. **Balaton airport** (☎ 83-354 256; www.flybalaton.hu) receives Ryanair flights from Düsseldorf, Frankfurt and London Stansted, and is 15km southwest of Keszthely near Lake Balaton. Hungary's national carrier is **Malév Hungarian Airlines** (MA; ☎ 06 40 212121; www.malev.hu).

Major airlines, aside from Malév, servicing Hungary:

Aeroflot (SU; ☎ 1-318 5955; www.aeroflot.com)
Air Berlin (AB; ☎ 06 800 17 110; www.airberlin.com)
Air France (AF; ☎ 1-483 8800; www.airfrance.com)
Alitalia (AZ; ☎ 1-483 2170; www.alitalia.it)
Austrian Airlines (OS; ☎ 1-296 0660; www.aua.com)
British Airways (BA; ☎ 1-777 4747; www.ba.com)
CSA (OK; ☎ 1-318 3045; www.csa.cz)
easyJet (EZY; www.easyjet.com)
El Al (LY; ☎ 1-266 2970; www.elal.co.il)
EgyptAir (MS; www.egyptair.com)
Finnair (AY; ☎ 1-296 5486; www.finnair.com)
germanwings (4U; ☎ 1-526 7005; www.germanwings.com)
LOT Polish Airlines (LO; ☎ 1-266 4771; www.lot.com)
Lufthansa (LH; ☎ 1-411 9900; www.lufthansa.com)
Ryanair (FR; www.ryanair.com)
SAS (SK; www.flysas.com)
Tarom (RO; www.tarom.ro)
Turkish Airlines (TK; ☎ 1-266 4291; www.thy.com)
Wizz Air (W6 ☎ 06 90 181 181; www.wizzair.com)

Land

Hungary's entry into the Schengen zone means that there are no border controls with Austria, Slovakia and Slovenia.

There are excellent land transport connections with Hungary's neighbours. Most of the departures listed are from Budapest, though other cities and towns closer to the various borders can also be used as springboards.

BUS

Most international buses arrive at the Népliget bus station in Budapest. **Eurolines** (www.eurolines.com), in conjunction with its Hungarian affiliate, **Volánbusz** (☎ 1-382 0888; www.volanbusz.hu), is the international bus company of Hungary.

Useful international buses include those from Budapest to Vienna; Bratislava, Slovakia; Subotica in Serbia; Rijeka in Croatia; Prague in the Czech Republic; and Sofia in Bulgaria. For more details, see p321.

CAR & MOTORCYCLE

Foreign driving licences are valid for one year after entering Hungary. Drivers of cars and riders of motorbikes also need the vehicle's registration papers. Third-party insurance is compulsory for driving in Hungary. If your car is registered in the EU, it's assumed you have it. Other motorists must show a Green Card or buy insurance at the border.

TRAIN

The Hungarian State Railways, MÁV (☎ 1-371 9449; www.mav.hu) links up with international rail networks in all directions, and its schedule is available online.

Inter-Rail (www.interrailnet.com) Global Passes cover much of Europe and can be purchased by nationals of European countries (or residents of at least six months). A pass offers 1st- and 2nd-class travel for five days within a 10-day period (€329/249), 10 days within a 22-day period (€489/359), 22 continuous days (€629/469), or one month (€809/599). Discounts are available for those aged under 26.

Eurail passes are also valid, but not sold, in Hungary. EuroCity (EC) and Intercity (IC) trains require a seat reservation and payment of a supplement. Most larger train stations in Hungary have left-luggage rooms open from at least 9am to 5pm. There are three main train stations in Budapest, so always note the station when checking a schedule online.

Some direct train connections from Budapest include Austria, Slovakia, Romania, Ukraine (continuing to Russia), Croatia, Serbia, Germany, Slovenia, the Czech Republic, Poland, Switzerland, Italy, Bulgaria and Greece. See p321 for details.

For tickets or more information about passes and discounts, ask at the MÁV Ticket Office in Budapest.

River

A hydrofoil service on the Danube River between Budapest and Vienna operates daily from late April to early October; passengers can disembark at Bratislava with advance notice. See p320 for more details.

GETTING AROUND

Air

Hungary does not have any scheduled internal flights.

Boat

In summer there are regular passenger ferries on Lake Balaton and on the Danube from Budapest to Szentendre, Vác, Visegrád and Esztergom. Details of the schedules are given in the relevant destination sections.

Bus

Domestic buses, run by Volánbusz (☎ 1-382 0888; www.volanbusz.hu) cover an extensive nationwide network.

Timetables are posted at stations and stops. Some footnotes you could come across include naponta (daily), hétköznap (weekdays), munkanapokon (on work days), munkaszüneti napok kivételével naponta (daily except holidays), and szabad és munkaszüneti napokon (on Saturday and holidays). A few large bus stations have luggage rooms, but these generally close by 6pm.

Car & Motorcycle

Many cities and towns require that you 'pay and display' when parking. The cost averages about 200Ft an hour in the countryside, and up to 400Ft on central Budapest streets.

AUTOMOBILE ASSOCIATIONS

The so-called 'Yellow Angels' of the Hungarian Automobile Club do basic breakdown repairs for free if you belong to an affiliated organisation such as AAA in the USA or AA in the UK. You can telephone 24 hours a day on ☎ 188 nationwide.

FUEL & SPARE PARTS

Ólommentes benzin (unleaded petrol 95/98 octane) is available everywhere. Most stations also have gázolaj (diesel).

HIRE

In general, you must be at least 21 years old and have had your licence for at least a year to rent a car. Drivers under 25 sometimes have to pay a surcharge.

ROAD RULES

The most important rule to remember is that there's a 100% ban on alcohol

HUNGARY

when you are driving, and this rule is *very* strictly enforced.

Using a mobile phone while driving is prohibited in Hungary. *All* vehicles must have their headlights switched on throughout the day outside built-up areas. Motorcyclists must have their headlights on at all times.

Hitching

In Hungary, hitchhiking is legal except on motorways. Hitchhiking is never an entirely safe way to travel and we don't recommend it, but if you're willing, **Kenguru** (Map p312; ☎ 1-266 5837; www.kenguru.hu; VIII Kőfaragó utca 15, Budapest; ☼ 10am-2pm Mon-Fri) is an agency that matches riders with drivers.

Local Transport

Public transport is efficient and extensive, with city bus and, in many towns, trolleybus services. Budapest and Szeged also have trams, and there's an extensive metro and a suburban commuter railway in Budapest. Purchase tickets at news-stands before travelling and validate them once aboard. Inspectors do check tickets, especially on the metro lines in Budapest.

Train

MÁV (☎ 06 40 494 949; www.mav.hu) operates reliable train services on its 8000km of tracks. Schedules are available online, and computer information kiosks are popping up at rail stations around the country. Second-class domestic train fares range from 125Ft for a journey of less than 5km, to 3830Ft for a 300km trip. First-class fares are usually 25% more. IC trains are express trains, the most comfortable and modern. *Gyorsvonat* (fast trains) take longer and use older cars; *személyvonat* (passenger trains) stop at every village along the way. Seat reservations *(helyjegy)* cost extra and are required on IC and some fast trains; these are indicated on the timetable by an 'R' in a box or a circle (a plain 'R' means seat reservations are available but not required).

In all stations a yellow board indicates departures *(indul)* and a white board arrivals *(érkezik)*. Express and fast trains are indicated in red, local trains in black. In some stations, large black-and-white schedules are plastered all over the walls.

Most train stations have left-luggage offices that are open at least from 9am to 5pm.

You might consider purchasing the Hungary pass from Eurail, available to non-European residents only, before entering the country. It costs US$104/147 for five/10 days of 1st-class travel in a 15-day period, and US$79/99 for youths in 2nd-class. Children aged five to 11 pay half-price. You would, however, need to use it a lot to get your money's worth.

HUNGARY

Liechtenstein

Liechtenstein makes a fabulous wine-and-cheese-hour trivia subject – *Did you know it is the sixth smallest country?… It's still governed by an iron-willed monarch who lives in a Gothic castle on a hill… Yes, it really is the world's largest producer of false teeth…* But if you're visiting this pocket-sized principality solely for the cocktail-party bragging rights, keep the operation covert. This theme-park micronation takes its independence seriously and would shudder at the thought of being considered for novelty value alone.

Liechtenstein prefers to be remembered for its stunning natural beauty. Measuring just 25km in length and 6km in width, it is barely larger than Manhattan, doesn't have an international airport and is reached by public bus from Switzerland. Vaduz is not the most soulful place on earth, but if you've come this far – coachloads of day trippers do simply for the souvenir passport stamp – it's worth venturing away from the capital. A riot of hiking and cycling trails offering spectacular views of craggy cliffs, quaint villages and lush green forests is what makes lovely Liechtenstein so appealing.

Liechtensteiners sing German lyrics to the tune of *God Save the Queen* in their national anthem and they sure hope the Lord preserves their royals. Head of state Prince Hans Adam II and his son, Crown Prince Alois, have constitutional powers unmatched in modern Europe and a business nous that keeps this landlocked sliver enviably prosperous.

FAST FACTS

- **Area** 150 sq km
- **Capital** Vaduz
- **Currency** Swiss franc (Sfr); €1 = Sfr1.53; US$1 = Sfr1.22; UK£1 = Sfr1.64; A$1 = €0.79; ¥100 = Sfr1.14; NZ$1 = Sfr0.64
- **Famous for** dentures, postcards stamped by the country's postal service
- **Official language** German
- **Phrases** *gruezi* (hello; good day); *merci vielmal* (thank you very much); *adieu* (goodbye); *Sprechen Sie Englisch?* (do you speak English?)
- **Population** 35,400
- **Telephone codes** country code ☎ 423; international access code ☎ 00
- **Visas** not required for holders of passports from the UK, Ireland, the EU, USA, Canada, Australia, New Zealand, South Africa, Norway and Iceland; see p586

LIECHTENSTEIN

LIECHTENSTEIN

retains the power to dissolve parliament and must approve every act before it becomes law. Prince Franz Josef II was the first ruler to live in the castle above the capital city of Vaduz. He died in 1989 and was succeeded by his son, Prince Hans-Adam II.

Liechtenstein has no military service and its minuscule army was disbanded in 1868. It is known for wine production, postage stamps, dentures and its status as a tax haven. In 2000 Liechtenstein's financial and political institutions were rocked by allegations that money laundering was rife in the country. In response to international outrage, banks agreed to stop allowing customers to bank money anonymously; however, the principality remains under pressure to introduce more reforms.

In 2003 Hans-Adam won sweeping powers to dismiss the elected government, appoint judges and reject proposed laws. The following year he handed the day-to-day running of the country to his son Alois.

Scandal rocked the principality again in 2008 when it was discovered that more than 1000 high-flying Germans had evaded tax by depositing large sums of money in trusts run by a Liechtenstein bank partly owned by the princely family. Liechtenstein didn't dispute that such money could have wound up in its banks (the principality doesn't consider tax evasion a crime) but accused Germany of spying.

FOOD & DRINK

Liechtenstein's cuisine borrows from its larger neighbours, and it is generally good quality but expensive. Basic restaurants provide simple but well-cooked food. Soups are popular and filling, and cheeses form an important part of the diet, as do rösti and wurst.

As in neighbouring Switzerland, restaurants are generally open five or six days a week for lunch and dinner (usually closed between 3pm and 6pm or 7pm). Cafes usually stay open all

HIGHLIGHTS

- Snap a picture of the royal castle with its stunning mountain backdrop in **Vaduz** (opposite).
- Get a souvenir **passport stamp** (opposite) and send a postcard home.
- Hit the slopes at **Malbun** (p367) to brag you've skied the Liechtenstein Alps.
- Test yourself with extreme hiking along the legendary **Fürstensteig trail** (p367).

CLIMATE & WHEN TO GO

Ski in Liechtenstein from December to April; sightsee and hike from May to October. Alpine resorts all but close down in late April, May and November.

HISTORY

A merger of the domain of Schellenberg and the county of Vaduz in 1712 by the powerful Liechtenstein family created the country. A principality under the Holy Roman Empire from the period 1719 to 1806, Liechtenstein finally achieved its full sovereign independence in 1866. A modern constitution was drawn up back in 1921, but even today the prince

---

CONNECTIONS: MOVING ON FROM LIECHTENSTEIN

Austria and Switzerland are the two obvious places to move on to from this millionaire ghetto: to cross the border, hop on a local bus (p367) at the Swiss border towns of Buchs or Sargans, or at Austrian next-door-neighbour Feldkirch.

day, and bars tend to open from lunchtime until some time around midnight.

VADUZ

pop 5160

Vaduz is the kind of capital city where the butcher knows the baker. With its tidy, quiet streets, lively patio cafes and a big Gothic-looking castle on a hill, it feels more like a village than anything else. It's also all that most visitors to Liechtenstein will see and at times it can feel like its soul has been sold to cater to the whims of tourist hordes alighting for 17 minutes on guided bus tours. Souvenir shops, tax-free luxury goods stores and cube-shaped concrete buildings dominate the small, somewhat bland town centre enclosed by Äulestrasse and the pedestrian-only Städtle.

INFORMATION

Liechtenstein Center (☎ 239 63 00; www.tourismus .li; Städtle; ☿ 9am-5pm) Sells souvenir passport stamps for Sfr3.

Post office (Äulestrasse 38; ☿ 7.45am-6pm Mon-Fri, 8-11am Sat)

SIGHTS & ACTIVITIES

Although **Schloss Vaduz** (Vaduz Castle) is not open to the public, its exterior graces many a photograph and it is worth climbing up the hill for. At the top, there's a magnificent vista of Vaduz with a spectacular mountain back-drop. There's also a network of walking trails along the ridge. For a peek inside the castle

grounds, arrive on 15 August (Liechtenstein's national day), when there are magnificent fireworks and the prince invites the entire country over to his place for a glass.

The well-designed **Liechtensteinisches Landesmuseum** (National Museum; ☎ 239 68 20; www .landesmuseum.li; Städtle 43; adult/concession Sfr8/5, incl Kunstmuseum Sfr18/8; ☿ 10am-5pm Tue-Sun, to 8pm Wed) provides an interesting romp through the principality's history.

The mainstay of the **Kunstmuseum Liechtenstein** (☎ 235 03 00; www.kunstmuseum.li; Städtle 32; adult/concession Sfr12/8, incl Landesmuseum Sfr18/8; ☿ 10am-5pm Tue-Sun, to 8pm Thu) is contemporary art, not the prince's collection of old masters, which have been relocated to the Liechtenstein Museum in Vienna.

The **Postmuseum** (☎ 236 61 05; Städtle 37; admission free; ☿ 10am-noon & 1-5pm), on the 1st floor, is mildly diverting. It showcases all national stamps issued since 1912.

To see how Vaduz once looked, head north-east from the pedestrian zone to **Mitteldorf**, a charming quarter of traditional houses and verdant gardens.

SLEEPING

Camping Mittagspitze (☎ 392 36 77, 392 23 11; www .campingtriesen.li; camp sites per adult/child/car Sfr9/4/5, per tent Sfr6-8; ☿ year-round; 🖵) A well-equipped ground in a leafy spot with a restaurant, TV lounge, playground and kiosk. Find it 3.5km outside Vaduz, south of Triesen.

SYHA Hostel (☎ 232 50 22; www.youthhostel.ch /schaan; Untere Rütigasse 6; dm/s/d Sfr33/57/84; ☿ Mar-Oct) This hostel caters particularly to cyclists and families. Halfway between Schaan and Vaduz, it's within easy walking distance of either. Reception is closed from 10am to 5pm.

Hotel Falknis (☎ 232 63 77; Landstrasse 92; s/d with shared bathroom Sfr55/110) Basic rooms located north of the centre – 15 minutes on foot or take the bus.

Landgasthof Au (☎ 232 11 17; Austrasse 2; s/d with shared bathroom Sfr68/110, with private bathroom Sfr90/140) A couple of bus stops south of Vaduz town centre (about a 10-minute walk), this sim-ple, family-run place is a reasonable budget option. A couple of the bigger doubles have terraces. Note that Landgasthof only accepts cash.

Landhaus am Giessen (☎ 235 00 35; www.giessen .li; Zollstrasse 16; s/d Sfr100/150; 🖵) Around the cor-ner from the Landgasthof Au, this is a fairly modern affair with comfortable and good-

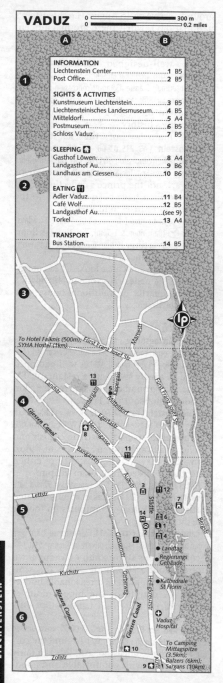

VADUZ

0 ———— 300 m
0 ———— 0.2 miles

To Hotel Falknis (500m);
SYHA Hostel (1km)

Landstr

Giessen Canal

Letitstr

Kirchstr

Binsen Canal

Zollstr

Hinterg.

Egertistr

Herrengasse

Bangarten

Aulestr

Städtle

Messt

Fürst Franz Josef Str

Bretscn

Heiligkreuzstr

Gerberweg

Giessen Canal

Mitteldorf

● Landtag
● Regierungs
  Gebäude

● Kathedrale
  St Florin

✚ Vaduz
  Hospital

To Camping
Mittagspitze
(3.5km);
Balzers (6km);
Sargans (10km)

sized, if comparatively charmless, rooms. It has a sauna and offers massages. There is wi-fi throughout.

our pick Gasthof Löwen (☎ 238 11 41; www.hotel-loewen.li; Herrengasse 35; s/d Sfr199/299) Historic and creakily elegant, this six-centuries-old guest house has eight spacious rooms with antique furniture and modern bathrooms. There's a cosy bar, fine-dining restaurant and a rear outdoor terrace overlooking grapevines.

EATING

Pedestrian-only Städtle has a clutch of footpath restaurants and cafes.

Cafe Wolf (☎ 232 23 21; Städtle 29; mains Sfr12.50-19.50) This relaxed cafe and restaurant has pavement tables in summer and a menu that mixes Swiss and international cuisine – anything from pizza to pseudo-Asian dishes.

Adler Vaduz (☎ 232 21 31; www.adler.li; Herrengasse 2; dishes Sfr17.50-46; ☽ Mon-Fri) A pleasant restaurant in the Hotel Adler offering a broad selection, from pasta to *Rindsfilet vom Grill auf Steinpilzrisotto mit Trüffel-Rotweinsauce nappiert* (beef steak fillet with mushroom risotto and a truffle and red-wine sauce).

Landgasthof Au (☎ 232 11 17; Austrasse 2; mains Sfr18-35; ☽ Wed-Sun) The Landgasthof Au (p365) garden restaurant has a good name for its local grub, which ranges from ham omelettes to a couple of vegetarian dishes and a kids' menu.

Torkel (☎ 232 44 10; Hintergasse 9; dishes Sfr42-58; ☽ lunch & dinner Mon-Fri, dinner Sat) Just above the prince's vineyards sits His Majesty's ivy-clad restaurant. The garden terrace enjoys a wonderful perspective of the castle above, while the ancient, wood-lined interior is cosy in winter. Food mixes classic with modern. The set lunch menu (Sfr64) gives a good overview.

AROUND VADUZ

Outside Vaduz the air is crisp and clear with a pungent, sweet aroma of cow dung and flowers. The countryside, dotted with tranquil villages and enticing churches set to a craggy Alps backdrop, is about as idyllic and relaxing as it gets.

Triesenberg, on a terrace above Vaduz, commands excellent views over the Rhine valley. It has a pretty onion-domed church and the **Walsermuseum** (☎ 262 19 26; www.triesenberg.li;

Jonaboda 2; adult/concession Sfr2/1; 7.45-11.45am & 1.30-5.45pm Mon-Fri, 7.45-11am & 1.30-5 Sat), devoted to the Walser community, whose members came from Switzerland's Valais to settle in the 13th century. Take bus 21 from Vaduz.

There are 400km of **hiking trails** through Liechtenstein (see www.wanderwege-llv.li), along with loads of well-marked **cycling routes** (look for signs with a cycle symbol; distances and directions will also be included). The most famous hiking trail is the **Fürstensteig trail**, a rite of passage for nearly every Liechtensteiner. You must be fit and not suffer from vertigo, as in places the path is narrow, reinforced with rope handholds and/or falls away to a sheer drop. The hike, which takes up to four hours, begins at the **Berggasthaus Gaflei** (take bus 22 from Triesenberg). Travel light and wear good shoes.

MALBUN
pop 35

Welcome to Liechtenstein's one and only ski resort: at the end of the road from Vaduz, the 1600m-high resort of Malbun feels – in the nicest possible sense – like the edge of the earth.

The road from Vaduz terminates at Malbun. There is an ATM by the lower bus stop. The **tourist office** (263 65 77; www.malbun .li; 9am-noon & 1.30-5pm Mon-Sat, closed mid-Apr–May & Nov–mid-Dec) is on the main street, not far from Hotel Walserhof.

Although rather limited in scope – the runs are mostly novice with a few intermediate and cross-country runs thrown in – the skiing is inexpensive for this part of the world and it does offer some bragging rights. Indeed, older British royals such as Princes Charles learnt to ski here.

A general ski pass (including the Sareis chair lift) costs per day/week Sfr45/205 for adults and Sfr29/127 for children. One day's equipment rental from **Malbun Sport** (263 37 55; www.malbunsport.li; 8am-6pm Mon-Fri, plus Sat & Sun in high season) costs Sfr58 including skis, shoes and poles.

Hotel Walserhof (264 43 23; d Sfr140) is a simple mountain house with four doubles and cheerful outdoor dining. For gob-smacking mountain views over dinner, it's hard to beat **Bergrestaurant Sareiserjoch** (268 21 01; www.sareis .li; mains Sfr20-35; Jun–mid-Oct & mid-Dec–Apr), at the end of the Sareis chair lift. Go for *Käsknöpfli* (cheese-filled dumplings).

LIECHTENSTEIN DIRECTORY

Liechtenstein and Switzerland share almost everything, so for more information about Liechtenstein basics, see p583.

Smoking in public places has yet to be banned in Liechtenstein, meaning you can freely smoke in hotels, restaurants and so on.

TRANSPORT IN LIECHTENSTEIN

GETTING THERE & AWAY
The nearest airports are Friedrichshafen (Germany) and Zürich (Switzerland), with train connections to the Swiss border towns of Buchs and Sargans. From each of these towns there are usually three buses to Vaduz (from Buchs Sfr2.40, Sargans Sfr3.60). Buses run

---

EMERGENCY NUMBERS

- Ambulance ☎ 144
- Fire ☎ 118
- Police ☎ 117

---

every 30 minutes from the Austrian border town of Feldkirch; you sometimes have to change at Schaan to reach Vaduz.

A few trains from Buchs to Feldkirch stop at Schaan (bus tickets are valid).

If you're travelling by road, the N16 from Switzerland passes through Liechtenstein via Schaan and ends at Feldkirch. The A13 follows the Rhine along the border; minor roads cross into Liechtenstein at each motorway exit.

GETTING AROUND

Bus travel is cheap and reliable; all fares cost Sfr2.40 or Sfr3.60, with the higher rate for journeys exceeding 13km (such as Vaduz to Malbun). Grab a timetable from the Vaduz tourist office.

Poland

If they were handing out prizes for 'most eventful history', Poland would be sure to get a gong. The nation has spent centuries at the pointy end of history, grappling with war and invasion. Nothing, however, has succeeded in suppressing the Poles' strong sense of nationhood and cultural identity, as exemplified by the ancient royal capital of Kraków, with its breathtaking castle, and bustling Warsaw, with its postwar reconstruction of its Old Town.

For the time being, at least, the time for resistance to oppressive regimes is over, as Poles enjoy the peaceful space provided by their membership of the EU. As investment flows into the country and the economy grows, Poles are visiting and working overseas like never before. The product is a younger generation that's more cosmopolitan and 'European' than its predecessors. As a result, regional centres such as urbane Gdańsk, cultured Wrocław and lively Poznań exude a sophisticated energy that's a heady mix of old and new.

Away from the cities, Poland is a diverse land, from its northern sandy beaches and magnificent southern mountains to the lost-in-time forest of Białowieża National Park in the east. And everywhere there are seldom-visited towns to discover, with their own ruined castles, picturesque squares and historic churches.

Although prices are rising as its economy gathers strength, Poland is still good value for travellers. As the Polish people work on combining their distinctive national identity with their place in the heart of Europe, it's a fascinating time to visit this beautiful country.

FAST FACTS

- **Area** 312, 685 sq km
- **Capital** Warsaw
- **Currency** złoty; €1 = 4.58zł; US$1 = 3.36zł; UK£1 = 4.87zł; A$1 = 2.33zł; ¥100 = 3.50zł; NZ$1 = 1.87zł
- **Famous for** Chopin, Copernicus, Marie Curie, Solidarity, vodka
- **Official language** Polish
- **Phrases** *dzień dobry* (good morning/afternoon); *dziękuję* (thank you); *proszę* (please)
- **Population** 38 million
- **Telephone codes** country code ☎ 48; international access code ☎ 00
- **Visas** not required for EU citizens; US, Canadian, New Zealand and Australian citizens do not need visas for stays of less than 90 days, see p446

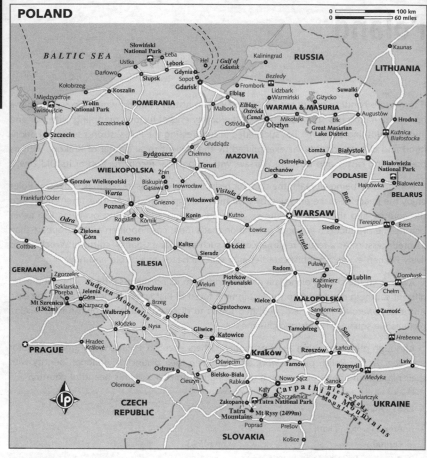

HIGHLIGHTS

- Experience the beauty and history of Kraków's **Wawel Castle** (p389).
- Meet European bison and other magnificent fauna at **Białowieża National Park** (p387).
- Soak up the cosmopolitan vibe of **Gdańsk** (p423) and take a dip in the Baltic at nearby **Sopot** (p429).
- Enjoy the skiing or hiking life of the **Tatra Mountains** (p409).
- Discover Warsaw's tragic wartime history at the **Warsaw Rising Museum** (p380).

ITINERARIES

- **One Week** Spend a day exploring Warsaw with a stroll round the Old Town and a stop at the Warsaw Rising Museum. The next day, head to Kraków for three days, visiting the Old Town, Wawel Castle, the former Jewish district of Kazimierz, and Wieliczka. Take a day trip to Oświęcim, then head on to Zakopane for two days.
- **Two Weeks** Follow the above itinerary, then on the eighth day travel to Wrocław for two days. Progress north to Toruń for a day, then onward to Gdańsk for two days, exploring the Old Town and visiting Westerplatte. Wind down with a couple of days at the seaside in Sopot.

CLIMATE & WHEN TO GO

Poland's weather can be unpredictable. Summer is usually warm and sunny, with July the hottest month, but it's also the season with the highest rainfall. Spring and autumn are pleasantly warm but can also be wet. Snow can fall anywhere in Poland between December and March, lingering until April or even May in the mountains.

The tourist season runs roughly from May to October, peaking in July and August. Many Polish families go on holidays during these two months, so transport is crowded and accommodation limited. From mid-autumn to mid-spring, outdoor activities are less prominent and many camping grounds and youth hostels are closed.

HISTORY

Poland's history started with the Polanians (People of the Plains). During the early Middle Ages, these Western Slavs moved into the flatlands between the Vistula and Odra Rivers. Mieszko I, Duke of the Polanians, adopted Christianity in 966 and embarked on a campaign of conquest. A papal edict in 1025 led to Mieszko's son Bolesław Chrobry (Boleslaus the Brave) being crowned Poland's first king.

Poland's early success proved fragile, and encroachment from Germanic peoples led to the relocation of the royal capital from Poznań to Kraków in 1038. More trouble loomed in 1226 when the Prince of Mazovia invited the Teutonic Knights to help convert the pagan tribes of the north. These Germanic crusaders used the opportunity to create their own state along the Baltic coast. The south had its own invaders to contend with, and Kraków was attacked by Tatars twice in the mid-13th century.

The kingdom prospered under Kazimierz III 'the Great' (1333–70). During this period, many new towns sprang up, while Kraków blossomed into one of Europe's leading cultural centres.

When the daughter of Kazimierz's nephew, Jadwiga, married the Grand Duke of Lithuania, Jagiełło, in 1386, Poland and Lithuania were united as the largest state in Europe, stretching from the Baltic to the Black Sea.

The Renaissance was introduced to Poland by the enlightened King Zygmunt during the 16th century, as he lavishly patronised the arts and sciences. By asserting that the earth travelled around the sun, Nicolaus Copernicus revolutionised the field of astronomy in 1543.

The 17th and 18th centuries produced disaster and decline for Poland. First it was subject to Swedish and Russian invasions, and eventually it faced partition by surrounding empires. In 1773 Russia, Prussia and Austria seized Polish territory in the First Partition; by the time the Third Partition was completed in 1795, Poland had vanished from the map of Europe.

Although the country remained divided through the entire 19th century, Poles steadfastly maintained their culture. Finally, upon the end of WWI the old imperial powers dissolved, and a sovereign Polish state was restored. Very soon, however, Poland was again at war. Under the command of Marshal Jozef Piłsudski, Poland defended its eastern territories from long-time enemy Russia, now transformed into the Soviet Union and determined to spread its revolution westward. After two years of impressive fighting by the outnumbered Poles, an armistice was signed, retaining Vilnius and Lviv within Poland.

Though Polish institutions and national identity flourished during the interwar period, disaster soon struck again. On 1 September 1939, a Nazi blitzkrieg rained down from the west; soon after, the Soviets invaded Poland from the east, dividing the country with Germany. This agreement didn't last long, as Hitler soon transformed Poland into a staging ground for the Nazi invasion of the Soviet

CONNECTIONS: MOVING ON FROM POLAND

Due to its central position, Poland offers plenty of possibilities for onward travel. The country is well-connected by train: there are direct connections to Berlin from both Warsaw (via Poznań) and Kraków; to Prague from Warsaw and Kraków; and to Kyiv from Warsaw and Kraków (via Przemyśl and Lviv). Trains also link Warsaw to Minsk and Moscow, and Gdańsk to Kaliningrad. International buses head in all directions, including eastward to the Baltic States, Belarus and Ukraine; see p385 for information on buses from Warsaw. From southern Zakopane (p409), it's easy to hop to Slovakia via bus, or even minibus. And from the Baltic coast ports of Gdańsk (p428), Gydania (p430) and Świnoujscie (p447), ferries head to various ports in Denmark and Sweden.

HOW MUCH?

- **Night in a hostel** 50zł
- **Night in a midrange double room** 250zł
- **Three-course restaurant meal for two** 150zł
- **Postcard** 1zł
- **Postage stamp** 3zł

LONELY PLANET INDEX

- **1L petrol** 3.80zł
- **1L bottled water** 2zł
- **Beer** 6zł to 8zł
- **Souvenir T-shirt** 35zł
- **Street snack (zapiekanka)** 4zł to 5zł

Union. Six million Polish inhabitants died during WWII (including the country's three million Jews), brutally annihilated in death camps. At the war's end, Poland's borders were redrawn yet again. The Soviet Union kept the eastern territories and extended the country's western boundary at the expense of Germany. These border changes were accompanied by the forced resettlement of more than a million Poles, Germans and Ukrainians.

Peacetime brought more repression. After WWII, Poland endured four decades of Soviet-dominated communist rule, punctuated by waves of protests, most notably the paralysing strikes of 1980–81, led by the Solidarity trade union. Finally, in the open elections of 1989, the communists fell from power and in 1990 Solidarity leader Lech Wałęsa became Poland's first democratically elected president.

The post-communist transition brought radical changes, which induced new social hardships and political crises. But within a decade Poland had built the foundations for a market economy, and reoriented its foreign relations towards the West. In March 1999, Poland was granted full NATO membership, and it joined the EU in May 2004.

In the 2007 parliamentary elections, Poles decisively rejected the Eurosceptic policies of the Law and Justice party's government, eccentrically headed by the twin Kaczyński brothers as president (Lech) and prime min-

ister (Jarosław). The new centrist government of prime minister Donald Tusk's Civic Platform is steering a pro-business, pro-EU course, although Lech Kaczyński's term as president runs to 2010.

PEOPLE

For centuries Poland was a multicultural country, home to large Jewish, German and Ukrainian communities. Its Jewish population was particularly large, and once numbered more than three million. However, after Nazi genocide and the forced resettlements that followed WWII, the Jewish population declined to 10,000 and Poland became an ethnically homogeneous country, with some 98% of the population being ethnic Poles.

More than 60% of the citizens live in towns and cities. Warsaw is by far the largest urban settlement, followed by Łódź, Kraków, Wrocław, Poznań and Gdańsk. Upper Silesia (around Katowice) is the most densely inhabited area, while the northeastern border regions remain the least populated.

Between five and 10 million Poles live outside Poland. This émigré community, known as 'Polonia', is located mainly in the USA (particularly Chicago).

Poles are friendly and polite, but not overly formal. The way of life in large urban centres increasingly resembles Western styles and manners. In the countryside, however, a more conservative culture dominates, evidenced by traditional gender roles and strong family ties. In both urban and rural settings, many Poles are devoutly religious.

The Poles' sense of personal space may be a bit cosier than you are accustomed to – you may notice this trait when queuing for tickets or manoeuvring along city streets. When greeting each other, Polish men are passionate about shaking hands. Polish women often shake hands with men, but the man should always wait for the woman to extend her hand first.

RELIGION

Roman Catholicism is the dominant Christian denomination, adhered to by more than 80% of Poles. The Orthodox church's followers constitute about 1% of the population, mostly living along a narrow strip on the eastern frontier.

The election of Karol Wojtyła, the archbishop of Kraków, as Pope John Paul II in 1978, and his triumphal visit to his homeland a year later, significantly enhanced the status of the church in Poland. The country was proud of the late Pope: even now his image can be seen in public places and private homes throughout the country.

The overthrow of communism was as much a victory for the Church as it was for democracy. The fine line between the Church and the state is often blurred in Poland, and the Church is a powerful lobby on social issues. Some Poles have grown wary of the Church's influence in society and politics, but Poland remains one of Europe's most religious countries, and packed-out churches are not uncommon.

ARTS
Literature
Poland has inherited a rich literary tradition dating from the 15th century, though its modern voice was shaped in the 19th century, during the long period of foreign occupation. It was a time for nationalist writers such as the poet Adam Mickiewicz (1798–1855), and Henryk Sienkiewicz (1846–1916), who won a Nobel Prize in 1905 for *Quo Vadis?* This nationalist tradition was revived in the communist era when Czesław Miłosz was awarded a Nobel Prize in 1980 for *The Captive Mind*.

At the turn of the 20th century, the avant-garde 'Young Poland' movement in art and literature developed in Kraków. The most notable representatives of this movement were writer Stanisław Wyspiański (1869–1907), also famous for his stained-glass work; playwright Stanisław Ignacy Witkiewicz (1885–1939), commonly known as Witkacy; and Nobel laureate Władysław Reymont (1867–1925). In 1996 Wisława Szymborska (b 1923) also received a Nobel Prize for her poetry.

Music
The most famous Polish musician was undoubtedly Frédéric Chopin (1810–49), whose music displays the melancholy and nostalgia that became hallmarks of the national style. Stanisław Moniuszko (1819–72) injected a Polish flavour into 19th-century Italian opera music by introducing folk songs and dances to the stage. His *Halka* (1858), about a peasant girl abandoned by a young noble, is a staple of the national opera houses.

On a more contemporary note, popular Polish musicians you might catch live in concert include the controversial Doda (pop singer); Feel (pop-rock band); Łzy (pop-rock band); Indios Bravos (reggae band); and Kasia Cerekwicka (pop singer). Poland's equivalent of the Rolling Stones is Lady Pank, a rock band formed in 1982 and still going strong.

Visual Arts
Poland's most renowned painter was Jan Matejko (1838–93), whose monumental historical paintings hang in galleries throughout the country. Wojciech Kossak (1857–1942) is another artist who documented Polish history; he is best remembered for the colossal painting *Panorama of Racławicka*, on display in Wrocław (p413).

A long-standing Polish craft is the fashioning of jewellery from amber. Amber is a fossil resin of vegetable origin that comes primarily from the Baltic region, and appears in a variety of colours from pale yellow to reddish brown. The best places to buy it are Gdańsk, Kraków and Warsaw.

Polish poster art has received international recognition; the best selection of poster galleries is in Warsaw and Kraków.

Cinema
Poland has produced several world-famous film directors. The most notable is Andrzej Wajda, who received an Honorary Award at the 1999 Academy Awards. *Katyń*, his moving story of the Katyń massacre in WWII, was nominated for Best Foreign Language Film at the 2008 Oscars. Western audiences are probably more familiar with the work of Roman Polański, who directed critically acclaimed films such as *Rosemary's Baby* and *Chinatown*. In 2002 Polański released the incredibly moving film *The Pianist*, which was filmed in Poland and set in the Warsaw Ghetto of WWII. The film went on to win three Oscars and the Cannes Palme d'Or. The late Krzysztof Kieślowski is best known for the *Three Colours* trilogy. The centre of Poland's movie industry, and home to its prestigious National Film School, is Łódź.

ENVIRONMENT
Poland covers an area of 312,685 sq km, approximately as large as the UK and Ireland put together, and is bordered by seven nations and one sea.

The northern edge of Poland meets the Baltic Sea. This broad, 524km-long coastline is spotted with sand dunes and seaside lakes. Also concentrated in the northeast are many postglacial lakes – more than any country in Europe, except Finland.

The southern border is defined by the mountain ranges of the Sudetes and Carpathians. Poland's highest mountains are the rocky Tatras, a section of the Carpathian Range it shares with Slovakia. The highest peak of the Polish Tatras is Mt Rysy (2499m).

The area in between is a vast plain, sectioned by wide north-flowing rivers. Poland's longest river is the Vistula (Wisła), which winds 1047km from the Tatras to the Baltic.

About a quarter of Poland is covered by forest. Some 60% of the forests are pine trees, but the share of deciduous species, such as oak, beech and birch, is increasing.

Poland's fauna includes hare, red deer, wild boar and, less abundantly, elk, brown bear and wildcat. European bison, which once inhabited Europe in large numbers, were brought to the brink of extinction early in the 20th century and a few hundred now live in Białowieża National Park (p387). The Great Masurian Lakes district (p439) attracts a vast array of bird life, such as storks and cormorants. The eagle, though rarely seen today, is Poland's national bird and appears on the Polish emblem.

Poland has 23 national parks, but they cover less than 1% of the country. No permit is necessary to visit these parks, but most have small admission fees. Camping in the parks is sometimes allowed, but only at specified sites. Poland also has a network of less strictly preserved areas called 'landscape parks', scattered throughout the country.

FOOD & DRINK
Staples & Specialities
Various cultures have influenced Polish cuisine, including Jewish, Ukrainian, Russian, Hungarian and German. Polish food is hearty and filling, abundant in potatoes and dumplings, and rich in meat.

Poland's most famous dishes are *bigos* (sauerkraut with a variety of meats), *pierogi* (ravioli-like dumplings stuffed with cottage cheese, minced meat, or cabbage and wild mushrooms) and *barszcz* (red beetroot soup, better known by the Russian word *borscht*).

Hearty soups such as *żurek* (sour soup with sausage and hard-boiled eggs) are a highlight of Polish cuisine. Main dishes are made with pork, including *golonka* (boiled pig's knuckle

served with horseradish) and *schab pieczony* (roast loin of pork seasoned with prunes and herbs). *Gołąbki* (cabbage leaves stuffed with mince and rice) is a tasty alternative.

Placki ziemniaczane (potato pancakes) and *naleśniki* (crepes) are also popular dishes.

Poles claim the national drink, *wódka* (vodka), was invented in their country. It's usually drunk neat and comes in a number of flavours, including *myśliwska* (flavoured with juniper berries), *wiśniówka* (with cherries) and *jarzębiak* (with rowanberries). The most famous variety is *żubrówka* (bison vodka), flavoured with grass from the Białowieża Forest. Other notable spirits include *krupnik* (honey liqueur), *śliwowica* (plum brandy) and *goldwasser* (sweet liqueur containing flakes of gold leaf).

Poles also appreciate the taste of *zimne piwo* (cold beer); the top brands, found everywhere, include Żywiec, Tyskie, Lech and Okocim, while regional brands are available in every city.

Where to Eat & Drink
The cheapest place to eat Polish food is a *bar mleczny* (milk bar), a survivor from the communist era. These no-frills, self-service cafeterias are popular with budget-conscious locals and backpackers alike. Up the scale, the number and variety of *restauracja* (restaurants) has ballooned in recent years, especially in the big cities. Pizzerias have also become phenomenally popular with Poles. And though Polish cuisine features plenty of meat, there are vegetarian restaurants to be found in most cities.

Menus usually have several sections: *zupy* (soups), *dania drugie* (main courses) and *dodatki* (accompaniments). The price of the main course may not include a side dish – such as potatoes and salads – which you choose (and pay extra for) from the *dodatki* section. Also note that the price for some dishes (particularly fish and poultry) may be listed per 100g, so the price will depend on the total weight of the fish or meat.

Poles start their day with *śniadanie* (breakfast); the most important and substantial meal of the day, *obiad*, is normally eaten between 2pm and 5pm. The third meal is *kolacja* (supper). Most restaurants, cafes and cafe-bars are open from 11am to 11pm. It's rare for Polish restaurants to serve breakfast, though milk bars and snack bars are open from early morning. In the Eating sections of this chapter, only nonstandard restaurant hours are listed.

Smoking is common in bars and restaurants, though there have been unsuccessful proposals to ban it from public spaces. It's becoming more common for hotels and restaurants to offer nonsmoking options.

WARSAW

pop 1.7 million

Warsaw (Warszawa in Polish, var-*shah*-va) may not be the prettiest of Poland's cities, but there's no mistaking its dynamism. As the bustling capital and business centre of the nation, Warsaw is home to an array of

dining and nightlife that's the equal of any European city its size.

It's true, however, that Warsaw can be hard work. The city centre sprawls across a wide area, quite separate from the attractive but tourist-heavy Old Town, and its traffic-choked streets lined with massive concrete buildings can be less than enthralling.

However, look at Warsaw with a historic perspective and you'll see the capital in an entirely new light. As a city that's survived everything fate could throw at it – including the complete destruction of its historic heart in WWII – Warsaw is a place with an extraordinary back story.

When you factor in its entertainment options; the beauty of its reconstructed Old

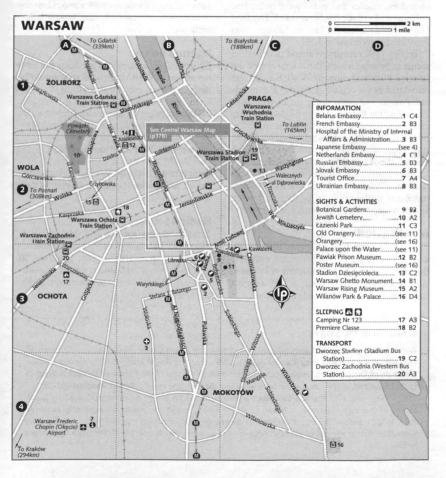

WARSAW

0 — 2 km
0 — 1 mile

INFORMATION
Belarus Embassy...................................1 C4
French Embassy....................................2 B3
Hospital of the Ministry of Internal Affairs & Administration......3 B3
Japanese Embassy..........................(see 4)
Netherlands Embassy.........................4 C3
Russian Embassy.................................5 D3
Slovak Embassy...................................6 B3
Tourist Office.......................................7 A4
Ukrainian Embassy..............................8 B3

SIGHTS & ACTIVITIES
Botanical Gardens...............................9 B3
Jewish Cemetery................................10 A2
Łazienki Park.....................................11 C3
Old Orangery.................................(see 11)
Orangery.......................................(see 16)
Palace upon the Water...................(see 11)
Pawiak Prison Museum......................12 B2
Poster Museum..............................(see 16)
Stadion Dziesięciolecia.....................13 C2
Warsaw Ghetto Monument...............14 B1
Warsaw Rising Museum.....................15 A2
Wilanów Park & Palace......................16 D4

SLEEPING
Camping Nr 123.................................17 A3
Premiere Classe.................................18 B2

TRANSPORT
Dworzec Stadion (Stadium Bus Station)...19 C2
Dworzec Zachodnia (Western Bus Station)...20 A3

ŻOLIBORZ
Warszawa Gdańska Train Station
Powązki Cemetery
WOLA
To Poznań (308km)
Warszawa Zachodnia Train Station
Warszawa Ochota Train Station
OCHOTA
Warsaw Frederic Chopin (Okęcie) Airport
To Kraków (294km)

To Gdańsk (339km)
Vistula River
Słomiński

To Białystok (188km)
PRAGA
Warszawa Wschodnia Train Station
To Lublin (165km)
See Central Warsaw Map (p378)
Warszawa Stadion Train Station

MOKOTÓW

POLAND

Town, Royal Way and former Royal Parks; and the history represented by the Stalinist-era Palace of Culture and the Warsaw Rising Museum, what emerges is a complex city that well repays a visit.

HISTORY

The Mazovian dukes were the first rulers of Warsaw, establishing it as their stronghold in the 14th century. The city's strategic central location led to the capital being transferred from Kraków to Warsaw in 1596, following the earlier union of Poland and Lithuania.

Although the 18th century was a period of catastrophic decline for the Polish state, Warsaw underwent a period of prosperity during this period. Many magnificent churches, palaces and parks were built, and cultural and artistic life blossomed. The first (short-lived) constitution in Europe was instituted in Warsaw in 1791.

In the 19th century Warsaw declined in status to become a mere provincial city of the Russian Empire. Following WWI, the city was reinstated as the capital of a newly independent Poland and once more began to thrive. Following the Warsaw Rising of 1944, the city centre was devastated, and the entire surviving population forcibly evacuated. Upon war's end, the people of Warsaw returned to the capital, and set about rebuilding its historic heart.

Since the fall of communism, and particularly since Poland's entry into the EU, Warsaw has been undergoing an economic boom, which has reshaped its commercial heart.

ORIENTATION

The Vistula River divides the city. The western left-bank sector features the city centre, including the Old Town, the historic nucleus of Warsaw. Almost all tourist attractions, as well as most tourist facilities, are on this side of the river.

If arriving by train, Warszawa Centralna station is, as the name suggests, within walking distance of the city centre and major attractions. If you arrive by bus at either major PKS bus station, you can take a train from an adjoining station into the centre.

INFORMATION

Bookshops

American Bookstore (Map p378; ☎ 022 827 4852; ul Nowy Świat 61) Books, including guidebooks, and maps.
EMPiK Galeria Centrum (Map p378; ul Marszałkowska 116/122); Royal Way (Map p378; ul Nowy Świat 15/17) Foreign books, newspapers and magazines.

Discount Cards

Warsaw Tourist Card (1/3 days 35/65zł) Free or discounted access to museums, public transport and some theatres, sports centres and restaurants. Available at the tourist office.

Internet Access

Expect to pay around 5zł per hour for internet access in Warsaw. Several convenient but dingy internet cafes are also within Warszawa Centralna train station.
Casablanca (Map p378; ul Krakowskie Przedmieście 4/6; ☉ 9am–1am Mon-Fri, 10am–2am Sat, 10am–midnight Sun) Enter from ul Oboźna.
Internet Café (Map p378; ul Nowy Świat 18/20; ☉ 9am–11pm Mon-Fri, 10am–10pm Sat & Sun)
Verso Internet (Map p378; ul Freta 17; ☉ 8am–8pm Mon-Fri, 9am–5pm Sat, 10am–4pm Sun) Enter from the rear, off ul Świętojerska.

Medical Services

Apteka Grabowskiego (Map p378; Warszawa Centralna; ☉ 24hr) Nonstop pharmacy at the train station.
Centrum Medyczne LIM (Map p378; ☎ 022 458 7000; www.cm-lim.com.pl; 3rd fl, Marriott Hotel, Al Jerozolimskie 65/79) Offers specialist doctors, laboratory tests and house calls.

WARSAW IN TWO DAYS

Wander through the **Old Town** (opposite) and tour the **Royal Castle** (opposite), having lunch afterwards at **Restauracja Przy Zamku** (p384). Walk along the **Royal Way** (p379) dropping into the **Museum of Caricature** (p379) en route. Take the lift to the top of the **Palace of Culture & Science** (p380) for views of the city, before promenading through the nearby **Saxon Gardens** (p379).

The next day, visit the **Warsaw Rising Museum** (p380) in the morning, followed by lunch at one of the many restaurants along ul Nowy Świat. Spend the afternoon exploring **Łazienki Park** (p380), before sipping a cocktail at **Sense** (p384). Finish off the day with a visit to the nightclub district around **ul Mazowiecka** (p384), or take in a concert at **Filharmonia Narodowa** (p384).

Dental-Med (Map p378; ☎ 022 629 5938; ul Hoża 27) A central dental practice.

Hospital of the Ministry of Internal Affairs & Administration (Map p375; ☎ 022 508 2000; ul Wołoska 137) A hospital preferred by government officials and diplomats.

Money

Foreign-exchange offices (kantors) and ATMs are easy to find around the city centre. Kantors open 24 hours can be found at Warszawa Centralna train station and the airport, but exchange rates at these places are about 10% lower than in the city centre. Avoid changing money in the Old Town, where the rates are even lower.

American Express (Map p378; Marriott Hotel, Al Jerozolimskie 65/79; ⏰ 7am-11pm)

Bank Pekao (Map p378; ul Krakowskie Przedmieście 1)

PBK Bank (Map p378; ground fl, Palace of Culture & Science Bldg)

PKO Bank (Map p378; Plac Bankowy 2)

Post

Main post office (Map p378; ul Świętokrzyska 31/33; ⏰ 24hr) also useful.

Tourist Information

Each tourist office provides free city maps and free booklets, such as the handy Warsaw in Short and the Visitor, and sells maps of other Polish cities; offices also help with booking hotel rooms.

Free monthly tourist magazines worth seeking out include Faces and Welcome to Warsaw. The comprehensive Warsaw Insider (8zł) and Warsaw in Your Pocket (5zł) are also useful.

Tourist office (☎ 9431; www.warsawtour.pl) Old Town (Map p378; 1st fl, Plac Zamkowy 10; ⏰ 8am-4pm); Royal Way (Map p378; ul Krakowskie Przedmieście 39; ⏰ 9am-8pm May-Sep, 9am-6pm Oct-Apr); Okęcie airport (Map p375; ⏰ 8am-8pm May-Sep, 8am-6pm Oct-Apr); main hall of Warszawa Centralna train station (Map p378; ⏰ 8am-8pm May-Sep, 8am-6pm Oct-Apr).

Warsaw tourist information centre (Map p378; ☎ 022 635 1881; www.wcit.waw.pl; pl Zamkowy 1/13; ⏰ 9am-6pm Mon-Fri, 10am-6pm Sat, 11am-6pm Sun) Helpful privately run tourist office in the Old Town.

Travel Agencies

Almatur (Map p378; ☎ 022 826 2639; ul Kopernika 23)

Orbis Travel (Map p378; ☎ 022 827 7265; ul Bracka 16)

Our Roots (Map p378; ☎ 022 620 0556; ul Twarda 6) Offers Jewish heritage tours.

Trakt (Map p378; ☎ 022 827 8068; www.trakt.com.pl; ul Kredytowa 6) Guided tours of Warsaw and beyond.

SIGHTS
Old Town

The main gateway to the Old Town is **Plac Zamkowy** (Castle Sq). All the buildings here were superbly rebuilt from their foundations after WWII, earning the Old Town a place on Unesco's World Heritage List. Within the square stands the **Monument to Sigismund III Vasa**, who moved the capital from Kraków to Warsaw in 1596.

The dominant feature of the square is the massive 13th-century **Royal Castle** (Map p378; Plac Zamkowy 4; adult/concession 20/13zł; free Sun Sep-May, free Mon Jun-Aug; ⏰ 11am-4pm Mon, 10am-4pm Tue-Sat, 11am-4pm Sun, closed Mon Oct-Apr), also reconstructed after the war. The highlight of the sumptuously decorated rooms is the Senators' Antechamber, where landscapes of 18th-century Warsaw by Bernardo Bellotto (Canaletto's nephew) are on show.

From the castle, walk down ul Świętojańska to Warsaw's oldest church, the 15th-century Gothic **St John's Cathedral** (Map p378; ul Świętojańska 8; crypt 1zł; ⏰ 10am-1pm & 3-5.30pm Mon-Sat). This street continues to the magnificent **Rynek Starego Miasta** (Old Town Market Sq).

Off the square is the **Warsaw Historical Museum** (Map p378; www.mhw.pl; Rynek Starego Miasta 42; adult/concession 6/3zł, free Sun; ⏰ 11am-6pm Tue & Thu, 10am-3.30pm Wed & Fri, 10.30am-4.30pm Sat & Sun). At noon it shows an English-language film depicting the wartime destruction of the city.

Nearby is the **Adam Mickiewicz Museum of Literature** (Map p378; Rynek Starego Miasta 20; adult/concession 5/4zł, free Sun; ⏰ 10am-3pm Mon, Tue & Fri, 11am-6pm Wed & Thu, 11am-5pm Sun), featuring exhibits on Poland's most revered literary figure and other leading writers.

Walk west for one block to the **Barbican**, part of the medieval city walls. North along ul Freta is the **Marie Skłodowska-Curie Museum** (Map p378; ul Freta 16; adult/concession 8/3zł; ⏰ 10am-4pm Tue-Sat, 10am-3pm Sun), which features unexciting displays about the great lady, who, along with husband Pierre, discovered radium and polonium, and laid the foundations for radiography, nuclear physics and cancer therapy.

Heading southwest, you'll reach the **Monument to the Warsaw Rising** (Map p378; cnr ul Długa & ul Miodowa). This striking set of statuary honours the heroic Polish revolt against German rule in 1944.

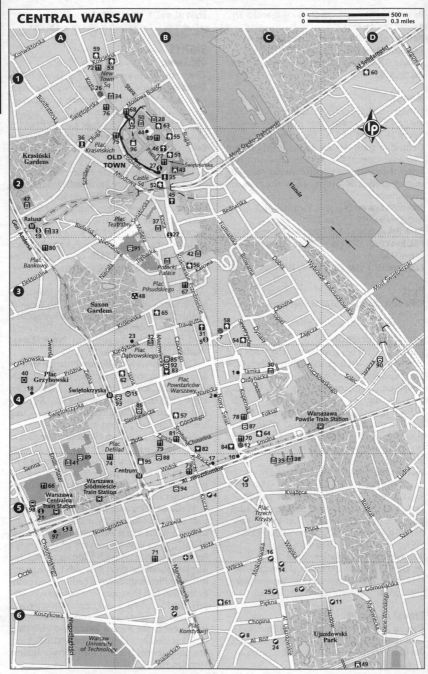

CENTRAL WARSAW

Not far from there, the **State Archaeological Museum** (Map p378; ul Długa 52; adult/concession 8/4zł, free Sun except 3rd Sun of month; 9am-4pm Mon-Wed & Fri, 11am-6pm Thu, 10am-4pm Sun, closed 1st & 3rd Sun each month) is located in a 17th-century former arsenal.

Royal Way (Szlak Królewski)

This 4km route links the Royal Castle with Łazienki Park (see p380) via ul Krakowskie Przedmieście, ul Nowy Świat and Al Ujazdowskie. Bus 180 runs along or near this route and continues south to Wilanów Park (Map p375). Bus 100 also runs on Saturday and Sunday from May to September, between Plac Zamkowy and Łazienki Park.

Just south of the Royal Castle is the ornate 15th-century **St Anne's Church** (Map p378; ul Krakowskie Przedmieście 68; daylight hr), with impressive views from its **tower** (adult/concession 3/2zł; 10am-6pm Tue-Sun).

Along nearby ul Kozia is the quirky **Museum of Caricature** (Map p378; www.muzeumkarykatury.pl; ul Kozia 11; adult/concession 5/3zł, free Sat; 11am-5pm Tue-Sun), exhibiting numerous original works by Polish and foreign caricaturists, created from the 18th century onwards.

Further south along ul Krakowskie Przedmieście you'll find **Radziwiłł Palace** (Map p378; not open to the public), the residence of the Polish president. To the west, beyond Plac Piłsudskiego, are the **Saxon Gardens** (admission free; 24hr). At the entrance is the small but poignant **Tomb of the Unknown Soldier** (Map p378), which stands within the only surviving remnant of the Saxon Palace that once stood here and was destroyed by the Nazis. The ceremonial changing of the guard takes place at noon on Sunday. At time of research, work had begun on rebuilding the palace, so access to the area may be limited when you visit.

South of the tomb is the **Ethnographic Museum** (Map p378; ul Kredytowa 1; adult/concession 8/4zł, Wed free; 9am-4pm Tue, Thu & Fri, 11am-6pm Wed, 10am-5pm Sat & Sun). It displays Polish folk costumes, and regional arts and crafts.

Back along the Royal Way is the 17th-century **Church of the Holy Cross** (Map p378; ul Krakowskie Przedmieście 3; erratic). Chopin's heart is preserved in the second pillar on the left-hand side of the main nave. It was brought from Paris, where he died of tuberculosis aged only 39. If you want to know more, head along ul Tamka to the small **Chopin Museum** (Map p378; ul Okólnik 1; adult/concession 8/4zł, free Wed; 10am-6pm Tue-Sat). On show are letters, hand-written musical scores and the great man's last piano.

East of the junction of ul Nowy Świat and Al Jerozolimskie is the **National Museum** (Map p378; www.mnw.art.pl; Al Jerozolimskie 3; adult/concession 12/7zł, incl temporary exhibitions 17/10zł, Sat free; 10am-4pm Tue-Fri, 10am-5pm Sat & Sun), with an impressive collection of Greek and Egyptian antiquities, Coptic frescos, medieval woodcarvings and Polish paintings; look out for the surrealistic fantasies of Jacek Malczewski. Next door is the **Museum of the Polish Army** (Map p378; Al Jerozolimskie 3; museum adult/concession 8/4zł, free Wed; 10am-5pm Wed-Sun May-Sep, 10am-4pm Wed-Sun Oct-Apr), with army vehicles outside and miscellaneous militaria within.

Go south along Al Ujazdowskie and cross busy ul Armii Ludowej. Over the road is the cutting-edge **Centre for Contemporary Art** (Map p378; www.csw.art.pl; Al Ujazdowskie 6; adult/concession 12/6zł, free Thu; 11am-7pm Tue-Sun). It's housed in the reconstructed **Ujazdów Castle** (Map p378), originally built during the 1620s. Further down (towards the south) are the small **Botanical Gardens** (Map p375; adult/concession 5/2.50zł; 10am-8pm Apr-Aug, 10am-6pm Sep-Oct).

Łazienki Park

This large, shady and popular **park** (admission free; daylight hr) is best known for the 18th-century **Palace upon the Water** (Map p375; adult/concession 12/9zł; 9am-4pm Tue-Sun). It was the summer residence of Stanisław August Poniatowski, the last king of Poland, who was deposed by the Russian army and confederation of Polish magnates in 1792. The park was once a royal hunting ground attached to Ujazdów Castle.

The **Old Orangery** (Map p375; adult/concession 6/4zł) contains a sculpture gallery and an 18th-century theatre. Between noon and 4pm every Sunday from May to September, piano recitals are held among the nearby rose gardens.

Wilanów Park

Another magnificent **park** (Map p375; ul Wisłostrada; adult/concession 5/3zł; 9am-dusk) lies 6km south-east of Łazienki Park. Its centrepiece is the splendid **Wilanów Palace** (Map p375; www.wilanow-palac.art.pl; adult/concession 16/8zł, free Sat; 9.30am-4.30pm Sun-Fri, 10.30am-6.30pm Sat), the summer residence of King Jan III Sobieski, who ended the Turkish threat to Central Europe by defeating the Turks at Vienna in 1683. In summer, be prepared to wait. The last tickets are sold one hour before closing time.

In the well-kept park behind the palace is the **Orangery** (Map p375; admission fee varies with exhibitions; 10am-6.30pm), which houses an art gallery. The **Poster Museum** (Map p375; adult/concession 9/5zł, free Wed; noon-4pm Mon, 10am-4pm Tue-Sun) in the former royal stables is a repository of Poland's world-renowned poster art.

To reach Wilanów, take bus 116 or 180 from ul Nowy Świat or Al Ujazdowskie.

Palace of Culture & Science

Massive, brooding and inescapable, this **towering structure** (Map p378; www.pkin.pl; Plac Defilad 1; 9am-8pm daily Sep-May, 9am-8pm Mon-Thu, to 11pm Fri-Sun Jun-Aug) has become an emblem of the city, as it's slowly rehabilitated from its Stalinist past. It has a particularly sinister aspect at dusk, though it's also a handy landmark. The palace was built in the early 1950s as a 'gift of friendship' from the Soviet Union (the kind of unwanted gift that's hard to hide away), and is still one of Europe's tallest buildings (over 230m). The clock faces were added to the building in the postcommunist period.

The **observation terrace** (adult/concession 20/15zł) on the 30th floor provides a panoramic view, though it can be very cold and windy.

Warsaw Rising Museum

This impressive **museum** (Map p375; ul Grzybowska 79; adult/concession 4/2zł, free Sun; 8am-6pm Mon, Wed & Fri, 10am-8pm Thu, 10am-6pm Sat & Sun) commemorates Warsaw's insurrection against its Nazi occupiers in 1944, which was destined to end in defeat and the destruction of much of the city and its population. The Rising was viciously suppressed by the Germans (while the Red Army stood by on the opposite bank of the Vistula), with more than 200,000 Poles dying by its conclusion.

The moving story of the Rising is retold here via photographs, exhibits and audiovisual displays. The centrepiece is a massive memorial wall emitting a heartbeat and selected audio recordings. At the end of the journey there's a replica 1944 cafe, underlining the fact that life went on, even in the worst days of the struggle. Captions are in Polish and English. Catch trams 8, 22 or 24 from Al Jerozolimskie, heading west.

Jewish Heritage

The suburbs northwest of the Palace of Culture & Science were once predominantly inhabited by Jewish Poles. During WWII the Nazis established a Jewish ghetto in the area, but razed it to the ground after crushing the Warsaw Ghetto Uprising in April 1943.

The **Warsaw Ghetto Monument** (Map p375; cnr ul Anielewicza & ul Zamenhofa) remembers the Nazis' victims via pictorial plaques. The nearby **Pawiak Prison Museum** (Map p375; ul Dzielna 24/26; admission free; ☾ 10am-4pm Wed-Sun) was a Gestapo prison during the Nazi occupation. Moving exhibits include letters and other personal items.

The most poignant remainder is Europe's largest **Jewish Cemetery** (Map p375; ul Okopowa 49/51; admission 4zł; ☾ 10am-5pm Mon-Thu, 9am-1pm Fri, 9am-4pm Sun). Founded in 1806, it has more than 100,000 gravestones. Visitors must wear a head-covering to enter, and it's accessible from the Old Town on bus 180, heading north from ul Nowy Świat.

The **Jewish Historical Institute** (Map p378; ☎ 022 827 9221; www.jewishinstitute.org.pl; ul Tłomackie 3/5; adult/concession 10/5zł; ☾ 9am-4pm Mon-Wed & Fri, 11am-6pm Thu) has permanent exhibits about the Warsaw Ghetto, as well as local Jewish artworks. Further south is the neo-Romanesque **Nożyk Synagogue** (Map p378; ul Twarda 6; admission 6zł; ☾ 9am-5pm Mon-Fri, 11am-4pm Sun), Warsaw's only synagogue to survive WWII.

FESTIVALS & EVENTS

International Book Fair (www.bookfair.pl) May
Mozart Festival (www.operakameralna.pl) June/July
Warsaw Summer Jazz Days (www.adamiakjazz.pl) July
Art of the Street Festival (www.sztukaulicy.pl) July
Warsaw Autumn International Festival of Contemporary Music (www.warsaw-autumn.art.pl) September
International Frédéric Chopin Piano Competition (www.konkurs.chopin.pl) October five-yearly, next due in 2010
Warsaw Film Festival (www.wff.pl) October

SLEEPING

Not surprisingly, Warsaw is the most expensive Polish city for accommodation, though there's a number of reasonably priced hostels around town. The tourist offices (p377) can help find a room.

Budget

Camping Nr 123 (Map p375; ☎ 022 822 9121; www.astur.waw.pl; ul Bitwy Warszawskiej 1920r 15/17; per person/tent 24/10zł; ☒) Set in extensive grounds near the Dworzec Zachodni bus station. Cabins (90zł) are also available from mid-April to mid-October and there's a tennis court nearby.

Smolna Youth Hostel (Map p378; ☎ 022 827 8952; www.hostelsmolna30.pl; ul Smolna 30; dm 36zł, s/d 65/120zł) Very central and very popular, though there's a midnight curfew (2am in July and August) and reception is closed between 10am and 4pm. It's simple but clean, and there's a lounge and kitchen area. Note that guests are separated into dorms according to gender, and reception is up four flights of stairs.

Hostel Helvetia (Map p378; ☎ 022 826 7108; www.hostel-helvetia.pl; ul Kopernika 36/40; dm 45-65zł, r 150-190zł) Bright hostel with an attractive combined lounge and kitchen. Dorms have lockers available, and there's one small women-only dorm. Bike hire is 25zł per day. Enter from the street behind, ul Sewerynów.

Nathan's Villa Hostel (Map p378; ☎ 022 622 2946; www.nathansvilla.com; ul Piękna 24/26; dm 45-65zł, r 170-180zł, apt 220zł) Nathan's sunlit courtyard leads to well-organised dorms, while private rooms are comfortable and decorated with monochrome photographs of Polish attractions. The kitchen is well set up, and there's a free laundry, a book exchange, and games to while away rainy days.

Hostel Kanonia (Map p378; ☎ 022 635 0676; www.kanonia.pl; ul Jezuicka 2; dm 50zł, r 190-240zł) Housed in a historic building in the heart of the Old Town, accommodation is mostly in dorms, with only one double and one triple. Some rooms have picturesque views onto the cobblestone streets, and there's a dining room with basic kitchen facilities.

Dom Przy Rynku Hostel (Map p378; ☎ 022 831 5033; www.cityhostel.net; Rynek Nowego Miasto 4; dm 55zł; ☾ Jul-Sep) Located in a quiet corner of the busy New Town, Przy Rynku is a neat, clean and friendly hostel occupying a 19th-century house. Its rooms accommodate two to five people, and there's a kitchen and laundry for guest use.

Oki Doki Hostel (Map p378; ☎ 022 826 5112; www.okidoki.pl; Plac Dąbrowskiego 3; dm 55-73zł, s/d 142/220zł) There are no drab dorms here. Each is decorated thematically using the brightest paints available; try the communist (red with a big image of Lenin). Lower bunks have good headroom, and the shared bathrooms are clean and bright. The hostel also has a bar, free washing machine and kitchen, and hires out bikes (25zł per day).

Midrange

Hotel Praski (Map p378; ☎ 022 818 4989; www.praski.pl; Al Solidarności 61; s/d from 150/230zł) The rooms of this inexpensive hotel vary in size, but have attractive high ceilings and comfortable beds. Bathrooms are clean, red carpets add old-fashioned charm, and some rooms have views of Praski Park. It's an easy walk across the river to the Old Town.

Premiere Classe (Map p375; ☎ 022 624 0800; www.campanile.com.pl; ul Towarowa 2; r 189zł) If you're not bothered too much by room size, this modern hotel makes a good base. Rooms are small but bright, and neatly set up with modern furnishings. Friendly staff is a plus. Guests can use the restaurants, bars and fitness centre in the neighbouring sister hotels.

Dom Literatury (Map p378; ☎ 022 828 3920; www.fundacjadl.com/hotele.html, in Polish; ul Krakowskie Przedmieście 87/89; s/d 220/370zł) Within a grand historic building, this accommodation features rambling halls and staircases bedecked with pot plants and sizeable paintings. There is a maze of comfortable rooms, many of which have excellent views of the Old Town and the Vistula. You're paying for the location, however, rather than the standard, and you can't expect too much English from the friendly staff.

our pick **Castle Inn** (Map p378; ☎ 022 425 0100; www.castleinn.pl; ul Świętojańska 2; s 250zł, d from 270zł) Progress up the stairs to the striking purple decor and shiny tiles of this Old Town accommodation, situated in a 17th-century tenement house. All rooms overlook either Castle Sq or St John's Cathedral, and come in a range of playful styles.

Hotel Gromada Centrum (Map p378; ☎ 022 582 9900; www.gromada.pl; Plac Powstańców Warszawy 2; s/d from 320/350zł) Centrally located, the Gromada is a big concrete box but also a great launching pad for exploring the central city. Upstairs from the funky green foyer, the featureless brown-carpeted corridors stretch out into the distance like an optical illusion. The rooms are plain, but clean and spacious.

Hotel Harenda (Map p378; ☎ 022 826 0071; www.hotelharenda.com.pl; ul Krakowskie Przedmieście 4/6; s/d/ste from 320/360/460zł) Boasting a great location just off the Royal Way, the Harenda's rooms are neat and clean, with solid timber furniture. There's an old-fashioned feel to the hotel's interiors, and an expensive antique shop just off the foyer if retail therapy is required. Breakfast is an additional 25zł.

Top End

Sofitel Victoria (Map p378; ☎ 022 657 8011; www.sofitel.com; ul Królewska 11; d/ste from €150/250; 🏊) The very model of a modern business hotel, with a spacious marble foyer, and a lounge area housing a small library of books on Polish culture and history. The rooms are conservatively decorated, with gleaming bathrooms. The cheaper doubles are great value.

Hotel Le Regina (Map p378; ☎ 022 531 6000; www.leregina.com; ul Kościelna 12; d/ste from €180/450; 🏊) It's not cheap, but the Le Regina is a jaw-dropping combination of traditional architecture and contemporary design. The enormous rooms feature king-size beds with headboards of dark, polished wood. Deluxe rooms also have timber floors, and terraces with courtyard views. All rooms sport spectacular bathrooms with marble benchtops.

Hotel Bristol (Map p378; ☎ 022 551 1000; www.warsaw.lemeridien.com; ul Krakowskie Przedmieście 42/44; r from 750zł; 🏊) Established in 1899 and restored to its former glory after a massive renovation, the Bristol is touted as Poland's most luxurious hotel. Its neoclassical exterior houses a feast of original art nouveau features, and huge, traditionally decorated rooms. Attentive staff cater to your every whim.

EATING

The most recent revolution to conquer the Polish capital has been a gastronomic one. A good selection of restaurants can be found in the Old Town and New Town, and in the area between ul Nowy Świat and the Palace of Culture & Science.

Budget

Tukan Salad Bar (Map p378; ☎ 022 531 2520; Plac Bankowy 2; mains from 5zł; ⏰ 8am-8pm Mon-Fri, 10am-6pm Sat) This place has several outlets around the capital offering a wide choice of salads. As the name suggests, look for the toucan on the door. This branch is hidden from the street in the arcade running parallel.

Bar Pod Barbakanem (Map p378; ul Mostowa 27/29; mains 5-8zł; ☀ 8am-5pm Mon-Fri, 9am-5pm Sat & Sun) Near the Barbican, this popular former milk bar that survived the fall of the Iron Curtain continues to serve cheap, unpretentious food in an interior marked by tiles: on the floor, walls and tabletops. Fill up while peering out through the lace curtains at the passing tourist hordes.

our pick **Cô tú** (Map p378; Hadlowo-Usługowe 21; mains 10-14zł; ☀ 10am-9pm Mon-Fri, 11am-7pm Sat & Sun) The wok at this simple Asian diner never rests, as hungry Poles can't get enough of the excellent dishes coming from the kitchen. The menu is enormous, covering seafood, vegetable, beef, chicken and pork, and you'll never have to wait more than 10 minutes for your food despite the queues. Duck through the archway at Nowy Świat 26 to find it.

Green Way (Map p378; ☎ 022 696 9321; ul Hoża 54; mains 10-13zł; ☀ 10am-8pm Mon-Fri, 11am-7pm Sat & Sun) Slicker than the usual outlets of this chain, with a cafe ambience and a good outdoor dining zone. Take your pick of the international menu, which includes goulash, curry, samosas and enchiladas. Portions are hefty, and there's no table service.

Dżonka (Map p378; ☎ 022 621 5015; ul Hoża 54; mains 10-30zł; ☀ 11am-7pm Mon-Fri, 11am-5pm Sat & Sun) This hidden gem serves a range of Asian dishes, covering Chinese, Japanese, Korean and Thai cuisine. Though small (just six tables), it has loads of personality, with dark timber surfaces, bamboo place mats and Japanese newspapers plastering the walls. There's some spicy food on the menu, including Sichuan cuisine, though it's been toned down a little for Polish palates.

Restauracja Pod Samsonem (Map p378; ☎ 022 831 1788; ul Freta 3/5; mains 10-30zł) Situated in the New Town, and frequented by locals looking for inexpensive and tasty meals with a Jewish flavour. Interesting appetisers include Russian pancakes with salmon, and 'Jewish caviar'. Spot the bas relief of Samson and the lion above the next door along from the entrance.

The most convenient places for groceries are the **MarcPol Supermarket** (Map p378; Plac Defilad) in front of the Palace of Culture & Science building, and the **Albert Supermarket** (Map p378; ul Złota 59) in the Złote Tarasy shopping centre behind Warszawa Centralna train station.

Midrange & Top End

Bar Bistro Bez Kantów (Map p378; ☎ 022 892 9800; ul Krakowie Przedmieście 11; mains 15-45zł; ☀ 6am-11pm) Informal, sunlit eatery on the Royal Way, with timber tables beneath sleek wooden panelling. Dishes involve pork, duck, veal and fish. Unusually for a Polish restaurant, it also serves breakfast.

Gospoda Pod Kogutem (Map p378; ☎ 022 635 8282; ul Freta 50; mains 17-40zł) Cosy eatery at the top of the New Town, presenting quality versions of Polish classics in a soothing dark green interior. Eat outside in summer. If you're game, try pig's trotters 'the Polish way'.

Bazyliszek Restauracja (Map p378; ☎ 022 831 1841; Rynek Starego Miasta 1/3; mains 19-40zł) Step beneath the basilisk into this restaurant in a prime spot on the Old Town Market Sq. It serves mainly Polish-style dishes, with forays into foreign cuisine like Argentinian steak.

Zgoda Grill Bar (Map p378; ☎ 022 827 9934; ul Zgoda 4; mains 22-45zł) A bright, informal place serving up a range of tasty Polish standards. There's also a decent salad bar available.

Podwale Piwna Kompania (Map p378; ☎ 022 635 6314; ul Podwale 25; mains 21-49zł; ☀ 11am-1am Mon-Sat, noon-1am Sun) The restaurant's name (The Company of Beer) gives you an idea of the lively atmosphere in this eatery just outside the Old Town's moat. The menu features lots of grilled items and dishes such as roast duck, Wiener schnitzel, pork ribs and steak. There's a courtyard for outdoor dining.

Tam Tam (Map p378; ☎ 022 828 2622; ul Foksal 18; mains 25-39zł) Housed in a colourful 'African-style' place with outdoor seating in the warmer months. The varied menu includes pasta, soups and salads, and a big list of teas and coffees. Pull up a bongo drum as a seat, and tuck in.

London Steakhouse (Map p378; ☎ 022 827 0020; Al Jerozolimskie 42; mains 28-78zł) You'll find it hard to convince yourself you're in London, but it's fun to spot the UK memorabilia among the cluttered decor, while being served by waitresses wearing Union Jack neckties and miniskirts. Steaks dominate the menu, which also includes fish and chips. A full English breakfast is served daily until 2pm.

Taqueria Mexicana (Map p378; ☎ 022 556 4720; ul Zgoda 5; mains 29-52zł) Brightly-hued place festooned with Mexican rugs, featuring a central bar. Varieties of tacos, enchiladas and fajitas adorn the menu, and there's a 22zł set lunch.

POLAND

Restauracja Przy Zamku (Map p378; ☎ 022 831 0259; Plac Zamkowy 15; mains 38-85zł) An attractive, old-world kind of place with hunting trophies on the walls and attentive, white-aproned waiters. The top-notch Polish menu includes fish and game and a bewildering array of entrées – try the excellent hare pâté served with cranberry sauce.

DRINKING

our pick Sense (Map p378; ul Nowy Świat 19; ☒ noon-late) A very modern venue with a mellow atmosphere. Comfortable banquettes sit beneath strings of cube-shaped lights, and there's an extensive wine and cocktail list, with some drinks measured in a 'Palace of Culture' (a tall scientific beaker). Try the house speciality, ginger rose vodka. There's also an impressive food menu if you're hungry.

Paparazzi (Map p378; ul Mazowiecka 12) This is one of Warsaw's flashest venues, where you can sip a bewildering array of cocktails under blown-up photos of Hollywood stars. It's big and roomy, with comfortable seating around the central bar.

Między Nami (Map p378; ul Bracka 20) A mix of bar, restaurant and cafe, 'Between You & Me' attracts a trendy set with its designer furniture, whitewashed walls, and excellent vegetarian menu. There's no sign over the door; look for the white awnings and chilled crowd.

ENTERTAINMENT
Nightclubs

There's no shortage of good clubs in Warsaw. Explore ul Mazowiecka, ul Sienkiewicza and the area around ul Nowy Świat for more nightclub action.

Enklawa (Map p378; www.enklawa.com, in Polish; ul Mazowiecka 12; ☒ 9pm-4am Tue-Sat) Funky red-and-orange space with comfy plush seating, mirrored ceilings, two bars and plenty of room to dance. Check out the long drinks list, hit the dance floor or observe the action from a stool on the upper balcony. Wednesday night is 'old school' night, with music from the '70s to '90s.

Foksal 19 (Map p378; ul Foksal 19; ☒ bar 5pm-1am Mon-Thu, 5pm-3am Fri & Sat, nightclub 11pm-5am Fri & Sat) Ultramodern playpen for Warsaw's bright young things. Downstairs is a cool drinking zone with a backlit bar, subdued golden lighting and comfy couches. Upstairs is the nightclub – a blue-lit contemporary space with DJs playing a variety of sounds.

Underground Music Café (Map p378; www.under .pl, in Polish; ul Marszałkowska 126/134) A swarm of students and backpackers pour into this basement club for its cheap beer, dark lighting and selection of music that varies from '70s and '80s to house, R&B and hip hop. Enter via the below-ground staircase facing McDonald's.

Tygmont (Map p378; ☎ 022 828 3409; www.tygmont .com.pl; ul Mazowiecka 6/8; ☒ 6pm-late) Hosting both local and international acts, the live jazz here is both varied and plentiful. Concerts start around 8pm but the place fills up early, so either reserve a table or turn up at opening time. Dinner is also available.

Free jazz concerts also take place in the Old Town's Rynek Starego Miasta on Saturday at 7pm in July and August.

Performing Arts

Advance tickets for most theatrical events can be bought at **ZASP Kasy Teatralne** (Map p378; ☎ 022 621 9454; Al Jerozolimskie 25; ☒ 9am-7pm Mon-Fri) or **EMPiK** Galeria Centrum (Map p378; ul Marszałkowska 116/122); Royal Way (Map p378; ul Nowy Świat 15/17) in the city centre.

Teatr Ateneum (Map p378; ☎ 022 625 7330; www .teatrateneum.pl, in Polish; ul Jaracza 2) This place leans towards contemporary Polish-language productions.

Teatr Wielki (Map p378; ☎ 022 692 0200; www.teatr wielki.pl; Plac Teatralny 1) The Grand Theatre hosts opera and ballet in its aptly grand premises.

Filharmonia Narodowa (Map p378; ☎ 022 551 7111; www.filharmonia.pl; ul Jasna 5) Classical-music concerts are held here.

Cinemas

To avoid watching Polish TV in your hotel room, catch a film at the central **Kino Atlantic** (Map p378; ul Chmielna 33) or enjoy a flick in socialist-era glory at **Kinoteka** (Map p378; Plac Defilad 1) within the Palace of Culture & Science.

SHOPPING

Galeria Centrum (Map p378; ul Marszałowska 104/122) is a sprawling modern shopping mall in the city centre.

There are also plentiful antique, arts and crafts shops around Rynek Starego Miasta in the Old Town, so brandish your credit card and explore. One of the most interesting is **Lapidarium** (Map p378; ☎ 022 635 6828; www.lapidarium .pl; ul Nowomiejska 15/7), which offers jewellery and communist-era collectibles.

GETTING THERE & AWAY
Air
The **Warsaw Frédéric Chopin airport** (Map p375; www.lotnisko-chopina.pl) is more commonly called Okęcie airport. The separate Etiuda terminal mostly handles discount airline departures.

The useful tourist office (p377) is on the arrivals level of Terminal 2.

At the arrivals level there are ATMs and several *kantors*. There are also car-rental companies, a left-luggage room and a newsagent where you can buy public transport tickets.

Domestic and international flights can be booked at the **LOT office** (Map p378; ☎ 0801 703 703; Al Jerozolimskie 65/79), or at any travel agency. Other airlines are listed on p446.

Bus
Warsaw has two major bus terminals for PKS buses. **Dworzec Zachodnia** (Western Bus Station; Map p375; Al Jerozolimskie 144) handles domestic buses heading south, north and west of the capital, including up to nine daily to Częstochowa (41zł, four hours), 10 to Gdańsk (50zł, six hours), nine to Kraków (43zł, six hours), 11 to Olsztyn (30zł, five hours), five to Toruń (37zł, four hours), four to Wrocław (51zł, seven hours), and five to Zakopane (57zł, eight hours). This complex is southwest of the city centre and adjoins the Warszawa Zachodnia train station. Take the commuter train that leaves from Warszawa Śródmieście station.

Dworzec Stadion (Stadium Bus Station; Map p375; ul Sokola 1) adjoins the Warszawa Stadion train station. It is also easily accessible by commuter train from Warszawa Śródmieście. Dworzec Stadion handles some domestic buses to the east and southeast, including 20 daily to Lublin (26zł, three hours), four to Białystok (30zł, 3½ hours) and three to Zamość (35zł, 4¾ hours).

Polski Express (Map p378) operates coaches from the airport, but passengers can also get on or off and buy tickets at the kiosk along Al Jana Pawła II, next to the Warszawa Centralna train station. Useful Polski Express services include those to Lublin (31zł, 3½ hours, five daily), Szczecin (63zł, 9½ hours, two daily) and Toruń (41zł, 3½ hours, eight daily).

International buses depart from and arrive at Dworzec Zachodnia or, occasionally, outside Warszawa Centralna. Tickets are available from the bus offices at Dworzec Zachodnia, from agencies at Warszawa Centralna or from any of the major travel agencies in the city, including Almatur (p377). **Eurolines Polska** (www .eurolinespolska.pl) operates a huge number of buses to destinations throughout Eastern and Western Europe; some sample routes include Amsterdam (20 hours, daily), Cologne (20½ hours, daily), London (27 hours, four weekly), Paris (24 hours, daily), Rome (28 hours, four weekly) and Vienna (13 hours, five weekly).

Train
Warsaw has several train stations, but the one that most travellers will use is **Warszawa Centralna** (Warsaw Central; Map p378; Al Jerozolimskie 54). Refer to the relevant destination sections in this chapter for information about services to/from Warsaw.

Warszawa Centralna is not always where trains start or finish, so make sure you get on or off promptly; and guard your belongings against pickpocketing and theft at all times.

The station's main hall houses ticket counters, ATMs and snack bars, as well as a post office, newsagents and a tourist office. Along the underground mezzanine level leading to the platforms are a dozen *kantors* (one of which is open 24 hours), a **left-luggage office** (⏰ 7am-midnight), lockers, eateries, outlets for local public transport tickets, internet cafes and bookshops.

Tickets for domestic and international trains are available from counters at the station (but allow at least an hour for possible queuing) or, in advance, from any major Orbis Travel office (p377). Tickets for immediate departures on domestic and international trains are also available from numerous, well-signed booths in the underpasses leading to Warszawa Centralna.

Some domestic trains also stop at Warszawa Śródmieście station, 300m east of Warszawa Centralna, and Warszawa Zachodnia, next to Dworzec Zachodnia bus station.

GETTING AROUND
To/From the Airport
The cheapest way of getting from the airport to the city centre is bus 175, which leaves every 10 to 15 minutes for the Old Town, via ul Nowy Świat and Warszawa Centralna train station. If you arrive in the wee hours, night bus N32 links the airport with Warszawa Centralna every 30 minutes.

The taxi fare between the airport and the city centre is from 35zł to 40zł. Official taxis displaying a name, telephone number and fares can be arranged at the official taxi counters at the international arrivals level.

Car

Warsaw traffic isn't fun, but there are good reasons to hire a car for jaunts into the countryside. Major car-rental companies are listed in the local English-language publications, and include **Avis** (☎ 022 650 4872; www.avis.pl), **Hertz** (☎ 022 500 1620; www.hertz.com.pl) and **Sixt** (☎ 022 511 1550; www.sixt.pl). For more details about car hire see p448.

Public Transport

Warsaw's public transport operates from 5am to 11pm daily. The fare (2.80zł) is valid for one ride only on a bus, tram, trolleybus or metro train travelling anywhere in the city.

Warsaw is the only place in Poland where ISIC cards get a public-transport discount (of 48%).

Tickets are available for 60/90 minutes (4/6zł), one day (9zł), three days (16zł), one week (32zł) and one month (78zł). Buy tickets from kiosks (including those marked 'RUCH') before boarding, and validate them on board.

A metro line operates from the Ursynów suburb (Kabaty) at the southern city limits to Słodowiec in the north, via the city centre (Centrum), but is of limited use to visitors. Local commuter trains head out to the suburbs from the Warszawa Śródmieście station.

Taxi

Taxis are a quick and easy way to get around – as long as you use official taxis and drivers use their meters. Beware of unauthorised 'Mafia' taxis parked in front of top-end hotels, at the airport, outside Warszawa Centralna train station and in the vicinity of most tourist sights.

MAZOVIA & PODLASIE

After being ruled as an independent state by a succession of dukes, Mazovia shot to prominence during the 16th century, when Warsaw became the national capital. The region has long been a base for industry, the traditional mainstay of Poland's second largest city, Łódź. To the east of Mazovia, toward the Belarus border, lies Podlasie, which means 'land close to the forest'. The main attraction of this region is the impressive Białowieża National Park.

ŁÓDŹ
pop 767,000

Little damaged in WWII, Łódź (pronounced woodge) is a lively, likeable place with a wealth of attractive art nouveau architecture, and the added bonus of being off the usual tourist track. It's also an easy day trip from Warsaw. Łódź became a major industrial centre in the 19th century, attracting immigrants from across Europe. Though its textile industry slumped in the post-communist years, the centrally-located city has had some success in attracting new investment in more diverse commercial fields.

Many of the attractions are along ul Piotrkowska, the main thoroughfare. You'll find banks and *kantors* here, and on ul Kopernika, one street west. You can't miss the bronze statues of local celebrities along ul Piotrkowska, including pianist Artur Rubenstein, seated at a baby grand. The helpful **tourist office** (☎ 042 638 5955; www.cityoflodz.pl; ul Piotrkowska 87; ⊙ 8am-7pm Mon-Fri, 9am-3pm Sat May-Oct, 8am-6pm Mon-Fri, 9am-2pm Sat Nov-Apr) hands out free tourist brochures.

As Łódź is famous for being the centre of Poland's cinema industry (giving rise to the nickname 'Holly-Woodge'), film buffs will find some attractions of interest here. Along ul Piotrkowska near the Grand Hotel, you can see **star-shaped plaques** honouring Polish stars and directors such as Roman Polański, and the **Cinematography Museum** (www.kinomuzeum.pl; Plac Zwycięstwa 1; adult/concession 5/3zł; ⊙ 9am-4pm Wed & Fri-Sun, 11am-5pm Tue & Thu) three blocks east of ul Piotrkowska's southern pedestrian zone is worth a look both for its collection of old cinema gear and its mansion setting.

The **Historical Museum of Łódź** (ul Ogrodowa 15; adult/concession 7/4zł, free Sun; ⊙ 10am-2pm Mon, 10am-4pm Tue & Thu, 2-6pm Wed, 10am-2pm Sat & Sun) is 200m northwest of Plac Wolności, at the northern end of the main drag. Close by is the fascinating **Manufaktura** (www.manufaktura.com; ul Karskiego 5), a shopping mall and entertainment centre constructed within a massive complex of historic red-brick factory buildings. **Dętka** (Plac Wolności 2; adult/concession 4/2zł; ⊙ noon-8pm Wed, Sat & Sun, Jun-Sep) is a new attraction operated by the Historical Museum, which features guided tours every half-hour through the old brick sewer system beneath the city's streets, with exhibits en route.

Herbst Palace (ul Przędalniana 72; adult/concession 7/4.50zł, free Thu; ⊙ 10am-5pm Tue, noon-5pm Wed & Fri, noon-7pm Thu, 11am-4pm Sat & Sun) has been converted into an appealing museum. It's accessible by bus 55 heading east from the cathedral at the southern end of ul Piotrkowska. The **Jewish Cemetery** (www.jewishlodzcemetery.org; ul Bracka 40; admission 4zł, free first Sun of month; 🕑 9am-5pm Sun-Thu, 9am-3pm Fri Apr-Oct, 9am-3pm Sun-Fri Nov-Mar) is one of the largest in Europe. It's 3km northeast of the city centre and accessible by tram 1 or 6 from near Plac Wolności. Enter from ul Zmienna.

The tourist office can provide information about all kinds of accommodation. The **youth hostel** (🕾 042 630 6680; www.yhlodz.pl; ul Legionów 27; dm 18-30zł, s/d/tr 45/71/120zł) is excellent, so book ahead. It features nicely decorated rooms in a spacious old building, with free laundry and a kitchen. It's 250m west of Plac Wolności.

The **Hotel Savoy** (🕾 042 632 9360; www.hotelsavoy .com.pl; ul Traugutta 6; s/d from 119/249zł) is well positioned just off central ul Piotrkowska. Don't be put off by the scuffed corridors and stencilled door numbers: they conceal spacious, light-filled rooms with clean bathrooms.

Around the corner, the **Grand Hotel** (🕾 042 633 9920; www.orbis.pl; ul Piotrkowska 72; s/d from 289/339zł) offers a touch of faded, if overpriced, fin de siècle grandeur.

Opposite the Grand, **Chłopska Izba** (🕾 042 630 8087; ul Piotrkowska 65; mains 15-39zł; 🕑 noon-11pm) is a restaurant with folksy decor, serving up tasty versions of all the Polish standards. **Esplanada** (🕾 042 630 5989; ul Piotrkowska 100; mains 19-39zł) is an excellent belle époque–style eatery serving quality Polish cuisine in a colourful venue.

From the **airport** (www.airport.lodz.pl), which can be reached by city buses 55, 65 and L (2.40zł, 20 minutes), there are flights via Ryanair to several British and Irish destinations, including London (at least daily) and Dublin (three weekly). Jet Air connects to other European cities, including Vienna (twice daily). The only domestic flights are twice-daily Jet Air services to Bydgoszcz, from where you can connect to other Polish and international cities.

From the convenient Łódź Fabryczna station, 400m east of the city centre, you can travel to Warsaw (31zł, 1½ hours, 15 daily) and Częstochowa (33zł, 2½ hours, three daily). From the Łódź Kaliska train station, 1.2km southwest of central Łódź, trains go to Warsaw (33zł, two hours, three daily), Wrocław (43zł, four hours, three daily), Poznań (43zł, 4½ hours, seven daily), Częstochowa (33zł, two hours, six daily), Toruń (34zł, three hours,

10 daily) and Gdańsk (51zł, seven hours, five daily). Buses head in all directions from the bus terminal, next to the Fabryczna train station.

BIAŁOWIEŻA NATIONAL PARK

Once a centre for hunting and timber-felling, Białowieża (Byah-wo-*vyeh*-zhah) is now Poland's oldest national park. Its significance is underlined by Unesco's unusual recognition of the reserve as both a Biosphere Reserve *and* a World Heritage site. The forest contains over 100 species of birds, along with elk, wild boars and wolves. Its major drawcard is the magnificent European bison, which was once extinct outside zoos, but has been successfully reintroduced to its ancient home.

The logical visitor base is the charming village of **Białowieża**. The main road to Białowieża from Hajnówka leads to the southern end of Palace Park (the former location of the Russian tsar's hunting lodge), then skirts around the park to become the village's main street, ul Waszkiewicza. At the western end of this street is the **post office** (🕑 7am-7pm Mon-Fri, 7am-2pm Sat).

Money can be changed at the Hotel Żubrówka; the hotel also has an ATM by the entrance and offers public internet access in its foyer.

You'll find the **PTTK** (Polskie Towarzystwo Turystyczno-Krajoznawcze, Polish Tourist Country Lovers Society; 🕾 085 681 2295; www.pttk.bialowieza.pl; ul Kolejowa 17; 🕑 8am-4pm) at the southern end of Palace Park. Serious hikers should contact the **National Park office** (🕾 085 682 9700; www.bpn .com.pl, in Polish; 🕑 9am-4pm) inside Palace Park. Most maps of the national park (especially the one published by PTOP – Północnopodlaskie Towarzystwo Ochrony Ptaków, North Podlasian Bird Protection Society) – detail several enticing hiking trails.

Sights & Activities

The elegant **Palace Park** (admission free; 🕑 daylight hr) is only accessible on foot, bicycle or horse-drawn cart across the bridge from the PTTK office. Over the river is the excellent **Natural & Forestry Museum** (adult/concession 12/6zł; 🕑 9am-4.30pm Apr-Sep, 9am-4pm Tue-Sun Oct-Mar), with displays on local flora and fauna, and beekeeping.

The **European Bison Reserve** (Rezerwat Żubrów; adult/concession 6/3zł; 🕑 9am-5pm May-Sep, 8am-4pm Tue-Sun Oct-Apr) is an open-plan zoo containing many of these mighty beasts, as well as

POLAND

wolves, strange horse-like tarpans and mammoth żubroń (hybrids of bison and cows). Entrance to the reserve is just north of the Hajnówka–Białowieża road, about 4.5km west of the PTTK office – look for the signs along the *żebra żubra* (bison's rib) trail, or follow the green or yellow marked trails. Alternatively, catch a local bus to the stop at the main road turn-off (3zł) and walk a kilometre to the entrance, but ask the driver first if the bus is taking a route past the reserve.

The main attraction is the **Strict Nature Reserve** (adult/concession 6/3zł; ☺ 9am-5pm), which starts about 1km north of Palace Park. It can only be visited on a three-hour tour with a licensed guide along an 8km trail (165zł for an English- or German-speaking guide). Licensed guides (in many languages) can be arranged at the PTTK office or any travel agency in the village. Note that the reserve does close sometimes due to inclement weather.

A comfortable way to visit the nature reserve is by horse-drawn cart, which costs 160zł in addition to guide and entry fees (three hours) and holds four people. Otherwise, it may be possible (with permission from the PTTK office) to visit the reserve by bicycle (with a guide). The Dom Turysty PTTK hires out bikes (25zł per day), as do several other hotels and pensions.

Sleeping & Eating
There are plenty of homes along the road from Hajnówka offering private rooms for about 40/70zł for singles/doubles.

Paprotka Youth Hostel (☎ 085 681 2560; www .paprotka.com.pl; ul Waszkiewicza 6; dm from 19zł, s/d 30/50zł) One of the best in the region. The rooms are light and spruce, with high ceilings and potted plants; the newly renovated bathrooms are clean, and the kitchen is excellent. There's a washing machine as well.

Dom Turysty PTTK (☎ 085 681 2505; dm from 25zł, d/tr/q from 80/105/128zł) Inexpensive accommodation inside Palace Park. It's seen better days, but the position and rates are hard to beat. It has a pleasant restaurant with a bison-head motif.

Pension Gawra (☎ 085 681 2804; www.gawra.bialow ieza.com; ul Polecha 2; d/tr from 60/90zł) A quiet, homely place with large rooms lined with timber in a hunting lodge–style, overlooking a pretty garden just behind the Hotel Żubrówka. The doubles with bathrooms are much more spacious than those without.

Pensjonacik Unikat (☎ 085 681 2774; www.unikat.bi alowieza.com; ul Waszkiewicza 39; s/d/tr/q 90/100/120/140zł) A bit too fond of dead creatures' hides as decor, but good value with its tidy woodpanelled rooms, one of which is designed for disabled access. The restaurant offers specialities such as Belarus-style potato pancakes, and has a menu in both German and English.

Hotel Żubrówka (☎ 085 681 2303; www.hotel -zubrowka.pl; ul Olgi Gabiec 6; s/d/ste from 340/380/500zł) Just across the way from the PTTK office, this is the town's best hotel. It's eccentrically decorated with animal hides, a working miniature water wheel, and pseudo cave drawings along the corridors. Rooms are predictably clean and comfortable, and there's a cafe, restaurant and nightclub on the premises.

Getting There & Away
From Warsaw, take the express train from Warszawa Centralna to Siedlce (1½ hours), wait for a connection on the slow train to Hajnówka (two hours), and then catch one of the nine daily PKS bus services to Białowieża (5zł, one hour). Two private companies, Oktobus and Lob-Trans, also run fairly squeezy minibuses between Hajnówka and Białowieża (5zł, one hour, 10 daily). For the latest timetable information, check out www .turystyka.hajnowka.pl, in Polish.

Four buses a day travel from the Dworzec Stadion station in Warsaw to Białystok (30zł, 3½ hours), from where two buses travel to Białowieża, at 6.30am and 3.10pm (15zł, 2½ hours). You may need to stay overnight in Białystok to catch these connecting services.

MAŁOPOLSKA

Małopolska (literally 'lesser Poland') is a stunning area, within which the visitor can spot plentiful remnants of traditional life amid green farmland and historic cities. The region covers a large swathe of southeastern Poland, from the former royal capital, Kraków, to the eastern Lublin Uplands.

KRAKÓW
pop 756,000
While many Polish cities are centred on an attractive Old Town, none can compare with Kraków for sheer, effortless beauty. With a charming origin involving the legendary defeat of a dragon by either Prince Krakus or a cobbler's apprentice (depending on which

story you believe), and with a miraculous escape from destruction in WWII, the city seems to have led a lucky existence.

As a result, Kraków is blessed with magnificent buildings and streets dating back to medieval times, and a stunning historic centrepiece, Wawel Castle.

Just south of the castle lies Kazimierz, the former Jewish quarter, reflecting both new and old. Its silent synagogues are a reminder of the tragedy of WWII, while the district's tiny streets and low-rise architecture have become home in recent years to a lively nightlife scene.

Not that you'll have trouble finding nightlife anywhere in Kraków, or a place to sleep. As the nation's biggest tourist drawcard, the city has hundreds of restaurants, bars and other venues tucked away in its laneways and cellars. Though hotel prices are above the national average, and visitor numbers high in summer, this vibrant, cosmopolitan city is an essential part of any tour of Poland.

Information
BOOKSHOPS
EMPiK (Map p390; Rynek Główny 5; 🕙 9am-10pm) Sells foreign newspapers, magazines, novels and maps.

Jarden Jewish Bookshop (Map p392; ul Szeroka 2) Located in Kazimierz.

Księgarnia Hetmańska (Map p390; Rynek Główny 17) An impressive selection of English-language books, including nonfiction on Polish history and culture.

Sklep Podróżnika (Map p390; ul Jagiellońska 6; 🕙 11am-7pm Mon-Fri, 10am-3pm Sat) The Traveller's Shop sells a wide selection of regional and city maps, as well as Lonely Planet titles.

DISCOUNT CARDS
Kraków Tourist Card (www.krakowcard.com; 2/3 days 50/65zł) Available from tourist offices, the card includes travel on public transport and entry to many museums.

INTERNET ACCESS
Greenland Internet Café (Map p390; ul Floriańska 30; per hr 4zł; 🕙 9am-midnight)

Klub Garinet (Map p390; ul Floriańska 18; per hr 4zł; 🕙 9am-midnight)

MONEY
Kantors and ATMs can be found all over the city centre. It's worth noting, however, that many *kantors* close on Sunday, and some located near Rynek Główny and the main train station offer terrible exchange rates –

check around before proffering your cash. There are also exchange facilities at the airport, with even less attractive rates.

Bank Pekao (Map p390; Rynek Główny 32) Centrally located financial institution.

POST
Main post office (Map p390; ul Westerplatte 20; 🕙 7.30am-8.30pm Mon-Fri, 8am-2pm Sat)

TOURIST INFORMATION
Two free magazines, *Welcome to Cracow & Małopolska* and *Visitor: Kraków & Zakopane* are available at upmarket hotels. The *Kraków in Your Pocket* booklet (5zł) is also very useful, packed with entertaining reviews of local sights and eateries.

Tourist office ul Św. Jana (Map p390; ☎ 012 421 7787; www.karnet.krakow.pl; ul Św. Jana 2; 🕙 10am-6pm Mon-Sat); town hall tower (Map p390; ☎ 012 433 7310; Rynek Główny 1; 🕙 9am-7pm Apr-Sep, 9am-5pm Oct-Mar); train station area (Map p390; ☎ 012 432 0110; ul Szpitalna 25; 🕙 9am-7pm May-Oct, 9am-5pm Nov-Apr); Kazimierz (Map p392; ☎ 012 422 0471; ul Józefa 7; 🕙 10am-6pm May-Sep, 11am-5pm Oct-Apr) Several helpful branches.

Małopolska tourism information centre (Map p390; ☎ 012 421 7706; www.mcit.pl; Rynek Główny 1/3; 🕙 9am-8pm May-Sep, 9am-5pm Oct-Apr) Helpful privately run tourist office centrally located in the Cloth Hall.

Sights & Activities
WAWEL HILL
Kraków's main draw for tourists is **Wawel Hill** (Map p390; grounds admission free; 🕙 6am-dusk). South of the Old Town, the hill is crowned with a castle and cathedral, both of which are enduring symbols of Poland.

You can choose from several attractions within the castle, each requiring a separate ticket, valid for a specific time. There's a limited daily quota of tickets for some parts, so arrive early if you want to see everything.

Within the magnificent **Wawel Castle** (Map p390; ☎ 012 422 5155; www.wawel.krakow.pl) are the **State Rooms** (adult/concession 15/8zł; free Mon Apr-Oct, free Sun Nov-Mar; 🕙 9.30am-1pm Mon, 9.30am-5pm Tue-Fri, 11am-6pm Sat & Sun Apr-Oct, 9.30am-4pm Tue-Sat Nov-Mar) and the **Royal Private Apartments** (adult/concession 20/15zł; 🕙 9.30am-5pm Tue-Fri, 11am-6pm Sat & Sun Apr-Oct, 9.30am-4pm Tue-Sat Nov-Mar). Entry to the latter is only allowed on a guided tour; you may have to accompany a Polish language tour if it's the only one remaining for the day. If you want to hire a guide who speaks English,

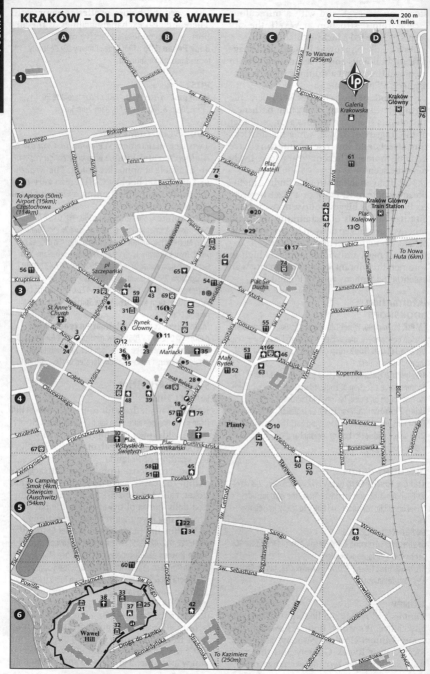

KRAKÓW – OLD TOWN & WAWEL

French or German, contact the onsite **guides office** (☎ 012 422 1697).

The 14th-century **Wawel Cathedral** (Map p390; adult/concession 10/5zł; 🕑 9am-5pm Mon-Sat, 12.15-5pm Sun) was the coronation and burial place of Polish royalty for four centuries, and houses **Royal Tombs**, including that of King Kazimierz Wielki. The **bell tower** of the golden-domed **Sigismund Chapel** (1539) contains the country's largest bell (11 tonnes).

Ecclesiastical artefacts are displayed in the small **Cathedral Museum** (Map p390; adult/concession 5/2zł; 🕑 10am-3pm Tue-Sun).

Other attractions include the **Museum of Oriental Art** (adult/concession 7/4zł; 🕑 9.30am-5pm Tue-Fri, 11am-6pm Sat & Sun Apr-Oct, 9.30am-4pm Tue-Sat Nov-Mar); the **Crown Treasury & Armoury** (adult/concession 15/8zł, free Mon; 🕑 9.30am-5pm Tue-Fri, 11am-6pm Sat & Sun Apr-Oct, 9.30am-4pm Tue-Sun Nov-Mar); the **Lost Wawel** (adult/concession 7/4zł, free Mon Apr-Oct, free Sun Nov-Mar; 🕑 9.30am-1pm Mon, 9.30am-5pm Tue-Fri, 11am-6pm Sat & Sun Apr-Oct, 9.30am-4pm Tue-Sat Nov-Mar), a well-displayed set of intriguing archaeological exhibits; and the atmospheric **Dragon's Cave** (Map p390; admission 3zł; 🕑 10am-5pm Apr-Oct). Go here last, as the exit leads out onto the riverbank.

OLD TOWN

The focus of the Old Town is **Rynek Główny** (Main Market Sq), Europe's largest medieval town square (200m by 200m). At its centre is the 16th-century Renaissance **Cloth Hall** (Sukiennice; Map p390), housing a large souvenir market. The upstairs **Gallery of 19th-Century Polish Painting** is closed for a renovation expected to take several years; if you're keen to see its works, you can catch a minibus from ul Starowiślna near the post office to its **temporary exhibition** (ul Zamkowa 2, Niepołomice; adult/concession 8/5zł; 🕑 10am-6pm) outside Kraków at the Royal Castle in Niepołomice.

The 14th-century **St Mary's Church** (Map p390; Rynek Główny 4; adult/concession 6/4zł; 🕑 11.30am-6pm Mon-Sat, 2-6pm Sun) fills the northeastern corner of the square. The huge main altarpiece by Wit Stwosz (Veit Stoss in German) of Nuremberg is the finest Gothic sculpture in Poland, and is opened ceremoniously each day at 11.50am. Every hour a *hejnał* (bugle call) is played from the highest tower of the church. The melody, played in medieval times as a warning call, breaks off abruptly to symbolise the moment when, according to legend, the throat of a 13th-century trumpeter was pierced by a Tatar arrow. Between May and August you can climb the **tower** (adult/concession 5/3zł).

Just south of St Mary's, the **English Language Club** (ul Sienna 5; admission 1.50zł; 6-8pm Wed) has met weekly since the dying days of communism, when local students wanted to make contact with foreign visitors. Their meetings are a fun way to meet a mixed bunch of Poles, expats and tourists in a relaxed setting.

West of the Cloth Hall is the 15th-century **town hall tower** (Map p390; adult/concession 6/4zł; 10.30am-6pm May-Oct), which you can climb. A little further west is the **Collegium Maius** (p390; ul Jagiellońska 15; adult/concession 12/6zł, Sat 6zł; 10am-2.20pm Mon-Fri, 10am-1.20pm Sat), the oldest surviving university building in Poland. Guided tours of its fascinating academic collection run half-hourly and there's usually a couple in English, at 11am and 1pm. Even if you don't go on a tour, step into the magnificent arcaded courtyard for a glimpse of the beautiful architecture.

On the northwest corner of the Rynek, the **Historical Museum of Kraków** (Map p390; www.mhk.pl; Rynek Główny 35; adult/concession 8/6zł, free Sat; 10am-5.30pm Wed-Sun May-Oct, 9am-4pm Wed & Fri-Sun, 10am-

5pm Thu Nov-Apr) has paintings, documents and oddments relating to the city.

From St Mary's Church, walk up (northeast) ul Floriańska to the 14th-century **Florian Gate**. This is a tourism hotspot, with crowds, buskers, and artists selling their work along the remnant section of the old city walls. Beyond it is the **Barbican** (Map p390; adult/concession 6/4zł; 10.30am-6pm Apr-Oct), a defensive bastion built in 1498. Nearby, the **Czartoryski Museum** (Map p390; ul Św Jana 19; adult/concession 10/5zł, free Sun May-Oct, free Thu Nov-Apr; 10am-6pm Tue-Sat, 10am-4pm Sun May-Oct, 10am-3.30pm Tue-Sun Nov-Apr) features an impressive collection of European art, including Leonardo da Vinci's *Lady with an Ermine*. Also on display are Turkish weapons and artefacts, including a campaign tent from the 1683 Battle of Vienna.

South of Rynek Główny, Plac Wszystkich Świętych is dominated by two 13th-century monastic churches: the **Dominican Church** (Map p390; ul Stolarska 12; admission free; 9am-6pm) to the east and the **Franciscan Church** (Map p390; Plac Wszystkich Świętych 5; admission free; 9am-5pm) to the west. The latter is noted for its stained-glass windows.

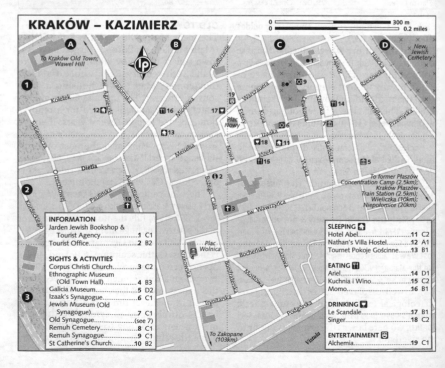

KRAKÓW – KAZIMIERZ

300 m
0.2 miles

To Kraków Old Town;
Wawel Hill

New Jewish Cemetery

To former Płaszów Concentration Camp (2.5km);
Kraków Płaszów Train Station (2.5km);
Wieliczka (10km);
Niepołomice (20km)

To Zakopane (103km)

INFORMATION
Jarden Jewish Bookshop &
   Tourist Agency.................................1 C1
Tourist Office......................................2 B2

SIGHTS & ACTIVITIES
Corpus Christi Church.......................3 C2
Ethnographic Museum
   (Old Town Hall)..............................4 B3
Galicia Museum..................................5 D2
Izaak's Synagogue.............................6 C1
Jewish Museum (Old
   Synagogue)...................................7 C1
Old Synagogue.............................(see 7)
Remuh Cemetery................................8 C1
Remuh Synagogue.............................9 C1
St Catherine's Church.......................10 B2

SLEEPING
Hotel Abel.......................................11 C2
Nathan's Villa Hostel.......................12 A1
Tournet Pokoje Gościnne.................13 B1

EATING
Ariel..14 D1
Kuchnia i Wino................................15 C2
Momo..16 B1

DRINKING
Le Scandale.....................................17 B1
Singer...18 C2

ENTERTAINMENT
Alchemia...19 C1

FREE THRILLS

If you're short of cash, take advantage of these *gratis* Kraków attractions:

■ Visit the beautiful courtyard of the **Collegium Maius** (opposite).

■ Soak up the heady historical atmosphere of the grounds of **Wawel Castle** (p389).

■ Examine the intriguing collection of the **Czartoryski Museum** (opposite) for free on certain weekdays.

■ Catch the historic *hejnał* (bugle call) being played from the tower of **St Mary's Church** (p391) each hour.

■ Take a walk from the bus 134 terminus through the Las Wolski woods to the monumental **Piłsudski Mound**.

To the south, you'll find the **Archaeological Museum** (Map p390; ul Poselska 3; adult/concession 7/5zł, free Sun; 9am-2pm Mon-Wed, 2-6pm Thu, 10am-2pm Fri & Sun), with displays on local prehistory and ancient Egyptian artefacts, including animal mummies.

Continuing south along ul Grodzka is the early 17th-century Jesuit **Church of SS Peter & Paul** (Map p390; ul Grodzka 64; dawn-dusk), Poland's first baroque church. The Romanesque 11th-century **St Andrew's Church** (Map p390; ul Grodzka 56; 9am-6pm Mon-Fri) was the only building in Kraków to withstand the Tatars' attack of 1241.

KAZIMIERZ

Founded by King Kazimierz the Great in 1335, Kazimierz was originally an independent town. In the 15th century, Jews were expelled from Kraków and forced to resettle in a small prescribed area in Kazimierz, separated by a wall. The Jewish quarter later became home to Jews fleeing persecution from throughout Europe.

By the outbreak of WWII there were 65,000 Jewish Poles in Kraków (around 30% of the city's population), and most lived in Kazimierz. During the war the Nazis relocated Jews to a walled ghetto in Podgórze, just south of the Vistula River. They were exterminated in the nearby **Płaszów Concentration Camp**, as portrayed in Steven Spielberg's haunting film *Schindler's List*.

Kazimierz's western Catholic quarter includes the 14th-century Gothic **St Catherine's Church** (Map p392; ul Augustian 7; admission free; only during services), with an imposing 17th-century gilded high altar, while the 14th-century **Corpus Christi Church** (Map p392; ul Bożego Ciała 26; admission free; 9am-7pm Mon-Sat) is crammed with baroque fittings. The **Ethnographic Museum** (Map p392; Plac Wolnica 1; adult/concession 8/4zł, free Sun; 11am-7pm Tue-Sat, 10am-3pm Sun May-Sep, 10am-6pm Mon, 10am-3pm Wed-Fri, 10am-2pm Sat & Sun Oct-Apr) in the Old Town Hall has a collection of regional crafts and costumes.

The eastern Jewish quarter is dotted with synagogues. The 15th-century **Old Synagogue** is the oldest Jewish religious building in Poland. It now houses the **Jewish Museum** (Map p392; ul Szeroka 24; adult/concession 7/5zł; 10am-2pm Mon, 9am-5pm Tue-Sun Apr-Oct, 10am-2pm Mon, 9am-4pm Wed-Sun Nov-Mar), with exhibitions on Jewish traditions.

Not far away, the **Galicia Museum** (Map p392; www.galiciajewishmuseum.org; ul Dajwór 18; adult/concession 12/6zł; 9am-7pm Mar-Oct, 10am-6pm Nov-Feb) features an impressive photographic exhibition, depicting modern-day traces of southeastern Poland's once thriving Jewish community.

A short walk north is the small 16th-century **Remuh Synagogue** (Map p392; ul Szeroka 40; adult/concession 5/2zł; 9am-4pm Sun-Fri), still used for religious services. Behind it, the **Remuh Cemetery** (admission free; 9am-4pm Mon-Fri) boasts some extraordinary Renaissance gravestones. Nearby, the restored **Izaak's Synagogue** (Map p392; ul Kupa 18; admission 5/2zł; 10am-4pm Sun-Fri) is decorated with impressive frescos from the 17th century.

It's easy to take a self-guided walking tour around Kazimierz with the *Jewish Kazimierz Short Guide* booklet, available from the Jarden Jewish Bookshop (see p389).

WIELICZKA SALT MINE

Wieliczka (vyeh-*leech*-kah), 15km southeast of the city centre, is famous for the **Wieliczka Salt Mine** (www.kopalnia.pl; ul Daniłowicza 10; adult/concession 64/49zł; 7.30am-7.30pm Apr-Oct, 8am-5pm Nov-Mar). It's an eerie world of pits and chambers, and every single element from chandeliers to altarpieces was hewn by hand from solid salt. The mine is included on Unesco's World Heritage list.

The highlight of a visit is the richly ornamented **Chapel of the Blessed Kinga**, a church measuring 54m by 17m, and 12m high. Construction of this underground temple took more than 30 years (1895–1927), resulting in the removal of 20,000 tonnes of rock salt.

POLAND

> **WORTH THE TRIP: NOWA HUTA**
>
> There's another side to Kraków that few tourists see. Catch tram 4, 15 or 22 east from Kraków Główny train station to Plac Centralny in Nowa Huta. This suburb was a 'workers' paradise' district built by the communist regime in the 1950s to counter the influence of the city's religious and intellectual traditions. Its immense, blocky concrete buildings stretch out along broad, straight streets, a fascinating contrast to the Old Town's delicate beauty.

The obligatory guided tour through the mine takes about two hours (a 2km walk). Tours in English operate approximately hourly between 9am and 5pm, increasing to half-hourly from 8.30am to 6pm in July and August. If you're visiting independently, you must wait for a tour to start. Last admission to the mine is shortly before closing time.

The best way to get to Wieliczka is by minibus (look for the 'Salt Mine' sign on the windscreen), departing frequently between 6am and 8pm from a location on ul Starowiślna, near the main post office in Kraków (2.50zł).

Tours

The following companies operate tours of Kraków and surrounding areas:

Almatur (Map p390; ☎ 012 422 4668; http://en .almatur.pl; Rynek Główny 27) Arranges various outdoor activities during summer.

Cracow Tours (Map p390; ☎ 012 619 2447; www .cracowtours.pl; Rynek Główny 41) Inside Orbis Travel, offering city tours, and tours of Auschwitz and the salt mines.

Crazy Guides (☎ 0500 091 200; www.crazyguides.com) Offers entertaining tours of the city's communist-era suburbs, in restored East German cars.

Jarden Jewish Bookshop & Tourist Agency (Map p392; ☎ 012 421 7166; www.jarden.pl; ul Szeroka 2) The best agency for tours of Polish Jewish heritage. Its showpiece, 'Retracing Schindler's List' (two hours by car), costs 60zł per person. All tours require a minimum of three and must be booked in advance. Tours are in English, but other languages can be arranged.

Festivals & Events

Organ Music Festival March
Krakow International Film Festival (www.cracow filmfestival.pl) May
Lajkonik Pageant In May/June, seven days after Corpus Christi.

Jewish Culture Festival (www.jewishfestival.pl) June/July
International Festival of Street Theatre (www .teatrkto.pl, in Polish) July
Summer Jazz Festival (www.cracjazz.com) July
Kraków Christmas Crib Competition December

Sleeping

Kraków is unquestionably Poland's major tourist destination, with prices to match. Booking ahead in the busy summer months is recommended.

BUDGET

Camping Smok (☎ 012 429 8300; ul Kamedulska 18; per person/tent 22/15zł) It's small, quiet and pleasantly located 4km west of the Old Town. To get here from outside the Kraków Główny train station building, take tram 2 to the end of the line in Zwierzyniec and change for any westbound bus (except bus 100).

Cracow Hostel (Map p390; ☎ 012 429 1106; www.cracow hostel.com; Rynek Główny 18; dm 35-80zł, ste 300zł) This place is perched high above the Rynek, with an amazing view of St Mary's Church from the roomy but comfortable lounge. There's also a kitchen and washing machine.

Stranger Hostel (☎ 012 432 0909; www.thestranger hostel.com; ul Dietla 97; dm 45-60zł, d/tr/q 140/210/240zł) This popular place is always jumping, via live music gigs, parties, barbecues and DVD films on a large screen. Most dorms have eight to 12 beds, though there are some private rooms available.

Greg & Tom Hostel (Map p390; ☎ 012 422 4100; www .gregtomhostel.com; ul Pawia 12; dm from 50zł, d 150zł) This well-run hostel is spread over two locations; the private rooms are a 10-minute walk away on ul Warszawska. The staff are friendly, the rooms are clean, and laundry facilities are included.

Mama's Hostel (Map p390; ☎ 012 429 5940; www .mamashostel.com.pl; ul Bracka 4; dm 50-65zł, d 200zł) Centrally located red-and-orange lodgings with a beautiful sunlit lounge overlooking a courtyard, with the aroma of freshly roasted coffee drifting up from a cafe below in the mornings. There's also table soccer and a washing machine.

our pick Nathan's Villa Hostel (Map p392; ☎ 012 422 3545; www.nathansvilla.com; ul Św. Agnieszki 1; dm/d from 50/160zł) Comfy rooms, sparkling bathrooms, free laundry and a friendly atmosphere make this place a big hit with backpackers, and its cellar bar, mini-cinema, beer garden and pool table add to the appeal. Conveniently located between the Old Town and Kazimierz.

MIDRANGE
An agency offering decent rooms around town is **Jordan Tourist Information & Accommodation Centre** (Map p390; ☎ 012 422 6091; www.jordan.krakow.pl; ul Pawia 8; ⏱ 8am-6pm Mon-Fri, 9am-2pm Sat; s/d around 130/150zł).

Apropo (☎ 0665 277 676; www.apropo.info; ul Karmelicka 36; d/tr 150/210zł) Set of comfortable rooms within a fully renovated old apartment, with access to shared bathrooms, a light-filled kitchen and laundry facilities. It's in a convenient location not far from the Old Town.

Tournet Pokoje Gościnne (Map p392; ☎ 012 292 0088; www.accommodation.krakow.pl; ul Miodowa 7; s/d/tr from 150/200/220zł) This is a neat pension in Kazimierz, offering simple but comfortable and quiet rooms. The bathrooms, however, are tiny.

AAA Kraków Apartments (☎ 012 426 5121; www.krakow-apartments.biz; apt from 180zł) Agency renting out renovated apartments in the vicinity of the Old Town, with a smaller selection in Kazimierz. Cheaper rates are available for longer stays.

Hotel Abel (Map p392; ☎ 012 411 8736; www.hotelabel.pl; ul Józefa 30; s/d/tr 180/250/270zł) Reflecting the character of Kazimierz, this hotel has a distinctive personality, evident in its polished wooden staircase, arched brickwork and age-worn tiles. The comfortable rooms make a good base for exploring the historic Jewish neighbourhood.

Hotel Royal (Map p390; ☎ 012 421 3500; www.royal.com.pl; ul Św. Gertrudy 26-29; s/d/ste from 180/330/460zł) Impressive art nouveau edifice with loads of old-world charm, just below Wawel Castle. It's split into two sections: the higher-priced two-star rooms are cosy, and far preferable to the fairly basic one-star rooms at the back.

Wielopole Guest Rooms (Map p390; ☎ 012 422 1475; www.wielopole.pl; ul Wielopole 3; s/d 250/378zł, ste 438-538zł) Smart and simple modern rooms in a renovated block on the eastern edge of the Old Town, with narrow beds but spotless bathrooms. The tariff includes an impressive buffet breakfast.

Hotel Wit Stwosz (Map p390; ☎ 012 429 6026; www.wit-stwosz.com.pl; ul Mikołajska 28; s/d/tr/ste 295/370/450/550zł) In a historic town house belonging to St Mary's Church, and decorated in a suitably religious theme. Rooms are compact and simply furnished, but tasteful and attractive.

TOP END
Hotel Amadeus (Map p390; ☎ 012 429 6070; www.hotel-amadeus.pl; ul Mikołajska 20; s/d/ste €190/200/300) Everything about this hotel says 'class'. The rooms are tastefully furnished, though singles are rather small given the price. One room has wheelchair access, and there's a sauna, a fitness centre, and a well-regarded restaurant. While hanging around the Amadeus' foyer, you can check out photos of famous guests.

Hotel Saski (Map p390; ☎ 012 421 4222; www.hotelsaski.com.pl; ul Sławkowska 3; s/d/tr/ste 330/410/460/490zł) The Saski occupies a historic mansion, complete with a uniformed doorman, rattling old lift and ornate furnishings. The rooms themselves are comparatively plain.

Hotel Wawel (Map p390; ☎ 012 424 1300; www.hotelwawel.pl; ul Poselska 22; s/d/ste 330/460/580zł; ⌨) Ideally located just off busy ul Grodzka, this is a pleasant place offering tastefully decorated rooms with timber highlights. It's far enough from the main drag to minimise noise.

Hotel Stary (Map p390; ☎ 012 384 0808; www.stary.hotel.com.pl; ul Szczepańska 5; s/d 800/900zł, ste from 1140zł; ⌨ ⌨) Setting new standards for accommodation in Poland, the Stary is housed in an 18th-century aristocratic residence that exudes charm. The fabrics are all-natural, the bathroom surfaces Italian marble, and there's a fitness centre, swimming pool and rooftop terrace to enjoy.

Eating
Kraków is a food paradise, tightly packed with restaurants serving a wide range of international cuisines.

One local speciality is *obwarzanki* (ring-shaped pretzels powdered with poppy seeds, sesame seeds or salt) available from street vendors dozing next to their barrows.

Self-caterers can stock up at the **supermarket** within the Galeria Krakowska shopping mall next to the main train station.

BUDGET
our pick **Momo** (Map p392; ☎ 0609 685 775; ul Dietla 49; mains 4-13zł; ⏱ 11am-8pm) Vegans will cross the doorstep of this Kazimierz restaurant with relief – the majority of the menu is completely animal-free. The space is decorated with Indian craft pieces, and serves up subcontinental soups, stuffed pancakes and rice dishes, with a great range of cakes. The Tibetan dumplings are a treat worth ordering.

Green Way (Map p390; ☎ 012 431 1027; ul Mikołajska 14; mains 7-15zł; ☯ 10am-10pm Mon-Fri, 11am-9pm Sat & Sun) The Green Way offers good value vegetarian fare such as vegie curry, enchiladas and salads.

Ariel (Map p392; ☎ 012 421 7920; ul Szeroka 18; mains 9-48zł) Atmospheric Jewish restaurant packed with old-fashioned timber furniture and portraits, serving a range of kosher dishes. Try the Berdytchov soup (beef, honey and cinnamon) for a tasty starter. There's often live music here at night.

Kuchnia i Wino (Map p392; ☎ 012 430 6710; ul Józefa 13; mains 11-49zł; ☯ noon-10pm) The name – 'Cuisine and Wine' – may not suggest this bistro has a lot of imagination, but just try one of its delightfully inspired Mediterranean dishes, such as veal with basil, and you'll be impressed. There's fresh seafood available from Thursday to Saturday.

Gruzińskie Chaczapuri (Map p390; ☎ 012 429 1131; ul Floriańska 26; mains 12-22zł) Cheap and cheerful place serving up tasty Georgian dishes. Grills, salads and steaks fill out the menu, and there's a separate vegetarian selection with items such as the traditional Georgian cheese pie with stewed vegetables.

Restauracja Pod Gruszką (Map p390; ☎ 012 422 8896; ul Szczepańska 1; mains 12-55zł; ☯ noon-midnight) A favourite haunt of writers and artists, this upstairs establishment is the eatery that time forgot, with its elaborate old-fashioned decor featuring chandeliers, lace tablecloths, age-worn carpets and sepia portraits. The menu covers a range of Polish dishes, the most distinctive being the soups served within small bread loaves.

MIDRANGE & TOP END

Ipanema (Map p390; ☎ 012 422 5323; ul Św. Tomasza 28; mains 14-115zł; ☯ 5pm-midnight Mon-Thu, 1pm-midnight Sat & Sun) A banana palm as decor may seem out of place in Poland, but this bright place pulls it off. The Brazilian menu features steaks, grills and a range of interesting Afro-Brazilian dishes.

Smak Ukraiński (Map p390; ☎ 012 421 9294; ul Kanonicza 15; mains 15-30zł; ☯ noon-10pm) This Ukrainian restaurant presents authentic dishes in a cosy little cellar decorated with provincial flair. Expect lots of dumplings, *borscht* and waiters in waistcoats.

Orient Ekspres (Map p390; ☎ 012 422 6672; ul Stolarska 13; mains 15-39zł) Hercule Poirot might be surprised to find this elegant eatery here,

well off the route of its railway namesake. The food is mainly Polish, with some international additions, accompanied by wine by the glass. Mellow music and candlelight make it a good place for a romantic rendezvous.

Casa della Pizza (Map p390; ☎ 012 421 6498; Mały Rynek 2; mains 16-46zł) This unpretentious place is away from the bulk of the tourist traffic, with a menu of pizzas and pasta. The downstairs bar section is the Arabian-styled Shisha Club, serving Middle Eastern food.

Nostalgia (Map p390; ☎ 012 425 4260; ul Karmelicka 10; mains 18-37zł; ☯ noon-11pm) A refined version of the traditional Polish eatery, Nostalgia features a fireplace, overhead timber beams, uncrowded tables and courteous service. Wrap yourself around Russian dumplings, a 'Hunter's Stew' of cabbage, meat and mushrooms, or vegie options such as potato pancakes. In warm weather there's an outdoor dining area.

Pod Aniołami (Map p390; ☎ 012 421 3999; ul Grodzka 35; mains 20-58zł; ☯ 1pm-midnight) This eatery 'under the angels' offers high-quality Polish food in a pleasant cellar atmosphere, though it can get a little smoky. Specialities include the huntsman's smoked wild boar steak.

Balaton (Map p390; ☎ 012 422 0469; ul Grodzka 37; mains 20-58zł; ☯ noon-10pm) Balaton, with its shabby decor and uninspired wait staff, may not look inviting, but it's a very popular place for simple Hungarian food and seems to fill up quickly every night.

Metropolitan Restaurant (Map p390; ☎ 012 421 9803; ul Sławkowska 3; mains 22-68zł; ☯ 7.30am-midnight Mon-Sat, 7.30am-10pm Sun) Attached to Hotel Saski, this place has nostalgic B&W photos plastering the walls, and is a great place for breakfast. It also serves pasta, grills and steaks, including luxurious items such as beef fillet flambé in a cognac sauce.

Drinking

There are hundreds of pubs and bars in Kraków's Old Town, many housed in ancient vaulted cellars, which get very smoky. Kazimierz also has a lively bar scene, centred on Plac Nowy and its surrounding streets.

Paparazzi (Map p390; ul Mikołajska 9; ☯ 11am-1am Mon-Fri, 4pm-4am Sat & Sun) If you haven't brought any reading material with you to this bar, look up – the ceiling is plastered with pages from racy tabloid newspapers. It's a bright, modern place, with B&W press photos covering the walls. The drinks menu includes cocktails such as the Polish martini, built around bison grass vodka. There's also inexpensive bar food.

Le Scandale (Map p392; Plac Nowy 9; 8am-3am) Smooth Kazimierz drinking hole with low black leather couches, ambient lighting and a gleaming well-stocked bar. Full of mellow drinkers sampling the extensive cocktail list.

Singer (Map p392; ul Estery 20; 9am-4am Sun-Thu, 9am-5am Fri & Sat) Laidback hang-out of the Kazimierz cognoscenti, this relaxed cafe-bar's moody candlelit interior is full of character. Alternatively, sit outside and converse over a sewing machine affixed to the table.

Pod Papugami (Map p390; Św. Jana 18; 1pm-2am Mon-Sat, 3pm-2am Sun) This is a vaguely Irish cellar pub decorated with old motorcycles and other assorted odds and ends. A good place to hide from inclement weather, with its pool table and tunnel-like maze of rooms.

Piwnica Pod Złotą Pipą (Map p390; ul Floriańska 30; noon-midnight) Less claustrophobic than other cellar bars, with lots of tables for eating or drinking. Decent bar food and international beers on tap.

Café Camelot (Map p390; Św Tomasza 17; 9am-midnight) For coffee and cake, try this genteel haven hidden around an obscure street corner in the Old Town. Its cosy rooms are cluttered with lace-covered candlelit tables, and a quirky collection of wooden figurines featuring spiritual or folkloric scenes.

Entertainment

The comprehensive Polish-English booklet *Karnet* (4zł), published by the tourist information centre (see p389), lists almost every event in the city.

NIGHTCLUBS

our pick **Piano Rouge** (Map p390; 012 431 0333; www.thepianorouge.com; Rynek Główny 46; 11am-2am) A sumptuous cellar venue decked out with classic sofas, ornate lampshades and billowing lengths of colourful silk. There's a dizzying array of nightly live jazz acts, and an in-house restaurant.

Łubu-Dubu (Map p390; ul Wielopole 15; 6pm-late) The name of this place (*wooboo-doo*boo) is as funky as its decor. It's a grungy upstairs joint that's an echo of the past, from the garish colours to the collection of objects from 1970s Poland. DJs spin 'old school' tracks, and a series of rooms creates spaces for talking or dancing as the mood strikes.

Alchemia (Map p392; ul Estery 5; 9am-3am) This Kazimierz venue exudes a shabby-is-the-new-cool look with rough-hewn wooden benches, candlelit tables and a companionable gloom. It hosts regular live music gigs and theatrical events through the week.

Black Gallery (Map p390; ul Mikołajska 24; 5pm-late) Underground pub-cum-nightclub with a modern aspect: split levels, exposed steel frame lighting and a metallic bar. It really gets going after midnight. It also has a more civilised courtyard, open from 2pm.

Rdza (Map p390; www.rdza.pl; ul Bracka 3/5; 7pm-late) This basement club attracts some of Kraków's more sophisticated clubbers, with its Polish house music bouncing off exposed brick walls and comfy sofas. Guest DJs start spinning at 9pm Friday and Saturday.

PERFORMING ARTS

Stary Teatr (Map p390; 012 422 4040; www.stary-teatr.pl, in Polish; ul Jagiellońska 5) This accomplished theatre company offers quality productions. To overcome the language barrier, pick a Shakespeare play you know well from the repertoire, and take in the distinctive Polish interpretation.

Teatr im Słowackiego (Map p390; 012 422 4022; www.slowacki.krakow.pl, in Polish; Plac Św. Ducha 1) This grand place, built in 1893, focuses on Polish classics and large productions.

Filharmonia Krakowska (Map p390; 012 422 9477; www.filharmonia.krakow.pl; ul Zwierzyniecka 1) Hosts one of the best orchestras in the country; concerts are usually held on Friday and Saturday.

CINEMAS

Two convenient cinemas are **Kino Sztuka** (Map p390; cnr Św. Tomasza & Św. Jana), and the tiny **Kino Pasaż** (Map p390; Rynek Główny 9).

Shopping

The place to start (or perhaps end) your Kraków shopping is at the large **souvenir market** within the Cloth Hall, selling everything from fine amber jewellery to tacky plush dragons.

Fascinating examples of Polish poster art can be purchased at **Galeria Plakatu** (Map p390; 012 421 2640; www.cracowpostergallery.com; ul Stolarska 8; noon-5pm Mon-Fri, 11am-2pm Sat).

Getting There & Away

For information on travelling from Kraków to Zakopane, Częstochowa or Oświęcim (for Auschwitz), refer to the relevant destination sections later.

AIR

The **John Paul II International airport** (www.lotnisko -balice.pl) is more often called Balice airport, after the suburb in which it's located, about 15km west of the Old Town. The airport terminal hosts several car-hire desks, along with currency exchanges offering unappealing rates. To get to the Old Town by public transport, step aboard the shuttle bus to the nearby train station, from the sign marked 'PKP' outside the airport. A conductor on board the train will sell you a ticket (8zł, 16 minutes) for the short journey to Kraków Główny station.

LOT flies between Kraków and Warsaw several times a day, and offers direct connections from Kraków to Frankfurt, Munich, Paris, Vienna and Tel Aviv, with flights to New York and Chicago during the summer months. Bookings for all flights can be made at the **LOT office** (Map p390; ☎ 0801 703 703; ul Basztowa 15). There are also domestic flights via Jet Air to Poznań (six times a week).

A range of other airlines, including several budget operators, connect Kraków to cities in Europe, including an array of destinations across Britain and Ireland. There are direct flights at least daily to and from London via British Airways, Centralwings, easyJet and Ryanair. Dublin is serviced daily by Ryanair and Aer Lingus.

BUS

If you've been travelling by bus elsewhere in Poland, Kraków's modern main **bus terminal** (Map p390; ul Bosacka 18) will seem like a palace compared to the usual facility. It's located on the other side of the main train station from the Old Town. Taking the train will generally be quicker, but buses of interest to visitors run to Lublin (38zł, five hours, hourly), Zamość (40zł, seven hours, five daily) and Cieszyn (17zł, three hours, 10 daily) on the Czech border.

TRAIN

The lovely old **Kraków Główny train station** (Map p390; Plac Dworcowy), on the northeastern outskirts of the Old Town, handles all international trains and most domestic rail services. The railway platforms are about 150m north of the station building, and you can also reach them from the adjacent Galeria Krakowska shopping mall.

Each day from Kraków, 22 trains head to Warsaw (48zł, three hours). There are also 14 trains daily to Wrocław (45zł, 4½ hours), 11 to Poznań (53zł, 7½ hours), two to Lublin (49zł, 5¼ hours), and 11 to Gdynia, via Gdańsk (62zł, 8¾ hours).

Advance tickets for international and domestic trains can be booked directly at the station or from Cracow Tours (p394).

OŚWIĘCIM
pop 40,800

Few place names have more impact than Auschwitz, which is seared into public consciousness as the location of history's most extensive experiment in genocide. Every year hundreds of thousands visit Oświęcim (osh-*fyen*-cheem), the Polish town that give its German name to the infamous Nazi death camp, to learn about its history and to pay respect to the dead.

Established within disused army barracks in 1940, Auschwitz was initially designed to hold Polish prisoners, but was expanded into the largest centre for the extermination of European Jews. Two more camps were subsequently established: Birkenau (Brzezinka, also known as Auschwitz II), 3km west of Auschwitz; and Monowitz (Monowice), several kilometres west of Oświęcim. In the course of their operation, between one and 1.5 million people were murdered in these death factories – about 90% of these were Jews.

GETTING THERE & AWAY

For most visitors, Auschwitz and Birkenau are an easy day trip from Kraków.

From Kraków Główny station, 13 mostly slow trains go to Oświęcim (11zł, 1½ hours) each day, though more depart from Kraków Płaszów station.

Far more convenient are the approximately hourly buses each day to Oświęcim (11zł, 1½ hours) departing from the bus station in Kraków, which either pass by or terminate at the museum. The return bus timetable to Kraków is displayed at the Birkenau visitors centre.

Every half-hour from 11.30am to 4.30pm between 15 April and 31 October, buses shuttle passengers between the visitor centres at Auschwitz and Birkenau (buses run to 5.30pm in May and September, and until 6.30pm from June to August). Otherwise, follow the signs for an easy walk (3km) or take a taxi. Auschwitz is also linked to the town's train station by buses 24, 25, 28 and 29 every 30 to 40 minutes.

Most travel agencies in Kraków offer organised tours of Auschwitz (including Birkenau), from 100zł to 130zł per person. Check with the operator for exactly how much time the tour allows you at Auschwitz, as some run to a very tight schedule.

Auschwitz

Auschwitz was only partially destroyed by the fleeing Nazis, so many of the original buildings remain as a bleak document of the camp's history. A dozen of the 30 surviving prison blocks house sections of the **State Museum Auschwitz-Birkenau** (☎ 033 844 8100; www .auschwitz.org.pl; admission free; ☉ 8am-7pm Jun-Aug, 8am-6pm May & Sep, 8am-5pm Apr & Oct, 8am-4pm Mar & Nov, 8am-3pm Dec-Feb).

About every half-hour, the cinema in the **visitors centre** at the entrance shows a 15-minute documentary film (adult/concession 3.50/2.50zł) about the liberation of the camp by Soviet troops on 27 January 1945. It's shown in several languages throughout the day; check the schedule at the information desk as soon as you arrive. The film is not recommended for children under 14 years old. The visitors centre also has a cafeteria, bookshops, a *kantor* and a left-luggage room.

Some basic explanations in Polish, English and Hebrew are provided on site, but you'll understand more if you buy the small *Auschwitz Birkenau Guide Book* (translated into about 15 languages) from the visitors centre. English-language tours (adult/concession 39/30zł, 3½ hours) of Auschwitz and Birkenau leave at 10am, 11am, 1pm and 3pm daily, and can also occur when a group of 10 people can be formed. Tours in a range of other languages can be arranged in advance.

Auschwitz is an easy day trip from Kraków. However, if you want to stay overnight, **Centre for Dialogue and Prayer** (☎ 033 843 10 00; www.cent rum-dialogu.oswiecim.pl; ul Kolbego 1; camping per person 23zł, s/d/tr/ste 95/190/285/270zł) is 700m southwest of Auschwitz. It's comfortable and quiet, and the price includes breakfast. Most rooms are en suite, and full board is also offered.

Birkenau

Birkenau (admission free; ☉ 8am-7pm Jun-Aug, 8am-6pm May & Sep, 8am-5pm Apr & Oct, 8am-4pm Mar & Nov, 8am-3pm Dec-Feb) was actually where the murder of huge numbers of Jews took place. This vast (175 hectares), purpose-built and grimly efficient camp had more than 300 prison barracks and four huge gas chambers complete with crematoria. Each gas chamber held 2000 people and electric lifts raised the bodies to the ovens. The camp could hold 200,000 inmates at one time.

Although much of the camp was destroyed by retreating Nazis, the size of the place, fenced off with barbed wire stretching almost as far as the eye can see, provides some idea of the scale of this heinous crime. The viewing platform above the entrance provides further perspective. In some ways, Birkenau is even more shocking than Auschwitz and there are fewer tourists.

CZĘSTOCHOWA
pop 245,000

Częstochowa (chen-sto-*ho*-vah), 114km northwest of Kraków, is an attractive pilgrimage town, dominated by the graceful Jasna Góra monastery atop a hill at its centre. The monastery, founded by the Paulites of Hungary in 1382, is the home of the Black Madonna, and owes its fame to a miracle. In 1430 a group of Hussites stole the holy icon, slashed it and broke it into three pieces. Legend has it that the picture bled, and the monks cleaned the retrieved panel with the aid of a spring, which rose miraculously from the ground. Though the picture was restored, the scars on the Virgin's face were retained in memory of the miracle.

The Madonna was also credited with the fortified monastery's resistance to the Swedish sieges of the 1650s. In 1717 the Black Madonna was crowned Queen of Poland.

From the train station, and adjacent bus terminal, turn right (north) up Al Wolności – along which are several internet cafes – to the main thoroughfare, Al Najświętszej Marii Panny (simplified to Al NMP). At the western end of this avenue is the monastery and at the eastern end is Plac Daszyńskiego. In-between you'll find the **tourist office** (☎ 034 368 2250; Al NMP 65; ☉ 9am-5pm Mon-Sat) and banks.

Sights

The **Paulite Monastery on Jasna Góra** (☎ 034 365 3888; www.jasnagora.pl; admission free; ☉ dawn-dusk) retains the appearance of a hilltop fortress. Inside the grounds are three **museums** (donations welcome; ☉ 9am-5pm May-Oct, 9am-4pm Nov-Apr): the **Arsenal**, with a variety of old weapons;

POLAND

the **600th-Anniversary Museum** (Muzeum Sześćsetlecia), which contains Lech Wałęsa's 1983 Nobel Peace Prize; and the **Treasury** (Skarbiec), featuring offerings presented by the faithful.

The **tower** (🕙 8am-4pm May-Oct) is the tallest (106m) historic church tower in Poland. The baroque church beneath is beautifully decorated. The image of the Black Madonna is on the high altar of the adjacent chapel, entered from the left of the church aisle. It's hard to see, so a copy is on display in the **Knights' Hall** (Sala Rycerska) in the monastery. Note that the Madonna is sometimes concealed by a silver cover; if so, check with the onsite information office for the next scheduled uncovering. It's quite an event, as priests file in, music plays and the image slowly emerges.

On weekends and holidays expect long queues for all three museums. The crowds in the chapel may be so thick that you're almost unable to enter, much less get near the icon.

In the town hall the **Częstochowa Museum** (Al NMP 45; adult/concession 4/3zł; 🕙 11am-5pm Tue-Sun Jun-Sep, 9am-3.30pm Tue, Thu & Fri, 11am-5.30pm Wed, 10am-4pm Sat & Sun Oct-May) features an ethnographic collection and modern Polish paintings.

Festivals & Events

The major Marian feasts at Jasna Góra are 3 May, 16 July, 15 August (especially), 26 August, 8 September, 12 September and 8 December. On these days the monastery is packed with pilgrims.

Sleeping & Eating

Dom Pielgrzyma (🕾 034 377 7564; ul Wyszyńskiego 1/31; dm 25zł, s/d/tr from 70/100/135zł) A huge place behind the monastery, it offers numerous quiet and comfortable rooms, and is remarkably good value.

Youth Hostel (🕾 034 324 3121; ul Jasnogórska 84/90; dm 27zł; 🕙 15 Jun-15 Sep) This hostel, two blocks north of the tourist office, has modest facilities. Look for the triangular green sign on the building's wall.

Plenty of eateries can be found near the Dom Pielgrzyma. Better restaurants are dotted along Al NMP.

Bar Viking (🕾 034 324 5768; ul Nowowiejskiego 10; mains 4-40zł; 🕙 10am-10pm) About 200m south of the Częstochowa Museum, this friendly place has a good range of dishes, including vegetarian choices.

Restaurant Cleopatra (🕾 034 368 0101; Al NMP 71; mains 15-20zł) The cheerfully out-of-place Cleopatra, near the tourist office, serves pizzas, kebabs and sandwiches among pillars painted with ancient Egyptian designs.

Getting There & Away

The **bus terminal** (Al Wolności 45) is next to the train station, but train travel is the superior option to most destinations.

From **Częstochowa Osobowa train station** (Al Wolności 21), 13 trains a day go to Warsaw (41zł, three hours). There are eight daily trains to Gdynia via Gdańsk (60zł, 9½ hours), six to Łódź (33zł, two hours), three to Olsztyn (56zł, seven hours), three to Zakopane (45zł, seven hours), nine to Kraków (31zł, 2½ hours) and four to Wrocław (34zł, three hours).

LUBLIN
pop 353,000

If the crowds are becoming too much in Kraków, you could do worse than jump on a train to Lublin. This attractive eastern city has many of the same attractions – a beautiful Old Town, a castle, good bars and restaurants – but is less visited by international tourists.

Though today the city's beautifully preserved Old Town is a peaceful blend of Gothic, Renaissance and baroque architecture, Lublin has an eventful past. In 1569 the Lublin Union was signed here, uniting Poland and Lithuania; and at the end of WWII, the Soviet Union set up a communist government in Lublin, prior to the liberation of Warsaw.

Information

Bank Pekao Old Town (ul Królewska 1); City centre (ul Krakowskie Przedmieście 64)

EMPiK (Galeria Centrum, 3rd fl, ul Krakowskie Przedmieście 16) Bookshop.

Main post office (ul Krakowskie Przedmieście 50)

Net Box (ul Krakowskie Przedmieście 52; per hr 4.50zł; 🕙 9am-9pm Mon-Fri, 10am-9pm Sat, 2-9pm Sun) Internet access in a courtyard off the street.

Tourist office (🕾 081 532 4412; www.lublin.pl; ul Jezuicka 1/3; 🕙 9am-6pm Mon-Fri, 10am-4pm Sat, 10am-3pm Sun May-Sep, 9am-5pm Mon-Fri, 10am-3pm Sat Oct-Apr) Lots of free brochures, including the city walking-route guide *Tourist Routes of Lublin*.

Sights
CASTLE

The substantial **castle**, standing on a hill northeast of the Old Town, has a dark history. It was

LUBLIN

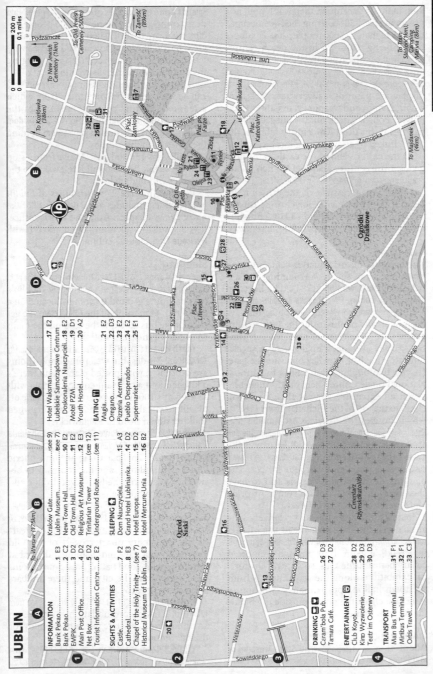

POLAND

built in the 14th century, then was rebuilt as a prison in the 1820s. During the Nazi occupation, more than 100,000 people passed its doors before being deported to the death camps. Its major occupant is now the **Lublin Museum** (www.zamek-lublin.pl; ul Zamkowa 9; adult/concession 6.50/4.50zł; 9am-4pm Wed-Sat, 9am-5pm Sun). On display are paintings, silverware, porcelain, woodcarvings and weaponry, mostly labelled only in Polish. Check out the alleged 'devil's paw-print' on the 17th-century table in the foyer, linked to an intriguing local legend.

At the eastern end of the castle is the gorgeous 14th-century **Chapel of the Holy Trinity** (adult/concession 6.50/4.50zł; 9am-3.45pm Tue-Sat, 9am-4.45pm Sun), accessible via the museum. Its interior is covered with polychrome Russo-Byzantine frescos painted in 1418 – possibly the finest medieval wall paintings in Poland.

OLD TOWN

The compact historic quarter centres on the **Rynek**, the main square surrounding the neoclassical **Old Town Hall** (1781). The **Historical Museum of Lublin** (Plac Łokietka 3; adult/concession 3.50/2.50zł; 9am-4pm Wed-Sat, 9am-5pm Sun) displays documents and photos inside the 14th-century **Kraków Gate**, a remnant of medieval fortifications. Daily at noon, a bugler plays a special tune atop the **New Town Hall** opposite the gate. (If you like bugling, don't miss the annual National Bugle Contest here on 15 August.)

For an expansive view of the Old Town, climb to the top of the **Trinitarian Tower** (1819), which houses the **Religious Art Museum** (Plac Katedralny; adult/concession 7/5zł; 10am-5pm Tue-Sun Apr-Oct, 10am-3pm Sat & Sun Nov-Mar). Nearby is the 16th-century **cathedral** (Plac Katedralny; dawn-dusk) and its impressive baroque frescos. The painting of the Virgin Mary is said to have shed tears in 1949, so it's a source of pride and reverence for local believers.

Beneath the city streets, a relatively new attraction is the **Underground Route** (Rynek 1; adult/concession 6/4zł; 10am-4pm Wed-Fri, noon-5pm Sat & Sun May-Oct), a 280m trail through connected cellars beneath the Old Town, with historical exhibitions along the way. Entry is from the town hall at approximately two-hourly intervals; check the notice outside the building for exact times.

MAJDANEK

About 4km southeast is the **State Museum of Majdanek** (www.majdanek.pl; admission free; 9am-

4pm). It commemorates one of the largest Nazi death camps, where some 235,000 people, including more than 100,000 Jews, were massacred. Barracks, guard towers and barbed wire fences remain in place; even more chilling are the crematorium and gas chambers.

A short explanatory film (admission 3zł) can be seen in the visitors centre, from which a marked 'visiting route' (5km) passes the massive stone **Monument of Fight & Martyrdom** and finishes at the domed **mausoleum** holding the ashes of many victims.

Trolleybus 156 and bus 23 leave from a stop near the Bank Pekao on ul Królewska, to the entrance of Majdanek.

Pick up the free *Tourist Routes of Lublin* guide, which includes a *Heritage Trail of the Lublin Jews* chapter, from the tourist office, if you want to walk along the marked **Jewish Heritage Trail** around Lublin.

Sleeping

Camping Marina (☎ 081 745 6910; www.graf-marina.pl, in Polish; ul Krężnicka 6; per tent 8zł, cabins from 55zł) Lublin's only camping ground is serenely located on a lake about 8km south of the Old Town. To get there, take bus 25 from the stop on the main road east of the train station.

Youth Hostel (☎ 081 533 0628; ul Długosza 6; dm/d/tr 32/72/108zł) Modest but well run. Simple rooms are decorated with potted plants, and there's a kitchen and a pleasant courtyard area with seating. It's 100m up a poorly marked lane off ul Długosza; take the second left turning when walking down from ul Racławickie.

Lubelskie Samorządowe Centrum Doskonalenia Nauczycieli (☎ 081 532 9241; www.lscdn.pl; ul Dominikańska 5; dm 52zł) This place is in an atmospheric Old Town building, and has rooms with between two and five beds. It's good value and often busy, so book ahead.

Dom Nauczyciela (☎ 081 533 8285; www.lublin .oupis.pl/hotel; ul Akademicka 4; s/d/tr from 90/110/195zł) Value-packed accommodation in the heart of the university quarter, west of the Old Town. Rooms have old-fashioned decor but are clean, with good bathrooms. Some rooms have views over the city, and there are bars and eateries nearby.

Motel PZM (☎ 081 533 4232; ul Prusa 8; s/d from 120/160zł) This accommodation is housed in an uninspiring concrete pile, but it's handy for the bus station. It's car-friendly too.

our pick **Hotel Waksman** (☎ 081 532 5454; www .waksman.pl; ul Grodzka 19; s/d 200/220zł, ste from 260zł)

This small gem is excellent value for its quality and location. Just within the Grodzka Gate in the Old Town, it offers elegantly appointed rooms with different colour schemes, and an attractive lounge with tapestries on the walls. One room has a waterbed.

Hotel Mercure-Unia (☎ 081 533 2061; www.orbis .pl; Al Racławickie 12; s/d from 265/295zł; ✵) This business hotel is big, central and convenient, and offers all modern conveniences, though it's lacking in atmosphere. There's a gym, bar and restaurant on the premises. Breakfast is 35zł extra per person.

Grand Hotel Lublinianka (☎ 081 446 6100; www .lublinianka.com; ul Krakowskie Przedmieście 56; s/d from 300/360zł; ✵) The swankiest place in town includes free use of a sauna and spa. The cheaper (3rd floor) rooms have skylights but are relatively small, while 'standard' rooms are spacious and have glitzy marble bathrooms. One room is designed for wheelchair access, and there's a good restaurant onsite.

Hotel Europa (☎ 081 535 0303; www.hoteleuropa .pl; ul Krakowskie Przedmieście 29; s/d from 380/420zł; ste 1150zł; ✵) Central hotel offering smart, thoroughly modernised rooms with high ceilings and elegant furniture, in a restored 19th-century building. Two rooms are designed for wheelchair access, and there's a nightclub downstairs.

Eating & Drinking

Pueblo Desperados (☎ 081 534 6179; Rynek 5; mains 6-24zł; ✵ 9am-10pm Mon-Thu, 9am-midnight Fri & Sat, 10am-10pm Sun) Takes a reasonable stab at Mexican cuisine in its tiny sombrero-decorated premises off the Old Town's central square. The usual suspects (burritos, tacos) are on the menu, along with so-called Mexican pizzas.

Pizzeria Acerna (☎ 081 532 4531; Rynek 2; mains 11-41zł) The Acerna is a popular eatery on the main square, serving cheap pizzas and pasta in dazzling variations.

our pick **Magia** (☎ 081 532 3041; ul Grodzka 2; mains 16-70zł; ✵ noon-midnight) Charming, relaxed restaurant with numerous vibes to choose from within its warren of dining rooms and large outdoor courtyard. Dishes range from tiger shrimps and snails to deer and duck, with every sort of pizza, pasta and pancake between.

Oregano (☎ 081 442 5530; ul Kościuszki 7; mains 20-45zł; ✵ noon-11pm) This pleasant, upmarket restaurant specialises in Mediterranean cuisine, featuring pasta, paella and seafood. There's a

well-organised English menu, and the chefs aren't scared of spice.

Tamara Café (ul Krakowskie Przedmieście 36) This cafe-bar takes its *vino* very seriously. Whether you're a cultured wine connoisseur, a courtyard cocktail fancier, or a hungry tippler who wants some vodka with (or in) your meal, pull up a chair.

Caram'bola Pub (ul Kościuszki 8; ✵ 10am-late Mon-Fri, noon-late Sat & Sun) This pub is a pleasant place for a beer or two. It also serves inexpensive bar food, including Lublin's ubiquitous pizzas.

There's a **supermarket** located near the bus terminal.

Entertainment

Club Koyot (ul Krakowskie Przedmieście 26; ✵ noon-late Mon-Fri, 4pm-late Sat & Sun) This club is concealed in a courtyard and features live music or DJs most nights.

Kino Wyzwolenie (ul Peowiaków 6; adult/concession 15/13zł) If you'd prefer a movie to music, this is a classic 1920s cinema in a convenient location.

Teatr im Osterwy (☎ 081 532 4244; ul Narutowicza 17) Lublin's main theatrical venue, which features mostly classical plays.

Getting There & Away

From the **bus terminal** (Al Tysiąclecia), opposite the castle, buses head to Białystok (27zł, three daily), Kraków (38zł, hourly), Olsztyn (72zł, one daily), Przemyśl (16zł, four daily) and Zakopane (63zł, one daily). Buses also leave approximately hourly to Zamość (15zł) and various destinations within Warsaw (26zł). From the same terminal, Polski Express offers five daily buses to Warsaw (31zł, three hours). Private minibuses head to various destinations, including Warsaw (30zł, every half-hour), from bus stops north and west of the bus terminal.

The **train station** (Plac Dworcowy) is 1.2km south of the Old Town and accessible by bus 1 or 13. When leaving the station, look for the bus stop on ul Gazowa, to the left of the station entrance as you walk down the steps (not the trolleybus stop). Alternatively, trolleybus 150 from the station is handy for the university area and the youth hostel. A dozen trains go daily to Warsaw (34zł, 2½ hours) and two travel to Kraków (49zł, 5¼ hours). Buy tickets from the station or **Orbis Travel** (☎ 081 532 2256; www.orbistravel.com.pl; ul Narutowicza 33a).

POLAND

AROUND LUBLIN

The hamlet of **Kozłówka** (koz-*woof*-kah), 38km north of Lublin, is famous for its sumptuous late-baroque **palace**, which houses the **Museum of the Zamoyski Family** (081 852 8310; www.muzeum zamoyskich.lublin.pl; adult/concession for entry to all sections 24/12zł; 10am-4pm Tue-Sun 15 Mar-Oct, 10am-3pm Nov-15 Dec). The collection in the **main palace** (adult/concession 16/8zł) features original furnishings, ceramic stoves and a large collection of paintings. You must see this area on a Polish-language guided tour, whose starting time will be noted at the top of your ticket. An English-language tour (best organised in advance) costs an extra 50zł. The entrance fee to this section also includes entry to the 1907 **chapel**.

Even more interesting is the incongruous **Socialist-Realist Art Gallery** (adult/concession 6/3zł; 10am-4pm Tue-Sun 15 Mar-Oct), decked out with numerous portraits and statues of communist-era leaders. It also features many idealised scenes of farmers and factory workers striving for socialism. These stirring works were originally tucked away here in embarrassment by the communist authorities, after Stalin's death led to the decline of this all-encompassing artistic style.

You can stay in some **palace rooms** and on an 'agrotourist' farm, **Agro Kozłówkie Rządcówke** (081 852 8220). Contact staff in advance about availability and current costs.

From Lublin, there's one morning bus to Kozłówka at 8.30am (7.50zł, 50 minutes). Alternatively, you can catch one of the frequent buses from Lublin to Lubartów, then take one of the regular minibuses that pass Kozłówka from there.

A bus heads back to Lublin from Kozłówka around 3.30pm, and another around 6.30pm. Double-check bus timetables before you visit the museum so you can plan your departure accordingly. If you get stuck, take a minibus to Lubartów, from where there is regular transport back to Lublin.

ZAMOŚĆ

pop 66,500

While most Polish cities' attractions centre on their medieval heart, Zamość (*zah*-moshch) is pure Renaissance. The streets of its attractive, compact Old Town are perfect for exploring, and its central market square is a symmetrical delight, reflecting the city's glorious 16th-century origins.

Zamość was founded in 1580 by Jan Zamoyski, the nation's chancellor and commander-in-chief. Designed by an Italian architect, the city was intended to be a prosperous trading settlement between Western Europe and the region stretching east to the Black Sea.

In WWII, the Nazis earmarked the city for German resettlement, sending the Polish population into slave labour or concentration camps. Most of the Jewish population of the renamed 'Himmlerstadt' was exterminated.

The splendid architecture of Zamość's Old Town was added to Unesco's World Heritage list in 1992. Since 2004, EU funds have been gradually restoring Zamość to its former glory.

Information

Bank Pekao (ul Grodzka 2)
K@fejka Internetowa (Rynek Wielki 10; per hr 3zł; 7.30am-5pm Mon-Fri, 9am-2pm Sat) Internet access.
Main post office (ul Kościuszki)
Tourist office (084 639 2292; Rynek Wielki 13; 8am-6pm Mon-Fri, 10am-5pm Sat & Sun May-Sep, 8am-5pm Mon-Fri, 9am-2pm Sat Oct-Apr) Sells *Along the Streets of Zamość* (2zł) and the glossy *Zamość – A Short Guidebook* (8.50zł).

Sights

The **Rynek Wielki** (Great Market Sq) is the heart of Zamość's attractive Old Town. The impressive Italianate Renaissance square (exactly 100m by 100m) is dominated by the lofty, pink **town hall** and surrounded by colourful arcaded burghers' houses, many adorned with elegant designs. The **Museum of Zamość** (ul Ormiańska 30; adult/concession 6/3zł; 9am-4pm Tue-Sun) is based in two of the loveliest buildings on the Rynek and houses interesting exhibits, including paintings, folk costumes, archaeological finds and a scale model of the 16th-century town.

Southwest of the square is the mighty 16th-century **cathedral** (ul Kolegiacka; dawn-dusk), which hosts the tomb of Jan Zamoyski in the chapel to the right of the high altar. The **belfry** (admission 1.50zł; May-Sep) can be climbed for good views of the historic cathedral bells and the Old Town. In the grounds, the **Sacral Museum** (admission 1.50zł; 10am-4pm Mon-Fri, 10am-1pm Sat & Sun May-Sep, 10am-1pm Sun Oct-Apr) features various robes, paintings and sculptures.

Zamoyski Palace (closed to the public) lost much of its character when it was converted into a military hospital in the 1830s. Today it's used for government offices. Nearby, the

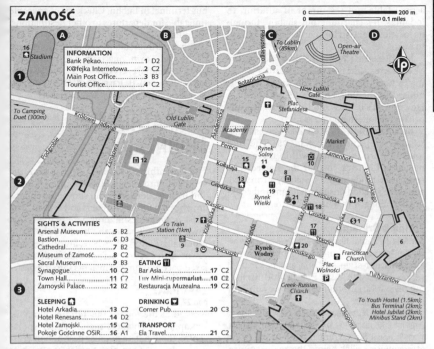

ZAMOŚĆ

0 — 200 m
0 — 0.1 miles

INFORMATION
Bank Pekao........................1 D2
K@fejka Internetowa.........2 C2
Main Post Office................3 B3
Tourist Office....................4 C2

SIGHTS & ACTIVITIES
Arsenal Museum................5 B2
Bastion.............................6 D3
Cathedral.........................7 B2
Museum of Zamość...........8 C2
Sacral Museum.................9 B3
Synagogue.......................10 C2
Town Hall........................11 C2
Żamoyski Palace..............12 B2

SLEEPING
Hotel Arkadia..................13 C2
Hotel Renesans...............14 D2
Hotel Zamojski................15 C2
Pokoje Gościnne OSiR......16 A1

EATING
Bar Asia..........................17 C2
Lux Mini-supermarket......10 C2
Restauracja Muzealna......19 C2

DRINKING
Corner Pub.......................20 C3

TRANSPORT
Ela Travel.........................21 C2

Arsenal Museum (ul Zamkowa 2; adult/concession 6/3zł; 9am-4pm Tue-Sun) holds an unremarkable collection of cannons, swords and firearms. To the north of the palace stretches a beautifully landscaped **park**.

Before WWII, Jewish citizens accounted for 45% of the town's population (of 12,000) and most lived in the area north and east of the palace. The most significant Jewish architectural relic is the Renaissance **synagogue** (ul Pereca 14; adult/concession 5/2zł; 9am-5pm Tue-Sat), built in the early 17th century. For some years it was used as a public library, but is now empty and awaiting transformation into a cultural centre. In the meantime you can visit and see its original wall and ceiling decoration, and a simple photo exhibition of Jewish life in the region.

On the eastern edge of the Old Town is the antiquated **Market Hall** (Hala Targowa), closed until 2010 due to a major renovation. Behind it is the best surviving **bastion** from the original city walls.

Sleeping

Youth Hostel (084 638 9500; ul Zamoyskiego 4; dm 15zł; Jul-Aug) You can find this hostel in a school

building 1.5km east of the Old Town, not far from the bus terminal. It's basic but functional and very cheap.

Pokoje Gościnne OSiR (084 638 6011; ul Królowej Jadwigi 8; dm 24zł; s/d/tr 90/125/150zł) Located in a sprawling sporting complex, a 15-minute walk west of the Old Town, and packed with old trophies and students playing table tennis. Rooms are plainly furnished, clean and comfortable, although the bathrooms fall short of the ideal.

Camping Duet (084 639 2499; ul Królowej Jadwigi 14; s/d/tr/q 75/90/120/150zł;) West of the Old Town, Camping Duet has neat bungalows, tennis courts, a restaurant, sauna and jacuzzi. Larger bungalows sleep up to six.

Hotel Jubilat (084 638 6401; www.hoteljubilat.pl; ul Kardynała Wyszyńskiego 52; s/d/ste from 136/177/292zł) An acceptable, if slightly drab, place to spend the night, right beside the bus station. It couldn't be handier for late arrivals or early departures, but it's a long way from anywhere else. It has a restaurant and fitness club.

Hotel Arkadia (084 638 6507; www.arkadia.zamosc .pl; Rynek Wielki 9; s/d/tr/ste from 140/160/200/250zł) With just nine rooms, this compact place offers

POLAND

a pool table and restaurant in addition to lodgings. It's charming but shabby, though its location right on the market square is hard to beat.

Hotel Renesans (☎ 084 639 2001; www.hotelrenesans .pl; ul Grecka 6; s/d/ste from 140/205/216zł) It's ironic that a hotel named after the Renaissance is housed in the Old Town's ugliest building. However, it's central and the rooms are surprisingly modern and pleasant.

Hotel Zamojski (☎ 084 639 2516; www.orbis.pl; ul Kołłątaja 2/4/6; s/d/ste 227/335/475zł; 🕸) The best joint in town is situated within three connected old houses, just off the square. The rooms are modern and tastefully furnished, and there's a good onsite restaurant and cocktail bar, along with a fitness centre.

Eating & Drinking

Bar Asia (ul Staszica 10; mains 5-9zł; 🕑 8am-5pm Mon-Fri, 8am-4pm Sat) For hungry but broke travellers, this old-style *bar mleczny* is ideal. It serves cheap and tasty Polish food including several variants of *pierogi*, in a minimally decorated space.

Restauracja Muzealna (☎ 084 638 7300; ul Ormiańska Ormianska 30; mains 10-25zł; 🕑 11am-10pm Mon-Sat, 11am-9pm Sun) Subterranean restaurant in an atmospheric cellar below the main square, bedecked with ornate timber furniture and portraits of nobles. It serves a better class of Polish cuisine at reasonable prices, and has a well-stocked bar.

Corner Pub (ul Żeromskiego 6) This cosy Irish-style pub is a good place to have a drink. It has comfy booths and the walls are ornamented with bric-a-brac such as antique clocks, swords and model cars.

For self-caterers, there's the handy **Lux minisupermarket** (ul Grodzka 16; 🕑 7am-8pm Mon-Sat, 8am-6pm Sun) near the Rynek.

Getting There & Away

Buses are usually more convenient and quicker than trains. The **bus terminal** (ul Hrubieszowska) is 2km east of the Old Town and linked by frequent city buses, primarily buses 0 and 3. Daily, buses go to Kraków (40zł, seven hours, five daily), Warsaw (35zł, 4¾ hours, three daily) and Lublin (15zł, two hours, hourly).

Quicker and cheaper are the minibuses that travel every 30 minutes between Lublin and Zamość (10zł, 1½ hours). They leave from the minibus stand opposite the bus terminal in Zamość and from a corner northwest of the

bus terminal in Lublin. Check the changeable timetable for departures to other destinations, including Warsaw and Kraków.

From the train station, about 1km southwest of the Old Town, one train heads to Lublin (28zł, 1½ hours) every day, and one to Warsaw (48zł, 5½ hours). **Ela Travel** (☎ 084 638 5775; ul Grodzka 18) sells international bus and air tickets.

CARPATHIAN MOUNTAINS

The Carpathians (Karpaty) stretch from the southern border with Slovakia into Ukraine, and their wooded hills and snowy mountains are a beacon for hikers, skiers and cyclists. The most popular destination here is the resort town of Zakopane in the heart of the Tatra Mountains (Tatry). Elsewhere, historic regional towns such as Przemyśl and Sanok offer a relaxed pace and unique insights into the past.

ZAKOPANE
pop 27,300
Nestled at the foot of the Tatra Mountains, Zakopane is Poland's major winter sports centre, though it's a popular destination year-round. It may resemble a tourist trap, with its overcommercialised, overpriced exterior, but it also has a relaxed, laid-back vibe that makes it a great place to chill out for a few days, even if you're not intending to ski or hike.

Zakopane also played an important role in keeping Polish culture alive during the long years of foreign rule in the 19th century. Many artistic types settled in the town, including composer Karol Szymanowski and the writer and painter, Witkacy. Witkacy's father, Stanisław Witkiewicz, was inspired by traditional local architecture to create the famous Zakopane style. Some of his buildings still stand.

Information
Bank Pekao (ul Krupówki 19)
Centrum Przewodnictwa Tatrzańskiego (Tatra Guide Centre; ☎ 018 206 37 99; ul Chałubińskiego 42a; 🕑 9am-3pm) Arranges English- and German-speaking mountain guides.
Księgarnia Górska (ul Zaruskiego 5) Bookshop in the reception area of the Dom Turysty PTTK, sells regional hiking maps.
Main post office (ul Krupówki; 🕑 7am-8pm Mon-Fri, 8am-2pm Sat)

Orbis Travel (☎ 018 201 5051; ul Krupówki 22) Offers the usual services, as well as accommodation in hotels and pensions. Also has an in-house *kantor*.

Tourist office (☎ 018 201 2211; ul Kościuszki 17; ⏱ 9am-5pm daily Jul & Aug, 9am-5pm Mon-Fri Sep-Jun) Offers advice, and sells hiking and city maps. The centre can also arrange rafting trips down the Dunajec River.

Widmo (ul Galicy 6; per hr 5zł; ⏱ 7.30am-midnight Mon-Fri, 9am-midnight Sat & Sun) Internet access.

Sights & Activities

Check out exhibits about regional history, ethnography and geology at the **Tatra Museum** (ul Krupówki 10; adult/concession 7/5.50zł, free Sun; ⏱ 9am-5pm Tue-Sat, 9am-3pm Sun), along with displays on local flora and fauna. Head southwest to **Villa Koliba** (ul Kościeliska 18), the first design (1892) by Witkiewicz in the Zakopane style. Fittingly, it now houses the **Museum of Zakopane Style** (adult/concession 7/5.50zł; ⏱ 9am-5pm Wed-Sat, 9am-3pm Sun).

About 350m southeast is **Villa Atma** (ul Kasprusie 19) with its **Szymanowksi Museum** (adult/concession 6/3zł, free Sun; ⏱ 10am-3.30pm Wed, Thu, Sat & Sun, 10am-6pm Fri), dedicated to the great musician who once lived there. There are piano recitals here in summer.

The **Tatra National Park Natural Museum** (ul Chałubińskiego 42a; admission free; ⏱ 8am-3pm Mon-Sat), near the Rondo en route to the national park, has some mildly interesting exhibits about the park's natural history.

A short walk northeast up the hill leads to **Villa Pod Jedlami** (ul Koziniec 1), another splendid house built in the Zakopane style (the interior

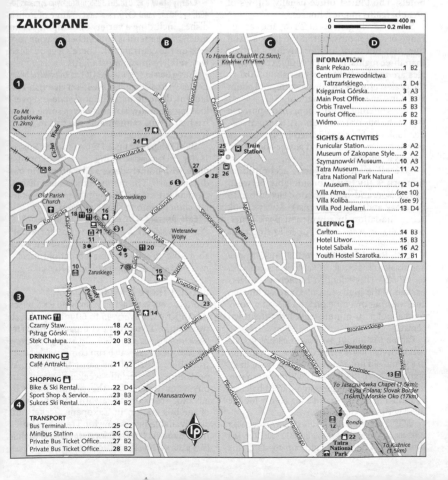

ZAKOPANE

0 ——— 400 m
0 ——— 0.2 miles

INFORMATION
Bank Pekao............................1 B2
Centrum Przewodnictwa
  Tatrzańskiego......................2 D4
Księgarnia Górska..................3 A3
Main Post Office....................4 B3
Orbis Travel..........................5 B3
Tourist Office........................6 B2
Widmo..................................7 B3

SIGHTS & ACTIVITIES
Funicular Station....................8 A2
Museum of Zakopane Style....9 A2
Szymanowski Museum..........10 A3
Tatra Museum......................11 A2
Tatra National Park Natural
  Museum............................12 D4
Villa Atma.......................(see 10)
Villa Koliba.......................(see 9)
Villa Pod Jedlami................13 D4

SLEEPING 🛏
Carlton...............................14 B3
Hotel Litwor........................15 B3
Hotel Sabała 16 A2
Youth Hostel Szarotka.........17 B1

EATING 🍴
Czarny Staw.........................18 A2
Pstrąg Górski.......................19 A2
Stek Chałupa.......................20 B3

DRINKING 🍷
Café Antrakt........................21 A2

SHOPPING 🛍
Bike & Ski Rental.................22 D4
Sport Shop & Service...........23 B3
Sukces Ski Rental................24 B2

TRANSPORT
Bus Terminal.......................25 C2
Minibus Station...................26 C2
Private Bus Ticket Office.......27 B2
Private Bus Ticket Office.......28 B2

cannot be visited). Perhaps Witkiewicz's greatest achievement is the **Jaszczurówka Chapel**, about 1.5km further east along the road to Morskie Oko.

Mt Gubałówka (1120m) offers excellent views over the Tatras and is a popular destination for tourists who don't feel overly energetic. The **funicular** (adult/concession one-way 10/8zł, return 16/12zł; 8am-10pm Jul & Aug, 8.30am-7.20pm Apr-Jun & Sep, 8.30am-6pm Oct & Nov) covers the 1388m-long route in less than five minutes, climbing 300m from the funicular station just north of ul Krupówki.

Sleeping

Given the abundance of private rooms and decent hostels, few travellers actually stay in hotels. The tourist office usually knows of great bargains in guest houses.

Some travel agencies in Zakopane can arrange private rooms, but in the peak season they may not want to offer anything for less than three nights. Expect a double room (singles are rarely offered) to cost about 70zł in the peak season in the town centre, and about 50zł for somewhere further out.

Locals offering private rooms may approach you at the bus or train stations; alternatively, just look out for signs posted in the front of private homes – *noclegi* and *pokoje* both mean 'rooms available'.

Like all seasonal resorts, accommodation prices fluctuate considerably between low season and high season (December to February and July to August). Always book accommodation in advance at peak times, especially on weekends. The following rates are for high season.

Youth Hostel Szarotka (018 201 3618; www .szarotkaptsm.republika.pl; ul Nowotarska 45; dm/d/tr 40/100/150zł) This friendly, homely place gets packed in the high season. There's a kitchen and washing machine on site. It's on a noisy road about a 10-minute walk from the town centre.

Carlton (018 201 4415; www.carlton.pl; ul Grun-waldzka 11; s/d/tr 100/200/300zł) Good value pension in a grand old house away from the main drag, featuring light-filled rooms with modern furniture. There's an impressive shared balcony overlooking the road, and a big comfy lounge lined with potted plants.

our pick **Hotel Sabała** (018 201 5092; www.sabala .zakopane.pl; ul Krupówki 11; s/d/ste from 310/400/520zł;) Built in 1894 but thoroughly up-to-date, this

striking timber building has a superb location overlooking the picturesque pedestrian thoroughfare. It offers cosy, attic-style rooms, and there's a sauna and solarium on the premises. A candlelit restaurant has views of street life.

Hotel Litwor (018 202 4200; www.litwor.pl; ul Krupówki 40; s/d/ste 488/613/838zł;) This sumptuous four-star place, with large, restful rooms, has all the usual top-end facilities, including a gym and sauna. A 20% discount applies to advance bookings. It also has an excellent restaurant serving classy versions of traditional dishes.

Eating & Drinking

The main street, ul Krupówki, is lined with all sorts of eateries.

Czarny Staw (018 201 3856; ul Krupówki 2; mains 10-46zł; 10am-1am) Offers a tasty range of Polish dishes, including a variety of dumplings, and much of the menu is cooked before your very eyes on the central grill. There's a good salad bar, and live music most nights.

Pstrąg Górski (018 206 4163; ul Krupówki 6; mains 16-30zł; 9am-10pm) This self-service fish restaurant, done up in traditional style and overlooking a narrow stream, serves some of the freshest trout, salmon and sea fish in town. It's excellent value.

Stek Chałupa (018 201 5918; ul Krupówki 33; mains 18-40zł; 8am-midnight) Big friendly barn of a place, with homely decor and waitresses in traditional garb. The menu features meat dishes, particularly steaks, though there are vegetarian choices among the salads and *pierogi*.

Café Antrakt (018 201 73 02; ul Krupówki 6; 11am-midnight) A mellow venue for an alcoholic or caffeine-laden drink, hidden away above the street with an ambient old-meets-new decor. It occasionally hosts live jazz.

Getting There & Away

From the **bus terminal** (ul Chramcówki), PKS buses run to Kraków every 45 to 60 minutes (16zł, two hours). Two private companies, **Trans Frej** (www.trans-frej.com.pl, in Polish) and **Szwagropol** (www .szwagropol.pl, in Polish), also run comfortable buses from here (18zł) at the same frequency. At peak times (especially weekends), you can buy your tickets for the private buses in advance from offices a short distance west of the bus station in Zakopane. Tickets are also available in Kraków for Trans Frej buses from **Biuro Turystyki i Zakwaterowania Waweltur** (Map p390; ul Pawia 8) and for Szwagropol buses from **Fogra Travel** (Map p390; ul Pawia 12). The minibus station opposite the bus terminal is most useful for journeys to towns within the Tatra Mountains.

From Zakopane, PKS buses also go once daily to Lublin (63zł, six hours), Sanok (39zł, 6½ hours), Przemyśl (42zł, 4½ hours) and Warsaw (60zł, eight hours). Two daily buses head to Poprad in Slovakia (21zł). PKS buses – and minibuses from opposite the bus terminal – regularly travel to Lake Morskie Oko and on to Polana Palenica. To cross into Slovakia, get off this bus/minibus at Łysa Polana, cross the border on foot and take another bus to Tatranská Lomnica and the other Slovak mountain towns.

From the **train station** (ul Chramcówki), trains for Kraków (33zł, 3½ hours) leave every two hours or so. Three trains a day go to Częstochowa (45zł, seven hours), three to Gdynia via Gdańsk (64zł, 13 hours), two to Łódź (53zł, nine hours), two to Poznań (56zł, 12 hours), and six head to Warsaw (53zł, nine hours).

TATRA MOUNTAINS

The Tatras, 100km south of Kraków, are the highest range of the Carpathian Mountains, providing a dramatic range of rugged scenery that's a distinct contrast to the rest of Poland's flatness. Roughly 60km long and 15km wide, this mountain range stretches across the Polish–Slovak border. A quarter is in Poland and is mostly part of the Tatra National Park (about 212 sq km). The Polish Tatras contain more than 20 peaks over 2000m, the highest of which is Mt Rysy (2499m).

Sights & Activities
CABLE CAR TO MT KASPROWY WIERCH
The **cable car** (adult/concession return 38/28zł; 7am-9pm Jul & Aug, 7.30am-5pm Apr-Jun, Sep & Oct, 8am-4pm Nov) from Kuźnice (3km south of Zakopane) to the summit of Mt Kasprowy Wierch (1985m) is a classic tourist experience enjoyed by Poles and foreigners alike. At the end of the trip, you can get off and stand with one foot in Poland and the other in Slovakia. The one-way journey takes 20 minutes and climbs 936m. The cable car normally shuts down for two weeks in May and November, and won't operate if the snow and, particularly, the winds are dangerous. Note that ticket prices are discounted significantly outside July and August.

The view from the top is spectacular (clouds permitting). Two chairlifts transport skiers to and from various slopes between December and April. A restaurant serves skiers and hikers alike. In summer, many people return to Zakopane on foot down the Gąsienicowa Valley, and the most intrepid walk the ridges all the way across to Lake Morskie Oko via Pięciu Stawów, a strenuous hike taking a full day in good weather.

If you buy a return ticket, your trip back is automatically reserved for two hours after your departure, so buy a one-way ticket to the top (28zł) and another one down (20zł), if you want to stay longer. Mt Kasprowy Wierch is popular; so in summer, arrive early and expect to wait. PKS buses and minibuses to Kuźnice frequently leave from Zakopane.

LAKE MORSKIE OKO
The emerald-green Lake Morskie Oko (Eye of the Sea) is among the loveliest lakes in the Tatras. PKS buses and minibuses regularly depart from Zakopane for Polana Palenica (30 minutes), from where a road (9km) continues uphill to the lake. Cars, bikes and buses are not allowed up this road, so you'll have to walk, but it's not steep (allow about two hours one way). Alternatively, take a horse-drawn carriage (35/20zł uphill/downhill, but very negotiable) to within 2km of the lake. In winter, transport is by horse-drawn four-seater sledge, which is more expensive. The last minibus to Zakopane returns between 5pm and 6pm.

HIKING
If you're doing any hiking in the Tatras get a copy of the *Tatrzański Park Narodowy* map (1:25,000), which shows all hiking trails in the area. Better still, buy one or more of the 14 sheets of *Tatry Polskie*, available at Księgarnia Górska (p406) in Zakopane. In July and August these trails can be overrun by tourists, so late spring and early autumn are the best times. Theoretically you can expect better weather in autumn, when rainfall is lower.

Like all alpine regions, the Tatras can be dangerous, particularly during the snow season (November to May). Remember the weather can be unpredictable. Bring proper hiking boots, warm clothing and waterproof rain gear – and be prepared to use occasional ropes and chains (provided along the trails) to get up and down some rocky slopes. Guides are not necessary because many of the trails are marked, but can be arranged in Zakopane (see p406) for about 230zł per day.

POLAND

There are several picturesque valleys south of Zakopane, including the **Dolina Strążyska**. You can continue from the Strążyska by the red trail up to **Mt Giewont** (1909m), 3½ hours from Zakopane, and then walk down the blue trail to Kuźnice in two hours.

Two long and beautiful forested valleys, the **Dolina Chochołowska** and the **Dolina Kościeliska**, are in the western part of the park, known as the Tatry Zachodnie (West Tatras). These valleys are ideal for cycling. Both are accessible by PKS buses and minibuses from Zakopane.

The Tatry Wysokie (High Tatras) to the east offer quite different scenery: bare granite peaks and glacial lakes. One way to get there is via cable car to **Mt Kasprowy Wierch**, then hike eastward along the red trail to Mt Świnica (2301m) and on to the Zawrat pass (2159m) – a tough three to four hours from Mt Kasprowy. From Zawrat, descend northwards to the Dolina Gąsienicowa along the blue trail and then back to Zakopane.

Alternatively, head south (also along the blue trail) to the wonderful **Dolina Pięciu Stawów** (Five Lakes Valley), where there is a mountain refuge 1¼ hours from Zawrat. The blue trail heading west from the refuge passes **Lake Morskie Oko**, 1½ hours from the refuge.

SKIING

Zakopane boasts four major ski areas (and several smaller ones) with more than 50 ski lifts. **Mt Kasprowy Wierch** (p409) and **Mt Gubałówka** (p408) offer the best conditions and the most challenging slopes in the area, with the ski season extending until early May. Lift tickets cost 8zł for one ride at Mt Kasprowy Wierch, and 5zł on the smaller lift at Mt Gubałówka. Alternatively, you can buy a day card (90zł) at Mt Kasprowy Wierch, which allows you to skip the queues. Purchase your lift tickets on the relevant mountain.

Another alternative is the **Harenda chairlift** (☎ 018 206 4029; www.harendazakopane.pl; ul Harenda 63; ⏰ 9am-6pm) just outside Zakopane, in the direction of Kraków. A one-way/return ticket is 4/6zł, and a day card is 70zł.

Ski equipment rental is available at all facilities except Mt Kasprowy Wierch. Otherwise, stop off on your way to Kuźnice at the **ski rental** place near the Rondo in Zakopane. Other places in Zakopane, such as **Sukces Ski Rental** (☎ 018 206 4197; ul Nowotarska 39) and **Sport Shop & Service** (☎ 018 201 5871; ul Krupówki 52a), also rent ski gear.

Sleeping

Tourists are not allowed to take their own cars into the park; you must walk in, take the cable car or use an official vehicle owned by the park or a hotel or hostel.

Camping is also not allowed in the park, but eight PTTK mountain refuges/hostels provide simple accommodation. Most refuges are small and fill up fast; in midsummer and midwinter they're invariably packed beyond capacity. No one is ever turned away, however, though you may have to crash on the floor if all the beds are taken. Do not arrive too late in the day, and bring along your own bed mat and sleeping bag. All refuges serve simple hot meals, but the kitchens and dining rooms close early (sometimes at 7pm).

The refuges listed here are open all year, but some may be temporarily closed for renovations or because of inclement weather. Check the current situation at the Dom Turysty PTTK in Zakopane or the regional **PTTK headquarters** (☎ 018 443 8610) in Nowy Sącz.

Dolina Pięciu Stawów Hostel (☎ 018 207 7607; dm 25-30zł) This is the highest (1700m) and most scenically located refuge in the Polish Tatras.

Hala Kondratowa Hostel (☎ 018 201 9114; dm 28zł) This place is about 30 minutes beyond Kalatówki on the trail to Giewont. It's in a terrific location and has a great atmosphere, but it is small.

Roztoka Hostel (☎ 018 207 7442; dm 28-30zł) Hikers wishing to traverse the park might want to begin here. It's accessible by the bus or minibus to Morskie Oko.

Morskie Oko Hostel (☎ 018 207 7609; dm 32-42zł) An early start from Zakopane would allow you to visit Morskie Oko in the morning and stay here at night.

Kalatówki Hotel (☎ 018 206 3644; s/d/tr/ste from 48/94/117/132zł) This large and decent refuge is the easiest to reach from Zakopane. It's a 40-minute walk from the Kuźnice cable-car station.

DUNAJEC GORGE

An entertaining and leisurely way to explore the Pieniny Mountains is to go **rafting** on the Dunajec River, which winds along the Polish–Slovak border through a spectacular and deep gorge.

The trip starts at the wharf (Przystan Flisacka) in Kąty, 46km northeast of Zakopane, and you can finish either at the spa town of

Szczawnica (adult/concession 39/19.50zł, 2¼ hours, 18km), or further on at Krościenko (adult/concession 48/24zł, 2¾ hours, 23km). The raft trip operates between April and October, but only starts when there's a minimum of 10 passengers.

The gorge is an easy day trip from Zakopane. Catch a regular bus to Nowy Targ (4zł, 30 minutes, hourly) from Zakopane to connect with one of five daily buses (10zł, 45 minutes) to Kąty. From Szczawnica or Krościenko, take the bus back to Nowy Targ (7zł, one hour, hourly) and change for Zakopane. Krościenko has frequent bus links with Szczawnica, and five buses travel daily between Szczawnica and Kraków (14zł, 2½ hours). You can also return to the Kąty car park by bus with the raftsmen.

To avoid waiting around in Kąty for a raft to fill up, organise a trip at any travel agency in Zakopane or at the tourist office. The cost is around 75zł to 80zł per person, and includes transport, equipment and guides.

SANOK
pop 39,400

Nestled in a picturesque valley in the foothills of the Bieszczady Mountains, Sanok has been subject to Ruthenian, Hungarian, Austrian, Russian, German and Polish rule in its eventful history. Although it contains an important industrial zone, it's also a popular base for exploring the mountains.

The helpful **tourist office** (☎ 013 464 4533; www .sanok.pl; Rynek 14; ☷ 9am-5pm Mon-Fri year-round, 9am-3pm Sat & Sun Oct-Apr) on the market square is the best place to find brochures on Sanok's attractions. The **PTTK office** (☎ 013 463 2512; www.pttk .avx.pl; ul 3 Maja 2; ☷ 8am-5pm Mon-Fri) also provides visitor information. There's a **Bank Pekao** (cnr ul Grzegorza & ul Kościuszki) nearby, and you can

check email at **Prox** (ul Kazimierz Wielkiego 6; per hr 3zł) further west.

Sanok is noted for its unique **Museum of Folk Architecture** (www.skansen.mblsanok.pl; ul Rybickiego 3; adult/concession 9/6zł; ☷ 8am-6pm May-Oct, 8am-2pm Nov-Apr), which features architecture from regional ethnic groups. Walk north from the town centre for 2km along ul Mickiewicza and ul Białogórska, then cross the bridge and turn right. The **Historical Museum** (ul Zamkowa 2; adult/ concession 10/7zł; ☷ 9am-3pm Tue-Sun, 8-10am Mon) is housed in a 16th-century castle and contains an impressive collection of Ruthenian icons, along with a modern art gallery.

Sanok's surrounding villages are attractions in their own right, as many have lovely old churches. The marked **Icon Trail** takes hikers or cyclists along a 70km loop, passing by 10 village churches, as well as attractive mountain countryside. Trail leaflets and maps (in English, German and French) are available from the tourist office, as well as information on other themed trails including a Jewish heritage route.

Convenient budget accommodation is available at **Hotel Pod Trzema Różami** (☎ 013 463 0922; www.podtrzemarozami.pl; ul Jagiellońska 13; s/d/tr/ste 80/100/120/140zł), about 300m south of the main square. Further south (another 600m) and up the scale is **Hotel Jagielloński** (☎ 013 463 1208; www.hoteljagiellonski.bieszczady24.pl; ul Jagiellońska 49; s/ d/tr/ste 115/150/195/230zł), with distinctive wooden furniture, parquetry floors and a very good restaurant. Sanok's most comfortable option is **Hotel Sanvit** (☎ 013 465 5088; www.sanvit.sanok.pl; ul Łazienna 1; s/d/tr/ste 110/150/190/250zł), just west of the square, with bright, modern rooms, shining bathrooms, and a restaurant.

Karczma Jadło Karpackie (☎ 013 464 6700; Rynek 12; mains 8-25zł) is an amenable, down-to-earth bar and restaurant on the main square. A good

---

WORTH THE TRIP: LAKE SOLINA

In the far southeastern corner of Poland, wedged between the Ukrainian and Slovak borders, lies **Lake Solina**. This sizeable reservoir (27km long and 60m deep) was created in 1968 when the San River was dammed. Today it's a popular centre for water sports and other recreational pursuits.

Polańczyk is the best place to base yourself. This pleasant town on the lake's western shore offers a range of attractions, including sailing, windsurfing, fishing and beaches. There are also numerous hotels and sanatoriums offering spa treatments.

There are regular buses from Sanok to Polańczyk each day. For more details, check out Lonely Planet's Poland country guide, visit www.karpaty.turystyka.pl or step into the local **tourist office** (☎ 013 470 3028; ul Wiejska 2).

place to have a drink, alcoholic or otherwise, is **Weranda Caffe** (ul 3 Maja 14; ☾ 10am-10pm), a cosy cafe-bar with a fireplace, and outdoor seating in summer.

The bus terminal and adjacent train station are about 1km southeast of the main square. Six buses go daily to Przemyśl (11zł, two hours), and one to Zakopane (39zł, 6½ hours). Buses also head regularly to Kraków and Warsaw. Train journeys to these destinations, however, may require multiple changes.

PRZEMYŚL
pop 67,100

Everything about Przemyśl (*psheh*-mishl) feels big: its sprawling market square, the massive churches surrounding it, and the broad San River flowing through the city.

Luckily the area of most interest to visitors – around the sloping **Rynek** (Market Sq) – is compact and easily explored. The **tourist office** (☎ 016 675 2164; www.przemysl.pl; ul Grodzka 1; ☾ 10am-6pm Mon-Fri, 9am-5pm Sat & Sun Apr-Sep, 9am-5pm Mon-Fri, 10am-2pm Sat Oct-Mar) is situated above the southwest corner of the square. Check your emails at the **public library** (ul Słowackiego 15; per hr 2zł; ☾ 10am-6pm Mon-Fri, 10am-4pm Sat), on the main road along the eastern edge of the Old Town.

About 350m southwest of the Rynek are the ruins of a 14th-century **castle** (ul Zamkowa), built by Kazimierz Wielki. In a modern building just northeast of Rynek, you can learn about the history of the surrounding region at the **National Museum of the Przemyśl Lands** (Plac Joselewicza; adult/concession 5/2.50zł; ☾ 9.30am-4.30pm Tue & Fri, 10am-2.30pm Wed, Thu & Sat, noon-6pm Sun).

For variety, visit the curious **Museum of Bells and Pipes** (ul Władycze 3; adult/concession 5/2.50zł; ☾ 9.30am-4.30pm Tue & Fri, 10am-2.30pm Wed, Thu & Sat, noon-6pm Sun) in the old Clock Tower, where you can inspect several floors worth of vintage bells, elaborately carved pipes and cigar cutters (the city has long been famous across Poland for manufacturing these items). From the top of the tower there's a great view.

Przemyśl has a selection of inexpensive accommodation, including the central **Dom Wycieczkowy Podzamcze** (☎ 016 678 5374; ul Waygarta 3; dm 23zł, d/tr/q 64/81/108zł), on the western edge of the Old Town. Its rooms have seen some wear, but it's pleasant enough for the price. **Hotelik Pod Basztą** (☎ 016 678 8268; www.hotelik-pod-baszta .w.interia.pl; ul Królowej Jadwigi 4; s/d/tr from 39/59/79zł) is

just below the castle. Rooms are a little old-fashioned, with shared bathrooms, but many have castle or city views.

More comfort is available at **Hotel Europejski** (☎ 016 675 7100; www.hotel-europejski.pl; ul Sowińskiego 4; s/d/tr/ste 110/140/170/210zł) in a renovated old building facing the attractive facade of the train station. An impressive staircase leads to simple, light rooms with high ceilings.

A worthy place to eat is **Restauracja Piwnica Mieszczańska** (☎ 016 675 0459; Rynek 9; mains 6-25zł), on Rynek. It must be Poland's only cellar restaurant with access to a skylight, and is decorated with mini-chandeliers and lace tablecloths. The bourgeoisie platter (three kinds of meat) will interest ardent carnivores, and there's a reasonable selection of soups and fish dishes.

Restauracja Karpacka (☎ 016 678 9057; ul Kościuszki 5; mains 10-30zł; ☾ 10am-10pm), just west of the tourist office, is an old-fashioned eatery featuring bow-tied waiters, a timber ceiling and yellow stucco walls. It serves a good range of Polish standards, and Ukrainian *borscht* as a nod to the neighbours just down the road.

If you fancy a drink, **Bistro Absynt** (Plac Dominikański 4), on the northwest corner of Rynek, is a relaxed space from which to sip and people-watch.

From Przemyśl, buses run to Lviv (95km) in Ukraine several times a day and regularly to all towns in southeastern Poland, including Sanok (11zl, two hours, six daily). Trains run to Lublin (41zł, four hours, two daily), Kraków (43zł, 3¾ hours, 11 daily) and Warsaw (53zł, 6¾ hours, four daily), and stop here on the way to/from Lviv. The bus terminal and adjacent train station in Przemyśl are about 1km northeast of the Rynek.

SILESIA

Silesia (Śląsk) is a fascinating mix of landscapes. Though the industrial zone around Katowice has limited attraction for visitors, beautiful Wrocław is a historic city with lively nightlife, and the Sudeten Mountains draw hikers and other nature lovers.

The history of the region is similarly diverse, having been governed by Polish, Bohemian, Austrian and German rulers. After two centuries as part of Prussia and Germany, the territory was largely included within Poland's new borders after WWII.

WROCŁAW

pop 640,000

When citizens of beautiful Kraków enthusiastically encourage you to visit Wrocław (*vrots-wahf*), you know you're onto something good. The city's delightful Old Town is a gracious mix of Gothic and baroque styles, and its large student population ensures a healthy number of restaurants, bars and nightclubs.

Wrocław has been traded back and forth between various rulers over the centuries, but began life in the year 1000 under the Polish Piast dynasty and developed into a prosperous trading and cultural centre. In the 1740s it passed to Prussia, under the German name of Breslau. Under Prussian rule, the city became a major textile manufacturing centre, greatly increasing its population.

Upon its return to Poland in 1945, Wrocław was a shell of its former self, having sustained massive damage in WWII. Though 70% of the city was destroyed, sensitive restoration has returned the historic centre to its former beauty.

Information

Bank Pekao (ul Oławska 2)

EMPiK (Rynek 50) Bookshop.

Internet Netvigator (ul Igielna 14; per hr 3zł; ⏱ 9am-midnight)

Księgarnia Świat Podróżnika (ul Wita Stwosza 19/20) Maps and guidebooks.

Main post office (Rynek 28; ⏱ 6.30am-8.30pm Mon-Sat)

Tourist office (☎ 071 344 3111; www.wroclaw.pl; Rynek 14; ⏱ 9am-9pm Apr-Oct, 9am-8pm Nov-Mar)

Tourist & Cultural Information Centre (☎ 071 342 0185; www.wroclaw-info.pl; ul Sukiennice 12; ⏱ 8am-7pm Mon-Fri, 9am-8pm Sat & Sun Apr-Oct) Handles cultural ticket sales and offers internet access.

W Sercu Miasta (ul Przejście Żelaźnicze 4; per hr 4zł; ⏱ 9am-midnight Mon-Sat, noon-midnight Sun) Internet access down a laneway in the middle of Rynek.

Sights

In the centre of the Old Town is the **Rynek**, Poland's second-largest old market square (after Kraków). The beautiful **town hall** (built 1327–1504) on the southern side plays host to the **City Dwellers' Art Museum** (adult/concession 7/5zł, free Wed; ⏱ 11am-5pm Tue-Sat, 10am-6pm Sun), with stately rooms on show, and exhibits featuring the art of gold and the stories of famous Wrocław inhabitants.

In the northwestern corner of the Rynek are two attractive small houses linked by a baroque gate. They're called **Jaś i Małgosia** (ul Św. Mikołaja), a couple better known to English speakers as Hansel and Gretel.

See if you can spot the diminutive statue of a gnome at ground level, just to the west of these houses; he's one of over 70 **Gnomes of Wrocław**, which are scattered through the city. Whimsical as they are, they're attributed to the symbol of the Orange Alternative, a communist-era dissident group that used ridicule as a weapon, and often painted gnomes where graffiti had been removed by the authorities.

Behind gate and gnome is the monumental 14th-century **St Elizabeth's Church** (ul Elżbiety 1; admission 5zł; ⏱ 9am-7pm Mon-Fri, 11am-5pm Sat, 1-6pm Sun May-Oct, 10am-5pm Mon-Sat, 1-5pm Sun Nov-Apr) with its 83m-high tower, which you can climb for city views. The southwestern corner of the Rynek opens into **Plac Solny** (Salt Sq), once the site of the town's salt trade and now home to a 24-hour flower market.

West of the Rynek is the **Arsenal**, a remnant of the town's 15th century fortifications. It now houses the **Military Museum** (ul Cieszyńskiego 9; adult/concession 7/5zł; ⏱ 11am-5pm Wed-Sat, 10am-6pm Sun), with the usual collection of old weapons.

One block east of the Rynek is the Gothic **St Mary Magdalene's Church** (ul Łaciarska; admission free; ⏱ 9am-4pm Mon-Sat) with a Romanesque portal from 1280 incorporated into its southern external wall. Climb the 72m high tower and its connected **bridge** (adult/concession 4/3zł, ⏱ 10am-8pm Apr-Oct) for a lofty view. Further east, the 15th-century former Bernardine church and monastery encompasses the **Museum of Architecture** (ul Bernardyńska 5; adult/concession 7/5zł; ⏱ 10am-4pm Tue, Wed, Fri & Sat, noon-6pm Thu, 11am-5pm Sun).

Slightly further east is Wrocław's pride and joy (and major tourist attraction), the giant **Panorama of Racławicka** (www.panoramaraclawicka.pl; ul Purkyniego 11; adult/concession 20/15zł; ⏱ 9am-5pm Tue-Sun May-Oct, 9am-4pm Tue-Sun Nov-Apr), a 360-degree painting of the 1794 Battle of Racławice, in which the Polish peasant army, led by Tadeusz Kościuszko, defeated Russian forces intent on partitioning Poland. Created by Jan Styka and Wojciech Kossak for the centenary of the battle in 1894, the painting is an immense 114m long and 15m high, and was brought here by Polish immigrants displaced from Lviv after WWII. Due to the communist government's uneasiness about glorifying a famous Russian defeat, however, the panorama wasn't re-erected until 1985, in a circular building east of the Old Town. Obligatory tours (with audio in

POLAND

WROCŁAW

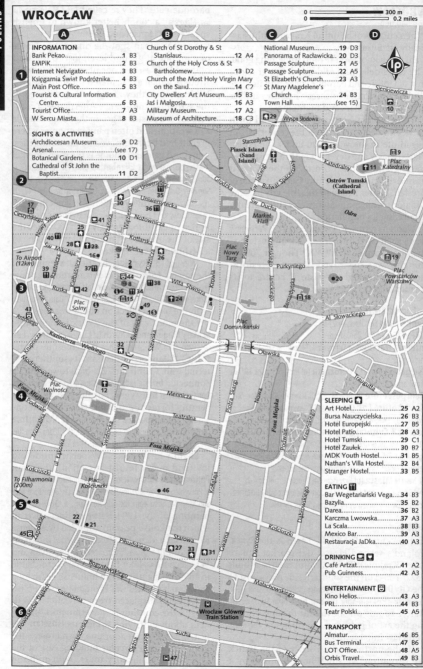

0 _____ 300 m
0 _____ 0.2 miles

INFORMATION
Bank Pekao.........................1 B3
EMPiK...............................2 B3
Internet Netvigator.............3 B3
Księgarnia Świat Podróżnika.. 4 B3
Main Post Office.................5 B3
Tourist & Cultural Information
  Centre.............................6 B3
Tourist Office.....................7 A3
W Sercu Miasta...................8 B3

SIGHTS & ACTIVITIES
Archdiocesan Museum..........9 D2
Arsenal.........................(see 17)
Botanical Gardens..............10 D1
Cathedral of St John the
  Baptist..........................11 D2

Church of St Dorothy & St
  Stanislaus......................12 A4
Church of the Holy Cross & St
  Bartholomew..................13 D2
Church of the Most Holy Virgin Mary
  on the Sand....................14 C2
City Dwellers' Art Museum....15 B3
Jaś i Małgosia....................16 A3
Military Museum.................17 A2
Museum of Architecture........18 C3

National Museum................19 D3
Panorama of Racławicka.. 20 D3
Passage Sculpture...............21 A5
Passage Sculpture...............22 A5
St Elizabeth's Church...........23 A3
St Mary Magdelene's
  Church..........................24 B3
Town Hall......................(see 15)

SLEEPING 🛏
Art Hotel.........................25 A2
Bursa Nauczycielska............26 B3
Hotel Europejski.................27 B5
Hotel Patio........................28 B3
Hotel Tumski......................29 C1
Hotel Zaułek......................30 B2
MDK Youth Hostel...............31 B5
Nathan's Villa Hostel...........32 B4
Stranger Hostel...................33 B5

EATING 🍴
Bar Wegetariański Vega.......34 B3
Bazylia.............................35 B2
Darea...............................36 B2
Karczma Lwowska...............37 A3
La Scala............................38 B3
Mexico Bar........................39 A3
Restauracja JaDka...............40 A3

DRINKING 🍸🍷
Café Artzat.......................41 A2
Pub Guinness.....................42 A3

ENTERTAINMENT 🎭
Kino Helios........................43 A3
PRL..................................44 B3
Teatr Polski........................45 A5

TRANSPORT
Almatur.............................46 B5
Bus Terminal......................47 B6
LOT Office.........................48 A5
Orbis Travel.......................49 B3

English, French, German, Spanish, Russian and other languages) run every 30 minutes between 9am and 4.30pm from April to November, and 10am and 3pm from December to March. The ticket also allows entry to the National Museum on the same day.

Located nearby, the **National Museum** (www .mnwr.art.pl; Plac Powstańców Warszawy 5; adult/concession 15/10zł, free Sat; ☾ 9am-4pm Wed-Fri & Sun, 10am-6pm Sat) exhibits Silesian medieval art, and a fine collection of modern Polish painting. Entry is included with a ticket to the Panorama.

North of the river is **Piasek Island** (Sand Island), where you'll find the 14th-century **Church of the Most Holy Virgin Mary on the Sand** (ul Św. Jadwigi; ☾ erratic) with lofty Gothic vaults and a year-round nativity scene. Cross the small bridge to **Ostrów Tumski** (Cathedral Island), a picturesque area full of churches, though it's no longer an island (an arm of the Odra River was reclaimed during the 19th century), and walk to the two-storey Gothic **Church of the Holy Cross & St Bartholomew** (Plac Kościelny; ☾ 9am-6pm), built between 1288 and 1350. Classical music concerts are often held in these two churches.

Further east is the Gothic **Cathedral of St John the Baptist** (Plac Katedralny; ☾ 10am-6pm Mon-Sat, except during services). Uniquely, there's a lift to whisk you to the top of the **tower** (adult/concession 5/4zł) for superb views. Next door is the **Archdiocesan Museum** (Plac Katedralny 16; adult/concession 3/2zł; ☾ 9am-3pm Tue-Sun). Nearby are the charming **Botanical Gardens** (ul Sienkiewicza 23; adult/concession 7/5zł; ☾ 8am-6pm Apr-Oct), where you can chill out among the chestnut trees and tulips.

To the south of the Old Town is the **Church of St Dorothy & St Stanislaus** (ul Świdnicka; ☾ dawn-dusk), a massive Gothic complex built in 1351. About 500m south of the church on the corner of ul Świdnicka and ul Piłsudskiego is a fascinating sculpture called **Passage** (Przejście), which depicts a group of pedestrians being swallowed by the pavement, only to re-emerge on the other side of the street.

Festivals & Events

Musica Polonica Nova Festival (www.musicapolonica nova.pl, in Polish) February

Jazz on the Odra International Festival (www .jnofestival.pl) April

Wrocław Non Stop (www.wroclawnonstop.pl) June/July

Wratislavia Cantans (www.wratislaviacantans.pl) September

Wrocław Marathon (www.wroclawmaraton.pl) September

Sleeping
BUDGET

MDK Youth Hostel (☎ 071 343 8856; www.mdk.kopernik .wroclaw.pl; ul Kołłątaja 20; dm/d from 22/29zł) Not far from the train station, this is a basic place, located in a grand mustard-coloured building. Some dorms are huge and beds are packed close together. It's almost always full, so book ahead.

Stranger Hostel (☎ 071 344 1206; www.thestranger hostel.com; ul Kołłątaja 16; dm 40-55zł) A tatty old staircase leads up to pleasant budget accommodation. Dorms are set in renovated apartment rooms with ornate lamps and decorative ceilings. Bathrooms are shiny clean, and guests have free access to a kitchen and washing machine. There's a games console and a DVD projector for rainy days.

Nathan's Villa Hostel (☎ 071 344 1095; www.nathans villa.com; ul Świdnicka 13; dm/r from 45/150zł) Sister to the successful Kraków hostel (p394), this comfortable 96-bed place is conveniently placed 150m south of the Rynek. It does accept noisy Polish school groups in addition to backpackers, so check before you check in.

Bursa Nauczycielska (☎ 071 344 3781; www.dodn .wroclaw.pl/bursa; ul Kotlarska 42; s/d/tr/q 65/110/105/120zł) A basic but clean hostel with shared bathrooms, ideally located just one block northeast of the Rynek. There's a lot of brown in the colour scheme, but the rooms are quite cosy.

MIDRANGE & TOP END

Old Town Apartments (Map p378; ☎ 022 351 2260; www .warsawshotel.com; Rynek Starego Miasta 12/14, Warsaw; apt from €85) Warsaw-based agency with modern, fully furnished one-bedroom apartments around Wrocław's main square. Weekly rates are available.

Hotel Zaułek (☎ 071 341 0046; www.hotel.uni.wroc .pl; ul Garbary 11; s/d from 260/330zł) Run by the university, this guest house accommodates just 18 visitors in a dozen homely rooms. The 1pm checkout is a plus for heavy sleepers, and weekend prices are a steal. Half and full board is available.

Hotel Tumski (☎ 071 322 6099; www.hotel-tumski .com.pl; Wyspa Słodowa 10; s/d/tr/ste from 260/380/420/530zł) This is a neat hotel in a peaceful setting overlooking the river, offering reasonable value for money. It's ideal for exploring the lovely ecclesiastical quarter, and there's a good restaurant attached.

Hotel Europejski (☎ 071 772 1000; www.silfor.pl; ul Piłsudskiego 88; s/d/ste 269/309/349zł) Apparently a leopard can change its spots – the formerly drab Europejski has recently been transformed into a smart business hotel. Rooms are clean and bright, and very handy for the train station.

Art Hotel (☎ 071 787 7100; www.arthotel.pl; ul Kiełbaśnicza 20; s/d/ste from 270/290/340zł; ⊠) Elegant but affordable accommodation in a renovated apartment building. Rooms feature tastefully restrained decor, quality fittings and gleaming bathrooms. Within the arched brick cellar is a top-notch restaurant, and there's a fitness room to work off the resultant calories.

Hotel Patio (☎ 071 375 0400; www.hotelpatio.pl; ul Kiełbaśniczna 24; s/d/ste from 300/330/500zł) Pleasant lodgings a short hop from the main square, housed within two buildings linked by a covered sunlit courtyard. Rooms are clean and light, sometimes small but with reasonably high ceilings. There's a restaurant, bar and hairdresser on site.

Eating & Drinking

Bar Wegetariański Vega (☎ 071 344 3934; Rynek 1/2; mains 5-6zł; ☯ 8am-7pm Mon-Fri, 9am-5pm Sat) This is a cheap cafeteria in the centre of the Rynek, offering vegie dishes in a light green space. Good choice of soups and crepes. Upstairs there's a vegan section, open from noon.

our pick Bazylia (Plac Uniwersytecki; mains 5-10zł; ☯ 8am-8pm) Inexpensive and bustling modern take on the classic *bar mleczny*, in a curved space with huge plate-glass windows overlooking the venerable university buildings. The menu has a lot of Polish standards such as *bigos* and *gołąbki*, and a decent range of salads and other vegetable dishes. Order and pay at the till before receiving your food.

La Scala (☎ 071 372 5394; Rynek 38; mains 12-140zł) Offers authentic Italian food and particularly good desserts. Some dishes are pricey, but you're paying for the location. The cheaper trattoria at ground level serves good pizza and pasta.

Mexico Bar (☎ 071 346 0292; ul Rzeźnicza 34; mains 13-38zł; ☯ noon-midnight) Compact, warmly lit restaurant featuring sombreros, backlit masks and a chandelier made of beer bottles. There's a small bar to lean on while waiting for a table. All the Tex-Mex standards are on the menu, but book at least two days ahead for a table on weekends.

Karczma Lwowska (☎ 071 343 9887; Rynek 4; mains 15-41zł; ☯ noon-midnight) Has a great spot on the main square, with outdoor seating in summer, and offers the usual meaty Polish standards in a space with a rustic rural look. It's worth stopping by to try the beer, served in ceramic mugs.

Darea (☎ 071 343 5301; ul Kuźnicza 43/45; mains 25-100zł; ☯ 11am-10pm) With management at the LG Electronics factory in nearby Kobierzyce top-heavy with Koreans, it was inevitable that Wrocław would produce a place serving dishes like *bibimbab* and *bulgogi*. You won't find better Korean anywhere in Poland.

Restauracja JaDka (☎ 071 343 6461; www.jadka.pl; ul Rzeźnicza 24/25; mains 38-81zł; ☯ noon-11pm) Arguably the best restaurant in town, presenting impeccable modern versions of Polish classics amid elegant table settings in delightful Gothic surrounds. The set lunch available Monday to Saturday is a snip at 35zł.

Pub Guinness (Plac Solny 5; ☯ noon-2am) No prizes for guessing what this pub serves. A lively, fairly authentic Irish pub, spread over three levels on a busy corner. The ground-floor bar buzzes with student and traveller groups getting together, and there's a restaurant and beer cellar as well. A good place to wind down after a hard day's sightseeing.

Café Artzat (ul Malarska 30) This low-key cafe just north of the Church of St Elizabeth is one of the best places in town to recharge the batteries over coffee or tea and a good book.

Entertainment

Check out the bimonthly *Visitor* (free and in English) for details of what's on in this important cultural centre. It's available from the tourist office and upmarket hotels.

our pick PRL (Rynek Ratusz 10; ☯ noon-late) The dictatorship of the proletariat is alive and well in this tongue-in-cheek venue inspired by communist nostalgia. Disco lights play over a bust of Lenin, propaganda posters line the walls, and red menace memorabilia is scattered through the maze of rooms. Descend to the basement – beneath the portraits of Stalin and Mao – if you'd like to hit the dance floor. Tuesday is karaoke night.

Teatr Polski (☎ 071 316 0777; www.teatrpolski .wroc.pl, in Polish; ul Zapolskiej 3) Wrocław's main theatrical venue stages classic Polish and foreign drama.

Filharmonia (☎ 071 342 2001; www.filharmonia .wroclaw.pl; ul Piłsudskiego 19) This place hosts concerts of classical music, mostly on Friday and Saturday nights.

Kino Helios (www.heliosnet.pl; ul Kazimierza Wielkiego 19a) If you're after a movie, head to this modern multiplex screening English-language films.

Getting There & Away

Orbis Travel (☎ 071 344 4408; Rynek 29) and **Almatur** (☎ 071 343 4135; ul Kościuszki 34) offer the usual services. If you're travelling to/from Wrocław at the weekend, you'll be in competition with thousands of itinerant university students, so book your ticket as soon as possible.

AIR

From **Copernicus airport** (www.airport.wroclaw.pl), LOT flies frequently between Wrocław and Warsaw. It also heads daily to Brussels, and twice daily to Frankfurt and Munich. Tickets can be bought at the **LOT office** (☎ 0801 703 703; ul Piłsudskiego 36).

A range of budget carriers connect Wrocław with other European cities, including a range of British and Irish regional destinations. Ryanair and Wizz Air fly daily to London; Ryanair heads five times a week to Dublin; and Cimber Air operates five flights a week to Copenhagen.

The airport is in Strachowice, about 12km west of the Old Town. The half-hourly bus 406 and infrequent night bus 249 link the airport with Wrocław Główny train station and the bus terminal.

BUS

The **bus terminal** (ul Sucha 11) is south of the main train station, and offers four daily buses to Warsaw (51zł, seven hours). For most other travel, however, the train is more convenient.

TRAIN

The **Wrocław Główny station** (ul Piłsudskiego 105) was built in 1856 and is a historical monument in itself. Every day, trains to Kraków (45zł, 4½ hours) depart every one or two hours, with similarly frequent services to Warsaw (102zł, 5¾ hours), usually via Łódź. Wrocław is also linked by train to Poznań (34zł, 2½ hours, at least hourly), Częstochowa (34zł, three hours, four daily) and Szczecin (51zł, five hours, eight daily).

SUDETEN MOUNTAINS

The Sudeten Mountains (Sudety) run for over 250km along the Czech–Polish border.

The Sudetes feature dense forests, amazing rock formations and deposits of semiprecious stones, and can be explored along the extensive network of trails for **hiking** or **mountain biking**. The highest part of this old eroded chain is Mt Śnieżka (1602m).

Szklarska Poręba, at the northwestern end of the Sudetes, offers superior facilities for **hiking** and **skiing**. It's at the base of Mt Szrenica (1362m), and the town centre is at the upper end of ul Jedności Narodowej. The small **tourist office** (☎ 075 754 7740; www.szklarskaporeba .pl; ul Pstrowskiego 1) has accommodation info and maps. Nearby, several trails begin at the intersection of ul Jedności Narodowej and ul Wielki Sikorskiego. The red trail goes to **Mt Szrenica** (two hours) and offers a peek at **Wodospad Kamieńczyka**, a spectacular waterfall.

Karpacz to the southeast has more nightlife on offer, though it attracts fewer serious mountaineers. It's loosely clustered along a 3km road winding through Łomnica Valley at the base of Mt Śnieżka. The **tourist office** (☎ 075 761 8605; www.karpacz.com.pl; ul Konstytucji 3 Maja 25a) should be your first port of call. To reach the peak of Mt Śnieżka on foot, take one of the trails (three to four hours) from Hotel Biały Jar. Some of the trails pass by one of two splendid postglacial lakes: **Mały Staw** and **Wielki Staw**.

The bus is the fastest way of getting around the region. Every day from Szklarska Poręba, about five buses head to Wrocław (29zł, three hours) and one train plods along to Warsaw (60zł, 11 hours). From Karpacz, get one of hourly buses to Jelenia Góra (7zł, one hour), where buses and trains go in all directions.

For the Czech Republic, take a bus from Szklarska Poręba to Jakuszyce (4zł, 15 minutes), cross the border on foot to Harrachov (on the Czech side) and take another bus from there.

WIELKOPOLSKA

Wielkopolska (Greater Poland) is the region where Poland came to life in the Middle Ages, and is referred to as the Cradle of the Polish State. As a result of this ancient eminence, its cities and towns are full of historic and cultural attractions.

The royal capital moved from Poznań to Kraków in 1038, though Wielkopolska remained an important province. Its historic significance didn't save it from international

POLAND

conflict, however, and the region became part of Prussia in 1793. Wielkopolska rose against German rule at the end of WWI and became part of the reborn Poland. The battles of WWII later caused widespread destruction in the area.

POZNAŃ
pop 565,000

No one could accuse Poznań of being too sleepy. Between its regular trade fairs, student population and visiting travellers, it's a vibrant city with a wide choice of attractions. There's a beautiful Old Town at its centre, with a number of interesting museums, and a range of lively bars, clubs and restaurants. The surrounding countryside is also good for cycling and hiking.

Poznań grew from humble beginnings, when 9th-century Polanian tribes built a wooden fort on the island of Ostrów Tumski. From 968 to 1038 Poznań was the de facto capital of Poland. Its position between Berlin and Warsaw has always underlined its importance as a trading town, and in 1925 a modern version of its famous medieval trade fairs was instituted. The fairs, filling up the city's hotels for several days at a time, are the lynchpin of the city's economy.

As it's at the heart of Wielkopolska, Poznań makes a good transport hub from which to explore the region.

Information

Bank Pekao Old Town (ul 23 Lutego); ul Św. Marcin (ul Św. Marcin 52/56)

City Information Centre (☎ 061 851 9645; ul Ratajczaka 44; ❧ 10am-7pm Mon-Fri, 10am-5pm Sat) Handles bookings for cultural events.

E24 (ul Półwiejska 42; per hr 4.50zł; ❧ 24hr) Inside the massive Stary Browar shopping centre.

EMPiK (Plac Wolności) Bookshop.

Globtroter Turystyczna (Stary Rynek 98/100) Sells maps and guidebooks. Enter from ul Żydowska.

Main post office (ul Kościuszki 77; ❧ 7am-8pm Mon-Fri, 8am-3pm Sat)

Tourist office (☎ 061 852 6156; Stary Rynek 59; ❧ 9am-8pm Mon-Sat, 10am-6pm Sun May-Sep, 9am-5pm Mon-Fri Oct-Apr)

Sights

If you're in the attractive **Stary Rynek** (Old Market Sq) at noon, keep an eye out for the goats in the Renaissance **town hall** (built 1550–60). Every midday two metal goats above its clock butt

their horns together 12 times, echoing an improbable centuries-old legend of two animals escaping a cook and fighting each other in the town hall tower. Inside the building, the **Poznań Historical Museum** (adult/concession 5.50/3.50zł, free Sat; ❧ 9am-4pm Tue, Thu & Fri, 11am-6pm Wed, 10am-3pm Sun) displays splendid period interiors.

Also within the square are the **Wielkopolska Military Museum** (Stary Rynek 9; adult/concession 3.50/2.20zł, free Sat; ❧ 9am-4pm Tue-Sat, 10am-3pm Sun) and the **Museum of Musical Instruments** (Stary Rynek 45; adult/concession 5.50/3.50zł, free Sat; ❧ 11am-5pm Tue-Sat, 10am-3pm Sun), along with the **Museum of the Wielkopolska Uprising** (Stary Rynek 3; adult/concession 4/2zł, free Sat; ❧ 10am-5pm Tue, Thu & Fri, 10am-6pm Wed, 10am-3pm Sat & Sun), which details the conflict in the region between German and Polish fighters after WWI.

The **Archaeological Museum** (ul Wodna 27; adult/concession 6/3zł, free Sat; ❧ 10am-4pm Tue-Fri, 10am-6pm Sat, 10am-3pm Sun) contains Egyptian mummies and displays on the prehistory of western Poland.

The 17th-century **Franciscan Church** (ul Franciszkańska 2; ❧ 8am-8pm), one block west of the Rynek, has an ornate baroque interior, complete with wall paintings and rich stucco work. Above the church, on a hill, is the **Museum of Applied Arts** (Gora Przemysła 1; adult/concession 5.50/3.50zł, free Sat; ❧ 10am-4pm Tue-Sat, 10am-3pm Sun), featuring glassware, ceramics, silverware and clocks.

The nearby **National Museum: Paintings & Sculpture Gallery** (Al Marcinkowskiego 9; adult/concession 10/6zł, free Sat; ❧ 10am-6pm Tue, 9am-5pm Wed, 10am-4pm Thu, 10am-5pm Fri & Sat, 10am-3pm Sun) displays mainly 19th- and 20th-century Polish paintings.

Two blocks south of Stary Rynek is the large, pink, baroque **Parish Church of St Stanislaus** (ul Gołębia 1; ❧ erratic) with monumental altars built in the mid-17th century. A short stroll southeast is the **Ethnographic Museum** (☎ 061 852 30 06; ul Grobla 25; adult/concession 5.50/3.50zł, free Sat; ❧ 10am-4pm Tue, Wed, Fri & Sat, 10am-3pm Sun), presenting a collection of woodcarving and traditional costumes.

The 19th-century Prussian **Poznań Citadel**, where 20,000 German troops held out for a month in February 1945, lies about 1.5km north of the Old Town. The fortress was destroyed by artillery fire but a park was laid out on the site, which incorporates both the **Poznań Army Museum** (Al Armii Poznań; admission free; ❧ 9am-4pm Tue-Sat, 10am-4pm Sun) and the nearby **Poznań Citadel Museum** (Al Armii Poznań; adult/concession 4/2zł, free Fri; ❧ 9am-4pm Tue-Sat, 10am-4pm Sun).

In a park in the area west of Stary Rynek, the emotive **Monument to the Victims of June 1956** commemorates the dead and injured of the massive 1956 strike by the city's industrial workers, which was crushed by tanks. Next door in the Cultural Centre, there's more detail to be uncovered in the **Museum of Poznań June 1956** (ul Św. Marcin 80/82; adult/concession 4/2zł, free Sat; ✆ 10am-6pm Tue-Fri, 10am-4pm Sat & Sun).

In **Park Wilsona**, 1km southwest of the train station, you'll find **Palm House** (ul Matejki 18; adult/concession 5.50/4zł; ✆ 9am-5pm Tue-Sat, 9am-6pm Sun). This huge greenhouse (built in 1910) contains 17,000 species of tropical and subtropical plants.

Ostrów Tumski is 1km east of the Old Town (take any eastbound tram from Plac Wielkopolski). This river island is dominated by the monumental, double-towered **Poznań Cathedral** (ul Ostrów Tumski), originally built in 968. The Byzantine-style **Golden Chapel** (1841) and the **mausoleums** of Mieszko I and Boleslaus the Brave are behind the high altar. Opposite the cathedral is the 15th-century Gothic **Church of the Virgin Mary** (ul Panny Marii 1/3).

Some 1.6km east of the Old Town is **Lake Malta**, a favourite weekend destination for Poles. It holds sailing regattas, outdoor concerts and other events in summer, and in winter there's a ski slope in operation.

A fun way to visit the lake is to take tram 3, 4 or 8 from Plac Wielkopolski to the Rondo Śródka stop on the other side of Ostrów Tumski. From the nearby terminus, you can catch a miniature train along the **Malta Park Railway** (ul Jana Pawła II; adult/concession 4.50/3zł; ✆ 10am-6.45pm Mon-Fri, 10am-6pm Sat & Sun May-15 Oct), which follows the lake's shore to the **New Zoo** (ul Krańcowa 81; adult/concession 9/6zł; ✆ 9am-7pm Apr-Sep, 9am-4pm Oct-Mar). This sprawling institution houses diverse species, including Baltic grey seals, in a pine forest environment.

Festival & Events
The largest trade fairs take place in January, June, September and October.

Poznań Jazz Festival (www.jazz.pl) March
St John's Fair Cultural event in June.
Malta International Theatre Festival (www.malta-festival.pl) June

Sleeping
During trade fairs, the rates of Poznań's accommodation dramatically increase. A room may also be difficult to find, so it pays to book

ahead. Prices given here are for outside trade fair periods.

Check out **Biuro Zakwaterowania Przemysław** (✆ 061 866 3560; www.przemyslaw.com.pl; ul Głogowska 16; s/d from 53/85zł, apt from 170zł; ✆ 8am-6pm Mon-Fri, 10am-2pm Sat), an accommodation agency not far from the train station. Rates for weekends and stays of more than three nights are cheaper than the prices quoted here.

Youth Hostel No 3 (✆ 061 866 4040; ul Berwińskiego 2/3; dm 30zł) Cheap lodgings about a 15-minute walk southwest of the train station along ul Głogowska, adjacent to Park Wilsona. It's a basic 'no frills' option, but fills up fast with students and school groups. There's a 10pm curfew.

Frolic Goats Hostel (✆ 061 852 4411; www.frolicgoats hostel.com; ul Wrocławska 16/6; dm/d/tr from 50/140/250zł) Named after the feisty goats who fight above the town hall clock, this hostel is aimed squarely at the international backpacker. There's a washing machine on the premises, bike hire is available for 25zł per day, and room rates are unaffected by trade fairs. Enter from ul Jaskółcza.

Mini Hotelik (✆ 061 633 1416; Al Niepodległości 8a; r 129-161zł) Like it says on the label, this is a small place in an old building between the train station and the Old Town. It's basic but clean, with colourfully painted chambers. Some rooms share a bathroom. Enter from ul Taylora.

Hotel Lech (✆ 061 853 0151; www.hotel-lech.poznan .pl; ul Św. Marcin 74; s/d/tr 172/264/366zł) Hotel Lech has standard three-star decor, but rooms are relatively spacious and the bathrooms are modern. Flash your ISIC card for a discount.

our pick **Rezydencja Solei** (✆ 061 855 7351; www.hotel-solei.pl; ul Szewska 2; s/d/ste 199/299/389zł) Temptingly close to Stary Rynek, this tiny hotel offers small but cosy rooms in an old-fashioned residential style, with wallpaper and timber furniture striking a homely note. The attic suite is amazingly large and can accommodate up to four people.

Hotel Stare Miasto (✆ 061 663 62 42; www.hotel staremiasto.pl; ul Rybaki 36; s/d 215/340zł; ✆) Elegant, value-for-money hotel with a tasteful chandeliered foyer and spacious breakfast room. Rooms can be small, but are clean and bright with lovely starched white sheets. Some upper rooms have skylights in place of windows.

Hotel Rzymski (✆ 061 852 8121; www.rzymskihotel .com.pl; Al Marcinkowskiego 22; s/d/tr from 245/300/405zł)

POLAND

POZNAŃ

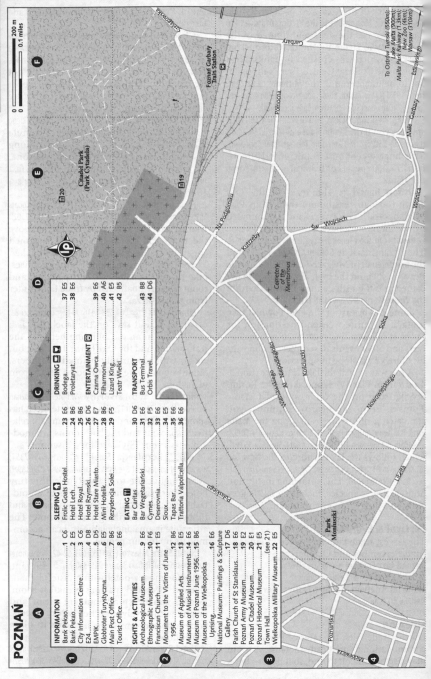

INFORMATION

Bank Pekao	1	C6
Bank Pekao	2	E5
City Information Centre	3	C6
E24	4	D8
EMPIK	5	D5
Globtroter Turystyczna	6	E5
Main Post Office	7	B6
Tourist Office	8	E6

SIGHTS & ACTIVITIES

Archaeological Museum	9	E6
Ethnographic Museum	10	F6
Franciscan Church	11	E5
Monument to the Victims of June 1956	12	B6
Museum of Applied Arts	13	E5
Museum of Musical Instruments	14	E6
Museum of Poznań June 1956	15	B6
Museum of the Wielkopolska Uprising	16	E6
National Museum: Paintings & Sculpture Gallery	17	D6
Parish Church of St Stanislaus	18	E6
Poznań Army Museum	19	E2
Poznań Citadel Museum	20	E1
Poznań Historical Museum	21	E5
Town Hall	(see 21)	
Wielkopolska Military Museum	22	E5

SLEEPING

Frolic Goats Hostel	23	E6
Hotel Lech	24	B6
Hotel Royal	25	B6
Hotel Rzymski	26	D6
Hotel Stare Miasto	27	E7
Mini Hotelik	28	B6
Rezydencja Solei	29	F5

EATING

Bar Caritas	30	D6
Bar Wegetariański	31	E6
Cymes	32	F5
Deserovnia	33	E6
Sioux	34	E5
Tapas Bar	35	E6
Trattoria Valpolicella	36	E6

DRINKING

Bodega	37	E5
Proletaryat	38	E6

ENTERTAINMENT

Czarna Owca	39	E6
Filharmonia	40	A6
Lizard King	41	E5
Teatr Wielki	42	B5

TRANSPORT

Bus Terminal	43	B8
Orbis Travel	44	D6

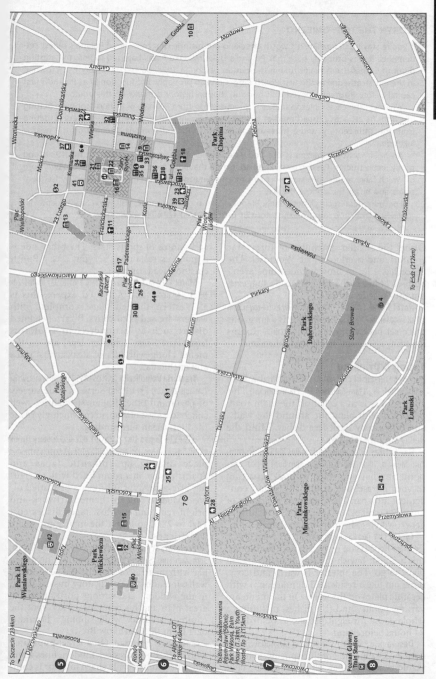

POLAND

WORTH THE TRIP: GNIEZNO

If you're staying in Poznań, it's worth checking out historic Gniezno, one of Poland's oldest settlements. It was probably here that Poland's Duke Mieszko I was baptised in 966, the starting point of Catholicism's major role in the nation's story. In 1025, Bolesław Chrobry was crowned in the city's cathedral as the first Polish king. Gniezno probably also functioned as Poland's first capital before Poznań achieved that honour, though history is murky on this point.

Whatever the case, Gniezno makes a good day trip from Poznań, or a short stopover. Setting out from its attractive broad **market square**, you can investigate its historic **cathedral**, dating from the 14th century, and a **museum** dedicated to Poland's origins, situated on the nearby lakeside.

An hour north of Gniezno is the Iron Age village of **Biskupin**, unearthed in the 1930s and partly reconstructed. Passing by it is a **tourist train** that links the towns of Żnin and Gąsawa, both of which have regular bus transport to Gniezno. Gniezno itself is linked to Poznań by frequent trains and buses throughout the day.

For more details, check out Lonely Planet's Poland country guide, visit www.turystyka.powiat -gniezno.pl, or drop into Gniezno's **tourist office** (☎ 061 428 4100; ul Tumska 12).

Offers the regular amenities of three-star comfort, and overlooks Plac Wolności. The decor has a lot of brown, and rooms aren't quite as grand as the elegant facade suggests, but they're a decent size.

Hotel Royal (☎ 061 858 2300; www.hotel-royal.com .pl; ul Św. Marcin 71; s/d 320/420zł) This is a gorgeous place set back from the main road. Rooms have huge beds and sparkling bathrooms.

Eating & Drinking

Bar Wegetariański (☎ 061 821 1255; ul Wrocławska 21; mains 5-10zł; ⏰ 11am-6pm Mon-Fri, 11am-3pm Sat) This cheap eatery is in a cellar off the main road, bedecked with plant life around the walls, and offers tasty meat-free dishes. Mind the decaying concrete steps.

Bar Caritas (Plac Wolności 1; mains 8-15zł; ⏰ 8am-7pm Mon-Fri, 10am-5pm Sat, noon-5pm Sun) You can point at what you want without resorting to your phrasebook at this cheap and convenient milk bar. There are many variants of *naleśniki* (crepes) on the menu. Lunchtimes get crowded, so be prepared to share a table.

Cymes (☎ 061 851 6638; ul Woźna 2/3; mains 18-26zł; ⏰ 11am-10pm) If you're tired of pork for dinner, this ambient Jewish restaurant is the logical place to go. The interior is warm and cosy, done out like a residential dining room with ceramic plates on the walls. On the menu are various poultry and fish dishes, including a whole goose for eight people, to be ordered 24 hours beforehand.

Deserovnia (☎ 061 852 5029; ul Świętosławska 12; mains 19-55zł) One side of this split-personality venue is a sporty bar, all dark timber, beer and photos of sports stars. The other side is a gracious restaurant serving classy Polish cuisine. Heads or tails?

Sioux (☎ 061 851 6286; Stary Rynek 93; mains 20-100zł; ⏰ noon-11pm) As you'd expect, this is a 'Western'-themed place, complete with waiters dressed as cowboys. Bizarrely named dishes such as 'Scoundrels in Uniforms from Fort Knox' (chicken legs) are on the menu, along with lots of steaks, ribs, grills and enchiladas.

Trattoria Valpolicella (☎ 061 855 7191; ul Wrocławska 7; mains 21-66zł; ⏰ 1-11pm) Serves a wide variety of pasta and other Italian specialities, well suited to a glass of vino, in convincingly rustic Mediterranean surroundings.

our pick **Tapas Bar** (☎ 061 852 8532; Stary Rynek 60; mains 32-62zł; ⏰ noon-midnight) Atmospheric place dishing up authentic tapas and Spanish wine, in a room lined with intriguing bric-a-brac including jars of stuffed olives, Mediterranean-themed artwork and bright red candles. Most tapas dishes cost 14zł to 22zł, so forget the mains and share with friends.

Proletaryat (ul Wrocławska 9; ⏰ 1pm-2am Mon-Sat, 3pm-2am Sun) Small red communist nostalgia bar with an array of socialist-era gear on the walls, including the obligatory bust of Lenin in the window, and various portraits of the great man and his comrades. Play 'spot the communist leader' while sipping a boutique beer from the Czarnków Brewery.

Bodega (ul Żydowska 4) On a street populated with cafes, Bodega's sleek modern lines stand out. The geometrically sharp interior is composed of mellow chocolate and gold tones, with candles on the tables. Good coffee is accompanied by sweet temptations.

Entertainment

Lizard King (Stary Rynek 86; ☾ noon-2am) Simultaneously happening and laid-back, this venue is in prime position on Stary Rynek. Friendly crowds sit drinking and eating in the split-level space, casting the occasional glance at the lizard over the bar. There's live music later in the week, mostly rock, jazz or blues, usually from 9pm.

Czarna Owca (ul Jaskółcza 13; ☾ noon-2am Mon-Fri, 5pm-2am Sat) Literally 'Black Sheep', this is a popular club with nightly DJs playing a mix of genres including R&B, house, rock, Latin, soul and funk. There's a disco night on Friday and a retro night on Tuesday.

Teatr Wielki (☎ 061 659 0280; www.opera.poznan.pl; ul Fredry 9) is the main venue for opera and ballet, while not far away, the **Filharmonia** (☎ 061 853 6935; www.filharmonia.poznan.pl; ul Św. Marcin 81) offers classical concerts at least weekly.

Getting There & Away

From **Poznań airport** (www.airport-poznan.com.pl), LOT flies at least six times a day to Warsaw, twice daily to Frankfurt, and at least three times daily to Munich. Tickets are available from the **LOT office** (☎ 0801 703 703) at the airport or from **Orbis Travel** (☎ 061 851 2000; Al Marcinkowskiego 21).

There are also domestic flights via Jet Air to Kraków (six times a week). A vast array of other European cities are serviced from Poznań, including London via British Airways, Wizz Air and Ryanair (at least daily); Dublin via Ryanair (three times a week); and Copenhagen via SAS (daily). The airport is in the western suburb of Ławica, 7km from the Old Town and accessible by buses 59 and L.

The **bus terminal** (ul Towarowa 17) is a 10-minute walk east of the train station. However, most destinations can be reached more comfortably and frequently by train.

The busy **Poznań Główny train station** (ul Dworcowa 1) offers services to Kraków (53zł, 7½ hours, 11 daily), Szczecin, some of which continue to Świnoujście (39zł, 2½ hours, 15 daily), Gdańsk and Gdynia (48zł, 5½ hours, seven daily), Toruń (33zł, 2½ hours, six daily) and Wrocław (34zł, 2½ hours, at least hourly). Nearly 20 trains a day head to Warsaw (95zł, 3½ hours).

POMERANIA

Pomerania (Pomorze) is an attractive region with diverse drawcards, from beautiful beaches to architecturally pleasing cities. It covers a large swathe of territory along the Baltic coast, from the German border in the west, to the lower Vistula Valley in the east. A sandy coastline stretches from Gdańsk to western Szczecin, and Toruń lies inland. Pomerania was fought over by Germanic and Slavic peoples for a millennium, before being incorporated almost fully within Poland after WWII.

GDAŃSK
pop 457,000

Port cities are usually lively places with distinctive personalities, and Gdańsk is no exception. From its busy riverside waterfront to the Renaissance splendour of its charming narrow streets, there's plenty to like about this coastal city.

And few Polish cities occupy such a pivotal position in history as Gdańsk. Founded more than a millennium ago, it became the focus of territorial tensions when the Teutonic Knights seized it from Poland in 1308. The city joined the Hanseatic League in 1361, and became one of the richest ports in the Baltic through its membership of the trading organisation. Finally, the Thirteen Years' War ended in 1466 with the Knights' defeat and Gdańsk's return to Polish rule.

This to-and-fro between Germanic and Polish control wasn't over, however – in 1793 Gdańsk was incorporated into Prussia, and after the German loss in WWI it became the autonomous Free City of Danzig. The city's environs are where WWII began, when the Nazis bombarded Polish troops stationed at Westerplatte. Gdańsk suffered immense damage during the war, but upon its return to Poland in 1945, its historic centre was faithfully reconstructed.

In the 1980s, Gdańsk achieved international fame as the home of the Solidarity trade union, whose rise paralleled the fall of communism in Europe. Today it's a vibrant city and a great base for exploring the Baltic coast.

Information
BOOKSHOPS
EMPiK (ul Podwale Grodzkie 8) Opposite the main train station.

GDAŃSK

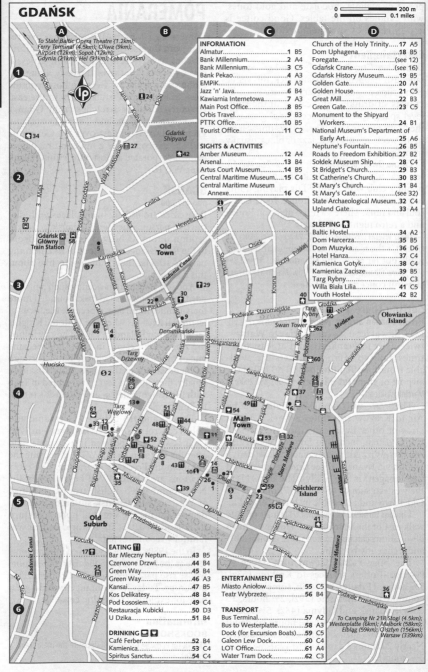

0 ――――――― 200 m
0 ――――――― 0.1 miles

ITERNET ACCESS

zz 'n' Java (ul Tkacka 17/18; per hr 5zł; ⏱ 10am-pm)

awiarnia Internetowa (Cinema City, ul Karmelicka 1; r hr 6zł; ⏱ 9am-1am Mon-Sat, 9.30am-1am Sun) Free ffee over 30 minutes access.

IONEY

ank Millennium Old Town (ul Wały Jagiellońskie /16); Main Town (ul Długi Targ 14/16)

ank Pekao (ul Garncarska 23)

OST

lain post office (ul Długa 22; ⏱ 8am-8pm Mon-Fri, m-3pm Sat)

OURIST INFORMATION

TTK office (☎ 058 301 1343; www.pttk-gdansk.pl; Długa 45; ⏱ 9am-6pm Mon-Fri, 8.30am-4.30pm Sat Sun)

ourist office (☎ 058 301 4355; www.got.gdansk.pl; Heweliusza 29; ⏱ 8am-4pm Mon-Fri) Well-concealed om the casual tourist, but helpful.

RAVEL AGENCIES

lmatur (☎ 058 301 2424; Długi Targ 11)

rbis Travel (☎ 058 301 4544; ul Podwale taromiejskie 96/97)

ights

AIN TOWN

The beautiful ul Długa (Long Street) and Długi Targ (Long Market) form the city's main historic thoroughfare, and are known collectively as the **Royal Way**. Polish kings traditionally paraded through the **Upland Gate** (built in the 1770s on a 15th-century gate), onward through the **oregate** (which once housed a torture chamber) and **Golden Gate** (1614), and proceeded east to the Renaissance **Green Gate** (1568).

Following the royal lead and starting from he Upland Gate, walk east to the Foregate. Within this structure, you can visit the **Amber Museum** (www.mhmg.gda.pl/bursztyn; adult/concession 0/5zł, free Tue; ⏱ 10am-2.30pm Tue, 10am-3.30pm Wed-Sat, 11am-3.30pm Sun), wherein you can marvel at the history of so-called 'Baltic gold'.

Further along ul Długa is the 18th-century **Dom Uphagena** (ul Długa; adult/concession 8/5zł, free Tue; ⏱ 10am-3pm Tue, 10am-4pm Wed-Sat, 11am-4pm Sun), featuring ornate furniture.

Proceed to the **Gdańsk History Museum** (ul Długa 47; adult/concession 8/5zł, free Tue; ⏱ 10am-3pm Tue, 10am-4pm Wed-Sat, 11am-4pm Sun), inside the towering Gothic **Main Town Hall**. On show are

photos of old Gdańsk, and the damage caused during WWII.

Not far past this point, behind **Neptune's Fountain** (1633), is the **Artus Court Museum** (ul Długi Targ 43/44; adult/concession 8/5zł, free Tue; ⏱ 10am-3pm Tue, 10am-4pm Wed-Sat, 11am-4pm Sun), where merchants used to congregate. The adjacent **Golden House** (1618) has a strikingly rich facade.

When you reach the Green Gate, step through and follow the riverside promenade north to the 14th-century **St Mary's Gate**, which houses the **State Archaeological Museum** (ul Mariacka 25/26; adult/concession 6/4zł, free Sat; ⏱ 10am-4pm Tue-Sun). It features an overly generous number of formerly diseased ancient human skulls, displays of amber, and river views from the adjacent **tower** (admission 3zł).

Through this gate, stroll along picturesque **ul Mariacka** (St Mary's St), lined with 17th-century burgher houses and amber shops. At the west end of ul Mariacka is the gigantic 14th-century **St Mary's Church** (admission free; ⏱ 8.30am-6pm, except during services) Watch little figures troop out at noon from its 14m-high astronomical clock, adorned with zodiacal signs. Climb the 405 steps of the **tower** (adult/concession 4/2zł) for a giddy view over the town. West along ul Piwna (Beer St) is the Dutch Renaissance **Arsenal** (1609), particularly attractive when its gilt is caught by the rays of the sun.

Back on the waterfront north of St Mary's Gate, you'll find the 15th-century **Gdańsk Crane**, the largest of its kind in medieval Europe and capable of hoisting loads of up to 2000kg. It's now part of the **Central Maritime Museum** (ul Ołowianka 9-13; one section adult/concession 6/4zł, all four sections 15/9zł; ⏱ 10am-6pm May-Oct, 10am-4pm Tue-Sun Nov-Apr). The museum offers a fascinating insight into Gdańsk's seafaring past, including the **Sołdek Museum Ship**, built here just after WWII.

OLD TOWN

Almost totally destroyed in 1945, the Old Town has never been completely rebuilt. However, among its gems are **St Catherine's Church** (ul Wielke Młyny; ⏱ 8am-6pm Mon-Sat), Gdańsk's oldest church (begun in the 1220s). Opposite, the **Great Mill** (ul Wielke Młyny) was built by the Teutonic Knights around 1350. It used to produce 200 tonnes of flour per day and continued to operate until 1945.

Right behind St Catherine's is **St Bridget's Church** (ul Profesorska 17; ⏱ 10am-6pm Mon-Sat).

POLAND

Formerly Lech Wałęsa's place of worship, the church was a strong supporter of the shipyard activists in the 1980s.

At the north end of the Old Town is the evocative **Roads to Freedom Exhibition** (ul Wały Piastowskie 24; adult/concession 6/4zł; ☺ 10am-4pm Tue-Sun). This excellent museum charts the decline and fall of Polish communism and the rise of the Solidarity trade union, and is a place that anyone interested in Gdańsk's history should visit.

A short walk further north, the soaring **Monument to the Shipyard Workers** (Plac Solidarności) stands at the entrance to the Gdańsk Shipyards. It was erected in late 1980 in memory of 44 workers killed during the riots of December 1970, and was the first monument in a communist regime to commemorate the regime's victims.

OLD SUBURB

The **National Museum's Department of Early Art** (ul Toruńska 1; adult/concession 10/6zł; ☺ 10am-5pm May-Sep, 9am-4pm Oct-Apr) is famous for its Dutch and Flemish paintings, especially Hans Memling's 15th-century *Last Judgment*.

Adjoining the museum is the former Franciscan **Church of the Holy Trinity** (ul Św. Trójcy; ☺ 10am-8pm Mon-Sat), built at the end of the 15th century.

OLIWA

Some 9km northwest is the lovely **Park Oliwski** (ul Cystersów), surrounding the towering **Oliwa Cathedral** (☺ 8am-8pm), built in the 13th century with a Gothic facade and a long, narrow central nave. The famous baroque organ is used for recitals each hour between 10am and 3pm Monday to Saturday in July and August. Nearby is the **Ethnographic Museum** (ul Cystersów 19; adult/concession 8/5zł; ☺ 10am-5pm Tue-Sun) in the Old Granary, and the **Modern Art Gallery** (adult/concession 9/6zł; ☺ 10am-5pm Tue-Sun) in the former Abbots' Palace.

To reach the park, take the commuter train to the Gdańsk Oliwa station (3.10zł). From there, it's a 10-minute walk; head (west) up ul Poczty Gdańsk, turn right (north) along the highway and look for the signs (in English) to 'Ethnographic Museum' and 'Cathedral'.

WESTERPLATTE

WWII began at 4.45am on 1 September 1939, when the German battleship *Schleswig-Holstein* began shelling the Polish naval post at Westerplatte, 7km north of Gdańsk Main Town. The 182-man Polish garriso held out against ferocious attacks for a wee before surrendering.

The enormity of this event is marke by a hilltop **memorial** (admission free; ☺ 24hr), small **museum** (ul Sucharskiego 1; adult/concession 3/2 ☺ 9am-4pm May-Sep) and **ruins** remaining fro the Nazi bombardment.

Bus 106 (25 minutes) goes to the pa every 15 minutes from a stop outside th main train station in Gdańsk. Alternativel excursion boats (22/45zł one way/return) and around Westerplatte leave from a doc near the Green Gate in Gdańsk between Apr and November.

Festivals & Events

International Organ Music Festival (www.gdanskie -organy.com, under Concerts) June to August.

International Street & Open-Air Theatre Festival (www.feta.pl) July

Sounds of the North Festival (www.nck.org.pl) July/August

St Dominic's Fair (www.mtgsa.pl, under Jarmark Św Dominika) Annual shopping fair in August.

International Shakespeare Festival (www.teatr -szekspir.gda.pl) August

Sleeping

Accommodation can be tight in the warme months. If you're having trouble finding ac commodation, check with the PTTK office Also consider staying in nearby Sopot (p429 or Gdynia (p430).

BUDGET

Camping Nr 218 Stogi (☎ 058 307 3915; www.campin -gdansk.pl; ul Wydmy 9; per person/tent 12/6zł, cabins 60 110zł; ☺ May-Sep) This camping ground is onl 200m from the beach in the seaside holida centre of Stogi, about 5.5km northeast o the Main Town. Tidy cabins sleep betwee two and five people, and facilities include volleyball court and children's playground Take tram 8 or 13 from the main train sta tion in Gdańsk.

Youth Hostel (☎ 058 301 2313; www.mokf.com.p ul Wałowa 21; dm/s/d/tr/q 18/31/62/63/84zł) Old-style hostel in a quiet, old building on the door step of the Gdańsk Shipyards, Lech Wałęsa' old stamping ground. Rooms are brown and basic, but clean. Book ahead, particularly ir summer. Smoking and drinking are strictly forbidden and there's a midnight curfew.

Dom Harcerza (☎ 058 301 3621; www.domharcerza
l; ul Za Murami 2/10; dm 34zł, s/d/tr/q 50/120/150/160zł) he rooms are small but cosy at this place, vhich offers the best value and location or any budget-priced hotel. It's popular so book ahead), and can get noisy when arge groups are staying here. There's a harming old-fashioned restaurant on the round floor.

Baltic Hostel (☎ 058 721 9657; www.baltichostel.com l; ul 3 Maja 25; dm 40zł, r 120zł) Readers have given nixed reviews of this hostel aimed at the inernational budget traveller. The dorms are a it crowded, but the lounge is good and it's andy to the bus and train stations. Save it for vhen the other hostels are full. The entrance is ight at the end of the long brown apartment lock, around to the right.

Apartments Poland (☎ 058 346 9864; www.apart nentpoland.com; apt €30-65) An agency with reno-ated properties scattered through the Tri-City Area (Gdańsk/Sopot/Gdynia), including a number in central Gdańsk. Some are big nough for families or other groups. Be aware of the additional electricity charge when checking out, based on a meter reading.

Targ Rybny (☎ 058 301 5627; www.gdanskhostel.com pl; ul Grodzka 21; dm 50zł, d/tr/q 150/180/240zł) A popu-ar modern hostel in a great central location overlooking the quay. It's a little cramped, but clean and sociable, with a comfy lounge area. It also offers bike rental (20zł per day).

MIDRANGE & TOP END

Kamienica Zacisze (☎ 0508 096 221; www.apartments gdansk.pl; ul Ogarna 107; apt €105-155) Set within a quiet courtyard off the street, this commu-nist-era workers' dormitory building has been transformed into a set of light, airy apart-ments for up to six people. Each apartment has high ceilings, a fully equipped kitchen and loads of space. Excellent value for the location and quality.

ourpick **Dom Muzyka** (☎ 058 326 0600; www .dom-muzyka.pl; ul Łąkowa 1/2; s/d/ste 220/310/460zł; ✿) Gorgeous white rooms with arched ceil-ings and quality furniture, inside the Music Academy some 300m east of the city centre. From July to August, a second wing of the building offers cheaper student-style accom-modation. It's hard to spot from the street; head for the door on the city end of the court-yard within the big yellow-brick building.

Willa Biała Lilia (☎ 058 301 7074; www.bialalilia .pl; ul Spichrzowa 16; s/d/apt 260/320/420zł) The White

Lily Villa is an attractive accommodation choice a short walk east of the Main Town on Spichlerze Island. Rooms are neat and clean, and the staff are helpful.

Kamienica Gotyk (☎ 0602 844 535; www.gotykhouse .eu; ul Mariacka 1; s/d 280/310zł) This Gothic guest house claims to be Gdańsk's oldest residence. Inside, the rooms are compact but neat, with clean bathrooms. The location is impressive, with St Mary's Church and the cafes and shops of ul Mariacka just outside the door.

Hotel Hanza (☎ 058 305 3427; www.hanza-hotel.com .pl; ul Tokarska 6; s/d/ste from 695/745/985zł; ✿) The Hanza is attractively perched along the wa-terfront near the Gdańsk Crane, and offers elegant, tasteful rooms in a modern build-ing. Some rooms have enviable views over the river.

Eating

Bar Mleczny Neptun (ul Długa 33/34; mains 2-13zł; ⏰ 7.30am-7pm Mon-Fri, 10am-6pm Sat & Sun) This joint is a cut above your run-of-the-mill milk bar, with potted plants, lace curtains, decorative tiling and old lamps for decor.

Green Way (☎ 058 301 4121; ul Garncarska 4/6; mains 7-10zł; ⏰ 10am-7pm Mon-Fri, noon-7pm Sat & Sun) Popular with local vegetarians, this eatery serves eve-rything from soy cutlets to Mexican goulash in an unfussy blue-and-yellow space. There's another, more central, branch at ul Długa 11.

U Dzika (☎ 058 305 2676; ul Piwna 59/61; mains 7-39zł; ⏰ 11am-10pm) Pleasant eatery with a nice outdoor terrace, specialising in *pierogi* (dumplings). If you're feeling adventurous, try the Fantasy Dumplings, comprising cottage cheese, cinnamon, raisins and peach.

Kansai (☎ 058 324 0888; ul Ogarna 124/125; mains 8-99zł; ⏰ noon-9pm Tue-Sat, noon-8pm Sun) You'd ex-pect fish to be served in a seaport, but Kansai adds an exotic twist by serving sushi in full-on Japanese ambience. Waiters are dressed in traditional robes, there's a samurai sword on the counter, and the menu has dishes made from tuna, salmon and butterfish, along with classic California rolls.

Czerwone Drzwi (☎ 058 301 5764; ul Piwna 52/53; mains 18-55zł; ⏰ noon-10pm) Step through the Red Door into a relaxed, refined cafe at-mosphere, which helps you digest the small but interesting menu of *pierogi*, pasta and Polish classics.

Restauracja Kubicki (☎ 058 301 0050; ul Wartka 5; mains 24-80zł) The Kubicki is a decent mid-priced place to try Polish food, especially seafood. It's

POLAND

one of the oldest eateries in Gdańsk, established in the Danzig days of 1918, and offers appropriately old-fashioned decor and service off a scenic laneway next to the river.

Pod Łososiem (☎ 058 301 7652; ul Szeroka 52/54; mains 55-90zł; ☉ noon-10pm) This is one of Gdańsk's oldest and most highly regarded restaurants, and is particularly famous for its salmon dishes and the gold-flecked liqueur *goldwasser*, which was invented here. Red leather seats, brass chandeliers and a gathering of gas lamps fill out the posh interior.

For self-catering, visit **Kos Delikatesy** (ul Piwna 9/10) in the Main Town.

Drinking

Spiritus Sanctus (ul Grobla I 13; ☉ 3-10pm) If you're tired of beer and vodka, head for this stylish wine bar opposite St Mary's Church. While you're enjoying your Slovenian white or Croatian red, you can marvel at the amazing decor, a jumble of abstract art and classic objets d'art.

ourpick Café Ferber (ul Długa 77/78; ☉ 8am-late) It's startling to step straight from Gdańsk's historic main street into this very modern cafe-bar, dominated by bright red panels, a suspended ceiling and boxy lighting. Partake of breakfast, well-made coffee, international wines, and cocktail creations such as the *szary kot* (grey cat). On weekends, DJs spin house and chill-out music into the wee small hours.

Kamienica (ul Mariacka 37/39) The best of the bunch on Mariacka is this excellent two-level cafe with a calm, sophisticated atmosphere and the best patio on the block. It's as popular for daytime coffee and cakes as it is for a sociable evening beverage.

Entertainment

Miasto Aniołów (www.miastoaniolow.com.pl, in Polish; ul Chmielna 26; admission 10zł; ☉ 9pm-late) The City of Angels covers all the bases – late-night revellers can hit the spacious dance floor, crash in the chill-out area, or hang around the atmospheric deck overlooking the Motława River. Nightly DJs play disco and other dance-oriented sounds.

State Baltic Opera Theatre (☎ 058 763 4912; www .operabaltycka.pl; Al Zwycięstwa 15) This place is in the suburb of Wrzeszcz, not far from the train station at Gdańsk Politechnika.

Teatr Wybrzeże (☎ 058 301 1328; ul Św. Ducha 2) Next to the Arsenal is the main city theatre. Both Polish and foreign classics (all in Polish) are part of the repertoire.

Getting There & Away

AIR

From **Lech Wałęsa airport** (www.airport.gdansk.pl LOT has at least five daily flights to Warsav and at least three daily to Frankfurt ani Munich. Tickets can be bought at the **LOT offic** (☎ 0801 703 703; ul Wały Jagiellońskie 2/4).

Gdańsk is also connected to a plethora c other European cities, including London vi Ryanair and Wizz Air (at least daily); Dubli via Ryanair and Centralwings (daily); an Copenhagen via SAS (up to three daily).

BOAT

Polferries (www.polferries.pl) offers services be tween Gdańsk and Nynäshamn (18 hours in Sweden every other day in summer (les frequently in the low season). The company uses the **ferry terminal** (ul Przemysłowa) in Now Port, about 5km north of the Main Town and a short walk from the local commuter trair station at Gdańsk Brzeżno. Orbis Travel and the PTTK Office in Gdańsk provide informa tion and sell tickets.

Between April and October, excursion boats leave regularly from the dock near the Green Gate in Gdańsk for Westerplatte (adult concession return 45/22/zł). Further north along the dockside, you can board the **Galeon Lew** (adult/concession return 35/20zł), a rep lica 17th-century galleon, for hourly cruises to Westerplatte. Just north of the galleon is the **Water Tram**, a ferry which heads to Sopot (adult/concession 10/5zł, three daily) and Hel (16/8zł, three daily) each weekend during May and June, then daily from July to August. Bicycles cost an extra 2zł to transport.

BUS

The **bus terminal** (ul 3 Maja 12) is behind the main train station and connected to ul Podwale Grodzkie by an underground passageway. Useful bus destinations include Warsaw (50zł, six hours, 10 daily) and Świnoujście (58zł, 8½ hours, one daily).

TRAIN

The city's main train station, **Gdańsk Główny** (ul Podwale Grodzkie 1), is conveniently located on the western outskirts of the Old Town. Most long-distance trains actually start or finish at Gdynia, so make sure you get on/off quickly there.

Each day nearly 20 trains (mainly express) head to Warsaw, (88zł, 4½ hours). There are rains to Olsztyn (34zł, three hours, seven aily), Kraków (62zł, 8¾ hours, 11 daily), 'oznań (48zł, 5½ hours, seven daily), Toruń 39zł, four hours, six daily) and Szczecin 51zł, 5½ hours, four daily). Trains also head o Białystok (53zł, 7½ hours, three daily) and ublin (56zł, eight hours, four daily).

ietting Around

'he airport is in Rębiechowo, about 12km orthwest of Gdańsk. It's accessible by bus 10 from the Gdańsk Wrzeszcz local commuter train station, or bus B from outside he Gdańsk Główny train station. Taxis cost 5zł to 55zł one way.

The local commuter train – the SKM – uns every 15 minutes between 6am and '.30pm, and less frequently thereafter, beween Gdańsk Główny and Gdynia Główna tations, via Sopot and Gdańsk Oliwa staions. (Note: the line to Gdańsk Nowy Port, ia Gdańsk Brzeżno, is a separate line that eaves less regularly from Gdańsk Główny.) 3uy tickets at any station and validate them n the yellow boxes at the platform entrance, or purchase them pre-validated from vendng machines on the platform.

AROUND GDAŃSK

Gdańsk is part of the so-called Tri-City Area ncluding Gdynia and Sopot, which are easy lay trips from Gdańsk.

Sopot

pop 39,600

Sopot, 12km north of Gdańsk, has been one of the Baltic coast's most fashionable seaside resorts since the 19th century. It has an easy-going atmosphere, good nightlife, and long stretches of sandy beach.

INFORMATION

The **tourist office** (☎ 058 550 3783; www.sopot.pl; ul Dworcowa 4; ✆ 9am-8pm Jun-Aug, 10am-6pm Sep-May) is about 50m from the main train station. A short walk to the east of the station is **Gamer** (ul Chopina 1; per hr 4.50zł; ✆ 9am-10pm), an internet cafe.

SIGHTS & ACTIVITIES

From the tourist office, head down ul Bohaterów Monte Cassino, one of Poland's most attractive pedestrian streets, past the surreal **Crooked House** (Krzywy Domek; ul Bohaterów

Monte Cassino 53) shopping centre to Poland's longest pier (515m), the famous **Molo** (www .molo.sopot.pl; adult/concession 3.80/2zł; ✆ 8am-8pm Apr-Sep). Various attractions and cultural events can be found near and along the structure.

Opposite Pension Wanda, **Museum Sopotu** (☎ 058 551 2266; ul Poniatowskiego 8; adult/concession 7/5zł; ✆ 10am-4pm Tue-Fri, noon-5pm Sat & Sun) has displays recalling the town's 19th-century incarnation as the German resort of Zoppot.

SLEEPING & EATING

There are no real budget options in Sopot, and prices increase during the busy summer season. Bistros and cafes serving a wide range of cuisines sprout up in summer along the promenades.

Willa Karat II (☎ 058 550 0742; ul 3 Maja 31; s/d/tr 150/270/290zł) Cosy budget lodgings a few blocks from the beach, with light, spacious rooms and clean bathrooms, and plants decorating the corridors. There's a kitchen and dining area for guest use. From the train station, walk right along ul Kościuszki, then left along ul 3 Maja towards the coast.

Hotel Eden (☎ 058 551 1503; www.hotel-eden.com .pl; ul Kordeckiego 4/6; s/d/tr/q/ste 200/300/360/420/480zł) One of the less expensive places in town. It's a quiet, old-fashioned pension with high ceilings, classic furniture and recently renovated bathrooms, overlooking a park one street from the beach.

Pension Wanda (☎ 058 550 3038; ul Poniatowskiego 7; s/d/tr 240/330/420zł, ste from 390zł) The Wanda is a homely place with light, airy rooms, in a handy location about 500m south of the pier. Some rooms have sea views.

Zhong Hua Hotel (☎ 058 550 2020; www.hotel chinski.pl; Al Wojska Polskiego 1; s/d 510/550zł, ste from 680zł) Attractive accommodation in a striking wooden pavilion on the seafront. The foyer is decked out in Chinese design, with hanging lanterns and beautiful timber furniture. The theme extends to the small but pleasant rooms, with views of the water.

Café del Arte (ul Bohaterów Monte Cassino 53) This classy cafe, within the Crooked House, is a great place to enjoy coffee, cake and ice cream surrounded by artistic objects in the combined cafe-gallery.

Mandarynka (ul Bema 6; ✆ noon-10pm) One street south of the main drag, this is a very cool confection of timber tables, scarlet lampshades and huge orange cushions. There's a food menu, and a DJ in action upstairs most nights.

POLAND

GETTING THERE & AWAY

From the **Sopot train station** (ul Dworcowa 7), local SKM commuter trains run every 15 minutes to Gdańsk Główny (4.50zł, 15 minutes) and Gdańsk Główna (3.10zł, 10 minutes) stations. Excursion boats leave several times a day (May to September) from the Sopot pier to Gdańsk and Hel. The Water Tram also links Sopot with Gdańsk (adult/concession 10/5zł, three daily) and Hel (12/6zł, three daily) each weekend during May and June, then daily from July to August.

Gdynia

pop 252,000

As a young city with a busy port atmosphere, Gdynia, 9km north of Sopot, is less atmospheric than Gdańsk or Sopot. It was greatly expanded as a seaport after this coastal area (but not Gdańsk) became part of Poland following WWI. However, it's worth dropping into on a day trip.

SIGHTS & ACTIVITIES

From the main Gdynia Główna train station on Plac Konstytucji, where there is a **tourist office** (☎ 058 721 2466; www.gdynia.pl; ♥ 8am-6pm Mon-Fri, 9am-4pm Sat, 9am-3pm Sun May-Sep, 10am-5pm Oct-Apr), follow ul 10 Lutego east for about 1.5km to the **Southern Pier**.

Moored on the pier's northern side are two interesting museum ships. First up is the curiously sky-blue destroyer **Błyskawica** (adult/concession 8/4zł; ♥ 9.45am-5pm Tue-Sun), which escaped capture in 1939 and went on to serve successfully with Allied naval forces throughout WWII.

Beyond it is the beautiful three-masted frigate **Dar Pomorza** (adult/concession 8/4zł; ♥ 9am-6pm daily Jul-Sep, 10am-4pm Tue-Sun May & Jun & Oct), built in Hamburg in 1909 as a training ship for German sailors. There's information in English on the dockside.

A 20-minute walk uphill (follow the signs) from Teatr Muzyczny on Plac Grunwaldzki (about 300m southwest of the start of the pier) leads to **Kamienna Góra**, a hill offering wonderful views.

SLEEPING & EATING

Gdynia is probably best visited as a day trip, but there are some reasonable accommodation options. There are several cheap eateries in the city centre, and upmarket fish restaurants along the pier.

China Town Hotel (☎ 058 620 9221; www.chinaho
.pl; ul Dworca 11a; s/d/tr/q 100/140/240/280zł) Inexpensiv lodgings can be found here, opposite the trai station. The rooms are plain but serviceabl for a night, though singles are very smal There's a Chinese restaurant in the sam building.

Hotel Antracyt (☎ 058 620 1239; ul Korzeniowskie 19; www.hotel-antracyt.pl; s/d 200/280zł) This place i further south, on a hill in an exclusive residen tial area, with fine views over the water.

our pick **Willa Lubicz** (☎ 058 668 4740; ul Orłowsk 43; www.willalubicz.pl; s/d/ste 380/410/690zł) If you'r looking for style you could try this quiet, up market place with a chic 1930s ambience a the southern end of town; Gdynia Orłowo i the nearest train station. Third-floor room have views of the sea.

Bistro Kwadrans (☎ 058 620 1592; Skwer Kościusz 20; mains 8-17zł; ♥ 9am-10pm Mon-Fri, 10am-10pm Sa noon-10pm Sun) One block north of the media strip along ul 10 Lutego, this is a great plac for tasty Polish food. It also serves up pizza including an improbable variant involvin banana and curry.

GETTING THERE & AWAY

Local commuter trains link Gdynia Główn station with Sopot (3.10zł) and Gdańs (4.50zł) every 15 minutes. From the sam station, trains run hourly to Hel (13zł, tw hours) and half-hourly to Lębork (12zł, on hour), where you can change for Łeba. Fron the small bus terminal outside, minibuses als go to Hel (12zł, two hours, six daily).

Stena Line uses the **Terminal Promowy** (u Kwiatkowskiego 60), about 5km northwest o Gdynia. It offers services between Gdynia an Karlskrona (10½ hours) in Sweden. Take bu 150 from ul Władysława IV.

Between May and September, excur sion boats leave Gdynia's Southern Pier t Hel (adult/concession one way 45/30zł, re turn 60/42zł), from a point beyond the Da Pomorza. The Water Tram also links Gdyni with Hel (adult/concession 10/5zł, four daily and Jastarnia (adult/concession 10/5zł, thre daily). Bikes cost 2zł extra to transport.

Hel

pop 3900

Never was a town more entertainingly named – English speakers can spend hours creating amusing twists on 'to Hel and back', or 'a col day in Hel'. In fact, this old fishing village a ie tip of the Hel Peninsula north of Gdańsk is a attractive place to visit, and a popular beach esort. The pristine, windswept **beach** on the altic side stretches the length of the peninula. On the southern side, the sea is popular or **windsurfing**; equipment can be rented in the illages of **Władysławowo** and **Jastarnia**.

The **Fokarium** (ul Morska 2; admission 2zł; ⏱ 8.30am-usk), off the main road along the seafront, is ome to endangered Baltic grey seals. It also as a good souvenir shop for those 'I'm in Hel' ostcards to send to friends back home. The 5th-century **Gothic church**, further along the eslanade, houses the **Museum of Fishery** (ul Nadmorksi adult/concession 5/3zł; ⏱ 10am-4pm Tue-Sun).

Visitors often stay in **private rooms** offered vithin local houses (mostly from May to eptember), at about 90zł per double. **Captain Morgan** (☎ 058 675 00 91; www.captainmorgan.hel.org.pl; Wiejska 21; d/tr 100/140zł) also offers plain, clean ooms, and good seafood in a quirky pub tuffed with maritime memorabilia.

To Hel, minibuses leave every hour or so rom the main train station in Gdynia (12zł, wo hours). Several trains depart from Gdynia ally (13zł, two hours, hourly), and from May o September from Gdańsk (20zł, three hours, ourly). Hel is also accessible by excursion oat from Gdańsk, Sopot and Gdynia – see he Getting There & Away section for each f these destinations for details.

Malbork
op 38,300
The magnificent **Malbork Castle** (☎ 055 647 800; www.zamek.malbork.pl; adult/concession 30/20zł; ⏱ 9am-7pm Tue-Sun May-Aug, 10am-5pm Tue-Sun Apr & ep, 10am-3pm Tue-Sun Oct-Mar) is the centrepiece f this town, 58km southeast of Gdańsk. It's he largest Gothic castle in Europe, and was once known as Marienburg, headquarters of he Teutonic Knights. It was constructed by he Order in 1276 and became the seat of their Grand Master in 1309. Damage sustained in WWII has been repaired since the conflict's end, and it was placed on the Unesco World Heritage List in 1997. The entry fee includes a compulsory Polish language tour; tours in English and other languages are available on request (195zł). On Mondays there's a limited tour for a bargain basement 5zł.

The **Youth Hostel** (☎ 055 272 2408; www.ssm malbork.webpark.pl, in Polish; ul Żeromskiego 45; dm/d 22/55zł) is a reasonable budget option in a local school about 500m south of the castle.

Hotel Zamek (☎ 055 272 3367; www.hotelprodus .pl; ul Starościńska 14; s/d/ste €63/72/170) is inside a restored medieval building in the Lower Castle. The rooms are a bit old-fashioned, but the bathrooms are up-to-date. The restaurant has character, but can be crowded with tour groups.

our pick **Hotel Grot** (☎ 055 646 9660; www.grothotel .pl; ul Kościuszki 22d; s/d/tr/ste 199/289/379/399zł) is classy for its price range, with contemporary furniture and an impressive restaurant. It's down an unnamed dead-end laneway opposite the unrecommended Hotel Zbyszko.

Restauracja Piwniczka (☎ 055 273 3668; ul Starościńska 1; mains 10-80zł; ⏱ 10am-7pm) is an atmospheric cellar restaurant beneath the west wall of the castle.

The castle is 1km west of the train and bus stations. Leave the train station, turn right, cut across the highway, head down ul Kościuszki and follow the signs. Malbork is an easy day trip by train from Gdańsk (12zł, 50 minutes, at least hourly). From Malbork, trains also go to Olsztyn (31zł, two hours, seven daily).

TORUŃ
pop 207,000
The first thing to strike you about Toruń, south of Gdańsk, is its massive red-brick churches, looking more like fortresses than places of worship. The city is defined by its striking Gothic architecture, which gives its Old Town a distinctive appearance and its promotional slogan: *gotyk na dotyk* (Touch Gothic). The city is a pleasant place to spend a few days, offering a nice balance between a relaxing slow pace and engaging entertainment diversions.

Toruń is also famous as the birthplace of Nicolaus Copernicus, a figure you cannot escape as you walk the streets of his home town – you can even buy gingerbread men in his likeness. The renowned astronomer spent his youth here, and the local university is named after him.

Historically, Toruń is intertwined with the Teutonic Knights, who established an outpost here in 1233. Following the Thirteen Years' War (1454–66), the Teutonic Order and Poland signed a peace treaty here, which returned to Poland a large area of land stretching from Toruń to Gdańsk.

Toruń was fortunate to escape major damage in WWII, and as a result is the best-preserved Gothic town in Poland. The Old

TORUŃ

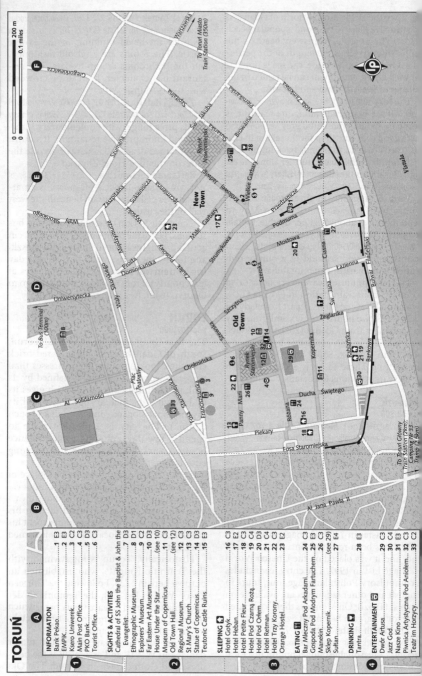

Town was added to Unesco's World Heritage List in 1997.

Information

Bank Pekao (ul Wielkie Garbary 11)
EMPiK (ul Wielkie Garbary 18) Bookshop.
Ksero Uniwerek (ul Franciszkańska 5; per hr 3zł;
🕑 8am-7pm Mon-Fri, 9am-4pm Sat) Internet access.
Main post office (Rynek Staromiejski; 🕑 6am-9pm)
PKO Bank (ul Szeroka)
Tourist office (☎ 056 621 0931; www.it.torun.pl;
Rynek Staromiejski 25; 🕑 9am-4pm Mon & Sat, 9am-6pm Tue-Fri, 9am-1pm Sun)

Sights

The starting point for any exploration of Toruń is the **Rynek Staromiejski** (Old Town Market Sq), the focal point of the Old Town. The **Regional Museum** (www.muzeum.torun.pl; Rynek Staromiejski 1; adult/concession 10/6zł; 🕑 10am-6pm Tue-Sun May-Sep, 10am-4pm Tue-Sun Oct-Apr) sits within the massive 14th-century **Old Town Hall**, featuring a fine collection of 19th- and 20th-century Polish art. Other displays recall the town's guilds, and there's an exhibition of medieval stained glass and religious paintings. Climb the 40m-high **tower** (adult/concession 10/6zł; 🕑 10am-4pm Tue-Sun Apr, 10am-8pm Tue-Sun May-Sep) for great views.

In front of the town hall is an elegant **statue** of Copernicus. Look for other interesting items of statuary around the square, including a dog and umbrella from a famous Polish comic strip, a donkey that once served as a punishment device, and a fabled violinist who saved Toruń from a plague of frogs.

The richly decorated, 15th-century **House Under the Star**, with its baroque facade and spiral wooden staircase, contains the **Far Eastern Art Museum** (Rynek Staromiejski 35; adult/concession 7/4zł; 🕑 10am-6pm Tue-Sun May-Sep, 10am-4pm Tue-Sun Oct-Apr).

Just off the northwestern corner of the square is the late-13th-century **St Mary's Church** (ul Panny Marii; 🕑 dawn-dusk), a Gothic building with magnificent 15th-century stalls.

Just around the corner is the **Explorers' Museum** (ul Franciszkańska 11; adult/concession 8/5zł; 🕑 11am-6pm Tue-Sun May-Sep, 10am-4pm Tue-Sun Oct-Apr), a small but interesting institution showcasing artefacts from the collection of inveterate wanderer Antonio Halik. There are hats, travel documents, and souvenirs of his journeys – including a vast array of hotel keys!

In 1473, Copernicus was allegedly born in the brick Gothic house (there's some doubt) that now contains the fairly dull **Museum of Copernicus** (ul Kopernika 15/17; adult/concession 10/7zł; 🕑 10am-6pm Tue-Sun May-Sep, 10am-4pm Tue-Sun Oct-Apr), presenting replicas of the great astronomer's instruments. More engaging, if overpriced, is the museum's short **audiovisual presentation** (adult/concession 12/7zł) regarding Copernicus' life in Toruń; and the extravagantly titled **World of Toruń's Gingerbread** (adult/concession 10/6zł). Visitors are guided by a costumed medieval townswoman and given the chance to bake their own *pierniki* (gingerbread). A combined ticket to any two of the three attractions costs 18/11zł.

One block east is the **Cathedral of SS John the Baptist & John the Evangelist** (ul Żeglarska; adult/concession 3/2zł; 🕑 9am-5.30pm Mon-Sat, 2-5.30pm Sun Apr-Oct), founded in 1233 and completed more than 200 years later, with its massive **tower** (adult/concession 6/4zl) and bell. There's no sightseeing allowed during services.

Further east are the ruins of the **Teutonic Castle** (ul Przedzamcze; adult/concession 4/2zł, free Mon; 🕑 10am-6pm), destroyed in 1454 by angry townsfolk protesting against the knights' oppressive regime.

In a park just north of the Old Town is the **Ethnographic Museum** (ul Wały Sikorskiego 19; adult/concession 8.50/4.50zł; 🕑 9am-4pm Wed & Fri, 10am-5pm Tue, Thu-Sun), showcasing traditional customs, costumes and weapons.

Sleeping

Toruń is blessed with a plentiful number of hotels within converted historic buildings in its Old Town; but as they're fairly small, it pays to book ahead.

Camping Nr 33 Tramp (☎ 056 654 7187; www.tramp.mosir.torun.pl; ul Kujawska 14; camping per person 8.50zł; tents 5.50-11zł, d/tr/q 50/70/90zł; 🕑 May-Sep) There's a choice of cabins or hotel-style rooms at this camping ground on the edge of the train line, along with an onsite snack bar. It's a five-minute walk west of the main train station.

Orange Hostel (☎ 056 652 0033; www.hostelorange.pl; ul Prosta 19; dm/s/d/tr 30/50/90/120zł) The wave of Polish hostels for the international backpacker has finally swept over sleepy Toruń. Orange is in a handy location, its decor is bright and cheerful, and its kitchen is an impressive place to practise the gentle art of self-catering.

Hotel Trzy Korony (☎ 056 622 6031; www.hotel3korony.pl; Rynek Staromiejski 21; s/d/tr/ste from 100/140/180/260zł) This budget hotel is by no means luxurious, but the simple rooms are neatly furnished with pine furniture, blue sofas and sunny yellow wallpaper. The hotel's glorious history includes stopovers by three distinguished monarchs (hence the 'three crowns' in the name).

Hotel Pod Orłem (☎ 056 622 5024; www.hotel.torun.pl; ul Mostowa 17; s/d/apt from 120/150/215zł) This hotel is great value, and although the rooms are smallish, have squeaky wooden floors, and some contain poky bathrooms, the service is good and it's central. The foyer and corridors are fun with their jumble of framed pop-art images and old photos.

Hotel Pod Czarną Różą (☎ 056 621 9637; www.hotel czarnaroza.pl; ul Rabiańska 11; s/d/tr/ste 170/210/250/320zł) 'Under the Black Rose' is spread between a historic inn and a new wing facing the river, though its interiors present a uniformly clean up-to-date look. Some doubles come with small but functional kitchens.

Hotel Retman (☎ 056 657 4460; www.hotelretman.pl; ul Rabiańska 15; s/d 190/250zł) Attractively decorated accommodation offering spacious, atmospheric rooms with red carpet and solid timber furniture. Downstairs is a good pub and restaurant.

Hotel Gotyk (☎ 056 658 4000; www.hotel-gotyk.com.pl; ul Piekary 20; s/d 190/270zł) Housed in a fully modernised 14th-century building just off the main square, rooms are very neat, with ornate furniture and high ceilings, and all come with sparkling bathrooms.

Hotel Heban (☎ 056 652 1555; www.hotel-heban.com.pl; ul Małe Garbary 7; s/d/ste from 190/300/350zł) This is a stylish, upmarket hotel occupying a historic 17th-century building in a quiet street. It also has a good restaurant, situated off a lavish foyer with painted wooden ceilings and a 24-hour bar.

Hotel Petite Fleur (☎ 056 621 5100; www.petite fleur.pl; ul Piekary 25; s/d 210/270zł) Just opposite the Gotyk, the Petite Fleur offers fresh, airy rooms in a renovated old town house, some with exposed original brickwork and rafters. It also has a French cellar restaurant.

Eating & Drinking

Bar Mleczny Pod Arkadami (ul Różana 1; mains 3–8zł; ⏰ 9am-7pm Mon-Fri, 9am-4pm Sat) This classic milk bar is just off the Old Town Sq, with a range of low-cost dishes. It also has a takeaway window serving a range of tasty *zapiekanki* (toasted rolls with cheese, mushrooms and ketchup) and sweet waffles.

Sułtan (☎ 056 621 0607; ul Mostowa 7; mains 8–12zł; ⏰ noon-midnight) A splash of Middle Eastern cuisine in northern Poland, in a cheerful venue decorated with colourful lanterns and Arabic script. The menu contains many variants of kebabs, along with soups, salads and pizzas.

Gospoda Pod Modrym Fartuchem (☎ 056 622 2626; Rynek Nowomiejski 8; mains 10–35zł; ⏰ 10am-10pm) This pleasant, unpretentious 15th-century pub on the New Town Sq has been visited by Polish kings and Napoleon. The usual meat-and-cabbage Polish dishes are joined by an array of Indian food, including a good vegetarian selection.

Manekin (☎ 056 621 0504; Rynek Staromiejski 16; mains 11–13zł) Vaguely Wild West decor adorns this inexpensive central restaurant specialising in *naleśniki* (crepes). It offers a variety of filled pancakes, including vegetarian options.

Tantra (ul Ślusarska 5) This astonishingly decorated bar is done out in an Indian and Tibetan theme and layered with cloth and other artefacts from the subcontinent. Sit on the cushion-strewn divans, order a drink from the long list, and meditate on the infinite.

Toruń is famous for its *pierniki*, which come in a variety of shapes, and can be bought at **Sklep Kopernik** (☎ 056 622 8832; Rynek Staromiejski 6).

Entertainment

Piwnica Artystyczna Pod Aniołem (Rynek Staromiejski 1) Set in a splendid spacious cellar in the Old Town Hall, this bar offers live music some nights. Check the posters outside for the latest gigs.

Jazz God (ul Rabiańska 17; ⏰ 5pm-2am Sun-Thu, 5pm-4am Fri & Sat) This is a lively cellar club with rock DJs most nights from 9pm.

Teatr im Horzycy (☎ 056 622 5222; Plac Teatralny 1) The main stage for theatre performances.

Dwór Artusa (☎ 056 655 4929; Artus Court, Rynek Staromiejski 6) This place often presents classical music.

Nasze Kino (www.naszekino.pl, in Polish; ul Podmurna 14; admission 12zł) Cool little art-house cinema embedded within part of the old city wall, its single screen showing a range of non-Hollywood films.

Getting There & Away

The **bus terminal** (ul Dąbrowskiego) is a 10-minute walk north of the Old Town. Polski Express has eight buses a day to Warsaw (41zł, 3½ hours) and two a day to Szczecin (59zł, six hours).

The **Toruń Główny train station** (Al Podgórska) is on the opposite side of the Vistula River and linked to the Old Town by bus 22 or 27 (get off at the first stop over the bridge). Some trains stop and finish at the more convenient Toruń Miasto train station, about 500m east of the New Town.

From the Toruń Główny station, there are trains to Poznań (33zł, 2½ hours, six daily), Gdańsk and Gdynia (39zł, four hours, six daily), Kraków (53zł, 7½ hours, three daily), Łódź (34zł, three hours, 10 daily), Olsztyn (34zł, 2½ hours, seven daily), Szczecin (49zł, five hours, up to three daily), Wrocław (48zł, 5½ hours, three daily) and Warsaw (41zł, three hours, nine daily). Trains travelling between Toruń and Gdańsk often change at Bydgoszcz, and between Toruń and Kraków you may need to get another connection at Inowrocław.

ŁEBA
pop 3800
Heading west from Gdańsk along the Pomeranian coast, Łeba (*weh*-bah) is the first major beach resort you encounter. Between May and September, this quiet fishing village transforms into a lively seaside destination.

The **tourist office** (☎ 059 866 2565; www.leba.pl; ul 11 Listopada 5a; ◷ 8am-8pm Mon-Fri, 8am-6pm Sat, 10am-4pm Sun Jul-Aug, 8am-4pm Mon-Fri Sep-Jun) is between the train station and the main street, ul Kościuszki. There are eateries on ul Kościuszki.

To reach the wide sandy **beach** from the train station, or adjacent bus stop, walk north along ul Kościuszki, ul Wojska Polskiego and ul Nadmorska for about 1.5km to the better eastern beach; if in doubt, follow the signs to the beachside Hotel Neptun.

SIGHTS
Beginning just west of Łeba, **Słowiński National Park** stretches along the coast for 33km. It contains a diversity of habitats, including forests, lakes, bogs and beaches, but the main attraction is the huge number of massive (and shifting) **sand dunes** that create a desert landscape. The wildlife and birdlife is also remarkably rich.

From Łeba to the sand dunes, follow the signs from near the train station northwest along ul Turystyczna and take the road west to the park entrance in the hamlet of Rąbka.

Minibuses ply this road in summer from Łeba (5zł); alternatively, it's a pleasant walk or bike ride (8km). No cars or buses are allowed beyond the park entrance.

SLEEPING & EATING
Many houses offer private rooms all year round, but finding a vacant room during summer can be tricky. There are plenty of decent eateries in the town centre and along ul Nadmorska.

Camping Nr 41 Ambre (☎ 059 866 2472; www.ambre .leba.pl; ul Nadmorska 9a; camping per adult/concession 13/8zł, cabins 240-400zł) This is a decent camping ground, but bring mosquito repellent if you don't want to be eaten alive.

Hotel Gołąbek (☎ 059 866 2175; www.hotel-golabek .leb.pl; ul Wybrzeże 10; s/d/tr/ste 240/350/410/700zł) This hotel exudes style on the edge of the wharf, with views of charming old fishing boats and the port. In summer the hotel hires out bicycles (5zł per hour).

GETTING THERE & AWAY
The usual transit point is Lębork, 29km south of Łeba. In summer there are several daily trains between the two destinations (8zł, 50 minutes). To Lębork, slow trains run every hour or two from Gdańsk, via Gdynia (16zł, 1½ hours). In summer (June to August), two trains run directly between Gdynia and Łeba (20zł, 2¼ hours), and four trains travel daily to/from Wrocław (55zł, eight hours).

SZCZECIN
pop 412,000
Szczecin (*shcheh*-cheen) is the major city and port of northwestern Poland. Massive damage in WWII accounts for the unaesthetic mishmash of new and old buildings in the city centre, but enough remains to give a sense of the pre-war days. The broad streets and massive historic buildings bear a strong resemblance to Berlin, for which Szczecin was once the main port as the German city of Stettin. Szczecin may not have the seamless charm of Toruń or Wrocław, but it's worth a visit if you're travelling to/from Germany.

Information
The **tourist office** (☎ 091 434 0440; Al Niepodległości 1; ◷ 9am-5pm Mon-Fri, 10am-2pm Sat) is helpful, as is the **cultural & tourist information office** (☎ 091 489 1630; ul Korsazy 34; ◷ 10am-6pm) in the castle. The **post office** and banks can be found along

WORTH THE TRIP: BALTIC BEACHES

Between Łeba and the German border, there are numerous seaside towns with unpolluted waters, offering fine sandy beaches during summer. Here are a few places for a sunbathing detour on your way west between Gdańsk and Szczecin:

■ **Ustka** Once the summer hang-out of German Chancellor Otto von Bismarck, this fishing port is full of atmosphere.

■ **Darłowo** A former medieval trading port with an impressive castle, and two beaches linked by a pedestrian bridge over a river.

■ **Kołobrzeg** This coastal city offers historic attractions, spa treatments and Baltic cruises.

■ **Międzyzdroje** A popular seaside resort and the gateway to Wolin National Park.

■ **Świnoujście** On a Baltic island shared with Germany, this busy port town boasts a long sandy shore and pleasant parks.

For more details, check out Lonely Planet's *Poland* country guide, or www.poland.travel.

Al Niepodległości, the main street. There's a handy internet cafe, **Portal** (Plac Zwyciestwa 3; per hr 5zł; ☉ 9am-11pm), in a big orange building 200m west of the tourist office.

Sights

The huge and austere **Castle of the Pomeranian Dukes** (ul Korsazy 34; admission free; ☉ dawn-dusk) lies 500m northeast of the tourist office. Originally built in the mid-14th century, it was enlarged in 1577 and rebuilt after major damage from airborne bombing in WWII. Its **Castle Museum** (adult/concession 6/3zł, free Thu; ☉ 10am-6pm Tue-Sun) explains the building's convoluted history, with special exhibitions mounted from time to time.

A short walk down (south) from the castle is the 15th-century **Old Town Hall** (ul Mściwoja 8), which contains the **Museum of the City of Szczecin** (adult/concession 6/3zł, free Thu; ☉ 10am-6pm Tue, 10am-4pm Wed-Sun). Nearby is the charmingly rebuilt **Old Town** with its cafes, bars and clubs. Three blocks northwest of the castle is the **National Museum** (ul Staromłyńska 27; adult/concession 6/3zł, free Thu; ☉ 10am-6pm Tue, Wed & Fri, 10am-4pm Thu, Sat & Sun), housing a historic art collection.

At the train station you can explore the city's newest attraction, **Szczecin Underground** (☎ 091 434 0801; www.schron.szczecin.pl; ul Kolumba 1/6; admission 15zł; ☉ noon). This guided tour takes you through a German-built bomb shelter that later became a Cold War fallout shelter. Pay at the Centrum Wynajmu i Turystyki office.

Sleeping & Eating

Camping PTTK Marina (☎ 091 460 1165; www.campingmarina.pl; ul Przestrzenna 23; per person/tent 15/9zł, s/d cabins 80/120zł) On the shore of Lake Dąbie –

get off at the Szczecin Dąbie train station and ask for directions (2km).

Youth Hostel PTSM (☎ 091 422 4761; www.ptsm.home.pl; ul Monte Cassino 19a; dm/d 24/50zł) This hostel has clean, spacious rooms and is 2km northwest of the tourist office. Catch tram 1 north to the stop marked 'Piotr Skargi', then walk right one block.

Hotelik Elka-Sen (☎ 091 433 5604; www.elkasen.szczecin.pl; Al 3 Maja 1a; s/d 140/180zł) Simple, light-filled rooms in a basement location in the centre of town. Just south of the tourist office, enter from the side street.

Hotel Podzamcze (☎ 091 812 1404; www.podzamcze.szczecin.pl; ul Sienna 1/3; s/d/ste 190/240/295zł) This hotel is in a charming location near the Old Town Hall. Its rooms are compact and its bathrooms tiny, but it's in a great location for the castle, the town hall and the train station.

Haga (☎ 091 812 1759; ul Sienna 10; mains 11-24zł) This informal place in the Old Town produces excellent Dutch-style filled pancakes from a menu listing more than 400 combinations.

Karczma Polska Pod Kogutem (☎ 091 434 6873; Plac Lotników 3; mains 12-62zł) Northwest of Al Niepodległości, this restaurant serves top-notch traditional Polish food. Roast rabbit in hazelnut sauce, anyone?

Getting There & Away

The **airport** (www.airport.com.pl) is in Goleniów, 45km northeast of the city. A shuttle bus (14zł) operated by **Interglobus** (☎ 091 485 0422; www.interglobus.pl) picks up from stops outside the LOT office and the train station before every flight, and meets all arrivals. Alternatively, a taxi should cost around 120zł.

LOT flies between Szczecin and Warsaw four times a day. Book at the **LOT office** (☎ 0801 703 703; ul Wyzwolenia 17), about 200m from the northern end of Al Niepodegłości. International flights on Ryanair include London (at least daily) and Dublin (three weekly). Oslo (five weekly) is reached via Norwegian.

The **bus terminal** (Plac Grodnicki) and the nearby **Szczecin Główny train station** (ul Kolumba) are 600m southeast of the tourist office. Bus departures are of limited interest, though Polski Express operates two services each day to Toruń (59zł, six hours) and Warsaw (63zł, 9½ hours) from a stand at the train station. Trains travel regularly to Poznań (39zł, 2½ hours, 15 daily), Gdańsk (51zł, 5½ hours, four daily) and Warsaw (56zł, seven hours, eight daily). Trains also head north to Świnoujście (28zł, two hours, hourly).

Another way to reach Świnoujście is via **ferry** (☎ 091 488 5564; www.wodolot-szczecin.pl; ul Jana z Kolna 7; adult/concession 50/25zł; ☼ mid-Jun–Oct), which travels daily from a quay north of the castle across the waters of the Szczeciński Lagoon (1¼ hours).

Advance tickets for trains and ferries are available from **Orbis Travel** (☎ 091 434 2618; Plac Zwycięstwa 1), about 200m west of the main post office.

WARMIA & MASURIA

The dominant feature of Warmia and Masuria is its beautiful postglacial landscape dominated by thousands of lakes, linked to rivers and canals, which host aquatic activities like yachting and canoeing. This picturesque lake district has little industry, and as a result remains unpolluted and attractive, especially in summer. Like much of northern Poland, the region has changed hands between Germanic and Polish rulers over the centuries.

ELBLĄG–OSTRÓDA CANAL

The longest navigable canal still used in Poland stretches 82km between Elbląg and Ostróda. Constructed between 1848 and 1876, this waterway was used to transport timber from inland forests to the Baltic. To overcome the 99.5m difference in water levels, the canal utilises an unusual system of five water-powered slipways so that boats are sometimes carried across dry land on rail-mounted trolleys.

Usually, **excursion boats** (☼ mid-May–Sep) depart from both Elbląg and Ostróda daily at 8am (adult/concession 85/65zł, 11 hours), but actual departures depend on available passengers. For information, call the **boat operators** (☎ Elbląg 055 232 4307, Ostróda 089 646 3871; www.zeglug a.com.pl).

Pensjonat Boss (☎ 055 239 3728; www.pensjonatboss .pl; ul Św Ducha 30; s/d/tr/ste 160/230/300/300zł) is one of several small hotels in Elbląg's Old Town, offering comfortable rooms above its own bar. **Camping Nr 61** (☎ 055 641 8666; www.camping61.com.pl; ul Panieńska 14; per person/tent 12/5zł, cabins d/q 60/100zł; ☼ May-Sep), right at Elbląg's boat dock, is a pleasant budget option. In Ostróda, try **Hotel Promenada** (☎ 089 642 8100; ul Mickiewicza 3; s/d/tr/ste from 140/180/240/300zł), 500m east of the bus and train stations.

Elbląg is accessible by frequent trains and buses from Gdańsk, Malbork, Frombork and Olsztyn. Ostróda is regularly connected by train to Olsztyn (8zł, 30 minutes, hourly) and Toruń (31zł, two hours, seven daily), and by bus to Olsztyn and Elbląg.

FROMBORK
pop 2500

It may look like the most uneventful town in history, but Frombork was once home to the famous astronomer Nicolaus Copernicus. It's where he wrote his ground-breaking *On the Revolutions of the Celestial Spheres*, which established the theory that the earth travelled around the sun. Beyond the memory of its famous resident, it's a charming, sleepy settlement that was founded on the shore of the Vistula Lagoon in the 13th century. It was later the site of a fortified ecclesiastical township, erected on Cathedral Hill.

The hill is now occupied by the extensive **Nicolaus Copernicus Museum** (ul Katedralna 8), with several sections requiring separate tickets. Most imposing is the red-brick Gothic **cathedral** (adult/concession 4/2zł; ☼ 9.30am-5pm Mon-Sat May-Sep, 9am-4pm Mon-Sat Oct-Apr), constructed in the 14th century. The nearby **Bishop's Palace** (adult/concession 4/2zł; ☼ 9am-4pm Tue-Sun) houses various exhibitions on local history, while the **belfry** (adult/concession 5/3zł; ☼ 9.30am-5pm May-Sep, 9am-4pm Oct-Apr) is home to an example of Foucault's pendulum. A short distance from the main museum, the **Hospital of the Holy Ghost** (adult/concession 4/2zł; ☼ 9am-4pm Tue-Sat) exhibits historical medical instruments and manuscripts.

POLAND

Camping Nr 12 (☎ 055 243 7744; ul Braniewska 14; per person/tent 7/10zł, dm/d/tr 25/58/87zł; ☽ May-Sep) is a privately owned camping ground at the eastern end of town, on the Braniewo road. It has basic cabins and a snack bar on the grounds.

Dom Familijny Rheticus (☎ 055 243 7800; www.domfamilijny.pl; ul Kopernika 10; s/d/ste 88/120/240zł) is a small, quaint old place with cosy rooms and good facilities, a short walk to the east of the bus stop. Breakfast is an extra 7zł.

The bus station is on the riverfront about 300m northwest of the museum. Frombork can be directly reached by bus from Elbląg (8zł, 40 minutes, hourly) and Gdańsk (18zł, three hours, two daily). The best place to get on and off is the bus stop directly below the museum on ul Kopernika.

OLSZTYN
pop 175,000

Olsztyn (ol-shtin) is a pleasant, relaxed city whose rebuilt Old Town is home to cobblestone streets, art galleries, cafes, bars and restaurants. As a busy transport hub, it's also the logical base from which to explore the region, including the Great Masurian Lakes district (opposite).

It's also another city on the Copernicus trail, as the great astronomer once served as administrator of Warmia, commanding Olsztyn Castle from 1516 to 1520. From 1466 to 1772 the town belonged to the kingdom of Poland. With the first partition of the nation, Olsztyn became Prussian Allenstein, until it returned to Polish hands in 1945.

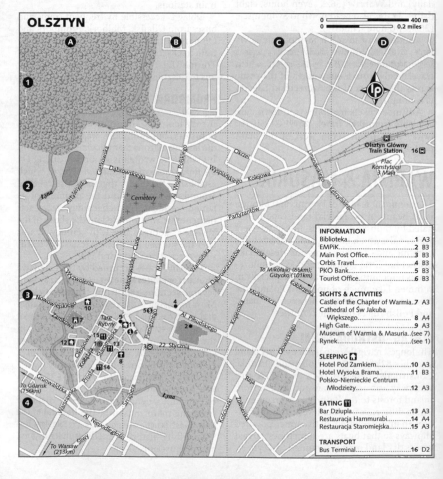

OLSZTYN

0 _____ 400 m
0 _____ 0.2 miles

INFORMATION
Biblioteka	1 A3
EMPiK	2 B3
Main Post Office	3 B3
Orbis Travel	4 B3
PKO Bank	5 B3
Tourist Office	6 B3

SIGHTS & ACTIVITIES
Castle of the Chapter of Warmia	7 A3
Cathedral of Św Jakuba Większego	8 A4
High Gate	9 A3
Museum of Warmia & Masuria	(see 7)
Rynek	(see 1)

SLEEPING 🏠
Hotel Pod Zamkiem	10 A3
Hotel Wysoka Brama	11 B3
Polsko-Niemieckie Centrum Młodzieży	12 A3

EATING 🍴
Bar Dziupla	13 A3
Restauracja Hammurabi	14 A4
Restauracja Staromiejska	15 A3

TRANSPORT
Bus Terminal	16 D2

The **tourist office** (☎ 089 535 3565; ul Staromiejska 1; 8am-4pm Mon-Fri) is next to the High Gate. Regarding money matters, try the **PKO Bank** (ul Pieniężnego).

For snail mail, go to the **main post office** (ul Pieniężnego); for cybermail, visit the **Biblioteka** (Library; ul Stare Miasto 33; per hr 3zł; 10am-7pm Mon-Fri, 9am-2pm Sat) in the centre of the Rynek, which offers internet access on its first floor. Books and maps are sold at **EMPiK** (ul Piłsudskiego 16) inside the Alfa Centrum shopping mall.

Sights

The **High Gate** is the remaining section of the 14th-century city walls. Further west, the 14th-century **Castle of the Chapter of Warmia** (ul Zamkowa 2) contains the **Museum of Warmia & Masuria** (adult/concession 9/7zł; 9am-5pm Tue-Sun May-Aug, 10am-4pm Tue-Sun Sep-Apr). Its exhibits star Copernicus, who made some astronomical observations here in the early 16th century, along with coins and art.

The **Rynek** (Market Sq) was rebuilt after WWII destruction. To the east, the red-brick Gothic **Cathedral of Św. Jakuba Większego** (ul Długosza) dates from the 14th century. Its 60m tower was added in 1596.

Sleeping

Hotel Wysoka Brama (☎ 089 527 3675; www.hotel wysokabrama.olsztyn.pl; ul Staromiejska 1; s/d/ste from 55/70/160zł) Offers cheap but basic rooms in a very central location next to the High Gate.

Hotel Pod Zamkiem (☎ 089 535 1287; www .hotel-olsztyn.com.pl; ul Nowowiejskiego 10; s/d/tr/ste from 160/220/260/250zł) Charmingly old-fashioned pension, featuring an extravagant stairwell constructed of dark timber carved with German text; but avoid the damp ground floor rooms. It's near the castle.

Polsko-Niemieckie Centrum Młodzieży (☎ 089 534 0780; www.pncm.olsztyn.pl; ul Okopowa 25; s/d/ste from 190/210/350zł) This place is situated next to the castle. The rooms (some with views of the castle) are plain, but have gleaming bathrooms. There's a sunlit restaurant off the foyer.

Eating

Bar Dziupla (☎ 089 527 5083; Rynek 9/10; mains 7-24zł; 8.30am-10pm) This small place is renowned among locals for its tasty Polish food, such as *pierogi*. It also does a good line in soups.

Restauracja Hammurabi (☎ 089 534 9467; ul Prosta 3/4; mains 10-32zł; 11am-11pm Fri & Sat, 11am-9pm Sun-Thu) The Hammurabi offers some inexpensive Middle Eastern choices in a cheerful Arabian setting, along with pizzas and steaks.

Restauracja Staromiejska (☎ 089 527 5883; ul Stare Miasto 4/6; mains 18-32zł; 10am-10pm) In classy premises on the Rynek, this restaurant serves quality Polish standards at reasonable prices. There's a range of *pierogi* and *naleśniki* on the menu.

Getting There & Away

From the **bus terminal** (ul Partyzantów), useful buses travel to Białystok (44zł, five hours, five daily) and Warsaw (30zł, five hours, 11 daily).

Trains depart from the **Olsztyn Główny train station** (ul Partyzantów) to Kętrzyn (20zł, 1½ hours, eight daily), Białystok (45zł, 4½ hours, three daily), Warsaw (41zł, four hours, seven daily), Gdańsk (34zł, three hours, seven daily) and Toruń (34zł, 2½ hours, seven daily). **Orbis Travel** (☎ 089 522 0613; Al Piłsudskiego) sells advance train tickets.

GREAT MASURIAN LAKES

The Great Masurian Lakes district east of Olsztyn has more than 2000 lakes, which are remnants of long-vanished glaciers, and surrounded by green hilly landscape. The largest lake is Lake Śniardwy (110 sq km). About 200km of canals connect these bodies of water, so the area is a prime destination for yachties and canoeists, as well as those who love to hike, fish and mountain-bike.

The detailed *Wielkie Jeziora Mazurskie* map (1:100,000) is essential for anyone exploring the region by water or hiking trails. The *Warmia i Mazury* map (1:300,000), available at regional tourist offices, is perfect for more general use.

ACTIVITIES

The larger lakes can be sailed from Węgorzewo to Ruciane-Nida, while canoeists might prefer the more intimate surroundings of rivers and smaller lakes. The most popular kayak route takes 10 days (106km) and follows rivers, canals and lakes from Sorkwity to Ruciane-Nida. Brochures explaining this route are available at regional tourist offices. There's also an extensive network of **hiking** and **mountain-biking** trails around the lakes.

Most travellers prefer to enjoy the lakes in comfort on **excursion boats**. Boats run daily (May to September) between Giżycko and Ruciane-Nida, via Mikołajki; and daily (June

POLAND

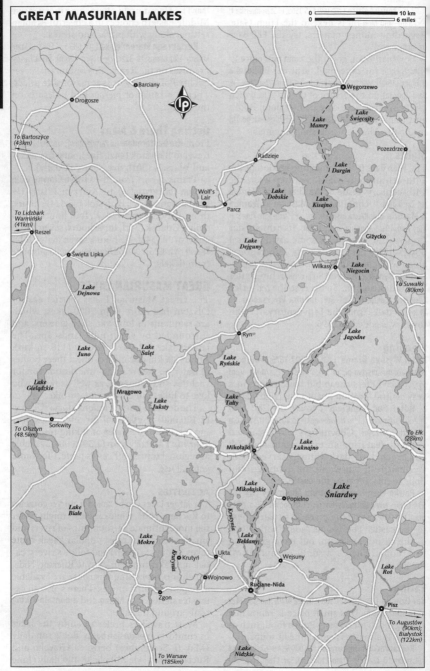

GREAT MASURIAN LAKES

0 — 10 km
0 — 6 miles

Barciany

Drogosze

Węgorzewo

To Bartoszyce
(43km)

Lake
Mamry

Lake
Święcajty

Radzieje

Pozezdrze

Lake
Dargin

Kętrzyn

Wolf's
Lair

Parcz

Lake
Dobskie

Lake
Kisajno

To Lidzbark
Warmiński
(41km)

Reszel

Lake
Dejguny

Giżycko

Święta Lipka

Wilkasy

Lake
Niegocin

Lake
Dejnowa

To Suwałki
(80km)

Ryn

Lake
Jagodne

Lake
Juno

Lake
Salęt

Lake
Ryńskie

Lake
Gielądzkie

Mrągowo

Lake
Juksty

Lake
Tałty

To Olsztyn
(48.5km)

Sorkwity

Mikołajki

Lake
Łuknajno

To Ełk
(28km)

Lake
Białe

Lake
Mikołajskie

Popielno

Lake
Śniardwy

Lake
Mokre

Krutynia

Krutyń

Ukta

Lake
Bełdany

Wejsuny

Lake
Roś

Wojnowo

Ruciane-Nida

Krutynia

Zgon

Pisz

To Augustów
(90km);
Białystok
(122km)

To Warsaw
(185km)

Lake
Nidzkie

to August) between Węgorzewo and Ruciane-Nida, via Giżycko and Mikołajki. However, services are more reliable from late June to late August. Schedules and fares are posted at the lake ports.

Święta Lipka

This village boasts a superb 17th-century **church** (7am-7pm), one of the purest examples of late-baroque architecture in Poland. Its lavishly decorated organ features angels adorning the 5000 pipes, and they dance to the organ's music. This mechanism is demonstrated several times daily from May to September, and recitals are held Friday nights from June to August.

Ask any of the regional tourist offices for a list of homes in Święta Lipka offering private rooms. There are several eateries and places to drink near the church.

Buses run to Kętrzyn every hour or so, but less often to Olsztyn.

Wolf's Lair

An eerie attraction at Gierłoż, 8km east of Kętrzyn, is the **Wolf's Lair** (Wilczy Szaniec; ☎ 089 752 4429; www.wolfsschanze.home.pl; adult/concession 10/5zł; 8am-dusk). This was Hitler's wartime headquarters for his invasion of the Soviet Union, and his main residence from 1941 to 1944.

In 1944 a group of high-ranking German officers tried to assassinate Hitler here. The leader of the plot, Claus von Stauffenberg, arrived from Berlin on 20 July for a regular military staff meeting. A frequent guest, he entered the meeting with a bomb in his briefcase. He placed it near Hitler and left to take a prearranged phone call, but the briefcase was then unwittingly moved by another officer. Though the explosion killed and wounded several people, Hitler suffered only minor injuries. Von Stauffenberg and some 5000 people allegedly involved in the plot were subsequently executed.

On 24 January 1945, as the Red Army approached, the Germans blew up Wolfsschanze (as it was known in German), and most bunkers were at least partly destroyed. However, huge concrete slabs – some 8.5m thick – and twisted metal remain. The ruins are at their most atmospheric in winter, with fewer visitors and a thick layer of snow.

A large map is posted at the entrance, with features of interest clearly labelled in English (Hitler's personal bunker, perhaps aptly, is unlucky number 13). Booklets outlining a self-guided walking tour are available in English and German at the kiosk in the car park. The services of English- and German-speaking guides are also available for 50zł.

Hotel Wilcze Gniazdo (☎ 089 752 4429; kontakt@wolfsschanze.pl; s/d/tr 70/80/130zł), situated in original buildings within the complex, is fairly basic but adequate for one night. A restaurant is attached.

Catch one of several daily PKS buses (3.50zł, 15 minutes) from Kętrzyn to Węgorzewo (via Radzieje, not Srokowo) and get off at the entrance. Between 10am and 4pm in July and August, a special bus marked *zielona linia* (green line) also runs from the train station in Kętrzyn to Wolf's Lair (Wilczy Szaniec; 3.50zł, 25 minutes, five daily). Contact the Kętrzyn **tourist office** (☎ 089 751 4765; Plac Piłsudskiego 1; 8.30am-3pm Mon-Fri) for updated transport details.

Giżycko
pop 29,600

Giżycko (ghee-*zhits*-ko) is the largest lakeside centre in the region, set on the northern shore of Lake Niegocin. A notable historic site is the 19th-century **Boyen Fortress** (ul Turystyczna 1; adult/concession 6/3zł; 9am-5pm), built by the Prussians to defend the border with Russia.

Near the main square (Plac Grunwaldzki) is the very helpful **tourist office** (☎ 087 428 5265; www.gizycko.turystyka.pl; ul Wyzwolenia 2; 9am-6pm Mon-Fri, 10am-4pm Sat & Sun Jul-Aug, 8am-5pm Mon-Fri, 10am-2pm Sat May & Jun & Sep, 9am-5pm Mon-Fri Oct-Apr) and **Bank Pekao** (ul Olsztyńska 15a). There are some *kantors* in the town centre, including one at **Orbis Travel** (☎ 087 428 3598; ul Dąbrowskiego 3), about 250m east of the main square.

Sailing boats are available from **Almatur** (☎ 087 428 5971; ul Moniuszki 24), 700m west of the fortress, and at **Centrum Mazur** (☎ 087 428 3871; ul Moniuszki 1) at Camping Nr 1 Zamek.

Wama Tour (☎ 087 429 3079; ul Konarskiego 1) rents out bicycles (30zł per day), and Hotel Zamek has kayaks (8zł per hour). **Żegluga Mazurska** (☎ 087 428 2578; ul Kolejowa 8) operates excursion boats, and you can arrange car rental through **Fiat Autoserwis** (☎ 087 428 5986; ul 1 Maja 21).

SLEEPING & EATING
Hotel Zamek (☎ 087 428 2419; www.cmazur.pl; camping per person 7.50zł; dm 25zł; r from 160zł; May-Sep) This combined hotel and camping ground provides a decent standard of accommodation for the price, and hires out bikes for 10zł per hour.

POLAND

Boyen Fortress Youth Hostel (☎ 087 428 2959; www .festeboyen.pl; dm 16-20zł) Has a character-packed location within the battlements, and offers the usual basic but clean facilities.

our pick **Hotel Cesarski** (☎ 087 428 1514; www .cesarski.pl; Plac Grunwalszki 8; s/d/ste 160/250/350zł) Formerly the German Kaiserhof, this newly renovated hotel is great value for its quality and central location.

Kuchnie Świata (☎ 087 429 2255; Plac Grunwaldzki 1; mains 9-39zł; Ⓨ 11am-11pm) A good dining choice is this cheery red-and-orange space serving up an eclectic range of dishes including pizza and pasta, along with *placki ziemniaczane* and other Polish favourites.

GETTING THERE & AWAY

From the train station, on the southern edge of town near the lake, trains run to Kętrzyn (8zł, 40 minutes, 11 daily), Olsztyn (28zł, two hours, eight daily) and Gdańsk (48zł, 4½ hours, four daily).

From the adjacent bus terminal, buses travel regularly to Mikołajki (10zł, one hour, hourly) and Olsztyn (20zł, three hours, at least hourly). Buses head to Warsaw every hour or two (39zł, five hours).

Mikołajki
pop 3800

Mikołajki (Mee-ko-*wahy*-kee), 86km east of Olsztyn, is a great base for exploring the lakes, and it's a picturesque little village in its own right. The **tourist office** (☎ 087 421 5507; www.mikolajki.pl; Plac Wolności 3; Ⓨ 9am-8pm Jul & Aug, 9am-5pm Tue-Sun May & Jun, Sep & Oct) is in the town centre. Nearby are *kantors* and ATMs.

Sailing boats and kayaks can be hired from **Cicha Zatoka** (☎ 087 421 5011; Al Spacerowa 1) at the waterfront on the other side of the bridge from the town centre, and also from the appropriately named **Fun** (☎ 087 421 6277; ul Kajki 82).

Lake Śniardwy and **Lake Łuknajno** are ideal for cycling. The tourist office can provide details and maps, and bikes can be rented from Pensjonjat Mikołajki (30zł per day).

SLEEPING & EATING

You'll find pensions and homes offering private rooms dotted along ul Kajki, the main street leading around Lake Mikołajskie; more pensions can be found along the roads to Ruciane-Nida and Ełk. There are plenty of eateries situated along the water-front and around the town square to cater for high-season visitors.

Camping Nr 2 Wagabunda (☎ 087 421 6018; www .wagabunda-mikolajki.pl; ul Leśna 2; per person/tent 13/13zł, cabins d/tr/q from 100/130/150zł; Ⓨ May-Oct) Across the bridge, this camping ground is 1km southwest of the town centre.

Pensjonat Mikołajki (☎ 087 421 6437; www.pens jonatmikolajki.prv.pl; ul Kajki 18; s/d/ste from 120/180/360zł) An attractive place to stay, with timber panelling and a prime lakefront location. Some rooms have balconies overlooking the water.

Pizzeria Królewska (☎ 087 421 6323; ul Kajki 5; mains 10-25zł; Ⓨ noon-10pm) A reasonable pizza restaurant open year-round, in cos cellar premises.

GETTING THERE & AWAY

From the bus terminal, next to the bridge at Plac Kościelny, up to seven buses go to Olsztyn (15zł, two hours) each day. Otherwise, get a bus (7zł, 40 minutes, hourly) to Mrągowo and change there for Olsztyn. Buses also go hourly to Giżycko (10zł, one hour), and four daily to Warsaw (38zł, 4½ hours). A private company, **Agawa** (☎ 0698 256 928) runs an express service daily to Warsaw year-round, departing from the bus terminal.

From the dozy train station, two slow trains shuttle along daily to Olsztyn (14zł, two hours), and two to Ełk (11zł, 1½ hours). In quiet times, the ticket office only opens 30 minutes (or less) before departures.

POLAND DIRECTORY

ACCOMMODATION

In this chapter, budget accommodation is defined as any place offering dorm beds, or hotels with double rooms costing up to 150zł per night. Midrange denotes accommodation offering doubles for between 150zł and 400zł per night; top-end is anything above that. All prices quoted are high season rates.

Unless otherwise noted, rooms have private bathrooms. Nearly every accommodation in every budget level offers internet access of some sort, even if it's just the computer in reception when the receptionist isn't too busy. Though there have been (so far unsuccessful) proposals to ban smoking from public spaces, it is becoming more common for hotels to offer nonsmoking options.

Camping

Poland has hundreds of camping grounds, and many offer good-value cabins and bungalows. Most open May to September, but some only open their gates between June and August.

Hostels

Schroniska młodzieżowe (youth hostels) in Poland are operated by Polskie Towarzystwo Schronisk Młodzieżowych (PTSM), a member of Hostelling International. Most only open in July and August, and are often very busy with Polish students; the year-round hostels have more facilities. Youth hostels are open to all, with no age limit. Curfews are common, and many hostels close between 10am and 5pm.

A growing number of privately-operated hostels operate in the main cities, and are geared towards international backpackers. They're open 24 hours and offer more modern facilities than the old youth hostels, though prices are higher. These hostels usually offer free use of washing machines, in response to the near-absence of laundromats in Poland.

A dorm bed can cost anything from 15zł to 75zł per person per night. Single/double rooms, if available, cost from about 80/100zł.

Hotels

Hotel prices often vary according to season, and are posted at hotel reception desks. Top-end hotels sometimes quote prices in euros, and discounted weekend rates are often available. Rooms with a private bathroom can be considerably more expensive than those with shared facilities. Most hotels offer 24-hour reception.

If possible, check the room before accepting. Don't be fooled by hotel reception areas, which may look great in contrast to the rest of the establishment. On the other hand, dreary scuffed corridors can sometimes open into clean, pleasant rooms.

Accommodation (sometimes with substantial discounts) can be reliably arranged via the internet through www.poland4u.com and www.hotels poland.com.

Mountain Refuges

PTTK runs a chain of *schroniska górskie* (mountain refuges) for hikers. They're usually simple, with a welcoming atmosphere, and serve cheap, hot meals. The more isolated refuges are obliged to accept everyone, so can be crowded in the high season. Refuges are normally open all year, but confirm with the nearest PTTK office before setting off.

Private Rooms & Apartments

Some destinations have agencies (usually called *biuro zakwaterowania* or *biuro kwater prywatnych*), which arrange accommodation in private homes. Rooms cost about 80/110zł per single/double. The most important factor to consider is location; if the home is in the suburbs, find out how far it is from reliable public transport.

During the high season, home owners also directly approach tourists. Prices are open to bargaining, but you're more likely to be offered somewhere out in the sticks. Also, private homes in smaller resorts and villages often have signs outside their gates or doors offering a *pokoje* (room) or *noclegi* (lodging).

In Warsaw, Kraków, Wrocław and Gdańsk, some agencies offer self-contained apartments, which are often an affordable alternative to hotels.

ACTIVITIES

Hikers and long-distance trekkers can enjoy marked trails across the Tatra Mountains (p409), where one of the most popular climbs is up the steep slopes of Mt Giewont (1894m). The Sudeten Mountains (p417) and the Great Masurian Lakes district (p439) also offer good walking opportunities. National parks worth hiking through include Białowieża National Park (p387), Kampinos National Park just outside Warsaw, Wielkopolska National Park outside Poznań, and the compact Wolin National Park east of Świnoujście. Trails are easy to follow and detailed maps are available at most larger bookshops.

As Poland is fairly flat, it's ideal for cyclists. Bicycle routes along the banks of the Vistula River are popular in Warsaw, Toruń and Kraków. Many of the national parks – including Wolin, Tatra (near Zakopane) and Słowinski (near Łeba) – offer bicycle trails, as does the Great Masurian Lakes district. For more of a challenge, try cycling in the Bieszczady ranges around Sanok (p411). Bikes can be rented at most resort towns and larger cities.

Zakopane (p410) will delight skiers from December to March, and facilities are cheaper than the ski resorts of Western Europe. Other sports on offer here include hang-gliding and paragliding. Another place to hit the snow is Szklarska Poręba (p417) in Silesia.

POLAND

Throngs of yachties, canoeists and kayakers enjoy the network of waterways in the Great Masurian Lakes district (p439) every summer; boats are available for rent from all lakeside towns, and there are even diving excursions. Windsurfers can head to the beaches of the Hel Peninsula (p431).

BOOKS

God's Playground: A History of Poland, by Norman Davies, offers an in-depth analysis of Polish history. The condensed version, *The Heart of Europe: A Short History of Poland,* also by Davies, has greater emphasis on the 20th century. *The Polish Way: A Thousand-Year History of the Poles and their Culture,* by Adam Zamoyski, is a superb cultural overview. The wartime Warsaw Rising is vividly brought to life in Norman Davies' *Rising '44,* and *The Polish Revolution: Solidarity 1980-82,* by Timothy Garton Ash, is entertaining and thorough. *Jews in Poland* by Iwo Cyprian Pogonowski provides a comprehensive record of half a millennium of Jewish life. Evocative works about rural life in interwar Poland include Bruno Schultz's *Street of Crocodiles* and Philip Marsden's *The Bronski House.*

BUSINESS HOURS

Most shops are open from 10am to 6pm Monday to Friday, and until 2pm on Saturday. Supermarkets and larger stores often have longer opening hours. Banks in larger cities are open from about 8am to 5pm weekdays (sometimes until 2pm on Saturday), but have shorter hours in smaller towns. *Kantors* generally follow shop hours.

Most restaurants, cafes and cafe-bars are open from 11am to 11pm. Nightclubs are often open from 9pm to the wee small hours of the next day.

DANGERS & ANNOYANCES

Poland is a relatively safe country, and crime has decreased significantly in recent years. Be alert, however, for thieves and pickpockets around major train stations, such as Warszawa Centralna. Robberies have been a problem on night trains, especially on international routes. Try to share a compartment with other people if possible.

Theft from cars is a widespread problem, so keep your vehicle in a guarded car park whenever possible. Heavy drinking is common and drunks can be disturbing, though rarely dangerous.

As Poland is an ethnically homogeneous nation, travellers who look racially different may attract curious stares from locals in outlying regions. Football (soccer) hooligans are not uncommon, so avoid travelling on public transport with them (especially if their team has lost!).

EMBASSIES & CONSULATES

All diplomatic missions listed are in Warsaw unless stated otherwise.

Australia (Map p378; ☎ 022 521 3444; www.australia .pl; ul Nowogrodzka 11)

Belarus (Map p375; ☎ 022 742 0990; www.belembassy .org/poland; ul Wiertnicza 58)

Canada (Map p378; ☎ 022 584 3100; www.canada.pl; ul Matejki 1/5)

Czech Republic (Map p378; ☎ 022 525 1850; www .mzv.cz/warsaw; ul Koszykowa 18)

France (Map p375; ☎ 022 529 3000; www.ambafrance -pl.org; ul Puławska 17); Kraków (Map p390; ☎ 012 424 5300; ul Stolarska 15)

Germany (Map p375; ☎ 022 584 1700; www.amba sadaniemiec.pl; ul Jazdów 12); Kraków (Map p390; ☎ 012 424 3000; ul Stolarska 7)

Ireland (Map p378; ☎ 022 849 6633; www.irlandia.pl; ul Mysia 5)

Japan (Map p375; ☎ 022 696 5000; www.pl.emb-japan .go.jp; ul Szwoleżerów 8)

Lithuania (Map p375; ☎ 022 625 3368; www.lietuva.pl; ul Ujazdowskie 14)

Netherlands (Map p375; ☎ 022 559 1200; www.nl embassy.pl; ul Kawalerii 10)

New Zealand (Map p378; ☎ 022 521 0500; www .nzembassy.com; Al Ujazdowskie 51)

Russia (Map p375; ☎ 022 621 3453; http://warsaw .rusembassy.org; ul Belwederska 49)

Slovakia (Map p375; ☎ 022 528 8110; emb.warsaw@ mzv.sk; ul Litewska 6)

South Africa (Map p378; ☎ 022 625 6228; warsaw .consular@foreign.gov.za; ul Koszykowa 54)

Ukraine (Map p375; ☎ 022 622 4797; www.ukraine -emb.pl; Al Szucha 7)

UK (Map p378; ☎ 022 311 0000; www.britishembassy .pl; Al Róż 1); Kraków (Map p390; ☎ 012 421 7030; ul Św. Anny 9)

USA (Map p378; ☎ 022 504 2000; http://poland.us embassy.gov; Al Ujazdowskie 29/31); Kraków (Map p390; ☎ 012 424 5100; ul Stolarska 9)

GAY & LESBIAN TRAVELLERS

Since the change of government in 2007, overt homophobia from state officials has declined;

though with the Church remaining influential in social matters, gay acceptance in Poland is still a work in progress. The gay community is becoming more visible, however, and in 2010 Warsaw is hosting **EuroPride** (www.europride .com), the first time this major gay festival has been held in a former communist country.

In general though, the Polish gay and lesbian scene remains fairly discreet. Warsaw and Kraków are the best places to find gay-friendly bars, clubs and accommodation. The free tourist brochure, the *Visitor,* lists a few gay nightspots, as do the **In Your Pocket** (www.inyourpocket.com) guides.

The best sources of information on gay Warsaw and Kraków are online at www .gayguide.net and www.gaypoland.pl. **Lambda** (☎ 022 628 5222; www.lambda.org.pl) is a national gay rights and information service.

HOLIDAYS

Poland's official public holidays:

New Year's Day 1 January
Easter Sunday March or April
Easter Monday March or April
State Holiday 1 May
Constitution Day 3 May
Pentecost Sunday Seventh Sunday after Easter
Corpus Christi Ninth Thursday after Easter
Assumption Day 15 August
All Saints' Day 1 November
Independence Day 11 November
Christmas 25 and 26 December

INTERNET ACCESS

Internet access is near-universal in Polish accommodation, from hostels through to every class of hotel: either as wireless access, via onsite computers, or both. As a result, individual accommodation with internet access has not been denoted as such in this chapter.

In the unlikely event that your lodgings are offline, you'll likely find an internet cafe nearby; expect to pay between 3zł and 5zł per hour. Also, some forward-thinking city councils have set up wireless access in their main market squares (eg Warsaw's Rynek Starego Miasta).

INTERNET RESOURCES

Commonwealth of Diverse Cultures (www.common wealth.pl) Outlines Poland's cultural heritage.
Poland.pl (www.poland.pl) News and a website directory.
Poland Tourism Portal (www.poland.travel) Useful travel site.

Polska (www.poland.gov.pl) Comprehensive government portal.
VirtualTourist.com (www.virtualtourist.com) Poland section features postings by travellers.
Visit.pl (www.visit.pl) Accommodation booking service.

MEDIA

The glossy, English-language *Poland Monthly* and the *Warsaw Business Journal* are aimed at the business community, while *Warsaw Insider* has more general-interest features, listings and reviews.

The free *Welcome to...* series of magazines covers Poznań, Kraków, Zakopane and Warsaw monthly. The free magazine *Poland: What, Where, When* covers Warsaw, Kraków and Gdańsk.

Recent newspapers and magazines from Western Europe and the USA are readily available at EMPiK bookshops, which are *everywhere,* and at news-stands in the foyers of upmarket hotels.

Poland has a mix of privately-owned TV channels, and state-owned nationwide channels. Foreign-language programs are painfully dubbed with one male voice covering all actors (that's men, women and children) and no lip-sync, so you can still hear the original language underneath. Most hotels offer English-language news channels.

Cinemas are present in all city centres, including modern multiplexes. English-language films are usually subtitled rather than dubbed into Polish, with the exception of children's movies.

MONEY

The Polish currency is the złoty (*zwo*-ti), abbreviated to zł. (The currency is also sometimes referred to by its international currency code, PLN). It's divided into 100 groszy (gr). Denominations of notes are 10, 20, 50, 100 and 200 złoty (rare), and coins come in one, two, five, 10, 20 and 50 groszy, and one, two and five złoty.

Bankomats (ATMs) accept most international credit cards and are easily found in the centre of all cities and most towns. Banks without an ATM may provide cash advances over the counter on credit cards.

Private *kantors* (foreign-exchange offices) are everywhere. *Kantors* require no paperwork and charge no commission. Rates at *kantors* in the midst of major tourist attractions, in top-end hotels and at airports are generally poor.

POLAND

The most widely accepted currencies are the euro, the US dollar and the pound sterling (in that order), though most *kantors* will change a range of other currencies. Foreign banknotes should be in good condition or *kantors* may refuse to accept them.

Travellers cheques are more secure than cash, but *kantors* rarely change them, and banks that do will charge 2% to 3% commission. A better option is a stored value cash card, which can be used in the same manner as a credit card; ask your bank about this before leaving home.

POST

Postal services are operated by Poczta Polska. Most cities have a dozen or more post offices, of which the Poczta Główna (main post office) has the widest range of services.

Letters and postcards sent by air from Poland take a few days to reach a European destination and a week or so to anywhere else. The cost of sending a normal-sized letter (up to 20g) or a postcard to other European countries is 3zł, rising to 3.50zł for North America and 4.50zł for Australia.

TELEPHONE

At the time of writing, landlines had 10 digits, incorporating the former three-digit area codes; however, the initial '0' will be phased out during the life of this book. To call Poland from abroad, dial the country code ☎ 48, then the last nine digits of the Polish number, dropping the initial '0'. The international access code from Poland is ☎ 00. For help, try the operators for local numbers (☎ 913), national numbers and codes (☎ 912) and international codes (☎ 908), but don't expect anyone to speak English.

The three mobile telephone providers are Orange, Era and Plus GSM. Prepaid accounts are cheap by Western European standards, and are quick and easy to set up at local offices of these companies. Reception is generally good and covers the whole country. Mobile numbers are often quoted as nine digits, but require an initial zero to be dialled from landline phones.

EMERGENCY NUMBERS

- Ambulance ☎ 999
- Fire ☎ 998
- Police ☎ 997
- Police (from mobile phones) ☎ 112

Most public telephones use magnetic phonecards, available at post offices and kiosks in units of 15 (9zł), 30 (15zł) and 60 (24zł) – one unit represents one three-minute local call. The cards can be used for domestic and international calls.

TRAVELLERS WITH DISABILITIES

Poland is not well set-up for people with disabilities, although there have been significant improvements over recent years. Wheelchair ramps are only available at some upmarket hotels, and public transport will be a real challenge for anyone with mobility problems. However, many top-end hotels now have at least one room specially designed for disabled access – book ahead for these. There are also some low-floor trams now running on the Warsaw and Kraków public transport networks. Information on disability issues is available from **Integracja** (☎ 022 635 1330; www.integracja.org).

VISAS

EU citizens do not need visas to visit Poland and can stay indefinitely. Citizens of Australia, Canada, Israel, New Zealand, Switzerland and the USA can stay in Poland up to 90 days without a visa.

However, since Poland's entry into the Schengen zone in December 2007, the 90 day visa-free entry period has been extended to all the Schengen countries; so if travelling from Poland through Germany and France, for example, you can't exceed 90 days in total. Once your 90 days is up, you must leave the Schengen zone for a minimum 90 days before you can once again enter it visa-free.

South African citizens do require a visa. Other nationals should check with Polish embassies or consulates in their countries for current visa requirements. Updates can be found at the website of the Ministry of Foreign Affairs, www.msz .gov.pl.

TRANSPORT IN POLAND

GETTING THERE & AWAY
Air

The majority of international flights to Poland arrive at Warsaw's Okęcie airport, while other important airports include Kraków Balice, Gdańsk, Poznań and Wrocław. The national carrier **LOT** (LO; www.lot.com; ☎ from mobiles 0801 703 703, 22 9572) flies to all major European cities.

Other major airlines flying to Poland:
Aeroflot (SU; ☎ 022 621 1611; www.aeroflot.com)
Air France (AF; ☎ 022 556 6400; www.airfrance.com)
Alitalia (AZ; ☎ 0801 107 700; www.alitalia.it)
British Airways (BA; ☎ 00 800 441 1592; www.ba.com)
Centralwings (C0; ☎ 022 420 5775; www.central
wings.com)
easyJet (U2; ☎ 0044 870 6 000 000; www.easyjet.com)
KLM (KL; ☎ 022 556 6444; www.klm.pl)
Lufthansa (LH; ☎ 022 338 1300; www.lufthansa.pl)
Malév (MA; ☎ 022 697 7472; www.malev.hu)
Ryanair (FR; ☎ 0300 703 007; www.ryanair.com)
SAS (SK; ☎ 022 850 0500; www.flysas.com)
SkyEurope (NE; ☎ 00 421 2 3301 7301; www.sky
europe.com)
Wizz Air (W6; ☎ 0300 503 010; www.wizzair.com)

Land

Since Poland is now within the Schengen zone, there are no border posts or border crossing formalities between Poland and Germany, the Czech Republic, Slovakia and Lithuania. Below is a list of major road border-crossings with Poland's non-Schengen neighbours that accept foreigners and are open 24 hours.
Belarus (South to north) Terespol, Kuźnica Białostocka.
Russia (West to east) Gronowo, Bezledy.
Ukraine (South to north) Medyka, Hrebenne, Dorohusk.

If you're heading to Russia or Lithuania and your train/bus passes through Belarus, be aware that you need a Belarusian transit visa and you must obtain it in advance.

BUS

International bus services are offered by dozens of Polish and international companies. They're cheaper than trains, but not as comfortable or fast.

One of the major operators is **Eurolines Polska** (☎ 032 351 2020; www.eurolinespolska.pl), which operates to a range of European destinations, including eastern cities such as Minsk, Brest, Vilnius, Tallinn and Riga.

CAR & MOTORCYCLE

To drive a car into Poland, EU citizens need their driving licence from home, while other nationalities must obtain an International Drivers Permit in their home country. Also required are vehicle registration papers and liability insurance (Green Card). If your insurance is not valid for Poland you must buy an additional policy at the border.

TRAIN

Trains link Poland with every neighbouring country and beyond, but international train travel is not cheap. To save money on fares, investigate special train tickets and rail passes (see p615). Domestic trains in Poland are significantly cheaper, so you'll save money if you buy a ticket to a Polish border destination, then take a local train.

Do note that some international trains to/from Poland have become notorious for theft. Keep a grip on your bags, particularly on the Berlin–Warsaw, Prague–Warsaw and Prague–Kraków overnight trains, and on *any* train travelling to/from Gdańsk.

Sea

For ferry services from Gdańsk and Gdynia see p428 and p430, respectively. There are also car and passenger ferries from the Polish town of Świnoujście, operated by the following companies:
Polferries (www.polferries.pl) Offers daily services from Świnoujście to Ystad (eight hours) in Sweden, every Saturday to Rønne (5¼ hours) in Denmark, and five days a week to Copenhagen (nine to 10½ hours).
Unity Line (www.unityline.pl) Runs ferries between Świnoujście and Ystad (6¾ hours).

Any travel agency in Scandinavia will sell tickets for these services. In Poland, ask at any Orbis Travel office. In summer, passenger boats ply the Baltic coast from Świnoujście to Ahlbeck, Heringsdorf, Bansin and Zinnowitz in Germany.

GETTING AROUND
Air

LOT (☎ 0801 703 703, from mobiles 22 9572; www.lot
.com) flies several times a day from Warsaw to Gdańsk, Kraków, Poznań, Szczecin and Wrocław. Another Polish airline, **Jet Air** (☎ 022 846 8661; www.jetair.pl) serves Warsaw, Łódź, Kraków, Poznań and Zielona Góra from its hub in Bydgoszcz.

Bicycle

Cycling is not great for getting around cities, but is often a good way to travel between villages. Major roads are busy but generally flat, while minor roads can be bumpy. If you get tired, it's easy to place your bike in the special luggage compartment of a train. These compartments are at the front or rear of slow passenger trains, but rarely found on fast or express trains, and never on InterCity or EuroCity services. You'll need a special ticket for your bike from the railway luggage office.

Bus

Buses can be useful on short routes and through the mountains in southern Poland; but usually trains are quicker and more comfortable, and private minibuses are quicker and more direct.

Most buses are operated by the state bus company, PKS. It provides two kinds of service from its bus terminals *(dworzec autobusowy PKS)*: ordinary buses (marked in black on timetables), and fast buses (marked in red), which ignore minor stops.

Timetables are posted on boards inside or outside PKS bus terminals. Additional symbols next to departure times may indicate the bus runs only on certain days or in certain seasons. Terminals usually have an information desk, but it's rarely staffed with English speakers. Tickets for PKS buses are usually bought at the terminal, but sometimes from drivers. Note that the quoted bus frequencies in this chapter are as per the summer schedule.

The largest private bus operator is **Polski Express** (www.polskiexpress.net), which operates long-distance routes to/from Warsaw (p385). Polski Express buses normally arrive and depart from PKS bus terminals – exceptions are mentioned in the relevant destination sections.

The price of bus tickets is determined by the length, in kilometres, of the trip. Prices start at roughly 3zł for a journey of up to 5km. Minibuses charge set prices for journeys, and these are normally posted in their windows or at the bus stop.

Car & Motorcycle

FUEL & SPARE PARTS

Petrol stations sell several kinds of petrol, including 94-octane leaded, 95-octane unleaded, 98-octane unleaded and diesel. Most petrol stations are open from 6am to 10pm (from 7am to 3pm Sunday), though some operate around the clock. Garages are plentiful. Roadside assistance can be summoned by dialling ☎ 981 or 022 9637.

HIRE

Major international car-rental companies, such as **Avis** (www.avis.pl), **Hertz** (www.hertz.pl) and **Europcar** (www.europcar.com.pl), are represented in larger cities and have smaller offices at airports. Rates are comparable to full-price rental in Western Europe.

Some companies offer one-way rentals, but no agency will allow you to drive their precious vehicle into Russia, Ukraine or Belarus.

Rental agencies will need to see your passport, your local driving licence (which must be held for at least one year) and a credit card (for the deposit). You need to be at least 21 or 23 years of age to rent a car; sometimes 25 for a more expensive car.

It's usually cheaper to prebook a car in Poland from abroad, rather than to front up at an agency inside the country.

ROAD RULES

The speed limit is 130km/h on motorways, 100km/h on two- or four-lane highways, 90km/h on other open roads and 50km/h in built-up areas. If the background of the sign bearing the town's name is white you must reduce speed to 50km/h; if the background is green there's no need to reduce speed (unless road signs indicate otherwise). Radar-equipped police are very active, especially in villages with white signs.

Unless signs state otherwise, cars may park on pavements as long as a minimum 1.5m-wide walkway is left for pedestrians. Parking in the opposite direction to traffic flow is allowed. The permitted blood alcohol level is a low 0.02%, so it's best not to drink if you're driving. Seat belts are compulsory, as are helmets for motorcyclists. Between October and February, all drivers must use headlights during the day (and night!).

Train

Trains will be your main means of transport. They're cheap, reliable and rarely overcrowded (except for July and August peak times). **Polish State Railways** (PKP; www.pkp.pl) operates trains to almost every place listed in this chapter.

InterCity trains operate on major routes out of Warsaw, including Gdańsk, Kraków, Poznań, Wrocław and Szczecin. They only stop at major cities and are the fastest way to travel by rail. These trains require seat reservations.

Down the pecking order but still quick are *pociąg ekspresowy* (express trains) and the similar but cheaper *pociąg TLK* (TLK trains). *Pociąg pospieszny* (fast trains) are a bit slower and more crowded, but will most likely be the type of train you most often catch. *Pociąg osobowy* (slow passenger trains) stop at every tree at the side of the track and should be used only for short trips. Express and fast trains do not normally require seat reservations except at peak times; seats on slow trains cannot be reserved.

Almost all trains carry two classes: *druga klasa* (2nd class) and *pierwsza klasa* (1st class), which is 50% more expensive. The carriages on long-distance trains are usually divided into compartments: 1st-class compartments have six seats; 2nd-class ones contain eight seats.

Note that the quoted train fares in this chapter are for a second class ticket on a *pospieszny* train, or the most likely alternative if the route is mainly served by a different type of train. Frequencies are as per the summer schedule.

In a couchette on an overnight train, compartments have four/six beds in 1st/2nd class. Sleepers have two/three people (1st/2nd class) in a compartment fitted with a washbasin, sheets and blankets. Most 2nd-class and all 1st-class carriages have nonsmoking compartments.

Train *odjazdy* (departures) are listed on a yellow board and *przyjazdy* (arrivals) on a white board. Ordinary trains are marked in black print, fast trains in red. An additional 'Ex' indicates an express train, and InterCity trains are identified by the letters 'IC'. The letter 'R' in a square indicates the train has compulsory seat reservation. The timetables also show which *peron* (platform) it's using. Be aware that the number applies to *both* sides of

the platform. If in doubt, check the platform departure board or route cards on the side of carriages, or ask a fellow passenger.

Be aware that signage is very poor at Polish train stations – there's often only one sign in the middle of the platform, making it hard to spot if you're at the rear of the train as it pulls in. If in doubt about your location, ask a fellow passenger.

Timetable and fare information in English is on the PKP website. *Miejsca sypialne* (sleepers) and *kuszetki* (couchettes) can be booked at special counters in larger train stations or from Orbis; pre-booking is recommended.

If a seat reservation is compulsory on your train, you will automatically be sold a *miejscówka* (reserved) seat ticket. If you do not make a seat reservation, you can travel on *any* train (of the type requested, ie slow, fast or express) to the destination indicated on your ticket on the date specified.

Your ticket will list the *klasa* (class); the *poc* (type) of train; where the train is travelling *od* (from) and *do* (to); the major town or junction the train is travelling *prez* (through); and the total *cena* (price). If more than one place is listed under the heading *prez* (via), find out from the conductor *early* if you have to change trains at the junction listed or be in a specific carriage (the train may separate later).

If you get on a train without a ticket, you can buy one directly from the conductor for a small supplement (8zł) – but do it right away. If the conductor finds you first, you'll be fined for travelling without a ticket. You can always upgrade from 2nd to 1st class for a small extra fee (about 8zł), plus the additional fare.

Slovakia

Yee! ha! yip! Exuberant, high-pitched squeals burst forth from folk dancers as they stomp round the floor. A field of fresh heather blooms on a Tatra mountain hillside once dominated by pine forest. A little old *babka* waits at the train station wearing kerchief and full village dress. Visiting Slovakia is not about earth-shattering sights or superlatives, it's more about experiencing the every day in a place where folkways and nature still hold sway.

That's not to say Bratislava doesn't bustle. As investment pours in, building cranes dominate the cityscape and a new and oh-so-trendy restaurant or hotel seems to open every second minute. The compact, rabbit-warren Old Town has to a certain extent gone commercial, but it's worth a day or two of distraction wandering the back streets.

Just make sure you also venture outside the capital to explore the ancient castles, traditional villages and national parks. Dense forests cover the low hills and fortress ruins top the cliffs of central Slovakia. Further east, medieval towns sit beneath the High Tatras peaks and a gondola swoops up to 2000m. You can hike beside a gorge waterfall one day and search out nail-less wooden churches in tiny villages the next.

Unfortunately, all is not pastoral bliss. You'll still see traces of the communist legacy – heavy industry and truly ugly concrete buildings. Thankfully the country's folksy spirit remains intact. So pull up a plate of *halušky* (dumplings) with *bryndza* (sheep's cheese) and drink a glass of *slivovice* (firewater-like plum brandy) for us – *nazdravie!*

FAST FACTS

- **Area** 49,035 sq km
- **Capital** Bratislava
- **Currency** euro (€); US$1 = €0.73; UK£1 = €1.06; A$1 = €0.50; ¥100 = €0.76; NZ$1 = €0.41
- **Famous for** ice hockey, beautiful women, mountain hiking, folk traditions
- **Official Language** Slovak
- **Phrases** *ahoj* (hello); *dovidenia* (goodbye); *ďakujem* (thank you); *este pivo prosím* (another beer please), *kde je WC* (veyt-say)? (where's the loo?)
- **Population** 5.44 million
- **Telephone Codes** country code ☎ 421; international access code ☎ 00
- **Visas** citizens of the UK, USA, Canada, Australia, New Zealand and Japan can enter Slovakia for 90 days without a visa; see p491

SLOVAKIA

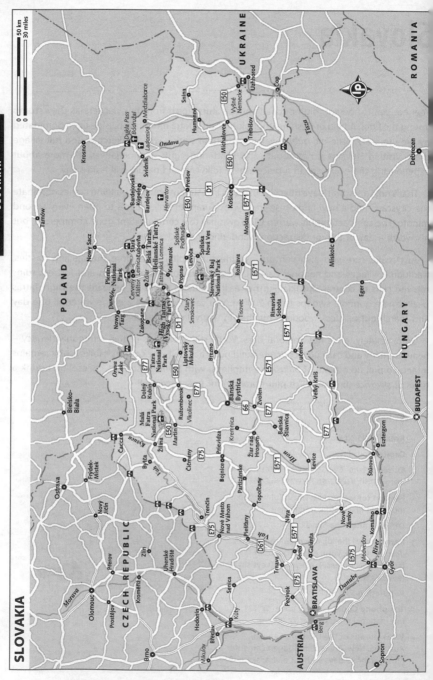

HIGHLIGHTS

- Hike between mountain huts among the crests of one Europe's smallest alpine mountain ranges, the 12km-long **High Tatras** (p471).
- Linger with friends over cake, coffee and drinks at one of the myriad sidewalk cafes in Old Town **Bratislava** (p456).
- At 4 hectares long, the ruins of **Spis Castle** (p480) are among the biggest in Europe.
- Go rural by staying in one of the traditional log-cottage villages like **Vlkolinec** (p467) or **Čičmany** (p468).
- Stay in a medieval burgher's house and visit the nation's most beautiful Gothic altar in **Levoča** (p478).

ITINERARIES

- **Three days** Entering from the east, either take the bus in from Kraków or fly to Poprad to get to the High Tatras. If rural bliss is your thing, make Ždiar your two-day mountain-hiking base, if you like more pampering after your exertion, stay in Tatranská Lomnica. On day three ride the rails west to the country's capital, Bratislava.
- **One week** Spend four nights in the Tatras, taking a day trip or two to see Spiš Castle, medieval Levoča or Kežmarok. Stop for a night in Trenčín to catch a torchlight tour of the hilltop fortress before venturing on to Old Town Bratislava for the last two nights.

CLIMATE & WHEN TO GO

Slovakia's moderate climate averages -2°C in January and 25°C in August. Spring floods are quite common, but autumn can be rainy, too. Snow blankets the mountains into April and the upper elevations of the High Tatras are covered well into June.

The tourist season runs from May through September. Lodging prices are lower outside those months, but many sights in outlying areas aren't open. September is still quite warm, young wine is being harvested and the mountains are snow-free (usually), making it one of the best times to visit. Rates skyrocket nationwide during the Easter and Christmas holidays.

HISTORY

Slavic tribes wandered west into what would become Slovakia sometime round about the 5th century; by the 9th, the territory was part of the short-lived Great Moravian empire. It was about then that the Magyars (Hungarians) set up shop next door and subsequently laid claim to the whole territory. In the early 16th century, the Turks moved into Budapest pushing the Hungarian monarchs to take up residence in Bratislava (known then as Pressburg, in German, or Pozsony, in Hungarian). Because Slovakia was the Hungarian frontierland, many fortresses were constructed during the Middle Ages, and can still be seen today.

At the turn of the 20th century, Slovak intellectuals cultivated ties with the Czechs and took their nation into the united Czechoslovakia post-WWI. A brief period of independence transpired when leaders declared Slovakia a German ally – the day before Hitler's troops invaded Czechoslovakia in March 1939. It was not a populist move and in August 1944 Slovak partisans instigated the ill-fated Slovak National Uprising (Slovenské Národné Povstanie, or SNP), a source of ongoing national pride (and innumerable street names).

After the communist takeover in 1948, power was again centralised in Prague until 1989, when the Velvet Revolution brought down the curtains on the communists. Elections in 1992 saw the left-leaning Movement for a Democratic Slovakia (HZDS) come to power with Vladimír Mečiar, a former boxer, as prime minister. By that summer the Slovak parliament had voted to declare sovereignty, and the federation dissolved peacefully on 1 January 1993.

Despite changing government leadership that first rejected and then embraced economic and social reforms, Slovakia was accepted into NATO and the EU by 2004,

CONNECTIONS: MOVING ON FROM SLOVAKIA

Though few airlines fly into Slovakia itself, Bratislava is just 60km from the well-connected Vienna International Airport. By train from Bratislava (p464), Budapest (three hours) and Prague (five hours) are easy to reach. Heading further east, buses become your best bet. You can connect to Zakopane, Poland (2½ hours) from Poprad (p477) near the Tatra Mountains, and to Uzhgorod, Ukraine (2½ hours) through Kosice (p487).

SLOVAKIA

HOW MUCH?

- **Night in hostel** €32
- **Double room in pension** €85
- **Day's ski hire** €10
- **Bicycle** €140
- **Postcard** €0.30

LONELY PLANET INDEX

- **1L petrol** €0.98
- **1L bottled water** €0.50
- **Beer** €1
- **Souvenir T-shirt** €10
- **Street snack (ice-cream scoop)** €0.40

---

and the Schengen member states in 2007. Amid some consternation over rising prices, the euro became the national currency in January 2009.

PEOPLE

A deeply religious and familial people, Slovaks have strong family circles and a deep sense of folk traditions. The young are warm and open, but there can be a reserve about older generations. Show interest in their country, or ask for help, and the shell cracks. Generosity and warmth lurk just behind the stoicism. Thankfully, surly service is now the exception rather than the rule in the tourist industry.

With such great scenery, it's not surprising that most Slovaks spend their weekends outdoors. Isť na prechadsku (going for a walk) is a national pastime so you will doubtless run into a backpack-toting Slovak wherever you trek in nature. About a quarter of the population lives in the five largest cities.

Government statistics estimate that Slovakia's population is 86% Slovak, 10% Hungarian and 1.7% Roma. This last figure is in some dispute as some groups estimate the Roma population as high as 3.5%. The minority Roma are still viewed with an uncompromising suspicion – at best.

RELIGION

Slovakia's first Christian church was founded in Nitra in AD 833 after SS Cyril and Methodius visited the Great Moravian empire. Despite 50 years of communist sup-

pression, the majority of Slovaks retained their strong beliefs. Today Roman Catholics form the majority (about 69%), but evangelicals are also numerous; East Slovakia has many Greek Catholic and Orthodox believers.

ARTS

Some city dwellers may have been put off by the clichéd image of the communist-era 'happy peasant', but traditional folk arts, from music to architecture, are still celebrated – especially during summer festivals.

Cinema

Slovak cinema first made its mark as part of the Czechoslovak New Wave of the 1960s, with classic films like Smrt si rika Engelchen (Death Calls Itself Engelchen, 1963) directed by Ján Kádar, and Obchod na korze (The Shop on the Main Street, 1965) by Elmar Klos. Martin Sulík was one of Slovakia's most promising new directors, winning an Oscar nomination for Všetko, čo mám rád (Everything I Like, 1992), and international acclaim for Krajinka (The Landscape, 2000). Unfortunately, lack of funding and the closing of the Koliba movie studios has meant there has been no serious Slovak movie-making since 2000, though there have been a few collaborations.

Music

Traditional Slovak folk instruments include the fujara (a 2m-long flute), the gajdy (bagpipes) and the konkovka (a strident shepherd's flute). Folk songs helped preserve the Slovak language during Hungarian rule, and in East Slovakia musical folk traditions are an integral part of village life.

In classical music, the 19th-century works of Ján L Bela and the symphonies of Alexander Moyzes receive world recognition. Slovakia's contemporary music scene is small, but vibrant. Modern musicians combine traditional lyrics or rhythms with a modern beat. Zuzana Mojžišová's music seems to have an almost Romany-like vibrancy, but stems from Slovak folk music. Marián Varga riffs on classical themes and the Peter Lipa band is the granddaddy of the Bratislava Jazz Days festival (p461).

Architecture

The wooden churches of East Slovakia, easily accessible from Bardejov (see p489) are some of the most interesting architectural gems in the country. You can see transplanted versions at a *skanzen* (open-air museum), like the one in Martin (p468), where vernacular village architecture is preserved. Levoča is known for its nearly complete medieval town walls and for the Gothic Church of St Jacob, and its 18m-high altar carved by Master Pavol. Of course you can't miss the brutal socialist-realist architecture of the communist epoch, as evidenced by the New Bridge (Nový most, p460) in Bratislava. Yes, it does resemble a UFO on a stick.

SPORT

Enter any bar or restaurant during puck-pushing season (September to April) and 12 large men and an ice rink will never be far from the TV screen, even at nice restaurants. Local club rivalries are heated, but the Olympic team showing has flagged in recent years. The announcement that Slovakia will host the 2011 World Championships surely perked up fans.

Slovak athletes did capture an Olympic slalom canoeing gold in 2008. But it's football that fills the summer months for most. The Slovaks have yet to attain the rabid fanaticism found elsewhere in Europe, but club games are a reliable source of red-blooded bravado. SK Slovan Bratislava is the nation's most successful team.

ENVIRONMENT
The Land

Slovakia sits in the heart of Europe, straddling the northwestern end of the Carpathian Mountains. This hilly country forms a clear physical barrier between the plains of Poland and Hungary. Almost 80% of Slovakia is more than 750m above sea level, and forests, mainly beech and spruce, cover 40% of the country.

Southwestern Slovakia is a fertile lowland stretching from the foothills of the Carpathians down to the Danube River, which, from Bratislava to Štúrovo, forms the border with Hungary.

Northern Slovakia is dominated by the High Tatras (Vysoké Tatry) mountains along the Polish border; Gerlachovský štít (2654m) being the highest peak. The forested ridges of the Low Tatras (Nízke Tatry) and the Malá Fatra are national park playgrounds. South are the gorges and waterfalls of Slovenský raj and the limestone caves of Slovenský kras. The longest river, the Váh, rises in the Tatras

and flows 390km west and south to join the Danube at Komárno.

Wildlife

Slovakia's national parks contain bears, marmots, wolves, lynxes, chamois, mink and otters, though they're rarely seen. Deer, pheasants, partridges, ducks, wild geese, storks, grouse, eagles and other birds of prey can be seen across the country.

National Parks

National parks and protected areas make up 20% of Slovakia. The parks in the High Tatras, Slovenský raj and Malá Fatra regions should not be missed.

Environmental Issues

Slovakia is a mixed bag in environmental terms. No doubt due to most Slovaks' penchant for all things outdoorsy, large swathes of the countryside are technically protected parkland. Watchdog groups like the International Union for the Conservation of Nature have protested that more and more development in the Tatras has put its national park status in question. And the communist legacy left more than its fair share of grimy, industrial factories. Big centres such as Bratislava and Košice do suffer from air pollution.

The controversial Gabčíkovo hydroelectric project, on the Danube west of Komárno, produces enough power to cover the needs of every home in Slovakia. But some believe it exacerbates the damage caused by annual floods and has damaged bird habitats.

Tens of thousands of hikers pass through Slovakia's parks and protected areas every year – try to do your bit to keep them pristine. Wherever possible, carry out your rubbish, avoid using detergents or toothpaste in or near watercourses, stick to established trails (this helps prevent erosion), cook on a kerosene stove rather than an open fire and do not engage in or encourage – by purchasing goods made from endangered species – unlawful hunting.

FOOD & DRINK
Staples & Specialities

Slovak cuisine is basic central European fare: various fried meat schnitzels with fries and hearty stews with potatoes. Soups like *cesnaková polievka* (garlic soup), either creamy or clear with croutons and cheese, and *kapustnica*

SLOVAKIA

(cabbage soup), with a paprika and pork base, start most meals. Slovakia's national dish is *bryndzové halušky*, gnocchi-like dumplings topped with soft sheep's cheese and bits of bacon fat. Don't pass up an opportunity to eat in a *salaš* or a *koliba* (rustic log-cabin eateries), where these traditional specialities are the mainstay.

For dessert, try *palacinka* (crepes) stuffed with jam or chocolate. *Ovocné knedličky* (fruit dumplings) are round balls filled with fruit and coated with crushed poppy seeds or breadcrumbs, dribbled with melted butter and sometimes accompanied by fruit purée and ice cream – yum.

Slovak wine is…what do oenophiles say…highly drinkable (ie good and cheap). The Modra region squeezes dry reds, like Frankovka and Kláštorné. Slovak Tokaj, a white dessert wine from the southeast, is trying to give the Hungarian version a run for its money (though it falls short).

Slovak *pivo* (beer) is as good as the Czech stuff – try full-bodied Zlatý Bažant or dark, sweet Martiner. *Borovička* (a potent berry-based clear liquor) and *slivovice* (plum-based) are consumed as shots and are said to aid digestion.

Where to Eat & Drink

Restaurants nationwide are generally open from 10am to 10pm. Self-service cafeterias (called *samoobsluha reštaurácie, jedáleň* or *bufet*) cater to office workers and are great places to eat during the day (but close early). Look for food stands near train and bus stations.

All manner of trendy world food has found a foothold in Bratislava, but most Slovak towns only have a pizzeria or a Chinese takeaway in addition to local staples. Cafes (spelled in English) are often as much bar and restaurant as coffee shop; *kaviareň* (cafes) may only serve beverages, but that includes alcohol; a *cukráreň* (pastry or sweet shop) is where you go to get cakes and ice creams with your java.

Most restaurants across the country have nonsmoking sections, but don't be surprised if these tables are right next to the smoking ones. Bars are definitely not nonsmoking.

Vegetarians & Vegans

It ain't easy being green in Slovakia. In this meat-lovers' haven even vegetable soups are made with chicken stock, and *bezmäsa* (meatless) dishes aren't always meatless (those bacon crumbles on the dumplings apparently don't count). Most menus have a pasta or a rice dish, and there's always the ubiquitous *vyprážaný syr* (fried cheese). Other than that, pizzerias are always an option.

Habits & Customs

Small tips (10%) are expected from foreigners, but your friends are likely to say you're spoiling the waiter. At least round up the bill to the next 10, like the locals do.

BRATISLAVA

☎ 02 / pop 426,091

Bratislava? Isn't that the town where some hostelling horror movies were set? Indeed. But the only scary things about Slovakia's capital are the no-longer-bargain-basement lodging prices, and the fact that the first international chain stores have appeared on the scene. Bath and Body Works – *gasp*!

The capital city is a host of contrasts – a charming Old Town across the river from a communist concrete-block city, an age-old castle sharing the skyline with the 1970s, UFO-like New Bridge. Still, narrow pedestrian streets, pastel 18th-century rococo buildings and sidewalk cafes galore make for a supremely strollable – if miniscule – historic centre. You may want to pop into a museum if it's raining, but otherwise the best thing to do is meander the mazelike alleys, stopping regularly for coffee or drinks. There's sure to be some chichi restaurant just opened. Try to ignore the gangs of inebriated English-speaking blokes roaming about on weekends. Ok, it's a little scary.

HISTORY

Founded in AD 907, Bratislava was already a large city in the 12th century. In 1467 the Hungarian Renaissance monarch Matthias Corvinus founded a university here, Academia Istropolitana. The city flourished during the reign of Maria Theresa of Austria (1740–80), when many of the imposing baroque palaces you see today were built. From the Turkish invasion until 1830, Hungarian monarchs were crowned in St Martin's cathedral, and Hungarian parliament met in Bratislava (then known as Pressburg or Poszony in German or Hungarian) until 1848.

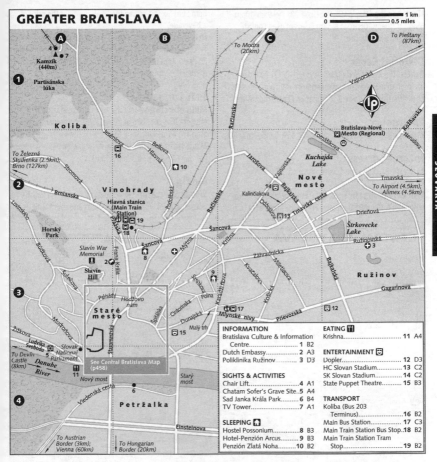

GREATER BRATISLAVA

INFORMATION		EATING 🍴	
Bratislava Culture & Information		Krishna......................... 11 A4	
Centre........................... 1 B2			
Dutch Embassy................. 2 A3		ENTERTAINMENT 🎭	
Poliklinika Ružinov........... 3 D3		Dopler............................ 12 D3	
		HC Slovan Stadium......... 13 C2	
SIGHTS & ACTIVITIES		SK Slovan Stadium......... 14 C2	
Chair Lift......................... 4 A1		State Puppet Theatre....... 15 B3	
Chatam Sofer's Grave Site. 5 A4			
Sad Janka Krála Park........ 6 B4		TRANSPORT	
TV Tower......................... 7 A1		Koliba (Bus 203	
		Terminus)........................16 B2	
SLEEPING 🛏		Main Bus Station.............. 17 C3	
Hostel Possonium............. 8 B3		Main Train Station Bus Stop.18 B2	
Hotel-Penzión Arcus......... 9 B3		Main Train Station Tram	
Penzión Zlatá Noha..........10 B2		Stop............................... 19 B2	

The communists did a number on the town's architecture and spirit, razing a large part of the Old Town (including the synagogue) to make way for the modern new second city of Czechoslovakia. Today, as the capital of one of the newer euro-currency members of the EU, Bratislava is a city under construction. Business complexes rise faster than mushrooms after a spring rain. Look for a new (and not cheap) hotel opening on a corner near you.

ORIENTATION
Bratislava's pedestrian centre starts south of Hodžovo nám. Follow Poštová south and you cross Obchodná (Shopping St) before getting to Nám SNP and the heart of the Old

Town, bounded by the castle in the west and Tesco department store in the east. The large, plaza-like Hviezdoslavovo nám is a convenient reference point, with the Old Town to the north, the Danube to the south, and the Slovak National Theatre on its east end.

The main train station, Hlavná stanica, is located just 1km north of the centre. The main bus station, called Mlynské Nivy by locals because of the street it's on, is a little over 1km east of the Old Town.

INFORMATION
Bookshops
Interpress Slovakia (Map p458; Sedlárska 2; 🕙 9am-10pm Mon-Sat, 2-10pm Sun) Foreign newspapers and local periodicals in English.

Next Apache (Map p458; Panenská 28; 9am-10pm Mon-Fri, 10am-10pm Sat & Sun) Loads of used English books and a comfy cafe.

Discount Cards
Bratislava City Card (1/2/3 days €6/10/12) Provides discounted museum admission and city transport; it's sold at the Bratislava Culture & Information Centre (opposite).

Emergency
Main police station (Map p458; 159; Gunduličova 10)

Internet Access
Hlavné and Hviezdoslavovo nám are free wi-fi zones.
Wifi Café (Map p458; ground fl, Tatracentrum, Hodžovo nám; 8.30am-9.30pm Mon-Fri, 10am-8pm Sat, 11am-8pm Sun) Six flat-screen terminals; wi-fi for the price of a beverage.
Internet Kaviaren (Map p458; 095248208; 1st fl, Tesco, Kamenné nám 1; per 15min €1; 9am-9pm Mon-Fri, 9am-7pm Sat & Sun) Ten terminals hidden behind the garden department in Tesco.

Left Luggage
Main bus station (autobusova stanica; Map p457; Mlynské Nivy; per bag per day €1.25; 5.30am-10pm Mon-Fri, 6am-6pm Sat & Sun)
Main train station (hlavná stanica; Map p457; per bag per day €1.50; 6.30am-11pm)

Media
Slovak Spectator (www.slovakspectator.sk) English-language weekly with current affairs and event listings.

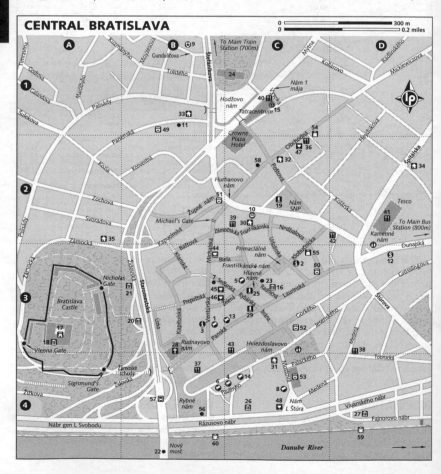

CENTRAL BRATISLAVA

BRATISLAVA IN TWO DAYS

Spend a day roaming the pedestrian streets, stopping for nibbles at one of Bratislava's many eateries like **Prašná Bašta** (p462). Ascend castle hill or the New Bridge, for a citywide view, contrasting the charming old town with the ugly new. The next day, trip out to **Devín Castle** (p464) at the confluence of two rivers and three countries.

Medical Services

Poliklinika Ruzinov (Map p457; ☎ 4823 4113; Ružinovská 10) Hospital with emergency services and a 24-hour pharmacy.

Money

Bratislava has an excess of banks and ATMs in the Old Town, with several branches on Poštova and around Kamenné nám. There are also ATMs and exchange booths in the train and bus stations, and at the airport.

Tatra Banka (Map p458; Dunajská 4) Has staff that speak exceptional English.

Post

Main post office (Map p458; Nám SNP 34-35)

Tourist Information

Bratislava Culture & Information Centre (BKIS; ☎ 16 186; www.bkis.sk) Airport (MR Štefánika; ☺ 8am-

7.30pm Mon-Fri, 10am-6pm Sat); Centre (Map p458; Klobučnícka 2; ☺ 8.30am-7pm Mon-Fri, 10am-5pm Sat); Main train station (Map p457; Hlavná stanica; ☺ 8am-4.30pm Mon-Fri, 10am-2pm Sat) Staff hide brochures behind the central tourist office counter and seem uninterested, but keep pressing and they'll help – a little.

Bratislava Tourist Service (BTS; Map p458; ☎ 2070 7501; www.bratislava-info.sk; Ventúrska 9; ☺ 10am-8pm) A tiny, tiny place, but it has a much more obliging staff than BKIS, and lots of maps and knick-knacks.

SIGHTS & ACTIVITIES
Old Town

Bratislava Castle (Bratislavský hrad; Map p458; admission free; ☺ 9am-9pm Apr-Sep, to 6pm Oct-Mar) lords over the west side of the Old Town on a hill above the Danube. Winding ramparts provide a great vantage point for comparing ancient and communist Bratislava. The castle looks a bit like a four-poster bed, a shape that was well established by the 15th century. During the Turkish occupation of Budapest, this was the seat of Hungarian royalty. A fire devastated the fortress in 1811; what you see today is a reconstruction from the 1950s. Except for a small archaeology exhibit, most of the interiors that make up the **Historical Museum** (Historické múzeum; Map p458; ☎ 5441 1441; www.snm.sk; adult/concession €3/1.50; ☺ 9am-5pm Tue-Sun) are closed for reconstruction until 2011. To see a more historically complete castle, take the bus beneath the New Bridge to Devín (p464), 8km outside the city.

SLOVAKIA

A series of old homes winds down the castle hill along Židovská in what was once the Jewish quarter. The **Museum of Clocks** (Múzeum hodín; Map p458; ☎ 5441 1940; Židovská 1; adult/concession €2/0.70; ☺ 10am-5pm Tue-Sun) is housed in the skinniest house in Slovakia. Further down, the **Museum of Jewish Culture** (Múzeum Židovskej kultúry; Map p458; ☎ 5441 8507; Židovská 17; adult/concession €6.70/2; ☺ 11am-5pm Sun-Fri) displays moving exhibits about the community lost during WWII. Black-and-white photos show the old ghetto and synagogue ploughed under by the communists to make way for a highway and bridge. The staff can help arrange a visit to **Chatam Sofer's grave site** (Map p457; www .chatamsofer.com; Žižkova at tram tunnel; donations accepted; ☺ by appointment only), the resting place of the much revered 19th-century rabbi.

A relatively modest interior belies the elaborate history of **St Martin's Cathedral** (Dóm sv Martina; Map p458; ☎ 5443 1359; Rudnayovo nám; admission €1.50; ☺ 8-11.30am & 1.30-4.30pm Mon-Sat). Eleven ruling monarchs (10 kings and one queen, Maria Theresa) were crowned in this 14th-century church. The busy motorway almost touching St Martin's follows the moat of the former city walls and is shaking the building to its core.

Further east along the Danube, the 1st-floor exhibits of the **Slovak National Museum** (Slovenské Národné múzeum; Map p458; ☎ 5934 9122; www.snm.sk; Vajanského nábr 2; adult/concession €3.30/1.70; ☺ 9am-5pm Tue-Sun) provide a super overview of the folk cultures and customs of Slovakia. Skip the tired natural-history stuff upstairs.

An 18th-century palace and a Stalinist-modern building make interesting co-hosts for the **Slovak National Gallery** (Slovenská Národná Galéria; Map p458; ☎ 5443 4587; www.sng.sk; Rázusovo nábr 2; adult/concession €3.30/1.70; ☺ 10am-5pm Tue-Sun). The nation's eclectic art collection ranges from Gothic to graphic design.

Two of Old Town's opulent theatres are off Hviezdoslavovo nám, a broad, tree-lined plaza. The gilt, neobaroque 1914 **Reduta Palace** hosts the nation's philharmonic orchestra (see p463), and the ornate 1886 Slovak National Theatre (p463) is the city's opera house. Neither is open for tours, but ticket prices aren't prohibitive.

Bustling, narrow **Rybárska brána** (Fisherman's Gate) street runs from Hviezdoslavovo nám to Hlavné nám, a main square which is filled with cafe tables in summer and a craft market that grows exponentially at Easter and Christmas times. **Roland's Fountain** (Map p458) at the centre may have been built in 1572 as an old-fashioned fire hydrant. Flanking one side of the square is the 1421 **old town hall** (Stará radnica; Map p458), and the city museum contained within, under indefinite reconstruction at the time of writing. The renovation of the nearby **Apponyi Palace** (Map p458; ☎ 5920 5112; Radničná 1; adult/concession €6.60/1.30; ☺ 10am-5pm Tue-Fri, 11am-6pm Sat & Sun) is complete, and it now serves as a museum of 18th- and 19th-century decorative arts.

Communist Bratislava

Forty-five years of communist rule was bound to leave a mark on Bratislava. Case in point: **Petržalka** (Map p457), the ugly, concrete-jungle housing estate across the river from the Old Town. (Can't you imagine going to the wrong flat in an identical adjacent building after drinking a few too many? Believe us, it happens.)

A sizeable chunk of the old city, including the synagogue, was demolished to create **New Bridge** (Nový most; Map p458; ☎ 6252 0300; www.u-f-o.sk; Viedenská cesta; observation deck adult/concession €6.70/3.30; ☺ 10am-11pm), colloquially called the UFO (pronounced ew-fo) bridge. This modernist marvel from 1972 has a viewing platform, an overhyped nightclub and a restaurant with out-of-this-world prices.

The communist-realist **Monument to the Slovak National Uprising** (Map p457; Nám SNP) actually celebrates partisans who fought Nazi fascism in WWII. The namesake square is where at midnight on 31 December 2002 hundreds of thousands danced – this author included – as Slovakia became an independent nation.

MAN AT WORK

The most photographed sight in Bratislava is a bronze statue called the **Watcher** (Čumil; Map p458). He peeps out of an imaginary manhole at the intersection of Panská and Rybarska, below a 'Man at Work' sign. But he's not alone. There are other quirky statues scattered around the pedestrian old town. Can you find them? The **Frenchman** leans on a park bench, the **Photographer** stalks his subject paparazzi-style around a corner and the **Schöner Náci** tips his top hat on a square. Look up for other questionable characters, like a timepiece-toting monk and a rather naked imp, decorating building facades.

SLOVAKIA

FREE THRILLS

Bratislava is chock-a-block full of free places to stroll:

- Wander along the pedestrian **old town** (p459) streets.

- Take in the formal French gardens behind the **Presidential Palace** (Map p458), open dawn till dusk.

- Meander along the riverfront promenade along Nábr arm gen L Svobodu, then cross the bridge to **Sad Janka Krála Park** (Map p457; Viedenská cesta). In addition to multiple paths, the 22-hectare park (dating back to 1775) has a large playground.

Still nostalgic for the good old days? Down a brewsky or two with Stalin, Lenin and the boys (or at least their statues) at Kréma Gurmánov Bratislavy (p462).

Hiking

To get out of the city and into the forest, take trolleybus 203 northeast from Hodžovo nám to the end of the line at Koliba, then walk up the road for about 20 minutes to the **TV tower** (Map p457) on Kamzík Hill (440m). Posted maps outline the many hiking possibilities in the forest surrounds and there are a couple of hotels with restaurants in the park. A **chair lift** (lanovka; Map p457; ☎ 5479 2503; adult/concession return €4/2.70; ☽ 10am-5pm Thu-Sun Oct-May) makes the 15 minute journey downhill to the picnic areas and playgrounds of Železná studienka and back.

FESTIVALS & EVENTS

Bratislava's best events are arts related. From June to September the **Cultural Summer Festival** (Kultúrne leto; ☎ 5441 3063; www.bkis.sk) brings a smorgasbord of operas, plays and performances to the streets and venues around town. Classical music takes centre stage at the **Bratislava Music Festival** (Bratislavské hudobné slávnosti; ☎ 5443 4546; www.bhsfestival.sk), which runs from late September to mid-October. **Bratislava Jazz Days** (Bratislavských jazzových dní; ☎ 5293 1572; www.bjd .sk) makes music for three days in September. The 26th of November is the usual start to the **Christmas market** with even more crafts and edibles for sale on Hlavné nám (Map p458). Try the *varene vino* (hot spiced wine), yum!

SLEEPING

Bratislava's lodging market is giving nearby Vienna's rates a run for its money these days, but don't expect comparable services. To book an apartment, check out www.bratislavahotels .com and www.apartmentsbratislava.com.

All hostels listed have free wi-fi, kitchens, laundries, and beer and wine for sale.

Hostel Possonium (Map p457; ☎ 2072 0007; www .possonium.sk; Šancová 20; dm €17-18, d €51; ☐) Mixed reviews have come in for Bratislava's newest hostel. Drawbacks include street noise and a 2km walk to the centre. Pluses: being across from the train station and having the lowest prices.

Hostel Blues (Map p458; ☎ 09204020; www.hostel blues.sk; Špitálska 2; dm €20, d €63; ☐) Friendly, professional staff not only help you plan your days, they offer free city sightseeing tours weekly. Jazz bands play some nights in the coffee house–like communal space (with free internet computers). Choose from single sex or mixed dorms, or those with double bunk beds. Apartments sleep four to six (from €108).

Downtown Backpackers (Map p458; ☎ 5464 1191; www.backpackers.sk; Panenská 31; dm €16-25, d €66; ☐) A boozy Bohemian classic (you enter through a bar). Red brick walls and tapestries add character, as does the fact you have to walk through some dorm rooms to get to others.

City Hostel (Map p458; ☎ 5263 6041; www.cityhostel .sk; Obchodná; s/d €40/60; ☐) More hotel than hostel really, cubicle-like singles and doubles all have their own bathrooms and TV. The super mod (leather and lime green) reception area has coffee and internet access, both of which are free.

Penzión Zlatá Noha (Map p457; ☎ 5477 4922; www .zlata-noha.sk; Bellova 2, Koliba hill; s/d €67/83; ☒ ☐) Tranquillity and family-run attention make up for distance at this comfy modern guest house above town. It's a great place for those with vehicles, and bus 203 regularly runs the 4km to the Old Town. For €7 you can add a buffet breakfast, and they'll cook other meals to order. Free wi-fi.

Hotel-Penzión Arcus (Map p457; ☎ 5557 2522; www.hotelarcus.sk; Moskovská 5; s/d incl breakfast €68/100) Because this family-run hotel was once an apartment building, rooms are quite varied in size (some with balcony, some with courtyard views). Flowery synthetic chairs seem a little outdated but bathrooms are new and sparkly white. Communal kitchens are available and some rooms have internet access.

SLOVAKIA

Penzión Chez David (Map p458; ☎ 5441 3824; www .chezdavid.sk; Zámocká 13; s/d incl breakfast €74/102; ⊠) With the cool blue colour scheme, great old photos of synagogues on the walls, and primo old-town location, you'll hardly even notice the building's boxiness (though the rooms are small). Kosher restaurant on site; free wi-fi in restaurant and garden.

Carlton Hotel (Map p458; ☎ 5939 0000; www.bratislava .radissonsas.com; Hviezdoslavovo nám 3; r €150-250; ⊠ 🖳) The Carlton, currently owned by Radisson, has been cruising like a luxury liner on one of the town's main squares since 1837. Walk from here across the street to the opera or symphony. Unfortunately some rooms have been outfitted in a jarringly modern aesthetic; ask for the classic if you prefer.

Arcadia Hotel (Map p458; ☎ 5949 0500; www.arcadia -hotel.sk; Františkánska 3; s/d incl breakfast €250/280; ⊠ 🖳) Pains were taken when turning a 13th-century palace into Bratislava's first five-star hotel: an ornate stained-glass skylight tops the interior courtyard, hand-painted designs grace the dining room's vaulted arches... Why not cuddle into the luxe robe and relax on a red-and-gold silk settee, or dip into the wellness whirlpool, before you dress for a decadent dinner?

EATING

The Old Town certainly isn't lacking for dining options or international cuisines. Most cater to visitors, and are priced accordingly. What's harder to find is reasonable Slovak food.

Student-oriented cheap eats, both sit-down and takeaway, are available all along Obchodná (Map p458). Cafeterias catering to workers (ie not open late, but you can order to go) are a great resource for budgeteers.

U Jakubu (Map p458; ☎ 5441 7951; Nám SNP 24; mains €2-5; ⌚ 8am-6pm Mon-Fri) Pile on the hearty fried and stewed classics in standard Slovak self-service style.

Presto (Map p458; ☎ 5464 8057; ground fl, Tatracentrum, Hodžovo nám 3; mains €3-6; ⌚ 8am-3pm Mon-Fri) Owned by the upscale Italian restaurant next door, this modern cafeteria has an international flavour – and lots of vegetables.

Verne (Map p458; ☎ 5443 0514; Hviezdoslavovo nám 18; mains €5-8; ⌚ 8.30am-midnight Mon-Fri, 11am-midnight Sat & Sun) Thoroughly reasonable prices, long hours (breakfast, too) and sidewalk seating attract expats and locals alike. Slovak-international food served.

U Remeselníka (☎ 5273 1357; Obchodná 64; mains €5-10) This folksy cafe, associated with the traditional craft store upstairs (see opposite), is a great place to try a trio of *halušky* – dumplings with sheep's cheese and bacon, with *klobasa*, and with cabbage.

Pizza Mizza (Map p458; ☎ 5296 5034; Tobrucká 5; mains €5-11) Word is the cooks might be resting on their accolades as of late, but Pizza Mizza is still a pleasant house-like restaurant with a long list of wood-fired options and pastas.

our pick Prašná Bašta (Map p458; ☎ 5443 4957; Zámočnicka 11; mains €8-15) The round, vaulted interior oozes old-Bratislava charm, but the hidden courtyard seating with a view of Michael's Gate is even better. Dishes range from traditional (potato dough–crusted schnitzel) to modern Eastern European (pork medallions with cream, leak and mustard sauce).

Also recommended:

City Vegetarian (Map p458; ☎ 5273 1381; Obchodná 58; mains €2-5; ⌚ 11am-4pm Mon-Fri) Vegetarian self-service.

Tesco (Map p458; ☎ 4446 4057; Kamenné nám 1; ⌚ 8am-9pm Mon-Fri, 9am-7pm Sat & Sun) Big supermarket for self-catering.

Of the many, many spiffy global food alternatives in Old Town – none priced for the average Slovak – **El Gaucho** (Map p458; ☎ 3212 1212; Hviezdoslavovo nám 13; mains €15-22) is one worth the dough. The Argentinean spices are good, but beef's really the thing here. You might also try **Krishna** (Map p457; ☎ 5464 1804; Botel Marina, Nábr arm gen L Svobodu; mains €10-18) for some decent tandoori.

DRINKING

From mid-April to October, sidewalk tables fill with friends settling in for a cocktail or two. Any one will do for a drink.

Čokoládovňa (Map p458; ☎ 5433 3945; Michalská 6; ⌚ 9am-9pm) This tiny 'chocolate cafe' has liqueurs, coffees and desserts made with the dark ambrosia.

Kréma Gurmánov Bratislavy (KGB; Map p458; ☎ 5273 1279; Obchodná 52; ⌚ 10am-2am Mon-Fri, 4pm-3am Sat, 4pm-midnight Sun) Drink a dark and smoky toast to a statue of Stalin under a Soviet flag at the cellar KGB bar.

Malecón (Map p458; ☎ 0910274583; Nám L Štúra 4) Where the pretty people go to sip and swill – mainly mojitos. Could owning a Beemer be a prerequisite for entry?

British themes are all the rage, but unless you want to only meet English speakers, steer clear of the touristy **Dubliner** (Map p458; ☎ 5441 0706; Sedlárska 6; ☺ 11am-3am Mon-Sat, to 1am Sun) and head to the more mixed crowd at **Greenwich Cocktail Bar** (Map p458; ☎ 0910760222; Zelená 10; ☺ 4pm-2am).

ENTERTAINMENT

Check **What's On** (www.whatsonslovakia.com) and **Kam do Mesta** (www.kamdomesta.sk) for the latest live bands and theatre events. We know of a few Brits who've been turned away by bouncers; backlash from stag party antics. Just be respectful, and know that Bratislavans themselves are pretty conservative.

Nightclubs

Café Štúdio Club (Map p458; ☎ 5443 1796; cnr Laurinská & Radničná; ☺ 10am-1am Mon-Wed, to 3am Thu & Fri, 4pm-3am Sat) Bop to the oldies, or chill out to jazz; most nights there's live music of some sort.

Channels (Map p458; ☎ 0911447323; Župné nám 2; ☺ 9.30am-4am) Each of two stories has a bar and a dance floor for grooving to a techno DJ beat.

Dopler (Map p457; ☎ 0903686707; Prievozská 18; ☺ 8pm-5am Fri & Sat) The city's biggest dance club, a taxi ride from the centre, draws in a college-age (and younger) crowd.

Apollon Club (Map p458; ☎ 091548031; www.apollon-gay-club.sk; Panenská 24; ☺ 6pm-3am Mon-Thu & Sun, 6pm-5am Fri & Sat) The only gay disco in town has two bars and three stages. Monday is karaoke; Sunday, boys only.

Sport

Home games of Bratislava's hallowed ice hockey team are held at **HC Slovan stadium** (Map p457; ☎ 4445 6500; www.hcslovan.sk, in Slovak; Odbojárov 3), while the hometown football team plays at **SK Slovan stadium** (Map p457; ☎ 4437 3083; www.slovan futbal.sk in Slovak; Viktora Tegelhoffa 4). You can buy tickets for both teams online at www.eventim.sk.

Performing Arts

Slovak National Theatre (Slovenské Národné Divadlo, SND; Map p458; www.snd.sk; Hviezdoslavovo nám; ☺ 8am-5.30pm Mon-Fri, 9am-1pm Sat) The local company stages both Slavic and international operas, along with ballets, at the state theatre. Buy tickets online, or at the ticket office around the back of the building.

Slovak Philharmonic (Slovenská Filharmónia; Map p458; ☎ 5920 8233; www.filharmonia.sk; cnr Nám L Štúra & Medená; ☺ ticket office 1-7pm Mon, Tue, Thu & Fri, 8am-2pm Wed) Listen to the state opera in gilt splendour at its Reduta Palace theatre home.

State Puppet Theatre (Štátne Bábkové Divadlo; Map p457; ☎ 5292 3668; www.babkovedivadlo.sk; Dunajská 36) Puppet shows here cater to the younger generation; some are even Shakespeare-inspired (age seven and older).

Folk dance and music ensembles, like **Sľuk** (☎ 6285 9125; www.sluk.sk) and **Lúčnica** (☎ 5292 0068; www.lucnica.sk), perform at various venues around town. Look for the schedules online.

SHOPPING

There are several crystal, craft and jewellery stores, as well as souvenir booths, in and around Hlavné nám. More and more artisan galleries are popping up in old-town alleys; check out the side streets.

ÚĽuv (Map p458; ☎ 5273 1351; www.uluv.sk; Obchodná 64) For serious folk-art shopping head to ÚĽuv, where there are two stores and a courtyard filled with artisans' studios.

Vinotéka Sv Urbana (Map p458; ☎ 5433 2573; Klobučnícka 4) Slovak and international wines for sample and sale.

GETTING THERE & AWAY

Slovakia's capital city, Bratislava is the main hub for trains, buses and airplanes heading into and out of the country. The best source for both domestic and international train and bus schedules is http://cp.atlas.sk.

Air

Most of the destinations from **MR Štefánika airport** (BTS; ☎ 3303 3353; Ivanska cesta 1; www.airportbratislava.sk), 7km northeast of the centre, are outside the region. You can fly between Bratislava and Košice, on **SkyEurope Airlines** (☎ 4850 1000; www.skyeurope.com), with up to five flights daily.

Boat

Plying the waters is a cruisy way to get to Bratislava from neighbouring Danube cities. From mid-April to September, **Slovenská plavba a prístavy** (☎ 5293 2226; www.lod.sk) runs one or two daily hydrofoils to Vienna (€22 one way, 1½ hours) and to Budapest (€79 one way, four hours) from the **hydrofoil terminal** (Map p458; Fajnorovo nábr 2). From June to October the **Twin City Liner** (☎ 0903610716; www.twincityliner.com) operates up to six boats a day between Vienna (€28 one way, 1½ hours) and the Bratislava **propeller terminal** (Map p458; Rázusovo nábr).

SLOVAKIA

Bus

The **main bus station** (autobusová stanica, AS; Map p457; ☎ reservations 5556 7349; www.slovaklines.sk; Mlynské Nivy) is 1.5km east of the Old Town. Buses leave from here heading to towns across Slovakia, including Žilina (€9, three hours, seven daily), Poprad (€15, seven hours, four daily) and Košice (€17, eight hours, nine daily).

Eurolines (☎ 5556 7349; www.eurolines.sk) runs direct buses between Bratislava and Prague (€12, four hours, daily) and Budapest (€19, 3½ hours, daily). It also connects Bratislava with many major Western European cities including Geneva, London (23 hours, five weekly), Munich, Paris (20 hours, three weekly), Rotterdam, Strasbourg and Vienna (one hour, hourly).

Train

At least 12 daily trains depart the **main train station** (Hlavná stanica; www.zsr.sk), 1km north of the centre, for Košice (€19, 5½ hours), most via Trenčín, (€6, two hours), Žilina (€10, 2¾ hours) and Poprad (€14, 4¾ to eight hours).

Direct trains connect Bratislava with Prague (€27, 4½ hours, six daily), Budapest (€21, three hours, seven daily) and Vienna (€9, one hour, 30 daily). Night departure trains link Bratislava with Kraków (€36, 7½ hours, daily) and Warsaw (€40, 8¼ hours, daily) in Poland.

GETTING AROUND
To/From the Airport

Bus 61 links the airport with the main train station (€0.75, 20 minutes). To get to the centre by taxi costs up to €15, services that operate out of the airport legitimately charge more than in town.

Public Transport

The main train station, Hlavná stanica, is located just 1km north of the centre. Tram 13 runs from the station to Nám L Štúra, immediately south of Hviezdoslavovo nám, and bus 93 stops at Hodžovo nám. The main bus station, called Mlynské Nivy by locals because of the street it's on, is a little over 1km east of the Old Town. If you arrive by bus, you can take bus 206 to Hodžovo nám, or bus 210 to the train station.

Dopravný Podnik Bratislava (DPB; ☎ 5950 5950; www.dpb.sk) runs an extensive tram, bus and trolleybus network. You can buy tickets (€0.50/0.60/0.75 for 10/30/60 minutes) at

news-stands and at the **DPB office** (Map p458; Obchodná 14; ⏰ 9am-5.30pm Mon-Fri). Validate on board. One-/two-/three-/seven-day *turistické cestovné lístky* (tourist travel tickets) cost €3/6/7/10 and are sold at the DPB office and train and bus stations. Check routes and schedules at www.imhd.sk.

The Bratislava City Card (one/two/three days for €6/10/12) includes all city transport, among other benefits. It's sold by Bratislava Culture & Information Centres; see p459 for details.

Car

Numerous international rental agencies have offices at the airport; **Alimex** (☎ 5564 1641; www .alimex.sk) is usually the most reasonable.

Taxi

Bratislava's taxis have meters, but there still seems to be a slight English-speaking surcharge. Within the Old Town a trip should cost no more than €10. Try **ABC Taxi** (☎ 16 100) or **Fun Taxi** (☎ 16 777).

AROUND BRATISLAVA

Hard-core castle aficionados should don their daypack and head to **Devín Castle** (☎ 02-6573 0105; Muranská; adult/concession €3/1.50; ⏰ 10am-5pm Tue-Fri, to 6pm Sat & Sun mid-Apr–Oct), 9km west of Bratislava. Once the military plaything of 9th-century warlord Prince Ratislav, the castle withstood the Turks but then was blown up in 1809 by the French. Peer at the older bits that have been unearthed and tour a reconstructed palace museum. Bus 29 links Devín with Bratislava's New Bridge stop, under the bridge. Austria is just across the river.

WEST SLOVAKIA

Snaking along the Small Carpathians on the main route northeast of Bratislava, watch for hilltop castle ruins high above the Váh River. Trenčín's magnificent, reconstructed castle is one of the most impressive along this once heavily fortified stretch.

TRENČÍN
☎ 032 / pop 56,850

The pretty pedestrian plazas and lively nightlife in this university town are attractive enough. But it's the mighty castle looming above the 18th- and 19th-century buildings that's really worth seeing. The form of today's fortress dates from around the 15th century but the city is much older than that. Trenčín Castle was first noted in a Viennese chronicle of 1069, and Roman legionnaires fancied the town's site (they called it Laugaricio) and stationed here in the 2nd century AD.

Orientation

From the adjacent bus and train stations walk west through Park MR Štefánika and beneath the highway past the Hotel Tatra, where a street bears left uphill to Mierové nám, the main square. The whole centre is easily walkable.

Information

Cultural Information Centre (☎ 161 86; www .trencin.sk; City Office, Sládkovičova; ☑ 10am-5pm Mon-Fri, 10am-noon Sat) Helpful, well-informed staff sell event tickets as well as giving out gobs of info.

Main post office (Mierové nám 21)

Mike Studio (Mierové nám 31; per 30min €1; ☑ 9am-10pm Mon-Sat, 10am-10pm Sun;) Just internet terminals, no cafe.

VUB Banka (Mierové nám 37) ATM and exchange.

Sights

Sitting high atop a rocky crag, **Trenčín Castle** (Trenčiansky hrad; ☎ 7435 657; www.muzeumtn.sk; adult/concession €4/2; ☑ 9am-5.30pm May-Sep, to 4.30pm Apr & Oct, to 3.30pm Nov-Mar) overshadows the town, as any good fortress should. Climb ever-more stairs to reach the lowest level of the castle fortifications, from there you already have commanding views of the Váh River plain. Two levels higher, you can enter the towers and palaces with one of the frequent tours. A complete visit of the reconstructed rooms takes about 75 minutes (in Slovak only, call two days ahead to arrange an English-speaking guide). At night, the green and purple spots light the exterior; the most evocative time to visit is summer evenings during a two-hour, torch-light tour, complete with medieval sword fighting, minstrels and staged frolics.

The town's unique claim to fame is the **Roman inscription** of AD 179, soldier's graffiti commemorating a battle against Germanic tribes. It is actually carved into the cliff behind the **Hotel Tatra** (☎ 6506 111; www.hotel-tatra .sk; Ul gen MR Štefánika 2) and can only be viewed through a window in the hotel's staircase; ask

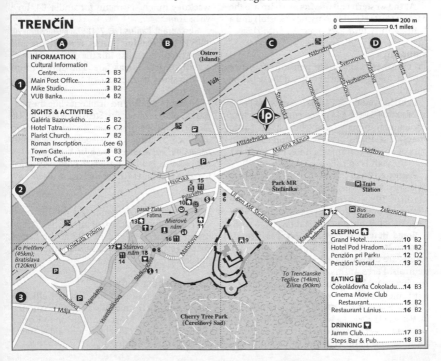

SLOVAKIA

WORTH THE TRIP: PIEŠŤANY

Thermal waters bubble under much of the country. Slovakia's premier spa site, **Piešťany** (☎ 33-775 7733; www.spa-piestany.sk), is only 87km northeast of Bratislava. A few years back Slovak spas were medical facilities requiring a doctor's note. Not so today. OK, there's still a slightly antiseptic look to some treatment rooms, but many of Piešťany's lovely 19th-century buildings sport a new coat of Maria-Theresa-yellow paint and others are under reconstruction. On Kúpeľne ostrov (Spa Island) you can swim in thermal pools, breathe seaside-like air in a salt cave or be wrapped naked in hot mud. Head to the *kasa* (cashier) at Napoleon 1 to book a service, or go online. There are several island hotels, which can be reserved on the spa website, and many more in town across the river. Trains from Bratislava take 1¼ hours (€4, 12 daily) and you can continue on the same line to Trenčín (€2, 45 minutes).

---

at reception. The translation reads: 'To the victory of the emperor and the army which, numbering 855 soldiers, resided at Laugaricio. By order of Maximianus, legate of the 2nd auxiliary legion'.

Temporary exhibits at the **Galéria Bazovského** (☎ 7436 858; www.gmab.sk, in Slovak; Palackého 27; adult/concession €1/0.80; ☉ 9am-5pm Tue-Sun) represent some of the best of 20th-century Slovak and Czech art. The main collection contains works by local painter Miloš Bazovský (1899–1968).

At the western end of Mierové nám are the baroque **Piarist Church** (Piaristický kostol) and a 16th-century **town gate** (*mestská brána*).

Sleeping

Trenčín has many more pensions than we can list, ask at the tourist office if those below are full.

Penzión Svorad (☎ 7430 322; www.svorad-trencin .sk; Palackého 4; dm €19-26) Frayed curtains, peeling linoleum, thin mattresses – but oh, the castle views. This dormitory-like pension resides in part of an old grammar school; maybe that's why the staff is so rule-obsessed.

Penzión pri Parku (☎ 7434 377; www.penzionpriparku .sk; Kragujevackých hrdinov 7; r €25-38) Ignore the mishmash of 1990s furnishings and admire the Victorian building in city park. Here you're close to both train and bus stations. Free wi-fi.

Grand Hotel (☎ 7434 353; www.grand-hotel.sk; Palackého 34; s/d €62/70; ☐) Soft contemporary rooms are awash in dark woods and upscale neutrals. Perks at this modern hotel include free bike rental, and whirlpool and sauna use. Wi-fi included.

Hotel Pod Hradom (☎ 7442 507; www.podhradom .sk; Matúšova 12; r incl breakfast €86-98; ☐) On a wee, winding street en route to the castle; a prime location and patio view are the main draws

at this 10-room lodging. Sloped ceilings and skylights add character to spartan rooms. Free broadband access.

Eating & Drinking

Čokoládovňa Čokoladu (☎ 0903480318; Štúrovo nám 7; cakes €1-3; ☉ 9am-8pm Mon-Sat, 1-8pm Sun) With a name like 'Chocolate Cafe Chocolate', what do you think they serve?

Cinema Movie Club Restaurant (☎ 0902898533; Palackého 33; mains €5-8) Chicken and risotto dishes are quite good here, but the real steal is the weekday lunch set menu for under €4. Free wi-fi zone.

Restaurant Lánius (☎ 7441 978; Mierové nám 20; mains €5-13) Creaking beams, wood floors and stone fireplaces make this the cosiest of places serving hearty Slovak fare. The dining room up the stairs at the rear of the courtyard is most fun.

Numerous cafes and drinkeries line the pedestrian plazas; check out **Steps Bar & Pub** (☎ 7446 252; Sládkovičova 4-6; ☉ 10.30am-1am Sun-Thu, to 4am Fri & Sat), which attracts a college-age crowd, and **Jamm Club** (Štúrovo nám 5; ☉ noon-1am Mon-Thu, noon-3am Fri, 2pm-3am Sat, 2pm-1am Sun), which hosts occasional live jazz and blues (other nights are disco).

Events

World music, jazz, rock, techno, hip hop, alternative; what kind of music isn't represented one weekend in July at the **Bazant Pohoda Festival** (www.pohodafestival.sk), the largest music festival in Slovakia.

Getting There & Away

Trains are the quickest and most cost-efficient way to get here from Bratislava (€6, two hours, at least 12 daily). Most continue on to Košice (€14, four hours). Twenty trains a day travel to Žilina (€6, 1½ hours).

CENTRAL SLOVAKIA

The rolling hills and forested mountain ranges of central Slovakia are home to the shepherding tradition that defines Slovak culture. Watch roadside for farmers selling local sheep's cheese. The beautiful Malá Fatra mountain range is where this nation's Robin Hood, Juraj Jánošík, once roamed.

ŽILINA

☎ 041 / pop 85,655

A Slavic tribe in the 6th century was the first to recognise Žilina's advantageous location at the intersection of several important trade routes, on the Váh River. Today it's still a convenient base for exploring the Malá Fatra National Park, surrounding fortresses and folk villages. That said, there isn't much to see in town besides the old palace-like castle on the outskirts.

Orientation

The train station is on the northeastern side of the Old Town, near the Váh River. A 700m walk along Národná takes you past Nám A Hlinku up to Mariánské nám, the main square. From the south end of the bus station, follow Jána Milca northeast to Národná.

Information

Net Café Pohoda (☎ 5640 099; Kukučínova 8; per hr €1.30; ☼ 9am-10pm Mon-Fri, 2-10pm Sat)

Main post office (Sládkovičova 1)

Tatra Banka (cnr Mariánské nám & Farská) ATM.

Tourist Information Office (TIK; ☎ 7233 186; www .zilina.sk\tik; Republiky 1; ☼ 9am-5pm Mon-Fri, 9am-2pm Sat & Sun) Loaded with info.

Sights

North across the Váh River, **Budatín Castle** (Budatínsky zámok; ☎ 5620 033; Topoľová 1; adult/concession €1.30/0.70; ☼ 9am-4.30pm Tue-Sun May-Aug, to 3.30pm Sep & Oct, to 1.30pm Nov-Apr) is more mansion than stronghold. The museum inside contains exhibits of 18th- and 19th-century decorative arts as well as wire figures made by area tinkers.

Other than that, you're left to stroll through the somewhat plain pedestrian squares.

Sleeping

The tourist office books accommodation, including private rooms, for a fee.

Kompas Cafe (☎ 0918481319; http://kompascafe .wordpress.com; Vojtecha Spanyola 37; dm €11) Two- to five-bed worker hostel rooms have wood beds, striped curtains, and not much else. At least there's a convivial cafe and a small kitchen here; 1km from the centre.

Penzlón Majovey (☎ 5624 152; www.slovanet.sk /majovey in Slovak; Jána Milca 3; s/d €36/62) A deep coral exterior is more interesting than the clean white room interiors, but the bathrooms are huge and tile floors keep things cool throughout. Very convenient.

Hotel Dubna Skala (☎ 5079 100; www.hoteldubna skala.sk; Hurbanova 8; s/d €119/144; 🖳) Hyper-modern lighted-glass murals as headboards seems an unlikely choice for a neoclassical building, but this stylish boutique hotel pulls it off. Check out the contemporary wine-cellar restaurant.

Eating & Drinking

Interchangeable bars and cafes lie around Mariánske and Hlinka squares.

Voyage Voyage (☎ 5640 230; Mariánske nám 191; mains €4-11) If the sleek neon and chrome don't convince you this isn't your typical Slovak eatery, menu items like chicken sauté with honey and chillis will.

02 (☎ 5640 320; Na Priekope 39; mains €5-11) Start with broccoli soup and move on to one of

---

WORTH THE TRIP: VLKOLÍNEC

The folksy mountain village of **Vlkolínec** (☎ 4321 023; www.vlkolinec.sk in Slovak; adult/student €2/1; ☼ 9am-3pm), about 71km east and south of Žilina, has long been considered a national treasure (and not just by Unesco). The pastel paint and steep roofs on the 45 traditional plastered log cabins are remarkably well maintained. It's easy to imagine a *vlk* (wolf) wandering through this wooded mountainside settlement arranged along a small stream. You pay entry to walk around, and one of the buildings has been turned into a small house museum, but this is still a living village – if just barely. Of the 35 residents, 12 are school children.

Driving or hiking the 6km up hill from Ružomberok is the only way to get to the village. Five direct trains a day stop in Ružomberok on their way from Bratislava (€12, 3½ hours) and Žilina (€3, 1½ hours) to Košice (€8, 2½ hours).

SLOVAKIA

WORTH THE TRIP: BOJNICE CASTLE

Bojnice Castle (Bojnice zámok; ☎ 046-5430 633; www.bojnicecastle.sk; adult/child €5.30/2.70; ☺ 9am-5pm daily Jul & Aug, 9am-5pm Tue-Sun Sep & May, 10am-3pm Tue-Sun Oct-Apr) comes straight out of a fairy-tale dream filled with towers and turrets and crenulated mouldings. The original 12th-century fortification got an early 20th-century redo by the Pálffy family, who modelled it on French romantic castles. (Original Gothic and Renaissance parts do survive within.) The time to visit is during the **International Festival of Ghosts & Ghouls** in May, which attracts thousands. Costumed guides re-enact legends and put on shows throughout the castle and grounds. The palace also gets decked out for Christmas, Valentine's Day and medieval events, among others; check the website. Bojnice, 3km from Prievidza (via local bus 3), is not on a main train line. A bus from Žilina to Prievidza takes 1½ hours (€2.60, eight daily), from Bratislava it's 3½ hours (€6.50, eight daily).

---

the traditional pork dishes, such as the cutlet grilled with bacon and topped with smoked sheep's cheese.

And then there's **Palacinkáreň** (☎ 0907297413; Dolný Val 9; mains €2-5; ☺ 9am-8pm Mon-Fri, 9am-2pm Sun) with savoury and sweet crêpes to order.

Pizzeria Carolina (☎ 5003 030; Národná 5; pizzas €3-8) is especially popular with university students.

Getting There & Away

Žilina is on the main railway line from Bratislava to Košice. At least 12 trains daily head to Trenčín (€6, one hour), Bratislava (€9, 2¾ hours), Poprad (€7, two hours) and Košice (€10, three hours).

AROUND ŽILINA

As well as nearby Malá Fatra National Park, a few folk culture sights within an hour of Žilina are well worth exploring.

The nearby town of **Martin** is an industrial centre with a **tourist information office** (☎ 4234 776; www.tikmartin.sk; Štefánika 9A) and the country's largest *skanzen* (open-air village museum). The **Museum of the Slovak Village** (Múzeum Slovenské Dediny; ☎ 043-4239 491; www.snm-em.sk; adult/concession €1.70/0.80; ☺ 9am-6pm Jul & Aug, 9am-5pm Tue-Sat Sep, Oct, May & Jun, 10am-2.30pm Tue-Sat Nov-Apr) comes complete with working *krčma* (village pub). Traditional buildings from all over the region have been moved here. Take the bus to Martin (€150, 40 minutes, half-hourly), 35km south of Žilina. The village museum is 4km southeast of the city. Take bus 10 from the bus station to the last stop, Ľadovaň, and walk the remaining 1km up through the forest (or hail a taxi).

Dark log homes painted with white geometric patterns fill the traditional village of **Čičmany** (www.cicmany.viapvt.sk, in Slovak), which is

50 minutes south of Žilina by bus (€1.80, five daily). If you've seen a brochure or postcard of Slovakia, you've probably seen a photograph of a Čičmany. Most houses are private residences, but **Radenov House** (No 42; adult/concession €1.60/0.80; ☺ 10am-4pm Tue-Sun) is a museum and there's a small restaurant in the long, narrow settlement. Return bus times allow hours to wander and photograph.

MALÁ FATRA NATIONAL PARK

☎ 041

Sentinel-like formations stand watch at the rocky gorge entrance to the valley filled with pine-clad slopes above. The Malá Fatra National Park (Národný park Malá Fatra) incorporates a chocolate box–pretty, 200-sq-km swathe of its namesake mountain range. The Vrátna Valley (Vrátna dolina), 25km east of Žilina, lies at the heart of the park. From here you can access the trailheads, ski lifts and a cable car to start your exploration. The long, one-street town of Terchová is at the lower end of the valley, Chata Vrátna is at the top. The small cluster of buildings in Štefanová lie east of the main valley road, 1km uphill from Terchová.

Information

For basic trails and ski runs, check out www.vratna.sk. For serious hiking, VKÚ's 1:50,000 *Malá Fatra – Vrátna* map (No 110) is best.

Mountain Rescue Service (Horská Záchranná služba; ☎ 5695 232; http://his.hzs.sk/; Štefanová)

Terchová tourist information centre (☎ 5695 307; www.ztt.sk; Sv Cyrila a Metoda 96, Terchová; ☺ 8am-5pm Mon-Fri, 9am-4pm Sat, 10am-3pm Sun) ATM next door.

Vrátna Infocentrum (☎ 5695 648; www.vratna.sk; Sv Maritina 294, Terchová; ☺ 8am-4pm) Focuses on Vrátna Valley.

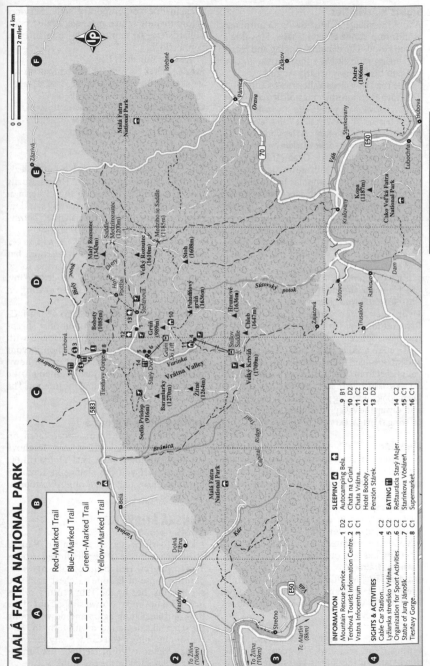

MALÁ FATRA NATIONAL PARK

Red-Marked Trail
Blue-Marked Trail
Green-Marked Trail
Yellow-Marked Trail

INFORMATION
Mountain Rescue Service............1 D2
Terchová Tourist Information Centre..2 C1
Vratna Infocentrum....................3 C1

SIGHTS & ACTIVITIES
Cable Car Station.........................4 C2
Lyžiarska stredisko Vrátna............5 C2
Organization for Sport Activities....6 C2
Statue of Juraj Jánošík................7 C1
Tiesňavy Gorge..........................8 C1

SLEEPING 🛏
Autocamping Bela......................9 B1
Chata na Grúni........................10 D2
Chata Vrátna..........................11 C2
Hotel Boboty..........................12 D2
Penzión Starek........................13 D2

EATING 🍴
Reštaurácia Starý Majer..............14 C2
Starinkova Vtelareň...................15 C1
Supermarket...........................16 C1

SLOVAKIA

Sights & Activities

Above the village of Terchová is an immense aluminium **statue of Juraj Jánošík**, Slovakia's Robin Hood. The dancing, singing and feasting during Jánošík Days folk festival go one beneath his likeness in early August.

The road to Vrátna Valley runs south from Terchová through the crags of **Tiesňavy Gorge** (Tiesňavy roklina), past picnic sites. A **cable car** (kabínkova lanovka; ☎ 5993 049; Chata Vrátna; return adult/concession €10/7; ◷ 8am-4pm) carries you from the top of the valley to **Snilov Saddle** (Snilovské sedlo; 1524m) below two peaks, **Chleb** (1647m) and **Velký Kriváň** (1709m). Both are on the red, ridge trail, one of the most popular in the park. A hike northeast from Chleb over **Poludňový grúň** (1636m), **Hromové** (1636m) and **Stoh** (1608m) to **Medziholie Saddle** (1185m) takes about 5½ hours. From there you can descend for an hour on the green trail to **Štefanová** village where there's a bus stop, and places to stay and eat.

You can rent mountain bikes (per day €8) from the **Organization for Sport Activities** (☎ 0903546600; www.splavovanie.sk) hut at Starý Dvor; they also organise two-hour Orava River rafting trips (from €15 per person) with two days' notice.

If you're a skier, the Vrátna Valley's tows and lifts are open from December to April. Buy your ticket from **Lyžiarska stredisko Vrátna** (☎ 5695 055; www.vratna.sk; day lift ticket adult/child €22/15) at Starý Dvor, look for the big parking lot on the left side midway up the valley. Nearby are several shacks offering **ski rental** (per pair €15; ◷ 8am-4pm).

Sleeping

Numerous private apartments and cottages are available for rent in the Terchová area, many are listed with pictures on the tourist-office website. No camping is allowed in the park.

Autocamping Bela (☎ 5621 478; per person/tent/car €3/3/3; ◷ May–mid-Oct; 🄿) Five kilometres west of the Vrátna Valley, this camping ground has 300 sites, a heated pool and a food stand. There's a bus stop out front.

Chata Vrátna (☎ 5695 739; http://chata.vratna .org; d/tr €23/30) Muddy hikers, giggling children and a fragrant wood-smoke aroma fill this well-worn, basic chalet at the top of Vrátna Valley.

ourpick Hotel Boboty (☎ 5695 228; www.hotel boboty.sk; Nový Dvor; s/d €56/102; 🖵 🄿) Skyscraping dining-room windows showcase tremendous vistas of the forests and mountains in a clean-line contemporary style. Services galore include sauna, massage, heated pool, billiards, free ski shuttle and in-room internet connections.

Also on our short list:

Penzión Stárek (☎ 5695 359; www.penzionstarek.sk; Štefanová 124; d incl breakfast €39; 🖵) Small log-cabin inn with good pizza restaurant and wi-fi.

Chata na Grúni (☎ 5695 324; www.chatanagruni.sk; dm €11) Hiker's hut at the top of Paseky chairlift; four- to six-bed dorms and self-service restaurant.

Eating

The food situation in the park is fairly bleak; most Slovaks bring their own. Hotels usually have restaurants, including the pizzeria at Penzión Stárek. There are takeaway stands at Starý Dvor and there's a supermarket (*potraviny*) at the valley turn-off in Terchová.

Starinkova Včeláreň (☎ 5993 130; A Hlinku 246, Terchová; snacks €1-4) This friendly tearoom has scones and homemade honey wine to go with its brew. From the 2nd-storey balcony, sip your cup and watch the sheep grazing on the hillside.

Reštaurácia Starý Majer (☎ 5695 419; mains €5-10; ◷ 10am-9pm) Tuck into traditional sheepherders' dishes surprisingly seasoned with fresh herbs. They even serve lemon in your water, a refreshing twist. Sit at rough-hewn picnic tables in the courtyard or among rustic farm implements decorating the interior. The best of the valley eateries.

Getting There & Around

At least every two hours, more often on weekdays, buses link Žilina with Terchová (€1.40, 45 minutes) and Chata Vrátna (€1.60, one hour). Or you can change in Terchová for local buses that make multiple stops in the valley.

BANSKÁ ŠTIAVNICA
☎ 045 / pop 10,674

Like a fossil preserved in amber, Banská Štiavnica is a medieval wonder frozen in time. The town grew rich in the Middle Ages, exploiting some of Europe's richest gold and silver veins, but by the 19th century mines had dried up, and the town slipped out of the flow of time. Climbing up and down among the steep hillsides terraced with 15th- to 18th-century buildings, you can see why the town made Unesco's World Heritage list (unless you're distracted by the exertion).

Orientation & Information

From the train station it's a 2km climb uphill through the factories and housing blocks to Nám sv Trojice, the main square in the Old Town. Buses stop 500m closer, at Križovatka. The **City Tourist Information Office** (☎ 6949 653; www.banskastiavnica.sk; Nám sv Trojice 3; ☑ 8am-5.30pm May-Sep, 8am-4pm Mon-Fri, 8am-2pm Sat Oct-Apr) doubles as a two-terminal internet cafe.

Sights

Wandering the steep streets gazing at old burghers' houses is the main attraction. Buildings aren't all in pristine condition, but the overall effect is still arresting. **Slovak Mining Museum** (Slovenské banské múzeum; ☎ 6949 422; ☑ 8am-5pm May-Aug, to 4pm Tue-Sun Sep-Apr) has several branches; most interesting is the **Open-air Mining Museum** (JK Hella 12; adult/concession €4/2; ☑ 8am-5pm May-Aug, to 4pm Tue-Sun Sep-Apr) where you can take a trip down into a former working mine. The umbrella organisation also manages the town history exhibits in the 16th-century **Old Castle** (Starozámocká 1; adult/concession €3/1.50; ☑ 8am-5pm May-Aug, to 4pm Tue-Sun Sep-Apr) and the 'History of the Struggle against the Turks' display at the **New Castle** (Novozámocká 1; adult/concession €3/1.50; ☑ 8am-5pm May-Aug, to 4pm Tue-Sun Sep-Apr) on an opposite hill. All are accessed by Slovak language tour, with English text available.

Sleeping & Eating

The info office keeps a long list of private rooms. There's a grocery store across from the bus stop.

Hostel 6 (☎ 0905106706; www.hostel6.sk; Andreja Slackovica 6; dm €13.30; ☐) Book ahead to snag one of the 14 beds in this tiny, hospitable backpackers hostel. The bathroom, kitchen and common room are similarly small but cosy; laundry available.

Penzión Príjemný Oddych (☎ 6921 301; www.prijemnyoddych.sk, in Slovak; Starozámocká 3; r €40) Yellow walls and framed folk embroidery keep the 17th-century building feeling light and, indeed, *prijemný* (pleasing). On-site restaurant, playground and a sauna.

For homemade Slovak food at its finest, try the *kapustnica* (cabbage and sausage soup) at **U Böhmna** (☎ 0903525022; Strieborná 7; mains €4-8) or anything on the menu at **Matej** (☎ 6912 051; Akademická 4; mains €5-10), not the grand hotel, but the little restaurant across the way from it.

Getting There & Away

Banská Štiavnica is not the easiest place to get to without your own transport. Only one direct bus daily departs from Bratislava (€7.60, 3½ hours), at 1pm. Otherwise, all bus and train arrivals require a change in Zvolen or Banská Bystrica. Check schedules at http://cp.atlas.sk.

EAST SLOVAKIA

Alpine peaks in Slovakia? As you look upon the snow-strewn jagged mountains rising like an apparition east of Liptovský Mikuláš, you may think you're imagining things, but there they are. Hiking the High Tatras is undoubtedly the highlight of the region, but in eastern Slovakia you can also admire ancient architecture, explore castle ruins, visit the second city and seek out small villages. Though it's a distance from Bratislava, once you get here, the area is fairly compact. And Poland is just the other side of the mountains.

HIGH TATRAS
☎ 052

OK, this isn't exactly Switzerland, but the High Tatras (Vysoké Tatry) is the tallest range in the Carpathian Mountains. The massif is only 25km wide and 78km long, about 600 of the 726 sq km area falls within Slovakia. Photo opportunities at higher elevations might get you fantasising about a career with *National Geographic* – pristine snowfields, ultramarine mountain lakes and crashing waterfalls. Lower elevations are still recovering from a massive windstorm in late 2004 that uprooted trees and turned a once-dense pine forest into meadow.

Since 1949 most of this jagged range has been included in the Tatra National Park (Tanap), complementing a similar park in Poland. But that hasn't arrested development (much to the chagrin of watchdog groups like International Union for Conservation of Nature). The three main resort towns – Štrbské Pleso, Starý Smokovec and Tatranská Lomnica – continue to grow. A €250-million project is underway to add four luxury hotels and new ski runs by 2011.

When planning your trip, keep in mind that the higher trails are closed from November to mid-June, and avalanches may close lower portions as well. There's snow by November,

SLOVAKIA

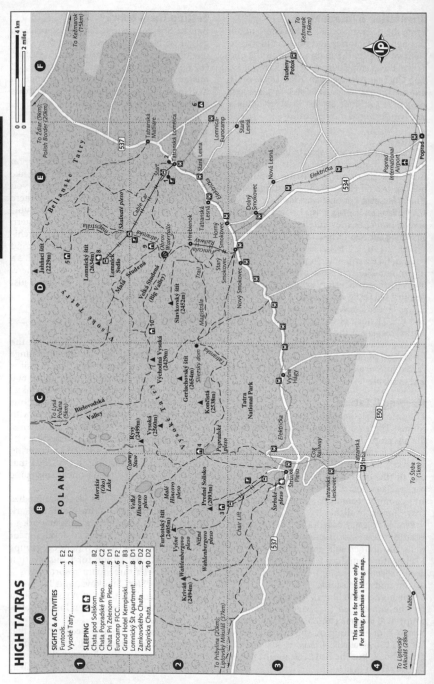

HIGH TATRAS

SIGHTS & ACTIVITIES
Funtools........................... 1 E2
Vysoké Tatry....................... 2 E2

SLEEPING 🛏
Chata pod Soliskom................. 3 B2
Chata Popradské Pleso.............. 4 C2
Chata Pri Zelenom Plese............ 5 D1
Eurocamp FICC...................... 6 F2
Grand Hotel Kempinski.............. 7 B3
Lomnický Šit Apartment............. 8 D1
Zamkovského Chata.................. 9 D1
Zbojnicka Chata.................... 10 D2

This map is for reference only.
For hiking, purchase a hiking map.

which lingers at least until May. June and July are especially rainy. July and August are the warmest (and most crowded) months. Hotel prices and crowds are at their lowest from October to April.

Orientation

Poprad is the nearest sizeable town (with main-line train station and airport), 15km south of Starý Smokovec. Tatranská Lomnica, the smallest and quaintest resort, lies 5km to the east of Smokovec and the bustling lakeside Štrbské Pleso is 11km west. A narrow-gauge electric train connects Poprad with Štrbské Pleso via Starý Smokovec, where you have to change to get to Tatranská Lomnica. Roads lead downhill from the resorts to less expensive villages.

MAPS

Our High Tatras map (Map p472) is intended for orientation only, not as a hiking guide. Buy the widely available, 1:25,000 VKÚ *Vysoké Tatry* (No 2) map. Green maps list summer hiking trails, blue ones show winter ski routes.

Information

All three main resort towns have ATMs.

Hotel FIS (☎ 4492 221; Areál FIS, Štrbské Pleso; per hr €4; ⏰ 24hr) Two lobby computers available for public rental.

Post office (off Cesta Slobody) Above Starý Smokovec train station.

Slovenská Sporiteľňa (☎ 4424 261; Cesta Slobody 24, Starý Smokovec) Central, with ATM and exchange.

Tatra Information Office (TIK) Starý Smokovec (☎ 4423 440; www.tatry.sk; Starý Smokovec 23; ⏰ 8am-8pm Mon-Fri, to 1pm Sat); Štrbské Pleso (☎ 4492 391; Hotel Toliar; ⏰ 8am-4pm); Tatranská Lomnica (☎ 4468 118; Cesta Slobody; ⏰ 10am-6pm Mon-Fri, 9am-1pm Sat) The Štrbské Pleso branch is good for trail information, Smokovec has the largest office, and overall, the staff in Lomnica are the most helpful.

T-Ski Travel (☎ 4423 200; www.slovakiatravel.sk; Starý Smokovec 46, Starý Smokovec; ⏰ 9am-4pm Mon-Thu, to 5pm Fri-Sun) Books lodging, including some hikers' huts, in person and online. Can arrange ski and mountain-bike programs. Located at the funicular station.

Townson Travel (☎ 4782 731; Tatranská Lomnica 94; per hr €3; ⏰ 9am-5pm Mon-Fri) A travel agency with one public computer.

U Michalka Café (Starý Smokovec 4; per hr €3; ⏰ 9am-midnight) Four terminals, great desserts (breakfast too).

Sights & Activities

A 600km network of trails reaches all the alpine valleys and some peaks, with mountain huts for hikers to stop at along the way. Routes are colour coded and easy to follow. Park regulations require you to keep to the marked trails and to refrain from picking flowers. Always wear hiking boots and layer clothing. Know that the assistance of the Mountain Rescue Service is not free and beware of sudden thunderstorms on ridges and peaks where there's no protection. For the latest weather and trail conditions stop by the **Mountain Rescue Service** (Horská Záchranná Služba; ☎ emergency 18 300; http://his.hzs.sk/; Starý Smokovec 23, Starý Smokovec).

STARÝ SMOKOVEC

From Starý Smokovec a **funicular railway** (☎ 4467 618; www.vt.sk; adult/concession return €7/5.50; ⏰ 7.30am-7pm), or a 55 minute hike on the green trail, takes you up to **Hrebienok** (1280m). From here you have a great view of the Velká Studená Valley and a couple of hiking options. Following the red trail, past the restaurant and lodging at Bilíkova chata, to **Obrov Waterfalls** (Obrovsky vodopad) takes about an hour. Continuing on from the falls, it's a 35-minute hike to Zamkovského chata, and Skalnaté pleso (see below), with its cable car and trails down to Tatranská Lomnica. An excellent day hike, this is part of the **Tatranská Magistrála Trail** that follows the southern slopes of the High Tatras for 65km.

Rent mountain bikes at **Tatrasport** (☎ 4425 241; www.tatry.net/tatrasport; per day €15; ⏰ 8am-noon & 1-6pm), above the bus-station parking lot.

TATRANSKÁ LOMNICA

While in the Tatras, you shouldn't miss the ride to the precipitous 2634m summit of **Lomnický štít** (bring a jacket!). From Lomnica, a large **gondola** (☎ 0903112200; www.vt.sk; adult/concession return €12/6; ⏰ 8.30am-7pm Jul & Aug, to 3.30pm Sep-Jun) stops at mid-station Štart before it takes you to the winter sports area, restaurant and lake at **Skalnaté pleso**. From there, a smaller **cable car** (☎ 0903112200; www.vt.sk; adult/concession return €20/16; ⏰ 8.30am-7pm Jul & Aug, to 3.30pm Sep-Jun) goes on to the summit where there's a viewing platform and Warhol-esque cafe-bar. Queues form early and timed tickets sometimes sell out.

Alternatively, you can yomp it up to Skalnaté by foot (2½ hours), where there's also a **chairlift** (☎ 0903112200; www.vt.sk; adult/concession €5/4; ⏰ 8.30am-5.30pm Jul & Aug, 8.30am-4.30pm Sep-Jun) running up to **Lomnické sedlo**, a 2190m saddle and ski area and trailhead below the summit.

Get off the cable car at Štart and you're at **Funtools** (☎ 0903112200; www.vt.sk; cable car plus 1 ride €9; ✆ noon-6.30pm May-Sep), from where you can take a fast ride down the mountain on a two-wheeled scooter, a luge-like three-wheel cart or on a four-wheel modified skate board.

ŠTRBSKÉ PLESO

Talk about development, if it's not a new condo-hotel going up, it's an old one being revamped. The big news is that in early 2009 Kempinski opened a five-star resort on the shores of Štrbské pleso, the glacial lake at 1346m. Day hikes are extremely popular here where you can follow the red-marked **Magistrála Trail** (uphill from the train station) for 3km (about an hour) to **Popradské pleso**, an even more idyllic pond at 1494m. From Popradské pleso the Magistrála zigzags steeply up the mountainside then traverses east towards **Sliezsky dom** and the Hrebienok funicular above Starý Smokovec (four hours).

There is also a year-round **chairlift** (☎ 4492 343; www.parksnow.sk; adult/concession return €7.50/5; ✆ 8am-3.30pm) up to Chata pod Soliskom, from where it's a 2km (one hour) walk north along the red trail to the 2093m summit of **Predné Solisko**.

MOUNTAINEERING

You can reach the top of **Slavkovský štít** (2452m) via the blue trail from Starý Smokovec (7.5km; seven to eight hours return), but to scale the peaks without marked hiking trails (Gerlachovský štít included), you must hire a mountain guide. Contact the **Mountain Guides Society Office** (☎ 4422 066; www.tatraguide.sk; Starý Smokovec 38, Starý Smokovec; ✆ 10am-6pm Mon-Fri, noon-6pm Sat & Sun Jun Sep, 10am-6pm Mon-Fri Oct-May), by the Hotel Smokovec. Guides cost from €150, and the society runs classes too.

WINTER SPORTS

Park Snow (☎ 4492 343; www.parksnow.sk; Areál FIS; day lift ticket adult/concession €26/18; ✆ 8.30am-3.30pm) in Štrbské pleso is the most poplar ski and snowboard area, with two chairlifts, four tow lines, 12km easy to moderate runs, one jump and a snow -tubing area.

But Tatranská Lomnica's ski resort, **Vysoké Tatry** (☎ 0903112200; www.vt.sk; Tatranská Lomnica 7, Tatranská Lomnica; day lift ticket adult/concession €27/22; ✆ 9am-3.30pm) is competing with a new high-speed quad lift that links to 6km of runs

(1300m drop). That brings the total to 8km of easy to moderate runs, two chairlifts, two cable cars and a tow line for beginner slopes. You can hire skis and snowboards at both resorts for about €15 per day.

Tow-assist snow sledging and tubing is to be had at **Snow Funpark** (☎ 0903112200; Hrebienok; per ride €1.50; ✆ 10.30am-4.30pm), at the top of the funicular above Starý Smokovec.

Sleeping

For the quintessential Slovak mountain experience, you can't beat hiking from one *chata* (a mountain hut, could be anything from shack to chalet) to the next, high up among the peaks. Food (optional meal service or restaurant) is always available. Beds in these hikers' huts fill up fast; reserve ahead.

No wild camping is permitted: there is a camping ground near Tatranská Lomnica. If you're looking for cheap sleeps, Ždiar (p476), east over the ridge, is a good option. It's best to reserve private rooms (per person €15 to €20) ahead of time via the internet (www.tatry .sk and www.tanap.sk/homes.html) as tourist offices don't do bookings and rooms fill fast.

STARÝ SMOKOVEC & AROUND

Penzion Gabriel (☎ 4422 332; www.jmg.sk; Nový Smokovec 68, Nový Smokovec; r €50-52) Steep dormer rooflines give alpine flare to this geodesic guest house. Inside rooms are just as mod, with cobalt blues and oranges. Refrigerators in-room, shared kitchen.

Bilíkova chata (☎ 4422 439; www.bilikovachata.sk, in Slovak; Hrebienok; r with shared bathroom €53) A 10 minute walk down hill from the upper funicular station brings you to the closest of the higher elevation (1220m) *chaty*. Stay among the clouds at this basic log-cabin hotel with a full-service restaurant.

Grand Hotel (☎ 4870 000; www.grandhotel.sk; Starý Smokovec 38; s/d €86/112; 🐾) More than 100 years of history are tied up in the most prominent lodging in Starý Smokovec. For full effect, splash out in the imperial grandeur of the royal suite (€230).

Other mountain huts:

Zbojnícka chata (☎ 0903638000; www.zbojnicka chata.sk; dm incl breakfast €15) Sixteen dorm-style beds, self-service eatery and small kitchen; at 1960m.

Zamkovského chata (☎ 4422 636; www.zamka.sk, in Slovak; dm €15-20) Twenty-eight beds in two- to four-bed rooms; full board available; at 1475m.

TATRANSKÁ LOMNICA & AROUND

Look for private room (*privat* or *zimmer frei*) signs on the back streets south and east of the train station.

Eurocamp FICC (☎ 4467 741; www.eurocamp-ficc .sk; per person/tent/car €4/3/3.50; ☯ year-round; ☒) Big and bustling, this 1500-capacity camping ground has two restaurants, a bar, billiards, a supermarket, a swimming pool… North of the Lomnica-Eurocamp tram station.

Penzión Encian (☎ 4467 520; www.tatry.sk/encian; Tatranská Lomnica 36; s/d €33/66) Owners Zdenka and Štefan Unák have created a warm and welcoming main-street inn. The small restaurant has a fire in the hearth and antique skiing memorabilia on display.

Grandhotel Praha (☎ 4467 941; www.grandhotel praha.sk; s/d incl breakfast €105/145; ☐ ☐ ☒) Remember when travel was elegant and you dressed for dinner? No? Well the 1899 Grandhotel does. Rooms are appropriately classic, if uninspired, and there's a snazzy spa.

From Skalnaté pleso above Tatranská Lomnica you could hike west 2½ hours to the huts listed under Starý Smokovec (opposite), or 2½ hours east to **Chata pri Zelenom plese** (☎ 4467 420; www.zelenepleso.sk; dm €13), a 50-bed lakeside lodge at 1540m.

ŠTRBSKÉ PLESO & AROUND

Rabid development and crowds make staying in Štrbské pleso a last choice, with one grand exception.

Grand Hotel Kempinski (☎ 3262 222; www.kemp inski-hightatras.com; Kupelna 6; r €255-300; ☒ ☐ ☒) After seamlessly blending several remodelled villas and new buildings, Kempinski opened its lap-of-luxury chateau lakeside in spring of 2009. Far and away the swankiest Tatra accommodation, the chain is hoping to entice high-end travellers into Poprad-Tatry airport with their Zen spa awaiting after the limousine service to the hotel.

Mountain huts above Štrbské pleso:

Chata pod Soliskom (☎ 0905652036; www.chata solisko.sk; dm €10) Nine beds, ugly concrete building, nice terrace. No hiking required – it's next to the chairlift; at 1800m.

Chata Popradské pleso (☎ 4492 177; www.poprad skepleso.sk; dm €15, d €53) Sizeable log lodge with restaurant and bar. Reserve ahead and you can drive here (road requires permission); at 1500m.

Eating & Drinking

The villages are close enough that it's easy to sleep in one and eat in another, but the restaurant offerings in general aren't great. All of the hotels, and some of the guest houses, have OK eateries; the grand ones have bars and discos. Look for the local *potraviny* (supermarket) on the main road in each village.

Samoobslužná Reštaurácia (☎ 4781 011; Hotel Toliar, Štrbské pleso 21; mains €2.50-6; ☯ 7am-10pm) This self-service cafeteria has one-dish meals (goulash, chicken stir-fry etc) and a few vegetarian options.

Reštaurácia Stará Mama (☎ 4467 713; shopping centre Sintra, Tatranská Lomnica; mains €5-12) Substantial soups and homemade *halušky* are the main reason to frequent this rustic fave; but the menu is actually quite extensive.

Tatry Pub (☎ 4422 448; Tatra Komplex, Starý Smokovec; ☯ 1pm-midnight) Refresh yourself at the official watering hole of the Mountain Guide Club. A full schedule of events includes DVD presentations, karaoke and DJ nights; pub food, too.

Scattered among the villages are numerous, often touristy, *koliba* restaurants. Our favourites are **Koliba Patria** (☎ 4492 591; Southern lake shore, Štrbske pleso; mains €6-15), for it's lakeside terrace, and **Zbojnícka Koliba** (☎ 4467 630; road to Grand Hotel Praha, Tatranská Lomnica; mains €10-20; ☯ 4pm-midnight), where some weekend evenings musicians play gypsy songs on the cimbalom while your chicken roasts over the open fire (it'll take an hour to cook).

Getting There & Around

The main road through the Tatras resorts is Rte 537, or Cesta Slobody (Freedom Way). Connect to it from the E50 motorway through Tatranská Štrba, Poprad or Velká Lomnica. To reach the Tatras by public transport from most destinations you need to switch in Poprad to an electric train that makes numerous stops along the main Tatra road, or buses that go to off-line destinations as well.

SLOVAKIA

BUS

Buses from Poprad travel to Starý Smokovec (€0.80, 20 minutes, every 30 minutes), Tatranská Lomnica (€1.20, 35 minutes, every 60 minutes) and Štrbské pleso (€1.50, 50 minutes, every 45 minutes).

At least every 1½ hours buses connect Tatranská Lomnica with Kežmarok (€1, 30 minutes) and Ždiar (€1, 25 minutes).

Local buses run between the resorts every 20 minutes and tend to be quicker than the train. Starý Smokovec to Tatranská Lomnica (€0.30) takes 10 minutes, and to Štrbské pleso (€1) takes 35 minutes.

TRAIN

A narrow-gauge electric train connects Poprad and the main High Tatra resort towns at least hourly. One line runs from Poprad via Starý Smokovec (30 minutes) to Štrbské Pleso (one hour), with frequent stops in between. Another line connects Starý Smokovec to Tatranská Lomnica (15 minutes). A third route from Tatranská Lomnica through Studeny Potok (15 minutes) loops south to Poprad (25 minutes). A €1.50 ticket covers up to a 29km ride, but it's easier to buy a one-/three-/seven-day pass for €3.30/6.70/12. If there's not a ticket window, buy tickets from the conductor; validate on board.

A cog railway runs between Tatranská Štrba (on the main Žilina–Poprad railway line) and Štrbské pleso (€1, 15 minutes, hourly).

BELÁ TATRAS

☎ 052

Travel east over the High Tatra mountain ridges and you start to hear Slovak spoken with a Polish accent. The Goral folk culture is an intricate part of the experience in the small *Belianské Tatry* (Belá Tatras). Traditional wooden cottages are still the building method of choice in the main village of Ždiar, giving the place a rustic, laid-back quality that the toney resort villages have always lacked. From here it's an easy day trip or journey on to Poland; heck, you can walk there!

Ždiar

Decorated timber cottages line long and narrow Ždiar, the only mountain settlement inhabited since the 16th century. Goral traditions have both been bolstered and eroded by tourism. Several sections of the village are historical reservations, including the **Ždiar House**

Museum (Ždiarsky dom; ☎ 4498 142; adult/concession €3/1.50; ☑ 10am-4pm Tue-Sun), a tiny place with colourful local costumes and furnishings.

Cross over the main road from the museum and a green trail skirts the river through Monkova Valley (880m) for a 2½-hour return hike with very little elevation change. You could also veer off to **Širkové sedlo** (1826m) and continue on to **Kopské sedlo** (1750m) in about three hours. At this point return, or cross over into the High Tatras. Chata pri Zelenom plese (p475) is an hour away, the cable car to Tatranská Lomnica (p473) is 2½ hours beyond that.

SLEEPING & EATING

Ždiar has a huge number of *privaty* (here they are large lodgings with shared facility rooms for rent, about €11 per person), so odds are good if you just show up and knock. Otherwise, check www.zdiar.sk (in Slovak), under *ubytovanie*. Pictures, prices and contact info is pretty straightforward.

our pick Ginger Monkey Hostel (☎ 4498 0844; www.gingermonkey.eu; Ždiar 294; dm/d €13/30; ☐) Crushing mountain views from an old Goral-style house, hot tea at any hour, laundry, wi-fi, a surprising sense of community among adventurous English-speakers… There's been some talk that this sort of writing will ruin things (remember the movie *The Beach*?) But how could we not mention the Monkey? There's a full kitchen, but most evenings the host leads the whole crew to a local restaurant for rousing conversations about social systems, life's purpose and what superhero could whoop which. Don't just book one night, you'll end up extending.

Goral Krčma (☎ 4498 138; Ždiar 460; mains €3-6) A traditional 'village pub' restaurant associated with an inn, this *krčma* serves all the regional specialities, like potato pancakes stuffed with a spicy sauté.

Other good eats:

Rustika Pizzeria (☎ 0908575050; Ždiar 334; pizza €4-6) Wood-fired pizza served in an old log house.

U Veroniky (☎ 0908575050; Ždiar 351; mains €5-10) Cute little romantic restaurant.

GETTING THERE & AWAY

There are up to six buses daily between Ždiar and Poprad (€1.80, 50 minutes) via Starý Smokovec (€1.10, 45 minutes) and Tatranská Lomnica (€1, 30 minutes). At least four daily buses travel between Ždiar and the Polish border, Tatranská Javorina, Lysá Poľana stop (€1, 30 minutes). From there you can walk across the bridge to the Polish side, where there are regular public buses and private minibuses to Zakopane (26km).

POPRAD

☎ 052 / pop 55,185

Poprad is an important air and land transfer point for the High Tatras. Otherwise, the modern, industrial city's attraction is limited. Oh, there is a HUGE water park here. From the adjacent train and bus stations, the central pedestrian square, Nám sv Egídia, is a five-minute walk south on Alžbetina.

Information

City Information Centre (☎ 7721 700; www.poprad .sk; Dom Kultúry Štefánikova 72; ☉ 8am-5pm Mon-Fri, 9am-noon Sat) Town info only.

Ex Cafe (J Curie 17; per hr €2; ☉ 8am-10pm Mon-Sat, from 1pm Sun) Internet terminals, no wi-fi.

Activities

Poprad's thermal water park, **Aqua City** (☎ 7851 222; www.aquacitypoprad.sk; Športová 1397; ☉ 9am-9pm), is admirably green. Among other initiatives, the water, heat and electricity here come from geothermal and solar sources. Prices for sauna, swim and slide zones differ; access to the outdoor thermal complex is €18/15 per day for adult/concession.

Sleeping & Eating

Numerous restaurants and cafes line Nám sv Egídia. The old Germanic village of Spišská Sobota, 2km northeast of the centre, is now part of Poprad. There are more than 10 lodging options on or near its medieval square.

Hotel Cafe Razy (☎ 7764 101; www.hotelcaferazy .sk; Nám Sv Egídia 58; s/d €36/56) Simple rooms with wood lofts are pretty sane (two have wi-fi), it's weekend evenings when the pizza cafe downstairs crowds up that get a little CRazy.

Caffe Filicori (☎ 0915962358; Nám Sv Egídia 42; small dishes €2-6) A modern cafe facade hides an excellent, vegetable-rich light menu. Try the 'zucchini' – baked mozzarella wrapped in the grilled green vegetable, sprinkled with balsamic vinegar and real shaved mozzarella on a bed of rocket lettuce. Free wi-fi zone.

Getting There & Away

Bus 12 travels between Poprad city centre and **Poprad-Tatry International airport** (☎ 7763 875;

www.airport-poprad.sk; Na Letisko 100), 5km west of the centre. **SkyEurope** (☎ 02-3301 7301; www.skyeurope .com) runs three flights per week between here and London's Luton Airport.

Intercity (IC) or Eurocity (EC) trains are the quickest way to get in and out of Poprad; four a day run to Bratislava (€16, four hours) and Košice (€6.50, one hour). For more on the electric trains that traverse the 13km or so to the High Tatras resorts, see opposite.

To reach Poland, you can take a bus from Poprad to Tatranská Javorina, Lysá Poľana stop (€2.50, 1½ hours, four daily). Walk across to the buses waiting to take you to Zakopane.

KEŽMAROK

☎ 052 / pop 17,383

Snuggled beneath the broody peaks of the High Tatras, Kežmarok's pocket-sized old-town square with resident castle seems especially quaint. The influence of the original 13th-century German settlers is evident in the architecture even today. Numerous distinct churches, and all those ice-cream shops, make it well worth an afternoon; and in July, the European Folk Craft Market comes to town.

Orientation & Information

Kežmarok is 14km east of Tatranská Lomnica and 16km northeast of Poprad – easy day-tripping distances. The bus and train stations are side by side, northwest of the Old Town; follow Dr Alexandra to the main square, Hlavné nám.

Alter Ego (☎ 4525 432; Hlavné nám 3) Great bookstore and map collection.

Kežmarok Information Agency (☎ 4524 047; www .kezmarok.net; Hlavné nám 46; ☉ 8am-5pm Mon-Fri, 9am-2pm Sat & Sun) Stocks heaps of brochures and souvenirs.

Sights

The imposing red-and-green, pseudo-Moorish **New Evangelical Church** (☎ 4526 314; cnr Toporcerova & Hviezdoslavovo; ☉ 10am-noon & 2-4pm Tue-Sat May-Oct), c 1894, dominates the south end of town. A €1.50 ticket also covers entry to the **Old Wooden Evangelical Church** (cnr Toporcerova & Hviezdoslavovo; ☉ 10am-noon & 2-4pm Tue-Sat May-Oct), next door. Built in 1717 without a single nail, it has an amazing interior of carved and painted wood.

The small, mansionlike **Kežmarok Castle** (☎ 4522 618; Hradne nám 45; adult/concession €2.30/1; ☉ by tour 9am-4pm Apr-Oct) dates back to the 15th century and is now a museum with period furniture and archaeology exhibits.

The second weekend in July, the **European Folk Craft Market** attracts traditional and modern artisans demonstrating and vending their wares. Plenty of food, drink and entertainment is to be had among the crowds then.

Sleeping & Eating

Penzión U Jakubu (☎ 4526 315; www.penzionujakuba.sk; Starý trh 39; mains €4-8) Take a seat at a big wooden bench near the open fire and be waited on by servers in traditional costume. An authentic, folksy Slovakness pervades both restaurant and guest house (rooms €30 to €40).

Sidewalk cafes abound in the pedestrian area around Hlavné nám. There are no fewer than six *cukráreň* (pastry cafes) serving cakes and ice cream, or you could stop at the tables on the square run by **Pizza Classica** (☎ 4523 693; cnr Hviezdoslavova & Hlavné nám; pizzas €3-8).

Getting There & Away

Buses are the way to get around locally; services run direct to Poprad (€1, 30 minutes, 16 daily), Tatranská Lomnica (€1, 30 minutes, 12 daily), Starý Smokovec (€1.30, 35 minutes, six daily) and Ždiar (€1.30, 40 minutes, three daily).

PIENINY NATIONAL PARK
☎ 052

With gently bubbling waters flowing between impressive 500m-tall cliffs, the 21-sq-km **Pieniny National Park** (Pieninský Národný Park) was created to protect the 9km **Dunajec Gorge**. The park combines with a similar one on the Polish side of the river and extends between the Slovak village of **Červený Kláštor** and Szczawnica, Poland. River floating is the main attraction here, but there's a riverside hiking trail and an ancient monastery, too.

At the mouth of the gorge is the fortified 14th-century **Red Monastery** (Červený Kláštor; ☎ 4822 955; adult/concession €2/1; ☯ 10am-5pm May-Oct). Mostly a park administrative centre, the monastery contains a fairly disappointing museum with statuary and old area prints. Two kilometres west, look for the small **information centre** (☎ 4822 122; www.pieniny.sk; Rte 543; ☯ 9am-5pm May-Oct).

There are two departure points along Rte 243 for a **river float trip** (☎ 4282 840; www.pltnictvo .sk; adult/concession €8.50/4; ☯ daylight May-Oct) in a *plté* (shallow, flat-bottom raft boats): one

opposite the monastery, and another 1km upriver west of the village. Don't be expecting white-water thrills – the Dunajec is a rather sedate 1½-hour experience terminating near the Slovak village of Lesnica.

To return to Červený Kláštor you can hike back the way you came, along the riverside trail through the gorge, in a little over an hour. It's an interesting walk even if you don't go water. Or, 500m southeast of the river drop off is Chata Pieniny in Lesnica. The lodging rents out bicycles (one way €4) and buses depart from there. Follow the yellow trail north of Lesnica (1.5km) and you reach a pedestrian border crossing into Poland.

Sleeping & Eating

Copious *privaty* and *zimmer frei* line the one road in Červený Kláštor. Food stalls stand between the monastery and the river launch.

Hotel Pltník (☎ 4822 525; www.hotelpltnik.sk; Červený Kláštor; per person/tent €2/1.70) Skip the ragged hotel and pitch your tent in the big river-front field next door.

Chata Pieniny (☎ 4397 530; www.chatapieniny.sk; Lesnica; dm €10) What a cheap and cheerful log lodge. Stay in a two- to six-bed dorm near the terminus of the raft trip. On-site restaurant, minimarket and bike rental (€4 per day).

Getting There & Away

Getting here is a challenge unless you have a car. Buses run to Červený Kláštor from Poprad (€3, two hours), via Kežmarok (€2, 1¼ hour) only two times a day Monday to Saturday and once on Sunday. From Košice (€6, three hours), there's one direct afternoon bus, otherwise you have to change in Stará Ľubovňa. Check schedules at http://cp.atlas.sk.

LEVOČA
☎ 053 / pop 14,677

High medieval walls surround ancient town buildings and cobblestone streets – so this is what Slovakia looked like in the 13th century. Today Levoča is one of the few Slovak cities to have its historic defences largely intact. At the old-town centre is the pride of the country's religious art and architecture collection, the Gothic Church of St Jacob and its 18m-high alter by Master Pavol. During the Middle Ages the king of Hungary invited Saxon Germans to colonise the eastern frontiers and Levoča became central to the resulting Slavo-Germanic Spiš cultural region.

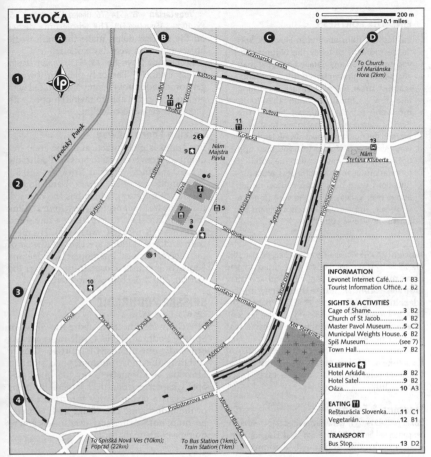

LEVOČA

SLOVAKIA

Orientation & Information

Levoča is on the main E50 motorway between Poprad (28km) and Košice (94km). The centre is 1km north of the train and bus stations. Both banks and post are on the small main square, Nám Majstra Pavla.

Levonet Internet Café (☎ 0908478700; Nám Majstra Pavla 38; per hr €2.50; ☯ 10am-10pm)

Tourist information office (☎ 4513 763; www .levoca.sk; Nám Majstra Pavla 58; ☯ 9am-6pm May-Sep, 9am-4pm Mon-Fri, 10am-2pm Sat Oct-Apr) Ask for the free photocopied map.

Sights

The spindles-and-spires **Church of St Jacob** (Chrám sv Jakuba; ☎ 4512 347; www.chramsvjakuba.sk; Nám Majstra Pavla; adult/concession €2/1; ☯ 1pm, 2pm,

3pm & 4pm Apr-Oct), built in the 14th and 15th centuries, elevates your spirit with its soaring arches, precious art and rare furnishings. Everyone comes to see the splendid golden Gothic altar (1517) created by Master Pavol of Levoča. On it the mysterious master carved and painted cherubic representations of the Last Supper and the Madonna and Child. (This Madonna's face appeared on the original 100Sk banknote.) Buy tickets at the **cashier** (kasa; ☯ 11am-5pm) inside the **Municipal Weights House** across the street from the north door. Entry is limited to certain hours, so check online or in person for additional times in the high season, we've listed the minimum.

Gothic and Renaissance eye candy abound on the main square, No 20 is the **Master Pavol**

FIND THE FORTRESS

Castles and ruins abound in Slovakia. Spiš Castle (right) is certainly the biggest, but you can pick up any detailed national map and see the ruin symbols dotting the landscape. A great day's adventure is tracking one down. Choose a symbol that looks promising to you, and start hiking. The nearest village is the best place to start, a marked hiking path almost always leads the way. At the top of your trek you may find only a hearth, or you may find the outlined foundations of an ancient fortress. Most fortifications were built along clifftop ridges above river valleys, so you're sure to get a work out, and a great view as a reward no matter what else you find.

Museum (☎ 4513 496; Nám Majstra Pavla 20; adult/concession €1.40/0.80; ☺ 9am-5pm Tue-Sun) dedicated to the city's most celebrated son. The 15th-century **town hall** (*radnica*), next to the church, houses a lacklustre **Spiš Museum** (☎ 4512 449; Nám Majstra Pavla; adult/concession €2.50/1.60; ☺ 9am-5pm Tue-Sun). The adjacent 16th-century **cage of shame** was built for naughty boys and girls.

From town you can see the **Church of Mariánska hora**, 2km north, where the largest Catholic pilgrimage in Slovakia takes place in early July.

Sleeping & Eating

Oáza (☎ 4514 511; www.ubytovanieoaza.sk; Nová 65; per person incl breakfast €10) Two-bed rooms with shared bathroom, and four-bed rooms with bathroom and kitchen, are just what the budget doctor ordered. There's a big shared garden (with lawn, caged chickens and vegetables) between the two parts of the house.

Hotel Arkáda (☎ 4512 372; www.arkada.sk; Nám Majstra Pavla 26; s/d €35/53; ☐) Pine timbers and furnishings are the norm, but you can upgrade to an apartment with antiques for just €67. The hotel restaurant (mains €5 to €8) serves heaping grilled meat platters and fondue for two among its offerings. Free wi-fi.

Hotel Satel (☎ 4512 943; www.hotelsatel.com; Nám Majstra Pavla 55; s/d €36/53) Vaulted arches come standard in any respectable 14th-century building, and the Hotel Satel is no exception. Just don't expect ornate – the Middle Ages were austere, as are the hotel's contemporary furnishings. Limited wi-fi available.

Vegetarián (☎ 4514 576; Uhoľná 137; mains €3-5; ☺ 10am-3.15pm Mon-Fri) The wholesome dishes on the no-fuss menu make this basic vegie buffet a hit with weekday workers.

Reštaurácia Slovenka (☎ 4512 339; Nám Majstra Pavla 66; mains €3-7) The only place in town to get homemade *pirohy* (dumplings stuffed with potato, somewhat akin to ravioli) topped with sheep's cheese and crackling.

Getting There & Away

Bus travel is most practical in the area; frequent services take you to Spišské Podhradie (€1, 20 minutes), Spišská Nová Ves (€0.80, 20 minutes, every 30 minutes) and Poprad (€1.60, 30 minutes), which has the onward, main-line train connections best for travelling to Bratislava. Two to five buses a day wend their way to Košice (€4, two hours). The main train and bus stations are 1km southeast of the centre; the local bus stop at Nám Štefana Kluberta is a little closer to town than the station, and most routes stop there.

SPIŠSKÉ PODHRADIE

☎ 053 / pop 3826

Stretching for 4 hectares above the village of Spišské Podhradie, Spiš Castle ruins are undoubtedly one of largest in Europe. They're certainly the most photographed sight in Slovakia. A kilometre away, the medieval Spiš Chapter ecclesiastical settlement, helps make this a favourite day trip from Levoča or the mountains. The village itself is pretty ho-hum, not worth a stay-over unless you're doing a castle night tour.

Sights

From the E50 motorway you catch glimpses of eerie outlines and stony ruins crowning the ridge on the eastern side of Spišské Podhradie. Can it really be that big? Indeed, **Spiš Castle** (Spišský hrad; ☎ 4541 336; www.spisskyhrad .com; adult/concession €4.50/2.50; ☺ 9am-5pm May-Oct) seems to go on forever. If the reconstructed ruins are this impressive, imagine what the fortress once was.

Chronicles first mention Spiš Castle in 1209, and the remaining central residential tower is thought to date from that time. From there defenders are said to have repulsed the Tatars in 1241. Rulers and noble families kept adding fortifications and palaces during the 15th and 16th centuries, but by 1780 the site had already lost military significance and much was destroyed in a fire that year. It wasn't until the 1970s that efforts were made to salvage and reconstruct what remained. Few structures are whole, but there's a cistern, a chapel and a rectangular Romanesque palace, which holds the museum. Descend to the dungeon to see the meaty bits; scary torture devices the human mind has invented. Night tours are available some summer weekends.

From the spur line train station, the castle is a healthy hike up. Cross the tracks near the station and follow the yellow markers. One kilometre south is Spišské Podhradie's bus stop. If you're driving or cycling, the easiest access is off the Prešov highway east of the castle.

On the west side of Spišské Podhradie, you'll find the still active **Spiš Chapter** (Spišská Kapitula; adult/concession €2/1), a 13th-century Catholic complex encircled by a 16th-century wall. Charming Gothic houses line the single street running between the two medieval gates. Buy tickets from the **information office** (☎ 0907300411; ⊗ 11.15am-2.45pm), where you can also pick up a guide. At the upper end is the magnificent **St Martin's Cathedral**, built in 1273, with twin Romanesque towers and a Gothic sanctuary. Inside are several trifold painted Gothic altars from the 15th century – quite impressive. On either side of the cathedral are the **seminary** and the Renaissance **bishop's palace** (1652). If you're travelling to Spiš Chapter by bus from Levoča, get off one stop before Spišské Podhradie, at Kapitula.

Sleeping & Eating

The castle has a food stand, and the village, a little grocery store.

Penzión Podzámok (☎ 4541 755; www.penzion podzamok.sk; Podzámková 28; s/d with shared bathroom €12/24; 🖵) Three family houses have been cobbled together to create a simple 42-bed guest house with a backyard view of the castle. Follow the street next to the bridge north. Full board available.

Spišsky Salaš (☎ 4541 202; www.spisskysalas.sk; Levočská cesta 11; mains €3-7) You can tell this is a local rustic specialities fave by the number of kids on the playground and the long wait for a table at the log restaurant and terrace on summer weekends. In addition to tasty lamb stew, the Salaš offers three simple wood-panel lodging rooms for rent (per person €13). It's on the road between E50 and Spišské Podhradie, 3km west of Spiš Chapter.

Getting There & Away

Buses connect with Levoča (€1, 20 minutes) and Poprad (€2.20, 50 minutes) at least hourly, services to Košice (€3, 1½ hours, 12 daily) are only slightly less frequent. A spur railway line heads to Spišské Podhradie from Spišské Vlachy (€0.50, 10 minutes), a station on the main line from Poprad to Košice, only three (inconvenient) times a day.

SLOVENSKÝ RAJ & AROUND
☎ 053

With rumbling waterfalls, steep gorges, sheer rockfaces, thick forests and hilltop meadows, Slovenský raj is a national park for the passionately outdoorsy. A few easier trails exist, but the one-way, ladder-and-chain ascents are the most dramatic. You cling to a metal rung headed straight up a precipice while an icy waterfall splashes and sprays you from a metre away. Oh, that's after you've scrambled horizontally across a log ladder to cross the stream down below. Pure exhilaration.

Orientation

The nearest town of any size is the lacklustre Spišská Nová Ves, 23km southeast of Poprad. The main trailheads on the northern edge of the national park are at Podlesok, on the outskirts of Hrabušice (16km southwest of Poprad), and Čingov, 5km west of Spišská Nová Ves. There are lodgings and eateries near northern trailheads. For full town services, you'll have to go into Spišská Nová Ves or Hrabušice. Dedinky, at the south end of the park, is a regular village with pub, supermarket, a lake and houses. Before you trek, make sure to buy VKÚ's 1:25,000 *Slovenský raj* hiking map (No 4), available at many tourist offices and bookshops countrywide.

Information

Your lodging place is often the best source of information; orientation maps are posted near trailheads. Procure money before you get to the park; there's an ATM and exchange at the Spišska Nová train station.

Internet Café (☎ 4299 402; Drevárska 2, Spišská Nová Ves; per hr €2; ⊗ 10am-10pm)

Mountain Rescue Service (Horská Záchranná Služba; ☎ emergency 183 00; http:// his.hzs.sk)

Tourist information centre (☎ 4428 292; www .slovenskyraj.sk; Letná 49, Spišská Nová Ves; ⊗ 8am-6pm Mon-Fri, 9am-1pm Sat, 2pm-6pm Sun May-Sep, 8am-5pm

SLOVAKIA

SLOVAKIA

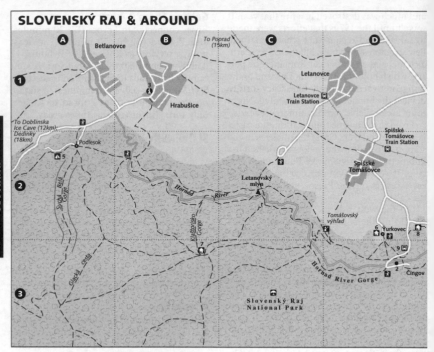

Mon-Fri Oct-May) Hit-or-miss help with area accommodation and info.

Tourist information (☎ 4299 854; Hlavná 171, Hrabušice; ☉ 8am-6pm Jun-Aug) Small, summertime office.

Sights & Activities

Slovenský raj National Park (Slovak Paradise; www.sloven skyraj.sk; admission €1), has numerous trails that include a one-way *roklina* (gorge) sections and take at least half a day. The shortest, **Zejmarská Gorge** hike, on a blue trail, starts at Biele Vody (15 minutes northeast of Dedinky via the red trail). The physically fit can run, clamber and climb up in 50 minutes; others huff and puff up in 90 minutes. To get back, you can follow the green trail down to Dedinky, or there's a **chairlift** (adult/concession €1/0.50; ☉ 9am-5pm) that works sporadically.

From Čingov a green trail leads up the **Hornád River Gorge** to **Letanovský mlyn** (1½ hours), from there the blue trail continues along the river to the base of the green, one-way, technically aided **Kláštorisko Gorge** hike (one hour). At the top, you can take a break at the lodge and restaurant, **Kláštorisko chata**

(☎ 4493 307; klastorisko@infosk.sk) before following another green trail back along the ridge towards Čingov. Allow at least six hours for the circuit, including lunch at Kláštorisko.

From Podlesok, an excellent day's hike (six to seven hours) heads up the **Suchá Belá Gorge** (with several steep ladders), then east to Kláštorisko on a yellow then red trail. From here, take the blue trail down to the Hornád River, then follow the river gorge upstream to return to Podlesok.

Six kilometres west of Dedinky is **Dobšinská Ice Cave** (Dobšinská Ľadová Jaskyňa; ☎ 7881 470; adult/ concession €7/5; ☉ 9am-4pm Tue-Sun Jun-Aug, 9.30am-2pm Tue-Sun May & Sep). The frozen formations are most dazzling in May, before they start to melt. Tours leave every hour or so.

Sleeping & Eating

Surrounding towns have private rooms (many listed at www.slovenskyraj.sk). All the park's hotels and pensions have restaurants. From May to September food stands open near the Podlesok trailhead. Stock up on provisions at the supermarket next to the bus station in Spišska Nová Ves.

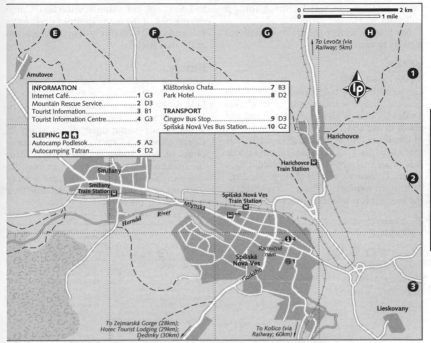

Autocamp Podlesok (☎ 4299 165; atcpodlesok@gmail.com; Podlesok; per person/tent €2/2, huts per person €9) Pitch a tent in the big field (600 capacity) or choose from A-frame cabins, small huts and cottages with two to 12 beds and a bathroom. Full restaurant on-site.

Autocamping Tatran (☎ 4297 105; www.durkovec.sk; per person/tent €3/2, dm €10, 2-person hut with shared bathroom €20; ⌨) Tents crowd together in the pasture surrounded by tiny huts and two big dormitories, neither are exactly new. Restaurant, game room and bike rental (per day €5) are available here, 2km west of Čingov.

Horec Tourist Lodging (☎ 0905742996; www.horec.xf.cz; Dobšinska Masa 62, Dedinky; s/d with shared bathroom €12/24) Eight clean, bright and basic two-bed rooms share two bathrooms, a common room and a kitchen. On the west side of the lake.

Park Hotel (☎ 4422022; www.hotelfloraslovenskyraj.sk; Hradisko, Čingov; s/d €55/34) Each of the renovated-in-'07 rooms has its own balcony overlooking a landscaped lawn, with plenty of chairs for lounging. Active types can appreciate the tennis court and sauna for post-hike recovery. A big summer terrace and even bigger menu

selection (mains €4 to €10) make this a good stop even if you're not sleeping over.

Getting There & Around

Off season especially, you may consider springing for a hire car in Košice; public transport connections can be a chore. Check schedules at http://cp.atlas.sk carefully. Four buses a day travel from Poprad to Dedinky (€2, 1¼ hours) and one (at 3.06pm) from Košice (€5, two hours).

Year-round from Spišska Nová Ves, six buses run weekdays and one on weekends (9.20am) to Čingov (€0.60, 12 minutes); two buses run weekdays only (6.35am and 2.30pm) to Hrabušice/Podlesok (€1.30, 35 minutes). You can reach Spišska Nová Ves by train from Poprad (€1.50, 25 minutes, 12 daily) and Košice (€4, 1½ hours, 12 daily), and by bus from Levoča (€0.80, 25 minutes, every half-hour). More buses (up to six) run from Spišska Nová Ves to the villages on weekends in July and August.

Weekdays there are two good connections from Poprad (6.25am and 2.25pm) to Hrabusice/Podlesok (€1.70, 50 minutes total), switching in Spišský Štrtok (only a half-hour wait).

No buses connect the trailhead villages directly to each other.

KOŠICE
☎ 055 / pop 235,300

Gather with the rest of Košice on the benches near the musical fountain, or to raise a glass at a sidewalk cafe. With so many locals out and about in the Old Town, you get a real sense of community in Slovakia's second city, one that's sorely lacking in the capital. An eclectic mix of architecture – from the Middle Ages Gothic Cathedral of St Elizabeth to the 20th-century art nouveau of Hotel Slávia – adds to the sense this is a living town worth getting

to know, not just a tourist attraction. Come during one of the many summer street festivals and you'll have plenty of opportunities to make new friends.

History

Košice received its city coat of arms in 1369 and for centuries was the eastern stronghold of the Hungarian kingdom. On 5 April 1945 the Košice Government Program – which made communist dictatorship in Czechoslovakia a virtual certainty – was announced here. Today US Steel girders form the backbone of the city; you can't miss the company's influence, from the ice-hockey stadium it sponsored to the factory flair stacks on the outskirts.

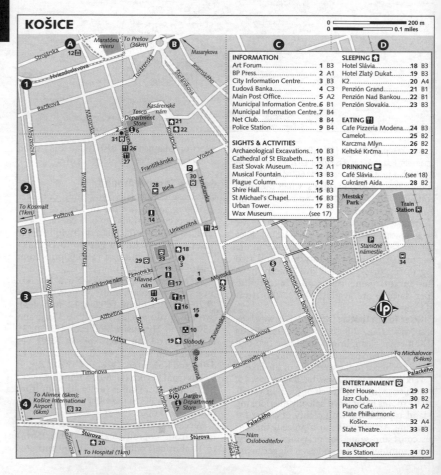

KOŠICE

INFORMATION
Art Forum..............................**1** B3
BP Press...............................**2** A1
City Information Centre...........**3** B3
Ľudová Banka........................**4** C3
Main Post Office.....................**5** A2
Municipal Information Centre...**6** B1
Municipal Information Centre...**7** B4
Net Club...............................**8** B4
Police Station.........................**9** B4

SIGHTS & ACTIVITIES
Archaeological Excavations..**10** B3
Cathedral of St Elizabeth......**11** B3
East Slovak Museum.............**12** A1
Musical Fountain..................**13** B3
Plague Column......................**14** B2
Shire Hall............................**15** B3
St Michael's Chapel..............**16** B3
Urban Tower........................**17** B3
Wax Museum.................(see 17)

SLEEPING 🏠
Hotel Slávia.........................**18** B3
Hotel Zlatý Dukat.................**19** B3
K2.......................................**20** A4
Penzión Grand......................**21** B1
Penzión Nad Bankou............**22** B1
Penzión Slovakia..................**23** B3

EATING 🍴
Cafe Pizzeria Modena....**24** B3
Camelot...............................**25** B2
Karczma Mlyn.....................**26** B2
Keltské Krčma......................**27** B2

DRINKING 🍷
Café Slávia....................(see 18)
Cukráreň Aida.....................**28** B2

ENTERTAINMENT 🎭
Beer House..........................**29** B3
Jazz Club............................**30** B2
Piano Café...........................**31** A2
State Philharmonic
  Košice...............................**32** A4
State Theatre.......................**33** B3

TRANSPORT
Bus Station..........................**34** D3

Orientation

The adjacent bus and train stations are just east of the Old Town. A five-minute walk along Mlynská brings you into Hlavná, which broadens to accommodate the squares of Nám Slobody and Hlavné nám.

Information

BOOKSHOPS

Art Forum (☎ 6232 677; Mlynská 6) Coffee-table pictorials and fiction in English; good selection by Slovak authors.
BP Press (☎ 6228 280; Hlavná 102) Foreign magazines and newspapers.

EMERGENCY

Police station (☎ 159; Pribinova 6)

INTERNET ACCESS

The City Information Centre (below) has five terminals at a cheap €0.50 per 20 minutes. Fast connections can be found at **Net Club** (☎ 6221 933; Hlavná 9; per hr €1.60; ☷ 9am-10pm).

MEDICAL SERVICES

Hospital (Fakultná Nemocnica L Pasteura; ☎ 6153 111; Rastislavova 43)

MONEY

Ľudová Banka (Mlynská 29) ATM and exchange; between the centre and transport stations.

POST

Main post office (Poštová 18)

TOURIST INFORMATION

City Information Centre (☎ 6258 888; www.kosice .sk; Hlavná 59; ☷ 9am-6pm Mon-Fri, 9am-1pm Sat, 1-5pm Sun Jun-Sep, closed Sun Oct-May) Large and official info office (read: less personable); internet access available.
Municipal Information Centre (MIC; ☎ 16 168; www.mickosice.sk) Dargov Department Store (Hlavná 2; ☷ 9am-7pm Mon-Sat, 9am-1pm Sun); Tesco Department Store (Hlavná 111; ☷ 8.30am-8.30pm Mon-Fri) Tiny info stands with a vibrant young staff and oodles of knick-knacks for sale.

Sights

Landscaped flower beds surround the **musical fountain** in the middle of Hlavná nám, across from the 1899 State Theatre. To the north stands a large baroque **plague column** from 1723.

The dark and brooding 14th-century **Cathedral of St Elizabeth** (Dóm sv Alžbety; ☎ 0908667093; adult/concession €4/2; ☷ 1-5pm Mon, 9am-5pm Tue-Fri,

9am-1pm Sat) wins the prize for sight most likely to grace your Košice postcard home. You can't miss Europe's easternmost Gothic cathedral dominating the square. Below the church, a **crypt** contains the tomb of Duke Ferenc Rákóczi, who was exiled to Turkey after the failed 18th-century Hungarian revolt against Austria. Don't forget to climb the church's **tower** for city views. To the south of the cathedral is the 14th-century **St Michael's Chapel** (adult/concession €1/0.50; ☷ 1-5pm Mon, 9am-5pm Tue-Fri, 9am-1pm Sat).

To check out the **Urban Tower** (originally built in the 14th century, rebuilt in the 1970s) you have to buy entry to the cheesy (and overpriced) **Wax Museum** (Múzeum voskových figurín; ☎ 6232 534; www.waxmuseum.sk; Hlavná 3; adult/concession €4/2.60; ☷ 11am-3pm Mon-Fri, noon-3pm Sat, 1-3pm Sun).

Get lost in the mazelike passages and tunnels of the **archaeological excavations** (☎ 6228 393; adult/concession €1/0.60; ☷ 10am-6pm Tue-Sun). The underground remains of medieval Košice – defence chambers, fortifications and waterways – weren't discovered until building work in 1996.

The 1945 Košice Government Program was proclaimed from the 1779 **Shire Hall** (Župný dom; Hlavná 27); today there's a minor art gallery inside.

The most intriguing part of the **East Slovak Museum** (Východoslovenské múzeum; ☎ 6220 309; Hviezdoslavova nám 3; adult/concession €1.30/0.70; ☷ 9am-5pm Tue-Sat, 9am-1pm Sun) is the gold treasure on display in the basement vault. During the renovation of the house at Hlavná 68 in 1935, this secret stash of 2920 gold coins dating from the 15th to 18th centuries was discovered. Anyone have a shovel?

Sleeping

The City Information Centre usually puts together a list of accommodation that includes summer dorms.

K2 (☎ 6230 909; Štúrova 32; s/d with shared bathroom €12/24) It's just a room, and a rather dowdy one at that. But what more do you want for this price in Old Town? No common room, no kitchen, no laundry.

our pick Penzión Slovakia (☎ 7289 820; www.penzion slovakia.sk; Orliá 6; s/d €48/54) A small, city guest house with loads of charm: guest quarters have wood-panelled ceilings, skylights and a mid-century mod aesthetic. Each room is named for a Slovak city. Free broadband connections, plus an excellent grill restaurant downstairs.

Penzión Grand (☎ 6337 546; www.penzionslovakia .sk; Kováčska 65; s/d/tr €46/52/66) These 2nd- and 3rd-floor lodgings (no elevator) ring an inviting interior courtyard with skylights above and a ground-floor cafe below (tasty salads). Furnishings are oddly mismatched. Wi-fi in some rooms.

Hotel Zlatý Dukat (☎ 7279 333; www.hotelzlatydukat .sk; Hlavná 16; s/d €121/131; 🖳) You'd never know from the classic contemporary design (dark wood and light linen, flat-screen TVs) that the building's history traces to the 13th century. Look through the glass floor near the reception desk to see the foundations of this story. Free wi-fi; room service available.

Yet more choices:

Penzión Nad Bankou (☎ 6838 221; Kováčska 63; s/d/tr €40/53/60) Three travelling together get quite a bargain at this guest house above a reasonable cafe.

Hotel Slávia (☎ 6224 395; www.hotelslavia.sk; Hlavná 63; s €78-80, d €90-125; 🍴 🖳) Flower-shape lights and candy-coloured pastels inside a 1902 art nouveau hotel and cafe.

Eating & Drinking

The 2nd floor of the train station has a surprising array of low-cost food options in a brightly lit, modern setting: sandwich bar, self-service Slovak food, pizza restaurant and pastry cafe. Any of the sidewalk cafes on the main square is a fine place to drink on a warm summer evening.

Cafe Pizzeria Modena (☎ 6222 788; Hlavná 40; pizza €2.50-5) A university crowd hangs out at the courtyard cafe tables here. You can also descend to the cellar restaurant to try the personal-sized pizzas and fresh salads.

Camelot (☎ 6854 039; Kovačka 19; mains €8-17) Cellar vaults and wooden trenchers certainly evoke the knightly spirit, but the food here is also darn good. Try the whole roast chicken or duck.

Practically next door to each other, both **Keltské Krčma** (☎ 6225 328; Hlavná 80; mains €7-12; 🕑 10am-11.30pm Mon-Thu, to 1am Fri & Sat, 3-11.30pm Sun) and **Karczma Mlyn** (☎ 6220 547; Hlavná 82; mains €3-8; 🕑 11am-midnight Sun-Thu, to 1am Sun) are pubs good for a pint, and for heaping portions of hearty food. The latter is more local-frequented; enter through the courtyard.

For coffee and sweets try turn-of-the-20th-century **Café Slaviá** (☎ 6233 190; Hotel Slaviá, Hlavná 63; 🕑 7am-11pm). For the most popular ice cream and cakes in town, head to **Cukráreň Aida** (☎ 6256 649; Hlavná 81; cakes €1-3; 🕑 8am-10pm).

Entertainment

The monthly publication **Kam do Mesta** (www .kamdomesta.sk) lists in Slovak the whats, wheres and whens of Košice's entertainment scene.

State Theatre (Štátne Divadlo Košice; ☎ 6221 231; www.sdke.sk; Hlavná 58; 🕑 box office 9am-5.30pm Mon-Fri, 10am-1pm Sat) Local opera and ballet companies stage performances in the 1899 neobaroque theatre from September to May.

State Philharmonic Košice (Štátna Filharmónia Košice; ☎ 6224 514; www.sfk.sk; House of the Arts, Moyzesova 66) The spring musical festival is a good time to catch performances of the city's philharmonic at the House of the Arts, but concerts take place year-round.

Beer House (☎ 0918807999; Hlavná 54; 🕑 11am-midnight Mon-Thu, 11am-2am Fri, 4pm-2am Sat, 4pm-midnight Sun) A regular schedule of live music includes rock, funk and '70s and '80s pop.

DJs spin house music most nights at both the **Jazz Club** (☎ 6224 237; Kováčska 39; 🕑 11am-midnight Mon-Thu, 11am-2am Fri, 4pm-2am Sat, 4pm-midnight Sun) and the **Piano Café** (☎ 0915517339; Hlavná 92; 🕑 10am-midnight Mon-Thu, 10am-1am Fri, 3pm-1am Sat, 3pm-midnight Sun). Watch for the occasional live jazz concert at each.

Shopping

Wander onto the alleylike 'Craftsman St' (Hrnčiarska) for some truly unique shopping – at a potter's workshop, an iron-works master, a herbalist and a gemstone studio. The leathermaker is around the corner and north on Kovačka street.

Getting There & Away

Check bus, plane and train schedules at http:// cp .atlas.sk.

AIR

Košice International airport (KSC; ☎ 6221 093; www .airportkosice.sk) is about 6km southwest of the centre. **SkyEurope** (☎ reservations 02-4850 4850; www .skyeurope.com) has up to four daily flights to/from Bratislava (one hour), one to Prague and several weekly flights to London. **ČSA** (Czech Airlines, OK; ☎ 6782 490; www.czechairlines.com) has up to five daily flights to and from Prague. **Austrian Airlines** (☎ 02-4940 2100; www.austrianairlines.com) runs a flight to Vienna every day except Saturday.

BUS

The **bus station** (☎ 6789 250; Staničné nám) sits beside the train station east of town. Buses are most efficient for getting to Levoča (€4, two hours, eight daily) or Bardejov (€3.60, two hours, 12 daily).

Eurobus (☎ 055-680 7306; www.eurobus.sk, in Slovak) handles routes in eastern Slovakia. There is one bus a day from Košice to Prague (€28, 11 hours), and one to Uzhhorod, Ukraine (€6, 2½ hours); a second, early morning bus runs from Friday to Sunday. Another option for getting to Uzhhorod is transferring to a bus in Michalovce (€2.50, one hour, four daily). Poland-bound by bus is not so easy: getting to Zakopane, for example, requires transfers in Poprad and Tatranská Javorina.

CAR
There are several big international car-rental representatives at the airport, but **Alimex** (☎ 7290 100; www.alimex.sk; Košice International Airport) is cheapest, if you're willing to drive around with adverts painted on the car.

TRAIN
The **train station** (☎ 2292 175; Staničné nám) is an easy walk from Hlavná nám. Express trains (R) run to/from Poprad (€6.50, 1¼ hours, up to 10 daily) and Žilina (€10.50, three hours, up to 14 daily). If you're commuting all the way to/from Bratislava, an IC or EC train (€19, five hours, four daily) is your best bet; even on an express train you could crawl along for more than seven hours with no dining car.

You can ride the rails from Košice to Miskolc (€4, 1½ hours, four daily) and Budapest (€25, four hours, four daily) in Hungary, and Kraków (€25, six hours, one daily). A sleeper train leaves Košice every night for Moscow (€57, 36 hours – *ugh!*) stopping in Lviv (€18, 12 hours) and Kyiv (€32, 22½ hours) in Ukraine. It also stops at Čop (€4, 2½ hours), 14km from Uzhhorod (not on the main train line), but arriving at 1am and finding a taxi isn't fun. It's easier to take a bus.

Getting Around
Transport tickets (€0.60, one zone) are good for buses and trams in most of the city; buy them from news-stands and public transport kiosks and validate on board. Bus 23 between the airport and the train station requires a two-zone ticket (€1).

BARDEJOV
☎ 054 / pop 33,374
Muted hues and intricately painted facades set apart each of Bardejov's Gothic-Renaissance

burgher houses. And yet the remarkable homogeneity of uniformly steep roofs and flat fronts helps make the main square the prettiest in Slovakia. Bardejov has been enthusiastically well preserved since the 15th century (there's always some scaffolding signalling upkeep) and deservedly made Unesco's World Heritage list in 2000. Today the quiet square is the tourist draw, but there are a few museums, including one that sheds light on this region's Eastern-facing religious art. Venture a couple of kilometres north of town to Bardejovské Kúpele, and you can take a cure at a thermal spa or explore traditional culture at an open-air village museum. Wooden churches in the area reflect the Carpatho-Rusyn heritage that the area shares with neighbouring parts of Ukraine and Poland.

History
Bardejov received its royal charter in 1376, and grew rich on trade between Poland and Russia. After an abortive 17th-century revolt against the Habsburgs, Bardejov's fortunes declined. In late 1944 heavy WWII fighting took place at the Dukla Pass on the Polish border, 54km northeast of Bardejov.

Orientation
The main square, Radničné nám, is a 600m walk southwest of the bus and train station. Some old town walls still encircle the city, enter through the gate off Slovenská at Baštová.

Information
ČSOB (Radničné nám 7) Exchange and ATM.
Golem Internet Café (Radničné nám 35; per hr €1; ☯ 9am-11pm Mon-Fri, 1-11pm Sat & Sun)
Main post office (Dlhý rad 14)
Tourist information centre (☎ 4723 013; www .bardejov.sk; Radničné nám 21; ☯ 9am-6.30pm Mon-Fri & 9am-4pm Sat & Sun May-Sep, 9am-5pm Mon-Fri, 9am-4pm Sat & 1-4pm Sun Oct-Apr) Loads of info, souvenirs and guide services.

Sights
There are two branches of the **Šariš Museum** (☎ 4724 966; www.muzeumbardejov.sk; ☯ 8am-noon & 12.30-4pm Tue-Sun) Icon Exposition (Expozícia ikony; Radničné nám 27; adult/concession €2/1); town hall (radnica; Radničné nám 48; adult/concession €2/1) worth seeing. In the centre square, the town hall contains altarpieces and a historical collection. Built in 1509, it was the first Renaissance building in

Slovakia. At the Icon Exposition more than 130 dazzling icons from the 16th to 19th centuries are on display. The religious art originally decorated Greek Catholic and Orthodox churches east of Bardejov.

The interior of the 15th-century **Basilica of St Egídius** (Bazilika Sv Egídia; Radničné nám; adult/concession €1/0.80; ☼ 10am-3.30pm Mon-Fri, to 2.30pm Sat) is packed with no fewer than 11 Gothic altarpieces, built from 1460 to 1510.

Sleeping & Eating

Penzión Semafor (☎ 0905830984; www.penzion semafor.sk; Kellerova 13; s/d €24/32, apt s/d €28/38) The five bright doubles in this family-run guest house share a communal kitchen and laundry; two more-spacious 'apartment' rooms have small kitchens of their own.

Hotel Bellevue (☎ 4728 404; www.bellevuehotel.sk; Mihalov 2503; s/d €64/84; ☒ ☐ ☒) Glass-enclosed pool, landscaped gardens and leafy surrounds are the main selling points for this hotel on a hill, 3km south of centre. There is a special-evening-out restaurant and great views.

el. Restaurant & Lodging (☎ 4728 404; www.el -restaurant.sk; Stöcklova 43; mains €3-9) An emphasis on fine ingredients make even the traditional Slovak dishes here seem fresh. The large variety of salads and vegetarian dishes is novel too. Access to room service is one of the best things about the three modern rooms for rent upstairs (single/double including breakfast €24/40).

Other eats:

Maja Sendvič (☎ 091941064; Radničné nám 15; sandwiches €1.50-3; ☼ 8am-9pm Mon-Fri, 1-11pm Sat, 3-9pm Sun) Big baguette sandwiches to go.

Reštaurácia Hubert (Radničné nám 4; mains €4-12) Game dishes and meaty fare.

Getting There & Away

Bardejov is on a spur train line from Prešov, so buses are most convenient. They run between Bardejov and Košice (€4, 1¾ hours, 13 daily) and to/from Poprad (€5, 2½ hours, eight daily). You can bus it to Bardejovské Kúpele (€0.40, five to 10 minutes) every half-hour or so.

Though you're close to Poland here, you're not near a main bus route. For those with a car, the E371 crosses into Poland north of Svidník, a town 35km east of Bardejov.

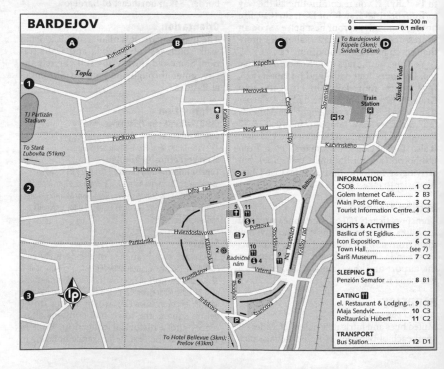

BARDEJOV

0 ——————— 200 m
0 ——————— 0.1 miles

INFORMATION
ČSOB.............................1 C2
Golem Internet Café.........2 B3
Main Post Office..............3 C2
Tourist Information Centre..4 C3

SIGHTS & ACTIVITIES
Basilica of St Egídius.........5 C2
Icon Exposition................6 C3
Town Hall..................(see 7)
Šariš Museum..................7 C2

SLEEPING
Penzión Semafor 8 B1

EATING
el. Restaurant & Lodging...9 C3
Maja Sendvič..................10 C3
Reštaurácia Hubert..........11 C2

TRANSPORT
Bus Station......................12 D1

WORTH THE TRIP: WOODEN CHURCHES

Travelling east from Bardejov, you come to the crossroads of Western and Eastern Christianity. The Greek Catholic (or Uniate) and Orthodox faithful living in the region in the 17th to 19th centuries built intricate onion-domed wooden churches (many without nails) and decorated them with elaborate icon screens and interior paintings. In July of 2008, eight eastern Slovak wooden churches were added to the Unesco World Heritage list, including one Catholic and two Protestant, but there are many more to see than that. (The Greek Catholic Presov Diocese website, www .grkatpo.sk/drevenecerk, has an extensive list.) Most of the churches are in isolated villages with limited bus connections and fewer services. Buy a *Wooden Churches Around Bardejov* booklet at the Bardejov tourist information centre (p487) for a self-driving tour of vernacular architecture in that area, including the oldest listed church at **Hervatov** (c 1500). Others, such as the listed churches at **Ladomirá** and **Bodružal** are closer to Svidník.

AROUND BARDEJOV

Three short kilometres to the north, with frequent local bus connections, you'll find the parklike spa town of **Bardejovské Kúpele**. If you want to book a service (mineral bath €10, 15-minute massage €7), you have to go in person to the **Spa House** (Kúpelny dom; ☎ 4774 225; ⏰ 8am-noon & 1-5pm Mon-Sat) at the top of the main pedestrian street. Across the way is the **Museum of Folk Architecture** (Múzeum Ľudovej Architektúry; ☎ 4722 070; adult/concession €1.30/0.70; ⏰ 9am-5pm Tue-Sun, to 3pm Oct-Apr), the oldest *skanzen* (open-air museum) in Slovakia. One of the Unesco-listed wooden churches is among the many traditional buildings relocated here. If you have a car, park in the lot by the bus station at the base of the village and walk up; the whole village is pedestrian-only.

SLOVAKIA DIRECTORY

ACCOMMODATION

For every season there is a price: May to September is considered tourist season, but prices top out around Christmas/New Year and Easter holidays. From October to April, rates drop dramatically (10% to 50%). We quote tourist-season prices. A midrange double room in Bratislava will run from €60 to €150, luxury digs upwards of that (often in the €250 range), and a dorm bed costs around €25. Reviews in this chapter are ordered according to price; a tourist tax of at least €1 is not included. Breakfast can usually be added for €4 to €8 and parking is widely available outside Bratislava. Rooms in this chapter include private bathroom unless otherwise stated. These days most lodgings have at least some nonsmoking rooms, though you'll still come across a few smoking-only accommodations.

Most camping grounds open from May to September and are accessible on public transport. Many have a restaurant and assorted cheap cabins. Wild camping is prohibited in national parks.

Outside Bratislava there are few backpacker-style hostels in Slovakia. Student dormitories throughout the country open to tourists in July and August. If you're looking for cheap sleeps outside those months, *ubytovňa* is the word to know. These are hostels for workers (in cities) or Slovak tourists (near natural attractions) that usually have basic, no-nonsense shared-bathroom singles and doubles or dorms.

Tourist towns outside the capital usually have private rooms, usually with shared facilities, for rent; look for signs reading '*privat*' or '*zimmer frei*' (from €10 per person). Information offices and websites sometimes have lists of renters.

Pensions are guest houses, with en-suite bathrooms, that have fewer services but more character than hotels.

ACTIVITIES

Slovakia is one of central Europe's best areas for hiking. You can take it relatively easy in the low mountains of Malá Fatra National Park (p470), hike higher elevation trails in the High Tatras (p473) or climb up ladders and foot holds through a challenging gorge ascent in Slovenský raj (p482). For even more adrenalin, sign up with one of the local mountain guides (p474) to scale the tallest peaks.

The High Tatras ski resorts (www.vt.sk and www.parksnow.sk) have some of Europe's cheapest alpine skiing, a day's lift ticket costs about €25. The season runs from December to April. See p474 for more.

BUSINESS HOURS

Restaurants nationwide are generally open from 10am to 10pm. Stand-alone shops open around 9am and close at 5pm or 6pm weekdays and at noon on Saturdays. The local *potraviny* (supermarket) hours are from 6.30am or 7am until 5pm or 6pm Monday to Friday and from 7am to noon on Saturday. Big-name chain grocery and department stores (Tesco, Billa etc) have longer hours, typically until 9pm for downtown branches and 24 hours for suburban hyper-markets.

Bank hours are from about 8am to 5pm Monday to Thursday, and until 4pm Friday. Post offices work from 8am to 7pm Monday to Friday and until 11am Saturday.

Most museums and castles are closed on Monday. Many tourist attractions outside the capital open only from May to September.

DANGERS & ANNOYANCES

Crime is low compared with Western Europe, but pickpocketing does happen. Just be aware. Never leave anything on the seat of an unattended vehicle, even a locked one; apparently that's advertising you don't want it any more.

EMBASSIES & CONSULATES

Australia and New Zealand do not have embassies in Slovakia; the nearest are in Vienna and Berlin respectively. The following are all in Bratislava:

Austria (Map p458; ☎ 02-5443 1334; www.embassy austria.sk; Ventúrska 10)
Czech Republic (Map p458; ☎ 02-5920 3303; www .mzv.cz/bratislava/; Hviezdoslavovo nám 8)
France (Map p458; ☎ 02-5934 7111; www.france.sk; Hlavné nám 7)
Germany (Map p458; ☎ 02-5920 4400; www.pressburg .diplo.de; Hviezdoslavovo nám 10)
Ireland (Map p458; ☎ 02-5930 9611; www.dfa.ie; Carlton Savoy Bldg, Mostová 2)
Netherlands (Map p457; ☎ 02-5262 5081; www .holandskoweb.com; Frana Kráľa 5)
UK (Map p458; ☎ 02-5998 2000; www.britishembassy .sk; Panská 16)
USA (Map p458; ☎ 02-5443 0861; http://slovakia .usembassy.gov; Hviezdoslavovo nám 4)

FESTIVALS & EVENTS

During summer months folk festivals take place all over Slovakia. In late June, early July, folk dancers and musicians gather at the biggest, **Východná Folklore Festival** (www.obec-vychodna

.sk, in Slovak), 32km west of Poprad. Weeks-long musical festivals with daily concerts are big in both Bratislava (p461) and Košice. The **Slovak Spectator** (www.slovakspectator.sk) newspaper lists events countrywide.

HOLIDAYS

New Year's & Independence Day 1 January
Three Kings Day 6 January
Good Friday & Easter Monday March/April
Labour Day 1 May
Victory over Fascism Day 8 May
SS Cyril & Methodius Day 5 July
SNP Day 29 August
Constitution Day 1 September
Our Lady of Sorrows Day 15 September
All Saints' Day 1 November
Christmas 24 to 26 December

INTERNET RESOURCES

Kompas (www.kompas.sk) Searchable countrywide map site.
Lodge Yourself (www.ubytujsa.sk) Places to stay in Slovakia.
Slovak Tourism Board (www.slovakiatourism.sk) Comprehensive overview and practicalities: history, culture, accommodation and restaurant listings.
Slovakia Document Store (www.panorama.sk) Great online bookstore, plus countrywide info.
What's On Slovakia (www.whatsonslovakia.com) Event listings.

MONEY

As of January 2009, Slovakia's currency is the euro. You'll still hear reference to the former currency, the Slovak crown, or Slovenská koruna (Sk).

Almost all banks have exchange desks and there are usually branches in or near the town square. ATMs are quite common even in smaller towns, but shouldn't be relied upon in villages. In Bratislava, credit cards are widely accepted. Elsewhere, Visa and MasterCard are accepted at most hotels and at higher category restaurants (though only if you announce before requesting the bill that you plan to pay with credit).

If you stay in a hostel in Bratislava, eat your meals in local pubs and use local transport, you can expect to spend €40 a day, if you're looking to bed down in pensions and dine in smarter eateries, count on €100 per day. You can get by on less out in the provinces, but there aren't many hostels. Concession admission prices are generally good for children younger than 12, students with ID, and seniors older than 65.

POST

Poste restante sent to Bratislava (c/o Poste restante, 81000 Bratislava 1), can be picked up at the **main post office** (Map p458; Nám SNP 34-35, Bratislava) and will be kept for one month.

TELEPHONE

Slovakia's country code is ☎ 421. Landline numbers can have either seven or eight digits. Mobile phone numbers are often used for business; they start with ☎ 09. When dialling from abroad, you need to drop the zero from both city area codes and mobile phone numbers.

To dial internationally from inside Slovakia, dial ☎ 00, the country code and the number.

Payphones require *telefónna karta* (telephone cards), purchased from newsagents, for local calls. International phone cards, like **EZ Phone** (www.ezcard.sk; per min to UK & USA €0.60) can also be bought.

TOURIST INFORMATION

The **Association of Information Centres of Slovakia** (AICES; ☎ 16 186; www.aices.sk) is an extensive network of city information centres. There's no Slovakia-wide information office; your best bet is to go online to the **Slovak Tourist Board** (www.slovakiatourism.sk).

TRAVELLERS WITH DISABILITES

Slovakia is behind many EU countries in terms of facilities for travellers with disabilities. Few hotels and restaurants have ramps or barrier-free rooms. **Slovak Union for the Disabled** (Slovenský zväz telesne postihnutých; ☎ 02-6381 4478; www.sztp.sk) works to change the status quo.

VISAS

Citizens of other EU countries do not require visas. Visitors from Australia, New Zealand, Canada, Japan and the US can enter visa-free for up to 90 days. South Africans need a visa. For a full list, see www.mzv.sk (under 'Ministry' and then 'Travel'). If you do require

---

EMERGENCY NUMBERS

- Ambulance ☎ 112
- Fire ☎ 112
- Police ☎ 112

---

a visa, it must be bought in advance – they are not issued on arrival.

TRANSPORT IN SLOVAKIA

GETTING THERE & AWAY

Air

Between June and September, SkyEurope runs flights from Bratislava to Split and Dubrovnik in Croatia. Czech Airlines shuttles regularly between Prague and both Bratislava and Košice.

Most of the other cities you can reach by air from Bratislava are within Western Europe; British destinations are particularly well represented by Ryanair and SkyEurope. SkyEurope also flies to London from Košice and Poprad.

Vienna International airport (VIE; www.viennaairport .com), 60km from Bratislava, is served by a vast range of flights. Buses connect to Bratislava's bus station and airport almost hourly.

Airlines flying to and from Slovakia:
Austrian Airlines (OS; ☎ 02-4940 2100; www.austrian airlines.com)
Czech Airlines (cOK; ☎ 02-5720 0710; www.czech airlines.com)
Ryanair (FR; ☎ 353-1 249 7791; www.ryanair.com)
SkyEurope Airlines (NE; ☎ 02-4850 1000; www.sky europe.com)

Land

After Slovakia became a member of the Schengen Agreement within the EU in 2007, land border crossings with other member states (Austria, Czech Republic, Poland and Hungary) were eliminated. This makes the check coming into Slovakia (and the EU) at the Ukraine border even more strenuous. Expect a delay as guards search for contraband cigarettes and vodka.

BUS

The best search engine for international and domestic bus schedules is http://cp.atlas.sk. The major hubs for departures to Eastern and Western Europe destinations are Bratislava (p456) and Košice (p484). There are also buses to Poland from Poprad (p477).

CAR & MOTORCYCLE

As well as your vehicle's registration papers, you need a 'green card', which shows you are covered by at least third-party liability insurance. Your vehicle must display a nationality sticker and carry a first-aid kit and warning triangle.

TRAIN

Direct trains connect Bratislava (p464) with the Czech Republic, Austria, Poland and Hungary, while trains from Košice (p487) head to Hungary, Poland, Russia and Ukraine. The website http://cp.atlas.sk has international and domestic schedules.

River

During spring and summer, Danube riverboats offer an alternative way to get between Bratislava and neighbouring Danube cities. See p463 for details.

GETTING AROUND
Bicycle

Roads are often narrow and potholed, and in towns cobblestones and tram tracks can prove dangerous for bike riders. Theft's a problem, so a lock is a must. Bike rental is uncommon outside the mountains. The cost of transporting a bike by rail is usually 10% of the train ticket.

Bus

National buses run by **Slovenská autobusová doprava** (SAD; www.sad.sk) are comparably priced to trains, but less convenient for most cities in this chapter. Search schedules at http://cp.atlas.sk. When looking at bus timetables in terminals, beware of the footnotes (fewer buses may go on weekends). It's helpful to know that *premáva* means 'it operates' and *nepremáva* means 'it doesn't operate'.

Car & Motorcycle

All foreign driving licences with photo ID are valid in Slovakia.

In order to use Slovakia's motorways (denoted by green signs), all vehicles must have a motorway sticker *(nálepka)*, which should be displayed in the windscreen. Rental cars come with them. You can buy stickers at petrol stations.

Parking restrictions are eagerly enforced with bright orange tyre boots. Always buy a ticket, either from a machine, or from the attendant wandering around with a waist pack, and put it on your dashboard.

Both Bratislava and Košice airports have international car-rental agencies.

Local Transport

City buses and trams operate from around 4.30am to 11.30pm daily. Tickets are sold at public transport offices and at news-stands. In Bratislava, some stops have ticket-vending machines. Validate tickets in the red machines on board or you could face a fine of up to €50.

Train

Slovak Republic Railways (Železnice Slovenskej Republiky or ŽSR; ☎ 18 188; www.zsr.sk) provides a cheap and efficient rail service. Most of the places covered in this chapter are on or near the main railway line between Bratislava and Košice. Check schedules at http://cp.atlas.sk.

Slovenia

It's a tiny place, about half the size of Switzerland, and counts just over two million people. But the only way to describe pint-sized Slovenia (Slovenija), an independent republic bordering Italy, Austria, Hungary, Croatia and the Adriatic Sea, is that it's 'a mouse that roars'.

Slovenia has been dubbed a lot of things since independence in 1991 – 'Europe in Miniature', 'the Sunny Side of the Alps', 'the Green Piece of Europe' – and, though they may sound like tourist-brochure blurbs, they're all true. From beaches, snow-capped mountains, hills awash in grapevines and wide plains blanketed in sunflowers, to Gothic churches, baroque palaces and art nouveau civic buildings, Slovenia offers more diversity than countries many times its size. Its incredible mixture of climates brings warm Mediterranean breezes up to the foothills of the Alps, where it can even snow in summer. With more than half of its total area covered in forest, Slovenia truly is one of the greenest countries in the world – and in recent years it has also become Europe's activities playground.

Among Slovenia's greatest assets, though, are the Slovenes themselves – welcoming, generous, multilingual, broad-minded. As far as they are concerned, they do not live emotionally, spiritually or even geographically in 'Eastern' Europe – their home is the very heart of the continent.

SLOVENIA

FAST FACTS

- **Area** 20,273 sq km
- **Capital** Ljubljana
- **Currency** euro (€); US$1 = €0.73; UK£1 = €1.06; A$1 = €0.50; ¥100 = €0.76; NZ$1 = €0.41
- **Famous for** hiking and skiing, Lake Bled, Lipizzaner horses, *pršut* (air-dried ham)
- **Official language** Slovene
- **Phrases** *dober dan* (hello); *živijo* (hi); *prosim* (please); *hvala* (thank you); *oprostite* (excuse me); *nasvidenje* (goodbye)
- **Population** 2.018 million
- **Telephone codes** country code ☎ 386; international access code ☎ 00
- **Visas** not required for most nationalities; see p528

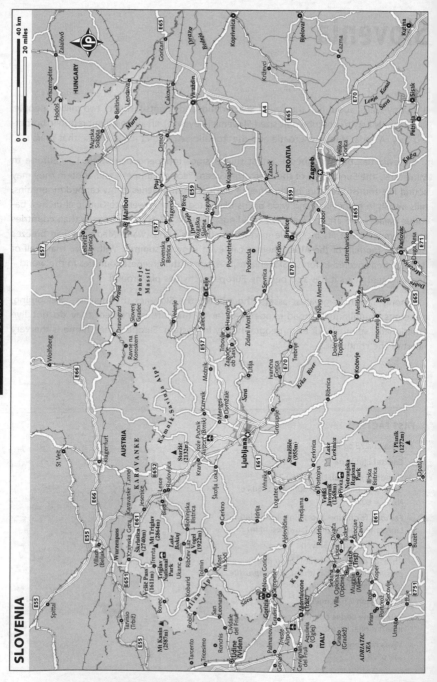

HIGHLIGHTS

- Experience the architecture, hilltop castle, green spaces and cafe life of **Ljubljana** (p497), Slovenia's capital.
- Wax romantic at the picture-postcard setting of **Bled** (p509): the lake, the island, the hilltop castle.
- Get into the outdoors or in the bluer-than-blue Soča in the majestic mountain scenery at **Bovec** (p514), arguably the country's best outdoor activities centre.
- Explore the series of karst caves at **Škocjan** (p517) a scene straight out of Jules Verne's *A Journey to the Centre of the Earth*.
- Swoon at wonderful Venetian architecture in the romantic port of **Piran** (p520).

ITINERARIES

- **Three days** Enjoy a long weekend in Ljubljana, sampling the capital's museums and nightlife, with an excursion to Bled.
- **One week** Spend a couple of days in Ljubljana, then head north to unwind in Bohinj or romantic Bled beside idyllic mountain lakes. Depending on the season take a bus or drive over the hairraising Vršič Pass into the valley of the vivid blue Soča River and take part in some extreme sports in Bovec or Kobarid before returning to Ljubljana.

CLIMATE & WHEN TO GO

The ski season generally lasts from December to March, though heavy snowfall can keep the Vršič Pass closed as late as May. Spring is a great time to be in the lowlands, though it can be pretty wet in May and June. At the same time, the days are getting longer and off-season rates apply. Hotel prices rise in summer, peaking in August, when rooms can be hard to come by on the coast. Warm September days are calm and ideal for hiking and climbing, while October and November can be rainy.

HISTORY

Slovenes can make a credible claim to have invented democracy. By the early 7th century their Slavic forebears had founded the Duchy of Carantania (Karantanija), based at Krn Castle (now Karnburg in Austria). Ruling dukes were elected by ennobled commoners and invested before ordinary citizens. This model was noted by the 16th-century French political theorist Jean Bodin, whose work was a key reference for Thomas Jefferson when he wrote the American Declaration of Independence in 1775–76. Carantania (later Carinthia) was fought over by Franks and Magyars from the 8th to 10th centuries, and later divided up among Austro-Germanic nobles and bishops. By 1335 Carantania and most of present-day Slovenia, with the exception of the Venetian-controlled coastal towns, were dominated by the Habsburgs.

Indeed, Austria ruled what is now Slovenia until 1918, apart from a brief interlude between 1809 and 1813 when Napoleon created six 'Illyrian Provinces' from Slovenian and Croatian regions and made Ljubljana the capital. Napoleon proved a popular conqueror as his relatively liberal regime de-Germanised the education system. Slovene was taught in schools for the first time, leading to a blossoming of national consciousness. In tribute, Ljubljana still has a French Revolution Sq (Trg Francoske Revolucije) with a column bearing a likeness of the French emperor.

Fighting during WWI was particularly savage along the Soča Valley – what would later become known as the Isonzo Front, which was occupied by Italy then dramatically retaken by German-led Austrian-Hungarian forces. The war ended with the collapse of Austria-Hungary, which handed western Slovenia to Italy as part of postwar reparations. Northern Carinthia, including the towns of Beljak and Celovec (now Villach and Klagenfurt), voted

---

CONNECTIONS: MOVING ON FROM SLOVENIA

As wonderful as Slovenia is, it is extremely well placed to leave. Border formalities with Slovenia's three European Union neighbours – Italy, Austria and Hungary – are almost nonexistent and all are accessible by train (p528) and (less frequently) bus (p528), as are many other European nations. Venice can also be reached by boat from Izola (p520) and Piran (p523). As a member state that forms part of the EU's external frontier, Slovenia must implement the strict Schengen border rules, so expect a somewhat closer inspection of your documents – national ID (for EU citizens) or passport and, in some cases, visa – when travelling by train or bus to/from Croatia.

SLOVENIA

to stay with Austria in a 1920 plebiscite. What remained of Slovenia joined fellow south (*jug*) Slavs in forming the Kingdom of Serbs, Croats and Slovenes, later Yugoslavia.

Nazi occupation in WWII was for the most part resisted by Slovenian partisans, though after Italy capitulated in 1943 the anti-partisan Slovenian Domobranci (Home Guards) were active in the west and, in a bid to prevent the communists from taking political control in liberated areas, threw their support behind the Germans. The war ended with Slovenia regaining Italian-held areas from Piran to Bovec, but losing Trst (Trieste) and part of divided Gorica (Gorizia).

Slovenia, with only 8% of the national population, was the economic powerhouse of Tito's Yugoslavia, producing up to 20% of the national GDP. By the 1980s the federation was becoming increasingly Serb-dominated, and Slovenes, who already felt taken for granted economically, feared losing their political autonomy. After free elections, Slovenia broke away from Yugoslavia on 25 June 1991. A 10-day war that left 66 people dead followed; rump Yugoslavia swiftly signed a truce in order to concentrate on regaining control of coastal Croatia. Slovenia was admitted to the UN in May 1992 and, together with nine other 'accession' countries, became a member of the EU in May 2004. In January 2007 Slovenia replaced the tolar with the euro as the national currency.

Slovenia shared the presidency of the EU Council with France in 2008, the same year

that saw the death of President Janez Drnovšek of cancer at age 57. In the national elections of October of that year, Janez Janša's coalition government was defeated by the Social Democrats under Borut Pahor, who was able to form a coalition with three minority parties.

PEOPLE

The population of Slovenia is largely homogeneous. More than 87% are ethnic Slovenes, with the remainder being Croats, Serbians, Bosnians and Roma; there are also small enclaves of Italians and Hungarians, who have special deputies looking after their interests in parliament. Slovenes are ethnically Slavic, typically multilingual and extroverts. Just under 58% of Slovenes identify themselves as Roman Catholics.

ARTS

Slovenia's most cherished writer is the Romantic poet France Prešeren (1800–49), whose statue commands Ljubljana's central square. Prešeren's patriotic yet humanistic verse was a driving force in raising Slovene national consciousness. Fittingly, a stanza of his poem *Zdravljica* (A Toast) comprise the lyrics of the national anthem.

Many of Ljubljana's most characteristic architectural features, including its recurring pyramid motif, were added by celebrated Slovenian architect Jože Plečnik (1872–1957), whose work fused classical architectural principles and folk-art traditions.

Slovenia has some excellent modern and contemporary artists, including Rudi Skočir, whose style reflects a taste for Viennese art nouveau. A favourite sculptor-cum-designer is Oskar Kogoj, whose work has become increasingly commercial in recent years.

Postmodernist painting and sculpture were more or less dominated from the 1980s by the multimedia group Neue Slowenische Kunst (NSK) and the artists' cooperative Irwin. It also spawned the internationally known industrial-music group Laibach, whose leader, Tomaž Hostnik, died tragically in 1983 when he hanged himself from a *kozolec*, the traditional (and iconic) hayrack found almost everywhere in Slovenia. Slovenia's vibrant music scene embraces rave, techno, jazz, punk, thrash-metal and *chanson* (torch songs from the likes of Vita Mavrič); the most popular local rock group is Siddharta, the only Slovenian band ever to appear on MTV. There's also a folk-music revival: listen for the groups Katice, Brina and Katalena, who play traditional Slovenian music with a modern twist. Terra Folk is the quintessential world music band.

Another way to hear traditional music is to attend the fun-filled Ljubljana-based 'Slovenian Evening' of folk music and dancing (audience participation mandatory) along with a four-course meal of Slovenian specialities plus wine run by an outfit called **Žídana Marela** (☎ 040-363 272; www.zidanamarela.si; €33). Groups depart from the Prešeren monument at 7.15pm on Wednesday and Friday year-round and proceed to the Skriti Kot (Hidden Corner), a restaurant in the shopping mall below Trg Ajdovščina. Just follow the guide with the red umbrella.

Well-received Slovenian films in recent years include *Kruh in Mleko* (Bread & Milk, 2001), the tragic story of a dysfunctional small-town family by Jan Cvitkovič, and Damjan Kozole's *Rezerni Deli* (Spare Parts, 2003) about the trafficking of illegal immigrants through Slovenia from Croatia to Italy by a couple of embittered misfits living in the southern town of Krško, site of the nation's only nuclear power plant. Much lighter is *Petelinji Zajtrk* (Rooster's Breakfast, 2007), a romance by Marko Naberšnik set in Gornja Radgona on the Austrian border in northeast Slovenia.

ENVIRONMENT

Slovenia is amazingly green; indeed, just under 57% of its total surface area is covered in forest. It is home to almost 3200 plant species – some 70 of which are indigenous. Triglav National Park is particularly rich in native flowering plants. Among the more peculiar endemic fauna in Slovenia is a blind salamander called *Proteus anguinus* that lives deep in karst caves, can survive for years without eating and has been called a 'living fossil'.

FOOD & DRINK

It's relatively hard to find such archetypal Slovenian foods as *žlikrofi* ('ravioli' filled with cheese, bacon and chives), *brodet* (fish soup) from the coast, *ajdovi žganci z ocvirki* (buckwheat 'porridge' with savoury pork crackling/scratchings) and salad greens doused in *bučno olje* (pumpkinseed oil); generally these are dishes eaten at home. A *gostilna* or *gostišče* (inn) or *restavracija* (restaurant), which are generally open 10am or 11am to 10pm or 11pm, more frequently serves *rižota* (risotto), *klobasa* (sausage), *zrezek* (cutlet/steak), *golaž*

(goulash) and *paprikaš* (piquant chicken or beef 'stew'). *Riba* (fish) is usually priced by the *dag* (100g). *Postrv* (freshwater trout) generally costs half the price of sea fish, though grilled squid *(lignji na žaru)* doused in garlic butter is usually a bargain.

Common in Slovenia are such Balkan favourites as *cevapčiči* (spicy meatballs of beef or pork), *pljeskavica* (spicy meat patties) and *ražnjiči* (shish kebabs), often served with *krompir* (potatoes).

You can snack cheaply on takeaway pizza slices or pieces of *burek* (€2 to €3), flaky pastry sometimes stuffed with meat, cheese or apple. Alternatives include *štruklji* (cottage-cheese dumplings) and *palačinke* (thin sweet pancakes).

Some restaurants have *dnevno kosilo* (set lunches), including *juha* (soup) and *solata* (salad), for as low as €5. This can be less than the price of a cheap main course, and usually one option will be vegetarian.

Tap water is safe to drink everywhere. Distinctively Slovenian wines include peppery red Teran made from Refošk grapes in the Karst region, Cviček, a dry light red – almost rosé – *vino* (wine) from eastern Slovenia and Malvazija, a straw-colour white wine from the coast that is light and dry. Slovenes are justly proud of their top vintages, but cheaper bar-standard 'open wine' *(odprto vino)* sold by the decilitre (0.1L) is often rot-gut.

Pivo (beer), whether *svetlo* (lager) or *temno* (dark), is best on *točeno* (draught).

There are dozens of kinds of *žganje* (fruit brandy) available, including *češnjevec* (made with cherries), *sadjevec* (mixed fruit), *brinjevec* (juniper), *hruška* (pears, also called *viljamovka*) and *slivovka* (plums).

Like many other countries in Europe, Slovenia bans smoking across the board in all public places, including restaurants, bars and hotels.

LJUBLJANA

☎ 01 / pop 216,200

Ljubljana is by far Slovenia's largest and most populous city. It is also the nation's political, economic and cultural capital. As such, virtually everything of national importance begins, ends or is taking place in Ljubljana.

But it can be difficult to get a grip on the place. In many ways the city whose name *almost* means 'beloved' (*ljubljena*) in Slovene

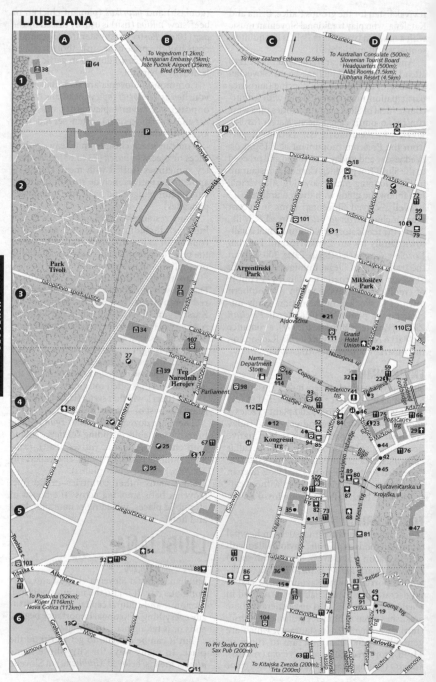

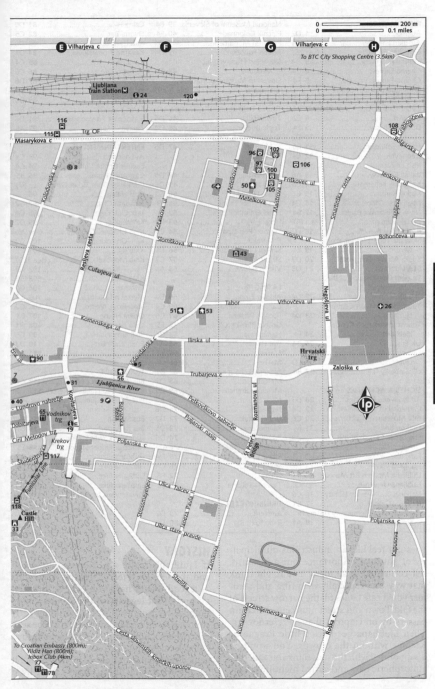

SLOVENIA

does not feel like an industrious municipality of national importance but a pleasant, self-contented small town. You might think that way too, especially in spring and summer when cafe tables fill the narrow streets of the Old Town and street musicians entertain passers-by on Čopova ul and Prešernov trg. Then Ljubljana becomes a little Prague or Kraków without the crowds. You won't be disappointed with the museums and galleries, atmospheric bars and varied nightlife either.

HISTORY

If Ljubljana really was founded by Jason and the Golden Fleece–seeking Argonauts as legend would have you believe, they left no proof. But legacies of the Roman city of Emona – remnants of walls, dwellings, early churches, even a gilded statuette – can be seen everywhere. Ljubljana took its present form as Laibach under the Austrian Habsburgs, but it gained regional prominence in 1809, when it became the capital of Napoleon's short-lived

'Illyrian Provinces'. Some fine art nouveau buildings filled up the holes left by a devastating earthquake in 1895, and architect Jože Plečnik continued the remake of the city up until WWII.

ORIENTATION

Prešernov trg, on the left bank of the Ljubljanica River, is the heart of Ljubljana. Just across delightful Triple Bridge is the picturesque – if bite-sized – Old Town, which follows the north and west flanks of Castle Hill. The bus and train stations are 800m northeast of Prešernov trg up Miklošičeva c.

Ljubljana's Jože Pučnik Airport, at Brnik near Kranj, is 27km north of the city.

Maps

Excellent free maps, some of which show the city's bus network, are available from the tourist offices (see p502). The more detailed 1:20,000-scale *Mestni Načrt Ljubljana* (Ljubljana City Map; €7.70) from Kod & Kam is available at news-stands and bookshops.

INFORMATION
Bookshops

Geonavtik (☎ 252 70 27; www.geonavtik.com; Kongresni trg 1; ☯ 8.30am-8.30pm Mon-Fri, 8.30am-4pm Sat) Stocks guides and books about Slovenia.
Knjigarna Behemot (☎ 251 13 92; www.behemot .si; Židovska steza 3; ☯ 10am-8pm Mon-Fri, 10am-3pm Sat) Pint-size English-language bookshop for bibliophiles.
Kod & Kam (☎ 200 27 32; www.gzs-dd.si/kod&kam; Trg Francoske Revolucije 7; ☯ 8am-8pm Mon-Fri, 8am-1pm Sat) Map specialists.

Discount Cards

The Ljubljana Card (€12.50), valid for three days (72 hours) and available from the tourist offices (p502), offers free admission to many museums, unlimited city bus travel and dis-counts on organised tours, accommodation and restaurants, hire cars etc.

Internet Access

Web connection is available at virtually all hostels and hotels, the Slovenia Tourist Information Centre (p502; €1 per half-hour), STA Ljubljana (p502; €1 per 20 minutes) and Student Organisation of the University of Ljubljana (p502; free). In addition:
Cyber Café Xplorer (☎ 430 19 91; Petkovškovo nabrežje 23; per 30min/hr/5hr €2.50/4/12; ☯ 10am-10pm Mon-Fri, 2-10pm Sat & Sun) Ljubljana's best internet cafe, with 10 superfast computers, wi-fi and international phone calls at €0.10 per minute.
DrogArt (☎ 439 72 70; Kolodvorska ul 20; 1st 15min free, then per 30min/hr €1/1.80; ☯ 10am-4pm Mon-Fri) Opposite the train station.
Portal.si Internet (☎ 234 46 00; Trg OF 4; per hr €3.80; ☯ 7am-8.30pm) In the bus station (get code from window No 4).

Internet Resources

City of Ljubljana (www.ljubljana.si) Comprehensive information portal on every aspect of life and tourism.

Laundry

Washing machines (€5 per load) are available, even to nonguests, at the Celica Hostel (p504). Commercial laundries, including **Chemo Express** (☎ 251 44 04; Wolfova ul 12; ☯ 7am-6pm Mon-Fri); Tabor (☎ 23107 82; Vidovdanska ul 2), charge from €4.20 per kg.

Left Luggage

Bus station (Trg OF 4; per day €2; ☯ 5.30am-10.30pm Sun-Fri, 5am-10pm Sat) Window No 3.
Train station (Trg OF 6; per day €2-3; ☯ 24hr) Coin lockers on platform No 1.

Medical Services

Central Pharmacy (Centralna Lekarna; ☎ 244 23 60; Prešernov trg 5; ☯ 7.30am-8pm Mon-Fri, 8am-1pm Sat)

LJUBLJANA IN TWO DAYS

Take the funicular up to **Ljubljana Castle** (p502) to get an idea of the lay of the land. After a seafood lunch at **Ribca** (p506), explore the Old Town then cross the Ljubljanica River via St James Bridge and walk north along bust-lined Vegova ul to Kongresni trg and **Prešernov trg** (p502). Over a fortifying libation at **Kavarna Tromostovje** (p506), plan your evening: low key at **Jazz Club Gajo** (p507), chichi at **Ultra** (p507) or alternative at **Metelkova Mesto** (p507).

On your second day check out some of the city's excellent **museums and galleries** (p503), and then stroll or cycle through Park Tivoli, stopping for a oh-so-local horse burger at **Hot Horse** (p506) along the way.

Community Health Centre Ljubljana (Zdravstveni Dom Ljubljana; www.zd-lj.si; ☎ 472 37 00; Metelkova ul 9; ◷ 7.30am-7pm) For nonemergencies.

University Medical Centre Ljubljana (Univerzitetni Klinični Center Ljubljana; ☎ 522 50 50; www3.kclj.si; Zaloška c 2; ◷ 24hr) Accident and emergency service.

Money

There are ATMs at every turn, including a row of them outside the main tourist information centre (TIC) office. At both the bus and train stations you'll find **bureaux de change** (◷ 7am-8pm) changing cash for no commission but not travellers cheques.

Abanka (☎ 300 15 00; Slovenska c 50; ◷ 9am-5pm Mon-Fri)

Nova Ljubljanska Banka (☎ 476 39 00; Trg Republike 2; ◷ 8am-6pm Mon-Fri)

Post

Main post office (Slovenska c 32; ◷ 8am-7pm Mon-Fri, to 1pm Sat) Holds poste restante for 30 days and changes money.

Post office branch (Pražakova ul 3; ◷ 8am-7pm Mon-Fri, to noon Sat) Just southwest of the bus and train stations.

Tourist Information

Slovenia Tourist Information Centre (STIC; ☎ 306 45 76; www.slovenia.info; Krekov trg 10; ◷ 8am-9pm Jun-Sep, 8am-7pm Oct-May) Internet and bicycle hire also available.

Student Organisation of the University of Ljubljana (Študentska Organizacija Univerze Ljubljani; ŠOU; ☎ 433 01 76; www.sou-lj.si; Trubarjeva c 7; ◷ 9am-6pm Mon-Thu, 9am-3pm Fri) Information and free internet.

Tourist Information Centre Ljubljana Old Town (TIC; ☎ 306 12 15; www.visitljubljana.si; Kresija Bldg, Stritarjeva ul; ◷ 8am-9pm Jun-Sep, 8am-7pm Oct-May); Train station (☎ 433 94 75; Trg OF 6; ◷ 8am-10pm Jun-Sep, 10am-7pm Oct-May)

Travel Agencies

Erazem (☎ 430 55 37; www.erazem.net; basement, Miklošičeva c 26; ◷ 10am-5pm Mon-Fri Jun-Sep, noon-5pm Mon-Fri Oct-May) Staff make flight and train bookings and sell student and hostel cards.

STA Ljubljana (☎ 439 16 90; www.staljubljana.com; 1st fl, Trg Ajdovščina 1; ◷ 10am-1pm & 2-5pm Mon-Fri) Discount airfares for students; go online at their internet cafe (open 8am to midnight Monday to Saturday).

SIGHTS

Ljubljana Castle (☎ 232 99 94; www.ljubljanafestival .si; admission free; ◷ 9am-11pm May-Sep, 10am-9pm Oct-

Apr) crowns a wooded hill that is the city's focal point. It's an architectural mishmash, including fortified walls dating from the early 16th century, a late-15th-century chapel and a 1970s concrete cafe. The best views are from the 19th-century **watchtower** (adult/student/child €3.50/2/2; ◷ 9am-9pm May-Sep, 10am-6pm Oct-Apr); admission includes a visit to the **Virtual Museum** below, a 23-minute, 3-D video tour of Ljubljana though the centuries. The fastest way to reach the castle is via the **funicular** (vzpenjača; adult/student/child return €3/2/2; ◷ 9am-11pm May-Sep, 10am-9pm Oct-Apr), which ascends from Krekov trg every 10 minutes, though you can also take the hourly **tourist train** (adult/child €3/2; ◷ up 9am-9pm, down 9.20am-9.20pm) from just south of the TIC on Stritarjeva ul. It takes about 15 minutes to walk to the castle from the Old Town.

Central Prešernov trg is dominated by the salmon pink, 17th-century **Franciscan Church of the Annunciation** (◷ 6.40am-noon & 3-8pm) and the **Prešeren monument** (1905), in honour of the national poet France Prešeren. Coyly observing Prešeren from a terracotta window at Wolfova ul 4 is a bust of his unrequited love (and poetic inspiration), Julija Primic. Wander north of the square along Miklošičeva c to admire the fine **art nouveau buildings**, including the landmark Grand Hotel Union at No 1, built in 1905, and the colourful former Cooperative Bank (1922) at No 8.

Leading southward from Prešernov trg is the small but perfectly formed **Triple Bridge**; prolific architect Jože Plečnik added two side bridges to the 19th-century span in 1931 to create something truly unique. The renovated baroque **Robba Fountain** stands before the Gothic **town hall** (1718) in **Mestni trg**, the 'City Square', that leads into two more: **Stari trg** (Old Sq) and **Gornji trg** (Upper Sq).

East of the Triple Bridge, the 18th-century **Cathedral of St Nicholas** (Dolničarjeva ul 1; ◷ 10am-noon & 3-6pm) is filled with pink marble, white stucco, gilt and a panoply of baroque frescoes. North and east of the cathedral is a lively open-air market (p506) selling both foodstuffs and dry goods, the magnificent riverside **Plečnik Colonnade** and the **Dragon Bridge** (Zmajski Most; 1901), a span guarded by four of the mythical creatures that are now the city's mascots.

The main building of **Ljubljana University** (Kongresni trg 12) was erected as a ducal palace in 1902. The more restrained Philharmonic Hall (p508) dates from 1898. South of the university building is the **National & University Library** (Gosposka ul 14; 9am-6pm Mon-Fri, 9am-2pm Sat), Plečnik's masterpiece completed in 1941, with its stunning main reading room. Diagonally opposite is the excellent **City Museum of Ljubljana** (241 25 00; www.mm-lj.si; Gosposka ul 15; adult/student & child €4/2.50; 10am-6pm Tue-Sun). The reconstructed Roman street dating back to the 1st century AD is worth a visit in itself.

Of several major galleries and museums west of Slovenska c, the best are the impressive **National Gallery** (241 54 18; www.ng-slo.si; Prešernova c 24 & Cankarjeva c 20; permanent collection free, temporary exhibits adult/student €7/3.50; 10am-6pm Tue-Sun), which contains the nation's historical art collection and the fascinating **National Museum of Contemporary History** (300 96 10; www.muzej-nz.si; Celovška c 23; adult/student €3.35/2.50; 10am-6pm) in Park Tivoli, with its imaginative look at 20th-century Slovenia through multimedia and artefacts. The inwardly vibrant (but outwardly drab) 1940s **Ljubljana Modern Art Museum** (241 68 00; www.mg-lj.si; Cankarjeva c 15) was undergoing extensive renovation at the time of research.

The **National Museum of Slovenia** (241 44 00; www.nms.si; Muzejska ul 1; adult/student €3/2.50, admission 1st Sun of month free; 10am-6pm Fri-Wed, 10am-8pm Thu), in an elegant 1888 building, has rich archaeological and coin collections, including a Roman lapidarium and a Stone Age bone flute discovered near Cerkno in western Slovenia in 1995. Joint entry to the National Museum and the attached **Slovenian Museum of Natural History** (241 09 40; www2.pms-lj.si; Muzejska ul 1; adult/student €3/2.50), which keeps the same hours, costs €5/4/10 per adult/student/family.

The **Slovenian Ethnographic Museum** (300 87 00; www.etno-muzej.si; Metelkova ul 2; adult/student €4.50/2.50; 10am-6pm Tue-Sun), housed in the 1886 Belgian Barracks on the southern edge of Metelkova, has a permanent collection on the top floor with traditional Slovenian trades and crafts – everything from beekeeping and blacksmithing to glass-painting and pottery making.

TOURS

Two-hour **walking tours** (adult/child 4-12yr €10/5; 10am, 2pm & 5pm Apr-Oct) that are combined with a ride up to the castle on the funicular or the tourist train or a cruise on the Ljubljanica are organised by the TIC (opposite). They depart daily from the town hall on Mestni trg in season.

FESTIVALS & EVENTS

There is plenty going on in and around the capital, including **Druga Godba** (www.drugagodba .si), a festival of alternative and world music at the Križanke in late May/early June; the **Ljubljana Festival** (www.ljubljanafestival.si), the nation's premier cultural event (music, theatre and dance) held from early July to late August; and the **Ljubljana Marathon** (www.ljubljanskimaraton .si) in late October.

SLEEPING

Ljubljana is not overly endowed with accommodation choices, though it has gained several new places in the budget and midrange levels in recent years.

Budget

The TIC (opposite) has comprehensive details of **private rooms** (€20-30 per person) and **apartments** (€50-95) though only a handful are what could be called central.

Ljubljana Resort (568 39 13; www.ljubljanaresort .si/eng; Dunajska c 270; camping adult €7.50-13.50, child €5.75-10.25; year-round;) Wait till you see the facilities at this attractive 6-hectare camping ground–cum–resort 4km north of the city centre. Along with a 50-room hotel (singles €71 to €111, doubles €112 to €152) and five bungalows (€105 to €150) accommodating up to five people, there's Laguna (www.laguna.si, admission adult/child from €8/10, open June to September), a 'city beach club' (read water park) with outdoor swimming pools, fitness studio with sauna, and badminton and volleyball courts. Take bus 6 or 8 to the Ježica stop.

Dijaški Dom Tabor (234 88 40; www.d-tabor.lj.edu s .si; dm/s/d €11/26/38; late Jun–late Aug;) In summer five colleges in Ljubljana open their halls of residence (dijaški dom) to visitors, but only this 300-bed one, a 10-minute walk southeast of the bus and train stations, is really central. Accommodation is in rooms with one to 10 beds. Enter from Kotnikova ul.

Simbol Castle Hostel (041-720 825; www.simbol.si; Petkovškovo nabrežje 47; dm/d/tr/q €16/50/54/68;) A favourite new place in Ljubljana, this five-room hostel wraps around a tiny courtyard bordering the Ljubljanica, and one room has views of the castle. Rooms, with two to six beds, have their own kitchens. Internet is free.

Alibi Hostel (251 12 44; www.alibi.si; Cankarjevo nabrežje 27; dm/d €20/50;) This well-situated 106-bed hostel on the Ljubljanica has brightly painted, airy dorms with four to 12 wooden bunks and five doubles. One room is air-conditioned and there's a private suite at the top for six people. Farther afield to the north in Bežigrad (bus 14 to Podmilščakova stop), Alibi Rooms (☎ 433 13 31; Kolarjeva ul 30) has eight rooms with between two and six beds (dorms €18, doubles €46) in an old villa with a lovely garden.

ourpick Celica Hostel (☎ 230 97 00; www.hostel celica.com; Metelkova ul 8; dm €21, s/d/tr cell €47/54/66, 4-to 5-bed room per person €27, 6-to 7-bed room per person €22; 🖳) This stylishly revamped former prison (1882) in Metelkova has 20 'cells', designed by as many different architects and complete with original bars; it also has nine rooms and apartments with three to seven beds; and a packed, popular 12-bed dorm. The ground floor is home to three cafes (set lunch €5 to €7; open 7.30am to midnight) and the hostel boasts its own gallery where everyone can show their own work.

Vila Veselova (☎ 059-926 721; www.v-v.si; Veselova ul 14; dm €21, d/q €68/102; 🗷 🖳) This very attractive bright yellow villa, with its own garden and 42 beds in the centre of the museum district, offers mostly hostel accommodation in five colourful rooms with four to eight beds. A double and two apartments with attached facilities and access to a kitchen make it an attractive midrange option, however. Some rooms face Park Tivoli across busy Tivolska c.

Midrange

Penzion Pod Lipo (☎ 031-809 893; www.penzion-podlipo .com; Borštnikov trg 3; d/tr/q €59/72/96; 🖳) Sitting atop one of Ljubljana's oldest *gostilne* and by a 400-year-old linden tree, this 10-room inn offers excellent value in a part of the city that is filling up with bars and restaurants. Fall in love with the communal kitchen, the original hardwood floors and the east-facing terrace that catches the morning sun.

Hotel Emonec (☎ 200 15 20; www.hotel-emonec.com; Wolfova ul 12; s €59-72, d €67-77, tr/q €90/105; 🖳) The decor is simple and functionally modern at this 39-room hotel and the staff is less than welcoming, but everything is spotless and you can't beat the central location.

Slamič B&B (☎ 433 82 33; www.slamic.si; Kersnikova ul 1; s €65-80, d €95-107; 🗷 🖳) It's a titch away from the action but Slamič, a B&B above a famous cafe and teahouse, offers 11 bright rooms with antique(ish) furnishings and parquet floors. Choice rooms include quiet No 1 looking on to a back garden and No 9 just

off an enormous terrace used by the cafe and made for smokers.

Pri Mraku (☎ 421 96 00; www.daj-dam.si; Rimska c 4; s €69-77, d €102-112, tr €121-131; 🗷 🖳) Although it calls itself a *gostilna*, 'At Twilight' is really just a smallish hotel (36 rooms) in an old building with no lift and a garden. Rooms on the 1st and 4th floors have air-con.

Hotel Park (☎ 300 25 00; www.hotelpark.si; Tabor 9; s €75-80, d €104-110; 🖳) A partial facelift inside and out has made this tower-block hotel an even better-value midrange choice in central Ljubljana. The 200 pleasant, well-renovated standard and comfort rooms are bright and unpretentiously well equipped. Cheaper 'hostel' rooms, some of which have shared facilities and others en-suite shower, cost €22/26 per person with shared/private bathroom in a double and €17/19 in a quad. Students with ISIC cards get a 10% discount.

Top End

Antiq Hotel (☎ 421 35 60; www.antiqhotel.si; Gornji trg 3; s €113-164, d €144-204; 🗷 🖳) Ljubljana's first (and still only) boutique hotel was cobbled together from a series of townhouses on the site of a Roman workshop. It has 16 rooms and apartments, most of which are very spacious, a small wellness centre next door and multitiered back garden. The decor is kitsch with a smirk and there are fabulous little nooks and touches everywhere: glassed-in medieval courtyard; vaulted ceilings; two noncarpeted, antiallergenic floors; and bath towels trimmed with Slovenian lace. Among our favourite rooms are enormous No 8 on the 2nd floor, with swooningly romantic views of the Hercules Fountain, and No 10, an even bigger two room suite on the top floor with a terrace and glimpses of Ljubljana Castle. The two cheapest rooms (singles/doubles €61/77, Nos 2 and 9, have their own bathrooms but they're on the corridor.

EATING

The Old Town has a fair number of appealing restaurants, but the majority of the venues here are cafes. For cheaper options, try the dull but functional snack bars around the bus and train stations, and both on and in the shopping mall below Trg Ajdovščina.

Restaurants

Harambaša (☎ 041-843 106; Vrtna ul 8; dishes €3.50-6; 🕙 10am-10pm Mon-Fri, noon-10pm Sat, noon-6pm Sun)

Here you'll find authentic Bosnian – Sarajevan to be precise – dishes like *čevapčiči* (spicy meatballs of beef or pork) and *pljeskavica* (meat patties) served at low tables in a charming modern cottage.

Kitajska Zvezda (☎ 425 88 24; Hrenova ul 19; mains €4.10-12.30; ☽ 11am-11pm) If you're looking for a fix of rice or noodles, try the 'Chinese Star' on the river just south of the Old Town. Szechuan dishes, including the *ma po doufu* (tofu with garlic and chilli), are good; they also do Cantonese and Shanghainese food.

Vegedrom (☎ 513 26 42; Vodnikova c 35; mains €5.60-12.60; ☽ 11am-10pm Mon-Fri, noon-10pm Sat) This appealing, if somewhat pricey, vegan restaurant at the northeastside edge of Park Tivoli now also dibble-dabbles (or is that nibble-nabbles?) in Indian food. The set lunch is good value at €6.90 and there's a salad bar (from €3.40).

Pri Škofju (☎ 426 45 08; Rečna ul 8; mains €7-15; ☽ 10am-midnight Mon-Fri, noon-midnight Sat & Sun) Still our off-the-beaten track favourite, this wonderful little place in tranquil Krakovo, south of the city centre, serves some of the best prepared local dishes and salads in Ljubljana, with an ever-changing menu. Weekday set lunches are good value at €5.30 to €6.90.

Sokol (☎ 439 68 55; Ciril Metodov trg 18; mains €7-20; ☽ noon-11pm) In this old vaulted house, traditional Slovenian food is served on heavy tables by costumed waiters. Along with traditional dishes like *obara* (veal stew, €7) and Krvavica sausage with cabbage and turnips (€8.50), there are the more esoteric deep-fried bull's testicles with tartare sauce and grilled stallion steak (€16).

Namasté (☎ 425 01 59; Breg 8; mains €7.50-15.50; ☽ 11am-midnight Mon-Sat, to 10pm Sun) Should you fancy a bit of Indian, head for this place on the left bank of the Ljubljanica. You won't get high street–quality curry but the thalis (from €7.50) and tandoori dishes (from €12.30) are good. The choice of vegetarian dishes is better than average and the set lunch is €8.

Cantina Mexicana (☎ 426 93 25; Knafljev prehod 3; mains €7.90-16.80; ☽ 10am-1am Sun-Tue, 10am-3am Wed-Fri, 9am-3am Sat) This stylish Mexican restaurant has an eye-catching red and blue exterior and hacienda-like decor inside. The fajitas (€7.90 to €12.90) are good.

Yildiz Han (☎ 426 57 17; Karlovška c 19; mains €8.50-15; ☽ noon-midnight Mon-Sat) If Turkish is your thing, head for authentic (trust us) 'Star House', which features belly dancing on Friday nights. Lunches are a snip at €5.

Taverna Tatjana (☎ 421 00 87; Gornji trg 38; mains €8.50-22; ☽ 3pm-midnight Mon-Sat) A wooden-beamed cottage pub with a nautical theme (think nets and seascapes), this is actually a rather exclusive fish restaurant with a lovely (and protected) back courtyard for the warmer months.

Gostilna Rimska XXI (☎ 425 20 29; Rimska c 21; mains €10-24; ☽ 12.30pm-1am Mon-Fri) This sleek new *gostilna* that changes its menu twice a day serves Mediterranean-inspired dishes till late. Set lunch is €16.

Špajza (☎ 425 30 94; Gornji trg 28; mains €14.60-22; ☽ noon-11pm Mon-Sat, to 10pm Sun) A welcome return to the Old Town is the 'Pantry', nicely decorated with its rough-hewn tables and chairs, wooden floors, frescoed ceilings and nostalgic bits and pieces. Try the 'Špajza filet' (€22), which is actually horseflesh, or a bit of *kozliček iz pečiče* (oven-roasted kid; €14.60); wines from a dozen different Slovenian producers are served. A three-course set lunch is only €10.

Pri Vitezu (☎ 426 60 58; Breg 18-20; mains €18-30; ☽ noon-11pm Mon-Sat) Located directly on the left bank of the Ljubljanica, 'At the Knight' is the place for a special meal (Mediterranean-style grills and Adriatic fish dishes), whether in the brasserie, the salon or the very cosy Knight's Room.

Ljubljana is awash in pizzerias, where pizza routinely costs €4 to €8.50. The pick of the crop includes **Foculus Pizzeria** (☎ 251 56 43; Gregorčičeva ul 3; ☽ 10am-midnight Mon-Fri, noon-midnight Sat & Sun), which boasts a vaulted ceiling painted with spring and autumn leaves; **Trta** (☎ 426 50 66; Grudnovo nabrežje 21; ☽ 11am-10.30pm Mon-Fri, noon-10.30pm Sat), on the right bank of the Ljubljanica; and **Mirje** (☎ 426 60 15; Tržaška c 5; ☽ 10am-10pm Mon-Fri, noon-5pm Sat), southwest of the city centre, which does some excellent pasta dishes, too.

Quick Eats

Nobel Burek (Miklošičeva c 30; burek €2, pizza slice €1.40; ☽ 24hr) This hole-in-the-wall serves Slovenian-style fast food round-the-clock.

Restavracija 2000 (☎ 476 69 25; Trg Republike 1; dishes €1.50-3, set lunch €6.50; ☽ 9am-7pm Mon-Fri, 9am-3pm Sat) In the basement of the Maximarket department store, this glass and chrome self-service eatery is surprisingly upbeat, and just the ticket if you want something quick while visiting the main museums.

Ajdovo Zrno (☎ 041-690 478; Trubarjeva c 7; soups & sandwiches €1.80-2, set lunch €6; ☺ 10am-7pm Mon-Fri) Vegetarian 'Buckwheat Grain' serves soups, sandwiches, fried vegetables and lots of different salads (self-service, €3 to €6). And they have terrific, freshly squeezed juices, including the unusual rose-petal juice with lemon. Enter from little Mali trg.

Paninoteka (☎ 041-529 824; Jurčičev trg 3; soups & toasted sandwiches €2.40-6; ☺ 8am-1am Mon-Sat, 9am-11pm Sun) Healthy sandwich creations on a lovely little square by the river.

Hot Horse (☎ 521 14 27; Park Tivoli; snacks & burgers €2.80-6; ☺ 9am-6am Mon, 10am-6am Tue-Sun) This place in a kiosk in the city's largest park supplies Ljubljančani with their favourite treat: horse burgers (€4). It's just down the hill from the National Museum of Contemporary History.

Ribca (☎ 425 15 44; Adamič-Lundrovo nabrežje 1; dishes €3-7.50; ☺ 8am-4pm Mon-Fri, 8am-2pm Sat) This basement seafood bar below the Plečnik Colonnade in Pogačarjev trg serves tasty fried squid, sardines and herrings to hungry market-goers. Set lunch is €7.50.

Self-Catering
Handy supermarkets include a large **Mercator** (Slovenska c 55; ☺ 7am-9pm) southwest of the train and bus stations and a smaller, more central **Mercator branch** (Kongresni trg 9; ☺ 7am-8pm Mon-Fri, 8am-3pm Sat & Sun) just up from the river.

The **Maximarket supermarket** (☎ 476 68 00; basement, Trg Republike 1; ☺ 9am-9pm Mon-Fri, 8am-5pm Sat) below the department store of the same name has the largest selection of food and wine in the city centre.

The open-air **market** (Pogačarjev trg & Vodnikov trg; ☺ 6am-6pm Mon-Fri, 6am-4pm Sat Jun-Sep, 6am-4pm Mon-Sat Oct-May), held across two squares north and east of the cathedral, sells mostly fresh fruit and vegetables.

DRINKING
Few cities of this size have central Ljubljana's concentration of inviting cafes and bars, the vast majority with outdoor seating.

Bars & Pubs
Kavarna Tromostovje (☎ 430 12 18; Prešernov trg 1; ☺ 7am-1am Apr-Oct) This cafe-bar on the southern side of Prešernov trg seems to change its name on an annual basis but remains one of the most popular places for a drink if you just want to sit outside and watch the passing parade.

Maček (☎ 425 37 91; Krojaška ul 5; ☺ 9am-1am) *The* place to be seen in Ljubljana on a sunny summer afternoon, the 'Cat' is Kavarna Tromostovje's rival on the right bank of the Ljubljanica. Happy hour is between 4pm and 7pm on weekdays.

Salon (☎ 439 87 64; Trubarjeva c 23; ☺ 9am-1am Mon-Wed, 9am-3am Thu-Sat, 3pm-1am Sun) Salon is a dazzling designer-kitsch cocktail bar featuring gold ceilings, faux leopard armchairs, heavy purple velvet drapes and excellent cocktails (€4.50 to €6.50).

Sax Pub (☎ 283 14 57; Eipprova ul 7; ☺ noon-1am Mon, 10am-1am Tue-Sat, 4-10pm Sun) Two decades in Trnovo and decorated with colourful murals and graffiti inside and out, the Sax has live jazz at 9pm or 9.30pm on Thursdays from late August to December and February to June. Canned stuff rules at other times.

Dvorni Bar (☎ 251 12 57; Dvorni trg 2; ☺ 8am-1am Mon-Sat, 8am-midnight Sun) This wine bar is an excellent place to taste Slovenian vintages; it stocks more than 100 varieties and has wine tastings every second Wednesday of the month.

Pr' Skelet (☎ 252 77 99; Ključavničarska ul 5; ☺ 10am-3am) It might sound like a one-joke wonder, but you'll shake, rattle and roll at this skeleton-themed basement bar, where cocktails are two for one throughout the day.

Žmavc (☎ 251 03 24; Rimska c 21; ☺ 7.30am-1am Mon-Fri, 10am-1am Sat, 6pm-1am Sun) A superpopular student hang-out west of Slovenska c, with comic-strip scenes and figures running halfway up the walls.

Pr' Semaforju (☎ 040-893 664; Slovenska c 5; ☺ 7am-midnight Mon-Fri) Student (and we're talking spotty teens here) hang-out par excellence, 'At the Traffic Light' (the name is translated into a dozen languages outside) is a slightly grotty cafe-bar that rocks later in the evening.

Cafes & Teahouses
Kavarna Zvezda (☎ 421 90 90; Kongresni trg 4 & Wolfova ul 14; ☺ 7am-11pm Mon-Sat, 10am-8pm Sun) The 'Star Café' is celebrated for its shop-made cakes, especially *skutina pečena* (€2.60), an eggy cheesecake.

Le Petit Café (☎ 251 25 75; Trg Francoske Revolucije 4; ☺ 7.30am-midnight) Just opposite the Križanke, this pleasant, studenty place offers great coffee and a wide range of breakfast goodies (€2.60 to €6.50).

Ambient (☎ 430 27 56; Čufarjeva ul 5; ☺ 7am-1am Mon-Fri, 9am-1am Sat, 6pm-1am Sun) This stylish cafe-cum-bistro hidden down a narrow side street just east of Miklošičeva c caters to a diverse crowd throughout the day.

Kafeterija Lan (Gallusovo nabrežje 27; ☻ 10am-midnight Mon-Thu, 10am-1am Fri, 11am-midnight Sat & Sun) A little greener-than-green cafe-bar on the river below Cobbler Bridge, Lan is something of a hipster gay magnet. There's a nice terrace under a spreading chestnut street.

Čajna Hiša (☎ 421 24 44; Stari trg 3; ☻ 9am-10.30pm Mon-Fri, 9am-3pm & 6-10pm Sat) If you take your cuppa seriously, come here; the appropriately named 'Teahouse' offers a wide range of green and black teas and fruit tisanes for €1.80 to €3.40 a pot.

Babo Juice Bar (☎ 040-533 334; Krojaška ul 4; juices & smoothies €1.95-4.40; ☻ 9am-9pm) Of the crop of juice bars that have sprouted all over Ljubljana, Babo is the best, with some excellent fruit and vegetable combinations.

Slaščičarna Pri Vodnjaku (☎ 425 07 12; Stari trg 30; ☻ 8am-midnight) For all kinds of chocolate of the ice cream and drinking kind, the 'Confectionery by the Fountain' will surely satisfy – there are almost three-dozen flavours (€1 per scoop), as well as teas (€1.60) and fresh juices (€0.80 to €3.35).

ENTERTAINMENT

The free quarterly **Ljubljana Life** (www.ljubljanalife.com) has practical information and listings. **Ljubljana in Your Pocket** (www.inyourpocket.com; €2.90), another quarterly, will cost you, but it's a thousand times more useful. *Where to? in Ljubljana*, available from the tourist offices (p502), lists cultural and sporting events.

Nightclubs

Inbox Club (☎ 428 96 90, 428 75 01; www.inbox-club .com; Jurčkova c 224; ☻ 9pm-dawn Thu-Sat) Ljubljana's biggest club is hidden in a shopping centre opposite the Leclerc Hypermarket (take bus 27 to NS Rudnik, the last stop) in the far southeastern suburbs

Klub K4 (☎ 438 02 61; www.klubk4.org; Kersnikova ul 4; ☻ 8pm-2am Tue, 8pm-4am Wed & Thu, 9pm-6am Fri & Sat, 10pm-4am Sun) This evergreen venue in the basement of the Student Organisation of Ljubljana University (ŠOU) headquarters features rave-electronic music on Fridays and Saturdays, with other styles of music on weeknights, and a popular gay and lesbian night on Sundays. It closes in July and August.

Bachus Center Club (☎ 241 82 44; www.bachus -center.com; Kongresni trg 3; ☻ 9pm-5am Mon-Sat) This place has something for everyone, including

a restaurant and bar-lounge, and attracts a pretty tame, pretty mainstream crowd.

As Lounge (☎ 425 88 22; www.gostilnaas.si; Čopova 5A but enter from Knafljev prehod; ☻ 9am-3am Wed-Sat) DJs transform this candlelit basement bar into a pumping, crowd-pulling nightclub four nights a week. The way the name sounds in Slovene might have you thinking you're going to get lucky. It just means 'ace', ace.

Ultra (☎ 070 818 979; www.ultra-club.si; Nazorjeva ul 6; ☻ 10pm-6am Wed-Sat) Ultra is a popular dance venue with four different theme nights and a switched-on, somewhat chichi crowd.

KMŠ (☎ 425 74 80; www.klubkms.si; Tržaška ul 2; ☻ 8am-5am Mon-Fri, 9pm-5am Sat) Located in the deep recesses of a former factory complex, the 'Maribor Student Club' is a raucous place with music and dancers all over the shop.

Metelkova Mesto (www.metelkova.org; Masarykova c 24) 'Metelkova Town', an ex-army garrison taken over by squatters after independence, is now a free-living commune – a miniature version of Copenhagen's Christiania. In this two-courtyard block, a dozen idiosyncratic venues hide behind brightly tagged doorways, coming to life generally after midnight, daily in summer and on Fridays and Saturdays the rest of the year. Entering the main 'city gate' from Masarykova c, the building to the right houses **Gala Hala** (www.galahala.com), with live bands and club nights, and **Klub Channel Zero** (www.ch0.org), with punk and hardcore. Easy to miss in the first building to the left are **Klub Tiffany** (www.ljudmila.org/siqrd/tiffany) for gay men and **Klub Monokel** (www.klubmonokel.com) for lesbians. Due south is the ever-popular **Jalla Jalla Club** (www.myspace.com/jallajallaclub), a congenial pub with concerts. Beyond the first courtyard to the southwest, **Klub Gromka** (www.metelkova .org/gromka) in the building with the conical roof has folk, live concerts, theatre and lectures. Next door is **Menza pri Koritu** (www.menzaprikoritu .org) under the strange E.T.-like figures with performances and concerts.

Live Music

Orto Bar (☎ 232 16 74; www.orto-bar.com; Graboličeva ul 1; ☻ 8am-4am Mon-Wed, 8am-5am Thu-Sat, 6-9pm Sun) A popular bar-club for late-night drinking and dancing with occasional live music, Orto is just five minutes' walk from Metelkova.

Jazz Club Gajo (☎ 425 32 06; www.jazzclubgajo.com; Beethovnova ul 8; ☻ 11am-2am Mon-Fri, 7pm-midnight Sat & Sun) Now in its 15th year, Gajo is the city's premier venue for live jazz and attracts both local and international talent (jam sessions 9pm Mondays).

Roxly Café Bar (☎ 430 10 21; www.roxly.si; Mala ul 5; ☯ 7am-2am Mon-Wed, to 3am Thu & Fri, 10am-3am Sat) New venue north of the Ljubljanica; there's live rock music from 10pm two or three nights a week.

Performing Arts

Philharmonic Hall (Filharmonija; ☎ 241 08 00; www.filhar monija.si; Kongresni trg 10) This century-old concert hall is home to the Slovenian Philharmonic Orchestra, founded in 1701.

Opera House (☎ 241 17 40; www.opera.si; Župančičeva ul 1) Opera and ballet are performed at the neo-Renaissance Opera House dating back to 1882.

Križanke (☎ 241 60 00, box office 241 60 26; Trg Francoske Revolucije 1-2) Hosts concerts of the Ljubljana Festival (p503) and other events both inside and out what was a sprawling monastic complex dating back to the 13th century.

Cankarjev Dom (☎ 241 71 00; www.cd-cc.si; Prešernova c 10) is Ljubljana's premier cultural centre and has two large auditoriums (the Gallus Hall has perfect acoustics) and a dozen smaller performance spaces offering a remarkable smorgasbord of performance arts. The **ticket office** (☎ 241 72 99; ☯ 11am-1pm & 3-8pm Mon-Fri, 11am-1pm Sat & 1hr before performances) is in the subway below Maximarket Supermarket.

Cinema

Kinoteka (☎ 434 25 20; www.kinoteka.si; Miklošičeva c 28) The 'Slovenian Cinematheque' screens archival art and classic films in their original languages.

GETTING THERE & AWAY
Bus

The **bus station** (☎ 234 46 00, information 090 93 42 30; www.ap-ljubljana.si; Trg OF 4; ☯ 5.30am-10.30pm Sun-Fri, 5am-10pm Sat) opposite the train station has bilingual info-phones; just pick one up and wait for the connection. Frequent buses serve Bohinj (€8.30, two hours, 86km, hourly) via Bled (€6.30, 1¼ hours, 57km). Most buses to Piran (€12, three hours, 140km, up to seven daily) go via Koper (€11.10, 2½ hours, 122km, up to 16 daily) and Postojna (€6, one hour, 53km, up to 36 daily).

International services from Ljubljana include Belgrade (€35, 7¾ hours, 536km, 10am and 10.25pm daily); Budapest (€8, six hours, 442km, 1pm Wednesday, Friday and Sunday), Frankfurt (€83, 12½ hours, 777km, 7.30pm Sunday to Friday, 9.30pm Saturday) via Munich (€48, 6¾ hours, 344km); Poreč (€17.50, 4½ hours, 162km, 1.45pm daily), Sarajevo (€38, 9½ hours, 570km, 3.15pm daily 4pm Wednesday and Sunday), Skopje (€50, 15 hours, 960km, 3pm Sunday to Friday); Split (€44, 10½ hours, 528km, 7.40pm daily) via Rijeka (€17, 2½ hours, 136km); Trieste (€11.60, 2¾ hours, 105km, 2.25pm Monday to Saturday); and Zagreb (€13.60, 2½ hours, 154km, 2.25am daily).

Train

Ljubljana's **train station** (☎ 291 33 32; www.slo -zeleznice.si; Trg OF 6; ☯ 5am-10pm) has daily services to Koper (€7.75 to €13, 2½ hours, 153km, up to five times daily). Alternatively you can take one of the more frequent Sežana-bound trains and change at Divača (€6.25 to €7.75, 1¾ hours, 104km).

Ljubljana–Vienna trains (€61.80, 6¼ hours, 385km, twice daily) via Graz (€31.40, 200km, three hours) are expensive, although Spar Schiene fares as low as €29 apply on certain trains at certain times. Otherwise save a little bit of money by going first to Maribor (from €7.70, 2½ hours, 156km, up to two dozen daily), where you can buy a Maribor–Graz ticket (€13, one hours, three daily) and then continue on domestic tickets from Graz to Vienna (€31.40, 2¾ hours, 214km). Similar savings apply via Jesenice and Villach and/or Klagenfurt.

Three trains depart daily from Ljubljana for Munich (€71.40, 6½ hours, 405km). The 11.50pm departure has sleeping carriages available.

Ljubljana–Venice trains (€25 to €47, four hours, 244km) via Sežana depart at 2.22am and 10.35am. It's cheaper to go first to Nova Gorica (€7.75, 3½ hours, 153km, five daily), cross over to Gorizia and then take an Italian train to Venice (€8.75, 2¼ hours).

For Zagreb there are seven trains daily from Ljubljana (€12.20, 2½ hours, 154km) via Zidani Most. Two trains from the capital serve Rijeka (€12.60, 2½ hours, 136km) via Postojna.

Ljubljana–Budapest trains (€57.80, 8¾ hours, 451km, twice daily) go via Ptuj and Hodoš; there are Budapest Special fares available for as low as €29 on certain trains at certain times. Belgrade (€25 to €44, 10 hours, 535km) is served by four trains a day.

GETTING AROUND

The cheapest way to Ljubljana's recently re-named **Jože Pučnik Airport** (LJU; www.lju-airport.si) at Brnik is by city bus from stop 28 (€4.10, 50 minutes, 27km) at the bus station. These run at 5.20am and hourly from 6.10am to 8.10pm Monday to Friday; on weekends there's a bus at 6.10am and then one every two hours from 9.10am to 7.10pm. A **private airport van** (☎ 041-792 865; €5) also links Trg OF near the bus station with the airport (30 minutes) up to 10 times daily between 5.20am and 10.30pm. A **taxi** (☎ 031-311 311, 041-445 406) from downtown Ljubljana will cost you about €38.

Ljubljana has an excellent network of city buses. Most operate every five to 15 minutes from 5am to 10.30pm, though some start as early as 3.15am and run till midnight. The central area is perfectly walkable, though, so buses are really only necessary if you're staying out of town. Buy metal tokens (*žetoni*; €0.80) from news-stands, or pay €1 on board.

Ljubljana Bike (per 2hr/day €1/5; ☺ 8am-7pm or 9pm Apr-Oct) has two-wheelers available from 10 locations around the city, including the train station, the STIC office (p502), Celica Hostel (p504) and opposite Antiq Hotel.

JULIAN ALPS

The Julian Alps – named in honour of Caesar himself – form Slovenia's dramatic north-west frontier with Italy. Triglav National Park, established in 1924, includes almost all of the Alps lying within Slovenia. The centre-piece of the park is, of course, Mt Triglav (2864m), Slovenia's highest mountain, but there are many other peaks here reaching above 2000m. Along with an embarrassment of fauna and flora, the area offers a wide range of adventure sports.

KRANJ
☎ 04 / pop 34,950

At the foot of the Kamnik-Savinja Alps, with the snow-capped peak of Storžič (2132m) and others looming to the north, Kranj is Slovenia's fourth-largest city. The attractive Old Town, perched on an escarpment above the confluence of the Sava and Kokra Rivers, barely measures 1km by 250m.

The frequent weekday buses between Kranj and Ljubljana airport at nearby Brnik make it possible to head straight to the Julian Alps

without first going to the capital. While waiting for your onward bus to Bled (€3.60, 30 minutes, 23km), have a look at the Old Town, starting with the art nouveau **former post office** (Koroška c 2) facing Maistrov trg and its rooftop cafe, a 600m walk south from the bus station. On your way you'll pass the 87-room **Hotel Creina** (☎ 281 75 00; www.hotel-creina.si; Koroška c 5; s/d €81/102; ☒ ☐), the only game in town and now getting a much needed refit. The **tourist office** (☎ 238 04 50; www.tourism-kranj.si; Glavni trg 2; ☺ 8am-7pm Mon-Sat, 9am-4pm Sun) can find you a private room from €25 or, in summer, a bed in a student dormitory (€15).

Most places of interest are along just three streets – pedestrianised Prešernova ul, Tavčarjeva ul and Tomišičeva ul – the first two of which lead to the **Church of St Cantianus**, with impressive frescoes and stained glass. Another 300m farther south, the Old Town dead-ends at the Serbian Orthodox **Plague Church**, built during a time of pestilence in 1470, and the 16th-century **defence tower** behind it. **Mitnica** (☎ 040-678 778; Tavčarjeva ul 35; ☺ 7am-11pm Mon-Wed, 7am-1am Thu, 7am-2am Fri & Sat, 3-11pm Sun) is a relaxing cafe-bar in the basement of a 16th-century toll house with a huge terrace backing on to the river.

From Kranj it's an easy excursion to **Škofja Loka** (population 12,275) whose main square, **Mestni trg**, contains beautifully painted houses and a **tourist office** (☎ 512 02 68; www.skofjaloka.info; Mestni trg 7). The fine **castle** (Grajska pot 13) has the **Loka Museum** (☎ 517 04 00; adult/child €3/2.10; ☺ 9am-6pm Tue-Sun Apr-Oct, 9am-5pm Sat & Sun Nov-Mar) with one of the best ethnographical collections in Slovenia. Buses for Škofja Loka (€2.30, 25 minutes, 13km) depart hourly from Kranj between 5.10am and 9.10pm.

BLED
☎ 04 / pop 5415

With an emerald-green lake, a picture-postcard church on a tiny island, a medieval castle clinging to a rocky cliff, and some of the highest peaks of the Julian Alps and the Karavanke as backdrops, Bled seems to have been designed by some god of tourism. As it is Slovenia's most popular destination, it can get pretty crowded in summer, but it's small, convenient and a delightful base from which to explore the mountains.

Information

À Propos Bar (☎ 574 40 44; Bled Shopping Centre, Ljubljanska c 4; per 15/30/60min €1.25/2.10/4.20; ☺ 8am-midnight) Internet access.

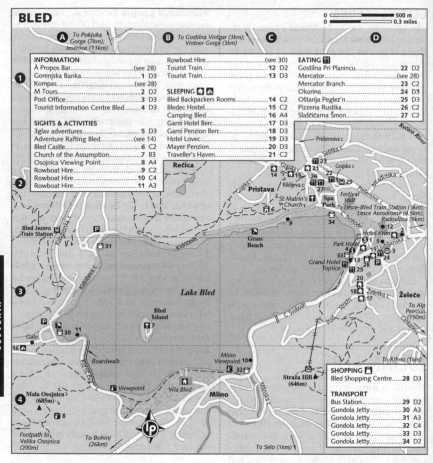

BLED

Gorenjska Banka (C Svobode 15; ☻ 9-11.30am & 2-5pm Mon-Fri, 8-11am Sat) North end of Park Hotel shop complex.

Kompas (☎ 572 75 00; www.kompas-bled.si; Bled Shopping Centre, Ljubljanska c 4; ☻ 8am-8pm Mon-Sat, 8am-noon & 4-8pm Sun Jul & Aug, 8am-7pm Mon-Sat Sep-Jun) Rents private rooms and bicycles.

M Tours (☎ 575 33 00; www.mtour.net; Ljubljanska c 7; ☻ 8am-8pm Mon-Sat, 8am-noon & 4-8pm Sun) Has private rooms.

Post office (Ljubljanska cesta 10; ☻ 8am-7pm Mon-Fri, 8am-noon Sat)

Tourist Information Centre Bled (☎ 574 11 22; www .bled.si; C Svobode 10; ☻ 8am-9pm Mon-Sat, 9am-5pm Sun Jul & Aug, 8am-7pm Mon-Sat, 11am-5pm Sun Mar-Jun & Sep-Oct, 9am-6pm Mon-Sat, noon-4pm Sun Nov, 8am-6pm Mon-Fri, 8am-1pm Sun Dec-Feb) Internet access is free for 15 minutes or pay €2.50/4 per 30/60 minutes

Sights

Sitting on its very own islet, the baroque **Church of the Assumption** (☻ 8am-dusk) is Bled's icon. Getting there by a piloted **gondola** (pletna; ☎ 041-427 155; per person €12) is the archetypal tourist experience. Gondola prices are standard from any jetty, and you'll stay on the island long enough to ring the 'lucky' bell; all in all, it's a 1½-hour trip. Ordinary row-yourself boats for three to four people cost €10 to €13 per hour.

Perched atop a 100m-high cliff, **Bled Castle** (☎ 572 9780; Grajska c 25; adult/student/child €7/6/3.50; ☻ 8am-8pm May-Oct, 8am-5pm Nov-Apr) is the perfect backdrop to a lake view. One of many access footpaths leads up from behind the Bledec Hostel. Admission includes entry to the recently revamped **museum collection**.

A short distance southeast of Bled and well served by bus (€1.80, 15 minutes, 7.5km, half-hourly), the sleepy town of **Radovljica** (population 6000) has a particularly delightful square called **Linhartov trg** in its Old Town, where there are restored and painted **manor houses**, an interesting **gallery**, the fascinating **Beekeeping Museum** (☎ 532 05 20; Linhartov trg 1; adult/student €3/2.50; ☘ 10am-1pm & 3-6pm Tue-Sun May-Oct, 10am-noon & 3-5pm Wed, Sat & Sun Mar, Apr, Nov & Dec) and, on the edge of the square, a **tourist office** (☎ 531 53 00; www.radovljica.si; Gorenjska c 1). The square lies 400m southeast of the bus station via Gorenjska c or just 100m up narrow Kolodvorska ul from the train station to the south.

Activities

The best way to see Lake Bled is on foot, the 6km stroll around the lake shouldn't take more than a couple of hours, including the short (but steep) climb to the brilliant **Osojnica viewing point** in the southwest. If you prefer, jump aboard the **tourist train** (adult/child €3/2; ☘ 9am-9pm May-mid-Oct, Sat & Sun Nov-Apr) for the 45-minute twirl around the lake, which departs from in front of the Sport Hall and, more centrally, from just north of the tourist office.

A popular and easy walk is to **Vintgar Gorge** (adult/student/child €4/3/2; ☘ 8am-7pm mid-May-Oct) 4km to the northwest. The highlight is the 1600m-long wooden walkway (1893) that criss-crosses the swirling Radovna River for the first 700m or so. Thereafter the scenery becomes tamer, passing a tall railway bridge and a spray-spouting weir, and the anticlimactic 13m-high **Šum Waterfall**. The easiest way to get to the gorge is via the appealing Gostilna Vintgar, an inn just three well-signed kilometres away on quiet, attractive roads from the Bledec Hostel. From early June to September, a daily bus (€3.50) leaves Bled bus station for Vintgar at 10am daily, arriving at 10.30am and returning at noon.

For something tougher, join one of the rafting or kayaking (€25 to €44) or paragliding (€85) trips on offer from **3glav adventures** (☎ 041-683 184; www.3glav-adventures.com; Ljubljanska c 1; ☘ 9am-7pm Apr-Oct); **Adventure Rafting Bled** (☎ 574 40 41, 051-676 008; www.adventure-rafting.si; Bled Backpackers Rooms, Grajska c 21; ☎ Apr-Oct) organises rafting and canyoning. Both the tourist office (opposite) and Kompas (opposite) rent **bikes** for €3.50/6 for one-/three-hours, or €8/11 for a half-/full day.

Sleeping

Bled is now blessed with several hostels, all within spitting distance of one another. Kompas (opposite) and M Tours (opposite) in the Hotel Krim have lists of private rooms, with singles/doubles starting at €24/38.

Camping Bled (☎ 575 20 00; www.camping-bled .com; Kidričeva c 10c; adult €8.50-11.50, child €5.95-8.05; ☘ Apr–mid-Oct) This popular 6.5-hectare site fills a small valley at the western end of the lake and boasts a popular restaurant.

Bled Backpackers Rooms (☎ 574 40 41, 051-678 008; www.bled-backpackersrooms.com; Grajska c 21; per person €17; ▢) With the attached George Best Bar open till at least midnight daily, this five-room place with 20 beds is Bled's party hostel. We love the room with the huge balcony and the storage lockers that open from the top.

Bledec Hostel (☎ 574 52 50; www.mlino.si; Grajska c 17; HI members/nonmembers dm €18/20, d €24/26; ▢) This official, somewhat old-fashioned hostel has dorms with four to seven beds and private bathrooms, a bar and an inexpensive restaurant. Laundry service (€8.50) and internet access (€2.10 per half-hour) is available.

Traveller's Haven (☎ 031-704 455, 041-396 545; www .travellers-haven.com; Riklijeva c 1; per person €19; ▢) This stunning new facility in a converted old villa (c 1909) has six rooms with between two and six beds, a great kitchen, free internet and laundry, and a chilled vibe.

Alp Penzion (☎ 576 74 50; www.alp-penzion.com; Cankarjeva c 20a; s €41, d €54-72) About 750m south of the town centre, the Alp is a bit away from the action but can be recommended for its tranquil location and lovely garden.

Garni Hotel Berc (☎ 576 56 58, www.berc-sp.si; Pod Stražo 13; s €40-45, d €65-70; ▢) This purpose-built place, reminiscent of a Swiss chalet, has 15 rooms on two floors in a quiet location above the lake. Just opposite is a second branch, Garni Penzion Berc (☎ 574 18 38; Želeška c 15; singles €35 to €40, doubles €60 to €55), with simpler rooms and cheaper rates.

Mayer Penzion (☎ 576 57 40; www.mayer-sp.si; Želeška c 7; s €45, d €70-75, apt €100; ▢) This delightful, flower-bedecked 12-room inn in a renovated 19th-century house is in the same neighbourhood as Garnic Hotel Berc. It's equally celebrated for its in-house restaurant.

Hotel Lovec (☎ 576 86 15; www.lovechotel.com; Ljubljanska c 6; s €110-151, d €128-225, ste from €245; ☒ ▢ ☒) A new favourite, the Lovec has been completely overhauled and now boasts 60 of some of the most attractive rooms in Bled.

We love the rooms with blonde-wood walls, red carpet and bath with jacuzzi in front of a massive window facing the lake.

Eating

Slaščičarna Šmon (☎ 574 16 16; Grajska c 3; ⏱ 7.30am-10pm) Bled's sweet of choice is *kremna rezina* (cream cake, €2.20), a layer of vanilla custard topped with whipped cream and sandwiched neatly between two layers of flaky pastry.

Gostilna Pri Planincu (☎ 574 16 13; Grajska c 8; mains €5-20.50; ⏱ 10am-10pm) 'At the Mountaineers' is a homey pub-restaurant just down the hill from the hostels, with Slovenian mains like sausage and *skutini štruklji* (cheese curd pastries) and grilled Balkan specialities such as *čevapčiči* (spicy meatballs of beef or pork; €7.40) and *pljeskavica z kajmakom* (Serbian-style meat patties with mascarpone-like cream cheese; €8.40).

Ostarija Peglez'n (☎ 574 42 18; C Svobode 19A; mains €8.50-22; ⏱ 11am-midnight) The best restaurant in Bled, the 'Iron Inn' is just opposite the landmark Grand Hotel Toplice, with attractively retro decor and some of the best fish dishes in town.

Okarina (☎ 574 14 58; Ljubljanska c 8; mains €9.80-24.80; ⏱ noon-midnight) This very upmarket restaurant has lots of colourful art spread over a modern dining room and serves both international favourites and decent Indian dishes like chicken *masala* and tandoori bass. There's a good choice of vegetarian dishes.

Pizzeria Rustika (☎ 576 89 00; Riklijeva c 13; pizza €5.70-9.50; ⏱ noon-midnight Tue-Sun) A marble-roll down the hill from the hostels, this place has its own wood-burning oven and seating on two levels plus an outside terrace.

You'll find a **Mercator** (Ljubljanska c 4; ⏱ 7am-8pm Mon-Sat, 8am-noon Sun) at the eastern end of Bled Shopping Centre. There's a smaller **Mercator branch** (Prešernova c 48; ⏱ 7am-8pm Mon-Sat, 8am-4pm Sun) close to the hostels.

Getting There & Around

Frequent buses to Bohinj (€3.60, one hour, 26km, hourly), Ljubljana (€6.30, 1¼ hours, 57km, hourly) and Kranj (€3.60, 30 minutes, 23km, half-hourly) via Radovljica (€1.80, 15 minutes, 7.5km) leave from the central bus station.

Bled has no central train station. Trains to Bohinjska Bistrica (€1.50, 20 minutes, 18km, seven daily) and Nova Gorica (€5.35, two hours, 79km, seven daily) use little Bled Jezero train station, which is 2km west of central Bled – handy for the camping ground but little else. Trains for Ljubljana (€4.10 to €7.60, 45 minutes to one hour, 51km, up to 17 daily) use Lesce-Bled train station, 4km to the east of town.

Book a taxi on ☎ 031-705 343.

BOHINJ

☎ 04 / pop 5275

Lake Bohinj, a larger and much less-developed glacial lake 26km to the southwest, is a world apart from Bled. Mt Triglav is visible from the lake and there are activities galore – from kayaking and mountain biking to hiking up Triglav via one of the southern approaches.

Bohinjska Bistrica, the area's largest village, is 6km east of the lake and only interesting for its train station. The main tourist hub on the lake is **Ribčev Laz** at the eastern end. Its miniscule commercial centre contains a supermarket, a post office (which changes money), an ATM and the **Bohinj tourist office** (☎ 574 60 10; www.bohinj-info.com; Ribčev Laz 48; ⏱ 8am-8pm Mon-Sat, to 6pm Sun Jul & Aug, 8am-6pm Mon-Sat, 9am-3pm Sun Sep-Jun), which can help with accommodation and sells **fishing licences** (€25 per day for the lake, €38.50 catch and release). **Alpinsport** (☎ 572 34 86; www.alpinsport.si; Ribčev Laz 53; ⏱ 9am or 10am-6pm or 8pm) organises a range of activities, and hires out kayaks, canoes, mountain bikes (per hour/day €4/14) and other equipment from a kiosk near the stone bridge. Next door is the delightful **Church of St John the Baptist**, which contains splendid 15th- and 16th-century frescoes, but is undergoing a protracted renovation.

The nearby village of **Stara Fužina** has an appealing little **Alpine Dairy Museum** (☎ 041-564 904; Stara Fužine 181; adult/child €2.10/1.60; ⏱ 11am-7pm Tue-Sun Jul & Aug, 10am-noon & 4-6pm Tue-Sun Jan-Jun, Sep & Oct). Just opposite is a cheesemonger called **Planšar** (☎ 572 30 95; Stara Fužina 179; ⏱ 1am-7pm Tue-Sun Jul & Aug, 10am-noon & 4-6pm Tue-Sun Jan-Jun, Sep & Oct), which specialises in homemade dairy products such as hard Bohinj cheese, cottage cheese and curd pie. Just 2km east is **Studor**, a village famed for its *toplarji*, the double-linked hayrack with barns or storage areas at the top, some of which date from the 18th and 19th centuries.

From June to late September, the inventively named **Tourist Boat** (☎ 041-434 986; adult/child/family one-way €8.50/6/18, return €10/7/23; ⏱ 10am-6pm) departs from the pier just opposite the Alpinsport kiosk every 30 to 40 minutes

---

HIKING MT TRIGLAV

The Julian Alps offer some of Europe's finest hiking. In summer some 170 mountain huts (planinska koča or planinski dom) operate, none more than five hours' walk from the next. These huts get very crowded, especially on weekends, so booking ahead is wise. If the weather turns bad, however, you won't be refused refuge.

At €27 per person in a room with up to four beds or €18 in a dormitory in a Category I hut (Category II huts charge €20 and €12 respectively), the huts aren't cheap, but as they serve meals (a simple meal should cost between €4.70 and €6.20 in a Category I hut, and €3.50 and €5 in a Category II hut) you can travel light. Sturdy boots and warm clothes are indispensable, even in midsummer. Trails are generally well marked with a white-centred red circle, but you can still get lost and it's very unwise to trek alone. It's best to engage the services of a qualified (and licensed) guide, who will cost from €50/150 per two-/eight-hour period.

The tourist offices in Bled (p510), Bohinj (opposite), Kranjska Gora (p514) and Bovec (p515) all have lots of hiking information, sell maps in a variety of scales and can help book huts and guides in their regions. You might also contact the Alpine Association of Slovenia (p526) directly.

(between four and six times a day at other times), terminating a half-hour later at the Ukanc jetty at the lake's far western end. Just 300m up from the Ukanc jetty and 5km west of Ribčev Laz, a **cable car** (☎ 572 97 12 adult/child one-way €8/6, return €12/8; ◷ 8am-6pm) whisks up half-hourly to 1540m; from here, paths continue up **Mt Vogel**.

In September, the **Cows' Ball** (www.bohinj.si) at Bohinj is a zany weekend of folk dance, music, eating and drinking to mark the return of the cows from their high pastures down to the valleys.

Sleeping & Eating

Private rooms (per person €10-15) and **apartments** (d €33-44, q €48.50-70) are available through the tourist office.

Autokamp Zlatorog (☎ 572 34 82; www.aaturizem .com; Ukanc 2; per person €7-12; ◷ May-Sep) This pine-shaded 2.5-hectare camping ground accommodating 500 guests is at the lake's western end, 4.5km from Ribčev Laz.

Hostel Pod Voglom (☎ 572 34 61; www.hostel-pod voglom.com; Ribčev Laz 60; per person with shared bathroom €19-21, with private bathroom €22-24, dm €16-18; 🖳) This welcome addition to Bohinj's budget accommodation scene some 3km west of the centre has 119 beds in 46 somewhat frayed rooms in two buildings. The so-called Hostel Building has doubles, triples and dormitory accommodation with shared facilities; rooms in the Rodica Annexe, with between one and four beds, are with en suite.

Penzion Gasperin (☎ 572 36 61; www.bohinj.si/gasp erin; Ribčev Laz 36A; per person €22-33; 🅿 🖳) This positively spotless chalet-style guest house with

20 rooms (nine of which are spanking new) is just 350m east of the tourist office and run by a friendly British/Slovenian couple. Some rooms (eg Nos 1, 2 and 3) have balconies.

Hotel Bellevue (☎ 572 33 31; www.hoteli-bohinj .si; Ribčev Laz 65, s €48-57, d €56-74; 🖳) The shabby Bellevue has a beautiful (if somewhat isolated) and atmospheric location on a hill about 700m south of the lake. Whodunit fans take note: Agatha Christie stayed in room No 204 for three weeks in 1967. Thirty-eight of the hotel's 59 rooms are in the unattractive Savica Annexe.

Gostilna Rupa (☎ 572 34 01; Srednja Vas 87; mains €7-15; ◷ 10am-midnight Jul & Aug, 10am-midnight Tue-Sun Sep-Jun) If you're under your own steam, head for this country-style restaurant in the next village over from Studor and about 5km from Ribčev Laz. Among the excellent home-cooked dishes are ajdova krapi, crescent-shaped dumplings made from buckwheat and cheese, various types of local klobasa (sausage) and Bohinj trout.

Getting There & Around

Buses run regularly from Ukanc ('Bohinj Zlatorog' on most schedules) to Ljubljana (€8.70, two hours, 91km, hourly) via Ribčev Laz, Bohinjska Bistrica and Bled (€4.10, one hour, 34km), with six extra buses daily between Ukanc and Bohinjska Bistrica (€2.70 20 minutes, 12km). From Bohinjska Bistrica, passenger trains to Nova Gorica (€4.70, 1¼ hours, 61km, up to seven daily) make use of a century-old tunnel under the mountains that provides the only direct option for reaching the Soča Valley. In addition there are daily

SLOVENIA

auto trains (*avtovlaki*) to Podbrdo (€7.50, eight minutes, 7km, five daily) and Most na Soči (€11.50, 25 minutes, 28km, three daily).

KRANJSKA GORA

☎ 04 / pop 1490

Nestling in the Sava Dolinka Valley, Kranjska Gora is Slovenia's largest and best-equipped ski resort. It's at its most perfect under a blanket of snow, but its surroundings are wonderful to explore at other times as well. There are endless possibilities for hiking and mountaineering in Triglav National Park, which is right on the town's doorstep to the south, and few travellers will be unimpressed by a trip over Vršič Pass (1611m), the gateway to the Soča Valley.

Kranjska Gora has lots of places offering ski tuition and hiring out equipment, including **ASK Kranjska Gora Ski School** (☎ 588 53 02; www .ask-kg.com; Borovška c 99A) in the same building as SKB Banka. Rent bikes from one of the **Sport Point** (☎ 588 48 83; www.sport-point.si; Borovška c 74; per hr/4hr/day €3.50/6.50/10; ☉ 9am-9pm) outlets. To watch the experts, the men's slalom and giant slalom **Vitranc Cup** (www.pokal-vitranc.com) is held in Kranjska Gora in late February and early March, and the **Ski-Jumping World Cup Championships** (www.planica.info) at nearby Planica (also in March).

Borovška c, 400m south of the bus stops, is the heart of the village, with the endearing **Liznjek House** (☎ 588 19 99; Borovška 63; adult/child €2.50/2; ☉ 10am-8pm Tue-Sat, 10am-5pm Sun May-Oct & Dec-Mar), an 18th-century museum house with a good collection of household objects and furnishings peculiar to Gorenjska province. At its western end is the **Tourist Information Centre Kranjska Gora** (☎ 580 94 40; www.kranjska -gora.si; Tičarjeva c 2; ☉ 8am-8pm Mon-Sat, 9am-6pm Sun Jun-Sep & mid-Dec–Mar, 8am-3pm Mon-Fri, 8am-4pm Sat, 9am-1pm Sun May, 8am-3pm Mon-Fri, 9am-4pm Sat Apr & Oct–mid-Dec).

Sleeping & Eating

Accommodation costs peak from December to March and in midsummer. **Private rooms** (per person €12-24) and **apartments** (d €34-50, q €68-108) can be arranged through the tourist office.

Hostel Pr' Tatko (☎ 031-479 087; Podkoren 72; www.prtatko.com; dm €13-17, q €56-76; ☐) One of Slovenia's nicest small hostels is in Podkoren, just 3km to the northwest of Kranjska Gora. It's a four-room affair in a traditional old farmhouse, each with between four (one en

suite) and eight beds. There's a decent-sized kitchen and common room. They'll teach you how to collect mushrooms in season.

Pension Borka (☎ 031-536 288; darinka2007@gmail .com; Borovška c 71; per person €20-30) Not a patch (operative word) on the Tatko but a lot more central, this very frayed property has some three-dozen rooms – mostly doubles and triples – crying out for a refit. There's a large cellar restaurant.

Hotel Kotnik (☎ 588 15 64; www.hotel-kotnik.si; Borovška c 75; s €50-59, d €60-78; ☐) If you're not into big high-rise hotels with hundreds of rooms, choose this charming, bright yellow low-rise property. It has 15 cosy rooms, a great restaurant and pizzeria, and it couldn't be more central.

Gostilna Pri Martinu (☎ 582 03 00; Borovška c 61; mains €4-12.50; ☉ 10am-11pm) This atmospheric tavern-restaurant in an old house opposite the fire station is one of the best places in town to try local specialities, such as *telečja obara* (veal stew; €4) and *ričet* (barley stew with smoked pork ribs; €5.90).

Getting There & Away

Buses run hourly on the half-hour to Ljubljana (€8.70, two hours, 91km) via Jesenice (€3.10, 30 minutes, 23km), where you should change for Bled (€2.70, 20 minutes, 16km). There's just one direct departure to Bled (€5.20, one hour, 40km) on weekdays at 9.05am. A service to Bovec (€6.70, two hours, 46km) via Vršič Pass departs five times daily (six on Sunday) in July and August, and on Saturday and Sunday at 8.27am in June and September.

SOČA VALLEY

The Soča Valley region is defined by the 96km-long Soča River coloured a deep, almost artificial turquoise. The valley has more than its share of historical sights, most of them related to one of the costliest battles of WWI, but the majority of visitors are here for rafting, hiking, skiing and other active sports.

Bovec

☎ 05 / pop 1760

Effectively the capital of the Soča Valley, Bovec has a great deal to offer adventure-sports enthusiasts. With the Julian Alps above, the Soča River below and Triglav National Park all around, you could spend a week here hiking, kayaking, mountain biking and, in winter, skiing at Mt Kanin (2587m), Slovenia's highest ski station, without ever doing the same thing twice.

The compact village square, **Trg Golobarskih Žrtev**, has everything you'll need. There are cafes, a hotel, the helpful **Tourist Information Centre Bovec** (☎ 389 64 44; www.bovec.si; Trg Golobarski Žrtev; ⏱ 8.30am-8.30pm Jul & Aug, 9am-5pm Mon-Fri, 9am-noon & 4-6pm Sat, 9am-noon Sun Sep-Jun) and a half-dozen adrenalin-raising adventure-sports companies.

ACTIVITIES

There's no shortage of activities on offer in and around Bovec. Possibilities include **canyoning** (€43 to €45 for two hours) at Sušec, or **caving** (€35 per person with guide). Or you could try your hand at **hydrospeed** (like riding down a river on a boogie board); you'll pay €45 to €55 for a 6km to 8km ride. A guided 10km **kayaking** tour costs from €39.50 to €41.50 per person, or a one-day training course from €45 to €53.50.

From April to October, you can go **rafting** (€35/45 for a 10/20km trip). And in winter you can take a tandem paraglider flight (ie as a passenger accompanied by a qualified pilot) from atop the Kanin cable car, 2000m above the valley floor. A flight costs from €110; ask Avantura for details.

Recommended operators:

Avantura (☎ 041-718 317; www.avantura.org)
Bovec Rafting Team (☎ 388 61 28, 041-338 308; www.bovec-rafting-team.com)
Outdoor Freaks (☎ 389 64 90, 041-553 675; www.outdoorfreaks.si)
Soča Rafting (☎ 389 62 00, 041-724 472; www.soca rafting.si)
Sport Mix (☎ 389 61 60, 031-871 991; www.sportmix.traftbovec.si)
Top Extreme (☎ 041-620 636; www.top.si)

SLEEPING & EATING

Alp Hotel (☎ 388 40 00; www.alp-chandler.si; Trg Golobarskih Žrtev 48; s €48-60, d €66-90; 🖥 🖳) This 103-room hotel is fairly good value and as central as you are going to find in Bovec. Guests get to use the swimming pool at the nearby Hotel Kanin.

Dobra Vila (☎ 389 64 00; www.dobra-vila-bovec.com; Mala Vas 112; s €58-105, d €88-135; 🖳) This positive stunner of a 12-room boutique hotel is housed in an erstwhile telephone-exchange building. It has its own small cinema, library, restaurant and wine cellar.

Martinov Hram (☎ 388 62 14; Trg Golobarskih Žrtev 27; mains €6.90-19.50; ⏱ 10am-10pm Tue-Thu, to midnight Fri & Sat) Traditional restaurant in an attractive inn specialising in game, Soča trout and mushroom dishes. During the winter, pizza rears its ugly head.

Private rooms (per person €15-30) are easy to come by in Bovec through the TIC.

Camping facilities are generally better in Kobarid (p516), but **Kamp Polovnik** (☎ 388 60 69; www.kamp-polovnik.com; Ledina 8; adult €5-7, child €3.75-5.25; ⏱ Apr–mid-Oct) about 500m southeast of the town centre is much more convenient.

GETTING THERE & AWAY

Buses to Nova Gorica (€7.50, two hours, 77km, up to five a day) go via Kobarid (€3.10, half-hour, 21km). A service to Kranjska Gora (€6.70, two hours, 46km) via the spectacular Vršič Pass departs five times daily (six on Sunday) in July and August, and on Saturday and Sunday at 3.35pm in June and September.

Kobarid

☎ 05 / pop 1235

Some 21km south of Bovec, quaint Kobarid (Caporetto in Italian) lies in a broad valley on the west bank of the Soča River. Although it's surrounded by mountain peaks higher than 2200m, Kobarid somehow feels more Mediterranean than alpine. The Italian border is just 9km to the west.

The **Tourist Information Centre Kobarid** (☎ 380 04 90; www.lto-sotocje.si; Gregorčičeva ul 8; ⏱ 9am-8pm Jul & Aug, 9am-12.30pm & 1.30-7pm Mon-Fri, 9am-1pm Sat Sep-Jun) is next door to the award-winning **Kobarid Museum** (☎ 389 00 00; Gregorčičeva ul 10; adult/student/child €4/3/2.50; ⏱ 9am-6pm Mon-Fri, 9am-7pm Sat & Sun Apr-Sep, 10am-5pm Mon-Fri, 9am-6pm Sat & Sun Oct-Mar), devoted almost entirely to the Isonzo (Soča) Front of WWI, which formed the backdrop to Ernest Hemingway's *A Farewell to Arms*. A free pamphlet and map titled *The Kobarid Historical Trail* outlines a 5km-long route that will take you past remnant WWI troop emplacements to the impressive **Kozjak Stream Waterfalls**. More ambitious is the hike outlined in the *Pot Miru/ Walk of Peace* brochure.

Kobarid is beginning to give Bovec a run for its money in extreme sports, and you'll find several outfits on or off the town's main square that can organise rafting, canyoning, canoeing and paragliding from April to October. They include the long-established

XPoint (☎ 388 53 08, 041-692 290; www.xpoint.si; Trg Svobode 6); the new and enthusiastic **Positive Sport** (☎ 040-654 475; www.positive-sport.com; Markova ul 2); and Apartma-Ra, which also organises two-hour quad-bike trips for €45.

The oldest (and, some would say, friendliest) camping ground in the valley, **Kamp Koren** (☎ 389 13 11; www.kamp-koren.si; Drežniške Ravne 33; per person €8.50-10; ☷ mid-Mar–Oct; ☐) is a small site about 500m northeast of Kobarid on the left bank of the Soča River and just beyond the Napoleon Bridge, built in 1750.

The welcoming little **Apartma-Ra** (☎ 041-641 899; apartma-ra@siol.net; Gregorčičeva ul 6C; per person €15-25; ☒) lies between the museum and Trg Svobode and has five rooms and apartments, some with terraces. The best place in town is the **Hotel Hvala** (☎ 389 93 00; www.hotelhvala.si; Trg Svobode 1; s €59-72, d €82-108; ☐), which has 31 rooms – some recently renovated to a level unseen in provincial Slovenia – linked by a snazzy new lift, a bar, a superb Restavracija Topli Val restaurant and a Mediterranean-style cafe in the garden.

In the centre of Kobarid you'll find two of Slovenia's best restaurants, both of which specialise in fish and seafood: the incomparable **Restavracija Topli Val** (☎ 389 93 00; Trg Svobode 1; mains €9.50-25; ☷ noon-10pm) and **Restavracija Kotlar** (☎ 389 11 10; Trg Svobode 11; mains €8.50-20; ☷ noon-11pm Thu, Sun & Mon, to midnight Fri & Sat).

Buses, which arrive at and depart from in front of the Cinca Marinca bar on Trg Svobode, link Kobarid with Nova Gorica (€6, 1½ hours, 55km, up to five daily) and Ljubljana (€11.50, three hours, 130km, up to four daily) passing Most na Soči train station, which is good for Bled and Bohinj. Buses that cross over the spectacular Vršič Pass to Kranjska Gora (€7.85, three hours, 68km) depart three times a day in July and August.

Nova Gorica
☎ 05 / pop 12,585

When the town of Gorica, capital of the former Slovenian province of Goriška, was awarded to the Italians after WWII, the new socialist government in Yugoslavia set itself to building a model town on the eastern side of the border. They called it 'New Gorica' and erected a chain-link barrier between the two towns. This rather flimsy 'Berlin Wall' was pulled down to great fanfare in 2004, leaving Piazza della Transalpina (or Trg z Mozaikom on this side) straddling the border right behind Nova

Gorica's train station. There you'll now find the esoteric **Museum of the Border in Gorica 1945–2004** (☎ 333 44 00; admission free; ☷ 1-5pm Mon-Fri, 9am-7pm Sat, 10am-7pm Sun). Nova Gorica is an easy way to get to/from Italy; Italian bus 1 (€0.98) will whisk you from Via G Caprin opposite the museum to Gorizia train station.

The helpful **Tourist Information Centre Nova Gorica** (☎ 330 46 00; www.novagorica-turizem.com; Bevkov trg 4; ☷ 8am-8pm Mon-Fri, 9am-1pm Sat & Sun Jul & Aug, 8am-6pm Mon-Fri, 9am-1pm Sat Sep-Jun) is in the lobby of the Kulturni Dom (Cultural House).

One of the few inexpensive accommodation options, **Prenočišče Pertout** (☎ 330 75 50, 041-624 452; www.prenociscepertout.com; Ul 25 Maja 23; s/d/tr €24/34/51) is a five-room B&B in Rožna Dolina, south of the town centre and scarcely 100m northeast of the Italian border. The Italian restaurant **Marco Polo** (☎ 302 97 29; Kidričeva ul 13; mains €8-17; ☷ 11am-11pm Mon-Thu, 11am-midnight Fri & Sat, noon-midnight Sun), with a delightful back terrace 250m east of the tourist office, is one of the town's best places to eat, serving pizza (€4.40 to €7.80), pasta (€5.50 to €10) and more ambitious dishes.

Buses travel hourly between Nova Gorica and Ljubljana (€10.70 2½ hours, 116km) via Postojna (€6.30, one hour, 53km), and up to five times daily to Bovec (€7.50, two hours, 77km) via Kobarid (€6, 1½ hours, 55km).

Trains link Nova Gorica with Bohinjska Bistrica (€4.70, 1¼ hours, 61km, up to seven daily), a springboard for Bled, with Postojna (€5.65, two hours, 61km, six daily) via Sežana and Divača, and with Ljubljana (€7.75, 3½ hours, 153km, five daily) via Jesenice.

KARST & COAST

Slovenia's short coast (47km) is an area of both history and recreation. Three important towns full of Venetian Gothic architecture – Koper, Izola and Piran – are the main drawcards here and the southernmost resort of Portorož has some decent beaches. En route from Ljubljana or the Soča Valley, you'll cross the Karst, a huge limestone plateau and a land of olives, ruby-red Teran wine, *pršut* (air-dried ham), old stone churches and deep subterranean caves. In fact, Slovenia's two most famous caverns – Postojna and Škocjan – are here.

POSTOJNA
☎ 05 / pop 8850

Slovenia's single most popular tourist attraction, **Postojna Cave** (☎ 700 01 00; www.postojnska-jama.si;

Jamska c 30; adult/student/child €20/16/13; ✆ tours hourly 9am-6pm Jul & Aug, to 5pm May, Jun & Sep, 10am, noon, 2pm & 4pm Apr & Oct, 10am, noon & 3pm Nov-Mar) is about 2km northwest of the town of that name. The 5.7km-long cavern is visited on a 1½-hour tour, but about 4km of it is covered by an electric train and the rest on foot. Inside, impressive stalagmites and stalactites stretch almost endlessly in all directions, as do the chattering crowds who pass them.

Close to the cave's entrance is the **Proteus Vivarium** (adult/student/child €7/6/4, with cave €24/19/14; ✆ 9.30am-5.30pm May-Sep, 10.30am-3.30pm Oct-Apr), a speliobiological research station with a video introduction to underground zoology. A 45-minute tour then leads you into a small, darkened cave to peep at some of the endemic *Proteus anguinus*, shy (and miniscule) creatures you've just learned about in the Postojna Cave.

Predjama (population 85), a village 9km northwest of Postojna, can claim the remarkable **Predjama Castle** (✆ 751 60 15; Predjama 1; www .turizem-kras.si; adult/student/child €8/7/5; ✆ 9am-7pm Jul & Aug, to 6pm May, Jun & Sep, 10am-5pm Apr & Oct, to 4pm Nov-Mar), which appears to grow out of a yawning cave. The partly furnished interior spread over four floors boasts costumed wax mannequins, one of which dangles from the dripping rock-roofed torture chamber. Beneath are stalactite-adorned **caves** (adult/student/child €7/6/4, cave & castle combination ticket €13/11/8; ✆ tours 11am, 1pm, 3pm & 5pm May-Sep), which lack Postojna's crowds but also much of its grandeur; tours last an hour.

Sleeping & Eating

Kompas Postojna (✆ 721 14 80; www.kompas-postojna .si; Titov trg 2A; r per person €18-20; ✆ 8am-7pm Mon-Fri, 9am-1pm Sat Jun-Aug, 8am-6pm Mon-Fri, 9am-1pm Sat May, Sep & Oct, 8am-5pm Mon-Fri, 9am-1pm Sat Nov-Apr) Has private rooms.

Hotel Sport (✆ 720 22 44; www.sport-hotel.si; Kolodvorska c 1; dm €20, s €55-65, d €70-90, tr 96-125, q €120-160; 🖳) A much more expensive proposition than when it opened a few short years ago, the Sport still offers reasonable value for money, with 32 spick-and-span and very comfortable rooms, including 40 hostel beds. It's just 300m north of the centre of Postojna. It rents mountain bikes (half-/full day €9/15) for exploring nearby Notranjska Regional Park.

Pizzeria Minutka (✆ 720 36 25; Ljubljanska c 14; pizza €4.90-7.10; ✆ noon-11pm) A pizzeria with a terrace, Minutka is a favourite with locals and is just south of the Hotel Sport.

Getting There & Away

Buses from Ljubljana to Koper, Piran and Nova Gorica all stop in Postojna (€6, one hour, 54km, half-hourly). The train is less useful, as the station is 1km east of town (ie almost 3km from the caves).

As close as you'll get by local bus from Postojna to Predjama (€2.30, 15 minutes, 9km, five daily Monday to Friday) and during the school year only is Bukovje, a village about 2km northeast of Predjama. A taxi from Postojna, including an hour's wait at Predjama Castle, will cost €30, which staff at Kompas Postojna can organise.

ŠKOCJAN CAVES
☎ 05

The immense system of **Škocjan Caves** (✆ 708 21 00; www.park-skocjanske-jame.si; Škocjan 2; adult/student/child €14/10/6), a Unesco World Heritage site since 1986, is far more captivating than the larger one at Postojna, and for many travellers a visit here will be a highlight of their trip to Slovenia. With relatively few stalactites, the attraction is the sheer depth of the awesome underground chasm, which you cross by a dizzying little footbridge. To see this you must join a shepherded walking tour, lasting 1½ to two hours and involving hundreds of steps and a funicular ride at the end. Tours depart hourly from 10am to 5pm from June to September, at 10am, 1pm and 3.30pm in April, May and October, and at 10am and 1pm Monday to Saturday, and 10am, 1pm and 3pm Sunday from November to March.

The nearest town with accommodation is **Divača** (population 1330), 5km to the northwest. **Gostilna Malovec** (✆ 763 12 25; Kraška 30a; per person €20) has a half-dozen basic but renovated rooms in a building beside its traditional **restaurant** (mains €5-15; ✆ 8am to 10pm). For something a bit more, well, 21st-century, cross the road to **Orient Express** (✆ 763 30 10; Kraška c 67; pizza €4.60-14; ✆ 11am-11pm Sun-Fri, 11am-2am Sat), a lively pizzeria and pub.

Bus services running from Ljubljana to Koper and the coast stop at Divača (€8, 1½ hours, 82km, half-hourly), as do trains (€6.25, 1½ hours, 104km, hourly). Staff at the train station ticket office can provide you with a photocopied route map for walking to the caves and there is a copy posted outside. Alternatively, a courtesy van meets incoming trains at 10am, 11.04am, 2pm and 3.35pm and will transport those with bus or train tickets to the caves.

LIPICA
☎ 05 / pop 95

Lipica is where Austrian Archduke Charles, son of Ferdinand I, established a stud farm to breed horses for the Spanish Riding School in Vienna in 1580. The snow-white beauties are still born and raised at the **Lipica Stud Farm** (☎ 739 15 80; www.lipica.org; Lipica 5; adult/student & child from €9/4.50), which offers equestrian fans a variety of tours, as well as riding and lessons. Tour times are complex; see the website for details.

Good value is the 80-room **Hotel Klub** (☎ 739 15 70; s/d €32/49; 🖵) near the stud farm with a sauna and fitness centre. The nearby **Hotel Maestoso** (☎ 739 15 80; s/d €80/120; 🖵 🏊) has 66 more modern rooms.

A van meets incoming trains at Divača, 9km to the northeast, at 10.19am, 11.24am, 2.24pm and 3.59pm and transports ticket holders to the stud farm.

KOPER
☎ 05 / pop 24,630

Coastal Slovenia's largest town, Koper (Capodistria in Italian and Aegida to the Greeks) at first glance appears to be a workaday city that scarcely gives tourism a second thought. Yet its central core is delightfully medieval and far less overrun than its ritzy cousin Piran, 17km down the coast. Koper grew rich as a key port trading salt, and was the capital of Istria under the Venetian Republic during the 15th and 16th centuries. It remains Slovenia's most important port.

Orientation

The joint bus and train station is about 1.5km southeast of central Titov trg. To walk into town, just head north along Kolodvorska c in the direction of the cathedral's distinctive campanile (bell tower). Alternatively, take bus 1 or 2 to Muda Gate.

Information

Banka Koper (Kidričeva ul 14; 🕑 8.30am-noon & 3-5pm Mon-Fri, 8.30am-noon Sat)
Kompas (☎ 663 05 81; Pristaniška ul 17; 🕑 8am-7pm Mon-Fri, 8am-1pm Sat) Private rooms.
Palma Travel Agency (☎ 663 36 60; Pristaniška ul 21; 🕑 8am-7pm Mon-Fri, 9am-noon Sat) Private rooms.
Pina (☎ 627 80 72; Kidričeva ul 43; adult/student per hr

€4.20/1.20; 🕑 4-10pm) Central internet cafe with 10 terminals.
Post office (Muzejski trg 3; 🕑 8am-7pm Mon-Fri)
Tourist Information Centre Koper (☎ 664 64 03; www.koper.si; Praetorian Palace, Titov trg 3; 🕑 9am-9pm Jul & Aug, 9am-5pm Mon-Fri, to 7pm Sat & Sun Sep-Jun)

Sights

You'll change centuries abruptly as you pass through **Muda Gate** (1516) leading into Prešernov trg. Continue north past the bridge-shaped **Da Ponte Fountain** (1666), and up Župančičeva ul and Čevljarska ul, the narrow commercial artery, to reach **Titov trg**. This fine central square is dominated by the 15th-century **City Tower** (adult/child €2/1.50; 🕑 9am-2pm & 4-9pm), which can be climbed, attached to the part-Gothic, part-Renaissance **Cathedral of the Assumption**. The Venetian Gothic and Renaissance **Praetorian Palace** (Titov trg 3; admission free) contains the town hall, with an old pharmacy and the tourist office on the ground floor and a ceremonial hall with exhibits on the 1st floor. Opposite, the splendid 1463 **Loggia** is now an elegant cafe (p520) and gallery. To the east of it is the circular Romanesque **Rotunda of St John the Baptist**, a baptistery dating from the second half of the 12th century.

The **Koper Regional Museum** (☎ 663 35 70; Kidričeva ul 19; adult/child €2.50/1.50; 🕑 9am-1pm & 6-9pm Tue-Sun Jul & Aug, 10am-6pm Tue-Fri, 9am-1pm Sat & Sun Sep-Jun), inside the Belgramoni-Tacco Palace, contains an Italianate sculpture garden. Kidričeva ul also has a few multicoloured medieval houses with beamed overhangs. It leads west into Carpacciov trg, the former fish market with a 15th-century **salt warehouse** and the stone **Column of St Justina** dating from 1571.

Sleeping

Both Kompas (left) and the Palma Travel Agency (left) can arrange **private rooms** (per person r €20-31) and **apartments** (2-person €32-40, 4-person €56-70), most of which are in the new town beyond the train station.

Motel Port (☎ 639 32 60; www.port-turizem.si; Ankaranska c 7; dm €15-17, s €29-40, d €43-48, tr €54-60; 🍴 🖵) Hidden on the 2nd floor of a shopping centre southeast of the Old Town, this place has 30 rooms, some of them en suite and air-conditioned and others dorm rooms with four to six beds. There's a breezy cafe-bar here as well.

Museum Hostel (☎ 626 18 70, 041-504 466; bozic .doris@siol.net; Muzejski trg 6; per person €20-25) This

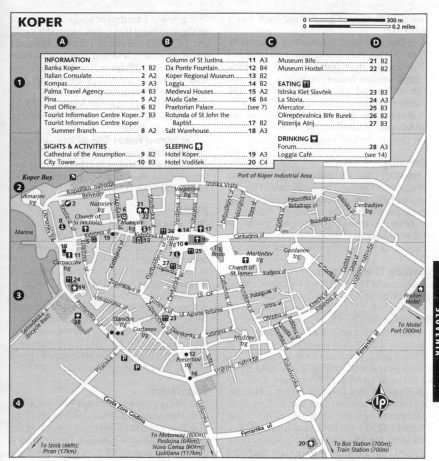

KOPER

0 — 300 m
0 — 0.2 miles

INFORMATION
Banka Koper.....................................1 B2
Italian Consulate.............................2 A2
Kompas...3 A3
Palma Travel Agency........................4 B3
Pina...5 A2
Post Office......................................6 B2
Tourist Information Centre Koper.7 B3
Tourist Information Centre Koper
   Summer Branch...........................8 A2

SIGHTS & ACTIVITIES
Cathedral of the Assumption........9 B2
City Tower.....................................10 B3

Column of St Justina.....................11 A3
Da Ponte Fountain........................12 B4
Koper Regional Museum...............13 B2
Loggia...14 B2
Medieval Houses...........................15 A2
Muda Gate....................................16 B4
Praetorian Palace......................(see 7)
Rotunda of St John the
   Baptist.......................................17 B2
Salt Warehouse.............................18 A3

SLEEPING 🏠
Hotel Koper..................................19 A3
Hotel Vodišek...............................20 C4

Museum Bife.................................21 B2
Museum Hostel.............................22 B2

EATING 🍴
Istrska Klet Slavček......................23 B3
La Storia..24 A3
Mercator.......................................25 B2
Okrepčevalnica Bife Burek...........26 B2
Pizzerija Atrij................................27 B3

DRINKING 🍷
Forum..28 A3
Loggia Café...............................(see 14)

SLOVENIA

---

good-value place is more a series of bright apartments with modern kitchens and bathrooms than a hostel. Reception is at the little Museum Bife, a cafe-bar on Muzejski trg; the rooms are actually at Mladinska ul 7.

Hotel Vodišek (☎ 639 24 68; www.hotel-vodisek.com; Kolodvorska c 2; s €45-60, d €68-90, tr €83-110; ⊠ 🖥) This hotel, with 32 small but reasonably priced rooms, is in a shopping centre halfway between the Old Town and the train and bus stations. Guests get to use the hotel's bicycles for free.

Hotel Koper (☎ 610 05 00; www.terme-catez.si; Pristaniška ul 3; s €76, d €120; ⊠ 🖥) This pleasant, 65-room property on the very edge of the historic Old Town is the only central hotel in Koper.

Eating

Okrepčevalnica Bife Burek (☎ 271 347; Kidričeva ul 8; snacks €1.70-2.50; ☯ 7am-10pm) Buy good-value *burek* here and enjoy it at Titov trg for a take-away snack.

Istrska Klet Slavček (☎ 627 67 29; Župančičeva ul 39; dishes €2.50-14; ☯ 7am-10pm Mon-Fri) This 'Istrian Cellar', situated below the 18th-century Carli Palace, is one of the most colourful places for a meal in Koper's Old Town. Filling set lunches go for less than €7, and there's local Malvazija and Teran wine from the barrel.

Pizzerija Atrij (☎ 627 22 55; Triglavska ul 2; pizza €3-6.70; ☯ 9am-10pm Mon-Fri, 10am-10pm Sat) This popular pizzeria down an alleyway no wider than your average quarterback's shoulder spread has a small covered garden out back and a salad bar.

La Storia (☎ 626 20 18; Pristaniška ul 3; mains €9.90-22.50; ☑ 11am-11pm Mon-Fri, noon-11pm Sat & Sun) This Italian-style trattoria with sky-view ceiling frescoes focuses on salads, pasta and fish dishes and has outside seating in the warmer months.

Mercator (Titov trg 2; ☑ 7am-8pm Mon-Fri, 7am-1pm Sat, 8am-noon Sun) Small branch of the supermarket giant in the Old Town.

Drinking

Loggia Café (☎ 621 32 13; Titov trg 1; ☑ 7.30am-10pm Mon-Sat, 10am-10pm Sun) This lovely cafe in the exquisite 15th-century Loggia is the best vantage point for watching the crowds on Titov trg.

Forum (Pristaniška ul 2; ☑ 7am-11pm) Cafe-bar at the northern side of the market and facing a little park and the sea; a popular local hang-out.

Getting There & Away

Buses run to Piran (€3.10, 30 minutes, 18km) every 20 minutes on weekdays and half-hourly on weekends. Up to nine buses daily head for Ljubljana (€11.10, 1¾ to 2½ hours, 120km), though the five daily trains are more comfortable, with IC services (€13, 2¼ hours) at 5.55am and 2.45pm, and local services (€7.75, 2½ hours) at 10.03am, 7.12pm and 8.13pm.

Buses to Trieste (€2.80, one hour, 23km, up to 10 per day) run along the coast via Ankaran and Muggia between 6am and 7.30pm from Monday to Saturday. Destinations in Croatia include Rijeka (€11.20, two hours, 84km, 10.10am Monday and Friday), Rovinj (€12, 129km, three hours, 3.50pm daily July and August) via Poreč (€10, two hours, 88km), plus three more to Poreč only at 7.30am, 2pm and 3.55pm Monday to Friday.

IZOLA
☎ 05 / pop 11,270

Overshadowed by more genteel Piran, Izola (Isola in Italian) has a certain Venetian charm, narrow old streets, and nice waterfront bars and restaurants. Ask the helpful **Tourist Information Centre Izola** (☎ 640 10 50; www.izola .eu; Sončno nabrežje 4; ☑ 9am-9pm Mon-Sat, 10am-5pm Sun Jun-Sep, 9am-5pm Mon-Fri, 10am-5pm Sat Oct-May) about **private rooms** (s €18-26, d €26-36) or, in July and August, check out the 174-bed **Riviera** (☎ 662 1740; branko.miklobusec@guest.arnes.si; Prekomorskih Brigad ul 7; dm €24), a student dormitory overlooking the marina. **Ribič** (☎ 641 83 13; Veliki trg 3; mains €8-18;

☑ 8am-1am) is a landmark seafood restaurant on the waterfront that is much loved by locals. Out in Izola's industrial suburbs, **Ambasada Gavioli** (☎ 641 8212, 041-353 722; www.ambasada-gavioli .com; Industrijska c; ☑ 8pm or 11pm-6am Fri & Sat) remains Slovenia's top club, showcasing a procession of international and local DJs.

Frequent buses between Koper (€1.80, 15 minutes, 6km) and Piran (€2.30, 20 minutes, 9.5km) go via Izola.

The **Prince of Venice** (☎ 05-617 80 00; www.kompas -online.net) catamaran serves Venice (€47 to €70, 2½ hours) at 7.30am or 8am between one and three times a week, and several times a week from April to October.

PIRAN
☎ 05 / pop 4430

Picturesque Piran (Pirano in Italian), sitting at the tip of a narrow peninsula, is everyone's favourite coastal town. Its Old Town is a gem of Venetian Gothic architecture, but it can be a mob scene at the height of summer. In April or October, though, it's hard not to fall in love with the winding Venetian Gothic alleyways and tempting seafood restaurants. It is believed that the town's name comes from the Greek word for fire (*pyr*) as fires were once lit at Punta, the tip of the peninsula, to guide ships to the port at Aegida (now Koper).

Orientation

Buses from everywhere except Portorož arrive at the bus station, a 300m stroll south of the Old Town's central Tartinijev trg, along the portside Cankarjevo nabrežje. Trying to drive a car here is insane; vehicles are stopped at a toll gate 200m south of the bus station, where the sensible choice is to use the huge Fornače car park (per hour/day €1/10) and ride the very frequent shuttle bus into town.

Information

Banka Koper (Tartinijev trg 12; ☑ 8.30am-noon & 3-5pm Mon-Fri, 8.30am-noon Sat)

Caffe Neptun (☎ 041-724 237; www.caffeneptun .com; Dantejeva ul 4; per 15min €1; ☑ 7am-1am Mon-Sat, 8am-10pm Sub) Modern cafe near bus station with internet access.

Maona Tourist Agency (☎ 673 45 20; www.maona.si; Cankarjevo nabrežje 7; ☑ 9am-8pm Mon-Sat, 10am-1pm & 5-7pm Sun) Rents private rooms and bikes, organises activities and cruises.

Post office (Cankarjevo nabrežje; ☑ 8am-7pm Mon-Fri, 8am-noon Sat)

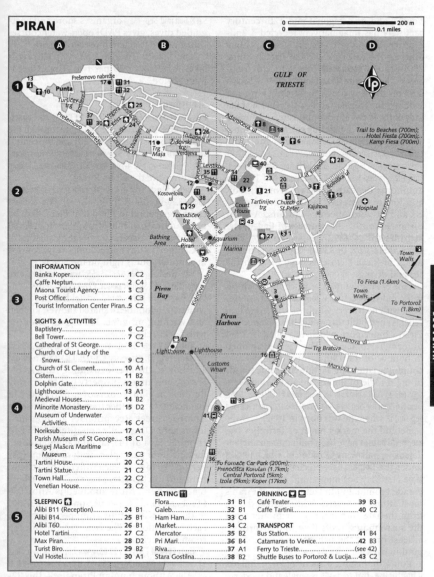

PIRAN

SLOVENIA

INFORMATION		
Banka Koper	1	C2
Caffe Neptun	2	C4
Maona Tourist Agency	3	C3
Post Office	4	C3
Tourist Information Center Piran	5	C2

SIGHTS & ACTIVITIES		
Baptistery	6	C2
Bell Tower	7	C2
Cathedral of St George	8	C1
Church of Our Lady of the Snows	9	C2
Church of St Clement	10	A1
Cistern	11	B2
Dolphin Gate	12	B2
Lighthouse	13	A1
Medieval Houses	14	B2
Minorite Monastery	15	D2
Museum of Underwater Activities	16	C4
Noriksub	17	A1
Parish Museum of St George	18	C1
Sergej Mašera Maritime Museum	19	C3
Tartini House	20	C2
Tartini Statue	21	C2
Town Hall	22	C2
Venetian House	23	C2

SLEEPING		
Alibi B11 (Reception)	24	B1
Alibi B14	25	B1
Alibi T60	26	B1
Hotel Tartini	27	C2
Max Piran	28	D2
Turist Biro	29	B2
Val Hostel	30	A1

EATING		
Flora	31	B1
Galeb	32	B1
Ham Ham	33	C4
Market	34	C2
Mercator	35	B2
Pri Mari	36	B4
Riva	37	A1
Stara Gostilna	38	B2

DRINKING		
Café Teater	39	B3
Caffe Tartinii	40	C2

TRANSPORT		
Bus Station	41	B4
Catamaran to Venice	42	B3
Ferry to Trieste	(see 42)	
Shuttle Buses to Portorož & Lucija	43	C2

Tourist Information Center Piran (☎ 673 44 40; www.portoroz.si; Tartinijev trg 2; ☑ 9am-7pm Jul-Sep, 9am-5pm Oct-Jun) In the impressive town hall.

Sights & Activities

Piran is watched over by the **Cathedral of St George** (Adamičeva ul 2) dating from the 16th and 17th centuries. If time weighs heavily on your hands, visit the attached **Parish Museum of St George** (☎ 673 34 40; admission €1; ☑ 10am-1pm & 3-5pm Mon & Wed-Fri, 10am-6pm Sat & Sun), which contains church plate, paintings and a lapidary. The cathedral's free-standing **bell tower** (admission €2; ☑ 10am-1pm & 6-9pm) dates back to 1608 and can be climbed. It was clearly modelled on the campanile at San Marco's Basilica in

Venice, and its octagonal mid-17th-century **baptistery** has imaginatively recycled a 2nd-century Roman sarcophagus as a baptismal font. To the east runs a 200m stretch of the 15th-century **town walls** complete with loopholes. The **Minorite Monastery** (☎ 673 44 17; Bolniška ul 30) on the way down to Tartinijev trg has a delightful cloister, and in the **Church of Our Lady of the Snows** almost opposite is a superb 15th-century arch painting of the Crucifixion. The **Sergej Mašera Maritime Museum** (☎ 671 00 40; Cankarjevo nabrežje 3; adult/student/child €/3.50/2.50/2.10; ☽ 9am-noon & 6-9pm Tue-Sun Jul & Aug, 9am-noon & 3-6pm Tue-Sun Sep-Jun) has 2000-year-old Roman amphorae beneath the glass ground floor, and lots of impressive antique ships' models and ex-voto offerings upstairs. A short distance south, the **Museum of Underwater Activities** (☎ 041-685 379; Župančičeva ul 24; adult/student/child €/3/2/2; ☽ 9.30am-10pm Jun-Sep) makes much of Piran's close association with the sea and diving.

One of Piran's most eye-catching structures is the red 15th-century **Venetian House** (Tartinijev trg 4), with its tracery windows and stone lion relief. When built this would have overlooked Piran's inner port, which was filled in 1894 to form Tartinijev trg. The square is named in honour of the 18th-century violinist and composer Giuseppe Tartini; his **statue** stands in the middle of the square and **Tartini House** (☎ 663 35 70; Kajuhova ul 12; adult/child €1.50/1; ☽ 9am-noon & 6-9pm Tue-Sun Jul & Aug, 11am-noon & 5-6pm Tue-Sun Sep-Jun) is where he was born in 1692.

Behind the market north of Tartinijev trg, **medieval houses** have been built into an ancient defensive wall along Obzidna ul, which passes under the **Dolphin Gate** erected in 1483. **Trg 1 Maja** (1st May Sq) may sound like a socialist parade ground, but in fact it's one of Piran's most attractive squares, with a **cistern** dating from the late 18th century. Rainwater from the surrounding roofs flow into it through at least one of the fish borne by the stone putti in back.

Punta, the historical 'snout' of Piran, still has a **lighthouse**, but today's is small and modern. Attached to it, the round, serrated tower of 18th-century **Church of St Clement** evokes the ancient beacon from which Piran got its name.

Most water-related activities take place in Portorož, but if you want to give diving a go, **Noriksub** (☎ 673 22 18, 041-746 153; www.skupina noriksub.si; Prešernovo nabrežje 24; shore/boat dive €30/40; ☽ 9am-noon & 1-6pm Tue-Sun Jun–mid-Sep, 10am-4pm Sat & Sun mid-Sep–May) organises shore and boat-guided dives, gives PADI open-water courses (beginners €240) and hires equipment.

The Maona Tourist Agency (p520) rents **bikes** for €6/9/15/20 per two-/five-/10-/24-hour period.

Sleeping

Private rooms (s €16-30, d €23-42, tr €32-55) and **apartments** (d €38-50, q €60-84) are available through the Maona Tourist Agency (p520) and the central **Turist Biro** (☎ 673 25 09; www.turistbiro-ag.si; Tomažičeva ul 3; ☽ 9am-1pm & 4-7pm Mon-Sat, 10am-1pm & 4-6pm Sun), opposite the Hotel Piran.

Kamp Fiesa (☎ 674 62 30; autocamp.fiesa@siol.net; adult €8.50-10, child €3.25; ☽ May-Sep) The closest camping ground to Piran is at Fiesa, 4km by road but less than 1km if you follow the coastal trail (*obalna pešpot*) east from the Cathedral of St George. It's tiny and becomes very crowded in summer, but is right on the beach.

Val Hostel (☎ 673 25 55; www.hostel-val.com; Gregorčičeva ul 38A; per person €22-25; ☐) This central, partially renovated hostel has 22 rooms, with two to four beds, shared shower, kitchen and washing machine. It's a great favourite with backpackers.

Alibi B11 (☎ 673 01 41; 031-363 666; www.alibi.si; Bonifacijeva ul 11; per person €20-22; ☐) The newest addition to the ever-expanding Alibi stable is not their nicest property but has mostly doubles in eight rooms over four floors in an ancient (and rather frayed) townhouse on a narrow street. Reception for all three hostels is here. Diagonally opposite is Alibi B14 (Bonifacijeva ul 14), an upbeat and colourful four-floor party place with six rooms (per person €20 to €22), each with two to six beds, bath and kitchenette. There's also a washing machine here. More subdued is Alibi T60 (Trubarjeva ul 60; per person €25 to €27.50) to the east with a fully equipped double on each of five floors. The view terrace of the top room is priceless.

Hotel Fiesa (☎ 671 22 00; www.hotelfiesa.com; Fiesa 57; park view d €58-78, tr €68-85, d sea view €69-98, tr €82-110) Although not in Piran itself, this 22-room pink-coloured hotel overlooking the sea near the Kamp Fiesa camping ground is one of the most atmospheric places to stay in the area.

Max Piran (☎ 673 34 36, 041-692 928; www.maxpiran .com; Ul IX Korpusa 26; s €35-40, d €60-70; ☐) Piran's most romantic accommodation option has just six rooms – each bearing a woman's name rather than a number – in a delightful coral-coloured 18th-century townhouse. It's just down from the cathedral.

Hotel Tartini (☎ 671 10 00; www.hotel-tartini-piran .com; Tartinijev trg 15; s €56-86, d €76-112, ste €128-192; ⊠ ☐) This attractive, 45-room property faces Tartinijev trg and manages to catch a few sea views from the upper floors. The staff are especially friendly and helpful. If you've got the dosh, splash out on suite No 40a; we're suckers for eyrie-like round rooms with €1-million views.

Eating & Drinking

One of Piran's major attractions is its plethora of fish restaurants, especially along Prešernovo nabrežje, though don't expect any bargains there.

Flora (☎ 673 12 58; Prešernovo nabrežje 26; pizza €4-7.50; ⊙ 10am-1am Jul & Aug, 10am-10pm Sep-Jun) The terrace of this simple pizzeria east of the Punta lighthouse has uninterrupted views of the Adriatic.

Galeb (☎ 673 32 25; Pusterla ul 5; mains €8-11; ⊙ 11am-4pm & 6pm-11pm or midnight Wed-Mon) This excellent family-run restaurant with seafront seating is east of the Punta lighthouse. The food is good but takes no risks.

Pri Mari (☎ 673 47 35, 041-616 488; Dantejeva ul 17; mains €7.50-16; ⊙ 10am-11pm Tue-Sun Jul & Aug, noon-10pm Tue-Sat, noon-6pm Sun Sep-Jun) This stylish Italian-owned restaurant south of the bus station serves the most inventive Mediterranean and Slovenian dishes in town. Try the fish paté and mussels in wine.

Stara Gostilna (☎ 673 31 65; Savudrijska ul 2; mains €7.50-17; ⊙ 9am-11pm) This delightful bistro in the Old Town serves both meat and fish dishes, and offers some of the best and most welcoming service in town.

Riva (☎ 673 221 80; Prešernovo nabrežje; mains €8-24; ⊙ 11.30am-midnight) The only seafood restaurant on Prešernovo nabrežje worth patronising is this classy place with the strip's best decor and sea views.

Café Teater (☎ 051-694 100; Stjenkova ul 1; ⊙ 7am-3am Mon-Fri, 9am-3am Sat & Sun) Anyone who's anyone in Piran can be found at this cafe with a waterfront terrace and troppo furnishings.

Caffe Tartini (☎ 673 33 81; Tartinijev trg 3; ⊙ 7am-3am) This cafe, housed in a classical building opposite the Venetian House, is a wonderful place for a cup of something hot and a slice of something sweet at almost any time of the day.

There's an outdoor **market** (Zelenjavni trg; ⊙ 7am-2pm Mon-Sat) in the small square behind the town hall. **Mercator** (Levstikova ul 5; ⊙ 7am-8pm Mon-Sat, 8am-noon Sun) has a branch in the Old Town. **Ham Ham** (Tomšičeva ul 41; ⊙ 7am-midnight) is a convenience store opposite the bus station.

Getting There & Away

From the bus station, buses run every 20 to 30 minutes to Koper (€3.10, 30 minutes, 18km) via Izola, while five head for Trieste in Italy (€10, 1¾ hours, 36km) between 6.45am and 6.55pm Monday to Saturday. Between three and five daily buses go to Ljubljana (€12, 2½ to three hours, 140km) via Divača and Postojna.

From the southern end of Tartinijev trg, a shuttle bus (€1) goes every 15 minutes to Lucija via Portorož.

Venezia Lines (☎ 05-674 71 61; www.venezialines .com) catamarans sail to Venice (one way/return €46/89, 2¼ hours) at 8.30am on Wednesday from May to mid-September. A new service run by **Trieste Lines** (www.triestelines.it) links Piran and Trieste twice a day Tuesday to Sunday from late April to late September. Buy tickets (one way/return €6.80/12.60) from the TIC in Piran.

PORTOROŽ

☎ 05 / pop 2900

Portorož (Portorose in Italian), the biggest resort in Slovenia, is actually quite classy for a seaside town, even along Obala, the main drag. And with the recent reopening of the 185-room Palace, the art nouveau hotel that put Portorož on the map, it may even start to relive its glory days. Portorož's sandy beaches are relatively clean, and there are pleasant spas and wellness centres where you can take the waters or cover yourself in curative mud.

At the same time, the vast array of accommodation options makes Portorož a useful fall back if everything's full in Piran. Full listings are available at the **Tourist Information Center Portorož** (☎ 674 22 20; www.portoroz.si; Obala 16; ⊙ 9am-7pm Jul & Aug, 9am-5pm Mon-Sat, 10am-2pm Sun Sep-Jun). Just off the main road between Piran and the centre of Portorož, the summer-only hostel **Prenočišča Korotan** (☎ 674 54 00; www.sd.upr .si/sdp/prenocisca; Obala 11; s €30-33, d €43-46, tr €57-60, q € €69-73; ⊙ Jul & Aug; ☐) has en-suite rooms. Be warned, though, that there is a 40/20% supplement for stays of just one/two nights. At the other end of the scale, the 48-room **Hotel Marko** (☎ 617 40 00; www.hotel-marko.com; Obala 28; s €56-96, d €70-120), with lovely gardens just opposite Portorož Bay is delightful.

There are dozens of decent pizzerias along Obala, but the place of choice is **Pizzeria Figarola** (☎ 674 22 00; Obala 14A; pizza €6.50-10.50; ☯ 10am-10pm), with a huge terrace just up from the main pier.

Papa Chico (☎ 677 93 10; Obala 26; mains €5.80-11.30; ☯ 9am-2am Mon-Sat, 10am-2am Sun) serves 'Mexican fun food' (go figure), including fajitas (€9.40 to €11.30).

Kavarna Cacao (☎ 674 10 35; Obala 14; ☯ 8am-1am Sun-Thu, to 3am Fri & Sat) wins the award as the most stylish cafe-bar on the coast and boasts a fabulous waterfront terrace.

Every 20 minutes, a shuttle bus (€1) from Piran trundles along Obala on its way to Lucija, passing by Prenočišča Korotan.

EASTERN SLOVENIA

The rolling vine-covered hills of eastern Slovenia are attractive but much less dramatic than the Julian Alps or, indeed, the coast. If you're heading by train to Vienna via Graz in Austria it saves money to stop in lively Maribor, Slovenia's second-largest city; international tickets are very expensive per kilometre, so doing as much travelling as possible on domestic trains saves cash. While there, consider visiting postcard-perfect Ptuj just down the road.

MARIBOR
☎ 02 / pop 89,450

Slovenia's light-industrial second city really has no unmissable sights but oozes with charm thanks to its delightfully patchy Old Town. Pedestrianised central streets buzz with cafes and student life, and in late June/early July the old, riverside Lent district buzzes with the two-week **Lent International Summer Festival** (http://lent.slovenija.net) extravaganza of folklore and culture.

Maribor Castle (Grajski trg 2), on the main square's northeast corner, contains a magnificent 18th-century **rococo staircase** visible from the street and the **Maribor Regional Museum** (☎ 228 35 51; adult/student & child €3/2.50; ☯ 9am-4pm Tue-Sat, 9am-2pm Sun), one of Slovenia's richest archaeological and ethnographical collections but undergoing a protracted renovation.

Two cafe-packed blocks to the southwest, the **Cathedral** (Slomškov trg) sits in an oasis of fountain-cooled calm. Follow little Poštna ul southward into **Glavni trg** with its extravagant **town hall** (Glavni trg 14) and **plague pillar**, a lovely column of saints erected by townspeople in gratitude for having survived the plague. A block farther south down Mesarski prehod is the Drava River's north bank, where you'll find the **Stara Trta** (Vojašniška 8), the world's oldest living grapevine. It's been a source of a dark red wine called Žametna Črnina (Black Velvet) for more than four centuries.

The helpful **Tourist Information Centre Maribor** (☎ 234 66 10; www.maribor.si; Partinzanska c 6A; ☯ 9am-7pm Mon-Fri, to 6pm Sat & Sun Jul & Aug, 9am-6pm Mon-Sat, to 1pm Sun Sep-Jun) has a complete listing of places to stay. At the budget end of the spectrum, try the new **Alibi C2** (☎ 051-663 555; www.alibi.si; Cafova ul 2; dm €17-20, d per person €20-25; ▯), a superswanky hostel with seven doubles and six dorms with six beds each in a beautifully renovated 19th-century building. Just around the corner is the **Grand Hotel Ocean** (☎ 234 36 73; www.hotelocean .si; Partizanska c 39; s €70-75, d €100; ▨ ▯), a stunning 23-room boutique hotel named after the first train to pass through the city in 1846 (and, well, the most exciting thing to happen here since).

Gril Ranca (☎ 252 55 50; Dravska ul 10; dishes €3-6; ☯ 8am-11pm Mon-Sat, noon-9pm Sun) serves simple but scrumptious Balkan grills in full view of the Drava. For something more, ahem, cosmopolitan try **Toti Rotovž** (☎ 228 76 50; Glavni trg 14 & Rotovški trg 9; mains €6-18; ☯ 9am-midnight Mon-Thu, 9am-2am Fri & Sat), a peculiar place behind the town hall that serves up just about every cuisine under the sun – from Slovenian to Thai and Greek to Mexican.

Buses run to Ljubljana (€12, three hours, 127km) two to four times a day. Also served are Celje (€6.30, 1½ hours, 55km, up to 10 a day) and Ptuj (€3.60, 45 minutes, 27km, hourly). There are daily buses to Munich (€46, 7½ hours, 453km) at 6.50pm and 9.50pm, and one to Vienna (€29, 4½ hours, 258km) at 5.45pm. Of the two-dozen daily trains to/from Ljubljana (€7.75, 2½ hours, 156km), five are IC express trains costing €19.60 and taking just under two hours.

PTUJ
☎ 02 / pop 18,950

Rising gently above a wide, almost flat valley, compact Ptuj (Poetovio to the Romans) forms a symphony of red-tile roofs best viewed from across the Drava River. Its pinnacle is the well-preserved **Ptuj Castle** (Na Gradu 1), containing the fine **Regional Museum Ptuj** (☎ 787 92 30; adult/student/child €4/2.50/2.50; ☼ 9am-6pm Mon-Fri, 9am-8pm Sat & Sun Jul & Aug, 9am-6pm daily May-Jun & Sep–mid-Oct, 9am-5pm mid-Oct–Apr).

For 10 days before Mardi Gras crowds come from far and wide to spot the shaggy Kurent straw men at Slovenia's foremost traditional carnival, **Kurentovanje** (www.kurento vanje.net). A 'rite of spring', it is celebrated for 10 days up to Shrove Tuesday (February or early March; the museum has some excellent Kurentovanje-related exhibits. The **Tourist Information Centre Ptuj** (☎ 779 60 11; www .ptuj-tourism.si; Slovenski trg 3; ☼ 9am-8pm May–mid-Oct, 9am-6pm mid-Oct–Apr), facing a medieval tower in the Old Town, has reams of information and lists of places to stay. If you're looking for budget accommodation, look no further than **Hostel Eva** (☎ 771 24 41, 040-226 522; info@bikeek.si; Jadranska 22; per person €12-17), a welcoming, up-to-date hostel connected to a bike shop (per day €10) with six rooms containing two to four beds and a large, light-filled kitchen. If you'd like more comfort, continue walking west on Prešernova ul past a parade of cafes and bars to the new **Park Hotel Ptuj** (☎ 749 33 00; www .parkhotel-ptuj.si; Prešernova ul 38; s €81-98, d €108-122, ste €110-126; ▯), a lovely new boutique hotel in an 18th-century townhouse with 15 individually designed rooms and lots of original artwork on the walls.

Eat next door at **Amadeus** (☎ 771 70 51; Prešernova ul 36; mains €6.50-20; ☼ noon-10pm Mon-Thu, noon-11pm Fri & Sat, noon-4pm Sun), a very pleasant *gostilna* above a cafe-bar serving *štruklji* (dumplings with herbs and cheese, €3.50), steak and pork dishes. More pleasant in the warmer months is **Ribič** (☎ 749 06 35; Dravska ul 9; mains €9-18; ☼ 10am-11pm Sun-Thu, to midnight Fri & Sat), the best restaurant in Ptuj, with a great riverside terrace and the ideal spot to have a fish dinner. Next to the town's open-air **market** (Novi trg; ☼ 7am-3pm) you'll find a large **Mercator** (Novi trg 3; ☼ 7.30am-7.30pm Mon-Fri, 7.30am-1pm Sat) supermarket.

Buses to Maribor (€3.60, 45 minutes, 27km) run at least hourly on weekdays but are less frequent on weekends. A half-dozen IC trains from Ljubljana (€9.20 to €13, 2½ hours, 155km) pass through Ptuj daily, two of which (10.08am and 7.03pm) are on their way to Budapest (€38.60, 4¼ hours, 313km).

SLOVENIA DIRECTORY

ACCOMMODATION

Accommodation listings throughout this guide have been ordered by price. Very roughly, budget accommodation means a double room under €50, midrange is €51 to €100 and top end is anything over €101. Accommodation is a little bit more expensive in Ljubljana. Unless otherwise indicated, rooms include en-suite toilet and bath or shower and breakfast. Smoking is banned in hotels.

Camping grounds generally charge per person, whether you're in a tent or caravan. Almost all sites close from mid-October to mid-April. Camping 'rough' is illegal in Slovenia, and this law is enforced, especially around Bled. Seek out the Slovenian Tourist Board's *Camping in Slovenia*.

Slovenia's growing stable of hostels includes Ljubljana's trendy Celica and the Alibi chain of hostels found in the capital, at Piran and now in Maribor. Throughout the country there are student dormitories (residence halls) moonlighting as hostels for visitors in July and August. Unless stated otherwise hostel rooms share bathrooms. Hostels usually cost from €15 to €22; prices are at their highest in July and August and during the Christmas break, when it can sometimes be difficult to find accommodation at any price.

Tourist information offices can help you access private rooms, apartments and tourist farms, or they can recommend private agencies that will. Such accommodation can appear misleadingly cheap if you overlook the 30% to 50% surcharge levied on stays of less than three nights. Also be aware that many such properties are in outlying villages with minimal public transport, and that the cheapest one-star category rooms with shared bathroom are actually very rare, so you'll usually pay well above the quoted minimum. Depending on the season you might save a little money by going directly to any house with a sign reading *sobe* (rooms). For more information check out the Slovenian Tourist Board's **Friendly Countryside** (www.slovenia.info/tour istfarms) pamphlet listing upwards of 200 farms with accommodation.

Guest houses, known as a *penzion, gostišče*, or *prenočišča*, are often cosy and better value than full-blown hotels. Nonetheless it can be difficult to find a double room in a hotel for under €50. Beware that locally listed rates are usually quoted per person assuming double occupancy. A tourist tax – routinely €0.50 to €1 (hotel) per person per day – is usually not included.

ACTIVITIES

Extreme Sports

Several areas specialise in adrenalin-rush activities, the greatest range being available at Bovec (p515), famous for rafting, hydro-speed, kayaking and canyoning, and increasingly at Bled (p511). Bovec is also a great place for paragliding; in winter you ascend Mt Kanin via ski lift and then jump off. Gliding costs are very reasonable from Lesce near Bled. Scuba diving from Piran (p522) is also good value.

Hiking

Hiking is extremely popular, with the **Alpine Association of Slovenia** (www.pzs.si) counting some 55,000 members and Ljubljančani flocking in droves to Triglav National Park (p513) on weekends. There are more than 7000km of marked trails and paths, and in summer as many as 170 mountain huts offer comfortable trailside refuge. Several treks are outlined in Lonely Planet's more comprehensive *Slovenia*.

Skiing

Skiing is a Slovenian passion, with slopes particularly crowded over the Christmas holidays and in early February. See the Slovenian Tourist Board's **Ski Centers of Slovenia** (www.slovenia.info/skiing) for more details.

Kranjska Gora (up to 1291m; p514) has some challenging runs, and the world record for ski-jumping was set at nearby Planica, 4km to the west. Above Lake Bohinj, Vogel (up to 1800m) is particularly scenic, as is Kanin (up to 2300m) above Bovec, which can have snow as late as May. Being relatively close to Ljubljana, Krvavec (up to 1971m), northeast of Kranj, can have particularly long lift queues.

Just west of Maribor in eastern Slovenia is a popular choice and the biggest downhill skiing area in the country. Although relatively low (336m to 1347m), the Mariborsko Pohorje is easily accessible, with very varied downhill pistes and relatively short lift queues.

Other Activities

Mountain bikes are available for hire from travel agencies at Bled, Bohinj, Bovec, Kranjska Gora and Postojna.

The Soča River near Kobarid and the Sava Bohinjka near Bohinj are great for fly-fishing April to October. Licences for the latter cost €55/38 (catch/catch and release) and are sold at the tourist office and certain hotels.

Spas and wellness centres are very popular in Slovenia; see **Slovenia Spas** (www.spa-slovenia.com) website for more information. Most towns have some sort of spa complex, and hotels often offer free or bargain-rate entry to their guests.

BUSINESS HOURS

All businesses post their opening times (*delovni čas*) on the door. Many shops close Saturday afternoons. A handful of grocery stores open on Sundays, including some branches of the ubiquitous Mercator supermarket chain. Most museums close on Mondays. Banks often take lunch breaks from 12.30pm to 2pm and only a few open on Saturday mornings.

Restaurants typically open for lunch and dinner until at least 10pm, and bars until midnight, though they may have longer hours on weekends and shorter ones on Sundays.

EMBASSIES & CONSULATES

Following are among the embassies and consulates in Slovenia. Unless noted otherwise, they are all in Ljubljana.

Australia (off Map pp498-9; ☎ 01-425 42 52; Dunajska c 50; ☒ 9am-1pm Mon-Fri)

Austria (Map pp498-9; ☎ 01-479 07 00; Prešernova c 23; ☒ 8am-noon Mon-Thu, 8-11am Fri) Enter from Veselova ul.

Canada (Map pp498-9; ☎ 01-252 44 44; 12th fl, Trg Republike 3; ☒ 9am-noon Mon-Fri)

Croatia Ljubljana (Map pp498-9; ☎ 01-425 62 20; Gruberjevo nabrežje 6; ☒ 9am-1pm Mon-Fri); Maribor (☎ 02-234 66 86; Trg Svobode 3; ☒ 10am-1pm Mon-Fri)

France (Map pp498-9; ☎ 01-479 04 00; Barjanska c 1; ☒ 8.30am-12.30pm Mon-Fri)

Hungary (off Map pp498-9; ☎ 01-512 18 82; ul Konrada Babnika 5; ☒ 8am-5pm Mon-Fri)

Ireland (Map pp498-9; ☎ 01-300 89 70; Palača Kapitelj, Poljanski nasip 6; ☒ 9.30am-12.30pm & 2.30-4pm Mon-Fri)

Italy Ljubljana (Map pp498-9; ☎ 01-426 21 94; Snežniška ul 8; ☒ 9-11am Mon-Fri); Koper (Map p519; ☎ 05-627 37 49; Belvedere 2; ☒ 8.30am-noon Mon-Fri)

Netherlands (Map pp498-9; ☎ 01-420 14 61; Palača Kapitelj, Poljanski nasip 6; ☒ 9am-noon Mon-Fri)

New Zealand (off Map pp498-9; ☎ 01-580 30 55; Verovškova ul 57; ☒ 8am-3pm Mon-Fri)

South Africa (☎ 01-200 63 00; Pražakova ul 4; ⏱ 3-4pm Tue) In Kompas building.
UK (Map pp498-9; ☎ 01-200 39 10; 4th fl, Trg Republike 3; ⏱ 9am-noon Mon-Fri)
USA (Map pp498-9; ☎ 01-200 55 00; Prešernova c 31; ⏱ 9-11.30am & 1-3pm Mon-Fri)

FESTIVALS & EVENTS

Major cultural and sporting events are listed under 'Events' on the website of the **Slovenian Tourist Board** (www.slovenia.info) and in the STB's comprehensive *Calendar of Major Events in Slovenia*, issued annually.

Slovenia's biggest open-air rock concert **Rock Otočec** (www.rock-otocec.com) is a three-day event held in late June/early July at Prečna airfield, 5km northwest of Novo Mesto in southeastern Slovenia.

GAY & LESBIAN TRAVELLERS

Roza Klub (☎ 01-430 47 40; Kersnikova ul 4) in Ljubljana is made up of the gay and lesbian branches of ŠKUC (Študentski Kulturni Center or Student Cultural Centre).

GALfon (☎ 01-432 40 89; ⏱ 7-10pm Mon-Fri) is a hotline and source of general information for gays and lesbians. The websites of **Slovenian Queer Resources Directory** (www.ljudmila.org/siqrd) and **Out in Slovenia** (www.outinslovenija.com) are both extensive and partially in English.

HOLIDAYS

Slovenia celebrates 14 holidays *(prazniki)* a year. If a holiday falls on a Sunday, then the following Monday becomes the holiday.
New Year 1 and 2 January
Prešeren Day (Slovenian Culture Day) 8 February
Easter March/April
Insurrection Day 27 April
Labour Days 1 and 2 May
National Day 25 June
Assumption Day 15 August
Reformation Day 31 October
All Saints Day 1 November
Christmas Day 25 December
Independence Day 26 December

INTERNET ACCESS

Virtually every hostel and hotel now has internet access – a computer for guests' use (free or for a small fee), wi-fi, or both. Most cities and towns have at least one cyber cafe but they usually only have a handful of terminals. Be advised that Slovenian keyboards are neither qwerty nor azerty but qwertz, reversing the y and z keys, but otherwise following the Anglophone norm.

INTERNET RESOURCES

The website of the **Slovenian Tourist Board** (www.slovenia.info) is tremendously useful, as is that of **Mat'Kurja** (www.matkurja.com), a directory of Slovenian web resources. Most Slovenian towns and cities have a website accessed by typing www.town.si (or sometimes www.town-tourism.si). Especially good are **Ljubljana** (www.ljubljana.si), **Maribor** (www.maribor.si) and **Piran-Portorož** (www.portoroz.si).

MONEY

Slovenia uses the euro as its official currency. Exchanging cash is simple at banks, major post offices, travel agencies and *menjalnice* (bureaux de change), although some of the latter don't accept travellers cheques. Major credit and debit cards are accepted almost everywhere, and ATMs are ubiquitous.

POST

Local mail costs €0.27 for up to 20g, while an international airmail stamp costs €0.45. Poste restante is free; address it to and pick it up from the main post office at Slovenska c 32, 1101 Ljubljana.

TELEPHONE

Slovenia's country code is ☎ 386. Public telephones require a phonecard *(telefonska kartica* or *telekartica)*, available at post offices and some news-stands. The cheapest card (€4, 25 units) gives about 20 minutes' calling time to other European countries; the highest value is €14.60 with 300 units. Local SIM cards with €5 credit are available for €12 from **SiMobil** (www.simobil.si) and for €15 from **Mobitel** (www.mobitel.si). Mobile numbers in Slovenia are identified by the prefix ☎ 031-, 040-, 041- and 051-.

TOURIST INFORMATION

The Ljubljana-based **Slovenian Tourist Board** (off Map pp498-9; ☎ 01-589 18 40; www.slovenia.info; Dunajska

SLOVENIA

EMERGENCY NUMBERS

- Ambulance ☎ 112
- Fire ☎ 112
- Police ☎ 113
- Roadside assistance ☎ 1987

c 156) has dozens of tourist information centres (TICs) in Slovenia, and overseas branches in a half-dozen European countries; see 'STB Representative Offices Abroad' on its website for details.

VISAS

Citizens of virtually all European countries, as well as Australia, Canada, Israel, Japan, New Zealand and the USA, do not require visas to visit Slovenia for stays of up to 90 days. Holders of EU and Swiss passports can enter using a national identity card.

Those who do require visas (including South Africans) can get them for up to 90 days at any Slovenian embassy or consulate – see the website of the **Ministry of Foreign Affairs** (www.mzz.gov.si) for a full listing. They cost €35 regardless of the type of visa or length of validity. You'll need confirmation of a hotel booking plus one photo, and you may have to show a return or onward ticket.

WOMEN TRAVELLERS

In the event of an emergency call the **police** (☎ 113) any time or the **SOS Helpline** (☎ 080 11 55; www.drustvo-sos.si; ⏰ noon-10pm Mon-Fri, 6-10pm Sat & Sun).

TRANSPORT IN SLOVENIA

GETTING THERE & AWAY
Air

Slovenia's only international airport receiving regular scheduled flights at present – Aerodrom Maribor does limited charters only – is Ljubljana's recently renamed **Jože Pučnik Airport** (LJU; www.lju-airport.si) at Brnik, 27km north of Ljubljana. From its base here, the Slovenian flag-carrier, **Adria Airways** (JP; ☎ 080 13 00, 01-369 10 10; www.adria-airways.com), serves some 28 European destinations on regularly scheduled flights, with just as many holiday spots served by charter flights in summer. Adria can be remarkably good value and includes useful connections to İstanbul, Ohrid (Macedonia), Pristina (Kosovo) and Tirana (Albania).

Other airlines with regularly scheduled flights to and from Ljubljana:

Air France (AF; ☎ 01-244 34 47; www.airfrance.com/si) Daily flights to Paris (CDG).

Austrian Airlines (OS; ☎ 01-202 01 00; www.aua.com) Multiple daily flights to Vienna.
Brussels Airlines (SN; ☎ 04-206 16 56; www.brussels airlines.com) Daily flights to Brussels.
ČSA Czech Airlines (OK; ☎ 04-206 17 50; www.czech airlines.com) Flights to Prague.
easyJet (EZY; ☎ 04-206 16 77; www.easyjet.com) Low-cost flights to London Stansted.
Finnair (AY; ☎ 080 13 00, 01-369 10 10; www.finnair .com) Flights to Helsinki.
JAT Airways (JU; ☎ 01-231 43 40; www.jat.com) Daily flights to Belgrade.
Malév Hungarian Airlines (MA; ☎ 04-206 16 76; www.malev.hu) Daily flights to Budapest.
Turkish Airlines (TK; ☎ 04-206 16 80; www.turkish airlines.com) Flights to İstanbul.

Land
BUS

International bus destinations from Ljubljana include Serbia, Germany, Hungary, Croatia, Bosnia and Hercegovina, Macedonia and Italy; see p508 for details. You can also catch buses to Italy and Croatia from coastal towns, including Piran (p523) and Koper (p520). Maribor (p524) also has buses to Germany and Austria.

TRAIN

It is possible to travel to Italy, Austria, Germany and Croatia by train; Ljubljana (p508) is the main hub, although you can, for example, hop on a train to Budapest at Ptuj (p525).

Train travel can be expensive. It is sometimes cheaper to travel as far as you can on domestic routes before crossing any borders. For example, you can travel on a Ljubljana–Vienna service but you will save a little bit of money by going first to Maribor; see p524 for details.

Seat reservations, compulsory on trains to and from Italy and on InterCity (IC) trains, cost €3.50, but it is usually included in the ticket price.

Sea

Piran despatches ferries to Trieste a couple of times a day and catamarans to Venice at least once a week; see p523 for details. There's also a catamaran between nearby Izola and Venice in summer months; see p520.

GETTING AROUND
Bus

It's worth booking long-distance buses ahead of time, especially when travelling on Friday afternoons. If your bag has to go in the luggage compartment below the bus, it will cost €1.50 extra. The online bus timetable, **Avtobusna Postaja Ljubljana** (www.ap-ljubljana.si), is extensive, but generally only lists buses that use Ljubljana as a hub.

Bicycle

Bicycles may be hired at some train stations, tourist offices, travel agencies and hotels.

Car

Hiring a car is recommended, and can even save you money as you can access cheaper out-of-centre hotels and farm or village homestays. Daily rates usually start at around €40/210 per day/week, including unlimited mileage, collision-damage waiver and theft protection. Unleaded petrol *(bencin)* costs €1.21 (95 octane) and €1.25 (98 octane), with diesel at €1.31. You must keep your headlights illuminated throughout the day. If you'll be doing a lot of driving consider buying Kod & Kam's 1:100,000 *Avtoatlas Slovenija* (€27).

A new law requires all cars to display a *vinjeta* (road-toll sticker) on the windscreen. They cost €35/55 for a half-/full year and are available at petrol stations, post offices and some kiosks; for a complete list consult the website www.cestnina.si. These will already be in place on a rental car but if you are driving your own vehicle, failure to display such a sticker risks a fine of €300 to €800.

Further information is available from the **Automobile Association of Slovenia** (☎ 01 530 53 00; www.amzs.si)

Hitching

Hitchhiking is fairly common and legal, except on motorways and a few major highways. Even young women hitch in Slovenia, but it's never totally safe and Lonely Planet doesn't recommend it.

Train

Slovenian Railways (Slovenske Železnice; ☎ 01-291 33 32; www.slo-zeleznice.si) has a useful online timetable that's easy to use. Buy tickets before boarding or you'll incur a €2.50 supplement. Be aware that EuroCity (EC) and InterCity (IC) trains carry a surcharge of €1.50 on top of standard quoted fares, while InterCity Slovenia ones cost €8.80/5.70 extra in 1st/2nd class.

SLOVENIA

Switzerland

What giddy romance Zermatt, St Moritz and other glitterati-encrusted names evoke: from the intoxicating chink of multimillionaires hobnobbing over cocktails served in ice-carved flutes to the comforting jangle of the cows coming home, seduction is head-over-heels. Ride a little red train between peak and pine, soak in mountain spas, snowshoe to your igloo, munch on chocolate, fall madly in love with painted bridges in Lucerne and know life in this snug, smug, truly ravishing enclave is good.

This is *Sonderfall Schweiz* ('special case Switzerland'), a rare and refined breed, a privileged neutral country set apart from others. Contemporary Switzerland is making moves towards international cooperation (ditching border controls for arrivals from Schengen countries in 2008 was a start), but Europe's bijou land of plenty is as proudly idiosyncratic, insular and unique as ever. Blessed with gargantuan cultural diversity, its four official languages alone (p585) say it all.

The Swiss don't do half-measures: Zürich, their most gregarious urban centre, has cutting-edge art, legendary nightlife and some of the world's highest living standards. The national passion for sweat, stamina and clingy Lycra takes 65 year olds across 2500m-high mountain passes for Sunday strolls, sees giggly three year olds skiing rings around grown-ups, prompts locals done with 'ordinary' marathons to sprint backwards up mountains – all in the name of good old-fashioned fun.

Join tourists at the postcard carousel trying to match their memories of Bern's chocolate-box architecture, the G-rated Matterhorn, the thundering Rheinfall et al, but understand that Switzerland is a place so outrageously beautiful it, simply put, has to be seen to be believed.

FAST FACTS

- **Area** 41,285 sq km
- **Capital** Bern
- **Currency** Swiss franc (Sfr); €1 = Sfr1.53; US$1 = Sfr1.22; UK£1 = Sfr1.64; A$1 = €0.79; ¥100 = Sfr1.14; NZ$1 = Sfr0.64
- **Famous for** cheese, yodelling, luxury watches, the Matterhorn, banking
- **Official languages** French, German, Italian, Romansch
- **Phrases** *gruezi* (hello, good day), *merci vielmal* (thank you very much), *adieu* (goodbye), *sprechen Sie Englisch?* (do you speak English?)
- **Population** 7,590,000
- **Telephone codes** country code ☎ 41; international access code ☎ 00
- **Visas** not required for holders of passports from the UK, Ireland, the EU, the USA, Canada, Australia, New Zealand, South Africa, Norway and Iceland; see p586)

SWITZERLAND

SWITZERLAND

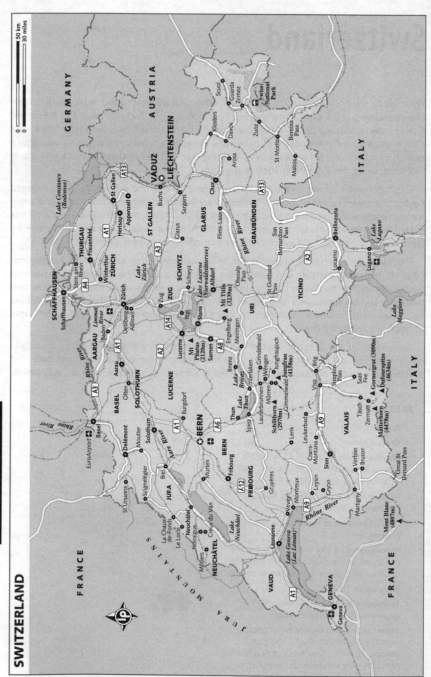

HIGHLIGHTS

- Be wowed by Eiger's monstrous north face, slaloming in the shadow of Mönch with a ride to what's known as the 'top of Europe', 3471m **Jungfraujoch** (p567).
- Get wet with a fountain dash beneath **Geneva's** Jet d'Eau (p540) or a soak in a white-chocolate bath.
- Party all night in one of Europe's hippest cities, **Zürich** (p567).
- Be surprised by Swiss capital **Bern** (p555): think medieval charm, folkloric fountains and pulsating party scene.
- Don your walking boots to hit the trails in the **Swiss National Park** (p582), where you're just as likely to encounter ibex, burrowing marmots and golden eagles as other walkers.
- Tread where few others go and sleep in hay in the mysterious green hills and thick, dark forests of the clover-shaped **Jura canton** (p552).

ITINERARIES

- **One week** Start in vibrant Zürich. Shop famous Bahnhofstrasse and hit the bars of Züri-West. Next, head to the Jungfrau region to explore some kick-ass (think James Bond racing an avalanche down a sheer snowy rock face) Alpine scenery. Take a pit stop in beautiful Lucerne before finishing up in country capital Bern.
- **Two weeks** As above, then head west for French immersion lessons in Geneva or lakeside Lausanne. Explore the Neuchâtel and Fribourg cantons, stopping in Gruyères to dip into a cheesy fondue and OD on meringues drowned in thick double cream. Zip to Zermatt or across to St Moritz to frolic in snow or green meadows then loop east to taste the Italian side of Switzerland.

CLIMATE & WHEN TO GO

Crystal-clear, sunny days abound year-round, though Swiss winters can be cold, snowy and sometimes rather grey (especially around Zürich), with temperatures hovering between 2°C and 6°C. Summers mix sun with rain and temperatures range from 20°C to 25°C, except in Ticino, the country's hot south, which has a more Mediterranean climate. At altitude, be prepared for a range of temperatures. See p595 for the Bern climate chart.

> ### CONNECTIONS: MOVING ON FROM SWITZERLAND
>
> A landlocked between France, Germany, Austria, Liechtenstein and Italy, Switzerland's a doddle to move on from. Geneva city buses run as far as the French border (a couple cross into France, continuing along the southern shore of Lake Geneva) and there's plenty of direct train connections from Geneva (p545) to Paris, as well as Hamburg, Milan and Barcelona. Cosmopolitan Zürich (p572) enjoys as many international rail connections, daily trains to/from Stuttgart, Munich and Innsbruck included. In northern Switzerland Basel (p576) is the major European rail hub, with separate train stations serving France and Germany. Then of course, there is Italy, a mere hop and a skip from Locarno in Italianate Ticino.

December to early April are the months to ski and snowboard; May to October is best for general sightseeing and hiking. Alpine resorts all but close down in late April, May and again in November.

HISTORY

The first inhabitants were a Celtic tribe, the Helvetii. The Romans arrived in 107 BC via the Great St Bernard Pass, but were gradually driven back by the Germanic Alemanni tribe, which settled in the region in the 5th century AD. Burgundians and Franks also came to the area, and Christianity was gradually introduced.

The territory was united under the Holy Roman Empire in 1032, but central control was never tight, and neighbouring nobles fought each other for local influence. Rudolph I spearheaded the Germanic Habsburg expansion and gradually brought the squabbling nobles to heel.

The Swiss Confederation

Upon Rudolph's death in 1291, local leaders saw a chance to gain independence. The forest communities of Uri, Schwyz and Nidwalden formed an alliance on 1 August 1291, which is seen as the origin of the Swiss Confederation (their struggles against the Habsburgs are idealised in the legend of William Tell). This union's success prompted

HOW MUCH?

- **Hostel dorm bed** Sfr29.50 to Sfr47
- **100g bar of Toblerone chocolate** Sfr2.50
- **100km by train** Sfr35
- **Public transport ticket** Sfr2
- **Half-/full-day bicycle hire** Sfr25/35

LONELY PLANET INDEX

- **1L unleaded petrol** Sfr1.38
- **1L bottled water** Sfr1.40
- **330ml bottle of beer** Sfr5 to Sfr10
- **Souvenir T-shirt** Sfr20 to Sfr30
- **Street snack (Wurst & pommes frites)** Sfr10

other communities to join: Lucerne (1332), followed by Zürich (1351), Glarus and Zug (1352), and Bern (1353).

Encouraged by successes against the Habsburgs, the Swiss acquired a taste for territorial expansion. More land was seized. Fribourg, Solothurn, Basel, Schaffhausen and Appenzell joined the confederation, and the Swiss gained independence from the Holy Roman Emperor Maximilian I after their victory at Dornach in 1499.

Eventually, the Swiss over-extended themselves. They took on a superior force of French and Venetians at Marignano in 1515 and lost. Realising they could no longer compete against better-equipped larger powers, they declared their neutrality. Even so, Swiss mercenaries continued to serve in other armies for centuries, and earned an unrivalled reputation for skill and courage.

The Reformation during the 16th century caused upheaval throughout Europe. The Protestant teachings of Luther, Zwingli and Calvin spread quickly, although the inaugural cantons remained Catholic. This caused internal unrest that dragged on for centuries.

The French Republic invaded Switzerland in 1798 and established the Helvetic Republic. The Swiss vehemently resisted such centralised control, causing Napoleon to restore the former confederation of cantons in 1803. Yet France still retained overall jurisdiction.

Following Napoleon's defeat by the British and Prussians at Waterloo, Switzerland finally gained independence.

The Modern State

Throughout the gradual move towards one nation, each canton remained fiercely independent, to the extent of controlling coinage and postal services. The cantons lost these powers in 1848, when a new federal constitution was agreed upon, with Bern as the capital. The Federal Assembly was set up to take care of national issues, but the cantons retained legislative (Grand Council) and executive (States Council) powers to deal with local matters.

Having achieved political stability, Switzerland could concentrate on economic and social matters. Poor in mineral resources, it developed industries dependent on highly skilled labour. A network of railways and roads was built, opening up previously inaccessible regions of the Alps and helping the development of tourism.

The Swiss carefully guarded their neutrality in the 20th century. Their only involvement in WWI was organising units of the Red Cross (founded in Geneva in 1863 by Henri Dunant). Switzerland did join the League of Nations after peace was won, but only on the condition that its involvement was financial and economic rather than military. Apart from some accidental bombing, WWII left Switzerland largely unscathed.

While the rest of Europe was still recovering from the war, Switzerland was able to forge ahead from an already powerful commercial, financial and industrial base. Zürich developed as an international banking and insurance centre, while the World Health Organization (WHO) and many other international bodies set up headquarters in Geneva. Its much-vaunted neutrality led it to decline joining either the UN or EU, and the country became one of the world's richest and most respected.

Then, in the late 1990s, a series of scandals forced Switzerland to begin reforming its famously secretive banking industry. In 1995, after pressure from Jewish groups, Swiss banks announced that they had discovered millions of dollars lying in dormant pre-1945 accounts, belonging to Holocaust victims and survivors. Three years later, amid allegations they'd been sitting on the money without seriously trying to trace its owners, the two largest banks, UBS and Credit Suisse agreed to pay US$1.25 billion in compensation to Holocaust survivors and their families.

Banking confidentiality, dating to the Middle Ages here, was enshrined in law in 1934 when numbered (rather than named) bank accounts were introduced. However, in 2004, the country made another concession to that veil of secrecy, when it agreed to tax accounts held in Switzerland by EU citizens.

The year 2001 was truly Switzerland's annus horribilis. The financial collapse of the national airline Swissair, a canyoning accident in the Bernese Oberland killing 21 tourists, an unprecedented gun massacre in the Zug parliament and a fatal fire in the Gotthard Tunnel within 12 months all prompted intense soul-searching. Four years on devastating floods prompted a more pragmatic debate on what should be done.

Since the new millennium, historically isolated Switzerland has recognised the universal challenges it faces and has slowly but surely started reaching out to the world. In 2002 it became the 190th member of the UN and in 2005 it finally joined Europe's 'Schengen' passport-free travel zone, a move that did not actually come into effect until December 2008 for overland arrivals and March 2009 for airport arrivals. Yet few expect the country to even consider joining either the EU –

something French-speaking cantons would welcome – or the euro single currency any time soon (if ever).

Much secrecy still reigns in the country's privileged banking sector which, in late 2008 even gave itself a scare. As the subprime mortgage scandal fired shock waves through the world's financial markets, Switzerland's two largest banks – UBS and Credit Suisse – were forced to admit heavy losses too. The government waded in with a US$60 billion package to bail out UBS, to the horror of most Swiss, who howled in protest at the huge bonuses paid in preceding years to those very bank managers who'd risked all – and cocked up.

In keeping with Western European trends, the Swiss banned smoking on public transport in 2005 and in 2007 Ticino became the first canton to outlaw smoking in all public places. Others hope to do the same.

PEOPLE

Switzerland's name may stand for everything from knives to watches, but don't expect this nation to take a stand for anyone other than itself. Militarily neutral for centuries, and armed to the teeth to make sure it stays that way, in Switzerland it's the Swiss Way or the highway.

With a population of almost 7.6 million, Switzerland averages 176 people per sq km.

IT ALL HAPPENED IN SWITZERLAND

■ Albert Einstein came up with his theories of relativity and the famous formula '$E=MC^2$' in Bern in 1905.

■ Switzerland gave birth to the World Wide Web at the acclaimed CERN (European Centre for Nuclear Research) institute outside Geneva.

■ The first acid trip took place in Switzerland. In 1943, chemist Albert Hofmann was conducting tests for a migraine cure in Basel when he accidentally absorbed the lysergic acid diethylamide, or LSD, compound through his fingertips.

■ Of the 800-or-so films a year produced by India's huge movie-making industry, more are shot in Switzerland than in any other foreign country. 'For the Indian public, Switzerland is the land of their dreams', film star Raj Mukherjee has said. Favourite destination shoots include the Bernese Oberland, Central Switzerland and Geneva.

■ Switzerland's central Alpine region possesses one of Europe's richest traditions of myth and legend. Pontius Pilate is said to rise out of the lake on Mt Pilatus, near Lucerne, every good Friday (the day he condemned Jesus Christ) to wash blood from his hands – and anybody who witnesses this event will allegedly die within the year. Tiny 'wild folk' with supernatural powers, called Chlyni Lüüt, were once reputed to inhabit Mt Rigi, also near Lucerne. Their children's spleens were removed at birth, giving them the ability to leap around mountain slopes.

Zürich is the largest city, followed by Geneva, Basel and Bern. Most people are of Germanic origin, as reflected in the breakdown of the four national languages (see p585). Around 20% of residents in Switzerland are not Swiss citizens.

The Swiss are polite, law-abiding people who usually see no good reason to break the rules. Living quietly with your neighbours is a national obsession. Good manners infuse the national psyche, and politeness is the cornerstone of all social intercourse. Always shake hands when being introduced to a Swiss, and kiss on both cheeks to greet and say goodbye to friends. Don't forget to greet shopkeepers when entering shops. When drinking with the Swiss, always wait until everyone has their drink and toast each of your companions, looking them in the eye and clinking glasses. Drinking before the toast is unforgivable, and will lead to seven years of bad sex…or so the superstition goes. Don't say you weren't warned.

In a few mountain regions such as Valais, people still wear traditional rural costumes, but dressing up is usually reserved for festivals. Yodelling, playing the alp horn and Swiss wrestling are also part of the Alpine tradition.

RELIGION

The split between Roman Catholicism (42%) and Protestantism (35%) roughly follows cantonal lines. Strong Protestant areas include Zürich, Geneva, Vaud, Bern and Neuchâtel; Valais, Ticino, Fribourg, Lucerne and the Jura are predominantly Catholic.

Just over 4% of the population is Muslim.

ARTS

Many foreign writers and artists, such as Voltaire, Byron, Shelley and Turner, have visited and settled in Switzerland. Local and international artists pouring into Zürich during WWI spawned its Dadaist movement.

Paul Klee (1879–1940) is the best-known native painter. He created bold, hard-lined abstract works. The writings of philosopher Jean-Jacques Rousseau (1712–78), in Geneva, played an important part in the development of democracy. Critically acclaimed postwar dramatists and novelists, Max Frisch (1911–91) and Friedrich Dürrenmatt (1921–90), entertained readers with their dark satire, tragi-comedies and morality plays. On the musical front, Arthur Honegger (1892–1955) is Switzerland's most recognised composer.

The Swiss have made important contributions to graphic design and commercial art. Anyone who's ever used a computer will have interacted with their fonts, from Helvetica to Fruitiger to Univers. The father of modern architecture, Le Corbusier (1887–1965), who designed Notre Dame du Haut chapel at Ronchamps in France, Chandigarh in India and the UN headquarters in New York, was Swiss. One of the most-acclaimed contemporary architectural teams on earth, Jacques Herzog and Pierre de Meuron, live and work in Basel. Winners of the prestigious Pritzker Prize in 2001, this pair created London's acclaimed Tate Modern museum building.

Gothic and Renaissance architecture are prevalent in urban areas, especially Bern. Rural Swiss houses vary according to region, but are generally characterised by ridged roofs with wide, overhanging eaves, and balconies and verandas enlivened by colourful floral displays, especially geraniums.

To the chagrin of many, Switzerland also sports some pretty artistic graffiti. Giant intricately spray-painted patterns (along with less savoury pieces) grace buildings scattered along railway tracks near train stations.

ENVIRONMENT

Mountains make up 70% of Switzerland's 41,285 sq km. Farming is intensive and cows graze on the upper slopes as soon as the retreating snow line permits.

Europe's highest elevations smugly sit here. The Dufourspitze (4634m) of Monte Rosa in the Alps is Switzerland's highest point, but the Matterhorn (4478m), with its Toblerone-shaped cap is better known. Then of course there's Mont Blanc (4807m), a hulk of a mountain – Europe's highest – shared with France and Italy.

Switzerland 1800 glaciers cover a 2000-sq-km area, but global warming means they're melting rapidly. The country's most famous mass of ice, rock and snow – the 23km-long Aletsch Glacier – shrunk 114.6m in 2006 alone and could shrink 80% by 2100 if things don't change say experts: 600 people posed nude on the glacier in 2007 for a photo by New Yorker Spencer Tunick as part of a Greenpeace campaign calling for governments worldwide to act quick.

BEHOLD THE ECO-ANGELS

Many Swiss resorts have been polishing their eco-halos recently in a bid to offset the impact of skiing. To further plan your environmentally friendly ski trip and reduce your carbon snowprint, see **Save our Snow** (www.saveoursnow.com) and the **Association of Car-Free Swiss Resorts** (www.gast.org, in German).

Whiter-than-white ski resorts in Graubünden include **Arosa** (www.arosa.ch), a one-hour train journey from Chur (p580), which runs on nearly 100% renewable energy, operates free shuttle buses and boasts Switzerland's first carbon offsetting policy; **Flims-Laax** (p580), which makes snow using hydroelectricity and recycled water; and **St Moritz** (p581), with its clean-energy policy, pedestrian zones and efficient public transport network.

Gstaad (www.gstaad.ch) has a pedestrianised centre, excellent public transport and makes huge efforts to preserve its natural surroundings in the Bernese Oberland. Valais skiers can carve with a clear conscience in **Verbier** (www.verbier.ch), where energy-efficient snow-grooming machines use biodiesel fuel. In the Jungfrau region, **Zermatt** (p552) is a whiter-than-white green classic with its car-free and eco-sound-building policies, free shuttle buses and 60% hydroelectricity. Other notable wholly car-free resorts include **Saas Fee** (www.saas-fee.ch) near Zermatt, **Wengen** and **Mürren** (p566) near Lauterbrunnen (p565), and Valais' **Bettmeralp** (www.bettmeralp.ch).

The St Gotthard Mountains in central Switzerland are the source of many lakes and rivers, including the Rhine and the Rhône. The Jura Mountains straddle the border with France, and peak at around 1700m. Between the two is the Mittelland, a region of hills also known as the Swiss Plateau criss-crossed by rivers, ravines and winding valleys.

The ibex, with its huge curved ridged horns is the most distinctive Alpine animal. In all some 12,000 of this type of mountain goat roam Switzerland and prime ibex-spotting terrain is the country's only national park (169 sq km), unimaginatively called the Swiss National Park.

Switzerland is extremely environmentally friendly: its citizens produce less than 400kg of waste each per year (half the figure for the USA), are diligent recyclers and are actively encouraged to use public transport. Moreover, pioneering green travel networks integrate the country's nonmotorised traffic routes: **SwitzerlandMobility** (www.switzerlandmobility.ch) maps out 169 routes for walkers (6300km), cyclists (8500km), mountain bikers (3300km), roller-bladers/skaters (1000km) and canoeists (250km) countrywide – all perfectly sign-posted and easy to follow.

Reinventing the Alps is the hot topic at higher altitudes. Most pressing is not so much how to be green, how to be ecological, how to burn clean energy – Swiss eco-angels have that sorted (above). Rather, it is what must be done to keep ski resorts sustainable as the globe warms: experts say you can forget sure-thing snow below 1500m by 2050.

FOOD & DRINK

Lactose intolerants will struggle in this dairy-obsessed country, which makes some of the world's most delectable chocolate and where cheese is a way of life. The best-known Swiss dish is fondue, in which melted Emmental and Gruyère are combined with white wine in a large pot and eaten with bread cubes. Another popular artery-hardener is raclette, melted cheese served with potatoes. Rösti (fried shredded potatoes) is German Switzerland's national dish, and is served with everything.

Many dishes are meaty, and veal is highly rated throughout the country. In Zürich it is thinly sliced and served in a cream sauce (*Gschnetzeltes Kalbsfleisch*). *Bündnerfleisch* is dried beef, smoked and thinly sliced. Like their northern neighbours, the Swiss also munch on a wide variety of Wurst (sausage).

Wine is considered an essential accompaniment to lunch and dinner. Local vintages are generally good quality, but you might never have heard of them, as they are rarely exported. The main growing regions are Italian- and French-speaking areas, particularly in Valais and by Lakes Neuchâtel and Geneva.

Buffet-style restaurant chains, such as Manora, have a huge selection of freshly cooked food at low prices. Migros and Coop are the main supermarket chains. Street stalls are a good place to pick up cheap eats – you'll find kebabs and sandwiches everywhere.

SWITZERLAND

ENDANGERED EDIBLES

For the ultimate authentic dining experience, sample products featured on Slow Food's Ark of Taste (www.slowfoodfoundation.com), a list of endangered world food products threatened with extinction by industrialisation, globalisation, hygiene laws and environmental dangers.

Travel your taste buds with a dozen-odd endangered species, including the fiery **Berduge eau de vie**, made from Berduge plums grown on the slopes of Mont Vully in the Fribourg canton, and sweet cherry **kirsch**: the Real McCoy Swiss version is feared for as fruit farmers replace ancient cherry varieties with less aromatic modern equivalents. Cherries also make **chriesimues**, syrup as thick as honey and used in baking or simply spread on bread. In Central Switzerland, the marked fall in the local Landrassen bee population could mean the end of **Landrassen bee honey**.

Sac (made from pork, liver, lard and spices aged for 12 months) and **fidighèla** (packed in veal intestine when straight, pork intestine if curved and aged for two to three weeks) are two types of salami worth a bite. Try them with the delightfully named, **hay-packed cheese**, a soft Alpine cheese that was indeed traditionally packed in hay, or grab a glass of wine and nibble **taillé aux greubons** (a type of pork-speckled savoury bread) from the Vaud canton instead.

Ticino **bona flour**, made from toasted corn, **rye bread** from the Val Müstair in Graubünden and **zincarlin** (a raw-milk, cup-shaped cheese unusually made from unbroken curds on the Swiss–Italian border) also appear on the threatened gastronomic-heritage list.

Bratwurst and pretzel stands (sometimes the pretzels are even stuffed with meats and cheeses) also abound in German cantons.

Restaurants sometimes close between meals (generally from 3pm to 5pm), although this is becoming rare in large cities, and tend to have a closing day, often Monday. Cafes usually stay open all day. Bars are open from lunchtime until at least midnight. Clubs get going after 10pm and close around 4am.

In cities and larger towns there are dedicated vegetarian restaurants. Most eateries offer a small selection of meatless options too, including large salad plates.

Nonsmokers are still waiting for the day that Switzerland imposes a nationwide ban on smoking in public places. Until then, ash trays remain firmly on the table in cafes and restaurants everywhere except Ticino – the first canton to impose a ban (in 2007).

GENEVA

pop 178,600

Supersleek, slick and cosmopolitan, Geneva (Genève in French, Genf in German) is a rare breed of city. It's one of Europe's priciest. Its people chatter in every language under the sun (184 nationalities comprise 45% of the city's population) and it's constantly thought of as the Swiss capital – which it isn't. This gem of a city superbly strung around the sparkling shores of Europe's largest Alpine lake is, in fact, only Switzerland's second-largest city.

Yet the whole world is here: the UN, International Red Cross, International Labour Organization, World Health Organization – 200-odd governmental and nongovernmental international organisations fill the city's plush hotels with big-name guests, feast on an incredulous choice of cuisine and help prop up the overload of banks, jewellers and chocolate shops for which Geneva is known. Strolling manicured city parks, lake sailing and skiing next door in the Alps are weekend pursuits.

ORIENTATION

The Rhône River divides Geneva into *rive droite* (right bank) – home to central train station Gare de Cornavin and the seedy Pâquis district – and *rive gauche* (left bank), where the Old Town overlooks Geneva's iconic landmark, the giant fountain of the Jet d'Eau.

INFORMATION

Emergency

Police station (Map p542; ☎ 117; Rue de Berne 6)

Internet Access

For a list of free access points in Geneva see www.freespot.ch.

Internet Café de la Gare (Map p542; ☎ 022 731 51 87; per hr Sfr10; ⏰ 7.30am-10.30pm Mon-Fri, 8.30am-10.30pm Sat & Sun) In the train station.

GENEVA

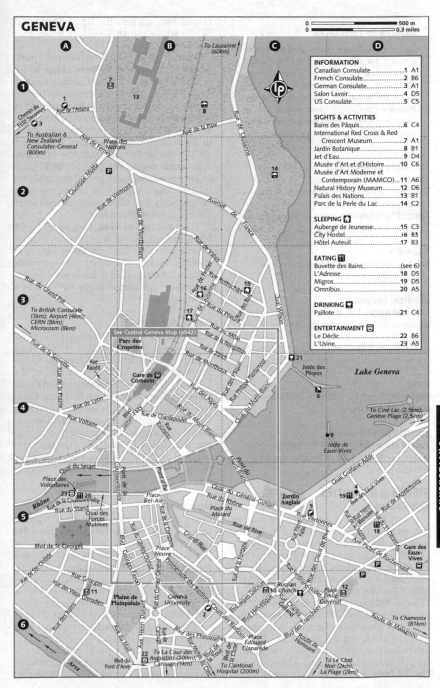

0 — 500 m
0 — 0.3 miles

INFORMATION
Canadian Consulate	1 A1
French Consulate	2 B6
German Consulate	3 A1
Salon Lavoir	4 D5
US Consulate	5 C5

SIGHTS & ACTIVITIES
Bains des Pâquis	6 C4
International Red Cross & Red Crescent Museum	7 A1
Jardin Botanique	8 B1
Jet d'Eau	9 D4
Musée d'Art et d'Histoire	10 C6
Musée d'Art Moderne et Contemporain (MAMCO)	11 A6
Natural History Museum	12 D6
Palais des Nations	13 B1
Parc de la Perle du Lac	14 C2

SLEEPING 🏠
Auberge de Jeunesse	15 C3
City Hostel	16 B3
Hôtel Auteuil	17 B3

EATING 🍴
Buvette des Bains	(see 6)
L'Adresse	18 D5
Migros	19 D5
Omnibus	20 A5

DRINKING 🍷
Paillote	21 C4

ENTERTAINMENT 🎭
Le Déclic	22 B6
L'Usine	23 A5

SWITZERLAND

GENEVA IN TWO DAYS

Explore the left-bank **parks**, **gardens** (opposite) and **Jet d'Eau** (right), then hit the **Old Town** (below) for lunch and a stroll. Tummy full, take in a **museum** (right) followed by a dip in the water and aperitif at **Bains des Päquis** (opposite). Day two: plan a tour of **CERN** (opposite) or **Palais des Nations** (right), followed by a spot of stylish shopping.

Internet Resources

City of Geneva (www.ville-ge.ch)
Glocals (www.glocals.com) Globals and locals share their tips and party.
Spotted by Locals (http://geneva.spottedbylocals.com) English-language blog.

Laundry

Salon Lavoir (Map p539; Rue du 31 Decembre 12; ⏱ 6am-midnight)

Medical Services

Cantonal Hospital (off Map p539; ☎ 022 372 33 11; emergency 022 372 81 20; www.hug-ge.ch; Rue Micheli du Crest 24)
SOS Médecins à Domicile (☎ 022 748 49 50; www.sos-medecins.ch, in French) Home/hotel doctor calls.

Post

Post office (Rue du Mont-Blanc 18; ⏱ 7.30am-6pm Mon-Fri, 9am-4pm Sat)

Tourist Information

Tourist office (☎ 022 909 70 00; www.geneve-tourisme.ch; Rue du Mont-Blanc 18; ⏱ 10am-6pm Mon, 9am-6pm Tue-Sat)

SIGHTS & ACTIVITIES
City Centre

The city centre is so compact it's easy to see many of the main sights on foot. Start with a coffee on **Île Rousseau** (Map p542), one of five islands to pierce Europe's largest alpine lake, where a statue honours the celebrated freethinker. Cross to the southern side of the lake and walk west along Quai du Général-Guisan to the **Horloge Fleurie** (Map p542; Flower Clock) in the **Jardin Anglais** (Map p542; Quai du Général-Guisan). Geneva's most photographed clock, crafted from 6500 flowers, has ticked since 1955 and sports the world's longest second hand (2.5m). Then dive into the **Old Town**, where the main street here,

Grand-Rue, shelters the **Espace Rousseau** at No 40 where the 18th-century philospher was born.

Nearby, the part-Romanesque, part-Gothic **Cathédrale de St-Pierre** (Map p542) is where Protestant John Calvin preached from 1536 to 1564; you can trace his life in the neighbouring **Musée Internationale de la Réforme** (International Museum of the Reformation; Map p542; ☎ 022 310 24 31; www.musee-reforme.ch; Rue du Cloître 4; adult/child/student Sfr10/7/free/5; ⏱ 10am-5pm Tue-Sun). Beneath the cathedral is an **archaeological site** (Map p542; ☎ 022 311 75 74; www.site-archeologique.ch; Cour St-Pierre 6; adult/child Sfr8/4; ⏱ 10am-5pm Tue-Sun), an interactive space safeguarding fine 4th-century mosaics and a 5th-century baptismal font.

The 140m-tall **Jet d'Eau** (Map p539) on the lake's southern shore is impossible to miss. At any one time there are seven tonnes of water in the air, shooting up with incredible force – 200km/h, 1360 horsepower – to create its sky-high plume, kissed by a rainbow on sunny days.

Palais des Nations

The art deco **Palais des Nations** (Map p539; ☎ 022 907 48 96; Ave de la Paix 14; tours Sfr10; ⏱ 10am-noon & 2-4pm Apr-Oct, 10am-5pm Jul & Aug, 10am-noon & 2-4pm Mon-Fri Nov-Mar) is the European arm of the UN and the home of 3000 international civil servants. You can see where decisions about world affairs are made on the hour-long tour. Afterwards check out the extensive gardens – don't miss the towering grey monument coated with heat-resistant titanium donated by the USSR to commemorate the conquest of space. ID or passport is obligatory for admission.

Museums

There are plenty of museums (many free) to fill rainy days. The **International Red Cross & Red Crescent Museum** (Musée Internationale de la Croix Rouge et du Croissant-Rouge; Map p539; ☎ 022 748 95 25; www.micr.org; Ave de la Paix 17; admission free; ⏱ 10am-5pm Wed-Mon) is a compelling multimedia trawl through atrocities perpetuated by humanity in recent history. Against the long litany of war and nastiness, documented in films, photos, sculptures and soundtracks, are set the noble aims of the organisation.

Konrad Witz's La pêche miraculeuse (c 1440–44) portraying Christ walking on water on Lake Geneva is a highlight of the **Musée d'Art**

et d'Histoire (Map p539; ☎ 022 418 26 00; http://mah.ville -ge.ch; Rue Charles Galland 2; permanent/temporary collection admission free/varies; ⊗ 10am-5pm Tue-Sun). The particularly well thought-out **Natural History Museum** (Musée d'Histoire Naturelle; Map p539; ☎ 022 418 63 00; Route de Malagnou 1; admission free; ⊗ 9.30am-5pm Tue-Sun) buzzes with kids ogling at pretty much every species known to man, stuffed for perpetuity.

Young, international, cross-media exhibitions fill the 1950s factory floor at **MAMCO** (Musée d'Art Moderne et Contemporain; Map p539; ☎ 022 320 61 22; www.mamco.ch; Rue des Vieux-Grenadiers 10; adult/student & child Sfr8/free; ⊗ noon-6pm Tue-Fri, 11am-6pm Sat & Sun, noon-9pm 1st Wed of month), while every Swatch watch ever designed ticks inside **La Cité du Temps** (Map p542; ☎ 022 818 39 00; www.citedutemps .com; 1 Pont de la Machine; ⊗ 9am-6pm), another old industrial space.

Parks & Gardens

Geneva has loads of parkland, much of it lakefront. Flowers, art installations and soul-stirring views of Mont Blanc on clear days make the northern lakeshore promenade a pleasure to walk: pass hip **Bains des Pâquis** (Map p539; ☎ 022 732 29 74; www.bains-des-paquis.ch; Quai du Mont-Blanc 30; ⊗ 9am-8pm mid-Apr–mid-Sep), where Genevans have frolicked in the sun

---

FREE THRILLS

Bags of fabulous things to see and do in Geneva don't cost a cent. Our favourite freebies:

■ Dashing like mad under the iconic the **Jet d'Eau** (opposite)

■ Getting lost in the **Old Town** (opposite)

■ Commiserating over the dark side of humanity at the **International Red Cross & Red Crescent Museum** (opposite)

■ Admiring every species of tiger known in man in the **Natural History Museum** (opposite)

■ Hobnobbing with big-bang scientists at **CERN** (right)

■ Going green in the **Jardin Botanique** (above)

■ Flopping on the beach on the **Bains de Pâquis** jetty (above)

■ **Pedalling** along the lake into France or towards Lausanne (p545)

---

since 1872 and continue to **Parc de la Perle du Lac** (Map p539). Further north, peacock-studded lawns ensnare the **Jardin Botanique** (Map p539; admission free; ⊗ 8am-7.30pm Apr-Oct, 9.30am-5pm Nov-Mar).

South of the Old Town, 4.5m-tall figures of Bèze, Calvin, Farel and Knox – in their nightgowns ready for bed – loom large in **Parc des Bastions** (Map p542).

CERN

The World Wide Web was one of the many creations to come out of the **European Organisation for Nuclear Research** (CERN; off Map p539; ☎ 022 767 84 84; visits-service@cern.ch; ⊗ tours 9am & 2pm Wed & Sat), a laboratory for research into particle physics funded by 20 nations, 8km west near Meyrin. The free three-hour guided visits need to be booked at least one month in advance, and you will need to present your ID or passport. Equally riveting is **Microcosm** (off Map p539; ☎ 022 767 84 84; http://microcosm.web.cern.ch; admission free; ⊗ 8.15am-5.30pm Mon-Fri, 8.30am-5pm Sat), CERN's on-site multimedia and interactive visitors centre.

From the train station take tram 14 or 16 to Avanchet then bus 56 to its terminus in front of CERN (Sfr3, 40 minutes).

FESTIVALS & EVENTS

August's two-week **Fêtes de Genève** (www.fetes-de -geneve.ch) ushers in parades, open-air concerts, lakeside merry-go-rounds and fireworks. On 11 December, the **Escalade** celebrates the foiling of an invasion by the Duke of Savoy in 1602 with a costumed parade, the smashing and eating of chocolate cauldrons, and a day of running races around the Old Town.

SLEEPING

When checking in, ask for your free public transport ticket covering unlimited bus travel for the duration of your hotel stay.

Budget

Hôme St-Pierre (Map p542; ☎ 022 310 37 07; www .homestpierre.ch; Cour St-Pierre 4; dm Sfr29, s/d with washbasin Sfr46/68; ⊗ reception 9am-noon & 4-8pm Mon-Sat, 9am-noon Sat; 🖵) This boarding house was founded by the German Lutheran Church in 1874. Women are its primary clientele – just six dorm beds are up for grabs for six lucky guys – and the rooftop terrace that crowns the place is magical.

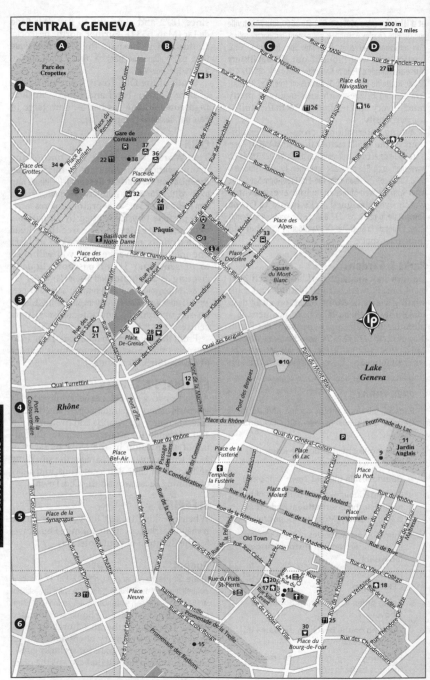

City Hostel (Map p539; ☎ 022 901 15 00; www.cityhostel.ch; Rue de Ferrier 2; dm Sfr32-36, s/d Sfr59/86; ☑ reception 7.30am-noon & 1pm-midnight; 💻) Spanking clean is the trademark of this organised hostel, where two-bed dorms give travellers a chance to double up cheaply. Rates include sheets, towels and use of the kitchen, TV room and a free locker.

Hotel St-Gervais (Map p542; ☎ 022 732 45 72; www.stgervais-geneva.ch; Rue des Corps-Saints 20; s/d with washbasin Sfr109/119, d with shower & toilet Sfr140; ☑ reception 7am-11pm) Travellers with jumbo-sized suitcases beware: scaling the seven floors in the pocket-handkerchief lift of this quaint choice near the train station is a squash and a squeeze. Renovated rooms kip on the 1st and 7th floors.

Also recommended:

Auberge de Jeunesse (Map p539; ☎ 022 732 62 60; www.yh-geneva.ch; Rue Rothschild 28-30; dm Sfr29, d from Sfr85; ☑ 6.30-10am & 2pm-1am Jun-Sep, 6.30-

10am & 4pm-midnight Oct-May; 💻) Dorms max out at 12 beds.

Midrange & Top End

our pick **Hôtel de la Cloche** (☎ 022 732 94 81; www.geneva-hotel.ch/cloche; Rue de la Cloche 6; s with shared bathroom Sfr65-90, with private bathroom Sfr90-120, d with shared bathroom Sfr95-118, with private bathroom Sfr110-148) Elegant fireplaces, bourgeois furnishings, wooden floors and the odd chandelier add a touch of grandeur to this old-fashioned one-star hotel.

Hôtel Bel'Esperance (☎ 022 818 37 37; www.hotel-bel-esperance.ch; Rue de la Vallée 1; s/d from Sfr98/154; ☑ reception 7am-10pm; 💻) This two-star hotel is a two-second flit to the Old Town. Rooms are quiet, cared for and those on the 1st floor share a kitchen. Ride the lift to the 5th floor to flop on a chair on a flower-filled rooftop terrace. Free wi-fi.

La Cour des Augustins (off Map p539; ☎ 022 322 21 00; www.lacourdesaugustins.com; Rue Jean-Violette 15; s/d from Sfr191/225; 💻) Disguised by a 19th-century facade, the crisp white interior of this 'boutique gallery hotel' sports the latest technology and screams cutting-edge.

Eidelweiss (☎ 022 544 51 51; www.manotel.com; Place de la Navigation 2; d Sfr290-390) Plunge yourself into the heart of the Swiss Alps *en ville* at this Heidi-style hideout, with its big cuddly St-Bernard, fireplace and chalet-styled restaurant.

Hôtel Auteuil (☎ 022 544 22 22; www.manotel.com; Rue de Lausanne 33; d from Sfr350; 📺 💻) The star of this design-driven hotel near the station is its collection of B&W photos of 1950s film stars in Geneva. Grab *The Book* from reception to find out precisely who's who where. Free wi-fi.

Hôtel Les Armures (☎ 022 310 91 72; www.hotel-les-armures.ch; Rue du Puits-St-Pierre 1; s/d from Sfr395/605; 📺 💻) This slumbering 17th-century beauty oozes history from every last beam. Beautifully placed in the heart of the Old Town, it provides an intimate and refined atmosphere. Wi-fi costs Sfr25 per day.

EATING

Geneva flaunts ethnic food galore. For the culinary curious with no fortune to blow, the Pâquis area cooks up cuisine from most corners of the globe in cheapish eateries.

Restaurants

In the Old Town, terrace cafes and restaurants crowd Geneva's oldest square, medieval Place

SWITZERLAND

du Bourg-de-Four. Near the station, Scandale (right) is a hot lunchtime spot. For quintessential Swiss fondue (Sfr32) and yodelling Eidelweiss (p543) is *the* address.

Les 5 Portes (☎ 022 731 84 38; Rue de Zürich 5; brunch Sfr10, mains Sfr15-20; ⏰ 9-2am Mon-Fri, 11-2am Sat, 11am-8pm Sun) The Five Doors is a fashionable Pâquis port of call that embraces every mood and moment.

Chez Ma Cousine (Map p542; ☎ 022 310 96 96; www.chezmacousine.ch; Place du Bourg-de-Four 6; lunch Sfr14.90; ⏰ 11am-10pm) *'On y mange du poulet'* (we eat chicken!) is the strap line of this student institution that appeals for one good reason – generously handsome, homely portions of chicken, potatoes and salad at an unbeatable price.

Buvette des Bains (Map p542; ☎ 022 738 16 16; www .bains-des-paquis.ch; Quai du Mont-Blanc 30; mains Sfr15; ⏰ 8am-10pm daily) Meet Genevans at this earthy beach bar at Bains des Pâquis (p541). Dining is on trays and in summer alfresco.

Omnibus (Map p539; ☎ 022 321 44 45; www.omnibus -café.ch; Rue de la Coulouvrenière 23; mains Sfr25-40; ⏰ 11-2am Mon-Fri, 5pm-2am Sat & Sun) Don't be fooled by the graffiti-plastered facade of this Rhône-side space. Inside, a maze of retro rooms seduces on first sight. Its business card is a recycled bus ticket.

our pick **L'Adresse** (Map p539; ☎ 022 736 32 32; www.ladresse.ch; Rue du 31 Decembre 32; mains Sfr25-35; ⏰ lunch & dinner Tue-Sat) An urban loft with rooftop terrace and hybrid lifestyle boutique-contemporary bistro, this hip address is at home in converted artist workshops. *The* address for lunch, brunch or (in their words) Saturday slunch…

Au Grütli (Map p542; ☎ 022 328 98 68; www.cafedu grutli.ch; Rue du Général Dufour 16; mains Sfr28-35; ⏰ 8am-

---

SPLURGE

It's a splurge all right but the water views at **RestO by Arthur's** (Map p542; ☎ 022 818 39 00; La Cité du Temps, 1 Pont de la Machine; mains Sfr35-46; ⏰ 9am-midnight Mon-Thu, 9am-1am Fri, 11am-1am Sat) are magnificent. One of the city's trendiest addresses, this designer-driven dining space squats on the 1st floor of an industrial building constructed in the 1840s to provide the city's public fountains with water. The cuisine style is world and every dish comes with its own wine recommendation.

11pm Mon-Fri, 4-11pm Sat & Sun) Indonesian lamb, moussaka, scallops with ginger and citrus fruits or Provençal chicken are among the international flavours at this razor-sharp theatre restaurant.

Café de Paris (Map p542; ☎ 022 732 84 50; Rue du Mont-Blanc 26; green salad, steak & chips Sfr40; ⏰ 11am-11pm daily) A memorable dining experience around since 1930. Everyone goes for the same thing here: green salad, beef steak with a killer-calorie herb and butter sauce and as many fries as you can handle.

Quick Eats & Self-Catering

Rue de Fribourg, Rue de Neuchâtel, Rue de Berne and the northern end of Rue des Alpes are loaded with kebab, falafel and quick-eat joints. Eat in or take away:

Mikado (Map p542; ☎ 022 732 47 74; Rue de l'Ancien Port 9; sushi Sfr2.50/piece, mains Sfr6.50; ⏰ 10am-6.30pm Tue-Fri, 10am-6pm Sat) If it's authenticity, speed and tasty fast food on a red lacquered tray you want, this Japanese delicatessen hits the spot.

Piment Vert (Map p542; ☎ 022 731 93 03; www.pim entvert.ch; Place De-Grenus 4; mains Sfr15-19; ⏰ 11.30am-2.45pm & 5.30-10pm Mon-Fri, noon-4pm Sat) Fast, fresh, and trendy sums up this hybrid Indian-Sri Lankan bar.

Central supermarkets:

Aperto (Map p542; train station; ⏰ 6am-midnight)
Migros (Map p539; 27 Rue des Eaux-Vives; ⏰ 8am-7pm Mon-Wed, 8am-7.30pm Thu & Fri, 8am-6pm Sat)

DRINKING & ENTERTAINMENT

The latest nightclubs, live-music venues and theatre events are well covered in the weekly *Genéve Agenda* (free at the tourist office). Pâquis, the district in between the train station and lake; is particularly well-endowed with bars. In summer the **paillote** (Map p539; Quai du Mont-Blanc 30; ⏰ to midnight), with wooden tables inches from the water, gets crammed.

Scandale (Map p542; ☎ 022 731 83 73; www.scandale .ch; Rue de Lausanne 24; ⏰ 11am-2am Tue-Fri, 5pm-2am Sat) Retro 1950s furnishings in a cavernous interior with comfy sofas ensures this lounge bar is never empty. Happenings include art exhibitions, Saturday-night DJs and bands.

La Bretelle (Map p542; ☎ 022 732 75 96; Rue des Étuves 17; ⏰ 6pm-2am daily) Little has changed since the 1970s, when this legendary bar opened. Live accordion-accompanied French chansons most nights.

La Clémence (Map p542; ☎ 022 312 24 98; www .laclemence.ch; Place du Bourg-de-Four 20; ⏰ 7-1am

> ### SPLURGE: THE ULTIMATE CHOCOLATE EXPERIENCE
>
> Soothe urban body and soul at **After the Rain Spa** (Map p542; ☎ 022 819 01 50; www .spa-aftertherain.ch; Passage des Lions 4; ⊗ 9am-9pm Mon-Sat) in downtown Geneva where the icing on the cake for chocolate fiends has to be a body wrap in creamy milk chocolate (45 minutes, Sfr140) or a good old soak in a white chocolate bath (30 minutes, Sfr180).

Mon-Thu & Sun, 7-2am Fri & Sat) Indulge in a glass of local wine or an artisanal beer at this venerable cafe-bar located on Geneva's loveliest square.

La Plage (off Map p539; ☎ 022 342 20 98; Rue Vautier 19; ⊗ 11-1am Mon-Thu, 10-2am Fri & Sat, 5pm-1am Sun) With bare wood tables, checked lino floor, green-wood shutters and tables outside, the Beach in Carouge is a timeless drinking hole.

L'Usine (Map p539; ☎ 022 781 34 90; www.usine.ch; Place des Volontaires 4) This grungy and youthful converted gold-roughing factory entertains with dance nights, art happenings, theatre, cabaret and club nights.

Le Chat Noir (off Map p539; ☎ 022 343 49 98; www .chatnoir.ch, in French; Rue Vautier 13; ⊗ Tue-Sat) Nightly jazz, rock, funk and salsa gigs.

Le Déclic (Map p539; ☎ 022 320 59 40; www.ledeclic .ch; Blvd du Pont d'Arve 28; ⊗ 5pm-2am Mon-Fri, 9pm-2am Sat) Gay nightclub.

Ciné Lac (off Map p539; www.cinelac.ch, in French; adult/under 14yr Sfr17/14; ⊗ Jul & Aug) Glorious summertime open-air cinema with a screen set up on the lakeside.

GETTING THERE & AWAY
Aéroport International de Genève (GVA; off Map p539; ☎ 0900 57 15 00; www.gva.ch), 4km from town, has connections to major European cities and many others worldwide. It is also an easyJet hub.

CGN (Compagnie Générale de Navigation; ☎ 0848 811 848; www.cgn.ch) operates a steamer service from its Jardin Anglais jetty to other villages on Lake Geneva. Many only sail May to September, including those to/from Lausanne (Sfr37.60, 3½ hours). Eurail and Swiss Pass holders are valid on CGN boats or there is a one-day CGN boat pass (Sfr49).

International buses depart from the **bus station** (☎ 0900 320 320, 022 732 02 30; www.coach-station .com; Place Dorcière).

Trains run to most Swiss towns including at least hourly to/from Lausanne (Sfr20.60, 40 minutes), Bern (Sfr46, 1¾ hours) and Zürich (Sfr80, 2¾ hours).

International daily rail connections from Geneva include Paris (Sfr127 by TGV, 3½ hours), Hamburg (Sfr276, 9½ hours), Milan (Sfr97, 4½ hours) and Barcelona (Sfr125, 10 hours).

GETTING AROUND
Getting from the airport is easy with regular trains into Gare de Cornavin (Sfr3, eight minutes). Slower bus 10 (Sfr3) does the same 5km trip. A metered taxi costs Sfr30 to Sfr50.

Pick up a bike at **Genève Roule** (Map p542; ☎ 022 740 13 43; www.geneveroule.ch; Place de Montbrillant 17; ⊗ 8am-6pm Mon-Sat) or its seasonal Jetée des Pâquis pick-up point for Sfr12/20 per day/weekend. May to October, borrow a bike carrying publicity for free.

Buses, trams, trains and boats service the city, and ticket dispensers are found at all stops. Tickets cost Sfr2 (within one zone, 30 minutes) or Sfr3 (two zones, one hour) and a city/canton day pass is Sfr7/12. The same tickets are also valid on the yellow shuttle boats known as Les Mouettes (the seagulls) that criss-cross the lake every 10 minutes between 7.30am and 6pm.

LAKE GENEVA REGION

East of Geneva, Western Europe's biggest lake stretches like a giant liquid mirror between French-speaking Switzerland on its northern shore and France to the south. Known as Lake Geneva by many and Lac Léman to Francophones, the Swiss side of the lake cossets the elegant city of Lausanne, pretty palm tree-studded Riviera resorts such as Vevey and Montreux, and the marvellous emerald spectacle of vines marching up steep hillsides in strict unison.

LAUSANNE
pop 119,200
In a fabulous location overlooking Lake Geneva, Lausanne is an enchanting beauty with several distinct personalities: the former

fishing village of Ouchy, with its summer beach-resort feel; Place St-François, with stylish, cobblestone shopping streets; and Flon, a warehouse district of bars, galleries and boutiques. It's also got a few amazing sights. One of the country's grandest Gothic cathedrals dominates its medieval centre.

The **tourist office** (☎ 021 613 73 21; www.lausanne -tourisme.ch; Place de la Navigation 4; ☼ 9am-6pm Oct-Mar, 9am-8pm Apr-Sep) neighbours Ouchy metro station and has a **branch office** (Place de la Gare 9; ☼ 9am-7pm) at the train station.

Sights & Activities
MUSÉE DE L'ART BRUT
This alluring **museum** (☎ 021 315 25 70; www.artbrut .ch; Ave des Bergières 11-13; adult/child/student Sfr10/free/5, free 1st Sat of month; ☼ 11am-6pm Tue-Sun Sep-Jun, daily Jul & Aug) showcases a fascinating amalgam of 15,000 works of art created by untrained artists – psychiatric patients, eccentrics and incarcerated criminals. The works offer a striking variety, at times a surprising technical capacity and in some cases an inspirational world-view. Biographies and explanations are in English. The museum is about 600m northwest of Place St François; take bus 2 or 3 to the Beaulieu stop.

CATHÉDRALE DE NOTRE DAME
This glorious Gothic **cathedral** (☼ 7am-7pm Mon-Fri, 8am-7pm Sat & Sun Apr-Aug, 7am-5.30pm Sep-Mar) is arguably the finest in Switzerland. Built in the 12th and 13th centuries, highlights include the stunningly detailed carved portal, vaulted ceilings and archways, and carefully restored stained-glass windows.

MUSÉE OLYMPIQUE
Lausanne is home to the International Olympic Committee, and sports aficionados can immerse themselves in archival footage, interactive computers and memorabilia at the information-packed **Musée Olympique** (☎ 021 621 65 11; www.museum.olympic.org; Quai d'Ouchy 1; adult/child/ student Sfr15/free/10; ☼ 9am-6pm daily Apr-Oct, 9am-6pm Tue-Sun Nov-Mar).

Sleeping
Hotel guests get a Lausanne Transport Card covering unlimited use of public transport for the duration of their stay.

Camping de Vidy (☎ 021 622 50 00; www.camping lausannevidy.ch; Chemin du Camping 3; camp sites per adult/car Sfr7.50/3.50, per tent €10-18) This camping ground is on the lake just to the west of the Vidy sports complex. Sites are well maintained and it's popular with families in summer. Get off bus 2 at Bois de Vaux.

Lausanne GuestHouse (☎ 021 601 80 00; www .lausanne-guesthouse.ch; Chemin des Épinettes 4; dm Sfr33-38, s/d with shared bathroom Sfr85/95, with private bathroom Sfr94/115; ▢) An attractive mansion converted into quality backpacking accommodation near the train station. Many rooms have lake views and some of the building's energy is solar.

Hôtel du Port (☎ 021 612 04 44; www.hotel-du -port.ch; Place du Port 5; s/d Sfr180/230) A perfect location in Ouchy, just back from the lake, makes this a good choice. The best doubles peep at the lake and suites slumber on the 3rd floor.

Eating
Café Romand (☎ 021 312 63 75; Place St François 2; mains Sfr18-28.50; ☼ 11am-11pm Mon-Sat) Bankers to punks flocks here to feast on the traditional food, ranging from fine fondue to *cervelle au beurre noir* (brains in black butter), cooked in this kitchen, which operates all day. Follow the tatty sign into the arcade.

our pick Café de Grancy (☎ 021 616 86 66; www .cafédegrancy.ch; Ave du Rond Point 1; mains Sfr18-35; ☼ 8am-midnight Mon & Wed-Thu, 8-1am Fri, 10-1am Sat, 10am-midnight Sun) An old-time bar resurrected with flair by young entrepreneurs, this spot is a hip hang-out with floppy lounges, wi-fi, weekend brunch and a tempting restaurant out back.

Café du Vieil Ouchy (☎ 021 616 21 94; Place du Port 3, Ouchy; mains Sfr18.50-38.50; ☼ Thu-Mon) A simple but charming location for fondue (Sfr23.50), rösti and other classics. Follow up with a meringue smothered in thick double Gruyère cream.

our pick Café les Alliés (☎ 021 648 69 40; www .lesallies.ch; Rue de la Pontaise 48; mains Sfr22-44; ☼ lunch & dinner Mon-Fri) It's not much to look at from the outside but inside a cosy, warm restaurant with creaky timber floors winds out back towards a pleasant summer garden. Imaginative salads precede mains such as *steak de veau poêlé au jus d'abricots* (pancooked steak in apricot sauce).

Also recommended:
Café-Restaurant du Vieux Lausanne (☎ 021 323 53 90; Rue Pierre Viret 6; mains from Sfr25-42; ☼ lunch & dinner Tue-Fri, dinner Sat) French and Swiss cuisine with a narrow pergola out back.

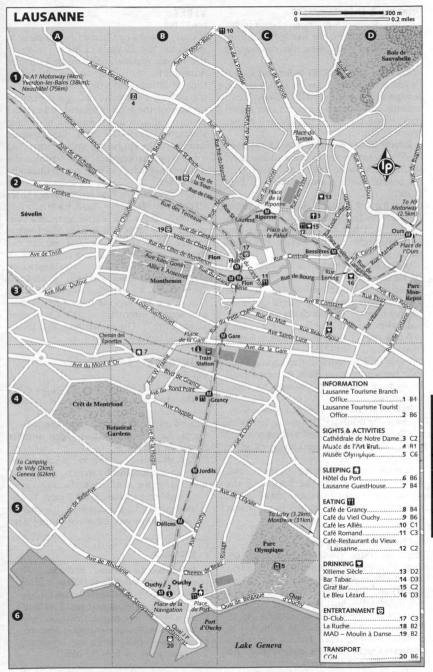

LAUSANNE

SWITZERLAND

INFORMATION

Lausanne Tourisme Branch Office	1 B4
Lausanne Tourisme Tourist Office	2 B6

SIGHTS & ACTIVITIES

Cathédrale de Notre Dame	3 C2
Musée de l'Art Brut	4 R1
Musée Olympique	5 C6

SLEEPING 🏠

Hôtel du Port	6 B6
Lausanne GuestHouse	7 B4

EATING 🍴

Café de Grancy	8 B4
Café du Vieil Ouchy	9 B6
Café les Alliés	10 C1
Café Romand	11 C3
Café-Restaurant du Vieux Lausanne	12 C2

DRINKING 🍷

XIIIeme Siècle	13 D2
Bar Tabac	14 D3
Girat Bar	15 C2
Le Bleu Lézard	16 D3

ENTERTAINMENT 🎭

D-Club	17 C3
La Ruche	18 B2
MAD – Moulin à Danse	19 B2

TRANSPORT

CGN	20 B6

Drinking & Entertainment

Lausanne is one of Switzerland's busier night-time cities. Look for the handy free listings booklet *What's Up* (www.whatsupmag.ch) in bars.

Bar Tabac (☎ 021 312 33 16; Rue Beau Séjour 7; ☿ 7am-9pm Mon-Wed, 7-1am Thu & Fri, 9-2am Sat, 9am-3pm Sun) Squeaky timber floors lend warmth and punters engage in animated chat around the bar at this spruced corner tavern of old.

XIIIeme Siècle (☎ 021 312 40 64; Rue Cité-Devant 10; ☿ 10pm-4am Tue-Sat) In a grand medieval setting with stone vaults and huge timber beams, this is a great place for a beer or six.

Giraf Bar (☎ 021 323 53 90; Escaliers du Marché; ☿ 8.30pm-1am Tue-Thu, to 2am Fri & Sat) This tiny smoke-filled bar fills up on Friday and Saturday night; dig the giraffe-skin motif on the lampshades.

Le Bleu Lézard (☎ 021 321 38 30; www.bleu-lezard .ch; Rue Enning 10; ☿ 7am-1am Mon-Thu, 7am-2am Fri, 8am-2am Sat, 9.30am-1am Sun) An oldie but a goodie, this corner bar-eatery cooks up Sunday brunch, wi-fi, a chatty atmosphere and a club-styled dance floor in the cellar.

D-Club (☎ 021 351 51 40; www.dclub.ch; Place de Centrale; admission Sfr10-25; ☿ 11pm-5am Wed-Sat) DJs spin funk to house at this heaving club. Take the stairs down from Rue du Grand Pont, turn right and descend to Place de Centrale.

MAD (☎ 021 340 69 69; www.mad.ch; Route de Genève 23; admission up to Sfr25; ☿ 11pm-4am Tue-Sun) With five floors of entertainment and every sound going, MAD throbs. Dress snappy and be 25 or older.

La Ruche (www.la-ruche.ch; Rue de la Tour 41; admission free-Sfr10; ☿ Thu-Sun) The Beehive is the last in the trio of Lausanne clubs of the moment, so hot even clubbers from Geneva trek here.

Getting There & Around

There are trains to/from Geneva (Sfr20.60, 33 to 51 minutes, up to six hourly), Geneva airport (Sfr25, 42 to 58 minutes, up to four hourly) and Bern (Sfr31, 70 minutes, one or two hourly). For boat services see p545.

Buses service most destinations (up to three stops Sfr1.90, one-hour unlimited in central Lausanne Sfr3). The m2 metro line connects Ouchy with the train station and costs the same as the buses.

VEVEY
pop 17,000

It's easy to see why Charlie Chaplin chose to spend the last 25 years of his life in Vevey (his former mansion will become a Chaplin museum in 2010). The swanky little place (one of Switzerland's two main Riviera resorts), with a colourful old square bumped up against the lake, is located in beautiful country. It also has a number of unique shops and lazy-day cafes. On summer Saturdays the sprawling square turns into a bustling marketplace with traditionally dressed merchants selling local handicrafts and wines.

For sleeping try **Yoba Riviera Lodge** (☎ 021 923 80 40; www.rivieralodge.ch; Place du Marché 5; dm Sfr32, s/d Sfr88/95; ▣), a fun, central hostel in a converted 19th-century mansion. The rooftop terrace offers great views and you can use the kitchen to reduce dining costs.

Le National (☎ 021 923 76 25; Rue du Torrent 9; mains Sfr25-32; ☿ 11am-midnight Mon-Tue, to 1am Wed-Thu, to 2am Fri & Sat) is a great place to eat and drink. One side is hip bar, the other side a restaurant serving international dishes and super salads (Sfr17). On sunny days, flop in the backyard beneath a tree.

MONTREUX
pop 23,200

In 1971 Frank Zappa was doing his thing in the Montreux casino when the building caught fire, casting a pall of smoke over Lake Geneva and inspiring the members of Deep Purple to pen their classic rock number *Smoke on the Water*.

The showpiece of the Swiss Riviera has been an inspiration to writers, artists and musicians for centuries. Famous one-time residents include Lord Byron, Ernest Hemingway and the Shelleys. It's easy to see why: Montreux boasts stunning Alps

---

SPLURGE

Restaurant Le Château (☎ 021 921 12 10; www.denismartin.ch; Rue du Château 2; tasting menu Sfr260; ☿ dinner Tue-Sun) is the place to head in Vevey should you have Sfr260 burning a hole in your pocket. Lunch à la Denis Martin, one the biggest names in Swiss contemporary cooking. Find it in a 17th-century residence a block from the lake.

WORTH THE TRIP: GRYON & LEYSIN

Trek off the beaten track to lap up Swiss Alpine charm in untouched Gryon (1130m), with great meadow hiking trials and **Chalet Martin** (☎ 024 498 33 21; Chalet Martin; www.gryon.com; dm/d from Sfr25/70; 🖳), a Swiss-Australian-run hostel that travellers give rave reviews. The vibe is strictly laid-back and the place organises dozens of activities – paragliding, skiing and chocolate tasting included. Take a train from Lausanne to Bex (Sfr17.40, 40 minutes, hourly), then the cogwheel train to Gryon (Sfr6.20, 30 minutes, hourly). The hostel is a five-minute signposted walk from the train stop.

Equally Zen is Leysin, a hub for skiers, boarders and hikers who can't sing the praises highly enough of **Hiking Sheep** (☎ 024 494 35 35; www.hikingsheep.com; dm/d Sfr30/80; 🗙 🖳). The tall, art deco house has a kitchen, great communal facilities, a pine-forested backyard and breathtaking views from its balconies. Find it a two-minute walk from Leysin-Grand Hôtel train station. Ride the cogwheel train from Aigle (Sfr10.80, 30 minutes, hourly), in turn linked by train with Lausanne (Sfr14.80, 30 minutes, hourly).

---

views, tidy rows of pastel buildings and Switzerland's most extraordinary castle.

Each year crowds throng to the **Montreux Jazz Festival** (www.montreuxjazz.com) for a fortnight in early July. Free concerts take place every day, but big-name gigs cost (Sfr40 to Sfr100).

Sights

Originally constructed on the shores of Lake Geneva in the 11th century, **Château de Chillon** (☎ 021 966 89 10; www.chillon.ch; Ave de Chillon 21; adult/student/child Sfr12/10/6; 🕑 9am-6pm Apr-Sep, 9.30am-5pm Mar & Oct, 10am-4pm Nov-Feb) was brought to the world's attention by Lord Byron, and the world has been filing past ever since. Spend at least a couple of hours exploring its myriad courtyards, towers, dungeons and halls filled with arms, period furniture and artwork.

The castle is a 45-minute lakefront walk from Montreux. Otherwise trolley bus 1 (Sfr2.30) passes every 10 minutes.

Sleeping & Eating

Auberge de Jeunesse (☎ 021 963 49 34; Passage de l'Auberge 8; Territet; dm from Sfr32; 🕑 mid-Feb–mid-Nov; 🖳) This chirpy hostel is a 30-minute walk along the lake clockwise from the tourist office (or take the local train to Territet or bus 1).

Hôtel La Rouvenaz (☎ 021 963 27 36; Rue du Marché 1; s/d Sfr130/190; 🖳) A simple, family-run spot with 12 rooms and its own Italian restaurant, you cannot get any closer to the lake or the heart of the action.

our pick **Hôtel Masson** (☎ 021 966 00 44; www .hotelmasson.ch; Rue Bonivard 5; s/d Sfr180/240) In 1829, this vintner's mansion was converted into a hotel. Its old charm has remained intact and the hotel, set in magnificent grounds, is on the Swiss Heritage list of most beautiful hotels in the country. Find it in the hills southeast of Montreux.

Montagnard (☎ 021 964 83 49; www.montagnard.ch; mains Sfr22-28; 🕑 Wed-Sun) For a taste of country fare in a timber farmhouse with gardens, head to the village of Villard-sur-Chamby, a 9.5km taxi ride from central Montreux.

Café du Grütli (☎ 021 963 42 65; Rue du Grand Chêne 8; mains up to Sfr30; 🕑 Wed-Mon) This cheerful little eatery is hidden in the old part of town and provides good home cooking. Think rösti with ham, hearty meat dishes, salads and the inevitable fondue.

Getting There & Away

There are trains to Geneva (Sfr28, 70 minutes, hourly) and Lausanne (Sfr10.20, 25 minutes, three hourly). Make the scenic journey to Interlaken via the GoldenPass Panoramic, with changes at Zweisimmen and Spiez (Sfr80, three hours, daily; rail passes valid).

FRIBOURG, NEUCHÂTEL & THE JURA

A far cry from the staggering Alpine scenes more readily associated with Switzerland, this gentle corner in the west of the country is a 'secret'. From the evocative medieval cantonal capitals of Fribourg and Neuchâtel to the mysterious green hills and deep dark forests of the Jura, it promises experiences and escapes off the beaten track. Be it marvelling at majestic ice creations or following the call of the

SWITZERLAND

devilish green fairy into the wayward Val de Travers, travel here is discovery.

NEUCHÂTEL
pop 32,300

Its Old Town sandstone elegance, the airy Gallic nonchalance of its cafe life and the gay lakeside air that breezes along the shoreline of its glittering lake makes Neuchâtel disarmingly charming. The small university town, complete with its own spirited *comune libre* (free commune), is compact enough to discover on foot, while the French spoken here is said be Switzerland's purest. Not just that: Neuchâtel's town observatory gives the official time-check for all of Switzerland.

The pedestrian zone and Place Pury (the local bus hub) are about 1km from the train station; walk down the hill along Ave de la Gare. The lakeside **tourist office** (☎ 032 889 68 90; www.neuchateltourism.ch; Hôtel des Postes, Pl du Port; ☻ 9am-noon & 1.30-5.30pm Mon-Fri, 9am-noon Sat Sep-Jun, 9am-6.30pm Mon-Fri, 9-4pm Sat, 10am-2pm Sun Jul & Aug) neighbours the post office.

Sights & Activities

The 15th-century **Chateau de Neuchâtel** (☎ 032 889 60 00; guided tours free; ☻ 10am-noon & 2-4pm Mon-Sat, 2-4pm Sun Apr-Sep) and the adjoining **Collegiate Church** are the centrepieces of the Old Town. The striking cenotaph of 15 statues dates from 1372. Scale the nearby **prison tower** (☎ 032 717 71 02; Rue Jehanne de Hochberg 5; admission Sfr1; ☻ 8am-6pm Apr-Sep) for broad views of town and lake.

Visit the **Musée d'Art et d'Histoire** (☎ 032 717 79 25; www.mahn.ch, in French; Esplanade Léopold Robert 1; adult/under 16yr Sfr8/free, Wed free; ☻ 11am-6pm Tue-Sun) to see beloved 18th-century clockwork figures.

Sleeping

L'Aubier (☎ 032 710 18 58; Rue du Château 1; s/d with washbasin Sfr80/110, with shower & toilet Sfr130/180; ☻ reception 11.45am-7pm Mon, 7.30am-7pm Tue-Fri, 8am-6pm Sat) Soulful sleeping above a green eating space is what this lovely cafe-hotel is about. Look for the diagonal-striped shutters peeping down on a knight.

Auberg'Inn (☎ 078 615 84 21; www.auberginn.ch, in French; Rue Fleury 1; s/d Sfr100/150; ☻ reception 8am-6pm Mon-Sat, 8am-noon Sun) Draw on the walls of the Blackboard room, sleep green in the Bamboo room or chill before a flat screen in the Cinema room at this atmospheric hostel-style place in a Renaissance town house. Free wi-fi.

Eating

Local specialities include tripe and *tomme neuchâteloise chaude* (baked goat cheese starter). Casual eating places dot pedestrian Rue des Moulins.

L'Aubier (☎ 032 710 18 58; Rue du Château 1; ☻ 11.45am-7pm Mon, 7.30am-7pm Tue-Fri, 8am-6pm Sat) This green-thinking cafe cooks up a healthy smattering of salads, quiches, tarts and so on – ideal for lunch.

our pick Famiglia Leccese (☎ 032 724 41 10; Rue de l'Ecluse 49; pasta Sfr15; ☻ dinner Tue-Sat, lunch & dinner Sun) With an entrance resembling a private apartment, this *bellissimo* slice of southern Italy is impossible to find unless you're local and know it. Look for the fairy lights behind Claude Cordey Motos.

Café du Jura (☎ 032 725 14 10; Rue de la Treille 7; mains Sfr25-35; ☻ lunch & dinner Mon-Sat) Food is cooked to fill and despite meaty mains such as tripe and *tête et langue de veau* (calf head and tongue), vegetarians are well catered for.

Coop (Rue de la Treille 4) Self-caterers stock up on local wine, cheese and absinthe at this supermarket.

Drinking & Entertainment

Le Bistrot du Concert (☎ 032 724 62 16; Rue de l'Hôtel de Ville 4; mains €20-25; ☻ 8am-midnight Mon-Thu, 8-1am Fri & Sat, 3pm-midnight Sun) A great all-round address, this industrial bar with buzzing pavement terrace has a soulful spirit, zinc bar and bistro menu chalked on the board.

Chauffage Compris (Rue des Moulins 37; ☻ 9-1am Mon-Thu, 9-2am Fri & Sat, 3pm-1am Sun) Its name – Heating Included – speaks volumes. This retro bar with a decorative tiled entrance that translates as 'heating and kitchen equipment' is one cool place to loiter. Weekend brunch Sfr10.

La Case à Chocs (☎ 032 721 20 56; www.case-a-chocs .ch, in French; Quai Philippe Godet 20; admission free-Sfr25; ☻ 9.30pm or 10pm-2am Fri-Sun) Alternative venue in a converted brewery with live music.

Getting There & Away

Trains serve Geneva (Sfr38, 70 minutes, hourly), Bern (Sfr18.20, 35 minutes, hourly) and other destinations.

VAL DE TRAVERS

Hikers come to the Travers Valley to marvel at the enormous **Creux du Van** abyss. This spectacular crescent-moon wall, a product of glacial erosion, interrupts the habitually green rolling countryside in startling fashion –

FAIRYLAND ABSINTHE

It was in the deepest darkest depths of the Val de Travers – dubbed the Pays des Fées (Fairyland) – that absinthe was first distilled in 1740 and produced commercially in 1797 (although it was a Frenchman called Pernod who made the first known bitter green liqueur just a few kilometres across the French–Swiss border in Pontarlier).

From 1910, following Switzerland's prohibition of the wickedly alcoholic and ruthlessly bitter aniseed drink, distillers of the so-called 'devil in the bottle' in the Val de Travers moved underground. In 1990 the great-grandson of a pre-prohibition distiller in Môtiers came up with Switzerland's first legal aniseed liqueur since 1910 – albeit one which was only 45% proof alcohol (instead of 50% to 75%) and which scarcely contained thujone (the offensive chemical found in wormwood, said to be the root of absinthe's devilish nature). An *extrait d'absinthe* (absinthe extract) quickly followed and in 2005, following Switzerland's lifting of its absinthe ban, the **Blackmint – Distillerie Kübler & Wyss** (☎ 032 861 14 69; www.blackmint.ch; Rue du Château 7) in Môtiers distilled its first true and authentic batch of the mythical *fée verte* (green fairy) from valley-grown wormwood. Mix one part crystal-clear liqueur with five parts water to make it green (and wait for light and floaty feelings to hit, as was the case after the first glass we shared with friends back home!).

Swilling the green fairy, aka absinthe, at the bar aboard an old steam train as it puffs the length of the Val de Travers is particularly evocative. Jump aboard in Neuchâtel with **Vapeur Val de Travers** (☎ 032 863 24 07; www.rvt-historique-ch; Rue de la Gare 19, Travers; day trips with lunch Sfr75).

it is just 1km long, but plunges 440m to the bottom (the first 200m is a sheer stony drop). The Creux is easiest reached on foot from **Noiraigue**, 22km southwest of Neuchâtel and accessible by hourly train from the latter (Sfr7, 20 minutes). The round-trip hike takes up to five hours route depending.

A green sleep in this valley is **L'Aubier** (☎ 032 732 22 11; www.aubier.ch; s/d from Sfr125/160), a designer eco-hotel on a biodynamic farm in Montézillon, 8km southwest of Neuchâtel. Light-flooded rooms overlook fields of grazing cows, whose milk is mixed with carrot juice to make carrot cheese sold in its eco-boutique.

Should absinthe tickle your fancy, discover all in **Môtiers** (see above), 35 minutes by train from Neuchâtel (Sfr10.80).

FRIBOURG
pop 33,400

Medieval Fribourg boasts the usual cathedrals and art museums, but for something different focus on the beer.

With two great breweries in town you can't go wrong. Head to **Brasserie du Cardinal** (www.cardinal.ch; Passage du Cardinal) to try one of Switzerland's best-known lagers, brewed since 1788. Two-hour **brewery tours** (☎ 058 123 42 58; adult Sfr12; ☽ advance reservation) demonstrate how water, malt and hops are turned into nine different types of Cardinal beer and include the **Musée de la Bière Cardinal** (☎ 084

812 50 00; www.cardinal.ch; Passage du Cardinal; adult/child Sfr10/5; ☽ 2-6pm Tue & Thu).

Small-time microbrewery **Brasserie Artisanale de Fribourg** (☎ 026 322 80 88; Rue de la Samaritaine 19; ☽ 8am-5pm Sat), run by a couple of mates as a Saturday hobby, produces just 50 hectolitres a year – of golden Barbeblanche, Barberousse with subtle caramel and honey aromas, and black Old Cat stout.

Imaginative, eight-room **Auberge aux 4 Vents** (☎ 026 347 36 00; www.aux4vents.ch; Res Balzli Grandfrey 124; s/d Sfr140/200, s/d/tr/q with shared bathroom from Sfr50/100/140/160; 🏠), just outside town, is our sleeping pick. Its four-bedded 'dortoir' is Switzerland's most luxurious dorm, and the dreamy Blue room sports flowery period furnishings and a bath tub that rolls out on rails through the window for a soak beneath stars. The highly recommended conservatory-style restaurant overlooks a stunning medieval Fribourg panorama. To find the 'Four Winds', drive north along Rue de Morat and turn right immediately before the train bridge.

Fribourg is easily accessible by train from Neuchâtel (Sfr19.60, 55 minutes), Geneva (Sfr32, 1½ hours) and Bern (Sfr12.80, 20 minutes).

GRUYÈRES

Cheese and featherweight meringues drowned in thick cream is what this village, so dreamy even Sleeping Beauty wouldn't wake up, is all about. A riot of 15th- to 17th-century

SWITZERLAND

houses tumble down a hillock. Its heart is cobbled, and an ab fab turreted **château** (☎ 026 921 21 02; www.chateau-gruyeres.ch; adult/child Sfr9.50/3; 🕑 9am-6pm Apr-Oct, 10am-4.30pm Nov-Feb) is its crowning glory.

The beans about its hard AOC-protected cheese, made for centuries in its surrounding Alpine pastures, are spilled at the **Maison du Gruyère** (☎ 026 921 84 00; www.lamaisondugruyere.ch; adult/under 12yr Sfr7/3; 🕑 9am-7pm Apr-Sep, 9am-6pm Oct-Mar) in Pringy, 1.5km away. The cheese-making takes place several times daily and can be watched through glass windows.

At the **Fromagerie d'Alpage de Moléson** (☎ 026 921 10 44; 🕑 9.30am-10pm mid-May–mid-Oct), a 17th-century mountain chalet 5km southwest of Gruyères in Moléson-sur-Gruyères (elevation 1100m), cheese is made a couple of times a day in summer using old-fashioned methods. Or hike through green Gruyères pastures to a couple of tiny mountain huts where shepherds make cheese in summer along the **Sentier des Fromageries** (7km to 8km, two hours); the **tourist office** (☎ 026 921 10 30; www.gruyeres.ch, in French; Rue du Bourg 1; 🕑 10.30am-noon & 1.30-4.30pm Mon-Fri year-round, 9am-5pm Sat & Sun Jul-mid-Sep) in Gruyères has details.

Back in town, fans of the *Alien* movies will relish the **Musée HR Giger** (☎ 026 921 22 00; adult/child Sfr10/5; 🕑 10am-6pm Apr-Oct, to 5pm Tue-Sun Nov-Mar), a shrine to HR Giger's expansive imagination in a 16th-century mansion. Finish with a drink in the Giger-style bar opposite.

Cheese fondue is the natural star of every menu, irrespective of season (locals only eat fondue in winter). Dip into a *motié-motié* (mix of Gruyère and soft local vacherin) at cosy, cowbell-strewn **Chalet de Gruyères** (☎ 026 921 21 54; www.chalet-gruyeres.ch, in French; Rue du Château 53; fondues & raclettes Sfr30; 🕑 lunch & dinner daily).

Gruyères can be reached by hourly bus or train (Sfr17.20, 40 minutes to one hour) from Fribourg to Bulle, then another hourly bus or train (Sfr3.50, 15 to 20 minutes). The village is a 10-minute walk uphill from the train station.

THE JURA

The grandest towns in this clover-shaped canton are little more than enchanting villages. Deep, mysterious forests and impossible green clearings succeed one another across the low mountains of the Jura and some 1200km of marked paths across the canton give hikers plenty of scope. This is the place to escape.

Its capital is **Delémont**, though there is little reason to linger. Head instead 12km northwest to stroll around contemporary art and installations at the open-air sculpture park **La Balade de Séprais** (www.balade-seprais.ch). Or feast on thin crisp *tartes flambées* and apple cake to die for at **Hôtel-Restaurant de la Demi Lune** (☎ 032 461 35 31; Place Roger Schaffter; s/d from Sfr95/100) in **St Ursanne**, a drop-dead-gorgeous medieval village with 12th-century Gothic church, 16th-century town gate, clusters of ancient houses and a lovely stone bridge crossing the Doubs River.

The **tourist office** (☎ 032 420 47 73; Place Roger Schaffter; 🕑 10am-noon & 2-5pm Mon-Fri, 10am-4pm Sat & Sun) has heaps of information on river kayaking, canoeing and walking.

From Delémont there are trains heading to St Ursanne (Sfr6.80, 20 minutes, hourly), from where you can continue to Porrentuy (Sfr4.80, 12 minutes).

VALAIS

Matterhorn country: an intoxicating land that seduces the toughest of critics with its endless panoramic vistas and breathtaking views. This is an earthy part of southern Switzerland where farmers were so poor a century ago they didn't have two francs to rub together, yet today it's a jet-set land where celebrities sip Sfr10,000 champagne cocktails from ice-carved goblets.

An area of extraordinary natural beauty, the outdoors here is so great it never goes out of fashion. Switzerland's 10 highest mountains – all over 4000m – rise to the sky here, while snow fiends ski and board in one of Europe's top resorts, Zermatt. When snows melt and valleys turn lush green, hiking opportunities are boundless.

ZERMATT
pop 5780

Since the mid-19th century, Zermatt has starred among Switzerland's glitziest resorts. Today it attracts intrepid mountaineers and hikers, skiers that cruise at snail's pace, spellbound by the scenery, and style-conscious darlings flashing designer togs in the lounge bars. But all are smitten with the Matterhorn (4478m), the Alps' most famous peak and an unfathomable monolith synonymous with

---

DETOUR: A GREEN TROT TOWARDS FRANCE

From Porrentuy one road leads west into France, 16km away. In Courtedoux, a village along this gently scenic stretch, pick up a mount to canter the gorgeous green cow-speckled countryside. Not only do David and Veronique at **Tourisme Équestre** (☎ 032 466 74 52; www.tourismeequestre .net; La Combatte 79a; ☺ Easter-Oct) organise guided horse treks (Sfr30/80/100 per hour/half-/full day); they also rent horse-drawn carriages equipped with BBQ, picnic table and chairs, plates and so on allowing you to explore the Jura by horse and cart – at a delightfully green average go-slow speed of 5km/h. Two- to six-day itineraries include a cosy overnight in a hay barns at **Ferme Montavon** (☎ 032 476 67 23; www.fermemontavon.ch; Réclère; sleeping in straw adult/child Sfr24/14; ☺ Easter-Oct), a cattle farm on the Swiss–French border in Réclère with a bed of straw in the eaves of a huge hay barn – stable to goats and cows in winter – to camp on. Advance reservations, including for a hearty dinner of farm produce (Sfr20 to Sfr30), are essential.

Switzerland that you simply can't quite stop looking at.

Orientation & Information

Zermatt is small, easy to navigate and car-free. The main street is Bahnhofstrasse, but street names are rarely used.

Surf (digitally) for free or hook your laptop up with wi-fi at **Papperla Pub** (☎ 027 967 40 40; www.papperlapub.ch).

The **tourist office** (☎ 027 966 81 00; www.zermatt .ch; Bahnhofplatz 5; ☺ 8.30am-6pm Mon-Sat, 8.30am-noon & 1.30-6pm Sun mid-Jun-Sep; 8.30am-noon & 1.30-6pm Mon-Sat, 9.30am-noon & 4-6pm Sun rest of year) has all the bumph.

Sights & Activities

Views from the cable cars and gondolas are uniformly breathtaking, especially from the cogwheel train to 3090m **Gornergrat** (Sfr38 one-way), which takes 35 to 45 minutes with two to three departures per hour. Sit on the right-hand side to gawp at the Matterhorn. Alternatively, hike from Zermatt to Gornergrat in five hours.

A walk in the **cemetery** is a sobering experience for any would-be mountaineer, as numerous monuments tell of untimely deaths on Monte Rosa and the Matterhorn: On 13 July 1865 Edward Whymper led the first successful ascent of the mountain. The climb took 32 hours but the descent was marred by tragedy when four team members crashed to their deaths in a 1200m fall down the North Wall. See the infamous rope that broke in the **Matterhorn Museum** (☎ 027 967 41 00; www .matterhornmuseum.ch; Kirchplatz; adult/under 10yr/10-16yr/student Sfr10/free/5/8; ☺ 11am-6pm Dec-Sep, 2-6pm Oct, closed Nov).

The **Alpin Center** (☎ 027 966 24 60; www.alpin center-zermatt.ch; Bahnhofstrasse 58; ☺ 8.30am-noon & 3-7pm mid-Nov-Apr & Jul-Sep) houses the ski school and mountain guides office. They arrange guided climbs to major 4000ers including Breithorn (Sfr165), Riffelhorn (Sfr257) and, for experts willing to acclimatise for a week, Matterhorn (Sfr998). Their program also covers multiday hikes, glacier hikes to Gorner (Sfr120), snowshoeing (Sfr140) and ice-climbing (Sfr175).

For skiers and snowboarders, Zermatt is cruising heaven, with mostly long, scenic red runs, plus a scattering of blues for ski virgins and knuckle-whitening black runs for experts. The three main skiing areas are **Rothorn**, **Stockhorn** and **Klein Matterhorn** – holding 300km of ski runs in all, with free buses shuttling skiers between areas. February to April is peak time. Snow can be sketchy in early summer but lifts are significantly quieter. Snowboarders make for Klein Matterhorn's freestyle park and halfpipe, while mogul fans enjoy a bumpy glide on Stockhorn.

Klein Matterhorn is topped by Europe's highest cable-car station (3820m), providing access to Europe's highest skiing, Switzerland's most extensive summer skiing (25km of runs) and deep powder at the Italian resort of Cervinia. Broad and exhilarating, the No 7 run down from the border is a must-ski. Don't forget your passport. If the weather is fine, take the lift up to the summit of Klein Matterhorn (3883m) for top-of-the-beanstalk views over the Swiss Alps (from Mont Blanc to Aletschhorn) and deep into Italy.

A day pass covering all ski lifts in Zermatt (excluding Cervinia) costs Sfr67/57/34

SWITZERLAND

per adult/student/child and Sfr75/64/38 including Cervinia.

Sleeping & Eating

Most places close May to mid-June and again October to mid-November.

Hotel Bahnhof (☎ 027 967 24 06; www.hotelbahnhof .com; Bahnhofstrasse; dm/s/d Sfr43/78/98) Opposite the station, these spruce budget digs have a lounge, a snazzy open-plan kitchen and proper beds that are a godsend after scaling or schussing down mountains all day. Free wi-fi.

Zermatt SYHA Hostel (☎ 027 967 23 20; Staldenweg 5; dm/d with half-board Sfr47.50/100; 🖳) Question: how many hostels have the Matterhorn peeking through the window in the morning? Answer: one. And if that doesn't convince you, the modern dorms, sunny terrace and first-rate facilities should.

our pick Berggasthaus Trift (☎ 079 408 70 20; dm/d with half-board Sfr63/150 ⏀ Jul-Sep) It's a trudge to this 2337m-high mountain hut but the hike is outstanding. The Alpine haven is run by Hugo (a whiz on the alphorn) and Fabienne, who serve treats such as home-cured beef and oven-warm apple tart on the terrace. Get the camera ready for when the sun sets over Monte Rosa.

Bayard Metzgerei (☎ 027 967 22 66; Bahnhofstrasse 9; sausages around Sfr6; ⏀ noon-6.30pm Jul-Sep, 4-6.30pm Dec-Mar) Follow your nose to this butcher's grill for to-go bratwurst, chicken and other carnivorous bites.

Whymper Stube (☎ 027 967 22 96; Bahnhofstrasse 80; mains Sfr23-42) The mantra at this Alpine classic serving the tastiest fondue in Zermatt (including variations with pears and gorgonzola): gorge today, climb tomorrow.

Drinking

Papperla Pub (☎ 027 967 40 40; Steinmattstrasse 34; ⏀ 11am-11.30pm) Rammed with sloshed skiers, this pub blends pulsating music with lethal Jägermeister bombs and good vibes. Squeeze in, slam shots, then shuffle downstairs to Schneewittchen club (open to 4am) for more of the same.

Hennu Stall (☎ 027 966 35 10; Klein Matterhorn; ⏀ 2-7pm) Last one down to this snow-bound 'chicken run' is a rotten egg. Hennu is the wildest après-ski shack on Klein Matterhorn. A metre-long 'ski' of shots will make you cluck all the way down to Zermatt.

Igloo Bar (Gornergrat; www.iglu-dorf.ch; ⏀ 10pm-4pm) Subzero sippers sunbathe, stare wide

mouthed at the Matterhorn and guzzle *glühwein* amid the ice sculptures at this igloo bar. It's on the run from Gornergrat to Riffelberg.

Getting There & Around

Zermatt is car-free. Dinky electric vehicles are used to transport goods and serve as taxis around town. Drivers have to leave their vehicles in one of the garages or the open-air car park in Täsch (Sfr13.50 per day) and take the train (Sfr7.60, 12 minutes) into Zermatt.

Trains depart roughly every 20 minutes from Brig (Sfr35, 1½ hours), stopping at Visp en route. Zermatt is also the starting point of the *Glacier Express* to Graubünden, one of the most spectacular train rides in the world.

LEUKERBAD

pop 1560

The road that zigzags up to Leukerbad past breathtakingly sheer chasms and wooded crags is a spectacular build-up: gazing up to an amphitheatre of towering rock turrets and canyon-like spires, Europe's largest thermal spa resort is pure drama.

There are 10-odd places to take to the waters: **Burgerbad** (☎ 027 472 20 20; www.burgerbad .ch; Rathausstrasse; 3hr baths adult/child/student Sfr20/12/16; ⏀ 8am-8pm) is the biggest and best, with its indoor and outdoor pools, whirlpools, jets, steam grottoes and water slides. The **tourist office** (☎ 027 472 71 71; www.leukerbad.ch; ⏀ 9am-noon & 1.15-6pm Mon-Fri, 9am-6pm Sat, 9am-noon Sun Jul-Nov & Dec-Apr, 9am-noon & 1.15-5.30pm Mon-Sat rest of year) has a full list.

When the skin starts to wrinkle, ride the cable car up the sheer side of the northern ridge of mountains to **Gemmi Pass** (2350m; single/ return Sfr19/28), a fantastic area for hiking. On foot, the steep hike up takes two hours.

Weisses Rössli (☎ 027 470 33 77; www.rossli.net; Tuftstrasse 4; s/d Sfr60/120) is a belle époque hotel run with *passione* by Italian-speaking Paolo and his son Jean-Pierre. The old-style rooms with washbasins and teeny balconies are basic but comfy.

Leukerbad is 16km north of Leuk, on the main rail route from Lausanne to Brig. An hourly postal bus goes from Leuk train station to Leukerbad (Sfrf10.80, 30 minutes); last departure is 7.20pm.

BERN

pop 122,400

One of the planet's most underrated capitals, Bern is a fabulous find. With the genteel, old soul of a Renaissance man and the heart of a high-flying 21st-century gal, the riverside city is both medieval and modern. The 15th-century Old Town is gorgeous enough to sweep you off your feet and make you forget the century (it's definitely worthy of its 1983 Unesco World Heritage site protection order). But edgy vintage boutiques, artsy-intellectual bars and Renzo Piano's futuristic art museum crammed with Paul Klee pieces slams you firmly back into the present.

INFORMATION

BernCard (per 24/48/72hr Sfr20/31/38) Discount card providing admission to permanent collections at 27 museums, free public transport, city-tour discounts.

Bern Tourismus (☎ 031 328 12 12; www.berninfo .com; Bahnhoftplatz; ☽ 9am-8.30pm Jun-Sep, 9am-6.30pm Mon-Sat, 10am-5pm Sun Oct-May) Street-level floor of the train station. City tours, free hotel bookings, internet access (Sfr12 per hour).

Internet Café (☎ 031 311 9850; www.pokerhill.ch, in German; Aarbergergasse 46; per hr Sfr8-10; ☽ 9.30am-12.30am Mon-Fri, noon-12.30am Sat) Internet access.

Post office (Schanzenstrasse 4; ☽ 7.30am-9pm Mon-Fri, 8am-4pm Sat, 4-9pm Sun)

Stauffacher (☎ 031 311 24 11; Neuengasse 25; ☽ 9am-7pm Mon-Fri, to 9pm Thu, to 5pm Sat) Bookshop with English titles on the 3rd floor.

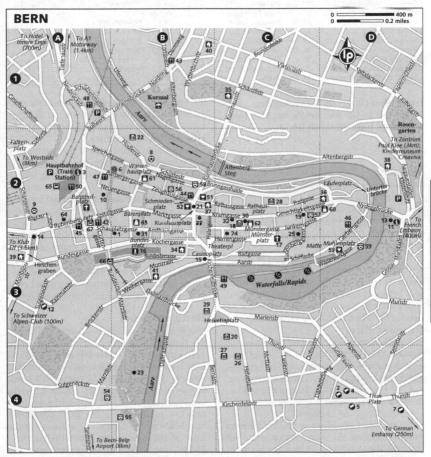

BERN

SWITZERLAND

Tourist office (☎ 031 328 12 12; Bärengraben; ✆ 9am-6pm Jun-Sep, 10am-4pm Mar-May & Oct, 11am-4pm Nov-Feb) Tourist office by the bear pits.

SIGHTS

Old Town

Bern's flag-bedecked medieval centre is an attraction in its own right, with 6km of covered arcades and cellar shops/bars descending from the streets. After a devastating fire in 1405, the wooden city was rebuilt in today's sandstone.

A focal point is Bern's **Zytglogge** (clock tower) that crowds congregate around to watch its revolving figures twirl at four minutes before the hour, after which the actual chimes begin. Tours enter the tower to see the clock mechanism May to October; contact the tourist office.

Equally enchanting are the 11 decorative **fountains** (1545) depicting historical and folkloric characters. Most are along Marktgasse as it becomes Kramgasse and Gerechtigkeitsgasse, but the most famous lies in Kornhausplatz: the **Kindlifresserbrunnen** (Ogre Fountain) of a giant snacking...on children.

Inside the 15th-century Gothic **Münster** (cathedral; audioguide Sfr5, tower admission adult/7-16yr Sfr4/2; ✆ 10am-5pm Tue-Sat, 11.30am-5pm Sun Easter-Nov, 10am-noon & 2-4pm Tue-Fri, to 5pm Sat, 11.30am-2pm Sun rest of year, tower closes 30 min earlier), a dizzying hike up the lofty spire – Switzerland's tallest – is worth the 344-step hike.

Bern was founded in 1191 by Berchtold V and named for the unfortunate bear (*bärn* in local dialect) that was his first hunting victim. The bear remains the city's heraldic mascot, hence the **Bärengraben** (bear pits; www.baerenpark-bern.ch, in German; ✆ 9.30am-5pm) where, to the dismay of some, Pedro has lived his entire life – 28 years. By autumn 2009 the 3.5m-deep stone pit will take the shape of a new, spacious, riverside park in either Pedro (if he makes it) or a new family of bears will live. Don't feed the bears; rather buy a paper cone of fresh fruit (Sfr3) from Walter, his keeper.

Einstein Museum

The world's most famous scientist developed his theory of relativity in Bern in 1905. Find out more at the **Einstein Haus** (☎ 031 312 00 91; www.einstein-bern.ch; Kramgasse 49; adult/student Sfr6/4.50; ✆ 10am-7pm Mon-Fri, to 4pm Sat Jeb-Dec), in the humble apartment where Einstein lived between 1903 and 1905 while working as a low-paid clerk in the Bern patent office. Multimedia displays now flesh out the story of the subsequent general equation – $E=MC^2$, or energy equals mass times the speed of light squared – which fundamentally changed humankind's understanding of space, time and the universe. Upstairs, a 20-minute biographical film tells his life story.

Paul Klee Centre

Bern's Guggenheim, the fabulous **Zentrum Paul Klee** (☎ 031 359 01 01; www.zpk.org; Monument in Fruchtland 3; adult/6-16yr Sfr16/6, audioguides Sfr5; ⓨ 10am-5pm Tue-Sun) is an eye-catching 150m-long building designed by Renzo Piano on the outskirts of town 3km east. Inside the three-peak structure, the middle 'hill' showcases 4000 rotating works from Paul Klee's prodigious and often playful career. Interactive computer displays built into the seating mean you can get the low-down on all the Swiss-born artist's major pieces and music audioguides (Sfr5) take visitors on one-hour DIY musical tours of his work.

In the basement of another 'hill' is **Kindermuseum Creaviva**, an inspired children's museum where kids can experiment with hands-on art exhibits (included in admission price) or sign up for a one-hour art workshop (Sfr15).

In the grounds, a walk through fields takes visitors past a stream of modern and contemporary sculptures, including works by Yoko Ono and Sol Lewitt.

Take bus 12 from Bubenbergplatz to Zentrum Paul Klee (Sfr3.80). By car the museum is right next to the Bern-Ostring exit of the A6.

Houses of Parliament

The 1902 **Bundeshäuser** (☎ 031 332 85 22; www.parliament.ch; Bundesplatz; admission free; ⓨ hourly tours 9am-4pm Mon-Sat), home of the Swiss Federal Assembly, are impressively ornate, with statues of the nation's founding fathers, a stained-glass dome adorned with cantonal emblems and a huge, 214-bulb chandelier. Tours are offered when the parliament is in recess; otherwise watch from the public gallery. Bring your passport to get in.

Kunstmuseum

The permanent collection at the **Museum of Fine Arts** (☎ 031 328 09 44; www.kunstmuseumbern.ch, in German; Hodlerstrasse 8-12; adult/student main collection Sfr8/5, temporary exhibitions Sfr8-18; ⓨ 10am-9pm Tue, to 5pm Wed-Sun) includes works by Italian artists such as Fra Angelico, Swiss artists such

as Ferninand Hodler and works by Picasso and Dalí.

SLEEPING

The tourist office makes hotel reservations (for free) and has information on 'three nights for the price of two' deals.

SYHA hostel (☎ 031 326 11 11; www.youthhostel.ch/bern; Weihergasse 4; dm Sfr33; ⓨ reception 7am-noon & 2pm-midnight; 🖳) Prettily set across from the river, this well-organised hostel sports clean dorms and a leafy terrace with red seating and ping-pong table. Free bike rental May to October (Sfr20 deposit).

Hotel Landhaus (☎ 031 331 41 66; www.landhausbern.ch; Altenbergstrasse 4; dm from Sfr33, d with shared/private bathroom Sfr120/160; 🖳) Backed by the grassy slope of a city park and fronted by the river and Old-Town spires, this historic hotel oozes character. Its soulful ground-floor restaurant, a tad bohemian, draws a staunchly local crowd.

Hotel Glocke Backpackers Bern (☎ 031 37 71; www.bernbackpackers.com; Rathausgasse 75; dm Sfr33-41; ⓨ reception 8-11am & 3-10pm; 🖳) Its Old Town location makes this many backpackers' first choice, although street noise might irritate light sleepers. Free wi-fi.

our pick Marthahaus Garni (☎ 031 332 41 35; www.marthahaus.ch; Wyttenbachstrasse 22a; dm Sfr45, s/d with shared bathroom, Sfr69/99, with private bathroom Sfr110/135; 🖳) Plum in a leafy residential location, this five-storey building feels like a friendly boarding house. Clean, simple rooms are very white with a smattering of modern art, plus there's a kitchen.

Hotel National (☎ 031 381 19 88; www.nationalbern.ch, in German; Hirschengraben 24; s/d with shared bathroom from Sfr60/120, with private bathroom Sfr95/140; 🖳) A quaint, charming hotel, the National wouldn't be out of place in Paris, with its wrought-iron lift, lavender sprigs and Persian rugs over creaky wooden floors.

Hotel Innere Enge (☎ 031 309 61 11; www.zghotels.ch; Engestrasse 54; d from Sfr240; 🖳) It might not be city centre, but this jazz hotel is unique. Run with passion by Bern Jazz Festival organiser Hans Zurbrügg and wife Marianne Gauer, a top Swiss hotel-interior designer, the place oozes panache. Don't miss its cellar jazz bar.

Hotel Belle Epoque (☎ 031 311 43 36; www.belle-epoque.ch; Gerechtigkeitsgasse 18; s/d from Sfr250/350; 🖳) A romantic hotel with art deco furnishings, standards here are so exacting that modern aberrations are cleverly hidden – dig the

TV in the steamer-trunk-style cupboard – so as not to spoil the look.

Bellevue Palace (☎ 031 320 45 45; www.bellevue-palace.ch; Kochergasse 3-5; s/d from Sfr360/390; ⊗ ☐) Bern's power brokers and international statesmen such as Nelson Mandela gravitate towards Bern's only five-star hotel. Near the parliament, it's *the* address to impress. Cheaper weekend rates.

EATING

Waterside or Old Town, Bern cooks up a delicious choice of dining handy for all budgets.

Altes Tramdepot (☎ 031 368 14 15; Am Bärengraben; set meals Sfr18-38, mains Sfr16-20; ⏲ 11am-12.30am, from 10am Sat & Sun) Even locals recommend this cavernous microbrewery by the bear pits. Swiss specialities snuggle up to wok-cooked stir-fries, pasta and international dishes on its bistro-styled menu.

Du Nord (☎ 031 332 23 38; www.dunord-bern.ch; Lorrainestrasse 2; mains Sfr20-35; ⏲ 8-11.30am Mon-Thu, to 12.30am Fri, 4pm-12.30am Sat) This gay-friendly space with good-value international kitchen and bar buzzes with Bern's hippest and the occasional gig. Find it crowned by a pretty pink, fairy-tale turret.

Terrasse & Casa (☎ 031 350 50 01; www.schwellen maetteli.ch; Damazziquai 11; mains Sfr28-45; ⏲ Terrasse 9am-11.30pm Mon-Sat, Sun 9am-10pm, Casa lunch & dinner Tue-Fri, 11.45am-11.30pm Sat & Sun) Dubbed 'Bern's Riviera', this twinset of classy hang-outs on the Aare is an experience. Terrasse is a glass shoebox with wooden decking over the water

and sun-loungers overlooking a weir, and Casa cooks Italian food in a country-styled timber-framed house.

Kornhauskeller (☎ 031 327 72 72; Kornhausplatz 18; mains Sfr32-52; ⏲ lunch & dinner Mon-Sat, dinner Sun, bar 5pm-1am Mon-Wed, 5pm-2am Thu-Sat, 5pm-12.30am Sun) Dress well and dine fine beneath vaulted frescoed arches at Bern's former granary, where beautiful people sip cocktails alongside historic stained-glass on the mezzanine above.

DRINKING & ENTERTAINMENT

For an earthy drink with old-generation locals, order one at the marble-topped bar inside **Markthalle** (below).

Silo Bar (☎ 031 311 54 12; www.silobar.ch, in German; Muhlenplatz 11; ⏲ 10pm-3.30am Thu-Sat) By the water in the hip Matte quarter, Bern's monumental 19th-century corn house throbs with mainstream hits and a lively predominantly student set – *the* place to drink, dance and party.

Café des Pyrénées (☎ 031 311 30 63; Kornhausplatz 17; ⏲ Mon-Sat) With its mix of wine-quaffing trendies and beer-loving students, this Bohemian joint feels like a Parisian cafe-bar. 'An essential stop on any bar crawl' was the verdict of most magazines writing about Bern in the Euro 2008 lead-up.

Wasserwerk (☎ 031 312 12 31; www.wasser werkclub.ch; Wasserwerkgasse 5; ⏲ 10pm-late Thu-Sat) Bern's main techno venue with bar, club and occasional live music.

Klub Elf (www.klubelf.ch; Ziegelackerstrasse 11a; ⏲ 11pm-late Fri & Sat) House, techno, trance and

---

TOP PICKS: QUICK EATS

This student-busy city has some super quick-eat options, oozing atmosphere and even a table thrown in for a highly affordable price.

- Munch between meals on a **brezel** smothered in salt crystals or sunflower, pumpkin or sesame seeds from kiosks at the train station; or a bag of piping **hot chestnuts** crunched to the tune of the astronomical clock striking.

- **Markthalle** (Bubenbergplatz 9; ⏲ 6.30am-11.30pm Mon-Wed, 6.30am-12.30am Thu & Fri, 7.30am-12.30am Sat) Buzzing in atmosphere and quick-snack action, this covered market arcade is jam-packed with eateries from around the world: curries, vegetarian, wok stir-fries, *bruschette*, noodles, pizza, south Indian, Turkish, middle Eastern…you name it, it's here. Eat standing at bars or around plastic tables.

- **Sous le Pont** (above) Grab fries, falafel or a *schnitzelb* from the graffiti-covered hole-in-the-wall next to the cafe-bar of the same name and dine at the graffiti-covered table in the graffiti-covered courtyard. Beer costs Sfr3.80/5.20 per 3/5dL glass.

- **Tibits** (☎ 031 312 91 11; Bahnhofplatz 10; ⏲ 6.30am-11.30pm Mon-Wed, 6.30am-midnight Thu-Sat, 8am-11pm Sun) This vegetarian buffet restaurant inside the train station is just the ticket for a quick healthy meal any size, any time of day. Serve yourself, get it weighed and pay accordingly.

minimal do the dance beat at this weekend club, where the real Saturday-night party kicks off after midnight and continues with an 'after' party from 5am on Sunday. Find flyers on MySpace.

Dampfzentrale (☎ 031 310 05 40; www.dampfzentrale.ch, in German; Marzilistrasse 47; ☺ varies) Host to far more than its action-packed Friday-night club (from 10pm), this industrial red-brick riverside building hosts concerts, festivals and contemporary dance; it also has a riverside restaurant terrace (☎ 031 312 33 00; open lunch and dinner Monday to Friday, dinner Saturday and Sunday).

Sous le Pont (☎ 031 306 69 55; www.souslepont.ch; Neubrückstrasse 8; ☺ 11.30am-2.30pm & 6pm-2.30am Tue-Thu, 11.30am-2.30pm & 7pm-2am Fri, 7pm-2.30am Sat) Delve into the grungy underground scene around the station in the bar of semichaotic alternative-arts centre, Reitschule. Find it in an old stone, graffiti-covered building – an old riding school built in 1897 – by the railway bridge.

SHOPPING

Revel in a lively atmosphere at Bern's open-air **vegetable, fruit & flower markets** (Bärenplatz, Bundesplatz, Schauplatz & Münstergasse; ☺ 6am-noon Tue & Sat); and **general market** (Waisenhausplatz; ☺ 8am-6pm Tue, to 4pm Sat Jan-Nov).

Mooching the Old Town boutiques, many hidden in bunker-style cellars or covered arcades, is delightful. Allow extra time for Gerechtigkeitsgasse, with its art and antique galleries, antiquarian bookshops, small shops specialising in interior design and fashion boutiques: **Alpin** (Gerechtigkeitsgasse 19) sells gorgeous knitwear and mix-and-match dresses by Zürich designer Nathalie Schweizer. Nearby **Olmo Shoes** (Zeughausgasse 14) sells funky footwear.

Bern's snappiest dresser is **Westside** (www.westside.ch), a state-of-the-art leisure and shopping centre west of the city centre, designed by Daniel Libeskind. Ride bus 14 from Bubenbergplatz (Sfr3.80).

If truly local souvenirs interest you, grab a Toblerone chocolate – it's made in Bern.

GETTING THERE & AROUND

Bern-Belp airport (BRN; ☎ 031 960 21 21; www.alpar.ch), 9km southeast of the city centre, is a small airport with direct flights to/from Munich (from where there are onward connections pretty much everywhere) with Lufthansa and Southampton in the UK with Fly Be. **Airport shuttles** (☎ 031 971 28 88, 079 651 70 70) coordinated with flight departures pick up/drop off at the train station (Sfr15, 20 minutes).

Hourly trains connect to most Swiss towns, including including Geneva (Sfr46, 1¾ hours), Basel (Sfr37, 70 minutes) and Zürich (Sfr46, one hour).

Walk around – perfectly manageable – or hop on a bus or tram; tickets, available from ticket machines at stops, cost Sfr2 (maximum six stops) or Sfr3.80 for a single journey within zones 1 and 2. **Moonliner** (☎ 031 321 88 12; www.moonliner.ch, in German) night buses transport night owls from Bahnhofplatz two or three times between midnight and 3.30am on Friday and Saturday nights. Fares start at Sfr5.

Or pedal around with a bike, microscooter or skateboard from **Bern Rollt** (☎ 079 277 28 57; www.bernrollt.ch; 1st 4hr free, then per hr Sfr1; ☺ 7.30am-9.30pm May-Oct), which has kiosks inside the train station, at the western end of Zeughausgasse and just off Bubenbergplatz on Hirschengrasse.

CENTRAL SWITZERLAND & BERNESE OBERLAND

The Bernese Oberland should come with a health warning – caution: may cause trembling in the north face of Eiger, uncontrollable bouts of euphoria at the foot of Jungfrau, 007 delusions at Schilthorn and A-list fever in Gstaad. Highly addictive, Mark Twain wrote that no opiate compared to walking through this landscape, and he should know. Though even when sober the electric green spruce forests, mountains so big they'll swallow you up, surreal china-blue skies, swirling glaciers and turquoise lakes seem hallucinatory. Up at Europe's highest station, Jungfraujoch, husky yapping mingles with Bollywood beats. Yet just paces away, the serpentine Aletsch Glacier flicks out its tongue and you're surrounded by 4000m turrets and frosty stillness.

LUCERNE
pop 58,400

Recipe for a gorgeous Swiss city: take a cobalt lake ringed by mountains of myth, add a medieval Old Town and sprinkle with

SWITZERLAND

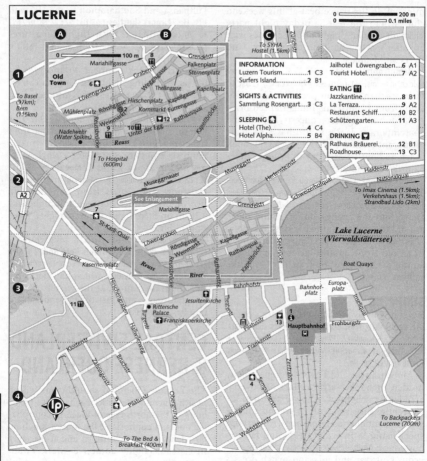

LUCERNE

See Enlargement

INFORMATION
Luzern Tourism..............1 C3
Surfers Island................2 B1

SIGHTS & ACTIVITIES
Sammlung Rosengart....3 C3

SLEEPING
Hotel (The)....................4 C4
Hotel Alpha...................5 B4

Jailhotel Löwengraben...6 A1
Tourist Hotel.................7 A2

EATING
Jazzkantine...................8 B1
La Terraza.....................9 A2
Restaurant Schiff..........10 B2
Schützengarten............11 A3

DRINKING
Rathaus Bräuerei...........12 B1
Roadhouse....................13 C3

---

covered bridges, sunny plazas, candy-coloured houses and waterfront promenades.
Lucerne is bright, beautiful and has been little Miss Popular since the likes of Goethe,
Queen Victoria and Wagner savoured her
views in the 19th century. Legend has it
that an angel with a light showed the first
settlers where to build a chapel in Lucerne,
and today it still has amazing grace.

Orientation & Information
The mostly pedestrian-only Old Town is
on the northern bank of the Reuss River.
The train station is centrally located on the
southern bank; from platform 3 access **Luzern
Tourism** (☎ 041 227 17 17; www.luzern.com; Zentralstrasse
5; ⏱ 8.30am-7.30pm Mon-Fri, 9am-7.30pm Sat & Sun mid-

Jun–mid-Sep, 8.30am-5.30pm Mon-Fri, 9am-1pm Sat & Sun
Nov-Apr, 9am-6.30pm daily rest of year). Get online at
Surfers Island (☎ 041 412 00 44; Weinmarkt 15; per hr
Sfr10; ⏱ 10am-7pm Mon-Fri, to 4pm Sat).

If you are planning to visit several museums, it's worth buying a **Lucerne Card** (24/48/72hr
Sfr19/27/33), available at the tourist office. It
gets you 50% discount on museum admissions, unlimited use of public transport and
other reductions.

Sights
OLD TOWN
Your first port of call should be the medieval
Old Town with ancient rampart walls and
towers, 15th-century buildings with painted
facades and the two much-photographed

covered bridges. **Kapellbrücke** (Chapel Bridge), dating from 1333, is Lucerne's best-known landmark. It's famous for its distinctive water tower and the spectacular 1993 fire that nearly destroyed it. Though it has been rebuilt, fire damage is still obvious on the 17th-century pictorial panels under the roof. In better condition, but rather dark and dour, are the *Dance of Death* panels under the roofline of **Spreuerbrücke** (Spreuer Bridge).

SAMMLUNG ROSENGART

Lucerne's blockbuster cultural attraction is the **Rosengart Collection** (☎ 041 220 16 60; www.rosengart .ch; Pilatusstrasse 10; adult/student Sfr18/16; 🕑 10am-6pm Apr-Oct, 11am-5pm Nov-Mar), occupying a graceful neoclassical pile. It showcases the outstanding stash of Angela Rosengart, a Swiss art dealer and close friend of Picasso. Alongside works by the great Spanish master are paintings and sketches by Cézanne, Klee, Kandinsky, Miró, Matisse and Monet. Standouts include Joan Miró's electric-blue *Dancer II* (1925) and Paul Klee's childlike *X-chen* (1938).

Complementing this collection are some 200 photographs by David Douglas Duncan of the last 17 years of Picasso's life with his family in their home on the French Riviera. It's a uniquely revealing series and principally a portrait of the artist as an impish craftsman, lover and father.

VERKEHRSHAUS

Planes, trains and automobiles are the name of the game in the huge, family-oriented **Transport Museum** (☎ 041 370 44 44; www.verkehr shaus.ch; Lidostrasse 5; adult/child Sfr24/12; 🕑 9am-6pm Apr-Oct, 10am-5pm Nov-Mar), east of the city centre, that's devoted to Switzerland's proud transport history. Space rockets, a communications display, simulators, a planetarium, an **IMAX cinema** (www.imax.ch; adult/child Sfr18/14) and the **Swiss Arena** – a gigantic 1:20,000 walkable map of Switzerland, taken from aerial photos, where you can delight in leaping over the Alps – all help make this Switzerland's most popular museum. Take bus 6, 8 or 24 from Bahnhofplatz.

Activities

Perfect for a splash or sunbathe is **Strandbad Lido** (☎ 041 370 38 06; www.lido-luzern.ch; Lidostrasse 6a; adult/child Sfr6/3; 🕑 9am-8pm mid-May-Sep), a lakefront beach with playground, volleyball court and heated outdoor pool. Or swim for free on the other bank of the lake by Seepark, off Alpenquai.

Outventure (☎ 041 611 14 41; www.outventure .ch; Stans) tempts adrenaline junkies with pursuits including tandem paragliding (for Sfr150), canyoning (from Sfr110), glacier trekking (Sfr150) and canoeing on Lake Lucerne (Sfr115).

If **cycling** is more you, check out the routes circumnavigating the lake. An easygoing and scenic option is the 16km pedal to Winkel via Kastanienbaum. The train station has **bike rental** (☎ 041 51 227 32 61; Sfr25/33 per half-/full-day).

Festivals & Events

Lucerne's six-day **Fasnacht** celebrations are more boisterous and fun than Basel's carnival. The party kicks off on 'Dirty Thursday' with the emergence of the character 'Tritschi' from a window in the town hall, when bands of musicians and revellers take to the streets. The carnival moves through raucous celebrations climaxing on Mardi Gras (Fat Tuesday), and is over on Ash Wednesday.

June's **Jodler Fest Luzern** (www.jodlerfestluzern.ch) is a classic Alpine shindig: think 12,000 Swiss yodellers, alphorn players and flag throwers.

Sleeping

Lucerne budget options rock!

Backpackers Lucerne (☎ 041 360 04 20; www.back packerslucerne.ch; Alpenquai 42; dm/d Sfr31/70; 🕑 reception 7-10am & 4-11pm; 🖳) Could this be backpacker heaven? Right on the lake, this soulful place has art-slung walls, bubbly staff, a well-equipped kitchen and immaculate dorms with balconies. It's a 15-minute walk southeast of the station.

SYHA hostel (☎ 041 420 88 00; www.youthhostel .ch/luzern; Sedelstrasse 12; dm/d Sfr32.50/82; 🕑 check-in 2pm-midnight summer, from 4pm winter; 🖳) These HI digs are modern, well run, clean and value-for-money meals are available throughout the day. Take bus 18 from the train station to Jugendherberge.

Hotel Alpha (☎ 041 240 42 80; www.hotelalpha.ch; Zähringerstrasse 24; s/d Sfr70/140; 🖳) Easy on the eye and wallet, this hotel is in a quiet residential area 10 minutes' walk from the centre. Rooms are simple, light and spotlessly clean.

Bed and Breakfast (☎ 041 310 15 14; www.theBandB .ch; Taubenhausstrasse 34; s/d Sfr80/120; 🕑 Mar-Oct) This friendly B&B feels like a private home, with stylish, contemporary rooms – crisp white bedding, scatter cushions and hot pink or lime accents. Unwind in the flowery garden or with a soak in the old-fashioned tub. Free wi-fi is another bonus. Take bus 1 to Eichof.

Tourist Hotel (☎ 041 410 24 74; www.touristhotel .ch; St-Karli-Quai 12; dm Sfr40-45, s/d with shared bathroom Sfr80/120, with private bathroom Sfr140/220; 🖳) Don't be put off by the uninspired name and pease pudding-green facade of this central, riverfront cheapie. Dorms are basic, but rooms cheery, with bold paint jobs, parquet floors and flatscreen TVs.

Jailhotel Löwengraben (☎ 041 410 78 30; www .jailhotel.ch; Löwengraben 18; s/d Sfr118/149) This former prison has novelty value, but you might get a jailhouse shock when you enter your cell to find barred windows, bare floorboards and a prefab bathroom. It's OK for a laugh, but not for quality shut-eye with thumping techno in Alcatraz club downstairs to 3am. Obligatory payment in cash on arrival? Daylight robbery!

our pick The Hotel (☎ 041 226 86 86; www.the -hotel.ch; Sempacherstrasse 14; ste Sfr430-570; 🗙 🖳) Streamlined and jet-black, 10 vampy suites reveal stainless-steel fittings, open-plan bathrooms peeking through to garden foliage, and stills from movie classics gracing the ceilings at this Jean Nouvel creation. Downstairs Bam Bou is one of Lucerne's hippest restaurants.

Eating & Drinking

Many places in Lucerne double as bars and restaurants. Places open for breakfast and stay open until late in the evening. Self-caterers should head to Hertensteinstrasse, where cheap eats are plentiful.

Jazzkantine (☎ 041 410 73 73; Grabenstrasse 8; mains Sfr15-22; ⏱ 7-12.30am Mon-Sat, 4pm-12.30am Sun) Stainless-steel bar, sturdy wooden tables and chalkboard menus – this is an arty haunt. Go for tasty *bruschette* or more ambitious dishes like penne vodka. Saturday-night gigs follow weeknight jazz workshops.

La Terraza (☎ 041 410 36 31; Metzgerrainle 9; mains Sfr17-45) Set in a 12th-century building that has housed fish sellers, dukes and scribes over the years, La Terraza oozes atmosphere. Think *bella Italia* with an urban edge. When the sun's out, sit on the riverfront terrace for favourites like clam and rocket spaghetti.

Schützengarten (☎ 041 240 01 10; Bruchstrasse 20; mains Sfr18.50-45; ⏱ Mon-Sat) As well as a cracking sense of humour, Schützengarten has smiley service, wood-panelled surrounds, appetising vegetarian and vegan dishes and

organic wine. Sit on the vine-strewn terrace in summer.

Restaurant Schiff (☎ 041 418 52 52; Unter der Egg 8; mains Sfr20-45) Under the waterfront arcades and lit by tealights at night, this restaurant has bags of charm. Try fish from Lake Lucerne and some of the city's most celebrated *Chögalipaschtetli* (vol-au-vents stuffed with meat and mushrooms).

Rathaus Bräuerei (☎ 041 410 52 57; Unter den Egg 2; ⏱ 8am-midnight Mon-Sat, to 11pm Sun) Sip homebrewed beer under the vaulted arches of this buzzy tavern, or nab a pavement table and watch the river flow.

Roadhouse (☎ 041 220 27 27; Pilatusstrasse 1; www .roadhouse.ch; ⏱ 11am-4am) Roadhouse plays solid rock to a young, fun crowd. Check out Wednesday night's jam sessions, where anyone with an instrument or voice (preferably both) can take the stand.

Getting There & Away

Frequent trains connect Lucerne to Interlaken West (Sfr33.40, two hours, via the scenic Brünig Pass), Bern (Sfr35, 1¼ hours), Lugano (Sfr55, 2¾ hours), Geneva (Sfr72, 3¼ hours, via Olten or Langnau) and Zürich (Sfr23, one hour).

INTERLAKEN
pop 5290

Once Interlaken made the Victorians swoon with its dreamy mountain vistas, viewed from the chandelier-lit confines of its grand hotels. Today it makes daredevils scream with its adrenaline-loaded adventures. Straddling the glittering Lakes Thun and Brienz and dazzled by the pearly whites of Eiger, Mönch and Jungfrau, the scenery here is mind-blowing. Particularly, some say, if you're abseiling waterfalls, thrashing white water or gliding soundlessly above 4000m peaks.

Though the streets are filled with enough yodelling kitsch to make Heidi cringe, Interlaken still makes a terrific base for exploring the Bernese Oberland. Its adventure capital status has spawned a breed of funky bars, party-mad hostels and restaurants serving flavours more imaginative than fondue.

Orientation & Information

Interlaken has two train stations: Interlaken West and Interlaken Ost; each has bike rental, money-changing facilities and a landing stage for boats on Lake Thun and Lake Brienz. The main drag, Höheweg, runs between the two stations. Walk from one to the other in less than 30 minutes.

Near Interlaken West is the **post office** (Postplatz; ⌚ 8am-noon & 1.45-6pm Mon-Fri, 8.30-11am Sat) and **tourist office** (☎ 033 826 53 00; www.interlakentourism.ch; Höheweg 37; ⌚ 8am-7pm Mon-Fri, 8am-5pm Sat, 10am-noon & 5-7pm Sun Jul-mid-Sep, 8am-noon & 1.30-6pm Mon-Fri, 9am-noon Sat rest of year).

Activities

Tempted to hurl yourself off a bridge, down a cliff or along a raging river? You're in the right place. Switzerland is the world's second-biggest adventure-sports mecca, nipping at New Zealand's sprightly heels, and Interlaken is its busiest hub.

Almost every heart-stopping pursuit you can think of is offered here (although the activities take place in the greater Jungfrau Region). You can white-water raft on the Lütschine, Simme and Saane Rivers, go canyoning in the Saxetet, Grimsel or Chli Schliere gorges, and canyon-jump at the Gletscherschlucht near Grindelwald (see p565). If that doesn't grab you, there's paragliding, glacier bungee jumping, skydiving, ice-climbing, hydro-speeding and, phew, much more. The latest craze, which you have to be crazy to try, is zorbing, where you're strapped into a giant plastic ball and sent spinning down a hill.

Prices are from Sfr90 for rock climbing, Sfr95 for zorbing, Sfr110 for rafting or canyoning, Sfr120 for hydro-speeding, Sfr130 for bungee jumping, Sfr160 for paragliding, Sfr195 for hang-gliding, and Sfr430 for skydiving. Most excursions are without incident, but there's always a small risk and it's wise to ask about safety records and procedures. Major operators able to arrange most sports include the following:

Alpin Center (☎ 033 823 55 23; www.alpincenter.ch; Hauptstrasse 16)

Alpinraft (☎ 033 823 41 00; www.alpinraft.ch; Hauptstrasse 7)

Outdoor Interlaken (☎ 033 826 77 19; www.outdoor-interlaken.ch; Hauptstrasse 15)

Swissraft (☎ 033 821 66 55; www.swissraft-activity.ch; Obere Jungfraustrasse 72)

Sleeping

RiverLodge & Camping TCS (☎ 033 822 44 34; Brienzstrasse 24; camp sites per adult/tent/car Sfr9/7/4, dm/s/d Sfr28/64/88; ⌚ May-mid-Oct) Facing the Aare River and handy for Interlaken Ost train station,

this camping ground and hostel duo offer first-class facilities, including a kitchen, laundry and wi-fi. Rent bikes and kayaks here.

Balmer's Herberge (☎ 033 822 19 61; www.balmers.ch; Hauptstrasse 23; dm Sfr27-30, d Sfr74-80; ▣) Adrenaline junkies hail Balmer's for its fun frat-house vibe. These party-mad digs offer beer garden happy hours, wrap lunches, pumping bar with DJs, and chill-out hammocks for nursing your hangover.

Schlaf im Stroh (☎ 033 822 04 31; www.uelisi.ch; Lanzenen 30; per person Sfr28; ⌚ May-Sep) Our readers sing the praises of this friendly farm. Bring your sleeping bag to snooze in the straw and wake up to a hearty breakfast. Kids adore the resident cats, goats and rabbits. It's 15 minutes' walk from Interlaken Ost station along the Aare River (upstream).

Funny Farm (☎ 033 828 12 81; www.funny-farm.ch; Hauptstrasse 36; dm Sfr30-38.50, s/d Sfr90/110; ▣ ▣) Funny Farm is halfway between a squat and an island shipwreck. The ramshackle art nouveau house, surrounded by makeshift bars and a swimming pool, is patrolled by Spliff, the lovably dopey St Bernard. Dorms are a bit faded and musty, but guests don't care; they're here for the party and revel in such anarchism.

Backpackers Villa Sonnenhof (☎ 033 826 71 71; www.villa.ch; Alpenstrasse 16; dm/d Sfr37/98; Jungfrau view extra Sfr5; ⌚ reception 7am-11pm; ▣) While most Interlaken hostels are charged with more energy than a Duracell bunny, this homely place recharges your batteries. The olive-fronted villa exudes Victorian flair with stucco and vintage steamer trunks, immaculate dorms, well-equipped kitchen and leafy garden.

our pick **Hotel Rugenpark** (☎ 033 822 36 61; www.rugenpark.ch; Rugenparkstrasse 19; s/d with shared bathroom Sfr65/105, with private bathroom Sfr85/130; ⌚ closed Nov-mid-Dec; ▣) Chris and Ursula have worked magic to transform this into a sweet B&B. Rooms are humble, but the place is spotless and has been enlivened with colourful butterflies, beads and travel trinkets. Quiz your knowledgeable hosts for local tips.

Post Hardmannli (☎ 033 822 89 19; www.post-hardermannli.ch; s/d Sfr100/155) An affable Swiss-Kiwi couple, Andreas and Kim, run this rustic chalet. Rooms are simple yet comfy, decorated with pine and chintzy pastels. Cheaper rooms forgo balconies and Jungfrau views. The home-grown farm produce at breakfast is a real treat.

Victoria-Jungfrau Grand Hotel & Spa (☎ 033 828 28 28; www.victoria-jungfrau.ch; Höheweg 41; s/d from Sfr560/680, d with Jungfrau views from Sfr780; 🖳 🏊) The reverent hush and impeccable service evoke an era when only royalty and the seriously wealthy travelled. A perfect melding of well-preserved Victorian features and modern luxury make this Interlaken's answer to Raffles.

Eating & Drinking

Am Marktplatz is scattered with bakeries and bistros with alfresco seating. The bars at Balmer's and Funny Farm are easily the liveliest drinking holes for revved-up 20-something travellers. You'll find a mixed crowd in the Happy Inn.

Sandwich Bar (☎ 033 821 63 25; Rosenstrasse 5; snacks Sfr4-8; 🕙 7.30am-7pm Mon-Fri, 8am-5pm Sat) This snack bar is an untouristy gem. Choose your bread and get creative with fillings (our favourite is *Bündnerfleisch* with sundried tomatoes and parmesan). Otherwise try soups, salads and locally made ice cream.

Belvéderè Brasserie (☎ 033 828 91 00; Höheweg 95; mains Sfr18-36) Yes it's attached to the boring-looking Hapimag, but this brasserie has an upbeat modern decor and terrace with Jungfrau views. It serves international favourites such as veal in merlot sauce, alongside a handful of Swiss stalwarts such as fondue and rösti.

Goldener Anker (☎ 033 822 16 72; www.anker.ch, in German; Marktgasse 57; mains Sfr18-38; 🕙 dinner) This beamed restaurant, locals will whisper in your ear, is the best in town. Globetrotters include everything from sizzling fajitas to red snapper and ostrich steaks. It also has a roster of live bands.

Benacus (☎ 033 821 20 20; www.benacus.ch; Stadthausplatz; mains Sfr20-30; 🕙 closed Sun, lunch Sat) Supercool Benacus is a breath of urban air with its glass walls, slick wine-red sofas, lounge music and street-facing terrace. The TV show, Funky Kitchen Club, is filmed here. The menu stars creative flavours like potato and star anise soup and Aargau chicken with caramelised pak choi.

Self-caterers stock up on beer and munchies at **Coop Pronto** (Höheweg 11; 🕙 6am-10.30pm).

Getting There & Away

The only way south for vehicles without a detour around the mountains is the car-carrying train from Kandersteg, south of Spiez.

Trains to Grindelwald (Sfr10.20, 40 minutes, hourly), Lauterbrunnen (Sfr7, 20 minutes, hourly) and Lucerne (Sfr30, two hours, hourly) depart from Interlaken Ost. Trains to Brig (Sfr41, 1½ hours, hourly) and Montreux via Bern or Visp (Sfr57 to Sfr67, 2¼ hours, hourly) leave from either Interlaken West or Ost.

JUNGFRAU REGION

If the Bernese Oberland is Switzerland's Alpine heart, the Jungfrau Region is where yours will skip a beat. Presided over by glacier-encrusted monoliths Eiger, Mönch and Jungfrau (Ogre, Monk and Virgin), the scenery stirs the soul and strains the neck muscles. A magnet for skiers and snowboarders with its 200km of pistes, a one-day ski pass for Kleine Scheidegg-Männlichen, Grindelwald-First, or Mürren-Schilthorn costs Sfr59. Come summer, hundreds of kilometres of walking trails allow you to capture the landscape from many angles, but it never looks less than astonishing.

The Lauterbrunnen Valley branches out from Interlaken with sheer rock faces and towering mountains on either side, attracting an army of hikers and mountain bikers. Cowbells echo in the valley and every house and hostel has a postcard-worthy view. Many visitors choose to visit this valley on a day trip from Interlaken.

Grindelwald

pop 3810

Once a simple farming village nestled in a valley under the north face of the Eiger, skiers and hikers cottoned onto Grindelwald's charms in the late 19th century, making it one of Switzerland's oldest and the Jungfrau's largest resorts. And it has lost none of its appeal over the decades, with archetypal Alpine chalets and verdant pastures set against an Oscar-worthy backdrop.

Grindelwald tourist office (☎ 033 854 12 12; www.grindelwald.ch; Dorfstrasse; 🕙 8am-noon & 1.30-6pm Mon-Fri, 9am-noon & 1.30-5pm Sat & Sun summer & winter, 8am-noon & 1.30-5pm Mon-Fri, 9am-noon Sat rest of year) is at the Sportzentrum, 200m from the train station.

Hourly trains link Grindelwald with Interlaken Ost (Sfr10.20, 40 minutes, hourly).

SLEEP SUSTAINABLY

Perched above Grindelwald village, eco-friendly chalet **Naturfreundehaus** (☎ 033 853 13 33; www.naturfreundehaeuser.ch; Terrassenweg; dm/s/d Sfr36/46/72; ☺ closed low season), whose name suitably translates as the House of Friends of Nature, is a green gem. Most folk have a cat or dog; Vreni and Heinz have Mono, a six-year-old trout, as family pet. Creaking floors lead up to cute pine-panelled rooms, including a shoebox single – Switzerland's smallest so they say. Try an Eiger coffee with amaretto or a home-made mint cordial in the quirky cafe downstairs. The garden has wonderful views to Eiger and Wetterhorn.

SIGHTS & ACTIVITIES

The shimmering, slowly melting **Oberer Gletscher** (Upper Glacier; adult/child Sfr6/3; ☺ 9am-6pm mid-May-Oct) is a 1½-hour hike from the village, or catch a bus (marked Terrasen Weg-Oberer Gletscher) to Hotel-Restaurant Wetterhorn. Walk 10 minutes from the bus stop, then pant up 890 log stairs to reach a terrace offering dramatic vistas. A crowd-puller is the vertiginous hanging bridge spanning the gorge.

Turbulent waters carve a path through the craggy **Gletscherschlucht** (Glacier Gorge; admission Sfr7; ☺ 10am-5pm May-Oct, to 6pm Jul & Aug), a 30-minute walk south of the centre. A footpath weaves through tunnels hacked into cliffs – a popular spot for canyon- and bungee-jumping expeditions.

First is the main **skiing** area, with runs stretching from **Oberjoch** at 2486m to the village at 1050m. In the summer it caters to **hikers** with 90km of trails about 1200m, 48km of which are open year-round. Catch the longest **cable car** (☎ 033 854 80 80; www.maennlichen.ch) in Europe from Grindelwald-Grund to Männlichen (single/return Sfr31/Sfr51), where there are more extraordinary views and hikes.

SLEEPING & EATING

SYHA hostel (☎ 033 853 10 09; www.youthhostel.ch/grindelwald; Terrassenweg; dm Sfr31.50-38.50, d with shared bathroom Sfr80, with private bathroom Sfr108; ☺ reception 7.30-10am & 4-10pm; ▢) The cosy wooden chalet housing this excellent hostel is perched high on a hill with magnificent views. Avoid the 20-minute slog from the train station by taking the Terrassenweg-bound bus to the Gaggi Säge stop.

Mountain Hostel (☎ 033 854 38 38; www.mountainhostel.ch; dm Sfr37-42, d Sfr92-102) Near the Männlichen cable-car station, this is a good base for sports junkies. Cyclists are especially welcomed. Rates include free ice-skating and swimming at a nearby facility.

Memory (☎ 033 854 31 31; mains Sfr16-28; Dorfstrasse; ☺ 11.30am-10.30pm) Always packed, the Eiger Hotel's unpretentious restaurant rolls out tasty Swiss grub such as rösti and fondue. Try to bag a table on the street-facing terrace.

C & M (☎ 033 853 07 10; mains Sfr20-36; ☺ 8.30am-11pm Wed-Mon) Just as appetising as the menu are the stupendous views to Unterer Gletscher from this gallery-style cafe's sunny terrace. Enjoy a salad, coffee and cake, or seasonally inspired dishes such as venison stew with dumplings and bilberry-stuffed apple.

Lauterbrunnen
pop 2480

Bijou Lauterbrunnen, with its cute main street chock-a-block with quintessential Swiss chalet architecture, is laid-back, down to earth and a hot spot with nature lovers happy to hike and climb. Goethe and Lord Byron penned poems to the ethereal beauty of its wispy **Staubbach Falls** (admission free; ☺ 8am-8pm Jun-Oct) – ultra-fine mist from a distance, torrent close up (you'll get wet). But the place is better known for the crash-bang spectacle of its **Trümmelbach Falls** (☎ 033 855 32 32; www.truemmelbach.ch; adult/child Sfr11/4; ☺ 9am-5pm Apr-Nov, 8.30am-6pm Jul & Aug). Up to 20,000L of water per second – drained from 24 sq km of Alpine glaciers and snow deposits – corkscrews through ravines and potholes shaped by the swirling waters inside the mountain. The falls are 4km out of town, linked by bus from the train station (Sfr3.40).

Lauterbrunnen's **tourist office** (☎ 033 856 85 68; www.wengen-muerren.ch; ☺ 9am-noon & 1-6pm daily May-Sep, 9am-noon & 1-6pm Mon-Fri rest of year) is opposite the train station. Two minutes away is **Valley Hostel** (☎ 033 855 20 08; www.valleyhostel.ch; dm/d Sfr25/70; ☺ reception 8am-noon & 3-10pm; ▢), a chilled hostel with open-plan kitchen, garden with waterfall views, free wi-fi and a chirpy team who can organise activities.

A few minutes' walk south of the centre, near the Staubbach Falls, **Camping Jungfrau** (☎ 033 856 20 10; www.camping-jungfrau.ch; camp sites per adult/tent/car Sfr11.60/10/3.50, dm Sfr27-30; ☺ year-round;

🔲) is a Rolls Royce of a camping ground, with cosy dorms, huts, kitchen, bike rental, wi-fi and dog shower for messy pups.

On the food front, hit **Airtime** (☎ 033 855 15 15; www.airtime.ch; 🕑 9am-8pm summer, 9am-noon & 4-8pm winter; 🔲), a funky cafe, book exchange, laundry and extreme sports agency inspired by Daniela and Beni's travels in New Zealand.

Gimmelwald
pop 120

Decades ago an anonymous backpacker scribbled these words in the Mountain Hostel's guest book: 'If heaven isn't what it's cracked up to be, send me back to Gimmelwald.' Enough said. When the sun is out in Gimmelwald, this pipsqueak of a village will take your breath away. Once a secret bolthole for hikers and adventurers keen to escape the region's worst tourist excesses, Gimmelwald gets a fair whack of foot traffic these days – though even crowds can't diminish its scintillating, textbook Swiss scenery and charm.

The surrounding hiking trails include one down from Mürren (30 to 40 minutes) and one up from Stechelberg (1¼ hours). Cable cars are also an option (Mürren or Stechelberg Sfr5.60).

After a long summer hike, bed down at **Pension Berggeist** (☎ 033 855 17 30; www.berggeist .ch; dm/d Sfr15/40), a dead-simple and rustic place with bargain rooms, priceless views and sandwiches sold by the centimetre to please every pocket. Book all kinds of activities here, from skydiving to llama trekking.

Or there's backpacking legend **Mountain Hostel** (☎ 033 855 17 04; www.mountainhostel.com; dm Sfr20; 🕑 reception 8.30am-noon & 6-11pm Apr-Nov; 🔲). A soak in its outdoor whirlpool with stunning views hits the spot every time. **Esther's Guest House** (☎ 033 855 54 88; www.esthers-guesthouse.ch; s/d Sfr45/100; 🔲) is a sweet B&B with tiny shop where you can stock up on local goodies like Gimmelwald salami and Stechelberg honey.

Surrounding hiking trails include one down from Mürren (30 to 40 minutes) and one up from Stechelberg (1¼ hours). Cable cars are also an option (Mürren or Stechelberg Sfr5.60).

Mürren
pop 440

Arrive on a clear evening when the sun hangs low on the horizon, and you'll think you've died and gone to heaven. Car-free Mürren *is* storybook Switzerland.

In summer, the **Allmendhubel funicular** (single/return Sfr12/7.40) takes you above Mürren to a panoramic restaurant. From here, you can set out on many walks, including the famous **Northface Trail** (1½ hours) via Schiltalp to the west, with spellbinding views of the Lauterbrunnen Valley and monstrous Eiger north face – bring binoculars to spy intrepid climbers. There's also a kid-friendly **Adventure Trail** (one hour).

The **tourist office** (☎ 033 856 86 86; www.wengen -muerren.ch; 🕑 8.30am-7pm Mon-Sat, to 8pm Thu, to 6pm Sun high season, to 7pm Mon-Sat, to 5pm Sun shoulder seasons, 8.30am-noon & 1-5pm Mon-Fri low season) is in the sports centre.

Sleeping options include **Eiger Guesthouse** (☎ 033 856 54 60; www.eigerguesthouse.com; dm Sfr40-70, d with shared/private bathroom Sfr120/160; 🔲), by the train station, with downstairs pub serving tasty grub; and **Hotel Jungfrau** (☎ 033 856 64 64; www.hoteljungfrau.ch; s Sfr88-110, d Sfr270-300; 🔲), overlooking the nursery slopes from its perch above Mürren. It dates to 1894 and has beamed lounge with open fire. Ten out of 10 to much-lauded chalet, **Hotel Alpenruh** (☎ 033 856 88 00; www.alpenruh-muerren.ch; s/d Sfr145/270; 🔲), for service, food and unbeatable views to Jungfrau massif.

Tham's (☎ 033 856 01 10; mains Sfr15-28; 🕑 dinner) serves Asian cooked by a former five-star chef who's literally taken to the hills to escape.

Schilthorn

There's a tremendous 360-degree panorama from the 2970m **Schilthorn** (www.schilthorn.ch). On a clear day, you can see from Titlis to Mont Blanc and across to the German Black Forest. Yet, some visitors seem more preoccupied with practising their delivery of the line 'The name's Bond, James Bond', than taking in the 200 or so peaks: this is where some scenes from *On Her Majesty's Secret Service* were shot in the 1960s as the fairly tacky **Touristorama** below the **Piz Gloria** revolving restaurant reminds you.

Buy a Sfr116 excursion trip (Half-Fare Card and Eurail Pass 50% off, Swiss Pass 65% off) going to Lauterbrunnen, Grütschalp, Mürren, Schilthorn and returning through Stechelberg to Interlaken. A return from Lauterbrunnen (via Grütschalp) and Mürren costs about Sfr100, as does the return journey via the Stechelberg cable car.

Jungfraujoch

Sure, the world wants to see Jungfraujoch (3471m) and yes, tickets are expensive, but don't let that stop you. It's a once-in-a-lifetime trip. And there's a reason why two million people a year visit this Holy Grail, Europe's highest train station. The icy wilderness of swirling glaciers and 4000m turrets that unfolds is truly enchanting.

Clear good weather is essential for the trip; check www.jungfrau.ch or call ☎ 033 828 79 31 and don't forget warm clothing, sunglasses and sunscreen. Up top, when you tire (is this possible?) of the view, dash downhill on a snow disc (free), zip across the frozen plateau on a flying fox (Sfr20), enjoy a bit of tame skiing or boarding (Sfr33), drive a team of Greenland dogs or do your best Tiger-Woods-in-moon-boots impersonation with a round of glacier golf. It isn't cheap at Sfr10 a shot, but get a hole-in-one and you win the Sfr100,000 jackpot (which, mysteriously, nobody has yet won).

From Interlaken Ost, journey time is 2½ hours each way (Sfr177.80 return, Swiss Pass/Eurail Sfr133). The last train back is at 5.50pm in summer, 4.40pm in winter. However, there's a cheaper 'good morning' ticket of Sfr153.80 (Swiss/Eurail Pass discounts available) if you take the first train (6am from Interlaken Ost) and leave the summit by 12.30pm. Between 1 November and 30 April the reduction is valid for both the 6am and 7.05am trains, and the 12.30pm restriction doesn't apply.

ZÜRICH

pop 350,100

Zürich is the epitome of Swiss efficiency, a savvy finance centre with possibly the densest public transport system in the world. Yet Switzerland's biggest city is also its most hip and creative: why else would Google (whose local employees shimmy into work each morning down a fire pole and go by the name of Zooglers) have located its European engineering centre here? This is a city where Berlin-style grunge jostles for space with swish posh quarters, where fashion fiends feel right at home in its bevy of clubs and lounge bars, where Europe's largest street party lets rip each August.

Trends aside, Zürich's river and lakeside location, with Alpine views, is a gift from nature. You could just about drink the water, it's so clean. Indeed, you will – 70% of Zürich's drinking water comes from the lake. Much of the ancient centre, with its winding lanes and tall church steeples, remains lovingly intact, while urban renovation has transformed the industrial wasteland of Züri-West into a happening space where everyone wants to be.

ORIENTATION

Zürich is at the northern end of Lake Zürich (Zürichsee), with the city centre split by the Limmat River. Like most Swiss cities it is compact and easy to navigate. The main train station (Hauptbahnhof) is on the western bank of the river, close to the old centre.

INFORMATION

Bellevue Apotheke (☎ 044 266 62 22; www.bellevue -apotheke.com; Theaterstrasse 14) A 24-hour chemist.

Orell Füssli (☎ 044 211 04 44; www.books.ch; Bahnhofstrasse 70; ☺ 9am-8pm Mon-Fri, to 6pm Sat) English language bookshop.

Police station (☎ 044 216 71 11; Bahnhofquai 3)

Post office (train station; ☺ 7am-9pm daily)

Quanta (☎ 044 260 72 66; Limmatquai 94, im Niederdorf; per hr Sfr10; ☺ 9am-midnight) Internet access.

University Hospital (☎ 044 255 11 11, 044 255 21 11; www.usz.ch; Rämistrasse 100) Casualty medical service.

Zürich Tourism (☎ 044 215 40 00; hotel reservations ☎ 044 215 40 40; www.zuerich.com; train station; ☺ 8am-8.30pm Mon-Sat, 8.30am-6.30pm Sun May-Oct; 8.30am-7pm Mon-Sat, 9am-6.30pm Sun Nov-Apr)

ZürichCard (per 24-/72hr Sfr17/24) Discount card available from the tourist office and airport train station; provides free public transport, free museum admission and more.

SIGHTS

Explore the cobbled streets of the pedestrian **Old Town** lining both sides of the river.

The bank vaults beneath **Bahnhofstrasse**, the city's most elegant street, are said to be crammed with gold and silver. Indulge in affluent Züricher-watching and ogle at the luxury shops selling watches, clocks, chocolates, furs, porcelain and fashion labels galore.

On Sundays it seems all of Zürich strolls around the lake. Do the same.

ZÜRICH

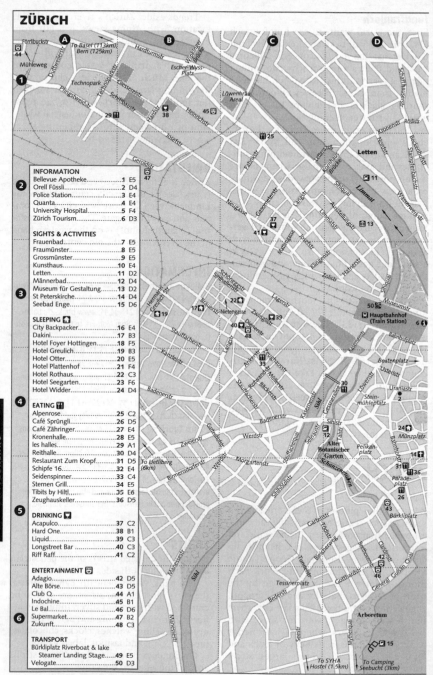

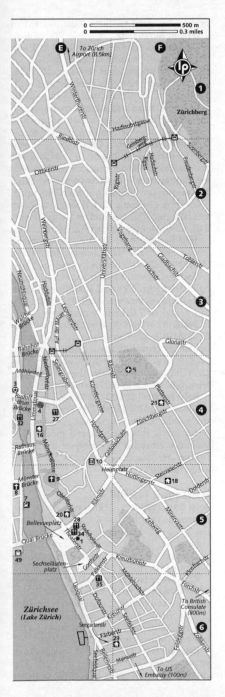

Churches

On the west bank of the Limmat River the 13th-century **Fraumünster** (cathedral; www.fraumuenster.ch; Münsterplatz; 9am-6pm May-Sep, 10am-5pm Oct-Apr) is Zürich's most noteworthy attraction, with some of the most distinctive and attractive stained-glass windows in the world.

Across the river is the dual-towered **Grossmünster** (Grossmünsterplatz; www.grossmuenster.ch; 9am-6pm daily mid-Mar–Oct, 10am-5pm Nov–mid-Mar, tower closed Sun morning mid-Mar–Oct & all Sun Nov–mid-Mar). This was where, in the 16th century, the Protestant preacher Huldrych Zwingli first spread his message of 'pray and work' during the Reformation – a seminal period in Zürich's history. The figure glowering from the south tower of the cathedral is Charlemagne, who founded the original church at this location.

From any position in the city, it's impossible to overlook the 13th-century tower of **St Peterskirche** (St Peter's Church; St Peterhofstatt; 8am-6pm Mon-Fri, 8am-4pm Sat, 11am-5pm Sun). Its prominent clock face, 8.7m in diameter, is Europe's largest.

Kunsthaus

Zürich's impressive **Fine Arts Museum** (044 253 84 84; www.kunsthaus.ch; Heimplatz 1; adult/child/student Sfr18/free/8, Sun free; 10am-8pm Wed-Fri, to 6pm Tue & Sat & Sun) boasts a rich collection of Alberto Giacometti stick-figure sculptures, Monets, Van Goghs, Rodin sculptures and other 19th- and 20th-century art. Swiss artist Ferdinand Hodler is also represented.

Museum für Gestaltung

The exhibitions at this **Design Museum** (043 446 67 67; www.museum-gestaltung.ch; Ausstellungstrasse 60; adult/student Sfr9/6; 10am-8pm Tue-Thu, to 5pm Fri-Sun) are consistently impressive and wide-ranging – anything from Bollywood to photographic short stories.

ACTIVITIES

Zürich comes into its own in summer when its green lakeshore parks buzz with bathers, sun-seekers, in-line skaters, footballers, lovers, picnickers, party animals, preeners and police patrolling on rollerblades! May to mid-September, **outdoor swimming areas** (admission Sfr6; 9am-7pm May & Sep, to 8pm Jun-Aug) – think a rectangular wooden pier partly covered by a pavilion – open around the lake and up the Limmat River. Many offer massages, yoga and saunas, as well as snacks. Our favourites

SWITZERLAND

GREEN DETOUR TO MARS

When the urban action gets too much, take a green breather with a half-day trip to Mars – or at least along the two-hour walking trail poetically known as **Planetenweg** ('Planetary Path'). From Zürich take the train (line S10) to Uetliberg (23 minutes, departures every 30 minutes), from where the planetary trial winds along the mountain ridge to Felsenegg. En route scale models of the planets are interspersed with fabulous lake views. At Felsenegg, a cable car descends every 10 minutes to Adliswil, from where frequent trains return to Zürich (line S4, 16 minutes). Buy the Sfr15.60 Albis-Netzkarte, which gets you to Uetliberg and back, including unlimited travel downtown.

---

are trendy **Seebad Enge** (☎ 044 201 38 89; www .seebadenge.ch; Mythenquai 95), where the bar opens until midnight in fine weather; and **Letten** (☎ 044 362 92 00; Lettensteg 10; admission free) where hip Züri-Westers swim, barbecue, skateboard, play volleyball or just drink and hang on the grass and concrete.

Along the river, 19th-century **Frauenbad** (Stadthausquai) is open to women only during the day, and **Männerbad** (Schanzengraben) is men-only. Both open their trendy bars to both sexes at night – leave shoes at the entrance and drink with feet dipped in the water!

For a month from mid-July, there's an extremely popular waterside **open-air cinema** (☎ 0800 078078; www.orangecinema.ch; Zürichhorn).

FESTIVALS & EVENTS

Zürich celebrates spring with **Sechseläuten** (www.sechselaeuten.ch), which sees guild members in historical costume parade down the streets on the third Monday in April, climaxing with the burning of a fireworks-filled 'snowman' (Böögg) to mark winter's end.

August's **Street Parade** (www.street-parade.ch) is Europe's largest street party in any given year, attracting well over half a million ravers.

SLEEPING
Budget
Camping Seebucht (☎ 044 482 16 12; www.camping -zurich.ch; Seestrasse 559; camp sites per 2 people, tent & car Sfr27; ☾ May-Sep) On the western shore of the lake, 4km from the city centre, this camping

ground has good facilities. Take bus 161 or 165 from Bürkliplatz.

City Backpacker (Hotel Biber; ☎ 044 251 90 15; www .city-backpacker.ch; Niederdorfstrasse 5; dm Sfr34, s/d Sfr71/104; ☾ reception closed noon-3pm; ☐) This youthful party hostel is friendly and well-equipped, if a trifle cramped. Overcome the claustrophobia in summer by hanging out on the roof terrace – the best spot in Zürich to wind down at sunset with a few cold beers.

Hotel Foyer Hottingen (☎ 044 256 19 19; www .hotel-foyer-hottingen.ch; Hottingerstrasse 31; dm Sfr40, s with shared bathroom Sfr110, with private bathroom Sfr125-145, d with shared bathroom Sfr145, with private bathroom Sfr165-185) Rooms are clinical but excellent value. Some have a balcony. Each floor has showers and communal kitchen and on the top floor is a dorm for women only with roof terrace.

SYHA hostel (☎ 043 399 78 00; www.youthhostel .ch; Mütschellenstrasse 114, Wollishofen; dm Sfr42, s/d Sfr106.50/127; ☐) This bulbous, purple-red hostel features a swish 24-hour reception/dining hall, flat-screen TVs and sparkling modern bathrooms. Dorms are small. Take tram 7 to Morgental, or S-Bahn to Wollishofen.

Dakini (☎ 044 291 42 20; www.dakini.ch; Brauerstrasse 87; s/d Sfr75/130; ☐) This relaxed B&B attracts a bohemian crowd of artists and performers, academics and trendy tourists who don't bat an eyelid at its location near the red-light district. Take tram 8 to Bäckeranlange.

Hotel Rothaus (☎ 043 322 10 58; www.hotelrothaus .ch; Sihlhallenstrasse 1; s/d from Sfr82/110) Smack in the middle of the Langstrasse action, you'd never guess this cheerful red brick place was once a brothel. A variety of fresh, airy rooms are complemented by a busy little eatery-bar downstairs.

Midrange & Top End
Hotel Otter (☎ 044 251 22 07; www.wueste.ch; Oberdorfstrasse 7; s/d from Sfr115/150) A true gem, the Otter has 17 rooms variously decorated with pink satin sheets and plastic beads, raised beds, wall murals and in one instance a hammock. A popular bar, the Wüste, is downstairs.

Hotel Seegarten (☎ 044 388 37 37; www.hotel-see garten.ch; Seegartenstrasse 14; s/d from Sfr190/240) Rattan furniture and vintage tourist posters give this place a rustic Mediterranean atmosphere, which is reinforced by the proximity to the lake and the on-site Restaurant Latino.

Hotel Greulich (☎ 043 243 42 43; www.greulich.ch; Hermann Greulich Strasse 56; s/d from Sfr190/255) The curving blue-grey walls lend these designer digs in a quieter part of Kreis 4 a retro art deco touch. Minimalist, off-white rooms are laid out in facing bungalows along two sides of an austere courtyard.

Hotel Plattenhof (☎ 044 251 19 10; www.plattenhof .ch; Plattenstrasse 26; s/d from Sfr205/245) This place manages to be cool without looking pretentious. It features a youthful, vaguely Japanese style, with low beds and mood lighting in its newest rooms. Even the older rooms are stylishly minimalist. Take tram 6 to Platte.

Hotel Widder (☎ 044 224 25 26; www.widderhotel .ch; Rennweg 7; s/d from Sfr523/725; ✂ ⌨) A stylish hotel in the equally grand Augustiner district, the Widder is a pleasing fusion of modernity and traditional charm. Rooms and public areas across the eight town houses that make up this place are stuffed with art and designer furniture.

EATING

Zürich has a thriving cafe culture and hundreds of restaurants – explore Niederdorfstrasse and its nearby backstreets.

Restaurants

Zeughauskeller (☎ 044 211 26 90; www.zeughauskeller .ch; Bahnhofstrasse 28a; mains Sfr17.50-33.50; ✆ 11.30am-11pm) The menu at this huge, atmospheric beer hall offers 20 different kinds of sausages in eight languages, as well as numerous other Swiss specialities of a carnivorous and vegetarian variety.

Café Zähringer (☎ 044 252 05 00; Zähringerplatz 11; mains Sfr18-32; ✆ 6pm-midnight Mon, 9am-midnight Tue-Sun) This very old-school alternative cafe serves up mostly organic, vegetarian food around communal tables. They have huge vegetarian and carnivores' breakfasts (Sfr20.50 and Sfr22.50).

Restaurant Zum Kropf (☎ 044 221 18 05; www.zum kropf.ch; In Gassen 16; mains Sfr21.50-45.50; ✆ 11.30am-11.30pm Mon-Sat) Notable for its historic interior, with marble columns, stained-glass and ceiling murals, Kropf has been favoured by locals since 1888 for its hearty Swiss staples and fine beers.

les halles (☎ 044 273 11 25; www.les-halles.ch; Pfingstweidstrasse 6; mains Sfr22-29; ✆ 11am-midnight Mon-Wed, to 1am Thu-Sat) One of several chirpy bar-restaurants in revamped factory buildings, this is the best place in town to tuck into *Moules mit Frites* (mussels and fries). Hang at the bustling bar and shop at the market.

Café Sprüngli (☎ 044 224 47 31; www.spruengli.ch; Bahnhofstrasse 21; ✆ 7am-6.30pm Mon-Fri, 8am-6pm Sat, 9.30am-5.30pm Sun) Indulge in cakes, chocolate and coffee at this epicentre of sweet Switzerland, in business since 1836. You can have a light lunch too but whatever you do, don't fail to check out the chocolate shop heaven around the corner on Paradeplatz.

Reithalle (☎ 044 212 07 66; www.restaurant-reithalle .ch; Gessnerallee 8; mains Sfr23.50-33.50; ✆ lunch & dinner Mon-Fri, dinner Sat & Sun) Fancy dining in stables in a former barracks complex? The walls at this boisterous, convivial spot are still lined with the cavalry horses' feeding and drinking troughs. Cuisine is copious Swiss and international, and tables are cleared at 11.30pm when the place morphs into dance club.

our pick Alpenrose (☎ 044 271 39 19; Fabrikstrasse 12; mains Sfr 24-42; ✆ Mon-Sat) With its timber-clad walls, No Polka-dancing warning and fine cuisine from regions all over Switzerland, this place makes for an inspired meal out. Try risotto from Ticino, *pizokel* (a kind of long and especially savoury *spätzli*, or dumpling) from Graubünden or freshly fished local perch filets.

Seidenspinner (☎ 044 241 07 00; www.seidenspinner .ch; Ankerstrasse 120; most mains Sfr29-56; ✆ lunch & dinner Tue-Fri, dinner Sat) A favourite with the media and fashion crowd, Silk-spinner boasts an extravagant interior with huge flower arrangements and shards of mirrored glass. European cooking dominates.

Kronenhalle (☎ 044 251 66 69; Rämistrasse 4; mains Sfr30-80; ✆ noon-midnight) Haunt of city movers and shakers in suits with an old-world feel, the Crown Hall is a brasserie where impeccably mannered waiters move discreetly beneath Chagall, Miro, Matisse and Picasso originals.

Quick Eats

Cheap eats abound around the train station, especially in the underground Shopville. Niederdorfstrasse has a string of snack bars offering pizza, kebabs and Asian food.

Tibits by Hiltl (☎ 044 260 32 22; www.tibits.ch; Seefeldstrasse 2; meals per 100g Sfr3.60-4.10; ✆ 6.30am-midnight daily, 8am-midnight Sat & 9am-midnight Sun) Tibits is where with-it, health-conscious Zürichers eat light. Think tasty vegetarian buffet, fresh fruit juices, coffees and cake – take your pick and pay at the counter.

Sternen Grill (Bellevueplatz/Theaterstrasse 22; snacks from Sfr5 12; ✆ 11.30am-midnight) This is the city's most famous – and busiest – sausage stand;

SWITZERLAND

just follow the crowds streaming in for a tasty greasefest.

Schipfe 16 (☎ 044 211 21 22; Schipfe 16; menus Sfr16-20; ☼ 10am-4pm Mon-Fri) Overlooking the Limmat River from the historic Schipfe area, Schipfe 16 is a good-natured canteen-style spot for a humble speed lunch.

DRINKING

Buzzing drinking options congregate in the happening Kreis 4 and Kreis 5 districts, together known as Züri-West. Langstrasse, directly behind the station, is a minor red-light district – safe to wander though you may be offered drugs or sex – with loads of popular bars quietly humming off its side streets. Mid-May to mid-September, Wednesday to Sunday, the trendy water bars at the **lake baths** (see p569) are hot places to hang bare-footed.

ourpick **Longstreet Bar** (☎ 044 241 21 72; www .longstreetbar.ch; Langstrasse 92; ☼ 8pm-3am Tue-Thu, to 4am Fri & Sat, to 2am Sun) Run by the guy seemingly behind half Zürich's nightlife, this purple-felt lined one-time cabaret is now a throbbing music bar with DJs. Count the thousands of light bulbs.

Liquid (☎ 079 446 73 66; www.liquid-bar.ch; Zwinglistrasse 12; ☼ 5pm-1am Mon-Thu, 5pm-3am Fri, 7pm-3am Sat) With its striped wallpaper and plastic chairs moulded in the shape of boiled eggs broken in half, this is kitsch at its best – a hip backdrop for lounge-oriented music nights.

Hard One (☎ 044 444 10 00; www.hardone.ch; Hardstrasse 260; admission free-Sfr15; ☼ 6pm-2am Tue-Thu, to 4am Fri & Sat) The punters flock to this glass cube of a lounge bar for great views and weekend gigs.

Acapulco (☎ 044 272 66 88; Neugasse 56; ☼ 5pm-1am Mon-Tue, 3pm-2am Wed-Thu, 5pm-3am Fri, 3pm-3am Sat, 3pm-2am Sun) is a retro hang-out, while the cinema-cum-bistro **Riff Raff** (☎ 044 444 22 05; Neugasse 57; ☼ from 8am Mon-Fri, from 10am Sat & Sun), is a counter-culture way to start the evening.

ENTERTAINMENT

Züritipp is the city's events magazine, available around town and from the tourist office. Also look for the quarterly *Zürich Guide*. Clubbers dress well and be prepared to cough up Sfr15 to Sfr30 admission.

Zukunft (www.zukunft.ch; Dienerstrasse 33; ☼ 11pm-late Thu-Sat) Look for a modest queue (there's no name) and head downstairs to this literally underground dance bar, where a broad

range of electro and other dance music keep a mixed crowd happy.

ourpick **Club Q** (☎ 044 444 40 50; www.club-q.ch; Förrlibückstrasse 151; admission up to Sfr30; ☼ 11pm-7am Fri, 11pm-8am Sat, 10pm-4am Sun) In a car park, Club Q is for serious dancers only, be it house, hip-hop or R&B. Ibiza nights don't quite match the Spanish rave island's mega-club vibe but for Zürich's club crowd it's the next best thing. The club's minor cousin, BBQ, is in the same car park.

Supermarket (☎ 044 440 20 05; www.supermarket.li; Geroldstrasse 17; ☼ 11pm-late Thu-Sat) Looking like an innocent little house, Supermarket boasts three cosy lounge bars around the dance floor, a covered back courtyard and an interesting roster of DJs playing house. The crowd is mid-20s.

Indochine (☎ 044 448 11 11; www.club-indochine .ch; Limmatstrasse 275; ☼ 10pm-late Thu-Sat) Models and rich kids mingle between the dimly-lit fat Buddhas of this faux opium den. It's Zürich's answer to Paris' Buddha Bar.

Alte Börse (www.alteboerse.com; Bleicherweg 5; ☼ 10pm-late Thu-Sat) In a respectable town-centre building, hundreds of dance fanatics cram in to this recently opened club for intense electronic sessions with DJs from all over the world. They also get in occasional live acts.

Two adjacent clubs for a well-dressed over-25 crowd lie just back from the northwest end of the lake: **Adagio** (☎ 044 206 36 66; www.adagio.ch; Gotthardstrasse 5; ☼ 9pm-2am Tue-Wed, to late Thu, to 4am Fri & Sat) seems like a scene from a medieval thriller with its vaulted and frescoed ceiling, while neighbouring **Le Bal** (☎ 044 206 36 66; www.lebal.ch; Beethovenstrasse 8; ☼ 9pm-2am Tue-Wed, to late Thu-Sat) swings between Latin and House.

GETTING THERE & AWAY

Zürich airport (ZRH; ☎ 043 816 22 11; www.zurich-airport.com), 10km north of the centre, is a small international hub with two terminals.

The A3 approaches Zürich from the south along the shore of Lake Zürich. The A1 is the fastest route from Bern and Basel.

Direct daily trains run to Stuttgart (Sfr76, three hours), Munich (Sfr104, 4½ hours) and Innsbruck (Sfr79, four hours) and many other international destinations. There are regular direct departures to most major Swiss towns, such as Lucerne (Sfr23, 46 to 50 minutes), Bern (Sfr46, 57 minutes) and Basel (Sfr31, 55 minutes).

GETTING AROUND

Up to nine trains an hour yo-yo between the airport and main train station between 6am and midnight (Sfr6, nine to 14 minutes).

There is a comprehensive, unified bus, tram and S-Bahn service in the city, which includes boats plying the Limmat River. Short trips under five stops are Sfr2.40. A 24-hour pass for the centre is Sfr7.80. For unlimited travel within the canton, including extended tours of the lake, a day pass costs Sfr30.40.

April to October **lake steamers** (☎ 044 487 13 33; www.zsg.ch) depart from Bürkliplatz.

City bikes (www.zuerirollt.ch) can be picked up at **Velogate** (train station; ☯ 8am-9.30pm) for free if you bring the bike back after six hours or pay Sfr5 per day.

NORTHERN SWITZERLAND

This region is left off most people's Switzerland itineraries – precisely why you should visit! Sure, it is known for industry and commerce, but it also has some great attractions. Breathe in the sweet (OK slightly stinky) odours of black-and-white cows as you roll through the bucolic countryside. Take time to explore the tiny rural towns set among green rolling hills and on Lake Constance (Bodensee) and the Rhine River on the German border.

BASEL

pop 163,100

Visit Basel in the summer. Strangely, given its northerly location, the city has some of the hottest weather in the country. When the mercury starts rising the city sheds its notorious reserve and just cuts loose. As locals bob along in the fast-moving Rhine (Rhein) River, cool off in the city's numerous fountains, whiz by on motor scooters and dine and drink on overcrowded pavements, you could almost be in Italy, rather than on the dual border with France and Germany.

Basel's (Bâle in French) idyllic Old Town and many enticing galleries and museums are top draws at any time of year. The famous Renaissance humanist, Erasmus of Rotterdam, was associated with the city and his tomb rests in the cathedral.

Orientation & Information

The pedestrian-only Old Town and most popular sights are all on the south bank in Grossbasel (Greater Basel).

Internet Dome (Steinenvorstadt 53; per hr Sfr9; ☯ noon-11pm Sun-Thu, to 1am Fri & Sat) Internet access.

Post office (Rüdengasse 1; ☯ 7.30am-6.30pm Mon-Wed, 7.30am-7pm Thu-Fri, 8am-5pm Sat)

Tourist office (☎ 061 268 68 68; www.basel.com; Stadt-Casino, Barfüsserplatz, Steinenberg 14; ☯ 8.30am-6.30pm Mon-Fri, 9am-5pm Sat, 9am-4pm Sun)

Sights & Activities

With its cobbled streets, colourful fountains, medieval churches and stately buildings, the Old Town is a wonderful place to wander. In Marktplatz check out the impressive rust-coloured **Rathaus** (town hall), with frescoed courtyard. The 12th-century **Münster** (cathedral), southeast from Marktplatz, is another highlight, with Gothic spires and Romanesque St Gallus doorway.

Theaterplatz is a crowd-pleaser, with a curious **fountain**, designed by Swiss sculptor Jean Tinguely. His madcap scrap-metal machines perform a peculiar water dance, delighting children and weary travellers alike. Also check out the 700-year-old **Spalentor** gate tower, a remnant of the town's old city walls, with a massive portal and grotesque gargoyles.

Art lovers can ogle at Switzerland's largest art collection, including works by Klee and Picasso, at the **Kunstmuseum** (Museum of Fine Arts; ☎ 061 206 62 62; www.kunstmuseumbasel.ch; St Alban-Graben 16; adult/child/student Sfr12/free/5, 1st Sun of the month free; ☯ 10am-5pm Tue-Sun).

But the art space to really knock your socks off is the **Fondation Beyeler** (☎ 061 645 97 00; www.beyeler.com; Baselstrasse 101, Riehen; adult/child/student Sfr23/6/12; ☯ 10am-6pm, to 8pm Wed), an open-plan building by Italian architect Renzo Piano. The quality of its 19th- and 20th-century paintings is matched only by the way Miró and Max Ernst sculptures are juxtaposed with similar tribal figures. Take tram 6 to Riehen.

Festivals & Events

Basel's huge **Fasnacht** spring carnival kicks off at 4am on the Monday after Ash Wednesday with the **Morgestraich**: streetlights are extinguished and a procession of masked, costumed revellers wends its way through town. Restaurants and bars stay open all night and the streets positively throb with festivities.

Sleeping

Hotels are often full during Basel's trade fairs and conventions; book ahead. Guests receive a free mobility pass upon checking in, meaning free travel on public transport.

Basel Backpack (☎ 061 333 00 37; www.basel backpack.ch; Dornacherstrasse 192; dm Sfr32, s/d Sfr80/98; 🖳) Converted from a factory, this inde

pendent hostel has cheerful, colour-coded eight-bed dorms and more sedate doubles and family rooms.

SYHA Basel City Youth Hostel (☎ 061 365 99 60; www.youthhostel.ch/basel.city; Pfeffingerstrasse 8; dm Sfr35.50, s/d Sfr79/95; 🕑 reception 7am-noon & 3-11pm; 🖳) A convenient hostel in former post office buildings, it's across from the train sta-

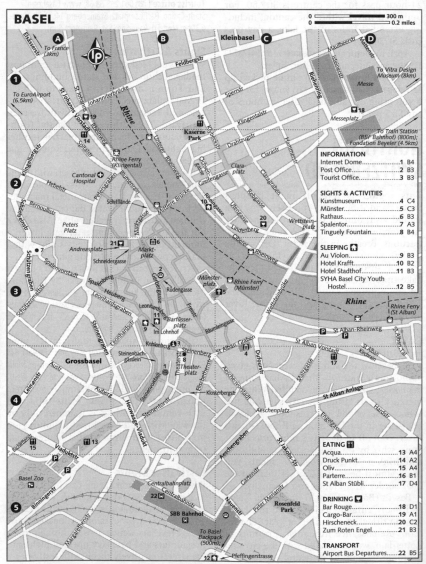

BASEL

0 —————— 300 m
0 —————— 0.2 miles

INFORMATION
Internet Dome.....................1 B4
Post Office...........................2 B3
Tourist Office.......................3 B3

SIGHTS & ACTIVITIES
Kunstmuseum......................4 C4
Münster................................5 C3
Rathaus................................6 B3
Spalentor.............................7 A3
Tinguely Fountain...............8 B4

SLEEPING 🏠
Au Violon............................9 B3
Hotel Krafft.......................10 B2
Hotel Stadthof...................11 B3
SYHA Basel City Youth
   Hostel.............................12 B5

EATING 🍴
Acqua.................................13 A4
Druck Punkt.......................14 A2
Oliv....................................15 A4
Parterre..............................16 B1
St Alban Stübli...................17 D4

DRINKING 🍷
Bar Rouge..........................18 D1
Cargo-Bar..........................19 A1
Hirscheneck.......................20 C2
Zum Roten Engel..............21 B3

TRANSPORT
Airport Bus Departures......22 B5

tion. Rooms have up to four beds and there's space a plenty – including a summertime interior courtyard.

Hotel Stadthof (☎ 061 261 87 11; www.stadthof.ch; Gerbergasse 84; s/d Sfr75/130) Book ahead to snag a room at this spartan but decent central hotel, above a pizzeria on an Old Town square. Nine rooms share loo and shower.

`our pick` **Au Violon** (☎ 061 269 87 11; www.au-violon .com; Im Lohnhof 4; s/d from Srf123/146) Quaint, atmospheric Au Violon was a prison from 1835 to 1995. Most of the rooms are two cells rolled into one and overlook a cobblestone courtyard or the cathedral. Sitting atop a leafy hilltop, its restaurant is equally appealing.

Hotel Krafft (☎ 061 690 91 30; www.hotelkrafft.ch; Rheingasse 12; s/d from Sfr145/230) Design-savvy urbanites adore this place. Sculptural chandeliers dangle in the creaky-floored dining room (for fine food) overlooking the Rhine, and stainless-steel water bars adorn each landing of the spiral stairs.

Eating

Our picks of Basel's rich dining scene all offer something a tad different.

`our pick` **Acqua** (☎ 061 564 66 66; www.acquabasilea .ch; Binningerstrasse 14; dishes Sfr15-42; ☿ lunch & dinner Tue-Fri, dinner Sat) For a glam post-industrial experience, head to these converted waterworks. Cuisine is Tuscan and Basel's beautiful people drink in the attached lounge bar. Summer terrace.

Druck Punkt (☎ 061 261 50 22; St Johanns Vorstadt 19; set menus Sfr17.50 & 22.50; ☿ Mon-Fri) This converted print shop makes an unpretentious bistro, with chalky walls and heavy wooden tables.

Parterre (☎ 061 695 89 98; www.parterre.net; Klybeckstrasse 1b; mains Sfr17-32; ☿ dinner Mon-Sat, snacks & light meals served 8am-midnight Mon-Fri, 10am-midnight Sat) Unusual dishes such as lake salmon in saffron sauce with potato gratin and cabbage stud the menu in this slightly alternative place overlooking a park.

Oliv (☎ 061 283 03 03; www.restaurantoliv.ch; Bachlettenstrasse 1; mains Sfr28 39; ☿ lunch & dinner Tue-Fri, dinner Sat) A trendy hang out not far from the zoo, Oliv leans towards fresh and varied Mediterranean cooking. Unusually, dainty appetites can order half portions.

St Alban Stübli (☎ 061 272 54 15; www.st-alban -stuebli.ch; St Alban Vorstadt 74; mains Sfr40-58; ☿ Mon-Fri) Set in a lovely quiet street, this is your quintessential cosy local tavern with dim

---

A CROSS-BORDER DETOUR

Design fiends have no choice. Nip across the German border to the **Vitra Design Museum** (☎ +49 7621 702 32 00; www.design-museum.de; Charles Eames Strasse 1, Weil am Rhein; adult/child/ student €8/free/6.50; ☿ 10am-6pm Mon-Sun, to 8pm Wed). Designed by Guggenheim creator Frank Gehry, the museum covers all aspects of interior design and sits amid the factory complex of furniture manufacturer Vitra – designed by a bunch of cutting-edge architects including Tadao Ando, Zaha Hadid and Álvaro Siza. Ride bus 55 from Claraplatz in Kleinbasel (30 minutes) to the Vitra stop. Take your passport.

---

yellow lighting, plenty of timber and fine linen. Food fuses local with French.

Drinking & Entertainment

Steinenvorstadt and Barfüsserplatz teem with teens and 20-somethings on the weekends. A faint whiff of grunge floats around Kleinbasel, the area around Rheingasse and Utengasse with a few watering holes and something of a red-light zone to lend it edge.

Bar Rouge (☎ 061 361 30 21; www.barrouge.ch; Level 31, Messeplatz 10; ☿ 5pm-1am Mon-Wed, Thu to 2am, to 4am Fri & Sat) This plush red bar with panoramic views from the 31st floor of the ugly glass *Messeturm* (trade fair tower) is the city's most memorable. Hipsters, and a few suits early on weekday evenings, come to appreciate the regular DJs and films.

Hirscheneck (☎ 061 692 73 33; Lindenberg 23; ☿ 9am-midnight Sun-Thu, 10am-2am Fri & Sat) A relaxed, grungy, almost knockabout place with an urban vibe (try to spot someone *without* piercings), this corner bar has tables on the footpath and regular gigs and DJs.

Zum Roten Engel (☎ 061 261 20 08; Andreasplatz 15; ☿ 9am-midnight Mon-Sat, 10am-10pm Sun) Spilling on to an irresistible, tiny cobblestone square, this student haunt is perfect for a latte by day or glass of wine come dusk.

Cargo-Bar (☎ 061 321 00 72; www.cargobar.ch; St Johanns Rheinweg 46; ☿ 4pm-1am Sun-Thu, to 2.30am Fri & Sat) A nice half-way house between cool and alternative, located in a tucked-away spot on the river. There are lots of art installations, live gigs, video shows and DJs.

Getting There & Away

The **EuroAirport** (BSL or MLH; ☎ 061 325 31 11; www.euro airport.com), 5km northwest of town, in France, is the main airport for Basel.

Basel is a major European rail hub with two main train stations, the Swiss-French SBB (south bank) and the BBF (north bank) for trains to/from Germany.

Destinations include Paris (Sfr69, five hours, seven times daily). Local trains to the Black Forest stop only at BBF, though fast EC services stop at SBB, too. Main destinations along this route are Amsterdam (Sfr180, eight hours, daily), Frankfurt (Sfr133, three hours, daily) and Hamburg (Sfr214, 6½ to 7½ hours, daily).

Services within Switzerland from SBB include Geneva (Sfr69, 2¾ hours, twice hourly) and Zürich (Sfr31, 55 minutes to 1¼ hours, twice hourly).

Getting Around

Bus 50 links the airport and SBB train station (Sfr6.60, 20 minutes). The trip by taxi (☎ 061 691 77 88) costs around Sfr40.

SCHAFFHAUSEN

pop 33,500

Schaffhausen is the kind of quaint medieval town one more readily associates with Germany (perhaps no coincidence given how close the border is). Ornate frescos and oriel windows adorn pastel-coloured houses in the pedestrian-only Altstadt (Old Town), home to the **tourist office** (☎ 052 632 40 20; www.schaff hausen-tourismus.ch or www.shtotal.info; Herrenacker 15; 9.30am-6pm Mon-Fri, to 4pm Sat Jun-Sep, to 2pm Sun Jun-Aug, to 5pm Mon-Fri, to 2pm Sat Oct-May).

Prime views preen their feathers atop the 16th-century **Munot fortress** (admission free; 8am-8pm May-Sep, 9am-5pm Oct-Apr), a 15-minute uphill walk through vineyards from town.

DETOUR: RIVERSIDE RECKY

The 45km **boat trip** (☎ 052 634 08 88; www .urh.ch or www.riverticket.ch; Freier Platz; single/return Sfr21/30; Mar-Oct) from Schaffhausen to Konstanz sails past one of the Rhine's more beautiful stretches. It passes by meadows, castles and ancient villages, including **Stein am Rhein**, 20km to the east, where you could easily wear out your camera snapping pictures of the buildings in the picture-perfect Rathausplatz.

Westward along the river on foot (40 minutes) or aboard bus 1 to Neuhausen is **Rheinfall** (Rhine Falls), waterfalls that, though only 23m tall, are deemed Europe's largest. The amount of water thundering down is extraordinary.

Set in leafy grounds the **SYHA hostel** (☎ 052 625 88 00; www.youthhostel.ch/schaffhausen; Randenstrasse 65; dm Sfr28; reception closed 10am-5pm, hostel closed mid-Nov–Feb;) is an old pile of a mansion with clean, modern bathrooms. It's 15 minutes by foot west of the train station or take bus 6 to Hallenbad. At the other extreme, the **Fischerzunft** (☎ 052 632 05 05; www.fischerzunft.ch; Rheinquai 8; s/d from Sfr210/295), one of Switzerland's most opulent hotels away from the big city, is known above all for its gourmet restaurant.

Direct hourly trains run to/from Zürich (Sfr18.20, 40 minutes).

APPENZELLERLAND

The Appenzellers are the butt of many a cruel joke by their fellow Swiss, a little like Tasmanians in Australia or Newfoundlanders in Canada. As Swiss Germans say, Appenzellers *hätte ä langi Laitig* (have a very long cable). It takes a while after you tug for them to get the message. And indeed, there's no denying that the Appenzellcanton is still firmly rooted in tradition: Innerrhoden continues to hold a yearly open-air parliament and didn't permit women to vote until 1991.

Such devotion to rural tradition has an upside. Locals go to great lengths to preserve their heritage and this area of impossibly green valleys, thick forests and impressive mountains is dotted with timeless villages and criss-crossed by endless hiking, cycling and mountain-biking.

The pastel-hued village of **Appenzell** is a feast for the eyes and the stomach. Behind the gaily decorative coloured facades of its traditional buildings lie cafes, cake shops, cheese shops, delicatessens, butchers and restaurants all offering local specialities. Don your lazy hat and enjoy a long slow lunch and wander!

The train station is 400m from the town centre, home to the **tourist office** (☎ 071 788 96 41; www.appenzell.ch; Hauptgasse 4; 9am-noon & 1.30-6pm Mon-Fri, 10am-noon & 2-5pm Sat & Sun Apr-Oct, 9am-noon & 2-5pm Mon-Fri, 2-5pm Sat & Sun Nov-Mar).

Hotel Appenzell (☎ 071 788 15 15; www.hotel -appenzell.ch; Landsgemeindeplatz; s/d Sfr130/220) sits in a brightly decorated, typical Appenzeller building and is a solid choice to both sleep and sample seasonal cuisine, including vege

---

THESE BOOTS ARE MADE FOR WALKING...NOT

Hiking trails abound around Appenzell. One more unusual one is the **Barefoot Path** from Gonten, 5km west of Appenzell, to Gontenbad (one hour), for which you really don't need shoes – think lush green moors and meadows. In Gontenbad, dip in mud-laden water from the moors at **Natur-Moorbad** (☎ 071 795 31 23; www.naturmoor bad.ch; admission Sfr20; Gontenbad), a moor bath, dating to 1740, whose wholly natural products relieve stress or skin conditions (adding in nettles, ferns and other plants) or simply serve to luxuriate loved ones with sweet rose baths (Sfr80 for two).

---

tarian dishes and the local strong-smelling Appenzell cheese.

There is a train to St Gallen (Sfr10.80, 50 minutes, twice hourly).

TICINO

This is the Switzerland that Heidi never mentioned: the summer air is rich, hot (and smokefree thanks to a cantonwide ban on smoking in public places since 2007) and the peacock-proud posers propel their scooters in and out of traffic. Italian weather, Italian style. And that's not to mention the Italian ice cream, Italian pizza, Italian architecture and Italian language.

South of the Alps, Ticino (Tessin in German and French) has a distinct look. The canton manages to perfectly fuse Swiss cool with Italian passion, as evidenced by a lusty love for Italian comfort food and full-bodied wines that's balanced by a healthy respect for rules and regulations.

BELLINZONA
pop 17,000

Ticino's capital is a quiet stunner. Strategically placed at the conversion point of several valleys leading down from the Alps, Bellinzona is visually unique. Inhabited since Neolithic times, it is dominated by three grey-stone, fairy-tale medieval castles that have attracted everyone from Swiss invaders to painters such as JMW Turner. Turner may have liked the place, but Bellinzona has a surprisingly low tourist profile, in spite of

its castles together forming a Unesco World Heritage site.

The **tourist office** (☎ 091 825 21 31; www.bellinzo naturismo.ch; Piazza Nosetto; 9am-6pm Mon-Fri, to noon Sat), in the restored Renaissance town hall, can provide information on Bellinzona and the whole canton.

You can roam the ramparts of the two larger castles, **Castelgrande** or **Castello di Montebello**, both of which are still in great condition and offer panoramic views of the town and countryside.

Housed in Villa Montebello, at the foot of the eponymous castle, the **Ostello della Gioventù** (☎ 091 825 15 22; www.youthhostel.ch/bellinzona; Via Noca 4; dm Sfr36.50, s/d Sfr65/90; reception closed 10am-3pm; hostel closed last 2 weeks Dec;) occupies what was a high-class girls' school for a century.

The only place to sleep just inside the Old Town (part of the city wall stands menacingly behind it) is **Albergo Croce Federale** (☎ 091 825 16 67; Viale della Stazione 12; s/d Sfr100/140). Rooms are straightforward but light, and the restaurant downstairs is cheerful.

A photographer runs the slightly chaotic **Osteria Zoccolino** (☎ 091 825 06 70; Piazza Governo 5; mains Sfr14-20; Mon-Sat), a cheery spot that bristles with happy diners at lunchtime. You never quite know what to expect here: a set lunch of Indian food, concerts on Thursday nights...and you may find he opens at night only when he has enough bookings. Don't worry, there are several alternatives along Via Teatro and Via Orico. Or seize the rare opportunity to dine in a Unesco World Heritage site at medieval **Castelgrande** (☎ 091 826 23 53; www.castelgrande.ch; Castelgrande; mains Sfr35-60; Tue-Sun).

Bellinzona is on the train route connecting Locarno (Sfr8.20, 20 to 25 minutes) and Lugano (Sfr11.80, 26 to 30 minutes).

LOCARNO
pop 15,000

The rambling red enclave of Italianate town houses, piazzas and arcades ending at the northern end of Lake Maggiore, coupled with more hours of sunshine than anywhere else in Switzerland, give this laid-back town a summer resort atmosphere. The lowest town in Switzerland, it seemed like a soothing spot to host the 1925 peace conference intended to bring stability to Europe after WWI.

Five minutes' walk west of the train station is the town's heart, Piazza Grande, and the tourist office (☎ 091 791 00 91; www.maggiore.ch; Largo Zorzi 1; ☺ 9am-6pm Mon-Fri, 10am-6pm Sat, 10am-1.30pm & 2.30-5pm Sun mid-Mar–Oct, 9.30am-noon & 1.30-5pm Mon-Fri, 10am-noon & 1.30-5pm Sat Nov–mid-Mar) nearby.

Sights & Activities

Don't miss the formidable **Madonna del Sasso**, located up on the hill, with panoramic views of the lake and town. The sanctuary was built after the Virgin Mary allegedly appeared in a vision in 1480. It features a church with 15th-century paintings, a small museum and several distinctive statues. There is a funicular from the town centre, but the 20-minute climb is not demanding (take Via al Sasso off Via Cappuccini) and you pass some shrines on the way.

In August more than 150,000 film buffs hit town for the two-week **International Film Festival** (www.pardo.ch). Cinemas are used during the day but at night films are shown in the open-air on a giant screen in the Piazza Grande.

Sleeping & Eating

Camping Delta (☎ 091 751 60 81; www.campingdelta.com; Via Respini 7; camp sites Sfr47-57, plus per adult/child/senior & student Sfr18/6/16; ☺ Mar-Oct) Although pricey, this camping ground has great facilities and is brilliantly located between the shores of Lago Maggiore and the Maggia River.

Vecchia Locarno (☎ 091 751 65 02; www.hotel-vecchia -locarno.ch; Via della Motta 10; s/d with shared bathroom Sfr55/100) Rooms are gathered around a sunny internal courtyard, evoking a Mediterranean mood, and some have Old Town views. Digs are simple but comfortable.

Lake Maggiore has a great variety of fresh and tasty fish, including *persico* (perch) and *corigone* (whitefish).

our pick **Osteria Chiara** (☎ 091 743 32 96; Vicolo della Chiara 1; pasta & mains Sfr16-32; ☺ Tue-Sat) Tucked away on a cobbled lane, this has all the cosy feel of a grotto. Sit at granite tables beneath the pergola or at timber tables by the fireplace for chunky pasta and mostly meat dishes. From the lake follow the signs up Vicolo dei Nessi.

Drinking

Bar Sport (Via della Posta 4; ☺ 8-1am Mon-Fri, 10-1am Sat, 2pm-1am Sun) A run-of-the-mill place by day, this rough-and-tumble bar with red-walled dance space out the back and beer garden is a huge hit with night owls. A few other bars loiter nearby.

Getting There & Away

The St Gotthard Pass provides the road link (A2) to central Switzerland. There are trains from Brig (Sfr51, 2½ hours, hourly) that pass through Italy en route; change trains at Domodóssola across the border and bring your passport.

LUGANO
pop 49,700

There is a distinct vibrant snappiness in the air in Lugano, Switzerland's southernmost tourist town, where visitors unravel the spaghetti maze of cobblestone streets while locals toil in stuffy banks – this is the country's third-most important banking centre.

A sophisticated slice of Italian life with colourful markets, upmarket shops, interlocking *piazze* and lakeside parks, lucky Lugano lounges on the northern shore of Lake Lugano, at the feet of Mounts San Salvatore and Brè. Read: a superb base for lake trips, water sports and hillside hikes.

The Centro Storico (Old Town) is a 10-minute walk down hill from the train station; take the stairs or the funicular (Sfr1.10). The **tourist office** (☎ 091 913 32 32; www.lugano-tourism .ch; Riva Giocondo Albertolli; ☺ 9am-7pm Mon-Fri, 9am-5pm Sat, 10am-5pm Sun Apr-Oct, 9am-noon & 2-5.30pm Mon-Fri, 10am-12.30pm & 1.30-5pm Sat Nov-Mar) runs a **booth** (☺ 2-7pm Mon-Sat) at the station.

Sights & Activities

Wander through the mostly porticoed lanes woven around the busy main square, Piazza della Riforma (which is even more lively when the Tuesday and Friday morning markets are held). Via Nassa is the main shopping street and indicates there is no shortage of cash in this town.

The simple Romanesque **Chiesa di Santa Maria degli Angioli** (St Mary of the Angels; Piazza Luini; ☺ 8am-5pm), against which a now-crumbling former hotel was built, contains two frescos by Bernardino Luini dating from 1529. Covering the entire wall that divides the church in two is a grand didactic illustration of the Crucifixion. The closer you look, the more scenes of Christ's Passion are revealed, along with others of him being taken down from the cross and the Resurrection. The power and vivacity of the colours are astounding.

Chomp on a chocolate-coated history lesson: watch the sweet substance made and taste for free at the **Museo del Cioccolato Alprose**

(☎ 091 611 88 88; www.alprose.ch; Via Rompada 36, Caslano; adult/child Sfr3/1; ⓨ 9am-5.30pm Mon-Fri, to 4.30pm Sat & Sun). Get there by the Ferrovia Ponte Tresa train (Sfr7).

Or take a **boat trip** to one of the photogenic villages hugging the shoreline – car-free **Gandria** is popular – and feast on traditional Ticinese dishes in your pick of quintessential Ticinese grottos.

Sleeping

Many hotels close for part of the winter.

Hostel Montarina (☎ 091 966 72 72; www.montarina .ch; Via Montarina 1; dm Sfr26) Hostel Montarina has simple rooms with four to 16 bunk beds. A buffet breakfast is available for Sfr12.

SYHA hostel (☎ 091 966 27 28; www.luganoyouth hostel.ch; Via Cantonale 13, Savosa; dm/s/d Sfr26/68/96; ⓨ mid-Mar-Oct; ⚑) Housed in Villa Savosa, this is one of Switzerland's more enticing youth hostels. Take bus 5 to Crocifisso.

Hotel Pestalozzi (☎ 091 921 46 46; www.pestalozzi -lugano.ch; Piazza Independenza 9; s/d with shared bathroom Sfr64/108, with private bathroom Sfr106/188; ⚑) This renovated art nouveau building is home to rooms with reds, blues and creams dominating the decor. Cheaper ones have a shared bathroom in the corridor.

Hotel Montarina (☎ 091 966 72 72; www.montarina. ch; Via Montarina 1; s/d Sfr85/125; ⚑) Behind the train station is this charming hotel with airy rooms, timber floors and antiques. Some rooms have kitchens and the garden is pool-clad.

Eating & Drinking

For pizza or overpriced pasta, any of the places around Piazza della Riforma are pleasant and lively enough.

Grand Café Al Porto (☎ 091 910 51 30; Via Pessina 3; ⓨ 8am-6.30pm Mon-Sat) This cafe, which began life way back in 1803, has several fine rooms for dining. Be sure to peek at the frescoed Cenacolo Fiorentino, once a monastery dining hall, upstairs.

Al Lido (☎ 091 971 55 00; Viale Castagnola; ⓨ brunch 11am-6pm; dinner Wed-Sat) Lugano's lakeside beach restaurant is hot for Sunday buffet brunch (Sfr36.50) and its Wednesday-evening version (same price), with DJ thrown in.

L'Antica Osteria del Porto (☎ 091 971 42 00; Via Foce 9; mains Sfr22-39; ⓨ Wed-Mon) Set back from the sailing club, this is the place to savour local fish and Ticinese dishes.

ourpick **Bottegone del Vino** (☎ 091 922 76 89; Via Magatti 3; mains Sfr28-42; ⓨ Mon-Sat) Favoured by the local banking brigade at lunchtime, this is a great place to taste fine local wines over a well-prepared meal. The menu changes daily and knowledgable waiters fuss around the tables, only too happy to suggest the perfect Ticino tipple.

Drinking & Entertainment

Soho Café (☎ 091 922 60 80; Corso Pestalozzi 3; ⓨ 7am-1am Mon-Fri, 4pm-1am Sat) So that's where they are! All those good-looking Lugano townies crowd in to this long, orange-lit bar for cocktails. Chilled DJ music creates a pleasant buzz. The problem might be squeezing through to the bar!

Another lively spot Thursday to Saturday night is **New Orleans Club** (☎ 091 921 44 77; www.neworleansclublugano.com; Piazza Indipendenza 1; ⓨ 5pm-1am Mon-Sat), with Latin, hip-hop and disco nights.

Getting There & Around

From **Agno airport** (☎ 091 612 11 11; www.lugano -airport.ch), **Darwin Airline** (www.darwinairline.com) flies to Rome (Fiumicino), Geneva and Olbia (in Sardinia). **Flybaboo** (www.flybaboo.com) flies regularly to Geneva and **Swiss** (www.swiss .com) to Zürich.

Lugano is on the same road and rail route as Bellinzona. To St Moritz, one postal bus runs direct via Italy at least Friday to Sunday (Sfr69, four hours, daily late June to mid-October and late December to early January). Reserve at the bus station, the train station information office or on ☎ 091 807 85 20. All postal buses leave from the main bus depot at Via Serafino Balestra, but you can pick up the St Moritz and some other buses outside the train station 15 minutes later.

GRAUBÜNDEN

Don't be fooled by Graubünden's diminutive size on a map. This is topographic origami at its finest. Unfold the rippled landscape to find an outdoor adventurer's paradise riddled with more than 11,000km of walking trails, 600-plus lakes and 1500km of downhill ski slopes – including super swanky St Moritz and back-packer mecca Flims-Laax. A cultural one-off, Graubünden thrives on contradictions: one minute it's Heidi cheese and fondue on the alm, the next high culture in Chur and risotto near the Italian border. Linguistically wired to flick from Italian to German to Romansch, locals keep you guessing too.

CHUR
pop 32,500

The Alps rise like an amphitheatre around Chur, Switzerland's oldest city, inhabited since 3000 BC. Linger more than a few minutes on your way to St Moritz and you'll soon warm to the capital of Graubünden. After a stint in the mountains its galleries, arty boutiques, appetising restaurants and vibrant bars are a refreshing tonic. The **tourist office** (☎ 081 252 18 18; www.churtourismus.ch; Bahnhofplatz 3; ☯ 7am-8pm Mon-Fri, 8am-6pm Sat & Sun) has stacks of info and maps on the region.

For an insight into the artistic legacy of Graubünden-born Alberto Giacometti (1877–1947) and his equally talented relatives, visit the **Bündner Kunstmuseum** (Museum of Fine Arts; ☎ 081 257 28 68; www.buendner-kunstmuseum.ch; Postplatz; adult/under 16yr/student Sfr8/free/6; ☯ 10am-5pm Tue-Sun) inside neoclassical Villa Planta.

Hurrah! Finally a backpacker gem in Chur's buzzy Welschdörfli district in the shape of **JBN** (☎ 081 284 10 10; www.justbenice.ch; Welschdörfli 19; dm Sfr33-40, d Sfr108-138, ste Sfr178; 🖳). Glammed up with original photography and quirky touches like dog's-backside coat hangers, the place has spacious dorms and a club that pumps up the volume at weekends (choose a mountain-facing room if decibels affect your slumber).

Another treat are the romantic loft rooms (not for tall people) at **Zunfthaus zur Rebleuten** (☎ 081 255 11 44; Pfisterplatz 1; s/d Sfr85/140), a Chur classic with 500 years of history behind it and a dozen fresh, inviting rooms.

Equally golden old is vaulted Gothic **Hofkellerei** (☎ 081 252 32 30; Hof 1; mains Sfr19-36; ☯ Tue-Sun), a 'ye olde inn' that has been sizzling and stirring since 1522. Wooden floorboards creak as you enter and regional flavours like *pizokel* with plums and *capuns* (rich mix of local *spätzli* pasta dough, beef, ham and herbs wrapped and baked in Swiss chard or spinach leaves) tickle tastebuds beneath wrought-iron chandeliers.

Chur is connected to Zürich (Sfr37, 85 minutes, hourly), Klosters (Sfr20.60, 1¼ hours) and Davos (Sfr27, 1½ hours).

FLIMS-LAAX

They say if the snow ain't falling anywhere else, you'll surely find some around Flims-Laax. These towns, along with tiny Falera,

20km west of Chur, form a single ski area known as the Weisses Arena (White Arena), with 220km of slopes catering for all levels. Laax in particular is known as a mecca for snowboarders, who spice up the local nightlife too. The resort is barely two hours by train and bus (less by car) from Zürich airport.

The main **tourist office** (☎ 081 920 92 00; www .flims.com summer, www.laax.com winter; Via Nova; ☯ 8am-6pm Mon-Fri, to noon Sat mid-Jun–mid-Aug, to 5pm Mon-Fri mid-Dec–mid-Apr) is in Flims-Dorf.

The ski slopes range as high as 3000m and are mostly intermediate or easy, although there are some 45km of more challenging runs. A one-day ski pass includes ski buses and costs Sfr62 (plus Sfr5 for the KeyCard that you use to access the lifts).

Laax was the first Swiss resort to allow snowboarders to use the lifts back in 1985, and remains a mecca for snowsurfers, with two huge half-pipes (one said to be the biggest in the world) and a freestyle park huddled around the unfortunately named Crap Sogn Gion peak. The season starts in late October on the glacier and, depending on snowfalls, in mid-December elsewhere.

In summer try **river rafting** on a turbulent 17km stretch of the Vorderrhein between Ilanz and Reichenau. It will take you through the **Rheinschlucht** (Rhine Gorge), somewhat optimistically dubbed Switzerland's Grand Canyon, but impressive enough for all that. **Swissraft** (☎ 081 911 52 50; www.swissraft.ch) offers half-/full day rafting for Sfr109/160.

Sleep? Dream on. It may resemble an over-sized Rubik's cube, but **Riders Palace** (☎ 081 927 97 00; www.riderspalace.ch; Laax Murschetg; dm Sfr50-60, d Sfr180-280) is a curious slice of designer cool with bare concrete walls and fluorescent lighting. Choose between basic five-bed dorms, slick rooms with Philippe Starck tubs or hi-tech suites complete with PlayStation and Dolby surround. Find it 200m from the Laax lifts.

Dining-wise, experience the raw funk of **La Vacca** (☎ 081 927 99 62; Plaun Station, Laax-Murschetg lifts; mains Sfr40-70; ☯ late Dec–mid-Apr), a tipi where cowhide-draped chairs surround a roaring open fire. Forget stringy fondue; the menu is as exciting as the design – think melt-in-your-mouth bison steaks paired with full-bodied Argentine wines.

In the drinking stakes, there's the too-cool lobby bar with DJs at **Riders Palace** (☯ 4pm-4am) or the **Crap Bar** (☎ 081 927 99 45; Laax-Murschetg lifts;

4pm-2am), the place to slam shots, check your email and shimmy in your snow-boots after a day pounding powder.

Postal buses run to Flims and the other villages in the White Arena area hourly from Chur (Sfr12.80 to Flims Dorf, 30 minutes). A free local shuttle bus connects the three villages.

ST MORITZ
pop 5060
Switzerland's original winter wonderland and the cradle of Alpine tourism, St Moritz (San Murezzan in Romansch) has been luring royals, the filthy rich and moneyed wannabes since 1864. With its smugly perfect lake and aloof mountains, the town looks a million dollars. Still waiting to make your first billion? Stay in St Moritz Bad.

Yet despite the Gucci set propping up the bars and celebs bashing the pistes (Kate Moss and George Clooney included), this resort isn't all show. The real riches lie outdoors with superb carving on Corviglia, hairy black runs on Diavolezza and miles of hiking trails when the powder melts.

Orientation & Information
Hilly St Moritz Dorf is above the train station, with luxury hotels, restaurants and shops. To the southwest, 2km around the lake is the more downmarket St Moritz Bad; buses run between the two. St Moritz is seasonal and becomes a ghost town during November and from late April to early June.

The **tourist office** (☎ 081 837 33 33; www.stmoritz .ch; Via Maistra 12; ☺ 9am 6.30pm Mon-Fri, 9am-noon & 1.30-6pm Sat, 4-6pm Sun Dec-Easter & mid-Jun–mid-Sep, 9am-noon & 2-6pm Mon-Fri, 9am-noon Sat rest of the year) has all the usual traveller info.

Activities
Skiers and snowboarders will revel in the 350km of runs in three key areas. For groomed slopes with big mountain vistas, head to **Corviglia** (2486m), accessible by funicular from Dorf. From Bad a cable car goes to Signal (shorter queues), giving access to the slopes of Piz Nair. A ski pass for both areas costs Sfr67 (child/youth Sfr23/45) for one day. Silhouetted by glaciated 4000ers, **Diavolezza** (2978m) is a must-ski for free-riders and fans of jaw-dropping descents.

Avid cross-country skiers can glide through snow-dusted woodlands and plains on 160km of groomed trails. See www.skien gadin.ch for the complete skiing low-down.

You can hike or try your hand at golf (including on the frozen lake in winter), tennis, in-line skating, fishing, horse riding, sailing, windsurfing and river rafting, to mention just a few. The tourist office has a list of prices and contacts.

Sleeping & Eating
Jugendherberge St Moritz (☎ 081 836 61 11; Stille Via Surpunt 60; www.youthhostel.ch/st.moritz; dm/d Sfr55/137; ☐) Budget beds are gold-dust rare in St Moritz, but you'll find one at this hostel edging the forest. The four-bed dorms and doubles are quiet and clean. There's a kiosk, games room and laundrette.

Chesa Chantarella (☎ 081 833 33 55; www.chesachan tarella.ch; Via Salastrains; s/d Sfr95/190; ☺ Jun-Sep & Dec-Apr) Sitting above the town, this is a lively choice with bright, modern rooms. Sip hot chocolate on the terrace, venture down to the wine cellar or dine on hearty local fare in the restaurant.

Hotel Waldhaus am See (☎ 081 836 60 00; www.wald haus-am-see.ch; s/d Sfr170/320; ☐) Overlooking the lake, this friendly pad has light-flooded rooms with pine furnishings and floral fabrics, many with enticing lake and mountain views. There's a sauna and a restaurant serving appetising grill specialities.

our pick **Hatecke** (☎ 081 864 11 75; www.hatecke .ch; snacks & mains Sfr15-25; ☺ 9am-6.30pm Mon-Fri, to 6pm Sat) Edible art is the only way to describe the organic, locally sourced delicacies at Hatecke. *Bündnerfleisch* and venison ham are carved into wafer-thin slices on a century-old slicing machine in this speciality shop. Sit on a sheepskin stool in the funky cafe next door to lunch on delicious Engadine beef carpaccio or *Bündnerfleisch* with truffle oil.

Engiadina (☎ 081 833 32 65; Plazza da Scuola 2; fondue Sfr29-46; ☺ Mon-Sat) A proper locals' place, Engiadina is famous for fondue, and that's the best thing to eat here. Champagne gives the melted cheese a kick. It's open year-round.

Drinking
Around 20 bars and clubs pulsate in winter. While you shuffle to the beat your wallet might also waltz itself wafer-thin, because nights out in St Moritz can be nasty on the banknotes.

Bobby's Pub (☎ 081 834 42 83; Via dal Bagn 50a; ☺ 9.30am-1.30am) This laid-back and friendly English-style watering hole serves 30 different brews and attracts young snowboarders in season. It's among the few places open year-round.

Roo Bar (☎ 081 837 50 50; Via Traunter Plazzas 7; ☺ 2-8pm Dec-Apr) After a hard day's skiing or boarding, snow bums fill the terrace of this après-ski joint at Hauser's Hotel. Hip-hop, techno and copious quantities of schnapps fuel the party.

Getting There & Away

The **Glacier Express** (www.glacierexpress.ch) plies one of Switzerland's most famous scenic train routes, connecting St Moritz to Zermatt (Sfr138 plus Sfr15 or Sfr30 reservation fee in summer, 7½ hours, daily) via the 2033m Oberalp Pass. It covers 290km and crosses 291 bridges. Novelty drink glasses in the dining car have sloping bases to compensate for the hills – remember to keep turning them around!

The *Palm Express* postal bus runs to Lugano (☎ 058 386 31 66; Sfr69 or Sfr20 with Swiss Travel pass, four hours, daily summer; Friday, Saturday and Sunday winter); advance reservations are obligatory.

SWISS NATIONAL PARK

The road west from Müstair stretches 34km over the Ofenpass (Pass dal Fuorn, 2149m), through the thick woods of Switzerland's only **national park** (www.nationalpark.ch; ☺ Jun-Oct) and on to **Zernez** and the brand-new, hands-on **Swiss National Park Centre** (☎ 081 851 41 41; www.nationalpark.ch; adult/child Sfr7/3; ☺ 8.30am-6pm Jun-Oct, 9am-noon & 2-5pm Nov-May), where you can explore a marmot hole, eyeball adders in the vivarium and learn about conservation and environmental change.

The national park was established in 1914 – the first such park in Europe – and spans 172 sq km. 'Nature gone wild' pretty much sums it up: think dolomite peaks, shimmering glaciers, larch woodlands, gentian-flecked pastures, clear waterfalls, and high moors strung with topaz lakes. Zernez **tourist office** (☎ 081 856 13 00; Chasa Fuchina) has hike details, including the three-hour tramp from S-chanf to Trupchun (popular in autumn when you might spy rutting deer) and the Naturlehrpfad circuit near **Il Fuorn**, where bearded vultures can be sighted.

NO LIONS, NO TIGERS, BUT BEARS, OH MY!

In recent years, brown bears with wanderlust and an appetite for a tasty Swiss sheep or three have frequently crossed the border from Italy into the Engadine. Their favourite place to cause havoc? The Swiss National Park, naturally, where they have less chance of being spotted. Bears made several cameo appearances in summer 2007, sticking their paws into beehives near Zernez and upsetting locals by killing a dozen or more sheep around the Albula Pass. One was captured and given a tracking device, which should at least put a stop to his Swiss escapades.

Entry to the park and its car parks is free. Walkers can enter by trails from Zernez, S-chanf and Scuol. Conservation is paramount here, so stick to footpaths and respect regulations prohibiting camping, littering, lighting fires, cycling, picking flowers and disturbing the animals.

Sleeping & Eating

There are several hotels and restaurants in Zernez and a couple in the park itself.

Hotel Bär & Post (☎ 081 851 55 00; www.baer-post .ch; dm/s/d Sfr118/85/170) Welcoming all-comers since 1905, these central digs have inviting rooms with lots of stone pine and downy duvets, plus basic bunk rooms. There's also a sauna and a rustic restaurant, dishing up good steaks and pasta.

Chamanna Cluozza (☎ 081 856 12 35; cluozza@hotmail. com; dm/d with half-board Sfr58/136; ☺ late Jun–mid-Oct) For peace and a cracking location, you can't beat this forest hideaway. Dorms are great for walkers eager to hit the trail first thing. It's a three-hour-odd hike from Zernez.

Il Fuorn (☎ 081 856 12 26; www.ilfuorn.ch; s/d from Sfr80/140, half-board extra Sfr30; ☺ May-Oct) In the heart of the national park, this guest house shelters light, comfy rooms with loads of pine. Trout and game are big on the *stübli* (cosy Swiss bistro) menu.

Getting There & Away

Trains run regularly from Zernez to St Moritz (Sfr17.40, 50 minutes), stopping at S-chanf, Zuoz and Celerina. For the latter and St Moritz, change at Samedan.

SWITZERLAND DIRECTORY

ACCOMMODATION

From palatial palaces and castles to mountain refuge, nuclear bunker, icy igloo or simple hayloft, Switzerland sports traditional and creative accommodation in every price range. Moreover, an increasing number of places are green when it comes to eco-friendly heating, lighting, waste disposal and so on.

Prices may seem steep – even the most inexpensive places are pricey compared with other parts of Europe. The upside is hostels, hotels and B&Bs almost always include a generous breakfast in their price and the standard of accommodation is high, divine fluffy feather duvet included.

In both Switzerland and Liechtenstein many budget hotels have cheaper rooms with shared toilet and shower facilities, and more expensive rooms with private bathroom. For a budget double with bathroom expect to pay up to Sfr150; midrange places will set you back anywhere from Sfr150 to Sfr250, while top-end places range from Sfr200 to pure unadulterated, time-honoured Swiss luxury, with gasp-worthy price tag to match. In both this chapter and Liechtenstein, prices include bathroom and are quoted at peak-season rates.

Rates in cities and towns stay constant most of the year. In mountain resorts prices are seasonal: low season (mid-September to mid-December, mid-April to mid-June), mid-season (January to mid-February, mid-June to early July, September); and high season (July to August, Christmas, mid-February to Easter).

Online, MySwitzerland.com is a great resource for tracking down accommodation.

Hay Barns

A fabulous way to experience life on a Swiss farm, **Aventure sur la paille/Schlaf im Stroh** (☎ 041 678 12 86; www.abenteuer-stroh.ch) is the ultimate adventure. When their cows are out to pasture in summer or indeed, even after they've been brought in for the winter come early October, farmers charge travellers Sfr20 to Sfr30 per adult and Sfr10 to Sfr20 per child to sleep on straw in their hay barns or lofts (listen to the jangle of cow or goat bells beneath your head!). Farmers provide cotton under-sheets (to avoid straw pricks) and woolly blankets for extra warmth, but guests need their own sleeping bags and pocket torch. Nightly rates include a farmhouse breakfast; shower and evening meals are extras.

Hostels

Switzerland has two types of hostels: **Swiss Youth Hostels** (SYHA; www.youthhostel.ch), affiliated with Hostelling International (HI), where nonmembers pay an additional 'guest fee' of Sfr6, and independent hostels which can be more charismatic. Prices listed in this book for SYHA hostels do not include the guest fee. On average a dorm bed in either type costs Sfr30 to Sfr40, including sheets.

There are another 80 hostels in the shape of Alpine chalet or rural farmhouse that offer hostel-style accommodation under the green umbrella group **Naturfreundehaus** (Friends of Nature; www.nfhouse.org).

ACTIVITIES

There are dozens of ski resorts throughout the Alps, pre-Alps and Jura, and 200-odd different ski schools. Equipment hire is available at resorts and ski passes allow unlimited use of mountain transport.

There is simply no better way to enjoy Switzerland's spectacular scenery than to walk through it. There are 50,000km of designated paths, often with a convenient inn or cafe located en route. Yellow signs marking the trail make it difficult to get lost, and each provides an average walking time to the next destination. Slightly more strenuous mountain paths have white-red-white markers. The **Schweizer Alpen-Club** (SAC; Map p555; ☎ 031 370 1818; www.sac-cas .ch, in German; Monbijoustrasse 61, Bern) maintains huts for overnight stays at altitude and can also help with extra information.

You can water-ski, sail and windsurf on most lakes. And there are more than 350 lake beaches. Rafting is possible on many Alpine rivers, including the Rhine and the Rhône.

Bungee jumping, paragliding, canyoning and other high-adrenalin sports are widely available throughout Switzerland, especially in the Interlaken area.

BUSINESS HOURS

Most shops are open from 8am to 6.30pm Monday to Friday with a one- to two-hour

SWITZERLAND

break for lunch at noon. In towns, there's often a late shopping day until 9pm, typically Thursday or Friday. Closing times on Saturday are usually 4pm or 5pm. Sunday sees souvenir shops and the odd supermarket at train stations open, but little else. Banks are open from 8.30am to 4.30pm Monday to Friday, with late opening usually one day a week. Eating and drinking establishments are open for lunch and dinner, unless otherwise noted in our reviews.

ELECTRICITY

Electrical supply is 220V, 50Hz. Swiss sockets are recessed, hexagonally shaped and incompatible with most plugs from abroad (including 'universal' adapters).

EMBASSIES & CONSULATES

Embassies are in Bern while cities such as Zürich and Geneva have several consulates. Neither Australia nor New Zealand has an embassy in Switzerland, but each has a consulate in Geneva. For a comprehensive list, see www.eda.admin.ch.

Australia (Map p539; ☎ 022 799 91 00; www.australia .ch; Chemin des Fins 2, Geneva)

Austria (Map p555; ☎ 031 356 52 52; www.ausse nministerium.at/bern, in German; Kirchenfeldstrasse 77-79, Bern)

Canada Bern (Map p555; ☎ 031 357 32 00; www .canada-ambassade.ch; Kirchenfeldstrasse 88); Geneva (Map p539; ☎ 022 919 92 00; 5 Ave de l'Ariana)

France Bern (Map p555; ☎ 031 359 21 11; www .ambafrance-ch.org, in German & French; Schosshalden-strasse 46); Geneva (Map p539; ☎ 022 319 00 00; www .consulfrance-geneve.org, In French; 2 Cours des Bastions)

Germany Bern (Map p555; ☎ 031-359 41 11; www .bern.diplo.de, in German & French; Willadingweg 83); Basel (☎ 061 693 33 03; Schwarzwaldallee 200); Geneva (Map p539; ☎ 022 730 11 11; Chemin du Petit-Saconnex 28c)

Italy (Map p555; ☎ 031 350 07 77; www.ambitalia.ch; Elfenstrasse 14, Bern)

New Zealand (Map p539; ☎ 022 929 03 50; Chemin des Fins 2, Grand-Saconnex, Geneva)

UK Bern (Map p555; ☎ 031 359 77 00; http://ukinswit zerland.fco.gov.uk/en; Thunstrasse 50); Geneva (Map p539; ☎ 022 918 24 00; Ave Louis Casai 50); Zürich (Map pp568-9; ☎ 01 383 65 60; Hegibachstrasse 47)

USA Bern (Map p555; ☎ 031 357 70 11; http://bern .usembassy.gov; Sulgeneckstrasse 19); Geneva (Map p539; ☎ 022 840 51 60; Rue François Versonnex 7); Zürich (Map pp568-9; ☎ 043 499 29 60; Dufourstrasse 101)

FESTIVALS & EVENTS

More events that we could possibly list happen; check www.switzerland.com for a complete listing.

February

Fasnacht A lively spring carnival of wild parties and parades is celebrated countrywide, but with particular enthusiasm in Basel and Lucerne.

March

Combats de Reines March to October, the lower Valais stages traditional cow fights known as the Combats de Reines.

April

Landsgemeinde On the last Sunday in April, the people of Appenzell gather in the main square to take part in a unique open-air parliament.

July

Montreux Jazz Festival Big-name rock/jazz acts hit town for this famous festival (www.montreuxjazz.com) held during the first two weeks of July.

August

National Day On 1 August, celebrations and fireworks mark the country's National Day.

Street Parade (www.streetparade.ch) Zürich lets its hair down in the second week of August with an enormous techno parade with 30 lovemobiles and more than half a million excited ravers.

October

Vintage Festivals Down a couple in wine-growing regions such as Neuchâtel and Lugano in early October.

November

Onion Market Bern takes on a carnival atmosphere for a unique market day held on the fourth Monday of November.

December

L'Escalade (www.escalade.ch) This historical festival held in Geneva on 11 December celebrates deliverance from would-be conquerors.

GAY & LESBIAN TRAVELLERS

Attitudes toward homosexuality are reasonably tolerant in Switzerland and the age of consent is 16. Zürich and Geneva have particularly lively gay scenes.

Online listing guides:

Cruiser magazine (www.cruiser.ch)
Pink Cross (www.pinkcross.ch)

HOLIDAYS

New Year's Day 1 January
Easter March/April; Good Friday, Easter Sunday and Monday
Ascension Day 40th day after Easter
Whit Sunday & Monday 7th week after Easter
National Day 1 August
Christmas Day 25 December
St Stephen's Day 26 December

INTERNET RESOURCES

Switzerland has a strong presence on the internet, with most tourist-related businesses having their own website; a good place to start is **Switzerland Tourism** (www.myswitzerland.com), with many useful links. Tune into the latest beat on **Glocals** (www.glocals.com), Switzerland's savviest urbanites tell you where the party is!

LANGUAGE

Located in the corner of Europe where Germany, France and Italy meet, Switzerland is a linguistic melting pot with three official federal languages: German (spoken by 64% of the population), French (19%) and Italian (8%). Swiss 'German' speakers write standard or 'high' German, but speak their own language: Schwyzertütsch has no official written form and is mostly unintelligible to outsiders.

A fourth language, Romansch, is spoken by less than 1% of the population, mainly in the canton of Graubünden. Derived from Latin, it's a linguistic relic that has survived in the isolation of mountain valleys. Romansch was recognised as a national language by referendum in 1938 and given federal protection in 1996.

English-speakers will have few problems being understood in the German-speaking parts. However, it is simple courtesy to greet people with the Swiss-German *grüezi* and to inquire *Sprechen Sie Englisch?* (Do you speak English?) before launching into English.

In French Switzerland you shouldn't have too many problems either, unlike in Italian-speaking Switzerland, where few speak anything other than Italian and a some French and/or German.

MONEY

Swiss francs are divided into 100 centimes (*Rappen* in German-speaking Switzerland). There are notes for 10, 20, 50, 100, 200 and 1000 francs, and coins for five, 10, 20 and 50 centimes, as well as for one, two and five francs.

All major travellers cheques and credit cards are accepted. Nearly all train stations have currency-exchange facilities open daily and ATMs are everywhere.

There's no need to tip in Switzerland, unless you feel the service was superlative. Tips are included in meal prices.

POST

Postcards and letters sent to Europe cost Sfr1.30/1.20 priority/economy; to elsewhere they cost Sfr1.80/1.40.

Post office opening times vary. Typically they open 7.30am to noon and 2pm to 6.30pm Monday to Friday and until 11am Saturday.

TELEPHONE

Area codes do not exist in Switzerland or Liechtenstein. Although the numbers for a particular city or town share the same three-digit prefix (for example Bern 031, Geneva 022), numbers always must be dialled in full, even when calling from next door – literally.

Mobile phone numbers start with the code 079. To find a phone number in Switzerland check the phone book – online at http://tel.local.ch/en; dial ☎ 1812 (connection charge 80c plus 10c a minute) to speak to a machine; or ☎ 1811 (connection charge Sfr1.50, Sfr0.70 for the first minute and Sfr0.22 per minute thereafter) for a real person; the latter also finds international telephone numbers.

National telephone provider **Swisscom** (http://fr.swisscom.ch) operates the world's densest network of public phone booths! Minimum charge for a call is Sfr0.50 and phones take Swiss franc or euro coins, and phonecards, sold at post offices, newsagencies etc. Many booths also accept major credit cards.

The normal/cheap tariff for international dialling to fixed-line phones is Sfr0.12/0.10

SWITZERLAND

LANGUAGE AREAS

- Romansch
- German
- French
- Italian

Basel · Zürich
☉ Bern · Lucerne · Chur
Lausanne · St Moritz
Geneva · Bellinzona

EMERGENCY NUMBERS

- Ambulance ☎ 144
- Fire ☎ 118
- Motoring breakdown assistance ☎ 140
- Police ☎ 117
- Swiss Mountain Rescue ☎ 1414

---

per minute for several countries, including Australia, Britain, Canada, New Zealand and the USA; and Sfr0.25/0.20 to countries including Ireland, Japan and the Netherlands.

Save money by buying a prepaid Swisscom card worth Sfr10, Sfr20, Sfr50 and Sfr100. Or look for prepaid cards from rival operators such as **Mobile Zone** (www.mobilezone .ch, in German, French & Italian).

Prepaid local SIM cards (Sfr30 to Sfr100) are available from the three network operators: **Orange** (www.orange.ch), **Sunrise** (www.sunrise .ch) and **Swisscom Mobile** (www.swisscom-mobile.ch). You'll need your passport when you buy.

TOURIST INFORMATION
Make the Swiss tourist board **Switzerland Tourism** (www.myswitzerland.com) your first port of call. Local tourist offices are extremely helpful and have reams of literature to give out, including maps (nearly always free).

VISAS
For up-to-date details on visa requirements, go to the **Swiss Federal Office for Migration** (www .eda.admin.ch) and click 'Services'.

Visas are not required for passport holders from the UK, EU, Ireland, the USA, Canada, Australia, New Zealand, South Africa, Norway and Iceland; see p601 for more.

TRANSPORT IN SWITZERLAND

GETTING THERE & AWAY
Air
The main international airports are **Zürich airport** (ZRH; ☎ 043 816 22 11; flight information by SMS ☎ send message ZRH plus flight number to 9292; www.zurich-airport.com) and **Geneva International airport** (GVA; ☎ 0900 57 15 00; www.gva.ch), and increasingly France-based **EuroAirport** (MLH or

BSL; ☎ +33 3 89 90 31 11; www.euroairport.com), serving Basel (as well as Mulhouse in France and Freiburg, Germany).

More than 100 scheduled airlines fly to/from Switzerland, including:

Air France (AF; ☎ 044 439 18 18; www.airfrance.com)
Alitalia (AZ; ☎ 044 828 45 40; www.alitalia.com)
American Airlines (AA; ☎ 044 654 52 56; www .aa.com)
Austrian Airlines (OS; ☎ 044 286 80 80; www .austrianairlines.com)
British Airways (BA; ☎ 0848 845 845; www.ba.com)
Continental Airlines (CO; ☎ 044 800 91 12; www .continental.com)
Lufthansa (LH; ☎ 0900 900922; www.lufthansa.com)
Singapore Airlines (SQ; ☎ 0900 88 18 18; www .singaporeair.com)
Swiss International Air Lines (LX; ☎ 0848 852 000; www.swiss.com) Switzerland's national carrier, commonly known as Swiss Air.
Thai Airways International (TG; ☎ 044 215 65 00; www.thaiairways.com)
United Airlines (UA; ☎ 044 212 47 17; www.ual.com)

In addition loads of budget operators fly in and out of Switzerland:

Air Berlin (AB; www.airberlin.com)
Air Transat (TS; www.airtransat.com)
Atlas Blue (8A; www.atlas-blue.com)
Baboo (F7; www.flybaboo.com)
bmibaby (WW; www.bmibaby.com)
easyJet (U2; www.easyjet.com)
Flybe (BE; www.flybe.com)
Flyglobespan (Y2; www.flyglobespan.com)
germanwings (4U; www.germanwings.com)
Helvetic (2L; www.helvetic.com)
Jet2.com (LS; www.jet2.com)
Ryanair (FR; www.ryanair.com)
Transavia.com (HV; www.transavia.com)

Boat
Switzerland can be reached by steamer from several lakes. From Germany, arrive via Lake Constance (Switzerland ☎ 071 466 78 88; www.sbsag .ch; Austria ☎ 05574 42868; www.bodenseeschifffahrt.at; Germany ☎ 07531 3640 389; www.bsb-online.com); from Italy via Lago Maggiore (☎ 091 751 61 40; www .navigazionelaghi.it); and from France along Lake Geneva (☎ 0848 811 848; www.cgn.ch).

Land
CAR & MOTORCYCLE
Roads into Switzerland are good despite the difficulty of the terrain, but special care is needed to negotiate mountain passes.

Upon entering Switzerland you will need to decide whether you wish to use the motorways: there is a one-off charge of Sfr40 payable in cash, including euros, at the border or, better still, in advance through Switzerland Tourism or a motoring organisation. The sticker (*vignette* in French and German, *contrassegno* in Italian) you receive is valid for a year and must be stuck on the windscreen. For more details, see www.vignette.ch.

Some Alpine tunnels incur additional tolls.

TRAIN

Located in the heart of Europe, Switzerland is a hub of train connections to the rest of the Continent. Zürich is the busiest international terminus, with two direct day trains and one night train to Vienna (seat/six-bed couchette Sfr123/148, 9½ hours); separate women-only compartments can be booked on overnight trains.

There are several trains daily from Paris to several cities including Geneva (€77, 3½ hours), Lausanne (€92 to €120, 3½ to four hours), Bern (€106 to €132, 4½ hours) and Basel (€91, 3¾ hours). Most connections from Germany, including from Frankfurt and Berlin, pass though Zürich or Basel.

Trains between Switzerland and Italy are operated by **Cisalpino** (CIS; ☎ 0900 300 300; www .cisalpino.com). Eurail and Interail passes are valid, and Swiss Pass holders get 20% discount. Nearly all connections to/from Italy pass through Milan before branching off to Zürich (Sfr97, 3¾ hour), Lucerne (Sfr97, 3½ hour), Bern (Sfr87.80, 3½ hour) or Lausanne (Sfr84, 3¾ hour).

GETTING AROUND
Air

Swiss International Air Lines (www.swiss.com) serves the major hubs of EuroAirport (Basel), Geneva and Zürich airports, with return fares fluctuating wildly in price – anything from Sfr70 to Sfr300; and Swiss nofrills carrier **Fly Baboo** (www.flybaboo.com) flies Geneva–Lugano.

Bicycle

You can hire bikes from most train stations with **Rent-a-Bike** (☎ 041 925 11 70; www.rent-a-bike .ch, in French & German; per day Sfr33) and return to any station with a rental office. Bikes can be transported on most trains; station-rented bikes travel free (maximum five bikes per train), otherwise you need a bike pass (one day Sfr15, with Swiss travel pass Sfr10). Bern, Geneva and Zürich offer free bike loans from their train stations.

Local tourist offices often have good cycling information.

Bus

Yellow postal buses are a supplement to the rail network, following postal routes and linking towns to the more inaccessible regions in the mountains. In all, routes cover some 8000km of terrain. Services are regular, and departures tie in with train arrivals. Postbus stations are next to train stations and offer destination and timetable information.

Car

The **Swiss Touring Club** (Touring Club der Schweiz; ☎ 022 417 24 24; www.tcs.ch), Switzerland's largest motoring organisation, is affiliated with the AA in Britain and has reciprocal agreements with motoring organisations worldwide.

You do not need an International Driving Permit to operate a vehicle in Switzerland. A licence from your home country is sufficient. There are numerous petrol stations and garages throughout Switzerland if you break down.

For the best deals on car hire, pre-book; particularly competitive rates are often found on **Auto Europe** (www.autoeurope.com).

When driving in Switzerland, be prepared for winding roads, high passes and long tunnels. Normal speed limits are 50km/h in towns, 120km/h on motorways, 100km/h on semimotorways (designated by roadside rectangular pictograms showing a white car on a green background) and 80km/h on other roads. Mountain roads are well-maintained but you should stay in low gear whenever possible and remember that ascending traffic has the right of way over descending traffic, and postbuses always have right of way. Snow chains are recommended during winter. Use dipped lights in *all* road tunnels. Some minor Alpine passes are closed from November to May – check with the local tourist offices before setting off.

Switzerland is tough on drink-driving; if your blood alcohol level is over 0.05% you face a large fine or imprisonment.

SWITZERLAND

PASSES & DISCOUNTS

Swiss public transport is an efficient, fully integrated and comprehensive system, which incorporates trains, buses, boats and funiculars. Convenient discount passes make the system even more appealing – on extensive travel within Switzerland the following national travel passes generally offer betters savings than Eurail or Inter Rail passes (p615). Find comprehensive information on all of them at http://traintickets.myswitzerland.com.

The **Swiss Pass** (www.swisstravelsystem.ch) is the best deal for big travellers, allowing unlimited travel on almost every train, boat and bus service in the country, and on trams and buses in 38 towns. Reductions of 50% apply on funiculars, cable cars and private railways, such as Jungfrau Railways. These passes are available for four days (Sfr260), eight days (Sfr376), 15 days (Sfr455), 22 days (Sfr525) and one month (Sfr578); prices are for 2nd-class tickets. If you are under 26, buy the **Swiss Youth Pass** equivalent, 25% cheaper in each instance. The **Swiss Flexi Pass** allows free, unlimited trips for three to six days within a month and costs Sfr249 to Sfr397 (2nd class). With either pass, two people travelling together get 15% off. Passes also allow you free admission to all Swiss museums, making them an even better bargain.

The **Swiss Card** allows a free return journey from your arrival point to any destination in Switzerland, 50% off rail, boat and bus excursions, and reductions on mountain railways. It costs Sfr182 (2nd class) or Sfr255 (1st class) and it is valid for a month. The **Half-Fare Card** is a similar deal, minus the free return trip. It costs Sfr99 for one month.

The **Family Card** gives free travel for children aged under 16 if they're accompanied by a parent and is available free to pass purchasers.

All these passes are best purchased online before arrival in Switzerland at www.swisstravelsystem.com or in the UK from the **Swiss Travel Centre** (☎ 0207 420 49 00; 30 Bedford St, London WC2E 9ED). In Switzerland larger train-station offices sell travel passes.

Train

The Swiss rail network consists of a combination of state-run and private lines, and covers 5000km. Trains are clean, reliable and frequent, and are as fast as the terrain will allow. Prices are high, and if you plan on taking more than one or two train trips it's best to purchase a travel pass (see above). All fares quoted in this chapter are for 2nd class; 1st-class fares are about 65% higher. All major stations are connected by hourly departures, but services stop from around midnight to 6am.

Most train stations offer luggage storage at a counter (around Sfr5 per piece) or in 24-hour lockers (Sfr3 to Sfr10), and have excellent information counters. Train schedules are revised yearly; double-check details before travelling either online with **Swiss Federal Railways** (www.rail.ch, www.sbb.ch/en), abbreviated to SBB/CFF/FFS in German/French/Italian. Or call its **Rail Service** (☎ 0900 300 300, per min Sfr1.19).

Regional Directory

CONTENTS

In addition to the country-specific information included at the end of each of the country chapters, we present you with this Regional Directory, chock-full of useful information about central Europe as a whole and sage advice for travellers to the region. This chapter should satisfy many of your questions or doubts as you go about planning your trip.

ACCOMMODATION

All of the accommodation listings in this book are presented according to price range, from budget to midrange listings and then top-end reviews. The cheapest places in which to rest your travel-weary head throughout the region are camping grounds, followed by hostels, university accommodation and private rooms. Guest houses, pensions and inns can also be good value.

Accommodation can be hard to find in popular tourist destinations and during peak holiday periods; it's advisable to book ahead in those cases where possible. If you arrive in a country by air, there is often an accommodation-booking desk at the airport, although it rarely covers the cheapest layer of hotels. Tourist offices often have extensive accommodation lists, and a few will help you book (sometimes for a small fee). Agencies offering private rooms and apartments can be good value; staying with a local family doesn't always mean that you'll lack privacy, but you'll probably have less freedom than in a hotel.

All rooms in this book come with a private bathroom unless otherwise stated, and all accommodation is quoted at high-season rates.

Camping

Camping is immensely popular and provides the cheapest accommodation across the region. It's particularly well catered for in Germany and Austria, slightly less so in the eastern countries. There's usually a charge per tent or site, per person and per vehicle. In the countries in the West, there are well-maintained areas at national parks and reserves for pitching a tent, and some grounds offer bungalows or wooden cabins. In the East, cabins are the norm, and local people often think of them when they hear the word 'camping'; these small bungalows cost double or triple the cost of pitching a tent on grounds that have minimal services.

BOOK YOUR STAY ONLINE

For more accommodation reviews and recommendations by Lonely Planet authors, check out the online booking service at www.lonelyplanet.com/hotels. You'll find the true, insider low-down on the best places to stay. Reviews are thorough and independent. Best of all, you can book online.

In large cities, most camping grounds will be some distance from the centre. For this reason, camping is most popular with people who have their own transport. If you're on foot, the money you save by camping can quickly be eaten up by the cost of commuting to/from a town centre. You may also need a tent, sleeping bag and cooking equipment.

It is, to all intents and purposes, illegal to camp anywhere but in designated areas or, with permission, on private property. Camping grounds may be open from April to October, from May to September, or perhaps only from June to August, when they are usually filled to capacity. A few private camping grounds are open year-round.

Farmhouses

Village or agrotourism (staying at a farmhouse) offers a distinctly local experience. It's like staying in a family's private room, except that the participating farms are in picturesque rural areas and some work may or may not be expected. In return, you might get fresh milk straight from the cow. Activities such as horse riding, kayaking, skiing and cycling are usually nearby, but reaching these remote outposts almost always requires having your own transport.

European Centre for Eco Agro Tourism (www.eceat .org) is a network of more than 1300 small-scale lodges and ecofriendly farms. **Country Holidays in Europe** (www.eurogites.org) also lists lodging options. You work a bit more for your supper with **World Wide Opportunities on Organic Farms** (www.wwoof.org), which facilitates farming work-stay opportunities in Austria, Germany, Switzerland and the Czech Republic. In Hungary check out the **Centre for Rural Tourism** (www.falutur.hu); in Poland the name to know is the **Federation for Village Tourism** (www.agroturystyka.pl).

Guest Houses & Pensions

Small private pensions (guest houses) are common in all parts of central Europe. Priced somewhere between hotels and private rooms, pensions typically have less than a dozen rooms. There's sometimes a small restaurant or bar on the premises, or you may be offered some sort of breakfast (for a fee, or included). You'll get much more personal service at a pension than you would at a hotel. Although the majority of pensions are simple affairs, there are more-expensive ones where you'll find saunas and other luxuries.

Homestays & Private Rooms

Renting a room in a private home is becoming less and less common regionwide, and you'll find fewer opportunities in the western countries of central Europe than in the eastern ones. Tourist offices usually have lists of available options, and travel agencies may book accommodation in local homes. You might also be approached at train and bus stations with offers of a room. Conditions vary greatly – try to see photos first or ask to see the place before you agree. Ask questions. Every so often you may get a host that rations toilet paper or wakes you super early to get you out before the next night-train passengers arrive. (Yes, that happened to us.)

You don't have to go through an intermediary, though. In holiday areas, look for houses with '*zimmer frei*', '*sobe*' or '*szoba kiadó*' displayed outside, advertising the availability of private rooms (these examples are in German, Slovene and Hungarian); just knock on the door and ask if any are available.

Hostels

Hostels offer the cheapest (secure) roof over your head in central Europe, and you do not have to be a youngster to take advantage of them. Many **Hostelling International** (HI; www.hihos tels.com) members and independent hostelries have moved away from an emphasis on 'youth' in an effort to attract a wider clientele. Note that in a few areas (Bavaria in Germany, for example), the strict maximum age for anyone, except group leaders or parents accompanying a child, may be 26. HI-affiliated hostels may cost a few extra euros a night if you're not a member; this extra charge can usually be set against the cost of future membership. Stay enough nights as a nonmember and you automatically become a member.

At a hostel, you get a bed for the night plus the use of communal facilities, which often include internet access and a kitchen where you can prepare your own meals. You are sometimes required to have your own sleeping sheet, but you can usually rent one for a small fee if required. Hostels are great places to meet fellow travellers and to crash for the night inexpensively.

Hostels vary widely in character, but the growing number of travellers and the in-

---

ROLL THE DICE, GET A ROOM

When maximising quality and minimising price is your main concern, consolidator websites such as **Hotwire** (www.hotwire.com) and **Priceline** (www.priceline.com) are an excellent gamble to take. They don't let you see the property name before you pay, but you can choose the neighbourhood, star level and amenities before you either bid or buy at up to 50% off the advertised rate. Want to splash out? Bid on a chichi resort at **Luxury Link** (www.luxurylink.com); some are a 'mystery' but quite a few of the hotels are named and described (with gorgeous photos to ogle).

---

creased competition, have prompted many to improve their facilities and cut back on rules and regulations. Increasingly, curfews and lock-outs are disappearing (with, unfortunately, some notable exceptions such as the official Polskie Towarzystwo Schronisk Młodzieżowych [PTSM] hostels in Poland, which shut their doors between 10pm and 5am). 'Wardens' with sergeant-major mentalities are, thankfully, an endangered species. Smaller dorms, with just four to six beds, are in favour and many places also provide single and double rooms.

Hotels

Categorisation varies from country to country and the hotels recommended in this book cater to every budget. Make sure to ask about discounts, which are often available for groups or for longer stays. If you think a hotel room is too expensive, ask if there's anything cheaper; often hotel owners may try to steer you into more expensive rooms. Cheaper rooms, with a washbasin in-room and toilet and shower down the hall, may be available. In the eastern countries in particular, hotel owners may be open to a little bargaining if times are slack.

Ask if breakfast is included in the price of a room; it may be extra – and mandatory. The higher the room price the more likely you'll get hot eggs and sausage instead of bread and jam in the morning.

More and more nonsmoking-only hotels and guest houses are opening up across the region. That said, the definition of 'nonsmoking room' in some hotels, particularly in Poland

and Hungary, can vary. Some older rooms designated as nonsmoking appear to have been so designated only the previous day – a smell may remain, and ashtrays might be provided.

Rental Accommodation

Apartment rental is an increasingly popular option in central Europe, particularly in the eastern part of the region. It may make sense if you're travelling with a family or a group of up to four persons, or planning to stay in one place for a week or longer. They are equipped with at least a kitchenette, which will save on the dining bill and allow you to peruse the neighbourhood markets and shops, and so eat like the locals do. Apartments can be rented from about €40 to €150 per day and can usually accommodate from two to four or five persons. Corporate apartments are the more upscale, with laundry facilities, parking, daily cleaning services and even a concierge. Internet access is not widely available in conjunction with rentals.

Vacation Rental By Owner (www.vrbo.com) and **Sublet.com** (www.sublet.com) are two international websites that often have good options in the region. Check the individual country chapters for destination-specific options. Also note that individual city websites sometimes list rentals under accommodation options.

University Accommodation

Some universities rent out space in student halls in July and August. Accommodation will sometimes be in single rooms but more commonly in doubles or triples, and cooking facilities may be available. Toilets and showers may or may not be shared. Inquire directly at local colleges or universities, at student information services or at local tourist offices.

ACTIVITIES

While the cities of central Europe offer nonstop entertainment, it's in the region's forests, on its lakes and rivers and atop its mountains where you'll get the biggest thrills – and lungfuls of fresh air. **Backroads** (www.backroads.com) is an ecosensitive tour company that organises a wide range of biking, hiking, multisport, single and multicountry trips across most of central Europe. See p33 for more destination suggestions.

Birdwatching

The countries of central Europe may not be the world's premier destination for spotting our feathered friends but there are good birding sites, in Hungary especially. Look for the endangered great bustard, Europe's largest bird, in Kiskunsági Nemzeti Park.

Budapest-based British author Gerard Gorman runs birdwatching tours in the Czech Republic, Slovakia, Slovenia, Poland and Hungary through his company **Probirder** (www.probirder.com). His books *Central and Eastern European Wildlife* and *Birding in Eastern Europe* are good resources. **Ecotours** (www.ecotours.hu) leads guided birding adventures in Hungary, Austria, Slovenia, Slovakia and Poland.

Canoeing, Kayaking & Rafting

Some of the region's best places for paddling include the Bavarian Alps in Germany, Dunajec River (p410) and the Great Masurian Lakes (p439) in Poland, Lake Balaton region (p336) in Hungary, Soča River (p515) in Slovenia, the Jura (p552) in Switzerland, and Vltava River (p137) in the Czech Republic.

Cycling

Cycling allows you to get up close to the scenery and the local people, keeping you fit in the process. It's a good way to get around many cities and towns and to see remote corners of a country you wouldn't ordinarily get to. In the mountainous regions it can be heavy going, but this is offset by the dense concentration of things to see. Particularly challenging – and rewarding – are the upper reaches of the Danube in southern Germany, and anywhere in the Alps (for those fit enough). Physical fitness is not a major prerequisite for cycling on the plains of eastern Hungary (they're flatter than French crêpes) but the persistent wind might slow you down. Other popular holiday cycling areas include the Danube Bend in Hungary and Slovenia's Karst region.

Look under the Getting Around sections in each country chapter for more specifics on riding and renting bicycles. See p609 for details on bringing a bike by air. Most long-distance bus companies transport bicycles. In the country chapters of this guide you'll find places listed where you can hire a bike.

There are travel agencies or sporting organisations that organise bicycle trips for single and multiple countries across central Europe.

A good bet is to ask at a local cycling club. **Backroads** (www.backroads.com) has itineraries for Slovenia, across Poland–Hungary–Slovakia, and through the Czech Republic and Austria. **Top Bicycle** (www.topbicycle.com) runs multicountry cycle tours through combinations of Germany, Austria, the Czech Republic, Poland, Slovakia and Hungary.

Hiking

Keen hikers can spend a lifetime exploring central Europe's many exciting trails. Probably the most spectacular are to be found in the mountains in Switzerland, Austria and Slovenia. The Alps are criss-crossed with clearly marked trails and offer rewarding challenges for everyone from beginners to experts; food and accommodation are available along the way, in season. There's also excellent hiking in the eastern part of the region, with well-maintained trails traversing forests, mountains and numerous national parks, especially in Slovakia.

Public transport will often take you to the trailheads. Hikers can find dorm accommodation and basic meals in chalets or mountain huts in almost all of these places. The best months for hiking are from June to September, especially late August and early September when rains have abated and summer crowds have largely disappeared.

Mountain paths have direction indicators and often markers indicating their level of difficulty. Those with a red-white-red marker mean you need sturdy hiking boots and a pole; a blue-white-blue marker indicates the need for mountaineering equipment.

UK-based **Ramblers Holidays** (www.ramblersholidays.co.uk) organises single-country hiking tours in Germany, Austria, Switzerland, Poland and Hungary.

Particularly recommended hiking destinations include Berchtesgaden National Park (p227) in Germany, the Valais region (p554) in Switzerland, Hohe Tauern National Park (p83) in Austria, the Tatra Mountains (p409, p473) in Poland and Slovakia, Mt Triglav (p513) in Slovenia, Malá Fatra National Park (p470) in Slovakia, and the Saxon Switzerland area (p191) in Germany.

Horse Riding

There are many places throughout the region to strap on a saddle and ride through lovely terrain – and then walk with a funny waddle after dismounting. Horse riding is particularly well organised in Hungary (p358), where a local folk saying claims that Hungarians 'were created by God to sit on horseback'. The best centres are at Szilvásvárad (p354) and Kecskemét. In Switzerland the riding area of choice is in St Moritz; in Germany head to tiny Sylt and Amrum in the North Frisian Islands. Horse riding is also very popular (and affordable) in the Czech Republic, Poland and Slovenia.

Skiing & Snowboarding

Central Europe is the continent's ski capital. The country chapters in this book are brimming with details on how to get your downhill thrills. The skiing season usually lasts from early December to late March, though at higher altitudes it may extend an extra month either way. Snow conditions can vary greatly from year to year and region to region, but January and February tend to be the best (and busiest) months. For comprehensive reports on ski conditions in Austria, Switzerland and Germany, log into www.onthesnow.com.

Ski resorts in the Swiss Alps offer world-class facilities – no place in the region can compete with the vistas – but they are also the most expensive. If you can afford it, a visit there is a must for any avid skier or fearless snowboarder. Zermatt (p553) and other resorts in the Valais region are among the best on the planet. Expect high prices, too, in the German Alps (p227), though Germany has cheaper (but far less spectacular) options in the Black Forest (p239) and Harz Mountains. Austria is generally slightly cheaper than Germany and Switzerland. A general rule of thumb as far as prices go is that the further east you travel, the less expensive the skiing. Expect to pay a bit less on the Slovenian slopes of the Julian Alps (p514) and, though facilities are limited, lift tickets in the High Tatras (p474) of Slovakia are a comparative give-away. Note that skiing holidays in central Europe often work out to be twice as expensive as a summer holiday of the same length for the same destination.

Thermal Baths

While 'taking the waters' used to be very serious business indeed, recent years have seen the rise of bathing as entertainment (and the proliferation of 'aqua parks'). Sure, some visitors still come for the cure, but for the most part these days bathers are just there to relax. A thermal bath, or spa, may be a hypermod-

ern pool complex with fountains that giggle and spurt, or intimate pools ensconced in a 14th-century Turkish *hammam* (bath house). Facilities usually offer both medical and aesthetic treatments. You can dive into the ritzy German spa town of Baden-Baden (p235), soak in fin de siècle spas of the Czech Republic's Karlovy Vary (Karlsbad; p128) and splash and slide at Slovakia's sprawling green-powered Aquacity in Poprad (p477). Hungary, however, remains the epicentre of spa culture in central Europe. Nearly 300 of its hot springs are used for public bathing – in thermal lakes, open-air pools, indoor spas and private hotel baths. If you're looking for a traditional experience, head to the art nouveau and neobaroque baths in Budapest (p310, p311). For something truly original, floating among water lilies in the thermal lake at Hévíz (p341) is not to be missed. Benefiting your health never felt so good.

BUSINESS HOURS

Central Europe tends to take Saturdays and Sundays as official days off, although only banks and offices are shut. Shops are usually open for at least part of the day on Saturdays, and most restaurants and cafes operate every day of the week.

Banks and post offices generally open from 9am to 5pm Monday to Friday, occasionally with an hour or two off for lunch. They may also be open on Saturday mornings. Local shops stay open until 6pm or 7pm; the megamarts such as Tesco never shut their doors. For more specific details, see the Directory in individual country chapters.

CHILDREN

Central Europe is a great place to bring the young ones along – and keep them interested (and tired) enough to avoid complaints. The region has well-established attractions geared toward children of all ages, particularly the more western countries. In countries such as Switzerland and Austria, it's also easy to find facilities for children in restaurants and hotels. In the more eastern countries of the region, such as Slovakia, finding such services is more of a challenge.

Many car-hire firms in the region have children's safety seats for hire at a small cost, but it is essential that you book them in advance. The same goes for high chairs and cots (cribs); they're standard in many restaurants and hotels but numbers are limited. The choice of baby food, infant formulas, soy and cow's milk, disposable nappies (diapers) and the like is generally good, though this is more true of large cities than smaller ones and especially towns and villages. If your baby or child requires special medicines or food, bring more than you think might be necessary, as availability when needed might be limited, particularly in the eastern countries of the region.

This book mentions places of interest to children (and their parents!) throughout the country chapters. Lonely Planet's *Travel with Children* is an excellent source of information and includes topics ranging from children's health to games that will keep the kids amused.

CLIMATE CHARTS

The climate charts opposite provide a snapshot of central Europe's weather patterns. See p20 for suggestions on when to visit the region.

COURSES

In central Europe you can enrol in courses on anything from language to alternative medicine to organic farming to skiing. Language courses are available to foreigners through universities or private schools. The individual country chapters give pointers on where to start looking for courses. In general, the best sources of detailed information are the cultural institutes maintained by many European countries around the world; failing that, try their national tourist offices or embassies. Student-exchange organisations, student travel agencies and organisations such as the YMCA/YWCA and HI can also help you.

Transitions Abroad (www.transitionsabroad.com) lists study abroad language courses in the Czech Republic, Austria, Germany and Switzerland. **Shaw Guides** (www.shawguides.com) not only lists language courses in some of the central European countries, but is also a clearing house for wine and cooking classes, photography workshops, art courses and writing workshops. You might take a one-week painting course in Slovenia, attend summer school in Poland or retreat to write in Switzerland.

CUSTOMS REGULATIONS

Duty-free goods are no longer sold to those travelling from one EU country to another. For goods that are purchased at airports or on ferries outside the EU, the usual allowances apply for tobacco (200 cigarettes, 50 cigars or 250g of loose tobacco), alcohol (1L of spirits or 2L of liquor with less than 22% alcohol by volume; and 2L of wine) and perfume (50g of perfume and 250ml of eau de toilette).

Do not confuse these allowances with duty-*paid* items (including alcohol and tobacco) bought at normal shops and supermarkets in another EU country. If bought for personal use, the allowances in this case are more than generous: 800 cigarettes, 200 cigars or 1kg of loose tobacco; 10L of spirits (more than 22% alcohol by volume), 20L of fortified wine or aperitif, 90L of wine or 110L of beer; and unlimited quantities of perfume. Unless you cross the border into non-EU countries, you are generally unlikely to be subjected to a search. But a few border or custom points do still exist in the eastern part of central Europe.

DANGERS & ANNOYANCES

Central Europe is as safe – or unsafe – as any other part of the developed world. If you can handle yourself in the big cities of Western Europe, North America or Australia, you'll have little trouble dealing with the less pleasant sides of travel to the region. It's never a bad idea, if possible, to work out a list of places where friends and relatives can contact you. For those planning to go hiking or skiing, it's best to leave plenty of clues as to your planned destination and date, as well as an expected return date or a time, so that people can go looking for you in case you run into trouble in the wild. This is best done at national-park headquarters or at your hotel or resort.

Drugs

Always treat drugs with a great deal of caution. There may be a lot of drugs available in some of the places you'll visit, but that doesn't mean they're legal. Even a little hashish can cause a great deal of trouble in some places.

Don't even think about bringing drugs home with you, either: if you have what energetic customs officials may think are stamps in your passport from 'suspect' places, they may well decide to take a closer look.

Racism

Nonwhite travellers should be aware that in some of these countries there are negative

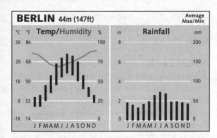

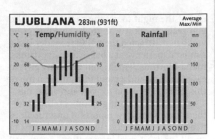

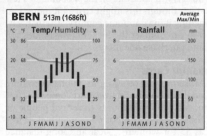

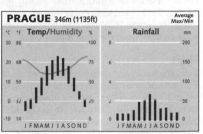

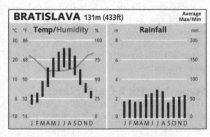

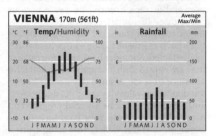

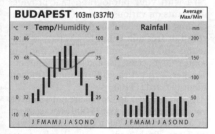

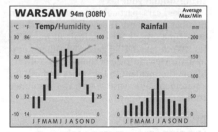

attitudes to immigrants, and that you may be mistaken for one and therefore a target for misguided discontent. Skinheads and neo-Nazis in parts of former East Germany and other areas have sometimes singled out the resident Roma, blacks, Asians and people of Middle Eastern descent as scapegoats for their own problems. In these days of 'War on Terror' alarm, people of African, Middle Eastern or Arab descent should be aware that

some locals may harbour knee-jerk negative feelings towards them.

Scams

Gentlemen, be wary of the attention of uber-gorgeous women who approach you on the street in eastern cities and want you to follow them to a club. The scam may be that the drinks are absurdly priced (€100-plus) and enforcers appear to walk you to the ATM at the end of the night to get the cash to pay. (Did you really think it was your charming good looks that attracted them?) One reader had a similar experience at a bar (expensive drinks, mafia-like musclemen), but no pretty girls to ease the pain, and a good thrashing on top of things. Pay attention to your surroundings.

A word of warning about credit cards: there have been a few reports of unscrupulous people making quick, hi-tech duplicates of credit- or debit-card information. Again, just be alert if your card leaves your possession for longer than you think necessary, and check your charges from the road if possible.

Theft

Petty theft is as common here as elsewhere in Europe and your wariness should extend to other travellers. The most important things to guard are your passport, papers, tickets and money – in that order. (Make copies of all important documents, such as your passport and driver's licence.) Be aware of your belongings in tourist centres; pickpockets target crowded transport and prime attractions such as Prague Castle – anywhere you'll be distracted. Shoulder bags and long camera bags are easy to slash and grab before you have a chance to react. A small day pack is better, but don't keep valuables in the outside pockets and watch your rear. Be especially vigilant on overnight trains; keep your bags locked and avoid those travel wallets that hang from a string around your neck.

Parked cars, particularly cars with foreign number plates and/or rental-agency stickers, are prime targets for criminals in most cities. Avoid leaving luggage and other items in plain view. In case of theft or loss, always report the incident to the police and ask for a statement; otherwise, your travel-insurance company won't pay.

DISCOUNT CARDS
Camping Card International

The **Camping Card International** (CCI; www.camp ingcardinternational.com) is a camping-ground ID valid for a year that can be used instead of a passport when checking into camping grounds and includes third-party insurance. Affiliated camping grounds will offer a small discount (usually 5% to 10%) if you have one. CCIs are issued by automobile associations, camping federations and, sometimes, at camping grounds. The CCI is also useful

as it can sometimes serve as a guarantee so that you don't have to leave your passport at reception.

Hostel Cards

A hostelling card is useful – if not always mandatory – for those staying at hostels. Many hostels in central Europe don't require that you be a hostelling association member, but they often charge less if you have a card. Many hostels will issue one on the spot or after a few stays, though this might cost a bit more than getting it in your home country. Alternatively, you can contact the local **HI** (www.hihostels.com) and purchase one there.

Senior Cards

Museums and other sights, public swimming pools and spas, and transport companies frequently offer discounts to retired people or those aged over 60 or 65 (sometimes as low as 55 for women). Local and long-distance travel is often cheaper as well. It's best to bring proof of age. European residents older than 60 are eligible for the Railplus Card, which provides discounts of around 25% for international train travel. Check at your domestic train station.

Student, Youth & Teacher Cards

The most useful of the available student/youth discount cards is the **International Student Identity Card** (ISIC; www.istc.org), a plastic ID-style card with your photograph that provides discounts on various forms of transport (including air travel and local public transport), cheap or free admission to a variety of museums and sights, and inexpensive meals in some student cafeterias and some restaurants. Teachers can get the International Teachers Identity Card (ITIC).

If you're under age 26 but are not a student, you can apply for a **Euro26 Card** (www.euro26.org) or an **International Youth Travel Card** (IYTC; www .myisic.com). Both cards give similar discounts and benefits as an ISIC; they are issued by student unions, hostelling organisations, youth-oriented travel agencies and online.

ELECTRICITY

All the countries of central Europe run on 220V, 50Hz AC. Check the voltage and cycle (usually 50Hz) used in your home country. Most appliances that are set up for 220V will handle 240V quite happily without modifications (and vice versa); the same goes for 110V and 125V combinations. It's preferable to adjust your appliance to the exact voltage if you can (modern battery chargers and computer power supplies will do this automatically). Don't mix 110/125V with 220/240V without a transformer, which will be built in if the appliance can, in fact, be adjusted.

Plugs throughout central Europe are the standard round two-pin variety, sometimes called the 'europlug'. If your plugs are of a different design, you'll need a simple adaptor.

EMBASSIES & CONSULATES

See the individual country chapters for the addresses of embassies and consulates in central Europe.

It's important to realise what your embassy can and cannot do to help you if you get into trouble while abroad. Generally speaking, it won't be much help in emergencies if the trouble you're in is remotely your own fault. Remember that you are bound by the laws of the country you are visiting. In genuine emergencies you might get some assistance, but only if other channels have been exhausted. For example, if you need to get home urgently, a free ticket home is exceedingly unlikely – the embassy would expect you to have insurance. If you have all your money and documents stolen, it might assist with getting a new passport, but a loan for onward travel is almost always out of the question.

GAY & LESBIAN TRAVELLERS

Homosexual activities are legal in every country covered by this book. Local attitudes towards public displays of same-sex affection vary widely among them, and between large, urban centres and smaller, rural areas. Wherever possible this guide lists in individual country Directory sections the contact addresses and websites of gay and lesbian organisations, as well as reviews of gay and lesbian venues in the Entertainment listings of major cities. While Berlin, Munich and Vienna have vibrant and active gay scenes, it's a different story in the eastern countries of the region: most capital cities have small gay scenes centred on one or two bars or clubs. Outside large population centres in the East, gay and lesbian venues are almost nonexistent.

Following are a few notable websites with up-to-date information for the European gay and lesbian community:

365Gay (www.365gay.com) A worldwide, daily gay and lesbian newspaper with a round-up of current events and articles.

Gay Journey (www.gayjourney.com) A mishmash of travel-related information including forums, booking engines, travel packages, regional bars and clubs, and write-ups of gay-friendly destinations.

International Gay & Lesbian Travel Association (www.iglta.org) Gay- and lesbian-friendly businesses (including accommodation and services) throughout the world, as well as a current newsletter and travel agency.

Mi Casa Su Casa (www.gayhometrade.com) The international home-exchange network service for gay and lesbian travellers. Membership costs US$75 for five years, and it provides listings for home-swapping vacation rentals around the world.

Spartacus International Gay Guide (www.sparta cusworld.com) A male-only directory of gay entertainment venues in Europe and the rest of the world.

HOLIDAYS

Throughout central Europe, children get the summer months off from school (usually mid-June through August), which is one reason why this is the busiest time to be out and about. There are also usually breaks for Easter and Christmas. See the relevant country's Directory for lists of local public holidays.

INSURANCE

The policies issued by **STA Travel** (www.statravel .com) and other student travel organisations are usually good value. Some policies offer different medical-expense options; the higher ones are chiefly for countries such as the USA that have extremely expensive medical costs. For this region it's best to take out the lower coverage. There is a wide variety of policies available, so check the fine print.

Emergency insurance from companies such as **Travel Guard** (www.travelguard.com) is for those who have coverage at home that does not extend to where they're travelling. More and more airline companies are offering trip-cancellation insurance when you get your tickets.

If you're an EU citizen, the European Health Insurance Card (EHIC) covers you for most medical care. The form is available from health centres. Note the EHIC will not cover you for nonemergencies or emergency repatriation. Citizens from other countries should find out if there is a reciprocal arrangement for free medical care between their country and the countries being visited.

Note that some insurance policies will specifically exclude 'dangerous activities', which can include scuba diving, motorcycling and even hiking. You may prefer a policy that pays doctors or hospitals directly rather than you having to pay on the spot and claim later. If you have to make a claim later, make sure you keep all documentation. Some policies ask you to call back (reverse charges) to a centre in your home country where an immediate assessment of your problem is made. Check that the policy covers ambulances and also an emergency flight home.

For information on car insurance, see p610.

INTERNET ACCESS

Every city and almost any decent-sized town in central Europe has internet access of some sort, though the same can't be said about all rural areas.

Wi-fi (WLAN in Germany) is increasingly becoming available across central Europe, most commonly in cafes, libraries, train stations and, of course, hotels. To find wi-fi hot spots, try sites such as www.jiwire.com. Often you'll find access is through large providers, such as **t-mobile** (www.t-mobile.com), which charge €8 or more per hour.

Some internet cafes may not be cafes at all. Sometimes you'll be limited to a monitor in a dark, smelly room full of teenage boys playing war games. But in the more-developed cities especially, internet cafes can be a social hub and a great way of meeting locals as well as fellow travellers. Make sure you have a web-based email account so that you can send and receive email on the road if you don't have a laptop or other web-enabled device with you.

If you're travelling with a notebook or a hand-held computer, be aware that there's a small chance your modem may not work once you leave your home country. The safest option is to buy a reputable 'global' modem before you leave home, or buy a local PC-card modem if you're spending an extended time in any one country. For more information on travelling with a portable computer, see www.teleadapt.com.

LEGAL MATTERS

Most central European police are friendly and helpful, especially if you have been a victim of a crime. You are required by law to prove your identity if asked by police, so always carry your passport, or an identity card if you're an EU citizen.

The age of consent for heterosexual and homosexual intercourse is generally between 16 and 18 across Europe. You can generally purchase alcohol by age 18. Although you are permitted to drive at 18, you might not be able to hire a car until you reach 25 years of age.

MAPS

Buying a good regional map will make things easier if you are planning a trip across more than a couple of countries. The *Central Europe* (1:2,000,000) map from Austrian publisher Freytag & Berndt is widely available. A larger atlas can be invaluable when driving or cycling.

In general, buying city and hiking maps in advance is unnecessary, as nearly all large towns produce them locally for a fraction of the price you'll pay at home. Nevertheless, maps of central European capitals and other major towns are widely available from travel bookshops if you want to do particularly detailed planning in advance.

MEDIA

The *International Herald Tribune* is widely available in larger towns, and most capitals have their own English-language weekly paper.

The English-language radio stations BBC World Service and Voice of America (VOA) are rebroadcast on local AM or FM radio stations. CNN International and Eurosport are found on cable and satellite TV systems across central Europe.

MONEY

At the time of publication, the countries in central Europe using the euro as their currency are Austria, Germany, Slovenia and Slovakia. The other countries use their own currencies, which are easily convertible, stable and reliable. Major international currencies such as the euro and the US dollar are easy to exchange. Hungary, Poland and the Czech Republic are expected to convert to the euro in years to come. A useful internet site for calculating exchange rates is www.xe.com/ucc.

ATMs & Credit Cards

Due to the onslaught of ATMs that accept most credit and cash cards, the hassle of trying to change travellers cheques at the weekend and dealing with rip-off *bureaux de changes* are a thing of the past throughout central Europe. If you're going to a small village, you'll want to find a bank machine before you get there.

Visa and MasterCard remain the most popular credit cards in the region, followed by Amex, which has offices in every country. While credit cards are accepted at an ever-growing number of places, in eastern countries you may need to announce that you intend to pay by card before requesting the cheque. Separate systems for processing the bill are used for cash and charge, and once the bill arrives, it may be too late to change.

Cash

This is, of course, the easiest way to carry money, but obviously not the most secure. The two most favoured currencies throughout the region are the euro and the US dollar. It is, however, easy to exchange virtually any other major world currency in big cities, though the exchange rates may be poor.

Tipping

In western central Europe, a tip of 10% to 15% is widely expected in restaurants, bars, taxis and hotels (porters etc). Increasingly it is included on the bill as an obligatory gratuity in restaurants – when this is the case, don't tip twice. In the eastern part of the region, except in places frequented by tourists, it is customary to round up the bill or leave about 10%. If, however, 'rounding up' means you're only giving honest waiters a pittance, consider adding a few more coins to keep all happy.

Travellers Cheques

The main advantage of carrying travellers cheques rather than cash is the protection they offer from theft, though they have lost their once enormous popularity as more and more travellers withdraw cash through ATMs as they go along. Banks usually charge from 1% to 2% commission to change travellers cheques. Amex and Thomas Cook representatives cash their own travellers cheques without commission, but both give rather poor rates of exchange. If you're changing more than US$20, you're usually better off going to a bank and paying the standard commission to change the cheques there.

Western Union

If all goes horribly wrong – your money, travellers cheques and credit cards are all stolen – then don't despair. As long as you know the phone number of an accommodating friend or relative back home, they will be able to get money wired to you anywhere in central Europe via **Western Union** (www.westernunion.com). We do not even bother listing Western Union representatives in this guide, as there are literally thousands of them. Just look for the distinctive yellow and black sign. The sender will be given a code that they then communicate to you and you take to the nearest office, along with your passport, to receive your cash.

PHOTOGRAPHY & VIDEO

For digital camera users, if you don't have your laptop to download photos onto regularly, bring as much memory as you can with you. Memory cards and sticks are often expensive to buy, especially when you need to get one quickly. Otherwise, many of the internet cafes listed throughout this book will be able to download your photos and burn them onto a CD for a small fee. Just to be on the safe side, bring along your USB cable and your camera's driver on a CD – unless the internet cafe runs XP on its computers (or uses Macs), they will probably need to download your camera's driver onto their system before being able to download your masterpieces.

If you're still shooting with 35mm film, know that they can safely pass through most airport X-Ray machines, supposedly up to at least 16 times (so says Kodak) without any loss of quality. Film and camera equipment are available everywhere in central Europe, but obviously shops in larger cities and towns have a wider selection. Avoid buying film at tourist sites; it may have been stored badly (by a window), or for a long time (perhaps even having reached its use-by date), and it will certainly be expensive.

Lonely Planet's *Travel Photography*, by Richard I'Anson, is a useful guide for people who want to get their shots just right.

Video-camera users should make sure they keep their batteries charged and have the correct charger, plugs and European transformer, if necessary. In most countries in central Europe it is possible to obtain video cartridges easily in large towns and cities, but make sure you buy one with the correct operating system. Like Australia and most of the rest of

Europe, central Europe usually uses the PAL format, which is incompatible with the North American and Japanese NTSC system. It is usually worth buying at least a few cartridges duty-free at the start of your trip. Similarly, if you want to buy prerecorded DVDs or videotapes to play back home, you won't get the picture if the systems (and, in the case of DVDs, the encoded regions) are different.

POST

Postal services can be considered reliable throughout central Europe. See the individual country chapters for details.

Poste restante (having letters sent to you care of local post offices) is still available across the region but is not the most reliable way of receiving letters, and seems rather redundant in the age of email and SIM cards. Express services such as **DHL** (www.dhl.com) or **FedEx** (www.fedex.com) are best for essential deliveries.

You can also have mail sent to you at American Express offices as long as you have an Amex card or are carrying its travellers cheques. When you buy Amex cheques, ask for a booklet listing all its office addresses worldwide. Amex will forward mail for a small fee, but what it won't do is accept parcels, registered letters, notices for registered letters, answer telephone inquiries about mail or hold mail longer than 30 days.

SOLO TRAVELLERS

There are a number of obvious advantages to solo travel: you do exactly what you want to do, see what you want to see and are more likely to meet locals and socialise with people you'd otherwise never speak to. However, it can also be lonely and less fun when things get frustrating. Fortunately, the European backpacking infrastructure is tailored to people travelling alone and hostels are great places to meet others. Indeed, you may find you'll spend a few days here and there with others you've met in hostels and who are heading in your direction and are keen to share the cost of a day trip or two. Most big cities in central Europe also have expat bars for those missing a slice of ersatz home. There are no specific dangers for solo travellers in central Europe, though you might find that you're not at the best table in restaurants as a lone diner. Women travelling solo should also check out the advice, p602.

TELEPHONE

You can ring abroad from almost any phone box in central Europe. Public telephones accepting stored-value phonecards (available from post offices, telephone centres, newsstands and retail outlets) are virtually the norm now; in some countries coin-operated phones are impossible to find. Both domestic rate phonecards and international discount cards are available.

Mobile Phones

Mobile phones have become essential communication devices throughout central Europe, which means you're likely to see a Slovenian farmer chatting on a mobile while leaning on a hayrack, and a granny thumbing a text message to her grandchildren while tottering down a laneway in rural Hungary. If you plan to spend more than a week or so in one country, seriously consider buying a SIM card to slip into your phone (but check with your provider at home before you leave that your handset has not been blocked). SIM cards can cost as little as €10 and can be topped up with cards available at supermarkets and any mobile-phone dealers. Alternatively, if you have roaming, your phone will usually switch automatically over to a local network. This can be expensive if you use the phone a great deal, but can be very useful for ad hoc use on the road. Check with your provider for any possible extra costs associated with receiving calls when in the region.

Phone Codes

International dialling codes and international access codes are given in the Fast Facts boxes at the beginning of each country chapter. Every town with a local area code has it listed directly underneath its heading.

TIME

All the countries covered in this book are on GMT+1 hour. They all employ daylight savings. Clocks are usually put forward an hour on the last Sunday in March. They are set back one hour on the last Sunday in October.

TOURIST INFORMATION

Tourist information is widely available throughout central Europe, with booths or offices set up in main cities and towns, usually in the tourist city centres but also at airports, train stations and sometimes bus stations. The services offered will differ but most of these places provide details about accommodation and other practical help – for example, basic town maps showing where to find toilets and internet cafes (among the most frequently asked questions!).

In each country chapter, tourist contacts are provided under specific city, town and village sections. Following is a list of official country websites that endeavour to provide up-to-date travel information:

Austria (www.austria.info)
Czech Republic (www.czechtourism.com)
Germany (www.cometogermany.com)
Hungary (www.hungary.com)
Liechtenstein (www.tourismus.li)
Poland (www.polandtour.org)
Slovakia (www.slovakia.travel)
Slovenia (www.slovenia.info)
Switzerland (www.myswitzerland.com)

TRAVELLERS WITH DISABILITIES

In the western countries of central Europe, you will find wheelchair ramps a common feature of midrange hotels and certainly of upmarket hotels, as well as most museums and many restaurants and cafes. Trains that accept Eurail passes in Germany and Switzerland are fitted for wheelchair access; these need prebooking but usually at no extra cost. In the eastern countries the lack of a dedicated infrastructure geared towards travellers with disabilities, plus the poorer state of many roads and pavements, make them more challenging destinations. In these countries, services catering to travellers with disabilities are rare, even in hotels.

If you have a physical disability, get in touch with your national support organisation and ask about the countries you plan to visit. These organisations often have complete libraries devoted to travel, and they can put you in touch with travel agents who specialise in tours for the disabled. Other excellent sources of helpful information and travel tips include **Disability World** (www.disabilityworld.com), the **Royal Association for Disability & Rehabilitation** (RADAR; www.radar.org.uk), **Access-Able Travel Source** (www.access-able.com) and the **Society for Accessible Travel & Hospitality** (www.sath.org).

VISAS

Travellers from EU countries, the USA, Canada, New Zealand and Australia need only a valid passport to enter any of the countries covered by this book. Non-EU citizens, however, are usually allowed only a three-month stay within any six-month period. Nationals of some other countries may need a visa in order to enter a specific country. Detailed visa regulations are given under Visas in the Directory section of each country chapter.

All countries in central Europe are part of the Schengen Agreement (though Switzerland and Liechtenstein are not members of the EU). Many – but not all – of the border posts between the countries of the region have disappeared. (The Czech Republic has protested the additional controlling at Austrian and German border posts, which have just moved inland instead of being reduced). Note that the countries comprising the Schengen zone are treated as one collective country in terms of the standard three-month stay.

Your most important travel document is your passport, which should be valid until well after you return home. If it's just about to expire, renew it before you travel. Some countries insist your passport remain valid for a specified period (usually at least three months) beyond the expected date of your departure from that country. In practice, this is rarely checked. Once you start travelling, carry your passport (or a copy of it) at all times and guard it carefully. The hassles created by losing your passport can be considerably reduced if you have a record of its number and issue date or, even better, photocopies of the relevant data pages. A photocopy of your birth certificate can also be useful.

For those who do require visas, it's important to remember that these will have a 'use-by' date, and you'll be refused entry after that period has elapsed. It may not be checked when entering these countries overland, but major problems can arise if it is requested during your stay or on departure and you can't produce a visa that's current.

Consulates sometimes issue visas on the spot, although some levy a 50% to 100% surcharge for 'express service'. If there's a choice between getting a visa in advance and on the border, go for the former option if you have the time. You can either do this in your home country or while on the road. Getting a visa from a neighbouring country, with the help of a travel agent, may spare you headaches and bureaucratic red tape. Also remember that most countries do not issue visas on their borders, or change their mind frequently about it. Carry spare passport photos; you may need from one to four photos every time you apply for a visa.

VOLUNTEERING

Organising a volunteer work placement is a great way to gain a deeper insight into local culture. If you're staying with a family, or working alongside local colleagues, you'll probably learn much more about life here than you would if you were continually on the move through the country. In some instances volunteers are paid a living allowance, sometimes they work for their keep, while other programs require the volunteer to pay. Lonely Planet's *Volunteer: A Traveller's Guide* is an overall introduction to the subject.

As well as searching general work-abroad websites (opposite), check out the **Coordinating Committee for International Voluntary Service** (www.unesco.org/ccivs). It's an umbrella organisation with more than 140 member organisations worldwide, useful if you want to find out about your target country's national volunteer-placement agency. The **International Willing Workers on Organic Farms** (WWOOF; www.wwoof.org) is an association of organisations in the western countries of central Europe. If you join a WWOOF organisation, you can arrange to live and work on a host's organic farm.

WEIGHTS & MEASURES

The metric system is in use throughout central Europe. In Germany, cheese and other food items are often sold per *Pfund* (500g).

WOMEN TRAVELLERS

Women travellers, in general, will find central Europe relatively enlightened and shouldn't often have to invent husbands that will be joining them soon or boyfriends that will be back any minute. Nevertheless, it is always wise to take some basic precautions. Avoid accepting drinks from strangers or consuming too much alcohol if you are out by yourself. Stick to well-lit, well-populated areas if walking on the streets alone after dark. Know where you're going and walk with purpose. In rare instances, a woman alone may receive comments or invitations, but this attention is rarely dangerous and is easily deflected with a shake of the head, a firm 'no' and an about-face walk. These precautions aside, most women will enjoy safe, hassle-free travel throughout the region.

Note that many women in eastern central Europe like to get dolled up, often donning high heels, short skirts and plenty of make-up for a night out. In fact, some clubs require these fancy duds to get past the bouncer.

WORK

European bosses aren't keen on giving jobs to foreigners when unemployment rates are what they are in some areas, particularly in the eastern part of the region. Officially, EU citizens are allowed to work in any other EU country, but the paperwork isn't always straightforward for long-term employment and after three months workers will probably need to apply for a residency permit. Other nationalities require special work permits that can be almost impossible to arrange, especially for temporary work. That doesn't prevent enterprising travellers from occasionally topping up their funds, however, by working in the hotel or restaurant trades at beach or ski resorts or teaching a little English, and they don't always have to do this illegally either.

Teaching English is the easiest way to make some extra cash in the ex-communist countries, but the market is saturated in places such as Prague and Budapest. You'll probably be much more successful in less popular places such as Ljubljana or smaller towns and cities throughout the region. If you do find a temporary job in central Europe, though, the pay is likely to be abysmally low. Do it for the experience – not to earn your fortune – and you won't be disappointed. Other typical tourist jobs (for example washing dishes in Alpine resorts) often come with board and lodging, and you'll probably have a good time partying with other travellers, although the pay often amounts to little more than pocket money.

Students will find that their national student-exchange organisations may be able to arrange temporary work permits to several countries through special programs. Call your local university or college for more information. For more details on working as a foreigner, look under Work in the individual country chapter Directory sections.

If you have a parent or grandparent who was born in an EU country, you may have certain rights you never knew about. Get in touch with that (and your) country's embassy and ask about dual citizenship (some countries may not allow this) and work permits. If you go for citizenship, also ask about any obligations, such as military service and residency.

If you play an instrument or have other artistic talents, you could try working the streets. As every Peruvian pipe player (and his fifth cousin) still knows, busking is fairly common in major central European cities such as Prague, Budapest, Frankfurt and Ljubljana. In most places, however, you are likely to require municipal permits for this sort of thing. It is illegal in some parts of Switzerland and Austria and not always well tolerated in Germany. Talk to other street artists before you start.

Selling goods on the street is generally frowned upon and can be tantamount to vagrancy, apart from at flea markets. It's also a hard way to make money if you're not selling something special. Most countries require permits for this sort of thing.

There are several references and websites that publicise specific positions across central Europe. **Transitions Abroad** (www.transitionsabroad .com) publishes *Work Abroad: The Complete Guide to Finding a Job Overseas* and the *Alternative Travel Directory: The Complete Guide to Studying, Traveling and Living Overseas*, as well as a colour magazine called *Transitions Abroad*. Its website, along with that of **Action Without Borders** (www.idealist.org) and **GoAbroad.com** (www.goabroad.com), lists hundreds of jobs and volunteer opportunities. *Work Your Way Around the World*, by Susan Griffith, gives practical advice, as does *Summer Jobs Abroad*, edited by David Woodworth.

Other, more specific, resources include the following:

Childcare International (www.childint.co.uk) Au pair and nanny jobs tending to little Europeans.

International Cooperative Education (www .icemenlo.com) Jobs for those with Teaching English as a Foreign Language (TEFL) credentials.

Jobs in the Alps (www.jobs-in-the-alps.com) Mainly service jobs like chambermaids, bar staff and porters. Some language skills required.

Season Workers (www.seasonworkers.com) Ski resort work and summer jobs; also has English-teaching jobs.

Transport in Central Europe

GETTING THERE & AWAY

Central Europe is well connected to the rest of the world by air. With intense competition between long-haul and no-frills carriers, there are plenty of tickets available to a variety of gateway cities. The westernmost capitals are likely to be the places where most transoceanic travellers begin their central European journey, but eastern capitals do receive some intercontinental flights. The proliferation of low-cost carriers has made short air hops across the region possible from Western Europe and the UK.

Taking the train (northwards from Turkey or Greece, for example, or eastwards from England, France or Spain) is a more invigorating and scenic (not to mention greener) way to enter central Europe than flying. The capitals of the westernmost central European countries are particularly well connected beyond the region, but you can get pretty much everywhere in this book by rail with a switch or two.

Bus, bicycle and car are other possible modes of transport that can be used to enter the region; each has its own distinct advantages and disadvantages. Whichever transport method you choose, you will find helpful practical information in the following sec-tions. Refer to the chapter Transport sections and the Getting There & Away sections at the end of gateway citys for specific details.

Flights, tours and rail tickets can be booked online at www.lonelyplanet .com/travel_services.

AIR

Air travel to central Europe has never been easier. Frankfurt and Zürich are major air hubs linked to points across the globe; Vienna is only slightly less connected. You can also reach Prague, Budapest and Warsaw from abroad. Airports in Ljubljana and Bratislava host intra-European flights only, while tiny Liechtenstein has no airport.

Airlines

Central European national carriers can help take you to and from a host of international cities, while a web of low-cost carrier routes connect Western Europe with smaller cities across the region. The rule of thumb is the further east you go, the fewer regional airports there are.

Most no-frills airlines specialise in certain countries or routes. SkyEurope, easyJet and Ryanair, for example, primarily fly from UK cities to central European destinations. Others have branched out: germanwings connects much of Europe (Moscow even) with numerous central European gateways.

The following list includes most of the major airlines servicing central Europe. See the Transport sections at the end of each country chapter for more specific information.

THINGS CHANGE...

The information in this chapter is particularly vulnerable to change. Check directly with the airline or a travel agent to make sure you understand how a fare (and ticket you may buy) works and be aware of the security requirements for international travel. Shop carefully. The details given in this chapter should be regarded as pointers and are not a substitute for your own careful, up-to-date research.

WHAT'S THAT BAG WORTH TO YOU?

Following the low-cost carrier trend, mainstream airlines have added fees for services that used to be free. Unless you're flying across an ocean, many will charge you for bringing checked luggage (from €12 per bag) and will impose strict limits on weight. If you're lugging a set of Czech crystal home, check your airline's policies – the supplemental payments could add up to *waaaay* more than your original ticket price. Other add-ons to watch for include phone-booking fees, assigned-seat fees, paper-ticket fees, priority-line fees, fresh-air fees… Oh, wait, they haven't started charging for oxygen – yet.

Adria Airways (JP; www.adria-airways.com) Intra-European flights only.

Air Berlin (AB; www.airberlin.de) Germany-based low-cost carrier.

Air Canada (AC; www.aircanada.ca)

Air France (AF; www.airfrance.com)

American Airlines (AA; www.aa.com)

Austrian Airlines (OS; www.aua.com)

British Airways (BA; www.britishairways.com)

Continental Airlines (CO; www.continental.com)

ČSA (OK; www.czechairlines.com)

Delta Air Lines (DL; www.delta.com)

easyJet (U2; www.easyjet.com) UK-based budget airline.

germanwings (4U; www.germanwings.com) German low-cost carrier.

KLM (KL; www.klm.nl)

LOT Polish Airlines (LO; www. lot.com)

Lufthansa (LH; www.lufthansa.com) National carrier of Germany.

Malév Hungarian Airlines (MA; www.malev.hu)

Qantas (QF; www.qantas.com.au)

Ryanair (1I; www.ryanair.com) British-based no-frills airline.

Singapore Airlines (SQ; www.singaporeair.com)

SkyEurope (NE; www.skyeurope.com) Low-cost airline based in central Europe.

Swiss International Air Lines (LX; www.swiss.com)

Wizzair (W6; www.wizzair.com) Cut-rate carrier based in Germany.

Tickets

You'll find cheaper fares are often available if you travel midweek, stay away at least one Saturday night or take advantage of promotional offers. You can track European airfares at **Airfare Watchdog** (www.airfarewatch dog.co.uk, www.airfarewatchdog.com) or sign up for sales alerts at individual airline websites. Unlike the full-service airlines, no-frills carriers often make one-way tickets available at around half the return fare, meaning that it is easy to put together an open-jaw ticket (ie flying to one place but leaving from another). Shop around but always make sure that the price you are quoted includes the relevant taxes *and* fees (see boxed text, left). The internet is obviously a great resource. Budget carriers such as Ryanair and SkyEurope do not participate in all search engines, but the following ticket booking agents are especially good for price shopping and buying:

Expedia (www.expedia.com) Full-service site.

FlyBudget.com (www.flybudget.com) Budget airlines only.

Fly Cheapo (www.flycheapo.com) Comprehensive low-cost-carrier site.

Kayak (www.kayak.com) Includes some discount airlines.

LastMinute.com (www.lastminute.com) Includes long-term planning options, too.

Opodo (www.opodo.com) Pan-European booking agent.

Orbitz (www.orbitz.com) Easy-to-understand fare charts.

Travelocity (www.travelocity.com) Great flexible search options.

COURIER FLIGHTS

Courier tickets are a great bargain if you're lucky enough to find one. You get cheap passage in return for accompanying packages or documents through customs and delivering them to a representative at the destination airport. You are permitted to bring along a carry-on bag, but often that's all. Be aware that this type of ticket is usually very restricted, so check carefully before purchasing.

Courier flights are occasionally advertised in newspapers. The **International Association of Air Travel Couriers** (IAATC; www.courier.org) offers access to its website and booking service for US$45.

SECONDHAND TICKETS

You'll occasionally see advertisements on youth-hostel bulletin boards and in newspapers from people who want to sell the unused portion of their air tickets. Don't ever shell out money for such tickets – if they're for international travel they're usually worthless, as the name on the ticket must match the name on the passport of the person checking in.

TRANSPORT IN CENTRAL EUROPE

CLIMATE CHANGE & TRAVEL

Climate change is a serious threat to the ecosystems that humans rely upon, and air travel is the fastest-growing contributor to the problem. Lonely Planet regards travel, overall, as a global benefit, but believes we all have a responsibility to limit our personal impact on global warming.

Flying & Climate Change

Pretty much every form of motor travel generates CO_2 (the main cause of human-induced climate change) but planes are far and away the worst offenders, not just because of the sheer distances they allow us to travel, but because they release greenhouse gases high into the atmosphere. The statistics are frightening: two people taking a return flight between Europe and the US will contribute as much to climate change as an average household's gas and electricity consumption over a whole year.

Carbon Offset Schemes

Climatecare.org and other websites use 'carbon calculators' that allow jetsetters to offset the greenhouse gases they are responsible for with contributions to energy-saving projects and other climate-friendly initiatives in the developing world – including projects in India, Honduras, Kazakhstan and Uganda.

Lonely Planet, together with Rough Guides and other concerned partners in the travel industry, supports the carbon offset scheme run by climatecare.org. Lonely Planet offsets all of its staff and author travel.

For more information check out our website: lonelyplanet.com.

STUDENT & YOUTH FARES

Full-time students and people aged under 26 sometimes have access to better deals than other travellers. The deals may not always be cheaper fares but can include more flexibility to change flights and/or routes. You have to show a document proving your date of birth and a valid International Student Identity Card (ISIC) or an International Youth Travel Card (IYTC) when buying your ticket and boarding the plane. See the **International Student Travel Confederation** (www.istc.org) for more information.

Asia

The cheapest option to central Europe will probably be a flight to the western capitals from one of the discount airfare capitals of Asia: Hong Kong, Singapore and Bangkok. From all three cities, Lufthansa flies to Frankfurt and Munich. Swiss International Air Lines connects Hong Kong and Bangkok with Zürich, and Austrian Airlines has direct flights from Bangkok to Vienna.

STA Travel offices proliferate in Asia, with branches in **Bangkok** (☎ 02-236 0262; www.statravel.co.th), **Singapore** (☎ 6737 7188; www.statravel.com.sg), **Hong Kong** (☎ 2736 1618; www.statravel.com.hk) and **Japan** (☎ 03 5391 2922; www.statra vel.co.jp).

Australia

Cheap flights from Australia to Europe generally connect via Southeast Asia, involving stopovers in Kuala Lumpur, Bangkok or Singapore. You can fly direct from Sydney to Frankfurt on Qantas and British Airways. There are quite a few travel agents that specialise in discount air tickets. Both **STA Travel** (www.statravel.com.au) and **Flight Centre** (www.flightcentre.com.au) have offices throughout Australia; online, try **travel.com.au** (www.travel.com.au).

Canada

Canadian fares tend to be at least 10% higher than those sold in the USA. Often the best way to reach central European destinations from Canada is via New York City or London, from where cheap airfares can often be found. Air Canada and Lufthansa connect Montreal, Calgary and Vancouver with Frankfurt. Swiss International Air Lines flies between Montreal and Zürich.

Travel CUTS (☎ 800-667-2887; www.travelcuts.com) is Canada's national student travel agency and has offices in all major cities.

New Zealand

The cheapest fares to Europe are routed through Southeast Asia and cost about the same as those from Australia. There are no direct flights to central Europe. The site **travel.co.nz** (www.travel.co.nz) is recommended for online bookings. **STA Travel** (☎ 0508 782 872; www.statravel.co.nz) and **Flight Centre** (☎ 0800 243 544; www.flightcentre.co.nz) are popular travel agents in New Zealand.

UK & Ireland
Discount air travel is big business in London. You can often find fares from here that either match or beat land-based alternatives in terms of cost. However, beware of the taxes and additional fees, which can be very high. In addition to British Airways, Ryanair, easyJet and SkyEurope connect to many destinations in central Europe – even far-flung ones such as Poprad in Slovakia.

STA Travel (☎ 0870 163 0026; www.statravel.co.uk) has some 70 branches throughout the UK and Ireland; it sells tickets to all travellers but caters especially to young people and students. Other recommended travel agencies include **Trailfinders** (www.trailfinders.co.uk) and **Travelbag** (☎ 0800 082 5000; www.travel bag.co.uk).

USA
Some cheap deals can be found from New York especially. National carriers including Lufthansa, Swiss International Air Lines and Austrian Airlines fly directly from at least their home capitals to one or more US destinations. New York is connected directly with Budapest by Malév Hungarian Airlines, and Prague by ČSA; you can fly LOT Polish Airlines from Chicago to Warsaw (June to August). Additionally, American Airlines connects Frankfurt and Zürich with Dallas and New York, while Continental Airlines flies direct to Frankfurt, Berlin, Hamburg, Zurich and Geneva from New York or Houston. Delta Air Lines has the most flights, connecting US cities such as Atlanta, Cincinnati, Los Angeles, Fort Lauderdale and New York with destinations including Prague, Frankfurt, Munich, Berlin.

Discount travel agents in the USA are known as consolidators (though you won't see any sign on the door that says so). If you're flexible, New York–based **Airhitch** (www.airhitch.org) might get you a great deal on a flight to/from Europe. The youth-oriented **STA Travel** (☎ 800 781 4040; www.statravel.com) has offices in all major cities.

Western Europe
Numerous national and low-cost carriers connect Western European cities to central Europe by air; see the Transport sections in the individual country chapters for details. Some recommended travel agencies in France include **OTU Voyages** (www.otu.fr) and **Nouvelles Frontières** (☎ 0825 000 747; www.nouvelles-frontieres.fr), both of which specialise in student fares and have branches countrywide. In Spain recommended agencies include **Barcelo Viajes** (☎ 902 116 226) and **Nouvelles Frontières** (☎ 902 170 979; www.nouvelles-frontieres.es).

LAND
Border Crossings
As almost every country covered in this book is an EU member (the exceptions are Switzerland and Liechtenstein), there will be few border crossings to deal with if you're entering from other EU countries to the west or from the north (for example, from Lithuania to Poland). However, travellers crossing from Belarus or Ukraine to Poland, Slovakia or Hungary can expect tighter-than-ever immigration and customs controls; make certain you have valid visas for Belarus and/or Ukraine if you need them, and no more than the allowable number of cigarettes. Crossing from Romania, Serbia or Croatia involves no great problems as long as you have the necessary visas and documents.

Bus
Every major urban centre in the region is well connected by international bus companies to destinations outside central Europe. Even if you're coming from far-flung locations such as London, İstanbul or Moscow, bus travel to the heart of Europe is possible with a connection or two (though it's hard on the backside and nerves, and not necessarily much cheaper than the train). See the Transport and Getting There & Away sections of individual country chapters for specific routes and prices.

Train
There are regular train services connecting central Europe with practically every corner of the European continent. Train travel could end up costing slightly more than bus travel, but it is generally more comfortable. See the Transport and Getting There & Away sections of individual country chapters for information on train travel to the region.

TRANSPORT IN CENTRAL EUROPE

SEA

Though it's not the most common way of getting to central Europe, ferries run from Sweden and Denmark to Germany (p206, 293) and Poland (p447). Compare prices and check routes at **Ferry Savers** (www .ferrysavers.com).

GETTING AROUND

AIR

Airlines in Central Europe

Flying lacks the flexibility and scenery of train transport and contributes to carbon emissions; it's therefore perhaps best saved for long-haul routes. That said, a wide range of no-frills carriers do fly even to smaller cities around the region. If you're travelling without checked luggage, booking at least two weeks ahead and are willing to travel to alternative airports, they can be quite a bargain. A number of cut-rate carriers operate from Germany in particular: Air Berlin will shuttle you between German cities and from there onto Austria, Poland, the Czech Republic and Hungary; Wizzair covers fewer cities, but has more destinations in Poland. See p604 for a list of airlines, and check out the individual country Transport sections for more-detailed information. **Fly Cheapo** (www.flycheapo .com) is an excellent web resource for finding out which low-cost carriers fly where.

Note that travelling light is essential when doing the low-cost bunny hop around the region as fees for bags can be exorbitant. For further information, see boxed text, p605.

Air Passes

The **Europebyair FlightPass** (www.europebyair.com) gives travellers from countries such as the USA, Canada, Australia and New Zealand one-way nonstop fares throughout Europe from US$99 per flight, with no blackout dates. Passes are good for 120 days.

Non-European residents can also get a **Star Alliance European Airpass** (www.staralliance .com), covering every central European nation (except Liechtenstein), in conjunction with an intercontinental round-trip ticket. Between three and 10 flight passes (starting at US$100 each) can be used within a three-

month period, but cities can only be visited once (unless changing flights).

BICYCLE

Crossing central Europe by bicycle is certainly doable. Where you go will depend on your skill and endurance levels – the region encompasses both Europe's highest mountain peaks and some of the flattest land this side of Kansas. See p592 for some recommended places to cycle and for bike tours in the region.

There are numerous proper bike routes in the western countries; the further east you go, the more you'll be relying on roadsides and rural routes. Be conscious of the fact that exhaust fumes can taint any bike trip anywhere.

The key to a successful trip is to travel light. What you carry should largely be determined by your destination and type of trip. It's worth carrying the tools necessary for repairing a puncture even for the shortest and most basic trip. Other things you might want to consider packing are spare brake and gear cables, spanners, Allen keys, spare spokes and strong adhesive tape. Before you set off ensure that you are competent at carrying out basic repairs – there's no point in weighing yourself down with equipment that you haven't got a clue how to use. Always check over your bike thoroughly each morning, and again at night when the day's touring is over. Take a good lock and always use it when you leave your bike unattended. The wearing of helmets is not compulsory but is certainly advised.

Hire

It is relatively easy to rent bicycles in the western countries – Austria, Germany and Switzerland – and you can often negotiate good deals. You might even be able to drop the bicycle off at a different location so you don't have to double back on your route. However, there are a dearth of bicycle-hire opportunities in the eastern portion of the region; the best hunting grounds will be organised camping areas and resort hotels in the high season. Local tourist offices have information on rental outlets. In villages, you might find a bike the old-fashioned, informal way – by asking around. Locals may be willing to lend their bike for a small fee. See individual country chapters for more details.

Purchase

For major cycling tours, it's best to have a bike you're familiar with, so consider bringing your own (see boxed text, right) rather than buying on arrival. If you can't be bothered with the hassle, there are plenty of possibilities for purchasing bikes in central Europe, from private vendors advertising in local papers to shops selling new and secondhand bicycles. If you're just interested in biking around a certain area and do not need an expensive bike, consider purchasing a preloved model from a secondhand shop or sporting-goods store – it might be cheaper than paying for several days' rental.

BOAT

Seasonal boat travel on central Europe's riverways is a cruisey, scenic – and sometimes slow – way to get around. You won't save any money plying the waters, but you will gain a unique perspective on the region. The Danube River serves as the region's main water-transport artery; from roughly April to October, ferries run from southern Germany to Austria, within Austria, and from Austria through Slovakia into Hungary. Vienna–Bratislava–Budapest is by far the most popular route. For more, see p29 and Getting There & Away in the individual city sections.

Various ferries cruise between towns on the Moselle (p244) and Rhine (p248) Rivers within Germany.

For more on organised boat tours, see p614.

BUS

Buses generally have the edge over trains in terms of cost, but are slower and less comfortable. They tend to be best for getting around cities and for reaching remote rural villages; they are often the only option in mountainous regions. International services tend to link major cities only. Note that even if two towns in different countries appear close together on the map, there may be no international bus service between them. For example, it takes several transfers to get between Košice in Slovakia and Debrecen in Hungary.

Europe's biggest network of international buses is provided by a group of bus companies that operates under the umbrella of **Eurolines** (www.eurolines.com). In almost every case its head office is located in a city's main bus station. Eurolines offers 15- and 30-day bus

---

> ### TRANSPORTING A BICYCLE
>
> If you want to bring your bicycle to central Europe, you should be able to take it on the plane. You can either take it apart and pack the pieces in a bike bag or box, or simply wheel it to the check-in desk, where it should be treated as a piece of luggage. You may have to remove the pedals and turn the handlebars sideways so that it takes up less space in the aircraft's hold. Be sure to check all this with the airline before you pay for your ticket. If your bicycle and other luggage exceed the weight allowance, ask about alternatives or you may suddenly find yourself being charged a fortune for excess baggage.

passes (around €345 and €445, respectively) that are cheaper than rail passes, but not as extensive or as flexible. Most trips must be international, though a few internal journeys are possible between major cities in Germany and Austria; as a result, you'll probably be better off buying single tickets as you go along. See Getting There & Away in individual city sections for more information about domestic and long-distance buses.

From April through October, **Flying Puli** (www.flyingpuli.com) operates a hop-on, hop-off continuous bus service circling clockwise through Austria, the Czech Republic, Poland, Slovakia and Austria. A 30-day pass costs €199, and city-to-city rates are available.

CAMPERVAN

A popular way to tour Europe is for two to four people to band together to buy or rent a campervan. The main advantage of going by campervan is flexibility, as it has transport, accommodation and storage all sewn up. Disadvantages include the cramped conditions, the necessity of finding parking, and having to leave your gear inside when you are exploring. Prices and facilities in camper ans vary considerably. Look for campervan rentals on websites such as **Worldwide-Motorhome-Hire .com** (www.worldwide-motorhome-hire.com). See below for more on driving in central Europe.

CAR

Though it's not always the most environmentally friendly alternative, travelling by vehicle allows wonderful flexibility, as well as the option to get off the beaten track and see what other travellers miss outside the cities. Cars can, however, be a major inconvenience in urban centres, where you may have to negotiate strange one-way systems or find somewhere to park in a confusing concrete jungle.

ViaMichelin (www.viamichelin.com) is excellent for planning routes.

Driving Licence & Documentation

Proof of ownership and insurance should always be carried when touring the region. An EU driving licence is acceptable for driving throughout central Europe, as are North American and Australian licences. To be on the safe side – or if you have any other type of licence – you could obtain an International Driving Permit (IDP) from your local motoring organisation. It's easy to get and could save you much hassle later on. Holders of old-style green UK licences must have them backed up with a German translation in Austria.

Fuel & Spare Parts

Fuel prices can vary enormously from country to country and may bear little relation to the general cost of living. Unleaded petrol of 95 or 98 octane, and diesel are widely available throughout central Europe.

Ireland's **Automobile Association** (www.aaroad watch.ie/eupetrolprices) maintains a good webpage of European fuel prices.

Hire & Lease

Hiring a vehicle is a relatively straightforward procedure. The minimum rental age is between 21 and 25, and you'll need a credit card. It is imperative to understand exactly what is included in your rental agreement (unlimited mileage? collision waiver?). Make sure you are covered by an adequate insurance policy. Ask in advance if you are allowed to drive a rented car across borders (and if so, which ones). Note that less than 4% of European cars have automatic transmissions, so if you need this, request ahead and expect to pay more for your car.

The big international firms will give you reliable service and a good standard of vehicle. You may have the option of returning the car to a different outlet at the end of the rental period (for a substantial fee). National or local firms often undercut the big companies. When comparing rates, beware of printed

tariffs intended only for local residents, as they may be lower than the prices foreigners are charged. When in doubt, ask.

You will find the most rental options near airports and in capital cities. Prices at airport rental offices are usually higher than at branches in the city centres, but in general rates range from €25 to €75 per day. Prebook for the lowest cost – you will pay more if you walk into an office and ask for a car on the spot, even allowing for special weekend deals. Smaller towns, especially in the east, may not have rental outlets. Check the Transport section of individual country chapters for more detail. You can make advance reservations online with the following international companies:

Avis (www.avis.com)
Budget (www.budget.com)
Europcar (www.europcar.com)
Hertz (www.hertz.com)

Brokers such as **Kemwel Holiday Autos** (www .kemwel.com) and **Auto Europe** (www.autoeurope.com) can arrange Europe-wide deals. If you're coming from North America, Australia or New Zealand, fly/drive packages may also be worth looking into. Ask your airline if it has any special deals for rental cars in Europe, or check the ads in the weekend travel sections of major newspapers.

Insurance

Third-party motor insurance is compulsory throughout Europe. Europeans should get the insurer of their private vehicle to issue a Green Card, which is an internationally recognised proof of insurance, and check that the card lists all the countries you intend to visit. You'll need this in the event of an accident outside the country where the vehicle is insured. The European Accident Statement is available from your insurance company and is copied so that each party at an accident can record identical information for insurance purposes. Never sign statements you can't read or understand – insist on a translation and sign that only if it's acceptable.

It's a good investment to take out a European breakdown-assistance policy, such as the Five Star Service offered by **AA** (www.theaa.com) or the European Motoring Assistance offered by **RAC** (www.rac.co.uk). Non-Europeans might find it cheaper to arrange for international coverage with their own national motoring organisation before leaving home. Ask your motoring organisation for details about free and reciprocal services offered by affiliated organisations around Europe.

Every vehicle travelling across an international border should display a sticker that shows the country of registration. It's compulsory to carry a red reflector warning triangle almost everywhere in Europe, which must be displayed in the event of a breakdown. Recommended accessories are a first-aid kit (compulsory in Slovenia), a spare-bulb kit and a fire extinguisher. Contact the RAC or the AA for more information about what is required in specific countries. Refer also to the Transport sections of individual country chapters in this book.

Road Conditions

Conditions and types of roads vary across the region, but it is possible to make some generalisations. The fastest routes are four- or six-lane highways (motorways, autobahns, autoroutes etc). These roads are great for speed, though some require a tariff for usage, often in the form of a motorway sticker or pass. There will usually be an alternative route you can take. Motorways and other primary routes are almost always in very good condition.

Road surfaces on minor routes are not perfect in some countries (such as Poland, Slovakia and Hungary), although normally they will be more than adequate. These roads are narrower and progress is generally much, much slower. To compensate, you can expect much better scenery and plenty of interesting villages along the way. Though it's a gross generalisation, minor roads tend to be in better condition in the western half of the region compared with the newer EU member states.

Driving at night can be especially hazardous in rural areas, as the roads are often narrow and winding, and you may encounter horse-drawn vehicles, cyclists, pedestrians and domestic animals.

Road Rules

You drive on the right-hand side of the road throughout the region and overtake on the left. Keep right except when overtaking, and use your indicators for any change of lane and when pulling away from the kerb. Take care with speed limits, as they vary from country to country. Speed limits are signposted, and are generally 110km/h or 120km/h on motorways, 100km/h on other highways, 80km/h on secondary and tertiary roads, and 50km/h or 60km/h in built-up areas. Motorcycles are usually limited to 90km/h on motorways, and vehicles with trailers to 80km/h. In towns you may only sound the horn to avoid having an accident. There is usually no speed limit on autobahns; exceptions are clearly signposted.

The use of seat belts is mandatory everywhere in central Europe. In most countries, children aged under 12 and intoxicated passengers are not permitted in the front seat. Driving after drinking any alcohol is a very serious offence – central European countries have a blood-alcohol-concentration (BAC) limit of between 0% and 0.08%. See the individual country chapters for more details on legal blood-alcohol limits.

Throughout Europe, when two roads of equal importance intersect, the vehicle coming from the right has right of way unless signs indicate otherwise. In many countries this also applies to cyclists, so take care. On roundabouts vehicles already in the roundabout have the right of way. Public transport vehicles pulling out from a stop also have right of way. Stay out of lanes marked 'bus' except when you're making a right-hand turn. Pedestrians have the right of way at marked crossings and whenever you're making a turn. In Europe it's prohibited to turn right against a red light, even after coming to a stop.

It's usually illegal to stop or park at the top of slopes, in front of pedestrian crossings, at bus or tram stops, on bridges or at level crossings. You must use a red reflector warning triangle when parking on a highway in an emergency. If you don't use the triangle and another vehicle hits you from behind, you will be held responsible.

Watch out for trams, as these have priority at crossroads and when they are turning right, provided they signal the turn. Don't pass a tram that is stopping to let off passengers until everyone is out and the tram doors have closed again (unless, of course, there's a safety island). Never pass a tram on the left or stop within 1m of tram tracks. A police officer who sees you blocking a tram route by waiting to turn left will flag you over.

You may be surprised at the apparent disregard of traffic regulations in some places, but as a visitor it is always best to be cautious.

In many countries, driving infringements are subject to an on-the-spot fine; always ask for a receipt.

In the event of an accident you're supposed to notify the police and file an insurance claim. If your car has significant body damage from a previous accident, point this out to customs upon arrival and have it noted somewhere, as damaged vehicles may only be allowed to leave the country with police permission.

Motoring organisations are able to supply their members with country-by-country information on motoring regulations, or they may sell motoring guidebooks.

HITCHING

Hitching is never entirely safe in any country, and we don't recommend it. Travellers who decide to hitch should understand that they are taking a small but potentially serious risk. People who do choose to hitch will be safer if they travel in pairs and let someone know where they plan to go. A man and woman travelling together is probably the best combination. Two or more men must expect some delays; two women together will make good time and should be relatively safe. Three people will have a very hard time getting a lift. Women travelling alone should never hitch.

Never let your pack be put in the boot, only sit next to a door that can be opened, and ask drivers where they are going before you say where you're going. Don't hesitate to refuse a ride if you feel at all uncomfortable, and insist on being let out at the first sign of trouble.

Don't try to catch a ride from city centres; take public transport to suburban exit routes. Hitching is usually illegal on motorways – stand on the slip roads or approach drivers at petrol stations and truck stops. Look presentable and cheerful, and make a cardboard sign indicating your intended destination in the local language. Never hitch where drivers can't stop in good time or without causing an obstruction. At dusk, give up and think about finding somewhere to stay. If your itinerary includes a ferry crossing, it might be worth trying to score a ride before the ferry rather than after, since vehicle tickets sometimes include all passengers free of charge.

It is sometimes possible to arrange a lift in advance: scan student notice boards in colleges, contact car-sharing agencies or click into chat rooms based in your destination and post a request. The useful **Hitchhikers** (www.hitchhikers.org) connects hitchhikers and drivers worldwide.

LOCAL TRANSPORT
Bus

Local buses are convenient for getting around. You can be more flexible when choosing destinations, as they travel not only around cities, but also to outlying towns and villages. One form of transport (both city- and nationwide) in eastern central Europe that sadly doesn't exist in the western countries is the shared minibus (sometimes called a maxitaxi). These convenient but cramped minibuses are used as a form of intercity and intracity transport.

Metro

Metros or intra-urban trains in cities such as Berlin, Vienna, Budapest and Prague are a great way to cover vast city distances for a small flat fare. Transfers between lines or zones may require additional tariffs; a single- or multiday pass is often the easiest way to avoid misunderstandings and pricey fines. Though metros rely on users to validate their tickets, officials do sometimes check tickets, especially in tourist areas.

Taxi

Good bus, rail, tram and underground train networks make the use of taxis all but unnecessary in much of the region. Taking a taxi in Switzerland, Austria and Germany will cost you a pretty penny for the ride, while costs in Poland, Hungary, Slovakia and other countries in the east of the region make taxis a much more viable option.

On some trips you may have to pay a supplement for things such as luggage, the time of day, whether you booked the taxi by phone or not, the location from which you boarded and whether there are extra passengers. Take care when catching taxis from airports or bus and train stations, as taxi companies have a monopoly on such places and either have a sanctioned higher per-kilometre fare or in-

---

MIND YOUR MANNERS

Giving up your seat for the elderly or mothers with young children is common courtesy on buses, trams and metros if you are young, male or able.

WHEN THE JOURNEY IS THE DESTINATION

A spectacular train or a boat ride in central Europe can be a destination all in itself. Below, the authors nominate some of their favourites:

■ **Rhine Valley** (p248) The hour-and-a-half train trip between Mainz and Koblenz in Germany is one of the world's great rides. Just fantastic. Out the windows you see castles, vineyard-covered hills and lots of interesting boat traffic on the river, about 5m from the train.

■ **Julian Alps** (p513) Slovenia's most scenic rail route runs from Jesenice to Nova Gorica via Bohinjska Bistrica. The two-hour trip skirts the Julian Alps along the Soča River; travelling south, sit on the right-hand side of the train to see the cobalt blue Soča at its most sparkling. It's a car train, too!

■ **Danube Valley** (p58) The boat trip from Melk to Krems in Austria's Danube Valley follows the river for three stunning hours as it winds through steep hills topped by crumbling castles and draped with grapevines.

■ **Berner Oberland** (p549, p567) Switzerland's GoldenPass Panoramic mountain train from Montreux to Lucerne (via Interlaken) takes in Alpine peaks and glacial lakes on its five-hour journey. But to get to the top of the world, or at least central Europe, you have to ride the rails from Interlaken up through the glacier to right below the peak at Jungfraujoch. Expect to pay big bucks, and don't go if it's cloudy.

■ **Great Masurian Lakes** (p439) In summer, excursion boats ply 200km worth of canals linking some 2000 lakes in this district in northern Poland. Start in Giżycko and cruise for four-and-a-half hours past forests and islands to Mikołajki.

---

dulge in all sorts of interesting tricks to make the meter speed up as soon as foreign accents are heard.

Trams & Trolleybuses

Trams and trolleybuses (electric buses) are also popular forms of public city transport. Again, validation of tickets once aboard is necessary. Some sleek new trams have electronic read-outs and stop indicators, but older cars also continue to operate.

MOTORCYCLE

Europe is ideal for motorcycle touring, with good-quality winding roads, stunning scenery and an active motorcycling scene. The weather is not always reliable, though, so make sure your wet-weather gear is up to scratch. The wearing of helmets for riders and passengers is compulsory throughout central Europe. Take note of local customs about parking motorcycles on footpaths. Though this is illegal in some countries, the police often turn a blind eye as long as the vehicle doesn't obstruct pedestrians. Motorcycle and moped rental is not very common in central Europe.

For useful tips from other motorcyclists who have crossed the region, check out the website of **Ride the World** (www.ridetheworld.com). Travellers interested in more-adventurous biking activities can scan **Horizons Unlimited** (www.horizonsunlimited.com).

See p609 for more on travelling by motor vehicle.

TOURS

A generic package holiday is worth considering only if your time is very limited. Most tour prices are for double occupancy, which means singles have to share a double room with a stranger of the same sex or pay a supplement to have the room to themselves.

US based **Homeric Tours** (☎ 212 753 1100; www.homerictours.com) hosts 1st-class (read: not cheap) multicountry and capital tours in central Europe. A British company highly experienced in travel to the eastern part of the region is **Regent Holidays** (☎ 0117-921 1711; www.regent-holidays.co.uk). Other British tour companies worth considering are **Exodus** (☎ 0870 240 5550; www.exodus.co.uk) and **Exploreworldwide** (☎ 0870 333 4001; www.exploreworldwide.com). From Australia, a good-value option is **Intrepid Travel** (☎ 1300 360 887; www.intrepidtravel.com).

Young (18- to 35-year-old) revellers can make merry on Europe-wide bus tours. **Contiki** (www.contiki.com) and **Top Deck** (www.topdecktravel.co.uk) offer both camping- and hotel-based bus tours throughout central Europe. They usually last for several weeks and can be a lot of fun –

if a bit hard on the liver. For people aged over 50, **Elder Hostel** (www.elderhostel.org) offers educational tours in the region.

Luxurious river cruises are another touring option. Ships generally hold 100 to 300 passengers, and meals are included. Though small, state rooms can be quite posh and usually have their own river views. **Viking River Cruises** (www.vikingrivercruises.com) has Danube, Rhine and multiriver itineraries in central Europe. For example, one eight-day excursion starts in Budapest, travelling through Bratislava, Vienna and the Danube Valley, and ending in Nuremburg (from US$1300). The superluxe new ships of **AMA Waterways** (www.amawaterways.com) follow similar courses, but the company also offers land options; for example, you could board in Trier, cruise to Nuremburg and detour to Prague (14 days from US$3000). **Cruise Locators** (www.cruiselocators.com) can help you compare and contrast companies.

National tourist offices in most countries offer organised trips to points of interest, be they within cities or in nearby rural areas. Organised tours will usually work out more expensive than going it alone, but are sometimes worth it if you are pressed for time. A short city tour, for example, will give you an overview of the place and can be a good way to begin your visit; afterwards, you'll know more precisely where you want to go again and where you want to avoid.

For information on activity-based tours see p591.

TRAIN

Trains are the most atmospheric, comfortable and fun way to make long overland journeys in central Europe. All of the major, and most of the minor, cities are on the rail network. It's perfectly feasible for train travel to be your only form of intercity transport. Overnight trains have the added benefit of saving you a night's accommodation. Think before you schedule, however – a daytime train journey through the Alps is definitely a trip highlight.

National rail websites often have searchable timetables in English. A particularly useful resource is the **Deutsche Bahn** (www.bahn.de) website, which covers the schedules of all the nations of central Europe (but only has prices for Germany). Train fares and schedules for the most popular routes in Europe,

plus information on rail and youth passes, can be found at **Rail Europe** (www.raileurope.com, www.raileurope.co.uk). As if all that online information isn't enough, you can check out the **European Rail Guide** (www.europeanrailguide.com) website for current timetables and fares.

The *Thomas Cook European Timetable*, which gives a complete listing of train schedules and indicates where supplements apply or where reservations are necessary, has long been the long-term travellers' bible. It is updated monthly and is available from **Thomas Cook** (www.thomascookpublishing.com).

Classes

Seats on most trains in central Europe come in 1st- and 2nd-class varieties. More and more train cars have a modern, aeroplane-like layout; 1st-class chairs are larger and often come equipped with laptop outlets. Dining cars are slowly being replaced by snack bars, but you'll still find sit-down meals and cabin compartments on some trains in the easternmost countries. In those countries, it often pays to stick to the faster, and generally newer, IC (Intercity) or EC (Eurocity) trains – especially if you're concerned with the condition of the bathrooms. Supplements usually apply on IC and EC express trains, and it is a good idea (and sometimes obligatory) to make seat reservations at peak times and on certain lines. The German ICE (Intercity Express) trains are the quickest in the region. Note that central European trains sometimes split en route so, even if you're on the right train, make sure you're also in the correct carriage. For more details on sleeping on overnight trains, see boxed text, opposite.

Costs

While reasonable, train travel is generally a bit pricier than bus travel. First-class tickets are about double the price of 2nd-class train tickets, and costs are significantly lower in the eastern part of the region for both international and domestic journeys. Train travel within Germany is particularly expensive.

Reservations

It is always advisable to buy a ticket in advance. Seat reservations are also advisable but only necessary if the letter 'R' is posted on the timetable next to your desired route. Outside the high season, reservations can be made pretty much up to your departure time, but never count on this. On busy routes and dur-

OVERNIGHT TRAINS

When you're travelling overnight (which is nearly always the case when going between the west and the east of the region), you'll get a bed reservation included in the price of your ticket, although you may have to pay a few euros extra for the bedding once on board. Each wagon is generally administered by an attendant who will look after your ticket and – crucially, if you arrive during the small hours – make sure that you get off at the correct stop. Each wagon has a toilet and washbasin at either end, although their cleanliness can vary massively. Be aware that toilets may be closed while the train is stopping in a station.

Western Central Europe

Trains in these countries will usually offer a choice of couchette or sleeper if you don't fancy sleeping in your seat with somebody else's elbow in your ear. Reservations are advisable, as sleeping options are allocated on a first-come, first-served basis.

Couchette bunks are comfortable enough, if lacking a bit in privacy. There are four per compartment in 1st class or six in 2nd class. For most international trains a bunk costs around €20 on top of the price of your ticket, irrespective of the length of the journey.

Sleepers are the most comfortable option, offering beds for one or two passengers in 1st class, and two or three passengers in 2nd class. Charges vary depending on the journey, but they are significantly more expensive than couchettes. Most long-distance trains have a dining (buffet) car or an attendant who wheels a snack trolley through carriages. If possible buy your food before travelling as on-board prices tend to be high.

Eastern Central Europe

Trains in these countries may offer third-class sleeping accommodation; it's not available everywhere, but it's the cheapest way to sleep. You may feel your privacy has been slightly invaded as the accommodation consists of six berths in each compartment.

Second class has four berths in a closed compartment. If there are three in your group, you'll often not be joined by anyone else.

First class is a treat, although you are paying for space rather than decor or service in most countries. You'll find two berths in a compartment, usually adorned with plastic flowers to remind you what you've paid for.

ing the summer, always try to reserve a seat several days in advance. For peace of mind, you may prefer to book tickets via travel agencies before you leave home, although this will be more expensive than booking on arrival in the region and is not necessary. You can book most routes in the region from any main station in central Europe.

Safety

You should be quite safe when travelling on trains in central Europe, but do be aware. Carry your valuables on you at all times – don't even go to the bathroom without taking your cash, wallet and passport. If you are sharing a compartment with others, you'll have to decide whether or not you trust them. If there's any doubt, be cautious with your belongings when leaving the compartment. At night, make sure your door is locked from the inside. If you have a compartment to yourself, you can ask the attendant to lock it while you go to the dining car or for a wander outside when the train is stopped. However, be aware that most criminals strike when they can easily disembark the train. Also note that overnight trains have a reputation as targets for theft.

Train Passes

European rail passes are worth buying if you plan to do a fair amount of intercountry travelling within a short space of time. Research your options before committing to a particular pass – find the one out there that most fits your plans and budget. Many passes also provide discounts on other modes of travel, as well as on entry to some tourist sites.

Try to plan at least some of your itinerary ahead so as to not overdo the overnight travelling. Although it can work out to be a great way of saving time and money, you don't want to be too tired to enjoy the next day of sightseeing.

Remember, even intercountry distances are relatively small in central Europe, and many of these overnight train rides are only five to seven hours long. After a few sleepless nights in a row, all the art on the walls of those museums you visit will start to look surreal.

When weighing up options, consider the cost of other cheap ticket deals, including advance-purchase reductions, one-off promotions or special circular-route tickets. International tickets are usually valid for two months, and you can make as many stops as you like en route; make your intentions known when purchasing and inform train conductors how far you're going before they punch your ticket.

Not all countries in central Europe are covered by rail passes, but most passes include a number of destinations. Pour yourself a cuppa or favourite drink and check out the excellent overview of rail passes at **The Man at Seat 61** (www.seat61.com/railpass.htm); you can also buy tickets here. Another agency that sells a multitude of passes, including the ones mentioned below, is **Rail Europe** (UK ☎ 08448 484 064; www.raileurope.co.uk; USA ☎ 877-257-2887; www.raileurope.com).

EURAIL

These passes can only be bought by residents of non-European countries, and are supposed to be purchased before arriving in Europe. They are valid for unlimited travel on national railways and some private lines in Switzerland, Austria, Germany, the Czech Republic, Poland, Hungary and Slovenia. Know your basic itinerary before you buy: **Eurail** (www.eurail.com) offers passes for a wide variety of areas and time periods.

The Eurail Global Pass is the standard pass for travellers aged 26 years and over. It provides unlimited 1st-class travel for periods ranging from 15 days (€510) to three months (€1400). Opt to travel just 10 days within two months and you'll pay about €600. Two or more people travelling together can get a 'saver' version of the pass, saving about 15%. For travellers under 26, the Global Pass offers the same options for 2nd-class travel only: 15 days to three months costs €330 to €930; 10 days within two months costs €390. This is the classic backpacker pass.

The Eurail Selectpass allows for travel between three to five contiguous countries for five, 10 or 15 days per two months. Options are myriad; as a guide, an adult can travel between Austria, Slovenia, the Czech Republic, Germany, Hungary and Switzerland for 10 days within two months for €515. Youth and 'saver' discounts still apply.

EUROPEAN EAST PASS

The European East Pass can be purchased by anyone not permanently resident in Europe (including the UK). The pass is valid for travel in Austria, Hungary, the Czech Republic, Slovakia and Poland, and also gives holders additional benefits, especially in Austria and Hungary (for example, discounted Danube River trips). The pass is sold by travel agents in North America, Australia and the UK. Rail Europe charges US$299 for five days of 1st-class travel within one month; extra rail days (maximum five) cost US$36 each.

INTER-RAIL

These passes are available to European residents (and to nationals of Turkey, Morocco, Tunisia and Algeria) of more than six months' standing; passport identification is required.

The **Inter-Rail pass** (www.interrailnet.com) is valid in Germany, Switzerland and Austria, Hungary, Slovakia, Poland, the Czech Republic and Slovenia, but is not valid on some high-speed services. Terms and conditions vary slightly from country to country, but there is only a discount of around 50% on normal fares when travelling in the country where you bought the pass. Special rules also apply for night-time train travel, so check the details carefully. The Inter-Rail pass is available in different classes at adult and youth (under 26) prices. A 1st-class adult ticket for five days' travel in 10 days is €329, 2nd-class adult is €249 and 2nd-class youth is €159. One continuous month will cost €809, €599 and €299, respectively. Single-country passes are available.

NATIONAL RAIL PASSES

Some discounted one-country rail passes are available from Eurail and Inter-Rail, as well as from the national train service itself. These are not always a great value, but they do save the time and hassle of having to buy individual tickets. In a large, expensive country such as Germany, a pass can make sense; in a small, relatively inexpensive country such as Slovakia, it makes none whatsoever.

Health

CONTENTS

Travel health depends on your predeparture preparations, your daily health care while travelling in central Europe and how you handle any medical problem that does develop. Few prepared travellers experience anything more than an upset stomach.

BEFORE YOU GO

Prevention is the key to staying healthy while abroad. A little planning before departure will save trouble later: see your dentist before a long trip and carry a spare pair of contact lenses or glasses. Bring medications in their original, clearly labelled containers. A signed and dated letter from your physician describing your medical conditions and medications, including generic names, is also a good idea. If carrying syringes or needles, be sure to have a physician's letter documenting their necessity.

INSURANCE

Make sure you have adequate health insurance. See p597 for general information.

RECOMMENDED VACCINATIONS

The World Health Organization (WHO) recommends that all travellers should be covered for diphtheria, tetanus, measles, mumps, rubella and polio. Travellers should also be aware that most vaccines don't produce immunity until at least two weeks after they're given.

IN TRANSIT

DEEP VEIN THROMBOSIS (DVT)

Blood clots may form in the legs during plane flights, chiefly because of prolonged immobility. The longer the flight, the greater the risk. The chief symptom of DVT is swelling or pain of the foot, ankle or calf, usually but not always just on one side. When a blood clot travels to the lungs, it may cause chest pain and breathing difficulties. Travellers with any of these symptoms should immediately seek medical attention.

To prevent the development of DVT on long flights you should walk about the cabin, contract the leg muscles while sitting, drink plenty of fluids and avoid alcohol and tobacco.

IN CENTRAL EUROPE

AVAILABILITY & COST OF HEALTH CARE

Good basic health care is readily available, and for minor illnesses pharmacists can give valuable advice and sell over-the-counter medication. They can also advise when more specialised help is required. The standard of dental care is usually good.

In the east of the region, medical care is not always readily available outside major cities, but embassies, consulates and five-star hotels can usually recommend doctors or clinics. In some cases, medical supplies required in hospital may need to be bought from a pharmacy, and nursing care may be limited.

INFECTIOUS DISEASES
HIV & AIDS

Infection with the human immunodeficiency virus (HIV) may lead to acquired immune deficiency syndrome (AIDS), which is a fatal disease. Any exposure to blood, blood products or body fluids may put the individual at risk. The disease is often transmitted through sexual contact or dirty needles – vaccinations, acupuncture, tattooing and body piercing can be potentially as dangerous as intravenous drug use. If you do need an injection, ask to see the syringe unwrapped in front of you, or take a needle and syringe pack with you.

Fear of HIV infection should never preclude treatment for serious medical conditions.

Sexually Transmitted Diseases

HIV/AIDS and hepatitis B can be transmitted through sexual contact. Other STDs include gonorrhoea, herpes and syphilis; sores, blisters or rashes around the genitals, and discharges or pain when urinating are common symptoms. In some STDs, such as wart virus or chlamydia, symptoms may be less marked or not observed at all, especially in women. Chlamydia infection can cause infertility in men and women before any symptoms have been noticed. Syphilis symptoms eventually disappear completely, but the disease continues and can cause severe problems in later years. While abstinence from sexual contact is the only 100% effective prevention, using condoms is also effective. The different sexually transmitted diseases each require treatment with specific antibiotics.

TRAVELLER'S DIARRHOEA

Simple things such as a change of water, food or climate can all cause a mild bout of diarrhoea, but a few rushed toilet trips with no other symptoms is not indicative of a major problem.

Dehydration is the main danger with any diarrhoea, particularly in children or the elderly, as dehydration can occur quite quickly. Under all circumstances fluid replacement (at least equal to the volume being lost) is the most important thing to remember. Weak black tea with a little sugar, soda water, or soft drinks allowed to go flat and diluted 50% with clean water are all good. With severe diarrhoea a rehydrating solution is preferable to replace lost minerals and salts.

Gut-paralysing drugs such as loperamide or diphenoxylate can be used to bring relief from the symptoms, although they do not actually cure the problem. Only use these drugs if you do not have access to toilets, eg if you must travel. Note that these drugs are not recommended for children aged under 12 years.

ENVIRONMENTAL HAZARDS
Altitude Sickness

Lack of oxygen at high altitudes (over 2500m) affects most people to some extent. The effect may be mild or severe, and occurs because less oxygen reaches the muscles and the brain at high altitude, requiring the heart and lungs to compensate by working harder. Symptoms of acute mountain sickness (AMS) usually develop during the first 24 hours at altitude but may be delayed up to three weeks. Mild symptoms include headache, lethargy, dizziness, difficulty sleeping and loss of appetite. AMS may become more severe without warning and can be fatal. Severe symptoms include breathlessness, a dry cough (which may progress to the production of pink, frothy sputum), severe headache, lack of co-ordination and balance, confusion, irrational behaviour, vomiting, drowsiness and unconsciousness. There is no hard-and-fast rule as to what altitude is too high: AMS has been fatal at 3000m, although 3500m to 4500m is the usual range.

Treat mild symptoms by resting at the same altitude until recovery, which usually takes a day or two. Paracetamol or aspirin can be taken for headaches. If symptoms persist or become worse, however, immediate descent is necessary; even 500m can help. Drug treatments should never be used to avoid descent or to enable further ascent. The risk of getting AMS can be reduced by taking the following measures:

- Ascend slowly. Have frequent rest days, spending two or three nights at each rise of 1000m. If you reach a high altitude by trekking, acclimatisation takes place gradually and you are less likely to be affected than if you fly directly to high altitude. It's wise to sleep at a lower altitude than the greatest height reached during the day. Also, once above 3000m, care should be taken not to increase the sleeping altitude by more than 300m per day.
- Drink extra fluids. The mountain air is dry and cold, and moisture is lost as you breathe. Evaporation of sweat may occur unnoticed and result in dehydration.
- Eat light, high-carbohydrate meals for more energy.
- Avoid alcohol, as it may increase the risk of dehydration.
- Avoid sedatives.

Cuts, Bites & Stings

Wash any cut well and treat it with an antiseptic such as povidone-iodine. Where possible, avoid bandages and Band-Aids, which can keep wounds wet.

Bee and wasp stings are usually painful rather than dangerous. However, in people who are allergic to them severe breathing difficulties may occur and require urgent medical care. Calamine lotion or a sting-relief spray will give relief, and ice packs will reduce the pain and swelling.

Hypothermia

Hypothermia occurs when the body loses heat faster than it can produce it and the core temperature of the body falls. It is surprisingly easy to progress from very cold to dangerously cold due to a combination of wind, wet clothing, fatigue and hunger, even if the air temperature is above freezing. If you are hiking at high altitudes, or are otherwise exposed to cold, wet and windy conditions, it is best to dress in layers. Silk, wool and some of the new artificial fibres are all good insulating materials. A hat is important, as a lot of heat is lost through the head. A strong, waterproof outer layer is essential, as is a 'space' blanket for emergencies. Carry basic supplies, including fluid to drink and food containing simple sugars to generate heat quickly.

Symptoms of hypothermia are exhaustion, numb skin (particularly toes and fingers), shivering, slurred speech, irrational or violent behaviour, lethargy, stumbling, dizzy spells, muscle cramps and violent bursts of energy. Irrationality may take the form of sufferers claiming they are warm and trying to take off their clothes.

To treat mild hypothermia, first get the person out of the wind and/or rain, remove their clothing if it's wet and replace it with dry, warm clothing. Give them hot liquids – not alcohol – and some high-kilojoule, easily digestible food. Do not rub victims: instead, allow them to slowly warm themselves. This should be enough to treat the early stages of hypothermia. The early recognition and treatment of mild hypothermia is the only way to prevent severe hypothermia, which is a critical condition.

Rabies

Rabies is spread through bites or licks on broken skin from an infected animal. It is always fatal unless treated promptly. Animal handlers should be vaccinated, as should those travelling to remote areas where a reliable source of postbite vaccine is not available within 24 hours. Three injections are needed over a month to be vaccinated. If you are bitten and have not been vaccinated, you will need a course of five injections starting as soon as possible after the injury. If you have been vaccinated, you will need fewer injections and have more time to seek medical help.

SEXUAL HEALTH

The **International Planned Parent Federation** (www.ippf.org) can advise about the availability of contraception in different countries. Contraception, including condoms, is widely available in the western part of the region. However, emergency contraception, which needs to be taken less than 24 hours after unprotected sex, may not be available throughout all of the region. When buying condoms, look for a European CE mark, which means they have been rigorously tested.

HEALTH

Language

CONTENTS

This language guide contains basic vocabulary and pronunciation guides to help you get around central Europe. For a more detailed guide to all the languages included here, get a copy of Lonely Planet's *Central Europe* phrasebook. For even more detail, check out Lonely Planet's *German, Czech, Hungarian* and *Polish* phrasebooks.

CZECH

PRONUNCIATION

Many Czech letters are pronounced in the same way as their English counterparts. Accents lengthen vowels and stress is always on the first syllable. Words are pronounced as they're written, so if you follow the guidelines below you'll have no trouble being understood. In indexes on Czech maps, **ch** comes after **h**.

c	as the 'ts' in 'bits'
č	as the 'ch' in 'church'
ch	as in Scottish 'loch'
ď	as the 'd' in 'duty'
ě	as the 'ye' in 'yct'
j	as the 'y' in 'you'
ň	as the 'ni' in 'onion'
ř	rolled 'r' plus ž
š	as the 'sh' in 'ship'
ť	as the 'te' in 'stew'
ž	as the 's' in 'pleasure'

ACCOMMODATION

hotel	hotel
guest house	penzión
youth hostel	ubytovna
camping ground	kemping
private room	privát
single room	jednolůžkový pokoj
double room	dvoulůžkový pokoj
Do you have any rooms available?	Máte volné pokoje?
How much is it?	Kolik to je?
Does it include breakfast?	Je v tom zahrnuta snídaně?

CONVERSATION & ESSENTIALS

Hello/Good day.	Dobrý den. (pol)
Hi.	Ahoj. (inf)
Goodbye.	Na shledanou.
Yes.	Ano.
No.	Ne.
Please.	Prosím.
Thank you.	Děkuji.
That's fine.	Není zač.
You're welcome.	Prosím.
Sorry.	Promiňte.
I don't understand.	Nerozumím.
What's it called?	Jak se to jmenuje?
How much is it?	Kolik to stojí?

DIRECTIONS

Where is it?	Kde je to?
left	vlevo
right	vpravo
straight ahead	rovně

EMERGENCIES – CZECH

Help!	Pomoc!
Call a doctor!	Zavolejte doktora!
Call an ambulance!	Zavolejte sanitku!
Call the police!	Zavolejte policii!
Go away!	Běžte pryč!
I'm lost.	Zabloudil jsem. (m)
	Zabloudila jsem. (f)

SHOPPING & SERVICES

the bank	banka
the chemist	lékárna
the church	kostel
the market	trh
the museum	muzeum
the post office	pošta
the tourist office	turistickáinformační kancelář
travel agency	cestovní kancelář

TIME, DAYS & NUMBERS

What time is it?	Kolik je hodin?
today	dnes

tonight	*dnes večer*
tomorrow	*zítra*
yesterday	*včera*
in the morning	*ráno*
in the evening	*večer*

SIGNS – CZECH

Vchod	Entrance
Východ	Exit
Informace	Information
Otevřeno	Open
Zavřeno	Closed
Zakázáno	Prohibited
Policie	Police Station
Záchody/WC/Toalety	Toilets
Páni/Muži	Men
Dámy/Ženy	Women

Monday	*pondělí*
Tuesday	*úterý*
Wednesday	*středa*
Thursday	*čtvrtek*
Friday	*pátek*
Saturday	*sobota*
Sunday	*neděle*

0	*null*
1	*jeden*
2	*dva*
3	*tři*
4	*čtyři*
5	*pět*
6	*šest*
7	*sedm*
8	*osm*
9	*devět*
10	*deset*
100	*sto*
1000	*tisíc*

TRANSPORT

What time does the ... leave/arrive?	*Kdy odjíždí/přijíždí ...?*
boat	*loď*
city bus	*městský autobus*
intercity bus	*meziměstský autobus*
train	*vlak*
tram	*tramvaj*

arrival	*příjezdy*
departure	*odjezdy*
timetable	*jízdní řád*

Where is the bus stop?	*Kde je autobusová zastávka?*

Where is the station?	*Kde je nádraží?*
Where is the left-luggage room?	*Kde je úschovna zavazadel?*
Please show me on the map.	*Prosím, ukažte mi to na mapě.*

GERMAN

PRONUNCIATION

Unlike English or French, German has almost no silent letters: you pronounce the **k** at the start of the word *Knie* (knee), the **p** at the start of *Psychologie* (psychology), and the **e** at the end of *Ich habe* (I have).

Vowels

As in English, vowels can be pronounced long, as the 'o' in 'pope', or short, as in 'pop'. As a general rule, German vowels are long before one consonant and short before two consonants, eg the **o** is long in *Dom* (cathedral), but short in *doch* (after all).

a	short, as the 'u' in 'cut', or long as in 'father'
au	as the 'ow' in 'vow'
ä	short as the 'e' in 'bet', or long as in 'care'
äu	as the 'oy' in 'boy'
e	short as in 'bet', or long as in 'obey'
ei	as the 'ai' in 'aisle'
eu	as the 'oy' in 'boy'
i	short as in 'it', or long as in 'marine'
ie	as in 'brief'
o	short as in 'not', or long as in 'note'
ö	as the 'er' in 'fern'
u	as in 'pull'
ü	like i but with tightly pursed lips

Consonants

Most German consonants sound similar to their English counterparts. One important difference is that **b**, **d** and **g** sound like 'p', 't' and 'k' respectively at the end of a word.

b	as in 'be'; as 'p' when end of word
ch	as in Scottish 'loch'
d	as in 'do'; as 't' when end of word
g	as in 'go'; as 'k' when end of word
j	as the 'y' in 'yet'
qu	as 'k' plus 'v'
r	can be trilled or guttural, depending on the region
s	as in 'sun'; as the 'z' in 'zoo' when followed by a vowel

sch	as the 'sh' in 'ship'
sp/st	as 'shp'/'sht' when first in word
-tion	the 't' is pronounced as the 'ts' in 'its'
v	as the 'f' in 'fan'
w	as the 'v' in 'van'
z	as the 'ts' in 'its'

ACCOMMODATION

hotel	Hotel
guest house	Pension/Gästehaus
youth hostel	Jugendherberge
camping ground	Campingplatz
a single room	ein Einzelzimmer
a double room	ein Doppelzimmer
one night	eine Nacht
two nights	zwei Nächte

Do you have any rooms available?	Haben Sie noch freie Zimmer?
How much is it per night/person?	Wieviel kostet es pro Nacht/Person?
Is breakfast included?	Ist Frühstück inbegriffen?

CONVERSATION & ESSENTIALS

Good day.	Guten Tag.
Hello.	Grüss Gott. (in Bavaria & Austria)
Goodbye.	Auf Wiedersehen.
Bye.	Tschüss. (inf)
Yes.	Ja.
No.	Nein.
Please.	Bitte.
Thank you.	Danke.
You're welcome.	Bitte sehr.
Excuse me/ Forgive me.	Entschuldigung.
Do you speak English?	Sprechen Sie Englisch?
How much is it?	Wieviel kostet es?
What's your name?	Wie heissen Sie?
My name is ...	Ich heisse ...

DIRECTIONS

Where is ...?	Wo ist ...?
Go straight ahead.	Gehen Sie geradeaus.
Turn left.	Biegen Sie links ab.

SIGNS – GERMAN

Eingang	Entrance
Ausgang	Exit
Auskunft	Information
Offen	Open
Geschlossen	Closed
Zimmer Frei	Rooms Available
Voll/Besetzt	Full/No Vacancies
Polizeiwache	Police Station
Verboten	Prohibited
Toiletten (WC)	Toilets
Herren	Men
Damen	Women

Turn right.	Biegen Sie rechts ab.
near/far	nahe/weit

SHOPPING & SERVICES

a bank	eine Bank
the chemist/ pharmacy	die Apotheke
the ... embassy	die ... Botschaft
the market	der Markt
the newsagent	der Zeitungshändler
the post office	das Postamt
the stationer	der Schreibwarengeschäft
the tourist office	das Verkehrsamt
What time does it open/close?	Um wieviel Uhr macht es auf/zu?

TIME, DAYS & NUMBERS

What time is it?	Wie spät ist es?
today	heute
tomorrow	morgen
yesterday	gestern
in the morning	morgens
in the afternoon	nachmittags

Monday	Montag
Tuesday	Dienstag
Wednesday	Mittwoch
Thursday	Donnerstag
Friday	Freitag
Saturday	Samstag/Sonnabend
Sunday	Sonntag

0	null
1	eins
2	zwei
3	drei
4	vier
5	fünf
6	sechs

7	*sieben*
8	*acht*
9	*neun*
10	*zehn*
100	*hundert*
1000	*tausend*

TRANSPORT

What time does ... leave?	*Wann fährt ... ab?*
What time does ... arrive?	*Wann kommt ... an?*
the boat	*das Boot*
the bus	*der Bus*
the intercity bus	*der überland Bus*
the tram	*die Strassenbahn*
the train	*der Zug*

What time is the next boat?	*Wann fährt das nächste Boot?*
I'd like to hire a car/bicycle.	*Ich möchte ein Auto/Fahrrad mieten.*
I'd like a one-way/ return ticket.	*Ich möchte eine Einzel-karte/ Rückfahrkarte.*

1st class	*erste Klasse*
2nd class	*zweite Klasse*
left-luggage locker	*Schliessfächer*
timetable	*Fahrplan*
bus stop	*Bushaltestelle*
tram stop	*Strassenbahnhaltestelle*
train station	*Bahnhof*
ferry terminal	*Fährhafen*

HUNGARIAN

PRONUNCIATION

Hungarian consonants can be simplified by pronouncing them much the same as in English; the exceptions are listed below. Double consonants **ll**, **tt** and **dd** are lengthened so you can almost hear them as separate letters. The letters **cs**, **dz**, **dzs**, **gy**, **ly**, **ny**, **sz**, **ty** and **zs** (consonant clusters) are separate letters in Hungarian and appear in separate sections in telephone books and other alphabetical listings, so *cukor* (sugar) appears in the dictionary before *csak* (only).

c	as the 'ts' in 'hats'
cs	as the 'ch' in 'church'
dz	as in 'adze'
dzs	as the 'j' in 'jet'
gy	as the 'du' in 'endure'
j	as the 'y' in 'yes'

ly	as the 'y' in 'yes'
ny	as the 'ni' in 'onion'
r	rolled like Scottish 'r'
s	as the 'sh' in 'ship'
sz	as the 's' in 'set'
ty	as the 'tu' in British English 'tube'
w	as 'v' (found in foreign words only)
zs	as the 's' in 'pleasure'

Vowels are a bit trickier: the difference in pronunciation between vowels with and without accent marks is important, eg *hát* means 'back' while *hat* means 'six'.

a	as the 'o' in hot
á	as in 'father'
e	a short 'e' as in 'set'
é	as the 'e' in 'they' with no 'y' sound
i	as in 'hit' but shorter
í	as in 'police'
o	as in 'open'
ó	a longer version of **o**
ö	as the 'u' in 'fur' with no 'r' sound
ő	a longer version of **ö**
u	as in 'pull'
ú	as the 'ue' in 'blue'
ü	similar to the 'u' in 'flute'; purse your lips tightly and say 'ee'
ű	a longer, breathier version of **ü**

ACCOMMODATION

hotel	*szálloda*
guest house	*panzió*
youth hostel	*ifjúsági szálló*
camping ground	*kemping*
private room	*fizetővendégszoba*
single room	*egyágyas szoba*
double room	*kétágyas szoba*

Do you have rooms available?	*Van szabad szobájuk?*
How much is it per night/person?	*Mennyibe kerül éjszakánként/ személyenként?*
Does it include breakfast?	*Az ár tartalmazza a reggelit?*

EMERGENCIES – HUNGARIAN

Help!	*Segítség!*
Call a doctor!	*Hívjon egy orvost!*
Call an ambulance!	*Hívja a mentőket!*
Call the police!	*Hívja a rendőrséget!*
Go away!	*Menjen innen!*
I'm lost.	*Eltévedtem.*

LANGUAGE

SIGNS – HUNGARIAN

Bejárat	Entrance
Kijárat	Exit
Információ	Information
Nyitva	Open
Zárva	Closed
Tilos	Prohibited
Rendőrőr-Kapitányság	Police Station
Toalett/WC	Toilets
Férfiak	Men
Nők	Women

CONVERSATION & ESSENTIALS

Hello.	Jó napot kivánok. (pol)
	Szia/Szervusz. (inf)
Goodbye.	Viszontlátásra. (pol)
	Szia/Szervusz. (inf)
Yes.	Igen.
No.	Nem.
Please.	Kérem.
Thank you.	Köszönöm.
Sorry/Forgive me.	Sajnálom/Elnézést.
Excuse me.	Bocsánat.
What's your name?	Mi a neve/neved? (pol/inf)
My name is ...	A nevem ...
I don't understand.	Nem értem.
Do you speak English?	Beszél angolul?
What's it called?	Hogy hívják?
How much is it?	Mennyibe kerül?

DIRECTIONS

Turn left.	Forduljon balra.
Turn right.	Forduljon jobbra.
Go straight ahead.	Menyen egyenesen elore.
Please show me on the map.	Kérem, mutassa meg a térképen.
near/far	közel/messze

SHOPPING & SERVICES

Where is ...?	Hol van ...?
a bank	bank
a chemist	gyógyszertár
the market	a piac
the museum	a múzeum
the post office	a posta
a tourist office	turistairoda
What time does it open?	Mikor nyit ki?
What time does it close?	Mikor zár be?

TIME, DAYS & NUMBERS

What time is it?	Hány óra?
today	ma
tonight	ma este
tomorrow	holnap
yesterday	tegnap
in the morning	reggel
in the evening	este
Monday	hétfő
Tuesday	kedd
Wednesday	szerda
Thursday	csütörtök
Friday	péntek
Saturday	szombat
Sunday	vasárnap
0	nulla
1	egy
2	kettő
3	három
4	négy
5	öt
6	hat
7	hét
8	nyolc
9	kilenc
10	tíz
100	száz
1000	ezer

TRANSPORT

What time does the ... leave/arrive?	Mikor indul/érkezik a ...?
boat/ferry	hajó/komp
city/intercity bus	város/varosközi
plane	repülőgép
train	vonat
tram	villamos
Where is ...?	Hol van ...?
the bus stop	az autóbuszmegálló
the station	az állomás
the left-luggage office	a csomagmegőrző
arrival	érkezés
departure	indulás
timetable	menetrend

POLISH

PRONUNCIATION

Written Polish is phonetically consistent, which means that the pronunciation of letters or clusters of letters doesn't vary from word to word. The stress almost always goes on the second-last syllable.

Vowels

a	as the 'u' in 'cut'
e	as in 'ten'
i	like the 'ee' in 'feet' but shorter
o	as in 'lot'
u	a bit shorter than the 'oo' in 'book'
y	similar to the 'i' in 'bit'

There are three vowels in Polish not found in English:

ą	a nasal vowel sound like the French *un*, similar to 'own' in 'sown'
ę	also nasalised, like the French *un*; pronounced as 'e' when last in word
ó	similar to **u**

Consonants

The consonants **b, d, f, g, k, l, m, n, p, s, t, v** and **z** are pronounced more or less as they are in English. The following consonants and clusters of consonants sound distinctly different to their English counterparts:

c	as the 'ts' in 'its'
ch	as the 'ch' in Scottish 'loch'
cz	as the 'ch' in 'church'
ć	much softer than Polish **c**; 'tsi' before vowels
dz	similar to the 'ds' in 'suds' but shorter
dź	as **dz** but softer; 'dzi' before vowels
dż	as the 'j' in 'jam'
h	as **ch**
j	as the 'y' in 'yet'
ł	as the 'w' in 'wine'
ń	as the 'ny' in 'canyon'; 'ni' before vowels
r	always trilled
rz	as the 's' in 'pleasure'
sz	as the 'sh' in 'show'
ś	as **s** but softer; 'si' before vowels
w	as the 'v' in 'van'
ź	softer version of **z**; 'zi' before vowels
ż	as **rz**

ACCOMMODATION

hotel	hotel
youth hostel	schronisko młodzieżowe
camping ground	kemping
single room	pokój jednoosobowy
double room	pokój dwuosobowy
private room	kwatera prywatna
Do you have any rooms available?	Czy są wolne pokoje?

How much is it?	Ile to kosztuje?
Does it include breakfast?	Czy śniadanie jest wliczone?

CONVERSATION & ESSENTIALS

Hello.	Cześć. (inf)
Hello/Good morning.	Dzień dobry. (pol)
Goodbye.	Do widzenia.
Yes.	Tak.
No.	Nie.
Please.	Proszę.
Thank you.	Dziękuję.
Excuse me./Sorry.	Przepraszam.
I don't understand.	Nie rozumiem.
What is it called?	Jak to się nazywa?
How much is it?	Ile to kosztuje?

DIRECTIONS

Please show me on the map.	Proszę pokazać mi to na mapie.
straight ahead	prosto
left	lewo
right	prawo

EMERGENCIES – POLISH

Help!	Pomocy!/Ratunku!
Call a doctor/ an ambulance!	Proszę wezwać lekarza/ karetkę!
Call the police!	Proszę wezwać policję!
I'm lost.	Zgubiłem się. (m)
	Zgubiłam się. (f)

SHOPPING & SERVICES

the bank	bank
the chemist	apteka
the church	kościół
the city centre	centrum miasta
the market	targ/bazar
the museum	muzeum
the post office	poczta
the tourist office	informacja turystyczna

What time does it open/close?	O której otwierają/zamykają?

TIME, DAYS & NUMBERS

What time is it?	Która jest godzina?
today	dzisiaj
tonight	dzisiaj wieczorem
tomorrow	jutro
yesterday	wczoraj
in the morning	rano
in the evening	wieczorem

SIGNS – POLISH

Wejście	Entrance
Wyjście	Exit
Informacja	Information
Otwarte	Open
Zamknięte	Closed
Wzbroniony	Prohibited
Posterunek Policji	Police Station
Toalety	Toilets
Panowie	Men
Panie	Women

Monday	*poniedziałek*
Tuesday	*wtorek*
Wednesday	*środa*
Thursday	*czwartek*
Friday	*piątek*
Saturday	*sobota*
Sunday	*niedziela*

0	*zero*
1	*jeden*
2	*dwa*
3	*trzy*
4	*cztery*
5	*pięć*
6	*sześć*
7	*siedem*
8	*osiem*
9	*dziewięć*
10	*dziesięć*
11	*jedenaście*
20	*dwadzieścia*
100	*sto*
1000	*tysiąc*

TRANSPORT

What time does the ... leave/arrive?	*O której godzinie przychodzi/ odchodzi ...?*
boat	*statek*
bus	*autobus*
plane	*samolot*
train	*pociąg*
tram	*tramwaj*

Where is the bus stop?	*Gdzie jest przystanek autobusowy?*
Where is the station?	*Gdzie jest stacja kolejowa?*
Where is the left-luggage office?	*Gdzie jest przechowalnia bagażu?*

arrival	*przyjazd*
departure	*odjazd*
timetable	*rozkład jazdy*

SLOVAK

PRONUNCIATION

The 43 letters of the Slovak alphabet have similar pronunciation to those of Czech. In words of three syllables or less, the stress falls on the first syllable. Longer words also have a secondary accent on the third or fifth syllable. There are 13 vowels (**a**, **á**, **ä**, **e**, **é**, **i**, **í**, **o**, **ó**, **u**, **ú**, **y** and **ý**), three semivowels (**l**, **ľ** and **r**) and five diphthongs (**ia**, **ie**, **iu**, **ou** and **ô**).

c	as the 'ts' in 'its'
č	as the 'ch' in 'church'
dz	as the 'ds' in 'suds'
dž	as the 'j' in 'judge'
ia	as the 'yo' in 'yonder'
ie	as the 'ye' in 'yes'
iu	as the word 'you'
j	as the 'y' in 'yet'
ň	as the 'ni' in 'onion'
ô	as the 'wo' in 'won't'
ou	as the 'ow' in 'know'
š	as the 'sh' in 'show'
y	as the 'i' in 'machine'
ž	as the 'z' in 'azure'

ACCOMMODATION

hotel	*hotel*
guest house	*penzión*
youth hostel	*mládežnícka ubytovňa*
camping ground	*kemping*
private room	*privát*
single room	*jednolôžková izba*
double room	*dvojlôžková izba*

Do you have any rooms available?	*Máte voľné izby?*
How much is it?	*Koľko to stojí?*
Is breakfast included?	*Sú raňajky zahrnuté v cene?*

EMERGENCIES – SLOVAK

Help!	*Pomoc!*
Call a doctor!	*Zavolajte doktora/lekára!*
Call an ambulance!	*Zavolajte záchranku!*
Call the police!	*Zavolajte políciu!*
Go away!	*Chod preč! (sg)*
	Chodte preč! (pl)
I'm lost.	*Nevyznám sa tu.*

CONVERSATION & ESSENTIALS

Hello.	*Ahoj.*
Goodbye.	*Dovidenia.*

Yes.	*Áno.*
No.	*Nie.*
Please.	*Prosím.*
Thank you.	*Ďakujem.*
Excuse me.	*Prepáčte mi.*
Forgive me.	*Odpuste mi.*
I'm sorry.	*Ospravedlňujem sa.*
I don't understand.	*Nerozumiem.*
What is it called?	*Ako sa do volá?*
How much is it?	*Koľko to stojí?*

DIRECTIONS

Please show me on the map.	*Prosím, ukážte mi to na mape.*
left	*vľavo*
right	*vpravo*
straight ahead	*rovno*

SHOPPING & SERVICES

the bank	*banka*
the chemist	*lekárnik*
the church	*kostol*
the city centre	*stred (centrum) mesta*
the market	*trh*
the museum	*múzeum*
the post office	*pošta*
the telephone centre	*telefónnu centrálu*
the tourist office	*turistické informačné centrum*

TIME, DAYS & NUMBERS

What time is it?	*Koľko je hodín?*
today	*dnes*
tonight	*dnes večer*
tomorrow	*zajtra*
yesterday	*včera*
in the morning	*ráno*
in the evening	*večer*

Monday	*pondelok*
Tuesday	*utorok*
Wednesday	*streda*
Thursday	*štvrtok*

Friday	*piatok*
Saturday	*sobota*
Sunday	*nedeľa*

0	*nula*
1	*jeden*
2	*dva*
3	*tri*
4	*štyri*
5	*päť*
6	*šesť*
7	*sedem*
8	*osem*
9	*deväť*
10	*desať*
100	*sto*
1000	*tisíc*

TRANSPORT

What time does the ... leave/arrive?	*Kedy odchádza/prichádza ...?*
boat	*loč*
city bus	*mestský autobus*
intercity bus	*medzimestský autobus*
plane	*lietadlo*
train	*vlak*
tram	*električka*

Where's the bus stop?	*Kde je autobusová zastávka?*
Where's the station?	*Kde je vlaková stanica?*
Where's the left-luggage office?	*Kde je úschovňa batožin?*

arrival	*príchod*
departure	*odchod*
timetable	*cestovný poriadok*

SLOVENE

PRONUNCIATION

Slovene pronunciation isn't difficult as most letters are very similar to English. The alphabet has 25 letters – 'q', 'w', 'x' and 'y' aren't used, but the following extra letters are used: **ê**, **é**, **ó**, **ò**, **č**, **š** and **ž**. Spelling is phonetically consistent. The letters **l** and **v** are both pronounced like the English 'w' when they occur at the end of syllables and before vowels.

c	as the 'ts' in 'its'
č	as the 'ch' in 'church'
ê	as the 'a' in 'apple'
e	as the 'a' in 'ago'
é	as the 'e' in 'they'

j	as the 'y' in 'yellow'
ó	as the 'a' in 'water'
ò	as the 'o' in 'soft'
r	a rolled 'r'
š	as the 'sh' in 'ship'
u	as in 'put'
ž	as the 's' in 'treasure'

ACCOMMODATION

hotel	hotel
guest house	gostišče
camping ground	kamping

Do you have a ...?	Ali imate prosto ...?
bed	posteljo
cheap room	poceni sobo
single room	enoposteljno sobo
double room	dvoposteljno sobo

How much is it ...?	Koliko stane ...?
per night/person	za eno noč/osebo
for one night	za eno noč/za dve noči
for two nights	za dve noči

Is breakfast included? Ali je zajtrk vključen?

CONVERSATION & ESSENTIALS

Hello.	Pozdravljeni. (pol)
	Zdravo/Žvivio. (inf)
Good day.	Dober dan.
Goodbye.	Nasvidenje.
Yes.	Da/Ja. (pol/inf)
No.	Ne.
Please.	Prosim.
Thank you.	Hvala.
You're welcome.	Prosim/Ni za kaj.
Excuse me.	Oprostite.
What's your name?	Kako vam je ime?
My name is ...	Jaz sem ...
Where are you from?	Od kod ste?
I'm from ...	Sem iz ...

SHOPPING & SERVICES

Where is the/a/an ...? Kje je ...?

bank/exchange	banka/menjalnica
consulate/embassy	konzulat/ambasada
post office	pošta
tourist office	turistični informa-cijski urad

TIME, DAYS & NUMBERS

today	danes
tonight	nocoj
tomorrow	jutri
in the morning	zjutraj
in the evening	zvečer

Monday	ponedeljek
Tuesday	torek
Wednesday	sreda
Thursday	četrtek
Friday	petek
Saturday	sobota
Sunday	nedelja

0	nula
1	ena
2	dve
3	tri
4	štiri
5	pet
6	šest
7	sedem
8	osem
9	devet
10	deset
100	sto
1000	tisoč

TRANSPORT

What time does ... leave/arrive?	Kdaj odpelje/pripelje ...?
boat/ferry	ladja/trajekt
bus	avtobus
plane	avion
train	vlak

| Can you show me on the map? | A mi lahko pokažete na mapi? |

timetable	spored
train station	železniška postaja
bus station	avtobusno postajališče
one way/return	enosmerna/povratna

The Authors

LISA DUNFORD   Coordinating Author, Slovakia

Lisa has been fascinated with Europe since childhood, probably because her grandfather came from a part of the Carpathian region that was Hungary, then Czechoslovakia and now Ukraine. She studied in Budapest during university, and after graduation worked in Bratislava. She learned the language, danced on the main square the night Slovakia became an independent nation, and made lifelong friends. Though she returns to Europe often, Lisa, her husband, and their dog currently call East Texas home. Lisa also wrote the Destination Central Europe, Experiencing Central Europe, Getting Started, Events Calendar, Itineraries, Regional Directory and Transport in Central Europe chapters.

BRETT ATKINSON   Czech Republic

Brett has been travelling to Europe for more than 20 years, and has honeymooned in Slovenia and Bosnia, written about Hungary's communist past, and island-hopped in Croatia. On his second extended research trip to the Czech Republic, he attempted to really get off the beaten track, especially if this meant seeking out interesting out-of-the-way microbreweries. When he's not on the road for Lonely Planet, Brett lives with Carol in Auckland, New Zealand. Fortunately his local microbrew emporium produces a damn fine Bohemian pilsner, ensuring the world's best beer is never far away.

NEAL BEDFORD   Austria

In his heart Neal will always be a New Zealander, but after living in Austria for the past decade he must finally admit that an ever increasing part of him now calls this land of mountains, valleys and rivers home. From his base in Vienna he has travelled the length and breadth of Austria on a number of occasions, searching for the boldest Feuerwehrfest, the biggest summer solstice bonfire, and the best local *Brauerei* (brewery). He is constantly amazed at the country's beauty, and at how grumpy the Viennese can be.

LONELY PLANET AUTHORS

Why is our travel information the best in the world? It's simple: our authors are passionate, dedicated travellers. They don't take freebies in exchange for positive coverage so you can be sure the advice you're given is impartial. They travel widely to all the popular spots, and off the beaten track. They don't research using just the internet or phone. They discover new places not included in any other guidebook. They personally visit thousands of hotels, restaurants, palaces, trails, galleries, temples and more. They speak with dozens of locals every day to make sure you get the kind of insider knowledge only a local could tell you. They take pride in getting all the details right, and in telling it how it is. Think you can do it? Find out how at **lonelyplanet.com**.

THE AUTHORS

STEVE FALLON   Slovenia

Steve has been travelling to Slovenia since the early 1990s, when a travel-publishing company initially refused his proposal to write a guidebook to the country because of 'the war going on' (it had ended two years before) and a US newspaper of record told him that their readers weren't interested in 'Slovakia'. Never mind, it was his own private Idaho for over a decade. Though he *still* hasn't reached the top of Mt Triglav (next time – *domen*, promise!), Steve considers at least part of his soul Slovenian and returns to the country as often as he can for a glimpse of the Julian Alps, a dribble of *bučno olje* (pumpkin-seed oil) and a dose of the dual.

TIM RICHARDS   Hungary, Poland

Having transferred with an international teaching organisation from a two-year stint in Egypt, Tim spent a year teaching English in Kraków in 1994–95. He was fascinated by the massive postcommunist transition affecting every aspect of Polish life, and by the surviving remnants of the Cold War days. He's since returned to Poland repeatedly for Lonely Planet, and has been delighted by his reacquaintance with this beautiful, complex country. When he's not on the road for Lonely Planet, Tim is a freelance journalist living in Melbourne, Australia, and writes on various topics: travel, lifestyle, the arts, technology and pets. You can see more of his writing at www.iwriter.com.au.

CAROLINE SIEG   Germany

Half-American and half-Swiss, Caroline Sieg has spent most of her life moving back and forth across the Atlantic Ocean, with lengthy stops in Zürich, Miami and New York City. When not cycling around Berlin's Tiergarten or Hamburg's waterways in an effort to work off a daily dose of *Kaffee und Kuchen* (coffee and cakes), Caroline can be found commissioning guidebooks in Lonely Planet's London office.

RYAN VER BERKMOES   Germany

Ryan Ver Berkmoes once lived in Germany. He spent three years in Frankfurt, during which time he edited a magazine until he got the chance for a new career – with Lonely Planet. One of his first jobs was working on the Germany chapter of an early edition of this very book. Later he worked on the 1st edition of Lonely Planet's *The Netherlands*, a country where they pronounce his name better than he can. These days he lives in Portland, Oregon. Learn more at ryanverberkmoes.com.

NICOLA WILLIAMS   Liechtenstein, Switzerland

Ever since Nicola moved to a village on the southern side of Lake Geneva, she has never quite been able to shake off that uncanny feeling that she is on holiday – a garden tumbling down the hillside towards that same glittering lake and the mysterious Jura mountains beyond is her wake-up call. Nicola has lived and worked in France since 1997, and when not flitting to Geneva, skiing or dipping into the Swiss countryside, she can be found writing at her desk. Previous Lonely Planet titles include *France; Provence & the Côte d'Azur; Languedoc-Roussillon; Tuscany & Umbria; Milan, Turin & Genoa;* and *Piedmont.*

Behind the Scenes

THIS BOOK

Central Europe is part of Lonely Planet's Europe series, which also includes *Western Europe, Eastern Europe, Mediterranean Europe, Scandinavian Europe* and *Europe on a Shoestring*. Lonely Planet also publishes phrasebooks to these regions.

This guidebook was commissioned in Lonely Planet's London office, and produced by the following:

Commissioning Editor Caroline Sieg
Coordinating Editors Susan Paterson, Laura Stansfeld
Coordinating Cartographer Valentina Kremenchutskaya
Coordinating Layout Designer Paul Iacono
Managing Editor Imogen Bannister
Managing Cartographer Mark Griffiths, Herman So
Managing Layout Designer Laura Jane, Indra Kilfoyle
Assisting Editors Nigel Chin, Jessica Crouch, Penelope Goodes, Carly Hall, Kim Hutchins, Amy Karafin, Helen Koehne, Rosie Nicholson, Sally O'Brien, Charlotte Orr, Simon Williamson, Helen Yeates
Assisting Cartographers Fatima Basic, Barbara Benson, Csanad Csutoros, Tony Fankhauser, David Kemp, Andy Rojas, Tom Webster
Assisting Layout Designer Cara Smith
Cover Designer Jane Hart

Project Manager Glenn van der Knijff
Language Content Coordinator Robyn Loughnane

Thanks to Lucy Birchley, Sally Darmody, Ryan Evans, Mark Germanchis, Katie Lynch, John Mazzocchi, Wayne Murphy, Trent Paton, Sarah Sloane, Gina Tsarouhas, Branislava Vladisavljevic, Juan Winata

THANKS
LISA DUNFORD

Dearest Saša, always being welcomed as a part of your family means more to me than I can say. Fero, Šimi, Sari Petriska – thank you, too. I appreciate the help of everyone who made suggestions and helped me along my way, including Martin Latal, Karen and Matuš Sulek, Zuzana Bielikova, Jimbo Holden and the Monkey.

BRETT ATKINSON

Hi and special thanks to Greg and Francie in Olomouc, and Tomáš in Wallachia – you all make returning to the Czech Republic a pleasure. Thanks also to Oldřiška and family in Český Krumlov, and to Doug in Loket. I'm sorry I wasn't around to see Jethro Tull under the castle; it looked pretty cool on YouTube. In Lonely Planet–ville, thanks to Mark Griffiths and the cartography team for mak-

---

THE LONELY PLANET STORY

Fresh from an epic journey across Europe, Asia and Australia in 1972, Tony and Maureen Wheeler sat at their kitchen table stapling together notes. The first Lonely Planet guidebook, *Across Asia on the Cheap,* was born.

Travellers snapped up the guides. Inspired by their success, the Wheelers began publishing books to Southeast Asia, India and beyond. Demand was prodigious, and the Wheelers expanded the business rapidly to keep up. Over the years, Lonely Planet extended its coverage to every country and into the virtual world via lonelyplanet.com and the Thorn Tree message board.

As Lonely Planet became a globally loved brand, Tony and Maureen received several offers for the company. But it wasn't until 2007 that they found a partner whom they trusted to remain true to the company's principles of travelling widely, treading lightly and giving sustainably. In October of that year, BBC Worldwide acquired a 75% share in the company, pledging to uphold Lonely Planet's commitment to independent travel, trustworthy advice and editorial independence.

Today, Lonely Planet has offices in Melbourne, London and Oakland, with over 500 staff members and 300 authors. Tony and Maureen are still actively involved with Lonely Planet. They're travelling more often than ever, and they're devoting their spare time to charitable projects. And the company is still driven by the philosophy of *Across Asia on the Cheap:* 'All you've got to do is decide to go and the hardest part is over. So go!'

ing sense of my multicoloured maps, and special thanks to the wonderfully tireless Will Gourlay for his undying energy and passion for the region. Finally, thanks to Carol for holding the fort in Auckland for a long 10 weeks, and for actually recognising me when I (eventually) got home. I promise to take you to Prague next time, OK?

NEAL BEDFORD

First and foremost, thanks and love to Karin for showing me her version of Salzburg and her former backyard, the Salzkammergut. In Vienna, the usual crowd needs special mention once again – you know who you are and how you've helped out. To all the people I met on the road who gave me their thoughts, advice, and guidance, special thanks.

STEVE FALLON

A number of people assisted in the research and writing of the Slovenia chapter, in particular my dear friends and fonts of all knowledge at the Ljubljana Tourist Board: Verica Leskovar, Tatjana Radovič and Petra Stušek. Others to whom I'd like to say *najlepša hvala* for assistance, inspiration, sustenance and/or a few laughs along the way include the boys (Miha Anzelc, Luka Esenko and Tomaž Marič) of Žīdana Marela in Ljubljana; Brina Čehovin and Tina Križnar of the Slovenian Tourist Board, Ljubljana; Marino Fakin of Slovenian Railways, Ljubljana; Aleš and Tanja Hvala of the Hotel Hvala and Restavracija Topli Val, Kobarid; Lado Leskovar of Unicef, based in Ljubljana; Tomaž Škofic of Adria Airways in Ljubljana; Robert Stan of Adventure Rafting Bled; and the staff at the Tourist Information Centre Ptuj for assistance (way beyond the call of duty) in helping me find an industrial-strength *klopotec* (wind rattle) on short notice as I whizzed in on a rainy morning from southwest Hungary. Goodbye pigeons! As always, my efforts here are dedicated to my partner, Michael Rothschild, who is way overdue a visit to God's own country.

CAROLINE SIEG

Thank you to my parents, who made sure I grew up truly bilingual and never let me forget where my roots truly come from. Thanks also to Andrea Schulte-Peevers for showing me a few bits of her Berlin and for sharing that historic election night. Last, *Prost!* to all the exceptional people I met along the way who provided me with insights, observations and recommendations.

RYAN VER BERKMOES

Big thanks to Lonely Planet authors Jeremy Grey (an old Germany colleague) and Neal Bedford (an old London colleague) as well as Simon Sellars and Zora O'Neill, whose brilliant work flavours my own. In Germany, Angela Cullen was a dear as always and I'm happy to see she still prefers Harry over a chihuahua. It was good to get back on track with Alan Wissenburg. Thanks to Birgit Borowski and Dr Eva Missler, who showed me the highs and the very few lows of Stuttgart. Kudos to the various Munich folk who thrilled me in bars and gave me nights out of *Pink Flamingos* that could have been produced by Samuel L Bronkowitz. And steins of lager to all my coauthors, who did fab jobs. Thanks to all those at Lonely Planet who gave support during a time of loss, and to Erin and Annah who always give me a home.

NICOLA WILLIAMS

Several friends recommended places to eat, not least my efficient army of Geneva-savvy volunteers: Carine Benetti, Lena Hagelstein, Sophie Lux, Stéphanie Nassenstein, Juraj Ondrejkovic, Tessema Tesfachew and party gal Ciara Browne. Appreciation in equal measure to man-around-town Alan Turner and to Sarah Garner for putting me in touch; to temporary New Yorker Claudia Rosiny for Bern talk; Elizabeth and Nicolas at

---

SEND US YOUR FEEDBACK

We love to hear from travellers – your comments keep us on our toes and help make our books better. Our well-travelled team reads every word on what you loved or loathed about this book. Although we cannot reply individually to postal submissions, we always guarantee that your feedback goes straight to the appropriate authors, in time for the next edition. Each person who sends us information is thanked in the next edition – and the most useful submissions are rewarded with a free book.

To send us your updates – and find out about Lonely Planet events, newsletters and travel news – visit our award-winning website: **lonelyplanet.com/contact**.

Note: we may edit, reproduce and incorporate your comments in Lonely Planet products such as guidebooks, websites and digital products, so let us know if you don't want your comments reproduced or your name acknowledged. For a copy of our privacy policy visit lonelyplanet.com/privacy.

Ferme Montavon for Jurassic farm pleasures; Nana/Omi for domestic reinforcement; and Niko, Mischa and Matthias for always travelling so happily. Last but far from least, sincere thanks to Damien Simonis and Kerry Walker, whose inspired Switzerland texts formed the bulk of the chapter.

OUR READERS

Many thanks to the travellers who used the last edition and wrote to us with helpful hints, useful advice and interesting anecdotes:

Sharlene Abela, Herve Blumenthal, Joe Bruckner, Jesse de Wit, Sam Holmes, Bob Hurley, E Hurst, Tony Jowett, Ana Liddie Navarro, Tony Mason, Paul Nordhaus, David Peck, Noreen Tai, Karen Wallace, Pat Yaros

ACKNOWLEDGMENTS

Many thanks to the following for the use of their content:

Globe on title page ©Mountain High Maps 1993 Digital Wisdom, Inc.

Internal photographs by Lonely Planet Images, and by Jon Davison p257 (#2), p258 (#3); Christer Fredriks p255 (#3), p260 (#1); Greg Gawlowski p259 (#2); Dennis Johnson p256 (#4); Martin Moos p254 (#1); Richard Nebesky p253, p254 (#4), p257 (#3), p258 (#1); Craig Pershouse p255 (#2); David Tomlinson p256 (#1).

All images are the copyright of the photographers unless otherwise indicated. Many of the images in this guide are available for licensing from Lonely Planet Images: www.lonelyplanetimages.com.

Index

INDEX

INDEX

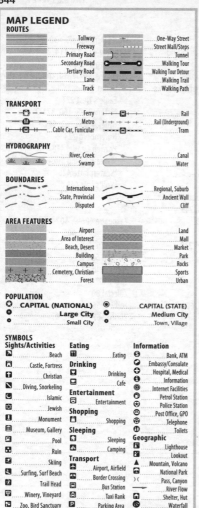

MAP LEGEND
ROUTES

Tollway
Freeway
Primary Road
Secondary Road
Tertiary Road
Lane
Track

One-Way Street
Street Mall/Steps
Tunnel
Walking Tour
Walking Tour Detour
Walking Trail
Walking Path

TRANSPORT

Ferry
Metro
Cable Car, Funicular

Rail
Rail (Underground)
Tram

HYDROGRAPHY

River, Creek
Swamp

Canal
Water

BOUNDARIES

International
State, Provincial
Disputed

Regional, Suburb
Ancient Wall
Cliff

AREA FEATURES

Airport
Area of Interest
Beach, Desert
Building
Campus
Cemetery, Christian
Forest

Land
Mall
Market
Park
Rocks
Sports
Urban

POPULATION

CAPITAL (NATIONAL)
Large City
Small City

CAPITAL (STATE)
Medium City
Town, Village

SYMBOLS
Sights/Activities
Beach
Castle, Fortress
Christian
Diving, Snorkeling
Islamic
Jewish
Monument
Museum, Gallery
Pool
Ruin
Skiing
Surfing, Surf Beach
Trail Head
Winery, Vineyard
Zoo, Bird Sanctuary

Eating
Eating

Drinking
Drinking
Cafe

Entertainment
Entertainment

Shopping
Shopping

Sleeping
Sleeping
Camping

Transport
Airport, Airfield
Border Crossing
Bus Station
Taxi Rank
Parking Area

Information
Bank, ATM
Embassy/Consulate
Hospital, Medical
Information
Internet Facilities
Petrol Station
Police Station
Post Office, GPO
Telephone
Toilets

Geographic
Lighthouse
Lookout
Mountain, Volcano
National Park
Pass, Canyon
River Flow
Shelter, Hut
Waterfall

LONELY PLANET OFFICES

Australia
Head Office
Locked Bag 1, Footscray, Victoria 3011
☎ 03 8379 8000, fax 03 8379 8111
talk2us@lonelyplanet.com.au

USA
150 Linden St, Oakland, CA 94607
☎ 510 250 6400, toll free 800 275 8555
fax 510 893 8572
info@lonelyplanet.com

UK
2nd fl, 186 City Rd,
London EC1V 2NT
☎ 020 7106 2100, fax 020 7106 2101
go@lonelyplanet.co.uk

Published by Lonely Planet Publications Pty Ltd
ABN 36 005 607 983

© Lonely Planet Publications Pty Ltd 2009

© photographers as indicated 2009

Cover photograph: Equestrian statue and dome of Theatinerkirche St Kajetan, Munich, Germany, David Borland/Lonely Planet Images. Many of the images in this guide are available for licensing from Lonely Planet Images: www.lonelyplanetimages.com.

Mixed Sources
Product group from well-managed forests and other controlled sources
www.fsc.org Cert no. SGS-COC-005002
© 1996 Forest Stewardship Council